# Planning and Environmental Law in I...

# Planning and Environmental Law in Ireland

John Gore-Grimes
BA, LLB, FCI Arb
*Solicitor*

Bloomsbury Professional

Published by
Bloomsbury Professional
Maxwelton House
41–43 Boltro Road
Haywards Heath
West Sussex
RH16 1BJ

Bloomsbury Professional
The Fitzwilliam Business Centre
26 Upper Pembroke Street
Dublin 2

ISBN 978 1 84766 365 8

© Bloomsbury Professional Limited 2011
Bloomsbury Professional, an imprint of Bloomsbury Publishing Plc

All rights reserved. No part of this publication may be reproduced in any material form (including photocopying or storing it in any medium by electronic means and whether or not transiently or incidentally to some other use of this publication) without the written permission of the copyright owner except in accordance with the provisions of the Copyright, Designs and Patents Act 1988 or under the terms of a licence issued by the Copyright Licensing Agency Ltd., Saffron House, 6–10 Kirby Street, London, EC1N 8TS, England. Applications for the copyright owner's written permission to reproduce any part of this publication should be addressed to the publisher.

Warning: The doing of an unauthorised act in relation to a copyright work may result in both a civil claim for damages and criminal prosecution.

This work is intended to be a general guide and cannot be a substitute for professional advice. Neither the authors nor the publisher accept any responsibility for loss occasioned to any person acting or refraining from acting as a result of material contained in this publication.

**British Library Cataloguing-in-Publication Data**
A catalogue record for this book is available from the British Library

Typeset by Marie Armah-Kwantreng, Dublin, Ireland
Printed and bound in the United Kingdom by CPI Antony Rowe, Chippenham, Wilts

# FOREWORD

Every member of the legal profession with an interest in the law of planning was grateful to John Gore-Grimes for sharing his extensive knowledge and experience of the topic, as a solicitor over many decades, with a wider audience in the book he wrote some years ago. Indeed, while lawyers were no doubt the primary group of readers he had in mind, I would be surprised if it did not also appeal to those many people outside the law, whether in the public or private field, who required speedy and reliable guidance on various aspects of planning.

I was happy to contribute a foreword to that work with its unusual but user-friendly dictionary format. Its sequel, which I am equally pleased to introduce, is a significantly more ambitious and comprehensive work. It reflects the extremely complex legal structures which now govern Irish planning and which demand treatment on this encyclopaedic scale. For those of us whose memories go back that far, the Local Government (Planning and Development) Act 1963, once seemed a veritable legislative monster: now, when we see what to-day's lawyers must master, we have almost fond memories of its relative simplicity.

Among the many changes, perhaps one of the most striking is the hugely important role now played in Irish planning by An Bord Pleanála. While that body has attracted much unfavourable comment over the years, some of it no doubt justified, even its most robust critics would probably concede that the vesting of so many planning functions in the Board rather than in the Minister for the Environment has been a healthy development. It is, of course, the case that the Minister is directly accountable to the Oireachtas, but that did not alter the perception that, during the period when he was effectively the 'overlord of planning', as it was put by Mr Justice Eamon Walsh, many of the decisions at that level were effectively made for political reasons rather than in the interests of good planning. The Board is now the ultimate arbiter, not merely of whether planning permissions should be granted, but whether particular developments are exempted from the need to have permission and whether developments of strategic infrastructural significance should go ahead. That is also the case where compulsory acquisitions of land are concerned.

While the advantages of having an independent body rather than the government exercising these vital and sensitive functions are obvious, it must be acknowledged that there are problematic features of the system as it now operates. It is not so much that the Board has made questionable decisions from time to time: that is hardly surprising, since it has been in existence in one form or another for over thirty years. But given the wide range of powers they enjoy and the serious consequences that can follow from their misuse, it is essential that the courts should be in a position to review their decisions where that is in the public interest. However, while the Board is, of course, subject to the judicial review jurisdiction of the High Court, that jurisdiction, as this book demonstrates, has been seriously circumscribed in two areas. First, the Oireachtas has sought to streamline the judicial review procedure so as to ensure that beneficial development is not unduly impeded by what are effectively 'appeals' to the High Court rather than judicial review applications in the proper sense. Those attempts, however well intentioned, have as often as not led to greater delays: it remains to be seen whether the latest changes will improve matters. Secondly, the courts have set the threshold for intervening in planning decisions at a remarkably high level. I have to accept that my own views on this have changed over the years: I think that there is much force in Mr Justice O'Sullivan's comment that the effect of the judgment in *The State (Keegan) v Stardust Victims' Compensation Tribunal* is that a decision would have to be regarded as 'mad' before the court could intervene. But to that I would add that the bar seems to have been raised even higher by the statement in *O'Keeffe v An Bord Pleanála* that the court could not interfere where there was *any* 'relevant material' to support the decision. While I fully accept that the courts should respect the decision of the Oireachtas to entrust planning decisions to persons with the appropriate expertise, it must be questionable whether that justifies a court in refraining from intervening where the material on which the body reached its decision is so tenuous and inconsequential that no body, addressing its collective mind to the issue properly, could reasonably have come to the particular conclusion.

Another major development has been the ever increasing influence of the European Union on Irish planning and environmental law. This is admirably dealt with in this book in a manner which emphasises the areas where our domestic laws – or the absence of them – have been unsparingly criticised at the EU level. An example is the Irish fondness for the 'retention' procedure, reflecting an indulgence towards those who cannot be bothered with the tedious formalities of applying for permission. That is a view manifestly not shared in Brussels, as witness the rejection of it as appropriate where an Environmental Impact Assessment is required.

One cannot help being depressed by the message which emerges from this book that, during the years of recent prosperity, the huge arsenal of planning measures spectacularly failed to ensure that planning decisions, particularly those involving the rezoning of land for housing, were taken in the public interest. Not only have we the dreadful legacy of the 'ghost estates' to remind us of that inexcusable failure: despite the enactment of Part V of the Planning and Development Act 2000, requiring local authorities to ensure that housing developments contained a specified level of social and affordable housing, the grim statistics in this book demonstrate that, even in the years of plenty, we miserably failed to ensure the provision of adequate housing for those with special needs.

I have no doubt that everyone concerned with our planning and environmental laws will find this book an invaluable guide through the frequently baffling labyrinths of which they now consist. I wish it every success.

Ronan Keane

20th April, 2011

# PREFACE

I was elated when Sandra Mulvey of Tottel Publishing, now Bloomsbury Professional, contacted me in early July 2008 to see if I would be writing a new edition on planning law. More than 2 years later I know how vanity has been bludgeoned to death by the reality and sheer drudgery of putting this second volume together. Nevertheless, it has been an interesting period to examine planning law in the post 'celtic tiger' era. Builders, developers, banks and international markets have all been found wanting and so too have some of the administrators of planning and development law. Undoubtedly planners and developers together did, to a significant extent, ignore the principles of sustainable development and sustainable zoning. The legislation has been strengthened by the provisions of the 2010 Act in the hopes that a repetition of what occurred will not happen again. But even prior to the 2010 Act you could nearly fill a house with the number of guidelines and white papers published by the Government to keep us on the right track. In spite of this, development occurred on flood plains, the principles of sustainable development were frequently overlooked and it appears that nobody thought to look at the figures (and they were available) to establish just how may dwelling houses were required by the market. Zoning was altered in many areas on the outskirts of the major residential clusters where there was insufficient infrastructure to sustain the planned development. These rezonings and developments pushed land prices up in an artificial way. The price of land must allow for generous infrastructure which will breathe sustainable life into the housing, office and production developments which occur. Many of the legislative measures were in place to foster sustainable development but they were often ignored by planners, by politicians and by developers. Sustainable development was parked as land prices and construction prices soared upwards leaving nothing to pay for or to provide the sustainable features which are the lung of any development. It is to be hoped that the new principle of a 'core strategy' will ensure that future development will be more controlled and will promote sustainable development and support economic renewal by harmonising development permission and directing it towards areas already targeted by the National Spatial Strategy for development and for investment in infrastructure. The concern must be as to whether or not the National Spatial Strategy has been sufficiently thought out and advanced to give best advantage to the 'core strategy' principle. All in all there is some recognition that land is becoming too scarce and too valuable to allow its worth to be assessed by the wild and irresponsible forces of a merry-go-round market economy. If we are to move towards a just and an integrated society in Ireland price control of land may become an inevitability, no matter how repugnant such a concept is to many of our citizens.

Having spent some 30 years examining ice, permafrost, glaciers and calving bergs I am convinced that the seawater levels are rising and will continue to do so until there is no more land ice left. If the ice should disappear completely we can expect that O'Connell Street may run from the Sugar Loaf mountain down to Roundwood. Although the rise in water levels will be gradual and spread over many years, now is the time to start building further up the hill. The map on the cover of this book represents the worst case scenario.

We are fortunate in Ireland to have some quality books on planning and environmental law. Garrett Simons SC, Prof Yvonne Scannell and Stephen Dodd BL are mighty giants in the planning and environmental planning business. The three volume edition of O'Sullivan and Shepherd now published by A&L Goodbody's Environment and Planning Law Unit under the watchful eye of its chief editor Alison Fanagan is a remarkable fountain of information. It may take a little time to learn your way around these volumes but it is rewarding when you persevere. I am greatly indebted to each of these authors and I am deeply respectful of the work and research which they have undertaken. They have allowed me to publish extracts from their works. My thanks are also due to Fintan Valentine SC and Noreen Gilheany Solicitor of McCann Fitzgerald, for allowing me to quote their work published in journals and in papers delivered at public lecture series.

I am grateful to Mr Justice Ronan Keane for his kindness in writing the Forward. My hope is that Ronan did not have to read every word of this exhausting manuscript.

I have a host of proof readers to thank including my brother Anthony, and Lisa O'Higgins, Sally Alford, Robert McDermott and Eoin Brereton. I am particularly grateful to Sandra Rochford who has laboured tirelessly to produce the manuscript which has been corrected, amended and changed on too many occasions. Sandra has also been willingly helped by Amanda Marron, Jennifer McDonald and Azelie Buttimore. Sandra Mulvey has been my contact in Bloomsbury and I am grateful to her for her patience, help and support.

My thanks are due also to Joe Kelly at A&L Goodbody for explaining the provisions of s 6 of the Acquisition of Land (Assessment of Compensation) Act 1919 in context of the new provisions of the Arbitration Act 2010.

A huge 'thanks' to my good friend Google. I could not have done it without you.

I sought and received great help and assistance from Jim O'Keeffe TD who used his own resources to find the answer to many questions which I had asked of the Department of Environment. I am most grateful to Jim for his tireless and prompt assistance and I wish him well in retirement.

John Gore Grimes Solicitor
The Shack
Baily
Co Dublin

June 2011

# CONTENTS

Foreword .................................................................................................. v
Preface .................................................................................................. vii
Contents ................................................................................................. ix
Table of Abbreviations ........................................................................ xxi
Table of Cases ................................................................................... xxiii
Table of Statutes ............................................................................... xxxv
Table of Statutory Instruments ......................................................... lxv
Table of European Legislation ....................................................... lxxiii
Table of Treaties and Conventions ................................................. lxxv
Table of Constitutions .................................................................... lxxvi

**Chapter 1 Plans, Policies, Guidelines and Directives** .................... 1
    Development Plans ............................................................................. 1
        Core strategy.................................................................................. 3
        Planning Guidelines No 15........................................................ 11
        Development plans and the Constitution................................. 16
        Development plans and the ECHR........................................... 18
        EU Directives and development plans .................................... 18
        Sustainability of development plans and strategic environmental
            assessment............................................................................... 19
        Permission for development ..................................................... 20
        Material contravention of development plans ......................... 21
        Applications for strategic infrastructure development ........... 32
        Interpretation of development plans/planning documents ......... 32
        Copies of development plans..................................................... 33
        Contents of development plans ................................................ 34
        Environmental assessment........................................................ 42
        Miscellaneous matters in relation to development plans........ 43
        Preparation and adoption of new development plans............. 44
        Making of development plan.................................................... 47
        Variation of development plans................................................ 51
        Ministerial directions regarding development plans
            and local area plans............................................................... 53
        Public right of way ..................................................................... 56
        Legal effects ................................................................................ 57
    Land Use Plans ................................................................................. 59
        Local area plans.......................................................................... 59
        Strategic development zones ..................................................... 64
        Architectural conservation area ................................................ 71
        Areas of special planning control ............................................. 73
        Areas of special amenity ........................................................... 79
        Landscape conservation areas .................................................. 83

Regional Planning Guidelines ........................................................................ 84
Ministerial Guidelines and Directives ............................................................ 94

**Chapter 2 Development and Exempted Development** ........................................ 99
When is Planning Permission Necessary? ..................................................... 99
'Development' ................................................................................................ 101
'Works' ........................................................................................................... 102
'Use' ............................................................................................................... 103
'Material Change in Use' ............................................................................... 103
    'Planning unit' ........................................................................................ 105
    'Abandonment of permission' ................................................................ 108
    'Abandonment of permission for use and/or for works' ........................ 109
    'Ancillary use' ......................................................................................... 111
    'Extinguishment/resumption of existing use rights' ............................... 113
    'Intensification of works/use' ................................................................. 116
    Material change in use as interpreted by the courts ................................ 122
'Structure' ....................................................................................................... 127
'Land' ............................................................................................................. 128
'Substratum of Land' ..................................................................................... 128
'Exempted Development' .............................................................................. 128
'Retention Permission' .................................................................................. 129
'Unauthorised Development' ......................................................................... 137
'Unauthorised Structure' ............................................................................... 137
'Unauthorised Use' ........................................................................................ 138
'Unauthorised Works' .................................................................................... 139
'Foreshore' ..................................................................................................... 139
'Exempted Development' .............................................................................. 142
    Statutory exempted development ............................................................ 143
    Local authority exempted development .................................................. 146
    Development by State authorities ........................................................... 164
    Development of the interior of a structure .............................................. 174
    Exempted forest and woodlands husbandry ........................................... 176
    Exempted development within the curtilage of a house ........................ 176
    Exempted development for casual trading areas .................................... 178
    Exempted development in relation to land reclamation .......................... 178
    Exempted development listed in the PDR 2001–2010 ........................... 179
    Exempted development provided for by regulations .............................. 180
    Exempted development under Sch 2, Pt 1 of PDR 2001 ........................ 187
    Exempted developments – advertisements ............................................. 241
    Exempted developments – rural .............................................................. 250
    Exempted developments under PDR 2001, arts 6–11 ............................ 266
    Exempted development under other enactments .................................... 278
    Further exempted development in PDA 2000 ........................................ 280
Declaration and Referral on Development and Exempted Development ........ 283

# Contents

**Chapter 3 Control of Development** .................................................. 289
    Control of Development .................................................................. 289
    General Obligation to Obtain Planning Permission ....................... 290
    Control of Development Regulations .............................................. 293
    Types of Planning Permission which may be Obtained on Application .......... 293
    Outline Planning Permission ........................................................... 293
    Outline Permission Regulations ...................................................... 297
    Restriction on Outline Application ................................................. 298
    Retention Permission ...................................................................... 298
        Substitute consent .................................................................... 300
    Applications Accompanied by EIS or Relating to Establishments
        to which Major Accident Regulations Apply ........................... 301
    Notice of Planning Application ....................................................... 302
        Newspaper notices .................................................................... 302
        Site notice ................................................................................. 303
    Consultations in Relation to Proposed Development ...................... 306
    Content of Planning Applications Generally .................................. 307
    Specified Additional Information .................................................... 309
    Requirements for Particulars to Accompany an Application
        under Article 22 ....................................................................... 310
    Legal Interest of Applicant in Land or Structure ............................ 312
    Plans and Particulars to Accompany an Application
        for Outline Permission ............................................................. 314
    Planning Application by Electricity Undertaking ........................... 314
    Procedure of Planning Authority on Receipt of Planning Application ........... 315
    Weekly List of Planning Applications ............................................ 318
    Notice to Certain Bodies ................................................................. 320
    Revocation or Modification of Permission ..................................... 320
    Submissions or Observations in Relation to a Planning Application ............. 322
    Allowance for Public Holidays, etc ................................................ 325
    Minimum Period for Determination of Planning Application ....... 325
    Maximum Period for Determination of Planning Application ...... 325
    Default Planning Permission ........................................................... 327
    Notification of Decision on Planning Application ......................... 331
    Notification of Grant of Permission ................................................ 332
    Weekly list of Planning Decisions .................................................. 333
    Permission Regulations – Further Information and Other Matters .......... 334
    Revised Plans .................................................................................. 336
    Notice of Further Information on Revised Plans ............................ 338
    Proper Planning and Sustainable Development of Area ................. 342
    'Proper Planning and Sustainable Development' ........................... 345
        Alternative sites ....................................................................... 345
        Amenity .................................................................................... 346
        Common good ......................................................................... 347
        Compulsory purchase orders ................................................... 348

Planning history of lands .................................................................. 348
Permission in material contravention of development plan....................... 348
Precedent............................................................................................ 349
Private interest ................................................................................... 349
Public health and safety ...................................................................... 350
*Res Judicata Pro Veritate Accipitur* ........................................................ 352
Planning Gain ............................................................................................. 353
Refusals for Past Failures ........................................................................... 354
Irrelevant Considerations ............................................................................ 356
    Compensation ..................................................................................... 356
    Licences or permission required as pre-condition
       under other legislation.................................................................... 357
    Ownership of land................................................................................ 358
    Personal circumstances ....................................................................... 358
    Other provisions limiting discretions of planning authorities................. 359
Conditions in Planning Permissions ............................................................ 365
    General conditions .............................................................................. 366
    Fair and reasonable ............................................................................ 367
    Relevant to planning policy ................................................................. 367
    Applicant not required to carry out planning authority's duties ............. 368
    Implementation not dependent on cooperation of third party................. 368
    Depriving landowner of existing use rights or uses................................ 369
    Conditions imposed by subsequent permission .................................... 369
    Enforceability...................................................................................... 370
    Precision............................................................................................. 371
    No abdication of jurisdiction of planning body .................................... 372
    Standard conditions............................................................................ 373
    Direct departure from application ....................................................... 373
    Fire conditions ................................................................................... 373
    Conditions requiring matters to be agreed........................................... 374
Statutory Planning Conditions Enumerated in PDA 2000, s 34(4) ............... 375
    Points of detail to be agreed between authority and developer.............. 383
    Social and affordable housing agreements.......................................... 385
    Transboundary environmental impacts............................................... 387
Conditions Restricting Use of Premises by Persons of a Particular Class
   or Description ......................................................................................... 387
    Sterilisation/planning agreements ...................................................... 387
Occupancy Conditions ................................................................................ 389
Development Contribution Schemes ........................................................... 393
    Formalities for drawing up a development contribution scheme........... 397
    Supplementary development contribution schemes............................. 400

# Chapter 4 Challenging Planning Decisions ............................................. 407
Part I: Appeals and Referrals to An Bord Pleanála ....................................... 407
    Jurisdiction of the Board to hear appeals............................................ 407
    Jurisdiction of the Board to hear referrals........................................... 408

## Contents

Who may appeal? ............................................................................ 410
Time limits for lodging an appeal to An Bord Pleanála ............................ 416
Circumstances in which Board may direct a material contravention
  of plan ..................................................................................... 417
An Bord Pleanála must determine the appeal *de novo* ........................... 418
Vexatious or frivolous appeals ........................................................... 418
Appeal against conditions only .......................................................... 419
Appeal against conditions requiring payment
  of a financial contribution ............................................................. 420
Prohibition against further planning applications pending appeal ............. 421
Rules and procedures in relation to appeals and referrals ........................ 422
Time limits within which Board must make its decision ......................... 423
Notice of postponement .................................................................. 423
Minister's entitlement to vary the time limit ........................................ 424
Provisions as to the making of appeals and referrals .............................. 424
Submission of documents, etc by planning authorities ........................... 428
Availability of documents relating to appeals and referrals ...................... 430
Submissions or observations by other parties ....................................... 430
Submissions or observations other than by parties
  to appeals or referrals ................................................................... 431
Power of Board to request submissions or observations ......................... 432
Power of Board to require submission of documents, etc ....................... 433
Power of Board where notice is served under ss 131 and 132 ................. 434
Oral hearings of appeals and referrals and applications .......................... 434
Matters other than those raised by parties ........................................... 443
Withdrawal of appeals, applications and referrals ................................. 444
Time for decisions on lodging appeals, etc .......................................... 445
The making of Regulations regarding appeals and referrals ..................... 445
Board to have regard to certain policies and objectives ........................... 446
Fees payable to the Board ................................................................ 447
Expenses of appeals and referrals ...................................................... 447
Reports and documents of the Board .................................................. 448
Documents to be made available to the public ..................................... 452
Planning Regulations dealing with appeals and referrals ........................ 453
Referrals to An Bord Pleanála .......................................................... 461
Part II: Statutory Judicial Review ....................................................... 469
  Article 10(a) of the EIA Directive – Judicial Review in Ireland ............... 469
  *Commission v Ireland* Case C–427/07 ........................................... 472
  What is statutory judicial review? .................................................. 480
  Leave to apply must be sought by *ex parte motion* .......................... 484
  Applications to stay proceedings ................................................... 495
  Time limits .............................................................................. 496
  Extension of time ...................................................................... 500
  Application for leave to apply ...................................................... 503
  Substantial interest .................................................................... 506

| | |
|---|---|
| Substantial grounds | 513 |
| Alternative remedies in judicial review cases | 518 |
| Case law examples of statutory judicial review | 521 |
| Undertaking as to damages | 523 |
| Appeals to the Supreme Court | 524 |
| Remittal | 531 |
| The quashing of part of a decision or act | 532 |
| Expeditious determination | 532 |

## Chapter 5 Enforcement and Planning Injunctions ... 535
### Part I: Enforcement ... 535
| | |
|---|---|
| Offence | 535 |
| Development carried out pursuant to a planning condition | 536 |
| Retention permission in relation to enforcement proceedings | 536 |
| Warning letter procedure | 545 |
| Contents of a warning letter | 548 |
| Decision on enforcement | 551 |
| Enforcement notice | 556 |
| Penalties for offences | 564 |
| Other provisions relating to enforcement | 566 |
| Challenging enforcement notices | 568 |

### Part II: The Planning Injunctions ... 570
| | |
|---|---|
| Enforcement by injunction in relation to unauthorised development | 570 |
| Discretion of the court | 572 |
| Procedure for application for injunction under PDA 2000, s 160 | 583 |
| Discretionary remedies – *Wicklow County Council v Forest Fencing Ltd* | 586 |
| Onus of proof | 587 |
| Hearsay | 590 |
| Undertakings as to damages | 591 |
| No damages payable in respect of s 160 application | 592 |
| Time limits | 593 |
| Costs of prosecutions and applications for injunctions | 595 |
| Proceedings against company directors | 597 |
| Permission not required for any works required under this Part | 599 |

## Chapter 6 Housing Supply – Social and Affordable Housing ... 601
| | |
|---|---|
| Introduction | 601 |
| Definitions of Social and Affordable Housing | 605 |
| Housing Strategies | 609 |
| Housing Strategies and Development Plans | 612 |
| Social and Affordable Housing Conditions and Agreements | 614 |
| Compensation for land transferred to local authority | 632 |
| Withering permissions | 640 |
| Exemption from social and affordable housing conditions | 643 |
| Refusal of Certificate under PDA 2000, s 97 | 647 |

## Contents

Offences for Non-compliance with the Provisions of PDA 2000, s 97 ........... 648
Allocation of Affordable Housing ..................................................................649
   Controls on subsequent sale or resale of certain houses............................ 650
   Section 99(3) clawback ............................................................................. 651
   PDA 2000, s 99 controls on resale of certain houses – clawback ............. 652
Part 5 of the Housing (Miscellaneous Provisions) Act 2009 ........................653
PDA 2000, s 100: Regulations under Part V – Housing Supply .....................658

### Chapter 7 Compensation and Compulsory Acquisition ...........................661
Part I: Compensation .....................................................................................661
   Introduction ................................................................................................ 661
   Compensation claims – time limits ............................................................ 663
   Determination of compensation claim....................................................... 664
   Arbitrator cases and the High Court........................................................... 665
   Regulations in relation to compensation .................................................... 667
   Prohibition of double compensation........................................................... 669
   Recovery of compensation from planning authority.................................. 669
   Registration of compensation ..................................................................... 669
   Recovery by planning authority of compensation
     on subsequent developments ................................................................. 669
   Right to compensation................................................................................. 671
   Determination of compensation in relation to decisions
     under PDA 2000, Part III ...................................................................... 673
   Restriction of compensation........................................................................ 677
   Notice preventing compensation ................................................................ 689
   Structures substantially replacing structures demolished
     or destroyed by fire ............................................................................... 694
   Restriction on assignment of compensation under s 190 ........................... 695
   Compensation where permission is revoked or modified .......................... 695
   Compensation regarding removal or alteration of a structure .................... 695
   Compensation regarding discontinuance of use.......................................... 696
   Compensation claim relating to area of special planning control .............. 696
   Compensation regarding cables, wires and pipelines................................. 697
   Compensation regarding creation of public rights of way ......................... 697
   Compensation regarding entry on land....................................................... 697
Part II: Compulsory Acquisition ....................................................................698
   Appropriation of land for local authority purposes.................................... 698
   Disposal of land by local authority............................................................. 700
   Development by planning authority ........................................................... 702
   Making the compulsory purchase order ..................................................... 704
   Transfer of Minister's functions to the Board............................................ 711
   Judicial review in relation to PDA 2000, Pt XIV....................................... 712
   Transfer of certain ministerial functions .................................................... 713
   Confirmation of compulsory purchase order where there are
     no objections......................................................................................... 714
   Time limits in respect of compulsory purchase of land ............................. 715

Transferred functions: supplemental provisions ............................................ 717
Section 217B: supplemental provisions ........................................................ 717
Board to make decision on transferred functions ......................................... 720
Oral hearings ................................................................................................. 721
Supplemental provisions relating to oral hearings ....................................... 722
Power to direct payment of certain costs ..................................................... 727
Certain procedures to run in parallel ............................................................ 728
Objective of the Board in relation to transferred functions ......................... 728
Amendment of s 10 of Local Government (No 2) Act 1960 ....................... 730
References to transferred functions in regulations, etc ................................ 731
Part IX, Ch 5 of the National Asset Management Agency Act 2009 .......... 731
Acquisition of land for open spaces ............................................................. 735

## Chapter 8 Additional Planning Controls on Land and on Buildings ........ 739
Advertisements ............................................................................................. 739
Archaeological Objects ................................................................................ 743
Control of Quarries ...................................................................................... 746
Derelict Sites/Derelict Land ......................................................................... 776
Licensing of Events and Funfairs ................................................................. 780
    Pre-application consultation .................................................................. 783
    Availability of documents ...................................................................... 785
    Consultation with prescribed bodies ...................................................... 786
    Making of submissions or observations by any other person ............... 786
    Further information ................................................................................ 786
    Decision on application .......................................................................... 786
    Grant of licence ...................................................................................... 787
    Codes of practice in relation to events ................................................... 788
    Service of notice in relation to events .................................................... 788
    General obligations with regard to safety at events ............................... 789
    Powers of inspection in connection with events ................................... 789
    Control of funfairs .................................................................................. 789
Major Accident Hazard Directive – Seveso II Directive ............................. 792
    PDR 2001 (as amended), Part 11 ........................................................... 795
Mineral Development .................................................................................. 808
Protected/Proposed Protected Structures ..................................................... 810
    Introduction ............................................................................................ 810
    Definitions .............................................................................................. 811
    Consequences of designation ................................................................. 818
    Duty of owners and occupiers to protect structures
        from endangerment ........................................................................... 821
    Notice to require works in relation to endangerment
        of protected structures ...................................................................... 822
    Notice to require restoration of character of protected structures ......... 822
    Damage .................................................................................................. 823
    Appeals against notices served on owner .............................................. 824

Notice to require restoration of character of protected structures
and other places ........................................................................... 825
Restoration notices and endangerment notices........................................ 826
Compulsory acquisition of protected structures and related matters.......... 829
CPO vesting orders................................................................................ 830
Refusal of Planning Permission for Past Failures to Comply ....................... 832
Removal or Alteration of a Structure ............................................................ 836
Statutory Planning Agreements ..................................................................... 838
Strategic Development Zones ........................................................................ 842
Taking Estates in Charge ................................................................................ 848
Tree Preservation Orders ................................................................................ 852

**Chapter 9 Substitute Consent and Appropriate Assessment** ..................... 857
Abolition of Retention Permission Where EIA is Required ........................... 857
Substitute Consent ......................................................................................... 858
   Natura 2000 sites and Natura impact statements..................................... 860
   Application for substitute consent where notice served
      by the planning authority ...................................................................... 862
   Application for substitute consent where notice not served
      by planning authority............................................................................ 863
   Application for substitute consent............................................................ 867
   Enforcement .............................................................................................. 874
Supplementary Provisions Relating to an Application
   for Substitute Consent ............................................................................... 875
What is Appropriate Assessment? ................................................................. 878
   Appropriate assessment............................................................................ 882
   'Candidate site of community importance' .............................................. 885
   'Candidate special protection area' ........................................................... 887
   Compensatory measures............................................................................ 887
   Competent authority.................................................................................. 888
   Consent for a proposed development ........................................................ 889
   European site ............................................................................................. 889
   Land use plan............................................................................................ 889
   Natura 2000 network ................................................................................ 890
   'Natura impact report' and 'Natura impact statement'............................. 890
   Proposed development.............................................................................. 892
   Screening for appropriate assessment ....................................................... 892
   Site of community importance .................................................................. 893
   Special area of conservation...................................................................... 893
   Wildlife site ............................................................................................... 894
   Draft land use plans and imperative reasons of overriding
      public interest........................................................................................ 894
   European site that does not host priority habitat or species
      and draft land use plan......................................................................... 895
   European site that hosts priority habitat type or species
      and draft land use plan......................................................................... 896

Making land use plans ............................................................. 898
Proposed development and IROPI ........................................... 898
European site that does not host priority habitat type
  or priority species ................................................................. 900
European site that hosts priority habitat or priority species ...... 901
Certain development carried out by or on behalf of local authorities ........ 901
Conclusion ................................................................................ 902

## Chapter 10 The EIA Directive ............................................ 903
Introduction .............................................................................. 903
Direct Effect ............................................................................. 907
  Irish courts and direct effect................................................... 924
Annex I Projects Distinguished from Annex II Projects ......... 925
Ruling of ECJ in Relation to Retention Permission ................. 929
Objectives of EIA ..................................................................... 932
Implementation of the EIA Directive into Irish law ................ 933
Exemptions from EIA .............................................................. 935
Meaning of 'Exceptional Cases' .............................................. 936
Project Splitting ....................................................................... 938
Scoping .................................................................................... 941
Transboundary Environmental Impacts .................................. 941
Transboundary Environmental Effects – Notification to the Minister ......... 942
Transboundary Environmental Effects – Information to the Minister ......... 943
Transboundary Consultation .................................................... 943
Notification of Board by Planning Authority .......................... 944
Request for Further Information .............................................. 944
Minimum Period for Determinations ....................................... 945
Inclusion of Notice of Transboundary Effects in Weekly List ...... 945
Notice of Decision ................................................................... 946
Public Notice of Information Received Pursuant to Request
  under PDA 2000, s 174(4) ..................................................... 946
EIA Distinguished from EIS .................................................... 947
Projects for Which EIA is Necessary ...................................... 952
Definition of 'Project' .............................................................. 954
Mitigating Measures ................................................................ 961
Development Consents ............................................................ 965
EIA and Outline Permission .................................................... 970
Decisions not to take Enforcement Action against
  Unauthorised Development ................................................... 972
EIA for Modification or Extension to Projects ........................ 973
'Significant Effects on the Environment' ................................. 974
EIA of Certain Developments Carried Out by or on Behalf
  of Local Authorities .............................................................. 978
EIA and State Authority Development .................................... 983
Approval of Certain State Developments Requiring EIA ........ 985
State Authority's Application for Approval to An Bord Pleanála ......... 986

## Contents

Approval of State authority's Proposed Development .................................. 988
*European Commission v Ireland* C–50/09 .................................................. 990

**Chapter 11 Structural Infrastructure Development** ................................. 997
Introduction ............................................................................................. 997
Synopsis of the Seventh Schedule ........................................................ 998
   Thresholds in the Seventh Schedule .................................................. 999
Cases of Strategic Infrastructure Other Than Those Listed
   in the Seventh Schedule ................................................................... 1000
Railway Orders and Roads .................................................................. 1008
Board's Jurisdiction in Relation to Certain Planning Applications ..... 1008
Pre-Application Consultation with An Bord Pleanála ........................ 1009
EIA of Strategic Infrastructure Development Applications ................ 1011
Public Notice ...................................................................................... 1012
Submissions and Observations in Relation to Applications
   to the Board for Strategic Infrastructure Development ................... 1013
Application to the Board for Structural Infrastructure Permission ..... 1015
   Supplemental provisions relating to the application .......................... 1015
The Board's Decision on Application under S 37E ............................ 1019
Costs .................................................................................................... 1023
Time Limits ......................................................................................... 1025
Nuclear Installations ............................................................................ 1027
Alteration by An Bord Pleanála of Strategic Infrastructure
   Development ..................................................................................... 1028
Preparation of EIS for Purposes of S 146B ......................................... 1030

**Chapter 12 Planning and Environmental Law for Conveyancers** ......... 1033
Planning History of the Development ................................................. 1033
Planning Warranty ............................................................................... 1038
Need for a Planning Amnesty .............................................................. 1041
Consequences of Planning Defects ..................................................... 1042
Building Energy Rating Certificates ................................................... 1044
Special Precautions when Dealing with Exempted Development ...... 1045
Special Precautions when Dealing with Protected Structures ............ 1047
Declarations and Referrals for Information ........................................ 1048
Requisitions Relating to Enforcement Procedures
   and Planning Injunctions ................................................................... 1049
Requisitions Relating to Tree Preservation Orders ............................. 1050
Requisitions Relevant to Public Rights of Way Created by Order ..... 1051
Requisitions Relevant to Outline Permission ...................................... 1052
   Special characteristics applying to outline permissions ..................... 1053
Requisitions Relating To Strategic Development Zone ...................... 1054
Requisitions Relevant to Architectural Conservation Areas
   and Areas of Special Planning Control ............................................. 1054
Requisitions Relevant to Landscape Conservation Orders ................. 1055
Requisitions Relating to Advertisement Structures ............................ 1056

Requisitions Relating to Cables, Wires, Pipelines and Appliances ............... 1056
Requisitions Relating to Major Accidents Directive ...................................... 1056
Requisitions Relating to Social and Affordable Housing .............................. 1058
Requisitions Relating to Taking Estates in Charge ........................................ 1059
General Requisitions Relating to Environmental Matters .............................. 1059
    Definitions.................................................................................................. 1059
General Pre-contract Enquiries/requisitions Concerning
    Environmental Matters ............................................................................. 1061
    Enquiries ................................................................................................... 1061
Pre-contract Enquiries/Requisitions Re Habitats Directive .......................... 1063
    Wildlife Acts 1976–2000 .......................................................................... 1063
    Birds Directive .......................................................................................... 1064
    Natural Heritage Areas.............................................................................. 1064
    Habitats Directive and European Communities (Natural Habitats)
        Regulations 1997.................................................................................. 1065
Life Span of Planning Permission ................................................................. 1066
Radon Gas Requisitions ................................................................................. 1068
Environmental Warranties .............................................................................. 1070
    Draft environmental warranty................................................................... 1070
Environmental Indemnities ............................................................................ 1074
Suggested Limited Indemnity in Respect of Environmental Issues
    given by Vendor and Counter-indemnity Given by Purchaser ................ 1074
Suggested List of Tenant's Covenants Dealing with Environmental
    Issues to be Contained in a Lease ............................................................ 1076
Suggested Landlord's Convenants Dealing with Environmental
    Issues Contained in a Lease ..................................................................... 1078
Suggested Loan Agreement Clauses Covering Environmental Issues .......... 1079

**Appendix of Planning Forms** .............................................................................. 1081

**Index** .................................................................................................................... 1103

# TABLE OF ABBREVIATIONS

## 1. Statutory Abbreviations

| | |
|---|---|
| BCA 1990 | Building Control Act 1990 |
| BCR 1991 | Building Control Regulations 1991 |
| BCR 1997 | Building Control Regulations 1997 |
| EPAA 1992 | Environmental Pollution Agency Act 1992 |
| LGA | Local Government Act |
| LG(PD)A 1963-1999 | Local Government (Planning and Development) Acts 1963-1999 |
| LG(PD)A 1963 | Local Government (Planning and Development) Act 1963 |
| LG(PD)A 1976 | Local Government (Planning and Development) Act 1976 |
| LG(PD)A 1982 | Local Government (Planning and Development) Act 1982 |
| LG(PD)A 1983 | Local Government (Planning and Development) Act 1983 |
| LG(PD)A 1990 | Local Government (Planning and Development) Act 1990 |
| LG(PD)A 1992 | Local Government (Planning and Development) Act 1992 |
| LG(PD)A 1993 | Local Government (Planning and Development) Act 1993 |
| LG(PD)A 1998 | Local Government (Planning and Development) Act 1998 |
| LG(PD)A 1999 | Local Government (Planning and Development) Act |
| LG(PD)R 1994 | Local Government (Planning and Development) Regulations 1994 |
| PDA 2000 | The Planning and Development Act 2000 |
| PD(A)A | Planning and Development (Amendment) Act |
| PDR 2001 | The Planning and Development Regulations 2001 |
| PD(SI)A | Planning and Development (Strategic Infrastructure) Act |
| WMA 1996 | Waste Management Act 1996 |

## 2. Other Abbreviations

| | |
|---|---|
| ASI | Area of Scientific Interest |
| CHP | Combined Heat and Power |
| CPO | Compulsory Purchase Order |
| ECHR | European Convention on Human Rights |
| EIA | Environmental Impact Assessment |
| EIS | Environmental Impact Statement |
| EPA | Environmental Protection Agency |
| ESA | Environmentally Sensitive Area |
| IPC | Integrated Pollution Control |
| IROPI | Draft land use plans and imperative reasons of overriding public interest |
| NAOSH | National Authority for Occupational Safety and Health |
| NHA | Natural Heritage Area |
| NSS | National Spatial Strategy |
| RPGs | Regional Planning Guidelines |

| | |
|---|---|
| SAAO | Special Amenity Area Order |
| SDZ | Strategic Development Zone |
| The Board | An Bord Pleanála |
| TPO | Tree Preservation Order |

# TABLE OF CASES

## A

AA v The Medical Council [2003] 4 IR 302 ................................................................4.283
Aannemersbedrijf PK Kraaijeveld BV EA v Gedeputeerde Staten Van Zuid-Holland
   (Case C–72/95) [1996] ECR I–5403 ............ 10.08, 10.11, 10.14, 10.15, 10.38, 10.126, 10.176
Abbeydrive Developments Limited v Kildare County Council
   [2005] IEHC 209 ..............................................................................................3.111, 7.23–7.25
Abraham v Région Wallonne (Case C–2/07) [2008] ECR I–1197 .......................................10.133
Aer Rianta CPT v An Bord Pleanála [2002] IEHC 69...............................................................1.72
Aer Rianta CPT v Commissioners for Aviation Regulation [2003] IEHC 12 ........................4.178
Allnatt London Properties Ltd v Middlesex County Council
   [1964] 62 LGR 304 .....................................................................................................2.49, 3.217
Altara Developments v Ventola Limited [2005] IEHC 312 ....................................................5.154
Ampleforth Ltd (t/a Fitzwilliam Hotel) v Cherating Ltd [2003] IESC 27................................2.35
An Blascaod Mór Teo v Commissioners of Public Works in Ireland [2000] 1 IR 6 ...............1.36
Ardagh Glass Ltd v Chester City Council [2009] EWHC 745 ................................................5.29
Ardoyne House Management Co Ltd v Dublin Corporation [1998] 2 IR 147 .............4.264, 4.270
Arklow Holidays Ltd v An Bord Pleanála
   [2005] IEHC 303 ...................................................................................................................4.111
Arklow Holidays Ltd v An Bord Pleanála and Wicklow County Council
   [2006] IEHC 15 .....................................................................................................................4.257
Arklow Holidays v An Bord Pleanála (No 3) [2006] IEHC 280 ................3.71–3.71, 4.286, 4.291
Arklow Holdings v An Bord Pleanála [2007] 4 IR 112 .........................................................4.278
Arklow Holidays Limited v An Bord Pleanála [2007] IEHC 327 ..............................4.283–4.283
Arklow Holidays Limited v An Bord Pleanála [2008] IEHC 2 .............................................4.284
Arthur v Kerry County Council [2000] 3 IR 407 ...........................................................7.68–7.70
Article 26 and the Illegal Immigrants (Trafficking) Bill, 1999, re [2000] 2 IR 360 ...............4.245
Article 26 and the Constitutionality of Part V of the Planning
   and Development Bill, 1999, re [2000] 2 IR 321 .................................6.12, 7.40, 7.102, 11.57
Article 26 and the Constitutionality of Part V of the Planning
   and Development Bill 1999, re [2001] ILRM 81 ..............................................................3.142
Ashbourne Holdings Ltd v An Bord Pleanála (No 3)
   [2001] IEHC 98 ........................................................................................................3.238, 4.285
Ashbourne Holdings v An Bord Pleanala [2003] 2 IR 114 ...................................................3.238
Associated Provincial Houses Ltd v Wednesbury Corporation [1947] 2 All ER 680 ............3.210
Athlone Woollen Mills Co Ltd v Athlone Urban District Council [1950] 1 IR 1 ...................4.28
Attorney General (McGarry) v Sligo County Council
   [1991] 1 IR 99 ............................................................... 1.04, 1.72, 1.75, 2.157–2.158, 6.24
Avenue Properties Limited v Farrell Homes Limited [1982] ILRM 21 ............5.112–5.113, 5.121

## B

BAA plc v Secretary of State for Transport, Local Government and the Regions
   [2003] JPL 610 .....................................................................................................................10.79
Ballintuber Heights Ltd v Cork County Council (unreported, 21 June 2002) HC ................11.42
Ballymac Designer Village Limited v Louth County Council [2002] 3 IR 247 .....................7.76
Begley and Clarke v An Bord Pleanála, South Dublin County Council
   (unreported, 14 January 2003) HC ......................................................................................8.265

Begley and Clarke v An Bord Pleanála, South Dublin County Council
 (unreported, 23 May 2003) HC .................................................................................. 4.285, 8.265
Bellway Urban Renewal Southern v Gillespie [2003] EWCA Civ 1408 ................. 10.151–10.156
Birmingham v Birr Urban District Council [1998] IEHC 190 ................................................ 5.105
Blessington Community and District Council v Wicklow County Council
 [1997] 1 IR 273 ........................................................................................................... 3.65, 4.246
Blessington Heritage Trust v Wicklow County Council [1999] 4 IR 571 ...................... 1.02, 4.238
Boland v An Bord Pleanála [1996] 3 IR 435 ................................... 3.228, 3.254, 3.251, 4.04, 11.60
Bord Na Móna v An Bord Pleanála [1985] IR 205 ................................................................. 3.244
Bradshaw and Faulkner v Bray UDC [1906] 1 IR 560 ........................................................... 7.127
British Telecommunications plc v Gloucester City Council
 [2001] EWHC Admin 1001 ...................................................................................................10.156
British Telecommunications plc v Gloucester City Council [2002] JPL 993 ........................ 10.184
Broadnet Ireland Ltd v Offices of the Director of Telecommunications Regulations
 and Eircom plc [2000] 2 ILRM 241 ........................................................................... 4.266–4.266
Browne v An Bord Pleanála [1991] 2 IR 209 .......................................................... 10.38, 10.171
Browne v Cashel UDC (unreported, 26 March 1993) HC ....................................................... 7.76
Browne v Kerry County Council [2009] IEHC 552 ........................................................ 8.78–8.81
Bund Naturschutz in Bayern BV v Freistaat Bayern [1994] ECR 1–3717 ............................. 10.80
Burdle v Secretary of State for Environment [1972] 1 WLR 1207 ................................... 2.23, 2.46
Butler v Dublin Corporation [1999] 1 IR 505, [1999] 1 ILRM 481 ............ 2.25, 2.68, 2.88, 2.291
Byrne v Dublin County Council [1983] ILRM 213 .................................................................. 7.69
Byrne v Fingal County Council [2001] 4 IR 565 ................................................................... 2.158

## C

Cablelink Limited v An Bord Pleanála [1999] 1 IR 596 ......................................................... 11.70
Cablelink v An Bord Pleanála (unreported, 19 November 1993) HC ........................... 3.175, 11.70
Cablelink v An Bord Pleanála [1999] 1 IR 596 ..................................................................... 3.175
Cairnduff v O'Connell [1986] IR 73 ............................................................................ 2.215, 5.130
Callan v Boyle [2007] IEHC 91 ............................................................................................. 5.157
Calor Teoranta v Sligo County Council [1991] 2 IR 267 ......................................................... 1.72
Campus Oil Limited v Minister for Industry and Commerce [1983] IR 88 ........................... 5.143
Carrick Hall Holdings Ltd v Dublin Corporation [1983] ILRM 268 ........................... 2.88, 2.515
Carroll and Colley (t/a Roger Green & Sons) v Brushfield Ltd
 (unreported, 9 October 1992) HC .......................................................................................... 2.40
Carroll v Brushfield Limited (unreported, 9 October 1992) HC ........................................... 2.289
Casey v An Bord Pleanála [2004] 2 IR 296 ........................................................................... 4.216
Cavan County Council v Eircell [1999] IEHC 125 ................................................................ 5.135
Central Dublin Development Association v Attorney General
 (1975) 109 ILTR 69 ......................................................................... 1.33–1.37, 7.05–7.08, 7.101
Chambers v An Bord Pleanála [1992] 1 IR 134 .................................................................... 4.238
Charles McHugh v Kildare County Council [2009] IESC 16 ................................................ 8.350
Chaulk v R [1990] 3 SCR 1303 .............................................................................................. 7.102
Chawke Caravans Limited v Limerick Corporation
 (unreported, 20 December 1991) HC ........................................................................ 1.37, 7.63
Chief Constable of North Wales Police v Evans [1982] 1 WLR 1155 ................................... 4.171
Child v Wicklow County Council [1995] IR 425 ..................................................................... 1.54
Clarke v Brady (unreported, 30 October 1990) HC ............................................................... 2.346

# Table of Cases

Clinton v An Bord Pleanála [2005] IEHC 84,
  [2007] 1 IR 272, [2007] 4 IR 701 ................................. 4.271, 7.114–7.123, 7.127–7.129,
  7.139–7.140, 7.198
Coll v Donegal County Council (No 2) (unreported, 29 March 2007) HC ......................... 4.267
Commission of European Communities v Ireland (Case C–215/06)
  [2008] ECR I–4911 ...................... 2.102–2.104, 3.29, 4.163, 5.13–5.19, 5.29, 5.57,
  5.181, 8.50, [9.03, [9.18, 10.51, 10.52, 10.56
Commission of European Communities v Ireland (Case C–427/07)
  15 January 2009 ................................................................. 4.168, 5.18–5.19, 5.28
Commission of European Communities v Ireland (Case C–427/07)
  (Second Chamber) 16 July 2009 ................................................. 4.162–4.164, 4.183
Commission of European Communities v Ireland (Case C–215/06)
  [2008] ECR I–4911 .................................................................... 5.19, 5.28
Commission v Belgium (Case C–133/94) [1996] ECR 1–2323 ............................... 10.76
Commission v Belgium [2001] ECR 1–4605 ................................................ 3.111
Commission v Germany (Case C–431/92) [1995] ECJ I–2189 ................... 10.177–10.179
Commission v Ireland (Case C–392/96)
  [1999] ECR I–5901 ............................................. 2.128, 10.76, 10.181–10.181
Commission v Ireland (Case C–427/07) [2009] ECR 1–6227 ..................... 4.163, 10.240
Commission v Ireland (Case C–50/09) (3 March 2011)
  (First Chamber) .......................................................... 10.227, 10.230–10.253
Commission v Italy (Case C–87/02) [2005] ENV LR 21,
  (unreported, 10 June 2004) ................................................... 10.120–10.124
Commission v Spain (Case C–332/04) [2006] ECR I–40 ...................................... 10.236
Commission v Spain (Case C–227/01) [2004] ECR I–8253 .......................... 10.81, 10.127
Commission v United Kingdom (Case C–508/03) [2006] ECR 1–3969 ............ 10.238, 10.171
Commission v United Kingdom [2000] Env LR 1 ............................................... 10.174
Construction Industry Federation v Dublin City Council [2005] 2 IR 496 ................... 3.288
Construction Industry Federation v Dublin City Council [2007] 1 IR 761 .................. 3.292
Convery v Dublin County Council [1996] 3 IR 161 .................................... 11.70–11.70
Convery v Dublin County Council [1996] 3 IR 153 ............................................ 11.70
Cooper v Cork County Council [2006] IEHC 353 ............................................... 7.64
Coras Iompair Éireann v An Bord Pleanála [2008] IEHC 295 ........................ 4.145, 8.277
Cork City Council v An Bord Pleanála [2007] 1 IR 761 ............................... 3.292, 4.22
Cork Corporation v O'Connell [1978] ILRM 85 ............................................... 2.88
Cork County Council v Ardfert Quarries (unreported, 7 December 1982) HC ............... 2.32
Cork County Council v Cliftonhall Limited [2001] IEHC 85 ...................... 5.119, 5.179
Cork County Council v Shackleton and Murphy Construction (Carrigtwohill) Ltd/
  Dun Laoghaire Rathdown County Council v Glenkerrin Homes
  [2007] IEHC 241 ............................................................ 6.13, 6.65–6.68, 6.72
Crodaun Homes Ltd v Kildare County Council [1983] ILRM ................................... 3.60
Crosbie v Custom House Dock Development Authority
  [1996] 2 IR 531 ............................................................ 7.126–7.138, 7.143, 7.165
Curley v Galway Corporation [1998] IEHC 231 ................................. 5.123, 5.134, 5.155
Curley v Galway Corporation [2001] IEHC 53 .................................. 5.123, 5.134, 5.177
Cusack v Minister for Local Government (unreported, 4 November 1980) HC ............. 2.76

**D**

Daly v Revenue Commissioners [1995] 3 IR1 .................................................. 7.102
DeFaoite v An Bord Pleanála [2000] IEHC 154 ..................................... 4.251–4.253

Derrybrien Cooperative Society Limited v Saorgus Energy Limited
 [2005] IEHC 485 ................................................................................5.16, 8.50, 9.03, 9.18
Devonshire County Council v Allens Caravans (Estates Limited) [1963] 612 LGR 57 ...........2.86
Dietacaron Ltd v An Bord Pleanála [2005] 2 ILRM 32 ..................................................3.128, 4.130
Dillon v Irish Cement Limited (unreported, 26 November 1984) SC ................2.352, 5.149, 5.150
Dolan & Dolan v Cooke [2000] IEHC 158 ........................................................................2.132
Donegal County Council v O'Donnell [1982] IEHC 12 ......................................................5.176
Dooley v Galway County Council [1992] 2 IR 136 ...............................................................3.61
Drogheda Corporation v Gantley [1983] IEHC 35 ..............................................................5.164
Drogheda Port Company v Louth County Council [1997] IEHC 61 ....................................3.222
Dublin City Council v Eighty Five Development Ltd (No 2) [1993] 2 IR 392 .......................7.56
Dublin City Council v Liffey Beat Limited [2005] IR 478 ....................................................5.114
Dublin Corporation v Bentham [1993] 2 IR 58 .......................................................2.216, 5.178
Dublin Corporation v Eircom plc, Eircell Limited and An Post [2002] 3 IR 327 ................2.479
Dublin Corporation v McGinley and Shackleton (unreported, 22 January 1996) HC ..........7.18
Dublin Corporation v Kevans (unreported, 14 July 1980) HC .......................................5.09, 5.126
Dublin Corporation v Langan [1982] IEHC 36 ....................................................................2.217
Dublin Corporation v Lowe and Signways Holdings Ltd [2000] IEHC 161 ................2.31, 8.10
Dublin Corporation v Lowe and Signways Holdings Ltd
 [2004] 4 IR 259 ..................................................................................5.127, 8.10, 8.14
Dublin Corporation v McGowan [1993] 1 IR 405 ........................................................5.129, 5.131
Dublin Corporation v McGrath [1978] ILRM 208 .............................................................5.58, 5.72
Dublin Corporation v Moore [1984] ILRM 339 ............................................2.88–2.88, 2.224, 2.260
Dublin Corporation v Mulligan (unreported, 6 May 1980) HC ...........................................5.126, 7.45
Dublin Corporation v O'Callaghan [2001] IEHC 22 ..............................................................5.54
Dublin Corporation v O'Dwyer Brothers (Mount St) Ltd [1997] IEHC 77 ...........................5.133
Dublin Corporation v O'Sullivan (unreported, 21 December 1984) HC ..............................5.151
Dublin Corporation v Regan Advertising [1986] IR 171 ...........................................2.23, 2.44, 2.515
Dublin Corporation v Regan Advertising [1989] IR 61 ..............................................8.09–8.09
Dublin Corporation v Smithwick [1976–1977] 1 ILRM 280 .............................7.39, 7.52, 7.83
Dublin Corporation v Sullivan (unreported, 21 December 1984) HC ................................5.158
Dublin County Council v Eighty-Five Developments Limited
 (unreported, 31 January 1992) HC ................................................................................7.52
Dublin County Council v Eighty-Five Developments Ltd (No 2)
 [1993] 2 IR 392 .......................................................................................3.172, 7.52, 7.58
Dublin County Council v Elton Homes Limited [1984] ILRM 297 ...........................5.184–5.184
Dublin County Council v Healy and Shackleton (unreported, 3 March 1984) HC ................7.19
Dublin County Council v Kirby [1985] ILRM 325 .....................................................5.140, 5.141
Dublin County Council v Marron [1985] ILRM 593 ....................................................2.158, 3.77
Dublin County Council v O'Riordan [1985] IR 159 ...................................................5.185–5.186
Dublin County Council v Sellwood Quarries Limited [1981] ILRM 23 ......................2.88, 5.132
Dublin County Council v Tallaght Block Co Ltd [1982] ILRM 534 ..................2.62, 2.515, 5.11
Dublin County Council v Tallaght Block Co Ltd [1985] ILRM 512 .......................................2.29
Dublin County Council v Tallaght Block Co Ltd (unreported, 17 May 1983) SC ................5.181
Dun Laoghaire Corporation v Frascati Estate [1982] ILRM 493 ........................................3.226
Dun Laoghaire Corporation v Parkhill Development [1989] IR 447 ..................................5.187
Dun Laoghaire Rathdown County Council v Glenkerrin Homes [2007] IEHC 334 ...............6.68
Dundalk Town Council v Lawlor [1988] ILRM 660 ......................................................5.67, 5.99
Dundalk Town Council v Lawlor [2005] 2 ILRM 106 .......................................5.67, 5.70, 8.286

# Table of Cases

Dunne (Frank Ltd) v Dublin County Council [1974] IR 45 ................................................3.211
Dunne and McKenzie v An Bord Pleanála [2006] IEHC 400 .............................................4.264
Dunne v Minister for the Environment, Heritage and Local Government (No 2)
   [2006] IESC 49, [2007] ILRM 264 .......................................................10.159–10.162, 10.167
Dyble v Minister of Housing and Local Government and Another [1966]
   Estates Gazette, 5 February ..............................................................................................2.60

## E

Earl of Mount Charles v Westmeath County Council [1996] 3 IR 417 .....................................2.79
East Donegal Co-Operative v Attorney General [1970] IR 317 ............................................7.131
East Wicklow Conservation Community Ltd v Wicklow County Council
   [1997] 2 ILRM 72 ..............................................................................................................1.70
Ebonwood Ltd v Meath County Council [2004] 3 IR 34 ........................................................7.63
Ebonwood Ltd v Meath County Council [2004] ILRM 305 ....................................................1.37
Ecologistas en Acciòn – CODA v Ayuntamiento de Madrid (Case C–142/07)
   [2008] ECR I–6097 ..........................................................................................10.136–10.137
Eighty-Five Developments Ltd v Dublin County Council (No 1) [1993] 2 IR 378 ..................7.52
Eircell Limited v Leitrim Co Co [2000] 1 IR 479 ....................................................................3.90
Ellis v Nolan and Bray Developments Limited (in Liquidation)
   [1983] IEHC 38 .....................................................................................................5.163, 5.185
Esat Digiphone Ltd v South Dublin County Council [2002] 3 IR 585 ....................2.43, 2.518
ESB v Cork County Council [2001] IEHC 190 .......................................................................3.89
Esdell Caravan Parks Limited v Hemmel Hempstead Rural District Council
   [1996] 1 QB 895 ...............................................................................................................2.60
European Commission v Federal Republic of Germany (Case C–301/95)
   [1995] ECR I–2189 ...............................................................................................10.05, 10.07
European Communities v Ireland C–392/96 [1999] ECR I–5901 ...........................2.455, 10.76

## F

Fairyhouse v An Bord Pleanála [2001] IEHC 106 ..................................................................2.247
Fawcett Properties v Buckingham County Council [1960] 3 All ER 503 .................3.209, 3.227
Ferryhouse Club v An Bord Pleanála [1997] 1 IR 497 ...........................................................4.91
Fingal Co Co v William P Keeling & Sons Ltd [2005] 2 IR 108 ..........................................12.01
Fingal County Council v RFS Limited [2000] IEHC 163 .........................................5.153, 5.179
Fingal County Council v William P Keeling & Sons Ltd
   [2005] 2 IR 108 ....................................................................................2.102, 5.11, 5.181
Finnegan v An Bord Pleanála [1979] ILRM 134 ....................................................................4.67
Flanagan v Galway City and County Manager [1990] 2 IR 66 ...............................1.59, 3.181
Frank Dunne v Dublin County Council [1974] IR 45 ..............................................................3.174
Frescati Estates Ltd v Walker [1975] IR 177 ..............................................................3.70–3.71
Friends of the Curragh Environment Ltd v An Bord Pleanála (unreported, 14 July 2006) HC,
   [2006] IEHC 390 .................................................................................................2.136, 4.168
Furlong v AF and GW McConnell [1990] IRLM 48 ............................................................3.178

## G

G v Director of Public Prosecutions [1994] 1 IR 374 ................................................4.243, 4.252
Galway Corporation v Lackagh Rock Co Ltd [1985] IR 120 ...............2.63–2.64, 2.88, 4.145
Galway County Council v Connaught Proteins (unreported, 28 March 1980) HC .................2.53
Geraghty v Minister for Local Government [1976] IR 153 .......................................4.106, 4.264
Glancre Teo v Cafferkey (No 2) [2004] 4 IR 22 ...................................................................2.276
Glancré Teo v An Bord Pleanála [2006] IEHC 205 ..............................................................4.275

Glencar Explorations plc v Mayo County Council [2002] 1 ILRM 481 .................................5.144
Glencar Explorations plc v Mayo County Council [2002] 1 IR 84 .........................................1.319
Glenkerrin Homes v Dun Laoghaire Rathdown County Council
  [2007] IEHC 298 ................................................................................................6.57–6.57, 6.65, 6.84
Goonery v Meath County Council (unreported, 1 July 2002) SC ...........................................4.202
Gormley v EMI Records (Ireland) Ltd [1997] IEHC 221 .......................................................4.116
Grampian Regional Council v Aberdeen UDC [1983] 47 P&CR 633 ....................................3.222
Grange Development Ltd v Dublin County Council [1986] IR 246 .......................................2.158
Grange Developments Ltd v Dublin County Council (No 2) [1989] IR 296 .........3.172, 7.39, 7.69
Graves v An Bord Pleanála [1997] 2 IR 2005 ..........................................................................4.48
Grealish v An Bord Pleanála [2006] 1 ILRM 140 ..................................................................3.162
Great Portland Estates plc v Westminster City Council [1985] AC 661 .............1.84, 3.181, 3.206
Greendale Building Co v Dublin County Council [1977] 1 IR 256 ........................................5.59
Grianán an Aileach Interpretive Centre Co Ltd v Donegal County Council
  [2004] 2 IR 625 ................................................................................... 2.516–2.517, [4.143–4.143
Griffin v Galway City and County Manager
  (unreported, 31 October 1990) HC ...........................................................................1.59, 3.180
Grimes v Punchestown Developments Co Limited and MCD Promotions Limited
  [2002] 1 ILRM 409, [2002] IESC 79 .....................................5.124, 5.137, 5.144, 5.159, 5.144
Guilford RDC v Fortiscue [1959] 2 QB 112 ............................................................................2.59

# H

Harding v Cork County Council (No 2) [2006] IEHC 295 ..........................................4.263–4.263
Harding v Cork County Council (No 3) (unreported, 30 November 2006) HC ......................4.285
Harding v Cork County Council [2006] IEHC 295 ..............................4.192, 4.224–4.228, 4.232
Harding v Cork County Council [2008] IESC 27 ......................................................4.168, 4.192,
  4.209, 4.224–4.232,
  4.263, 5.62, 8.394
Harrington v An Bord Pleanála (No 1) [2005] IEHC 388 ......................................................4.207
Harrington v An Bord Pleanála (No 2) (unreported, 16 March 2006) HC ............................4.285
Hartley v Minister for Housing and Local Government [1970] 1 QB 413 ..............................2.30
Heaney v Ireland [1994] 3 IR 593 ...........................................................................6.12, 7.102, 7.130
Henderson v Henderson (1843) 3 Hare 100 ..................................................................4.283–4.286
Hickey v An Bord Pleanála [2004] IEHC 226 ..........................................................................4.63
Hoburn Homes Limited and Gortalough Holding Ltd v An Bord Pleanála
  [1993] ILRM 368 .............................................................................................................7.51, 7.59
Hogan v St Kevin's Company and Purcell [1986] IR 80 ..........................................................7.16
Hogan v Waterford County Manager (unreported, 30 April 2003) HC ................................4.217
Horne v Freeney [1982] IEHC 20 ............................................................................................2.214
Howard v Commissioner of Public Works [1994] 1 IR 101 ..................................................10.207
Huntstown Air Park Ltd v An Bord Pleanála [1999] 1 ILRM 281 ..................................4.85–4.85
Hynes v Wicklow County Council and Arklow UDC [2003] 3 IR 66 ..................................4.206

# I

Iarnród Éireann v Ireland [1996] 3 IR 312 ............................................................................7.102
Illium Properties Ltd v Dublin City Council [2004] IEHC 327 .............................................3.125
Illium Properties Ltd v Dublin City Council [2004] IEHC 403 ..............................................3.81
Irish Asphalt v An Bord Pleanála [1996] 1 ILRM 81 ...........................................................4.280
Irish Cement Ltd v An Bord Pleanála [1998] IEHC 30 ..........................................3.223, 4.249
Irish Hardware Association v South Dublin County Council [2001] 2 ILRM 291 .......3.151, 4.280

Irish Wildbird Conservancy v Clonakilty Golf and Country Club Ltd
(unreported, 23 July 1996) HC .................................................................................................2.131

## J

JA Pye (Oxford) Limited v South Gloucestershire DC [2001] EWCA Civ 450 ..........8.351, 8.352
Jackson Way Properties Ltd v Minister for the Environment
[1999] 4 IR 608 .....................................................................................................4.247, 4.270, 4.272
Jeffers v Louth County Council (unreported, 2 May 2004) HC ................................................1.72
Jerry Beades Construction Ltd v The Right Honourable Lord Mayor Aldermen
and Burgesses of the City of Dublin [2005] IEHC 406 ........................................................4.210
Johnson and Staunton Limited v Esso (Ireland) Limited [1990] 1 IR 289 ............................5.188

## K

Keane v An Bord Pleanála (unreported, 20 June 1995) HC ....................................................4.246
Keane v An Bord Pleanála (unreported, 23 May 2005) HC .....................................................4.82
Keane v An Bord Pleanála [1997] 1 IR 184 ..............................................................................4.276
Keane v An Bord Pleanála [1998] 2 ILRM 241 .............................3.70–3.71, 3.148, 3.201, 10.04
Keane v An Bord Pleanála [1998] 2 ILRM 401 .............................................................3.156–3.159
Keelgrove Properties Ltd v An Bord Pleanála [2000] I IR 47 ................................................4.206
Kelly v County Council of Leitrim and An Bord Pleanála [2005] 2 IR 404,
[2005] IEHC 11 .........................................................................................................................4.214
Kelly v Roscommon County Council [2006] IEHC 30 .............................................................3.40
Kelo v City of New London 545 US 469 (2005) ......................................................................7.132
Kenney Construction Ltd v An Bord Pleanála [2005] IEHC 306 ................................4.42, 4.110
Kenny and Hussey v An Bord Pleanála (unreported, 20 December 1984) SC .......................2.26
Kenny Homes & Co Ltd v Galway City and County Manager [1995] IR 178 ...............1.62, 2.158
Kenny v An Bord Pleanála (No 1) [2001] 1 IR 565 ..........................................3.35, 4.248, 4.256
Kenny v An Bord Pleanála [2008] IEHC 320 ..........................................................................4.185
Kenny v Dublin City Council [2004] IEHC 381 .....................................................................4.215
Keogh v Galway Corporation [1995] 3 IR 457 ...............................................................1.85, 6.25
Kerry County Council v Kerins [1996] 3 IR 493 .......................................................................6.42
Kerry County Council v Lovatt [2003] IR 589 ..........................................................................1.64
Kildare County Council v An Bord Pleanála [2006] IEHC 73 ....................................7.143, 7.178
Kildare County Council v Goode [1999] 2 IR 495 ..........................................2.07, 2.61, 2.66, 8.27
Killiney and Ballybrack Development Association Ltd v Minister
for Local Government (No 2) [1978] ILRM 78 .................................3.215, 4.107, 11.47, 4.264
Killiney and Ballybrack Development Association Ltd v Minister
Local Government and Templefinn Estates Ltd (No 1) [1978] 112 ILTR 69 ..................4.107
Kinsella v Dundalk Town Council [2004] 1 IR 545 ................................................................3.135
Kinsella v Dundalk Town Council [2004] IEHC 373 ...................................................3.135, 4.263
Klohn v An Bord Pleanála [2008] IEHC 111 ..............................................................10.110, 10.192
Kraaijeveld V Gedeputeerde Staten van Zuid-Holland (Case–72/95)
[1996] ECR 1–5403 ..................................................................................................................10.76
KSK Enterprises Ltd v An Bord Pleanála [1994] 2 IR 128 ....................................................4.189

## L

Lally v Mayo County Council (unreported, 8 February 1985) Circuit Court .......................2.158
Lambert v Lewis [1982] IEHC 24 ............................................................................................2.276
Lancefort Ltd v An Bord Pleanála
(unreported, 23 July 1997) HC ...........................................4.83, 4.108, 4.237, 4.239, 4.277, 4.285
Lancefort Ltd v An Bord Pleanála (unreported, 31 March 1998) HC ..................................4.285

Lancefort Ltd v An Bord Pleanála [1998] 2 ILRM 401 .................................................................4.83
Lancefort Ltd v An Bord Pleanála [1998] 2 IR 511 ...................................................................4.108
Lancefort Ltd v An Bord Pleanála [1999] 2 IR 270 .........................................................4.237, 4.239
Langarth Properties Ltd v Bray UDC (unreported, 25 June 2001) HC ...............3.269, 8.354–8.355
Lanigan t/a Tullamaine Castle Stud v Michael Barry t/a Tipperary Recovery
    and Tipperary County Council [2008] IEHC 29 ..................................................................5.170
Law v Minister for Local Government (unreported, 30 May 1974) HC ...................................4.264
Lee v O'Riordan (unreported, 10 February 1995) HC .......................................................2.33, 8.30
Leech v Reilly [1983] IEHC 65 ..................................................................................................5.116
Leen v Aer Rianta [2003] 4 IR 394 .............................................................................................5.136
Lennon v Kingdom Plant Hire Limited (unreported, 13 December 1991) HC ..........................2.230
Lennon v Limerick County Council [2006] IEHC 112 ................................................................4.40
Liddy v Minister for Public Enterprise, Irish Aviation Authority,
    Aer Rianta Teoranta Ireland and the Attorney General [2004] 1 ILRM 9 .........................7.101
Limerick County Council v Tobin (unreported, 15 August 2005) HC .......................................5.161
Limerick County v Joseph Tobin t/a Harry Tobin Sand and Gravel
    [2005] IEHC 281 .......................................................................................................5.143–5.145
Linehan v Cork County Council [2008] IEHC 76 ................................................4.83, 4.202, 4.258
Lucas (F) & Sons Ltd v Dorking and Horley RDC [1960] 59 LGR 132 ...................................3.221
Luggalla (Byrne v Commissioners of Public Works)
    (unreported, 3 December 1994) HC .....................................................................................2.181
Luxembourg v Linster (Case C287/98) [2000] ECR I–6917 .........................................2.133, 10.73
Lynch v Dublin City Council (unreported, 25 July 2003) HC .............................3.99, 4.15, 4.218

## M

MacPharthalain v Commissioners of Public Works [1992] 1 IR 111,
    [1994] 3 IR 353 ............................................................................................................7.03] 7.03
Maher v An Bord Pleanála [1993] 1 IR 439 ...............................................................................3.146
Maher v An Bord Pleanála [1999] 2 ILRM 198 .............................................2.135, 10.40, 10.132
Mahon v Butler [1997] 3 IR 369, [1998] 1 ILRM 284 .....................................5.104, 5.140, 8.142
Mahon v Irish Rugby Football Union [1997] ILRM 446 ................................................5.104, 5.162
Marry v Connaughton [1984] IEHC 74 ..........................................................................5.117, 5.180
Marshall v Arklow Town Council [2004] 4 IR 92 ..............................................3.44, 4.208, 4.215
Martin v An Bord Pleanála [2007] IESC 23 ....................................................10.10, 10.232, 10.242
Mason and McCarthy v KTK Sand and Gravel Ltd [2004] IEHC 183 .......................................5.03
Max Developments Ltd v An Bord Pleanála [1994] 2 IR 121] ........................................4.84, 4.85
McAnenley v An Bord Pleanála and Monaghan County Council [2002] 2 IR 763 ........4.50, 4.264
McBride v Galway Corporation [1998] 1 IR 485 ...........................................................10.11, 10.36
McCabe v CIÉ and Irish Rail [2007] 2 IR 392 ..............................................................2.214, 8.278
McCabe v Harding Investments Ltd [1984] ILRM 763 ...............................................................3.70
McCann v An Bord Pleanála [1997] 1 ILRM 264 .....................................................................4.206
McDonagh and Sons Ltd v Galway Corporation [1995] 1 IR 191 ............................................3.165
McEvoy and Smith v Meath County Council
    [2003] 1 IR 208 ...................................................................1.305, 4.101, 4.187, 7.180, 8.272
McGoldrick v An Bord Pleanála [1997] IR 497 ........................................................................4.264
McGrath Limestone Works Ltd v Galway County Council [1989] ILRM 602 ..........................8.32
McMahon v Dublin Corporation [1996] 3 IR 509 .......................................................................2.77
McMahon v Dublin Corporation [1997] 1 ILRM 227 ................................................................4.143
McNamara v An Bord Pleanála [1995] 2 ILRM 125 .................................................................4.244

## Table of Cases

Meath County Council v Beachmount Homes and Thomas McCluskey
 (unreported, 11 May 1987) HC .................................................................................. 5.187
Meath County Council v Daly [1987] IR 391 ............................................................... 2.34
Meath County Council v Shiels [2008] IEHC 355 ........................................... 4.146, 4.150
Methuen-Campbell v Walters [1979] 1 All ER 606 ......................................... 8.266–8.266
MF Quirke & Sons v Maher [2008] IEHC 428 ............................................................. 8.87
MF Quirke and Ors v An Bord Pleanála [2009] IEHC 429 ............................... 8.82–8.86
Minister for Housing and Local Government v Hartnell [1965] 1 All ER 490 ......... 2.50, 3.219
Molloy & Walsh v Dublin County Council [1990] ILRM 633 ................................... 3.113
Molloy v Minister for Justice, Equality and Law Reform [2004] 2 IR 493 ................ 2.26
Molloy v Dublin County Council (unreported, 16 July 2005) HC .......................... 3.111
Molloy v Dublin County Council [1990] 1 IR 90 .......................................... 3.78, 3.110
Molumby v Kearns [1999] IEHC 86 ...................................................... 2.37, 2.271, 5.153
Monaghan County Council v Brogan [1987] IR 333 ................................ 2.14, 2.64, 2.81, 2.82
Monaghan UDC v Alf-a-Bet Promotions Ltd [1980] ILRM 64, 249 ................. 3.68, 3.78
Monopower v Monaghan County Council [2006] IEHC 253 ..................................... 4.220
Morris v Garvey [1983] IR 319 ..................................................................................... 5.122
Mount Charles (Earl of) v Meath County Council [1996] 3 IR 417 ........................... 8.141
Mountbrook Homes Limited v Oldcourt Developments Limited [2005] IEHC 171 ......... 5.120
Mulcreevy v Minister for the Environment, Heritage and Local Government
 [2004] 1 IR 72 ........................................................................................................... 8.269
Mulhall v An Bord Pleanála (unreported, 10 June 1996) HC ...................................... 4.246
Mulholland and Kinsella v An Bord Pleanála (No 1) [2005] IEHC 188 .................... 4.182
Mulholland and Kinsella v An Bord Pleanála (No 2) [2005] 1 ILRM 287 ................. 4.109
Mulholland v An Bord Pleanála (No 2) [2006] 1 IR 453 ............................................ 4.246
Mullaghmore (Howard v Commissioners of Public Works) [1994] 3 IR 394 .............. 2.181
Murphy v Cobh Town Council and Anor [2006] IEHC 324 ........................................ 4.45
Murphy v Wicklow County Council [1999] IEHC 225 .............................................. 4.234

### N

Neville v An Bord Pleanála (No 2) [2001] IEHC 145 ................................................ 4.274
Ní Ghruagain v An Bord Pleanála (unreported, 19 June 2003) HC ............................ 4.281
North Wall Quay Property Holdings Co Ltd v Dublin Docklands Development Authority
 [2008] IEHC 305 ...................................................................................................... 4.194

### O

Ó Nualláin v Dublin Corporation [1999] 4 IR 137 ................................... 10.126, 10.184
O'Brien v Dun Laoghaire/Rathdown County Council [2006] IEHC 177 ................... 4.240
O'Callaghan v Commissioners of Public Works in Ireland [1993] ILRM 391,
 [1995] ILRM 364 ............................................................................................ 8.25, 8.407
O'Connell v Environmental Protection Agency [2002] 1 ILRM 1 ............................. 4.269
O'Connell v Environmental Protection Agency [2003] 1 IR 530 .................... 10.232, 10.241
O'Connor v An Bord Pleanála [2008] IEHC 13 ................................... 2.521, 4.35, 4.43
O'Connor v Clare County Council (unreported, 11 February 1994) HC ............ 1.72, 7.61–7.62
O'Connor v Dublin Corporation [2000] IEHC 68 ....................................... 10.49, 11.61
O'Connor v Frank Hetherington Limited (unreported, 28 May 1987) HC ................ 5.130
O'Connor's Downtown Properties Ltd v Nenagh UDC [1993] 1 IR 1 ............. 3.80, 3.130
O'Dea v The Minister for Local Government and Dublin County Council
 [1991] 91 ILTR 169 ................................................................................................... 4.28
O'Keefe v An Bord Pleanála [1993] 1 IR 39 ........................ 1.65, 4.18, 4.143, 4.176–4.178,
 4.221, 5.54, 7.178–7.178, 8.77, 10.192, 11.52

O'Leary v Dublin County Council [1998] IR 150 .................................................................2.158
O'Reilly Brothers (Wicklow) Ltd v Wicklow County Council [2006] IEHC 363 .........2.520, 4.39
O'Reilly v Cassidy [1995] 1 ILRM 306 ..................................................................4.252–4.255
O'Shea v Kerry County Council [2003] 4 IR 143 ........................................................4.214, 4.231
Openneer v Donegal County Council [2006] 1 ILRM 150 ......................................................4.215

## P

P v Minister for Justice Equality and Law Reform [2002] I ILRM 16 ..................................4.255
Palmerlane Ltd v An Bord Pleanála [1999] 2 ILRM 514 .......................................................4.143
Patterson v Murphy and Trading Services Limited [1978] ILRM 85 ......................................2.61
Pearce v Westmeath County Council (unreported, 19 December 2008) HC ............................8.77
Peter Sweetman v Shell E & P Ireland Limited [2006] IEHC 85 .........................................5.152
Petticoat Lane Rentals Limited v Secretary of State for the Environment
    [1971] 1 All ER 793 ............................................................................................................2.51
Pine Valley Developments Ltd) v Dublin County Council [1994] IR 407 ............................2.158
Pioneer Aggregates Limited v Secretary of State for the Environment [1985] AC 132 .........2.26
Power Securities Ltd v Daly [1984] IEHC 88 ..........................................................................7.17
Prest v Secretary of State for Wales (1982) 81 LGR 193 ......................................................7.140
Pyx Granite v Minister for Housing and Local Government [1958] 1 QB 554 ....................3.208

## R

R (on the application of Delena Wells) v Secretary of State for Transport,
    Local Government and the Regions (Case C–201/02)
    [2004] ECR I–723 .............................................................................10.165, 10.168–10.171
R (Blewett) v Derbyshire County Council [2004] Env LR 29 ..............................................10.145
R (Lebus) v South Cambridgeshire District Council [2002] EWHC 2009 Admin ...............10.156
R (on the application of Edwards) v Environmental Agency [2008] UKHL 22,
    [2006] EWCA Civ 877 .....................................................................................10.138–10.146
R (on the application of Dickens) v Aylesbury DC [2008] JPL 1575 ..................................10.149
R (on the application of Porkopp) v London Underground Limited
    [2003] EWCA Civ 961, [2004] 1 P&C R 479 ....................................................10.161, 10.175
R (Wells) v Secretary of State for Transport, Local Government and the Regions
    (Case C–201/02) [2004] ECR 1–723 ..............................................................................10.161
R v Derbyshire County Council ex parte North East Derbyshire District Council
    [1997] 77 LGR 389 ............................................................................................................5.03
R v Hillingdon LBC Exp Royco Homes Ltd (No 2) [1974] 2 All ER 643 .............................3.214
R v North Yorkshire County Council ex parte Browne [2000] 1 AC 397 ..............10.161, 10.170
R v Rochdale Metropolitan Borough Council ex parte Milne [2001] JPL 470 ...................10.173
Radio Tara Ltd [1992] ILRM 237 ...........................................................................................2.83
Raiu v Refugee Appeals Tribunal [2003] 2 IR 63 .......................................................4.278, 4.285
Readymix (Eire) v Dublin Co Co (unreported, 30 July 1974) SC ............................................2.72
Rehabilitation Institute v An Bord Pleanála [1988] 6 ILT 193 ...................2.42, 2.88, 2.137, 2.271
Rehabilitation Institute v Dublin Corporation (unreported, 14 January 1988) HC ..................2.25
Roadstone Provinces Ltd v An Bord Pleanála [2008] IEHC 210 (4 July 2008) ....................4.145
Roughan v Clare County Council (unreported, 18 December 1996) HC ................1.56–1.57, 6.26
Rugby Football Union v Secretary of State for Transport [2003] JPL 96 ..........................2.282
Ryan v Roadstone [2006] IEHC 53..........................................................................................5.149
Ryanair v An Bord Pleanála [2004] 2 IR 334 ..............................................................3.254, 4.62
Rylands v Fletcher (1868) LR 3 HL 330 ..................................................................................2.07

# Table of Cases

## S

Salafia v The Minister for the Environment, Heritage and Local Government
 (unreported, 1 March 2006) HC ..................................................................................4.235
Sandyford Environmental Planning & Road Safety Group Ltd v Dun Laoghaire
 Rathdown County Council [2004] IEHC 133 ..............................................................1.109
Sanofi-Aventis Belgiu (Case C–472/07) ..........................................................................4.164
Scarrif v Commissioners of Public Works (unreported, 15 March 1995) HC ..................5.128
Scott v An Bord Pleanála [1995] 1 ILRM 424 ............................................2.07, 4.250, 4.271
Seery v An Bord Pleanála (unreported, 26 November 2003) HC ......................................3.77
Seery v An Bord Pleanála [2001] 2 ILRM 151 ....................................................4.266–4.266
Shannon Regional Fisheries Board v An Bord Pleanála [1994] 3 IR 449 .......................10.09
Sharpe (P & F) Ltd v Dublin City and County Manager [1989] IR 701,
 [1989] ILRM 565 .........................................................1.50–1.55, 1.61, 2.158, 3.169, 4.262
Sherwin v An Bord Pleanála [2007] IEHC 227 ................................................................8.271
Simonovich v An Bord Pleanála (unreported, 23 April 1993) HC ...................................4.264
Simonovich v An Bord Pleanála (unreported, 24 July 1998) HC .....................................1.110
Sinclair-Lockhart's Trustees v Central Land Board [1950] 1 P&CR 195, (1951) SC 258 .....2.223,
 8.265
Sligo County Council v Gavin Martin [2007] IEHC 178 (24 May 2007) ........................2.07
Sloan v An Bord Pleanála, Louth County Council and National Roads Authority
 [2003] 2 ILRM 61 ..........................................................................................................4.83
Slough Estates Ltd v Slough Borough Council [1962] 2 All ER 988 .............................3.221
Smyth v Colgan [1999] 1 IR 548 ....................................................................................2.225
South Dublin County Council v Balfe
 (unreported, 3 November 1995) HC ..........................................................5.147, 5.158, 5.172
South Dublin County Council v Fallowvale Ltd [2005] IEHC 408 ........2.327, 2.343, 5.148, 5.150
Stack v An Bord Pleanála [2000] IEHC 155 .....................................................................4.91
Stack v An Bord Pleanála, Kerry County Council and McKiernan
 (unreported, 7 March 2003) HC ...................................................................................4.90
Stafford and Bates v Roadstone Limited [1980] ILRM 221 ..........................................2.515
Stafford v Roadstone Ltd [1980] ILRM 1 .......................................................5.113, 2.88, 8.31
State (Abenglen Properties Ltd) v Dublin Corporation
 [1984] IR 381 ..................................................................................3.127, 4.260–4.261, 10.133
State (Boyd) v Cork County Council [1983] IEHC 8 ....................................................3.155
State (Conlon Construction Ltd) v Cork County Council
 (unreported, 31 July 1975) HC ..........................................................................3.80, 3.131
State (Davidson) v Farrell [1960] IR 438 .......................................................................4.259
State (Finglas Industrial Estates) v Dublin County Council
 (unreported, 17 March 1983) SC ..................................................................................3.66
State (Fitzgerald) v An Bord Pleanála [1985] ILRM 117 .................................2.102, [9.02
State (Havarty) v An Bord Pleanála [1987] IR 485 ........................................................4.64
State (Keegan) v Stardust Compensation Tribunal [1986] IR 642 ...................2.83, 4.176–4.177
State (Keegan) v Stardust Compensation Tribunal [1987] ILRM 202 ..........................1.53
State (Kenny and Hussey) v An Bord Pleanála and Meenan
 (unreported, 20 December 1984) SC ..........................................................................3.151
State (Lynch) v Cooney [1982] IR 337 ...........................................................................5.51
State (NCE Ltd) v Dublin County Council [1979] ILRM 249 ............................3.64, 3.132
State (Pine Valley Development Ltd) v Dublin County Council [1984] 1 IR 407 ........3.113
State (Sweeney) v Minister for the Environment [1979] ILRM 35 ..............................3.149

xxxiii

State (Tern Houses (Brennanstown) Ltd) v An Bord Pleanála [1985] IR 725 .........................3.161
State (Toft) v Galway Corporation [1981] ILRM 439 ................................................................3.65
Sweetman v An Bord Pleanála (No 1) [2007] 2 ILRM 328 ......................................................4.185
Sweetman v An Bord Pleanála [2007] IEHC 361 ....................................................................4.168
Swords Cloghran Properties v Fingal County Council (unreported, 29 June 2006) HC ...........4.26

## T

Talbot v An Bord Pleanála [2009] 1 ILRM 356 ........................................................................4.292
Tennyson v Dun Laoghaire Corporation [1991] 2 IR 527 ......................................1.72, 1.75, 2.158
Times Newspapers Limited v United Kingdom (1979) 2 EHRR 245 ......................................7.102
Tralee UDC v Stack [1984] IEHC 106 .......................................................................................2.229
Trentham v Gloucestershire County Council [1996] 1 WLR 506 .............................................2.23

## U

Usk and District Residents Association Ltd v An Bord Pleanála [2007] 2 ILRM 378 ............4.288
Usk and District Residents Association Ltd v An Bord Pleanála,
  Ireland and the Attorney General [2009] IEHC 346 .............................................................4.195
Usk and District Residents Association v Environmental Protection Agency
  [2007] IEHC 30 .....................................................................................................................4.185

## V

Veolia Water UK plc v Fingal County Council [2006] IEHC 137 ...........................................4.185
Village Residents Association Limited (No 2) [2000] 4 IR 321, [2001] 2 ILRM 22 ..............4.285
Village Residents Association Limited v An Bord Pleanála [2000] 1 IR 65 ..................4.256, 9.02

## W

Waddington v An Bord Pleanála [2000] IEHC 110 ..................................................................10.48
Waterford County Council v John A Wood Ltd [1999] 1 IR 556 .......................5.140, 8.29, 8.33
Webb v Ireland [1988] IR 353 .....................................................................................................8.22
Webber v Minister of Housing and Local Government [1968] ILR 29 ....................................2.25
Weir v Dublin Corporation [1983] IR 242 .......................................................................11.70–11.70
Westmeath County Council v Quirke & Sons (unreported, 23 May 1996) HC .........................2.81
Westmeath County Council v Quirke & Sons
  (unreported, 28 June 1996) HC .........................................................................2.36, 2.70, 2.271
Weston v An Bord Pleanála [2008] IEHC 71 ..............................................................................3.26
Westport UDC v Golden [2002] 1 ILRM 439 ................................................................5.105, 5.152
Westport Urban District Council v Golden [2002] 1 ILRM 439 ..............................................2.288
White v Dublin City Council [2004] 1 IR 545 ..........................................................................4.210
White v Dublin Corporation [2002] IEHC 68 ...............................................................4.98, 4.130
White v McInerney Construction Limited [1995] ILRM 374 ...................................................5.113
Wicklow County Council v Forest Fencing Limited t/a Abwood Homes
  [2007] IEHC 242 ....................................................................................................................5.146
Wicklow Heritage Trust Ltd v Wicklow County Council
  [1998] IEHC 19 ..............................................................................................................1.76, 6.26
Williams v Minister for Housing and Local Government [1967] 65 LGR 495 Dib CT ............2.47
Wilson v West Sussex County Council [1963] 2 QR 764 ..........................................................2.86
Wood (J) & Co Limited v Wicklow County Council [1995] ILRM 51 ....................................7.58
Wood v Secretary of State for the Environment [1973] 1 WLR 707 ........................................2.24
World Wildlife Fund (WWF) v Autonome Provinz Bozen
  (Case C–435/97) [1998] ECR I–5613 .......................10.14, 10.36–10.38, 10.67–10.72, 10.156

## X

XJ's Investments Ltd v Dun Laoghaire Corporation [1996] IR 750 ..........................................1.75

# TABLE OF STATUTES

## A

Acquisition of Land (Assessment of
  Compensation) Act 1919 ............ 2.183,
             6.81, 7.10, 7.205, 8.312

   s 2   (2) ........................................ 6.80
   6 .......................................... 7.12, 7.13

Air Navigation and Transport
  Act 1950 ........................................ 7.101
   s 14 ............................................... 7.101

Air Navigation and Transport (Amendment)
  Act 1998 ............................. 7.141, 7.145

Air Pollution Act 1987 .............. 3.158, 8.71,
                    12.08, 12.48
   s 26 ............................................... 2.345

Arbitration Act 2010 ............................ 7.13
   s 29   (1) ........................................ 7.14
   34 ................................................. 6.88
   Sch .................................................. 7.13

Arterial Drainage Act 1945
  Pt II ............................................... 2.477

Arterial Drainage (Amendment)
  Act 1995 ....................................... 2.477

Auctioneers and House Agents
  Act 1947–1973 ............................. 2.226

## B

Betting Act 1931 ...................... 2.235, 2.275

Blascaod Mór National Historic Park
  Act 1989 .......................................... 1.36

British–Irish Agreement
  Act 1999 ........................................ 2.166
  Annex 1 Pt 1 .................................. 4.12

Building Control
  Act 1990 ........................... 12.01, 12.04
   s 22 ............................................... 12.17

Building Control Acts
  1990–2007 ......................... 12.08, 12.48

## C

Capital Acquisitions Tax Act 1976 ....... 6.75
   s 15 .................................................. 6.75
      (1) ................................................ 6.76
   25 .................................................... 6.76

Casual Trading Act 1995 .................... 2.226
   s 1–2 .............................................. 2.226
   6 ..................................................... 2.226

City and County Management
  (Amendment) Act 1955 ......... 1.49, 1.70
   s 3 .................................................... 1.70
   4 ............................................. 1.45, 1.50

Civil Liability and Courts Act 2004
   s 53 ................................................ 5.107
      (1) ..................................... 1.244
      (2) ................................................ 5.107

Companies Act 1990
   s 26   (3) ........................................ 8.328
   27   (1) ........................................ 8.328
   140   (5) ...................................... 8.328

Companies Acts 1963–2009 ................. 3.64

Control of Dogs Acts 1986
  and 1992 ...................................... 3.241

Credit Institutions (Financial Support)
  Act 2008 ....................................... 7.201

## D

Dangerous Substances Acts
  1972–1979 .................................... 12.48

Data Protection Acts 1998
  and 2003 ........................... 3.118, 4.113

Derelict Sites Act 1990 ............. 2.93, 2.110,
                2.484, 7.134, 8.125, 8.137
   s 3 ..................................... 8.127–8.127
   6   (4) ........................................ 8.133
   8 ..................................................... 8.128
      (5) ................................................ 8.129

Derelict Sites Act 1990 (contd)
    s 9 .................................................. 8.130
    10 .................................................. 8.131
    11 ................... 2.484, 8.128–8.134,
                                   8.140, 8.314
    12 .................................................. 8.140
    13 .................................................... 7.58
    14 .................................................. 8.138
    15 ........................................ 8.138, 8.139
    16 ........................................ 8.138, 8.139
    22 .................................................. 8.135
    23 .................................................. 8.136
    24 .................................................. 8.136
    28   (1) .......................................... 8.133
           (2) .......................................... 8.134
    29 .................................................. 8.133
    30   (4) .......................................... 8.133
    32   (3) .......................................... 8.133
    Pt III .............................................. 8.135

Derelict Sites Acts 1990–2000 ............ 12.08

Dublin Corporation Act 1890 .............. 12.17

Dublin Docklands Development Authority
    Act 1997 .................. 2.93, 2.110, 7.134
    s 25 ....................... 2.484, 3.296, 4.194
    26 .................................................. 2.484

Dublin Transport Authority
    Act 2008 ............................ 1.160, 1.327
    s 31B ................................................ 1.144
    31C .................................................. 1.144
    86 .................................................... 1.185
    89 .................................................... 1.276
    91 ........................................ 1.298, 1.300
    93 .................................................... 1.160
    94 .......................................... 7.58, 7.58
    95 .................................................... 1.144

Public Transport Regulation Act 2009
    s 44 .................................................. 1.300

### E

Education Act 1998 ............................. 2.235

Electricity Regulation
    Act 1999 ................ 2.235, 11.06, 11.11
    s 2   (1) .......................................... 11.06
    13A (1) ........................................... 11.11
    13A (1) ........................................... 11.11
    13AA ............................................... 11.11

    13I .................................................... 11.11
    13J .................................................... 11.11
    s 13L ............................................... 11.11
    13N .................................................. 11.11
    13P .................................................. 11.11
    13Z .................................................. 11.11
    13I–13J............................................ 11.11

Environment and Local Government
(Performance of Certain Functions)
Act 2002 ........................................ 3.255

Environmental Protection Act
1990 (UK) .................................... 10.139

Environmental Protection Agency
    Act 1992 ................ 3.138, 3.157, 3.241
    s 84   (4) (a) ..................... 2.476, 2.483
    86   (8) ........................................ 2.237
    98 .................................................... 3.156
    99   (f) ........................................ 3.137
    107 .................................................. 3.241
    Pt IV ............................................... 2.237

European Communities
    Act 1972 ..................... 3.23, 9.60, 9.90

European Communities
    Acts 1972–2007 ........................... 12.48

Environmental Protection Agency
    Acts 1992–2003 ............... 10.125, 12.08

European Convention on Human Rights
    Act 2003 ........................... 3.205, 5.102

### F

Factories Act 1955 ............................... 12.48

Finance (1909–1910)
    Act 1910 ........................... 2.235, 2.273

Fisheries (Consolidation)
    Acts 1959–2003 ............................ 12.48

Fisheries Acts 1959–1990 .................... 12.08

Fisheries and Foreshore (Amendment)
    Act 1998 ........................................ 2.370

Fisheries (Amendment) Act 1997 ........ 2.370

Foreshore Act 1933 ................... 2.113, 2.116
    s 1 ....................................... 2.113, 2.116
    1A ...................................................... 2.116

# Table of Statutes

Foreshore Acts
   1993–1998 ........................ 2.113, 2.115

Forestry Act 1946
   s 19 .............................................. 12.50
      21 .............................................. 12.50

Freedom of Information Act 1997 ....... 4.113

## G

Gas Act 1976 ................. 3.202, 7.141, 7.144
   s 8 ................................................ 2.317
      26 .............................................. 11.07
      40 ............................................... 2.317

Gas (Amendment) Act 1987
   s 2 ................................................ 2.317

Gas (Amendment) Act 2000
   s 20 .............................................. 11.07

Grangegorman Development Agency
   Act 2005
   s 42 .............................................. 1.193

## H

Harbours Act 1946 ............................... 7.45
   s 134 ........................................... 2.316

Harbours Act 1996 ............................. 7.146
   s 16 ............................................. 7.147
   Sch 4 ........................................... 7.147

Harbours (Amendment) Act 2009 ....... 7.146
   s 7    (3) ..................................... 7.147

Health Act 1970 ................................... 7.45

Housing of Working Classes
   Acts 1890–1958 .......................... 7.194

Housing Act 1966 .............................. 7.154
   s 76 ............................................. 7.134
      77 ............................................. 7.134
      78 ............................................. 7.134
      78 ............................................. 7.160
          (1) .................................... 7.156
          (2), (4) ............................. 4.193
      80 ............................................. 7.134
      86 .................................. 7.120, 7.134
   Sch 3 ................................ 7.134, 7.154

Housing Act 1988
   s 9    (2) .............................. 6.20, 6.27,
                                    6.29, 6.104
      13 ................................................ 6.20

Housing (Miscellaneous Provisions) Act
   1992
   s 2 ................................................ 6.128
      6 ....................................... 6.89, 6.104

Housing (Miscellaneous Provisions)
   Act 2004
   s 2 ................................................ 3.255

Housing (Miscellaneous Provisions) Act
   2009
   s 2 .................................................. 6.52
      7 ................................................ 6.140
      78 .............................................. 6.140
      78–96 ........................................ 6.138
      79 ................................... 6.140–6.145,
                                 6.157–6.160
      80 ................................... 6.145, 6.160
      81 ................................. 6.152–6.162
      82 .............................................. 6.140
      83 ................................. 6.143–6.143
      84 ................................. 6.145–6.149
      85 .............................................. 6.156
      86 .............................................. 6.144
      90 .............................................. 6.143
      94 .............................................. 6.140
      95    (1) ..................................... 6.152
      99    (4) ..................................... 6.159
   Pt 5 ................................. 6.137–6.140
      V ................................................ 6.153
      5 ................................... 6.139, 6.149

Housing (Traveller Accommodation)
   Act 1998 ....................................... 2.159

Housing Acts 1966–1998 .................... 6.165

Housing Acts 1966–2002 ........... 6.92, 6.102

## I

Interpretation Act 1937
   s 11    (h) ........................................ 4.83

Interpretation Act 2005
   s 18    (a) ...................................... 11.62

## L

Land and Conveyancing Law Reform
Act 2009
s 8 (1) ..................................... 3.255

Land Reclamation
Act 1949 ........................... 2.227–2.229
s 1 ................................................. 2.228

Landlord and Tenants Acts
1967–1994 ................................... 7.111

Lands Clauses Consolidation Act 1845
s 123 ............................................ 7.157

Local Government (Ireland)
Act 1898
s 10 .................................. 7.114, 7.134

Local Government Act 1925
s 68 .............................................. 7.134
Sch 6 ............................................ 7.134

Local Government Act 1941 ................. 7.45

Local Government (No 2)
Act 1960 ....................................... 7.194
s 10 ...................... 7.120, 7.134, 7.194
  (2) .................................... 7.194
11 .............................................. 7.114

Local Government (Planning and
Development)
Act 1963 .................... 2.03, 2.71, 2.110,
2.128, 2.219, 2.236,
2.482, 3.04, 3.15, 3.90,
4.67, 4.82, 4.259,
4.264, 5.129, 7.05,
7.54, 7.101, 8.11–8.13,
8.26–8.28, 8.39,
8.59, 8.69, 8.83, 8.104, 12.57
s 2 ...................................... 8.11
3 ................................................ 8.11
4 .................. 2.03–2.03, 2.109–2.111,
2.219, 2.229
  (1) (g) ............................... 8.13
5 ................................................ 12.19
7 ................................................ 5.72
24 ............................................... 2.181
  (f) ........................................ 8.29
26 ............................................... 3.238
  (3) ..................................... 1.254

s 28 (2) ....................................... 2.102
30 ................................................ 3.89
36 ................................................ 3.238
38 ................................................ 8.350
42 ................................................ 3.182
43 ................................................ 3.182
45 ................................................ 8.401
55 ....................................... 7.49, 7.54
56 ................................................ 7.55
57 ................................................ 7.69
82 ................................................ 4.259
  (3B)(a) (i) ............................ 4.211
92 ................................................ 2.03
Pt IV ............... 2.03, 2.61, 2.109–2.112,
2.474, 3.10, 3.167, 8.41,
8.42, 8.69, 8.93–8.101,
8.117–8.122, 8.144, 8.185,
8.320, 8.384, 8.393
VI ............................ 7.47, 7.58–7.58

Local Government (Planning and
Development)
Act 1976 ................... 2.289, 3.04, 3.202,
4.67, 4.210, 5.139, 5.172
s 5 ............................. 3.201, 4.101
25 ................................................ 7.209
27 .................... 2.53, 2.61, 2.88, 2.288,
5.104, 5.111–5.113, 5.129,
5.137–5.140, 5.158, 5.163,
5.184, 8.31, 8.142, 9.01
  (1) ................... 2.88, 5.141, 8.272
  (2) ....................................... 5.163
40 ................................................ 3.182

Local Government (Planning
and Development)
Act 1990 .......................... 7.06, 7.38
s 1 (1) ...................................... 8.265
13 ......................................... 7.58, 7.76
21 ................................................ 8.406
45 ................................................ 8.406
Sch 3–5 ....................................... 7.07

Local Government (Reorganisation)
Act 1985
s 9 ................................................ 2.473

Local Government (Sanitary Services)
Act 1964
s 3 (1) ...................................... 8.314
7–9 ......................................... 7.134

# Table of Statutes

Local Government (Sanitary Services)
Act 1964 (contd)
s 16 ............................................... 7.134
34 ............................................... 2.345

Local Government (Water Pollution)
Act 1977 ............................... 8.71, 12.48
s 11 .................................................... 7.49
12 .................................... 2.345–2.346

Local Government Act 1991
s 43 ................................................. 1.269
45 ................................................. 1.254
50 ...................................... 3.294, 5.77

Local Government (Planning and
Development) Act 1992
s 19 (3) ....................................... 4.259

Local Government (Planning and
Development) Act 1993
s 4 (1) ....................................... 2.181

Local Government Act 1994
s 65 ................................................. 4.114

Local Government (Water Pollution)
Act 1997 ........................................ 3.158

Local Government (Planning and
Development) Acts
1963–1999 .................................... 3.138

Local Government (Planning
and Development)
Acts 2000–2010 ........................... 12.48

Local Government
Act 2001 ......... 1.29, 1.45, 1.49–1.50,
1.61, 2.180, 4.71, 7.98–
7.102, 9.70, 9.113
s 18 (1) (b) ............................... 7.104
43 ....................... 9.102, 9.113, 10.66
139 .............................................. 1.68
140 1.45, 1.49–1.53, 1.59–1.68, 1.254
(1) .............................. 1.50, 4.09
(2) (a) ................................. 4.09
(10) ..................................... 1.67
183 ................................. 7.104–7.108
247 ............................... 1.112, 2.102,
2.147, 2.211, 4.174,
4.218, 5.06, 5.46,
5.79–5.80, 5.97,
5.157, 7.110
(d) ........................................ 4.95
(k) .......................... 7.186, 7.193
(m) .............................. 7.58, 7.58
Sch 4 ....................... 1.71, 1.170, 2.211

Local Government (No 2) Act 2003
s 5 ................. 3.255, 6.105, 6.109, 6.116

Litter Act 1982 ..................................... 12.48

## M

Maritime Safety Act 2005
s 60 ................................................ 2.116

Mineral Development Act 1940
s 44–47 .......................................... 8.251

Minerals Development Act 1979 ......... 8.247

Minerals Development Acts
1940–1955 ...................................... 4.12

Minerals Development Acts
1940–1999 ................ 2.166, 2.434, 4.12

Mines and Quarries Act 1965
s 3 (2) .......................................... 8.72

Minister for the Environment and Local
Government (Performance of Certain
Functions) Act 2002 ..................... 1.325
s 1 ................................................. 1.324

Ministers and Secretaries (Amendment)
Act 1939
s 6 (1) ....................................... 1.325

## N

National Asset Management Agency Act
2009 ............................................. 7.198
s 2 ................................................ 7.201
10 (1) ..................................... 7.202
158 ............................... 7.198–7.199
(1)–(2) ....................... 7.202
159 ............................................ 7.198
238 ............................................ 2.101

National Monuments Act 1930
s 2 ................................................ 8.15
14 (1) ................................... 10.250
23 ............................................... 8.18
25 ............................................... 8.16

xxxix

National Monuments Act 1930 (contd)
  s 26 ...................... 2.240, 2.348, 2.479,
                                    8.16–8.21
    (3) ........................................ 8.15

National Monuments (Amendment)
  Act 1987
  s 2 ........................................... 8.23
    5 .................. 2.166, 4.12, 7.58, 7.126
    10 (2) (c) ................................ 7.58

National Monuments (Amendment)
  Act 1994 ................. 8.15–8.20
  s 4 ............................................... 8.20
    5 ................................................ 8.20
    10 .............................................. 8.21
    12 ..................................... 2.166, 4.12
      (1) ........................................ 8.23
    14 .............................................. 8.15
    19 .............................................. 8.18
    21 .............................................. 8.16
    26 .............................................. 8.16
    82 ............................................ 2.240

National Monuments (Amendment)
  Act 2004
  s 8 ..................... 8.25, 10.159

National Monuments Acts
  1930–1994 ............... 2.166, 4.12, 12.49

Nursing Home Support Scheme Act 2009
  s 3 ............................................. 11.04

## O

Open Spaces Act 1906
  s 20 ............................................ 7.208

Organisation of Working Time
  Act 1997 ............................. 3.100, 4.95

## P

Petroleum (Exploration and Extraction)
  Safety Act 2010
  s 3 ................................................. 11.11

Petroleum and Other Minerals Development
  Act 1960 ...................................... 2.434
  s 2 ................................................ 8.252

s 8 ................................................. 8.253
  5 .................................................. 8.252
  36 ................................................ 8.252

Petroleum and Other Minerals Development
  Acts 1960–1995 ................. 8.245–8.252

Planning and Compensation Act 1991
  s 22 .............................................. 10.166
  Sch 2 ........................................... 10.166

Planning and Development
  Act 2000 ...................... 1.40–1.49, 1.58,
                          1.71, 1.77–1.80, 1.91–1.95,
                          1.131–1.139, 1.161, 1.165–
                          1.176, 1.254, 1.316, 2.05–
                          2.08, 2.55, 2.72, 2.88, 2.89–
                          2.91, 2.102–2.102, 2.109–
                          2.113, 2.121–2.128, 2.141–
                          2.143, 2.171, 2.180, 2.183–
                          2.187, 2.225, 2.236, 2.299,
                          2.384–2.390, 2.411, 2.457,
                          2.479–2.479, 2.481, 2.508–
                          2.514, 3.01–3.04, 3.14–3.15,
                          3.50, 3.69, 3.113–3.113,
                          3.135–3.142, 3.147–3.150,
                          3.155–3.161, 3.166, 3.242,
                          3.255, 3.261–3.268, 3.278–
                          3.280, 3.288–3.288, 3.295,
                          4.58, 4.123–4.124, 4.148,
                          4.175, 4.200, 5.07–5.13,
                          5.30, 5.42–5.44, 5.53–5.60,
                          5.72, 5.92, 5.103, 5.157,
                          5.162–5.170, 6.10–6.12,
                          6.19, 6.42, 6.50, 6.95–6.101,
                          7.07, 7.26, 7.47, 7.58, 7.120,
                          8.27, 8.82, 8.104–8.106,
                          8.132, 8.187, 8.221, 8.276,
                          8.311–8.317, 8.330–8.337,
                          8.355, 8.388, 8.401, 9.15,
                          10.51, 10.61, 10.109, 10.165,
                          10.200–10.205, 10.230,
                          11.02, 12.01, 12.01, 12.17–
                                       12.18, 12.36,
                                       12.49, 2.124
  s 1 ................................................. 8.265
  1A ............................................... 10.66

# Table of Statutes

Planning and Development
Act 2000 (contd)
  s 2 ......................... 1.212, 2.109, 2.132,
                      2.225–2.227, 2.312, 3.69,
                      3.126, 4.136, 5.106, 6.42,
                      7.200, 8.01, 8.130, 8.258,
                      8.263, 8.274, 8.284,
                      10.109, 12.40
    (1) ..................... 2.03, 2.06–2.08,
                  2.89–2.91, 2.107–
                  2.111, 2.125, 2.133,
                  2.141–2.143, 2.181,
                  2.225, 2.299, 2.341,
                  2.411, 2.481, 4.55
    (8) ............................ 1.48, 12.55
        (h) ............................... 1.320
  3 .............. 2.04–2.05, 2.10, 8.02, 8.11
    (1) ..................... 2.04, 8.02, 8.10
    (3) ........................................ 2.05
  4 ................. 1.52–1.62, 1.222, 1.236,
                      2.03–2.03, 2.92, 2.109,
                      2.112, 2.117, 2.122, 2.132,
                      2.490, 3.181, 8.275–8.277
    (1) .............. 1.236, 2.123–2.142,
                  2.160, 2.214–
                  2.218, 2.229, 2.492–
                  2.496, 3.196,
                  8.273–8.274
        (a) ..................... 2.124–2.131
        (g) ...................... 2.145, 8.14
        (h) .................. 2.213–2.216,
                  2.471, 2.491,
                  8.277–8.278
        (i) .................... 2.220, 8.274,
                  8.397
        (ia) ............................. 8.274
        (j) .................... 2.221–2.224
        (k) .................................. 2.226
        (l) ................................... 2.227
    (2) .............. 1.236, 2.127, 2.181,
                  2.214, 2.231, 2.492–
                  2.496, 3.196, 8.273
    (4) ............... 2.133, 2.232, 8.275
    (5) ...................................... 2.233
        (b) ................................ 5.01
        (l) ................................. 2.227

s 5 ............... 2.247, 2.471, 2.508–2.522,
                    3.196, 4.03, 4.55,
                    4.67, 4.91, 4.119–
                    4.123, 4.136, 4.142–
                    4.145, 4.264, 5.99,
                    8.221, 12.12,
                    12.19–12.24
    (1) ......................... 2.247, 2.512,
                  2.518, 4.137
    (2) ...................................... 4.137
        (a) ............................... 2.526
        (b) .................... 2.526–2.527
    (3) ...................................... 4.138
    (4) ................. 2.513–2.513, 4.139
    (5) ........................ 2.513, 4.140
    (6) ........................ 4.141–4.141
  7 ............................................... 3.196
    (2) (a) ................................... 1.01
        (r) ..................................... 5.38
  9 ............................................... 1.125
    (1) ........................................ 1.46
  10 ................. 1.01, 1.06, 1.28, 1.133,
                      2.457, 6.25, 7.200, 8.188
    (1) ..................... 1.01, 1.20–1.23,
                  1.80, 3.140, 8.21
        (a) ................................. 7.120
    (2) ..................... 1.07, 1.24–1.24,
                  1.80, 1.88, 7.75
        (c) ............. 1.39, 1.49, 2.456,
                  3.136, 3.186, 4.21,
                  7.58, 7.64, 8.56,
                  9.44, 11.06, 11.36,
                  11.53, 11.91
        (e) ..................... 1.253, 2.503
        (f) .................................. 8.266
        (i) ................................... 2.159
        (k) ...................... 1.39, 8.188
        (m) .................................. 3.11
        (o) .................................... 1.83
    (2A) ...................................... 1.25
    (5) ........................................ 1.97
    (5A) ...................................... 1.28
    (6) ...................................... 1.103
    (7) ......................... 1.104, 1.178
    (8) ......................... 1.02, 1.104
        (c) ................................ 2.457
  11 ................... 1.11, 1.22–1.22, 1.105,
                    1.309–1.312,
                    3.264, 6.36, 8.351

Planning and Development
Act 2000 (contd)
   s 11 (contd)
      (1) ................. 1.46, 1.106–1.107
      (1A) ........................ 1.47, 1.107
         (a) ............ 1.46–1.47, 1.107
         (b) ................................ 1.109
         (c) ..................... 1.109, 1.111
            (iii) ....................... 1.110
      (2) ..................................... 1.108
         (b) ................................ 1.109
      (3) ..................................... 1.109
      (4) (a) ............................... 1.109
         (c)–(d) ......................... 1.110
      (5) ..................................... 1.110
         (b) (ii) ......................... 1.111
   12 ................. 1.11, 1.22, 1.95, 1.112,
               1.136–1.144, 1.202, 1.229,
               1.327,
               6.36, 7.63, 8.06
      (1) .......................... 1.112, 1.312
      (3) .......................... 8.258, 1.113
      (4) ..................................... 1.116
         (a) ................................ 1.114
      (5) (2) ................................ 1.114
         (a) ................................ 1.117
      (6) ..................................... 1.119
      (7) (a) ..................... 1.120–1.121
         (b) ................................ 1.121
      (8) ..................................... 1.123
      (10) ................................... 1.126
         (a) ................................ 1.124
         (b) ................................ 1.125
      (11) ................................... 1.127
      (12) ................................... 1.128
      (12C).................................. 5.06
      (13) ................................... 1.129
      (14) ........................ 1.46, 1.130
      (16) ...................... 1.132, 4.173
      (17) ................................... 1.135
   13 ................. 1.11, 1.21, 1.92, 1.105,
               1.132–1.144, 1.327,
               2.471, 6.20, 6.36
      (1) .......................... 1.136, 1.315
      (2) ..................................... 1.315
   14 ..................... 1.163, 12.28
      (1) ..................................... 1.161

      (2) ..................................... 1.162
      (3)–(5) .............................. 1.162
   15 ........................................... 1.165
      (1) ............................. 2.157, 6.22
      (2) ............................ 1.174, 6.38
   16 ............................................. 1.77
   17 ........................................... 3.280
      (1) ....................................... 1.78
      (2) ....................................... 1.79
   18 ............... 1.175, 3.190, 7.63, 8.06
      (3) (a) ............................... 1.175
         (b) ................................ 1.176
      (4) ..................................... 1.177
         (a) ................................ 1.176
      (5) ........................... 1.177–1.182
      (6) ..................................... 1.177
   19 ............. 1.175–1.179, 1.186–1.188
      (1) (a) ............................... 1.179
         (b) ................... 1.180, 2.473
      (2)–(2A) ........................... 1.185
      (2B) ........................ 1.175–1.182
      (3) ..................................... 1.185
   20 ......................... 1.144, 1.175, 1.189,
               1.327, 7.63, 8.06
      (2) ..................................... 1.189
   21 .................................. 1.277, 1.284
      (1) ..................................... 1.269
      (2) ..................................... 1.270
   21–27 ...................................... 1.269
   22 ........................................... 1.302
   23 ................... 1.269, 1.272, 1.278
      (1) ..................................... 1.270
      (2) ..................................... 1.271
      (3A) .................................. 1.273
      (4) ..................................... 1.274
   24 ............ 1.160, 1.269, 1.278, 1.284–
               1.287, 1.302
      (1) ................. 1.277, 1.285–1.286
      (4) ..................................... 1.283
      (6) ........................... 1.287–1.292
      (6A) .................................. 1.293
      (6B) .................................. 1.294
      (7) (a) .................... 1.283, 1.295
         (b) ................................ 1.296
   25 ..................... 1.293–1.300, 4.194
      (3A) .................................. 1.298
      (3B) .................................. 1.299

## Table of Statutes

Planning and Development
Act 2000 (contd)
- s 26 .............................................. 1.160
  - (1), (4) ................................ 1.301
  - (6) ....................................... 1.306
    - (b) ................................ 1.292
- 27 ....................... 1.269, 1.303–1.314,
  3.306, 5.113, 5.162
  - (1) ............... 1.303–1.305, 8.272
  - (2) (a) ............................... 1.312
  - (4) ...................................... 1.304
    - (a) ................... 1.111, 1.307
    - (b) ............................. 1.315
- 27A ............................................. 1.308
  - (4) ..................................... 1.311
- 27B ............................................. 1.312
  - (1)–(2) .............................. 3.313
  - (4) ..................................... 3.314
- 27C ............................................. 1.315
- 28 .................. 1.14, 1.18, 1.62, 1.316,
  1.323, 3.152, 4.16,
  7.58, 12.32
  - (1) ...................................... 1.317
  - (2) ...................................... 1.318
- 29 ............... 1.62, 1.323, 3.152, 4.09,
  4.16, 7.58
- 30 ................................................ 1.324
  - (1)–(2) .............................. 1.323
- 31 ................................................ 1.160
- 34 ................................................ 9.113
  - (5) ...................................... 4.136
- 35 ................................................ 9.113
  - (6)–(6C) ........................... 3.168
  - (7)(c) ................................ 8.328
- 37 (5) ....................................... 4.136
- 37A, 37H ................................... 9.113
- 31 ....................... 1.144, 1.303, 1.326,
  10.209
  - (1) ...................................... 1.327
  - (2) ......................................... 7.58
    - (c) ................................ 1.115
- 31A ..................................... 1.45–1.60
- 31C ................................. 1.144, 1.327
- 31D ................................. 1.144, 1.327
- 31G ............................................. 1.298
- 31GG .......................................... 1.299
- 32 ................... 2.01–2.04, 2.92–2.95,
  2.117, 3.04, 7.37
  - (1) .................. 2.04, 2.121, 5.02

- (a) ............................... 2.109
- (b) ........ 2.94, 2.109–2.112
- (2) ................. 2.02, 2.121, 2.479,
  3.06, 5.02
- 32–50 ................................. 3.03, 9.113
- 33 ...................................... 3.10, 3.167
  - (2) ........................... 8.320, 10.66
  - (3)–(4) ................................. 3.11
- 34 ................... 1.43, 1.49, 1.93, 1.175,
  1.213, 2.03–2.03,
  2.97, 2.106–2.111,
  3.14–3.17, 3.23,
  3.83, 3.97, 3.111,
  3.195, 3.207,
  3.254, 3.278, 3.296–3.297,
  3.300, 4.07–4.10, 4.14, 4.94,
  4.129, 4.147, 7.205, 8.284,
  8.377–8.384, 8.393, 9.53,
  10.233, 11.06, 11.18
- 34 (1) .............. 3.136, 3.207–3.208,
  3.229, 6.54
  - (2) (a) ..................... 1.43, 3.136,
    3.207, 4.21,
    10.05, 11.36
    - (ii) .............. 1.252, 3.182
    - (iii) ....................... 3.186
    - (iv) ....................... 3.187
    - (v) ........................ 3.188
    - (vi) ....................... 3.189
  - (b) .................... 3.136, 10.05
  - (c) ............ 3.137, 3.159, 4.07
  - (3) ................. 3.96, 3.118, 3.199,
    4.129, 10.78
  - (4) ............... 3.114, 3.159, 3.188,
    3.236, 4.21, 7.64,
    8.59–8.63,
    9.44, 11.56
    - (a) ................... 3.237–3.239,
      4.07, 8.61
    - (b) .......... 3.240, 3.245, 8.62
    - (c) ............ 3.174, 3.241, 8.63
      - (ii) ........................ 3.211
    - (d) .............................. 3.242
    - (e) .............................. 3.243
    - (f) .............................. 3.244
    - (g) ....................... 3.18, 3.245,
      8.387–8.389
    - (h)–(l) ........................ 3.245

xliii

Planning and Development
Act 2000 (contd)
  s 34 (contd)
    (4) (m) ................. 2.166, 3.245,
                    4.12, 8.394
        (n) .............................. 3.246
        (o) .............................. 3.247
        (p) .............................. 3.248
        (q) .............................. 3.249
    (5) .............. 3.229, 3.250, 3.254,
                4.03–4.07, 4.55,
                4.112, 4.147, 4.193
    (6) ................. 1.58–1.61, 1.170,
                3.111
        (a) ....................... 1.48, 4.07
        (b) ................................ 1.48
        (c) ................................. 1.49
        (d) ................................ 1.49
    (7) ........................................ 1.71
    (8) ............. 3.104–3.108, 3.126,
                4.07, 8.327, 10.99
        (a) .................... 3.103, 3.108
        (b) ................... 3.104, 3.124
        (f) ............ 3.108–3.112, 4.07
    (9) ....................................... 3.126
    (10) ..................................... 3.152
    (11) ..................................... 3.116
    (12) ............... 2.96, 2.106, 3.30,
                5.08–5.10, 5.46,
                5.156, 5.181,
                9.01–9.04,
                10.52–10.57
        (c) .................................. 5.06
    (12A) ................................. 10.53
    (12B) ................................. 10.54
    (12C) .............. 2.102, 5.08–5.10,
                5.157, 10.55
    (13) ....................... 3.155, 3.173,
                8.354–8.355
    (14) ....................................... 6.54
  34F ............................................. 11.42
  35 ... 3.25, 3.166, 3.168, 3.178, 3.245,
                7.58, 8.318–8.320,
                8.327–8.329
    (1) .......................... 8.320, 8.326
    (2) .......................... 3.168, 8.324
    (3) .......................... 3.168, 8.325
    (4) .......................... 3.168, 8.326
    (5) .......................... 3.168, 8.327

    (6) ...................................... 8.327
    (6A) .................................... 8.327
    (7) ............................. 3.10, 8.328
  36 ............................ 3.11–3.14, 3.24,
                3.160, 12.32
    (1)–(2) ................................. 3.15
    (3) ...................................... 12.32
        (a) .................................. 3.15
        (b) .................................. 3.15
            (viii) ..................... 3.255
        (c) .................................. 3.15
    (4) ........................................ 3.16
    (5) ........................................ 3.16
    (6) ............................. 3.14–3.17
  37 ............... 2.183, 2.519, 3.21–3.23,
                3.98, 3.152, 3.160, 3.195,
                4.07, 4.35, 4.46–4.49,
                4.59, 4.126–4.130,
                8.378, 9.60
    (1) ............................... 4.07, 4.49
        (a) ............... 4.02, 4.10, 4.15
        (b) ..................... 3.136, 4.18
        (d) ................................ 4.15
    (2) ............................... 4.16, 4.38
        (a) ............. 1.61, 3.150, 11.55
        (b) ............. 1.62, 3.152, 4.17,
                11.55
            (iv) ........................ 3.150
        (c) ........................ 4.16, 11.55
    (4) ............................... 4.11, 4.13
        (c)–(e) ......................... 4.222
    (5) ............................. 4.55, 4.102,
                4.149–4.149
        (a) ........................ 4.25–4.28
        (b) ................................ 4.25
        (c) ................................. 4.03
    (6) .................... 3.97, 4.14, 4.35
        (a) ............... 3.97, 4.14, 4.49
        (d) (i) ........................... 4.49
        (f) .................................. 4.37
        (h) ................................. 4.31
        (e) ......................... 4.29, 4.123
        (G) ........................... 2.03–2.03
  37A ........................ 2.183, 3.08, 4.07,
                11.02, 11.06,
                11.14–11.18
    (2) ......................... 11.06, 11.15,
                11.20–11.25
    (4) ....................................... 11.18

## Table of Statutes

Planning and Development
Act 2000 (contd)
- s 37A–37I .................................... 2.183
- 37A–37K ................................... 2.186
- 37B ...................... 2.186, 3.08, 11.02,
  11.06, 11.18–11.28,
  11.41, 11.66–11.71
  - (3) ...................................... 11.20
- 37C ............................................ 11.19
  - (1) ...................................... 11.21
  - (2) ...................................... 11.24
- 37D .............................. 11.19, 11.31,
  11.66–11.71
  - (1) ...................................... 11.29
  - (3) ...................................... 11.30
  - (4) ...................................... 11.31
- 37E ............. 4.67–4.69, 4.123, 11.27,
  11.37–11.40,
  11.66–11.71
  - (1) ............... 11.27, 11.40, 11.53
  - (2) ............... 11.28–11.34, 11.41
  - (3) .......................... 11.34, 11.53
    - (a) .................... 11.34–11.37
      - (ii) ........................ 11.35
      - (iv) ....................... 11.38
    - (d) .............................. 11.37
  - (4) .............. 11.36, 11.53–11.53
  - (6) .......................... 11.39–11.39
- 37F ............................... 11.46, 11.52
  - (1) .......................... 11.42, 11.53
  - (2) ...................................... 11.43
  - (3) .......................... 11.44, 11.53
  - (4) ...................................... 11.45
  - (5) ...................................... 11.71
- 37G .................... 2.109–2.111, 11.06,
  11.38, 11.46, 11.53,
  11.65–11.71
  - (5) ...................................... 11.54
  - (6) ...................................... 11.55
  - (7) ...................................... 11.56
    - (d) .................... 11.56–11.57
  - (8) .......................... 11.56–11.58
  - (9) ...................................... 11.59
  - (10) .................................... 11.60
  - (11) .................................... 11.62
- 37H ............................................ 11.64
  - (2) ...................................... 11.65
    - (c) ............................... 11.66
  - (4) ...................................... 11.67

- (5) ...................................... 11.68
- (6) ...................................... 11.69
- 37H–37J ................................... 11.62
- 37I ............................................ 11.71
- 37J ............................................ 11.73
  - (2)–(3) ............................... 11.72
- 37K ............................... 11.74–11.80
- 38 ....................... 4.112–4.115, 9.113
  - (1) ...................................... 4.114
  - (1A) ................................... 4.113
  - (2) ...................................... 4.113
  - (3)–(5) ............................... 4.114
  - (6) ...................................... 4.115
  - (7) ...................................... 4.115
- 39 ............................................... 8.352
  - (1) ...................................... 3.177
  - (2) ................. 2.72, 3.204–3.205,
    3.261, 3.271,
    3.273, 3.276
  - (4) ........................................ 3.05
- 40 ................... 2.99, 2.102, 3.15–3.17,
  5.88, 5.165, 6.16,
  6.96–6.100, 8.386,
  8.396, 12.32
- 41 ................... 2.26, 2.99, 2.102, 3.15–
  3.17, 5.165, 6.16,
  6.96–6.100, 8.388,
  12.32
- 42 ............... 1.218, 2.26, 2.100–2.102,
  3.15–3.18, 4.193,
  5.165, 6.16, 6.96–6.100,
  8.382–8.386, 9.60, 12.32–
  12.32, 12.55–12.55
  - (4) ........................................ 3.20
    - (a) ............................... 1.218
- 42A ............................... 8.382, 9.113
- 43 ..................................... 2.102, 12.57
- 44 .................... 3.89–3.93, 4.02, 4.55,
  4.193, 7.84
  - (6) ............................... 3.92, 4.02
- 45 ................. 3.242, 4.55, 7.203–7.204
  - (3) ........................................ 4.02
  - (8) ...................................... 7.205
- 46 .................... 4.02, 4.55, 7.01, 7.11,
  7.86, 8.332–8.347
  - (1) ........................... 5.103, 8.333
  - (2) ............................. 7.87, 8.335
  - (4) ...................................... 8.337
  - (5) ...................................... 8.338

xlv

Planning and Development
  Act 2000 (contd)
  s 46 (contd)
    (6) ............................ 4.02, 8.336
    (7) ........................................ 8.339
    (8) ........................................ 8.340
    (9) ........................................ 8.341
    (10) ...................................... 8.342
    (11) ...................................... 8.343
    (12) ...................................... 8.344
    (13) ...................................... 8.345
  47 ...................... 2.479, 3.204–3.205,
                3.261, 3.273, 8.348–
                8.355, 12.01
    (1) ............................ 3.263, 8.349
    (2) ............................ 3.264, 8.351
    (3) ............................ 3.265, 8.353
    (4) ............................ 3.268, 8.355
    (5) ............................ 3.266, 8.356
  48 ...................... 3.236, 3.277–3.288,
                3.294–3.300, 4.22,
                4.193, 9.45, 9.113,
                11.56
    (1) ................ 3.278, 3.283, 3.292
    (2) ........................................ 3.279
      (c) .................... 3.281–3.283,
                  3.293
    (3) ........................................ 3.284
    (4) ........................................ 3.287
    (5) ........................................ 3.288
    (6)–(7), (9) .......................... 3.289
    (10) ........................................ 4.22
      (a)–(b) ........................... 3.290
      (c) .................... 3.290, 4.23
    (11) ...................................... 3.291
    (12) ...................................... 3.283
      (a) ................................ 3.293
      (b) .................... 3.283, 3.293
      (c) ................................ 3.294
    (13) ...................................... 3.297
      (a)–(b) ............................. 4.24
    (14)(a) ................................ 3.294
    (15) ...................................... 3.295
    (17) ...................................... 3.280
  49 ...................... 3.236, 3.277–3.283,
                3.296–3.300, 4.193,
                7.133–7.134, 9.45,
                9.113, 11.56
    (1) .......................... 3.296–3.299
    (4) ........................................ 3.298
    (5) ........................................ 3.299
    (7) ............................ 3.280, 3.300
  50 ............... 4.83, 4.144, 4.168, 4.168,
                4.168–4.175, 4.180,
                4.189–4.193, 4.197–
                4.200, 4.207, 4.215–
                4.217, 4.219, 4.222–
                4.229, 4.244, 4.254,
                4.261, 4.265, 4.270,
                4.284, 4.291–4.293,
                5.77, 5.143–5.145, 6.87
    (1) ................ 2.514, 4.174, 7.139
    (1A) ...................................... 1.197
    (2) .............. 4.175, 4.184, 4.190,
                4.202–4.204, 4.219–4.219,
                4.290, 7.139
      (a) ................................ 4.204
      (c) ................................ 4.193
    (3) ............................ 4.175, 4.193
    (4) ........................................ 4.198
      (d) ................................ 4.232
    (5) ........................................ 4.199
    (6) ........................................ 4.204
    (7) ................. 4.204–4.205, 4.271
    (8) ........................ 4.204–4.204,
                4.211–4.212
    (11)(a) ............................... 4.271
  50A ................... 4.171, 4.180, 4.184–
                4.184, 4.189, 4.217, 4.222,
                4.254, 4.291, 5.143, 9.113
    (1) ........................................ 4.219
    (2) ........................................ 4.171
    (3) (a) ...................... 4.222, 4.242
      (b) .................... 4.222, 4.232
        (i) ......................... 4.168
        (ii) .............. 4.165, 4.241
    (4) ........................................ 4.223
    (6) ........................................ 4.265
    (7) ............... 4.270–4.272, 4.278,
                4.284
    (8) .......................... 4.270–4.272
    (9) ........................................ 4.289
    (10) ...................................... 4.291
    (11) ...................................... 4.292
      (a) .................... 4.271, 4.292
    (12) ...................................... 4.293
  50B ................... 4.168–4.170, 4.183,
                4.184, 4.188

## Table of Statutes

Planning and Development
  Act 2000 (contd)
  s 51 ................................ 8.259, 8.266
    (1) ............................................ 8.267
    51–80 ............................. 1.89, 8.257
    52 ................................. 8.280, 8.298
    (1) ............................................ 8.268
    (2) ............................. 8.268, 8.270
    (3) ............................................ 8.271
  s 53 ....................... 5.107, 8.280, 8.298
    55 .......................... 7.54, 8.258, 8.294
    56 .................................................. 7.54
    57 ........................ 2.471–2.471, 2.492,
        3.191, 4.136, 4.150, 8.270–
        8.273, 8.279
    (1) .............. 2.214, 2.267, 2.471,
        3.191, 4.136, 4.150,
        8.273–8.277
    (1)–(2) ............................... 4.150
    (2) ............... 8.280, 12.18, 12.36
    (3) ........................... 8.280–8.284
    (4) ......................................... 4.150
    (5) ......................................... 8.280
    (6) ............................. 3.193, 8.280
    (7) ............................. 4.150, 8.281
    (8) ............................... 4.55, 4.150
    (9) ......................................... 8.282
    (10) ........................... 3.192, 8.283
    58 ........................ 5.103, 8.284, 8.289
    (4) ................. 5.79, 5.103, 8.285
    (5) ......................................... 8.285
    59 .......................... 8.286–8.289, 8.296,
        12.18
    (1) ............. 2.494, 5.103, 8.293–
        8.293, 8.301–8.301, 8.314
    (2) ......................................... 8.287
    (3) ............... 8.287, 8.293, 8.301
    (4) ......................................... 8.293
    60 ........................ 2.102, 5.158, 8.286–
        8.288, 8.295–8.299, 12.18
    (1) ......................................... 8.296
    (2) ........................ 2.493, 8.293–
        8.295, 8.301
    (3) ......................................... 8.297
    (4) ......................................... 8.298
    (5) ........................... 5.107, 8.298
    (6) ............................. 8.293, 8.299
    (7) ......................................... 8.300
    61 ................................. 8.293, 8.301

  s 62 ................................ 8.296, 8.302
    63 ........................... 5.79, 5.103, 8.303
    64 .................................................. 8.303
    65 .................................................. 8.302
    (1) ............................................ 8.296
    67 ................................. 8.305, 12.18
    68 .................................. 2.494, 8.306
    69–70 ........................................ 8.307
    71 ............................... 7.07–7.07, 8.308
    71–78 ........................................ 1.225
    71–80 ........................................ 8.308
    72 ................................. 8.309, 12.18
    73 .................................................. 8.310
    74–76 ........................................ 8.311
    77 ..................................... 8.311–8.312
    77AC ........................................ 9.141
    78 .................................................. 8.313
    79 .................................................. 8.315
    (2) ............................................ 6.158
    (3) ............................................ 6.159
    80 .................................. 6.160, 8.316
    81 .................................................. 1.92
    (1)–(2) ............................... 1.221
    82 ..................... 2.471, 2.479, 2.495
    (1) ............................. 1.222, 3.194
    (2) ............................. 1.222, 3.194
    83 .................................................. 1.224
    (3) ............................................ 1.225
    84 .................................................. 2.496
    (1) ............................. 1.93, 1.226
    (2)–(3) ............................... 1.227
    (4) ......................................... 1.228
    85 ............... 1.229–1.237, 7.01, 7.09–
        7.11, 7.91
    (5) (a) .................................. 1.231
        (b) .................................. 1.232
    (6) ......................................... 1.232
    (7) ......................................... 1.233
    86 .................................. 1.235, 3.196
    87 ............... 1.94, 2.190, 2.496, 3.196
    (1)–(2) ..................... 1.93, 1.236
    (3) ............................. 1.95, 12.36
    88 ............ 1.94, 1.238–1.244, 2.497,
        4.02, 4.55, 7.01, 7.09–7.11,
        7.91, 12.36
    (1) ......................................... 1.238
    (2) ............................. 1.238, 7.91
    (3) ......................................... 1.238

Planning and Development
Act 2000 (contd)
  s 88 (contd)
    (4) ..................................... 1.239
    (5) ..................................... 1.240
    (7) ..................................... 1.241
    (8) ..................................... 1.241
  89 ............................................. 1.242
  90 ........................... 1.244, 2.497
  91 ............................................. 1.243
  92 ................. 1.245, 2.109, 2.498
  93 ............................................. 6.125
    (1) ............................ 3.255, 6.14
    (2) ........................................ 6.16
    (3) .................... 6.17, 6.55, 6.126
      (d) ..................................... 6.59
    (4) ..................... 3.197, 3.255, 6.18
  93–101 ........................... 3.255, 6.10
  94 .................... 1.82, 6.16, 6.21, 6.36,
                                  7.120
    (1) .................... 1.95, 6.22, 6.141
    (2) ........................................ 6.27
    (3) ............................ 1.96, 6.28
    (4) ........................................ 6.29
    (5) (a) ............. 3.258, 6.33, 6.45,
                    6.89, 6.153–6.160
      (b) ..................................... 6.33
      (c) ..................................... 6.45
      (d) ..................................... 6.30
  95 ........................................ 1.82, 6.34
    (1) ........................................ 6.36
      (a) ..................................... 6.35
      (c) ..................................... 6.45
      (d) ..................................... 6.37
    (3) (a) ................................ 6.38
      (b) ..................................... 6.39
  96 ............... 3.55, 3.255, 4.03, 4.151,
       6.40–6.50, 6.55, 6.76, 6.109,
                                  12.45
    (2) ............... 3.255–3.259, 4.55,
                  6.48–6.49, 6.54,
                6.55, 6.55, 6.153–6.160,
                                12.45
    (3) .............................. 6.55, 6.59
      (a) ........................... 6.55–6.55
      (b) ............. 6.52, 6.55–6.55,
                  6.55–6.55, 6.78
      (c) ............. 3.258, 6.53–6.55
      (d) ........................ 6.55–6.59

      (da) .................................3.255
      (e) ...................................6.60
      (f) ....................................6.61
      (g) .............. 6.55, 6.62–6.65
      (h) ....................... 6.55, 6.63
      (i) .....................................6.64
    (4) .................... 3.198, 6.55, 6.69
96  (5) ..............................4.55, 4.136,
                              4.151, 6.71
    (6) .................. 6.73, 6.78, 6.95,
                                 6.110
      (a)....................................6.75
      (b) .............. 6.59–6.67, 6.75
    (7) ...................................6.112
      (a) ...................................6.78
        (ii).....................3.255
        (iia) .......................6.78
      (b) ...................................6.78
      (c) ....................................6.82
    (8) .................. 3.255, 6.83, 6.110
    (9) ....................................6.89
      (b) ..................................6.165
    (10) .................................6.113
      (a) ...................................6.90
    (11) ...........................6.91–6.93
    (12) ......................... 6.71, 6.92
    (13) ....................... 6.104, 6.135
    (15) ........................ 6.95–6.96
    (16) ......................... 6.77, 6.95
96A ..................... 3.255, 4.03, 6.100
96B .......................... 3.255, 4.03, 6.16,
                             6.100–6.102
    (8) .................................. 6.100
97 .......................... 3.55, 6.105–6.119,
                              6.163, 12.45
    (1) ................................... 6.106
    (2) (a) ............................. 6.107
      (b) ................................ 6.108
    (3) ............... 3.255, 6.105–6.109,
                                 6.116
    (5) .......................... 6.115, 6.164
    (6) ................................... 6.111
    (7) ................................... 6.112
    (11) ................................. 6.114
    (12) ................................. 6.116
      (b) ........... 3.255, 6.105, 6.116
    (13) ................................. 6.117
    (14) ................................. 6.117
    (15) ................................. 6.117

# Table of Statutes

Planning and Development
  Act 2000 (contd)
  s 97 (contd)
    (16) ................................. 6.119
    (17) ............ 6.105, 6.120–6.122
      (b) ............................... 6.105
    (19) ................................. 6.121
    (20) ................................. 6.121
    (21) ................................. 6.122
    (22) ................................. 6.123
  98 ..................................... 6.124, 6.129
    (2) ................................... 6.129
    (3) ................................... 6.129
    (6) ................................... 6.130
    (7) ................................... 6.125
  99 ..................... 6.130–6.133, 12.45
    (3) ................................... 6.131
      (d) ...................... 6.134, 6.79
        (i) ........................... 6.78
    (3A) .................................. 3.255
      (c) ............................... 3.255
  100 ................................... 6.39, 6.163
    (1) (a) ................. 6.15, 6.125
        (b) ............................. 6.16
  101 ..................................... 6.166
  105 ..................................... 12.35
  112 ......................... 7.191, 11.01
    (4) .................................... 11.01
  112A .................................... 11.01
  117X(2) ................................. 9.122
  119 ....................................... 7.141
  125 ........................................ 4.09
    (a)–(b) ........................... 4.29
  125–146D ............................. 4.09
  126 ............. 4.14, 4.31, 7.186, 9.58
    (1) .............................. 4.30–4.32
    (2) .................................... 4.30
    (3) .................................... 4.33
  127 ............................. 2.519–2.522
    (1) .......................... 4.39, 4.46
      (a)–(g) ......................... 4.35
      (b) .............................. 4.41
      (e) .............................. 3.98
      (g) .............................. 4.47
    (5) .................................... 4.47
  128 .............. 4.09, 4.49, 4.126, 4.264,
                          8.211, 8.223, 10.95
    (1) ........................ 4.49, 4.264

  s 129 .................................. 4.55
    (2) ................................... 4.55
      (a) ................................. 4.68
    (3) ................................... 4.55
    (4) ............................ 4.55–4.59
  130 ................. 3.23, 4.56–4.60, 9.59
    (3) ...................... 4.58–4.60, 9.59
    (4) ................................... 4.81
    (5) .................... 3.23, 4.56–4.59,
                                    9.60
  131 .......................... 4.25, 4.60–4.63,
                                    9.61–9.63
  132 .......................... 4.25, 4.60–4.66,
                                    4.111, 9.62
  132. ..................................... 4.25
  133 ................... 3.116, 4.25, 4.66,
                                    4.149, 9.63
  134 .............. 2.524, 4.09, 4.19, 4.60,
                     4.67, 4.102, 4.123–4.124,
                     7.175–7.176, 11.51
    (1) .......................... 2.524, 4.124
    (2) .................................... 4.67
      (a) ............................... 2.524
    (3) .................................... 4.69
    (4) .................................... 4.69
    (5) .................................... 4.124
      (a) ................................. 4.09
  134A ..................... 4.67–4.69, 4.123
  135 ................ 1.260, 4.09, 4.67–4.70,
                     4.72, 7.175–7.175, 7.182,
                                    9.64
    (2A) ................................. 4.70
    (2AE) ............................... 4.71
    (2B)(dd) ........................... 4.72
    (3) .................................... 4.72
    (4) .................................... 4.74
    (5) .................................... 4.75
      (a) ........... 4.09, 7.175–7.176
        (ii) ......................... 4.111
      (b) .............................. 4.75
    (6) .................................... 4.76
    (7) .......................... 5.79, 7.178
    (8) ............................ 4.77–4.78
  135AB–135AD ...................... 4.71
  137 ............................... 4.87–4.89
  138 .............. 1.69, 3.116, 4.19–4.19,
                                    4.25, 4.149

Planning and Development
Act 2000 (contd)
s 139 ............... 1.61, 1.68, 3.116, 4.20,
    4.53, 4.125–4.129, 10.101
  (2) ........................................ 4.21
140 ........................ 1.51, 1.61, 4.92
  (1) ........................................ 4.92
  (3) ........................................ 4.94
141 ............................... 4.95–4.99
  (1) ........................................ 4.95
  (2) ............................... 4.93–4.95
  (3 ......................................... 4.96
142 ........................................... 4.97
  (2) ........................................ 4.98
  (3) ........................................ 4.98
  (4) .................... 4.58, 4.99, 8.226
143 ..................... 3.200, 4.09, 4.100,
    7.175, 7.179, 9.44, 11.06,
    11.53, 11.91
  (1) ........................................ 7.179
  (2) ........................................ 7.180
144 ............... 2.519, 4.35, 4.56, 4.67,
    4.102, 9.65, 11.66
  (1) ............................... 4.09, 4.36
  (1A) ..................................... 4.36
145 .......................................... 4.104
  (1) (b) ................................... 4.09
146 ............ 4.09, 4.71, 4.105–4.106,
    7.175–7.176, 7.181, 11.47–
    11.49, 11.53, 11.85
  (3) ...................................... 11.48
  (5) ........................... 4.111, 11.50
    (B) ............................. 4.102
    (C) ............................. 4.102
    (c) .............................. 10.90
146A ....................................... 11.81
146A–146D ............................. 4.09
146B ....................................... 11.84
  (1) ...................................... 11.81
  (2) (a) ................................ 11.82
    (b) ............................. 11.83
  (3) ...................................... 11.84, 11.90
    (b) ............................. 11.85
  (6) ...................................... 11.85
146C ............................. 10.93, 11.81,
    11.84–11.88
  (3) ...................................... 11.88
  (4) ...................................... 11.89

(5) ........................................ 11.90
(6) ........................................ 11.91
(7) ........................................ 11.92
147 (1) (b) (ii) ........................ 2.174
151 ................................ 5.02, 5.79
151–164 ................................... 5.01
152 ................. 2.102, 5.05, 5.35–5.48,
    5.53, 5.64, 5.78, 5.156,
    10.57, 12.25
  (1) ............................... 5.31–5.34
    (a) ................. 5.32, 5.53, 5.61
  (2) ........................................ 5.32
  (3) ........................................ 5.35
  (4) ........................................ 5.41
    (b) ................................ 5.53
153 .................. 5.42, 5.47, 5.51–5.61,
    5.77–5.78
  (1) ..................... 5.01, 5.48–5.51
  (2) ........................................ 5.52
    (a) ......................... 5.49–5.52
    (b) ................................ 5.51
  (3) ............................... 5.53, 5.65
  (4) ........................................ 5.53
  (5) ...................... 5.35, 5.53, 5.78
  (6) ............................... 5.01, 5.60
  (7) ............................... 5.01, 5.60
154 ................. 2.499, 5.47, 5.67–5.70,
    5.73, 5.86, 5.98, 8.93, 8.102,
    8.114, 8.119–8.122, 9.54
  (1) ............................... 5.61, 5.75
    (a) ................................ 5.62
    (b) ................................ 5.63
  (2) ............................... 5.36, 5.64
  (3) (b) ................................. 5.75
  (4) ........................................ 5.65
  (5) ............................... 5.66–5.67
    (b) ......................... 5.66–5.71
  (7) (b) ................................. 5.73
  (8) ............................... 5.73, 5.79
  (9) ............................... 5.73, 5.79
    (d) ................................ 5.66
  (10) ...................................... 5.73
  (11) ...................................... 5.74
  (12) ...................................... 5.75
  (13) ...................................... 5.76
  (14) ...................................... 5.77
155 ................. 2.102, 5.05, 5.46, 5.61,
    5.78–5.78, 5.156

## Table of Statutes

Planning and Development
Act 2000 (contd)
  s 156 ................ 4.76, 5.01, 5.02, 5.66,
                    5.79–5.82, 10.56
    (1) ........................................ 5.79
    (2) ........................................ 5.80
    (3) ........................................ 5.81
    (4) ........................................ 5.82
    (5) ........................................ 5.83
    (6) ........................................ 5.84
    (7) ........................................ 5.85
    (8) ........................................ 5.86
    (9) ........................................ 5.87
  157 ................. 5.01, 5.42, 5.77, 5.89
    (4) ............................. 5.44, 8.212
      (a) ................................... 5.88
      (aa) ...................... 5.42, 5.89
      (b) ....................... 5.43, 5.90
      (c) ..................... 5.91, 5.147
    (5) ........................................ 5.92
  157–171 ................................... 7.198
  158 ............................................ 5.93
    (1) ...................................... 5.183
  159 ............................................ 5.94
  160 ............... 2.88, 2.500, 4.146, 5.01,
              5.06–5.09, 5.42, 5.54–5.60,
              5.77, 5.95–5.98, 5.104,
              5.110, 5.120, 5.138–5.169,
              5.174–5.182, 5.189, 6.04,
              10.57, 12.25
    (1) ............... 5.104, 5.106, 5.183
    (2) ...................................... 5.109
    (3) ......................... 5.138, 5.161
    (4) ...................................... 5.139
    (6) (a) ............................... 5.165
      (i)–(ii) .................... 5.127
      (aa) ........................ 5.166
      (b) ........................... 5.167
    (7) ......................... 5.168, 5.182
  161 ......................... 5.96, 5.138, 5.174
  162 ....................... 5.97, 5.147–5.148,
              5.156, 10.57
    (1) ............................. 2.102, 5.147
    (2) ................. 2.102, 5.05, 5.46–
              5.48
    (3) ................. 2.102, 5.01, 5.06–
              5.10, 5.157, 5.181
    (5) ........................................ 4.09

s 163 ........................ 2.501, 5.98, 5.189
164 ................................................ 5.189
165 ...................................... 1.193, 8.357
165–171 ......................... 1.191, 8.357,
              9.102, 9.113
166 ................................. 1.194–1.201,
              8.357–8.368
  (1) .............. 1.191–1.195, 8.359
  (2) ................. 1.191, 1.196, 8.360
  (3) ............................. 1.196, 8.361
    (a)–(c) ........................... 1.194
  (4) ............................. 1.194, 8.362
  (5) ............................. 1.194, 8.363
  (6) ...................................... 8.364
167 .................................... 8.365, 12.35
  (1)–(2) .............................. 1.195
168 ...................... 1.197, 1.203, 8.143,
              8.357–8.361, 9.102
  (1) ............................. 1.197, 8.366
  (1A) .................................. 1.197
  (2) ............... 1.198, 8.367–8.367
    (a)–(g) .......................... 8.368
  (3) ...................................... 1.199
  (4) ...................................... 1.200
  (5) ............................. 1.201, 9.101
  (50)(2) .............................. 1.199
169 ...................... 1.193, 1.202–1.211,
              4.02, 4.55, 8.357–8.358,
              8.369, 9.102
  (1) ............................. 1.203, 8.369
  (2) ............................. 1.203, 8.369
  (3) ............................. 1.204, 8.370
  (4) (b) ............................. 8.371
  (5) ............................. 1.210, 8.373
  (6) .................. 1.211, 4.02, 8.374
  (7) (a) ............................. 8.375
  (8) ............................. 1.212, 8.376
  (9) ............................. 1.91, 1.212
170 ...................... 3.195, 8.357, 8.377,
              9.102, 11.18
  (1) ...................................... 1.213
  (2) ............................. 1.214, 8.377
  (3) ............................. 1.215, 8.378
  (4) ............................. 1.216, 8.379
171 ............................................. 8.381
  (1)–(3), (4) ....................... 1.218
  (5) ........................... 1.217, 8.382
    (A) ............................. 10.109

Planning and Development
Act 2000 (contd)
s 172 ...................... 2.139–2.139, 2.480,
              3.199, 4.13, 4.117, 8.56,
              9.113, 10.01, 10.50, 10.62,
              10.231, 10.239
    (1) ............. 8.56, 10.239, 10.253
    (1A) ............................... 10.239
    (3) ...................................... 10.70
    (5) ........................................ 4.58
172–177 ........................ 10.01, 10.61,
              10.64, 10.226
173 ................ 10.84, 10.229, 10.239
    (1) ......................... 3.199, 10.78
    (2) ........................ 10.84, 10.229
174 ..................... 9.113, 10.01, 10.64,
              10.87–10.88
    (3) .......................... 3.260, 10.87
    (4) ....................... 10.87, 10.102
    (6) ........................................ 10.87
175 ....................... 2.147, 2.180, 7.149,
              7.172, 7.184, 8.212, 10.197,
              10.204, 11.02
    (1) ...................... 2.148, 10.187,
              11.02, 11.06
    (2) .................................... 10.188
    (3) ................ 2.149, 4.53, 4.129,
              4.129
    (4) ............ 2.174, 8.212, 10.189
        (a)–(b) ......................... 2.150
    (5) (a) ............................. 10.190
        (ii) ...................... 10.191
    (6) ................................. 10.193
    (7) ................................. 10.194
    (8) ................................. 10.71
        (a) ........................... 10.195
        (b) ................ 10.71, 10.195
        (c) ............................ 10.196
    (9) ........................................ 7.172
    (10) ................................ 10.199
    (11) ................................ 10.201
    (12) ................................ 10.202
    (13) ................................ 10.203
    (14) ................................ 10.204
176 .................... 2.117, 2.148–2.154,
              2.318, 2.361–2.365, 4.222,
              9.113, 10.01, 10.45–10.50,
              10.64, 10.110, 10.187,
              10.207, 10.216, 11.02, 11.86
    (1) ............... 2.153, 10.44, 11.02
    (2) ...................................... 2.154
    (e) ................................... 8.56
    (3) ...................................... 2.156
    (6) (a) .............................. 8.189
177 ....................... 2.139–2.139, 9.52,
              9.110, 11.41, 11.88
    (3) ...................................... 9.119
    (e) .................... 8.117, 8.120
177A .............................................. 9.15
    (5) ...................................... 9.131
177A–177AE ................ 2.139–2.139,
              10.16
177AA .................. 9.99, 9.131–9.133
    (1) ............................. 9.131, 9.140
    (2) ............................ 9.131–9.138
    (d) ................... 9.139, 9.140
    (7) ...................................... 9.132
    (8) ........................................ 9.98
177AB .................. 9.99, 9.133–9.144
    (1) ...................................... 9.135
    (2) ............................ 9.136–9.139
    (3) ............................ 9.137–9.139
    (4) ...................................... 9.139
177AC .................. 9.99, 9.133–9.140
177AD ........................................ 9.142
177AD. ...................................... 9.111
177AE ........................................ 9.145
    (1) ...................................... 9.143
    (4) ...................................... 9.146
    (7) ...................................... 9.148
    (10) .................................... 9.149
    (11) .................................... 9.150
    (13) .................................... 9.151
    (14) .................................... 9.145
177B ............. 9.17–9.19, 9.54, 9.131
    (2) ........................................ 9.31
    (8) ........................................ 9.18
177C .............................................. 9.19
    (1) ........................................ 9.21
    (2) ........................................ 9.19
177D ....................... 9.24, 9.32, 9.47
    (2) ............................... 9.07, 9.15
    (7) ........................................ 9.32

# Table of Statutes

Planning and Development  
Act 2000 (contd)  
  s 177E ........... 8.100, 8.113, 8.117, 9.41  
    (2) ......................................... 9.33  
  177F ................................................ 9.15  
    (1) ......................................... 9.36  
  177G .................................... 9.15, 9.39  
  177H ............................................... 9.40  
  177I ....................................... 9.41, 9.44  
  177J ................................................ 9.47  
    (1) ......................................... 9.42  
  177K .......................... 9.15, 9.44, 9.56  
    (6) ......................................... 9.47  
  177L ...................................... 9.47, 9.56  
  177M .............................................. 9.32  
  177N ............... 9.32–9.40, 9.44, 9.65  
  177O ............................................... 9.53  
  177P ................................................ 9.57  
    (1) ......................................... 9.58  
    (2) ......................................... 9.59  
    (3) ......................................... 9.61  
    (4) ......................................... 9.62  
    (5) ......................................... 9.63  
    (6) ......................................... 9.64  
  177Q ..................................... 9.65–9.67  
  177R ............................................. 9.118  
    (1) ....................................... 9.103  
  177R–177AE ........................... 1.199  
  177S(1) ........................................ 9.100  
    (2) ....................................... 9.101  
  177T .............................................. 9.106  
    (2)–(3) ............................... 9.110  
    (7) ....................................... 9.111  
  177U ............................................. 9.114  
    (8) ....................................... 9.102  
  177V .................................... 9.70, 9.79  
    (2) ......................................... 9.87  
  177W ................. 9.98, 9.119–9.121  
    (1) ........................... 9.119, 9.129  
    (4) ....................................... 9.119  
      (d) .................... 9.123, 9.124  
    (6) ....................................... 9.120  
    (7) ............................. 9.98, 9.121  
  177X ...................... 9.98, 9.121–9.122  
    (3) ....................................... 9.128  
  177Y ......... 9.98, 9.121, 9.124–9.126  
    (1)–(2) ............................... 9.124  
    (3) ....................................... 9.125  

    (4) ....................................... 9.128  
  s 177Z ............................... 9.122–9.127  
    (1) ....................................... 9.128  
    (3) ....................................... 9.129  
    (4) ....................................... 9.130  
  178 ...................... 1.171, 2.117, 2.139,  
        2.157, 2.159, 2.211, 2.502,  
        6.23  
  178–182 ........................ 9.102, 9.113  
  179 ..................... 2.117, 2.139–2.139,  
        2.160, 2.173–2.180, 2.211,  
        8.189, 8.215, 9.102, 9.113  
    (3) ............................... 2.171, 8.217  
      (a) ................................. 2.176  
      (b) ..................... 2.171, 2.177  
    (4) ................ 2.172, 2.179, 8.219  
      (a) ................................. 2.172  
      (b) ..................... 2.172, 8.219  
    (6) ..................... 2.117, 8.189  
      (a) ..................... 2.172, 2.180  
      (c) ..................... 2.172, 2.180,  
          8.189  
  180 ..................... 3.242, 8.384, 8.393,  
        9.102, 9.113, 12.46  
    (1) ............................. 8.384–8.385  
    (2A) ................................., 8.392  
    (3) ....................................... 8.390  
    (4) ....................................... 8.391  
    (6) ............................. 8.392, 8.396  
  181 ..................... 2.182–2.182, 2.197–  
        2.200, 10.205, 10.222  
    (1) (a) ......... 2.184, 2.187, 2.208,  
        10.216  
      (b) ................................. 10.209  
      (a) ................................. 10.206  
      (B) (1) ........................... 10.222  
  181A ................. 2.182, 2.201, 2.205,  
        10.214, 10.222–10.224,  
        11.02, 11.06  
    (1) ........................ 10.217, 10.222  
      (b) ................................... 11.06  
    (2) ..................................... 10.212  
    (3) ........... 8.220, 10.217–10.218  
      (a) (ii) ......................... 11.06  
      (b) ................................. 10.219  
      (c) ................................. 10.219  
      (iii) ............................. 10.218  
    (4) ............ 2.201, 10.220, 10.222

Planning and Development
Act 2000 (contd)
- s 181A–181C ................ 2.184, 9.102, 9.113
  - 181B ............... 2.182, 2.203, 10.214–10.218, 10.224
    - (2) ...................... 2.203, 10.222
    - (3) ...................... 2.204, 10.222
    - (4) .................................. 10.222
    - (5) .................................. 10.223
    - (6) ...................... 2.204, 10.224
    - (7) .......................... 2.206, 7.172
    - (8) ....................................2.206
    - (13) ..................................2.207
  - 181C ............. 2.182, 2.208–2.208, 10.214
    - (2) ...................................2.208
    - (3) ..................... 2.208, 10.216
    - (7) ................................10.216
  - 182 ........... 2.317, 2.479, 4.122, 7.01, 7.11, 7.92, 11.02, 11.06
    - (1) ....................................2.317
    - (4) (b) ............ 4.02, 4.29, 4.122
      - (A) .............................2.318
      - (B) .............................2.318
      - (C) .............................2.318
      - (D) .............................2.318
  - 182 A–182E ............................ 2.479
  - 182A ................ 2.318, 11.06–11.06, 11.08
    - (1) ....................................11.06
    - (5) ....................................11.06
  - 182A–182D ................ 9.102, 9.113
  - 182A–182E ............................11.06
  - 182A–182E .................... 2.318, 11.12
  - 182B ............. 11.06–11.06, 11.12–11.15
  - 182C ................ 11.02, 11.06–11.08
    - (1) ....................................11.06
    - (9)–(9F) ...........................11.08
    - (9E) ..................................11.11
  - 182D ........................ 11.06, 11.12
  - 182E ........................ 11.06, 11.06, 11.12–11.12
  - 183 ......................... 7.22, 12.36
    - (2) ........................... 7.09, 7.22
  - 183 (1) ...................................7.09
  - 183–189 ................................7.01
  - 184 ......................... 7.10–7.11, 7.43
- s 185 ..............................................7.20
- 186 ..............................................7.26
- 187 ..................................6.82, 7.27
- 188 ..............................................7.28
- 189 ...................................7.29–7.32
  - (1) ..............................................7.35
  - (5) ..............................................7.33
  - (6) ...................................7.34–7.34
  - (7) ..............................................7.35
- 190 ................3.170, 7.01, 7.09–7.09, 7.38, 7.42, 7.48, 7.63, 7.72, 8.06
- 190–195 ...........................7.01, 7.36
- 191 .................2.55, 7.02, 7.38–7.38, 7.48, 7.57, 7.71, 8.06
  - (1) ...........................3.171, 7.64
  - (2) ...........................7.01, 7.63
  - (3) ...........................7.64, 7.64
  - (4) ...........................2.99, 7.66
- 192 ...............7.01, 7.38, 7.46, 7.58–7.58, 7.67–7.77
  - (1) ...........................7.31, 7.67
  - (2) ..................7.30, 7.46, 7.73
  - (3) ...........................7.67, 7.78
  - (4) ..............................................7.70
  - (5) ..................7.32, 7.72, 7.79
  - (6) ..............................................7.79
- 193 ..............2.55, 4.55, 4.154–4.154
  - (1) ..............................................7.81
  - (2) ..................4.03, 4.136, 7.82
- 194 ..............................................7.83
- 195 ...................................7.01, 7.09
  - (1) ..............................................7.84
  - (2) ..............................................7.85
- 195–201 ....................................7.09
- 196 ........................7.09, 7.11, 8.346
- 196–201 ....................................7.01
- 197 ..........................7.09–7.11, 7.88, 8.59–8.63, 8.347
  - (2) ..............................................7.89
  - (3) ..............................................7.90
- 198 ...........................7.09–7.11, 7.91
- 199 ...................................7.09, 7.93
- 200 ...................................7.09, 7.94
- 201 ...................................7.09, 7.96
- 202 .....................1.247–1.258, 2.240, 2.480, 3.182–3.185
  - (1) ...........................1.248, 3.182
  - (5) ...........................1.250, 3.185

# Table of Statutes

Planning and Development
Act 2000 (contd)
- s 202–209 ................................. 2.480
- 203 ............... 1.259–1.262, 3.184, 4.123–4.124
  - (1) ........................ 1.258, 3.183
  - (2) ............................... 1.258
  - (3) ............................... 1.258
- 204 .................. 1.261–1.267, 2.503, 12.37
- 205 .................. 3.243, 5.79, 8.397–8.405, 12.26
  - (1) (b) ............................ 8.397
  - (2) ............................... 8.398
  - (3) ............................... 8.403
  - (4)–(5) ........................... 8.404
  - (11) .............................. 8.400
  - (12) .............................. 8.399
- 206 ........................... 12.29–12.31
- 207 ............... 4.55, 7.01, 7.11, 7.94–7.94, 12.28–12.31
  - (5) ............................... 4.02
- 208 ................................... 7.94
  - (2) (b) ........................... 5.103
- 209 ................... 8.03–8.05, 12.38
- 210 ......................... 7.97–7.102
- 211 .................. 6.94, 7.103–7.107
  - (4) ............................... 7.110
  - (5) ............................... 7.111
- 212 ........... 7.112–7.119, 7.128–7.129
- 213 ......................... 7.114–7.121
  - (2) ......................... 7.120–7.122
  - (4) ......................... 7.120–7.121
- 214 .................. 4.124, 4.134, 4.174, 4.193, 4.200–4.205, 7.133, 7.139, 7.170–7.173, 7.182–7.195
  - (1) ........................ 7.121, 7.134
  - (3) ............................... 7.135
  - (4) ............................... 7.136
- 215 .................. 3.202, 4.53, 4.124–4.129, 4.129, 4.134, 7.136, 7.141, 7.164, 7.170–7.173, 7.182–7.195, 11.13
  - (B) ......................... 7.141–7.145
  - (C) ......................... 7.141–7.146
- 215A .................. 3.202, 7.141, 7.162, 7.170–7.173, 7.182–7.195

- s 215B ..................... 7.141, 7.173, 7.182–7.195
- 216 ......................... 4.193, 7.136
  - (1) ............................... 7.148
  - (2) ............................... 7.149
- 217 ......................... 7.150–7.157
  - (6A) .............................. 7.158
  - (7) (a) ........................... 7.159
      (b) ........................... 7.160
- 217A ................................. 7.162
  - (3) ............................... 7.163
- 217A– 217C ......................... 7.161
- 217B ......................... 7.164, 7.169
  - (3) ............................... 7.163
  - (4) ......................... 7.165–7.165
  - (5) ............................... 7.166
  - (6) ............................... 7.167
  - (7) ............................... 7.168
  - (8) ............................... 7.169
- 217C ................................. 7.170
  - (3) ............................... 7.171
  - (4) ............................... 7.172
- 218 .................. 4.123–4.124, 4.134
  - (1) ............................... 7.173
  - (4) ............................... 7.175
- 219 ................................... 7.182
  - (3) ............................... 7.183
- 220 ................................... 7.184
- 221 ......................... 7.186, 7.192
  - (1) ......................... 7.187–7.188
  - (2) ......................... 7.188–7.188
  - (3) ............................... 7.189
  - (5) ............................... 7.190
  - (7) ......................... 7.191–7.191
  - (8) ............................... 7.192
  - (9) ......................... 7.186, 7.193
- 222 ................................... 7.194
- 223 ................................... 7.196
  - (1) ............................... 7.195
  - (2) ............................... 8.172
- 224 ......................... 2.113–2.114
- 224–228 ................... 9.102, 9.113
- 225 ......................... 2.113–2.114
- 226 ......................... 2.113, 2.117
  - (6) ......................... 11.02, 11.06
- 227 ................................... 2.118
- 228 ................................... 2.120

Planning and Development
Act 2000 (contd)
- s 229 ................................ 8.147–8.151
- 229) ............................................ 5.103
- 229–241 .................................... 8.141
-     (5) ........................................ 7.117
- 230 ................................ 8.144, 8.153
-     (3) ................................ 5.79, 5.103
-     (4) .......................................... 8.175
- 230–239 .................................... 5.125
- 231 ..................... 7.129, 8.151, 12.12
-     (2)–(3) .................................... 8.169
-     (4) .......................................... 8.170
- 232 .............................................. 8.171
-     (2) (e) .................................... 8.169
- 233 .............................................. 8.172
-                             234 8.173–8.177
- 235 .............................................. 8.174
- 238 .............................................. 8.175
- 239 ........................ 5.79, 8.144–8.149,
-                             8.177, 8.183, 12.12
-     (1) ......................... 8.177–8.177
-     (4) .......................................... 8.179
-         (b) .................................. 5.103
-     (5) .......................................... 8.180
-     (6) .......................................... 8.182
-     (6A) ........................................ 8.184
-     (7) .......................................... 8.185
-     (8) .......................................... 8.186
-         (a)–(c) .......................... 5.103
- 240 ........................ 5.125, 8.144, 8.176
- 241 .............................................. 8.147
- 246 .................................. 3.28, 12.12
-     (2) .............................. 3.28, 12.12
- 247 .............. 2.208, 3.45–3.49, 3.234,
-                             5.79, 5.103, 6.55
-     (1) .......................................... 3.46
-     (2) .......................................... 3.47
-     (3) .......................................... 3.48
-     (4) .......................................... 3.49
-     (5) .......................................... 3.51
-     (6) ................................ 3.52, 5.103
- 249 (2) ...................................... 4.218
- 250 ................................................ 5.72
-     (1) ............................................ 5.72
-     (2) ............................................ 5.72
-     (9) ............................................ 5.72
- 251 ................................................ 8.81
- s 252 ........................ 1.242, 5.103, 7.01,
-                                          7.95, 8.307
- 253 ................................................ 7.95
- 254 .................................... 2.504, 4.55,
-                                          12.12, 12.39
-     (6) ............................................ 4.02
-     (7) .................................... 2.506, 4.02
- 256 .............................................. 3.203
- 257 .............................................. 3.137
- 258 .............................................. 12.12
- 259 .............................................. 12.12
- 261 .3.33, 5.15, 8.28–8.28, 8.31–8.45,
-         8.65– ........ 8.104, 8.115–8.122
-     (6) ................................ 8.39–8.43,
-                                          8.82–8.86
-     (7) ................................ 8.34, 8.56–
-                                          8.63, 8.82
-     (8) .................................. 8.59–8.65
-     (9) ............................................ 8.66
-         (A) .......................... 8.31, 8.89
-     (10) ................................ 8.67–8.71
-     (11) .......................................... 8.69
-     (12) .......................................... 8.70
-     (13) .......................................... 8.71
- 261A ................ 8.43–8.44, 8.88–8.89,
-                             8.96, 8.110, 8.119, 8.124,
-                             9.32, 9.54, 10.59
-     (1) .............................. 8.91, 8.107
-         (b) .................................. 8.93
-     (2) (a) ............ 8.96, 8.107–8.123
-         (b) .................................. 8.96
-     (3) ............................................ 8.99
-         (a) ............ 8.98–8.100, 8.113
-         (c) .................................. 8.100
-         (d) .................................. 8.100
-     (4) .......................... 8.101–8.102
-         (a) ...................... 8.101, 8.116
-     (5) .......................................... 8.104
-         (a) .............................. 8.104,
-                                          8.118–8.119
-             (i)–(ii) .................... 8.120
-         (b)–(c) ........................ 8.105
-         (d) .............................. 8.106
-     (6) .......................................... 8.112
-         (a) .............................. 8.111
-         (f) ...................... 8.113–8.119
-     (7) .......................................... 8.113
-     (8) .......................................... 8.114
-     (9) .......................................... 8.115

## Table of Statutes

Planning and Development
Act 2000 (contd)
  s 261A (contd)
    (10) .................................... 8.117
    (11) .................................... 8.118
    (12) .................................... 8.120
      (a) .............................. 8.121
    (13) .................................... 8.121
      (c) .............................. 8.122
    (14) .................................... 8.123
  261A (4)(a) .............................. 8.116
  268 (1) (c) .................... 1.257, 2.166
  270 ............................................ 2.490
  Pt I ................................................ 1.83
    II ........................ 1.83, 3.35, 4.117,
                        4.193, 8.81
      Ch II ................................. 1.175
    III ....................... 1.83, 2.501, 4.193,
                      5.189, 7.01, 7.11,
                      7.32–7.37, 7.49–7.49, 7.72,
                      8.93, 8.98–8.101, 8.117–
                      8.122, 8.135, 8.185, 9.113,
                      10.66
    IV .............. 1.83, 4.29, 4.150, 4.193,
                      8.257, 12.50
      Ch 6 .......................... 8.257
    V ................ 1.83, 1.200, 3.46, 3.142,
                     3.164, 3.198, 3.255–3.257,
                     4.151, 6.01–6.04, 6.10–6.12,
                     6.14–6.17, 6.22, 6.30, 6.36,
                     6.39, 6.41–6.49, 6.55–6.57,
                     6.65–6.68, 6.72, 6.92, 6.97,
                     6.105, 6.125, 6.140, 6.145,
                     6.153–6.161, 6.166
    VI ............................................ 4.174
      Ch III ................................ 4.02
    VIII ................... 1.214, 2.139, 4.193,
                      5.01, 5.05, 5.51, 5.103,
                      5.182, 7.203, 11.06, 12.25
    IX ..................... 1.201, 4.193, 8.357,
                      9.102, 9.113, 10.66
    X ....................... 2.139–2.147, 2.240,
                      2.480, 3.23, 3.112, 4.117,
                      10.01, 10.43, 10.61, 10.63,
                      10.88, 10.226
    XA .................... 1.214, 3.195, 8.106,
                      8.124, 8.377, 9.09, 9.15,
                      9.102, 10.01, 10.1610.66

    Pt XAB ................. 1.214, 3.112, 3.195,
                      8.106, 8.377, 9.05, 9.09,
                      9.144, 10.01, 10.16
    XI ..................... 2.176, 2.211, 9.102,
                      9.113, 10.66
    XII ...................... 3.170, 4.193, 6.82,
                      7.01, 7.09
      Ch II ................................... 7.36
    XIII ............................... 2.480, 4.193
    XIV ................... 4.174, 4.193, 4.200,
                      4.205, 7.97, 7.102, 7.114–
                      7.119, 7.195
    XV .................... 2.113, 2.116, 9.102,
                      9.113, 10.66
    XVI .................................. 2.25, 4.193,
                      8.141–8.155
    XIX ........................................... 2.490
    Sch 1 .................. 1.15–1.16, 1.83, 1.87,
                      3.147, 12.50
      2 ..................... 2.235, 2.240, 2.243,
                      2.479, 7.10–7.11, 7.43, 7.45–
                      7.46, 8.55
      3 ..................... 1.256, 3.147, 3.171,
                      7.02, 7.47, 7.58, 7.61, 8.06
      4 ....................... 1.172, 1.173, 1.268,
                      3.147, 3.153, 3.171, 7.02,
                      7.04, 7.47, 7.57, 7.58–7.58,
                      7.64, 7.101, 12.50
      5 ............... 3.147, 7.02, 7.32, 7.49,
                      7.64, 7.64, 7.72,
                      7.79, 12.30
      7 ............... 2.183, 2.484, 3.08–3.08,
                      11.02–11.05, 11.15–11.18,
                      11.37, 11.93

Planning and Development (Amendment)
  Act 2001 ........................................ 8.328
  s 4 .................................................. 2.88
  Pt XA ............................................. 9.05
    XAB ........................................ 9.18

Planning and Development (Amendment)
  Act 2002 .................. 1.89, 1.185, 3.142,
                3.198, 3.255–3.256, 3.300,
                4.150, 6.10, 6.16–6.16, 6.48–
                6.53, 6.56, 6.96–6.100,
                6.105, 9.113

Planning and Development (Amendment)
Act 2002 (contd)
   s 3 ................... 3.255, 4.151, 6.16, 6.40,
                   6.50–6.55, 6.59, 6.69, 6.96,
                   12.45
      9 .................................................. 1.189
      4 ....... 2.111, 3.255, 6.16, 6.96–6.102,
                   6.165, 12.45
      5 ............................ 3.255, 6.105, 6.116
      6   (a) .................................................. 4.55
           (b) .................................................. 4.136
      7 ...................................... 1.132, 4.173
      8 .................................................. 1.188
      9 .................................................. 1.189
     10 ............................ 1.136, 3.97–3.97,
                   4.35, 4.49
     11 .................................................. 3.282
     13 ...................................... 4.136, 4.150
         (a) .................................................. 4.150
         (b) .................................................. 8.280
         (c) ............................ 4.150, 8.281
     14 .................................................. 8.184
     38 .................................................. 6.43

Planning and Development (Amendment)
Act 2006
   s 36 .............................................. 11.06

Planning and Development
(Strategic Infrastructure)
   Act 2006 ...................... 1.73–1.74, 2.93,
                   2.180, 2.183–2.186, 2.197,
                   2.204, 2.317, 2.484–2.489,
                   3.08, 3.36, 3.207, 4.13,
                   4.148, 4.165, 4.168, 4.175–
                   4.175, 4.201, 4.222–4.224,
                   4.271, 4.292, 8.320–8.321,
                   9.102, 9.113, 10.216–10.224,
                   10.233, 11.01, 11.13, 11.24,
                   11.36–11.37
   s 3 ................. 2.186, 3.09, 11.06, 11.24,
                   11.27–11.34, 11.38,
                   11.40–11.43, 11.53–11.74
      4 ............. 2.318, 2.479–2.479, 11.02,
                   11.06, 11.06–11.06, 11.12–
                   11.15
         (3) .................................................. 11.07
      5 ........................... 3.08, 11.02–11.04
      6   (d) .................................................. 2.03

s 8   (1) ................. 3.237–3.239, 4.07,
                   8.61
      (2) ............... 3.229, 3.250, 3.254,
                   4.03–4.07, 4.147
  9 ..... 3.168, 3.169, 3.178, 8.320–8.327
  10 ............................... 4.07, 4.13, 4.49
  11 .................................................. 4.113
  12 .................................................. 2.99
  13 ........... 4.144, 4.165, 4.168, 4.171–
                   4.175, 4.189–4.193, 4.197–
                   4.204, 4.219–4.223, 4.241,
                   4.265, 4.270, 4.284, 4.289–
                   4.293, 5.143
  18 .................................................. 11.01
  19 .................................................. 11.01
  20 ........................................ 4.09, 4.29
  21 ................. 4.09, 4.49, 4.264, 8.211,
                   10.95
  22 ..................... 4.09, 4.60, 4.67–4.69,
                   4.123, 7.175, 7.176
  23 ............................................ 4.67, 4.70
      (a) ............................... 4.09, 4.72
      (b) ................. 4.09, 7.175–7.176
  24 ...................................... 4.19, 4.149
  25 .................................. 4.07, 4.09, 4.92
  26 ..................... 3.200, 4.09, 4.100,
                   7.179, 11.06
      (6) .................................................. 2.210
  28 .................................. 4.09, 4.104
  29 ..................... 4.09, 4.105–4.106,
                   4.111, 11.48
  30 ............................... 4.09, 11.81–11.92
  31 .......................................... 5.79, 5.87
  32 ..................... 10.84–10.84, 10.228
  33  (c) .................................................. 3.260
  34 ..................... 2.147, 10.193–10.197
      (a) .................................................. 10.190
      (c) .................................................. 7.172
  35 .................................................. 2.182
      (a) .................................................. 10.205
  36 ..................... 2.182, 2.201–2.208,
                   7.172, 10.206, 10.212–
                   10.218, 11.02
  37 ...................................... 3.202, 7.141
  38 .................................................. 7.169
  39  (a) ............................... 4.134, 7.173
      (b) .................................................. 4.123

# Table of Statutes

Planning and Development (Strategic Infrastructure) Act 2006 (contd)
  s 38–39 .................................................. 4.174
    40 ......................................................... 7.182
    41 ............................. 7.186–7.191
    42 ......................................................... 7.197
    47 ......................................................... 2.490
    50A (11) ........................................... 4.292
    130 (5) ................................................ 4.09
    270A ................................................... 2.490

Planning and Development (Amendment) Act 2007
  s 67 ....................................................... 7.63

Planning and Development (Amendment) Act 2010 ...................... 1.01, 1.09–1.16,
    1.111, 1.170, 1.182,
    1.313, 2.55, 2.88, 2.93, 2.97,
    2.102, 2.384, 3.01, 3.34,
    3.140, 3.207, 4.168–4.169,
    4.181, 5.01, 5.13, 5.42, 7.01,
    7.112, 7.201, 8.31, 8.65–
    8.69, 8.89, 8.101–8.106,
    8.118, 8.188, 8.384, 8.394,
    9.08, 9.71, 10.16, 10.53,
    10.58, 10.66, 10.226, 11.02,
    12.32
  s 2 ....................................................... 10.109
    3 .......................................................... 4.183
    4 ................... 1.08, 1.18, 2.133, 2.481,
        4.03, 11.06
      (1) (b) (iv) ............................... 12.40
          (c) ......................................... 1.01
    5 ................... 2.03, 2.92, 2.123, 8.275
        (a) ........................ 2.227, 2.218,
          8.274, 8.397
        (b) ...................................... 2.232
    7 ..................... 1.01, 1.07, 1.08, 1.11,
        1.20, 1.22, 1.24–1.29,
        6.25, 7.64
    8 ........................ 1.22, 1.107, 1.309,
        8.351
    8–10 ............................................... 1.105
    9 ............................................ 1.22, 1.112,
        1.130–1.136, 1.202
      (b) (i) ................................... 1.114
      (c) (aa) ............................ 1.118
      (d) ......................... 1.120–1.121
      (e) ....................................... 1.124

      (ii) ............................... 1.126
    (f) ..................................... 1.130
      (a) ................................ 1.46
      (ii) ............................... 1.116
  10 ......... 1.21, 1.22, 1.136, 1.142, 4.49
  11 ...................................................... 1.175
    (b) ................................................. 1.177
      (i) ............................................ 1.185
  12 ........................................ 1.175–1.182
    (2B) ............................................. 1.182
    (a) (ii) ....................................... 1.181
    (b) (ii) ...................................... 1.185
  13 ........................ 1.175, 1.189, 4.232
  14 ....................................... 1.269–1.270
    (2) (j) ......................................... 1.271
    (b) (1) ....................................... 1.271
      (k) ........................................ 1.271
  15 ........................ 1.160, 1.269, 1.287
  16 ...................................................... 1.269
    (a) ................................................. 1.303
    (b) ................................................. 1.306
  17 ........................ 1.111, 1.307, 1.311
    (2) ................................................. 1.308
    (4) ................................................. 4.188
  18 ....................................... 1.312–1.314
  19 ...................................................... 1.185
  20 ................ 1.14, 1.18, 1.317, 12.32
    (4) (c) .......................................... 8.328
  21 ....................... 1.144, 1.155–1.160,
      1.326–1.327, 4.07
  23 .......................... 1.43, 1.48, 1.170,
      2.03, 2.96, 2.106, 3.31, 3.83,
      3.97, 3.108–3.111,
      4.07, 9.03, 10.99
    (a) ..................................... 1.48, 1.61
      (i)–(iv) ......................... 4.07
    (b) ......................... 3.104, 3.124
      (ii) ...................... 3.108, 4.07
    (c) ................. 4.07, 5.181, 10.52
    (12) ................................................. 3.30
    (3A) ............................................. 1.272
    (12) ..................................... 5.13, 9.04
    (12B) ........................................... 10.53
    (12C) ................ 10.54–10.56
    (f) .................................................. 3.112
  23–32 ................................... 9.113, 3.03
  24 .............. 3.166, 8.29, 8.320, 8.330
    (b) ................................................ 8.326
  25 ..................................... 3.09, 11.18

Planning and Development (Amendment)
Act 2010 (contd)
- s 26 .................................................. 11.66
- 27 ....................................................4.112
  - (b) ......................... 1.314, 4.113
  - (c) ....................................4.114
- 28 .............. 1.218, 2.26, 2.100–2.101,
  3.18, 3.20, 8.388, 12.55
  - (1) ..................................... 12.32
  - (2) .......................... 2.101, 12.32
  - (3) ............................ 3.19, 12.56
  - (4) ............................ 2.100, 3.20
- 29 ........................ 1.218, 2.26, 2.101
- 30 ............. 3.236, 3.277–3.280, 4.193
  - (a) .......................... 3.283, 3.293
  - (c) .......................... 3.280
- 31 .............. 3.236, 3.277, 3.296, 4.193
  - (1A) .................................. 3.296
  - (b) .................................... 3.297
  - (c) .................................... 3.300
- 32 ............. 4.168–4.171, 4.184, 4.219
- 33 ....................... 4.168–4.170, 4.184
- 34 ............ 2.214, 2.492, 3.191, 4.136,
  4.150, 8.273, 8.277
  - (12) ..................................... 4.07
- 35 ........................ 1.222, 2.495, 3.194
- 36 ........................ 1.236, 2.496, 3.255
- 37 ................. 3.196, 3.255, 6.16, 9.70
  - (G) ..................................... 2.03
- 38 ....................................................4.03
  - (a) (i) ...................... 3.255, 6.52
    - (ii) ............................... 3.255
    - (iii) ..................... 3.255, 6.59
  - (b) ............................ 3.255, 6.78
- 42 ................... 3.23, 4.09, 4.56–4.59,
  9.60
- 43 ............................... 1.260, 4.09
  - (a) .......................... 7.175–7.176
  - (b) .................... 4.71, 7.175–7.176
  - (c) ................. 4.72, 7.175–7.176
- 44 ................. 4.09, 4.67, 4.102, 11.66
  - (1) ......................................... 4.36
  - (1A) .................................... 4.36
  - (1B) .................................... 4.36
- 45 .................... 5.01, 5.47, 5.48, 5.51
  - (a) ...................................... 5.42
  - (b) ............................ 5.60–5.60
- 46 ........... 4.76, 5.01, 5.02, 5.66, 5.79
  - (f) ....................................... 5.86

- s 47 ................................................5.01
  - (a) ............................ 5.42, 5.89
  - (b) ....................................5.43
- 48 ................5.01, 5.166, 12.25
- 49 .................2.102, 5.01, 5.06–5.10,
  5.157, 10.57
  - (c) ................................3.255, 6.83
- 50 ............. 1.197, 8.357, 8.366, 9.102
  - (a) .....................................1.197
  - (b) .....................................1.198
  - (c) .....................................8.368
- 50A ............................................4.181
- 51 ....................... 1.202–1.211, 4.02,
  8.357, 8.371,
  8.369, 9.102
  - (b) .....................................8.375
- 52 ....................... 1.214, 3.195, 8.357,
  8.377–8.377, 9.102
- 53 ..............2.139, 9.113, 10.01, 10.64
- 54 ........................ 2.139–2.139, 8.56,
  9.113, 10.01,
  10.50, 10.62
  - (a) ....................... 4.118, 10.231,
    10.239, 10.253
- 55 ............................10.87, 10.102
- 56 ....................... 2.139–2.139, 9.113,
  10.01, 10.64
- 57 ..............................9.17, 9.32
- 56 ........................ 2.153, 2.365, 10.44,
  10.50, 10.110, 11.02
- 57 ........ 2.139–2.139, 9.07, 9.15–9.24,
  9.103, 9.110, 10.01, 10.64
- 58 ........................ 2.117, 2.139, 8.189
  - (a) .................. 2.172, 2.180, 8.189
  - (b) .................. 2.172, 2.180, 8.189
- 58–66 ............................. 9.102, 9.113
- 59 ................................8.384–8.385,
  8.393, 12.46
  - (a) ............................ 3.242, 8.384
  - (b) ............................ 3.242, 8.386
  - (c) ................. 3.242, 8.389, 12.46
  - (d) ............................ 3.242, 8.390
  - (e) ............................ 3.242, 8.390
  - (f) ............................ 3.242, 8.391
  - (g) ............................ 3.242, 8.396
- 60 ........................ 2.182, 2.197–2.201,
  10.206, 10.217–10.220
  - (a)–(b) .............................. 11.06

## Table of Statutes

Planning and Development (Amendment) Act 2010 (contd)
- s 61 .................... 2.182, 2.197, 2.203, 10.222
  - (c) ............................... 2.204
- 62 ............... 2.182, 2.208–2.208
- 63 ........................ 2.318, 11.06
  - (a) .............................. 11.02
- 64 ............. 2.318, 2.479, 11.06
- 65 ............. 2.318, 2.479, 11.02
  - (e)–(f) ........................ 11.08
- 65E ................................ 11.08
- 66 ......................... 2.318, 2.479
- 67 ................... 7.01, 7.57, 8.06
- 68 ........................ 7.112, 7.119
  - (b)–(c) ........................ 7.117
- 69 ........................ 7.157, 7.158
- 72 .................................... 8.81
- 74 .......................... 8.42, 8.65
  - (a) ............ 8.34, 8.42, 8.52
  - (b) ...................... 8.56–8.58
  - (c) ...................... 8.59–8.65
  - (d) .............................. 8.67
  - (e) .............................. 8.71
- 75 ............ 8.43–8.44, 8.88–8.89, 8.96–8.104, 8.111–8.123, 10.59
- 77 ........................... 1.15, 1.83
  - (3) ............................... 1.83
    - (a) ............................. 1.16
    - (b) ............................. 1.83
- 78 (a) ............................ 11.04
  - (b) ............................ 11.05
  - (c) ................... 11.03–11.04
- 177B(1) ........................... 9.18
  - (2) ............................... 9.31
- 177C .............................. 9.28
  - (1)–(2) ........................ 9.19
  - (3) ............................... 9.21
  - (4) ............................... 9.22
  - (5) ............................... 9.23
- 177D(1) .......................... 9.24
  - (5)–(6) ........................ 9.28
  - (7) ...................... 9.29–9.31
  - (8) ............................... 9.30
- 177E ............................... 9.31
  - (3) ............................... 9.33
  - (4) ............................... 9.34
  - (5) ............................... 9.35
- s 177F(2) ........................ 9.38
- 177G ............................. 9.39
- 177K(2) .......................... 9.44
  - (3) ............................... 9.45
- 177L ...................... 9.48–9.49
  - (6) ............................... 9.50
  - (7) ............................... 9.51
  - (8) ............................... 9.52
- 177N ............................. 9.36
- 177O ............................. 9.53
- 177P(1) .......................... 9.58
  - (2) ............................... 9.59
- 177R–177AE ................. 2.98
- 177S ............................. 9.100
- 177V .............................. 9.88
  - (1) ............................... 9.81
  - (2) ............................... 9.87
  - (3) ............................... 9.87
  - (4) ............................... 9.88
- 261A(1) .......................... 8.93
  - (f) ............................... 8.94
  - (g) .............................. 8.95
  - (2) (a) ....................... 8.110
- Pt XA ..................... 2.106, 9.18
- Pt XAB .................. 1.199, 2.98, 2.106, 9.142

Planning and Development Acts 2000–2002 ............................... 1.29

Planning and Development Acts 2000–2006 ................. 5.107, 6.55

Planning and Development Act 2000–2010 ......................... 12.52

Property Values (Arbitration and Appeals) Act 1960
- s 2 ............................. 6.71, 6.81

Protection of the Environment Act 2003 ......... 1.90, 2.159, 3.157, 3.203, 10.233
- s 4 (1) ............................ 3.157
  - (2) ............................. 3.158
- 61 ................................... 4.07

Public Health (Ireland) Act 1878 ......... 12.48
- s 203 ............................. 7.134

Public Transport Regulation Act 2009
- s 41 (1) ......................... 1.299

## R

Referendum Act 1994 .............. 2.300, 2.413

Registration of Title
  Act 1964 ............................... 5.73, 7.204

Roads Act 1933
  s 47 ................................................ 7.149

Roads Act 1993 .............. 1.254, 2.91, 2.110,
  3.202, 3.138, 4.129, 4.272,
  7.58, 7.134, 7.141, 7.142,
  7.149, 7.171, 8.394, 10.187,
  10.204, 11.13
  s 2 .............................. 1.25, 2.166, 4.12
  5    (1) ..................................... 10.66
  10 ................................................. 1.25
  11 ............. 8.384–8.389, 8.392, 8.395
      (1) ................ 8.391–8.391, 12.46
  18 ................................................ 1.254
  19   (6) ..................................... 2.484
  20 ................................... 1.254, 2.159
  47 ................................................ 7.149
  47–52 .......................................... 7.134
  48 ................................................ 7.155
  49 ....................... 7.142, 7.149, 7.166
  50 ..................... 7.142, 7.166, 10.187
  51 ............. 4.71, 7.142, 7.149, 7.166,
        9.102, 9.113, 10.66, 10.187
      (3) ..................................... 7.168
  52 ................................................ 7.160
  73 .................................................. 1.28

Roads (Amendment)
  Act 1998 ...... 3.202, 4.129, 7.133–7.134,
        7.142, 11.13s 5 7.160

Roads Act 2007 ....................... 4.129, 7.133,
        7.134, 7.141, 7.143

Road Traffic Act 1961
  s 45 ..................................... 2.166, 4.12

Road Traffic Act 1993 ........................ 4.272
  s 11 ............................................... 8.385

Road Traffic Act 1994
  s 49   (3) ..................................... 1.254

Roads Acts 1993–1998 ........... 3.202, 10.159

Roads Acts 1993–2007 ................ 9.70, 9.87,
        9.145

## T

Telecommunications (Miscellaneous
  Provisions) Act 1996 .................... 2.235

Town and Regional Planning
  Act 1934 ......................................... 7.38

Transport (Dublin Light Rail)
  Act 1996 ....................................... 2.110
  s 4 ................................................ 2.484

Transport (Railway Infrastructure)
  Act 2001 .................. 2.93, 2.110, 2.183,
        2.488, 9.87,
        9.102, 9.113, 10.66
  s 38 ............................................... 2.315

## U

Urban Renewal (Amendment) Act 1987
  s 5 ................................................ 7.126

Urban Renewal Act 1986 ......... 2.110, 7.126
  s 9 ................................. 7.126–7.127
  12 ................................................ 2.484

Urban Renewal Act 1987 ..................... 7.126

Urban Renewal Act 1998 ......... 1.176, 1.241,
        3.190

## V

Valuation Act 1988
  s 2 ................................................ 8.135

Vocational Education Act 1930 ............. 7.45

## W

Waste Management (Amendment)
  Act 2001 ............................... 1.90, 2.159

Waste Management Act 1996 ..... 1.08, 3.138
  s 10   (A) ....................................... 1.90
  22 ................................................ 2.159
  54 ................................... 3.137, 3.156
      (4) (a) ................... 2.238, 2.476,
        2.483
  55 ................................................ 2.345
  Pt V ............................................. 2.483

## Table of Statutes

Waste Management Acts
1996–2001 ..................... 2.159

Waste Management Acts
1996–2003 ......................... 12.08, 12.48

Waste Management Acts
1996–2008 .................................. 12.48

Water Pollution Acts 1977–1990 ........ 12.08

Water Services Act 2007 .......... 8.384, 8.392
   s 2 ................................................. 8.391
   95 ................................................. 8.392

Water Supplies Act 1942 ..................... 7.134
   s 6 ................................................. 7.152

Wildlife Act 1976 ..................... 12.08, 12.49
   s 15 .............. 2.152, 2.337, 7.117, 8.56,
                             9.118, 10.47
   16 .......................... 2.152, 7.117, 8.56,
                          9.118, 10.47, 12.50
   17 .......................... 2.152, 7.117, 8.56,
                          9.118, 10.47, 12.50
   21 ............................................... 12.50
   27 .................................... 5.151, 5.185
      (2) ........................................ 5.129
   57 ............................................... 12.50
   60 ............................................... 12.50
   61 ............................................... 12.50

Wildlife (Amendment)
Act 2000 ............................12.08, 12.49
   s 11 ............................................... 12.50
   15 ................................................ 12.52
   16 ................................................ 12.52
      (1) ............................ 7.117, 9.118
      (2) (b) .................... 2.152, 2.456,
                               10.47
   18 ......................... 2.152, 2.456, 7.117,
               9.118, 10.47, 12.50–12.52
   21 ................................................ 12.52
   26 ........................ 2.152, 2.337, 7.117,
                         9.118, 10.47
   27 ........................ 2.152, 2.337, 7.117,
                       9.118, 10.47, 12.50
   28 ........................ 2.152, 7.117, 9.118,
                         10.47, 12.50
   29 ................................................ 12.50
   29 ................................................ 12.50

Wildlife Amendment Acts
1976 and 2000 ............................. 2.455

### S

Safety Health and Welfare at Work Acts
1989–2005 ................................... 12.48

Safety in Industry Act 1980 ................. 12.48

# TABLE OF STATUTORY INSTRUMENTS

Affordable Homes Partnership (Establishment) Order 2005 (SI 383/2005) .................................. 6.159

Building Regulations 1997 (SI 497/1997) .................................. 2.474

Building Control Regulations 1997 ..... 2.474 (SI 496/1997)
Pt III .............................................. 2.345

Environmental Protection Agency Act 1992 (Noise) Regulations 1994 (SI 179/1994) .................................. 3.241

European Communities Act 1972 (Access to Information on the Environment) Regulations 1998 (SI 125/1998) .................................. 4.113

European Communities (Construction Products) Regulations 1992 (SI 198/1992) .................................. 12.66

European Communities (Control of Major Accident Hazards Involving Dangerous Substances) Regulations 2000 (SI 476/2000) .................................. 8.212

European Communities (Control of Major Accident Hazards Involving Dangerous Substances) Regulations 2006 (SI 74/2006) ............. 8.187, 8.244

European Communities (Environmental Assessment of Certain Plans and Programmes) Regulations 2004 (SI 435/2004) ..................... 1.41, 1.186, 1.199, 1.272, 8.357
art 4 ..................................... 1.97, 1.133
5 ................................................ 1.141

European Communities (Environmental Impact Assessment) (Amendment) Regulations 1999 (SI 93/1999) .... 10.61
Sch 2 .......................................... 10.115
3 .............................................. 10.182

European Communities (Environmental Impact Assessment) (Amendment) Regulations 2001 (SI 538/2001) ................................. 2.450

European Communities (Environmental Impact Assessment) (Amendment) Regulations 2006 (SI 659/2006) ......... 2.147, 2.174, 2.180, 10.195
art 4 .............................................. 10.70
6 (2) ........................ 10.71, 10.195

European Communities (Environmental Impact Assessment) Regulations 1989 (SI 349/1989)
art 2 (4) ....................................... 2.156
24 ................................................ 10.45

European Communities (Environmental Impact Assessment) Regulations 2006 (SI 659/2006)

European Communities (Environmental Assessment of Certain Plans and Programmes) Regulations 2004 (SI 435/2004)
art 6 .............................................. 1.188

European Communities (Ground Water) Regulations 2010 (SI 9/2010) ............................. 1.08, 7.64

European Communities (Major Accident Hazards of Certain Industrial Activities) (Amendment) Regulations 1989 (SI 194/1989)
art 39 .......................................... 8.211

European Communities (Natural Habitat) Regulations 1997 (SI 94/1997) ................................. 2.455
art 4 .............................................. 12.53
6 ................................................ 12.53
12 ................................................ 12.50
art 14A(6) ................................... 12.53

European Communities (Natural Habitat)
Regulations 1997 (SI 94/1997) (contd)
   art 7 .................................................. 12.53
      8, 10 ........................................ 12.53
      12 ............................................. 12.50
      15 (2) ........................... 12.53–12.53
      17–18 ....................................... 12.53
      19 (1) (a) ............................... 12.53
      27 (11) ..................................... 12.53
      31 ................... 2.242, 2.480, 10.255
      32 ................................. 12.53–12.53

European Communities (Natural Habitats)
(Amendment) Regulations 1998
(SI 233/1998) ............................... 12.52

European Communities (Natural Habitats)
(Amendment) Regulations 2005
(SI 378/2005) ............................... 12.52
   art 3 .................................................. 12.53
      4 ................................................. 12.53
      14A(8) ..................................... 12.53

European Communities (Natural Habitat)
Regulations 1997–2005 ............... 12.49

European Communities (Surface Waters)
Regulations 2009
(SI 272/2009) ........................ 1.08, 7.64

European Communities (Water Policy)
Regulations 2003 (SI 722/2003)
   art 13 ...................................... 1.08, 7.64

Heritage (Transfer of Departmental and
Ministerial Functions) Order 2002
(SI 356/2002) ............................... 8.268

Irish Aviation Authority (Aerodromes and
Visual Ground Aids) Order 1998
(SI 487/1998) ............................... 2.326

Local Government (Planning and
Development) Regulations 1994
(SI 86/1994) ................................ 10.126
   art 9 .................................................. 2.479
      20(2) ........................................ 10.172
      35 ............................................. 3.135
   Pt 1 ................................................. 2.479
   Sch 8 ............................................. 7.101

Local Government (Planning and
Development) (Fees) Regulations 2001
(SI 525/2001) ....................... 4.67, 4.102

Local Government Planning and
Development (Amendment)
Regulations 2001
(SI 539/2001) ............................... 2.450

Planning and Development (No 2)
Regulations 2007 (SI 135/2007)
   art 11 (2) (b) ................................. 3.83

Planning and Development Act 2000
(Certification of Fairground
Equipment) Regulations 2003
(SI 449/2003) ............................... 8.183

Planning and Development Act 2000
(Commencement) (No 3) Order 2001
(SI 599/2001) ................................. 3.15

Planning and Development Regulations 2000
(SI 350/2000) .................... 4.132, 10.231
   art 5  (1) ........................... 2.307, 2.309
      87 (1) ........................................ 2.189
      90 ............................................. 10.211
      103 ........................................... 10.50
      132(2) ..................................... 10.103
      133 ............................................. 8.201
   Sch ................................................ 11.02

Planning and Development
Regulations 2001
(SI 600/2001) ................... 1.174, 1.255,
           2.149, 2.122, 2.219, 2.236,
           2.273–2.286, 2.327, 2.362–
           2.363, 2.390–2.392, 2.456,
           2.467, 2.482, 3.12, 3.53,
           3.76, 3.129, 3.133, 4.124,
           6.55, 8.181, 8.277, 10.230
   art 2 .................................. 2.242, 10.129
      3 ............................................... 10.232
        (3) ...... 2.347–2.352, 2.390, 2.456
      5 ......................... 2.235, 2.243, 2.285
        (1) ................... 2.273, 2.286,
             2.288–2.288, 2.309–2.311,
             2.389–2.392, 2.481
        (f) ........................................ 1.234

## Table of Statutory Instruments

Planning and Development Regulations 2001
(SI 600/2001) (contd)
- art 6 ............ 1.255, 2.236, 2.286, 2.385, 2.425, 2.467–2.471, 2.479, 2.479, 2.480–2.480, 8.07
  - (3) ............ 2.473
  - (4) (a) ............ 2.474
    - (b) ............ 2.475
- 7 ............ 2.236, 2.469, 2.476, 2.483
  - (1) ............ 2.237
  - (2) ............ 2.238
- 8 ............ 2.236, 2.441, 2.477–2.478, 10.21
- 9 ............ 2.236, 2.244, 2.286–2.286, 2.385, 2.423, 2.471–2.473, 2.479, 2.480, 8.232, 8.238, 10.255
  - (1) .... 2.240, 2.479, 2.267, 8.238
  - (2) (ii) ............ 2.409
    - (a) (x) ............ 2.257, 2.266, 2.433
    - (b) ............ 1.255, 2.480
      - (i) ........ 2.252, 2.267, 2.293, 2.308, 2.323, 2.350, 2.363, 2.480
      - (ii) ....... 2.396–2.400, 2.415–2.418, 2.480
      - (iii) ............ 2.429, 2.436–2.439, 2.444–2.448, 2.480
      - (iv) ............ 1.255, 2.480
    - (c) ............ 2.480, 9.06
    - (d) ............ 2.480
  - (10)(b)(ii) ............ 2.389
  - (2) ............ 2.241, 2.480
  - (3) ............ 2.480
  - (4) ............ 10.110
    - 8 2.236
- 9 ............ 2.236
- 10 ............ 2.236, 2.243, 2.269–2.272, 2.286–2.288, 2.481
  - (1) ............ 2.270, 2.481
  - (2) ............ 2.481
    - (a) ............ 2.284, 2.481
    - (b) ............ 2.285, 2.481
  - (3) ............ 2.481
  - (4) ............ 2.235, 2.481
  - (5) ............ 2.286, 2.235, 2.481
- 11 ............ 2.236, 2.482
- 12 ............ 2.456
- 13 ............ 8.351
- 13J ............ 1.174
- 15 ............ 1.279
  - (a) ............ 1.285
  - (b) ............ 1.283
  - (c) ............ 1.286
  - (e) ............ 1.282
  - (g)–(h) ............ 1.283
- 16–47 ............ 3.35
- 17 ............ 3.38, 8.201
  - (1) ............ 8.201
    - (a) ............ 3.77
    - (b) ............ 3.38, 3.44, 3.55, 3.74–3.77
- 18 ............ 2.425, 3.74–3.77, 8.201
  - (1) ............ 3.37
- 19 ....... 2.425, 3.38, 3.44, 3.74–3.77, 4.215, ............ 8.201
  - (1) ............ 3.74
    - (a) ............ 3.38, 3.74
    - (b) ............ 3.39
    - (c) ............ 3.41
  - (2) ............ 3.41
  - (3) ............ 3.42
  - (4) ............ 3.39
- 20 ............ 3.43, 3.74
- 21 ............ 2.99, 3.24, 10.172
- 22 ............ 3.54, 3.57, 3.74–3.77, 8.203
  - (1) (a) ............ 3.77
  - (2) ............ 3.55, 3.72
  - (3) ............ 3.55
  - (4) ............ 3.56, 3.73
    - (a) (1) ............ 3.77
- 22A ............ 3.57
- 23 ............ 3.56–3.57
  - (1) ............ 3.73
  - (5) ............ 3.58

Planning and Development Regulations 2001
(SI 600/2001) (contd)
- art 24 .................................. 3.72–3.77
- 25 ............................................ 3.74
  - (1)–(3) ................................ 3.73
- 26 ........................ 3.57, 3.76, 3.122
  - (1) ....................................... 3.74
  - (1)–(8) ................................ 3.75
  - (2)–(3) ................................ 3.74
  - (4) ...................... 3.44, 3.74–3.76
  - (5) ..................... 3.75–3.75, 3.84
  - (7) ....................................... 3.76
- 27 ..................... 3.83, 8.204, 10.101
  - (1) ............................. 3.82, 3.84
  - (2) ................... 3.82, 3.84, 3.118
  - (3) ....................................... 3.84
  - (4) ....................................... 3.85
- 28 ..................... 3.86, 3.114, 3.134,
      4.218, 8.205, 10.103
  - (1) ....................................... 3.86
    - (d) .................................. 3.87
  - (2) ............................. 3.75, 3.88
- 29 ............................. 3.94, 3.100,
      3.114, 4.218
  - (1) ..................................... 3.133
    - (b) .................................. 3.95
  - (2) ............................. 3.98, 4.44
  - (3)–(4) ................................ 3.95
- 30 ......................................... 3.102
- 31 .... 3.24, 3.43, 3.114, 3.122, 4.218
- 32 (1)–(2) .............................. 3.117
  - (3) ..................................... 3.119
  - (4) ..................................... 3.120
- 33 ........................ 3.125, 6.55, 6.55
  - (2) ..................................... 10.96
  - (3) ..................................... 3.122
  - (4) ..................................... 3.123
- 33–39 .................................... 3.121
- 33 ............................................ 3.84
- 34 ................ 3.84, 3.126, 6.55, 6.88
  - (2) ..................................... 3.126
- 35 ................................. 3.133–3.134,
      4.263, 6.55
  - (1) ..................................... 3.129
  - (2) ..................................... 3.133
- 36 (4) ...................................... 3.74
- 48–50 .................................... 6.163
- art 49 ..................................... 6.164
- 50 .......................................... 6.125
- 51 ............................... 8.260–8.261
- 66 (1) .................................... 4.117
  - (2) ..................................... 4.119
- 66–78 .................................... 4.117
- 67 .............................. 4.121–4.124
  - (a) ..................................... 4.133
- 68 ................................ 4.54, 4.125
- 69 ................................ 4.53, 4.126
  - (1) ....................................... 4.51
  - (2) ....................................... 4.52
- 70 ................................ 4.53, 4.127
- 71 ................................ 4.53, 4.128
- 72 ................... 4.52, 4.129, 8.225,
      10.101–10.101
- 73 .......................................... 4.130
- 74 .......................................... 4.131
- 75 .................... 4.106–4.108, 4.132
- 76 .......................................... 4.133
- 77 .......................................... 4.134
- 78 .......................................... 4.135
- 80 .......................................... 2.173
- 81 ............................... 2.161–2.163
- 82 ................................. 2.165, 2.172,
      2.174, 8.219
  - (3) ........................... 2.165–2.166
  - (4) ..................................... 2.166
- 83 .......................................... 2.167
  - (1) ..................................... 2.169
  - (2) ..................................... 2.170
- 84 .......................................... 8.219
- 86 .................................. 1.169, 2.187,
      2.189–2.193, 10.212
  - (1) ........................... 2.187–2.189,
        10.207, 10.210
  - (2) ..................................... 2.188
- 86–91 .................................... 2.187
- 87 ................................. 2.187–2.189,
      2.198–2.199, 8.220, 10.207
  - (3) ..................................... 2.190
  - (4) ..................................... 2.191
- 88 ....................... 2.187, 2.193, 10.208
- 89 ....................... 2.187, 2.194, 10.209
- 90 .......................................... 2.195
- 91 .......................................... 2.196
- 92–132 ............. 4.118, 10.50, 10.61

Planning and Development Regulations 2001 (SI 600/2001) (contd)

| | |
|---|---|
| 93 | 10.45 |
| 94 | 10.111, 10.230, 10.239 |
| (b) | 10.113 |
| (c) | 10.114 |
| 95 | 2.149, 10.85 |
| 96 | 3.22, 10.172 |
| (1)–(4) | 3.23 |
| 109 | 2.456 |
| 103 | 2.456, 10.47 |
| 104 | 10.50 |
| 108 | 10.230 |
| 111 | 10.110 |
| 117–118 | 2.149 |
| 120 | 2.456 |
| (1) | 2.151 |
| (2) | 2.152 |
| 121 | 8.213, 10.189 |
| 124–132 | 10.61 |
| 126(1) | 10.99 |
| 133 | 8.201, 8.209 |
| 133–155 | 4.120 |
| 134 | 8.202 |
| 135 | 8.203 |
| 136 | 8.204 |
| 137 | 8.205, 8.211 |
| (1) | 8.206 |
| (2) | 8.205, 8.206 |
| (3) | 8.205 |
| 138 | 4.117, 8.208 |
| 139 | 8.209 |
| 140 | 8.210 |
| 142 | 2.174, 8.212 |
| 143 | 2.174, 8.213 |
| (2) | 8.213 |
| 144 | 8.214 |
| 145 | 2.174, 8.189, 8.215 |
| 146 | 8.216 |
| 147 | 2.174, 8.217 |
| (1) | 8.219 |
| 148 | 8.218 |
| 149 | 8.219 |
| 150(1) | 8.220 |
| (a) (ii) | 8.219 |
| 151 | 8.220–8.222 |
| 152 | 8.223 |
| 153 | 8.224 |
| art 154 | 8.225 |
| 155 | 8.226 |
| (1) | 3.35 |
| 174 | 7.21 |
| (2) | 7.22 |
| 175 | 7.24 |
| 176 | 7.25 |
| 177 | 7.71–7.72 |
| (c) | 7.75 |
| 182 | 8.154 |
| 183 | 8.153 |
| 183–199 | 8.176 |
| 184–199 | 8.155 |
| 185 | 8.159–8.161 |
| 186 | 8.160 |
| 187 | 8.160 |
| 188 | 8.162 |
| 189 | 8.157, 8.163 |
| 190 | 8.164 |
| 191 | 8.167 |
| 192 | 8.168 |
| 206 | 7.107 |
| (1)–(2) | 7.108 |
| (3) | 7.109 |
| 210 | 11.23 |
| Pt 2 | 2.236 |
| 3 | 1.174, 2.467 |
| 4 | 3.12, 3.35–3.35 |
| 5 | 2.275 |
| 7 | 4.117 |
| 8 | 2.162, 2.175, 8.189, 8.215 |
| 9 | 2.187 |
| 11 | 8.200 |
| 16 | 8.176 |
| 10 | 3.23, 4.118, 8.213 |
| 11 | 2.480, 4.120, 8.199, 8.207, 8.216 |
| 13 | 7.21 |
| Sch 2 | 2.128, 2.145, 2.229–2.234, 2.235, 2.236, 2.244, 2.249, 2.252–2.268, 2.269, 2.284–2.286, 2.290–2.300, 2.307, 2.310–2.324, 2.326–2.373, 2.382, 2.385, 2.423–2.431, 2.455, 2.468–2.479, 2.480–2.481, 7.42, 7.47, 7.11, 10.46 |

Planning and Development Regulations 2001
(SI 600/2001) (contd)
  Sch 2B ........................................ 1.280
    Pt 1 ..................... 2.246, 2.286–
                                    2.288, 2.467
    3 ........................ 2.423, 2.437
    3 .......... 3.38, 3.59, 3.60, 3.98, 4.44
    5 ......................... 2.480, 3.23, 3.23,
                                    8.54, 10.45
      Pt 1 ..................................... 10.44
      Pt 2 ..................................... 10.47
      Pt 2 ..................................... 10.46
    6 ..................... 3.35, 3.144, 10.110–
                          10.115, 10.230, 10.239
    7 ..................... 2.186, 2.456, 2.480,
                          2.485–2.487, 9.05, 10.182,
                                    11.86
    8 ............................... 8.206, 8.207,
                                    8.220, 8.211
    9 ............................................... 3.55

Planning and Development Regulations 2003
  (SI 90/2003) .................................. 6.125
  art 3 .............................................. 6.163
  4 ..................................... 1.274, 6.16
  5 ............................................... 6.165

Planning and Development (Strategic
  Environmental Assessment)
  Regulations 2004
  (SI 436/2004) .......... 1.41, 1.134, 1.199,
                                    1.280, 2.182
  art 7 .............................................. 1.174
  art 10 ............................................ 1.282
  Sch 2 (a) ...................................... 1.100

Planning and Development Regulations 2005
  (SI 364/2005) .................... 2.122, 2.128,
                                    2.453, 2.455

Planning and Development Regulations 2006
  (SI 685/2006) ................... 2.102, 2.165,
                                    2.122, 3.12, 3.35–3.43,
                                    3.53–3.57, 3.72–3.75, 3.82,
                                    3.84, 3.94–3.100, 3.122,
                                    3.129–3.133, 4.44, 4.118,
                                    10.88, 10.189, 11.23
  art 4 .............................................. 2.236
  8 ................................................ 3.35
  12 ..................................... 4.124, 4.133
  12–16 ........................................ 4.117

art 13 ................................. 4.54, 4.125
  14 ................................... 4.53, 4.129
  15 ............................................ 4.131
  16 ............................................ 4.133
  16–32 ......................................... 3.12
  17 ................................ 2.161–2.163
    (3) .............................................. 3.36
  18 .............................................. 2.166
    (2) .............................................. 3.37
  19 ................................ 2.167–2.170
  20 .................... 2.187, 2.198–2.199,
                                    10.207
    (1) ............................................ 2.189
  21 .................... 2.187, 2.193, 10.208
    (1) (a) ...................................... 1.257
  22 ................................. 2.187, 2.194,
                                    3.57, 10.210
    (1) .............................................. 3.55
  23–132 .................................... 10.50
  24 ........................ 2.149, 3.74, 10.85
  25 .................................. 3.74, 10.47
  26 .............................................. 3.76
  27 ............................................ 10.101
    (5) .............................................. 3.83
  28 .................................. 3.134, 4.11
  29 (1) ........................................... 4.11
    (2) .............................................. 3.98
  31 ................................ 3.114, 10.102
  32 .............................................. 8.200
  32–37 ....................................... 8.199
  33 .............................................. 8.205
    (2) ................................. 3.122, 8.211
    (3) .............................................. 3.123
  33–37 ....................................... 4.120
  33–39 ......................................... 3.12
  34 .................................. 3.126, 8.211
  35 .................................. 3.133, 8.213
  36 .................................. 2.174, 8.217
  37 .............................................. 8.219
  124 ............................... 10.93–10.95
    (1) ............................................ 10.93
      (a) .......................................... 10.89
      (b) .......................................... 10.90
    (2) ............................................ 10.90
  124–132 .................................. 10.88
  125 ............................... 10.92–10.95
  126 ........................................... 10.93
  127 ........................................... 10.95
  128 ............................... 10.96–10.98

## Table of Statutory Instruments

Planning and Development Regulations 2006 (SI 685/2006) (contd)
- art 130 .................................................. 10.101
- 132(1) ................................................ 10.103
- (3) .................................................... 10.104
- (4) .................................................... 10.105
- (5) .................................................... 10.106
- (6) .................................................... 10.107
- (7) .................................................... 10.108
- 219(2) ................................................. 11.23
- Pt 4   3.12
- Sch 2 ............................................... 2.272, 2.285
- 3 ........................................................ 3.53

Planning and Development Regulations 2007 (SI 83/2007) ............... 2.102,, 2.122, 2.249–2.249 3.12, 3.94, 3.95
- art 4 ...................................................... 8.211
- 9 ......................................................... 3.83
- 11 ....................................................... 3.118

Planning and Development (No 2) Regulations 2007 (SI 135/2007) ................. 2.122, 3.83

Planning and Development Regulations 2008 (SI 235/2008) ............... 2.122, 2.301, 2.360, 2.364, 2.373, 2.382, 2.384, 2.425, 2.458, 2.466, 4.118, 10.230, 10.239
- art 108 ................................................ 10.231
- 124(3) ................................................ 10.91
- Sch 6 .................................................. 10.231

Planning and Development (Amendment) Regulations 2008 ................... 2.305
(SI 256/2008) ............... 2.122, 2.242, 2.480, 10.255

Planning and Development (Amendment) Act 2010 (Commencement) Order 2010 (SI 405/2010) ............................ 10.253

Planning and Development Regulations 2001–2007
- art 32 .................................................... 3.83

Planning and Development Regulations 2001–2008 ............... 2.122, 2.167, 2.459, 2.466, 11.01

Planning and Development Regulations 2001–2010 .......................... 2.182, 2.231
- Pt 8 ....................................................... 2.160

Planning and Development (Amendment) Act 2010 (Commencement) Order 2010 (SI 502/2010) ......................................... 8.91

Planning and Development (Amendment) Act 2010 (Commencement) (No 2) Order 2010 (SI 451/2010) ................ 8.91

Planning and Development (Amendment) Act 2010 (Commencement) (No 3) Order 2010 ........................................... 8.91

Planning and Development Amendment) Act 2010 (Commencement) Order 2011 (SI 132/2011) ........................................... 8.91

Planning and Development Regulation 2010 (SI 406/2010) ........ 9.32

Rules of the Superior Courts
................................................. 4.210, 4.265
- O 63A, r 1(g) ............................... 4.182
- O 84 ............................ 4.174, 4.193, 4.206–4.210, 7.139
- O 84, r 20 (4) ............................... 4.243
- O 84, r 21 (1) ............................... 4.217
- O 84, r 20 (4) ............................... 4.230
- (b) ........................................ 4.265
- O 84, r 21 ...................................... 4.207
- O 84, r 26 ...................................... 4.220
- O 84, r 6 (4) .................................. 4.287
- O 63   (a) ..................................... 4.182
- O 63A ........................................... 4.182
- O 84 .............................................. 4.204
- O 84, r 21 (1) ............................... 4.243

Town and Country Planning (Assessment of Environmental Effects) Regulations 1988 ......................................... 10.150
- art 2 ............................................ 10.150
- 4 ................................................ 10.150

Wireless Telegraphy (Wired Broadcast Relay Licence) Regulations 1974 (SI 67/1974) .................................... 2.359

# TABLE OF EUROPEAN LEGISLATION

Council Directive 75/442/EEC ........... 10.32
    Annex IIA ..................... 10.32

Council Directive
79/409/EEC ............... 1.39, 4.155, 9.11,
    9.68, 9.78–9.78, 9.86, 9.105,
    10.34, 10.182, 12.08
    art 4 ................. 1.212, 4.166, 7.58, 7.64,
        9.96, 12.51
    (2) ............................ 5.26, 10.41
    Annex 1 ....................... 12.51

Council Directive
82/501/EEC ............ 8.189, 8.229, 11.23

Council Directive
85/337/EEC ............... 2.102, 3.23, 4.59,
    4.155, 4.160–4.167, 4.184,
    4.186, 5.13–5.19, 5.57, 8.27,
    8.73–8.74, 8.92, 8.96, 9.05–
    9.07, 9.24–9.24, 9.40, 9.60,
    10.03–10.14, 10.38, 10.51,
    10.60–10.61, 10.67, 10.74–
    10.77, 10.87, 10.120–10.135,
    10.137, 10.150, 10.158,
    10.166, 10.175, 10.182,
    10.212, 10.225–10.232,
    10.241, 10.249–10.255
    1 ....................... 4.188, 10.16, 10.67
        (1) ...................................... 10.15
        (2) .......... 10.26, 10.125, 10.133,
        10.158, 10.166, 10.174–
        10.174, 10.249
        (2)............................ 10.166
        (4) ....................................... 10.67
        (5) .......................... 10.68–10.73
    2 ............................... 5.19, 10.08,
        10.17, 10.40, 10.131
        (1) ................. 5.18, 5.29, 10.06–
        10.07, 10.15, 10.36, 10.76,
        10.126, 10.150, 10.166,
        10.174–10.174
        (2) ........................ 4.157, 10.16,
        10.21–10.22

    (3) ...................... 5.19–5.19, 9.24,
        10.19, 10.41, 10.69, 10.73
    (c) ....................................... 3.144
    (d) ....................................... 3.144
    2–4 ............ 10.225, 10.227, 10.245,
        10.252, 10.254
    2–6 ..........................................
    3 ......................... 2.242, 5.19, 10.13,
        10.18, 10.20, 10.131,
        10.225–10.252
    4 ......................... 5.19–5.21, 10.13,
        10.17–10.19, 10.237
        (1) ......................... 10.32, 10.177
        (2) ................ 5.19, 10.06–10.07,
        10.15, , 10.27, 10.36, 10.76,
        10.119–10.126, 10.166,
        10.174–10.174
        (3) ................ 5.19, 10.34, 10.42,
        10.119, 10.182
        (4) ................................... 10.120
    4–11 ................. 5.19, 10.18, 10.235
    5 ............. 5.21–5.24, 8.237, 10.15,
        10.20–10.23, 10.86, 10.178,
        12.53
        (1) .................. 7.14, 10.35, 10.74
        10.84
        (2) ........................ 10.84, 10.131
    5–10 .................... 5.19–5.19, 10.19,
        10.76, 10.124
    6 ................ 5.22, 5.24, 10.21, 10.86
        (1) ............... 10.15, 10.20, 10.22,
        10.23
        (2) ........................ 10.22, 10.131
        (3) ................................... 10.22
    7 ................... 5.19, 5.23–5.25, 10.17,
        10.21–10.25, 10.86–10.88,
        10.237
    8 ....................... 5.24, 10.23, 10.227
    9 ....................... 5.25, 10.24, 10.60,
        10.227
    11 ......................................... 10.237

Council Directive 85/337/EEC (contd)
  art 10 ...................... 5.26, 10.25, 10.237
    (a) ............. 4.160, 4.167–4.169,
      4.183, 4.184–4.188, 10.60
    10a ............... 4.183, 10.26, 10.60
    11 ...................... 8.235, 10.13, 10.27
    12 ...................... 10.07, 10.28, 10.76
      (2) ...................................... 10.06
    13 ............................................. 10.29
    14 ............................................. 10.30
  Pt IV ............................................... 7.49
  Annex I ..................... 5.19, 8.238, 9.05,
    9.25, 9.96, 9.117, 10.19,
    10.31, 10.32–10.33, 10.44,
    10.76, 10.117, 10.128–
    10.134, 10.161, 10.176–
    10.180, 10.212
    II .................. 5.19, 5.26, 8.233,
    9.05, 9.25, 9.78, 9.117,
    10.06–10.07, 10.31, 10.33,
    10.36, 10.42–10.46, 10.76,
    10.119–10.124, 10.126–
    10.134, 10.150, 10.161,
    10.176–10.180, 10.212
    III ..... 5.19, 10.20, 10.31, 10.34,
    10.119, ......... 10.178, 10.182
    IV ............................ 9.26, 10.31
    H ......................................... 5.19

Council Directive 85/437/EEC
  arts 2–6, 8 and 9 ........................ 10.233

Council Directive 89/106/EEC ............ 12.66

Council Directive
  91/271/EEC ........................ 1.39, 4.155
  art 2   (6) .................................... 10.32

Council Directive
  91/676/EEC ....................... 1.39, 4.155

Council Directive 91/689/EEC ............ 10.32

Council Directive
  92/43/EEC ................. 1.39, 4.155, 5.14,
    8.90, 9.07, 9.24, 9.48, 9.68,
    9.78, 9.86, 9.100, 10.34,
    10.182, 12.08
  art 2 ................................................. 9.89

art 3 ............................................9.105
  4 ......................................9.96, 9.117
    (1) ....................................9.89–9.91
  5 ..................................................9.90
    (1) ....................................9.91–9.95
    (2) ..................................................9.92
    (3) ................................9.93–9.95
    (4) ..................................................9.94
  6 ..........................8.45, 9.101, 9.107,
    10.185
    (2) ..........................................2.470, 9.95
    (3) ...................9.05, 9.70, 9.73–
    9.78, 9.79
    (4) .....................9.12, 9.73–9.76,
    9.83–9.85
  7 ..............................................9.101
  10 ................................1.08, 6.25, 7.64
  11 ..................................................9.89
  15 ..................................................8.240
  21 ...................................9.89, 9.116
  Annex III ................................9.89–9.89

Council Directive 93/37/EEC ................6.64

Council Directive 94/31/EC .................10.32

Council Directive
  96/61/EC ................4.162, 4.183, 4.184,
    4.186, 10.17, 10.139
  15 ..................................................4.168
    (a) ................4.167, 4.168, 4.168

Council Directive
  96/82/EC ....................1.08, 1.39, 3.159,
    4.155, 8.187–8.196, , 8.227–
    8.229, 8.244, 12.40, 12.41
  art 1   (7) ......................................8.237
  4 .....................................8.227–8.229
  7 .....................................8.230–8.234
  8 ..................................................8.231
  9 .....................................8.232–8.234
  10 ..................................................8.234
  11 ..................................................8.236
  12 ..................................................8.237
  13 ..................................................8.238
  14 ..................................................8.239
  16 ..................................................8.241

Council Directive 96/82/EC (contd)
 art 17 ............................................ 8.242
 18 ............................................ 8.243
 19 ............................................ 8.244
 Sch 3 ............................................ 8.203
 Annex II ...................... 8.233
 III ............................................ 8.232
 IV ............................................ 8.236
 V ............................................ 8.238

Council Directive
 97/11/EC ............... 4.155, 4.162, 4.164,
 5.13, 5.19–5.20, 8.27, 9.25,
 10.03, 10.10–10.14, 10.137,
 10.159, 10.182, 10.225
 1–5 .......................................... 10.60
 3 .................................................. 5.27

Council Directive
 2000/60/EC .......................... 1.39, 4.159

Council Directive
 2001/42/EC ............... 1.41, 1.97, 1.141,
 1.187, 1.199, 1.272, 4.159,
 4.184
 art 1 ................................................ 1.41
 3 (8) ...................................... 10.73

EU Directive 2001/91/EC ................... 12.15

Council Directive 2003/4/EC ............... 10.21

Council Directive 2003/5/EC ............... 4.164

Council Directive
 2003/35/EC .............. 4.13, 4.157, 4.160,
 4.165–4.168, 4.168, 4.168,
 4.183, 4.184, 9.25, 10.03,
 10.14, 10.60, 10.225
 art 1 (2) ..................................... 4.160
 (6) ............................................ 10.60
 2 (1) ..................................... 4.157
 (1)–(5) .............................. 4.159
 3 (1) ..................... 4.157, 4.165
 (3)–(6) ............................. 4.166
 (7) ........................... 4.168, 10.60
 4 (4) ..................................... 4.168
 7 ............................................... 4.183
 10 (3) (a) ..................... 4.160, 4.186

Council Directive
 2003/105/EC .................. 8.188, 8.209,
 8.227–8.232, 12.40
 art 1 .................................... 8.228, 8.229
 (6) ............................................ 8.236
 Annex III ................................... 10.182

Council Directive 2008/1/EC .............. 4.184
 art 16 ............................................ 4.184

Council Directive
 2009/31/EC .............. 9.25, 10.03, 10.14,
 10.32–10.33

Council Regulation 974/98/EC ............. 5.79,
 5.81–5.84, 6.121, 7.28

European Communities (Environmental
Impact Assessment) Regulations 1989
(SI 349/1989)
 art 24 ............................................. 2.156

# TABLE OF TREATIES AND CONVENTIONS

EC Treaty ............................................. 10.76
 art 5 ............................................ 10.177
 10 ............................... 10.07, 10.166
 169 ............................................ 10.76
 189 ............................................ 10.177
 226 ............................. 10.76, 10.121
 249 ......................................... 10.234

European Convention
 on Human Rights ............... 5.101, 8.198
 art 6 ..................................... 1.38, 7.174
 (1) ..................................... 5.102

First Protocol 1 ........................ 7.41

Transboundary Convention ........ 2.203, 3.23,
 4.59, 9.40, 9.60, 10.70,
 10.71, 10.87, 10.103, 10.193,
 10.195, 10.201, 10.217,
 10.218, 10.222, 11.06, 11.34,
 11.34, 11.89, 11.91

UN ECE Espoo Convention
 on EIA ..................... 9.25, 10.70, 10.71

# TABLE OF CONSTITUTIONS

Constitution of Ireland ................... 5.101
    Art 5 ........................................... 10.159
        10 ........................................ 10.159
        15 ........................................ 10.159
        26 ................................(2)(i) 3.142
        26.2.1° ............................ 6.12, 6.93
        40 ........................................ 10.159
        40.1 .............................. 1.36, 7.101
        40.3 ........................................ 1.36
        40.3 ................................ 7.02, 7.40
        40.3.2° ................................. 7.102
        43 ............................................ 7.02
        43 ................. 1.30, 7.02, 7.40, 8.78
        43.1 ........................................ 1.31
        43.2 ........................................ 1.32

# Chapter 1
# PLANS, POLICIES, GUIDELINES AND DIRECTIVES

**DEVELOPMENT PLANS**

**[1.01]** At the outset it should be recognised that perhaps the most significant amendments made in the planning legislation as contained in the Planning and Development (Amendment) Act 2010 (PD(A)A 2010) relate to development plans and to local area development plans. PD(A)A 2010, s 7 has inserted an additional subsection into the Planning and Development Act 2000 (PDA 2000), s 10(1) being s 7(a)(1A), which provides that the written statement referred to in PDA 2000, s 10(1) will include a core strategy to demonstrate that the development objectives in the development plan are consistent, as far as practicable, with the national and regional development objectives set out in the National Spatial Strategy (NSS) and in the regional planning guidelines (RPGs). Both the NSS and the RPGs have been frequently overlooked or ignored entirely. A 'core strategy' is defined in PD(A)A 2010, s 4(c) and 'it shall be construed in accordance with s 10 (inserted by s 7 of the PD(A)A 2010)'.[1]

**[1.02]** A development plan is a written statement and a plan or plans setting out the overall strategy for the proper planning and sustainable development of the area of the development plan.[2] It indicates the development objectives for the area of the planning authority. Each planning authority is required to make a development plan every six years for the whole of its area. The requirement to make a development plan is mandatory, not discretionary.[3] Although the development plan is, in a sense, limited to the functional area of the planning authority, nevertheless the planning authority must have regard to plans of adjoining authorities. A planning authority may also, at its choice, make any number of local area plans in respect of particular areas within its own functional area. If a local area plan, or parts of it, as drawn up by a planning authority is in conflict with the development plan, it is the development plan that will prevail. Significantly there is no presumption in law that any land zoned in a particular development plan (including a development plan which has been varied) shall remain so zoned in any subsequent development plan.[4]

**[1.03]** During the balmy years of the Celtic tiger it is known that some 40,000+ hectares of land in Ireland was zoned for residential development. The actual requirement for residentially zoned land were reliably estimated as 12,000 hectares and that is, by all accounts, a reasonably generous estimate for a period of eight years from 2008. The over-zoning, in terms of dwelling unit numbers, amounts to enough zoned land for

---
1. See para **1.06**.
2. PDA 2000, s 10(1).
3. See *Blessington Heritage Trust v Wicklow County Council* [1999] 4 IR 571.
4. PDA 2000, s 10(8).

1,500,000 houses and apartments at a time when the estimate for dwellings or dwelling units up to the year 2016 is 400,000. Some 28,000 hectares will have to be de-zoned or rezoned if this imbalance is to be corrected and the rezoning is scheduled to occur as each new development plan comes into place. It is a matter of absolute priority to ensure that residential zoning is reduced throughout Ireland and to ensure that it keeps pace with but does not exceed demand for residential housing. The over-estimate of residential housing needs was a significant contributor to the collapse of the property market and all that fell with it. It was an inevitable, but mainly unpredicted, reaction to such a widely generous over-estimate of Ireland's housing needs.

**[1.04]** The Supreme Court has defined the development plan as 'an environmental contract' made between the planning authority and the public.[5] In *Attorney General (McGarry) v Sligo County Council*[6] an often quoted definition of the meaning of the development plan was given by McCarthy J as follows:

> The plan is a statement of objectives; it informs the community, in its draft form, of the intended objectives and affords the community the opportunity of inspection, criticism and, if thought proper, objection. When adopted it forms an environmental contract between the planning authority, the Council, and the community, embodying a promise by the Council that it will regulate private development in a manner consistent with the objectives stated in the plan and, further, that the Council itself shall not affect any development which contravenes the plan materially. The private citizen, refused permission for development on such grounds based upon such objectives, may console himself that it will be the same for others during the currency of the plan, and that the Council will not shrink from enforcing these objectives itself. He would be further assured by the requirement of consultation with important and highly qualified independent bodies such as the National Monuments Advisory Council, An Taisce etc.

**[1.05]** *Attorney General (McGarry) v Sligo County Council*[7] concerned Sligo County Council's proposal to develop and operate a dump in the immediate vicinity of what is one of the largest groups of megalithic remains in Western Europe located at Carrowmore outside Sligo town. The Carrowmore burial ground was described in the relevant development plan and the development plan acknowledged its unique importance. It was an objective of the development plan that structures would not be permitted to be built which would conflict with the preservation of this amenity. The proposal to develop a dump in the vicinity was challenged on the grounds that the operation would be in material contravention of the development plan and as such would be illegal. The plaintiff was unsuccessful in the High Court before McWilliam J but was successful before the Supreme Court where McCarthy J held that the dumping proposal did constitute a material contravention of the local authority's development plan.

---

5. See *Attorney General (McGarry) v Sligo County Council* [1991] 1 IR 99 *per* McCarthy J.
6. See *Attorney General (McGarry) v Sligo County Council* [1991] 1 IR 99 *per* McCarthy J.
7. See *Attorney General (McGarry) v Sligo County Council* [1991] 1 IR 99 *per* McCarthy J.

## Core strategy

**[1.06]** PDA 2000, s 10 deals with the content of development plans and sub-s (1) provides that a development plan shall set out the overall strategy for the proper planning and sustainable development of the area of the development plan.

**[1.07]** The development plan must contain the matters listed in PDA 2000, s 10(2). That section has been substantially added to and amended by PD(A)A 2010, s 7.

**[1.08]** Before dealing with the new 'core strategy' principles as introduced by PD(A)A 2010, s 7(1A) it is important to list the objectives that a development plan must include as provided by PDA 2000, s 10(2)(a)-(p), as inserted by PD(A)A 2010, s 7, namely the following:

- (a) the zoning of land for the use solely or primarily of particular areas for particular purposes (whether residential, commercial, industrial, agricultural, recreational, as open space as otherwise or a mixture of those uses), where and to such extent as the proper planning and sustainable development of the area in the opinion of the planning authority requires the uses to be indicated;

- (b) the provision or facilitation of the provision of infrastructure including transport, energy and communication facilities, water supplies, waste recovery and disposal facilities (regard having been had to the waste management plan for the area made in accordance with the Waste Management Act 1996), waste water services and ancillary facilities;

- (c) the conservation and protection of the environment including, in particular, the archaeological and natural heritage and the conservation and protection of European sites and any other sites which may be prescribed for the purposes of this paragraph;

- (ca) the encouragement, pursuant to Article 10 of the Habitats Directive, of the management of features of the landscape, such as traditional field boundaries, important for the ecological coherence of the Natura 2000 network and essential for the migration, disbursal and genetic exchange of wild species.

- (cb) the promotion of compliance with environmental standards and objectives established —
    - (i) for bodies of surface water, by the European Communities (Surface Waters) Regulations 2009;
    - (ii) for ground water, by the European Communities (Ground Water) Regulations 2010;
  
  Which standards and objectives are included in river basin management plans (within the meaning of Regulation 13 of the European Communities (Water Policy) Regulations 2003);[8]

---

8. Paragraphs (ca) and (cb) have been inserted by PD(A)A 2010, s 7(b).

(d) the integration of the planning and sustainable development of the area with the social, community and cultural requirements of the area and its population;

(e) the preservation of the character of the landscape, where, and to the extent that, in the opinion of the planning authority, the proper planning and sustainable development of the area requires it, including the preservation of views and prospects and the amenities of places and features of natural beauty or interest;

(f) the protection of structures, or parts of structures, which are of special architectural, historical, archaeological, artistic, cultural, scientific, social or technical interests;

(g) the preservation of the character of architectural conservation areas;

(h) the development and renewal of areas in need of regeneration;

(i) the provision of accommodation for travellers, and the use of particular areas for that purpose;

(j) the preservation, improvement and extension of amenities and recreational amenities;

(k) the control, having regard to the provisions of the Major Accidents Directive and any regulations, under any enactment, giving effect to that Directive, of —

  (i) siting of new establishments,

  (ii) modification of existing establishments, and

  (iii) development in the vicinity of such a establishments, for the purpose of reducing the risk, or limiting the consequences, of major accident;

(l) the provision, of or facilitation of the provision, of services for the community including, in particular, schools, crèches, and other education and childcare facilities;[9]

(m) the protection of the linguistic and cultural heritage of the Gaeltacht including the promotion of Irish as the community language, where there is a Gaeltacht area in the area of the development plan;[10]

(n) the promotion of sustainable settlement and transportation strategies in urban and rural areas including the promotion measures to —

  (i) reduce energy demand in response to the likelihood of increases in energy and other costs due to long-term decline in non-renewable resources;

  (ii) reduce anthropogenic[11] greenhouse gas emissions, and

  (iii) address the necessity of adaptation to climate change;

---

9. As substituted by PD(A)A 2010, s 7(b)(ii).
10. As substituted by PD(A)A 2010, s 7(b)(ii).
11. PD(A)A 2010, s 4 defines 'anthropogenic' in relation to greenhouse gas emissions as meaning those emissions that result from or are produced by human activity or intervention.

in particular, having regard to location, layout and design of new development;

(o) the preservation of public rights of way which give access to seashore, mountain, lakeshore, riverbank or other place of natural beauty or recreation utility, which public rights of way shall be identified both by marking them on at least one of the maps forming part of the development plan and by indicating their location on a list appended to the development plan, and

(p) landscape, in accordance with relevant policies or objectives for the time being of Government or any Minister of the Government relating to providing framework for identification, assessment, protection, management and planning of landscapes and developed having regard to the European Landscape Convention done at Florence on 20 October 2000.[12]

[1.09] Prior to the commencement date of PD(A)A 2010 planning authorities only had to 'have regard to' the National Spatial Strategy (NSS) and to regional planning guidelines (RPGs). This discretionary rather than mandatory wording allowed for powerful lobbying which resulted in seriously damaging over-zoning of inappropriate land. Effectively, the NSS and the RPGs were ignored by property developers and planning authorities most thoroughly and destructively during the four year period prior to 2006. Housing development and population increases were not directed primarily at the nine major growth 'gateways' planned for in the NSS. Almost half of all national growth in the first four years since the publication of the NSS took place in the commuter belts of Dublin, Cork and Galway. The NSS had identified Dublin and the regional cities as the preferred place for growth. They also highlighted four new 'gateways' to include the towns of Dundalk and Sligo and the linked gateways of Letterkenny/Derry and the midland towns of Athlone, Tullamore and Mullingar as places where preferred growth should occur. The NSS required that government spending on infrastructure such as schools, healthcare and transport links, should be concentrated on the preferred growth areas. The objective of the NSS was to build up critical mass within the gateways and nine 'hubs' identified in the NSS.

[1.10] The need to re-establish the NSS and the RPGs is self evident. The uncontrolled potential for profit making and the requirement for general sustainable development are poor bed fellows. That is not to say that developers are not valuable contributors to the economy but if we are to attempt to avoid the constant fluctuations of high peaks and low troughs the community of developers must work within the boundaries of sustainable development. Local authority planners, some of whom clearly took their eye off the ball, will have to play their part and for the moment they will be forced to do so at least in relation to the NSS and the RPGs, as a consequence of the implications of the core strategy provisions in the PD(A)A 2010. All future development plans are required to include a core strategy to ensure that both development plans and local area plans will run together and to ensure harmonisation between the development plan and the NSS.

---

12. Subsections (c)-(p) have been inserted by PD(A)A 2010, s 7(ii).

All zoning decisions must be taken within the framework of the NSS and within the RPGs. The core strategy is being put in place to ensure that State investment in infrastructure and the provision of services by the State will be utilised in order to obtain the most sustainable outcome. Once the core strategy is in place, local authorities will be bound to adhere to the NSS and to the RPGs. If that adherence is not demonstrated, local authorities will be required to vary their development plans. Local authorities will also be required to carry out ministerial directions.

**[1.11]** Local area plans have been reined in by the provisions of the PD(A)A 2010. They can no longer be used as a backdoor method for the introduction of new zoning during the lifetime of a development plan without offering any opportunity of intervention by the Minister for the Environment, Heritage and Local Government to direct a planning authority to take specific action to amend their plan in the interests of proper planning and sustainable development. Local area plans also are subject to the core strategy contained in the development plan and if any inconsistency appears the Minister has power to direct the planning authority to take specific action in the interests of proper planning and sustainable development. Local authorities are required to comply with ministerial directions to ensure consistency between development plans, local area plans and environmental protection and conservation legislation, particularly in relation to the Habitats Directive. All of this has been achieved through PD(A)A 2010, s 7 and by the addition of four subsections to the PDA 2000, which read as follows:

> (1A) the written statement referred to in subsection (1) shall include a core strategy which shows that the development objectives in the development plan are consistent, as far as practicable, with national and regional development objectives set out in the National Spatial Strategy and regional planning guidelines.
>
> (1B) a planning authority shall prepare a core strategy, other than where subsection (1C) applies, as soon as practicable and in any event not later than a period of one year after the making of regional planning guidelines under Chapter III which affect the area of the development plan, and shall accordingly vary the development plan under section 13 to include the core strategy.
>
> (1C) where a period of more than 4 years has expired since the making of the development plan when regional planning guidelines under Chapter III which affect the area of the development plan are made, the planning authority shall prepare a core strategy for inclusion in the new development plan under section 11 and 12.
>
> (1D) the written statement referred to in subsection (1) shall also include a separate statement which shows that the development objectives of the development plan are consistent, as far as practicable, with the conservation and protection of the environment.

**[1.12]** The PD(A)A 2010 has openly set about controlling the autonomy of both elected members and officials in local authorities in relation to the granting of planning permissions which conflict with the NSS and the RPGs. The Explanatory and Financial

Memorandum published with the first edition of this much altered piece of legislation[13] reads as follows:

> The Bill is driven by the overreaching ambition to strengthen local democracy and accountability, a key objective in accordance with the ongoing process of local government reform being pursued in the context of the White Paper on Local Government, by maintaining the central role of local government in the planning process.

**[1.13]** The 'core strategy' requires planning authorities to provide evidenced based information statements to demonstrate how both the development plan and the housing strategy are consistent with RPGs and with the NSS. The housing strategy has been around, in one way or another, for some time and it has developed and continues to do so. Nevertheless, in terms of the provision of social and affordable housing it has been spectacularly ineffective. As a 'housing strategy' it has also been ignored by wild card zoning decisions and wild card planning permissions which have been put in place to accommodate strategically unsuited sites some of which are frequently under water in the month of November and others located in over-zoned desert areas which when developed will offer poor value and very little hope in terms of sustainable development. The NSS is a younger concept first produced in 2002. Until the commencement of PD(A)A 2010, the NSS was more or less a toothless youngster. The teeth are taking root and sharpening up with the assistance of the 'core strategy' and the new and more powerful use of ministerial directives and ministerial guidelines. The NSS is a document which must and will be improved.

**[1.14]** When making a draft development plan the planning authorities are now compelled to demonstrate by written statement how the policies and objectives contained in ministerial guidelines are implemented in the draft development plan. If the planning authority is of the opinion that because of the nature and characteristics of the area it has not been possible to implement certain objectives and/or the policies of the Minister as set out in the guidelines, the planning authority must provide reasons in writing as to why the policies and objectives of the Minister have not been implemented.[14]

**[1.15]** In making a start, the PD(A)A 2010, s 77 amends the First Schedule to the Principal Act (ie, the PDA 2000) by the deletion of para 2 of the First Schedule. The First Schedule of PDA 2000 sets out the purposes for which objectives may be indicated in a development plan. Under the heading Location and Pattern of Development, para 2 of the First Schedule (Part I) read:

> To promoting sustainable settlement and transportation strategies in urban and rural areas.

---

13. The Planning and Development (Amendment) Bill was substantially amended and altered between the date of its first publication and the date when the Act as passed by both Houses was signed into law by President McAleese. It is regrettable that there was no publication of a revised Explanatory and Financial Memorandum in circumstances where fundamental revisions and amendments occurred.
14. See PDA 2000, s 28 as amended by the insertion of sub-ss (1A) and (1B) by PD(A)A 2010, s 20.

That seems to be a fairly inoffensive statement but one way or another it has been deleted.

**[1.16]** On a more positive note PD(A)A 2010 has added three new paragraphs to the First Schedule of PDA 2000, Pt 1, namely:

6. Carrying out flood risk assessment for the purpose of regulating, restricting and controlling development in areas at risk of flooding ... (whether inland or coastal).[15]

12. Regulating, restricting and controlling development in areas at risk of erosion and other natural hazards.

13. Reserving land for use and cultivation as allotments in regulating, promoting, facilitating or controlling the provision of land for that use.[16]

The real question is whether or not the core strategy principle will work. Linking core strategy to the NSS has the potential of creating a new planning synergy. The NSS was first published in 2002 when it was heralded as 'a coherent national planning framework for Ireland for the next twenty years'.

It is to be hoped that the NSS of 2022 will be so improved as to be completely unrecognisable when compared with today's NSS.

**[1.17]** The next question is, whether the Minister and the Department of Environment, Heritage and Local Government will keep Planning Authorities in line by the use of ministerial directives and ministerial planning guidelines. This is an enormous task as successive draft development plans are rolled out. These draft plans would have to be thoroughly and objectively scrutinised and the temptation for a Minister to promote one political ideology or another must be stamped out should it occur, when, otherwise the plans are consistent with proper planning and sustainable development. Just as the draft development plan should be directed towards achieving proper planning and sustainable developments, so too should ministerial guidelines and directives be issued in a way which is objective and solely motivated by proper planning and sustainable development.

**[1.18]** In fact, the central role of local government in the planning process has not been dealt a fatal blow. The decisions to adopt, alter or vary a development plan remain a reserved function of local elected representatives. However, the practice of producing last minute amendments to development plans and to local area plans, which have commonly involved additional zoning and the delisting of protected structures, will come under public scrutiny and if they deviate from the NSS and RPGs, they will have to be fully justified. The paramount requirement of the core strategy principle, as stated in the memorandum is 'to ensure a closer alignment between National Spatial Strategy, regional planning guidelines, development plans and local area plans'. If this is achieved at a cost of halting unwarranted interference in specialist planning and environmental issues by largely untrained elected representatives, it will be well worthwhile. If officials in the planning authorities respect the synergies which can so readily be achieved in

---

15. Paragraph 6 has been substituted by PD(A)A 2010, s 77(a)(ii).
16. Paragraphs 12 and 13 have been inserted by PD(A)A 2010, s 77(a)(iii).

terms of saving scarce resources and providing permissions which are environmentally alert and genuinely sustainable, progress will be made. It is always a good time to stop developing structures on identified flood plains and, indeed, that particular matter will be attended to by flood risk assessment[17] and by firm ministerial guidelines issued under PDA 2000, s 28 as amended by s 20 of PD(A)A 2010. It is a good time to insist upon sustainable development in terms of strategic planning and in terms of strategic environmental assessment. Implementation of the core strategy provisions will help Ireland to cope more effectively with the uncertainties which are threatened by climate change.

[1.19] Best practice guidance documents have been issued by the Minister on flood risk management, on sustainable rural housing and on sustainable urban residential development. Section 20 of PD(A)A 2010 provides that in having regard to the guidelines issued by the Minister a planning authority shall consider the Minister's policies and objectives contained in the guidelines when preparing the draft development plan and the development plan. A statement is to be attached showing how the planning authority has implemented the policies and objectives of the Minister's guidelines or, if applicable, that it is not possible to implement the policies and objectives contained in the Minister's guidelines, giving reasons as to why the policies and objectives in the Minister's guidelines have not been implemented.[18]

[1.20] The written statement referred to in PDA 2000, s 10(1) shall include a core strategy which demonstrates that the development objectives in the development plan are consistent, as far as practicable, with national development objectives contained in the NSS and with regional development objectives contained in the RPGs.[19]

[1.21] Each planning authority is required to prepare a core strategy as soon as practicable and in any event not later than one year after the making of regional planning guidelines under Chapter III which affect the area of the development plan. The core strategy prepared by the local authority will vary the development plan as a variation in accordance with PDA 2000, s 13 as amended by Planning and Development (Amendment) Act 2010, s 10.

[1.22] If a period of more than four years has expired since the making of the development plan and the making of regional planning guidelines under Chapter III which affect the area of the development plan, the planning authority must prepare a core strategy for inclusion in the new development plan under PDA 2000, ss 11 and 12. Section 11 (as amended by PD(A)A 2010, s 8) deals with the preparation of a draft development plan. PDA 2000, s 12 (as amended by s 9 of PD(A)A 2010) deals with the making of a development plan.[20]

---

17. PD(A)A 2010, s 4 defines 'flood risk assessment' as meaning an assessment of the likelihood of flooding, the potential consequences arising and measures, if any, necessary to manage those consequences.
18. PD(A)A 2010, s 20 amending PDA 2000, s 28.
19. PD(A)A 2010, s 7(1A).
20. PD(A)A 2010, s 7(1C).

**[1.23]** To confirm the purpose of the core strategy provision another new subsection has been added to s 10(1), namely (1D), which reads as follows:

> The written statement referred to in subsection (1) shall also include a separate statement which shows that the development objectives in the development plan are consistent, as far as practicable, with the conservation and protection of the environment.

**[1.24]** PDA 2000, s 10(2), as amended, deals with the contents of development plans. The section has been extended by PD(A)A 2010, s 7(c) which sets out the contents of a core strategy in sub-ss (2A), (2B) and (2C) of the main Act. The purpose of the core strategy is to ensure that development will be controlled as to its type, location and size by the principles laid down in the NSS, the RPGs and any policies of the Minister in relation to national and regional population targets. The planning authority's core strategy in its development plan will give details of the amount of land already zoned for residential use or land zoned for a mixture of residential and other uses, in terms of its size and in terms of the number of units proposed. The core strategy will contain a statement to demonstrate how the zoning proposals are consistent with the NSS and the RPGs and with Ministerial directions.

**[1.25]** The core strategy in a local authority's development plan will set out a settlement hierarchy and provide details of:

(i) whether a city or town referred to in a hierarchy is designated as a gateway or a hub for the purposes of the National Spatial Strategy;

(ii) other towns referred to in the hierarchy;

(iii) any policies or objectives for the time being of the Government or any Minister of the Government in relation to national and regional population targets that apply to towns and cities referred to in the hierarchy;

(iv) any policies or objectives for the time being of the Government or any Minister of the Government in relation to national and regional population targets that apply to the areas or classes of areas not included in the hierarchy;

(v) projected population growth of cities and towns in the hierarchy;

(vi) aggregate projected population, other than population referred to in sub-para (v), in —

    (I) Villages and smaller towns with a population of under 1,500 persons, and

    (II) Open countryside outside of villages and towns;

(vii) Relevant roads that have been classified as national, primary or secondary roads under s 10 of the Roads Act 1993 and relevant regional and local roads within the meaning of s 2 of that Act;

(viii) Relevant inter-urban and commuter rail routes; and

(ix) Where appropriate, rural areas in respect of which planning guidelines relating to sustainable rural housing issued by the Minister under s 28 apply.[21]

**[1.26]** In the case of the development plan for a city or town council the details to be provided are as follows:

(i) the city or town centre concerned,

(ii) the areas designated for significant development during the period of the development plan, particularly areas for which it is intended to prepare a local area plan,

(iii) the availability of public transport within the catchment of residential or commercial development, and

(iv) retail centres in that city or town centre.[22]

**[1.27]** The meaning of 'settlement hierarchy' is defined as meaning a rank given by a planning authority to a city or town which is located within its administrative area. The settlement hierarchy involves ranking cities or towns with a population in excess of 1,500 and then identifying future population growth of those cities or towns in the hierarchy. The ranking is based not only on projected population increase but also on the proposed role and function of that city or town. Thus the settlement hierarchy ranking will take account of the potential of economic development and it will also take account of the potential for social development as, for example, a necessary gateway development which is strategically located in the neighbourhood of a city.[23]

**[1.28]** Another new provision inserted into PDA 2000, s 10(5A) provides that strategic environmental assessment or an appropriate assessment, as the case may be, of a draft development plan shall be carried out where required.[24] The final amendment of PDA 2000, s 10 deals with rights of way and provides that nothing in PD(A)A 2010, s 7 shall affect the existence or validity of any public right of way and further that no objective included in a development plan under this section shall be construed as affecting the power of a local authority to extinguish a public right of way as provided in s 73 of the Roads Act 1993.[25]

## Planning Guidelines No 15

**[1.29]** During 2007 the Department of the Environment, Heritage and Local Government issued planning guidelines dealing with development plans. These guidelines were prepared in order to assist planning authorities in the preparation of their development plans. For a full and clear understanding of the purpose, content and

---

21. PDA 2000, s 10(2A)(f)(i)-(ix) as inserted by PD(A)A 2010, s 7(c) inclusive.
22. PDA 2000, s 10(2A)(g) as inserted by PD(A)A 2010, s 7(c).
23. PDA 2000, s 10(2C) as extended by PD(A)A 2010, s 7(c).
24. Inserted by PD(A)A 2010, s 7(d).
25. PDA 2000, s 10(9) & (10) inserted by PD(A)A 2010, s 7(e).

the objectives of development plans the Department's planning guidelines no 15 are instructive. The guidelines start with an overview and this is reproduced below:[26]

(a) **Overview**

High quality development plans lie at the heart of a high quality planning system. These guidelines set out a framework within which development plans will achieve high standards in:

- how they set out their aims and objectives;
- how they are produced;
- how they are presented; and
- how they are implemented and monitored.

Building upon the legislative framework established by the Planning and Development Acts 2000–2002, as well as past experience, these guidelines set out in detail, how, within the legislative framework for planning, Ireland can develop a more dynamic, objective and inclusive planning system to structure future development that meets wider economic, social, environmental and heritage objectives.

The guidelines have a number of key messages.

(b) **Development plans should be strategic**

Planning and development issues today are complex and frequently overlap with other policy areas such as economic development, transport and education provision. The development plan must recognise the wider policy context and set out a strategic spatial framework – a clear view ahead in development terms – for the area which the development plan covers. This spatial framework, while acknowledging wider social, economic and environmental trends, needs to focus on the 'big picture' of planning issues, possibilities and considerations that will underpin how the development process in that area is to be structured in order to achieve the plan's objectives for the wider community.

(c) **Development plans should be a catalyst for positive change and progress**

Development plans must recognise and be responsive to the fact that Ireland's population and economy are continuing to grow rapidly. Ireland is one of only four countries out of the 25 member states of the European Union where a pattern of significant upward increase in population is predicted to the year 2020 and beyond. The latest population projections from the Central Statistics Office indicate that the population will by then exceed 5 million. Up to 1 million homes could be needed to cater for the demand for housing to which this level of population increase and the reducing size and composition of households may

---

26. Paragraphs (a)–(j) are taken from a Department of the Environment, Heritage and Local Government publication entitled 'Development Plans: Guidelines for Planning Authorities', (June 2007). These guidelines must now be read in conjunction with the provisions made by PD(A)A 2010, s 7. It is likely that new guidelines will be issued to take account of the 'core strategy' and increased environmental awareness.

give rise.[27] Substantial retail development and development of educational, health and leisure facilities and other services, offices, enterprise and commercial development will also be needed to cater for this scale of projected growth. All of this will need to be underpinned by substantial investment by both the public and private sectors in modern infrastructure to catch up with the country's infrastructural deficit and continue to up-grade, modernise, provide and expand infrastructure such as roads, public transport, energy and telecommunications.

The making and implementation of the development plan provides an opportunity for Planning Authorities to ensure that new development is promoted and structured in a way that achieves high standards, in terms of architectural quality and urban design and in the development of a high quality of public realm and compact towns and cities. The competitiveness of places will in the future increasingly depend on their attractiveness in terms of urban design, quality of amenities and efficiency of circulation. The development plan has the key role in ensuring that all of these objectives are met, thereby bolstering regional competitiveness.

The National Spatial Strategy (NSS) sets out a strategic planning framework to cater for the scale of anticipated development in Ireland for the period up to 2020. Gateways, hubs and other towns will see significant growth. The NSS also stresses the importance of creating places that will attract and sustain both people and jobs.

The development plan is central to achieving greater balance in regional development and enabling all areas to develop to their maximum potential. The plan creates the vision for the area it covers, specifies the type, amount and quality of development needed to achieve that vision and seeks to protect and enhance the environment and amenities. It creates the policy framework and necessary degree of certainty within which individual development decisions can be made over the life of the plan.

**(d) Development plans should anticipate future needs on an objective basis**

Development plans, based on an objective, needs driven assessment of future development requirements including the amount of land that needs to be zoned for particular purposes, will help to build public confidence in the preparation of those plans and their implementation. Zoning that is not responsive to or justifiable by reference to reasonable needs, or which substantially exceeds such needs, is not consistent with proper planning and sustainable development.[28]

**(e) Role in protecting the environment and heritage**

Development plans play a central role in the identification and protection of the natural and the built environment. The development plan will set out policies for the protection of the environment and heritage and is an important source of information for landowners, developers, communities and members of the public in this regard. Development plan policies affecting protected sites should be clearly compatible with their long-term protection and sustainable use.

---

27. In view of the economic situation in existence as this book goes to press these figures are likely to be revised downwards.
28. This paragraph was written in 2007 or earlier. Someone, at least, was aware of the dangers of over-zoning.

**(f) Development plans as a framework within which sustainable development can be achieved**

As the blueprint for development for their areas, development plans are the overarching strategic framework document for sustainable development. Sustainable development means ensuring that all development is sustainable in economic, social and environmental terms. As such, the development plan must offer clear guidance on sustainable development policies and objectives, both national and local, which address the various issues involved, such as climate change, waste management, transport, urban development, sustainable communities, use of natural resources and so on.

Development plans should be consistent with the objectives of *The National Climate Change Strategy 2007–2012,* which builds on the commitment to sustainable development set out in *Towards 2016* and the *National Development Plan 2007–2013.* This is one of a number of inter-related Government initiatives that will address energy and climate change issues.

**(g) Consistency between plans and strategies at different levels is essential**

New frameworks for planning at national, regional, county and city levels have been provided with the National Spatial Strategy, regional planning guidelines and the revised arrangements for preparing development plans under the provisions of the Planning and Development Act 2000. However, to be effective each layer of the planning system must reinforce and support the others. Development plans should take on board and implement relevant national and regional policies in a manner consistent with the NSS and regional guidelines if the planning system as a whole is to function effectively. Similarly, good development plans will inform policies at regional and national level. It is intended that guidance will also be prepared for planning authorities on Local Area Plans which will complete the suite of guidance for each layer in the planning framework.

**(h) Ownership of the development plan is central to effective implementation**

The development plan is a framework for both initiating and influencing the process of change in our surroundings in order to support the wider economic, social and environmental objectives of the community. Building ownership of the plan by the elected members who adopt it, and by wider public and sectoral interests is essential to facilitating the plan's effective implementation. This will make the ongoing planning process, including the assessment of planning applications more transparent and efficient.

**(i) Diverse community needs should be addressed**

The mix of different people in many areas, particularly in cities and towns, is changing rapidly. New communities are being established, made up of a diverse range of people of varying age, sex, race and ethnic background, physical ability and faith. Research into why certain cities and regions have a competitive economic advantage indicates that cultural diversity is one of the factors involved. In this broad sense, immigration is likely to continue playing a significant role in supporting Ireland's economic development in the years ahead.

The planning process should be responsive to the planning issues arising from growing cultural diversity and should seek, where possible, to actively affirm and support the needs of the new local communities which are emerging. The areas where immigrants settle have the potential to develop a new local diversity which can re-vitalise them and support urban regeneration. New approaches to work practices, new types of entrepreneurship, links with home countries and other innovative approaches which immigrants may bring can become a basis for stimulating new local economic activity. Development plans may need to specifically recognise these changes and seek to create conditions which enable the potential for local initiatives to be realised. Views on the acceptability of different types and mixes of retail, commercial and other business activities at neighbourhood or community level should be teased out and reviewed, taking account of input from immigrant communities.

Effective data analysis combined with local knowledge from sources such as social services and educational establishments can help identify planning needs. In particular, planning authorities should seek to pro-actively engage with the Department of Education and Science to identify existing and future education requirements and plans from the national perspective. Greater liaison with the Department of Education and Science should also enable planning authorities to exploit the synergies involved in planning for educational provision.

In addition, consultation should reach out to those whose views may not have been canvassed in the past, and not just to those who have traditionally participated in the process. Different methods and techniques may be required for different sections of the population. Local planning authorities should involve the community at an early stage in the preparation of development plans. The community should also be involved in the monitoring process to help assess the impact of the development plan for different people in the community.

**(j) Codes of Conduct must be observed in making the development plan**

In making and adopting the development plan, the elected council, acting in the interests of the common good and the proper planning and sustainable development of the area,[29] must, in accordance with the *Code of Conduct for Councillors* prepared under the Local Government Act 2001, carry out their duties in this regard in a transparent manner, and must follow due process, and make their decisions based on relevant considerations, while ignoring that which is irrelevant within the requirements of the statutory planning framework. Equally, local authority employees involved in the preparation of the development plan should perform their duties objectively and should have no vested interest in the contents of the plan – see the *Code of Conduct for Employees* prepared under the Local Government Act 2001. Development plans should be user friendly, logical, internally consistent, up-to-date and in a format which is suitable for hardcopy, Internet and CD versions.[30]

---

29. It is manifestly the case that the interests of the common good and proper planning and sustainable development are principles which come into head-on conflict with profitability. Profit making must never be denied but it needs to be controlled if 'sustainable development' and common good policies are to survive.
30. Extracted from Guidelines for Planning Authorities, published by Department of Environment, Heritage and Local Government.

## Development plans and the Constitution

**[1.30]** Article 43 of the Constitution guarantees to defend and vindicate, as far as is practicable, the rights to private property.

**[1.31]** Article 43.1 reads:

> 1° The State acknowledges that man, in virtue of his rational being, has the natural right, antecedent to positive law, to private ownership of external goods.
>
> 2° The State accordingly guarantees to pass no law attempting to abolish the right of private ownership or the general right to transfer, bequeath, and inherit property.

The Constitution does, however, concede that limits can be placed on property rights in the interests of social justice and in the interests of common good.

**[1.32]** Article 43.2 reads:

> 1° The State recognises, however, that the exercise of the rights mentioned in the foregoing provisions of this Article ought, in civil society, to be regulated by the principles of social justice.
>
> 2° The State, accordingly, may as occasion requires delimit by law the exercise of the said rights with a view to reconciling their exercise with the exigencies of the common good.

**[1.33]** The relationship between the development plan of a local authority and the constitutional guarantee of property rights was scrutinised in *Central Dublin Association v The Attorney General*[31] where the court upheld the constitutionality of development plans. The court's main reasons for so doing may be summarised as follows.

**[1.34]** Development plans are constitutional because:

(i) They are for the common good.

(ii) Property owners are made aware that their property rights may be adversely affected by development plans, but they are given a right within the system to make objections. Due process is available to objectors who may make their views known.

(iii) Where there is undue interference with property rights, compensation can be claimed.

**[1.35]** The court recognised that the making of a development plan could cause a serious reduction in the value of property in some cases while in others a rezoning, for example, from agricultural to housing development would cause a substantial increase in value. The court held that a plan of development throughout all the administrative areas of Ireland is necessary for the common good even if, in some cases, it might lead to

---

31. *Central Dublin Association v Attorney General* (1975) 109 ILTR 69.

reduction in value of certain property. Because it is necessary to control development in a structured and thought-out manner and because development plans are for the common good they could not be said to be an unjust attack on the property rights of citizens.

**[1.36]** The effect of the decision in *Central Dublin Association v The Attorney General*[32] was to strengthen and recognise the concept of and the necessity for development plans. The reasons given in (i) and (ii) in para **1.34** above are generally sound but reason (iii) gives rise to questions as to what is or is not 'undue interference' or perhaps an 'unjust attack' on one's property rights. For example, a special amenity area order might very well reduce the value of a property owner's land either by a considerable amount or indeed to nothing at all; nevertheless there is no provision for compensation for a landowner who is affected by such an order. In the High Court, Budd J demonstrated how the courts may be willing to find that the manner in which the property rights were restricted may, on occasions, be unconstitutional. In *An Blascaod Mór Teo v Commissioners of Public Works in Ireland*,[33] the Supreme Court upheld the views of Budd J in the High Court by declaring that the Blascaod Mór National Historic Park Act 1989 was unconstitutional because the provisions of that Act provided for compulsory acquisition of lands depending on the pedigree of the landowners. The decision established the principle that there may be some circumstances where a court will find that the restriction of property rights imposed by the planning process is unconstitutional. In this case, the Act[34] had provided that the Commissioners of Public Works could not compulsorily acquire lands owned by persons or their relatives or their lineal descendants who are ordinarily resident on the Great Blascaod Island prior to 17 November 1953. In fact, none of the plaintiffs nor their lineal descendants were pre–53 residents and, in consequence, the lands were subject to compulsory purchase order (CPO). Barrington J held that the Act of 1989[35] introduced an unusual and dubious classification with ethnic and racial overtones. The classification imposed by the Act[36] was based on a principle of pedigree which, outside the law of succession, had no place in a democratic society committed to the principle of equality. In making a distinction between persons from whom land could be acquired compulsorily and persons from whom land could not be so acquired, the Act[37] in its entirety was contrary to the provisions of Art 40.1 and 40.3 and as such was deemed to be unconstitutional. The High Court also ruled that although property rights may be restricted in the interests of the common good, the State (and perhaps local authorities) can be required to give reasoned justifications for imposing limitations to ensure that these limitations are neither discriminatory nor disproportionate. The equality provisions in the Constitution are paramount and land use plans cannot influence them.

---

32. *Central Dublin Association v The Attorney General* (1995) 109 ILTR 69.
33. *An Blascaod Mór Teo v Commissioners of Public Works in Ireland* [2000] 1 IR 6.
34. Blascaod Mór National Historic Park Act 1989.
35. Blascaod Mór National Historic Park Act 1989.
36. Blascaod Mór National Historic Park Act 1989.
37. Blascaod Mór National Historic Park Act 1989.

**[1.37]** Although the status of a development plan can be considered reasonably secure in the light of the decision in *Central Dublin Development Association v The Attorney General*[38] the same cannot be said for the draft development plan, particularly in relation to objectives which are contained within it and which did not appear or which are materially different from those in the development plans which preceded the draft. Thus, in *Ebonwood Ltd v Meath County Council*[39] Peart J held that compensation for refusal of a planning permission could not be excluded for reasons based on provisions in a draft development plan. The learned judge laid emphasis on the importance of the public's participation rights in the planning process. While the plan was still a draft plan that process had not been exhausted. The draft plan is, after all, a mere proposal. It is not a development plan. It is likely that if the local authority had made a variation of the plan to include the objectives which were proposed in the draft plan then that variation, provided it had gone through all the processes laid down in the Act, would be sufficient to deny compensation to the plaintiff in that case because the variation, once confirmed, is part of the development plan. Peart J referred to *Chawke Caravans Limited v Limerick County Council*[40] and found that it was beyond doubt that any reference in the Act to a development plan is a reference only to the development plan currently in force and not to any draft plan.

## Development plans and the ECHR

**[1.38]** Planning authorities, in preparing a development plan, must ensure that any person affected by the plan must be afforded a right to participate by being offered a fair hearing before an impartial tribunal. The planning authority must also have genuine regard to any submissions made by participants. In making a decision in relation to a development plan or other land use plan the planning authority is bound to give reasons for its decisions. Article 6 of the European Convention on Human Rights makes provision for rights to a fair hearing before an impartial tribunal and compels planning authorities to give a proper opportunity to all persons likely to be affected by the development plan to make their views known to the planning authority during the course of the process and before the development plan is voted as the accepted development plan by the elected members of the local authority.

## EU Directives and development plans

**[1.39]** There are a number of EU directives which must be taken into consideration by a local authority in preparing its development plan. Member States are required to draw up appropriate management plans to take care of the following:

(a) Directive 79/409/EC requires the preparation of management plans for habitats of wild birds.

---

38. *Central Dublin Development Association v The Attorney General* (1975) 109 ILTR 69.
39. *Ebonwood Ltd v Meath County Council* [2004] ILRM 305 HC.
40. *Chawke Caravans Limited v Limerick County Council* (unreported, 20 December 1997) HC.

(b) Directive 92/43/EEC requires that account must be taken for the management of wild flora and fauna.

(c) PDA 2000, s 10(2)(c) requires that a development plan must include the conservation and protection of the environment including, in particular, the archaeological and natural heritage and the conservation and protection of European sites and other sites which may be prescribed for the purposes of the paragraph.

(d) Directive 91/271/EEC dealing with the treatment of disposal of urban waste water must be taken into account.

(e) Directive 91/676/EEC dealing with the protection of waters from pollution by agricultural nitrate must be taken into account.

(f) Directive 96/82/EC (the Seveso Directive) dealing with the control of major accident hazards resulting from the manufacture or use of dangerous substances must be taken into consideration. In particular, Member States are required to ensure that 'land use policies' provide objectives for the prevention of major accidents and for the limitation of their consequences. The siting of new establishments (a place where dangerous substances are used and/or manufactured) and the modification of existing establishments, must be controlled in such a manner as to rule out, as far as is possible, danger to human life and danger to other developments in the surrounding area. This is specifically dealt with as a mandatory objective for development plans in PDA 2000, s 10(2)(k) which provides for the control, having regard to the provisions of the Major Accidents Directive and any regulations under any enactment giving effect to that Directive of:

   (i) the siting of a new establishment;

   (ii) the modification of an existing establishment;

   (iii) development in the vicinity of such establishment for the purpose of reducing risk or limiting the consequences of a major accident.

(g) Directive 2000/60/EC requires that good water management and land use policies must be taken into consideration by a local authority in preparing its development plan.

## Sustainability of development plans and strategic environmental assessment

[1.40] The definition of 'development plan' requires that the plan must set out the overall strategy for the proper planning and *sustainable development* for the area of the planning authority. The development plan must indicate development objectives. The concept of sustainable development first received statutory recognition in PDA 2000. Sustainable development is widely understood as a concept which promotes environmental issues but it goes further than that. While the concept of sustainable development does include environmental sustainability it also includes economic sustainability, social sustainability, cultural sustainability and educational and recreational sustainability.

**[1.41]** Most importantly, in relation to environmental sustainability, the requirements of Directive 2001/42/EC of 27 June 2001 on the assessment of the effects of certain plans and programmes on the environment has been transposed into Irish law by virtue of the European Communities (Environmental Assessment of Certain Plans and Programmes) Regulations 2004 (SI 435/2004), and the Planning and Development (Strategic Environmental Assessment) Regulations 2004 (SI 436/2004). Directive 2001/42/EC is commonly known as the SEA Directive, and art 1 of the SEA Directive states:

> The objective of this Directive, is to provide for a high level of protection of the environment and to contribute to the integration of environmental considerations into the preparation for adoption of plans and programmes with a view to promoting sustainable development, by ensuring that, in accordance with this Directive, an environmental assessment is carried out of certain plans and programmes which are likely to have significant effects on the environment.

**[1.42]** Guidelines for regional authorities and planning authorities comprising assessment of the effects of certain plans and programmes on the environment were issued in November 2004 dealing with the implementation of the SEA Directive. The guidelines relate to the application of the SEA Directive to certain plans prepared under PDA 2000 and are particularly addressed to:

(a) regional authorities, in relation to the preparation or review of regional planning guidelines;

(b) planning authorities, in relation to the preparation or review of development plans and local area plans;

(c) relevant development agencies, in relation to the preparation of a planning scheme in respect of a strategic development zone (SDZ).

The range of environmental issues to be addressed in an SEA is similar to the environmental impact assessment (EIA) regime for the protection of such matters as air, water, flora and fauna and animal life, etc. In effect, an SEA requires strategic environmental assessment of development plans, local area plans and regional and planning guidelines and the development of strategic development zones.

**Permission for development**

**[1.43]** PDA 2000, s 34, as amended,[41] deals with the application for planning permission and it goes without saying that full account of a development plan must be taken in preparing an application for planning permission. PDA 2000 requires that the planning authority, when making its decision in relation to an application under s 34, shall have

---

41. PDA 2000 has been substantially amended by PD(A)A 2010, s 23 and both the section and the amendments of it are dealt with comprehensively in **Ch 2**.

regard to the provisions of the development plan. In making its decision in relation to an application the planning authority is also restricted to considering the proper planning and sustainable development of the area.[42] PDA 2000 lists a number of matters, including the provisions of the development plan, to which the planning authority must have regard and these are dealt with below.

## Material contravention of development plans

**[1.44]** A planning authority cannot legally grant permission for a development which is in material contravention of its own development plan. For example, if an application for permission relates to land which is zoned for agricultural use, a planning authority cannot grant a permission for the building of a residential housing estate on that land unless it adopts the procedure set out in PDA 2000, as amended by PD(A)A 2010, s 23. The section and the amendment set out the procedures to be followed by a planning authority when a planning permission would materially contravene its own development plan. If the permission is to survive, the planning authority must follow the material contravention procedure meticulously.

**[1.45]** The functions of a planning authority are divided into executive functions (those exercisable by the manager of a planning authority) and reserved functions (those which may be implemented only by resolution of the elected members of the planning authority). In a planning context, it should be noted that the determination of planning applications is generally an executive function subject, however, to the provisions of s 140 of Local Government Act 2001 (LGA 2001).[43]

**[1.46]** The making of a development plan or variation to a development plan is a reserved function unless the elected members of the local authority do not decide to make the plan within a period of two years from the giving of notice under PDA 2000, s 11(1), as amended.[44] Section 11(1) provides that notice of intention to review the local authority's existing development plan and to make a new development plan must be given not later than four years after the making of its development plan. Thus, the elected members have a maximum period of six years in which to make a new development plan and if they fail to do so the manager will be required to make the plan at the end of that time which may not be a full six years.[45] Notice may be given some time before the expiration of four years and the time in which to make the development plan is the date of the notice within the four year period plus two years. If the manager is required to make the plan at the end of the correct time the plan must include all elements of the plan already agreed by the elected members.[46]

---

42. PDA 2000, s 34(2)(a).
43. See below at paras **1.50–1.52**. This part of the material contravention procedure was previously legislated for in the City and County Management (Amendment) Act 1955, s 4.
44. See PD(A)A 2010, s 8.
45. PDA 2000, s 9(1).
46. PDA 2000, s 12(14) as amended by PD(A)A 2010, s 9(f)(a).

**[1.47]** PDA 2000, s 11(1A), as inserted by PD(A)A 2010, s 8(a) requires that any review of a development plan or the making of a new development plan must be strategic in nature to ensure that what will be delivered is consistent with an overall strategy for the proper planning and sustainable development of the area covered by the development plan. The review of or the making of a new draft plan must also be strategic in nature for the purposes of the core strategy. The newly inserted s 11(1A) requires that the development plan must take account of any statutory obligations of any local authority in the area and must also take account of the relevant policies and objectives of the government or of its Ministers.

**[1.48]** PDA 2000,[47] as amended, allows the planning authority, by means of the material contravention procedure, to grant permission even though the development proposal concerned would contravene materially the development plan or the local area plan, provided the following requirements are strictly adhered to before permission is granted, namely:

    (i)    notice in the prescribed form of the intention of the planning authority to consider deciding to grant the permission shall be published in at least one daily newspaper circulating in its area and the notice shall specifically state which objective of the development plan would be materially contravened by granting this permission,

    (ii)   copies of the notice shall be given to each of the following —

        (I)    the applicant,

        (II)   a prescribed body which has been notified of the application by the planning authority, and

        (III)  any person who has submitted a submission or observation in writing in relation to the development to which the application relates,

    (iii)  any submission or observation as regards the making of a decision to grant permission and which is received by the planning authority not later than 4 weeks after the first publication of the notice shall be duly considered by the authority,

    (iiia) not later than 6 weeks from the publication of the notice under subparagraph (i), the manager shall prepare a report for the planning authority advising the authority of his or her opinion regarding the compliance or otherwise of the proposed development under any relevant Ministerial guidelines under section 2(8) or any relevant policies or objectives of the Government or Minister of the Government or with any regional planning guidelines and the report shall be considered by the authority before a resolution is passed under subparagraph (iv), and

    (iv)  a resolution shall be passed by the authority requiring that a decision to grant permission be made.

The section continues by providing that it shall be necessary for the passing of a resolution referred to in para (a) that the number of the members of the planning

---

47.    PDA 2000, s 34(6) as amended by PD(A)A 2010, s 23(a).

authority voting in favour of the resolution is not less than three-quarters of the total number of the members of the planning authority or where the number so obtained is not a whole number, the whole number next below the number so obtained shall be sufficient, and the requirement of this paragraph is in addition to and not in substitution for any other requirement applying in relation to such resolution. Minister Gormley appears to have considered that a two-thirds majority should be required. That proposal appears to have vanished and the required majority remains at three-quarters. The three-quarters majority which represents 75% is preferable to the two-thirds majority which represents 66.6% recurring. It is perhaps to be regretted that the Minister did not abolish this provision altogether. Material contravention has been frequently, but not exclusively, operated by elected representatives in a manner which is incompatible with the concept of sustainable development.

**[1.49]** PDA 2000[48] provides that where:

    (i)    notice is given pursuant to section 140 of the Local Government Act 2001 of intention to propose a resolution which, if passed, would require the manager to decide to grant permission under this section; and

    (ii)    the manager is of the opinion that the development concerned would contravene materially the development plan;

he or she shall within one week of receiving the notice, make by order, a declaration stating his or her opinion (a copy of which shall be furnished by him or her to each of the signatories of the notice) and thereupon the provisions of sub-paragraphs (i), (ii) and (iii) of paragraph (a) shall apply and have effect and shall operate to cause the notice to be of no further effect.[49]

If a resolution shall be passed by the authority, requiring that a decision to grant permission be made in material contravention of the authority's development plan, the manager shall decide to grant the relevant permission.[50] Subparagraphs (i), (ii) and (iii) of s 34(2)(a), deal with matters to which the planning authority shall be restricted to considering in making its decision in accordance with proper planning and sustainable development of the area, regard being had to:

    (i)    the provisions of the development plan;

    (ii)    the provision of any special amenity area order relating to the area;

    (iii)    any European site or any other area prescribed for the purposes of s 10(2)(c).

**[1.50]** The LGA 2001 has amended and replaced s 4 of the City and County Management (Amendment) Act 1955. Section 140(1) of LGA 2001 reads:

    (i)    In this section 'local authority' includes a joint body.

    (ii)    Subject to this section, an elected council or joint body may by resolution require any particular act, matter or thing specifically mentioned in the

---

48.    PDA 2000, s 34(6)(c).

49.    See PDA 2000, s 34(6)(c)(i) and (ii). Note that the City and County Management (Amendment) Act 1955 has been replaced by LGA 2001.

50.    PDA 2000, s 34(6)(d).

resolution and which the local authority or the manager concerned can lawfully do or effect, to be done or effected in the performance of the executive functions of the local authority.[51]

In effect, this section allows elected members to exercise a degree of control over the officials of a planning authority in the performance of their executive functions. Although this principle was accepted in *Sharpe (P&F) Limited v Dublin City and County Manager*,[52] that case imposed an obligation on elected members to act in a judicial manner. The question can always be asked of the decision made by the elected members of a planning authority, as to whether or not the decision was reached in a judicial manner.

[1.51] Section 140 decisions are by no means uncommon, and councillors have frequently compelled their manager to grant permission for a particular development in contravention of the development plan. In reaching their decision, the councillors must take into consideration the principles of proper planning and of sustainable development.

[1.52] There has always been some speculation, as to just how effective s 140[53] motions are, in directing a manager as to how he/she should exercise his/her executive functions in deciding on planning matters. As seen, the decision in *Sharpe (P&F) Ltd v Dublin City and County Manager* supported the proposition that a s 4 motion could direct a county manager to grant or refuse a planning permission. In that case the Supreme Court held that a county manager, served with a s 4 resolution (now a s 140 resolution) to grant planning permission which materially contravenes the development plan, must comply with that resolution provided:

(1) that the elected members acted in a judicial manner;

(2) that parties affected by the decision received a fair and proper opportunity to have their views conveyed to the elected members and that the elected members acted fairly in all respects in arriving at the decision;

(3) that the resolution is valid and lawful.

[1.53] A heavy burden is placed on the elected representatives in that:

(i) the elected members are obliged to act in a judicial manner, that is to say that they must have regard to all relevant and legitimate factors before them and they must disregard all irrelevant and illegitimate factors;

(ii) they must consider and take account of invited planning objections or representations and they cannot proceed to ignore these planning objections or representations or to pay them no heed;

---

51. The remainder of the procedures required for initiating material contravention are set out in s 140(3)–(11) inclusive of LGA 2001 under the heading 'Requirement for a particular thing to be done.'
52. *Sharpe (P & F) Limited v Dublin City and County Manager* [1989] ILRM 565.
53. These were commonly referred to as 's 4 motions' being the City and County Management (Amendment) Act 1955, s 4 as now amended by LGA 2001, s 140.

(iii) if they do not allow the planning objections or representations made to them to influence the decision to adopt or not to adopt the resolution directing the manager to give permission, then the whole procedure could be declared invalid on judicial review. At the very least, there is a good deal of uncertainty in relation to the s 140 procedure which, in many cases, may provide an objector with adequate grounds for judicial review.

A resolution which is 'unreasonable' would be illegal and need not be obeyed by the county manager.[54]

**[1.54]** *Child v Wicklow County Council*,[55] is another important case which shows a fairly determined attempt by the judiciary to insist that the operation of, what were then, s 4 resolutions are conducted strictly within the principles as laid down. The court in that case held that decisions of the elected members which failed to take account of proper planning and development of the area or which ignored or rejected the advice of expert officials, and which failed to take previous refusals of permission for the same development into account, were *ultra vires*.

**[1.55]** *Sharpe (P&F) Ltd v Dublin City and County Manager*[56] also required that in the case of what were then s 4 motions, the elected members are obliged to ensure that 'an adequate note is taken and not necessarily verbatim, but of sufficient detail to permit a court on judicial review to be able to ascertain the material on which the decision was reached' (*per* Finlay CJ).

**[1.56]** There are many examples of cases where the court has ruled on circumstances which amounted to a material contravention. In *Roughan v Clare County Council*,[57] the respondents proposed to develop a halting site for the travelling community in an area which had been classified as a special development zone. The proposal was held to be in material contravention of the county council's own development plan which contained a designation as a special development zone, and in consequence the proposal was ruled to be *ultra vires*. Barron J stated that he did not accept that it was unnecessary for a local authority to include all of its development objectives in its development plan. If that were the case a local authority would be allowed to override not only the plan but also the important consultative procedures which pre-empt the making of the development plan. Barron J, in making his decision, also attempted to provide a definition of 'material contravention' as follows:

> It has been submitted on behalf of the applicants that what is or is not a material contravention has to be considered in the light of the substance of the proposed development; whether or not any change of use would be significant; the location of the proposed development; the planning history of the site or area; and the objectives of the development plan. I accept that all these matters must be taken into account when considering whether or not any proposed contravention of the

---

54. See *State (Keegan) v Stardust Compensation Tribunal* [1987] ILRM 202.
55. *Child v Wicklow County Council* [1995] IR 425.
56. *Sharpe (P & F) Limited v Dublin City and County Manager* [1989] ILRM 565.
57. *Roughan v Clare County Council* (unreported, 18 December 1996) HC.

development plan is material. What is material depends upon the grounds upon which the proposed development is being, or might reasonably be expected to be, opposed by local interests. If there are no real or substantial grounds, in the context of planning law, for opposing the development then, it is unlikely to be a material contravention. In the present case it seems clear that no development involving more than two units would be permitted by the local authority. It is also clear from previous applications for permission in special development zones that the local authority regards the exceptions laid down in the plan as being the only grounds upon which developments may be permitted. I am satisfied that in the present case the proposed development is one which would be a material contravention of the development plan. There is a statutory procedure for the making of development plans which involves consultation with the local population and advising the local population of the local authority's proposals by advertisement. The local population are entitled to the rights of such consultation and it seems to me that to allow any alteration of the plan which would not have been anticipated by those reading the plan would be in breach of the rights of the local population to such consultation.

**[1.57]** In *Roughan v Clare County Council*,[58] it was of course always open to the councillors of the county council to pass a s 4 (as it then was) resolution directing the manager to grant the permission.

**[1.58]** It is clear to some (but not all) lawyers and planners alike that PDA 2000 would have greatly benefited the planning process if PDA 2000, s 34(6) had been left out altogether. Looking at the cases cited, it is suggested that it is highly unlikely that all of the requirements laid down in the various decided cases are followed in all instances of material contravention procedures initiated by the elected members, when deciding to pass a resolution directing the manager as to how he/she should decide on planning matters. Elected representatives are mainly concerned with the worries and anxieties of their constituents. They are not, for the most part, trained or skilled in planning practice. If sustainable development is to be achieved it is far better to leave matters, which strictly concern planning issues, in the hands of planning experts. The democratic process is closely related to the material concerns and aspirations of members of the public. It is unsuited to the making of objective and sustainable planning decisions as to whether or not a development proposal should proceed, in circumstances where it is clearly in material contravention of the development plan. The elected representatives must, in some cases at least, find it hard to remain objective when dealing with two issues which are often in conflict with each other, namely:

(i) the hopes and aspirations of the developer applicant;

(ii) the hopes and aspirations of the development plan.

**[1.59]** There have been a number of successful challenges, including *Flanagan v Galway City and County Manager*,[59] where the county manager refused to obey a s 4

---

58. *Roughan v Clare County Council* (unreported, 18 December 1996) HC.
59. *Flanagan v Galway City and County Manager* [1990] 2 IR 66 HC.

resolution. The elected members sought an order of *mandamus* but their application was refused because it was shown that the elected members had been motivated by the personal circumstances of the applicant. Similar circumstances arose in *Griffin v Galway City and County Manager*,[60] where the manager refused to obey a s 140 resolution and an order for *mandamus* was refused because the elected members had taken into account the personal circumstances of the applicant. The elected members are confined to a consideration of the proper planning and sustainable development of their area but, naturally, as elected public representatives, they are bound to consider hardship, injustice and other right-minded matters. If they do so, and if those deliberations and thoughts can be shown to have influenced the decision, the order directing the city or county manager to grant permission may be ignored.

**[1.60]** These two cases illustrate how elected members, in arriving at their decisions to direct the county manager to materially contravene a development plan for County Galway, were motivated by concerns which may have been humanitarian/political but which were not purely planning considerations.

**[1.61]** Assuming that evidence can be obtained from the notes taken, as required in *Sharpe (P&F) Ltd v Dublin City and County Manager*,[61] a high proportion of s 4 (now s 140) resolutions are potentially open to challenge by way of judicial review. Not everyone would wish to involve themselves with the cost of High Court applications of this nature. A more satisfactory way of dealing with, what may be, an unnecessary and unwanted political interference with the planning process, would be to remove both s 139 and s 140 motions from the legislation in relation to planning matters, as provided in the LGA 2001 and to remove PDA 2000, s 34(6), as amended by PD(A)A 2010, s 23(a). Where the elected representatives are of the opinion that a development should be allowed to proceed by way of material contravention of the development plan, a preferable procedure would be that elected members should pass a resolution submitting any question of material contravention by way of referral in any particular case, to An Bord Pleanála for its ultimate decision. The constitution and day to day working of the board are better designed to deal with the planning principles involved in material contravention, within the constraints of 'fairness' which the courts have imposed. The board may, in any case, decide to grant permission on appeal even if the proposed development materially contravenes the development plan relating to the area of the planning authority to whose decision the appeal relates.[62]

**[1.62]** The right of the board to grant permission on appeal even though it materially contravenes the development plan is curtailed in that the board may only grant permission under PDA 2000, s 37(2)(a) where it considers that:

(i) the proposed development is of strategic or national importance,

(ii) there are conflicting objectives in the development plan or the objectives are not clearly stated, insofar as the proposed development is concerned, or

---

60. *Griffin v Galway City and County Manager* (unreported, 31 October 1990) HC, *per* Blayney J.
61. *Sharpe (P & F) Limited v Dublin City and County Manager* [1989] ILRM 565.
62. PDA 2000, s 37(2)(a).

(iii) permission for the proposed development should be granted having regard to regional planning guidelines for the area, guidelines under s 28, policy directives under s 29, the statutory obligations of any local authority in the area, and any relevant policy of the Government, the Ministers or any Minister of the Government, or

(iv) permission for the proposed development should be granted having regard to the pattern of development, and the permissions granted, in the area since the making of the development plan.[63]

If necessary, s 37(2)(a) could be altered. Perhaps, the most definitive case on the question of material contravention of a development plan is *Kenny Homes & Co. Ltd v Galway City and County Manager*.[64] In that case, Blaney J concluded that elected representatives cannot really make material contraventions, because they cannot frame the conditions, or at least they cannot frame them in advance of hearing the objections and representations. The implication here is that s 140 of the LGA 2001 can only be invoked by the elected members to compel the performance of executive functions which do not have to be exercised in a judicial manner.

> While it is clear from the decision of the Supreme Court in *Sharpe*, that a direction to grant permission may be the subject of a s 4 resolution, in my opinion that section is not an appropriate instrument for such direction. (*Per* Blaney J.)

**[1.63]** In *Kenny Homes v Galway City and County Manager*,[65] the manager refused to obey a s 4 resolution. An order for *mandamus* was refused by Blaney J because:

(i) The manner in which it was phrased did not leave it open to the councillors to consider what conditions they would attach to the permission.

(ii) Councillors had heard an oral presentation by the applicant but none from the objectors. Blaney J said that he considered that s 4 is not an appropriate instrument for directing county managers in relation to their function of deciding on planning applications.

**[1.64]** In *Kerry County Council v Lovatt*,[66] Keane J held that a direction from the elected members to the county manager to grant a planning permission is not a decision to grant planning permission. It is no more than a direction but the decision to grant planning permission is an executive function which remains vested in the county manager.

**[1.65]** In *O'Keefe v An Bord Pleanála*,[67] the court held that a city or county manager is bound to comply with a valid direction given by the elected members. If the manager does not comply with the direction but decides, in any case, to make a decision to grant or to refuse to grant permission, that decision is appealable to the An Bord Pleanála.

---

63. PDA 2000, s 37(2)(b).
64. *Kenny Homes & Co Ltd v Galway City and County Manager* [1995] IR 178.
65. *Kenny Homes & Co Ltd v Galway City and County Manager* [1995] IR 178.
66. *Kerry County Council v Lovatt* [2003] IR 589.
67. *O'Keefe v An Bord Pleanála* [1993] 1 IR 39.

**[1.66]** The remaining provisions of s 140 are summarised as follows.

The elected members must give notice of their intention to propose a resolution in writing to the manager signed by at least three members and setting out the text of the proposed resolution. The section calls for a special meeting to be held within seven days of the date on which the notice is received by the manager. Where a resolution is received the manager notifies all of the elected members of the local authority and gives notice of the date of the special meeting. A provision is made so that if an ordinary meeting of the councillors should take place within a period of 14 days after the date on which the special meeting has been fixed the entire resolution may be considered at the ordinary meeting and there is no requirement for the special meeting. At least one-third of the total number of elected members must vote in favour of the resolution if it is received. Where a resolution is passed in accordance with s 140 by the elected members and if and when and insofar as money for its purpose is or has been provided, the manager shall cause the act, matter or thing mentioned in the resolution to be implemented.

**[1.67]** LGA 2001, s 140(10) provides circumstances where a resolution will not apply, namely:

(a) to the performance of any function of a local authority generally,

(b) to every case or occasion of the performance of any such function or to a number or class of such cases or occasions so extended as to be substantially or in effect every case or occasion on which any such function is performed,

(c) to every case or occasion of the performance of such function in a particular area or to any number or class of such cases or occasions so extended as to be substantially or in effect every case or occasion on which any such function is performed in that area, or

(d) so as to prevent the performance of any function of a local authority which the authority or the manager is required by law or by order of a Court to perform, and

any resolution claiming to be passed under this section which contravenes this subsection is void.

**[1.68]** Section 140 motions[68] are motions which are designed to allow the elected members to direct a county or a city manager to do some particular thing. Section 139 motions[69] are motions which are designed to allow the elected members to direct a county or a city manager not to do some particular thing. They are far less common, in practice, than the s 140[70] motions, because the elected members cannot direct a county manager or a city manager not to do a particular thing which he/she is obliged to do by statute.

---

68. LGA 2001, s 140.
69. LGA 2001, s 139.
70. LGA 2001, s 140.

**[1.69]** Section 139 of LGA 2001 provides:

> (1) Where the elected council or joint body is informed in accordance with s 138 of any works (not being any works which the local authority or joint body are required by or under statute or by order of a Court to undertake), the elected council or joint body, as the case may be, may by resolution, direct that those works shall not proceed.
>
> (2) The manager shall comply with a resolution of an elected council or joint body duly and lawfully passed under this section.

**[1.70]** In *East Wicklow Conservation Community Ltd v Wicklow County Council*,[71] the county manager refused to be bound by the resolution of the council directing him not to locate a landfill site at a particular location. Costello P in the High Court held that the provision of a site for waste disposal was something that the local authority was required to undertake by or under statute, and therefore the elected members had no power under s 3 (as it then was) of the City and County Management (Amendment) Act 1955 to direct the county manager not to proceed with the work. This case was appealed to the Supreme Court where Costello J's decision was upheld.

**[1.71]** PDA 2000[72] makes the distinction between s 140 notices which relate to land wholly within the local authority's functional area and cases where the land, the subject matter of the planning application, is situate in more than one local electoral area. If the land is located in more than one electoral area, then not less than three-quarters of the elected members of all relevant areas must vote in favour of the resolution if the resolution is to be carried.

**[1.72]** By way of illustration a number of cases are listed below in which courts have considered material contraventions:

1. *Aer Rianta CPT v An Bord Pleanála*.[73] In this case the board gave planning permission for development of a car park and ancillary developments in an area within what is known as the 'red safety area' at Dublin Airport. Aer Rianta sought judicial review proceedings after they had lost an appeal before An Bord Pleanála. Aer Rianta made the case that the location of this car park was in a dangerous area and that its proposed location involved safety issues. The proposed car park development was close to an approach area of a runway at the airport. Aer Rianta also made the case that the proposal was in material contravention of the development plan. Kelly J held that Aer Rianta had not made a sufficient case to show the court that there would be a material contravention of the development plan if the development proceeded. The learned judge also noted that evidence had been given at the planning appeal by

---

71. *East Wicklow Conservation Community Ltd v Wicklow County Council* [1997] 2 ILRM 72.
72. See PDA 2000, s 34(7) as amended by LGA 2001 (Sch 4).
73. *Aer Rianta CPT v An Bord Pleanála* [2002] IEHC 69, Kelly J. Note: the full title of this case is *Aer Rianta CPT v An Bord Pleanála and Gannon Homes Ltd, Irish Aviation Authority and Fingal County Council*. The case had significant commercial implications in that Aer Rianta's position was compromised.

the Irish Aviation Authority (the statutory body responsible for the safety of aircraft and for safe, efficient navigation) stating that it did not oppose the development. The court supported the board's decision in dismissing Aer Rianta's objection.

2. *Tennyson v Dun Laoghaire Corporation*.[74] Dun Laoghaire Corporation's density proposals for housing were specifically set out in its development plan. A proposal to develop residential units received planning permission but the court set aside the planning permission on the basis that the density of the proposed residential units was in excess of, and in conflict with, the standards specified in the local authority's development plan and as such the proposal constituted a material contravention of the plan.

3. *Calor Teoranta v Sligo County Council*.[75] Sligo County Council's development plan included a general objective which prohibited any development which would give rise to concerns as to the existence of fire hazards or potential fire hazards. Calor Teoranta wished to develop a liquid petroleum gas tank but failed to include any details of thermal insulation as a means of reducing the tank's potential to explode in the event of fire. This omission constituted a material contravention of the local authority's development plan.

4. *Attorney General (McGarry) v Sligo County Council*.[76] Sligo County Council in its development plan had listed a site at Carrowmore, containing one of the largest groups of megalithic remains in Western Europe, as a listed site. Sligo County Council proposed to operate a dump in the immediate vicinity of those remains. The Sligo County Council proposal was held to be a material contravention of its own development plan. In this case the status of the development plan was considered in detail. The development plan is a statement of objectives which informs the public, in its draft form, of the intended objectives of the relevant local authority. Members of the public are afforded an opportunity to inspect the plan and to lodge objections or criticisms. Once adopted, the development plan forms an environmental contract between the planning authority and the community to an extent which amounts to a promise on behalf of the local authority that it will regulate development in a manner which is consistent with the objectives stated in the development plan and furthermore that the council itself will not contravene its own development plan.

5. *O'Connor v Clare County Council*.[77] Clare County Council's development plan specified that an area be developed as an integrated visitor facility. It specifically noted that use of any part of the site as a shop or storage units would materially contravene the development objectives specified in the

---

74. *Tennyson v Dun Laoghaire Corporation* [1991] 2 IR 527.
75. *Calor Teoranta v Sligo County Council* [1991] 2 IR 267.
76. *Attorney General (McGarry) v Sligo County Council* [1991] 1 IR 99.
77. *O'Connor v Clare County Council* (unreported, 11 February 1994) HC Murphy J.

development plan. An application for permission for a shop and storage units was refused and the refusal was upheld.

6. *Jeffers v Louth County Council.*[78] The Jeffers family lived at Drumleck, Castlebellingham, Co Louth and objected to Louth County Council's proposal to develop part of their lands as a temporary halting site. Gilligan J held that the proposal was a material contravention of the local authority's own development plan in that the proposal breached the council's own regulations and standards on road safety as set out in the development plan.

## Applications for strategic infrastructure development

**[1.73]** The Planning and Development (Strategic Infrastructure) Act 2006 (PD(SI)A 2006) created a single stage consent procedure. The Act became law on 16 July 2006. Parts of the Act were commenced in October and November 2006 but the final and most relevant commencement occurred on 31 January 2007,[79] when the 'strategic infrastructure' provisions came into being. The purpose of this legislation is to promote development of strategic, economic or social importance or development[80] that would contribute significantly to the fulfilment of many objectives of the National Spatial Strategy for Ireland 2002–2020 and/or objectives in regional planning guidelines. If a development qualifies under the terms of PD(SI)A 2006 an application in the first instance for permission is made to a new division within An Bord Pleanála. The planning authority is bypassed.

**[1.74]** An Bord Pleanála is not in any way restrained from granting a permission for strategic infrastructure development even though the development materially contravenes the relevant planning authority's development plan. An Bord Pleanála, in dealing with an application for a strategic infrastructure development, may also ignore the objectives contained in the NSS for Ireland 2002–2020 or any recommendation contained in any RPGs. A high proportion of development contemplated within the terms of PD(SI)A 2006 would indeed contravene the objectives of a planning authority in its development plan and/or the objectives of the NSS for Ireland or RPGs.

## Interpretation of development plans/planning documents

**[1.75]** A development plan is a written statement that indicates the development objectives within the functional area of the planning authority concerned. The purpose of a development plan is to inform persons who are contemplating development within the planning authority's functional area as to what types of development may or may not be permitted. In order to ensure consistent interpretation of a development plan, and its success and survival, it must be written in a manner which will be understood by reasonably intelligent persons who have no particular expertise in either legal matters or

---

78. *Jeffers v Louth County Council* (unreported, 2 May 2004) HC Gilligan J.
79. SI 684/2006.
80. See also **Ch 11** on strategic infrastructure development.

planning matters. In *Tennyson v Dun Laoghaire Corporation*,[81] Barr J held that 'residential units' were housing units and that the density proposed was in conflict with the standards specified in the plan such that the proposed development constituted a material contravention of the development plan. The purpose of the development plan is to provide an understandable guide to the public. A development plan must not be an intricate document that can only be read and understood by trained lawyers and trained planners. In *XJ's Investments Ltd v Dun Laoghaire Corporation*,[82] the Supreme Court held that planning documents are not Acts of the Oireachtas or subordinate legislation emanating from skilled draftsmen and inviting the accepted cannons of construction applicable to such material. In *Attorney General (McGarry) v Sligo County Council*,[83] McCarthy J in the Supreme Court concluded that the courts were well qualified to interpret a development plan without feeling any necessity to defer to the views or the expertise of either the planning authority or An Bord Pleanála.

[1.76] In *Wicklow Heritage Trust Ltd v Wicklow County Council*,[84] McGuinness J examined a proposal to develop a large waste disposal site with all its ancillary facilities in an area of rural amenity and high quality agricultural ground in County Wicklow. The test which the learned judge used in interpreting the objectives of the development plan was the test as to whether a reasonably intelligent person without any particular planning expertise would permit such a development in the proposed location. McGuinness J held that no responsible planning authority would grant planning permission for a waste disposal facility of the size and type proposed on the selected site. Examples had been given to the court where Wicklow County Council had refused permission for similar developments on comparable sites in County Wicklow on the basis that, at the very least, they constituted an unpleasant intrusion on the landscape. At the time Wicklow County Council's development plan was completely silent on the question of waste disposal facilities and no waste plan had been adopted. Nevertheless, in the circumstances of the case the court held that the proposed development would constitute a material contravention of the plan if it were permitted to proceed.

## Copies of development plans

[1.77] PDA 2000[85] provides that a planning authority must make its development plan available for inspection and for purchase by members of the public, and allow for purchase of copies of the development plan and of variations of a development plan and extracts therefrom. It must also make available, for inspection and for purchase, copies of the reports to the manager, in the making of the development plan. Copies of the development plan and variations of it, together with reports for the manager and extracts therefrom, shall be made available for purchase on payment of a specified fee not exceeding the reasonable cost of making a copy.

---

81. *Tennyson v Dun Laoghaire Corporation* [1991] 2 IR 527.
82. *XJ's Investments Ltd v Dun Laoghaire Corporation* [1996] IR 750.
83. *Attorney General (McGarry) v Sligo County Council* [1991] 1 IR 99.
84. *Wicklow Heritage Trust Ltd v Wicklow County Council* [1998] IEHC 19, McGuinness J.
85. PDA 2000, s 16(1), (2) and (3).

**[1.78]** PDA 2000[86] provides that a document purporting to be a copy of a part or all of a development plan and to be certified by an officer of a planning authority as a correct copy shall be evidence of the plan or part, unless the contrary is shown, and it shall not be necessary to prove the signature of the officer or that he or she was in fact such an officer.

**[1.79]** PDA 2000[87] provides that evidence of all or part of a development plan may be given by production of a copy thereof certified in accordance with this subsection and it shall not be necessary to produce the plan itself.

## Contents of development plans

**[1.80]** PDA 2000[88] defines the contents of a development plan as follows:

> A development plan shall set out an overall strategy for the proper planning and sustainable development of the area of the development plan and shall consist of a written statement and a plan or plans indicating the development objectives for the area in question.

PDA 2000[89] continues by providing mandatory objectives which must be included without prejudice to the generality of sub-s (1).

**[1.81]** This list of objectives has already been fully set out at para **[1.08]**.

**[1.82]** An additional mandatory objective, which must be included in all local authority development plans, is a housing strategy for the purposes of ensuring that the proper planning and sustainable development of the area of the development plan provides for the housing of the existing and future population of the area in the manner set out in the strategy.[90]

**[1.83]** Apart from the mandatory objectives, which must be included in a development plan, there are, in addition, objectives listed in PDA 2000, Sch 1 which are 'discretionary' objectives and these are set out below. There are five parts to the First Schedule:

> Part I deals with location and pattern of development;
>
> Part II deals with control of areas and structures;
>
> Part III deals with community facilities;
>
> Part IV deals with environment and amenities;
>
> Part V deals with infrastructure and transport.

---

86. PDA 2000, s 17(1).
87. PDA 2000, s 17(2).
88. PDA 2000, s 10(1).
89. PDA 2000, s 10(2).
90. See PDA 2000, s 94(1) to (5) inclusive. See also PDA 2000, s 95 which deals with the content of the housing strategy within the context of the development plan.

The First Schedule to PDA 2000 provides as follows:

FIRST SCHEDULE[91]

Purposes for which objectives may be indicated in Development Plan

Part I

Location and pattern of development

1. Reserving or allocating any particular land, or all land in any particular area, for development of a specified class or classes, or prohibiting or restricting, either permanently or temporarily, development of any specified land.

2. Promoting sustainable settlement and transportation strategies in urban and rural areas. [This paragraph has been deleted by PD(A)A 2010, s 77.]

3. Preserving the quality and character of urban or rural areas.

4. Regulating, restricting or controlling retail development.

5. Regulating, promoting or controlling tourism development.

6. Carrying out flood risk assessment for the purposes of regulating, restricting and controlling development in areas at risk of flooding (whether inland or coastal).[92]

7. Regulating, restricting and controlling the development of coastal areas and development in the vicinity of inland waterways.

8. Regulating, restricting and controlling development on the foreshore, or any part of the foreshore.

9. Giving effect to the European Spatial Development Perspective towards balanced and sustainable development of the territory of the European Union, adopted at the meeting of Ministers responsible for Regional/Spatial Planning of the European Union at Potsdam, 10 and 11 May, 1999.

10. Regulating, restricting or controlling development in order to reduce the risk of serious danger to human health or the environment.

11. Regulating, promoting or controlling the exploitation of natural resources.

12. Regulating, restricting and controlling development in areas at risk of erosion and other natural hazards.

13. Reserving land for use and cultivation as allotments and regulating, promoting, facilitating or controlling the provision of land for that use.

Part II

Control of Areas and Structures

1. Regulating and controlling the layout of areas and structures, including density, spacing, grouping and orientation of structures in relation to roads, open spaces and other structures.

---

91. PD(A)A 2010, s 77 amends the First Schedule to PDA 2000 in the following respects: deletion of para 2 and insertion of a new para 6; the new text appears in **1.16**. PD(A)A 2010, s 77(3) inserts new paras 11 and 12 as shown in the same para.
92. Controlling development on flood plains is now a mandatory objective under EU law. Flood risk assessment must also be carried out in appropriate cases.

2. Regulating and controlling the design, colour and materials of structures and groups of structures, including streets and townscapes, and structures and groups of structures in rural areas.

3. Promoting design in structures for the purposes of flexible and sustainable use, including conservation of energy and resources.

4. Limiting the number of structures, or the number of structures of a specified class, which may be constructed, erected or made on, in or under any area.

5. Regulating and controlling, either generally or in particular areas, all or any of the following matters:

   (a)   the size, height, floor area and character of structures;

   (b)   building lines, coverage and the space about houses and other structures;

   (c)   the extent of parking places required in, on or under structures of a particular class or size, or services or facilities for the parking, loading, unloading or fuelling of vehicles;

   (d)   the objects which may be affixed to structures;

   (e)   the purposes for and the manner in which structures may be used or occupied, including, in the case of a house, the letting thereof in separate units.

6. Regulating and controlling in accordance with the principles of proper planning and sustainable development, the following:

   (a)   the disposition or layout of land and structures or structures of any specified class, including the reservation of sufficient open space in relation to the number, class and character of structures in any particular development proposal, road layout, landscaping and planting;

   (b)   the provision of water, waste water, waste and public lighting facilities;

   (c)   the provision of service roads and the location and design of means of access to transport networks, including public transport;

   (d)   the provision of facilities for parking, unloading, loading and fuelling of vehicles on any land.

7. The removal or alteration of structures which are inconsistent with the development plan.

Part III

Community Facilities

1. Facilitating the provision and siting of services and facilities necessary for the community, including the following:

   (a)   hospitals and other healthcare facilities;

   (b)   centres for social, economic, recreational, cultural, environmental, or general development of the community;

   (c)   facilities for the elderly and for persons with disabilities;

   (d)   places of public worship and meeting halls;

(e) recreational facilities and open spaces, including caravan and camping parks, sports grounds and playgrounds;

(f) shopping and banking facilities.

2. Ensuring the provision and siting of sanitary services.

3. Reserving of land for burial grounds.

Part IV

Environment and Amenities

1. Protecting and preserving the quality of the environment, including the prevention, limitation, elimination, abatement or reduction of environmental pollution and the protection of waters, groundwater, the seashore and the atmosphere.

2. Securing the reduction or prevention of noise emissions or vibrations.

3. Prohibiting, regulating or controlling the deposit or disposal of waste materials, refuse and litter, the disposal of sewage and the pollution of waters.

4. Protecting features of the landscape which are of major importance for wild fauna and flora.

5.. (a) Preserving and protecting flora, fauna and ecological diversity.

(b) Preserving and protecting trees, shrubs, plants and flowers.

6. Protecting and preserving (either *in situ* or by record) places, caves, sites, features and other objects of archaeological, geological, historical, scientific or ecological interest.

7. Preserving the character of the landscape, including views and prospects, and the amenities of places and features of natural beauty or interest.

8. Preserving public rights of way other than those referred to in section 10(2)(o).[93]

9. Reserving land as open spaces, whether public or private, (other than open spaces reserved under Part II of this Schedule) or as a public park, public garden or public recreation space.

10. Prohibiting, restricting or controlling, either generally or in particular places or within a specified distance of the centre line of all roads or any specified road, the erection of all or any particular forms of advertisement structure or the exhibition of all or any particular forms of advertisement.

11. Preventing, remedying or removing injury to amenities arising form the ruinous or neglected condition of any structure or from the objectionable or neglected condition of any land.

Part V

Infrastructure and Transport

1. Reserving land for transport networks, including roads, rail, light rail and air and sea transport, for communication networks, for energy generation and for

---

93. This amendment has been inserted by PD(A)A 2010, s 77(b).

**[1.84]** Planning and Environmental Law in Ireland

energy networks, including renewable energy and for other networks, and for ancillary facilities to service those networks.

2. Facilitating the provision of sustainable integrated transport, public transport and road traffic systems and promoting the development of local transport plans.

3. Securing the greater convenience and safety of users of all transport networks and of pedestrians and cyclists.

4. Establishment of public rights of way and extinguishment of public and private rights of way.

5. Construction, alteration, closure or diversion of roads, including cycleways and busways.

6. Establishing:

   (a) the line, width, level and construction of,

   (b) the means of access to and egress from, and

   (c) the general dimensions and character of,

roads, including cycleways and busways, and, where appropriate, other transport networks, whether new or existing.

7. Providing for the management and control of traffic, including the provision and control of parking areas.

8. Providing for works incidental to making, improvement or landscaping of any transport, communication, energy or other network.

**[1.84]** The general rule is that all of the local authority's objectives must be included in its development plan. This principle was strongly supported by Lord Scarman in *Great Portland Estates plc v Westminster City Council*:[94]

> If a local planning authority has proposals of policy for the development and use of land in its area which it chooses to exclude from the plan, it is, in my judgement, failing to do its duty ... It was the duty of the Council to formulate in plan its development and land use proposals. It deliberately omitted some. There was therefore a failure on the part of the Council to meet the requirement of the schedule. By excluding from the plan its proposals in respect of office development outside the central activities zone the Council deprived persons such as the Respondents from raising objections and securing a public enquiry into such objections.

**[1.85]** In *Keogh v Galway Corporation*,[95] Galway Corporation wished to develop a halting site for the travelling community in Salthill. The development proposal had not been mentioned in the local authority's development plan and it was contended by the applicants that the proposal was therefore a material contravention of the local authority's own development plan and that the corporation had no jurisdiction to carry out the proposed development. Galway Corporation argued that it was not required to

---

94. *Great Portland Estates plc v Westminster City Council* [1985] AC 661.
95. *Keogh v Galway Corporation* [1995] 3 IR 457.

specify every projected development of halting sites in the plan and referred to a general provision in the plan which provided for the carrying out of objectives not included as specific objectives where such works become necessary. In fact, the only reference to providing halting sites in the Galway County Borough Development Plan 1991 related to a specific objective of the corporation to provide halting sites for travellers at Tuam Road, Headford Road, Doughiska and along the access road to Silver Strand. The Bishopsfield in Salthill did not fall within any of those locations:

> It is central to the scheme of the Act that a citizen is to be given notice of a development which might affect him in a substantial way and have the opportunity of stating his case in relation to what is projected. The provision of halting sites is a matter of clear interest to adjoining householders and is also frequently a matter of great concern and controversy (*per* Carney J).

The learned judge held in favour of the applicants on the basis that the council's plans sought to bypass the mandatory consultation process provided for in the Act and as such the proposal materially contravened the council's own development plan.

[1.86] Although the First Schedule objectives are discretionary, if circumstances indicate that they should be included, there is an obligation on the local authority to consider whether or not those objectives should in fact be included. If a local authority plans to carry out a development that is likely to affect people living in the vicinity in a substantial way these types of developments should be included in a development plan in order to provide for transparency and to enable persons affected to make their views known. In such cases, members of the public who are affected by the proposal should be allowed a right to object if they should wish to do so.

[1.87] All of the matters referred to in PDA 2000, Sch 1, Pts I to V inclusive, are discretionary. The Minister is given power to add additional objectives which shall or may be incorporated in development plans.

[1.88] 'Development objectives' are a combination of the mandatory objectives listed in PDA 2000, s 10(2) and the discretionary objectives listed in PDA 2000, Sch 1.

Other objectives, examples of which are listed below, form a part of the local authority's development plan or any variation or renewal of that plan, although they may not be specifically included in the development plan.

## *Protected structures*

[1.89] The record of protected structures[96] is recorded in the local authority's record of protected structures within its functional area. The record of protected structures forms part of the local authority's development plan.

---

96. See PDA 2000, ss 51–80 inclusive; s 57 is amended by PD(A)A 2002, s 13.

## Waste management

**[1.90]** A local authority development plan is deemed to include a waste management plan which operates within its functional area. The Waste Management Act 1996, s 10(a), as substituted by the Waste Management (Amendment) Act 2001, and the Protection of the Environment Act 2003, makes it clear that if a conflict arises between a development plan and a development objective in the waste management plan, it is the waste management plan which will prevail.

## Strategic development zones

**[1.91]** Where an area is of economic or social importance to the State, the site may be designated as a strategic development zone (SDZ) which may be compulsorily acquired by the relevant planning authority. Once the site is designated as a strategic development zone it shall be included as part of the planning authority's development plan. If there is a conflict between the development objectives in the development plan and the development objectives in the scheme applicable to the strategic development zone, PDA 2000 provides that a planning scheme made under this section[97] shall be deemed to form part of any development plan in force in the area of the scheme until the scheme is revoked and any contrary provisions of the development plan shall be superseded.

## Architectural conservation area

**[1.92]** PDA 2000[98] provides that:

> (1) A development plan shall include an objective to preserve the character of a place, area, group of structures or townscape, taking account of building lines and heights, that:
>
> > (a) is of special architectural, historical, archaeological, artistic, cultural, scientific, social or technical interest or value; or
> >
> > (b) contributes to the appreciation of protected structures, if the planning authority is of the opinion that its inclusion is necessary for the preservation of the character of the place, area, group of structures or townscape concerned and any such place, area, group of structures or townscape shall be known as and is in this Act referred to as an 'architectural conservation area'.
>
> (2) Where a development plan includes an objective referred to in sub-s (1), any development plan that replaces the first mentioned development plan shall, subject to any variation thereof under s 13, also include that objective.

---

97. PDA 2000, s 169(9).
98. PDA 2000, s 81(1) and (2).

## Areas of special planning control

**[1.93]** PDA 2000[99] provides that if a planning authority considers that all or part of an architectural conservation area is of special importance to, or as respects, the civic life or the architectural, historical, cultural or social character of a city or town in which it is situated, it shall prepare a scheme setting out development objectives for the preservation and enhancement of that area, or part of that area, and providing for matters connected therewith. PDA 2000[100] provides that any development within an area of special planning control shall not be exempted development where it contravenes an approved scheme applying to that area. PDA 2000[101] provides that where an area has been designated as a special control area and an application for permission is made, a planning authority, or the board on appeal, shall, in addition to the matters set out in s 34, have regard to the provisions of the approved scheme.

**[1.94]** Another legal effect which arises in the situation where land is affected by a special planning control scheme is provided by s 88[102] which is a comprehensive section enabling the planning authority to serve notice requiring each person who is the owner or occupier of land to which a development objective of an approved scheme applies to specify measures required to be undertaken, including:

(i) the restoration, demolition, removal, alteration, replacement, maintenance, repair or cleaning of any structure, or

(ii) the discontinuance of any use or the continuance of any use subject to conditions.

Section 87[103] continues by setting up a discussion forum with the planning authority and the section also provides a right of appeal against the notice to An Bord Pleanála.

## Social and affordable housing[104]

**[1.95]** PDA 2000[105] provides that:

> Each planning authority shall include in any development plan it makes in accordance with s 12 a strategy for the purpose of ensuring that the proper planning and sustainable development of the area of the development plan provides for the housing of the existing and future population of the area in the manner set out in the strategy.

---

99. PDA 2000, s 84(1).
100. PDA 2000, s 87(1).
101. PDA 2000, s 87(2).
102. See PDA 2000, s 88(1) to (8) inclusive, particularly sub-s (2) which makes detailed provisions for the contents of the notice and also sub-s (6) which deals with the appeal procedures where an appeal against the notice is lodged with An Bord Pleanála.
103. PDA 2000, s 87(3).
104. This subject is dealt with comprehensively in **Ch 6**.
105. PDA 2000, s 94(1).

[1.96] PDA 2000[106] provides that a housing strategy shall take into account:
- (a) the existing need and likely future need for housing to which sub-s (4)(a) applies [sub-s (4)(a) requires a housing strategy to include an estimate of the amount of housing required for social housing and for affordable housing],
- (b) the need to ensure that housing is available for persons who have different levels of income,
- (c) the need to ensure that a mixture of house types and sizes is developed to reasonably match the requirements of the different categories of households, as may be determined by the planning authority, and including the special requirements of elderly persons and persons with disabilities, and
- (d) the need to counteract undue segregation in housing between persons of different social backgrounds.

In effect, each planning authority must include objectives in its development plan estimating the amount of social and/or affordable housing required in their area. Also, it must estimate the amount of land required to be zoned for social and/or affordable housing. The amount of land to be zoned for social and/or affordable housing should equate to a maximum of 20% of the total requirement for lands zoned for housing.

## Environmental assessment

[1.97] Section 10(5) of PDA 2000 has been restructured by the European Communities (Environmental Assessment of Certain Plans and Programmes) Regulations 2004 (SI 435/2004) (reg 4). The amended subsection now reads as follows:

> The Minister may, for the purposes of giving effect to Directive 2001/42/EC of the European Parliament and Council of 27 June 2001 on the assessment of the effects of certain plans and programmes on the environment (No 2001/42/EC, OJ No L197, 21 July 2001 P.0030–0037), by regulations make provision in relation to consideration of the likely significant effects on the environment of implementing a development plan.

Clearly, the making of certain development plans is subject to mandatory environmental assessment in the first instance. The mandatory environmental assessment is required where the area of the development plan has a population of 10,000 persons or more.

[1.98] An environmental assessment is also mandatory in circumstances where the planning authority determines that the implementation of its development plan would be likely to have significant effects on the environment. In those circumstances, additional public notice requirements apply. If the planning authority concludes that its development plan is likely to have any significant effects on the environment it is bound to give notice to and invite submissions from the Environmental Protection Agency, the Minister for the Environment, Heritage and Local Government (in circumstances where significant effects apply in relation to architectural or archaeological heritage or to

---

106. PDA 2000, s 94(3).

nature conservation) and to the Minister for Communications, Marine and Natural Resources (where the planning authority concludes that its plan may have significant effects on either fisheries or the marine environment).

**[1.99]** Both the Environmental Protection Agency and the Minister are entitled to make submissions to the planning authority within a period of four weeks from the date of the notice and the planning authority must then consider the submissions and, where applicable, must give a reasoned decision as to whether or not the planning authority intends to implement environmental assessment.

**[1.100]** If the population is less than 10,000 persons the planning authority is still required to carry out a form of screening. If the planning authority concludes that its development would be likely to have significant effects on the environment, taking into consideration the contents of Sch 2(a) of the Planning and Development (Strategic Environmental Assessment) Regulations 2004, a separate environmental assessment will have to be prepared and placed with the development plan before the development plan takes effect. Any environmental assessment published by the planning authority whether because the population is in excess of 10,000 or because the planning authority concludes that its development will be likely to have significant effects on the environment shall be made available for public inspection at the office of the planning authority during office hours.

## Miscellaneous matters in relation to development plans

**[1.101]** Each planning authority is required to make a development plan in relation to the entire of its area. However, county boroughs, towns and urban districts may make development plans in conjunction with an adjoining county council. This is a sensible provision to ensure an integrated planning policy. With the expansion of towns, a development plan which was restricted to the town boundaries, and which did not take account of new developments within the county council area outside the town boundaries, would defeat the purpose of the development plan which is to set out an overall strategy for proper planning and sustainable development.

**[1.102]** Planning authorities are also required to have regard to development plans of adjoining planning authorities, and to coordinate, by consultation, the objectives in development plans for adjoining areas where practicable. The development plan is also required, so far as is practicable, to be consistent with such national plans, policies or strategies as the Minister for the Environment and Local Government determines and which relate to proper planning and sustainable development. The Minister also has power to require two or more planning authorities to coordinate their development plans for their areas.

**[1.103]** Where a planning authority proposes to include in a development plan any development objective the responsibility for the effecting of which would fall on another local authority, the planning authority shall not include that objective in the plan except after consultation with the other local authority.[107]

**[1.104]** A development plan may indicate that specified developments in a particular area will be subject to the making of a local area plan.[108] There shall be no presumption in law that any land zoned in a particular development plan (including a development plan that has been varied) shall remain so zoned in any subsequent development plan.[109]

## Preparation and adoption of new development plans

**[1.105]** PDA 2000, ss 11–13, as amended and added to by PD(A)A 2010, ss 8–10, deal with the preparation and adoption of a new development plan, and the variation of existing development plans. The detailed procedure is set out in detail in PDA 2000 and in PD(A)A 2010 and what follows is a summary which should not discourage a reading of the full text of those sections.

**[1.106]** The planning authority must give notice of its intention to review its existing development plan, and to prepare a new development plan for its area within four years from the adoption of the existing plan.[110] The completed new plan must be available within six years which allows a period of two years for the completion of and the adoption of the new development plan.

**[1.107]** PD(A)A 2010, s 8 has inserted a new sub-s (1A) after PDA 2000, s 11(1), which requires that:

> The review of the exiting development plan and the preparation of a new development plan shall be strategic in nature for the purposes of developing —
> 
> (a) The objectives and policies to deliver an overall strategy for the proper planning and sustainable development of the area of the development plan, and
> 
> (b) The core strategy,
> 
> and shall take account of the statutory obligations of any local authority in the area and any relevant policies or objectives for the time being of the Government or any Minister of the Government.[111]

**[1.108]** The notice issued by the local authority stating its intention to review its existing development plan and to prepare a new development plan will invite submissions and observations and will be sent to the Minister, to any prescribed authority, to any adjoining planning authorities, to the board, to any relevant regional authority and to any town commissioners and city and county development boards within the functional area

---

107. PDA 2000, s 10(6).
108. PDA 2000, s 10(7).
109. PDA 2000, s 10(8).
110. PDA 2000, s 11(1).
111. PD(A)A 2010, s 8(a).

of the authority. The notice must be published in one or more newspapers circulating in the area.[112]

**[1.109]** That notice will invite submissions and observations regarding objectives and policies to deliver an overall strategy for the proper planning and sustainable development of the areas within the development plan. Submissions and observations may be made in writing to the planning authority within a specified period which shall not be less than eight weeks.[113] The notice shall also indicate that children or groups or associations representing the interests of children are entitled to make submissions or observations.[114] Significantly, the notice states that the planning authority intends to review the zoning of the area of the development plan for the purposes of developing objectives and policies to deliver an overall strategy for the proper planning and sustainable development of the area and for the purpose of developing the core strategy. The subsection provides that any requests or proposals for zoning of particular lands for any purpose will not be considered at that stage.[115] The planning authority then goes through a consultation procedure which can involve oral hearings, written submissions and liaison with interested bodies.[116] Within 16 weeks of the initial notice, the manager of the planning authority is required to prepare a report on the consultations held, and submissions and observations received.[117] The manager does not have to comment on every single submission made and, in appropriate cases, he only has to summarise the issues raised and give his opinion on them. The statutory requirement is to 'summarise' the issues and it does not require a manager to summarise the contents. In *Sandyford Environmental Planning & Road Safety Group Ltd v Dun Laoghaire Rathdown County Council*,[118] McKechnie J did sound a note of warning. The case concerned a variation of the development plan. The manager's comments on the submissions made were, in the opinion of the applicants, misleading and meaningless. In the event, the learned judge ruled in favour of the manager but he had this to say:

> ... I wish to emphasise that, in my view, a local authority should not have or adopt a minimalist standard to the contents of such a notice and, if anything, should err on the side of an expansive approach. If, for example, the true reasons for this proposal were the Council's Housing Strategy and/or the Strategic Guidelines, then, whilst these would have to be referred to, I doubt strongly if a mere reference to such documents, and no more, would have conveyed in recognisable language the meaningful information which, in my opinion, the public are entitled to expect from such a notice. So, whilst I believe that the notice in this case did contain reasons which were proper, intelligible and adequate, I would caution strongly against any practice or policy, used or designed, directly or indirectly to limit,

---

112. PDA 2000, s 11(2).
113. PDA 2000, s 11(2)(b) as amended by PD(A)A 2010, s 8(b).
114. As inserted by PD(A)A 2010, s 8(b) para (b).
115. As inserted by PD(A)A 2010, s 8(b) paras (b), (c).
116. PDA 2000, s 11(3)(a), (b) and (c).
117. PDA 2000, s 11(4)(a). Note also subpara (b) as amended by PD(A)A 2010, s 8(c)(i), (ii) and (iii).
118. *Sandyford Environmental Planning & Road Safety Group Ltd v Dun Laoghaire Rathdown County Council* [2004] IEHC 133 (30 June 2004).

**[1.110]**                      Planning and Environmental Law in Ireland

whether by omission, phraseology or otherwise, information which should be supplied to the public.

**[1.110]** Professor Yvonne Scannell at a planning seminar delivered on 8 and 9 December 2008 had this to say:

> In general, great care should be taken to address and respond to issues raised and to explain why serious arguments made were not accepted, particularly where they could have involved a conflict with statutory obligations or policy considerations binding the planning authority. It is probably safe to disregard frivolous or vexatious arguments or those without substance or foundation. Special care should be taken for observations by property owners, distinguished experts,[119] NGOs and statutory bodies with environmental responsibilities.'[120]

This report is submitted to the council members, or to a committee of the council members if the council so decides.[121] The council members may issue directions to the manager regarding the draft plan and any such directions shall be strategic in nature consistent with the draft core strategy and must take account of the statutory obligations of any local authority in the area, any relevant policies or objectives of the time being of the government or any Minister of the government and the manager shall comply with any such directions.[122] The manager then has 12 weeks within which to prepare the draft development plan and submit it back to the council members for consideration.[123] The planning authority has a further eight weeks within which to make further amendments to the plan.[124]

**[1.111]** PD(A)A 2010, s 8(c), dealing with the necessity to summarise the issues, replaces PDA 2000, s 11(b)(ii) with the following subparagraph:

> (ii)    summarise the issues raised in submissions and during the consultations, where appropriate, but shall not refer to submissions relating to a request or proposal for zoning of particular land for any purpose.

This provision is very much in line with other provisions in PD(A)A 2010 where the Act sets out to ensure that zoning proposals are strictly controlled within the sphere of influence of the Minister, the planning authorities and, where appropriate, the board. Also, PD(A)A 2010, s 8(c)(ii) inserts a new paragraph after para (bb):

> (bc)   A report under paragraph (a) shall summarise the issues raised and recommendations made by the relevant regional authority in a report prepared in accordance with section 27(a) (inserted by section 17 of the Act of 2010) and outline the recommendations of the manager in relation to the manner in which those issues and recommendations should be addressed in the draft development plan.

---

119. See *Simonovich v An Bord Pleanála* (unreported, 24 July 1998) HC.
120. Lecture given by Scannell entitled, 'Development and Other Land use Plans in the 2000 Act' in Intensive Course on Planning Law – School of Law, TCD, 9 December 2008.
121. PDA 2000, s 11(4)(c).
122. PDA 2000, s 11(4)(d) as amended by PD(A)A 2010, s 8(c)(iii).
123. PDA 2000, s 11(5)(a).
124. PDA 2000, s 11(5)(b) and (c).

## Making of development plan

**[1.112]** Once the draft development plan has been proposed and a period of eight weeks has elapsed without further amendments being made the planning authority will notify and serve copies of the draft development plan on the board, the relevant regional authority and the prescribed authorities within two weeks. The planning authority will also publish notice of the draft development plan in one or more newspapers circulating in the area.[125] PDA 2000, s 12 (as amended by PD(A)A 2010, s 9) provides further that if there are no amendments to the draft development plan, that plan as submitted to them is deemed to be the draft development plan.[126] This draft is then put on public display for a period of not less than 10 weeks, and public notices of its existence are issued.[127] Written submissions or observations are invited within the stated period.

**[1.113]** Where the new draft development plan proposes the addition or deletion of protected structures, then the planning authority is required to serve notice on the owners or occupiers of such structures.[128]

**[1.114]** Within 22 weeks of the notice advising that the draft development plan is on public display the manager is required to prepare a report on submissions and observations received and submit it to the council members for their consideration.[129] The manager's report lists the persons and bodies who have made submissions and observations and in particular the report summarises any issues raised by the Minister and thereafter it summarises any issues raised by other bodies or persons.[130]

**[1.115]** Any planning authority situated within the greater Dublin area shall make a report summarising the issues raised and the recommendations of the Dublin Transport Authority in its written submission prepared in accordance with s 31(c) and outline the recommendations of the manager in relation to the manner in which those issues and recommendations should be addressed in the development plan.[131]

**[1.116]** Planning and Development Amendment Act 2010 has also added one new subsection to PDA 2000, s 12(4), namely sub-s (bc), which requires that the manager's report on any submissions or observations received as submitted to the council members must summarise the issues raised and recommendations made by the relevant regional authority in its written submissions and outline the recommendations of the manager in relation to the manner in which those issues and recommendations should be addressed in the development plan.[132]

---

125. PDA 2000, s 12(1)(a) and (b) as amended by PD(A)A 2010, s 9(a).
126. PDA 2000, s 12(2)(a) as amended by LGA 2001, s 247.
127. PDA 2000, s 12(2)(b).
128. PDA 2000, s 12(3)(a).
129. PDA 2000, s 12(4)(a).
130. PDA 2000, s 12(5)(2) as amended by PD(A)A 2010, s 9(b)(i).
131. See para (bb) as inserted by the Dublin Transport Authority Act 2008, s 84.
132. See para (bc) as inserted by PD(A)A 2010, s 9(ii).

**[1.117]** The members of the planning authority shall consider the draft plan and the report of the manager.[133]

**[1.118]** Having considered the draft plan and the manager's report and having considered submissions and observations or recommendations of the Minister or of a regional authority made to the planning authority, if the planning authority decides not to comply with such recommendation the planning authority must inform the Minister and/or the regional authority, as the case may be, as soon as practicable by notice in writing stating the reasons why the recommendation was not accepted.[134]

**[1.119]** The planning authority may either accept and adopt the draft development plan as the development plan, or propose alterations.[135]

**[1.120]** If the proposed amendment would amount to a material alteration of the draft development plan the planning authority has three weeks after the passing of its resolution to publish a notice of the proposed amendment in at least one newspaper circulating in its area. The planning authority must also send notice of the proposed amendment to the Minister, the board and the prescribed authorities. This provision is subject to what is stated in sub-paras (aa)–(ae), as set out below.[136]

**[1.121]** PDA 2000, s 12(7)(a) has been further extended by PD(A)A 2010, s 9(d)(ii) by the insertion of the following paragraphs:

(aa) The planning authority shall determine if a strategic environmental assessment or an appropriate assessment or both such assessments, as the case may be, is or are required to be carried out as respects one or more than one proposed material alteration of the draft development plan.

(ab) The manager, not later than two weeks after a determination under paragraph (aa) shall specify such a period as he or she considers necessary following the passing of a resolution under sub-section (6) as being required to facilitate an assessment referred to in paragraph (aa).

(ac) The planning authority shall publish notice of the proposed material alteration, and where appropriate in the circumstances, the making of a determination that an assessment referred to in paragraph (aa) is required, in at least one newspaper circulating in its area.

(ad) The notice referred to in paragraph (ac) shall state —

(i) That a copy of the proposed material alteration and of any determination by the authority that an assessment referred to in paragraph (aa) is required may be inspected at a stated place or places and at stated times and on the authority's website, during a stated period of not less than 4 weeks (and that copies will be kept for inspection accordingly) and

---

133. PDA 2000, s 12(5)(a).
134. PD(A)A 2010, s 9(c)(aa).
135. PDA 2000, s 12(6).
136. PDA 2000, s 12(7)(a) as substituted by PD(A)A 2010, s 9(d)(1).

(ii) That written submissions or observations with respect to the proposed material alteration or an assessment referred to in paragraph (aa) and made to the planning authority within a stated period shall be taken into account by the authority before the development plan is made.

(ae) The planning authority shall carry out an assessment referred to in paragraph (aa) of the proposed material alteration of the draft development plan within the period specified by the manager.

A notice under paragraph (a) or (ac) (inserted by s 9 of the Act of 2010) shall state that:

(i) A copy of the proposed amendment of the draft development plan may be inspected at a stated place and at stated times during a stated period of not less than four weeks (and the copy shall be kept available for inspection accordingly), and

(ii) Written submissions or observations with respect to the proposed amendment of the draft made to the planning authority within the stated period shall be taken into consideration before the making of any amendment.[137]

**[1.122]** If an amendment of the draft development plan would be a material alteration, the manager of the planning authority shall, within eight weeks of publishing notice of the proposed amendment, prepare a report on any submissions or observations received for consideration by members of the planning authority.

**[1.123]** The manager's report lists the persons or bodies who have made submissions or observations and summarises the issues raised by them. The report will also contain the manager's response to the issues raised taking account of the proper planning and sustainable development of the area, the statutory obligations of the planning authority and the policies or objectives of the government or of any Minister of the government.[138]

**[1.124]** New wording is contained in PD(A)A 2010, s 9(e), to replace PDA 2000, s 12(10)(a), as follows:

The members of the authority shall, by resolution, having considered the manager's report, make the plan with or without the proposed amendment that would, if made, be a material alteration except that where they decide to accept the amendment they may do so subject to any modifications, to the amendments as they consider appropriate, which may include the making of a further modification to the alteration and paragraph (c) shall apply in relation to any further modification.

**[1.125]** Where a material contravention has occurred, a statement of this fact must be entered in the planning register and the obligations in relation to time and other matters specified in PDA 2000, s 9 shall apply.[139]

---

137. PDA 2000, s 12(7)(b) as amended by PD(A)A 2010, s 9(d)(iii).
138. PDA 2000, s 12(8).
139. PDA 2000, s 12(10)(b).

**[1.126]** An additional subsection has been added to PDA 2000, s 12(10) after para (b) above, namely as follows:

    (c)    A further modification to the alteration —

        (i)    May be made where it is minor in nature and therefore not likely to have significant effects on the environment or adversely affect the integrity of European site,

        (ii)    Shall not be made where it relates to —

            (I)    An increase in the area of land zoned for any purpose, or

            (II)    An addition to or deletion from the record of protected structures.[140]

**[1.127]** The councillors, in considering the development plan, are restricted to considering the proper planning and sustainable development of the area to which that development plan relates, the statutory obligations of any local authority in the area and any relevant policies or directives for the time being of the government or any Minister of the government.[141]

**[1.128]** Where a planning authority makes a development plan notice it must publish notice in at least one newspaper circulating in the area stating that a copy of the plan is available for inspection at a stated place or places and the planning authority is also required to send a copy of the development plan to the Minister, the prescribed authorities and any adjoining planning authorities, to the board and any town commissioners and city and county development boards within its area.[142]

**[1.129]** When the plan is made, the planning authority must serve notice on the owner and occupier of any protected structure that has been added to or deleted from the record of protected structures in the development plan.[143]

**[1.130]** New provisions have been made by PD(A)A 2010, s 9(f), replacing the old s 12(14) of PDA 2000, as follows:

    (a)    Notwithstanding any other provision of this Part, where a planning authority fails to make a development plan within a period referred to in paragraph (b), the manager shall make the plan provided that so much of the plan as had been agreed by the members of the planning authority shall be included as part of the plan as made by the manager.

    (b)    The period referred to in paragraph (a) is —

        (i)    not more than 2 years from the giving of notice under section 11(1), or

        (ii)    where sub-section (7)(aa) (inserted by section 9 of the Act of 2010) applies —

            (I)    Not more than 2 years and 4 weeks, or

---

140. PD(A)A 2010, s 9(e)(ii).
141. PDA 2000, s 12(11).
142. PDA 2000, s 12(12).
143. PDA 2000, s 12(13).

(II) If appropriate in the circumstances, such longer period than 2 years and 4 weeks as is specified under sub-section (7)(ab) (inserted by section 9 of the Act of 2010) by the manager as being required to facilitate an assessment referred to in sub-section (7)(aa).

If the planning authority fails to make the development plan within two years from publication of the notice of intention to review the plan, then the manager must make the plan. In doing so he must include so much of the plan as has already been agreed by the council members.[144]

[1.131] A development plan is not open to challenge by reason only of the fact that the time scales for each of the procedures set out in PDA 2000 have not been complied with.

[1.132] PDA 2000, s 12(16) (as amended by PD(A)A 2002, s 7) provides that a person shall not question the validity of the development plan by reason only that the procedures as set out under s 11(3)–(5), and s 11(1), (4), (5), (6), (7), (8) and (9) were not completed within the time required under the relevant subsection. PDA 2000, s 13(10), in the context of a variation of the development plan, provides that a person shall not question the validity of a variation in the development plan by reason only that the procedures as set out in PDA 2000, s 13 were not completed within the time required.

[1.133] The development plan must indicate the fact that there is likely to be significant environmental impact, if that is the case. It must also take into account, in terms of a potential environmental impact assessment, the likely effects that the planning authority's plan will have on neighbouring local authorities. A planning authority must have regard to any submissions made to it by a neighbouring local authority in relation to likely significant environmental effects.[145]

[1.134] The Planning and Development (Strategic Environment Assessment) Regulations 2004 require that a planning authority, in making a development plan, must take into account the assessment of the effects of certain plans and programmes on the environment. In many cases certain development plans are subject to environmental assessment. (See paras **1.97** to **1.100**.)

[1.135] The development plan comes into effect four weeks from the day that it is made.[146]

## Variation of development plans

[1.136] PDA 2000, s 13, as amended by PD(A)A 2010, s 10, sets out the procedures for variations. The procedure is similar to the procedures proscribed by PDA 2000, s 12, as

---

144. PDA 2000, s 12(14).
145. PDA 2000, s 10 as restructured by European Communities (Environmental Assessment of Certain Plans and Programmes) Regulations 2004 (SI 435/2004), reg 4.
146. PDA 2000, s 12(17).

amended by PD(A)A 2010, s 9, for the preparation of new development plans. PDA 2000, s 13(1) expressly provides that a planning authority may at any time, for stated reasons, decide to make a variation to a development plan which is for the time being in force. The ensuing provisions in s 13(2)–(8) inclusive (as amended by Planning and Development (Amendment) Act s 10) are similar to those already set out in relation to the making of the development plan. It again involves the manager preparing a report on the submissions and observations and submitting the proposed variation and report to the councillors for adoption. Any variation made to the development plan has effect from the day that the variation is made.

**[1.137]** PDA 2000 provides that when considering a variation of a development plan in accordance with this section, a planning authority may invite such persons as it considers appropriate to make oral submissions regarding the variation. Oral submissions may, in certain circumstances, be received in relation to the making of a variation but there is no corresponding provision for oral submissions in relation to the making of a development plan.[147]

**[1.138]** PDA 2000 provides that a person shall not question the validity of a variation in a development plan by reason only that the procedures as set out in the section were not completed within the time required.[148]

**[1.139]** PDA 2000 provides that a variation made to a development plan shall have effect from the day that variation was made.[149]

**[1.140]** In making a variation or variations to the development plan, any new significant likely environmental impact or impacts within this area or within an area of an adjoining planning authority, having regard, in particular, to any submissions which were made by adjoining planning authorities, must be taken into account.

**[1.141]** PDA 2000, in relation to a variation of an existing development plan, provides that the Minister may, for the purpose of giving effect to Directive 2001/42/EC of the European Parliament and Council of 27 June 2001 on the assessment of the effects of certain plans and programmes on the environment ([2001] OJ L197/0030–0037), by regulations make provision in relation to consideration of the likely significant effects on the environment of implementing a variation of a development plan.[150]

**[1.142]** An additional subsection, sub-s (13), has been added by PD(A)A 2010, s 10 which reads as follows:

> An appropriate assessment of a draft variation of a development plan shall be carried out in accordance with Part XAV.

---

147. PDA 2000, s 13(9).
148. PDA 2000, s 13(10).
149. PDA 2000, s 13(11).
150. PDA 2000, s 13(12) inserted by the European Communities (Environmental Assessment of Certain Plans and Programmes) Regulations 2004 (SI 435/2004), reg 5.

## Ministerial directions regarding development plans and local area plans

**[1.143]** The Minister has always, under previous legislation, had power to issue directions to a planning authority regarding the contents of its draft development plan and existing development plans in certain circumstances. Those powers mainly relate to circumstances where the development plan failed to set out an overall strategy for the proper planning and sustainable development of the area or otherwise where it significantly failed to comply with the provisions of PDA 2000.

**[1.144]** PDA 2000, s 31 has been substituted by s 21 of PD(A)A 2010. Section 21 empowers the Minister, for stated reasons, to direct a planning authority to take such steps as the Minister shall require in relation to the plan. In order to give such a direction to the planning authority there are a number of pre-conditions which must be satisfied. The Minister must be of the opinion that, in making a development plan or a variation to a development plan:

1. the planning authority has ignored or not taken sufficient account of submissions or observations made by the Minister under s 12 (relating to making of a development plan), s 13 (relating to a variation of a development plan) or s 20 (relating to consultation and adoption of local area plans);
2. the development plan or local area plan fails to set out an overall strategy for the proper planning and sustainable development of the area;
3. the plan does not comply with the requirements of this Act;
4. where applicable if submissions have been made and received under s 31C or s 31D (inserted by s 95 of the Dublin Transport Authority Act 2008)[151] to the effect that a planning authority's plan in the Greater Dublin Area is inconsistent with the strategy of the national transport authority;

the Minister's direction will require the planning authority to take specified measures in relation to the plan.

**[1.145]** If such a direction is issued by the Minister, and provided it falls within one or more of the matters set out in paras 1 to 4 above, the planning authority, to include the manager, the executives and the elected members, must comply with that direction. It cannot use material contravention or any other ruse to avoid complying with the Minister's directions.[152]

**[1.146]** Four weeks notice in writing of the Minister's intention to issue a direction under this section must be given to the planning authority.[153]

**[1.147]** The contents of the notice are specified in s 21(4) of PD(A)A 2010.

---

151. The Dublin Transport Authority Act 2008, s 31B deals with the Dublin Transport Authority's role in the preparation of a draft development plan. The Dublin Transport Authority Act 2008, s 31C deals with the DTA's role in the making of a development plan.
152. PDA 2000, s 31A(2), as amended.
153. PDA 2000, s 31A(3), as amended.

**[1.148]** Notice under sub-s (3) shall be furnished by the Minister to the manager and the cathaoirleach of the planning authority and if there are regional planning guidelines in force notice must also be served on the regional planning authority concerned. Notice must also be served on the Dublin Transport Authority where relevant.[154]

**[1.149]** The date of the commencement of the development plan will be postponed, in relevant cases, until such time as the Minister's direction has been complied with.[155]

**[1.150]** Within two weeks of the receipt of the notice from the Minister the planning authority must publish a copy of the draft ministerial direction in one or more newspapers circulating in the area setting out the reasons for the direction and stating where and when it may be inspected and those actions must be taken within a period of two weeks from the date of the notice. The notice also invites written submissions or observations to be made to the Minister which submissions and observations must be taken into consideration by the Minister before issuing the engrossed or final ministerial direction.[156]

**[1.151]** Within four weeks after the expiry of the two week period mentioned above the manager of the planning authority is required to prepare a report dealing with the submissions and observations received and that report shall be furnished to the Minister and to the elected members of the planning authority.[157]

**[1.152]** The manager's report above referred to shall summarise the views of anyone who made submissions or observations and shall also summarise the views of the elected members and the recommendations (if any) of the elected members and recommendations (if any) made by the regional authority.

**[1.153]** The manager's report must make recommendations in relation to the best manner in which to give effect to the draft ministerial direction.[158]

**[1.154]** The elected members are entitled to make submissions to the Minister directly in relation to the notice issued by the Minister provided they are made within two weeks of the date of the Minister's notice.[159]

**[1.155]** Having considered the manager's report and any submissions made directly by elected members the Minister may, within three weeks of the date of receipt of the manager's report, issue the direction with minor amendments or the Minister may decide not to issue the direction. If the Minister believes that a material amendment to the draft direction is required or if amendments are necessary for any other reason the Minister can, for stated reasons, appoint an inspector within three weeks of the date of the receipt of the manager's report. The inspector appointed, having consulted with all parties, shall make a report to the Minister containing his/her recommendations. Copies of the

---

154. PDA 2000, s 31A(5), as amended.
155. PDA 2010, s 31A(6), as amended.
156. PDA 2010, s 31A(7), as amended.
157. PDA 2010, s 31A(8), as amended.
158. PDA 2010, s 31A(9), as amended.
159. PDA 2010, s 31A(10), as amended.

inspector's report will be furnished by the Minister to the manager, to the elected members and to any other parties who have made submissions or observations as quickly as possible. Any person or body furnished with the inspector's report is entitled to make further submissions or observations to the Minister within 10 days of the date that the inspector's report was received by them.[160]

**[1.156]** Within a period of three weeks from the date of receipt of a report or such other period extending the three week period as the Minister may direct the Minister having considered the report, recommendations or submissions as the case may be shall decide for stated reasons either to issue a ministerial direction, not to issue a ministerial direction or to issue an amended ministerial direction to take account of the recommendations contained in the inspector's report or any submissions made by persons furnished with the inspector's report.[161]

**[1.157]** Having made a ministerial direction the Minister is required to lay a copy of the direction before each House of the Oireachtas.[162]

**[1.158]** As soon as may be after the ministerial direction has issued to the planning authority the planning authority shall make the direction available for inspection by members of the public during office hours at the offices of the authority and shall also make it available by placing the direction on the authority's website or otherwise in electronic form.[163]

**[1.159]** An obligation is also placed on the Minister to publish or cause to be published the direction in such manner as the Minister considers appropriate.[164]

**[1.160]** PDA 2000, s 31, apart from being substantially amended by PD(A)A 2010, s 21, also had a new s 31A added to it by s 93 of the Dublin Transport Authority Act 2008. The new s 31A, as inserted by the Dublin Transport Authority Act 2008, has been substituted again by the new provisions contained in PD(A)A 2010, s 22. The new s 31A allows the Minister, for stated reasons, to direct a regional authority or authorities to take such specified measures as he or she may require in relation to the making of regional planning guidelines. Again, if the Minister is of the opinion that:

1. a regional authority or authorities in making regional planning guidelines have ignored or not taken sufficient account of submissions or observations made by the Minister under PDA 2000, s 24 (as amended by PD(A)A 2010, s 15) or under PDA 2000, s 26; or

2. the regional planning guidelines fail to provide a long term strategic planning framework for development of the regional regions if the regional authority's area or part thereof is within the Greater Dublin Area (GDA) that the guidelines

---

160. PDA 2000, s 31A(11) to (15), as amended.
161. PDA 2000, s 31A(16), as amended.
162. PDA 2000, s 21(18), as amended.
163. PDA 2000, s 21(19), as amended.
164. PDA 2000, s 21(20), as amended.

are not consistent with the transport strategy of the National Transport Authority.

The remaining subsections of the amending section, PD(A)A 2010, s 22(2) to (20), are similar to the same numbered subsections in PD(A)A 2010, s 21.

## Public right of way

**[1.161]** PDA 2000 provides that where a planning authority proposes to include, for the first time, a provision in a development plan relating to the preservation of a specific public right of way, it shall serve notice (which shall include particulars of the provision and a map indicating the right of way) of its intention to do so on any owner or occupier of the land over which the right of way exists[165] or, where appropriate, the direction may constitute the plan.[166]

**[1.162]** The notice states that the planning authority proposes to include a provision in the development plan relating to the preservation of a public right of way and invites written submissions or observations. The notice requires that such written submissions or observations shall be submitted within a period of not less than six weeks and that submissions or observations will be taken into consideration by the planning authority.[167] Once the decision is made, notice of that decision or recommendation must be published in a daily newspaper circulating in the area. It must also be served on the person(s) affected by it.[168] Such notice must be served even if the recommendation is against the inclusion of the specified right of way in the development plan. Any person served with such notice has a right to appeal to the Circuit Court within 21 days and the court, if satisfied that no public right of way exists, shall so declare and the provisions shall accordingly not be included:[169]

(a) the taking of an appeal shall not prejudice the making of a development plan except in regard to the inclusion of the proposed provision which is before the court;

(b) where a development plan has been made and the court, having considered an appeal, decides that the public right of way exists, the proposed provision under this section shall be deemed to be part of the development plan.[170]

**[1.163]** Where an existing development plan contains any provisions relating to the preservation of a public right of way, the provision may be included in any subsequent development plan without the necessity to comply with s 14:[171]

(a) nothing in this section shall affect the existence or validity of any public right of way which is not included in the development plan;

---

165. PDA 2000, s 14(1).
166. PD(A)A 2010, s 21(17).
167. PDA 2000, s 14(2)(a) and (b).
168. PDA 2000, s 14(3).
169. PDA 2000, s 14(4).
170. PDA 2000, s 14(5)(a) and (b).
171. PDA 2000, s 14(6).

(b) the inclusion of a public right of way in a development plan shall be evidence of existence of such a right unless the contrary is shown.[172]

## Legal effects

**[1.164]** Professor Yvonne Scannell in *Environmental and Land Use Law* places the importance of development plans in context:

> The impact of development objectives listed in the development plan is felt throughout all aspects of planning law. The plan sets the framework for all future development in the planning authority's area for stated periods. Section 15 provides that it is the duty of the planning authority to take such steps within its powers as may be necessary to secure the objectives of the development plan. This obligation may have been regarded as something in the nature of a policy statement in the past but in a modern planned economy, where plans are made to give effect to important national and strategic development objectives, development plans have assumed a far greater significance than in the past. The Act envisages that many objectives in development plans will be accomplished by the private sector and/or by public private partnership. So, for example, objectives must be set to facilitate the provision of infrastructure by, inter alia, the private sector.[173]

**[1.165]** PDA 2000 provides a general duty for a planning authority to secure the objectives of the development plan by providing that it shall be the duty of the planning authority to take such steps within its powers as may be necessary for securing the objectives of the development plan. The Act provides that the manager of a planning authority shall, not more than two years after the making of a development plan, give a report to the members of the authority on the progress achieved in securing the objectives referred to in s 15(1).[174]

**[1.166]** The obligation imposed on a planning authority to secure the objectives of the development plan by PDA 2000 is no more than a general duty. It is a qualified duty in that the section states that the planning authority is only required to take such steps as are 'within its powers'. The addition of the words in inverted commas first appeared in PDA 2000.

**[1.167]** The first question is whether the legislature seriously intended that a planning authority should secure and achieve the objectives which it lays out in its development plan. The answer to that question must be a qualified 'no', as reasoned below:

(i) no time limit is set in the development plan for the achievement of the planning authority's objectives. The absence of a time limit means that objectives may role over from one development plan to the next;

---

172. PDA 2000, s 14(7)(a) and (b).
173. Scannell, *Environmental and Land Use Law* (Round Hall, 2006) at p 55, para 2.42.
174. PDA 2000, s 15(1) and (2).

(ii) as a matter of practicality, a planning authority, at one time or another, may not have the resources to finance the full list of the aspirations set out in the development plan;

(iii) many of the objectives of a planning authority's development plan are more suited to the portfolio of the private sector which cannot be compelled, in relatively free market conditions, to get to work at any particular time or to undertake or complete a particular development, except of course the normal stipulation regarding the life of a planning permission or such extended period as the planning authority may agree.

**[1.168]** The second question is whether the legislature envisaged that the role of the planning authority was, at least in part, a 'watchdog' role to ensure that the objectives of the development plan are not materially contravened either by the State, by the private sector or by the local authorities themselves, save in accordance with the specific statutory exemption provisions. The answer to the second question must be a qualified 'yes', acknowledging, of course, the role of the local authorities in carrying out substantial development on their own initiative within their own functional areas.

**[1.169]** The State, however, does not require permission for a host of developments prescribed in Planning and Development Regulations 2001 (PDR 2001) (SI 600/2001), Pt 9, art 86 which makes provision with respect to certain developments by or on behalf of the State to include, by way of example, garda stations, prisons, council houses, barracks and in connection with the defence forces. Local authorities do not require permission to carry out development within their own functional areas but they cannot undertake a development which will materially contravene their own development plan.

**[1.170]** PDA 2000, as amended by PD(A)A 2010, sets out the procedures to be followed by a planning authority where planning permission would materially contravene its development plan. PDA 2000, s 34(6) as amended by PD(A)A 2010, s 23(a)(i) and (iv) provides that, in a case in which the development concerned contravenes materially the development plan, a planning authority may, notwithstanding any other provision of this Act, decide to grant permission under this section, provided that the following requirements are complied with before the decision is made. It then goes on to list the requirements and these are dealt with at para **1.44** to **1.72** inclusive.[175]

**[1.171]** PDA 2000, s 178(1), (2) and (3) provide that a local authority shall not affect any development in its functional area which materially contravenes the development plan. A planning authority or An Bord Pleanála, on appeal, must take into consideration the objectives of the planning authority's development plan to ensure that the application does not seek to materially contravene that plan. If a development proposal comes within the scope of the exempted development regulations or the statutory provisions

---

175. PDA 2000, s 34(6)(a), (b), (c) and (d) as amended by LGA 2001, Sch 4 and as amended by PD(A)A 2010, s 23. These sections set out the material contravention procedures available to a local authority. Note: This section sets out the material contravention procedures available to a local authority.

providing for exempted development and if the development is contrary to an objective in the development plan, the exempted development becomes de-exempted.

**[1.172]** PDA 2000, Sch 4 deals with reasons for refusals of permission which exclude compensation. Paragraph 3 provides that compensation will be excluded if development of the kind proposed would be premature by reference to the order of priority, if any, for development indicated in the development plan or pending the adoption of a local area plan in accordance with the development plan. That is adequate reason for a refusal to grant planning permission. Where permission is refused because it materially contravenes the development plan, no claim for compensation can be made.

**[1.173]** PDA 2000, Sch 4, para 20 excludes payment of compensation where permission is refused on the grounds that the development would contravene materially the development objective in the development plan for the zoning of land for use solely or primarily of particular areas for particular purposes (whether residential, commercial, industrial, agriculture, recreational, as open space or otherwise, or a mixture of such uses).

**[1.174]** Part 3 of PDR 2001, as amended by art 7 of the Planning and Development (Strategic Environmental Assessment) Regulations 2004, which inserted art 13(J)(I) into Pt 3, provides that the planning authority shall monitor the significant environmental effects of implementation of the development plan in order, *inter alia*, to identify at an early stage unforeseen adverse effects and to be able to undertake appropriate remedial action and, for this purpose, existing monitoring arrangements may be used, if appropriate, with a view to avoiding duplication of monitoring. PDR 2001, as so amended by art 13J(2), provides that the report required of the manager under s 15(2) of the Act shall include information in relation to progress on, and the results of, monitoring the significant environmental effects of implementation of the development plan.

## LAND USE PLANS

### Local area plans

**[1.175]** PDA 2000, s 18(1) as amended by PD(A)A 2010, s 11 provides subject to s 19(2B) (as inserted by PD(A)A 2010, s 12) that a planning authority may at any time, and for any particular area, within its functional area, prepare a local area plan[176] in respect of that area.[177] Two or more planning authorities may cooperate in preparing a local area plan in respect of an area which lies within the combined functional area of the authorities concerned.[178] PDA 2000, s 18(3)(a) reads as follows:

> When considering an application for permission under section 34, a planning authority, or the Board on appeal, shall have regard to the provisions of any local

---

176. PDA 2000, Part II, Ch II comprises PDA 2000, ss 18, 19 and 20 as amended respectively by PD(A)A 2010, ss 11, 12 and 13.
177. PDA 2000, s 18(1) as amended by PD(A)A 2010, s 11.
178. PDA 2000, s 18(2).

area plan prepared for the area to which the application relates, and the planning authority or the Board may also consider any relevant draft local plan which has been prepared but not yet made in accordance with section 20.

**[1.176]** It is probable that s 18(3)(a) may be subject to legal challenge in the courts. It seems completely unreasonable to grant status to a draft local plan at a time when it has not yet been democratically adopted. The concept in the section of giving approval to a draft local area plan as something which the planning authority or the board may also consider contradicts much of the other legislation dealing with draft development plans and other draft plans in the Act of 2000 as amended. It is submitted that the contradiction is an unhappy one and one which should not be safely relied upon by the planning authority and/or the board. When considering an application for permission, a planning authority, or the board on appeal, shall also have regard to any integrated area plan (within the meaning of the Urban Renewal Act 1998) for the area to which the application relates.[179] A local area plan prepared under this section shall indicate the period for which the plan is to remain in force.[180]

**[1.177]** A local area plan may remain in force, in accordance with this section, notwithstanding the variation of a development plan or the making of a new development plan affecting the area to which the local area plan relates except that, where any provision of the local plan conflicts with the provisions of the development plan as varied or the new development plan, the provisions of the local area plan shall cease to have effect.[181] Subject to s 19(2B) (inserted by s 12 of PD(A)A 2010) a planning authority may at any time amend or revoke a local area plan.[182] The planning authority may enter into an arrangement with any suitably qualified person or local community group for the preparation, or the carrying out of any aspect of the preparation, of a local area plan.[183]

**[1.178]** PDA 2000, s 10(7) provides that a development plan may indicate that specified development in a particular area will be subject to the making of a local area plan. That provision implies that for a local area plan to be effective it must be entirely consistent with the objectives of the development plan.

**[1.179]** PDA 2000, s 19, as amended by PD(A)A 2010, s 12, deals with the application and content of local area plans. This section provides that the planning authority may make a plan in any area, including a Gaeltacht area, or an existing suburb of an urban area, which the planning authority considers suitable and, in particular, plans for those areas requiring economic, physical and social renewal and for areas likely to be the subject to large scale development within the lifetime of the development plan.[184]

---

179. PDA 2000, s 18(3)(b).
180. PDA 2000, s 18(4)(a).
181. PDA 2000, s 18(4)(b).
182. PDA 2000, s 18(5) as amended by PD(A)A 2010, s 11(b).
183. PDA 2000, s 18(6).
184. PDA 2000, s 19(1)(a).

**[1.180]** The planning authorities are required to make local area plans in respect of areas which are designated as towns in the most recent census of population (other than a town designated as a suburb or environs in that census), having a population in excess of 5,000 people, and where the town is situate in a county council's functional area.[185]

**[1.181]** PDA 200, s 19 has been amended by the insertion of a new sub-s (1)(bb) inserted by PD(A)A 2010, s 12(a)(ii) which provides that:

> (bb) Notwithstanding paragraph (b), a local area plan shall be made in respect of a town with a population that exceeded 1,500 persons (in the census of population most recently published before a planning authority makes its decision under subparagraph (i)) except where—
>
> > (i) the planning authority decides to indicate objectives for the area of the town in its own development plan under section (2), or
> >
> > (ii) a local area plan has already been made in respect of the area of the town or objectives for that area have already been indicated in the development plan under section 10(2).

**[1.182]** Subject to paras (d) and (e) below and notwithstanding the provision of s 18(5), as amended by PD(A)A 2010 (which provides that subject to s 19(2B)[186] (inserted by s 12 of PD(A)A 2010)), a planning authority may at any time amend or revoke a local area plan. A planning authority shall send notice of the proposal to make, amend or revoke a local area plan to the board and to the prescribed authorities (and where applicable it shall enclose a copy of the proposed plan or amended plan) at least every six years after the making of the previous local area plan.

**[1.183]** Subject to para (e) below and not more than five years after the making of the previous local area plan, a planning authority may, as it considers it appropriate, by resolution, defer sending a notice of the proposal to make, amend or revoke a local area plan to the board and to the prescribed authorities and publishing notice of the proposal in one or more newspapers circulating in the area for a further period not exceeding five years.

**[1.184]** The resolution in para (d) above cannot be passed by a planning authority until members of the authority have notified the manager of the decision of the authority to defer sending and publishing the notices and giving reasons therefore and the members of the authority have sought and obtained from the manager:

> (I) an opinion that the local area plan remains consistent with the objectives and core strategy of the relevant development;

---

185. PDA 2000, s 19(1)(b)(i), (ii) and (iii).
186. PD(A)A 2010, s 12(2B) provides that where an objective of a local area plan is no longer consistent with the objectives of a development plan for the area, the planning authority shall as soon as may be and in any event not later one year following the making of a development plan amend the local area plan so that its objectives are consistent with the objectives of the development plan.

(II) an opinion that the objectives of the local area plan have not been substantially secured; and

(III) confirmation that the sending and publishing of a notice may be deferred and the period for which they may be deferred.

Where a resolution is passed under para (d) that resolution shall be published in a newspaper circulating in the area of the local area plan within two weeks after the resolution has passed and the notice shall also be made available for inspection by members of the public during office hours at the office of the planning authority and made available in electronic form by placing the notice on the authority's website.

**[1.185]** PD(A)A 2002 added a new s 19(2) to PDA 2000 which provides that a local area plan shall be consistent with the objectives of the development plan *its core strategy and any regional planning guidelines that apply to the area of the plan*[187] and shall consist of a written statement and a plan or plans which may include:

(a) objectives for the zoning of land for the use solely or primarily of particular areas for particular purposes; or

(b) such other objectives in such detail as may be determined by the planning authority for the proper planning and sustainable development of the area to which it applies including *the objective of the development of land on a phased basis*,[188] detail on community facilities and amenities and on standards for the design of development and structures.

PDA 2000, s 19(2) has been further amended by s 86 of the Dublin Transport Authority Act 2008 and by the insertion of a new s 19(2A) which reads:

> Each planning authority within the GDA (Greater Dublin Area) shall ensure that its local area plans are consistent with the transport strategy of the DTA (Dublin Transport Authority).

A new paragraph PDA 2000, s 19(c)(2B) has been added by s 19 of PD(A)A 2010 which reads as follows:

> Where any objective of a local area plan is no longer consistent with the objectives of a development plan for the area, the planning authority shall as soon as may be (and in any event not later than one year following the making of the development plan) amend the local area plan so that its objectives are consistent with the objectives of the development plan.

The section continues by providing that the Minister may provide in regulations that local area plans shall be prepared in respect of certain classes of areas or in certain circumstances and a planning authority shall comply with any such regulations.[189]

---

187. The words in italics have been inserted by PD(A)A 2010, s 12(b)(i).
188. Note that the words in italics have been inserted by PD(A)A 2010, s 12(b)(ii).
189. PDA 2000, s 19(3).

**[1.186]** The European Communities (Environmental Assessment of Certain Plans and Programmes) Regulations 2004 have added a new sub-s (4) to PDA 2000, s 19.

**[1.187]** PDA 2000 (as amended), s 19(4) provides that the Minister may, for the purpose of giving effect to Directive 2001/42/EC of the European Parliament and Council of 27 June 2001 on the assessment of the effects of certain plans and programmes on the environment ([2001] OJ L197/0030–0037), by regulations make provision in relation to consideration of the likely significant effects on the environment of implementing a local area plan.

**[1.188]** Two new additional subsections after s 19(4) (as amended) have been inserted by reg 6 of the European Communities (Environmental Assessment of Certain Plans and Programmes Regulations) 2004, as follows:

> (5) an appropriate assessment of a draft local area plan shall be carried out in accordance with Part XAB;

> (6) there shall be no presumption in law that any land zoned in a particular local area plan shall remain so zoned in any subsequent local area plan.

As a consequence of the amendment of s 19 of PDA 2000 by s 8 of PD(A)A 2002 a local area plan may now include zoning objectives for land use solely or primarily of particular areas for particular purposes.

**[1.189]** PDA 2000, s 20, as amended by the PD(A)A 2002, s 9 and as further amended by PD(A)A 2010, s 13, deals with consultation and adoption of local area plans including the level of consultation that must take place. A planning authority shall take whatever steps it considers necessary to consult with the Minister and the pubic before preparing, amending or revoking a local area plan to include consultations with local residents, public sector agencies, non-governmental agencies, local community groups and commercial and business interests within the area.[190] If a local authority is to make, amend or revoke a local area plan in a Gaeltacht area it shall consult with Údarás na Gaeltachta.[191] The provisions of the section are similar to those which relate to the adoption of development plans in providing a process for adopting, amending or revoking local area plans. For a full understanding of the consultation and adoption procedures relating to local area plans s 20 should be read carefully together with the amendments provided in s 9 of the PD(A)A 2002 and s 13 of PD(A)A 2010.

**[1.190]** In summary, it could be said of local area plans that they are similar to development plans. They cover a much smaller area but the provisions are more detailed, especially in relation to standards of design of housing and standards of design of layout and other buildings. Much of the plan is concerned with community facilities and amenities.

---

190. PDA 2000, s 20 as amended by PD(A)A 2010, s 13.
191. PDA 2000, s 20(2).

## Strategic development zones

**[1.191]** Strategic Development Zones (SDZs) were introduced into Irish law by PDA 2000, Pt IX (ss 165–171). The government, on foot of a proposal from the Minister for Environment, Heritage and Local Government may designate a particular site or sites for the establishment of an SDZ to facilitate such development. The government must be of the opinion that the specified development is of economic or social importance to the State.[192] Before proposing the designation of the site the Minister is required to consult with any relevant development agency or planning authority on the proposed designation.[193]

**[1.192]** 'Development agency' means the Industrial Development Agency (Ireland), Enterprise Ireland, the Shannon Free Airport Development Company Limited, Údarás na Gaeltachta, the National Building Agency Limited, the Grangegorman Development Agency, a local authority or other such person as may be prescribed by the Minister for the purposes of this part.

**[1.193]** 'Strategic development zones' means a site or sites to which a planning scheme made under s 169 applies.[194]

**[1.194]** The government order must specify the following:

(a) The particular development agency or agencies which will be responsible for the preparation of the draft planning scheme.[195]

(b) The type or types of development which are to be facilitated by the establishment of the SDZ.[196] Development, which is ancillary to or necessary for the specified types of development, is deemed to be included in the order, even if not expressly stated to be included by the government. This may include any necessary infrastructural and community facilities and services.[197]

(c) The reasons why the type or types of development had been specified and the site or sites designated by the government.[198]

The Minister is required to send a copy of any order made under s 166 to any relevant development agency, planning authority, regional authority and to the board.[199] Receiving a copy of the order made by the government would appear to be the only function which An Bord Pleanála has in relation to SDZs. The application for permission is made to the local authority and there is no appeal to the board against the local authority's decision.

---

192. PDA 2000, s 166(1).
193. PDA 2000, s 166(2).
194. PDA 2000, s 165 as amended by the Grangegorman Development Agency Act 2005, s 42.
195. PDA 2000, s 166(3)(a).
196. PDA 2000, s 166(3)(b)(c).
197. PDA 2000, s 166(5).
198. PDA 2000, s 166(3)(c).
199. PDA 2000, s 166(4).

[1.195] The acquisition of the site for an SDZ may be carried out by the planning authority which can use any powers available to it to acquire land, including, where necessary, the local authority's powers of compulsory acquisition, in order to provide secure or facilitate the provision of the site or sites which have been designated under s 166. Acquisition powers exercised by the planning authority may be used either before or after the making of a planning scheme in accordance with s 166(1).[200] The development agency, which is or will be involved in the preparation of the draft planning scheme may enter into an agreement with the owner or owners of the lands specified in the government order under s 166 for the establishment of an SDZ to facilitate the development of the land.[201]

[1.196] Any agreement made under s 166(2) with any person having an interest in land may be enforced by the relevant development agency against persons deriving title under that person in respect of that land.[202]

## Planning scheme for SDZs

[1.197] PDA 2000, s 168 has been amended by Planning and Development (Amendment) Act 2000, s 50. Section 168(1) of PDA 2000 provides that subject to s 50(1A),[203] and as soon as may be after the making of the order designating under s 166:

(a) The relevant development agency (other than a local authority) or any person who has entered into an agreement with the relevant development agency shall prepare a draft planning scheme for all or any part of the site and submit it to the relevant planning authority.[204]

(b) Where the local authority is the development agency, the local authority and any person who has entered into an agreement with the development agency shall prepare a draft planning scheme for all or any part of the said site.

[1.198] PDA 2000, s 168(2), as amended, provides that a draft planning scheme shall consist of a written statement and a plan indicating how the site is to be developed and in particular:

(a) the type or types of development which may be permitted to be established on the site (subject to the order of the government under s 166),

(b) the extent of any such proposed development,

(c) proposals in relation to the overall design or the proposed development, including the maximum heights, the external finishes of structures and the general appearance and design,

---

200. PDA 2000, s 167(1).
201. PDA 2000, s 167(2).
202. PDA 2000, s 166(3).
203. PDA 2000, s 168(1A), as inserted by PD(A)A 2010, s 50(a) provides that the first draft of a planning scheme for all or part of a site designated as an STZ must be prepared within a period of two years from the date of making of the order designating the site.
204. PD(A)A 2010, s 50(a) and (b) which substitute PDA 2000, s 168(1).

(d) proposals relating to transportation, including, public transportation, the roads layout, the provision of parking spaces and traffic management,

(e) proposals relating to the provision of services on the site, including the provision of waste and sewerage facilities and water, electricity and telecommunications services, oil and gas pipelines, including storage facilities for oil or gas,

(f) proposals relating to minimising any adverse effects on the environment, including the natural and built environment, and on the amenities of the area, and

(g) where the scheme provides for residential development, proposals relating to the provision of amenities, facilities and services for the community, including schools, crèches and other education and childcare services.

## Environmental assessment

**[1.199]** The Minister may, for the purpose of giving effect to Directive 2001/42/EC of the European Parliament and Council of 27 June 2001 on the assessment of the effects of certain plans and programmes on the environment ([2001] OJ L197/0030–0037), by regulations make provision in relation to consideration of the likely significant effects on the environment of implementing a planning scheme.[205] The Planning and Development (Strategic) Environmental Assessment Regulations 2004 now require environmental assessment in the case of the preparation of a draft planning scheme in respect of SDZs. Also a new sub-s (3A) has been inserted after PDA 2000, s 168(50)(3). It reads:

> An appropriate assessment of a draft planning scheme shall be carried out in accordance with Part XAB.[206]

## SDZs and social and affordable housing

**[1.200]** Where a draft scheme relates to residential development it must be consistent with the housing strategy prepared by the planning authority in accordance with PDA 2000, Pt V. If land within an SDZ is to be used for residential development, a specific objective reserving land for the provision of social and affordable housing must be included in the scheme.[207]

---

205. PDA 2000, s 168(3), which provided that a planning scheme would also contain information of any likely significant impacts on the environment of implementing the planning scheme, has been replaced by this new subsection inserted by European Communities (Environmental Assessment of Certain Plans and Programmes) Regulations 2004 (SI 435/2004).
206. PDA 2000, Pt XAB comprises ss 177R–177AE and sets out the detailed procedures dealing with 'appropriate assessment'. See **Ch 10**.
207. PDA 2000, s 168(4)(a) and (b).

## SDZs in adjoining local authority areas

**[1.201]** Where designated sites under PDA 2000, s 166 are situate in two or more planning authorities' functional areas, the functions conferred under PDA 2000, Pt IX, including the approval or the making of a planning scheme, may be performed jointly by the authorities in question or performed by one, having obtained the consent of the other authority or authorities in advance of the making of the scheme.[208]

## Making of planning scheme

**[1.202]** This section lays out the procedure for the adoption of a draft planning scheme.[209] There are some similarities in the manner in which a draft planning scheme is adopted when compared with the adoption of a development plan under PDA 2000, s 12, as amended by PD(A)A 2010, s 9.

**[1.203]** Where a draft planning scheme for an SDZ has been prepared and submitted to the planning authority by the development agency and any person who is a party to an agreement under PDA 2000, s 168, the planning authority shall as soon as may be practicable send notice and copies of the draft scheme to the Minister, the board and prescribed authorities. The development agency is also required to publish a notice for the preparation of the draft scheme in one or more newspapers circulating in the area.[210] The notice shall state that a copy of the draft plan may be inspected at stated places and at stated time for a period of not less than six weeks and that written submissions and observations with respect to the draft scheme may be made to the planning authority within the stated period and that these will be taken into consideration in deciding upon the scheme.[211]

**[1.204]** Within a period of and not later than 12 weeks after giving the notice, the manager shall prepare a report on any submissions or observations received and submit the report to the members of the authority for their consideration. The report shall:

    (i) list the persons or bodies who made submissions or observations under the section,

    (ii) summarise the issues raised by the persons or bodies in the submissions or observations,

    (iii) give the response of the manager to the issues raised, taking account of the proper planning and sustainable development of the area, the statutory obligations of any local authority in the area and any relevant policies or objectives for the time being of the Government or of any Minister of the Government.[212]

---

208. PDA 2000, s 168(5)(a) and (b).
209. PDA 2000, s 169 as amended by PD(A)A 2010, s 51.
210. PDA 2000, s 169(1)(a) and (b).
211. PDA 2000, s 169(2)(a) and (b).
212. PDA 2000, s 169(3)(a) and (b).

**[1.205]** The members of the planning authority shall consider the draft scheme and report to the manager. The draft planning scheme shall be deemed to be made six weeks after the submission of that draft planning scheme and report to the elected members in accordance with s 169(3) unless the planning authority decides by resolution either to make the draft planning scheme subject to variations and modifications or not to make the draft planning scheme.[213] If the planning authority decides by resolution to make the draft planning scheme subject to variations and modifications that resolution shall be subject to a determination by the planning authority as to whether or not one or more of the proposed variations should be subject to the carrying out of environmental assessment or of appropriate assessment as the case may be.[214]

**[1.206]** If environmental assessment or appropriate assessment is required, the manager of the planning authority shall specify the time required to facilitate the relevant assessment. The manager's determination as to the time required shall be made within two weeks of the planning authority's determination that assessment is required.[215]

**[1.207]** Notice of the proposed material alterations together with the fact, where applicable, that the planning authority has determined to undertake an environmental assessment or an appropriate assessment, as applicable, must be published by the planning authority in at least one newspaper circulating in this area.[216]

**[1.208]** The newspaper notice also invites members of the public to make submissions and observations within a stated period and the newspaper notice also states that any submissions or observations received will be taken into consideration.[217]

**[1.209]** The planning authority shall carry out the assessment being either an environmental assessment or an appropriate assessment, as applicable, of the proposed material alteration of the draft planning scheme within a period to be specified by the manager, and:[218]

 (i) make, subject to variations and modifications, the draft planning scheme; or

 (ii) decide not to make the draft planning scheme.

Where the draft planning scheme is made, it will have effect four weeks from the date on which it is made unless an appeal is brought to the board under s 169(6).

**[1.210]** Following the decision of the planning authority the authority shall, as soon as may be, and in any case not later than six working days following the making of a decision:

 (i) give notice of the decision to the Minister, the Board and prescribed authorities and any person who made written submissions or observations, and

---

213. PDA 2000, s 169 as amended by PD(A)A 2010, s 51(a)(ba).
214. PDA 2000, s 169 as amended by PD(A)A 2010, s 51(a)(b)(i) and (ii).
215. PDA 2000, s 169 as amended by PD(A)A 2010, s 51(a)(bb).
216. PDA 2000, s 169 as amended by PD(A)A 2010, s 51(a)(bc).
217. PDA 2000, s 169 as amended by PD(A)A 2010, s 51(a)(bd)(i) and (ii).
218. PDA 2000, s 169 as amended by PD(A)A 2010, s 51(a)(be).

(ii) publish a notice of the decision in one or more newspapers circulating in the area.

The notice shall:

(i) give the date of the decision of the planning authority in respect of the draft planning scheme,

(ii) state the nature of the decisions,

(iii) state that a copy of the planning scheme is available for inspection at a stated place or places (and the copy shall be kept available for inspection accordingly),

(iv) state that any person who made submissions or observations regarding the draft scheme may appeal the decision of the planning authority to the Board within 4 weeks of the date of the planning authority's decision, and

(v) contain such other information as may be prescribed.[219]

[1.211] The development agency or any person who made submissions or observations in respect of the draft planning scheme may, for stated reasons, within four weeks of the date of the decision of the planning authority appeal the decision of the planning authority to the board.[220] If there are modifications which have been made by the board on appeal those modifications may be made where they are minor in nature and therefore not likely to have significant affects on the environment or adversely affect the integrity of a European site.[221]

[1.212] In considering a draft scheme under this section, a planning authority or the board, as the case may be, shall consider the proper and sustainable development of the area and consider the provisions of the development plan, the provisions of the housing strategy, the provisions of any special amenity area order or the conservation and preservation of any European Site[222] and, where appropriate:

(a) the effect the scheme would have on any neighbouring land to the land concerned,

(b) the effect the scheme would have on any place which is outside the area of the planning authority, and

(c) any other consideration relating to development outside the area of the planning authority, including any area outside the state.[223]

A planning scheme made under this section shall be deemed to form part of any development plan in force in the area of the scheme until the scheme is revoked, and any contrary provisions of the development plan shall be superseded.[224]

---

219. PDA 2000, s 169(5)(a) and (b).
220. PDA 2000, s 169(6).
221. PDA 2000, s 169 as amended by PD(A)A 2010, s 51(b)(a) and (aa).
222. For interpretation of a European site, see PDA 2000, s 2. It includes, for example, a site of importance for the purposes of art 4(2) of the Habitats Directive, a special area of conservation within the meaning of the European Communities (Natural Habitats) Regulations 1997 and an area classified under the Birds Directive, art 4(1) and (2).
223. PDA 2000, s 169(8)(a)(b) and (c).
224. PDA 2000, s 169(9).

## Application for development in an SDZ

**[1.213]** The application procedure is familiar in the sense that some of the normal planning permission provisions of PDA 2000, s 34 are applicable and also the permission regulations apply and must be adhered to.[225]

**[1.214]** However, a planning authority, subject to the provisions of Pt XA or Pt XAB, or both of those Parts, as appropriate, shall grant permission in respect of an application for a development in an SDZ where it is satisfied that the development, where carried out in accordance with the application or subject to any conditions which the planning authority may attach to a permission, would be consistent with any planning scheme in force for the land in question, and no permission shall be granted for any development which would not be consistent with such a planning scheme.[226] Accordingly, the enforcement provisions under PDA 2000, Pt VIII will apply to any development which is not carried out in a manner which is consistent with the planning scheme. Conversely, permission must be refused for development which would not be consistent with the planning scheme.

**[1.215]** Most importantly, there is no right of appeal to An Bord Pleanála against a decision of a planning authority on the application for permission in respect of development in an SDZ.[227] Some lawyers and planners have expressed concerns about the denial of the right to appeal a grant of permission for development within an SDZ provided for in PDA 2000, s 170(3) and those concerns are certainly justified. The only challenge available against a decision of a planning authority on the application for permission for development in an SDZ is a challenge by way of judicial review.

**[1.216]** Having regard to the fact that no appeal is permitted against a decision by a planning authority to grant permission for development within an SDZ, any such grant of permission shall come into force immediately on the date of the grant.[228]

**[1.217]** The 'life' or duration of a planning permission granted within an SDZ is normally five years unless another duration period is specifically specified in the grant of permission. It is also possible to apply to have the duration or life of a planning permission extended where substantial works were carried out pursuant to the planning permission before the expiration of the life of a planning permission, and where the development will be completed within a reasonable time.[229]

## Revocation of planning scheme

**[1.218]** A planning authority may by resolution, with the consent of the relevant development agency, amend or revoke a planning scheme.[230] Notice of revocation of a

---

225. PDA 2000, s 170(1).
226. PDA 2000, s 170(2) as amended by PD(A)A 2010, s 52.
227. PDA 2000, s 170(3).
228. PDA 2000, s 170(4).
229. PDA 2000, s 171(5).
230. PDA 2000, s 171(1).

planning scheme shall be given in at least one newspaper circulating in the area of the planning authority.[231] The amendment or revocation of a planning scheme shall not prejudice the validity of any planning permission granted or anything done in accordance with the terms of the scheme before it was amended or revoked except in accordance with the terms of the Act.[232] It may be necessary to amend a planning scheme if the circumstances relating to the scheme have changed having regard to the implementation of the scheme. It may be necessary to revoke the planning scheme where, for example, the site or sites to which the scheme relates have been developed in accordance with the scheme.

[1.219] The decision to revoke or amend is a reserved function for the members of the authority to vote upon. The planning authority, having received the consent of the development agency concerned, may not amend or revoke a planning scheme on its own initiative because such amendments and/or revocations are 'reserved functions'.

## Architectural conservation area

[1.220] Architectural conservation areas must be included as an objective of a development plan.

[1.221] A development plan shall include an objective to preserve the character of a place, area, group of structures or township, taking account of building lines and heights that:

    (a)    is of special architectural, historical, archaeological, artistic, cultural, scientific, social or technical interest or value; or

    (b)    contributes to the appreciation of protected structures.

If the planning authority is of the opinion that its inclusion is necessary for the preservation of the character of the place, area, group of structures or townscape concerned and any such place, area, group of structures or townscapes shall be known as and is in the Act referred to as an 'architectural conservation area'.[233] If a development plan does include an objective to preserve the character of a place, area, group of structures or townscape, etc, any development plan that replaces the first mentioned development plan shall, subject to any variation thereof, include that objective.[234]

[1.222] Notwithstanding s 4(1)(a), (h), (i), (j), (k), or (l), the carrying out of works to the exterior of a structure located in an architectural conservation area shall be exempted development only if those works would not materially affect the character of the area.[235] If the planning authority is considering an application for permission in relation to land

---

231. PDA 2000, s 171(3). See also PD(A)A 2010, s 28 dealing with the power to extend the appropriate period under PDA 2000, s 42 and also PD(A)A 2010, s 29 amending PDA 2000, s 42(a).
232. PDA 2000, s 171(4).
233. PDA 2000, s 81(1)(a) and (b).
234. PDA 2000, s 81(2).
235. PDA 2000, s 82(1) as amended by PD(A)A 2010, s 35.

situated in an architectural conservation area, a planning authority, or the board on appeal, shall take into account the material effect (if any) that the proposed development would be likely to have on the character of the architectural conservation area.[236]

**[1.223]** In looking at the criteria for an architectural conservation area, Simons makes a useful analysis which explains the concept very clearly:

> It would seem to follow from these criteria that it is not necessary that any particular structure within an architectural conservation area be a protected structure. In other words, whereas none of the individual structures might be of sufficient special architectural, historical, archaeological, artistic, cultural, scientific, social or technical interest as to justify designation, in its own right, as a protected structure, the importance of the sum may be greater than the individual parts and, accordingly, a group of structures might properly be designated as an architectural conservation area.[237]

## Power to acquire structure or other land

**[1.224]** Such acquisition by a planning authority may take place either by agreement, or in default of agreement, compulsorily, if the planning authority is of the opinion that:

(a) it is necessary to do so in order to preserve the character of the architectural conservation area and

    (i) the condition of the land or the use to which the land or any structure on the land is being put, detracts, or is likely to detract, to a material degree from the character or appearance of the architectural conservation area or

    (ii) the acquisition of the land is necessary for the development or renewal of the architectural conservation area or for the provision of amenities in the area.[238]

The planning authority is prohibited from compulsorily acquiring any land within an architectural conservation area that is lawfully occupied as a dwelling house by any person other than a person employed therein as a caretaker.[239]

**[1.225]** PDA 2000, ss 71 to 78 deal with the power to acquire a protected structure and make provisions for compulsory acquisition, the objection against compulsory acquisition, the vesting of the protected structure in the planning authority where the compulsory acquisition proceeds and compensation payable to a person who has property, estate or interest in a protected structure which has been compulsorily acquired by the planning authority. These procedures, as outlined in those sections, apply to the compulsory acquisition of land situate in an architectural conservation area.[240]

---

236. PDA 2000, s 82(2).
237. See Simons, *Planning and Development Law* (2nd edn, Thomson Round Hall, 2007) at p 359, para 8.64.
238. PDA 2000, s 83(1)(a) and (b).
239. PDA 2000, s 83(2).
240. PDA 2000, s 83(3).

## Areas of special planning control

**[1.226]** In a sense, areas of special planning control are a land use plan within a land use plan. Thus, a special planning control scheme is a scheme setting out development control objectives for the preservation and enhancement of an architectural conservation area. The scheme can be for all or for part of the architectural conservation area but the area must first be designated as an architectural conservation area before a special control scheme can be applied to it. A planning authority may, if it considers that all or part of an architectural conservation area is of special importance to the civic life or architectural, historical, cultural or social character of a city or town in which it is situated, prepare a scheme setting out development objectives for the preservation and enhancement of that area or part of that area, and providing for matters connected therewith.[241]

**[1.227]** Matters to be taken into consideration in preparing a scheme declaring an area to be an area of special planning control include:

(a) the promotion of a high standard of civic amenity and civic design;

(b) the preservation and protection of the environment, including the archaeological and natural heritage;

(c) the renewal, preservation, conservation, restoration, development or re-development of streetscape, layout and building pattern, including coordination and upgrading of shop frontages;

(d) the control of the layout of areas, density, building lines and height of structures and the treatment of spaces around and between structures;

(e) the control of the design, colour and material structures in particular the type or quality of building materials used in the structures;

(f) the promotion of the maintenance, repair or cleaning of structures;

(g) the promotion of an appropriate mix of uses of structures or other land;

(h) the control of any new or existing uses of structures or other land;

(i) the promotion of the development or re-development of derelict sites or vacant sites; or

(j) the regulation, restriction or control of the erection of advertisement structures and the exhibition of advertisements.[242]

The scheme prepared by the planning authority shall be in writing and shall be consistent with the objectives of the relevant development plan and any local area plan or integrated area plan in force relating to the area to which the scheme relates.[243]

**[1.228]** The prepared scheme shall indicate the period for which it is to remain in force. A scheme may indicate the order in which it is proposed that the objectives of the scheme or the provisions for its furtherance or attainment will be implemented.[244]

---

241. PDA 2000, s 84(1).
242. PDA 2000, s 84(2)(a)–(j).
243. PDA 2000, s 84(3).
244. PDA 2000, s 84(4)(a) and (b).

[1.229] PDA 2000, s 85 sets out the procedure for adopting a special planning control scheme in relation to an architectural conservation area. Many of the procedures in this section are similar to the procedures for adopting a development plan under PDA 2000, s 12. A planning authority must pass a resolution concerning the proposal of a special planning control scheme. Notices in writing dealing with the preparation of the scheme must be served on the Minister, the board and such other persons as may be prescribed. A newspaper notice in one or more newspapers circulating the area must be published giving notice of the preparation of the scheme. The notice must indicate the place or places and the period (not less than eight weeks) at which times the scheme may be inspected and the notice must also invite submissions or observations in relation to the scheme within a period (being not less than eight weeks) as specified in the notice.[245] Where the scheme prepared includes an objective or provision relating to:

    (i)    the co-ordination, upgrading or changing of specified shop frontages,

    (ii)   the control of the layout of specified areas, the density, building lines and height of specified structures and the treatment of spaces around and between specified structures,

    (ii)   the control of the design, colour and materials of specified structures,

    (iii)  the promotion of the maintenance, repair or cleaning of specified structures,

    (iv)  the control of the use or uses of any specified structure or other land in the area,

    (v)   the discontinuance of the existence of use of any specified structure or other land,

    (vi)  the development or re-development of specified derelict or vacant sites, or

    (vii) the control of specified advertisement structures or of the exhibition of specified advertisements,

the planning authority shall, as soon as may be after the making of a resolution, notify in writing each person who is the owner or occupier of land thereby affected, of the objective or provision concerned.[246]

[1.230] The notice is served on the owners or occupiers of premises affected by the objective and the notice must advise the owner or occupier of the measures that are required to be undertaken in respect of the structure and other land to ensure compliance with the proposed objective or objectives. The notice will also indicate where the scheme may be inspected and the times at which it may be inspected and it will invite submissions or observations in relation to the proposed objective as specified in the notice.[247]

[1.231] Within 12 weeks from the date on which the last notice was sent, the manager of the planning authority must prepare a report on any submissions or observations

---

245. PDA 2000, s 85(2) and (3).
246. PDA 2000, s 85(4)(a).
247. PDA 2000, s 85(4)(b).

received in relation to the scheme and submit that report to the members of the authority for their consideration.[248]

**[1.232]** The manager's report shall:

(i) list the persons who made submissions or observations in relation to the scheme;

(ii) give a summary of the matters raised in those submissions or observations; and

(iii) include the response of the manager to the submissions or observations.[249]

In responding to submissions or observations made in relation to a scheme prepared by the manager, the manager shall take into account the proper planning and sustainable development of the area, the statutory obligations of any local authority in the area and any relevant policies or objectives of the government or of any Minister of the government.[250]

**[1.233]** A planning authority may, after considering the report of the manager, by resolution, approve the scheme with or without modifications, or refuse to so approve, and a scheme so approved shall be known as and is referred to as 'an approved scheme'.[251]

**[1.234]** Where a planning authority approves a scheme, it shall publish a notice thereof in one or more newspapers circulating in the city or town concerned. The notice shall indicate the place or places at which, and the times during which, the approved scheme may be inspected (and a copy thereof shall be kept available for inspection accordingly). A planning authority shall send a copy of the scheme to the Minister, the board and such other persons as may be prescribed.[252&253]

**[1.235]** The planning authority has an obligation to review a special planning control scheme from time to time but not later than six years after its approval or its last review, as appropriate. The scheme may be reviewed and may by resolution be amended or revoked. The provisions of PDA 2000, s 85 shall apply to any amendment of an approved scheme. Notice of revocation of an approved scheme must be published in a newspaper circulating in the city or town concerned and the amendment or revocation of an approved scheme shall be without prejudice to the validity of anything previously done thereunder.[254]

---

248. PDA 2000, s 85(5)(a).
249. PDA 2000, s 85(5)(b).
250. PDA 2000, s 85(6).
251. PDA 2000, s 85(7).
252. PDA 2000, s 85(7), (8) and (9).
253. In relation to 'such other persons as may be prescribed' these, under art 5(f) of the planning regulations, are the Minister for Arts and Heritage, Gaeltacht and the Islands, the Heritage Council, An Taisce An Chomhairle Ealaíon, Bord Fáilte Éireann and the appropriate Chamber of Commerce.
254. PDA 2000, s 86.

## Development in special planning control areas

**[1.236]** PDA 2000, s 4 is the section which defines exempted development and, notwithstanding the provisions of s 4(1)(a), (b), (i), (j), (k) or (l) and/or any regulations made under s 4(2), any development within an area of special planning control shall not be exempted development where it contravenes an approved scheme applying to that area.[255] A planning authority, in considering an application for permission, or the board, on considering an appeal, shall have regard to the provisions of any approved scheme.[256]

**[1.237]** An owner or occupier of land situated in an area of special planning control may make a written request to the planning authority seeking a declaration as to:

(a) those developments or classes of development that it considers would be contrary or would not be contrary, as the case may be, to the approved scheme concerned;

(b) the objectives or provisions of the approved scheme that apply to the land; or

(c) the measures that will be required to be undertaken in respect of the land to ensure compliance with such objectives or provisions.

The planning authority must issue its declaration within 12 weeks or such other period as may be prescribed by the Minister. The declaration may, at any time, be rescinded or varied and the rescission of variation of a declaration shall not affect any development commenced prior thereto in reliance on the declaration concerned. Any declaration made by a planning authority shall be entered in the register kept by the authority. A copy of the declaration shall be made available to members of the public for inspection.[257]

## Notices under PDA 2000, s 88

**[1.238]** The planning authority may serve notice on the owner or occupier of land in an area of special planning control. The s 88 notice served on an owner or occupier may require that certain measures be undertaken to include restoration, demolition, removal, alteration, replacement, maintenance, repair or cleaning of any structure or the discontinuance of any use or the continuance of any use, subject to conditions. A notice served under PDA 2000, s 88(1) shall:

(a) refer to the structure or land concerned,

(b) specify the date on which the notice shall come into force,

(c) specify the measures required to be undertaken on the coming into force of the notice including, as appropriate, measures for:

(i) the restoration, demolition, removal, alteration, replacement, maintenance, repair or cleaning of any structure or

---

255. PDA 2000, s 87(1) as amended by PD(A)A 2010, s 36.
256. PDA 2000, s 87(2).
257. PDA 2000, s 85(3)–(8).

(ii) the discontinuance of any use or the continuance of any use subject to conditions,

(d) invite the person on whom the notice is served, within such period as is specified in the notice (being not less than 8 weeks from the date of service of the notice) to make written representations to the planning authority concerning the notice,

(e) invite the person to enter into discussions with the planning authority, within such period as is specified in the notice (being not less than 8 weeks from the date of service of the notice) concerning the matters to which the notice refers and in particular concerning —

(i) the period within which the measure specified in the notice are to be carried out, and

(ii) the provision by the planning authority of advice, materials, equipment, the services of the authority's staff or other assistants required to carry out the measures specified in the notice,

(f) specify the period within which, unless otherwise agreed in the discussions entered into pursuant to an invitation in the notice in accordance with *paragraph (e)*, the measures specified in the notice shall be carried out, being a period of not less than 8 weeks from the date of the coming into force of the notice,

(g) state that the planning authority shall pay any expenses that are reasonably incurred by that person in carrying out the steps specified in the notice, other than expenses that relate to unauthorised development carried out not more than 7 years prior to the service of the notice, and

(h) state that the planning authority shall, by way of compensation, pay, to any person who shows that as a result of complying with the notice —

(i) the value of an interest he or she has in the land or part thereof existing at the time of the notice has been reduced, or

(ii) he or she, having an interest in the land at that time, has suffered damage by being disturbed in his or her enjoyment of the structure or of the land,

a sum equal to the amount of such reduction in value or a sum in respect of the damage suffered.[258]

If the invitation to enter into discussions is accepted, the planning authority shall take all such measures as may be necessary to enable the discussions concerned to take place.[259]

**[1.239]** After considering any representations made and any discussions held, the planning authority may confirm, amend or revoke the notice and shall notify in writing the person to whom the notice is addressed.[260]

---

258. PDA 2000, s 88(2)(a)–(h).
259. PDA 2000, s 88(3).
260. PDA 2000, s 88(4).

## Appeal to An Bord Pleanála

**[1.240]** Any person served with a notice under s 88 may, within eight weeks from the date of notification of the confirmation or amendment of the notice, appeal to An Bord Pleanála against the notice.[261]

**[1.241]** The Board must take the following into account when an appeal is brought to it against a notice:

- (a) the proper planning and sustainable development of the area,
- (b) the provisions of the development plan for the area,
- (c) any local plan or integrated area plan (within the meaning of the Urban Renewal Act 1998) in force relating to the area to which the scheme relates, and
- (d) the provisions of the approved scheme concerned and having taken those matters into account the Board may confirm the notice with or without modification or it may annul the notice.

A notice served by a planning authority under s 88 may, for stated reasons, be withdrawn by notice in writing.[262] A notice under this section (other than a notice that has been withdrawn) shall not come into force —

- (a) until the expiry of any period within which an appeal against the notice may be brought, or
- (b) where an appeal is taken against the notice, when the appeal has been withdrawn or decided,

as may be appropriate.[263]

## Implementation of the notice under s 88

**[1.242]** If, within eight weeks from the date of coming into force of the notice or such longer period as may be agreed by the planning authority and the person to whom the notice is addressed, the restoration, demolition, removal, alteration, replacement, maintenance, repair or cleaning required by the notice has not been effected, the planning authority may, subject to s 252, enter the structure or land and may effect such restoration, demolition, removal, alteration, replacement, maintenance, repair or cleaning as is specified in the notice.[264&265]

---

261. PDA 2000, s 88(5).
262. PDA 2000, s 88(7).
263. PDA 2000, s 88(8)(a) and (b).
264. PDA 2000, s 89.
265. PDA 2000, s 252 enables an authorised person to enter onto land during daytime or during business hours of any premises that is open at other times, following notification of the owner or occupier or, if necessary, following an application to the District Court. The authorised person may also request a member of the Garda Síochána to accompany them on the inspection.

## *Enforcement of s 88 notices*

**[1.243]** Where a person served with a notice under s 88 fails to comply with a requirement of the notice, or causes or permits a person to fail to comply with such requirement, he or she shall be guilty of an offence.[266]

**[1.244]** The court may compel compliance by a person served with a notice under s 88 where that person fails to comply with a requirement of the notice, or cause or permits a person to fail to comply with a requirement of the notice on the application of the planning authority. The application is made to the High Court or the Circuit Court seeking an order to compel any person to comply with the notice or to do, or refrain from doing or continuing to do, anything that the court considers necessary or expedient to ensure compliance with all the terms of the said notice. The order may also direct positive action such as restoration, demolition, removal, alteration, replacement, maintenance, repair or cleaning of any structure or other feature or the discontinuance of any use or continuance thereof subject to conditions specified in the order. Any order made by the court, however, is contingent on the right of the owner or occupier to the payment of compensation. Questionably, a s 88 notice would be regarded as a significant interference with the property rights of the owner or occupier under the Constitution. Any order made in relation to s 88 notices by the court should be conditional on the payment of compensation by the planning authority. The Circuit Court has jurisdiction to hear and determine applications where the market value of the land, the subject of the application, does not exceed €3,000,000. Where the market value of the land subject to the application under this section exceeds €3,000,000, the Circuit Court shall, if an application is made to it, transfer proceedings to the High Court but any order made or act done in the course of such proceedings before the Circuit Court before the transfer has taken place shall be valid unless discharged or varied by the High Court.[267]

**[1.245]** Permission shall not be required in respect of a development required by notice under s 88 or an order made under s 90. A development required by a s 88 notice or order under s 90 is exempted development.[268]

## Areas of special amenity

**[1.246]** While architectural conservation areas and areas of special planning control will more commonly be applicable to cities, towns and villages, areas of special amenity will predominately relate to less developed areas.

**[1.247]** Areas of special amenity are specifically defined in PDA 2000, s 202(1) and (2). The planning authority may designate an area as an area of special amenity and the Minister may also direct the local authority to make a special amenity area order

---

266. PDA 2000, s 91.
267. See generally the provisions of PDA 2000, s 90 and provisions of the Civil Liability and Courts Act 2004, s 53(1) in relation to courts' jurisdiction.
268. PDA 2000, s 92.

(SAAO), setting out the objectives and the directions which the local authority is obliged to obey.

**[1.248]** The local authority has the power to declare an area of special amenity where, in its opinion, by reason of (a) its outstanding natural beauty, or (b) its special recreational value, and having regard to any benefits for nature conservation, an area should be declared under this section to be an area of special amenity. It may, by resolution, make an order to do so and the order may state the objective of the planning authority in relation to the preservation or enhancement of the character or special features of the area, including objectives for the prevention or limitation of development in the area.[269]

**[1.249]** Where it appears to the Minister that an area should be declared to be an area of special amenity by reason of (a) its outstanding natural beauty, or (b) its special recreational value, and having regard to any benefits for nature conservation, he or she may, if he or she considers it necessary, direct the planning authority to make an order in relation to an area specified in the direction and may, if he or she thinks fit, require that the objective specified in the direction be included by the planning authority in the order in respect of matters and in a manner so specified, and if the Minister gives a direction the planning authority concerned shall comply with that direction. Any direction given by the Minister can only be revoked with the consent of the Minister.[270]

**[1.250]** Where the functional areas of two planning authorities are contiguous, either authority may, with the consent of the other, make an order under this section in respect of an area in or partly in the functional area of the other.[271]

**[1.251]** Any order may be revoked or varied by a subsequent order and a planning authority may, from time to time, review an order made (excepting any order merely revoking a previous order), for the purpose of deciding whether it is desirable to revoke or amend the order.[272]

**[1.252]** An SAAO will have significant effects on the planning potential for the area which it covers. The planning authority and An Bord Pleanála are required to have regard to the provisions of any SAAO relating to the area in determining an application for planning permission.[273]

**[1.253]** One of the mandatory objectives which must be included in a development plan is:

> the preservation of the character of the landscape where, and to the extent that, in the opinion of the planning authority, the proper planning and sustainable development of the area requires it, including the preservation of views and prospects and the amenities of places and features of natural beauty or interest.[274]

---

269. PDA 2000, s 202(1).
270. PDA 2000, s 202(2) and (3).
271. PDA 2000, s 202(5).
272. PDA 2000, s 202(6) and (7).
273. PDA 2000, s 34(2)(a)(ii).
274. PDA 2000, s 10(2)(e).

**[1.254]** Under previous legislation no permission for development could be granted if the permission was in material contravention either of the development plan or of an SAAO.[275] There is no express provision in PDA 2000 to state unequivocally that development within an area affected by an SAAO would be a material contravention. The aims of an SAAO and the wording of the order would coincide closely to the provisions of PDA 2000, s 10(2)(e) and for that reason, and by implication at least, it may be argued that development within an area covered by an SAAO is a material contravention which cannot proceed unless the special material contravention procedure is invoked involving the passing of a special resolution by three-quarters of the total number of elected members.[276] The Roads Act 1993 requires the National Roads Authority to have regard to the provisions of an SAAO when performing functions in relation to the construction or maintenance of a national road although the National Roads Authority has power to direct a road authority to carry out specified works where the works are in material contravention of an SAAO but if they give such a direction they are required to give public notice and to initiate the public participation procedures set out in the Roads Act.[277]

**[1.255]** There is a specific prohibition against development in an area affected by an SAAO contained in the Planning Regulations 2001. Exempted development, as defined in art 6 of PDR 2001 and art 9(1)(b), exempts development to which art 6 relates in an area to which an SAAO relates. PDR 2001 then lists the development to be de-exempted and the de-exempted classes include the construction, erection, lowering, repair or replacement of any fence or wall of brick, stone, blocks with decorative finish, other concrete blocks or mass concrete; certain industrial development; development by statutory undertakers; and certain use of land for the exhibition of advertisements. Furthermore, PDR 2001, art 9(1)(b)(iv) sanctions a planning authority to specify any other class of exempted development which may be prevented, in the sense of de-exempted or limited, when making the SAAO.

**[1.256]** Compensation is not payable where planning permission is refused in respect of a development proposal in an area to which an SAAO applies.[278]

**[1.257]** The provisions of Planning and Development Regulations 2006 (PDR 2006), art 21(1)(a) are also relevant:

> Where it appears to the authority that the land or structure is situate in an area of special amenity, whether or not an order in respect of that area has been confirmed under section 203 (or deemed to be so confirmed under section 268(1)(c)) of the Act), or that the development or retention of the structure might obstruct any view or prospect of special amenity value or special interest – the planning authority must send notice as soon as may be after the receipt of the application to An Chomhairle Ealaíon, Fáilte Ireland, and An Taisce – the National Trust for Ireland.

---

275. Local Government (Planning and Development) Act 1963, s 26(3) (as amended by the Local Government Act 1991, s 45).
276. See LGA 2001, s 140.
277. Roads Act 1993, ss 18 and 20 as amended by Road Traffic Act 1994, s 49(3).
278. PDA 2000, Sch 3 para 6.

## Confirmation of order under s 202

[1.258] The procedure for confirming an order passed by resolution designating an area as an area of special amenity requires the planning authority to publish a notice in one or more newspapers circulating in the area stating the following:

- (a) the fact of the order having been made, and describing the area to which it relates,
- (b) naming the place where a copy of the order and any map referred to therein may be seen during office hours,
- (c) specifying the period (not being less than four weeks) within which and the manner in which objections to the order may be made to the planning authority, and
- (d) specifying that the order requires confirmation by the Board and that where any objections are duly made to the order and are not withdrawn, an oral hearing will be held and the objections will be considered before the order is confirmed.[279]

As soon as may be after the period for making objections has expired, the planning authority may submit the order made under s 202 to the Board for confirmation, and, when making any such submission, it shall also submit to the Board any objections to the order which have been duly made and have not been withdrawn.[280]

If no objection is duly made to the order, or if all objections so made are withdrawn, the Board may confirm the order made under s 202, with or without modifications, or refuse to confirm it.

Where any objections to the order are not withdrawn, the Board shall hold an oral hearing and shall consider the objections, and may then confirm the order, with or without modifications or refuse to confirm it.[281]

[1.259] Apart from publishing a notice in the newspaper as required by PDA 2000, s 203 there is no specific requirement, in relation to SAAOs, to serve owners of lands and premises within the area affected by the SAAO. Although few people other than contractors and the persons who caused the notice to be published trouble to read public notices in newspapers it is likely that the 'word' that an SAAO was to be made would spread around the area like wildfire. Nevertheless, the SAAO procedure would be strengthened and improved if it required the planning authority to serve owners and occupiers of lands and premises affected by the order.

[1.260] Where objections are made within four weeks of the date of the confirmation of the SAAO and provided they are not withdrawn An Bord Pleanála will hold an oral hearing to consider the objection before confirming the order. Having considered any submission and objection the board may confirm the order with or without modification

---

279. PDA 2000, s 203(1)(a) to (d).
280. PDA 2000, s 203(2).
281. PDA 2000, s 203(3)(a) and (b).

or it may refuse the order. The conduct of the oral hearing before the board is regulated by the provisions of PDA 2000, s 135 as amended by PD(A)A 2010, s 43.

## Landscape conservation areas

**[1.261]** A planning authority may designate an area as a landscape conservation area for the purposes of preserving the landscape. The purpose behind this provision is to authorise planning authorities to exercise planning control in these areas in respect of developments which would normally be exempted, such as the removal of hedges and ditches, the division of commonage, afforestation and land reclamation. The loss of exempted development status is not automatic in the sense that it does not accompany the order when it is made unless the Minister for Environment, Heritage and Local Government specifically prescribes the kind of development which is de-exempted within the landscape conservation area. The local authority may then make an order specifying that any development prescribed by the Minister is not exempted in all or part of the landscape conservation area. Both the Minister, when making the regulations under this section, and the planning authority when designating the landscape conservation area, will be obliged to consult with any State authority in circumstances where the regulations or order relate to the functions of that authority.[282]

**[1.262]** The requirements for making a landscape conservation area order are less demanding than the requirements under s 203 PDA 2000 for making an SAAO. Notably, there is no requirement for confirmation of the order by the board. Two or more planning authorities may propose to jointly designate an area or place as a landscape conservation area in which case the functions for making the order must be performed jointly.

### Landscape conservation area order procedure

**[1.263]** Where a planning authority proposes to make a land conservation area order it shall cause notice of the proposed order to be published in one or more newspapers circulating in the area of the proposed landscape conservation area. The notice shall state that the planning authority proposes to make an order designating a landscape conservation area, indicating the place or places and times at which a map outlining the area may be inspected, and shall give details of the location of the area and any prescribed development which it proposes to specify in the order, that submissions or observations regarding the proposed order may be made to the planning authority within a stated period of not less than six weeks, and that the submissions and observations will be taken into consideration by the planning authority.[283]

**[1.264]** Elected members of the planning authority, having considered any submissions, may by resolution make an order with or without modifications or may refuse to do so.[284]

---

282. PDA 2000, s 204(1)–(3).
283. PDA 2000, s 204(5)(a) and (b).
284. PDA 2000, s 204(6).

[1.265] A planning authority shall give notice of any order in at least one newspaper circulating in the functional area and the notices shall give details of any prescribed development which is specified in the order. Notice shall also be given to the board and to any other prescribed body which in the opinion of the planning authority has an interest in such notice.[285]

[1.266] Particulars of any landscape conservation area order made by a planning authority shall be entered in the planning authority's register.[286]

[1.267] Provisions are also made for amendment or revocation of a landscape conservation area order made by a planning authority, which require the procedure of publishing a newspaper notice of the proposal and inviting submissions.[287]

[1.268] The principal drawback for persons living in an area affected by a landscape conservation area order is the potential loss of exempted development. The order does not de-exempt development within a landscape conservation area unless the development to be de-exempted is specifically mentioned in the order as having been prescribed by the Minister. To date, the Minister has made no such regulations by way of de-exempting exempted development in a landscape conservation area. The entitlement to compensation where an application for permission is refused on the basis that the proposed development would adversely affect a landscape conservation area is excluded.[288] The payment of compensation is also excluded where the reason for refusal is that the development would interfere with the character of the landscape or with a view or prospect of special amenity value or natural interest or beauty, any of which it is necessary to preserve even though the particular feature may not have been specifically identified in the landscape conservation area order.[289]

## REGIONAL PLANNING GUIDELINES

[1.269] Regional planning authorities were established under s 43 of the Local Government Act 1991. The provisions relating to them are to be found in PDA 2000, Pt 2, Ch III, ss 21–27 inclusive.[290] PDA 2000, s 21(1) provides that a regional planning authority may, after consultation with the planning authorities within its region, or in the case of regional authorities within the Greater Dublin Area, after consultation with the planning authorities within their regions and the Dublin Transport Authority or, at the direction of the Minister, shall make regional planning guidelines (RPGs). The section gave statutory recognition to regional guidelines for the first time.

---

285. PDA 2000, s 204(12)(a) and (b).
286. PDA 2000, s 204(14).
287. PDA 2000, s 204(7)–(10).
288. PDA 2000, Sch 4 para 17.
289. PDA 2000, Sch 4 para 8.
290. Note that PDA 2000, ss 23, 24 and 27 have been amended by PD(A)A 2010, ss 14, 15 and 16 respectively.

**[1.270]** RPGs may be made for the whole region or for one or more parts of the region[291] but, in the case of the Greater Dublin Area, may be made jointly by the regional authorities within the Greater Dublin Area:

    1(a)    the objective of regional planning guidelines shall be to support the implementation of the National Spatial Strategy by providing a long term strategic planning framework for the development of the region for which the guidelines are prepared which shall be consistent with the National Spatial Strategy.

    1(b)    the planning framework referred to at paragraph (a) shall consider the future development of the region for which the guidelines are prepared for a period of not less than twelve years and not more than twenty years.[292]

**[1.271]** The guidelines shall address, for the whole of the region to which the guidelines relate and in accordance with the principles of proper planning and sustainable development, the following matters:

    (a)    any policies or objectives for the time being of the Government or any Minister for the Government, or any policies contained in the National Spatial Strategy in relation to national and regional population targets;[293]

    (b)    economic and employment trends;

    (c)    the location of industrial and commercial development;

    (d)    transportation, including public transportation;

    (e)    water supply and waste water-facilities;

    (f)    waste disposal;

    (g)    energy and communications networks;

    (h)    the provision of educational, healthcare, retail and other community facilities;

    (i)    the preservation and protection of the environment and its amenities, including the archaeological, architectural and natural heritage;

    (j)    landscape, in accordance with relevant policies or objectives for the time being of the Government or any Minister of the Government relating to providing a framework for identification, assessment, protection, management and planning of landscapes and developed having regard to the European Landscape Convention done at Florence on the 20th October 2000;[294]

    (k)    the promotion of sustainable settlement and transportation strategies in urban and rural areas, including the promotion of measures to reduce anthropogenic greenhouse gas emissions and address the necessity of adaptation to climate change;[295]

    (l)    such other matters as may be prescribed.

---

291. PDA 2000, s 21(2).
292. PDA 2000, s 23(1)(a)(b). Note that s 23(1)(a) has been amended by PD(A)A 2010, s 14.
293. PDA 2000, s 23(2)(a) has been amended by PD(A)A 2010, s 14(b)(1).
294. PDA 2000, s 23(2)(j) has been amended by PD(A)A 2010, s 14(2)(j).
295. PDA 2000, s 23(2) has been extended by the addition of a new subpara (k) by the provisions of PD(A)A 2010, s 14(b)(k).

**[1.272]** A new s 23(3) has been inserted into the old s 23 of PDA 2000 and the amendment comes from the European Communities (Environmental Assessment of Certain Plans and Programmes) Regulations 2004 (SI 435/2004), as further amended by PD(A)A 2010, s 23(c)(3A). The regulations provide that the Minister may, for purposes of giving effect to Directive 2001/42/EC of the European Parliament and Council of 27 June 2001 on the assessment of the effects of certain plans and programmes on the environment ([2001] OJ L197/0030–0037), by regulations make provision in relation to consideration of the likely significant effects on the environment of implementing regional planning guidelines.

**[1.273]** Section 23(3A) as inserted provides that:

> An appropriate assessment of draft regional planning guidelines shall be carried out in accordance with Part XAB.[296]

**[1.274]** PDA 2000, s 23(4)(a), (b) and (c) provides that in making RPGs the regional authority must take into account the proper planning and sustainable development of the whole region to which the guidelines relate, the statutory obligations of any local authority in the region and any relevant policies or objectives at the time being of the government or of any Minister of the government, including any national plans, policies or strategies specified by the Minister to be of relevance to the determination of strategic planning policies. It may be noted that the Planning and Development (Regional Planning Guidelines) Regulations 2003, art 4 provides that the National Spatial Strategy 2002–2020 published on 28 November 2002 is specified to be of relevance to the determination of strategic planning policies.

**[1.275]** When making planning guidelines which affect the Gaeltacht, the regional authority must have regard to the need to protect the linguistic and cultural heritage of the Gaeltacht.

**[1.276]** When making RPGs, the regional planning authorities within the Greater Dublin Area shall ensure that the guidelines are consistent with the transport strategy of the DTA.[297]

**[1.277]** PDA 2000, s 24(1) deals with consultation regarding RPGs. Subsection 1 provides that a regional authority shall give notice of its intention to make the RPGs as soon as may be after making the necessary arrangements under s 21.

**[1.278]** The notice required shall be given to the Minister, the board, the prescribed authorities and any town commissioners in the area and shall be published in one or more newspapers circulating in the region for which the RPGs are prepared and shall:

(a) state that the regional authority intends to make regional planning guidelines;

(b) indicate the matters to be considered in the guidelines having regard to s 23;

---

296. Part XAB regulates the conditions of 'appropriate consent'.
297. This provision is made by the Dublin Transport Authority Act 2008, s 89.

(c) include that submissions regarding the making of regional planning guidelines may be made in writing to the regional authority within a specified period (which shall not be less than eight weeks).[298]

[1.279] PDR 2001, arts 15(a)–15(h) inclusive provide that the notice advising that draft regulations are about to be made by the regional authority must also state that it proposes to carry out an environmental impact assessment (EIA) as part of the making of RPGs. The regional authority must prepare an environmental report on the likely significant effects on the environment to be affected by the RPGs. Draft RPGs must also be accompanied by an environmental report. The draft environmental report must be available to be inspected by interested parties for a period of not less than ten weeks and submissions and observations are invited in relation to the environmental report which accompanies the draft RPGs.

[1.280] The information to be contained in an environmental report is set out in Sch 2B of PDR 2001 (SI 600/2001) as inserted by the Planning and Development (Strategic Environmental Assessment) Regulations 2004 (SI 436/2004). There are 10 matters contained in Sch 2(B) and all are mandatory and must be included in the report. The Sch 2(B) information to be included in the report comprises the following:

(a) an outline of the contents and main objectives of the plan and relationship of other relevant plans;

(b) the relevant aspects of the current state of the environment and the likely evolution thereof without implementation of the plan;

(c) the environmental characteristics of areas likely to be significantly affected;

(d) any existing environmental problems which are relevant to the plan including, in particular, those relating to any areas of a particular environmental importance, such as areas designated pursuant to the Birds Directive or Habitats Directive;

(e) the environmental protection objectives, established at international, European Union or national level which are relevant to the plan and the way those objectives and any environmental considerations have been taken into account during its preparation;

(f) the likely significant effects on the environment, including issues such as bio-diversity, population, human health, flora, fauna, soil, water, air, climatic factors, material assets, cultural heritage including architectural and archaeological heritage, landscape and the interrelationship between the above factors;

(g) the measures envisaged to prevent, reduce and as fully as possible offset any significant adverse effects on the environment of implementing the plan;

(h) an outline of the reasons for selecting the alternatives dealt with, and a description of how the assessment was undertaken including any

---

298. PDA 2000, s 24(1) and (2)(a), (b), (c).

(i) a description of the measures envisaged concerning monitoring of the significant environmental effects of the implementation of the plan;

(j) a non-technical summary of the information provided under the above headings.

Schedule 2(B), in general, mirrors the type of information required in relation to an EIA but the need to include information on monitoring measures is a specific addition.

**[1.281]** A regional authority must take account of any submissions or observations received on the draft regional plan as prepared and it shall make the RPGs subject to any modifications considered necessary. Once the guidelines have been made a notice must be published of the making of the guidelines in at least one newspaper circulating in the area and once again they must invite inspection of the guidelines.

**[1.282]** Where the regional authority considers that implementation of the guidelines is likely to have significant effects on the environment of another member state or where a member state is likely to be significantly affected and that member state requests consultation, the regional authority must enter into consultation with the state concerned in relation to the transboundary environmental effects of implementing the guidelines and the method envisaged to reduce or eliminate the effects. Detailed provisions of the full special procedures concerning transboundary environmental effects are contained in PDR 2001, art 15(e) (as inserted by the Planning and Development (Strategic Environmental Assessment) Regulations 2004, art 10).

**[1.283]** PDR 2001, art 15(g), as inserted by the Planning and Development (Strategic Environmental Assessment) Regulations 2004, art 10, provides that a notice under PDA 2000, s 24(7)(a) shall state that a statement is also available summarising: (a) how environmental considerations have been integrated into the guidelines; (b) how (i) the environmental report prepared pursuant to art 15(b), (ii) submissions and observations made to the regional authority in response to a notice under PDA 2000, s 24(4), and (iii) any consultation under art 15(e), have been taken into account during the preparation of the guidelines; (c) the reasons for choosing the guidelines, as adopted, in light of the other reasonable alternatives dealt with; and (d) the measures decided upon to monitor, in accordance with art 15(h), the significant environmental effects of implementation of the guidelines.

**[1.284]** PDA 2000, s 24 (as amended) sets out the full procedure for making RPGs. A regional authority having consulted with or made arrangements with the relevant planning authority in its area under PDA 2000, s 21 shall give notice of its intention to make RPGs. The regional authority's guidelines shall be given to the Minister, the board, the prescribed authorities and any town commissioners in the area and also it must be published in one or more newspapers circulating in the area. A notice of intention to make RPGs shall include a statement of intent to make the guidelines, and it shall detail the matters to be included in the guidelines. The notice will also invite parties, to include members of the public, to make submissions to it within a period of eight weeks from the date of publication of the notice.

**[1.285]** Art 15(a) of PDR 2001 provides that the s 24(1) notice, in addition to the requirements of s 24(2), shall state that:

1. the regional authority proposes to carry out an environmental assessment as part of the making of the regional planning guidelines; and

2. for this purpose the regional authority will prepare an environmental report of the likely significant effects on the environment of implementing the regional planning guidelines.

**[1.286]** PDR 2001, art 15(c) provides that as soon as is practicable, having given notice under s 24(1), the regional authority shall give notice to the Environmental Protection Agency and to the Minister for the Environment, Heritage and Local Government if it appears to the regional authority that the plan might have significant effects in relation to archaeological heritage or to nature conservation. Notice must be given to the Minister for Communications, Marine and Natural Resources where it appears to the regional authority that the plan might have significant effects on fisheries or the marine environment.

**[1.287]** A new sub-s (6), has been added to PDA 2000, s 24.[299] Section 24(6)(a) provides that the regional authority shall, subject to any amendments which it considers necessary, make the RPGs subject also, however, to compliance with s 24(6)(b) and (e) below, and having considered any submissions or observations made by members of the public or any other specified parties, make the RPGs.

**[1.288]** Section 24(6)(b) provides that before completing the RPGs the regional authority must determine whether any strategic environmental assessment or appropriate assessment or both such assessments are required in relation to one or more of any proposed material amendments to the draft RPGs.

**[1.289]** Section 24(6)(c) provides that within two weeks of making a determination as to whether or not strategic environmental assessment or appropriate assessment is required the director of the regional authority shall specify such period as may be necessary to facilitate such assessment.

**[1.290]** Section 24(6)(d) states that if material amendments are made and where, as appropriate, a determination is made that strategic environmental assessment or appropriate assessment or both is required, notices of those facts must be published in a newspaper circulating in the area in which the regional authority operates.

**[1.291]** Section 24(6)(e) sets out details of any proposed material amendment or any new determination in relation to assessment and states that further details may be inspected stating the place and times where such inspection can take place and also stating that the authority's website will carry these details for a period of not less than

---

299. PD(A)A 2010, s 15. The new sub-s (6) comprises s 24(6)(a)–(e)(i), (e)(ii), (f) and (6A) and (6B).

four weeks. Further, s 24(6)(e) invites written submissions or observations with respect to any proposed material amendment or any assessment required to be submitted to the regional authority within a period specified in the notice.

**[1.292]** Section 24(6)(f) provides that an assessment referred to in s 26(6)(b) of proposed material amendment(s) of the draft RPGs shall be carried out within a period to be specified by the director of the regional authority.

**[1.293]** Section 24(6A) provides that having considered submissions or observations under s 24(6) and subject to the provisions of s 25 (dealing with the procedure for making RPGs and dealt with below) the regional authority shall make the RPGs with or without the proposed material amendments and subject to any minor modifications considered necessary.

**[1.294]** Section 24(6B) provides that minor modifications referred to in s 24(6A) can be made where they are of such a nature that they would be unlikely to have any significant effects on the environment or unlikely to adversely affect the integrity of a European site.

**[1.295]** Section 24(7)(a) provides that as soon as the RPGs have been made the regional authority is required to publish the guidelines in at least one newspaper circulating in the functional area of each planning authority in the region for which the guidelines are prepared.

**[1.296]** Section 24(7)(b) provides that the newspaper notice shall also state the place and times where the new guidelines may be inspected.

**[1.297]** PDA 2000, s 25 sets out the statutory requirements in relation to the making of RPGs and deals with the nature of the cooperation required between the regional development authority and the planning authorities in the making of the guidelines. Those procedures for the making of the guidelines and for cooperation on the making of the guidelines should be agreed with the planning authorities once notice of intention of making the guidelines has been served.[300]

**[1.298]** PDA 2000, s 25(3A) has been inserted by the Dublin Transport Authority Act 2008, s 91 to provide that regional authorities in the Greater Dublin Area (GDA) in making RPGs shall include a statement of the actions being taken or proposed to ensure effective integration of transport and land use planning, including, in particular:

(a) a statement explaining how the regional authorities propose to address the matters identified in the report of the Dublin Transport Authority (DTA) prepared in accordance with s 31G; and

(b) where the regional authorities do not propose to address or propose only to partial address, any matter identified in the report of the DTA prepared in accordance with s 31G, a statement of the reasons for that course of action.

---

300. PDA 2000, s 25(1), (2), (3), (4) and (5).

**[1.299]** PDA 2000, s 25(3B) has been inserted by the Public Transport Regulation Act 2009, s 41(1) and the subsection provides that where a regional authority (other than a regional authority situate within the GDA) makes RPGs it shall include in the guidelines a statement of the actions being taken or proposed to ensure effective integration of transport and land use planning, including, in particular:

(a) a statement explaining how it proposes to address the matters identified in the report of the DTA prepared in accordance with s 31GG; and

(b) where it does not propose to address, or proposes only to partial address, any matter identified in the report of the DTA prepared in accordance with s 31GG, a statement of the reasons for that course of action.

**[1.300]** PDA 2000, s 26 specifically provides that any guidelines made under this section shall supersede any previous RPGs for the relevant area. Also, the Minister may make regulations or issue guidelines with regard to procedures to be adopted under this section and also in relation to the number, membership and functions of committees set up in accordance with s 25(2).[301]

**[1.301]** PDA 2000, s 26 deals with the review of RPGs. RPGs must be reviewed not later than six years after the making of such guidelines and not less than once in every period of six years thereafter. Where new guidelines are made under the provisions of PDA 2000, s 26(1) they shall supersede any RPGs for the relevant area.[302]

**[1.302]** PDA 2000, s 26 also provides that before any planning guidelines are revoked by a regional authority, other than for the purpose of making new RPGs, the regional authority must consult with the planning authorities within its region. Where new regional guidelines are made the regional authority must follow the procedures laid down in ss 22, 24 and 25.[303]

**[1.303]** PDA 2000, s 27(1)[304] provides that a planning authority shall ensure when making a development plan or a local area plan that that plan is consistent with any RPGs in force for its area. The Minister may require a planning authority in making its development plan to comply with RPGs or the Minister may issue a direction regarding development plans under PDA 2000, s 31 to ensure that the planning authority does comply with any RPGs in force for its area. Any such order made may be made in respect of either the entire RPGs generally or in respect of specified guidelines or specific elements of those guidelines.[305]

**[1.304]** As RPGs can be made during the term of a development plan, once the RPGs are made the planning authority must review the existing development plan and consider

---

301. Please refer to PDA 2000, s 25 (as amended by the Dublin Transport Authority Act 2008, s 91 and Public Transport Regulation Act 2009, s 44).
302. PDA 2000, s 26(4).
303. PDA 2000, s 26(2) and (3).
304. As amended by PD(A)A 2010, s 16(a).
305. PDA 2000, s 27(2) and (3).

whether any variation of the development plan is necessary in order to achieve the objectives of the RPGs made since the development plan came into operation.[306]

**[1.305]** As seen, a planning authority shall have regard to RPGs in force when making and adopting a development plan. In *McEvoy and Smith v Meath County Council*,[307] Quirke J held that the obligation to have regard to strategic planning guidelines as set out in s 27(1) PDA 2000 is more permissive than mandatory. Quirke J held that the obligation was one which committed the planning authority to informing itself fully of and giving reasonable consideration to any regional planning guidelines which are in force in the area with the aim of accommodating the objectives and policies contained in the guidelines. However, it appears that the local authority is not bound to comply with the guidelines and that it may depart from them for *bona fide* reasons consistent with the proper planning and development of the area.

**[1.306]** Regulations may be made by the Minister concerning the procedures and administration to be adopted by regional planning authorities in performing their functions in relation to the preparation of a draft development plan, the making of a development plan or the variation of a development plan as the case may be.[308]

**[1.307]** An additional s 27(a) has been added to PDA 2000, s 27 by PD(A)A 2010, s 17 dealing with the report of the regional authority for preparation of the local authority's draft development plan.

**[1.308]** Regional authorities are required to prepare submissions or observations to the planning authority or to the planning authorities within or partly within the regional authority's area. The submissions or observations are presented in a report dealing with matters that the regional authority is of the opinion require to be considered in relation to the development plan being made by the planning authority.[309]

**[1.309]** The submission of the regional authority's report is initiated by the service of notice of the planning authority's intention to prepare a new development plan for its area within a period of four years from the making of the development plan.[310]

**[1.310]** The submission and observations are contained in a report prepared by the regional authority concerning matters that the regional authority considers to require consideration by the planning authority concerned which should include but shall not be limited to the following matters:

    (a)    Any policies or objectives for the time being of the Government or any Minister of the Government in relation to national and regional population

---

306. PDA 2000, s 27(4).
307. *McEvoy and Smith v Meath County Council* [2003] 1 IR 208.
308. PDA 2000, s 27(6) as inserted by PD(A)A 2010, s 16(b).
309. PDA 2000, s 27A as inserted by PD(A)A 2010, s 17(2).
310. PDA 2000, s 11 as amended by PD(A)A 2010, s 8.

targets, and the best distribution of residential development and related employment development with a view to —

    (i) Promoting consistency as far as possible, between housing, settlement and economic objectives in the draft development plan and core strategy and regional planning guidelines, and

    (ii) Assisting in drafting the core strategy of the draft development plan;

(b) The objectives of providing physical, economic or social infrastructure in a manner that promotes balanced regional development;

(c) Planning for the best use of lands having regard to location, scale and density of new development to benefit from investment of public funds in transport, infrastructure and public transport service; and

(d) Collaboration between the planning authority and the regional authority in respect of integrated planning for transport and land use, in particular in relation to large scale developments and the promotion of sustainable transportation strategies in urban and rural areas, including the promotion of measures to reduce anthropogenic greenhouse gas omissions and address the necessity of adaptation to climate change.

[1.311] Where one or more regional authorities share a part of the area controlled by a planning authority they shall make joint submissions and observations and shall submit a joint report to the Minister.[311]

[1.312] Another new section has been inserted in PDA 2000, s 27 by PD(A)A 2010, s 18, namely s 27B. Where a regional authority receives a notice from a planning authority under PDA 2000, s 12(1) indicating that the draft development plan has been prepared in accordance with s 11 the planning authority shall send notice and a copy of the draft development plan to the board, the relevant regional authority and the prescribed authorities, any town commissioners and city and county development boards within the area and it will publish a notice of the preparation of a draft in one or more newspapers circulating in the area. The s 12(1) notice states that the draft plan may be inspected at a time and place stated for a period of 12 weeks and that written submissions or observations with respect to the draft can be made to the planning authority within the period stated in the notice and they will be taken into consideration before making the plan. Similar to s 27(2)(a), the submissions or observations made by the regional authority shall contain a report setting out the matters which in the opinion of the authority require consideration by the planning authority concerned in the making of its development plan.

[1.313] If it is the regional authority's opinion as made in the submissions and observations, and the report is to the effect that the draft development plan and its core strategy are not consistent with the regional planning guidelines, the submissions, observations and the report shall include recommendations as to what amendments are

---

311. PDA 2000, s 27A(4) as inserted by PD(A)A 2010, s 17.

**[1.314]** Planning and Environmental Law in Ireland

required in the opinion of the regional authority to ensure that the draft development plan and its core strategy are consistent.[312]

**[1.314]** A copy of the submissions or observations and the report of the regional authority shall be sent to the Minister and again when more than one regional authority is affected joint submissions and observations and joint reports will be submitted to the Minster.[313]

**[1.315]** PDA 2000, s 27C, deals with the role of the authority in variation of development plan. Where a regional authority receives notice from a planning authority under s 13(1), it shall prepare submissions and observations for the purpose of s 13(2). Section 13(1) allows a planning authority at any time, for stated reasons, to decide to make a variation of the development plan which for the time being is in force. Section 13(2) provides that if the planning authority proposes to make a variation it shall notify the board, the relevant regional authority and, where appropriate, any adjoining planning authority, the prescribed authority, and any town commissioners and city and county development boards within the area of the development plan. Notices of the proposed variation of the development plan will be published in one or more newspapers circulating in the area. The remaining subsections of s 27C, namely s 27C(2), (3), (4), (5), are precisely the same as the similarly numbered subsections in 27(b).

## MINISTERIAL GUIDELINES AND DIRECTIVES

**[1.316]** PDA 2000 permits the Minister to issue guidelines to planning authorities regarding any of the functions under the Act and the planning authority shall have regard to those guidelines in the performance of its functions. Where applicable, the board shall have regard to any guidelines issued to planning authorities in performance of its functions.[314]

**[1.317]** Subsections (1A) and (1B) inserted after PDA 2000, s 28(1) by PD(A)A 2010, s 20 are important subsections, presumably designed to keep planning authorities in control in relation to conforming to ministerial guidelines and directives.

> (1A) provides that without prejudice to the generality of subsection (1) and for the purposes of that subsection a planning authority in having regard to the guidelines issued by the Minister under that subsection shall —
>
> (a) Consider the policies and objectives of the Minister contained in the guidelines when preparing and making a draft development plan and the development plan, and
>
> (b) Append a statement to the draft development plan and the development plan which shall include information referred to in subsection (1B).

---

312. PDA 2000, s 27B(2) and (3) as inserted by PD(A)A 2010, s 18.
313. PDA 2000, s 27B(4) as inserted by PD(A)A 2010, s 18.
314. PDA 2000, s 28(1) and (2).

(1B) sets out the information required in the planning authority's statement to be appended to the draft development plan and the development plan namely to demonstrate —

(a) How the planning authority has implemented the policies and objectives of the Minister contained in the guidelines when considering their application to the area or part of the area of the development plan and the development plan, or

(b) If applicable, that the planning opinion has formed the opinion that it is not possible, because of the nature and characteristics of the area or part of the area of the development plan, to implement certain policies and objectives of the Minister contained in the guidelines when considering the application of those policies in the area or part of the area of the draft development plan or the development plan and shall give reasons for the forming of the opinion and why the policies and objectives of the Minister have not been so implemented.

A heavy onus is placed on planning authorities either to comply with ministerial guidelines and directives or, if they do not comply with them, to furnish convincing reasons as to why they have not been able to comply with ministerial guidelines and directives.

**[1.318]** PDA 2000, s 28(2) also compels the board to have regard to any guidelines issued to the planning authorities in the performance of its functions – in other words, when dealing with appeals from a decision of the planning authority.

**[1.319]** The meaning of 'to have regard to' was discussed in *Glencar Explorations plc v Mayo County Council*[315] where the Chief Justice stated as follows:

The fact that they are obliged to have regard to policies and objectives of the government or a particular Minister does not mean that, in every case, they are obliged to implement the policies and objectives in question. If the Oireachtas had intended such an obligation to rest on the planning authority in a case such as the present, it will have said so.

The term 'to have regard to' does not imply that the guidelines or recommendations must be followed 'slavishly' or complied with to the letter. Rather, the obligation on the planning authority and the board in relation to guidelines and recommendations is to inform themselves fully of them and to give reasonable consideration to them.

**[1.320]** The Minister also has a power to revoke or amend guidelines and the guidelines shall be made available for inspection by members of the public by planning authorities.[316]

**[1.321]** Examples of guidelines are the *Development Management Guidelines for Planning Authorities* issued of June 2007, the *Sustainable Residential Development in Urban Areas Guidelines* of February 2008 and the *Urban Design Manual – A Best*

---
315. *Glencar Explorations plc v Mayo County Council* [2002] 1 IR 84 *per* Keane CJ.
316. PDA 2000, s 2(h).

*Practice Guide*, which is a companion document to the planning guidelines on *Sustainable Residential Development in Urban Areas*. Consultation draft guidelines for planning authorities dealing with the planning system and with flood risk management were issued in 2008 after a very wet summer which produced some spectacularly damaging flooding. Increased flooding may be a consequence of progressive global warming and in some locations it is certainly a consequence of developers receiving permission from planning authorities to carry out development on flood planes. It is also the case that considerable development has been completed with inadequate facilities for safe and comprehensive disposal of surface water.

**[1.322]** Nevertheless, the guidelines issued by the Department of Environment, Heritage and Local Government are thoughtful and well written documents. If anyone has any doubt as to the real meaning of sustainable development or the reality of global warming, a read of these informative documents will put them on the right track. It is clear, already, that far reaching programmes of sustainable development are no longer an aspiration. They are a pressing necessity. It is also clear that rising seawater levels are slowly progressive but inevitable. Already the spring tides are damaging the decorative portions of O'Connell Bridge in Dublin which were not designed to resist tidal pressure. If all the land-based glacial ice in the northern and southern hemispheres turns into water in the next 90 to 150 years there will be a startling rise in water levels which could well be anything between 20 and 30 metres. The accuracy of these predictions is difficult to measure but it is quite clear that a lot of first class agricultural land with good alluvial soil will be submerged. Perhaps O'Connell Street may eventually be re-located on the Calary Bog road in County Wicklow. One day Dublin's main thoroughfare could be located somewhere between the Sugarloaf Mountain and Roundwood.

**[1.323]** Limitations are placed on ministerial power by PDA 2000, s 30(1) which provides that notwithstanding PDA 2000, s 28 (as amended) or s 29 and subject to s 30(2) of PDA 2000, the Minister shall not exercise any power of control in relation to any particular case with which the planning authority or the board is or may be concerned. The guidelines and directives must be of a general nature and cannot concern any particular case.

**[1.324]** PDA 2000, s 30(1) and (2) has been substituted by the Minister for the Environment and Local Government (Performance of Certain Functions) Act 2002, s (1) which provides that notwithstanding ss 28 and 29 and subject to PDA 2000, s 30(2) the Minister shall not exercise any power or control in relation to any particular case in which a planning authority or the board is or maybe concerned.

**[1.325]** PDA 2000, s 30(2) provides that s 30(1) shall not affect the performance by the Minister of functions transferred (whether before or after the passing of the Minister for the Environment and Local Government (Performance of Certain Functions) Act 2002) to him or her from the Minister for Community Rural and Gaeltacht Affairs by an order under s 6(1) of the Ministers and Secretaries (Amendment) Act 1939.

**[1.326]** PDA 2000, s 31 provides for Ministerial directions regarding development plans, variations of development plans and local area plans.[317] The section provides a supervisory role for the Minister for Environment, Heritage and Local Government in relation to development plans. The directions may be made either before or after the making of a development plan.

**[1.327]** PDA 2000, s 31(1), as substituted by PD(A)A 2010, s 21, provides that if the Minister is of the opinion that:

- (a) A planning authority, in making a development plan, a variation of a development plan, or a local area plan (in this section referred to as a 'plan') has ignored, or has not taken sufficient account of submissions or observations made by the Minister to the planning authority under section 12, 13 or 20,
- (b) In the case of a plan, the plan fails to set out an overall strategy for the proper planning and sustainable development of the area,
- (c) The plan is not in compliance with the requirements of this Act, or
- (d) If applicable, having received a submission prepared under section 31C or s 31D (inserted by section 95 of the Act of 2008)[318] that a plan of a planning authority in the Greater Dublin Area (GDA) is not consistent with the transport strategy of the National Transport Authority,

The Minister may in accordance with this section, for stated reasons, direct a planning authority to take such specified measures as he or she may require in relation to that plan.

---

317. PDA 2000, s 31 has been substituted by PD(A)A 2010, s 21.
318. The Act 2008 means the Dublin Transport Authority Act 2008.

# Chapter 2

# DEVELOPMENT AND EXEMPTED DEVELOPMENT

## WHEN IS PLANNING PERMISSION NECESSARY?

**[2.01]** Section 32 of PDA 2000 is a central provision of the planning code which requires that planning permission must be obtained, subject to the provisions of the Act, (a) in respect of any *development* of *land*, not being *exempted development*, and (b) in the case of development which is unauthorised, for the *retention* of that *unauthorised development*, provided that unauthorised development has not offended certain environmental concerns. If it has, retention permission may not be available.[1]

**[2.02]** A person shall not carry out any development in respect of which permission is required by s 32(1), except under and in accordance with a permission granted under this part.[2]

**[2.03]** The requirement to obtain planning permission was first introduced as a statutory requirement in the Local Government (Planning and Development) Act 1963. The commencement date of that Act was 1 October 1964. It is commonly, but perhaps wrongly, believed that any development which was substantially completed on 1 October 1964 did not require planning permission and does not require retention permission. In fact, PDA 2000, s 32(1)(b) requires that permission is needed by way of retention in the case of development which is unauthorised. The section quoted does not provide any exemption for the necessity to obtain planning permission in respect of pre-1 October 1964 development. Specific definitions are contained in PDA 2000, s 2(1) and the relevant definitions, in this context, are as follows:

> 'unauthorised development' means, in relation to land, the carrying out of any unauthorised works (including the construction, erection or making of any unauthorised structure) or the making of any unauthorised use;
>
> 'unauthorised structure' means a structure other than—
>
> (a) a structure which was in existence on the 1 October 1964, or
>
> (b) a structure, the construction, erection or making of which was the subject of a permission for development granted under Part IV of the Act of 1963 or deemed to be such under section 92 of that Act or under section 34 or 37(G) of this Act, being a permission which has not been revoked, or which exists as a result of the carrying out of exempted development (within the meaning of s 4 of the Act of 1963 or s 4 of this Act);[3]

---

1. The new provisions for retention permission are dealt with below at paras **2.94–2.106**.
2. PDA 2000, s 32(2).
3. Part of this definition has been amended by PD(SI)A 2006, s 6(d).

'unauthorised use' means in relation to land, use commenced on or after the 1 October 1964, being a use which is a material change in use of any structure or other land being development other than—

(a) exempted development within the meaning of section 4 of the Act of 1963 or section 4 of this Act, or

(b) development which is the subject of a permission granted under Part IV of the Act of 1963 or under section 34 (as amended by s 23 of PD(A)A 2010) or 37(G) of this Act, being a permission which has not been revoked, and which is carried out in compliance with that permission or any condition to which that permission is subject;[3]

'unauthorised works' means any works on, in, over or under land commenced on or after the 1 October 1964, being development other than—

(a) exempted development (within the meaning of section 4 of the Act of 1963 or section 4 of this Act), or

(b) development which is the subject of a permission granted under Part IV of the Act of 1963 or under section 34 or 37(G) of this Act, being a permission which has not been revoked, and which is carried out in compliance with that permission or any condition to which that permission is subject.[3]

**[2.04]** The procedures laid down in s 32 of PDA 2000 may appear to be easy to follow but to understand the section fully a detailed definition of key words in the section and in PDA 2000, s 3(1) and (2), which defines 'development', must be examined. The key words in PDA 2000, s 32 and PDA 2000, s 3(1) and (2) are highlighted in italics below. The highlighted words which require a full explanation are as follows:

2. *Development;*
2a. *Works;*
2b. *Use;*
2c. *Material change in use;*
2d. *Structures;*
3. *Land;*
3a. *Substratum of land;*
4. *Exempted Development;*
5. *Retention Permission;*
6. *Unauthorised Development;*
7. *Unauthorised Works;*
8. *Unauthorised Use*
9. *Unauthorised Structure;*
10. *Foreshore.*[4]

---

4. Foreshore is not a key word used in PDA 2000, s 32(1) or in s 3(1), but it is, nevertheless, a key word in the context of the meaning of 'development'.

## 'DEVELOPMENT'

**[2.05]** At its simplest, development is activity which requires planning permission unless expressly exempted.

PDA 2000 defines development as follows:

> (1) In this Act 'development' means, except where the context requires, the carrying out of any *works* on, in, over or under land or the making of any material change in the use of any structures or other land.[5]
>
> (2) For the purposes of subsection (1) and without prejudice to the generality of that subsection —
>
> > (a) where any structure or other land or any tree or other object on the land becomes used for the exhibition of advertisements, or
> >
> > (b) where land becomes used for any of the following purposes—
> >
> > > (i) the placing or keeping of any vans, tents, or other objects, whether or not moveable and whether or not collapsible for the purpose of caravanning or camping or habitation or the sale of goods,
> > >
> > > (ii) the storage of caravans or tents, or
> > >
> > > (iii) the deposit of vehicles whether or not usable for the purpose for which they were constructed or last used, old metal, mining or industrial waste, builder's waste, rubbish or debris, the use of the land shall be taken as having materially changed.[6]
>
> (3) For the avoidance of doubt, it is hereby declared that, for the purposes of this section, the use as two or more dwellings of any house previously used as a single dwelling involves a material change in use of the structure and of each part thereof which is so used.[7]

Development, as defined by s 3, is divided into two distinct categories, namely:

(a) the carrying out of works on, in, over or under land; or

(b) the making of a material change in the use of any structures or other land.

Development is no more or no less than that and the attempt in the section to single out only some of the circumstances where material change in use occurs by referring to advertisements, vans, tents, old vehicles, metal, mining or industrial waste and builders waste, rubbish or debris, does little to assist an understanding of the complete meaning of 'development'. In fact, it is positively confusing in its failure to provide a comprehensive definition of 'material change in use'. A 'continuing use' is not a development. Development, in that context, can only occur where there is a material change in use.

---

5. PDA 2000, s 3(1).
6. PDA 2000, s 3(2).
7. PDA 2000, s 3(3).

## 'WORKS'

**[2.06]** PDA 2000 defines 'works' as including:

> any act or operation of construction, excavation, demolition, extension, alteration, repair or renewal and, in relation to a protected structure or proposed protected structure, includes any act or operation involving the application or removal of plaster, paint, wallpaper, tiles or other material to or from the surfaces of the interior or exterior of a structure.[8]

The definition of the word 'alteration', which is included in the definition of 'works', above, is separately defined as follows:

> 'alteration' includes —
> 
> (a) plastering or painting or the removal of plaster or stucco, or
> 
> (b) the replacement of a door, window or roof,
> 
> that materially alters the external appearance of a structure so as to render the appearance inconsistent with the character of the structure or neighbouring structures.[9]

**[2.07]** A number of cases are cited below which illustrate the meaning of 'works' in a planning context.

In *Scott v An Bord Pleanála, Arcon Mines*,[10] the act of draining off water from land as a necessity prior to excavating an ore body was held not to be development on the basis that development means 'carrying out works on land' but it does not extend to the consequences of those works on other land. There may be other common law remedies available to persons whose land is affected by water draining from other lands.[11]

In *Kildare County Council v Goode*,[12] the argument was made that because quarrying operations are in the nature of 'works' the concept of 'intensification' cannot apply to quarrying. It was held that 'abandonment' is a good indication of the fact that development has ceased on a particular site but that conversely, 'intensification' is a good indication that development is continuing on a site. In *Kildare County Council v Goode*,[13] works had ceased and when they were recommenced the works comprised the extraction of sand and gravel which were 'works' of a completely different nature to the works which had been carried out prior to the abandonment. A new permission was required.

In *Sligo County Council v Gavin Martin*,[14] the respondent removed a mobile home and a concrete base with pipe work attached, pursuant to an order. The respondent replaced the old mobile home with a smaller one and that replacement was held to constitute 'works' and as such it required planning permission.

---

8. PDA 2000, s 2(1).
9. PDA 2000, s 2(1).
10. *Scott v An Bord Pleanála, Arcon Mines* [1995] 1 ILRM 424.
11. See *Rylands v Fletcher* (1868) LR 3 HL 330.
12. *Kildare County Council v Goode* [1999] 2 IR 495, SC.
13. *Kildare County Council v Goode* [1999] 2 IR 495, SC.
14. *Sligo County Council v Gavin Martin* [2007] IEHC 178 (24 May 2007).

## 'USE'

**[2.08]** PDA 2000[15] interprets 'use' in relation to land and the definition does not include the use of the land by the carrying out of any works thereon. This definition implies two separate concepts, the first being 'use' and the second being 'works'. Because a structure has a particular 'use', for example as a residence, the use cannot be expanded by carrying out works unless either those works are exempted development or, if they are not exempted development, planning permission has been obtained for those works. Conversely, because a structure has a particular use (such as a dwelling house) that use cannot be changed except in very limited circumstances where a change is allowed under exempted development regulations or provisions or unless planning permission for the new use is obtained. The use of land is no more or no less than a factual description of the activities which are being carried out on the land at any given time.

## 'MATERIAL CHANGE IN USE'

**[2.09]** There is no complete statutory definition of 'material change in use' in PDA 2000, and preceding planning legislation never attempted to define it.

**[2.10]** PDA 2000[16] defines 'development' and the definition has two separate principles. The first part of 'development' is defined as the carrying out of any works on, in, over or under land. The second part is the making of any material change in the use of any structure or other land. PDA 2000, s 3 gives five separate examples of circumstances where the use of land shall be taken as being materially changed.[17]

**[2.11]** The meaning of material change in use goes well beyond the specific PDA 2000, s 3 definitions and for a fuller understanding of the concept an examination of the terms and principles which constitute a material change in use may be helpful.

**[2.12]** The concept of material change in use embraces the following planning concepts:

(i) planning unit;

(ii) abandonment of permission;

(iii) abandonment of planning permission for use and/or for works;[18]

(iv) ancillary use;

(v) extinguishment/resumption of existing use rights;

(vi) intensification of works/use.

These concepts are defined below.

---

15. PDA 2000, s 2(1).
16. PDA 2000, s 3.
17. PDA 2000, s 3(1), (2) and (3).
18. Abandonment of use is also referred to as discontinuance of use.

**[2.13]** For a material change in use to occur there must be an existing use which is a material existing use. Although it is usually a simple matter to identify a change in use, the difficulty occurs in determining whether or not that change in use is a 'material change in use'.

**[2.14]** Keane J in *Monaghan County Council v Brogan*[19] held that 'material' in the context of 'material change in use' must mean 'material for planning purposes'.

**[2.15]** The law on what is a 'material change' has developed considerably but the definitions are not always as clear as they might be. In practical terms, the first question to ask is what is the permitted or established use of a particular property? If the use has remained the same since 1 October 1964 then the use is an established use. If the use has changed since 1 October 1964 and permission for a new use was obtained from the planning authority, it is a permitted use.

**[2.16]** There will, however, be no 'development' unless the change is 'material' that is to say 'material' in the sense that the change is of such a character that it matters, having regard to the objects of planning control. In some cases it will be obvious that a particular change in use is 'material' as, for example, a proposal to change a dwelling house to offices or to change a seaside field into a caravan park. In other cases, as will be seen, a decision as to whether or not change in use is or is not material, is much more difficult to determine. Again, at its simplest, it can be asked if the new use is the same as the old use and if they are different it may be safely concluded that there is a change in use. The next and more difficult question is whether the new use and the old use are materially different. There are two separate concepts here:

(a) the concept of an 'existing use'; and
(b) the concept of 'materiality' in assessing the degree of change.

Distinguishing the different categories of use is not always an easy matter and there is little or no help to be found in the statutory definitions.

**[2.17]** The planning impact of the proposed change in use must, necessarily, play a part. The concept that 'material', in the context of proposed change in use, constitutes development only if the new use is substantially different from the old use, is only relevant in a negative way, that is to say, by the application of the principle of *de minimis non curat lex* (the law has no regard for trivial matters). In effect, the courts have sought to exclude from planning control development activities which are un-important either because they are insignificant or small, or because of their infrequent occurrence.

**[2.18]** A change in use may constitute development but not every change in use is development. It is only development when the change is a material change. It may be difficult to determine when the change has taken place. If, for example, a farmer has a field beside the river and occasionally hauls out boats and stores them there, it does not necessarily mean that there has been development by change from agricultural use to use as a boat yard. It is to these types of cases that the principle of *de minimis* is applied.

---

19. *Monaghan County Council v Brogan* [1987] IR 333.

[2.19] The question of materiality in the change in use, therefore, is one of fact and of degree.

[2.20] Before examining the court decisions that deal with the meaning of 'material change in use' in the context of use change, there are a number of planning concepts closely connected with the principle of material change in use which should be explained.

## 'Planning unit'

[2.21] In determining whether a material change in use may or may not occur the planning unit must be considered. In setting a previous use against a current use, it is important to consider the appropriate physical site of the relevant use or, in other words, the planning unit. Planning statutes do not offer any definition or guidance on the subject. Case law does, however, provide a clearer understanding of the meaning of 'planning unit'.

[2.22] Where part only of a structure or portion only of a site of land is subject to a change in use, it may be difficult to decide what is the appropriate planning unit in determining whether a material change in use has occurred. One must consider the whole of the premises and not merely part of it and the question to be asked is whether the character of the whole existing use will be substantially affected by a change which is proposed in part only of the building. Clearly, for example, the use of part of a dwelling house as a shop would be a material change in use because it involves a change in the kind of use.

[2.23] The leading English case where the meaning of 'planning unit' was examined is *Burdle v Secretary of State for Environment*.[20] In that case, Bridge J formulated the principles which can be applied in determining the proper 'planning unit'. The principles are set out in paras (a), (b) and (c) below:

> (a) Whenever it is possible to recognise a single main purpose of the occupier's use of his land to which secondary activities are incidental or ancillary, the whole unit of occupation should be considered. This proposition emerges clearly from the case of *G Percy Trentham v Gloucestershire County Council*[21] where Diplock LJ stated:
>
> 'What is the unit which the local authority are entitled to look at and deal with in an enforcement notice for the purpose of determining whether or not there has been a material change in the use of any building or other land? As I suggested in the course of the argument I think that for the purpose, what the local authority are entitled to look at is the whole of the area which was used for a particular purpose including any part of that area whose use was incidental to or ancillary to the achievement of that purpose.'

---

20. *Burdle v Secretary of State for Environment* [1972] 1 WLR 1207.
21. *G Percy Trentham v Gloucestershire County Council* [1996] 1 WLR 506.

(b) It may be equally apt to consider the entire unit of occupation even though the occupier carries on a variety of activities and it is not possible to say that one is incidental or ancillary to another. This is well settled in the case of a composite use where the component activities have fluctuated in their intensity from time to time, but the different activities are not confined within separate and physical distinct areas of land.

(c) It may frequently occur that within a single unit of occupation, two or more physically separate and distinct areas are occupied for different and related purposes. In such a case, each area used for a different main purpose together with its incidental and ancillary activities, ought to be considered as a separate planning unit.

These three criteria were endorsed in Ireland by Blaney J in *Dublin Corporation v Regan Advertising*.[22] In that case, an advertisement had been placed on the front of a building advertising the nature of the business carried on in the premises. When the advertisement was changed to an advertisement for other products and services not connected with the trade being carried out in the building it was held that planning permission was required on the grounds that a material change in use had occurred.

**[2.24]** In *Wood v Secretary of State for the Environment and Others*,[23] the issue was as to whether there had been a material change in use caused by an increase in sales of produce from a small holding, because produce was brought in from outside. The local authority's enforcement notice related to the farm house and to a small conservatory attached to it. The Secretary of State, on appeal, found that looking at the farm house, apart from the conservatory, there was no material change but looking at the conservatory on its own, as he held he was entitled to do, there was a material change which related to the conservatory only. The matter came before the Divisional Court which held that the Secretary of State had been wrong to divide the farm house and the conservatory. Lord Widgery CJ said:

> In no case known to me, however, has it been said that, unless the circumstances are highly special, it is permissible to dissect a single dwelling house into separate parts and treat them as different planning units for this purpose. Indeed, so far as authority goes, it all seems to me to go the other way.

The learned judge concluded that it would be most unusual to regard a dwelling house as more than one planning unit.

**[2.25]** The following five points may assist, by example, in understanding the meaning of a planning unit:

(i) **Predominant Use, Ancillary Use and Multiple Uses**

A premises may be described as a 'hotel' but if the activities within the hotel are analysed, it will be seen that there are a variety of different activities taking place inside it. There will be retail sales in the dining room and bars, there will be storage, there will be undoubtedly car parking, pay accommodation,

---

22. *Dublin Corporation v Regan Advertising* [1986] IR 171, HC.
23. *Wood v Secretary of State for the Environment and Others* [1973] 1 WLR 707.

conference facilities, entertainment, staff accommodation and offices. The predominant use comes under the term 'hotel' and this permits a level of ancillary activity associated with what one would normally understand as being the activities of a hotel. The planning unit is the whole unit of occupation devoted to the primary use but, clearly, the hotel owner could not argue that no material change in use took place if he/she was to close the door of his/her hotel and open a retail store even though retail activities had taken place in the hotel.

(ii) **Composite Use**

A particular planning unit may have two or more separate uses which are carried out within the same four walls without any clear physical barriers of separation. As there is no physical separation it may not be possible to divide the unit into two or more separate planning units but any changes in use which occur within the planning unit must be measured for materiality against the site as a whole. There may, therefore, be a material change in use if one of the component uses absorbs the entire site to the exclusion of the other. In *Rehabilitation Institute v Dublin Corporation*,[24] the main part of a building was used as offices but an area on one floor of the three storey building was used for training handicapped trainees in a specially fitted out workshop. Subsequently, the training floor was converted into offices. As the training operation was a use which was an ancillary use to the main use of the building (namely offices) the change was not a material change in use for which planning permission was required.

(iii) **Dual Use**

A site may have one use in one part and another use in another part with no ancillary link. For example, one portion of the site may be used for the storage of scrap metal and other portion for the sale of motor cars. In this case, as distinct from para (ii) above, where a division can be made the planning unit will be considered as two separate planning units each with different single primary uses.

(iv) **Recurrent or Seasonal Uses**

A ski resort in Switzerland may operate as ski resort during winter months when snow is on the ground but the entire operation will be closed down in the summer months and the lands will be used for grazing cattle and/or for tourist walkers, etc. In *Webber v Minister of Housing and Local Government*,[25] the Court of Appeal ruled that the 'purpose' for which land was 'normally' used, in the terms of the Act, could include two seasonal uses, such as the existing use of a field for camping in the summer months and grazing of cattle in the winter. The two uses amount to a single planning unit.

---

24. *Rehabilitation Institute v Dublin Corporation* (unreported, 14 January 1988) HC *per* Barron J.
25. *Webber v Minister of Housing and Local Government* [1968] ILR 29.

### (v) Transient Use

A transient or short term use may not amount to a material change in use. In *Butler v Dublin Corporation*,[26] it was held that the staging of concerts at Lansdowne Road was merely a continuance of the existing use of land as a public stadium and that the change from sport fixtures to pop concerts was not a material change in use because it was for a minimal duration which would not give rise to any infrastructural planning considerations.[27]

## 'Abandonment of permission'

**[2.26]** A planning permission cannot be abandoned. If an applicant applies for and obtains a permission for, say, a block of flats and a year later obtains a further permission on the same site for an office development, the first permission is not considered to be abandoned by the fact that a second permission has been granted for a different type of development. In *Pioneer Aggregates Limited v Secretary of State for the Environment*,[28] the House of Lords held that planning permission for works cannot, as a general principle, be abandoned. The matter has also been decided in Ireland in *Kenny and Hussey v An Bord Pleanála*,[29] where it was held that the idea of abandonment of a planning permission is inconsistent with the time limits/life-time which apply to the life of all planning permissions (generally five years). Each permission has a set time limit (normally five years, unless extended or varied under s 41 or s 42 respectively of the PDA 2000 or by s 28 or s 29 of PD(A)A 2010 by the local authority or by An Bord Pleanála) and no matter how many permissions are granted for different developments of the same piece of land, provided the time limit has not expired, none of the permissions can be said to have been abandoned. If a planning permission ceases after five years in respect of a portion of a development which has not been completed, the expiration of the time limit will not affect the continuance of any use in accordance with the planning permission. In *Molloy and Ors v Minister for Justice, Equality and Law Reform*,[30] the respondent purchased a property from the Franciscan Fathers for use as a hostel for asylum seekers. It was agreed that the use as a hostel for asylum seekers was a material change in use which required planning permission in circumstances where the Franciscans had used the building for administration purposes since 1977. There was, however, an earlier planning permission of 1969 which granted permission for use as a hostel. Gilligan J held that the grant of the planning permission enured for the benefit of the building concerned and as there was an existing planning permission for use of the building as a hostel, and since no other use permission had been granted, the use as a hostel was still extant and valid. The valid use granted by the 1969 permission had not

---

26. *Butler v Dublin Corporation* [1999] 1 ILRM 481, SC.
27. These types of transient events are now covered by special licensing arrangements under PDA 2000, Pt XVI.
28. *Pioneer Aggregates Limited v Secretary of State for the Environment* [1985] AC 132.
29. *Kenny and Hussey v An Bord Pleanála* (unreported, 20 December 1984) SC.
30. *Molloy and Ors v Minister for Justice, Equality and Law Reform* [2004] 2 IR 493.

been lost or abandoned by reason of the material and unauthorised change in use which had occurred in 1977.

## 'Abandonment of permission for use and/or for works'

**[2.27]** The concept of abandonment applies both to development in the sense of carrying out works and to development in the sense of the making of any material change in the use of any structures or other land.

**[2.28]** Discontinuance of works and/or discontinuance of use may constitute abandonment. Temporary suspension of development either in the sense of carrying out works or in the sense of making a material change in use would not usually constitute abandonment. For abandonment to occur there must be an actual ending of development works coupled with an intention not to resume the development in question. If the development has ceased for a very long time and if it can be safely assumed or, if it has been openly admitted, that development will not be recommenced, it is likely that abandonment has taken place and that a new planning permission will be required if development is to start again. In all cases, abandonment is decided depending on the facts and the circumstances of the interruption of the development. The intention of the developer is a relevant factor also and that intention may be either expressed or, in some cases, implied by matters such as the length of time during which the development has been suspended.

**[2.29]** Abandonment of a particular use can, in certain circumstances, disentitle a landowner to re-commence that use without planning permission on the basis that to do so would amount to a material change in use. A useful explanation of the concept is contained in the judgment of Hederman J in *Dublin County Council v Tallaght Block Co Ltd*:[31]

> Where a previous use of land has not been merely suspended for a temporary and determined period, but has ceased for a considerable time, with no evidenced intention of resuming it at any particular time, the tribunal of fact was entitled to find that the previous use had been abandoned, so that the resumption constituted a material change of use.

In that case, a site for block manufacturing had not been used for eight years and when the use was resumed it was decided that planning permission was required. The two elements of abandonment were established in the case, namely:

(i) cessation of the use for a considerable period of time;

(ii) no evidence of intention to resume the use during that period.

**[2.30]** In *Hartley v Minister for Housing and Local Government*,[32] Lord Denning stated:

> The question in all such cases is simply this; had the cessation of use (followed by non use) been merely temporary or did it amount to an abandonment? If it was

---

31. *Dublin County Council v Tallaght Block Co Ltd* [1985] ILRM 512.
32. *Hartley v Minister for Housing and Local Government* [1970] 1 QB 413.

merely temporary, the previous use can be resumed without planning permission being obtained. If it amounted to abandonment, it cannot be resumed unless planning permission is obtained. Abandonment depends on the circumstances. If the land has remained unused for a considerable time, in such circumstances that a reasonable man might conclude that the previous use had been abandoned, the tribunal may hold it to have been abandoned.

**[2.31]** In *Dublin Corporation v Lowe and Signways Ltd*,[33] the facts disclosed that an advertising hoarding was taken down from the exterior of a building by one advertising company when its licence agreement with the owner of the building expired. When another advertising hoarding was erected three days later that development was considered to be a material change in use for which planning permission was required. The first removal of the advertising hoarding was permanent in the sense that the advertising company's licence had come to an end and accordingly the removal of the advertisement amounted to abandonment, in the sense that the advertisement was removed with no intention of replacing it. This case illustrates that, although the time gap between one development being discontinued and the same or a very similar development being commenced is a relevant factor in deciding whether or not a particular development has been abandoned, the time gap need not be lengthy, as seen in the *Lowe and Signways Ltd* case,[34] and there are circumstances where the time gap can be very short indeed.

**[2.32]** In *Cork County Council v Ardfert Quarries*,[35] a building was used for bagging and loading cement for sale. The use of the building was established as 'general industrial use'. There was a four year period when the bagging and loading of cement ceased and, in consequence, it was held that the use had been abandoned and that any resumption of that use would require planning permission. In that case, the court inferred that there was a lack of intention on the part of Ardfert Quarries to resume the general industrial use.

**[2.33]** In *Lee v O'Riordan*,[36] a sand and gravel pit was closed for 12 years with no evidenced intention of resumption. While closed, the pit had been sold at a price which was consistent with the value of a worked-out sand and gravel pit. When the new owners resumed the sand and gravel business without applying for planning permission it was held that their actions amounted to a material change in use for which planning permission was required.

**[2.34]** In *Meath County Council v Daly*,[37] a garage car repair premises with attendant petrol pumps was changed firstly to a timber manufacturer, secondly to a sales room and thirdly to a manufacturing premises for lighting equipment. Throughout the transformation there was no evidence of any intention to resume the lawful garage repair

---

33. *Dublin Corporation v Lowe and Signways Ltd* [2000] IEHC 161.
34. *Dublin Corporation v Lowe and Signways Ltd* [2000] IEHC 161.
35. *Cork County Council v Ardfert Quarries* (unreported, 7 December 1982) HC.
36. *Lee v O'Riordan* (unreported, 10 February 1995) HC.
37. *Meath County Council v Daly* [1987] IR 391.

shop with petrol pumps but, when the owner did resume the garage repairs and petrol sales, it was held to be a material change of use which required planning permission.

**[2.35]** In *Ampleforth Ltd (t/a Fitzwilliam Hotel) v Cherating Ltd*,[38] the use of a room as a bar had been changed to use as a restaurant on foot of a grant of permission. The bar use had been abandoned for five years. The use as a bar could not be re-established without planning permission. The change back to a bar premises would have been a material change in use for which planning permission was required.

**[2.36]** In *Westmeath County Council v Quirke & Sons*,[39] between 1912 and 1965 land had been used as a stone quarry where intermittent blasting and quarrying was carried out. The operation of the quarry at that time was small scale and as such the effects which the quarry had on local residents and on the local area were not significant. The use ceased in 1965. In the 1970s, the lands were used for the production of ground limestone pursuant to a permission granted for that operation. Later, the quarry was used intensively for limestone extraction. By 1990 the large-scale operation of the quarry, in terms of dust, noise levels and volume and size of machinery and trucks, had increased to such an extent that the operation did have a significant effect on the local residents and on the local area. Budd J held that the original use had been abandoned and the scale of the latest operation amounted to intensification. The test applied by the learned judge in this case was whether a reasonable man looking at a converted cattle shed or farm supplies store in the disused-looking quarry would have concluded that the use had been abandoned?

**[2.37]** In *Molumby v Kearns*,[40] O'Sullivan J held that where there had been a significant increase in commercial activity in an industrial estate involving more and larger vehicles and significantly increased noise and traffic volume, there was a material change in use for planning purposes by reason of intensification. In making his decision the learned judge had regard to the effects in planning and/or environmental terms of such intensification in order to assess whether it was a material change for planning purposes.

**[2.38]** A use may also be abandoned if the use is inconsistent with the use which is authorised by a planning permission and that planning permission has been implemented. Also, a use may be abandoned where the land or structure has been utterly changed, such as by excavation or demolition, etc.

## 'Ancillary use'

**[2.39]** Uses of land and premises which are subordinate or incidental to the main use are referred to as 'ancillary uses'.

**[2.40]** One or more uses may be incidental or subordinate to the main use and these are referred to as ancillary uses. For example, the land on which, or the structure within

---

38. *Ampleforth Ltd (t/a Fitzwilliam Hotel) v Cherating Ltd* [2003] IESC 27.
39. *Westmeath County Council v Quirke & Sons* (unreported, 28 June 1996) HC.
40. *Molumby v Kearns* [1999] IEHC 86.

which, an ancillary activity takes place is deemed to have the same use as the primary use of the land as a whole. An ancillary use, as such, does not amount to a material change in use. See *Carroll and Colley (t/a Roger Green & Sons) v Brushfield Ltd*.[41] In that case, a garage attached to a hotel was converted to use as a public bar. Uses such as bars, bedrooms, restaurants, kitchens, store rooms, etc, are all ancillary uses to the overall use of a hotel. When the garage was converted to a public bar that was acceptable within the overall context of the use as a hotel and no material change in use had occurred. The entire hotel constituted the planning unit.

[2.41] So, a planning unit may have a number of uses in addition to its primary use. Where one or more uses are incidental or subordinate to the main use, the ancillary use is deemed to have the same use as the primary use and a change in the ancillary use will not amount to a material change in use.

[2.42] Cessation of an ancillary use does not give rise to a material change in use.[42] Each case will be examined as matters of fact to be determined by the relevant planning authority or by An Bord Pleanála.

[2.43] Ancillary use as distinguished from primary use was dealt with in *Esat Digifone Ltd v South Dublin Co Co*.[43] In that case, a public house owner allowed Esat Digifone to erect telephone aerials and boosters on his premises. South Dublin County Council commenced enforcement proceedings on the basis that no planning permission had been obtained and the plaintiff argued that the installation of the aerials and boosters were ancillary to the primary use of the premises as a public house. The court did not accept the plaintiff's argument and held that the aerials and boosters were not a use ordinarily incidental to the use of the premises as a public house. The aerials in this case were by no means for the exclusive use of the public house and they served a much larger area in and around the neighbourhood.

[2.44] A further example of the definition of ancillary use is cited in *Dublin Corporation v Regan Advertising*,[44] where premises in York Road, Dun Laoghaire, County Dublin, had been used for industrial purposes since 1938. An advertisement for the business was painted on the premises in 1954 and re-painted in 1972. In 1984, the owners made a contract with Regan Advertising allowing them to use the painted facade for advertising purposes unconnected with the occupier's business. The Supreme Court held that the use of the facade to advertise other business was a material change in use for which planning permission was required.

[2.45] Planning permission will be required in the following circumstances:
(i) if the length between the primary or main use and the ancillary use is broken, to such an extent that the ancillary use becomes an independent, or a non-ancillary use;

---

41. *Carroll and Colley (t/a Roger Green & Sons) v Brushfield Ltd* (unreported, 9 October 1992) HC.
42. See *Rehabilitation Institute v An Bord Pleanála* [1988] 6 ILT 193.
43. *Esat Digifone Ltd v South Dublin Co Co* [2002] 3 IR 585.
44. *Dublin Corporation v Regan Advertising* [1986] IR 171.

(ii) if the ancillary use is intensified to such an extent that it becomes a material change in use;

(iii) if the main or primary use ceases so as to leave the ancillary use as an isolated or independent use.

Ancillary uses are not recognised as uses in their own right. Clearly a shop such as Clerys in O'Connell Street, Dublin may have offices, a cafeteria and food store, luggage and garment sales outlets, etc. From time to time, within the area of the shop, the offices or food store may be changed to sales areas without the necessity for obtaining planning permission because the uses are ancillary to the main use which is, undeniably, 'shop use'.

[2.46] In the *'Burdle'* case[45] referred to above, an egg vending machine measuring six foot two inches high and two foot seven inches square was placed, free-standing, adjoining a licensed premises, in a garage forecourt which had a road frontage of 120 feet and a depth of 15 feet. The garage had four petrol pumps. The local authority served an enforcement notice requiring the removal of the egg vending machine. It was held that although the space occupied by the machine was small in comparison with the total area of the forecourt, it did introduce a material change in use. The use was not ancillary to the main use.

[2.47] In *Williams v Minister for Housing and Local Government and Another*,[46] a shop in a nursery garden was being used for selling produce from the garden. The planning unit was held to be the whole of the nursery garden and not just the shop alone so that the use of the whole unit, including the shop, was 'agricultural use'. When the owners changed that use by discontinuing growing their own produce and by selling imported produce from the shop it was held to be a material change in use requiring planning permission.

## 'Extinguishment/resumption of existing use rights'

[2.48] The concept of extinguishment is akin to the concept of abandonment but in the case of extinguishment the intention of the party or parties is of much less importance. A use may be extinguished if a structure or land perishes. Extinguishment of existing use rights which attach to land or to structures may occur when re-development takes place by the implementation of a permission and the erection of a new building. If a warehouse is demolished and re-developed with planning permission as an office block, the warehouse use is extinguished. Existing use rights may also be extinguished by the imposition of an appropriate condition in a planning permission. Once an existing use has been extinguished, its resumption requires planning permission because without it a material change of use occurs.

---

45. *Burdle v Secretary of State for Environment* [1972] 1 WLR 1207; see para **2.23**.
46. *Williams v Minister for Housing and Local Government and Another* [1967] 65 LGR 495 Dib CT.

**[2.49]** In *Allnatt London Properties Limited v Middlesex County Council*,[47] permission was granted for the extension of an existing factory subject to two conditions, namely:

(a) that the new extension should be used only in conjunction with the main existing factory as one industrial unit so as to avoid multiplication of industrial uses; and

(b) that until 1971 the site was to be used by a person or a firm occupying at the date of the permission as a light or general industrial building in the County of Middlesex.

In effect, these conditions potentially deprived the plaintiff of an existing use right in its main factory and it was held that the applicant had the right to continue his existing use or, that if it was to be withdrawn it could only be done if the withdrawal was accompanied by the payment of compensation.

**[2.50]** In *Minister for Housing and Local Government v Hartnell*,[48] the defendant owned a five acre field and kept six caravans on three-quarters of an acre. When it became necessary to apply for permission he applied for a licence to station 94 caravans on the entire five acre site but the permission which issued contained a condition that not more than six caravans should be stationed on the land at any time. The defendant's existing use right in respect of the three-quarters of an acre had not been limited to six caravans and it was held that he could, on the three-quarter acre area, bring such a number of caravans as the site could take so as not to amount to a material change in use by intensification of use. It was held that the defendant could not be deprived of existing use rights.

**[2.51]** In *Petticoat Lane Rentals Limited v Secretary of State for the Environment*,[49] application was made for comprehensive re-development of an area which had been used for market trading. The owners of the redeveloped buildings allowed Sunday market trading in a car park beneath the building, but it was held that the local authority was not required to expressly extinguish, by condition, a pre-existing right and that it was clear from the permission granted that the car park area was to be used as a car park. If the owners now wished to permit Sunday market trading, it amounted to a change in use in respect of which a further permission would have to be obtained.

**[2.52]** The conclusion from the case law would seem to be that express conditions can validly revoke or modify existing use rights provided:

(a) they reasonably relate to the permitted development;

(b) they are not so unreasonable that no reasonable local authority would have imposed them;

(c) they have been imposed by the planning authority for a planning purpose.

---

47. *Allnatt London Properties Limited v Middlesex County Council* [1962] 62 LGR 304.
48. *Minister for Housing and Local Government v Hartnell* [1965] 1 All ER 490.
49. *Petticoat Lane Rentals Limited v Secretary of State for the Environment* [1971] 1 All ER 793.

**[2.53]** Where premises are destroyed by fire or by some other catastrophe, the use permission also perishes. In *Galway County Council v Connaught Proteins*,[50] Galway County Council applied to the High Court under s 27 of the Local Government (Planning and Development) Act 1976 for an order prohibiting unauthorised use of land by the respondent who used the premises as an animal by-product processing plant. In 1966, the former owners of a disused corn store mill sought permission to use the premises for the extraction of oils and fats from slaughterhouse offal. The applicant, Galros, did not propose to make any structural alterations and the applications lodged did not refer to change in use but referred to alterations only. The county council granted permission for alterations only, although they were aware that the application was really an application for change in use. The council conceded that permission should really be regarded as a permission for change in use. The premises were completely destroyed by fire in 1968, though the respondent did not concede that the destruction was complete. Permission was not applied for to rebuild the mill and, in fact, it was not rebuilt for several years. Galros used the site to store lorries and Mr McGann, a director of Galros, carried on some limited operation of extraction of oils and fats from slaughterhouse offal. Galros then sold the site to Connaught Proteins. Mr McGann joined the new company and it was conceded that he carried out some limited business of offal rendering between 1969 and the date of sale in 1973. In 1973, the council noticed that some building work had commenced and it issued a warning notice stating that all works must cease immediately. Later the council wrote another letter claiming that the respondent's use of the premises was unauthorised use and that any use now being carried on should cease immediately. In May 1973, Connaught Proteins's architects did apply for retention permission but, in the meantime, a second fire took place on the premises and the company, after the second fire, once again started construction work. The council objected and advised the company that it was carrying out unauthorised work and called upon it to cease immediately. The company, in fact, built and completed an entirely new factory and application for retention of the structure was lodged in June 1975. Permission for retention was refused but the county council did not seek to enforce this point in the High Court. Instead, the council applied to the High Court for an order prohibiting an unauthorised use. The manner in which Connaught Proteins conducted its business was shown to be entirely unsatisfactory and the conditions of the factory were proved to be a health hazard and a nuisance to the people in the surrounding neighbourhood. Connaught Proteins's record in relation to development was also unsatisfactory and no permission existed for the building which constituted its present factory.

**[2.54]** Mr Justice Barrington held that when the mill perished in the first fire, the permission to use those premises for a specified purpose also perished.

> It could be argued that the permission to use the mill for a specified purpose, implied a permission to use the outbuildings for ancillary purposes. When the mill itself perished it appears to me that one could not apply for a permission to use the outbuildings for the principal business (*per* Barrington J).

---

50. *Galway County Council v Connaught Proteins* (unreported, 28 March 1980) HC *per* Barrington J.

Connaught Proteins had attempted a comprehensive redevelopment, albeit without permission, but the pre-existing use was deemed by the learned judge to have been extinguished when the premises were, in the first instance, destroyed by fire.

[2.55] PDA 2000[51] does make a special provision for payment of compensation where planning permission is refused for a development which substantially replaces structures demolished or destroyed by fire or otherwise than by an unlawful act by the owner or occupier. This is a valuable provision, and the section reads:

(1) Nothing in s 191[52] shall prevent compensation being paid —
   (a) in a case in which there has been a refusal of permission for the erection of a new structure substantially replacing a structure (other than an unauthorised structure) which has been demolished or destroyed by fire or otherwise than by an unlawful act of the owner or of the occupier with the agreement of the owner within the 2 years preceding the date of application for permission, or there has been imposed a condition in consequence of which the new structure may not be used for the purpose for which the demolished or destroyed structure was last used, or
   (b) in a case in which there has been imposed a condition in consequence of which the new structure referred to in para (a) or the front thereof, or the front of an existing structure (other than an unauthorised structure) which has been taken down in order to be re-erected or altered, is set back or forward.
(2) Every dispute and question as to whether a new structure would or does replace substantially within the meaning of subsection (1) a demolished or destroyed structure shall be referred to the Board for determination.

## 'Intensification of works/use'

[2.56] The concept of intensification in planning law reflects the definition of development in that it has two categories, namely:

1. intensification of works;
2. intensification of use.

Intensification of works arises where the works become works of sufficient intensity to amount, as such, to the carrying out of works on, in or under lands, and in that sense it may amount to development for which planning permission is required.

[2.57] Intensification of use arises where a use becomes use of sufficient intensity to amount to a material change in use and, in that sense, it may amount to development for which planning permission is required.

[2.58] Intensification, whether of use or of works, has no statutory origin but a number of court decisions both in Ireland and in England are of assistance in understanding the underlying principles.

---

51. PDA 2000, s 193.
52. PDA 2000, s 191 has been amended by PD(SI)A 2010. The amendment does not alter PDA 2000, s 193 which section has not been amended.

**[2.59]** In *Guilford RDC v Fortiscue*,[53] Lord Evershed in the course of his judgment said:

> Mere intensity of user may, (as it seems to me), but I must not be taken as deciding this point, affect the definable character of the land and of its use or one of them. An example was taken during the argument of some housing estate, or part of a housing estate, on which houses had been erected on a certain density per acre. If the density of the houses on that part of the estate is greatly increased, it seems to me that it may – I say no more – affect the material nature of the housing estate as such, or that part of it and, therefore, the user of that part of land. I refer also to another example taken during the argument – that of a cricket ground. If the Kennington Oval Cricket Ground were used to provide continuously a great number of pitches, on which boys and others could contemporaneously play cricket during the summer, no doubt the Kennington Oval would remain a cricket ground but it would be a cricket ground materially changed – it would no longer be a First Class County Cricket Ground but would be a cricket ground of a different kind. It is also, as it seems to me, obvious that increasing intensive use or occupation may involve a sensational increase in the burden of services which the local authority has to supply and that, in truth, might in some cases at least, be material in considering whether the use of the land has been materially changed.

**[2.60]** In *Dyble v Minister of Housing and Local Government and Another*,[54] a change in intensity of use constituted a material change where a part time vehicle repair man took on the job full time. Again, intensification is a question of degree. Many of the cases seem to concern caravan sites and quarries. In *Esdell Caravan Parks Limited v Hemmel Hempstead Rural District Council*,[55] Lord Denning MR stated that an increase of the order of 24 to 78 caravans might well amount to a material change in use.

**[2.61]** One of the earlier Irish cases on intensification is *Patterson v Murphy and Trading Services Limited*.[56] In that case, shale had been taken from a quarry field prior to 1 October 1964 and it was carried away on a fairly casual basis. From 1977, operations increased and heavy machinery was brought onto the site for crushing and grading. Blasting operations were also carried on in the quarry. These operations were found to differ materially from those carried on prior to 1977. It was further held that a different product was being quarried using different methods and producing substantially greater quantities. The court recognised the very considerable change which had taken place in 1977, namely that a different product was being produced, which was manufactured stone as opposed to shale. The product was used for a different purpose in the building industry and fetched a very different price. The method of production was different and the raw material (rock) for the end product was obtained by means of blasting on a regular basis. Large crushing and screening plant was installed and used to produce stones of the correct dimensions. Considerable ancillary equipment was used and additional labour force was employed. The scale of the operation became a

---

53. *Guilford RDC v Fortiscue* [1959] 2 QB 112.
54. *Dyble v Minister of Housing and Local Government and Another* [1966] *Estates Gazette*, 5 February, 457.
55. *Esdell Caravan Parks Limited v Hemmel Hempstead Rural District Council* [1996] 1 QB 895.
56. *Patterson v Murphy and Trading Services Limited* [1978] ILRM 85.

substantial one and bore no resemblance to the scale of operations carried on before 1 October 1964. In answering the question as to whether this intensification amounted to a material change in use, Costello J had this to say:

> It seems to me that the concept of material change of use is a correct one, and it applies whether the Court is considering 'development' under the second limb of the definition (ie material change of use) or under the first limb (ie carrying out of works on land), which was commenced prior to the appointed day, so if it appears that the scale of operations had so intensified as to render contemporary operations materially different to those carried on before the appointed day, this fact can be taken into account in considering whether, what is at present being done, commenced prior to the 1st October 1964. If present day 'development' differs materially from the 'development' being carried on prior to the 1st October 1964 I do not think it can be said that it was commenced prior to the appointed day. This is the situation in the present case. The development, I am now considering, was in fact not commenced until the summer of last year. Thus it was and is development which requires permission under Part IV of the 1963 Act and in my opinion I should prohibit its use under s 27 [note s 27 here refers to the Local Government (Planning and Development) Act 1976]. I should add that if the case fell to be considered as one of 'development' arising from making a material change in the use of land I would have reached the same conclusion.

In the foregoing passage cited by Costello J it is clear that the learned judge did recognise both the concept of carrying out of works and the concept of material change in use as two separate 'limbs' of the definition but that that distinction, in the learned judge's opinion, applied only to the concept of material change in use. It was not extended to the definition of intensification. Costello J's opinion in this case was later overruled.[57]

**[2.62]** The doctrine of intensification was further approved by the Supreme Court in *Dublin County Council v Tallaght Block Co*[58] and in that case also the distinction between intensification of works and intensification of use was not recognised. In *Tallaght Block*, the land had been used for the screening of clay and gravel. Subsequently, the use was changed to the manufacture of concrete blocks. The latter operation involved the installation of a cement storage structure, the provision of a concrete mixing plant and the building of additional premises. In the first instance, there was a material change in use from clay and gravel screening to block manufacturing and secondly, there was intensification because of the extra raw material, machinery, buildings and personnel on site. The use of the lands for block manufacturing was held to be an unauthorised use.

**[2.63]** In *Galway County Council v Lackagh Rock Limited*,[59] the county council had operated a quarry from 1950 to 1973 and the respondent took a lease of the quarry in December 1976. The quarry had been operating between 1973 and 1976. The quarry had been actively worked by the county council but the respondent increased the

---

57. See *Kildare County Council v Goode* [1999] 2 IR 495.
58. *Dublin County Council v Tallaght Block Co* [1982] ILRM 534.
59. *Galway County Council v Lackagh Rock Limited* [1985] IR 20.

operation by bringing a mobile primary crusher onto the site, and there was a continuous build up of plant and machinery together with the erection of ancillary buildings. Diesel generators were used to power the graders and an office, weigh-bridge, canteen, oil storage tanks and garage work shops were placed on the site to include loading bays and storage. The number of employees increased from six to fourteen, and the court accepted that the site was being used in a different manner to its use on the appointed day, but it did not think that the difference in this case amounted to material change of use. The evidence showed that at the height of its operation the county council had been drawing out large volumes of stone amounting to some 144 loads a day. The respondent's operation produced levels slightly below the county council's output and the evidence showed that no objections had been made by local people. The council acknowledged that it had not objected to the presence of the building on the site. In this case, Barron J held that there had not been an intensification of use such as to constitute a material change in use on the grounds that for a material change in use to have occurred it must be demonstrated that the change which has occurred has affected the proper planning and development of the area and the test to be applied is to compare matters which the planning authority would have considered if a planning application had been made in respect of the quarrying operation on the appointed day, and the matters to be considered if an application were to be made for the contemporary operations.

**[2.64]** In *Monaghan County Council v Brogan*,[60] Keane J disagreed with Barron J's 'test' in *Lackagh Rock* on the basis that it gave the planning authority the power to decide what did or did not constitute development and that that decision was stronger than a decision of the High Court. *Monaghan County Council v Brogan* concerned a slaughter house where activities between 1940 and 1950 had been carried out on the respondent's farm in a small way in order to provide feed for greyhounds owned by the respondent's brother. In 1983, a newspaper advertisement appeared, looking for casualty cattle and offering highest prices. The telephone number was disclosed. As a result of this advertisement in the *Northern Standard*, the scale of slaughtering increased and the county council brought an application to restrain this unauthorised use of the farm. Brogan's lawyers relied heavily on the decision in *Lackagh Rock* where Barron J held that the question of materiality in relation to change of use was one to be decided by the courts and not by the county council. Keane J had this to say:

> The extent or scale in which the slaughtering is being carried on, the appearance of the newspaper advertisement and the violent methods employed by the respondents to prevent any access to their premises, satisfies me beyond any doubt that, not merely had there been a significant increase in the amount of slaughtering going on, but that the object of the operation now, is the supply of food for human consumption. It is also clear that the activity now being carried on is essentially a commercial operation in contrast to the relatively modest and intermittent slaughtering which went on prior to 1983. The question accordingly resolved itself into one as to whether a change of use which involves the slaughtering of animals in a scale significantly greater than before, forming part

---

60. *Monaghan County Council v Brogan* [1987] IR 333.

of a commercial operation established for the first time on a particular farm, is 'material in the context of planning'. Were such an operation to be established in an urban environment, there could not be the slightest doubt that it would be a material change of use of the land. It is true, that in the present case, it had been established in a rural area but I am satisfied that, it, is none the less a material change in the use of land in the context of the proper planning and development of the area.

**[2.65]** 'Material change' in the context of a change of use means 'material' for planning purposes and must be determined by the court as a matter of fact. There is no necessity for the court to seek the views of the planning authority.

**[2.66]** In *Kildare County Council v Goode*,[61] the Supreme Court made a clear statement to the effect that the concepts of intensification and of abandonment both have two separate limbs, namely, intensification of and abandonment of development by works and intensification by way of, and abandonment by way of, material change in use.

**[2.67]** That decision ended a controversy and it is now clear that an intensification of use or an intensification of works may represent development. It is also clear that if intensification is to amount to a development requiring planning permission, the intensification must be significant in the context of planning law.

**[2.68]** In *Butler v Dublin Corporation*,[62] Keane J provided a useful definition of 'intensification of use', as follows:

> Although the expression 'intensification of use' is not to be found in our planning code or in its English equivalent, the legislatures in both jurisdictions must have envisaged that a particular use could be so altered in character by the volume of activities or operations being carried on that the original use must be regarded as having been materially changed. One man digging up stones in a field and carrying them away in a wheelbarrow for a few hours each week may be succeeded by fleets of bulldozers, JCBs and lorries extracting and carrying away huge volumes of rock from the same site. The use in both instances may properly be described as 'quarrying', but that its intensification to a particular degree may constitute a material change in the original use is, I think, not merely borne out by the authorities to which I have referred but is consistent with the underlying policy of the Act of 1963 and the amending legislation of ensuring that significant changes in the physical characteristics of the environment are subjected to planning control.

**[2.69]** In referring to the now accepted fact that intensification of use can amount to development which requires planning permission, Simons sums it up well:

> To put the matter in somewhat simplistic terms, more of the same can, in certain circumstances, represent a fresh act of development.[63]

---

61. *Kildare County Council v Goode* [1999] 2 IR 495.
62. *Butler v Dublin Corporation* [1999] 1 IR 505.
63. See Simons, *Planning and Development Law* (2nd edn, Thomson Round Hall, 2007) at para 2.52, p 82.

**[2.70]** Intensification of use, if it is to amount to a material change in use, must give rise to fresh planning considerations. In *Westmeath County Council v Quirke*,[64] in determining whether intensification had occurred, the court had regard to:

(iii) the object of the operation;

(iv) the difference between production methods;

(v) the scale of the operation;

(vi) the levels and size of trucks;

(vii) dust and noise levels;

(viii) the effect on local residents;

(ix) the area of the operation.

Other significant factors which should be taken into consideration would include the extent of the methods used, such as blasting and increased traffic to and from the site.

**[2.71]** Intensification can also occur where the use and/or the works greatly exceed the use and/or the works permitted by a planning permission. Arguably any development which had occurred prior to 1 October 1964 did not require planning permission and now does not require retention permission. When the Local Government (Planning and Development) Act 1963 was commenced it became necessary to obtain planning permission for all development other than exempted development. It is clear that where works or use are carried on prior to 1 October 1964, they may not require either planning permission or retention permission if those works or use are continued after 1 October 1964. But if works or use commenced prior to 1 October 1964 are intensified, that intensification, depending on its degree, may amount to development requiring planning permission or retention permission as appropriate.

**[2.72]** Intensification of works and/or of use can arise if the works and/or the use greatly exceed the works and/or use permitted by the planning permission. Furthermore, if the application for permission specified a particular use for a development when permission was granted, the particular use will be the only authorised use. In *Readymix (Eire) v Dublin Co Co*,[65] Henchy J stated:

> It is the combined effect of the permission and other documents that must be looked at in determining the proper scope of a permission.

From this it can be readily seen that if the use and/or the works envisaged in the application or envisaged by the terms of a permission granted are exceeded during the course of development, intensification may arise. A permission may contain a condition limiting the scope and/or the scale of the proposed development. For example, a permission can limit excavation to a specified tonnage *per* day. Even in cases where there are no special conditions limiting the use and/or the works, the application for

---

64. *Westmeath County Council v Quirke* (unreported, 28 June 1996) HC.
65. *Readymix (Eire) v Dublin Co Co* (unreported, 30 July 1974) SC.

permission may itself describe the use of the works and, in that sense, it may give an indication to the planning authority and to potential third party objectors of the scale of the proposed use or works. If, in either case, the actual development exceeds the scale of a limiting condition contained in a planning permission or if it exceeds the scale of the description of the development set out in the application for planning permission, an intensification may occur which would require a separate planning permission or, as applicable, a separate retention permission. PDA 2000[66] provides that where planning permission is granted for a structure the grant may specify the purposes for which this structure may or may not be used. The effect of intensifying the use to a use which exceeds the limits set down in a planning permission may be a breach of condition.

[2.73] No attempt has ever been made to establish a doctrine of dis-intensification and to date even the complete abandonment of a use does not constitute development, notwithstanding that a reduction in the level of activity may itself have significant planning and sustainability implications.

## Material change in use as interpreted by the courts

[2.74] A change in use must be 'material' to constitute development. If a change in use is a material change in use, planning permission will be required unless the change is exempted by the exempted development regulations or by any exemption which arises under some other statutory provision.

[2.75] The courts have approached the interpretation of the materiality of change in use in two ways.

[2.76] Firstly, they have looked at the character of the use both before the change in use and after it. In *Cusack v Minister for Local Government*,[67] where a dentist's surgery was changed to a solicitor's office, McWilliam J held that this change was a material change in use because the character of the use as a solicitor's office differs from the character of use as a dentist's surgery. The nature of these two professions is entirely different. However, if a change in use from dentist's surgery to solicitor's office is scrutinised more carefully and regard is had only to considerations which are strictly planning considerations, it will be seen that dentists and solicitors are two separate professions but, in pure planning terms, the question is whether or not that change is material. What impact does such a change have on the immediate neighbourhood and on the surrounding area? The dentist and the solicitor carry on their work in a building and patients or clients, respectively, call to see them. Both generally operate during day time hours and they do not usually operate at night-time. The ebb and flow of callers would not be substantially different between the dentist and the solicitor and traffic movements would be in or around the same volume. Would the solicitor's or the dentist's neighbours notice much difference? Probably not.

---

66. PDA 2000, s 39(2).
67. *Cusack v Minister for Local Government* (unreported, 4 November 1980) HC.

**Development and Exempted Development** [2.80]

[2.77] In *McMahon v Dublin Corporation*,[68] a conversion of a residential use of a dwelling to a use for commercial short term lettings amounted to a material change in use which required planning permission. The change in use in *McMahon* can be contrasted with the change of use in *Cusack* in that changing a single residential use to a number of short term lettings for commercial user is a change from one situation to an entirely different situation.

[2.78] Secondly, the courts have approached the interpretation of the materiality of a change in use by examining the impact which the change in use has on the immediate neighbourhood and the surrounding area. This second approach is now the preferred approach. If this second approach had been applied in *Cusack v Minister for Local Government*,[69] it is likely that the outcome would have been different whereas the planning impact on the immediate neighbourhood resulting from the change in use in *McMahon v Dublin Corporation*[70] must have been noticeable in a negative sense only.

[2.79] The matter of material change in use came before the courts in *Earl of Mount Charles v Westmeath County Council*,[71] where the applicant argued that the use of the lands at Slane Castle as a rock concert venue during five previous years, had turned the rock concert into a use which the plaintiff claimed was a part of the normal use of the land and castle. The plaintiff claimed that the use did not amount to material change in use. Budd J disagreed on the grounds that rock concerts were occasional and infrequent events at Slane Castle. They could not be described as being part of the normal use of the land. The use of Slane Castle and the lands of Slane Castle for a rock concerts was an ancillary use. If, however, that use changed to such an extent that it was no longer ancillary to the dominant use, that change in itself may become a material change in use for which planning permission is required. In the course of his judgment, the learned judge concentrated more on the substantive impacts of the use in planning terms and, in particular, the impact rock concerts would have in the neighbourhood and on the surrounding area in terms of noise, crowds, traffic, litter, etc.

[2.80] What emerges from the decisions both in the English and Irish courts is that the test based on the character of a change in use (eg, from solicitor's office to dentist's surgery) is not a conclusive test in establishing material change in use. Rather, the courts prefer a more detailed examination dealing specifically, in planning terms, with the impact which a change in use will have on the surrounding area. Such factors as increased noise, more traffic (in the sense of both people and vehicles), more litter, more airborne dust or dirt and similar environmental dis-improvements to include working night-time hours instead of day-time hours, and other physical impact factors are matters to be taken into account in deciding whether or not a change in use is material.

---

68. *McMahon v Dublin Corporation* [1996] 3 IR 509.
69. *Cusack v Minister for Local Government* (unreported, 4 November 1980) HC.
70. *McMahon v Dublin Corporation* [1996] 3 IR 509.
71. *Earl of Mount Charles v Westmeath County Council* [1996] 3 IR 417.

**[2.81]** In *Westmeath County Council v Quirke & Sons*,[72] Budd J stated as follows:

> Many alterations in the activities carried on land constitute a change in use; however not all alterations will be material. Whether such changes amount to a material change in use is a question of fact as is explained in *Monaghan County Council v Brogan* [[1987] IR 333]. Consideration of the materiality of a change in use means assessing not only the use itself but also its effects.

**[2.82]** Whether a change in use amounts to a material change in use is a question both of fact and of degree. In *Monaghan County Council v Brogan*,[73] Keane J held that 'material change' in the context of a change of use means 'material' for planning purposes which must be determined by the court as a matter of fact. It was not necessary to adduce evidence as to the views of the planning authority on the question, nor was the absence of objections to the development by other persons crucial in determining whether there has been a material change in use.

**[2.83]** It is for the courts to decide on the question of materiality of a change in use. If the change of use is material, planning permission or retention permission[74] will be required if the development is to proceed or to survive. The question as to whether or not planning permission may or may not be granted is entirely a matter for the relevant planning authority and a careful line should be drawn to ensure that the courts do not trespass on planning authority territory. In fact, the courts have shown a marked reluctance to overturn decisions made by planning authorities and by An Bord Pleanála.[75] They have mainly left decisions as to whether works or material change in use amount to development to the planning authorities and to An Bord Pleanála. Mainly, the courts will only intervene where the planning authority or An Bord Pleanála has misinterpreted the meaning of development or of exempted development in making a decision as to whether any particular activity constitutes development or exempted development. The courts may also intervene where the decision of the planning authority or of An Bord Pleanála is wholly unreasonable or wrong as a matter of fact.

**[2.84]** The primary responsibility in making a decision as to whether or not any particular activity amounts to development or exempted development rests with the planning authority or with An Bord Pleanála.

**[2.85]** The importance of the planning impact of a change in use as opposed to a mere change in the character of the use, in assessing whether or not a change in use is or is not material, has been dealt with by the courts in England. The English decisions have paid particular attention to the possible consequences which the development proposal would have for local amenities. Early on, the English courts considered that the assessment of planning impact is an all-important concept in determining materiality.

---

72. *Westmeath County Council v Quirke & Sons* (unreported, 23 May 1996) HC.
73. *Monaghan County Council v Brogan* [1987] IR 333.
74. See definition of 'retention permission' and note the provisions precluding an application for retention permission where there are relevant environmental concerns.
75. See *Denis O'Keefe v An Bord Pleanála and O'Brien and, by order of the Court, Radio Tara Ltd* [1992] ILRM 237 and *State (Keegan) v Stardust Compensation Tribunal* [1986] IR 642.

**[2.86]** The courts will have regard, in particular, to the possible effects of a development proposal on local amenities. The following two extracts from judgments may be of assistance in helping to identify the factors which are to be taken into account in considering 'materiality' apart from the physical facts of the case:

1. 'The materiality to be considered is a materiality from the planning point of view and, in particular, the question of amenities' *per* Lord Parker CJ in *Devonshire County Council v Allens Caravans (Estates Limited)*.[76]

2. 'Considerations which are relevant, are planning considerations and the persons concerned in determining whether there was a material change of use would have to consider such matters as the development plan for the area, the declared policy of the planning authority, the circumstances in which the permission was granted and the terms of the permission' *per* Diplock LJ in *Wilson v West Sussex County Council*.[77]

From the foregoing it can be seen that it is possible that, for example, a change in use might be thought to be material in a town but not in a rural area. A change in use in one place may be a material change while an identical change in another place may not be a material change. The extract from Diplock LJ's judgment illustrates the importance of the terms of a permission where an existing use is permitted under a planning permission. The terms of the permission must be carefully scrutinised.

**[2.87]** The development of quarries has, in many cases, dealt with the question of material change in use resulting from intensification. Not all intensification amounts to material change in use.

**[2.88]** In numerous quarry cases in Ireland, development, in the sense of extraction of materials or quarrying, commenced before 1 October 1964 and, accordingly, it was considered that permission was not required. At least, until the passing of PDA 2000, 'pre-64' development was not unauthorised development. At times quarrying operations were interrupted temporarily and then recommenced. The courts were asked to decide, in cases of recommencement, where the quarrying activity was greatly increased or 'intensified', whether or not the intensification amounted to a material change in use:[78]

(i) In *Stafford v Roadstone Ltd*,[79] the plaintiffs applied for an order under s 27(1) of the Local Government (Planning and Development) Act 1976 to prohibit the quarrying activities of the defendants.[80] The defendants pleaded that quarrying had commenced prior to 1 October 1964 and as such the development which they were carrying out did not require permission. It was not unauthorised

---

76. *Devonshire County Council v Allens Caravans (Estates Limited)* [1963] 612 LGR 57, 58.
77. *Wilson v West Sussex County Council* [1963] 2 QR 764, 85.
78. Note that the environmental impacts of quarrying activities play a significant role in deciding whether or not quarry is operating legally and this is dealt with, in terms of the provisions of EIA legislation and the provisions of PD(A)A 2010, in **Ch 9**.
79. *Stafford v Roadstone Ltd* [1980] ILRM 1.
80. Note that the clearer terms of PDA 2000, s 160 have replaced Local Government (Planning and Development) Act 1976, s 27 since the decision in *Stafford v Roadstone Ltd* [1980] ILRM 1. See also Planning and Development (Amendment) Act 2001, s 48.

development. Barrington J, in the course of his judgment, considered that the work being carried out in the quarry prior to 1964 and shortly afterwards was materially different to the works being carried out in 1980 when the case was heard. Barrington J held:

a. that there had been an unauthorised development in the quarry;
b. that the use of the quarry and adjoining lands had been intensified to such a point as to amount to a material change in use;
c. that the purpose of the unauthorised development was to bring about the unauthorised use.

(ii) In *Dublin County Council v Sellwood Quarries*,[81] where land was formerly used for sand and gravel extraction but was changed for use as a quarry, it was held by Gannon J that this was a material change in use because gravel removal was a relatively simple procedure whereas the removal of rock involved heavy machinery and blasting.

(iii) In *Butler v Dublin Corporation*,[82] the use of Lansdowne Road Rugby Football grounds was held to be materially altered in planning terms by its use as a venue for pop concerts by Costello J in the High Court but that argument was rejected the Supreme Court which held that the use could not be regarded as being materially altered in planning terms by fleeting changes in the use of the stadium and grounds for pop concerts.

(iv) In *Carrick Hall Holdings Ltd v Dublin Corporation*,[83] the High Court held that a change in use from a hotel licence with a public bar to an ordinary seven day licensed premises was a material change in use in terms of intensification because of the effects which such change would have on the neighbouring area. There were and still are occasions when the noise and disturbance generated by a public bar with a seven day licence, particularly at closing time, would have a greater impact on the neighbouring area compared with a residents bar in a hotel. Social conditions have changed since the hearing of the *Carrick Hall Holdings* case in 1983. Most hotels in residential areas operate as public bars with an ordinary seven day licence. The effect of enforcement of the drink driving laws has, undoubtedly, lessened the impact to some extent at least.

(v) In *Galway Corporation v Lackagh Rock Co Ltd*,[84] Barron J stated that intensification *per se* would not constitute a material change in use unless the intensification of activity was material in that it gave rise to fresh planning considerations:

> The importance of this principle lies, not so much in the intensification of the use itself, but in the fact that such use may impose burdens on the local

---

81. *Dublin County Council v Sellwood Quarries* [1981] ILRM 23.
82. *Butler v Dublin Corporation* (unreported, 22 January 1999) SC.
83. *Carrick Hall Holdings Ltd v Dublin Corporation* [1983] ILRM 268.
84. *Galway Corporation v Lackagh Rock Co Ltd* [1985] IR 120.

authority or otherwise infringe, in a materially different manner, upon the proper planning for the area.

(vi) In *Cork Corporation v O'Connell*,[85] it was held that a change in use from retail hardware store to amusement arcade did involve material change in use. Both the use as a retail hardware store and the use as an amusement arcade were commercial uses but undoubtedly the customers visiting a retail hardware store and the customers visiting an amusement arcade would be substantially different with the latter having a greater potential for making an adverse impact on the surrounding area or in the neighbourhood.

(vii) In *Rehabilitation Institute v An Bord Pleanála*,[86] Barron J held that trivial or temporary changes in use may be ignored for planning purposes. The learned judge further held that a cessation of an ancillary use does not give rise to a material change in use.

(viii) In *Dublin Corporation v Moore*,[87] the Supreme Court reversed a High Court decision when the corporation attempted to injunct the parking of two ice cream sales vans in the driveway of a dwelling house and the maintenance of a refrigerating process by connection to the electricity mains. The corporation argued that there was a material change in use of the driveway being the change in use ancillary to residential use, to a commercial use. The Supreme Court held that this change in use did not amount to unauthorised development. The use was ancillary to the main use of the dwelling house and was a use within the curtilage of the dwelling house.

The Supreme Court also held that the character of an area cannot be considered in the determination of such an issue as this would offend against the rights of equality provided for in the Constitution.[88]

## 'STRUCTURE'

[2.89] PDA 2000[89] defines 'structure' as:

any building, structure, excavation, or other thing constructed or made on, in or under any land, or any part of a structure so defined, and—

(a) where the context so admits, includes the land on, in or under which the structure is situate, and

(b) in relation to a protected structure or a proposed protected structure includes —

(i) the interior of such structure,

---

85. *Cork Corporation v O'Connell* [1978] ILRM 85.
86. *Rehabilitation Institute v An Bord Pleanála* [1988] 6 ILT 193.
87. *Dublin Corporation v Moore* [1984] ILRM 339, SC.
88. The decision in *Dublin Corporation v Moore* [1984] ILRM 339 might very well upset the rationale applied in *Cork Corporation v O'Connell* [1978] ILRM 85.
89. PDA 2000, s 2(1).

> (ii) the land lying within the curtilage of the structure,
> 
> (iii) any other structures lying within that curtilage and their interiors, and
> 
> (iv) all fixtures and features which form part of the interior or exterior of any structure or structures referred to in sub-para (i) or (iii).

Part of a structure comes within the definition of a structure and as such part of a structure is a structure. A structure also includes excavation on, in or under any land and where the context so admits the structure includes the land on, in or under which it is situate. An object may, however, be placed on land and not attached to it and it may not have been constructed on the site. Thus a large concrete mixer on wheels which remains in the one position for many years is not a structure within the definition. Also other industrial implements such as large conveyors on wheels for moving grain or coal, etc, from place to place and mobile cranes are not structures.

## 'LAND'

[2.90] PDA 2000[90] defines 'land' as including any structure and any land covered with water (whether inland or coastal).

## 'SUBSTRATUM OF LAND'

[2.91] PDA 2000[91] defines 'substratum of land' as meaning:

> any subsoil or anything beneath the surface of land required—
> 
> (a) for the purposes of a tunnel or tunnelling or anything connected therewith, or
> 
> (b) for any other purpose connected with a scheme within the meaning of the Roads Act 1993.[92]

## 'EXEMPTED DEVELOPMENT'

[2.92] PDA 2000[93] provides that permission is required for the development of land not being exempted development. Section 4 of PDA 2000[94] sets out a list of categories of exempted development. Further details of s 4 exemptions and of categories of exempted development are contained in regulations made under PDA 2000 as amended and this topic is dealt with in detail below at paras **2.121** to **2.233**.

[2.93] Exempted development does not require planning permission. Legislation, apart from PDA 2000, as amended by PD(A)A 2010, provides for further exempted

---

90. PDA 2000, s 2(1).
91. PDA 2000, s 2(1).
92. PDA 2000, s 2(1).
93. PDA 2000, s 32.
94. PDA 2000, s 4 as amended by PD(A)A 2010, s 5.

development and this legislation includes the Dublin Docklands Development Authority Act 1997, the Derelict Sites Act 1990, the Roads Act 1993, the Transport (Railway Infrastructure) Act 2001 and PD(SI)A 2006.

## 'RETENTION PERMISSION'

[2.94] At the outset it must be stated that retention permission is no longer available in cases where an EIA should have been undertaken in the first instance or in cases where an EIS is lodged with the application for retention permission. That said, where EIA or EIS was not relevant, planning permission shall be required in the case of development which is unauthorised, for the retention of the unauthorised development. PDA 2000[95] imposes an obligation to obtain retention permission for the retention of that unauthorised development:

  (a)  where unauthorised development has or is being carried out;

  (b)  in order to continue an existing unauthorised use, or to continue a use which has been brought into being without permission; or

  (c)  where there is non-compliance with a condition or with conditions in a planning permission.

[2.95] Section 32 reads:

> (1) Subject to the other provisions of this Act, permission shall be required under this Part —
>
>   (a)  in respect of any development of land not being exempted development, and
>
>   (b)  in the case of development which is unauthorised for the retention of that unauthorised development.

[2.96] PDA 2000, s 34(12) has now been substituted by PD(A)A 2010, s 23 and now reads as follows:

> (12) A planning authority shall refuse to consider an application to retain unauthorised development of land where the authority decides that if an application for permission had been made in respect of the development concerned before it was commenced the application would have required that one or more than one of the following was carried out—
>
>   (a)  an environmental impact assessment,
>
>   (b)  a determination as to whether an environmental impact assessment is required, or
>
>   (c)  an appropriate assessment.

From this it can be seen that if an application for grant of retention permission is for sub threshold projects and if the works commenced without a prior screening exercise and

---

95.   PDA 2000, s 32(1)(b).

had been carried out, then retention permission is no longer available. The non-availability of retention permission remains even if it can be shown that if a screening exercise had been carried out the project would have been found to have no significant effects on the environment and as such it would not have triggered the requirement for formal assessment under the EIA Directive. It is the failure to carry out the prior screening exercise which precludes subsequent retention permission. Undeniably the provision will motivate developers to ensure, in cases where there is the slightest doubt, that planning applications are screened by the planning authority.

**[2.97]** Two *de minimis* exceptions are provided in the newly inserted s 34(12A), (12B) and (12C)[96] which read:

> (12A) For the purposes of subsection (12), if an application for permission has been made in respect of the following development before it was commenced, the application shall be deemed not to have required a determination referred to at subsection (12)(b);[97]
>
> > (a) a development within the curtilage of a dwellinghouse, for any purpose incidental to the enjoyment of the dwellinghouse as a dwellinghouse;
> >
> > (b) modifications to the exterior of a building.
>
> (12B) Where a planning authority refuses to consider an application for permission under subsection (12) it shall return the application to the applicant, together with any fee received from the applicant in respect of the application, and shall give reasons for its decision to the applicant.
>
> (12C) Subject to subsections (12) and (12A), an application for development of land in accordance with the permission regulations may be made for the retention of unauthorised development, and this section shall apply to such an application, subject to any necessary modifications.

Although the potential for an application for retention permission is abolished where it is in conflict with the EIA Directive, PD(A)A 2010 makes provision for the grant of 'substitute consent' which is discussed in **Ch 9**.

**[2.98]** Retention permission is required in the case of unauthorised/non-conforming development (to include use) other than an unauthorised/non-conforming development which would have required that one or more of the following was carried out:

> (a) an environmental impact assessment,
>
> (b) a determination as to whether an environmental impact assessment is required, or
>
> (c) an appropriate assessment.[98]

The obtaining of it can be enforced by the courts. The standard provisions relating to planning applications apply to an application for retention permission.

---

96. Inserted by PD(A)A 2010, s 23.
97. The sub-s 12(b) determination is a determination as to whether an EIA is required.
98. For definition of and operation of 'appropriate assessment' see PD(A)A 2010, Pt XAB, s 177R to s 177AE inclusive.

**[2.99]** There are a number of special features which attach to retention permission and these are listed below:

(i) No application for compensation can be made in respect of a refusal by the local authority or by An Bord Pleanála to grant retention permission.[99]

(ii) An application for retention permission cannot be preceded by an application for outline permission.[100]

(iii) A developer who has developed a development which is either wholly or partly unauthorised/non-conforming may not be compelled to apply for retention permission after the expiration of seven years, in a case where no application for planning permission was made, or after the expiration of seven years plus the life of the planning permission in a case where planning permission has been granted. The normal life of a planning permission is five years but in the case of a large development which has no prospect of being completed within the five year period, the planning authority has power to extend the life-time or duration of a planning permission at the time when the permission is granted. In such a case, the number of years will appear both in the notification of decision to grant planning permission and in the notification of grant of planning permission. Even after the permission has been granted, the planning authority may grant a further extended period beyond the five year or other life span of the permission to enable the developer to complete the development. The normal five-year life span of a planning permission or any other life span is not usually stated in a grant of permission. If a permission does not specify its own life span, the presumption is that it has a life span of five years from the date of the grant. If the life span of a five-year permission has to be extended by a planning authority during the course of the development because the development has not been completed and an application is made to it for an extension of time, the documentation should, in appropriate cases, be accompanied by further documents issued by the planning authority demonstrating that the appropriate period has been extended by such additional period as the planning authority considers requisite to enable the development to which the permission relates to be completed. PDA 2000, s 41 allows a planning authority or the board, in the first instance, to grant a planning permission for a longer period than the five years duration permitted by PDA 2000, s 40. In making a decision to grant a longer period than five years the planning authority or the board shall have regard to the nature and extent of the relevant development and to any other material considerations. Section 41 time extensions would usually be granted, in the first instance, for developments which are anticipated to take more than five years to complete. The section was amended by s 12 of PD(SI)A 2006 and the potential extension applicable under s 31 applies to permissions granted for strategic infrastructure under the

---

99. PDA 2000, s 191(4).
100. PDR 2001, art 21 (as substituted by the 2006 Regulations).

2006 Act most of which comprises substantial development which might be take more than five years to complete.

**[2.100]** PDA 2000, s 42, as amended by PD(A)A 2010, s 28, deals with the power to extend the appropriate period and it offers a once only opportunity[101] to extend the life of the planning permission by a further period of up to, but not exceeding, five years. PDA 2000, s 42 allowed a planning authority to extend the life of the planning permission by whatever period it deemed was necessary to enable a development to be completed. The amended section allows for the extension of five years and no more than five years. The period of the extension, which must not, in any case, exceed five years, is determined by the local authority on the basis of the amount of time that it considers is necessary to enable the development, to which the permission relates, to be completed. The granting of an extension is subject to the following conditions, namely:

- (a) Either—
  - (i) the authority is satisfied that—
    - (I) the development to which the permission relates was commenced before the expiration of the appropriate period sought to be extended,
    - (II) substantial works were carried out pursuant to the permission during that period, and
    - (III) the development will be completed within a reasonable time,

  or
  - (ii) the authority is satisfied—
    - (I) that there were considerations of a commercial, economic or technical nature beyond the control of the applicant which substantially militated against either the commence of development or the carrying out of substantial works pursuant to the planning permission,
    - (II) that there have been no significant changes in the development objectives in the development plan or in regional development objectives in the regional planning guidelines for the area of the planning authority since the date of the permission such that the development would no longer be consistent with the proper planning and sustainable development of the area,
    - (III) that the development would not be inconsistent with the proper planning and sustainable development of the area having regard to any guidelines issued by the Minister under section 2(8), notwithstanding that they were so issued after the date of the grant of permission in relation to which an application is made under this section, and
    - (IV) where the development has not commenced that an environmental impact assessment, or an appropriate assessment, or both of those

---

101. PD(A)A 2010, s 28(4).

assessments, if required, was or were carried out before the permission was granted.[102]

The application for retention permission must be in accordance with the regulations under the Act and all requirements of the regulations must be complied with as regards the application. The application must be made before the appropriate period, in other words, before the existing planning permission has expired.[103]

[2.101] PD(A)A 2010, s 28(2) provides that a planning authority may attach conditions to retention permission providing for the payment by the applicant of adequate security to ensure satisfactory completion of the proposed development. The section also allows the planning authority to add to or vary any condition contained in the original grant of permission. Any decision by the planning authority to extend the life of the planning permission shall be made as expeditiously as possible and it shall be the objective of the planning authority to give notice of its decision within eight weeks.[104] A new s 42(a) was inserted after PDA 2000, s 42 by Pt 8, s 238 of the National Asset Management Agency Act 2009 dealing with the power to extend the appropriate period of an application made by the National Assets Management Agency (NAMA). That section has been amended by PD(A)A 2010, s 29 and the wording of that section is the same as the wording in s 28. The difference being that s 28 applies generally to applicants and s 29 applies specifically to NAMA in circumstances where NAMA wishes to apply for an extension of the life of a planning permission.

[2.102] PDA 2000, s 43 has not received any attention from PD(A)A 2010. The section enables the making of regulations in relation to matters of procedure and other matters as the Minister deems necessary to give full effect to the provisions of PDA 2000, ss 40, 41 and 42, as amended by PD(A)A 2010.[105]

(iv) Fees payable for an application for retention permission are considerably more expensive than similar fees paid for an application for planning permission. The amount of the fees payable for an application for retention permission should always be checked before the application is lodged. The fee amount is changed from time to time and invariably the change is upwards. The purpose of charging a higher fee for retention permission applications is to encourage developers, in the first instance, to apply and obtain planning permission before works on the development commence. The possibility of obtaining retention permission is not something that should be encouraged but rather the circumstances in which a developer can apply for planning permission in the first instance should be normal procedure. Retention permission is a fall-back mechanism which should only be applied and granted in a genuine case and in exceptional circumstances. Retention permission was never intended to assist a fairly common practice in Ireland of 'build now and obtain retention

---

102. PD(A)A 2010, s 28(1)(a).
103. PD(A)A 2010, s 28(1)(b), (c) and (d).
104. PD(A)A 2010, s 28(2) and (3).
105. PDR 2001, Pt III as amended by PDR 2006 and further amended by PDR 2007.

[2.102]

permission later'. The effect of paying a higher fee for retention application, used as a deterrent for applying for retention permission in exceptional circumstances, was commented upon by the European Court of Justice (ECJ) in *Commission v Ireland*.[106] The ECJ considered that there should be a qualitative distinction between retention permission and conventional planning permission so as to discourage developers from applying for retention permission in circumstances where it is fairly obvious that the conventional permission application procedure was the proper procedure. The ECJ considered that the higher fees charged in Ireland for retention applications were not set at a level which amounted to a sufficient deterrent.

(v) Retention permission is not available for developments which comprise the demolition of buildings.

(vi) The Supreme Court in *State (Fitzgerald) v An Bord Pleanála*[107] has clearly decided that neither the planning authority nor An Bord Pleanála is entitled to take into account the fact that if retention permission is not granted, costly demolition could be required by enforcement proceedings taken by the planning authority. The fact that the developer may be put to expense or may endure difficulties and hardships cannot be taken into account.

(vii) PDA 2000[108] provides that the onus of proving the existence of any permission granted under Part III of the Act shall be on the defendant where proceedings are taken for an offence under the Act.

(viii) PDA 2000[109] provides that notwithstanding s 162(1) it shall not be a defence to a prosecution if the defendant proves that he or she has applied for or has been granted retention permission —

(a) Since the initiation of proceedings under this Part,

(b) Since the date of the sending of a warning letter under s 152, or

(c) Since the date of service of an enforcement notice in the case of urgency in accordance with s 155.

(ix) PDA 2000[110] also provides that no enforcement action under this Part (including an application for an injunction under PDA 2000, s 60) shall be stayed or withdrawn by reason of an application for permission for retention of unauthorised development under s 34(12C) or the grant of that permission. In *Commission v Ireland*,[111] Ireland, in its defence, made reference to the provisions of PDA 2000, s 162(3), as amended, but the ECJ took the view that

---

106. *Commission v Ireland* (Case C–215/06) [51].
107. *State (Fitzgerald) v An Bord Pleanála* [1985] ILRM 117, SC.
108. PDA 2000, s 162(1).
109. PDA 2000, 162(2).
110. PDA 2000, s 162(3) as amended by LGA 2001, s 247 and further amended by PD(A)A 2010, s 49.
111. *Commission v Ireland* (Case C–215/06).

although no enforcement action would be stayed or withdrawn because of an application for or a grant of retention permission, effectively, the planning authority, as enforcers, would defer taking enforcement proceedings in those circumstances.

(x) Retention permission, as provided for in PDA 2000, differs slightly in the definition from the provisions which previously applied under s 28(2) (Local Government (Planning and Development) Act 1963). Under the 1963 Act, permission for retention could be granted to take effect retrospectively, in other words back to the date when the development took place. Under the 1963 Act, if retention permission was obtained the status of the development in question was changed from unauthorised to authorised and the effect of the permission was backdated to the date when the development took place. Under the provisions of PDA 2000, the grant of retention for planning permission does not have any retrospective effect.

(xi) Before the decision in *Fingal County Council v William P Keeling and Sons Ltd*,[112] many conveyancers and planners believed that if an application for retention permission was applied for in circumstances where immunity from enforcement had been gained due to the passage of time, that immunity would be waived by the mere fact that the applicant had applied for retention permission. Normally a permission has a five year life span and immunity from enforcement is achieved seven years after the expiration of the life of permission, which is usually 12 years. If development in respect of which no application for permission was made has been *in situ* without any enforcement action being taken against it, the immunity is obtained seven years from the date of commencement of that development. The court in *Fingal County Council v William P Keeling and Sons Ltd*[113] held that a developer is not estopped from claiming that a development is in fact immune from enforcement proceedings by reason only of having made an application for planning permission for retention of development. This decision was made on the basis that to allow estoppel would deprive a developer of a right in law simply because he had exercised a different right. It seems, therefore, that once the immunity against enforcement has been obtained (12 years in the case of development with permission which infringes the permission or seven years in the case of development with no permission), the planning authority cannot commence enforcement proceedings even though it may have refused a subsequent application for retention permission.

(xii) Most significantly, the ECJ ruled that the provisions made under PDA 2000 for the grant of retention permission are inconsistent with the requirements of the Environmental Impact Assessment Directive (EIA Directive). The ruling of the

---

112. *Fingal County Council v William P Keeling and Sons Ltd* [2005] 2 IR 108.
113. *Fingal County Council v William P Keeling and Sons Ltd* [2005] 2 IR 108.

**[2.103]**  Planning and Environmental Law in Ireland

ECJ was made in the context of infringement proceedings taken against Ireland by the European Commission in *Commission v Ireland*.[114]

**[2.103]** While the ECJ agreed with the argument put forward by Ireland that a member state should be entitled to regularise the status of unauthorised development by the grant of retention development consent, the Commission emphasised that any such regularisation must be confined to 'exceptional circumstances':

> While Community law cannot preclude the application of national rules from allowing, in certain cases, the regularisation of operations or measures which are unlawful in the light of Community law, such a possibility should be subject to the conditions that it does not offer the persons concerned the opportunity to circumvent the Community rules or to dispense with applying them, and that it should remain the exception.[115]

The Commission considered that retention permission in Ireland was too easily obtained and that the legislative provisions should make it unattractive for developers to have resort to retention planning permissions. The fact that a higher fee is payable in connection with the retention application was not a sufficient deterrent in the Commission's view. The Commission also complained that there was no requirement under Irish law to establish or prove 'exceptional circumstances' before an application for retention planning permission can be made and that Irish law requires amendment to take account of the 'exceptional circumstances' principle.

**[2.104]** The ECJ judgment was delivered on 8 July 2008.[116] The ECJ concluded that the Irish enforcement system is inadequate and deficient. The court was critical of the fact that the taking of enforcement action is discretionary. The ECJ ruled that Ireland had failed to transpose the EIA Directive properly by allowing retention permission to be granted after development had been carried out in whole or in part. In allowing this Ireland undermined the preventative objectives of the EIA Directive. The court also ruled that Ireland's enforcement regime did not guarantee the effective application of the EIA Directive and in the course of the hearing a number of cases were cited where effective enforcement action was not taken against unauthorised development.

**[2.105]** In many cases there is no real possibility of investigating the planning history of a building back to 1 October 1964. What is clearly required is a planning amnesty to provide that once a development has been completed and a period of, say, 15 years has passed since completion, the development should be deemed to be planning compliant in all cases. It would even be acceptable if the 15-year period applied to cases where development had been commenced without planning permission.

**[2.106]** As seen, PDA 2000, s 34(12) has now been substituted by the four new subsections detailed above in s 23 of PD(A)A 2010 being s 34(12), (12A), (12B) and (12C) and, in effect, application for retention permission can no longer be applied for if

---

114. *Commission v Ireland* (Case C–215/06) [51].
115. *Commission v Ireland* (Case C–215/06) [51].
116. *Commission v Ireland* (Case C–215/06) [51].

the development is one which would require environmental assessment. A new consent procedure is in place and this is dealt with in detail in **Ch 10**. This procedure is known as 'substitute consent', legislated for in PD(A)A 2010, Pt XA, and 'appropriate assessment', legislated for in PD(A)A 2010, Pt XAB.

## 'UNAUTHORISED DEVELOPMENT'

**[2.107]** The interpretation of unauthorised development first appeared in s 2(1) PDA 2000. This section provides that unauthorised development means, in relation to land, the carrying out of any unauthorised works (including the construction, erection or making of any unauthorised structure) or the making of any unauthorised use. Significantly, no reference is made in this definition to:

(i) pre-1 October 1964 development;

(ii) exempted development;

(ii) development carried out in compliance with planning permission and any conditions to which that permission is subject.

**[2.108]** The s 2(1) definition breaks down 'unauthorised development' into three separate issues, namely 'unauthorised structure', 'unauthorised use' and 'unauthorised works'. All three of those phrases respectively do make specific reference to:

(a) structures in existence on 1 October 1964;

(b) use commenced on or after 1 October 1964;

(c) works commenced on or after 1 October 1964.

## 'UNAUTHORISED STRUCTURE'

**[2.109]** This term is referred to in the definition of 'unauthorised development', PDA 2000, s 2(1).

Section 2 of PDA 2000[117] interprets 'unauthorised structure' as meaning a structure other than:

(a) a structure which was in existence on 1 of October 1964, or

(b) a structure, the construction, erection or making of which was the subject of a permission for development granted under Part IV of the Act of 1963 or deemed to be such under s 92 of that Act or under s 34 or 37G[118] of this Act, being a permission which has not been revoked or which exists as a result of the carrying out of exempted development (within the meaning of s 4 of the Act of 1963 or s 4 of this Act).

It can be seen from this interpretation that express provision is made for any structure erected prior to 1 October 1964. This interpretation indicates that a pre-1 October 1964

---

117. PDA 2000, s 2.
118. This amendment is inserted into PDA 2000 by the provisions of PD(SI)A 2006.

is excluded from the definition of 'unauthorised structure' and as such one might conclude that it is a structure which does not require planning permission. Furthermore, the section could be taken as meaning that a pre-1964 structure does not require retention permission. The interpretation of 'unauthorised structure' lies uncomfortably beside the PDA 2000, s 32(1)(b) which unequivocally states that 'subject to the other provisions of this Act, permission shall be required under this Part':

> (b) in the case of development which is unauthorised for the retention of that unauthorised development.

PDA 2000, s 32(1)(a) also states that permission shall be required in respect of any development of land, not being exempted development. The lengthy provisions in PDA 2000 and in other statutory provisions and regulations do not, in any case, specifically include pre-1 October 1964 development as 'exempted' development.

**[2.110]** After 1 October 1964, to be authorised, structures must either be erected with permission or carried out under the exempted development provisions provided for in the Local Government (Planning and Development) Act 1963 or, if the structure is to be erected after the commencement of PDA 2000 (11 March 2002) it must be carried out under the exemptions provided for in that Act and in the regulations made under that Act or in accordance with other 'exempted development' provisions in other statutes, to include the Urban Renewal Act 1986, the Derelict Sites Act 1990, the Roads Act 1993, the Transport (Dublin Light Rail) Act 1996, the Dublin Docklands Development Authority Act 1997 and the Transport (Railway Infrastructure) Act 2001.

## 'UNAUTHORISED USE'

**[2.111]** This term is also referred to in the definition of 'unauthorised development'. PDA 2000[119] interprets 'unauthorised use' as meaning, in relation to land, use commenced on or after 1 October 1964, being a use which is a material change in use of any structure or other land and being a development other than:

> (a) exempted development (within the meaning of s 4 of the Act of 1963 or s 4 of this Act), or
>
> (b) development, which is the subject of a permission granted under Pt IV of the Act of 1963 or s 34 or 37G of PDA 2000, being permission which has not been revoked and which was carried out in compliance with that permission or any condition to which that permission is subject.

An unauthorised use or a material change in use which, in either case, was in being on 1 October 1964, does not appear to require planning permission nor does it appear to require retention permission. However, the same problem arises here as in para **2.109** above. Does this interpretation mean, as it should properly mean, that an authorised use or a material change in use which, in either case, was established prior to 1 October 1964 is not 'unauthorised use' and that it does not require planning permission or retention permission? There can be no conclusive answer to that question because PDA

---

119. PDA 2000, s 2(1).

2000, s 32(1)(b) provides that retention permission is required for all 'unauthorised development'.

## 'UNAUTHORISED WORKS'

**[2.112]** This term is also part of the definition of 'unauthorised development'. PDA 2000[120] provides that 'unauthorised works' means any works carried on, in, over or under land commenced on or after 1 October 1964, being development other than:

> (a) exempted development (within the meaning of s 4 of the Act of 1963 or s 4 of the Act of 2000); or
>
> (b) development, which is the subject of a permission granted under Part IV of the Act of 1963 or under s 34 or 37G of the Act of 2000, being a permission which has not been revoked, and which is carried out in compliance with that permission or any condition to which that permission is subject.

It can be seen from the use of the words 'works on, in, over or under land commenced on or after 1 October 1964' that it is clearly stated that 'works' carried out before 1 October 1964 are not 'unauthorised works'. Again this interpretation comes into conflict with the unequivocal provisions of PDA 2000, s 32(1)(b) which requires retention permission for all 'unauthorised development'.

## 'FORESHORE'

**[2.113]** Part XV of PDA 2000 deals with development on the foreshore. It provides two relevant definitions in the context of 'foreshore development', namely:[121]

> (i) 'development' includes development consisting of the reclamation of any land on the foreshore;
>
> (ii) 'foreshore' has the meaning assigned to it by the Foreshore Act 1933,[122] but includes land between the line of high water of ordinary or medium tides and land within the functional area of the planning authority concerned, that adjoins the first-mentioned land.

PDA 2000[123] also imposes an obligation:

> (1) Subject to the provisions of this Act, permission shall be required under Part III in respect of development on the foreshore not being exempted development, in circumstances where, were such development carried out, it would adjoin—
>
> (a) the functional area of a planning authority, or
>
> (b) any reclaimed land adjoining such functional area

---

120. PDA 2000, s 2(1).
121. PDA 2000, s 224.
122. The Foreshore Act 1933 defines 'foreshore' as 'the bed and shore below the line of high water, of ordinary or medium tides, of the sea and every tidal river and tidal estuary'. As distinct from the 'foreshore', the 'seashore' is defined in the Foreshore Act 1923, s 1 as encompassing the foreshore, with all beaches, banks, cliffs, sand and rocks contiguous to the foreshore.
123. PDA 2000, s 225(1), (2), (3) and (4).

and accordingly, that part of the foreshore on which it is proposed to carry out the development shall for the purposes of making an application for permission in respect of such development be deemed to be within the functional area of that planning authority.

(2) That part of the foreshore on which a development has been commenced or completed pursuant to a permission granted under Part III shall, for the purposes of this Act or any other enactment whether passed before or after the passing of this Act, be deemed to be within the functional area of the planning authority that granted such permission.

(3) This section shall not apply to —

(a) developments to which s 226 applies,[124] or
(b) development consisting of underwater cables, wires, pipelines or other similar apparatus used for the purpose of —
  (i) transmitting electricity or telecommunication signals, or
  (ii) carrying gas, petroleum, oil or water,

or development connected to land within the functional area of the planning authority solely by means of any such cable, wire, pipe-line or apparatus.

(4) This section is in addition to and not in substitution for the Foreshore Acts 1993 to 1998.

**[2.114]** PDA 2000, s 225 provides an obligation to obtain permission in respect of development on the foreshore. The foreshore is defined in PDA 2000, s 224 and it is an area which adjoins the functional area of the planning authority or which adjoins any reclaimed land. Although the functional area itself is not extended, the Act deems that, where any development is to be carried out on the foreshore, it is carried out within the functional area of the relevant planning authority. The notional extension of the planning authority's functional area is only extended for the purposes of dealing with a planning application. In effect, therefore, any development on the foreshore is treated in the same way as development on the mainland with all the necessary requirements for application for planning permission and the consequent enforcement provisions for any default.

**[2.115]** PDA 2000, s 225 effectively requires that, apart from obtaining planning permission in respect of development of the foreshore, it will also be necessary to obtain such licences as are required under the provisions of the Foreshore Acts 1993–1998.

**[2.116]** The bed and shore below the line of high water include the bed and shore exposed at low water and, in general, this is the property of the State and not the property of a landowner whose boundary will go to the high tide mark only. Prior to the Foreshore Act of 1933, the expressions 'seashore' and 'foreshore' meant one and the same thing, namely, that portion of Ireland which lies between the high water mark of the ordinary medium tides and the low water mark of ordinary medium tides. The definition under s 1 of the Foreshore Act 1933 embraces the whole shore from and including the sea banks and cliffs contiguous thereto and, in addition, the whole of the

---

124. PDA 2000, s 226 applies to local authority development on the foreshore.

foreshore and all sands and rocks contiguous thereto. No seaward limit is prescribed by the Act as to the extent of the foreshore seawards from the high water mark and, therefore, it appeared to extend seawards, at least to territorial limits, and possibly even beyond. A definition has now been amended by the insertion of s 1A under s 60 of the Maritime Safety Act 2005 which provides that:

> The outer limit of the foreshore is and shall be deemed always to have been and to be, coterminous with the seaward limit of the territorial seas of the State as provided, from time to time, by Act of the Oireachtas.

The definition of 'foreshore', for the purposes of Pt XV of PDA 2000, includes the land within the functional area of the planning authority concerned, which extends above and beyond the high tide mark of ordinary or medium tides but not, apparently, of spring tides, nor neap tides. High tide, for the purposes of this section, is half way between high water springs and high water neaps.

[2.117] PDA 2000, s 4 exempts local authorities from the necessity of obtaining planning permission for the carrying out of development within the boundaries of its functional area. There are some limitations to that general principle and, for example, a local authority cannot carry out development within its functional area if that development would be in material contravention of its down development plan.[125] When a local authority proposes to carry out development which requires environmental impact assessment under the provisions of PDA 2000, s 176 that development is subject to assessment by An Bord Pleanála. Because of the natural environmental sensitivity of 'foreshore', PDA 2000, s 226 requires a local authority to apply to the board for approval where it proposes to carry out development on the foreshore either on its own or jointly with some other party. Section 226(3) deals with the requirement of a local authority and with the requirements of any other party to prepare an environmental impact statement in respect of certain classes of development on the foreshore. However, the restrictions placed on a local authority under PDA 2000, s 179[126] and the conditions imposed by PDA 2000, s 32, providing a general obligation to obtain planning permission for development other than exempt development, do not apply to local authority development on the foreshore. An Bord Pleanála may grant permission either with or without conditions or it may refuse it. Specifically the board may attach conditions for or in connection with the protection of the marine environment (including the protection of fisheries) and it may also impose conditions to secure the safety of navigation.[127]

[2.118] PDA 2000, s 227 enables a local authority, in special circumstances, to use its compulsory acquisition powers to acquire foreshore which is in private ownership. The local authority's compulsory acquisition powers extend to the acquisition of foreshore which is in the ownership of the State.[128]

---

125. PDA 2000, s 178.
126. PDA 2000, s 179(6) as amended by PD(A)A 2010, s 58(a) and (b).
127. PDA 2000, s 226(2)(a) and (b).
128. See PDA 2000, s 227(10).

[2.119] The general rule is that land in the ownership of the State may not be acquired by compulsory acquisition but an exception is made in the case of foreshore acquisition.

[2.120] PDA 2000, s 228 provides a procedure, which must be followed by a local authority before carrying out site investigations,[129] to include a requirement that the local authority must publish a notice in one or more newspapers circulating in the area four weeks before carrying out any proposed site investigations. Such notice must also be served on the Minister for the Marine and Natural Resources and on any prescribed bodies.

## 'EXEMPTED DEVELOPMENT'

[2.121] PDA 2000[130] provides that subject to the other provisions of this Act, permission shall be required under Pt III:

(a) in respect of any development of land, not being exempted development, and

(b) in the case of development which is unauthorised, for the retention of that unauthorised development.

PDA 2000[131] further provides that a person shall not carry out any development in respect of which permission is required by s 32(1), except under and in accordance with a permission granted under Pt III.

[2.122] Previous paragraphs in this chapter have dealt with the meaning of 'development'. Listed below are the various ways in which 'exempted development' arises. Planning permission is not required for exempted development:

(A) **Statutory exempted development** comprises development within the terms of PDA 2000, s 4.

(B) **Planning Regulations exempted development** comprises exempt development listed in the Planning and Development Regulations (PDR) 2001–2008 consisting of the following statutory instruments: PDR 2001 (SI 600/2001) as amended by SI 364/2005, SI 685/2006, SI 83/2007, SI 135/2007, SI 235/2008 and SI 256/2008.

The categories of exempted development are constantly being expanded and amended by new regulations and this is a progression which is likely to increase in future years as greater efforts are made to encourage sustainable development and to reduce carbon emissions and combat the effects of global warming in terms of rising sea levels and the probability of drought. New planning and environmental regulations are likely to be in place by the time

---

129. For a more detailed examination of 'foreshore' see Scannell, *Environmental and Land Use Law* (Round Hall, 2006) under heading 'N-Coastal Development', paras 4.107 to 4.127, pp 345–352 and also see Dodd, *The Planning Acts 2000–2007 – Annotated and Consolidated* (Round Hall, 2008) paras 1.267 to 1.271, pp 558–566.
130. PDA 2000, s 32(1).
131. PDA 2000, s 32(2).

this volume first reaches the bookshelves, so a visit to www.environ.ie is always worthwhile in order to check the amending legislation or regulations in planning law and in environmental law.

(C) **Exempted development under other non-planning enactments.**

(D) **Other miscellaneous exempted development.**

(E) **Circumstances where exempted development is de-exempted.**

The main reason for exempting certain developments from the requirement to obtain planning permission is usually stated to be the fact that there are a whole host of relatively small and unimportant works and changes in use which would simply clog up the system if permission had to be obtained for all of them. When cases of permitted exempt development are examined it will also be noted that there is a strong case for greatly expanding the list of exempt developments because there are still very many relatively small and unimportant works which now require planning permission but which should be exempted. Professor Yvonne Scannell has this to say:

> It is a regrettable feature of Irish planning law that overworked and under-resourced planning authorities have to deal with so many applications for so many minor developments which should be exempted or regulated in some less cumbersome manner. A review of the nature and extent of exempted development is long overdue.[132]

It will also have been seen that the reasons for exempting development frequently go beyond exemption for small and unimportant works or uses. In particular, exempted development regulations are used to promote and encourage certain developments. A growing number of exempted developments relate to the promotion of heating and other pumping and mechanical systems which are designed to lessen or, indeed, to exclude carbon emissions. Again this is an area which is expanding and which will become more significant as the effects of global warming become progressively and fatally evident.

## Statutory exempted development

**[2.123]** Statutory exempted development comprises exempted development which is defined in PDA 2000, as amended.[133] Statutory exempted development includes agricultural use development:

## *Agricultural use development*[134]

**[2.124]** The following shall be exempted development for the purposes of PDA 2000:

> Development consisting of the use of any land for the purpose of agriculture and development consisting of the use for that purpose of any building occupied together with the land so used.

---

132. See Scannell, *Environmental and Land Use Law* (Thomson Round Hall, 2006) para J1, p 91.
133. PDA 2000, s 4(1)(a) to (l) inclusive as amended by PD(A)A 2010, s 5.
134. PDA 2000, s 4(1)(a).

**[2.125]** PDA 2000[135] defines 'agriculture' to include horticulture, fruit growing, seed growing, dairy farming, the breeding and keeping of livestock (including any creature kept for the production of food, wool, skins or fur or for the purpose of its use in the farming of land), the training of horses and rearing of bloodstock, the use of land as grazing land, meadow land, osier land, market gardens and nursery ground, and 'agricultural' shall be construed accordingly.

**[2.126]** 'Osier land' is perhaps an unfamiliar term and it refers to land used for the growing of willow trees for the making of baskets.

**[2.127]** PDA 2000, s 4(1)(a) to (l) provides a useful guideline as to the meaning of statutory exempted development.[136] PDA 2000, s 4(2)(a) and (c) provides that the Minister may by regulation provide for any case of development to be exempted development for the purposes of this Act where he or she is of the opinion that:

> (i) by reason of the size, nature or limited effect on its surroundings, of development belonging to that class, the carrying out of such development would not offend against principles of proper planning and sustainable development, or
>
> (ii) the development is authorised, or is required to be authorised, by or under any enactment (whether the authorisation takes the form of the grant of a licence, consent, approval or any other type of authorisation) where the enactment concerned requires there to be consultation (howsoever described) with members of the public in relation to the proposed development prior to the granting of the authorisation (howsoever described).

**[2.128]** The use of land for turbary and the use of land for woodlands were included in the definition of 'agriculture' contained in the Local Government (Planning and Development) Act 1963. They have been deliberately excluded from the definition of 'agriculture' in PDA 2000 because the European Court of Justice ruled that EIS requirements apply to the use of land for turbary and for woodlands.[137]

**[2.129]** The words used in s 4(1)(a) are explicit. The statutory agricultural exemption relates only to the *use* of land for agriculture or the *use* for agricultural purposes of any building occupied together with land so used. Use in relation to land does not include the use of the land by the carrying out of any works thereon, and a use in itself is not a development. Development only occurs when there is a material change in use. For the purpose of s 4(1) the material change in use must be a change in use to an agricultural use. Land reclamation, when the land was not previously used for agriculture but which is being reclaimed for agricultural purposes would be a good example of what is

---

135. PDA 2000, s 2(1).
136. PDA 2000, s 4(1)(a) to (l) inclusive as amended by PD(A)A 2010, s 5.
137. *Commission v Ireland* Case 392/96 [1999] ECR I–5901. Limited exemption applies to extraction of turf in an area of less than 10 hectares or where peat extraction includes the drainage of bog land which was commenced prior to 14 April 2007 subject to certain conditions. See PDR 2001, Sch 2, class 17 as amended by PDR 2005 (SI 364/2005).

envisaged under PDA 2000, s 4(1)(a) provided that no environmental impact assessment (EIA) is required. The use must, prior to the material change in use, be a non-agricultural use. If the 'development' resulting from a material change in use requires an environmental impact statement (EIS), it is not exempted development and planning permission is required.

[2.130] For the exemption under s 4(1)(a) to operate the material change in use of land or of any buildings to agricultural use will only be exempt where they are 'occupied together with the lands so used' and where no EIS is required in order for the material change in use to occur.

[2.131] The interpretation of s 4(1)(a) was considered by Costello P in *Irish Wildbird Conservancy v Clonakilty Golf and Country Club Ltd*,[138] where the golf club wished to extend its golfing facilities by cleaning drains, improving drainage and securing the river bank of a stream which flowed through the golf course. In doing so they used some heavy machinery to clear away scrub and trees. It was held that works of reclamation could not be exempted development within the meaning of s 4(1)(a) because the development undertaken by the golf club comprised works and did not refer to the use of any land for the purpose of agriculture or the use for that purpose of any building occupied together with land so used.

[2.132] In *Dolan & Dolan v Cooke*,[139] the respondent wished to construct a pathway or roadway through woodlands to provide access to his lands on the far side of the woodlands. In effect, he wished to create a shortcut to his lands. Morris J held that such development was not exempted development under s 4. Having carefully examined the words in the s 2 definition of 'agriculture', it was clear to the learned judge that this development did not come within that definition and that accordingly planning permission was necessary. This decision was upheld in the Supreme Court. The exemption provided by s 4(1)(a) is strictly limited. The extent of those limitations, in the context of agricultural exemptions, is frequently either not understood or conveniently overlooked.

[2.133] Where a proposed agricultural development requires EIA, the environmental impact of the proposed development must be assessed before it can proceed.[140] The Act provides that the Minister may prescribe development or classes of development which, notwithstanding s 2(1)(a), shall not be exempted development.[141] A consent procedure is necessary in cases where an EIA is required. This is effectively achieved by de-exempting PDA 2000, s 4(1) development in relation to agricultural material change in

---

138. *Irish Wildbird Conservancy v Clonakilty Golf and Country Club Ltd* (unreported, 23 July 1996) HC *per* Costello P.
139. *Dolan & Dolan v Cooke* [2000] IEHC 158 (20 January 2000) Morris P.
140. PDA 2000, s 4(4).
141. PDA 2000, s 2(1) has been amended by PD(A)A 2010, s 4 by the deletion of the definition of 'Council Directive' and by the substitution of separate definitions for (i) Birds Directive, (ii) European Site, (iii) Habitats Directive, (iv) Major Accidents Directive, and (v) planning application.

use where EIA is required. Ireland now accepts that the EIA Directive is binding in Irish law even though it may not have been fully transposed into Irish law. Entire classes of projects cannot be exempted in cases where EIA is required. It is not permissible for a country to set thresholds at such a low level that, effectively, EIA would never be required. Ireland has been criticised by the ECJ where it held that Ireland had set thresholds which concentrated on the size only of the development. Ireland had omitted to take the nature and location of the development into consideration and these are essential factors which may not be overlooked.[142]

**[2.134]** Thresholds must embrace all aspects of a development which may impact on the development or which may impact on the environment to the extent that negative impacts must not just be disclosed but must be eliminated. The development proposal must be environmentally acceptable.

**[2.135]** The Irish courts have, in general, been supportive of the Directive and have frequently enforced compliance with it. In *Maher v An Bord Pleanála*,[143] the applicant maintained that the board should not have granted permission for development of a 200 sow, pig rearing building because there was no EIA. It was held that the interpretation by the board of the threshold requirements was legally incorrect. An EIS was a requirement and, in its absence, the court set aside the board's decision to grant permission.

**[2.136]** In *Friends of the Curragh Environment Limited v An Bord Pleanála and Ors*,[144] it was held that a planning authority must assess not only the impact which the development will have on the environment as it is at the date of the application but it should also take into account the impact which it will have on the future of proposed related developments in respect of which no permission has been granted, when they are considering whether or not an EIA is necessary.

**[2.137]** In *Rehabilitation Institute v An Bord Pleanála*,[145] the board granted permission for a slaughter house. The Board failed to give the applicants an opportunity to submit a report on the impact which their development would have on the residents of an adjoining premises. Although the respondents did deal with the impact on human beings, they did not take account of the vulnerable group in the adjoining premises and consequently the court set aside the permission.

## Local authority exempted development

**[2.138]** Although much of the work undertaken by a local authority is exempted development, local authorities are not completely free to act without any restraint whatsoever.

---

142. *Luxembourg v Linster* (Case C287/98) [2000] ECR I–6917.
143. *Maher v An Bord Pleanála* [1999] 2 ILRM 198.
144. *Friends of the Curragh Environment Limited v An Bord Pleanála and Ors*[2006] IEHC 390.
145. *Rehabilitation Institute v An Bord Pleanála* [1988] 6 ILT 193.

**[2.139]** Local authority development may be categorised under five headings, namely:

(i) Exempted development under PDA 2000, s 4(1) sub-paras (b)–(g) inclusive.

(ii) Where development proposed by a local authority is subject to EIA, the development must be approved by An Bord Pleanála in accordance with the provisions of Pt X of PDA 2000 (as amended).[146]

(iii) PDA 2000, s 178 provides that local authorities shall not effect any development which materially contravenes its own development plan.

(iv) PDA 2000, s 179[147] allows the Minister to prescribe a development or a class of development if he or she is of the opinion that by reason of the likely size, nature or effect of the surroundings of such development or class of development there should, in relation to any such development or development belonging to such class of development, be compliance with the provisions of PDA 2000, s 179 and Pt VIII of PDR 2001, as amended, before it can be lawfully carried out.

(v) Occasionally, a local authority may have to obtain planning permission for its development. This would normally be the case where a local authority undertakes development outside its own functional area provided that the development undertaken is not otherwise exempted.[148]

**[2.140]** The following types of local authority development comprise the exempted development exclusions as listed in PDA 2000, s 4(1):

(b) development by the council of a county in its functional area, exclusive of any borough or urban district;

(c) development by the corporation of a county or other borough in that borough;

(d) development by the council of an urban district in that district;

(e) development consisting of the carrying out by the corporation of a county or other borough or the council of a county or an urban district of any

---

146. Part X deals with the requirement for an environmental impact statement in PDA 2000 (as amended), ss 172 to 177. The amendments and insertions are made to Pt X by PD(A)A 2010, ss 53, 54, 55, 56 and 57. Section 57 inserts the lengthy 'substitute consent' procedure in ss 177A to 177AE inclusive.

147. PDA 2000, s 179 has been amended by PD(A)A 2010, s 58 which provides for a special procedure which must notify prescribed bodies and members of the public of certain large development to be undertaken by a local authority affecting the surrounding area. See PD(A)A 2010, s 58 and the regulations made under that section (not yet made at the time this book went to press).

148. Part X deals with the requirement for an environmental impact statement in PDA 2000 (as amended), ss 172 to 177. The amendments and insertions are made to PDA 2000, Pt X by PD(A)A 2010, ss 53, 54, 55, 56 and 57. Section 57 inserts the lengthy 'substitute consent' procedure in ss 177A to 177AE inclusive.

works required for the construction of a new road or the maintenance or improvement of a road;

(f) development carried out on behalf of, or jointly or in partnership with, a local authority that is a planning authority, pursuant to a contract entered into by the local authority concerned, whether in its capacity as a planning authority or in any other capacity;

(g) development consisting of the carrying out by any local authority or statutory undertaker of any works for the purpose of inspecting, repairing, renewing, altering or removing any sewers, mains, pipes, cables, overhead wires, or other apparatus, including the excavation of any street or other land for that purpose.

**[2.141]** PDA 2000[149] defines a 'statutory undertaker' as meaning a person, for the time being, authorised by or under any enactment or instrument under an enactment to:

(a) construct or operate a railway, canal, inland navigation, dock, harbour or airport;

(b) provide, or carry out works for the provision of gas, electricity or telecommunications services, or

(c) provide services connected with, or carry out works for the purposes of the carrying on of the activities of, any public undertaking.

**[2.142]** Development by a local authority which gains exemption under the provisions of s 4(1)(b), (c) and (d) is development which must be carried out within the functional area of that local authority. If development is carried on outside the local authority's functional area, planning permission must be obtained unless the development is carried out within the terms of s 4(1)(e), (f) and (g).

**[2.143]** PDA 2000[150] defines 'functional area' as being, in relation to a planning authority:

(a) in the case of the council of a county, its administrative county, excluding any borough or urban district,

(b) in the case of any other planning authority, its administrative area.

**[2.144]** Development which is undertaken by a local authority specified in s 4(1)(e), (f) and (g) gains exemption from the requirement to obtain planning permission, even though the development is carried on outside its functional area. A local authority can, without planning permission, develop a new road and maintain or improve an old road although the road is not within its functional area. A local authority can also carry out development, without planning permission, in another local authority's functional area, if it undertakes the development on behalf of or jointly or in partnership with the local authority in whose functional area the work is to be carried out.

---

149. PDA 2000, s 2(1).
150. PDA 2000, s 2(1).

**[2.145]** Section 4(1)(g) is the third exception where a local authority can carry out development outside its own functional area, but the wording in that exemption deals only with inspecting, repairing, renewing, altering or removing any sewers, mains, pipes, cables, overhead wires, or other apparatus outside its own functional area, including the excavation of any street or other land for that purpose. Clearly, planning permission will be required when a local authority wishes to lay new sewers, mains, pipes, cables, overhead wires, or other apparatus, unless that work is exempted under Sch 2 of PDR 2001 or unless the work is carried out on behalf of, or jointly or in partnership with, a local authority that is a planning authority, pursuant to a contract entered into by the local authority concerned, whether in its capacity as a planning authority or in any other capacity.

**[2.146]** The exempted development categories offered to local authorities may appear to be unacceptably wide. They are, however, subject to numerous controls and restrictions.

**[2.147]** The exemption provisions that benefit local authorities are restricted by the provisions of PDA 2000, Pt X,[151] which deal with EIA, which is required in respect of certain developments carried out by or on behalf of local authorities.

**[2.148]** PDA 2000, s 175(1) provides that where development is carried out by a local authority or a person on behalf of or jointly or in partnership with a local authority pursuant to a contract entered into by that local authority whether in its capacity as planning authority or in any other capacity with the purpose of carrying out development in the local authority's jurisdiction for which an EIS would be required under s 176 of the Act, the local authority must submit the development proposal accompanied by an EIS for the approval of An Bord Pleanála. Work may not commence on the proposed development unless the board has approved the application with or without modifications.

**[2.149]** PDR 2001[152] provides that before making an application for approval to the board under PDA 2000, s 175(3), a local authority may, in accordance with art 95, as amended by PDR 2006, art 24, request the board to provide a written opinion on the information to be contained in the EIS. This is known as a scoping request.

**[2.150]** The following documents must be accompanied with the documents to be lodged on application to the board for approval, namely:

(a) three copies of plans and particulars of the proposed development,

(b) three copies of the EIS for the proposed development,

(c) one copy of the notice published under s 175(4)(a) of the Act, and

---

151. PDA 2000, s 175(1) to (14) as amended by the European Communities (Environmental Impact Assessment) (Amendment) Regulations 2006 (SI 659/2006) and by PD(SI)A 2006, s 34(a), (b) and (c) and LGA 2001, s 247.
152. PDR 2001 arts 117 and 118.

(d) a list of the bodies to which notice was sent under s 175(4)(b) of the Act and an indication of the date on which the notice was sent.

**[2.151]** PDR 2001[153] requires that where a local authority proposes to carry out a sub-threshold development and where it considers that the development would be likely to have significant effects on the environment, it shall prepare, or cause to be prepared, an EIS in respect thereof.

**[2.152]** PDR 2001[154] provides that where a local authority proposes to carry out a sub-threshold development which would be located on or in:

(a) a European site;

(b) an area the subject of a notice under s 16(2)(b) of the Wildlife (Amendment) Act 2000;

(c) an area designated as a natural heritage area under s 18 of the Wildlife (Amendment) Act 2000;

(d) land established or recognised as a nature reserve within the meaning of s 15 or 16 of the Wildlife Act 1976 as amended by ss 26 and 27 of the Wildlife (Amendment) Act 2000; or

(e) land designated as a refuge for flora or as a refuge for fauna under s 17 of the Wildlife Act 1976, as amended by s 28 of the Wildlife (Amendment) Act 2000.

The local authority concerned shall decide whether the development would or would not be likely to have significant effects on the environment of such site, area or land, as appropriate.

## Development which is subject to EIA

**[2.153]** PDA 2000, s 176(1) now reads as follows:

> The Minister shall, for the purpose of giving effect to the Environmental Impact Assessment Directive, make regulations—[155]
>
> (a) identifying development which may have significant effects on the environment, and
>
> (b) specifying the manner in which the likelihood that such development would have significant effects on the environment is to be determined.

**[2.154]** PDA 2000, s 176(2) provides a detailed list of the matters in respect of which regulations may be made. If local authority development comes within a class of development prescribed by PDA 2000, s 176 (as amended) for the purposes of an EIA the local authority's development is subject to approval of the development by An Bord Pleanála. This approval must be sought by the local authority whether or not the development is being carried out by the local authority on its own initiative or by the

---

153. PDR 2001, art 120(1).
154. PDR 2001, art 120(2).
155. PDA 2000, s 176(1) has been amended by PD(A)A 2010, s 56.

local authority with any other party and it also applies whether or not the development is carried out within or outside its own functional area.

**[2.155]** PDA 2000, s 176(2) reads:

> Without prejudice to the generality of subsection (1), regulations under that subsection may provide for all or any one or more of the following matters:
>
> (a) the establishment of thresholds or criteria for the purpose of determining which classes of development are likely to have significant effects on the environment;
>
> (b) the establishment of different such thresholds or criteria in respect of different classes of areas;
>
> (c) the determination on a case-by-case basis, in conjunction with the use of thresholds or criteria, of the developments which are likely to have significant effects on the environment;
>
> (d) where thresholds or criteria are not established, the determination on a case-by-case basis of the developments which are likely to have significant effects on the environment;
>
> (e) the identification of selection criteria in relation to —
>
>   (i) the establishment of thresholds or criteria for the purpose of determining which classes of development are likely to have significant effects on the environment, or
>
>   (ii) the determination on a case-by-case basis of the developments which are likely to have significant effects on the environment.

**[2.156]** PDA 2000, s 176(3) provides that:

> Any reference in an enactment to development of a class specified under Article 24 of the European Communities (Environmental Impact Assessment) Regulations 1989 (SI 349/1989), shall be deemed to be a reference to a class of development prescribed under this section.

## Local authority development which contravenes the materiality of its own development plan

**[2.157]** PDA 2000, s 178 provides that local authority development materially contravening that local authority's own development plan is not exempted development even where the development is proposed within its own functional area. The courts can and do prevent local authorities from carrying out development which is in material contravention of that local authority's own development plan. PDA 2000, s 15(1) imposes a general duty on a planning authority to secure the objectives of its development plan noting that 'it shall be the duty of a planning authority to take such steps within its powers as may be necessary for securing the objectives of the development plan'. The circumstances in which action can be taken as a means of enforcing statutory provisions may give rise to difficulty. A breach of statutory duty will not always give rise to a cause of action. In *Attorney General (McGarry) v Sligo County*

*Council*,[156] McCarthy J steered away from any attempt to directly enforce PDA 2000, s 15(1); rather, he considered that the development plan:

> forms an environmental contract between the planning authority, the council and the community, embodying a promise by the council that it will regulate development in a manner consistent with the objective stated in the plan and, further, that the council itself shall not affect any development which contravenes the plan materially.

**[2.158]** The development plan as an environmental contract is a concept which, in one way or another, has found favour in the courts and many cases of material contravention imply that there is an environmental contract between the local authority and the community or, at the very least, that the development plan, as a document which is developed for the common good, is a document which cannot be tampered with and which must be interpreted strictly in accordance with the published plan. A development plan is a document which sometimes offers enormous gains and you do not see too many examples of landowners or developers rushing to court to contradict it where their land has been re-zoned for housing or other valuable development. Conversely, because the development plan is for the good of the community it can and does, undoubtedly, impose hardship on many people who are affected adversely by it. See *Byrne v Fingal County Council*,[157] where an applicant sought to prevent the development of a local authority traveller's halting site on the basis that the development involved a material contravention of the local authority's development plan. McKechnie J held that the provision of halting sites was a clear objective of the local authority and that in those circumstances there could be no material contravention of the development plan. It is the plan as a whole which must be considered and not necessarily a single or a particular provision of the plan. There is no definition of 'material contravention' of a development plan but Professor Yvonne Scannell[158] has researched and listed a number of helpful examples of what the courts have considered as material contraventions and these are reproduced here with the kind permission of the author.

(a) Granting outline permission for a housing estate in an area zoned to provide for the further development of agriculture and to preserve open space amenity: see *State (Pine Valley Developments Ltd) v Dublin County Council*.[159]

(b) Granting planning permission for a bungalow to be built in close proximity to a national monument listed for preservation in the development plan: see *Dublin County Council v Marron*.[160]

(c) Developing a landfill near a site containing archaeological remains which the development plan had listed for preservation: see *Attorney General (McGarry) v Sligo County Council*.[161]

---

156. *Attorney General (McGarry) v Sligo County Council* [1991] 1 IR 99.
157. *Byrne v Fingal County Council* [2001] 4 IR 565 *per* McKechnie J.
158. Scannell, *Environmental and Land Use Law* (Thomson Round Hall, 2005), p 146.
159. *State (Pine Valley Developments Ltd) v Dublin County Council* [1994] IR 407.
160. *Dublin County Council v Marron* [1985] ILRM 593.
161. *Attorney General (McGarry) v Sligo County Council* [1991] 1 IR 99.

(d) Undertaking to permit industrial buildings, as a hotel and entertainment structure, on lands zoned for agricultural uses: *Grange Development Ltd v Dublin County Council*.[162]

(e) Building a traveller halting site on lands zoned high amenity and along side a national primary route: *O'Leary v Dublin County Council*[163] (halting site and land zoned high amenity) and *Lally v Mayo County Council*[164] (building a halting site along side a national primary route).

(f) Directing that planning permission be granted for a new access to a dual carriageway: *Sharpe v Dublin City and Council Manager*[165] (access to a dual carriageway) and *Griffin v Galway County Manager*[166] (access to national primary route).

(g) Directing the grant of planning permission for houses, a hotel and offices on lands zoned for industrial use: *Kenny Homes v Galway City Manager.*[167] And,

(h) Granting planning permission for a housing scheme which contravened the density provisions of the development plan: *Tennyson v Dun Laoghaire Corporation.*[168]

**[2.159]** The prohibition against material contravention of a local authority's development plan contained in PDA 2000, s 178 has been dis-applied under the provisions of other legislation, to include:

(a) The Housing (Traveller Accommodation) Act 1998, which contains an express requirement that a housing authority shall include objectives in relation to the provision of accommodation for travellers in its development plan.

(b) PDA 2000, s 10(2)(i) provides that a development plan shall include objectives for the provision of accommodation for travellers and the use of particular areas for that purpose.

(c) Under s 20 of the Roads Act 1993, the National Roads Authority (NRA) may direct a local authority to carry out road works under the Act even though those road works are in material contravention of its own development plan. Nevertheless, the NRA must think carefully before giving such a direction because where a direction is given to a local authority directing it to carry out certain road works which are in material contravention of that local authority's own development plan, in those circumstances, s 20(2) of the Roads Act 1993

---

162. *Grange Development Ltd v Dublin County Council* [1986] IR 246.
163. *O'Leary v Dublin County Council* [1998] IR 150.
164. *Lally v Mayo County Council* (unreported, 8 February 1985) Circuit Court, Osmond J.
165. *Sharpe v Dublin City and Council Manager* [1989] IR 701.
166. *Griffin v Galway County Manager* (unreported, 31 October 1990) HC, Blaney J.
167. *Kenny Homes v Galway City Manager* [1995] 1 IR 178.
168. *Tennyson v Dun Laoghaire Corporation* [1991] 2 IR 527.

requires the NRA to follow a specific procedure and to attend to the following matters:

(i) In making such a direction the NRA must publish notice in a newspaper circulated in the area where the works are to be carried out stating that it proposes to issue a direction and that objections or representations may be made in writing to the NRA in relation to the proposed direction within a period of not less than one month of the date of publication of the notice.

(ii) The NRA must also serve notice on the road authority and if the road authority is not the planning authority it must serve notice on the planning authority as well stating that it proposes to issue a direction and that objections and representations may be made in writing to it within a period of one month from the date of its notice. In each case it is within a period of not less than one month from the date of its notice.

(iii) If objections or representations are received and are not withdrawn the NRA must consider those objections and representations.

(d) Another circumstance in which the material contravention procedure is disapplied arises under the Waste Management Acts 1996–2001 (as amended by the Protection of the Environment Act 2003). Section 22 of the Waste Management Act 1996, which has been specifically amended by the Waste Management (Amendment) Act 2001,[169] provides that the manager of the local authority may decide to proceed with development which is inconsistent with the development plan but is necessary for the proper implementation of a waste management plan in force in relation to the area concerned. Before taking such a step the manager must publish notice of the local authority's intention to carry out the proposed development in one or more newspapers circulating in that functional area and it must invite submissions and observations which submissions and observations, if received, must be considered by the manager. Submissions and observations in writing in relation to the proposal must be received not later than four weeks after the publication of the newspaper notice.

## *Public consultation procedure*

**[2.160]** At first sight the amount of exempted development which is permitted to local authorities under PDA 2000, s 4(1) would seem to offer the local authorities a very easy passage. When PDA 2000, s 179 and the provisions of Pt 8 of PDR 2001–2010 are taken into account, it will be appreciated that local authorities will have to think carefully about whether or not their development proposal is or is not exempted, before proceeding with development.

---

169. See Waste Management Act 1996, s 22(10)(c) as inserted by the Waste Management (Amendment) Act 2001.

**[2.161]** The public consultation procedure is not dissimilar to the statutory procedure providing for the application for planning permission. PDR 2001, art 81, as amended by PDR 2006, art 17, deals with the notice to be given in respect of development proposals made by a local authority

**[2.162]** 'Proposed development' is defined in Pt 8. It consists of development to be carried out by a local authority which is de-exempted. Where local authority development does not have the benefit of the exemption provided for in PDA 2000, s 4(1), art 81 of PDR 2001 provides that the local authority must give notice of the proposed development in an approved newspaper.[170] It must also erect a site notice, or notices on the land where the proposed development is to take place.[171] The notice shall state that the local authority intends to carry out development and indicate the location, townland or postal address of the proposed development, as appropriate. It also indicates the nature and the extent of the development.[172]

**[2.163]** If the proposed development consists of the carrying out of works which would materially affect the character of a protected structure or a proposed protected structure, or if it comprises the carrying out of works to the exterior of a structure which is located within an architectural conservation area or an area specified as an architectural conservation area in a draft of a proposed development plan or a proposed variation of a development plan and the development would materially affect the character of the area concerned, that fact must be indicated. The local authority must state that the plans and particulars in relation to the development will be available for inspection during office hours at the offices of the local authority and that copies may be purchased at a price not exceeding the reasonable cost of making such copies. The plans and particulars are open for inspection and for purchase, at a fee not exceeding the reasonable costs of making a copy, for six weeks beginning on the day that the newspaper notice is published. The notices published by the local authority in relation to the application invite submissions or observations with respect to the proposed development, dealing with the proper planning and sustainable development of the area in which the development would be situated. Submissions and observations may be made in writing to the local authority before a date specified in the notice (which date shall not be less than two weeks after the end of the inspection period which is a six week period).[173]

**[2.164]** Article 81 also provides that the site notice must be inscribed in indelible ink and affixed on rigid durable material and be secured against damage from bad weather or other causes. The site notice must be securely erected or affixed in a conspicuous position near the main entrance to the land concerned from a public road or if there is more than one entrance from the public roads at each entrance or near all such entrances or on any other part of the land or structure adjoining a public road so that it can be

---

170. PDR 2001, art 81(1)(a).
171. PDR 2001, art 81(1)(b).
172. PDR 2001, art 81(2)(a) and (b).
173. PDR 2001, art 81(2)(c)(i) and (ii), and (d)(i) and (ii). See amendments of art 81 in PDR 2006, art 17.

easily visible and legible by persons using the public road. It shall not be obscured or concealed at any time. Where the land does not adjoin a public road a site notice must be erected or affixed in a conspicuous position on the land as to be easily visible and legible by persons outside the land. A site notice shall be erected or affixed on the land or structure concerned not later than the day of publication of the newspaper notice and it must be left in position for a period of at least four weeks after publication of the newspaper notice. If it is removed, or becomes defaced or illegible, it must be renewed and replaced.[174]

**[2.165]** Article 82 deals with the notice of proposed development to certain bodies. A notice of proposed development must be sent to various bodies in different circumstances and these are set out in art 82(3) which has been significantly amended and extended by PDR 2006. Article 82(3) must be used in the context of the 2006 amendments and additions. The notice to be served under art 82(1) by the local authority shall indicate the location, townland or postal address of the proposed development and indicate its nature and extent. The notice invites submissions and observations from the recipient dealing with the proper planning and sustainable development of the area to be submitted to the authority within a time limit specified by it which shall be not less than two weeks after the end of the inspection period. The notice served is accompanied by the plans and particulars of the proposed development.[175]

**[2.166]** PDR 2001, art 82(3) is substituted by PDR 2006, art 18 as follows:

18(1) Article 82(3) of the Regulations is substituted by the following:

(3)(a) where it appears to the authority that the land or structure is situated in an area of special amenity, whether or not an order in respect of that area has been confirmed under s 203 (or deemed to be so confirmed under s 268(1)(c)) of the Act or that the development or retention of the structure might obstruct any view or prospect of special amenity value or special interest – to An Chomhairle Ealaíon, Fáilte Ireland, and An Taisce – The National Trust for Ireland,

(b) where it appears to the authority that the development might obstruct or detract from the value of any tourist amenity or tourist amenity works – to Fáilte Ireland,

(c) where it appears to the authority that the development —

   (i) would involve the carrying of out of works to a protected structure or a proposed protected structure, or to the exterior of a structure which is located within an architectural conservation area,

   (ii) might detract from the appearance of a structure referred to in sub-paragraph (i),

---

174. PDR 2001, art 81(3), (4) and (5).
175. See PDR 2001, art 82(2)(a) and (b).

(iii) might effect or be unduly close to —

    (I) a cave, site, feature or other object of archaeological, geological, scientific, ecological or historical interest,

    (II) a monument or place recorded under s 12 of the National Monuments (Amendment) Act 1994 (No 17 of 1994),

    (III) a historic monument or archaeological area entered in the Register of Historic Monuments under s 5 of the National Monuments (Amendment) Act 1987 (No 17 of 1987),

    (IV) a national monument in the ownership or guardianship of the Minister under the National Monuments Acts, 1930–1994 or

(iv) might obstruct any scheme for improvement of the surroundings of, or any means of access to, any structure, place, feature or object referred to in sub-paragraph (iii),

to the Minister, the Heritage Council and An Taisce – The National Trust for Ireland, and in the case of development of a type referred to in sub-paragraph (i) or (ii) An Chomhairle Ealaíon and Fáilte Ireland,

(d) where it appears to the authority that the area of another local authority might be affected by the development – to that local authority,

(e) where it appears to the authority that the development would not be consistent with or would materially contravene any regional planning guidelines (or any objective thereof) of a regional authority – to that regional authority.

(f) where it appears to the authority that if permission were granted, a condition should be attached under s 34(4)(m) of the Act – to any local authority (other than the planning authority) who would be affected by such condition.

(g) where it appears to the authority that —

    (i) the development might cause the significant abstraction or additional of water either to or from surface or ground waters, whether naturally occurring or artificial,

    (ii) the development might give rise to significant discharges of polluting matters or other materials to such waters or be likely to cause serious water pollution or the danger of such pollution, or

    (iii) the development would involve the carrying out of works in, over, along or adjacent to the banks of such waters, or to any structure in, over or along the banks of such waters which might materially affect the waters,

– to the appropriate Regional Fisheries Board and, in any case where the waters concerned are listed in Part I of Annex I of the Schedule to the British – Irish Agreement Act 1999 (No 1) of 1999, to Waterways Ireland,

(h) where it appears to the authority that the development might endanger or interfere with the safety of, or the safe and efficient navigation of aircraft – to the Irish Aviation Authority,

(i) where it appears to the authority that the development might interfere with the operation and development of a licensed airport whose annual traffic is not less than one million passenger movements – to the airport operator,

(j) where the development may have an impact on bus or rail-based transport – to Córas Iompair Éireann and the Railway Procurement Agency, as appropriate,

(k) where it appears that —

    (i) the development consists of or comprises the formation, laying or material widening of an access to a national road within the meaning of section 2 of the Roads Act 1993 (No 14 of 1993), not being a national road within a built-up area within the meaning of section 45 of the Road Traffic Act 1961, or

    (ii) the development might give rise to a significant increase in the volume of traffic using a national road,

– to the National Road Authority

(l) where the development might significantly impact on surface transport in the Greater Dublin Area, the Dublin Transportation Office (or any body that replaces that office),

(m) where the development comprises or is for the purposes of an activity requiring an integrated pollution control licence or a waste licence – to the Environmental Protection Agency,

(n) where it appears to the authority that the development might have significant effects in relation to nature conservation – to the Heritage Council, the Minister and An Taisce – the National Trust for Ireland,

(o) where the development is in a Gaeltacht area and it appears to the authority that it might materially affect the linguistic and cultural heritage of the Gaeltacht, including the promotion of Irish as the community language – to the Minister for Community, Rural and Gaeltacht Affairs and Údarás na Gaeltachta,

(p) where the development is in the vicinity of an explosive factory, storage magazine or local authority explosives store – to the Minister for Justice, Equality and Law Reform,

(q) where it appears to the authority that the development might have significant effects on public health – to the Health Service Executive,

(r) where the application relates to extraction of minerals within the meaning of the Minerals Development Acts, 1940 to 1995 – to the Minister for Communications, Marine and Natural Resources,

(s) where it appears to the authority that the development might impact on the foreshore – to the Minister for Communications, Marine and Natural Resources,

(t) where the development might —

    (i) give rise to a significant increase in the volume or type of traffic, (including construction traffic) passing under a height restricted railway bridge or using a railway level crossing, or a bridge over a railway,

(ii) because of its proximity to a railway, impact on the structural integrity of railway infrastructure during construction of the development, or

(iii) endanger or interfere with the safe operation of a railway, during or after construction,

– to the railway operator, the Railway Safety Commission, and, in the case of development which might impact on a light railway or metro, the Railway Procurement Agency,

(u) where the application relates to —

(i) the extraction of minerals, other than minerals within the meaning of the Minerals Development Acts 1940–1999, whether by surface or underground means,

(ii) the development of, or extensions to, quarries, including sand or gravel pits, for the extraction of earth materials, or

(iii) a development which, for other purposes, requires excavation of earth materials greater than a total volume of 50,000 m3 or the excavation of earth materials on a site area greater than 1 hectare

– to the Minister for Communications, Marine & Natural Resources

(2) Article 82(4) of the Regulations is amended by the substitution of "Fáilte Ireland" for "Bord Fáilte Éireann".

[2.167] PDR 2001–2008, art 83[176] provides that the local authority must make available for inspection the documents, particulars and plans describing the nature of the proposed development and the principal features thereof including:

(i) where the proposed development would consist of or comprise the provision of houses, the number of house to be provided,

(ii) where the proposed development would relate to a protected structure or a proposed protected structure, an indication of that fact,

(iii) where the proposed development would comprise or be for the purposes of an activity requiring an integrated pollution control licence or a waste licence, an indication of that fact.[177]

[2.168] The location map must be drawn on a scale of not less than 1:1,000 in built up areas and 1:1,250 in all other areas. The scale must be shown on the map and the map must be coloured or marked clearly to identify the land on which it is proposed to carry out the proposed development.

[2.169] Except in the case of development of new roads or widening of existing roads or in the case of the construction of a bridge or tunnel,[178] the documents must include a site layout plan drawn on a scale of not less than 1:500 showing the boundary of the site on which it is proposed to carry out the proposed development and the buildings or other

---

176. PDR 2001, art 83 as amended by PDR 2006, art 19.
177. PDR 2001, art 83(1)(a).
178. PDR 2001, art 83(1)(b) and (c).

structures, and roads or other features, in the vicinity of the site, and also such other plans and drawings, drawn to a scale of not less than 1:100, as are necessary to describe the proposed development. If the proposed development consists of the construction of new roads of widening or realignment of existing roads, etc, the plans and drawings must be drawn to a scale of not less than 1:2,500 and if the proposed development comprises the construction of a bridge or tunnel the plans and drawings must be drawn to a scale of not less than 1:200.

[2.170] A local authority shall make available for inspection or purchase on payment of a specified fee not exceeding the reasonable cost of making such a copy, a copy of the documents referred to above and a copy of any submissions or observations received by the authority in respect of the proposed development during office hours at the offices of the authority.[179]

[2.171] PDA 2000[180] requires the manager of a local authority to prepare a written report in relation to the proposed development and to submit it to the members of the authority. The report is prepared after the time for receipt of submissions and observations has expired. It must comply with the requirements of PDA 2000, s 179(3)(b) and it shall:

(i) describe the nature and extent of the proposed development and the principal features thereof, and include an appropriate plan of the development and appropriate map of the relevant area,

(ii) evaluate whether or not the proposed development, would be consistent with the proper planning and sustainable development of the area to which the development relates, having regard to the provisions of the development plan and giving the reasons and the considerations for the evaluation,

(iii) list the persons or bodies who made submissions or observations with respect to the proposed development in accordance with the regulations under subsection (2),

(iv) summarise the issues, with respect to the proper planning and sustainable development of the area in which the proposed development would be situated, raised in any such submissions or observations, and give the response to the manager thereto, and

(v) recommend whether or not the proposed development should be proceeded with as proposed, or as varied or modified as recommended in the report, or should not be proceeded with, as the case may be.

[2.172] PDA 2000, s 179(4)(a) requires the members of a local authority, as soon as may be, to consider the proposed development and the report of the manager. Following consideration of the manager's report, the proposed development may be carried out as recommended in the manager's report, unless the local authority, by resolution, decides to vary or modify the development, otherwise than as recommended in the manager's report or decides not to proceed with the development. A resolution under PDA 2000,

---

179. PDR 2001, art 83(2) as amended by PDR 2006, art 19.
180. PDA 2000, s 179(3)(a) and (b).

s 179(4)(b) must be passed not later than six weeks after receipt of the manager's report. A notice must be sent out to the persons or bodies notified under art 82 or to the persons or bodies making submission or observations indicating, as the case may be, that the proposed development will be carried out, or will not be carried out, or will be carried out subject to variations and modifications, and that notice must be sent out as appropriate after the making of a resolution under s 179(4)(b) of the Act or after the expiration of a period of six weeks after receipt of the manager's report in the said section.[181]

(6) This section shall not apply to proposed development which —

- (a) consists of works of maintenance or repair other than works to a protected structure, or a proposed protected structure, which would materially affect the character of —
    - (i) the structure, or
    - (ii) any element of the structure which contributes to its special architectural, historical, archaeological, artistic, cultural, scientific, social or technical interest,[182]
- (b) is necessary for dealing urgently with any situation which the manager considers is an emergency situation calling for immediate action,
- (c) consists of works which a local authority is required to undertake —
    - (i) by or under any enactment,
    - (ii) by or under the law of the European Union, or a provision of any act adopted by the institution of the European Union, or
    - (iii) by order of a court[183]
- (d) is development in respect of which an environmental impact statement is required under section 175 or under any other enactment.

## Development prescribed for the purposes of PDA 2000, s 179[184]

[2.173] The following classes of proposed local authority development are prescribed for the purposes of s 179 and these classes are subject to the s 179 public consultation process:

- (1)(a) the construction or erection of a house,
- (b) the construction of a new road or the widening or realignment of an existing road, where the length of the new road or of the widened or realigned portion of the existing road, as the case may be, would be—
    - (i) in the case of a road in an urban area, 100 metres or more, or
    - (ii) in the case of a road in another area, 1 kilometre or more,
- (c) the construction of a bridge or tunnel,

---

181. PDA 2000, s 179(4)(a), (b) and (c).
182. Section 179(6)(a) has been substituted by PD(A)A 2010, s 58(a).
183. Section 179(6)(c) has been substituted by PD(A)A 2010, s 58(b).
184. See PDR 2001, art 80(1) and (2).

(d) the construction or erection of pumping stations, treatment works, holding tanks or outfall facilities for waste water or storm water,

(e) the construction or erection of water intake or treatment works, overground aqueducts or dams or other installations designed to hold water or to store it on a long-term basis,

(f) drilling for water supplies,

(g) construction of a swimming pool,

(h) the use of land, or the construction or erection of any installation or facility, for the disposal of waste, not being —

   (i) development which comprises or is for the purposes of an activity in relation to which a waste licence is required or

   (ii) development consisting of the provision of a bring facility which comprises not more than 5 receptacles,

(i) the use of land as a burial ground,

(j) the construction or erection of a fire station, a library or a public toilet and

(k) any development other than those specified in paragraphs (a) to (j) the estimated cost of which exceeds €126,000, not being development consisting of the laying underground of sewers, pipes, mains or other apparatus.

(2). (a) Subject to paragraph (b), this Part shall not apply to proposed development that a local authority that is a planning authority proposes to carry out outside its functional area.

(b) This Part shall apply to development of a class specified in sub-art (1)(b) or (c) that a local authority that is a planning authority proposes to carry out outside its functional area.

(c) This Part shall also apply to development which is carried out within the functional area of a local authority that is a planning authority, on behalf of, or in partnership with the local authority, pursuant to a contract with the local authority.

[2.174] Part 11, Ch 3, art 142 of PDR 2001 provides that where a local authority development requires EIA which relates to the provisions of, or modification to, an establishment, notice as required by PDA 2000, s 175(4)[185] shall indicate that fact. In cases where the Major Accident Hazards Directive is relevant, the National Authority for Occupational Safety and Health (NAOSH) must be notified. In those circumstances the PDA 2000, s 179 procedure set out in s 179(3) and (4) will not apply but, rather, the notice requirements provided for in PDR 2001, art 143 are applicable in that NAOSH must be notified of the proposed development where there is risk of a major accident.[186]

[2.175] In a case where local authority development does not require EIA but where the development proposal relates to the provision of, or modification to an establishment

---

185. PDA 2000, s 175(4) has been amended by the European Communities (Environmental Impact Assessment) (Amendment) Regulations 2006 (SI 659/2006).

186. See PDR 2001, Ch 4, art 145 and PDR 2001, art 147 which provide additional notice requirements to those set out in art 82. See also PDR 2006, art 36 amending art 147(1)(b)(ii) by the substitution of 'article 27' for 'article 29'.

which could have significant repercussion, the major accident hazards shall be prescribed for the purposes of PDA 2000, s 179 and the provisions of Pt 8 shall apply.[187]

[2.176] To comply with the provisions of PDA 2000, Pt XI the manager of the local authority shall, having either received submissions or observations or, if no submissions or observations were made or the time for receipt of such have expired, prepare a report of the proposed development for consideration by the local councillors.[188]

[2.177] The manager's report shall describe the nature and extent of the proposed development and the principal features of it and the report must include an appropriate plan of the development and a map of the relevant area. The manager's report must also evaluate whether or not the proposed development would be consistent with the proper planning and sustainable development of the area to which the development relates, having regard to the provisions of the development plan. The report must give reasons and considerations for the evaluation.[189]

[2.178] The manager's report must also list the persons or bodies who have made submissions and observations with respect to the proposed development and it must summarise the issues, with respect to proper planning and sustainable development of the area in which the proposed development will be situated, raised in any submissions or observations, and give the response of the manager to such submissions and observations. Finally, the manager must make a recommendation as to whether or not the proposed development should be proceeded with as proposed, should be varied or modified as recommended in his report or should not be proceeded with at all.

[2.179] The local councillors then are required to consider the manager's report and the proposed development as soon as may be. Following the consideration of the report, the proposed development may be carried out as recommended in the manager's report, unless the local authority, by resolution, decides to vary or modify the development, otherwise then as recommended in the manager's report, or decides not to proceed with the development. The local councillors' resolution must be passed not later than six weeks from the date of receipt of the manager's report.[190]

[2.180] Certain works are excepted from the procedural requirements relating to a local authority's own development provided by PDA 2000, s 179 and the section shall not apply to a proposed development which:

    (a) consists of works of maintenance or repair, other than works to a protected structure or to a proposed protected structure which would materially affect the character of:

        (i) the structure or

---

187. See PDR 2001, Ch 4, art 145 and PDR 2001, art 147 which provide additional notice requirements to those set out in art 82. See also PDR 2006, art 36 amending art 147(1)(b)(ii) by the substitution of 'article 27' for 'article 29'.
188. PDA 2000, s 179(3)(a).
189. PDA 2000, s 179(3)(b)(i) to (v) inclusive.
190. PDA 2000, s 179(4)(a) to (c) inclusive.

　　　　　(ii) any element of the structure which contributes to its special architectural, historical, archaeological, artistic, cultural, scientific, social or technical interest.

(b) is necessary for dealing urgently with any situation which the manager considers is an emergency situation calling for immediate action,

(c) consists of works which a local authority is required to undertake:

　　　　　(i) by or under any enactment

　　　　　(ii) by or under the law of the European Union or a provision of any act adopted by an Institution of the European Union or

　　　　　(ii) by order of a court.[191]

(d) is development in respect of which an environmental impact statement is required under section 175 or under any other enactment.

Environmental impact assessment must be undertaken by and submitted by the local authority to An Bord Pleanála in relevant cases. PDA 2000[192] does not exempt the local authority from undertaking EIA and preparing an EIS for submission to An Bord Pleanála for decision. The requirement to obtain the approval of An Bord Pleanála of the local authority's EIS may be necessary even though there is no requirement to obtain planning permission as a result of the exempted development provisions. This is dealt with in more detail in considering EIA in **Ch 10**.

## Development by State authorities

**[2.181]** PDA 2000, s 2(1) defines 'State authority' as meaning:

(a) a Minister of the government, or

(b) the Commissioners;

'Commissioners' means the Commissioners of Public Works in Ireland.

It had been generally accepted that State authorities were exempted from the necessity to obtain planning permission under the Local Government (Planning and Development) Act 1963, s 24, but that there was an obligation on them to consult with the planning authority and if the planning authority raised objections the State authority would then have to consult with the Minister. The concept of automatic State exemption from the necessity to apply for planning permission was challenged in two cases:

(a) *Mullaghmore (Howard v Commissioners of Public Works)*,[193] and

(b) *Luggalla (Byrne v Commissioners of Public Works)*.[194]

---

191. PDA 2000, s 179(6)(a) substituted by PD(A)A 2010, s 58(a) and PDA 2000, s 179(6)(c) as substituted by PD(A)A 2010, s 58(b).
192. PDA 2000, s 175 as amended by LGA 2001, by PD(SI)A 2006 and by the European Communities (Environmental Impact Assessment) (Amendment) Regulations 2006.
193. *Mullaghmore (Howard v Commissioners of Public Works)* [1994] 3 IR 394.
194. *Luggalla (Byrne v Commissioners of Public Works)* (unreported, 3 December 1994) HC.

The *Mullaghmore* case concentrated solely on the argument as to whether or not exemption applied to State authorities. The Supreme Court held that development by a State authority is subject to a requirement to obtain planning permission. To allow the State to carry out development without planning permission was held to be incompatible with the Constitution. The decision in this case might also have implied that the State would have to obtain retention permission for all developments carried out by it since 1 October 1964. The Local Government (Planning and Development) Act 1993, s 4(1) provided an amnesty in respect of all State developments carried out since 1 October 1964, and s 4(2) extended that period for one year beginning on the commencement date of s 4. That time limit expired on 15 June 1994. Since that date all development carried out by State authorities requires permission for development other than exempted development.

[2.182] In general, State authorities do have to obtain planning permission for developments in the same manner as private citizens and private sector developers subject to exceptional provisions contained in PDA 2000, s 181, as amended by the PD(SI)A 2006, s 35(a) and (b), which allows the Minister to make regulations exempting certain developments from the necessity of obtaining planning permission. Strictly speaking, development exempted by the regulations made by the Minister in pursuance of PDA 2000, s 181 (as amended) is not exempted development as such. Many of these developments would only be subject to the requirements of PDR 2001–2010 and the provisions of the relevant articles contained in the Planning and Development (Strategic Environmental Assessment) Regulations 2004 (SI 436/2004). PDA 2000, s 181 has been extended considerably by the provisions of s 36 of the PD(SI)A 2006 by the addition of s 181A, which deals with approval of certain State development requiring EIS,[195] and s 181B, which provides criteria for decisions in respect of a proposed development subject to an application under ss 181A and 181C dealing with procedures in advance of seeking approval under s 181B.[196]

[2.183] PD(SI)A 2006 amends PDA 2000 in an effort to provide for the introduction of a streamlined planning consent procedure for strategic infrastructure developments, determined by a new strategic infrastructure division established within An Bord Pleanála, and to make consequential changes to the Act of 2000. As will be seen,[197] the PD(SI)A 2006 provides for a specialised planning consent procedure for major transmission lines. It also amends the Transport (Railway Infrastructure) Act 2001 to provide that An Bord Pleanála will approve railway orders, and it amends the Acquisition of Land (Assessment of Compensation) Act 1919 to provide for compensation that will be assessed for the sub-stratum of land. PDA 2000, s 37 has been expanded by the insertion of new ss 37A to 37I providing for a new strategic consent procedure for those types of infrastructure listed in a new Sch 7 which has been added to PDA 2000. Under the new strategic consent procedure, persons or bodies seeking permission for those types of strategic infrastructure apply directly to An Bord Pleanála.

---

195. Section 181A has been further amended by PD(A)A 2010, s 60.
196. Sections 181B and 181C have been further amended by PD(A)A 2010, ss 61 and 62.
197. See **Ch 11**.

**[2.184]**

If the board determines that the project in question is of strategic importance, having regard to the criteria set out in s 37A, an application, accompanied by an EIS, may be made directly to the board. The additional ss 37A to 37I inclusive set out the procedures for the initial consultations with the board, which include the making of an application, notification of the application to various persons including the planning authority or authorities, as the case may be, for the relevant area/areas and the procedures and considerations to be applied by the board in determining the application.

**[2.184]** PDA 2000, s 181(1)(a) allows the Minister, by regulation, to provide that, except for this section and ss 181A to 181C, the provisions of this Act shall not apply to any specified class or classes of development by or on behalf of a State authority where the development is, in the opinion of the Minister, in connection with or for the purposes of public safety or order, the administration of justice or national security or defence and, for so long as the regulations are in force, the provisions of this Act shall not apply to the specified class or classes of development.

**[2.185]** The Minister may then, entirely at his/her discretion, require that any class of development specified under the extended s 181 of PDA 2000 be subject to a form of public consultation. Where the development is likely to have significant effects on the environment, an EIA will be required.

**[2.186]** The new streamlined planning consent procedure for strategic infrastructure developments is, in effect, application for consent for a Sch 7 development. The permissions procedure for strategic infrastructure developments in accordance with PDA 2000, ss 37A to 37K inclusive is extended by PD(SI)A 2006, s 3. Section 37B requires that anyone applying for permission for a Sch 7 development shall, before making an application, enter into consultations with the board in relation to the proposed development.

**[2.187]** PDR 2001, Pt 9 is headed 'Provisions with Respect to Certain Developments by or on behalf of State Authorities' and comprises arts 86–91.[198] In particular, art 86 is authorised by PDA 2000, s 181(1)(a), and comprises a list of classes of development to which the permission provisions of PDA 2000 do not apply. Part 9 of PDR 2001, art 86(1), in accordance with s 181(1)(a) of PDA 2000, excludes the following classes of development from the provisions of that Act:

    (a)    development consisting of the provision of—

        (i)    Garda stations or other buildings, or other premises or installations, or other structures or facilities, used for the purposes of or in connection with the operations of An Garda Síochána,

        (ii)    prisons or other places of detention,

        (iii)    courthouses or other buildings, or other premises or installations, or other structures or facilities, whether provided on a permanent or a temporary basis, used for the purposes of or in connection

---

198. Note that PDR 2001 arts 87, 88 and 89 have been amended by PDR 2006, arts 20, 21 and 22 respectively.

with the transaction of any business relating to courts, tribunals, inquiries or inquests established by statute,

(iv) barracks or other buildings, or other premises or installations (including air fields and naval yards), or other structures or facilities, used for the purpose of or in connection with the operations of the Defence Forces,

(v) office buildings or other premises used for the purposes of or in connection with the business of Uachtarán Na hÉireann, Dáil Éireann, Seanad Éireann, the Department of the Taoiseach, the Office of the Tánaiste, the Department of Defence, the Department of Foreign Affairs, the Department of Justice, Equality and Law Reform, the Court Service, the Office of the Attorney General, the Chief State Solicitor's Office and the Office of the Director of Public Prosecutions,

(b) (i) development consisting of the provision of an extension of any building referred to in paragraph (a) where such extension will be situated, in whole or in part, outside the curtilage of the existing building or where building is situated within a premises or other installation referred to in the said paragraph outside the curtilage of premises or other installation,

(ii) development consisting of the provision of an extension of a premises or other installation, other than a building, referred to in paragraph (a) which will extend the premises or other installation beyond the curtilage of the existing premises or other installation;

(c) subject to paragraph (e), where any building, premises or other installation referred to in paragraph (a) is a protected structure or a proposed protected structure any works which would materially affect the character of the protected structure or proposed protected structure;[199]

(d) development consisting of the carrying out of any works within, or bounding the curtilage of a building, premises or other installation referred to in paragraph (a), insofar as the works are incidental to the use of such building, premises or installation;

(e) (i) development consisting of the carrying out of any works, for reasons of national security, within, or bounding, the curtilage of any building, premises or other installation occupied by, or under the control of a State authority, other than a building, premises or other installation referred to in paragraph (a),

(ii) development consisting of the carrying out by or on behalf of a State authority, for reasons of national security, of any works within, or bounding, the curtilage of the residence of a holder, or

---

199. It is hard to see how there can be any justifiable reason for exempting protected structures or proposed protected structures which are government owned structures. Many of the structures and buildings mentioned in art 86(1)(a) are in fact protected structures or proposed protected structures and there is no justifiable reason as to why protection should not be afforded to those structures and buildings also.

former holder, of public office or any public servant or former public servant,

(iii) development consisting of the carrying out, by or on behalf of a State authority in connection with the administration of justice, of any works within, or bounding, the curtilage of the residence of a person in receipt of protection of An Garda Síochána

**[2.188]** Article 86(2):

For the purposes of this article, a building, premises, installation, structure or facility may be provided by the carrying out of works or by the making of a material change in the use of a building, premise, installation, structure or facility.

**[2.189]** Article 87 deals with public notice required for proposed developments undertaken by or on behalf of State authorities being developments contemplated within the scope of art 86(1)(a), (b) and (c).[200] PDR 2000, art 87(1), as substituted by PDR 2006, s 20, now reads as follows:

(1) This article shall apply to classes of development specified in article 86(1)(a), (b) or (c) other than —

(a) Development consisting of the construction or erection of such temporary structures for the purposes of or in connection with the operations of the Defence Forces or An Garda Síochána as are urgently required for reasons of national security, or

(b) Development identified as likely to have significant effects on the environment in accordance with section 176 of the Act,

and the development to which this article applies is hereafter in this Part referred to as 'proposed development'.

(2) Articles 87(3)(c)(ii) and (4)(a)(iv)(II) of the Regulations are amended by the deletion of 'or an area specified as an architectural conservation area in a draft of a proposed development plan or a proposed variation of a development plan.

Developments contemplated by art 86(1)(d) and (e) are not subject to the notification requirements. Temporary structures erected for the purposes of or in connection with operations of the Defence Forces and An Garda Síochána as are urgently required for reasons of national security are also excluded from the notification requirement.

**[2.190]** Article 87(3)(d) requires that drawings and particulars of the proposed development are made available for inspection at the head offices of the State authority and at a specified location in the area in which the proposed development will be situated to be viewed at specified times for a period of six weeks beginning from the date of publication of the notice. The s 87 notice also invites submissions and observations dealing with the proper planning and sustainable development of the area to be made in writing within a period of six weeks beginning on the date of publication of the notice.

---

200. Note that art 87(1) of the regulations has been substituted by PDR 2006, art 20(1).

**[2.191]** Article 87(4)(a) requires that a site notice be affixed giving details of the location of the development proposal, its nature and extent and the times at which the drawings and other documents may be inspected. If works have to be carried out that would materially affect the character of a protected structure or of a proposed protected structure that must be mentioned in the site notice. Also if the carrying out of works to the exterior of the structure, which is located within an architectural conservation area or an area specified as an architectural conservation area, will materially affect the character of the area concerned, that too must be mentioned on the site notice. That notice must also specify that submissions and observations may be made stating the time in which they must be lodged with the State authority.

**[2.192]** Article 87(4)(b) provides that the notice must be secured against the weather. It must be in a conspicuous position near the main entrance and visible from a public road at or near all entrances to the site or structure if the structure concerned does not adjoin a public road, the site notice must be erected in a conspicuous position on the land or structure so as to be easily visible and legible by persons outside the land or structure and it must not be either obscured or concealed at any time. A site notice must be in position for at least four weeks from the date of publication of a newspaper notice and if removed or damaged must be renewed or replaced.

**[2.193]** Article 88, as amended by PDR 2006, art 21, deals with notice of proposed development which is to be given to certain bodies in relation to art 86 structures and premises.

**[2.194]** Article 89, as amended by PDR 2006, art 22, deals with the availability for inspection of plans and particulars in relation to art 86 structures and premises.

**[2.195]** Article 90 requires a State authority to 'have regard' to certain matters in relation to art 86 structures and premises.

**[2.196]** Article 91 deals with the notice of decision in respect of proposed development of State building and structures within the meaning of art 86. Under the 1994 Regulations, notice of the decision with respect to the proposed development had to be furnished within three days from the date of the decision. That has been replaced by that awful and indefinite phrase 'as soon as may be' after the making of the decision.

## Approval of certain State developments requiring EIA

**[2.197]** Where a State authority development is likely to have significant effects on the environment or adverse effects on the integrity of a European site as the case may be, an assessment procedure will be performed by An Bord Pleanála and the proposed development will not be carried out unless the board has approved it.[201] The relevant State authority shall submit an EIS or a Natura[202] impact statement or both of those

---

201. PDA 2000, s 181(1)(a) and (b) as inserted by PD(SI)A 2006 and amended by PD(A)A 2010, ss 60 and 61.
202. Natura 2000 is a network of protected areas covering private and national habitat sites and species of particular importance for the conservation of biodiversity within the EU.

statements, as the case may be, to An Bord Pleanála. On receipt of the EIS, the board will conduct an EIA on the development, and if the board invites the State authority to alter the terms of the proposed development then a further notice is required together with a revised EIS or a revised Natura impact statement or both of those documents as the case may be.

**[2.198]** Development undertaken by State authorities, unlike local authority development, is not generally exempt from the requirement to obtain planning permission. However, PDR 2001, art 86 lists specific developments, mainly involving security issues, which are exempt, to include such things as prisons, barracks, garda stations, courthouses, etc. Article 87[203] provides that the State authority must give public notice of the development proposal as described in PDR 2001, art 86 other than development of temporary structures for the Defence Forces or An Garda Síochána as are urgently required for reasons of national security.

**[2.199]** The notice required must be published in an approved newspaper and must be exhibited on a site notice where the proposed development is to be located. The notices shall identify the State authority which will carry out the development and also indicate the location, townland and address of the proposed development. The notice shall also describe (briefly) the nature and extent of the proposed development.[204]

**[2.200]** If the proposed development relates to a protected structure or to a proposed protected structure or if it relates to the exterior of a structure located in an architectural conservation area and the development would materially affect the character of the area concerned, that state of affairs must be indicated in the notices published. The notices shall also invite submissions from members of the public to be lodged within six weeks of the date of the newspaper notice.[205]

**[2.201]** PDA 2000, s 181A[206] provides that State authority development which will have adverse effects on the environment or adverse effects on the integrity of a European site will require approval from An Bord Pleanála and the application to the board must include an EIS or a Natura impact statement or both as the case may be. A copy of the application and the EIS must be sent to the local authority or, as necessary, to the local authorities in whose area the proposed development will occur. Similar notices must also be given to prescribed bodies where relevant and any body which receives such notice is invited to make submissions to the board in relation to:

(I) The implication of the proposed development for the proper planning and sustainable development in the area concerned, and

---

203. PDR 2001, art 87 as amended by PDR 2006, art 20.
204. PDR 2001, art 87 as amended by PDR 2006, art 20.
205. Note that the regulations above referred to are part of the specific regulations made by the relevant Minister under the provisions of PDA 2000, s 181.
206. PDA 2000, s 181A was inserted by PD(SI)A 2006, s 36 and amended by PD(A)A 2010, s 60.

(II) The likely effects on the environment and on the integrity of a European site as the case may be.

If the board is of the opinion that permission for the proposed development should be granted subject to alteration the board may request submission of further information and it may invite the State authority to alter the proposed development and to submit further information concerning the alteration along with a revised EIS, if required.[207]

[2.202] If the board is of the opinion that any further information received by it from the State authority contains significant information concerning affects on the environment or adverse effects on the integrity of a European site as the case may be or the likely consequences for the proper planning and sustainable development of the area where the proposed development will be located, the board will require the State authority to publish further notice to the public and send further notice to the local authority and to prescribed bodies inviting further submissions and observations within a period of not less than three weeks from the date of the notice.

[2.203] PDA 2000, s 181B[208] sets out the criteria for the board to consider in making a determination on the application of a State authority for permission to develop where the proposed development requires either an EIS or a Natura impact statement, or both of these statements as the case may be. In carrying out EIA under s 181B the board must consider:

(a) The environmental impact statement or Natura impact statement or both of those statements as the case may be submitted pursuant to section 181(A)(1) or (4), any submissions or observations made in accordance with section 181(A)(3) or (7) and any other information furnished in accordance with section 181(A)(4) relating to—

(i) the likely consequences for proper planning and sustainable development in the area in which it is proposed to situate the proposed development of such development, and

(ii) the likely effects on the environment or adverse effects on the integrity of a European site,

and

(b) The report of any recommendations of a person conducting any oral hearing relating to the proposed development.[209]

In exceptional circumstances (which are not defined) the board may grant a State authority an exemption from the requirement to prepare an EIS or a Natura impact statement or both of those statements as the case may be. No such exemption can be granted by the board if another Member State or a State which is a party to the

---

207. PDA 2000, s 181A(4) as inserted by PD(SI)A 2006, s 36.
208. PDA 2000, s 181B inserted by PD(SI)A 2006, s 36 as amended by PD(A)A 2010, s 61.
209. PDA 2000, s 181B inserted by PD(SI)A 2006, s 36 and as amended by PD(A)A 2010, s 61(a), (b) and (c).

Transboundary Convention[210] has indicated that it wishes to express views on the effects on the environment which the proposed development will have in that State.[211]

[2.204] In granting an exemption in exceptional circumstances the board shall consider whether:

    (a)  The effects, if any, of the proposed development on the environment or adverse effects, if any, of the proposed development on the integrity of a European site should be assessed in some other manner, and

    (b)  The information arising from such assessment should be made available to members of the public, and it may apply such requirements regarding these matters in relation to the application for approval as it considers necessary or appropriate.[212]

The Minister for Defence may grant exemption for State authority developments both in relation to Board approval and in relation to the necessity to submit an EIS in circumstances where the application to the board and the submission of an EIS would have adverse effects on national defence. Notice of any such exemption granted must be published in *Iris Oifigiúil* and in one daily newspaper circulating in the area. Notice of such exemption, together with details of any information given to members of the public, must be furnished to the Commission of the European Communities.[213]

[2.205] The Board in making a decision on the application under s 181A may:

    (a)  approve the proposed development,

    (b)  make such modifications to the proposed development as it specifies in the approval and approve the proposed development as so modified,

    (c)  approve, in part only, the proposed development (with or without specified modifications of it of the foregoing kind), or

    (d)  refuse to approve the proposed development,

and may attach to an approval under paragraph (a), (b) or (c) such conditions as it considers appropriate.[214]

[2.206] PDA 2000, s 181B(7), as inserted by PD(SI)A 2006, permits the board to include a condition which would amount to a substantial planning gain for the community. This reward for the community can either be in the form of a construction of a facility or the provision of a service. There is, however, a limit placed on the substantial gain to the community and s 181B(8) provides that the substantial community gain shall not require the developer to commit an amount of financial resources as would substantially deprive him/her of the benefits likely to accrue from the grant of approval. No substantive guidance is offered by the legislation either as to the cost of the community gain to be provided by the developer other than it should be a

---

210.  PDA 2000, s 181B(2) as inserted by PD(SI)A 2006, s 36 and amended by PD(A)A 2010, s 61(a) and (b).

211.  PDA 2000, s 181B(2) as inserted by PD(SI)A 2006, s 36 and amended by PD(A)A 2010, s 61(a) and (b).

212.  PDA 2000, s 181B(3)(a) and (b) as amended by PD(A)A 2010, s 61(c).

213.  PDA 2000, s 181B(6) as inserted by PD(SI)A 2006.

214.  PDA 2000, s 181B(6)(a) to (d) inclusive, as inserted by PD(SI)A 2006.

'substantial gain' or as to the level of deprivation which a developer must suffer before he can cry:

> You have gone too far. If I pay that much there will be nothing or very little left for me.

However, sub-ss (9) and (10) allow for regulations to be made.

[2.207] Section 181B(13) protects both the State and the board from having to disclose any details of the internal arrangements for development which might facilitate unauthorised entry or exit to and from the premises to be developed. Thus it would not be possible to obtain copies of the plans for, for example, a prison which has been constructed or which is proposed to be constructed.

[2.208] PDA 2000, s 181C, as inserted by PD(SI)A 2006, s 36 and as amended by PD(A)A 2010, s 62, requires State authorities to have pre-planning consultations with the board before the application and the accompanying EIS are lodged. Unlike the pre-planning consultations for planning applications under PDA 2000, s 247, which are discretionary, the s 181C pre-planning consultations are mandatory. The Board may give advice generally or it may advise, in particular, regarding:

(a) the procedures involved in making the application, and

(b) what considerations, related to proper planning and sustainable development, the environment or a European site, may, in the opinion of the Board have a bearing on its decision in relation to the application.[215]

Section 181C(3)[216] is helpful in that it allows a prospective applicant to request the board to make a determination as to whether development of a class specified in regulations made under s 181(1)(a), which the developer intends to carry out or to have carried out, is likely to have significant effects on the environment or adverse effects on the integrity of a European site as the case may be. When the determination has been made the applicant will be informed of it.

[2.209] The applicant may also seek an opinion in writing prepared by the board as to the information required in an EIS or a Natura impact statement or both as the case may be. The applicant can obtain guidance from the board as to the contents of the environmental or Natura impact statements which they have to prepare for submission to the board.

[2.210] If consultations are held or if the board furnishes an opinion as to the contents in the EIS or the Natura impact statement those statements or the advice given by the board cannot be relied upon in the formal planning process or in legal proceedings.[217]

---

215. PDA 2000, s 181C(2) as inserted by PD(SI)A 2006, s 36 and amended by PD(A)A 2010, s 62.
216. PDA 2000, s 181C as inserted by PD(SI)A 2006, s 36 and amended, in relation to sub-ss (2) and (3)(a) and (b) by PD(A)A 2010, s 62(a), (b)(i) and (b)(ii).
217. PDA 2000, s 181C as inserted by PD(SI)A 2006, s 36(6)(a) and (b) and amened by PD(A)A 2010, s 65.

**[2.211]** The exemption provisions which benefit local authorities are further restricted by the provisions of PDA 2000, Pt XI,[218] which deals with the restrictions on development by certain local authorities where the development contravenes the local authorities' development plan.

**[2.212]** The significant de-exemption provision relating to local authority development in PDA 2000, s 178 provides the following three subsections:

> (1) The council of a county council shall not effect any development in its functional area, exclusive of any borough or urban district, which contravenes materially the development plan.
>
> (2) The corporation of a county or other borough shall not effect any development in the borough which contravenes materially the development plan.
>
> (3) The council of an urban district shall not effect any development in the district which contravenes materially the development plan.

### Development of the interior of a structure

**[2.213]** Exempted development arises under the provisions of PDA 2000, s 4(1)(h) where the development consists of the carrying out of works for the maintenance, improvement or other alteration of any structure, being works which affect only the interior of the structure or which do not materially affect the external appearance of the structure so as to render the appearance inconsistent with the character of the structure or of neighbouring structures. Internal works within structures are very common and the planning system would almost certainly grind to a halt if permission was required every time someone wished to paint their bedroom or make any other internal alterations and improvements. The section carefully refers to works as opposed to use. A material change in use of a premises will require planning permission.

**[2.214]** The benefit of exempted status under s 4(1)(h) is qualified where the premises is a protected structure or a proposed protected structure. PDA 2000, s 57(1), as amended by PD(A)A 2010, s 34, provides that notwithstanding s 4(1)(a), (h), (i), (j), (k) or (l) and any regulations made under s 4(2), the carrying out of works to a protected structure, or a proposed protected structure, shall be exempted development only if those works would not materially affect the character of:

> (a) the structure, or
>
> (b) any element of the structure which contributes to its special architectural, historical, archaeological, artistic, cultural, scientific, social or technical interest.

If planning permission has been obtained, showing the interior layout of a structure, it is not open to a developer to change that interior in a way that is not indicated on the plans lodged, because the planning permission must be implemented in its entirety or not at all. In *Horne v Freeney*,[219] the applicant submitted for planning permission and obtained

---

218. PDA 2000, s 178 (1)–(3) and s 179(1)–(5) as amended by LGA 2001, s 247 and Sch 4.
219. *Horne v Freeney* [1982] IEHC 20 (7 July 1982) Murphy J.

a grant of permission which permitted a concrete roof, but the applicant developed a stainless steel roof and other structural alterations which had not been included in the application. An open area was enclosed and used for dodgem cars and part of the first floor of the premises was used for a games room for amusement which had not been authorised in the grant of permission. Murphy J held that the planning permission granted was indivisible and it authorised the carrying out of the totality of the works for which permission was granted and not some of them only. It was not open to the applicant to choose part of the work only from the approved plans and to miss out on other parts. In *McCabe v CIÉ and Irish Rail*,[220] CIE had to renew and reconstruct a railway bridge which had become unsafe. The work undertaken by CIE did not amount to a total replacement of the original bridge. The external appearance of the bridge was not inconsistent with its character. The bridge, however, had been an arched bridge and the replacement changed the arch beneath the bridge to a rectangle. The change was the plaintiff's main complaint but Herbert J held that the change of shape was only one of the features of the bridge and that, in effect, there was no objective basis for considering that a change of the space beneath the bridge from arched to rectangular affected the character of the structure.

[2.215] In *Cairnduff v O'Connell*,[221] a balcony and outside staircase (possibly serving as a fire escape) were built at the rear of a terraced house in Waterloo Road, Dublin. A window, which had been closed off at the side of the house, was reopened. The Supreme Court held that these developments were not inconsistent with the character of the structure or with the character of neighbouring structures as many of the adjoining houses had similar features.

[2.216] In *Dublin Corporation v Benthem*,[222] the High Court held that the replacement of timber framed Georgian windows with aluminium windows without sashes in houses in Belgrave Square, Rathmines, Dublin could not benefit from the exemption in s 4(1)(h). The new windows were manifestly out of character with the neighbouring premises from the square which had retained the timber framed Georgian windows.

[2.217] In *Dublin Corporation v Langan*,[223] the interior of 29 Bachelors Walk, Dublin was entirely replaced. The front of the premises was demolished and the replacement was moved forward of the building line. The basement was filled in and pillars were constructed capable of supporting an entirely different structure from the one which had existed prior to the demolition works. The entire development could not have been described as repair and maintenance works but went well beyond that. Gannon J held that the works carried out greatly exceeded the limits of exempted development and that the entire premises were one structure so that the works carried out therein might partly be exempted development and partly development which required planning permission.

---

220. *McCabe v CIÉ and Irish Rail* [2007] 2 IR 392 Herbert J.
221. *Cairnduff v O'Connell* [1986] IR 73, SC.
222. *Dublin Corporation v Benthem* [1993] 2 IR 58, HC.
223. *Dublin Corporation v Langan* [1982] IEHC 36 (14 May 1982).

The premises was to be treated as one development and as such the entire development was held to be unauthorised.

## Exempted forest and woodlands husbandry

**[2.218]** Exemption for forestry maintenance is dealt with in s 4(1)(i) and (ia), as amended by PD(A)A 2010, s 5(a)(i) and (ii), which provides that exemption will apply to development consisting of the thinning, felling or replanting of trees, forests or woodlands or works ancillary to that development, but not including the replacement of broadleaf high forest by conifer species. Exemption for forestry maintenance will also apply to development (other than where the development consists of provision of access to a public road) consisting of the construction, maintenance or improvement of a road (other than a public road) or works ancillary to such road development, where the road serves forests and woodlands.

**[2.219]** Under the Local Government (Planning and Development) Act 1963, turbary and initial planting of forests were exempted development. Initial planting of forests and turbary are no longer exempted under the general exemption for agriculture, and Ireland was criticised by the EU because such activities can have significant environmental effects. There is an ongoing dispute between the Government and the turf – harvesters which may very well be resolved eventually by the European Court of Justice. The likelihood, if not the certainty, is that the dispute settlement will not favour the turf harvesters. The s 4 exemption is now limited to felling, thinning and maintenance of forests and woodlands and some further exemptions appear in PDR 2001.

**[2.220]** Section 4(1)(i) generally allows for husbandry in forest and woodlands and for the construction, maintenance and improvements of non-public roads within them. Specifically, however, replanting does not include the replacement of broadleaf high forest by conifer species. The replacement of broadleaf high forest by conifer species is a development and it is a development which will require an EIS.

## Exempted development within the curtilage of a house

**[2.221]** Section 4(1)(j) exempts development consisting of the use of any structure or other land within the curtilage of a house for any purpose incidental to the enjoyment of the house as such.

**[2.222]** The first thing to note about this exemption is that it applies strictly to use and not to the carrying out of works. The Act does not assist with a definition of the word 'curtilage'. The meaning of 'curtilage' is defined in the *Oxford English Dictionary* as 'a small court, yard, garth or piece of ground attached to a dwelling house and forming one enclosure with it, or so regarded by the law; the area attached to and containing a dwelling house and its outbuildings'. The curtilage of a house is ground which serves the purpose of the house or building in some necessary or reasonably useful way. It does not have to be physically enclosed. Curtilage of a house, in the context of the exemption provided for in PDA 2000, s 4(1)(j), applies only to the incidental use of land which is already within the curtilage of a dwelling house. The use of any structure or other land within the curtilage of a house must be for a purpose incidental to the enjoyment of the house as such. It seems from the case law that the yard stick is always one of reasonableness. It has been held, for example, that the storage of a replica Spitfire aeroplane in the garden of a dwelling house was not incidental to the enjoyment of the dwelling house as such. Using a flat patch in a garden as a helipad for flying to and from the house by helicopter might or might not be a use of land within the curtilage of a house which is incidental to the enjoyment of the house as such. There have, however, been several decisions which asked the question: 'what is the nature and scale of the activity which was said to be incidental to the enjoyment of the dwelling house as such?' The more dominant the activity, the less likely it was to be described as incidental. The indulgence of a hobby is more likely to qualify than some commercial activity. Perhaps helicopter flying is a hobby and undoubtedly the owner of the dwelling house might consider it as such but his/her neighbours might consider that the noise and intrusion of helicopters flying in and out of a residential garden in a relatively built up area is not a reasonable use and that it could not, in the ordinary sense, be described as being incidental to the enjoyment of the house as such. These are the sort of questions which are difficult to answer but by way of a general statement it is clear that the ordinary use of land or premises within the curtilage of a dwelling house, in general, does not require planning permission. Fingal County Council refused to serve a notice on a householder who used his side garden to land his helicopter, on the grounds that such use of the land within the curtilage of a house is incidental to the enjoyment of the house as such and is therefore exempt. That ruling by Fingal County Council is probably unsafe and it would be unlikely to survive if challenged in the courts. Indeed, County Kerry and County Cork planning authorities have refused similar applications.

[2.223] The curtilage of a house was usefully defined by Lord Mackintosh in *Sinclair-Lockhart's Trustees v Central Land Board*.[224] It was described thus:

> Ground which is used for the comfortable enjoyment of a house or other building may be regarded in law as being within the curtilage of that house or building and thereby is an integral part of same although it has not been marked off or enclosed in any way. It is enough that it serves the purpose of the house or building in some necessary or reasonably useful way.

[2.224] In *Dublin Corporation v Moore*,[225] the Supreme Court held by a majority of two to one that the parking of two ice-cream sales vans in the driveway of a dwelling house and the maintaining of the refrigeration process by connecting the van to the electricity mains amounted to unauthorised development. It was not exempted development under s 4(1)(j).

[2.225] Prior to PDA 2000, planning legislation had not defined the word 'house' in any interpretation sections. PDA 2000, s 2(1) defines a house as follows:

> 'house' means a building or part of a building which is being or has been occupied as a dwelling or was provided for use as a dwelling but has not been occupied and,

---

224. *Sinclair-Lockhart's Trustees v Central Land Board* (1951) SC 258.
225. *Dublin Corporation v Moore* [1984] ILRM 339.

where appropriate, includes a building which was designed for use as two or more dwellings or a flat, an apartment or other dwelling within such a building.

Even prior to the commencement of PDA 2000, s 2, the Supreme Court held in *Smyth v Colgan*[226] in relation to an exempted extension at the rear of the premises, where the applicant argued that the exemption could not be relied upon because the house had not been lived in at the date when the extension was commenced, that it was not necessary that the house had been lived in prior to the exempted extension being developed. Even if the house was uninhabited at the time that the extension was developed, the absence of occupants would not affect the statutory exempted status of the extension provided, of course, that it otherwise qualified for exemption. The decision in *Smyth v Colgan*[227] has been confirmed by the provisions of PDA 2000, s 2(1). Although the house need not be occupied it must be in existence prior to the commencement of the exempted extension. To extend the analogy further, a house with planning permission cannot be built at the same time as an exempted extension, if the extension is to benefit from the exemption regulations. The house must be completed before the building of the exempted extension is started.

## Exempted development for casual trading areas

[2.226] Section 4(1)(k) of the PDA 2000 exempted development comprises of the use of land for the purpose of a casual trading area (within the meaning of the Casual Trading Act 1995). Section 1 of the Casual Trading Act 1995 defines casual trading area as 'land designated by bye-laws under s 6 of the Act as an area where casual trading may be carried out'. Casual trading is defined in s 2(1) of the Act as 'selling goods at a place (including a public road) to which the public have access as of right or at any other place that is a casual trading area'. A number of exceptions are provided in s 2(2), to include: selling by auction (other than by Dutch auction (ie, sale of goods by auction where the price is reduced by the auctioneer until a purchaser is found) by a holder of a licence or permit under the Auctioneers and House Agents Act 1947–1973; selling to a person at his home or place of business; or selling where the seller shows that the profits from the sale are for use for charitable purposes or for other purposes from which no private profit is derived and that no remuneration, emolument, gain or profit will accrue to the seller or his servants or agents therefrom.

## Exempted development in relation to land reclamation

[2.227] Section 4(1)(l)[228] exempts development consisting of the carrying out of any works referred to in the Land Reclamation Act 1949, not being works comprised in the fencing or enclosure of land which has been open to or used by the public within the 10 years preceding the date on which the works are commenced or works consisting of land reclamation of estuarine marshland and callows,[229] referred to in s 2 of the Act.

---

226. *Smyth v Colgan* [1999] 1 IR 548 SC.
227. *Smyth v Colgan* [1999] 1 IR 548 SC.
228. As amended by PD(A)A 2010, s 5(a)(iii).
229. 'Callows' comprise low lying land which is liable to flooding.

**[2.228]** The works referred to in the Land Reclamation Act 1949, s 1, include the following words:

(a) field drainage;

(b) land reclamation;

(c) the construction and improvement of watercourses;

(d) the removal of unnecessary fences;

(e) the construction of new fences and the improvement of existing ones;

(f) the improvement of hill grazing;

(g) the reclamation of estuarine marsh land and of callows;

(h) any operations ancillary to the foregoing.

**[2.229]** In *Tralee UDC v Stack*,[230] the respondent started to fill in a pond in order to reclaim the area for agricultural use. The development was partly carried out and no planning permission was applied for. The respondent claimed exemption under the equivalent of PDA 2000, s 4(1)(a) and 4(1)(l). Barrington J held that where land reclamation is contemplated under the terms of the Land Reclamation Act 1949 the reclamation is carried out by the Minister either at the request of the occupier of the lands or on the Minister's own initiative. Class 11 of Pt III of the Second Schedule of PDR 2001 extends a similar exemption to the general public. In this case, however, Barrington J held that the respondent could not rely on the reference in the Land Reclamation Act 1949 contained in s 4 of the Local Government (Planning and Development) Act 1963 and that accordingly the development proposed to be carried out or completed was not exempted development and required planning permission.

**[2.230]** In *Lennon v Kingdom Plant Hire Limited*,[231] Morris J considered the meaning of the word 'reclamation'. In that case, the real purpose of the works was to gather boulders for coastal protection. The landscape was materially defaced in a manner which was inconsistent with genuine land reclamation. The learned judge held that the 'development' in that case went far beyond the ordinary reclamation in that a landscape of high amenity was seriously scarred and boulders were removed. It was held that the works carried out were not exempted development.

## Exempted development listed in the PDR 2001–2010

**[2.231]** Section 4(2) PDA 2000 empowers the Minister by regulations to provide for any class of development to be exempted development for the purposes of the Act. In making the regulations, however, the Minister must be of the opinion that either:

(a) (i) by reason of the size, nature or limited effect on its surroundings, of development belonging to that class, the carrying out of such development would not offend against the principles of proper planning and sustainable development, or

---

230. *Tralee UDC v Stack* [1984] IEHC 106 (13 January 1984) *per* Barrington J.
231. *Lennon v Kingdom Plant Hire Limited* (unreported, 13 December 1991) HC *per* Morris J.

(ii) the development is authorised or is required to be authorised by or under any enactment (whether the authorisation takes the form of the grant of a licence, consent, approval or any other type of authorisation) where the enactment concerned requires there to be consultation (howsoever described) with members of the public in relation to the proposed development prior to the granting of the authorisation (howsoever described).

[2.232] Section 4(4) PDA 2000[232] provides:

(a) Notwithstanding sub-ss (1)(a), (i) or (l) and any regulations made under sub-s (2) development commenced on or after the coming into operation of this section shall not be exempted development if an environmental impact assessment of the development is required.

(b) The Minister may, for the purposes of giving further effect to the Habitats Directive and requirements of efficiency and effectiveness in the control of proper planning and sustainable development, prescribe development or classes of development (whether or not by reference to an area or a class of areas in which the development is carried out) which, notwithstanding sub-s (1)(a) and (h) to (j), and any regulations made under sub-s (2), shall not be exempted development.

In effect, all development which requires EIA will require a planning permission before it can proceed.

[2.233] Section 4(5) PDA 2000 requires the Minister before making regulations under this section to consult with any other State authority where he or she, or that other State authority considers that any such regulation relates to the functions of that State authority.

## Exempted development provided for by regulations

[2.234] Schedule 2 of PDR 2001 divides exempted developments into four parts:

(a) PDR 2001, Sch 2, Pt 1 deals with with general exempted development.

(b) PDR 2001, Sch 2, Pt 2 deals with exempted developments in relation to advertisements.

(c) PDR 2001, Sch 2, Pt 3 deals with rural exempted developments.

(d) PDR 2001, Sch 2, Pt 4 deals with exempted development in relation to classes of use.

### *Interpretation of terms*

[2.235] PDR 2001, art 5 deals with the interpretation of terms used in Pt 2 of the regulation:

(i) 'aerodrome' means any definite and limited area (including water) intended to be used, either wholly or in part for or in connection with the landing or departure of aircraft;

---

232. As substituted by PD(A)A 2010, s 5(b).

(ii) 'airport' means an area of land comprising an aerodrome and any buildings, roads and car parks connected to the aerodrome and used by the airport authority in connection with the operation thereof;

(iii) 'airport operational building' means a building other than a hotel, required in connection with the movement or maintenance of aircraft, or with the embarking, disembarking, loading, discharge or transport of passengers, livestock or goods at an airport;

(iv) 'amusement arcade' means premises used for the playing of gaming machines, video games or other amusement machines;

(v) 'betting office' means premises for the time being registered in the register of bookmaking offices kept by the Revenue Commissioners under the Betting Act 1931 (No 27/1931);

(vi) 'biomass' means the biodegradable fraction of products, waste and residues from agriculture (including vegetal and animal substances), forestry and related industries, as well as the biodegradable fraction of industrial and municipal waste;

(vii) 'business premises' means—

  (a) any structure or other land (not being an excluded premises) which is normally used for the carrying on of any professional, commercial or industrial undertaking, or any structure (not being an excluded premises) which is normally used for the provision therein of services to persons,

  (b) a hotel or public house,

  (c) any structure or other land used for the purposes of, or in connection with, the functions of a State authority;

(viii) 'care' means personal care, including help with physical, intellectual or social needs;

(ix) 'childminding' means the activity of minding no more than six children, including the children, if any, of the person minding, in the house of that person, for profit or gain;

(x) 'CHP' has the meaning assigned to it by the Electricity Regulation Act 1999;

(xi) 'day centre' means non-residential premises used for social or recreational purposes or for the provision of care (including occupational training);

(xii) 'Director of Telecommunications Regulation' means the Director of Telecommunications Regulation appointed under the Telecommunications (Miscellaneous Provisions) Act 1996;

(xiii) 'excluded premises' means—

  (a) any premises used for the purposes of a religious, educational, cultural, recreational or medical character,

- (b) any guest house or other premises (not being a hotel) providing overnight guest accommodation, block of flats or apartments, club, boarding house or hostel,
- (c) any structure which was designed for use as one or more dwellings, except such a structure which was used as business premises immediately before 1 October 1964 or is so used with permission under the Act;

(xiv) 'fish counter' means a device capable of mechanically or electrically enumerating fish as they pass a specific point or area;

(xv) 'Greater Dublin Area' means the area comprising the County Borough of Dublin and the administrative counties of Dun Laoghaire/Rathdown, Fingal, Kildare, Meath, South Dublin and Wicklow;

(xvi) 'house' does not, as regards development of Classes 1, 2, 3, 4, 6(b) (ii), 7 or 8 specified in Column 1 of Part 1 of Schedule 2, or development to which articles 10(4) or 10(5) refer, include a building designed for use or used as two or more dwellings or a flat, an apartment or other dwelling within such a building;

(xvii) 'illuminated' in relation to any advertisement, sign or other advertisement structure means illuminated internally or externally by artificial lighting, directly or by reflection for the purpose of advertisement, announcement or direction;

(xviii) 'industrial building' means a structure (not being a shop, or a structure in or adjacent to and belonging to a quarry or mine) used for the carrying on of any industrial process;

(xix) 'light industrial building' means an industrial building in which the processes carried on or the plant or machinery installed are such as could be carried on or installed in any residential area without detriment to the amenity of that area by reason of noise, vibration, smell, fumes, smoke, soot, ash, dust or grit;

(xx) 'industrial process' means any process which is carried on in the course of trade or business, other than agriculture, and which is—
- (a) for or incidental to the making of any article or part of an article, or
- (b) for or incidental to the altering, repairing, ornamenting, finishing, cleaning, washing, packing, canning, adapting for sale, breaking up or demolition of any article, including the getting, dressing or treatment of minerals,

and for the purpose of this paragraph, 'article' includes:
- (i) a vehicle, aircraft, ship or vessel, or
- (ii) a sound recording, film, broadcast, cable program, publication and computer program or other original database;

(xxi) 'industrial undertaker' means a person by whom an industrial process is carried on and 'industrial undertaking' shall be construed accordingly;

(xxii) 'mobile telephony' means public mobile telephony;

(xxiii) 'painting' includes any application of colour;

(xxiv) 'repository' means a structure (excluding any land occupied therewith) where storage is the principal use and where no business is transacted other than business incidental to such storage;

(xxv) 'school' has the meaning assigned to it by the Education Act 1998;

(xxvi) 'shop' means a structure used for any or all of the following purposes, where sale, display or service is principally to visiting members of the public:

    (a) for the retail sale of goods,

    (b) as a post office,

    (c) for the sale of tickets or as a travel agency,

    (d) for the sale of sandwiches or other food or of wine for consumption off the premises, where the sale of such food or wine is subsidiary to the main retail use, and 'wine' is defined as any intoxicating liquor which may be sold under a wine retailers off-licence within the meaning of the Finance (1909–1910) Act 1910,

    (e) for hairdressing,

    (f) for the display of goods for sale,

    (g) for the hiring out of domestic or personal goods or articles,

    (h) as a launderette or dry cleaners,

    (i) for the receipt of goods to be washed, cleaned or repaired.

but does not include any use associated with the provision of funeral services or as a funeral home or as a hotel, restaurant or public house, or for the sale of hot food for consumption off the premises, except under para (d) above, or any use to which class 2 or 3 of Part 4 of Schedule 2 applies;

(xxvii) 'supermarket' means a self service shop selling mainly food;

(xxviii) 'telecommunications network' means the whole of telecommunications infrastructure and any associated physical infrastructure of any network operator;

(xxix) 'telecommunications service' means services which consist wholly or partly in the transmission or routing of signals on a telecommunications network or both transmission and routing;

(xxx) 'wholesale warehouse' means a structure where business, principally of a wholesale nature is transacted and goods are stored or displayed incidentally to the transaction of that business.

In Sch 2, unless the context otherwise requires, any reference to the height of a structure, plant or machinery shall be construed as a reference to its height when measured from ground level, and for that purpose 'ground level' means the level of the ground immediately adjacent to the structure, plant or machinery, or where the level of the ground where it is situated or is to be situated is not uniform, the level of the lowest part of the ground adjacent to it.

## Summary of exempted development regulations in PDR 2001, Pt 2

**[2.236]** Article 6 of PDR 2001 defines exempted development under the regulations by reference to Pts 1, 2 and 3 of Sch 2 of the said regulations. Exempted status under art 6 is subject to arts 7, 8 and 9 of PDR 2001. Article 7, as amended by PDR 2006, art 4, in summary, deals with developments under other enactments which are exempted developments. Article 8 deals with work specified in drainage schemes which are exempt. Article 9 presents a comprehensive list of restrictions on developments, which are dealt with below. Article 10 deals with the change of use in the context of exempted development and this is specifically dealt with below. Article 11 provides a saver for certain developments commenced prior to the coming into operation of Pt 2 of PDR 2001 which development was exempted development for the purposes of the Act of 1963 or the Regulations of 1994. Notwithstanding the repeal of the Act and the replication of those regulations, such development continues to be exempted development for the purposes of the PDA 2000.

## Development under other enactments

**[2.237]** Article 7(1) refers to development works comprising the carrying out of development referred to in s 86(8) of the Environmental Protection Agency Act 1992 (as amended)[233] for the purpose of giving effect to a condition attached to a licence or revised licence granted by the EPA under Pt IV of the said Act. Such development shall be exempted development.

**[2.238]** Article 7(2) deals with development works comprising the carrying out of development referred to in s 54(4)(a) of the Waste Management Act 1996 for the purpose of giving effect to a condition attached to a licence or revised licence granted by the EPA under Pt V of the said Act. Such development shall be exempted development.

## Works specified in a drainage scheme

**[2.239]** Article 8 exempts any work that is required under a drainage scheme from the necessity of obtaining planning permission. In addition to works specified in the scheme being exempted, if additional works are required during the course of the works they too will be exempted.

## Restrictions on exempted development to which art 6 relates

**[2.240]** Article 9(1) exempts certain development to which art 6 relates:

(a) If the carrying out of such development would —

(i) contravene a condition attached to a permission under the Act or be inconsistent with any use specified in a permission under the Act;

---

233. PDR 2006, art 4.

(ii) consist of or comprise the formation, laying out or material widening of a means of access to a public road the surface carriageway of which exceeds 4 metres in width;

(iii) endanger public safety by reason of traffic hazard or obstruction of road users;

(iv) except in the case of a porch to which class 7 specified in column 1 of Part 1 of Schedule 2 applies and which complies with the conditions and limitations specified in column 2 of the said Part 1 opposite the mention of that class in the said column 1, comprise the construction, erection, extension or renewal of a building on any street so as to bring forward the building, or any part of the building, beyond the front wall of the building on either side thereof or beyond a line determined as the building line in a development plan for the area or, pending the variation of a development plan or the making of a new development plan, in the draft variation of the development plan or the draft development plan;

(v) consist of or comprise the carrying out under a public road of works other than a connection to a wired broadcast relay service, sewer, water mains, gas main or electricity supply line or cable, or any works to which class 25, 26 or 31(a) specified in column 1 of Part 1 of Schedule 2 applies;

(vi) interfere with the character of a landscape, or a view or prospect of special amenity value or special interest, the preservation of which is an objective of a development plan for the area in which the development is proposed or, pending the variation of a development plan or the making of a new development plan, in the draft variation of the development plan or the draft development plan;

(vii) consist of or comprise the excavation, alteration or demolition (other than peat extraction) of places, caves, sites, features or other objects of archaeological, geological, historical, scientific or ecological interest, the preservation of which is an objective of a development plan for the area in which the development is proposed or pending the variation of a development plan or the making of a new development plan, in the draft variation of the development plan or the draft development plan, save any excavation, pursuant to and in accordance with a licence granted under s 26 of the National Monuments Act 1930;

(viii) consist of or comprise the extension, alteration, repair or renewal of an unauthorised structure or a structure the use of which is an unauthorised use;

(ix) consist of the demolition or such alteration of a building or other structure as would preclude or restrict the continuance of an existing use of a building or other structure where it is an objective of the planning authority to ensure that the building or other structure would remain available for such use and such objective has been specified in a development plan for the area or, pending the variation of a development plan or the making of a new development plan, in the draft variation of the development plan or the draft development plan;

 (x) consist of the fencing or enclosure of any land habitually open to or used by the public during the 10 years preceeding such fencing or enclosure for recreational purposes or as a means of access to any seashore, mountain, lakeshore, riverbank or other place of natural beauty or recreational utility;

 (xi) obstruct any public right of way;

 (xii) further to the provisions of s 82 of the Act, consist of or comprise the carrying out of works to the exterior of a structure, where the structure concerned is located within an architectural conservation area or an area specified as an architectural conservation area in a development plan for the area or, pending the variation of a development plan or the making of a new development plan, in the draft variation of the development plan or the draft development plan and the development would materially affect the character of the area;

(b) in an area to which a special amenity area order relates, if such development would be development —

 (i) of class 1, 3, 11, 16, 21, 22, 27, 28, 29, 31 (other than paragraph (a) thereof), 33(c) (including the laying out and use of land for golf or pitch and putt or sports involving the use of motor vehicles, aircraft or firearms), 39, 44 or 50(a) specified in column 1 of Part 1 of Schedule 2; or

 (ii) consisting of the use of a structure or other land for the exhibition of advertisements of class 1, 4, 6, 11, 16 or 17 specified in column 1 of Part 2 of the said Schedule or the erection of an advertisement structure for the exhibition of any advertisement or any of the said classes; or

 (iii) of class 3, 5, 6, 7, 8, 9, 10, 11, 12 or 13 specified in column 1 of Part 3 of the said Schedule;

 (iv) of any class of Parts 1, 2 or 3 of Schedule 2 not referred to in sub-paragraphs (i), (ii) and (iii) where it is stated in the order made under s 202 of the Act that such development shall be prevented or limited;

(c) if it is development to which Part 10 applies, unless the development is required by or under any statutory provision (other than the Act or these Regulations) to comply with procedures for the purpose of giving effect to the Council Directive;

(d) if it consists of the provision of, or modification to, an establishment and could have significant repercussions on major accident hazards.

**[2.241]** Article 9(2) provides that sub-art (1)(a)(vi) shall not apply where the development consists of construction by any electricity undertaking of an overhead line or cable not exceeding 100 metres in length for the purpose of conducting electricity from a distribution or transmission line to any premises.

**[2.242]** For the avoidance of doubt, sub-art (1)(a)(vii) shall not apply to any operation or activity in respect of which a Minister of the government has granted consent or approval in accordance with the requirements of reg 31 of the Habitats Regulations 1997, and where reg 31(5) does not apply.[234]

## Exempted development under Sch 2, Pt 1 of PDR 2001

**[2.243]** This part deals with general exemptions to include exempted development to or within a house or amenity or structure adjoining the house, bearing in mind that the interpretation of the word 'house' under PDR 2001, art 5, does not include, as regards development of classes 1, 2, 3, 4, 6(b)(ii), 7 or 8 specified in PDR 2001, column 1 of Part 1 of Sch 2, or development to which PDR 2001, art 10(4) or 10(5) refer, a building designed for the use or used as two or more dwellings or a flat, an apartment or other dwelling within such building.

**[2.244]** All exempted developments listed in PDR 2001, Sch 2, Pt 1 are subject to the restrictions contained in PDR 2001, art 9 and also to the column 2 limitations imposed in PDR 2001, Sch 2, Pt 1. This part contains 57 classes of exemption.

**[2.245]** Classes 1–14 are classes of development within the curtilage of a house. We have seen from the definition of 'house' that this class is not applicable to the extension of an apartment.

### Class 1 exemptions

**[2.246]** PDR 2001, Sch 2, Pt 1, class 1 exemptions deal specifically with developments carried out at the rear or side of a house. Houses can be extended, including the construction of a conservatory, provided the development takes place to the rear of the dwelling house or provided the development consists of conversion for use as part of the dwelling house of any garage, store, shed or other similar structure attached to the rear or to the side of the house. The following conditions and limitations are imposed on PDR 2001 Sch 2, Pt 1, class 1 development:

1  (a)   Where a house has not been extended previously, the floor area of any such extension (this is limited to ground floor extensions) shall not exceed 40m² in floor area. (Note: the extension may be a building or may be a conservatory.)

    (b)   Subject to para (a) above, if the house is a terraced or semi-detached house, the floor area of any extension above ground floor level shall not exceed 12m².

---

234. Note: art 3 has been inserted after art 2 by Planning and Development (Amendment) Regulations 2008.

(c) Subject to para (a) above, if the house is a detached house, the floor area of any extension above ground floor level shall not exceed 20m².

2  (a) If the house has been previously extended, the floor area of any of those extensions must be taken together with the floor area of the proposed extension or extensions constructed or erected after the 1 October 1964, including those for which planning permission has been obtained, such extensions shall not, cumulatively, exceed 40 m².

(b) Subject to para (a) where the house is terraced or semi-detached and has been extended previously, the floor area of any extension above ground level taken together with the floor area of any previous extension or extensions above ground level constructed or erected after 1 October 1964, including those for which planning permission has been obtained, shall not exceed 12m².

(c) Subject to para (a) where the house is detached and has been extended previously, the floor area of any extension above ground level, taken together with the floor area of any previous extension or extensions above ground level constructed or erected after 1 October 1964, including those for which planning permission has been obtained, shall not exceed 20m².

3 Any above ground floor extension must be distanced not less than 2m from any party boundary.

4  (a) Where the rear wall of a house does not include a gable, the height of the walls of any such extension shall not exceed the height of the rear wall of the house.

(b) Where the rear wall of the house includes a gable, the height of the wall of any such extension shall not exceed the height of the side walls of the house.

(c) The height of the highest part of the roof of any such extension shall not exceed, in the case of a flat roofed extension, the height of the eaves or parapet, as may be appropriate, or in any other case, shall not exceed the height of the highest part of the roof of the dwelling.

5 Extensions to the rear of the house must not reduce the area of private open space, reserved exclusively for the use of the occupants of the house, to the rear of the house, to less then 25 m².

6  (a) Any window proposed at ground level in any extension must not be less than 1m from the boundary it faces.

(b) Any window in or above ground level extension must be not less than 11m from the boundary it faces.

(c) Any window in a first floor extension of a detached house which is an extension above ground level, which is larger than 12m² in area, shall be not less than 11m from the boundary it faces.

7 The roof of any extension shall not be used as a balcony or roof garden.

## Planning declarations and referrals under PDA 2000, s 5

**[2.247]** The foregoing seven paragraphs are generally the paragraphs which are most commonly used for exempted development in urban areas (but they are not restricted to urban areas) and they are also the ones which cause the most trouble. Section 5 of PDA 2000 provides a procedure to settle any doubt which may arise as to whether or not the development proposal is or is not an exempted development. An application for a declaration is made, in the first instance, to the planning authority. Section 5(1) of PDA 2000 allows 'any person' to seek a declaration from the planning authority and in doing so they must give reasons and considerations as to why they, as applicant, consider that the development proposal is exempted development. The planning authority's declaration will specify what is or is not exempted development. In circumstances where the planning authority's declaration is either unsatisfactory or is not forthcoming, a referral can be made within four weeks to An Bord Pleanála. The Board in making its decision must give reasons and considerations for that decision but the reasons and considerations need not be extensive. They must, however, be sufficient to enable a person to commence a claim for judicial review. In *Fairyhouse v An Bord Pleanála*,[235] it was held that the board must comply with fair procedures and those fair procedures may include requesting the applicant to comment on any submissions received on the reference.

**[2.248]** The two most common categories of exempted development under class 1 are:

(a) the extension to the rear of a house, or

(b) the conversion of a garage, store, shed or other structure to the rear or the side of a house.

In order to qualify as an extension which will obtain exemption under class 1 it is essential that the extension structure is physically connected internally to the house. Any development to which class 1 refers in relation to development at the side of a house would be a garage or store which is connected to the house. No exempted extensions can be placed in front of the house except the addition of a limited-sized porch which is dealt with below. Rear extensions must be entirely at the rear of the house and it is important to remember that although the extension can be as large as 40m$^2$, an area of 25m$^2$ must remain as private open space reserved exclusively for the use of the occupants of the house to the rear of the house. That immediately requires a rear garden of at least 65m$^2$ if the entire 40m$^2$ is to be used in the rear extension. Garages, stores and sheds or other structures attached either to the rear or side of the house may be converted for use as part of the house.

The use of the extension cannot simply be any use and generally the use must relate to the use of the house. For example, the occupation of an extension that is a separate self-contained residential unit to the main unit was held by An Bord Pleanála to

---

235. *Fairyhouse v An Bord Pleanála* [2001] IEHC 106.

constitute a material change in use but where the extension became part of the main house and was used for family accommodation, the board held that that did not involve a material change in use.

## *Class 2 exemptions*

[2.249] PDR 2001, Sch 2, Pt 1, class 2 exemptions have been amended and extended by SI 83/2007.[236] The revised class 2 exemption refers to:

(a) *Heating systems:* the provision as part of a heating system of a house of a chimney or flue, boiler house or fuel storage tank or structure where the capacity of the oil storage tank shall not exceed 3,500 litres.

(b) *Wind turbines:* the construction, erection or placing within the curtilage of a house of a wind turbine. To gain the class 2 exemption in relation to the erection or placing of a wind turbine within the curtilage of a house, the following column 2 conditions and limitations must be complied with:

(1) The turbine shall not be erected on or attached to the house or any building or other structure within its curtilage.

(2) The total height of the turbine shall not exceed 13m.

(3) The rotor diameter shall not exceed 6m.

(4) The minimum clearance between the lower tip of the rotor and the ground level shall not be less than 3m.

(5) The supporting tower shall be a distance of not less than the total structure height (including the blade of the turbine at the highest point of its arc) plus 1m from any party boundary.

(6) Noise levels must not exceed 43db(A) during normal operation, or in excess of 5db(A) above the background noise, whichever is the greater, as measured from the nearest neighbouring inhabited dwelling.

(7) No more than one turbine shall be erected within the curtilage of a house.

(8) No such structure shall be constructed, erected or placed forward of the front wall of a house.

(9) All turbine components shall have a matt, non-reflective finish and the blade shall be made of material that does not deflect telecommunication signals.

(10) No sign, advertisement or object, not required for the functioning or safety of the turbine, shall be attached to or exhibited on the wind turbine. (Note: This prohibits the attachment of aerials or satellite dishes to the mast.)

---

236. The heating systems, wind turbines and solar panel provisions are contained in PDR 2007 (SI 83/2007).

(c) *Solar panels:* exemption will apply to the installation or erection of a solar panel on, or within the curtilage of, a house, or any buildings within the curtilage of a house. That exemption must comply with the following column 2 conditions and limitations:

   (1) The total aperture area of any such panel, taken together with any other such panel previously placed on or within the said cartilage, shall not exceed 12m$^2$ or 50% of the total roof area, whichever is the lesser.

   (2) The distance between the plane of the wall or a pitched roof and the panel shall not exceed 15cm.

   (3) The distance between the plane of a flat roof and the panel shall not exceed 50cm.

   (4) The solar panel shall be a minimum of 50cm from any edge of the wall or roof on which it is mounted.

   (5) The height of a free-standing solar array shall not exceed 2m, at its highest point, above ground level.

   (6) A free-standing solar array shall not be placed on or forward of the front wall of a house.

   (7) The erection of any free-standing solar array shall not reduce the area of private open space, reserved exclusively for the use of the occupants of the house, to the rear or to the side of the house to less than 25m$^2$.

(d) *Ground heat pump systems:* exemption will also be available for the installation on or within the curtilage of a house of a ground heat pump system (horizontal and vertical) or an air source heat pump. To obtain an exemption the following column 2 conditions and limitations must be complied with:

   (1) The level of the ground shall not be altered by more than 1m above or below the level of the adjoining ground.

   (2) The total area of such heat pump, taken together with any other such pump previously erected, shall not exceed 2.5m$^2$.

   (3) The heat pump shall be a minimum of 50cm from any edge of the wall or roof on which it is mounted.

   (4) No such structure shall be erected on, or forward of, the front wall or roof of the house.

   (5) Noise levels must not exceed 43db(A) during normal operation, or in excess of 5db(A) above the background noise, whichever is greater, as measured from the nearest neighbouring inhabited dwelling.

Class 2 exemptions, as amended and extended by SI 83/2007, are cases which may stray beyond the requirement for exempted developments for small or insignificant developments.

**[2.250]** The main motivation for including the possibility of erecting wind turbines, solar panels and ground heat pump systems or air source heat pump is, undoubtedly, to encourage the use of green energy. Nevertheless, it will be seen from the column 2 conditions and limitations applying to each type of heating system that considerable efforts have been made to make these generating systems as un-intrusive as possible on neighbouring premises. The windmills must be erected at the rear or at the side of a house but never in the front of a house. The size is strictly controlled and sound levels are strictly controlled.

**[2.251]** Solar panels are probably less intrusive than windmills and they are now becoming a common sight on the roofs of houses. The lighthouses and the floating navigational aids of Ireland are mainly solar powered but in the case of a major lighthouse the array of solar panels which they require would not fit on the roof of a normal residential house. Unless further developments occur in relation to solar panels a large array of panels is required in order to make a meaningful contribution to the energy used in an average dwelling house. As things develop the mix of ground heat and solar panels are becoming popular ways to build and heat dwellings. Again the column 2 conditions and limitations are strict in relation to solar panels and, in particular, a free-standing solar panel array shall not exceed 2m in height. Allowing for the fact that solar panels have to catch sunlight or indeed sky light during day time hours, panels at 2m off the ground in a residential area will have severe limitations. If you do erect a free-standing solar array in your garden it, in some ways, resembles the column 2 conditions and limitations which apply to exempted development at the rear of a dwelling house or at the side of a dwelling house in that an area of not less than 25m$^2$ must be kept available for the amenity use by the residents. If a 40m$^2$ extension has been added on to the rear of the premises it will leave very little room, if any, for a free-standing solar array in the back garden because of the provision that a minimum of 25m$^2$ open space must be retained. If there is a good-sized south facing pitched roof this is probably the best place for solar panels.

## *Class 3 exemptions*

**[2.252]** PDR 2001, Sch 2, Pt 1, class 3 exemptions relate to tents, awnings, shades, greenhouses, garages or sheds. The construction, erection or placing within the curtilage of a house of any garage, store, shed, tent, awning, shade or other object or similar structure is exempt development subject to the following column 2 conditions and limitations:

1. they are not placed forward of the front wall of the house;

2. the total area of such structures constructed, erected or placed within the curtilage of a house shall not, taken together with any other such structures previously constructed, erected or placed within the said curtilage, exceed 25m$^2$;

3. the construction, erection or placing within the curtilage of a house of any such structure shall not reduce the amount of private open space reserved

exclusively for the use of the occupants of the house to the rear or to the side of the house to less than 25m²;

4. the external finish of any garage or any structure will conform with those of the house and that the roof covering, where such structure has a tiled or slated roof, shall conform with those in the house;

5. the height of the structure shall not exceed, in the case of a tiled or slated pitch roof, 4m or in any other case, 3m;

6. the structure shall not be used for human habitation or for the keeping of pigs, poultry, pigeons, ponies or horses or for any other purpose other than a purpose incidental to the enjoyment of the house as such.

If you live in an area to which a special amenity area order (SAAO) relates, class 1 and class 3 exemptions will not apply as exemptions, as provided by the provisions of PDR 2001, art 9(1)(b)(i). An Bord Pleanála, in particular, has attempted to limit the class 3 exemption in a reasonably strict manner.

[2.253] Exemption will be obtained if a tent, awning, shade or other object, greenhouse, garage, store, shed or other similar structure is erected within the curtilage of a house. The positioning of the commas is important and 'shade or other object' clearly relates to another object which has the purpose of shading light or sunshine. Similarly a 'shed or other similar structure' means a similar structure to a shed but the construction of a children's den in a garden was held by An Bord Pleanála not to be an exempted development as it did not come within the definition. As can be commonly observed, there are many children's dens in gardens, as indeed, there should be, but strictly speaking they are developments which require planning permission unless, like children themselves, they are of a temporary nature.

## Class 4 exemptions

[2.254] PDR 2001, Sch 2, Pt 1, class 4 contains exemptions dealing with antenna or other satellite dishes, etc. Class 4 permits wireless or television antennae on the roof of the house provided the antennae shall not exceed 6m above the roof. The column 2 conditions and limitations relating to satellite dishes either for transmitting or receiving satellite signals are as follows:

1. There is not to be more than one such antenna erected on or within the curtilage of a house. This is frequently ignored and terrestrial and satellite systems often exist side by side in circumstances where it is fairly certain that no permission has been obtained.

2. The diameter is not in excess of 1m.

3. The antenna may not be erected on, or forward of, the front wall of the house.

4. The antenna cannot be erected on the front roof slope of the house or higher than the highest part of the roof (that presumably excludes chimneys) of the house.

The orientation of a satellite dish in Europe is south-east (this is a useful compass reference if you find that you are lost in a building estate and are trying, for example, to make your way northwards on a sunless day). Because the orientation of the dish must be south-east it causes problems for aerial erectors, depending on size and orientation of a particular house. The satellite dish can be placed on a shed or garage in a rear garden or it can be placed on the side of a garage or gable wall provided it does not protrude beyond the front wall. It should be noted, however, that no dishes can be erected on a protected structure or on a proposed protected structure without planning permission. Observation will show that there are a good number of satellite dishes which are non-compliant with the column 2 conditions and limitations. If you are a TV addict and are in the market for a dwelling house it might be worth looking at the orientation to see if it is possible to erect a dish aerial in compliance with the conditions and limitations in column 2 of class 4. There are some houses where it is impossible to achieve compliance for the very simple reason that there is no unobstructed space facing to the south-east to which the dish aerial can be secured.

## Class 5 exemptions

[2.255] PDR 2001, Sch 2, Pt 1, class 5 exemptions deal with gates, railings, fences and walls. The construction, erection or alteration within or bounding the curtilage of a house, of gates, gateways, railings or wooden fences or walls of brick, stone, blocks with decorative finish, other than concrete blocks or mass concrete, is exempted development. These structures may be constructed without permission provided, if they are in front of the house, any such structure must not exceed 1.2m in height. In any other case the height of such structure must not exceed 2m. This does not assume a right to increase the height of a party wall without the consent of the adjoining owner. No such structure shall be a metal palisade or other security fence.

[2.256] Every wall other than a dry or natural stone wall bounding any garden or other space must be capped. The face of any wall of concrete or concrete block (other than blocks with decorative finish) which will be visible from any road, path or public area, including public open space, must be rendered or plastered.

[2.257] Class 5 development will not be exempt if it 'consists of the fencing or enclosure of any land habitually open to or used by the public during the 10 years preceding such fencing or enclosure for recreational purposes or as a means of access to any seashore, mountain, lakeshore, riverbank or other place of natural beauty or recreational utility'. This useful de-exemption is provided in PDR 2001, art 9(1)(a)(x).

[2.258] Class 5 does not only deal with the construction or erection of a gate, gateway, railing, wooden fence or a wall, stone, blocks with decorative finish, other concrete blocks or mass concrete. It also deals with the alteration but not with the demolition of them.

## Class 6 exemptions

**[2.259]** PDR 2001, Sch 2, Pt 1, class 6 exemptions deal with the construction of paths, drains or ponds, landscaping, provision for hard surfaces within the curtilage of a residence but to the rear of the house and provision for car parking in the front or side of the house. Class 6 allows for paths, drains and ponds to be constructed and landscaping works, all of which are within the curtilage of a house to be developed without the necessity of planning permission. Patios or other hard surfaces may be made in the rear garden, provided their use is incidental to the enjoyment of the house, but in all cases, the level of the ground cannot be raised more than one metre above the adjoining ground. A hard surface in front of the house for the parking of not more than two vehicles 'used for a purpose incidental to the enjoyment of the house as such' may be installed without permission. This exemption does not imply that you can widen a pedestrian gate or that you can dish a footpath or provide ramps onto a roadway without permission. You cannot open vehicle access to your house from any roadway which is more than 4m wide. The use of a vehicle must be for a purpose incidental to the enjoyment of the house, as such, so that it is unlikely that you would be allowed to park two articulated trucks in your front garden.

**[2.260]** Interestingly, no limitation appears in the column 2 conditions and limitations as to the area of any hard surface to be provided to the rear of a house or even to the side or front of a house. As long as the hard surfaces are all incidental to the enjoyment of the house as such, no size limitation is imposed. Perhaps a hard surface for parking of not more than two motor vehicles to the front or side of a house does indicate some size restriction but it is unspecified. The probable limitation in these cases is that the hard surface should not be larger than what is required for parking of one, two or more cars depending on the size of the house, to include reasonable pedestrian circulation between and around the cars. In other words, the hard surface must reasonably serve, in a proportionate way, the number of cars which the house can accommodate. Although 'hard surface' is not defined it would seem from some An Bord Pleanála decisions that it includes both a concrete or tarmac surface and timber decking. In *Dublin Corporation v Moore*,[237] the defendant parked two commercial vehicles within the front driveway of the dwelling house in a place which was intended for parking. That was held to be exempted development although some lawyers and planners would have doubts about the decision in this case. At the same time, a separate An Bord Pleanála case[238] held that where two oil delivery trucks, which were also commercial vehicles, were parked on a residential site, the board considered that that was not a use which was incidental to the enjoyment of the dwelling, particularly in this instance, since one of the trucks was owned by somebody who did not even reside in the dwelling.

**[2.261]** A common feature of the modern garden is timber decking for barbeques and for sitting out in sunlight on the few occasions when it is available. These timber decks are almost invariably permanent and as they come under class 6 exemptions and since

---

237. *Dublin Corporation v Moore* [1984] ILRM 339.
238. 24 RL 2135 (Waterford County, 26 November 2004).

the only column 2 conditions and limitations in class 6 exemptions disallow the raising/lowering of ground level above or below one metre higher or lower than the adjoining ground, it would appear that there is no limitation as to the size of the decking and no requirement to leave open space area of 25m². If that is the case, and it would appear to be so, it is surely an oversight!

## Class 7 exemptions

[2.262] PDR 2001, Sch 2, Pt 1, class 7 contains exemptions relating to porches. The construction or erection of a porch outside any external door of a house is exempted development subject to some limiting conditions, namely:

1. The porch must be at least 2m from any road.
2. The floor area must not exceed 2m².
3. The height of such structure with a tiled or slated pitched roof must not be more than 4m or in any other case, 3m.

## Class 8 exemptions

[2.263] PDR 2001, Sch 2, Pt 1, class 8 contains exemptions dealing with caravans, campers or boats. The keeping and storing of not more than one caravan, camper-van or boat within the curtilage of the house is exempted development, provided it is not used for display, advertisement or sale of goods or for the purposes of any business. No caravan, camper-van or boat shall be kept or stored for more than *nine months* in any year and they shall not be occupied as a dwelling while so kept or stored.

The words here are carefully construed to mean that you can keep either one caravan, one camper van or one boat but not one of each within the curtilage of a house for a period of not more than nine months in any one year. The nine months restriction is one which is commonly ignored.

## Classes 9–13 exemptions

### Class 9 deals with gates and gateways

[2.264] PDR 2001, Sch 2, Pt 1, class 9 exemptions deal with gates and gateways. Planning permission to construct, erect, renew or replace any gate or gateway other than a gate or gateway within or bounding the curtilage of the house, is exempted development. The height for a complying construction, erection or renewal of such gate or gateway must not exceed 2m. Where barriers at the entrance to a car park were erected at Monaghan General Hospital they were held to constitute gates within the meaning of this class.[239]

---

239. 72 RF 1002 (Monaghan Urban District, 5 November 2001).

## Class 10 deals with plastering or capping walls

[2.265] PDR 2001, Sch 2, Pt 1, class 10 exemptions provide that the plastering or capping of any wall of concrete blocks or mass concrete is exempted development. The exemption applies to boundary walls and to internal walls such as walls within, for example, an orchard. The exemption is not restricted to walls within the curtilage of the house. If the walls are a protected structure the works to it are de-exempted.

## Class 11 deals with fences, etc

[2.266] PDR 2001, Sch 2, Pt 1, class 11 exemptions deal with fences, etc, other than hoarding or sheet metal fence. The construction, erection, lowering, repair or replacement, other than within or bounding the curtilage of a house, of any fence, (not being a hoarding or sheet metal fence) or any wall of brick, stone, blocks with decorative finish, other concrete blocks or mass concrete, is exempted development. This exemption is subject to the following column 2 conditions and limitations:

1. The height of the new structure shall not exceed 1.2m or the height of the structure being replaced, whichever is the greater and in any event shall not exceed 2m.

2. Every wall other than a dry or natural stone wall, constructed or erected abounding a road shall be capped and the face of any wall or concrete blocks (other than blocks of a decorative finish) which would be visible from any road, path or public area, including public open space, shall be rendered or plastered.

A restriction on this exemption is provided in PDR 2001, art 9(1)(a)(x) which is likely to apply to this class. It provides that such development will not be exempt if it 'consists of the fencing or enclosure of any land habitually open or used by the public during the 10 years preceding such fencing or enclosure for recreational purposes or as a means of access to any seashore, mountain, lakeshore, riverbank or other places of natural beauty or recreational utility'.

## Class 12 deals with painting external parts of buildings or structures

[2.267] PDR 2001, Sch 2, Pt 1, class 12 exemptions deal with the painting of external parts of the building or structure. You can paint your house whatever colour you choose. There are many notable examples of this including Jeremy Irons's splendid Norman Keep overlooking Roaring Water Bay in West Cork. PDR 2001, art 9(1)(b)(i) de-exempts class 12 exemptions if the fences or walls are situated in an area affected by a SAAO. There is also a limitation which prohibits the painting of murals on a house.[240] 'Painting'[241] includes any application of colour. Painting the exterior of a structure

---

240. Murals may be painted on hoardings or other temporary structures bounding land on which development is permitted under a temporary permission or, in some circumstances, where it is exempted development. See PDR 2001, Sch 2, Pt 2 dealing with exempted advertisements.
241. See definition PDR 2001, art 5(1).

where the structure is located within an architectural conservation area and where the painting, in the sense of development, would have materially affected the character of the area is de-exempted under PDR 2001, art 9(1)(a)(xii). PDA 2000, s 57(1) provides that 'notwithstanding s 49(1)(h) the carrying out of works to a protected structure or a proposed protected structure shall be exempted development only if those works would not materially affect the character of:

(a) the structure; or

(b) any element of the structure which contributes to its special, architectural, historical, archaeological, artist, cultural, scientific, social or technical interest.

## Class 13 deals with exemptions concerning repairs of private streets, roads or footpaths

[2.268] PDR 2001, Sch 2, Pt 1, class 13 exemptions deal with the repair or improvement of a private street, road, way or footpath. The repair or improvement of any private street, road or way where the work is being carried out or within the boundary of the street, road or way and the construction of any private footpath or private paving may be carried out without the necessity of planning permission as it is exempted development. The column 2 conditions and limitations provide that the width of such private footpaths or paving shall not exceed 3m. The limitation of 3m in width only applies to construction. It does not include repair or improvement of any private street or roadway. Also the demolition of a private street or road or way would not be included as exempted development.

## Classes 14–22 exemptions

## Class 14 exemptions deal with certain types of change in use which will not require planning permission

[2.269] PDR 2001, Sch 2, Pt 1, class 14 exemptions deal with certain types of change in use which will not require planning permission. The whole question of change in use within the meaning of the concept of exempted development is also dealt with in art 10 and in Pt 4, Sch 2 of the PDR 2001. To understand class 14 exemptions, it is useful to first examine both art 10 and Pt 4, Sch 2.

[2.270] Article 10(1) PDR 2001 provides that development which consists of a change in use within any one of the classes of use specified in Pt 4 of Sch 2, shall be exempted development for the purposes of the Act, provided that the development, if carried out would not:

(a) involve the carrying out of any works other than works which are exempted development;

(b) contravene a condition attached to a permission under the Act;

(c) be inconsistent with any use specified or included in such permission; or

(d) be a development where the existing use is an unauthorised use, save where such change in use consists of the resumption of a use which is not unauthorised and which has not been abandoned.

## Change of use comprising exempted development under art 10

**[2.271]** In practical terms, art 10 allows that it is usually permissible, without permission for change of use, to convert from one use within a particular class to another use within that class. For example, in the case of a shop, you can change the use of a hairdresser to a post office without permission unless:

(a) the conversion from a hairdressers shop to a post office involves building works which amount to a development (other than exempted development) in which case permission for that development must be obtained;

(b) the permission for the hairdressers shop restricted the use to a hairdressing shop only;

(c) if the change from hairdressers shop to post office is inconsistent with any use specified or included in such permissions; or

(d) the use of a hairdressers shop is an unauthorised use, then, unless the change is to the resumption of a use which was not unauthorised and which has not been abandoned, permission must be obtained, ie, if change for a hairdressers shop to post office was to occur where the hairdressers shop was an unauthorised use and the premises had never been a post office or had been a post office so long ago that the use was now abandoned, then the change would require permission.

A change in use from one use within a particular class to another use within a particular class is exempt development. Conversely, a change in use from a use within one class to a use within another class is not exempted development. For a change in use to amount to 'development' the change in use must be material. It is a question of fact as to whether a change in use is or is not material. The first step to take is to establish the use class into which the current activity belongs. The second step is to examine the proposed change in use to establish whether or not that proposed activity can be found. The third step involves an examination of the facts to establish whether or not the change in use is a material change in use, bearing in mind that intensification in use may amount to a material change in use.[242] Where a use is incidental or ancillary to a main use the change in use will not be a material change in use.[243] If a change in use is merely transient or temporary it is not a material change in use.[244]

---

242. *Molumby and Others v Kearns* (unreported, 19 January 1999) HC *per* O'Sullivan J.
243. *Westmeath County Council v Quirke and Sons* (unreported, 28 May 1996) HC.
244. *Rehabilitation Institute v An Bord Pleanála* [1988] 6 ILT 193.

## Exempted developments under Sch 2, Pt 4

**[2.272]** Part 4 of Sch 2 of PDR 2001 lists and distinguishes 11 different classes of use and varying types of use that fit within each class. Part 4 must be read in conjunction with the provisions of art 10.

## Exempted development – classes of use – Sch 2, Pt 4

**[2.273]** *Class 1* – use as a shop. PDR 2001[245] defines shop as meaning, a structure used for any or all of the following purposes, where the sale, display or service is principally to visiting members of the public:

(a) for the retail sale of goods,

(b) as a post office,

(c) for the sale of tickets or as a travel agency,

(d) for the sale of sandwiches or other food or wine for consumption off the premises, where the sale of such food or wine is subsidiary to the main retail use, and 'wine' is defined as any intoxicating liquor which may be sold under a wine retailer's off-licence (within the meaning of the Finance (1909–1910) Act 1910),

(e) for hairdressing,

(f) for the display of goods for sale,

(g) for the hiring out of domestic or personal goods or articles,

(h) as a launderette or dry cleaners,

(i) for the reception of goods to be washed, cleaned or repaired,

but does not include any use associated with the provision of funeral services or as a funeral home, or as a hotel, a restaurant or a public house, or for the sale of hot food or intoxicating liquor for consumption off the premises except under para (d), or any use to which class 2 or 3 of Part 4 of Sch 2 applies.

**[2.274]** *Class 2* – use for the provision of:

(a) financial services; not defined but they include banks, building societies, mortgage shops, credit unions, etc;

(b) professional services (other than health or medical services). Again professional services are not defined but they would include such professions as solicitors, accountants, architects, engineers, etc;

(c) any other services (including use as a betting office), where the services are provided principally to visiting members of the public. This is a catch-all definition for services generally which are principally provided to visiting

---

245. PDR 2001, art 5(1).

members of the public such as tourist offices, information centres, travel agencies, etc.

**[2.275]** *Class 3* – use of an office, other than a use to which class 2 of this Part of this Schedule applies. This is a catch all definition for class 2 developments but, 'office' is not defined in the regulations. 'Office' in this context would cover a broad range of uses to include betting offices. PDR 2001 defines 'betting office'[246] as meaning premises for the time being registered in the Register of Bookmaking Offices kept by the Revenue Commissioners under the Betting Act 1931.

**[2.276]** *Class 4* – use as a light industrial building. PDR 2001 defines 'light industrial building'[247] as meaning an industrial building in which the processes carried on or the plant and machinery installed are such as could be carried on or installed in any residential area without detriment to the amenity of that area by reason of noise, vibration, smell, fumes, smoke, soot, ash, dust or grit. See *Glancre Teo v Cafferkey and Others (No 2)*.[248] In that case, a change of use involved a change from the drying of peat and the manufacture of fuel to treatment of sewage. The High Court held that the development was not an exempted development because there were significant differences between the two uses to such an extent that the change in use did constitute a material change in use of the facility and, as such, it amounted to 'development' within the meaning of the planning Acts. Furthermore, the new use required the operator to obtain a waste permit. Application for permission for a change in use was necessary. See also *Lambert v Lewis*,[249] where several changes of use occurred in a premises which, in the first instance, was used as a workshop for five years. Thereafter the premises were used for the storage and slicing of potatoes for a period of six years. The next use was for storage and cutting animal carcasses and after that the premises were let out for storage purposes. The final use of the premises was for woodworking purposes and it was held that the changes in use were material changes and that the uses were of a general industrial nature and not 'light industrial' use. Permission was required.

**[2.277]** *Class 5* – use as a wholesale warehouse or as a repository. PDR 2001[250] defines 'wholesale warehouse' as meaning a structure where business, principally of a wholesale nature is transacted, and goods are stored or displayed incidentally to the transaction of that business. 'Repository' means a structure (excluding any land occupied therewith) where storage is the principal use and where no business is transacted other than business incidental to such storage.[251]

**[2.278]** *Class 6* – use as a residential club, a guest house or a hostel (other than a hostel where care is provided). Class 6 would include buildings, other than hotels, which offer temporary residence.

---

246. PDR 2001, Part 5(1).
247. PDR 2001, Part 5(1).
248. *Glancre Teo v Cafferkey and Others (No 2)* [2004] 4 IR 22.
249. *Lambert v Lewis* [1982] IEHC 24.
250. PDR 2001, art 5(1).
251. PDR 2001, art 5(1).

**[2.279]** *Class 7* – use:

(a) for public worship or religious instruction;

(b) for the social or recreational activities of a religious body;

(c) as a monastery or convent.

Class 7 use applies to buildings which are used for a religious purpose. The exemption would not apply to, for example, a disused church which is used as a community centre. The use within the building must be a religious use.

**[2.280]** *Class 8* – use:

(a) as a health centre or clinic or for the provision of any medical or health services (but not the use of the house of a consultant or practitioner, or any building attached to the house or within the curtilage thereof, for that purpose);

(b) as a crèche;

(c) as a day nursery;

(d) as a day centre.

The only one of these four uses which is defined in PDR 2001[252] is a 'day centre', meaning non-residential premises for social or recreational purposes or for the provision of care (including occupational training).

**[2.281]** *Class 9* – use:

(a) for the provision of residential accommodation and care[253] to people in need of care (but not for the use of a house for that purpose);

(b) as a hospital or nursing home;

(c) as a residential school, residential college or residential training centre.

**[2.282]** *Class 10* – use as:

(a) an art gallery (but not for the sale or hire of works of art);

(b) a museum;

(c) a public library or public reading room;

(d) a public hall;

(e) an exhibition hall;

(f) a social centre, community centre or non-residential club, but not as a dance hall or concert hall.

---

252. PDR 2001, art 5(1).
253. See definition in PDR 2001, art 5(1) where care is defined as personal care, including help with physical, intellectual or social needs.

PDR 2001 does not define any of these class 10 buildings but a hall is a building or a part of a building enclosed both vertically and horizontally – ie, walls and roof. In *Rugby Football Union v Secretary of State for Transport*,[254] it was held that Twickenham rugby football grounds was not a hall because it was not enclosed horizontally.

[2.283] *Class 11* – use as:
- (a) a theatre;
- (b) a cinema;
- (c) a concert hall;
- (d) a bingo hall;
- (e) a skating rink or gymnasium for other indoor sports or recreation not involving the use of motor vehicles or firearms.

All the buildings described at (a) to (e) inclusive must be enclosed both vertically and horizontally.

## ARTICLE 10 OF PDR 2001

[2.284] PDR 2001, art 10(2)(a) provides that a use which is ordinarily incidental to any use specified in Pt 4 of Sch 2 is not excluded from that use as an incident thereto merely by reason of it being specified in the said Part of the Schedule as a separate use. This subsection provides for what is a normal and acceptable principal use which takes account of the concept of ancillary use.

[2.285] Part 4 of Sch 2 does include some general definitions of use but in all cases the interpretation article (art 5) should be examined to understand the meanings attributed to the words used. For avoidance of doubt, art 10(2)(b) of PDR 2001 makes it clear that nothing in any class of Pt 4 Sch 2 shall include any use:
- (i) as an amusement arcade;
- (ii) as a motor service station;
- (iii) for the sale or leasing, or display for sale or leasing of motor vehicles;
- (iv) for a taxi or hackney business or for the hire of motor vehicles;
- (v) as a scrap yard, or a yard for the breaking of motor vehicles;
- (vi) for the storage or distribution of minerals;
- (vii) as a supermarket, the total net retail sales space of which exceeds 3,500m$^2$ in the greater Dublin Area and 3,000m$^2$ in the remainder of the State;
- (viii) as a retail warehouse, the total gross retail sales space of which exceeds 6,000m$^2$ including ancillary garden centre; or
- (ix) as a shop, associated with a petrol station, the total net retail sales space of which exceeds 100m$^2$.

---

254. *Rugby Football Union v Secretary of State for Transport* [2003] JPL 96.

**[2.286]** PDR 2001, art 10 provides for three special classes of exempted development in sub-paras (3), (4) and (5), namely:

> (3) Development consisting of the provisions within a building occupied by, or under the control of, a State authority of a shop or restaurant for visiting members of the public shall be exempted development for the purposes of the Act.
>
> (4) Development consisting of the use of not more than four bedrooms in a house, where each bedroom is used for the accommodation of not more than four persons as overnight guest accommodation, shall be exempted development for the purposes of the Act, provided that such development would not contravene a condition attached to a permission under the Act or be inconsistent with any use specified or included in such permission.

This was a new provision when PDR 2001 was commenced and it limits the use of each of the four bedrooms to the accommodation of not more than four persons. It is the restriction of not more than four persons *per* bedroom which is the addition to PDR 2001 but, otherwise, this exempted development of small bed and breakfast accommodation comprising four bedrooms has been with us for some time and it does not seem to have caused many of the problems which were anticipated. There had been concern that changing the use of the average sized suburban house could have an injurious impact on the residential amenities in the immediate vicinity, particularly if they were located in a purpose built estate. To put it to its extreme limits, there was nothing in the legislation to stop each and every four bedroom house on such estates offering guest accommodation, with consequent problems in terms of traffic movements, parking, noise, etc. Such an extreme example of this type of development could entirely change the residential character of urban roads or streets. Many critics feel that the exemption for four bedroom B & B exempted development should have been more properly limited to rural areas where the problems of signage, parking, intensification of traffic movement, noise, etc, were unlikely to arise. Bearing in mind that art 6 relates to the lists of exempted developments contained in Pts 1, 2 and 3 of Sch 2, it is specifically stated in art 9 that it is only development to which art 6 relates that is affected to the extent that it shall not be exempted development if it is in breach of the contents of that article. Most of the art 9 restrictions on exemption are eminently sensible but, because the B & B exemption is not contained in Pts 1, 2 or 3 of Sch 2, but appears in sub-para 4 of art 10, it is not subject to a threat that its exempted development status will be lost if it does not comply with the restrictions on exemption contained in art 9. The art 9 restrictions include such matters as endangering public safety by reason of traffic hazard or obstruction of other road users and obstructing any public right of way. It would be more satisfactory if art 10 sub-para 4, which deals with B & B accommodation, had been published with the full qualifications of art 9, in a part of the Second Schedule of PDR 2001.

Article 10(5) exempts development consisting of the use of a house for childminding. 'Childminding', in Article 5(1) of Part 2 of PDR 2001, means an activity of minding no more than six children, including the children (if any) of the person minding, in the house of that person, for profit or gain.

It is noted how the exemptions contained in class 14 of Sch 2, Pt 1 of PDR 2001 are influenced by the provisions of art 10 and Pt 4 of Sch 2 of PDR 2001.

**[2.287]** Class 14 of Pt 1 of Sch 2 deals with six specific cases where development consisting of a change in use, will, subject to the provisions of art 10, not require planning permission.

**[2.288]** Exempted development consisting of a change in use referred to in class 14 comprises the following:

(a) Change in the use of premises used for the sale of hot food for consumption off the premises or for the sale or leasing or display for sale or leasing of motor vehicles, to use as a shop.

(b) Change in use as a public house to use as a shop.

(c) Change in the use of a premises used for the direction of funerals or as a funeral home or as an amusement arcade[255] or restaurant to use as a shop.

(d) Change in the use of a premises used for the provision of financial services, professional services (other than health or medical services) or any other services (including use as a betting office), where those services are provided principally to visiting members of the public, to use as a shop.

(e) Change in the use of a house from two or more dwellings to use as a single dwelling provided the house was used as a single dwelling previously.

(f) Since 1997, there has been a welcome and now well established change in the policy towards care[256] in the community. The aim has been to move away from institutions which house physically and mentally handicapped people. In recent years, people with intellectual or physical disabilities are frequently housed in houses within residential areas. From time to time this policy has caused some alarm among various residents associations but when the regulations are examined it must be appreciated that the impact of such houses in a residential area must be minimal because the number of persons with intellectual or physical disability living in any such residence shall not exceed six, and the number of resident carers shall not exceed two. Permission is not required for change of use from a house to use as a residence for persons with intellectual or physical disability or mental illness and persons providing care for such persons subject to the limitation in numbers above stated.

As seen, if one of the restrictions contained in PDR 2001, art 10[257] applies to the Sch 2, Pt 1, class 14 developments consisting of a change of use, the exempted development status will also be lost. For class 14 development to be exempted, the change of use must

---

255. PDR 2001, art 5(1) defines 'amusement arcade' as a premises used for the playing of gaming machines, video games or other amusement machines.
256. PDR 2001, art 5(1) defines 'care' as meaning personal care, including help with physical, intellectual or social needs.
257. These restrictions are listed at para **2.285**.

be a 'material change of use'. Effectively, any change of use from a use specified in sub-paras (a)–(d) above to a use coming within the definition of a shop,[258] will be within this class of exemption. The reverse does not exempt development and if a shop is changed to other uses as specified in sub-paras (a)–(d), that development is not exempted. In *Westport Urban District Council v Golden*,[259] the respondent obtained permission to use a building as a restaurant part of which contained seated accommodation and part of which was self service with a take-away facility. Later, the seated accommodation part of the building was converted into a Supermac fast food take-away outlet and no permission was obtained. The court granted an injunction under s 27 of the Local Government (Planning and Development) Act 1976. The new use involved more late night services with the consequent increase in traffic, noise and litter and as such the development was not exempted development.

**[2.289]** See also *Carroll v Brushfield Limited*,[260] where a garage at the rear of the Clarence Hotel in Dublin was converted to a bar, replacing another back bar in the hotel. The applicant for a s 27 injunction under the Local Government (Planning and Development) Act 1976 was unsuccessful because he could not establish that a nuisance in law had been created by this development. Also it was held that the hotel, as a whole, was a single planning unit and as such change of use from garage to bar was authorised within the general planning unit.

## Classes 15–20 exemptions

**[2.290]** PDR 2001, Sch 2, Pt 1, classes 15–20 provide for temporary structures and uses which do not require planning permission.

## Class 15 exemptions

**[2.291]** PDR 2001, Sch 2, Pt 1, class 15 exemptions deal with occasional use for social or recreational purposes of any school, hall, club, art gallery, museum, library, reading room, gymnasium or other structure normally used for public worship or religious instruction. Where these are occasionally used for social or recreational purposes, no permission is required. This is an interesting exemption because to gain exemption a development must have taken place. The development would be a material change in use, but in *Butler v Dublin Corporation*[261] it was held that a material change in use will not amount to development where the change in use is merely a temporary or transient one. Therefore, 'occasional use' must be more than a temporary or transient change if it is to come within the exemption in class 15. If the occasional use is less than a mere temporary or transient change in use it may not require planning permission in any case, because it is not a material change in use.

---

258. See definition of 'shop' in PDR 2001, art 5(1).
259. *Westport Urban District Council v Golden* [2002] 1 ILRM 439, HC.
260. *Carroll v Brushfield Limited* (unreported, 9 October 1992) HC.
261. *Butler v Dublin Corporation* [1999] 1 IR 505 *per* Keane J.

## Class 16 exemptions

**[2.292]** PDR 2001, Sch 2, Pt 1, class 16 exemptions deal with the erection, construction or placing on land on, in, over or under which, or on land adjoining which, development consisting of works (other than mining) is being or is about to be carried out pursuant to permission under the Act, or as exempted development, of structures, works, plant or machinery needed temporarily in connection with that development during the period in which it is being carried out. The column 2 conditions and limitations provide that such structures, works, plants or machinery shall be removed at the expiration of the period and the land shall be reinstated save to such extent as may be authorised or required by a permission under the Act.

**[2.293]** Foreman's huts, wash rooms, enclosed storage areas or sealed containers may be placed in or about a site during the course of development. Similarly, plant and machinery may be parked there and used during the development works. Excavation may be necessary to provide temporary drainage on site and there are a host of other incidental activities which may take place during the development which are exempted under class 16. If the development is being carried out in an area to which an SAAO applies then, under the provisions of PDR 2001, art 9(1)(b)(i), the class 16 exemption will not apply. Emphatically, the planning permission must be in being before any preparatory works are undertaken and before huts, storage areas and machinery, etc, are brought to the site. The items which are brought on to the site are only exempt if they are needed in connection with the development. They must be needed temporarily, that is to say, only for the period during which the development takes place. For example, where a temporary structure was erected on a site where house building was in the course of development, that temporary structure (used as a sales office) was not exempted development within the meaning of a class 16 exemption, because it was not required for the purposes of development. Selling a house is not 'development'.[262]

## Class 17 exemptions

**[2.294]** PDR 2001, Sch 2, Pt 1, class 17 exemptions deal with the erection, construction or placing on land on, in, over or under which, or on land adjoining which, development (other than mining) is being, or is about to be carried out pursuant to any permission, consent, approval or confirmation granted under the Act, or any other enactment or as exempted development, of temporary on-site accommodation for persons employed, or otherwise engaged, in connection with carrying out development during the period in which it is being carried out. The column 2 conditions and limitations provide that such accommodation shall be removed at the expiration of the period and the lands shall be reinstated save to such extent as may be authorised or required by a permission, consent, approval or confirmation granted under the Act or any other enactment.

**[2.295]** Accommodation is not defined here but this class captures temporary, on-site accommodation for persons who are employed by the contractor either as employees or

---

262. See 27 RL 2129 (Wicklow County).

possibly also as sub-contractors. The accommodation must be close to the site where the development is taking place and can only be used by persons working on the site. It would typically include caravans, temporary kitchen and dining facilities and portacabins. All of these must be removed as soon as the development has been completed.

## Class 18 exemptions

[2.296] PDR 2001, Sch 2, Pt 1, class 18 exemptions deal with temporary structures, works, plant or machinery needed for site preparation in mining operations. In the case of mining operations, where permission has been granted under the Act, no additional permission is required for structures, works, plant or machinery needed temporarily in connection with the preparation of the site for development. The column 2 conditions and limitations provide that such structures, works, plant or machinery shall be removed when commissioning of the mine and any ancillary structures or facilities have been completed pursuant to a permission under the Act.

[2.297] Again it will be seen that once the preparation works have been completed, the structures, works, plant or machinery must be removed. The time for removal envisaged here would not necessarily coincide with the commencement of mining operations. Once the preparation of the development has been completed, that is the time when the temporary structures, works, plant and machinery should be taken from the site. Those items cannot be brought on to the site unless the mining operation has been granted planning permission under the Act.

## Class 19 exemptions

[2.298] PDR 2001, Sch 2, Pt 1, class 19 exemptions deal with temporary structures and facilities erected by or on behalf of the State authority for visiting dignitaries or delegations. Temporary structures and other temporary facilities erected on behalf of the State authority and required in connection with a visit of a dignitary or delegation will not require permission.

[2.299] The column 2 conditions and limitations provide that such temporary structures and other temporary facilities erected on behalf of the State authority which are required in connection with the visit of dignitaries or delegations will not require permission provided that they are removed after the visit has been completed and provided the land is reinstated. PDA 2000[263] interprets 'State Authority' as meaning:

(a) A Minister of the government, or

(b) The Commissioners (meaning the Commissioners of Public Works in Ireland).

The wording in the column 1 description of development is probably deliberately unrestrictive, to enable a State authority to have a fairly free hand. There is, for example,

---

263. PDA 2000, s 2(1).

no definition of 'dignitaries' nor of 'delegations'. The exemption is not restricted to temporary structures or other temporary facilities for dignitaries and delegations from another country and the word 'foreign' has been omitted in PDR 2001.

## Class 20 exemptions

[2.300] PDR 2001, Sch 2, Pt 1, class 20 exemptions deal with premises temporarily used for political elections to the office of President of Ireland, an election of members of Dáil Éireann, the Parliament of the European Communities, a local authority or Údarás Gaeltachta, or a referendum within the meaning of the Referendum Act 1994. These will not require planning permission. This class would include temporary offices of candidates in elections and also places where votes are collected and counted. The column 2 conditions and limitations provide that the use shall be discontinued after a period not exceeding 30 days.

## Class 20a exemptions

[2.301] PDR 2008 (SI 235/2008) has amended the regulations by the insertion after class 20 of new classes 20a, 20b and 20c.

[2.302] The erection of a mast for mapping meteorological conditions is now exempted development subject to the following column 2 conditions and limitations:

1. No such mast shall be erected for a period exceeding 15 months in any 24 month period.

2. The total mast height shall not exceed 80m.

3. The mast shall be a distance of not less than:

    (a) the total structure height plus:

    (i) 5m from any party boundary.

    (ii) 20m from any non-electrical overhead cables.

    (iii) 20m from any 38kV electricity distribution lines.

    (iv) 30m from the centre line of any electricity transmission line of 110kV or more.

    (b) 5km from the nearest airport or aerodrome, or any communication, navigation and surveillance facilities designed by the Irish Aviation Authority, save with the consent in writing of the Authority and compliance with any conditions relating to the provision of aviation obstacle warning lighting.

4. Not more than one such mast shall be erected within the site.

5. All mast components shall have a matt, non-reflective finish and the blade shall be made from material that does not deflect telecommunication signals.

6. No sign, advertisement or object not required for the functioning or safety of the mast shall be attached to or exhibited on the mast.

The stringent conditions in column 2 should be noted here. If an 80ft mast collapsed from its base during high winds it is at least conceivable that it might travel more than 5m in its fall. A safety margin of 5m seems unsafe especially if the boundary is the boundary of a dwelling house. Even if the mast did not travel 5m in its fall, equipment attached to the mast might become detached on impact. There must be a case for extending that 5m safety area in relation to these masts, especially in relation to their proximity to dwelling units.

## Class 20b exemptions

**[2.303]** The erection on land on which development consisting of the construction of a school is to be carried out pursuant to a permission or outline permission under the Act of temporary on-site school structures is exempted subject to the following column 2 conditions and limitations:

1. No such structure shall be erected for a period exceeding five years.
2. The gross floor area of such structure shall not exceed 50% of the gross floor area of the school to be constructed pursuant to the permission under the Act.
3. No such structure shall be above the ground floor.
4. Such structure shall comply with the Department of Education and Science Primary and Post Primary Technical Guidance Documents for the time being in force.

## Class 20c exemptions

**[2.304]** Temporary use as a school of any structure formerly used as a school, hall, club, art gallery, museum, library, reading room, gymnasium or any such structure normally used for religious instruction is exempted, subject to the following column 2 conditions and limitations:

1. The use shall be discontinued after a period not exceeding two years;
2. Such structure shall comply with the Department of Education and Science Primary and Post Primary Technical Guidance Documents for the time being in force.

**[2.305]** PDR 2008 (SI 235/2008), inserting classes 20b and 20c, was a rather hurried piece of legislation put in place to provide a temporary solution to a problem which has been created by developers and planners who neglected to make proper provision, in several areas, for sites for schools in residential developments. They probably also failed to make provision for adequate provision for other infrastructural necessities. The meaning of the words 'sustainable development' is beginning to be understood by some planning authorities. It appears to be an uncomfortable concept for some developers who see it as harmful to profitability. There have been too many cases where development, particularly residential development, has been completed with little or no accompanying infrastructure for shopping, open space and for the provision of schools. Each September we read of cases where parents are unable to obtain a placing for their children in the local schools because of overcrowding. It is hoped that both developers and planners will come to terms with the concept of sustainable development and that, in future, an application which does not take proper account of sustainability issues will be refused.

[2.306] Certain types of development for industrial purposes are exempt from the necessity of requiring planning permission if they come within the terms as set out under classes 21 and 22.

## Class 21 exemptions

[2.307] PDR 2001, Sch 2, Pt 1, class 21 exemptions deal with certain works carried out by an industrial undertaker within the curtilage of that site.

(a) Developments of the following description shall be exempted development when carried out by an industrial undertaker[264] on land occupied and used by such undertaker for the carrying on and for the purpose of any industrial process, or on land used as a dock, harbour, quay for the purposes of any industrial undertaking—

    (i) The provision, rearrangement, replacement or maintenance of private ways or private railways, sidings or conveyors.

    (ii) The provision, rearrangement, replacement or maintenance of sewers, mains, pipes, cables or other apparatus.

    (iii) The installation or erection by way of addition or replacement of plant, machinery, or structures of the nature of plant or machinery.

(b) Any work for the provision of a hard surface within the curtilage of an industrial building to be used in connection with an industrial process carried on in the building.

[2.308] Column 2 conditions and limitations provide that:

1. Any such development shall not materially alter the appearance of the premises of the undertaking.

2. The height of any plant or machinery or any structure in the nature of plant or machinery shall not exceed 15m above ground level or the height of the plant, machinery or structure replaced, whichever is the greater.

It is sometimes difficult to see precisely what type of development comes within the description of class 21 and the column 2 conditions and limitations attached to it.

---

264. PDR 2000, art 5(1): an 'industrial undertaker' means a person by whom an industrial process is carried on and 'industrial undertaking' shall be construed accordingly.

Article 9(1)(b)(i) de-exempts this type of development for industrial purposes where the development is situate in an area where an SAAO applies. In one case the installation of an effluent treatment plant within the confines of a tannery was held to fall within class 19(a)(iii), now class 21(a)(iii), because effluent treatment is an 'industrial' process. The wording must be strictly understood, in that class 21(a)(iii) only refers to the installation or erection by way of addition or replacement of plant and machinery. This means that before the works were undertaken there must have been an effluent plant which was either added to or replaced.[265] By contrast, the construction of racks for the purpose of storing steel at Chadwicks Building Centre did not come within the definition of industrial process and accordingly that development was not exempted development.[266] Where a quarry owner constructed an asphalt plant within the confines of his quarry, although the asphalt was an 'industrial process' it was a separate industrial process to the work which had traditionally been carried out in the quarry and as such it was not exempted development within class 21(a)(iii).[267] As the various decisions made by planning authorities relating to what are now the class 21 exemptions are examined, it is easy to pick out inconsistencies and a recognition of what is or is not exempted development within class 21 is often problematic.

**[2.309]** 'Industrial process' is defined in PDR 2001,[268] art 5(1), as any process which is carried on in the course of trade or business other than agriculture, which is:

(a) for or incidental to the making of an article or part of an article or,

(b) for or incidental to the altering, repairing, ornamenting, finishing, cleaning, washing, packing, canning, adapting for sale, breaking up or demolition of any article, including the getting, dressing or treatment of minerals, and

(c) for the purpose of this paragraph 'article' includes:

   (i) a vehicle, aircraft, ship or vessel, or

   (ii) a sound recording, film, broadcast, cable programme, publication and computer programme or other original database.

## *Class 22 exemptions*

**[2.310]** PDR 2001, Sch 2, Pt 1, class 22 exemptions deal with storage within the curtilage of an industrial building which is not visible from the roadway. Storage within the curtilage of an industrial building in connection with the industrial process carried on in the building, of raw materials, products, packing materials or fuel or the deposit of waste arising from industrial process, provided they are not visible from the adjacent roadway, is exempted development. The column 2 conditions and limitations state that

---

265. See 56 IF 673 (Dungarvan Urban District Council, 7 June 1994).
266. See 29 N RF 0856 (Dublin County Borough, 26 November 1998).
267. See 04 RL 223 (County Cork, 24 August 2005).
268. PDR 2000, s 5(1).

the raw materials, products, packing materials, fuel or waste stored shall not be visible from any public road contiguous or adjacent to the curtilage of the industrial building.

[2.311] The proviso prohibiting storage of stock or materials on ground surrounding industrial buildings, if they are visible from the roadway, was first introduced in the Regulations of 1994, and it has caused difficulties, particularly in the warehousing industry where the main business is storage. Warehousing frequently may not involve an 'industrial process'. Storage by warehousing companies, etc, is frequently undertaken without an application for planning permission even though the on-site storage is outside the warehouse and in view of the roadway. The class 22 exemption only applies where there is an 'industrial process' being carried on on the site. Permission should be obtained in cases where materials are stored on site which are visible from the roadway. It will be noted that the word 'industrial process' is used again in class 21 and, as seen, the definition appears in PDR 2001, art 5(1).[269]

## Classes 23–32 exemptions

### Classes 23–25 exemptions

[2.312] A 'statutory undertaker' is defined in PDA 2000, s 2[270] as a person, for the time being, authorised by or under any enactment or instrument under any enactment to:

(a) construct or operate a railway, canal, inland navigation, dock, harbour or airport;

(b) provide, or carry out works for the provision of gas, electricity, telecommunications services; or

(c) provide services connected with or carry out works for the purposes of the carrying on of the activities of any public undertaking.

### Class 23 exemptions

[2.313] PDR 2001, Sch 2, Pt 1, class 23 exemptions deal with the carrying out by any railway undertaking of development required in connection with the movement of traffic by rail in, on, over or under the operational land of the undertaking. These are exempted developments, except:

(a) the construction or erection of a railway station or bridge, or any residential structure, office or other structure to be used for,

(b) manufacturing or repairing work, which is not situated wholly within the interior of a railway station, or

(c) the reconstruction or alterations of any of the aforementioned structures so as materially to affect the design or external appearance thereof.

---

269. PDR 2001, art 5(1).
270. PDA 2000, s 2.

**[2.314]** The column 2 conditions and limitations provide that any car park provided or constructed shall incorporate parking spaces for not more than 60 cars.

**[2.315]** This exemption is made very wide by the use of the words 'development required in connection with the movement of traffic by rail, other than the construction of a railway station, a bridge, or a residential structure or office structure used for manufacturing or repair work not situated wholly within the interior of the railway station'. Section 38 of the Transport (Railway Infrastructure) Act 2001 exempts certain development which is specified in a 'railway order'. If the Minister makes a railway order under s 38, two types of exempted development come into being, namely:

(i) development comprising the carrying out of railway works, including the use of the railway works or any part thereof for the purposes of the operation of a railway or any incidental temporary works connected with such development;

(ii) development comprising the carrying out of railway works for maintenance, improvement or repair of a railway that has been built pursuant to a railway order.

The general public must be encouraged to use railways as a matter of public policy and as a means of decreasing the size of Ireland's carbon footprint. Therefore, it is essential that adequate car park spaces are made available close to the railway station. The limit of 60 car park spaces seems too restrictive at a time when every effort should be made to increase low charge or no charge car parking close to railway stations.

*Class 24 exemptions*

**[2.316]** PDR 2001, Sch 2, Pt 1, class 24 exemptions deal with harbour works, etc.

(a) 'Exemption' benefits harbour authorities in developing harbour works authorised under s 134 of the Harbours Act 1946 comprising construction, reconstruction or extension or removal of docks, graving docks, quays, wharves, jetties, piers, embankments, breakwaters, roads, viaducts, tram-ways, railways or aerodromes (but not the construction or erection of sheds, transit sheds, trans-shipment sheds, silos, stores or other structures or the reconstruction or alteration of such excepted structures so as materially to affect the design or external appearance thereof), or

(b) The exemption also extends to the cleaning, scouring, deepening, improving or dredging of the harbour or approaches thereto and the removal of any obstruction within the limits of the harbour and the use of land for the disposal of dredged material in accordance with an objective within a development plan for the area in which the land is situated.

*Class 25 exemptions*

**[2.317]** PDR 2001, Sch 2, Pt 1, class 25 exemptions deal with the carrying out:

(a) pursuant to and in accordance with a consent given by the Minister for Public Enterprise under s 8 of the Gas Act 1976 by the Irish Gas Board of

**Development and Exempted Development** [2.318]

   development consisting of the construction of underground pipelines for the transmission of gas (but not the construction or erection of any apparatus, equipment or other thing ancillary to such pipe line save cathodic protection equipment and marker posts);

(b) pursuant to and in accordance with an order made by the Minister for Public Enterprise under s 2 of the Gas (Amendment) Act 1987, by the Irish Gas Board of development consisting of the laying underground of mains, pipes, cables and other apparatus;

(c) in accordance with any requirements of the Minister for Public Enterprise or the Marine and Natural Resources, as the case may be, under s 40 of the Gas Act 1976, of development consisting of the construction of an underground pipeline for the transmission of gas (but not the construction or erection of any apparatus, equipment or other thing ancillary to such pipeline save cathodic protection equipment and marker posts); or

(d) by any gas undertaking (other than the Irish Gas Board) of development consisting of the laying underground of mains, pipes, cables or other apparatus for the purpose of the undertaking.

The Irish Gas Board is given general power to lay underground gas pipes for transmission of gas without the necessity of having to obtain planning permission. Similar exemption exists in favour of any gas undertakings (other than the Irish Gas Board). The PD(SI)A 2006 is dealt with below. Sections of this Act also affect the provisions of the class 25 exemption. Also, under the provision of s 182(1) of PDA 2000 a local authority may, with the consent of the owner and occupier of any land not forming part of a public road, place, construct or lay, as may be appropriate, cables, wires or pipelines (including water pipes, sewers or drains) and any ancillary apparatus on, under or over land and may, from time to time, inspect, repair, alter, renew or remove any such cables, wires or pipelines. It is not absolutely clear if s 182 was intended to deal with gas pipelines but the reference to pipelines is, in that sense, non-specific, so it may refer to all pipelines. Perhaps that assumption is taking the meaning outside the intent of s 182, particularly since the laying of gas pipelines is not within the normal remit of a local authority and there are significant safety issues in laying gas pipes because it is a high pressure system which requires careful and specific engineering.

*Classes 26–29 exemptions*

[2.318] PDR 2001, Sch 2, Pt 1, classes 26–29 exemptions deal with the carrying out of development by any electricity undertaking. Where development is carried out by an electricity undertaking, such undertakers benefit from a number of exemptions. However, those exemptions must be read in the context of PDA 2000, ss 182A to 182E, which were inserted by s 4 of PD(SI)A 2006, as further amended by PD(SI)A 2006, s 4,[271] which introduced a requirement to obtain approval from An Bord Pleanála for the

---

271. Note that s 182(B) as inserted by PD(SI)A 2006, s 4 has been amended by PD(A)A 2010, ss 63, 64, 65 and 66 in relation to s 182(A), 182(B), 182(C) and 182(D) of PDA 2000.

purposes of transmission of electricity. If the development of electricity transmission lines belongs to a class of development identified for the purposes of PDA 2000, s 176 then the developer/undertaker shall prepare, or cause to be prepared, an EIS in respect of the development. The development shall not be carried out unless the board has approved it with or without modifications.[272]

## Class 26 exemptions

**[2.319]** Class 26 exempts the carrying out by an electricity undertaking of development consisting of the laying of underground mains, pipes, cables or other apparatus for the purpose of the undertaking. There are no column 2 conditions and limitations attached to class 26.

## Class 27 exemptions

**[2.320]** Class 27 exempts the carrying out by an electricity undertaking of certain development consisting of the construction of overhead transmission or distribution lines for conducting electricity at a voltage not exceeding a nominal value of 20kV. There are no column 2 conditions and limitations attached to class 27. The 20kV line is for normal domestic use. The voltage limit is included in class 27 exemptions because overhead lines are considered more dangerous than underground cables.

## Class 28 exemptions

**[2.321]** Class 28 exempts the carrying out by an electricity undertaking of certain development consisting of the construction or erection of an overhead transmission line not more than 40m from a position in respect of which permission for such line was granted and which otherwise complies with such permission, but not a line in respect of which a condition attached to the relevant permission imposed a contrary requirement. There are no column 2 conditions and limitations attached to class 28.

## Class 29 exemptions

**[2.322]** Class 29 exempts the carrying out by an electricity undertaking of certain development consisting of the construction or erection of a unit substation for the distribution of electricity at a voltage not exceeding a nominal value of 20kV. The column 2 conditions and limitations provide that the volume above ground level of any such unit substation shall not exceed 11 $m^3$, measured externally.

**[2.323]** PDR 2001, art 9(1)(b)(i) provides that where exempted development under classes 27, 28 and 29 is carried out in an area to which an SAAO relates, such development is not exempted development. That provision does not apply to class 26 which, of course, relates to underground cables.

---

272. PD(SI)A 2006, s 4 inserting s 182A(1), (2) and (3) and see also s 4(4) to (9) inclusive as amended by PD(A)A 2010, s 66.

## Class 30 exemptions

**[2.324]** PDR 2001, Sch 2, Pt 1, class 30 exemptions deal with certain developments carried out by An Post – The Post Office, to include provision of:

(a) pillarboxes or other forms of letter box,

(b) roadside boxes for the delivery of mail,

(c) deposit boxes for temporary storage of mail for local delivery, or

(d) machines for the supply of stamps or printed postage labels.

All are exempted from the necessity of obtaining planning permission.

## Class 31 exemptions

**[2.325]** PDR 2001, Sch 2, Pt 1, class 31 exemptions deal with works of statutory undertakers in providing telecommunications services. There are a number of exemptions which will benefit a statutory undertaker authorised to provide a telecommunications service and class 31 specifically exempts development consisting of the provision of:

(a) underground telecommunications structures or other underground telecommunications works (including the laying of mains and cables and the installation underground of any apparatus or equipment);

(b) overhead telecommunications.

There are three column 2 conditions and limitations for (b):

1 Poles carrying overhead lines shall not exceed 10m in height.

2 Poles carrying other equipment shall not exceed 10m in height and 0.6m in diameter measured at the widest point, where 'other equipment' means one transmitting or receiving dish (the diameter of which shall not exceed 0.3m), or one panel antenna (the dimension of which shall not exceed 0.5m in length x 0.3m in width x 0.2m in depth) used for the provision of a specific telecommunications service the provision of which would otherwise require an additional pole route carrying overhead wires.

3 Where a pole or poles carry radio transmitting or receiving apparatus, the field strength of the non-ionising radiation emissions from that installation shall not exceed the limits specified by the Director of Telecommunications Regulation (ComReg).

(c) Telecommunication undertakers can also provide telephone kiosks or other telephone facilities in a public place not being on, over or along a public road. Column 2 conditions and limitations for (c) provide that no such kiosk or facility shall be situated within 10m of the curtilage of any house, save with the consent in writing of the owner or occupier thereof.

(d) Telecommunication undertakers may also provide equipment for transmitting or receiving signals from satellites in space. Column 2 conditions and limitations provide:

1 No such equipment shall exceed 10m in height.

2 The diameter of any antenna shall not exceed 2m.

3 No such equipment shall be situated within 10m of the curtilage of any house save with the consent in writing of the owner occupier thereof, or within 10m of a window of a workroom or other structure.

(e) Telecommunication undertakers may provide permanent telecommunications exchange and radio station containers. The following column 2 conditions and limitations apply:

1 The equipment housed in the container shall be used exclusively for the purposes of concentrating and re-routing calls and the container shall not have attached to it or within it, whether visible or not, any antennae for the direct transmission or reception of mobile telephony or other telecommunications signals in such a way that the container would act as an antennae support structure.

2 No such container shall exceed 10m in length, 3m in width or 3m in height.

3 No such container shall be situated within 10m of the curtilage of a house save with the consent in writing or the owner or occupier thereof, or within 10m of the window of a workroom of any other structure.

4 The field strength of the non-ionising radiation emissions from the radio station contained shall not exceed the limits specified by ComReg.

(f) Telecommunication undertakers may provide cabinets forming part of a telecommunications system. Column 2 conditions and limitations provide that the volume above the ground level of any such cabinet shall not exceed $2m^3$ measured externally.

(g) Telecommunication undertakers may also provide transportable radio installations subject to the following column 2 conditions and limitations:

1 The structure for such an installation shall not exceed 15m in height and 2m in width at its widest point.

2 The installation may only be used:

(a) to provide anticipated additional coverage at a sporting, social or other event, provided that the structure is not in place for more than two weeks before the event nor for a period exceeding eight weeks which shall include assembly and dismantling,

## Development and Exempted Development [2.325]

      (b) for demonstration or simulation purposes, whether to demonstrate the visual effects of such structure in a particular location or to measure the output, and such structure shall be in place for a period of not more than 12 weeks, or

      (c) as a temporary replacement for a structure, which has been accidentally or otherwise incapacitated, and such structure shall be in place for a period of not more than 12 weeks.

  3 The planning authority in whose functional area the installation is placed shall be notified by the statutory undertaker in writing of the provision and purpose of such installation before it is made operational.

(h) Telecommunication undertakers may also provide attachments of additional antennae to an existing antenna support structure subject to the following column 2 conditions and limitations:

  1. The total number of such antennae shall not exceed 12, of which not more than eight shall be dish type (whether shielded or not).

  2.. (a) The dimensions of any such antenna provided shall not exceed the greatest length, width or depth of any antenna for mobile telephony of corresponding type already attached to the structure.

      (b) In any other case, the dimensions of any such antenna provided shall not exceed:

          (i) in the case of any panel type antenna, 1.5m in length x 0.4m in width x 0.15m in depth,

          (ii) in the case of any co-linear type antenna, 5m in length x 0.1m in diameter, and

          (iii) in the case of any dish type antenna (whether shielded or not), 1.8m in diameter.

  3 The attachment of such antennae shall not result in the field strength of the non-ionising radiation emissions for the site exceeding limits specified by ComReg.

  4 The attachment of such antennae may be carried out by way of a platform only where the antennae support structure already incorporates a platform.

  5 The height of the existing structure (including any antenna thereon) shall not be exceeded.

(i) Telecommunications undertakers may also provide antennae for high capacity transmission links by way of attachment to existing high capacity antennae support structures, subject to the following column 2 conditions and limitations:

  1. The addition shall be of the dish type antennae used for the sole purpose of point to point communication.

2. The additional antennae shall not exceed the number provided for in the existing design capacity of the support structure.

3. No new member shall be added to the structure save by way of brackets or other fixing systems used for the attachment of the additional antennae.

4. The maximum diameter of any added antenna shall not exceed the width of the support structure at the point at which the additional antenna is attached.

5. The planning authority in whose functional area the support structure exists shall be notified by the statutory undertaker in writing of the attachment of any such additional antennae at least four weeks before the antenna or antennae are attached.

6. The attachment of such antenna shall not result in the field strength of the non-ionising radiation emissions from the radio installation on the site exceeding the limits specified by ComReg.

(j) Telecommunication undertakers may also provide an antenna support structure in place of an existing antenna support structure subject to the following column 2 conditions and limitations:

1 The replaced structure shall be removed no later than four weeks following its decommissioning.

2 Where, for reasons of the integrity of the network or other operational reasons, the structure to be replaced remains in use during the construction of the replacement structure, the replacement structure shall be located as near as possible to the existing structure having regard to the construction activity and safety requirements and, in any case, no replacement structure shall be located more than 20m from the replaced structure (measured from the base).

3 (a) The height of the replacement structure shall not exceed the height of the replaced structure.

(b) (i) Subject to sub-para (ii), the width of the replacement structure shall not exceed the width of the replaced structure.

(ii) Where the replaced structure was 2m or less in width, the width of the replacement structure may not be more than twice the width of the replaced structure, all measurements to be taken at the widest point.

(c) Where the replaced structure did not incorporate an antenna platform, the replacement shall not incorporate such a platform.

4 (a) Subject to sub-para (b), the antennae to be attached to the replacement structure shall not exceed the number of antennae on the replaced structure.

## Development and Exempted Development [2.325]

    (b) An additional 12 antennae for mobile telephony may be attached to the replacement structure, of which not more than eight of the additional 12 shall be of the dish type (whether shielded or not).

  5 (a) The dimensions of any additional antenna for mobile telephony shall not exceed the greatest length, width or depth of any antenna for mobile telephony of corresponding type on the replaced structure.

    (b) In any other case, the dimensions of any antenna provided shall not exceed:

      (i) in the case of any panel type antenna, 1.5m in length x 0.4m in width x 0.15m in depth,

      (ii) in the case of any co-linear type antenna, 5m in length x 0.1m in diameter, and

      (iii) in the case of any dish type antenna (whether shielded or not), 1.8m in diameter.

  6 The replacement of an antenna support structure together with any replaced or additional antenna shall not result in the field strength of the non-ionising radiation emissions from the radio installations on the site exceeding the limits specified by ComReg.

(k) Telecommunications undertakers may provide antennae attached to the following existing structures:

  (i) public or commercial buildings (other than educational facilities, child care facilities or hospitals) by way of attachment to roofs, facades, chimneys, chimney pots or vent pipes;

  (ii) telegraph poles, lamp posts, flagpoles, CCTV poles;

  (iii) electricity pylons,

all of which at (i), (ii) and (iii) are subject to the following column 2 conditions and limitations:

  1 The antenna shall be attached directly to the structure (other than a structure with a flat roof) and not by way of a supporting fixture.

  2 In the case of a structure with a flat roof, a supporting fixture may be used provided that:

    (a) the fixture does not exceed the height of any existing parapet or railing on the roof by more than 2m, and

    (b) access to the roof is not available to any person other than a person authorised by the statutory undertaker.

3. When an antenna is attached to the façade of a building or the exterior of a chimney or vent, the colour of the antenna shall match and blend with the colour of such façade, chimney or vent pipe.

4. Where the antenna is hidden inside a chimney pot the existing chimney pot may be replaced by a chimney pot in a suitable material which shall be the same colour, size and shape as the replaced pot, and the antenna shall not protrude beyond the top of the chimney pot.

5. The planning authority, in whose functional area the structure on which the antennae will be attached is situated, shall be notified by the statutory undertaker in writing of the proposed location of any such structure at least four weeks before such attachment.

6. The field strength of any such antenna shall not result in the field strength of the non-ionising radiation emission form the radio installations on the site exceeding the limits specified by ComReg.

In relation to class 31 development it shall not be exempted where it is situated within an area to which an SAAO relates. In that case planning permission must be obtained.

## *Class 32 exemptions*

**[2.326]** PDR 2001, Sch 2, Pt 1, class 32 exemptions deal with certain exempted developments for persons who have an aerodrome licence. The carrying out by any person to whom an aerodrome licence within the meaning of the Irish Aviation Authority (Aerodromes and Visual Ground Aids) Order 1998 (SI 487/1998) has been granted, of development consisting of:

(a) the construction or erection of an extension of an operational building within the airport, subject to the following column 2 conditions and limitations:

1. Where the building has not been extended previously, the floor area of any such extension shall not exceed 500m$^2$ or 15% of the existing floor area, whichever is the lesser.

2. Where the building has been extended previously, the floor area of any such extension, taken together with the floor area of any previous extension or extensions, shall not exceed 15% of the original floor area or 500m$^2$, whichever is the lesser.

3. The planning authority for the area shall be notified in writing not less than four weeks before such development takes place.

(b) the construction, extension, alteration or removal of aprons, taxiways or airside roads used for the movement of aircraft and the distribution of vehicles and equipment on the airside, within an airport;

(c) the construction, erection or alteration of visual navigational aids on the ground including taxiing, guidance, signage, inset and elevated airfield lighting or apparatus necessary for the safe navigation of aircraft, within an airport;

(d) the construction, erection or alteration of security fencing and gates, security cameras and other measures connected with the security of an airport infrastructure within an airport; and

(e) the erection or alteration of directional, locational or warning signs on the ground, within an airport.

[2.327] In *South Dublin County Council v Fallowvale Limited and Weston Limited*,[273] McKechnie J held, *inter alia*:

1. That because the aerodrome operators had secured a licence to operate Weston Airport from the Irish Aviation Authority, they were not relieved from the obligation of obtaining planning permission.

2. That a control tower at Weston Airport was not a 'visual navigation aid' within the meaning of that term in PDR 2001, class 32(c) and it accordingly did require planning permission.

3. That demolishing a hanger and replacing it with another structure did not constitute an 'extension' within the meaning of PDR 2001, class 32(a), since an extension must relate to a building that already exists.

## Classes 33–37 exemptions

[2.328] PDR 2001, Sch 2, Pt 1, classes 33–37 exemptions deal with certain development which is exempted development where it is for amenity or recreational purposes.

## Class 33 exemptions

[2.329] PDR 2001, Sch 2, Pt 1, class 33 exemptions deal with the provision of roadside shrines and certain sports grounds, etc.

Development consisting of the laying out of the use of land:

(a) as a park, private open space, ornamental garden,

(b) as a roadside shrine,

(c) for athletics, sports (other than golf, pitch and putt or sports involving the use of motor vehicles, aircraft or firearms) where no charge is made for admission of the public to the land.

---

273. *South Dublin County Council v Fallowvale Limited and Weston Limited* [2005] IEHC 408 (28 April 2005).

**[2.330]** There are many examples of roadside shrines throughout the country, but column 2 conditions and limitations provide that the size of these must not exceed 2m$^2$ and must not be more then 2m in height above the centre of the road. Shrines may not be illuminated without planning permission. One might well wonder how many gigantic grottos were sanctioned by the grant of a planning permission but, of course, many of these pre-date 1 October 1964.

**[2.331]** Although there is no definition of a roadside shrine it would include the ever increasing number of memorials to fatal road traffic accidents which appear on roadsides and so on.

**[2.332]** It was held that the excavation of land and the deposition of soil on adjoining grounds for the purpose of making a large man-made lake did not amount to an exempted development under class 33 as it did not involve the laying out and use of land as a park, private open space or ornamental garden.[274]

**[2.333]** The most important part of this exemption is the laying out and use of land for athletics or sports. Provided there is no charge to participate for participants in athletics or sports and provided the athletics or sports do not come within the specific exemptions to include golf, pitch and putt and sports involving motor vehicles, aircraft or firearms, such development will be exempted development. If the laying out of lands requires either the raising of the level or indeed the excavation below ground level and such is to a scale which would constitute reclamation, it is likely that permission is required.

## Class 34 exemptions

**[2.334]** PDR 2001, Sch 2, Pt 1, class 34 exemptions deal with golf courses and pitch and putt courses. PDR 2001 in class 34 has greatly limited the exemptions which are available to golf courses. In the 1970s and 1980s considerable numbers of new golf courses were laid out and the impact on landscape, flora, fauna and wildlife habitats created by these new courses did not go unnoticed by environmentalists. To golfers they are beautiful green meadows and lawns with trees and holes filled with sand. Every green has a flag. To others they are environmental black spots devoid of flora and fauna and offering very little to the wildlife community.

**[2.335]** Class 34 does provide that works which are incidental to the maintenance and management of any golf course or pitch and putt courses, including alterations to the layout thereof, excluding any extension to the area of a golf course or pitch and putt course, are exempted. The construction and layout of a new golf course or pitch and putt course requires full planning permission and may require an EIA. The alteration of the layout in an existing golf course is allowed provided the area of the course is not increased. There are no column 2 conditions and limitations attached to class 34.

---

274. 09 RL 2175 (Kildare County Council, 10 November 2004).

## Class 35 exemptions

**[2.336]** PDR 2001, Sch 2, Pt 1, class 35 exemptions deal with inland waterways. Exemptions, which greatly assist recreation on inland waterways, are provided in class 35 comprising development consisting of:

(a) the carrying out of works by or on behalf of a statutory undertaker for the maintenance, improvement, reconstruction or restoration of any watercourse, canal, river, lake or other inland waterways or any lock, quay, mooring, harbour, pier, dry-dock or other structure forming part of the inland waterways or associated therewith, and any development incidental thereto. Such works are exempted.

(b) So too is the erection or construction by or on behalf of a statutory undertaker of facilities required in connection with the operation, use or management of a watercourse, canal, river, lake or other inland waterway.

There are some restrictions placed on this exemption by the column 2 conditions and limitations, which will apply to para (b) only. The column 2 conditions and limitations are as follows:

1. Any building erected shall not have a floor area in excess of 40 m$^2$.
2. Houses or such building with a pitched roof shall not exceed 6m in height or, in any other case, 3m in height.
3. Car parks provided shall not exceed more than 24 spaces.

## Class 36 exemptions

**[2.337]** PDR 2001, Sch 2, Pt 1, class 36 exemptions deal with public parks and nature reserves.

(a) Development works carried out by or on behalf of a State authority or other public body on land used by the authority or public body as a public park consisting of works incidental to that use, including construction or erection of any structure used for the purpose of enjoyment of the park or which is required in connection with the management and operation of the park are exempt. If such structures are constructed or erected they are subject to the following column 2 conditions and limitations:

1. The floor area of any building shall not exceed 40m$^2$.
2. The height of the building shall not exceed 10m.
3. Any car park provided shall not exceed 40 car park spaces.

(b) Class 36 also provides for exemption where development consisting of the carrying out of works by or on behalf of a State authority or other public body on nature reserves established in accordance with s 15 of the Wildlife Act 1976, as amended by ss 26 and 27 of the Wildlife (Amendment) Act 2000 (including the provision, construction or erection of structures), in connection with or for the purpose of the enjoyment of the reserve which are required in connection with the management or operation of the reserve.

The purpose of class 36 exemptions is to provide exemption for maintenance works to the park. The structures which are referred to and which may be constructed as exempted structures would probably include normal furniture to be found in the park to include pathways, signage, gates, sheds for lawnmower storage, etc.

## Class 37 exemptions

[2.338] Development consisting of the use of land for any fair, funfair, bazaar or circus or any local event of a religious, cultural, educational, political, social, recreational or sporting character, and the placing or maintenance of tents, vans or other temporary or movable structures or objects on the land in connection with such use, is exempt. The column 2 conditions and limitations provide:

1. That such events must not last for more than 15 days on a single occasion or more than 30 days in any one year, where the events are reoccurring events.

2. Once the event is over or the use is discontinued the land shall be reinstated save to such extent as may be authorised or required by a permission under the Act.

## Classes 38–57 exemptions

### Classes 38–55 exemptions

[2.339] PDR 2001, Sch 2, Pt 1, classes 38–55 exemptions bring together and list a number of miscellaneous exemptions, and these allow exemption for the following.

### Class 38 exemptions

[2.340] PDR 2001, Sch 2, Pt 1, class 38 exemptions deal with flags and banners. Development consisting of the placing or erection on, or within the curtilage of, a building, or any other land, occupied by, or under the control, of a State authority or an institution of the European Union, of flags, banners or national emblems and any structures for the display of flags, banners, or national emblems, is exempt.

[2.341] This exemption only applies to using flags, banners or emblems or placing flag poles on buildings or lands so long as they are occupied or under the control of a State authority or institution of the European Union. Section 2(1) PDA 2000 defines a State authority as a Minister of government or the Commissioners of Public Works.

### Class 39 exemptions

[2.342] PDR 2001, Sch 2, Pt 1, class 39 exemptions deal with lighthouses and navigational aids. Development which comprises the erection, placing or keeping on land of any lighthouse, beacon, buoy or other aid to navigation on water or in the air is exempt. In direct response to the public outcry in relation to the Commissioners of Irish

Lights proposal to erect a 700 foot high Loran C mast at Loophead, the exemption does not apply to lighthouses, buoys, beacons and other navigational aids (including aerials) which exceed 40m in height. A high proportion of Irish lighthouses are now protected structures. The Baily lighthouse in Howth, County Dublin, is located within an area to which an SAAO relates. It is also a protected structure. In the case of a protected structure, one cannot assume that exemption applies but if a structure is located within an area to which an SAAO relates, further development of that structure or development on the site on which it stands is not exempted development.

[2.343] In *South Dublin County Council v Fallowvale Ltd*,[275] a control tower within an aerodrome was held not to be a lighthouse and as such was not exempted under class 39, even though it had a revolving light on its roof.

## Class 40 exemptions

[2.344] PDR 2001, Sch 2, Pt 1, class 40 exemptions deal with burial grounds, monuments, fair greens, school grounds and show grounds. Under the Regulations of 1977, a blanket exemption existed for burial grounds, but the use of land as a burial ground was de-exempted in the Regulations of 1994. The State did not wish to encourage burials in back gardens, public parks, etc. Class 40 does, however, exempt works incidental to the use and maintenance of any burial ground, church yard, monument, fair green market, school grounds or show grounds except:

(a) the erection or construction of any wall, fence or gate bounding or abutting on the public road;

(b) the erection or construction of any building, other than a stall or store which is wholly enclosed within the market building; or

(c) the reconstruction or alteration of any building, other than a stall or store which is wholly enclosed within a market building.

## Class 41 exemptions

[2.345] PDR 2001, Sch 2, Pt 1, class 41 exemptions comprise a miscellaneous mop-up of statutory exemptions including works consisting of or incidental to:

(a) the carrying out of any works on land to comply with a licence granted under s 34 of the Local Government (Sanitary Services) Act 1948 is exempt, but not the building of any hut, chalet or the construction of any road or hard-standing;

(b) the removal of any structure or object or the carrying out of works required by a planning authority under the provisions of the Act or any other enactment;

(c) developments carried out in compliance with a notice under s 12 of the Local Government (Water Pollution) Act 1977;

(d) the carrying out of development in compliance with a notice under s 26 of the Air Pollution Act 1987;

---

275. *South Dublin County Council v Fallowvale Ltd* [2005] IEHC 408 (28 April 2005).

(e) the carrying out of development in compliance with the condition or conditions attached to a fire safety certificate granted in accordance with Part III of the Building Control Regulations 1997, other than construction or erection of an external fire escape or water tank; or

(f) the carrying out of development in compliance with a notice under s 55 of the Waste Management Act 1996.

**[2.346]** In *Clarke v Brady*,[276] notice was served by the planning authority under the provisions of the Local Government (Water Pollution) Act 1977, s 12 requiring the provision of properly designed sealed holding tanks for contaminated farm effluent and also requiring uncontaminated surface water to be directed to the nearest stream in properly designed pipes. The recipient of the notice had plans drawn up by his engineer and these were submitted to the local authority for approval. In its letter of approval the local authority advised that planning permission may be required for the development. Hamilton P noted that the works to be carried out and being carried out were in excess of those required by the Water Pollution Act notice. The learned judge directed that all of the work on the site should cease until planning permission was granted. The letter served by the local authority approving the works was not deemed to be an amendment of the Water Pollution Act notice and because the works required were in excess of the Water Pollution Act notice, planning permission was required.

## Class 42 exemptions

**[2.347]** PDR 2001, Sch 2, Pt 1, class 42 exemptions deal with use of land as a bring-facility. Development consisting of the use of land as a bring-facility is exempt. A 'bring-facility' is defined in PDR 2001, art 3(3) as 'a facility of purpose-built receptacles in which segregated domestic waste may be deposited by the public, provided in an area to which the public have access'. The column 2 conditions and limitations on the use of land as a bring-facility being exempt provide that:

1. no more than five receptacles shall be provided;
2. the capacity of each receptacle shall not exceed 4.5m$^3$;
3. the receptacles may not be positioned on a public road;
4. nor within 50m of any house, other than with the consent in writing of the owner or occupier thereof.

This exemption applies to use only of a 'bring-facility', it does not apply to the works required to carry out the development of a bring-facility. Planning permission is required for the work of construction of a bring-facility.

## Class 43 exemptions

**[2.348]** PDR 2001, Sch 2, Pt 1, class 43 exemptions deal with excavation for the purpose of research and discovery. Excavation for the purpose of research or discovery,

---

276. *Clarke v Brady* (unreported, 30 October 1990) HC *per* Hamilton P.

pursuant to and in accordance with a licence under s 26 of the National Monuments Act 1930 of a site, feature or other object for archaeological or historical interest or excavation of a site, feature or object of geological interest are both exempt. If excavation within class 43 is to be exempted, it must be for the purposes of research and discovery. If excavation is for commercial purposes, it is not exempted development.

## Class 44 exemptions

[2.349] PDR 2001, Sch 2, Pt 1, class 44 exemptions deal with the drilling of wells and the erection of pump-houses. The sinking of a well, drilling of a bore hole, erection of a pump or construction of a pump house for the purpose of providing a domestic water supply, or a group water supply scheme in accordance with a plan or proposal approved by the Minister or a local authority for the purpose of making a grant towards the cost of such work, are all exempt.

[2.350] PDR 2001, art 9(1)(b)(i) provides that if the sinking of a well, drilling of a hole, erection of a pump, or construction of a pump house occurs within an area to which an SAAO relates it will not be exempted.

## Class 45 exemptions

[2.351] PDR 2001, Sch 2, Pt 1, class 45 exemptions deal with drilling for survey purposes (other than drilling for minerals). Any drilling and excavation for the purpose of surveying land or examining the depth and nature of subsoil is exempt. Column 1 specifically excludes drilling or excavation for mineral prospecting.

[2.352] 'Minerals' are defined in PDR 2001, art 3.3 as meaning 'all minerals and substances in or under land of a kind ordinarily worked by underground or by surface working for the removal but does not include turf'. In *Dillon v Irish Cement*,[277] it was held that the excavation of 10,500 tonnes of shale for the purpose of ascertaining its quality for the making of cement did not come within the equivalent class of the 1977 Regulations.

## Class 46 exemptions

[2.353] PDR 2001, Sch 2, Pt 1, class 46 exemptions deal with the equipment or structures erected for measuring levels, volumes or flows in rivers, etc. Development, consisting of the provision, construction or erection by the Commissioners or the Environmental Protection Agency (EPA) or a local authority outside its functional area, of equipment or structures for the purpose of collection of information on levels, volumes or flows of water in rivers or other watercourses, lakes or ground waters and any development incidental thereto, is exempt. The column 2 conditions and limitations imposed prevent the construction of any accompanying buildings or other structure with a gross floor area in excess of 8m$^2$ and with a height in excess of 4m.

---

277. *Dillon v Irish Cement* (unreported, 26 November 1996) HC.

**[2.354]** Clearly, there is no requirement to exempt a local authority from carrying out measurement within its own functional area as this would be an exempt development in any case. This exemption is to facilitate monitoring of waters for purposes of pollution control.

## Class 47 exemptions

**[2.355]** PDR 2001, Sch 2, Pt 1, Class 47 exemptions deal with equipment or structures erected to measure air quality and air pollution. Developments consisting of the provision, construction, installation, or erection by the EPA, or a local authority outside it's functional area, of any equipment or structure for or in connection with the collection of information on air quality including, on the level of pollutants in, or the constituents of the atmosphere, and any development incidental thereto, are exempt.

**[2.356]** The column 2 conditions and limitations provide:

1. Any equipment provided, constructed or installed which is erected on or attached to an existing structure shall not protrude more than 2m in front of the building line or 2m above the highest point of the roof.

2. The gross floor space of any building or other structure provided, constructed, installed or erected shall not exceed 20m$^2$ and the height of any building or other structure shall not exceed 3m.

The measuring of air quality and of air pollution by a local authority in its functional area would, of course, be exempt in any case.

## Class 48 exemptions

**[2.357]** PDR 2001, Sch 2, Pt 1, class 48 exemptions deal with connecting premises to services such as telephone, cable TV, sewers, water, gas and electricity. The connection of any premises to a wired broadcast relay service, sewer, water main, gas main or electricity supply line or cable, including the breaking open of any street or land for that purpose, is exempt.

**[2.358]** The exemption allows premises to be connected to the various services listed. The connection is subject to restrictions and other legislation including, where necessary, the obtaining of a licence from the local authority to open up a street or pavement with conditions for reinstatement, etc. There are no column 2 conditions or limitations.

## Class 49 exemptions

**[2.359]** PDR 2001, Sch 2, Pt 1, class 49 exemptions deal with the erection of a cabinet as part of a wired broadcast relay service. The construction or erection by a person licensed under the Wireless Telegraphy (Wired Broadcast Relay Licence) Regulations 1974 of a cabinet as part of a wired broadcast relay service is exempt. The column 2 conditions and limitations provide that the volume above ground level of such cabinet shall not exceed 1m³ measured externally.

## Class 50 exemptions

**[2.360]** PDR 2001, Sch 2, Pt 1, class 50 has been substituted by a new column 1 description of development and new column 2 conditions and limitations. PDR 2008 (SI 235/2008) has substituted the old class 50 with a new class 50. The wording in both column 1 and column 2 has been altered by this substitution. Class 50 is a most important exemption dealing with demolition of a building within the curtilage of a house or other structures:

    (a)    The demolition of a building or buildings within the curtilage of:

        (i)    a house,

        (ii)    an industrial building,

        (iii)    a business premises, or

        (iv)    a farmyard complex.

    (b)    The demolition of part of a habitable house in connection with the provisions of an extension or porch in accordance with class 1 or 7, respectively, of this Part of this Schedule or in accordance with a permission for an extension or porch under this Act.

**[2.361]** Class 50 column 2 conditions and limitations provide as follows:

    1. No such building or buildings shall abut on another building in separate ownership.

    2. The cumulative floor area of any such building or buildings shall not exceed:

        (a)    in the case of a building or buildings within the curtilage of a house 40m², and

        (b)    in all other cases 100m².

    3. No such demolition shall be carried out to facilitate development of any class described for the purpose of s 176 of the Act. (Note: s 176 of PDA 2000 prescribes classes of development requiring EIA and is dealt with below.)

**[2.362]** Class 50 under PDR 2001, column 1 read as follows:

    (a)    the demolition of a building or other structure, other than:

        (i)    a habitable house,

        (ii)    a building which forms part of a terrace of buildings, or

        (iii)    a building which abuts on another building in separate ownership.

**[2.363]** Paragraph (b) of column 1 under PDR 2001, class 50 remains the same. There were no column 2 conditions and limitations to class 50 in PDR 2001. The development by demolition referred to in para (a) will not be exempted development where the building or buildings are located within an area to which an SAAO relates, as provided by PDR 2001, art 9(1)(b)(i). Clearly, the demolition of the house itself, the industrial building, the business premises or the farmyard complex requires planning permission but another building or buildings within the curtilage of those four categories may be demolished without permission provided they are not located within an area to which an SAAO relates.

[2.364] The new strict column 2 conditions and limitations as provided by PDR 2008 must be carefully noted. The maximum size of a building or buildings which can be demolished without permission within the curtilage of a house is 40m$^2$, and 100m$^2$ in the case of an industrial building, business premises or farmyard complex.

[2.365] PDA 2000, s 176[278] prescribes certain classes of development which may require an EIA. The section permits the Minister, for the purpose of giving effect to the EIA Directive, to make regulations:

(a) identifying developments which may have significant effects on the environment; and

(b) specifying the manner in which the likelihood that such development would have significant effects on the environment is to be determined.

The section also deals with the establishment of thresholds or criteria for the purpose of determining which classes of development are likely to have significant effects on the environment. The regulations made under s 176 of PDA 2000 permit regulations to establish different thresholds or criteria in respect of different classes of areas and to determine on a case-by-case basis, in conjunction with the use of thresholds or criteria of developments, which are likely to have significant effects on the environment. Where thresholds or criteria are not established, the determination on a case-by-case basis of developments which are likely to have significant effects on the environment may also be dealt with by regulations. Regulations may also be made concerning the identification of selection criteria in relation to the establishment of thresholds and in relation to the determination on a case-by-case basis.

*Class 51 exemptions*

[2.366] PDR 2001, Sch 2, Pt 1, class 51 exemptions deal with drainage works by the OPW including the carrying out by the Commissioners of any works for the maintenance of works and structures for which, by virtue of the Arterial Drainage Act 1945 or any order made thereunder, the Commissioners are responsible, and any development incidental thereto.

[2.367] There are no column 2 conditions and limitations in this class, and effectively class 51 allows the Commissioners of Public Works to carry out works under the Arterial Drainage Act 1945 or any order made thereunder without obtaining planning permission.

---

278. Section 176(1) as amended by PD(A)A 2010, s 56.

## Class 52 exemptions

**[2.368]** PDR 2001, Sch 2, Pt 1, class 52 exemptions deal with construction of a footbridge, fish pass, walkway, fish stand, etc:

> Development consisting of the construction or erection by a Regional Fisheries Board of:
> 
> (a) a footbridge,
> 
> (b) a fish pass,
> 
> (c) a fish screen or barrier,
> 
> (d) a walkway or fishing stand, or
> 
> (e) a fish counter,
> 
> are exempt.

**[2.369]** The column 2 conditions and limitations applicable to class 52(a) provide that any footbridge shall not exceed 1.2m in width or 8m in length. The column 2 conditions and limitations applicable to class 52(d) provide that any such walkway shall not exceed 1.2m in width, and any such fishing stand shall not exceed 10m$^2$ in area. There are no conditions or limitations in relation to the provision of a fish counter.

## Class 53 exemptions

**[2.370]** PDR 2001, Sch 2, Pt 1, class 53 exemptions deal with development, below the high water mark, in accordance with the licence granted. The carrying out of development below high water mark pursuant to and in accordance with a licence granted under the Fisheries (Amendment) Act 1997, including a licence deemed to be granted under that Act or under the Fisheries and Foreshore (Amendment) Act 1998, shall be exempted development. There are no column 2 conditions and limitations applying to this. There was no similar exemption in the 1994 Regulations. This exemption specifically exempts mussel rafts and fish farms from the necessity of obtaining planning permission provided they are licensed. This has always been the case but many mussel rafts and fish farms around the coast of Ireland were not licensed as the licensing function of the Department of Communications Marine and Natural Resources was, at the start, poorly administered. The licensing function by the Department is now fully and effectively operated but there are still many fish farms which are unlit at night and which are a hazard to navigation. On occasions, they have been positioned in anchorages of natural refuge shown on the official charts as such. Fish farms, and more particularly mussel rafts, with their lines of blue barrels, are frequently visually intrusive. It is a vexed question as to whether the fish farms are the cause of water and sea bed pollution and although a recent study, commissioned by the fish farmers, gives fish farms a clean bill of health in terms of environmental pollution, many would argue that this is not the case. Anyone who has looked beneath a fish farm will have seen a dead sea-bed which is devoid of any life. The reason is simple. The preservative in the pellets used to feed fish in fish farms is highly toxic. A case can be made for including fish farms and mussel lines within the planning process but the larger forms of these installations do require an EIS where the output is one which would exceed one hundred tonnes *per annum*. Because reference is made to 'the high water mark', the licence which issues for class 53 exempted development refers to sea water fish breeding only. Fish breeding in lakes and inland waterways is not exempted under the regulations and will require an EIS where fish breeding takes place in lakes and in installations upstream of drinking water intakes, and other fresh-water fish breeding installations which would exceed 1 million smolts and with less than 1m$^3$ *per* second *per* 1 million smolts low flow diluting water.

## Class 54 exemptions

**[2.371]** PDR 2001, Sch 2, Pt 1, class 54 exemptions deal with reclamation of foreshore for protection of piers and slipways, etc. This provision provides that reclamation of an area, not exceeding 100m$^2$ of foreshore, for the purposes of protecting a pier, slip way or other structure on the foreshore shall be exempted development. There are no column 2 conditions and limitations.

## Class 55 exemptions

**[2.372]** PDR 2001, Sch 2, Pt 1, class 55 exemptions deal with satellite dishes within the curtilage of business premises. This provision has made a sensible rationalisation. Previously business premises to include pubs, TV retail outlets, etc, were required to apply for planning permission to erect satellite dishes and other aerials. In most cases they did not do so but now the exemption applicable to satellite dishes for dwelling houses (see class 4 above) has been extended to business premises, by permitting the erection on or within the curtilage of business premises of a satellite dish for receiving or transmitting signals from satellites. The column 2 conditions and limitations provide:

1. Not more than one such antenna shall be erected on or within the curtilage of a business premises.
2. The diameter of any such antenna shall not exceed 2m.
3. No such antenna shall be erected on, or forward, of the front wall of the business premises.
4. No such antenna shall be erected on the front roof slope of the business premises or higher than the highest part of the roof of the business premises.

## Class 56 exemptions

COMBINED HEAT AND POWER UNIT SYSTEMS FOR INDUSTRIAL BUILDING

**[2.373]** PDR 2001, Sch 2, Pt 2 has had a new class added by SI 235/2008, being class 56. The exemptions deal with:

(a) The construction, erection or placing within the curtilage of an industrial building of a structure for the purposes of housing a (fully enclosed) Combined Heat and Power system.

The column 2 conditions and limitations relating to para (a) are:

1. The gross floor area of the structure shall not exceed 500m².
2. No such structure shall exceed 10m in height or 50m in length.
3. No such structure shall be within:
    (a) 10m of any public road;
    (b) 200m of the nearest habitable house or residential building or school, hospital, church or building used for public assembly (other than a house or building of persons providing the structure) save with the consent in writing of the owner, as appropriate, the occupier or person in charge thereof.
4. No such structure within 100m of any public road shall exceed 8m in height.
5. No such structure shall have more than two flues, neither of which shall exceed 20m in height from ground level.
6. The diameter of any flue shall not exceed 1m.
7. Noise levels must not exceed 43db(A) during normal operation, as measured at the nearest party boundary.
8. Not more than one such structure shall be erected.
9. The structure shall be used for the purposes of housing a Combined Heat and Power unit only.

## COMBINED HEAT AND POWER UNIT SYSTEMS FOR A LIGHT INDUSTRIAL BUILDING

[2.374] (b) The construction, erection or placing within the curtilage of a business premises, or a light industrial building, of a structure for the purpose of housing a (fully enclosed) combined heat and power unit system.

The column 2 conditions and limitations relating to para (b) of class 56 are as follows:

1. The gross floor area of the structure shall not exceed 300m².
2. No such structure shall exceed 8m in height or 40m in length.
3. No such structure shall be within:
    (a) 10m of any public road;
    (b) 200m of the nearest habitable house or residential building or school, hospital, church or building used for public assembly (other than a house or building of persons providing the structure) save with the consent in writing of the owner, as appropriate, the occupier or person in charge thereof.
4. No such structure shall have more than 2 flues, neither of which shall exceed 16m in height from ground level.
5. The diameter of any flue shall not exceed 1m.
6. Noise levels must not exceed 43db(A) during normal operation, as measured at the nearest party boundary.
7. Not more than one such structure shall be erected within the curtilage of such premises or building.

8. The structure shall be used for the purposes of housing a combined heat and power unit only.

## WIND TURBINES FOR INDUSTRIAL BUILDINGS

**[2.375]** 2(c) The construction, erection or placing within the curtilage of an industrial building or light industrial building, or business premises of a wind turbine.

The column 2 conditions and limitations are as follows:

1. The turbine shall not be erected on or attached to the premises or building of any structure within the curtilage of the building or premises.
2. The total height of the turbine shall not exceed 20m.
3. The rotor diameter shall not exceed 8m.
4. The minimum clearance between the lower tip of the rotor and ground level shall not be less than 3m.
5. The supporting tower shall be a distance of not less than the total structure height (including the blade of the turbine at the highest point of its arc) plus:
    (i) 5m from any party boundary;
    (ii) 5m from any non-electrical overhead cables;
    (iii) 20m from any 38kV electricity distribution line;
    (iv) 30m from the centre line of any electricity transmission line of 110kV or more.
6. The turbine shall not be located within 5km of the nearest airport or aerodrome or any communication, navigation and surveillance facilities designated by the Irish Aviation Authority, save with the consent in writing of the Authority and in compliance with any conditions relating to the provision of aviation obstacle warning lighting.
7. Noise levels must not exceed 43db(A) during normal operation, as measured from the nearest party boundary.
8. Not more than one turbine shall be erected within the curtilage of the premises or building.
9. All turbine components shall have a matt, non-reflective finish and the blade shall be made of material that does not deflect telecommunication signals.
10. No sign, advertisement or object, not required for the functioning or safety of the turbine shall be attached to or exhibited on the wind turbine.
11. The turbine shall not be located within an architectural conservation area.

## SOLAR PANELS FOR AN INDUSTRIAL BUILDING

**[2.376]** (d) The installation or erection on or within the curtilage of an industrial building or any ancillary buildings within the curtilage of an industrial building of solar panels (thermal collector or photo-voltaic).

The column 2 conditions and limitations provide as follows:

1. The distance between the plane of the wall or a pitched roof and the panel shall not exceed 1m.
2. The distance between the plane of a flat roof and the panel shall not exceed 2m.
3. The solar panels shall be a minimum of 50cm from the edge of the wall or roof on which it is mounted.
4. The total aperture area of any wall mounted panel, or free-standing solar array shall not exceed 50m$^2$.
5. Any equipment associated with panels, including water tanks, shall be located within the roof space of the building. The height of a free-standing solar array shall not exceed 2m, at its highest point, above ground level.
6. No sign, advertisement or object, not required for the functioning or safety of the panel shall be attached to or exhibited on the panels.

## SOLAR PANELS FOR A LIGHT INDUSTRIAL BUILDING

[2.377] (e) The installation or erection on a business premises or light industrial building or, any ancillary buildings within the curtilage of any such premises or buildings, of solar thermal collector panels shall be exempt.

The column 2 conditions and limitations provide as follows:

1. Such solar panel may not be installed or erected on a wall of such premises or building.
2. The total aperture of any such panel, taken together with any other such panel previously placed on or within the said curtilage, shall not exceed 50m$^2$ or 50% of the total roof area whichever is the lesser.
3. The distance between the plane of a pitched roof and the panel shall not exceed:
    (a) 50cm in the case of a light industrial building;
    (b) 15cm in the case of a business premises.
4. The distance between the plane of a flat roof and the panel shall not exceed:
    (a) 2m in the case of a light industrial building;
    (b) 1m in the case of a business premises.
5. The solar panel shall be a minimum of 50cm from the edge of the roof on which it is mounted, or 2m in the case of a flat roof.
6. Any equipment associated with the panels, including water tanks, shall be located within the roof space of the building.
7. The total aperture area of any free-standing solar array shall not exceed 25m$^2$.
8. The height of a free-standing solar array shall not exceed 2m, at its highest point, above ground level.

9. A free-standing solar array shall not be located forward of the front wall of the building premises.
10. No sign, advertisement or object, not required for the function or safety of the panel shall be attached to or exhibited on the panels.

## PHOTO-VOLTAIC SOLAR PANELS FOR BUSINESS PREMISES OR LIGHT INDUSTRIAL BUILDINGS

**[2.378]** (f) The installation or erection on a business premises or light industrial building, or any ancillary buildings within the curtilage of such building, of photo-voltaic solar panels shall be exempt.

The column 2 conditions and limitations read as follows:

1. The total aperture of any such panel, taken together with any other such panel previously placed on or within the said curtilage, shall not exceed 50m$^2$ or 50% of the total roof area whichever is the lesser.
2. The distance between the plane of the wall and the panel shall not exceed 15cm.
3. The distance between the plane of a pitched roof and the panel shall not exceed:
    (a) 50cm in the case of light industrial building;
    (b) 15cm in the case of a business premises.
4. The distance between the plane of a flat roof and the panel shall not exceed:
    (a) 2m in the case of a light industrial building;
    (b) 1m in the case of a business premises.
5. The solar panel shall be a minimum of 50cm from the edge of a wall or pitched roof on which it is mounted or 2m in the case of a flat roof.
6. The total aperture area of any wall mounted panel or free-standing solar array shall not exceed 25m$^2$
7. Any equipment associated with panels, including water tanks, shall be located within the roof space of the building.
8. The height of any free-standing solar array shall not exceed 2m at it highest point, above ground level.
9. A free-standing solar array shall not be located forward of the front wall of the building or premises
10. No sign, advertising or object, not required for the functioning or safety of the turbine shall be attached to or exhibited on the panels.

## GROUND SOURCE HEAT PUMP SYSTEM FOR INDUSTRIAL BUILDINGS

**[2.379]** (g) The installation on or within the curtilage of an industrial building, or any ancillary buildings within the curtilage of an industrial building, of a ground source heat pump system (horizontal and vertical) or any air source pumps shall be exempt.

The column 2 conditions and limitations are as follows:

1. The level of the ground shall not be altered by more than 1m above or below the level of the adjoining ground.
2. The total area of any air source heat pumps shall not exceed 15m².
3. The air source heat pump shall be a minimum of 50cm from the edge of the wall or roof on which it was mounted.
4. Noise levels must not exceed 43db(A) during normal operation as measured from the nearest party boundary
5. Distance from party boundaries and from foundations of any structure or building shall be maintained in line with the Sustainable Energy Ireland Renewable Energy Information Office Procurement Guidelines on Heat Pump Systems for the time being in force.

## GROUND SOURCE HEAT PUMP SYSTEM FOR A LIGHT INDUSTRIAL BUILDING

[2.380] (h) The installation on or within the curtilage of a business premises or light industrial building, or any ancillary buildings within the curtilage of such premises or building, of a ground source heat pump system (horizontal and vertical) or air source heat pump shall be exempt.

The column 2 conditions and limitations provide as follows:

1. The level of the ground shall not be altered by more than 1m above or below the level of the adjoining ground.
2. The total area of any air source heat pump shall not exceed 10m².
3. No such structure shall be constructed, erected or placed forward of the front wall of the building.
4. The heat pump shall be a minimum of 50cm from the edge of the wall or roof on which it is mounted.
5. Noise levels must not exceed 43db(A) during normal operation, as measured from the nearest party boundary.
6. Distances from party boundaries and from the foundations of any structure or building shall be maintained in line with the Sustainable Energy Ireland Renewable Energy Information Office Procurement Guidelines on Heat Pump Systems for the time being in force.

## BIOMASS BOILERS AS PART OF A HEATING SYSTEM FOR INDUSTRIAL BUILDINGS OR LIGHT INDUSTRIAL BUILDINGS

[2.381] (i) The provision as part of a heating system for an industrial building or light industrial building or business premises of a biomass boiler, including a boiler house, flues mounted on the boiler house, and over ground flues storage tank or structure shall be exempt.

The Column 2 conditions and limitations provide as follows:

1. The gross floor area of the boiler house shall not exceed 20m².
2. The capacity of such fuel tan or structure shall not exceed 75m³.

3. The height of a boiler house or such a fuel storage tank or structure shall not exceed 3m.
4. The height of a flue mounted on a biomass unit shall not exceed 16m, measured from ground level.
5. Not more than two flues shall be erected.
6. Not more than one such structure shall be erected within the curtilage of the site.
7. The diameter of any flue shall not exceed 1m.
8. The boiler house shall not be located within:
   (i) 10m of any public road;
   (ii) 100m of the nearest habitable house or residential building or school, hospital, church or building used for public assembly (other than a house or building of the person providing the structure) save with the consent in writing of the owner, and, as appropriate, the occupier or person in charge thereof.
9. Noise levels must not exceed 43db(A) during normal operation as measured from the nearest party boundary.

In effect, class 56 is a class which provides incentives by exempting the necessity for obtaining planning permission in relation to the installation of alternative heating systems. The aim here is to discourage the use of carboniferous fuels. Combined heat and power systems, wind turbines, solar panels, ground source heat pumps, air source heat pumps and biomass boilers may be installed at various classes of industrial buildings, light industrial buildings and business premises, without planning permission if they are within class 56 and if they comply with the column 2 conditions and limitations in class 56.

## Class 57 exemptions

**[2.382]** PDR 2001, Sch 2, Pt 2, class 57 has been added to that list of exemptions by the provisions of SI 235/2008. Exemption is provided for the extension of a school where the school has not been previously extended by the construction or erection of an extension to the side or rear of the school.

**[2.383]** The column 2 conditions and limitations provide:
1. The floor area of any such extension which shall not exceed;
   (a) 160m$^2$, or
   (b) 40% of the gross floor area of the school,
   whichever is the lesser.
2. No such structure shall be above the ground floor.
3. Any extension shall be a distance of not less than 2m from any party boundary.
4. Such structure shall comply with the Department of Education and Science Primary and Post Primary Technical Guidance Documents for the time being in force.

**[2.384]** PDR 2008 hastily inserted the new class 57 when the extent to which developers and planners had ignored the requirement for necessary social infrastructure and common-sense engineering, was realised. The message of sustainability in terms of development has not travelled very far since the introduction of PDA 2000. What is provided for in class 57 is temporary and unsatisfactory. There are many areas where planners and developers have not come to terms with sustainable development. In relation to house building there are at least two examples which stand out as remarkable examples of ignoring the concept of sustainable development on the part of planners and developers and these are:

1. The provisions of new schools and other necessary infrastructure in residential development.

2. Taking measures to avoid, as far as possible, the carrying out of intensive development on recognised geographical flood plains and the provision of adequate surface water drains to prevent flooding.

It is to be hoped that the 'core strategy' provisions contained in PD(A)A 2010 will address these two points effectively.

## Exempted developments – advertisements

**[2.385]** PDR 2001, art 6, Sch 2, Pt 2 contains exemptions for certain developments consisting of the erection of advertising structures for the exhibition of an advertisement. Part 2 contains classes 1–18. With the exception of classes 3, 7, 8 and 12 all other classes have column 2 conditions and limitations. The developments in this schedule are also subject to PDR 2001, art 9.

**[2.386]** 'Advertisement' is defined PDA 2000[279] as meaning any word, letter, model, balloon, inflatable structure, kite, poster, notice, device or representation employed for the purpose of advertisement, announcement or direction.

**[2.387]** 'Advertisement structure' is also defined in PDA 2000 as meaning any structure which is a hoarding, scaffold, framework, pole, standard device or sign (whether illuminated or not) and which is used or intended for use for exhibiting advertisements or any attachment to a building or structure used for advertisement purposes.

## *Class 1 exemptions*

**[2.388]** Class 1 exemptions deal with advertisements, other than those in classes 2, 3 or 5, exhibited on business premises. Advertisements (other than those specified in classes 2, 3 or 5) exhibited on business premises, wholly with reference to the business or other activity carried on or the goods or services provided on those premises, are exempt, subject to nine column 2 conditions and limitations, namely:
    1    The total area of such advertisements exhibited on or attached or affixed to the front of any building on the premises shall not exceed an area equal

---

279. PDA 2000, s 2(1).

to 0.3m² for every metre length of such front, less the total area of any such advertisements exhibited on the premises but not exhibited on or attached or affixed to a building, and in any event shall not exceed 5m².

2. The total area of such advertisements exhibited on or attached or affixed to any face of a building on the premises other than the front thereof shall not exceed 1.2m² and the total area of any such advertisements on such face which are illuminated shall not exceed 0.3m².

3. The total area of such advertisements which are not exhibited on or attached or affixed to a building on the premises shall not exceed 3m², of which not more than 1.5m² shall consist of advertisements which are illuminated.

4. (a) No part of any such advertisement which is not exhibited on or attached or affixed to a building on the premises, or of an advertisement structure on which it is exhibited, shall be more than 2.5m in height.

   (b) No part of any such advertisement which is exhibited on or attached or affixed to a building on the premises shall be more than 4m in height above ground level.

5. Where any such advertisement projects more than 5cm over any public road, the sign or other advertisement structure on which it is exhibited shall not be less than 2m above the level of such road[280] and shall not project more than 1m over such road.

6. Where any such advertisement consists of a circular sign and projects more than 5cm over any public road, the diameter of such sign shall not exceed 1m and no other such advertisement shall be exhibited on a sign or other advertisement structure projecting more than 5cm over such road.

7. Where any one or more such advertisements are exhibited on a swinging or fixed sign or other advertisement structure (other than a circular sign) projecting more than 5cm from any external face of a building, the total area of such advertisements shall not exceed 1.2m² and the area of any face of any such advertisement shall not exceed 0.4m².

8. No such advertisement shall contain or consist of any symbol, emblem, model, logo or device exceeding 0.6m in height or any letter exceeding 0.3m in height.

9. No such advertisement shall cover any part of any window or door of any building on which the advertisement is exhibited or to which it is attached or affixed.

There are many blatant examples where many of the column 2 limitations and conditions are not complied with, but who is to say whether or not planning permission has been obtained for the numerous advertisements which are not compliant with the column 2 conditions and limitations?

---

280. 2m above the level of such roads seems dangerously low allowing some trailers or 5.4m approx above the surface of the road.

**[2.389]** Class 1 also deals with advertisements on business premises which refer either to the business or other activity carried on or to the goods and services provided on that premise. The column 2 conditions and limitations are self-explanatory. If the business premises is situated within an area to which an SAAO relates, the exemption will not apply.[281] 'Business premises' is defined in PDR 2001[282] as meaning:

(a) any structure or other land (not being an excluded premises) which is normally used for the carrying on of any professional, commercial or industrial undertaking or any structure (not being an excluded premises) which is normally used for the provision therein of services to persons;

(b) a hotel or public house;

(c) any structure or other land used for the purposes of, or in connection with, the functions of a State authority.

**[2.390]** 'Excluded premises' is also defined under PDR 2001[283] as meaning:

(a) any premises used for the purpose of religious, educational, cultural, recreational or medical character;

(b) any guest house or other premises (not being a hotel) providing overnight guest accommodation, block of flats or apartments, club, boarding house or hostel;

(c) any structure which was designed for use as one or more dwellings, except such a structure which was used as business premises immediately before 1 October 1964 or is so used with permission under PDA 2000.

## Class 2 exemptions

**[2.391]** Class 2 exemptions relate to illuminated advertisements in shop windows or on display at business premises. The column 1 description of development relating to class 2 exemptions provides that illuminated advertisements exhibited as part of any shop or other window display on business premises and other advertisements affixed to the inside of the glass surface of a window of a business premises or otherwise exhibited through a window of such premises are exempt. The column 2 conditions and limitations provide that the total area of any advertisement so exhibited shall not exceed one-quarter of the area of the window through which the advertisements are exhibited.

**[2.392]** The word 'illuminated' is defined under PDR 2001:[284] illuminated in relation to any advertisement, sign or other advertisement structure means illuminated internally or externally by artificial lighting, directly or by reflection, for the purpose of advertisement, announcement or direction.

---

281. See PDR 2001, art 9(10)(b)(ii).
282. PDR 2001, art 5(1).
283. PDR 2001, art 3(3).
284. PDR 2001, art 5(1).

## Class 3 exemptions

**[2.393]** Any advertisements displayed within a business premises and which are not visible from outside the premises are exempt. There are no column 2 conditions and limitations in class 3, so, by implication, there is no limit to the size of these interior advertisements.

## Class 4 exemptions

**[2.394]** An advertisement in the form of a flag, which is attached to a single flagstaff fixed in an upright position on the roof of a business premises and which bears no inscription or emblem other than the name, device or logo of a person or business occupying the business premises, is exempted development.

**[2.395]** There is one column 2 condition and limitation which provides that only one flag advertisement attached to a single flag pole shall be exhibited on a business premises. Observation would seem to indicate that this restriction on flag advertising is breached more often than it is observed. Also, the question might be asked as to what number of flags, which are not fixed in an upright position, can be displayed before the necessity to obtain planning permission is dealt with by enforcement. These flag advertisements must be on the roof and must be on a vertical pole, not a slanted flag pole.

**[2.396]** If the business premises, from which the single flag advertisement is exhibited from a single flag pole, is situated within an area to which an SAAO relates the exemption will not apply.[285]

## Class 5 exemptions

**[2.397]** Advertisements, exhibited at the entrance to any premises, relating to any person, partnership or company carrying on a public service or a profession, business or trade at the premises, are exempt.

**[2.398]** This exemption is subject to two column 2 conditions and limitations, namely:

1. No such advertisement shall exceed $0.3m^2$ in area.
2. Not more than one such advertisement, or, in the case of premises with entrances on different road frontages, one such advertisement for each such frontage, shall be exhibited in respect of each such person, partnership or company on the premises.

## Class 6 exemptions

**[2.399]** Advertisements relating to any institution of a religious, educational, cultural, recreational or medical or similar character, any guesthouse or other premises (other than a hotel) providing overnight guest accommodation or any public house, block of

---

285. See PDR 2001, art 9(1)(b)(ii).

flats, club, boarding house or hostel, situated on the land on which any such advertisement is exhibited, are exempt.

[2.400] There are three column 2 conditions and limitations on this exemption:
1. No such advertisement shall exceed 0.6m$^2$ in area.
2. No part of any such advertisement or an advertisement structure on which it is exhibited shall be more than 2.5m in height above ground level.
3. Not more than one such advertisement or, in the case of premises with entrances on different road frontages, one such advertisement for each such frontage, shall be exhibited in respect of any such premises.

Class 6 development is de-exempted where it is situated in an area to which an SAAO relates.[286]

## Class 7 exemptions

[2.401] Advertisements exhibited on land wholly or for the most part enclosed within a hedge, fence, wall or similar screen or structure (not being land which is a public park, public garden or other land held for the use and enjoyment of the public, or a part of a railway undertaking's enclosed land normally used for the carriage of passengers or goods by rail) and not readily visible from land outside the enclosure wherein it is exhibited, are exempt.

[2.402] There are no column 2 conditions and limitations affecting this class and consequently there is no limit as to the size of these advertisements. The advertisement must not be 'readily visible' from land outside the hedged, fenced, walled or screened area. The term 'readily' is not defined but it is presumed to mean that the advertisements are not generally visible from the outside but that they may be either partially or wholly visible from certain limited viewing points.

## Class 8 exemptions

[2.403] Advertisements exhibited within a railway station, bus station, airport terminal or ferry terminal and which are not readily visible from outside the premises are exempt. As there are no column 2 conditions and limitations there is no limitation as to the size of these advertisements. The meaning of 'readily visible' is the same as in the class 7 exemption which, as has been seen, has neither a statutory nor a case law definition.

## Class 9 exemptions

[2.404] Advertisements relating to the sale or letting of any structure or other land (not being an advertisement structure) on which they are exhibited are exempt.

---

286. See PDR 2001, art 9(1)(b)(ii).

**[2.405]** The three column 2 conditions and limitations on these exemptions are as follows:

1. The area of any such advertisement shall not exceed:
    (a) in the case of an advertisement relating to the sale or letting of a house, 0.6m$^2$;
    (b) in the case of an advertisement relating to the sale or letting of any other structure or land, 1.2m$^2$.
2. Not more than one such advertisement shall be exhibited on the structure or other land.
3. No such advertisement shall be exhibited, and no advertisement structure erected for the purpose of exhibiting such advertisement shall remain on the structure or land, for more than seven days after the sale or letting to which the advertisement relates.

As will be seen from observation, these provisions are sometimes ignored. They cover the usual 'for sale' or 'to let' advertisements which are often placed by auctioneers in some prominent place which is visible from the roadway abutting the premises for sale or for letting. These selling or letting advertisements must be removed within seven days after the sale or letting in accordance with the column 2 conditions and limitations. It is not altogether clear as to whether this means seven days after the sale has been completed or the letting agreement signed and exchanged or whether it means seven days after the contract for purchase or the contract for letting has been exchanged or has come into being. The usual practice would seem to be that after an auction or a private treaty the 'for sale' sign is changed to a 'sold' or a 'sale agreed' sign which remains in place between the date of exchange of contract and the date of closing the sale which is usually something between four and eight weeks later.

## *Class 10 exemptions*

**[2.406]** Advertisements relating to the sale on or before a date specified therein of goods or livestock, and exhibited on land where such goods or livestock are situated or where such sale is held, not being land which is normally used, whether at regular intervals or otherwise, for the purpose of holding sales of goods or livestock, are exempt.

**[2.407]** The three column 2 conditions and limitations imposed on this exemption are as follows:

1. No such advertisement shall exceed 0.6m$^2$ in area.
2. Not more than one such advertisement shall be exhibited on the land concerned.
3. No such advertisement shall be exhibited, and no advertisement structure erected for the purpose of exhibiting such advertisement shall remain on the land for more than seven days after the date specified.

To obtain exemption, the date on which the livestock sale is to take place must be specifically displayed in the advertisement.

## Class 11 exemptions

**[2.408]** Advertisements relating to the carrying out of building or similar works on the land on which they are exhibited, not being land which is normally used, whether at regular intervals or otherwise, for the purpose of carrying out such works, are exempt subject to the following three column 2 conditions and limitations:

1. Where only one advertisement is exhibited, such advertisement shall not exceed 3.5m² in area and shall not be exhibited more than 6m above ground level.

2. Where more than one advertisement is exhibited, no such advertisement shall exceed 0.6m² in area, the total area of such advertisement shall not exceed 3.5m² and no such advertisement shall be exhibited more than 4m above ground level.

3. No such advertisement shall be exhibited, and no advertisement structure erected for the purpose of exhibiting such advertisement shall remain on the land, for more than seven days after the completion of the works.

One might wonder if contractors' advertisements on cranes, which are exhibited at a height greatly in excess of 6m, have the benefit of exemption.

**[2.409]** PDR 2001, art 9(1)(2)(ii) provides that development within this class is not exempt if it is situate within an area to which an SAAO relates.

## Class 12 exemptions

**[2.410]** Advertisements for the purposes of announcement or direction or warning exhibited by a statutory undertaker in relation to the operations of the statutory undertaking, are exempt.

**[2.411]** PDA 2000[287] defines a 'statutory undertaker' as meaning a person, for the time being, authorised by or under an enactment or instrument under an enactment to:

(a) construct or operate a railway, canal, inland navigation, dock, harbour or airport,

(b) provide, or carry out works for the provision of, gas, electricity or telecommunications services, or

(c) provide services connected with, or carry out works for the purposes of the carrying on of the activities of, any public undertaking.

There are no column 2 conditions and limitations affecting class 12.

## Class 13 exemptions

**[2.412]** Advertisements for the purposes of identification, direction or warning with respect to the land or structures on which they are exhibited, are exempt. The only column 2 condition and limitation provides that no such advertisement shall exceed 0.3m² in area.

---

287. PDA 2000, s 2(1).

## Class 14 exemptions

**[2.413]** Advertisements relating to an election to the office of President of Ireland, an election of members of Dáil Éireann, the Parliament of the European Communities, a local authority or Údarás na Gaeltáchta, or a referendum within the meaning of the Referendum Act 1994, are exempt.

**[2.414]** The only column 2 condition and limitation provides that no such advertisement shall be exhibited, and no advertisement structure erected for the purpose of exhibiting such advertisement shall be left in place, for more than seven days after the date of the election or referendum to which the advertisement relates.

**[2.415]** In practice, fines have been imposed after elections where candidates have failed to remove election posters and the political parties have paid heed to this so that, in general, the vast majority of posters are removed within the seven-day period. The problem is that the plastic tiers are left on lamp poles and they continue to accumulate in an unsightly fashion, election after election. Perhaps these plastic tiers should be controlled in the same way as the posters, although identifying offenders would be a problem unless each party was compelled to use a nominated colour for the plastic tiers. The column 2 condition and limitation does not provide any limit on the size or location of these advertisements and perhaps that is something that should be considered in future legislation. At the very least these election posters should not be exhibited in an area to which an SAAO applies.[288]

## Class 15 exemptions

**[2.416]** Advertisements required to be exhibited by or under any enactment, including advertisements the exhibition of which is so required as a condition of the valid exercise of any power, or proper performance of any function, given or imposed by such enactment, or for compliance with any procedure prescribed by or under any enactment, are exempt. There are no column 2 conditions and limitations affecting class 15. This category includes advertisements required under any Act or regulation, including the exhibition of a notice of planning application.

## Class 16 exemptions

**[2.417]** Advertisements, other than advertisements specified in class 17 of this Part of this Schedule, announcing any local event of a religious, cultural, educational, political, social, recreational or sporting character, and advertisements relating to any temporary matter in connection with any local event of such a character, not in either case being an event promoted or carried on for commercial purposes, are exempt.

---

288. See PDR 2001, art 9(1)(b)(ii).

**[2.418]** There are three column 2 conditions and limitations imposed on this exemption, namely as follows:

1. No such advertisement shall exceed 1.2m² in area.
2. No such advertisement shall be exhibited more than 2.5m above ground level or be glued, pasted or otherwise affixed to any structure other than an advertisement structure.
3. No such advertisement shall be exhibited, and no advertisement structure erected for the purpose of exhibiting such advertisement shall be left in place, for more than seven days after the conclusion of the event or matter to which it relates.

As is stated these advertisements must not promote events which are promoted or carried on for commercial purposes. There is some doubt as to whether an entry fee which is paid as a means of collecting money for charity is or is not paid for commercial purposes. The exemption will not apply if the advertisements are exhibited in an area to which an SAAO relates.[289]

## Class 17 exemptions

**[2.419]** Advertisements consisting of placards, posters or bills relating to the visit of any travelling circus, funfair, carnival, show, musicians, players or other travelling entertainment, are exempt.

**[2.420]** There are three column 2 conditions and limitations which are as follows:

1. No such advertisement shall exceed 1.2m² in area.
2. No such advertisement shall be exhibited more than 2.5m above ground level or be glued, pasted or otherwise affixed to any structure other than an advertisement structure.
3. No such advertisement shall be exhibited, and no advertisement structure erected for the purpose of exhibiting such advertisement shall be left in place, for more than seven days after the last performance or closing of the entertainment.

This is another case of an exemption which is de-exempted if the advertisements are exhibited in an area to which an SAAO relates. The advertisements are limited to placards, posters or bills and they must relate to the visit of a travelling circus, funfair, carnival show, musicians, players or other travelling entertainment. Clearly any permanent as opposed to 'passing' performance advertisements are not considered to be exempted development under class 17.

## Class 18 exemptions

**[2.421]** An advertisement relating to any demonstration of agricultural methods or processes on the land on which the advertisement is exhibited, is exempt.

---

289. See PDR 2001, art 9(1)(b)(ii).

[2.422] There are three column 2 conditions and limitations affecting this exemption, as follows:

1. No such advertisement shall exceed 0.6m$^2$ in area.
2. Not more than one such advertisement shall be exhibited on the land concerned.
3. No such advertisement shall be exhibited, and no advertisement structure erected for the purpose of exhibiting such advertisement shall remain on the land, for more than seven days after the date of the demonstration to which it relates.

Demonstrations envisaged in class 18 must be related to agricultural matters but presumably they can be promotional in terms of sales, and educational in terms of teaching the use of processes or of agricultural methods.

## Exempted developments – rural

[2.423] PDR 2001, Sch 2, Pt 3 deals with exemptions in the context of rural development. All exempted developments listed in Sch 2, Pt 3 are subject to the restrictions, where appropriate, contained in PDR 2001, art 9, and to the column 2 conditions and limitations imposed by PDR 2001, Sch 2, Pt 3.

[2.424] There are 17 classes of exempted rural development in PDR 2001, Sch 2, Pt 3 and some changes have been introduced since 1994 which mainly reflect a reduction in the size of exempted agricultural structures and reduction of certain thresholds dealing with the housing of bovines, sheep, goats, donkeys, horses, deer, rabbits, pigs and poultry.

[2.425] Article 6, Pt 3 of Sch 2 of PDR 2001 has been extended by the addition of new arts 18 (dealing with renewable technologies) and 19 (dealing with temporary structures and uses).[290]

### Class 1 exemptions

[2.426] Temporary use of any land for the placing of any tent, camper van, caravan or for the mooring of any boat, barge or other vessel used for the purpose of camping is exempted development. The column 2 conditions and limitations state as follow:

1. Not more than one tent, camper van or caravan shall be placed within 100m of another tent, camper van or caravan at any time.
2. No tent, camper van, caravan or vessel shall remain on the land for a period greater than 10 days.
3. No tent, camper van, caravan or vessel shall be used for the storage, display, advertisement or sale of goods or for the purposes of any business.

---
290. See Planning and Development Regulations 2008 (SI 235/2008).

4. No tent, camper van or caravan shall be placed on land within 50m of any public road unless the land is enclosed by a wall, bank or hedge, or any combination thereof, having an average height of not less than 1.5m.

Class 1 relates to temporary use only. The provision that a camper van, caravan or even a tent must not be placed within a radius of 100m from another camper van, caravan or tent at any time, means that there certainly is plenty of space and indeed it is a rather extravagant gap which is sometimes, or often, ignored in rural areas where music and other festivals occur during the summer months. 'Temporary' means temporary in the sense of use so that taking up all the tents and removing all the camper vans and caravans within 10 days and replacing them on the 11th day with new camper vans, caravans and tents would not be exempted development because the use is continuing for a period which exceeds 10 days.

## Class 2 exemptions

[2.427] PDR 2001, Sch 2, Pt 3, class 2 provides that the temporary use of land by a scouting organisation for a camp is exempted development. The column 2 conditions and limitations state that the land shall not be used for such purposes for any period or periods exceeding 30 days in any year.

## Class 3 exemptions

[2.428] PDR 2001, Sch 2, Pt 3, class 3 exempts works relating to the construction or maintenance of any gully, drain, pond, trough, pit or culvert, the widening or deepening of watercourses, the removal of obstructions from watercourses and the making or repairing of embankments in connection with any of the foregoing works.

[2.429] There are no column 2 conditions and limitations affecting class 3. If the works carried out within an area to which an SAAO relates, the works will require planning permission.[291]

[2.430] The works in class 3 all relate to reclamation works or other works to assist the passage of water from one place to another and to prevent flooding. It is, however, limited to field drainage works in the context of agriculture and therefore when the Kiltiernan-Ballindereen Flood Relief group carried out certain works to prevent flooding in their area, the planning authority in County Galway decided that these works were not exempted under class 3 because the works did not have any connection with agriculture as such.[292] Making agricultural lands available for agriculture by removing flood waters from it would appear to be works which do have a connection with agriculture as such.

---
291. See PDR 2001, art 9(1)(b)(iii).
292. See 07 RF 0820 (County Galway, 18 November 1997). It would be preferable if all *bona fide* attempts to prevent flooding in an area were encouraged, subject to supervision by the local authority to ensure that the parties involved were not simply passing the water on from their backyard into somebody else's backyard.

## Class 4 exemptions

**[2.431]** PDR 2001, Sch 2, Pt 3, class 4 categorises the construction or erection of any wall or fence, other than a fence of sheet metal or a wall or fence within or bounding the curtilage[293] of a house, as exempt.

**[2.432]** The column 2 conditions and limitations provide as follows:
1. the height of the wall or fence, other than a fence referred to in para 2, shall not exceed 2m;
2. the height of any fence for the purpose of deer farming or conservation shall not exceed 3m.

The column 2 conditions and limitations are self-explanatory but it should be noted that this exemption does not include a fence of sheet metal and it does not include a wall or fence within or bounding the curtilage of a house. A wire fence or an electric fence would be permitted under this exemption and it is common practice for farmers to fence off areas of grass for new grazing on a rotation basis so that when one area has been exhausted the cattle, sheep or other animals will be moved to another area.

**[2.433]** Fencing or enclosure of lands habitually open to or used by the public during the 10 years preceding such fencing or enclosure, for recreational purpose or as a means of access to any seashore, mountain, lakeshore, riverbank or other place of natural beauty or recreational utility is de-exempted in accordance with the provisions of PDR 2001, art 9(1)(a)(x). There have been many examples of this type of de-exempted fencing along the coastlines of Ireland. In Donegal, the removal of a stile which allowed the public access to a beach over a fence and the replacement of it by a locked gate, was held to fall within the restrictions of PDR 2001, art 9(1)(a)(x).[294]

## Class 5 exemptions

**[2.434]** PDR 2001, Sch 2, Pt 3, class 5 exemptions deal with:

(a) The carrying out of works on any land for the purpose of mineral prospecting and the erection or placing on land of any structures required for that purpose, where the prospecting is carried out pursuant to and in accordance with the terms and conditions of a licence, lease or permission granted by the Minister for the Marine and Natural Resources under the Minerals Development Act 1940 to 1999.

(b) The carrying out of works on land for the purpose of searching for petroleum and the erection or placing on land of any structures required for that purpose, where searching is carried out pursuant to and in accordance with the terms and conditions of an exploration licence, a petroleum prospecting licence, or a reserved area licence granted by the

---

293. The use of the word 'curtilage' is unfortunate, given that curtilage may not be equivalent to 'boundary'.
294. See 05 RL 2011 (Donegal County, 14 March 2003).

Minister for the Marine and Natural Resources under the Petroleum and Other Minerals Development Act 1960.

**[2.435]** There are no column 2 conditions and limitations affecting class 3 but it will be noted that the class covers two types of works, namely:

1. Work directly related to the activity of prospecting or searching for minerals and petroleum.
2. The erection and placing of structures on land and in accordance with the necessary licence to bring the prospecting to a stage further where the results are promising.

All works carried out in connection with (a) or (b) must be done strictly in conformity with the terms and conditions of the lease or licence which issues if they are to achieve exempted development status.

**[2.436]** If the work envisaged by class 5 is carried out in an area to which an SAAO relates, such work is de-exempted under the provisions of PDR 2001, art 9(1)(b)(iii).

## Class 6 exemptions

**[2.437]** Works consisting of the provision of a roofed structure for the housing of cattle, sheep, goats, donkeys, horses, deer or rabbits having a gross floor area not exceeding 200m$^2$ (whether or not by extension of an existing structure), and any ancillary provision for effluent storage, are exempt. There are, however, strict limitations imposed in column 2 conditions and limitations, namely:

1. No such structure shall be used for any purpose other than the purpose of agriculture.
2. The gross floor space of such structure together with any other such structures situated within the same farmyard complex or within 100m of that complex shall not exceed 300m$^2$ gross floor space in aggregate.
3. Effluent storage facilities adequate to serve the structure having regard to its size, use and location shall be constructed in line with Department of Agriculture, Food and Rural Development and Department of the Environment and Local Government requirements and shall have regard to the need to avoid water pollution.
4. No such structure shall be situated, and no effluent from such structure shall be stored, within 10m of any public road.
5. No such structure within 100m of any public road shall exceed 8m in height.
6. No such structure shall be situated, and no effluent from such structure shall be stored, within 100m of any house (other than the house of the person providing the structure) or other residential building or school, hospital, church or building used for public assembly, save with the consent in writing of the owner and, as may be appropriate, the occupier or person in charge thereof.
7. No unpainted metal sheeting shall be used for roofing or on the external finish of the structure.

Curiously, the class 6 exemption refers to the 'provision' of a roofed structure. Such a provision could include both the construction *de novo* of such structure or the conversion of an existing structure. The provision or construction or conversion of a roofed structure for the housing of the list of animals mentioned above, must be served by an effluent storage facility of adequate size, use and location in accordance with the relevant departmental requirements. Any construction or conversion which seeks to gain the benefit of exemption under class 6 will not do so if the effluent storage facilities are either inadequate or not provided at all. Bearing in mind that all of the classes within Sch 2, Pt 3 are agricultural exemptions, if a structure were built for the housing of horses and it otherwise complied with the conditions in Class 6, it would not be exempted development if the horses were race horses or show jumping horses. The animals housed within the roof structure must be animals used for agricultural purposes.

[2.438] If development envisaged for exemption under class 6 occurs in an area to which an SAAO relates it is de-exempted.[295]

## Class 7 exemptions

[2.439] Class 7 exempts works for the provision of a roofed structure for the housing of pigs, mink or poultry, having a gross floor area not exceeding 75m$^2$ (whether or not by an extension of an existing structure) and ancillary provision for effluent storage. Although the limitations are similar to the limitations imposed in class 6, there are some minor differences and the class 7, column 2 conditions and limitations are as follows:

1. No such structure shall be used for the any purpose other than the purpose of agriculture.

2. The gross floor space area of such structure together with any other such structures situated within the same farmyard complex or within 100m of that complex shall not exceed 100m$^2$ gross floor space in aggregate.

3. Effluent storage facilities adequate to serve the structure having regard to its size, use and location shall be constructed in line with Department of Agriculture, Food and Rural Development and Department of the Environment and Local Government requirements and shall have regard to the need to avoid water pollution.

4. No such structure shall be situated and no effluent from such structure shall be stored, within 10m of any public road.

5. No such structure within 100m of any public road shall exceed 8m in height.

6. No such structure shall be situated, and no effluent from such structure shall be stored, within 100m of any house (other than the house of the person providing the structure) or other residential building or school, hospital, church or building or used for public assembly, save with the consent in writing of the owner and, as may be appropriate, the occupier or person in charge thereof.

---

295. See PDR 2001, art 9(1)(b)(iii).

7. No unpainted metal sheeting shall be used for roofing or on the external finish of the structure.

8. Boundary fencing on any mink holding must be escape-proof for mink.

It will be noted that the word 'provision' of a roofed structure is used, and includes either construction *de novo* or conversion of an existing structure. If development envisaged for exemption under Class 7 is located in an area to which an SAAO relates the development is de-exempted under PDR 2001, art 9(1)(b)(iii).

## Class 8 exemptions

[2.440] Class 8 exempts works providing for roofless cubicles, open loose yards, self feed silo or silage areas, feeding aprons, assembly yards, milking parlours or structures for the making and storage of silage or any other structures of a similar character or description, having an aggregate gross floor area not exceeding 200m$^2$, and any ancillary provision for effluent storage.

[2.441] The column 2 conditions and limitations in class 8 are precisely the same as the limitations numbered 1 to 7 in class 6. If development, envisaged for exemption under art 8, is carried out in an area to which an SAAO relates it is de-exempted by PDR 2001, art 9(1)(b)(iii).

## Class 9 exemptions

[2.442] Class 9 exempts works consisting of the provision of any store, barn, shed, glasshouse or other structure not being a type specified in classes 6, 7 or 8 above and having a gross floor space not exceeding 300m$^2$.

[2.443] The column 2 conditions and limitations are similar in places to those in class 6 but there are some differences and to avoid confusion the limitations are listed below as follows:

1. No such structure shall be used for any purpose other than the purpose of agriculture or forestry, but excluding the housing of animals or the storing of effluent.

2. The gross floor space of such structures together with any other such structures situated within the same farmyard complex or complex of such structures or within 100m of that complex shall not exceed 900m$^2$ gross floor space in aggregate.

3. No such structure shall be situated within 10m of any public road.

4. No such structure within 100m of any public road shall exceed 8m in height.

5. No such structures shall be situated within 100m of any house (other than the house of the person providing the structure) or other residential building or school, hospital, church or building used for public assembly, save with the consent in writing of the owner and, as may be appropriate, the occupier or person in charge thereof.

6. No unpainted metal sheeting shall be used for roofing or on the external finish of the structure.

Class 9 is a class which covers structures not covered by classes 6, 7 and 8 and includes such structures as sheds, barns, glass-houses or stores. Whereas the use in classes 6, 7 and 8 is strictly limited to agriculture, the use in class 9 includes both agriculture and forestry. The main difference between this and the preceding classes is that class 9 structures may not be used for the storage of animals. Again, if development envisaged for exemption under class 9 occurs in an area to which an SAAO relates, it is de-exempted.

## Class 10 exemptions

[2.444] Class 10 is the final class dealing with exempted agricultural structures in rural areas. It provides for an exemption for the erection of an unroofed fenced area for the exercising or training of horses or ponies together with a drainage bed or soft surface material to provide an all-weather surface. The column 2 conditions and limitations are as follow:

1. No such structure shall be used for any purpose other than the exercising or training of horses or ponies.

2. No such area shall be used for the staging of public events.

3. No such structure shall be situated within 10m of any public road, and no entrance to such area shall be directly off any public road.

4. The height of any such structure shall not exceed 2m.

It should be noted that the word used here is not 'provision' of an unroofed fenced area. It refers to the 'erection' of an unroofed fenced area (eg, a show jumping arena), which limits this development to construction *de novo*. Another limitation here is that if the land before the development was agricultural land, the change in use of agricultural land to use as a riding stable has been held to be a material change in use.[296] The 3 April 2003 decision is not the final word on this matter and in many, if not in most, cases a show jumping arena, for example, would be likely to be developed on agricultural land even though that might not always happen. If material change in use (from agricultural to show jumping arena) does de-exempt class 10, the class, as a rural exemption class, is practically useless. The question which a court might ask is whether de-exemption in the case of that type of material change in use was intended by the legislators. It is suggested that it might not have been so intended. The structure is limited strictly to the use of training horses and if the staging of public events is involved, it is not included if the exemption is to apply. If development envisaged for exemption under class 10 occurs in an area to which an SAAO relates it is de-exempted under the provisions of PDR 2001, art 9(1)(b)(iii).

---

296. 06D RL 2023 (Dun Laoghaire-Rathdown County, 3 April 2003).

## Class 11 exemptions

**[2.445]** Class 11 deals with exemption for land reclamation works in rural areas. The following works are exempt if carried out on land used for agriculture or forestry purposes only:

- (a) field drainage;
- (b) land reclamation;
- (c) the removal of fences;
- (d) the improvement of existing fences;
- (e) the improvement of hill grazing; or
- (f) the reclamation of estuarine marsh land or of callows, where the preservation of such land or callows is not an objective of a development plan for the area.

There are no column 2 conditions and limitations attached to class 11.

**[2.446]** If exemption is to be obtained under class 11, the land on which the works are carried out must have been used for agricultural or forestry prior to the works being carried out. Also, if, after the works have been carried out, the land is to be used for additional purposes other than agricultural or forestry, the exemption will not apply. The works or land reclamation must be solely for the purpose of agricultural or forestry. If not the change in use will be a material change in use for which permission is required and in this class, as opposed to class 10, the legislators did intend to de-exempt class 11 exemptions where the land is not strictly limited to use for agricultural or forestry purposes. If development seeking exemption under class 11 is carried out in an area to which an SAAO relates it will not be exempted.[297]

## Class 12 exemptions

**[2.447]** Class 12 exempts works consisting of the provision of a roof structure for the housing of greyhounds, having a gross floor area not exceeding 50m² (whether or not by extension of an existing structure), and any ancillary provisions for effluent storage. The column 2 conditions and limitations are as follows:

1. No such structure shall be used for any purpose other than the keeping of greyhounds.
2. The gross floor space of such structure together with any other such structures situated within a premises or within 100m of that premises shall not exceed 75m² gross floor space in aggregate.
3. Effluent storage facilities adequate to serve the structure having regard to its size, use, location and the need to avoid water pollution shall be provided.
4. No such structure shall be situated, and no effluent from such structure shall be stored, within 10m of any public road.

---

297. See PDR 2001, art 9(1)(b)(iii).

5. No such structure within 100m of any public road shall exceed 8m in height.

6. No such structure shall be situated and no effluent from such structure shall be stored, within 100m of any house (other than the house of the person providing the structure) or other residential building or school, hospital, church or building used for public assembly, save with the consent in writing of the owner and, as may be appropriate, the occupier or person in charge thereof.

Class 12 uses the word 'provision' and not 'erection' so that the exemption will apply whether or not a roofed structure for greyhounds is to be constructed *de novo* or whether an existing structure is to be altered or converted. If development as envisaged for exemption under class 12 is carried out in an area to which an SAAO relates, the development will not be exempted development.[298]

## *Class 13 exemptions*

**[2.448]** Class 13 exempts works consisting of the provision, for any purpose in connection with keeping of greyhounds, of a roofless hard surface yard or of a roofless hard surface enclosed area, where the area does not exceed 100m$^2$ (whether or not by extension of an existing yard or area), and any ancillary provisions for effluent storage. The column 2 conditions and limitations for class 13 are as follows:

1. The gross floor space of such structure or structures together with any other such structures situated within the same complex or within 100m of that complex shall not exceed 150m$^2$ gross floor space in aggregate.

2. Effluent storage facilities adequate to serve the structure having regard to its size, use, location and the need to avoid water pollution shall be provided.

3. No such structure shall be situated and no effluent from such structure shall be stored, within 10m of any public road.

4. No such structure shall be situated, and no effluent from such structure shall be stored, within 100m of any house (other than the house of the person providing the structure) or other residential building or school, hospital, church or building used for public assembly, save with the consent in writing of the owner and, as may be appropriate, the occupier or person in charge thereof.

Class 13 relates to the provision of a roofless hard surfaced yard or enclosed area in connection with the keeping of greyhounds. The word 'provision' is used which will allow for development de novo or alterations or conversions of existing structures. Again, the Class 13 exemption will not apply where development seeking exemption is envisaged in an area to which an SAAO relates.[299]

---

298. See PDR 2001, art 9(1)(b)(iii).
299. See PDR 2001, art 9(1)(b)(iii).

## Class 14 exemptions

**[2.449]** Class 14 provides exemption for the use of uncultivated land or semi-natural areas for intensive agricultural purposes. The column 2 conditions and limitations provide that the area involved shall be less than 100 hectares. If an EIA is required for this development then it is not exempted development.

## Class 15 exemptions

**[2.450]** Class 15 exempts initial afforestation. There are no column 2 conditions and limitations.

This exemption may only refer to reasonably small scale afforestation developments. The use of the word 'initial' would indicate that, before planting, the lands had not been used as an afforestation development previously. If the area exceeds 50 hectares it is possible that an EIA would be required. If an EIA is required, the development is not exempted. The European Court of Justice ruled against Ireland on 21 September 1999 in relation to the thresholds adopted by Ireland concerning afforestation, which had been 70 hectares. In the case of peat extraction it had been 50 hectares. The view taken by the European Court was that these limits exceeded the discretion available to Ireland and that developing forestry in an area of 70 hectares or peat extraction in an area of 50 hectares would have an effect on the nature of the landscape which could be detrimental.

Two new pieces of legislation were introduced to ensure that Ireland's position in relation to initial afforestation and peat extraction would conform with the European Community legislation. This legislation comprised the European Communities (Environmental Impact Assessment) (Amendment) Regulations 2001[300] and the Local Government Planning and Development (Amendment) Regulations 2001[301]. A new 'forest consent' system is now in operation which requires that all initial afforestation proposals must receive the approval from the Minister for Marine and Natural Resources. The consent system also involves a consultation process with prescribed bodies including the local authority for the area. Public consultation is also required to ensure that such matters as habitats, archaeology and other environmental considerations are taken into account. If initial afforestation is to cover an area in excess of 50 hectares or more, it almost certainly will require an EIA and in that event the development is not exempted development.

## Class 16 exemptions

**[2.451]** Class 16 exempts the replacement of broadleaf high forest by conifer species. The column 2 conditions and limitations in class 16 require that the area involved shall be less than 10 hectares.

**[2.452]** An EIA would be required if replacement of broad-leaf high forest by conifer species were to occur in an area which is greater than 10 hectares. In that case there is no

---

300. European Communities (Environmental Impact Assessment) (Amendment) Regulations 2001 (SI 538/2001).
301. Local Government Planning and Development (Amendment) Regulations 2001 (SI 539/2001).

**[2.453]** possibility of exemption. In fact both turbary and initial planting of forest are now excluded from the definition of 'agriculture'; nevertheless the exempted development regulations do exempt initial afforestation and the replacement of broad-leaf high forest by conifer trees. The limitations in the case of initial afforestation are dealt with above and the limitation in relation to replacement of broad-leaf high forest by conifer trees provides that such development will only be exempted development if it is carried out on an area of less than 10 hectares.

## Class 17 exemptions

**[2.453]** Class 17 dealing with peat extraction has now been amended by the substitution of a new class 17 provided in the PDR 2005 (SI 364/2005).

**[2.454]** The exemption provided in class 17 will only apply to:
  (a) Peat extraction in a new or extended area of less than 10 hectares; or
  (b) Peat extraction in a new or extended area of 10 hectares or more, where the drainage of the bogland commenced prior to the coming into force of these regulations (ie, 21 January, 2002).

**[2.455]** The column 2 conditions and limitations which have been inserted by PDR 2005 are as follows:
  1. No such peat extraction shall be likely to have significant effects on the environment by reference to the criteria set out in Sch 7.
  2. Paragraph 1 shall not apply to peat extraction:
     (i) on a European site where such a development is regulated by the European Communities (Natural Habitat) Regulations 1997, or any regulation or enactment amending or replacing those regulations; or
     (ii) on a site prescribed under article 12 where such development is regulated by the Wildlife Amendment Acts 1976 and 2000 or any enactment amending or replacing those acts.

The ECJ ruling on 27 June 2010[302] also ruled against exempted extraction of peat of an area up to 50 hectares because it did not take proper account of environmental issues. Although the exemption in PDR 2001, Sch 2, Pt 3, class 17 permitted exempted peat extraction in a new or extended area of less than 10 hectares, or peat extraction in a new or extended area of 10 hectares or more where drainage of the bog land commenced prior to the coming into force of these regulations, there were no column 2 conditions and limitations.

**[2.456]** PDR 2001, art 3(3) interprets 'peat extraction' as including any related drainage of bogland. If the drainage of bogland commenced prior to the commencement date of PDR 2001 (21 January 2002), there is no limit to the extent of the area where peat extraction can occur. The 10 hectare area is a safe area in terms of the requirement of an EIA. If peat extraction over an area of 30 hectares is planned, an EIA is a necessary

---

302. *Commission v Ireland* (Case C–392/96).

requirement and therefore the development could not in any case be exempted development. Sch 7 of PDR 2001 relates to arts 103, 109 and 120. This schedule sets out the criteria for determining whether a development would or would not be likely to have significant effects on the environment. If peat extraction is likely to have significant effects on the environment by reference to Sch 7 it will not be exempted as stated in para 1 of the column 2 conditions and limitations. If peat extraction is to occur on a site which is a European site regulated by the Habitats Regulations, the extraction will not be exempted development even though it is on an area of less than 10 hectares. Also, PDR 2001, art 12 prescribes sites for the purpose of s 10(2)(c) of PDA 2000 in the following circumstances:

(a) any area designated as a natural heritage area under s 18 of the Wildlife (Amendment) Act 2000; and

(b) any area the subject of a notice under s 16(2)(b) of the Wildlife (Amendment) Act 2000.

If either (a) and/or (b) apply, peat extraction within these areas will require permission.

[2.457] PDA 2000[303] deals with the content of development plans and, specifically, s 10(c) requires that apart from what is required in sub-s (1) in relation to a development plan, account must be taken of:

> The conservation and protection of the environment including, in particular, the archaeological and natural heritage and the conservation and protection of European sites and any other sites which may be prescribed for the purpose of this paragraph.

## Classes 18 exemptions

[2.458] Classes 18 and 19 have been added by PDR 2008 (SI 235/2008).

[2.459] PDR 2001–2008, Sch 2, Pt 3, class 18 exemptions are very similar to the exemptions which have been set out in full under the description of development in column 1 and under the conditions and limitations in column 2 of class 56 of Sch 2, Pt 1 of these Regulations. The column 1 description of development in class 18 refers to an agricultural holding in class 18(a), (b), (c) and (d). The column 1 description of development in class 18(e) refers to an agricultural building. Class 56, on the other hand, deals with 'industrial buildings', 'light industrial buildings', 'business premises' and, as appropriate, 'ancillary buildings within the curtilage of those buildings'.

[2.460] The purpose of class 18 is to provide exemptions for the following:

(a) Combined heat and power systems in relation to agricultural holdings.

(b) Wind turbines in relation to agricultural holdings.

(c) Solar panels (thermal collector or photo-voltaic) in relation to agricultural holdings.

---

303. PDA 2000, s 10.

(d) Ground source heat pump systems (horizontal and vertical), or air source heat pumps in relation to agricultural holdings.

(e) Biomass boilers, including a boiler house, flues mounted on the boiler house and over ground fuel storage tanks or structures in relation to agricultural buildings.

The heating power sources described in 18(a) to 18(e) are exempted development provided the column 2 conditions and limitations are complied with. Because of slight differences and in order to prevent too much confusion it is worthwhile setting out the column 2 conditions applying to 18(a) to 18(e) inclusive. They are as follows.

## Combined heating power system within agricultural holdings

**[2.461]** *Column 1 of class 18(a)* provides that the construction, or erection or placing within an agricultural holding of a structure for the purpose of housing a (fully enclosed) combined heating power system is exempted development subject to the following Column 2 conditions and limitations.

1. The gross floor area of a structure shall not exceed 300m$^2$.
2. No such structure shall exceed 8m in height, or 40m in length.
3. No such structure shall be within
   (a) 10m of any public road;
   (b) 100m of the nearest habitable house (other than the house of the person providing the structure) or any other residential building or school, hospital, church or building used for public assembly, save with the consent in writing of the owner and as appropriate, the occupier or person in charge thereof.
4. No such structure shall have more than two flues, neither of which shall exceed 16m in height from ground level.
5. The diameter of any flue shall not exceed 1m.
6. Noise levels must not exceed 43db(A) during normal operation, as measured at the party boundary.
7. Not more than one such structure shall be erected within the agricultural holding.
8. The structure shall be used for the purpose of housing a combined heat and power unit only.

## Wind turbines within agricultural holdings

**[2.462]** Column 1 of class 18(b) provides that the construction or erection or placing within an agricultural holding of a wind turbine is exempted development subject to the following column 2 conditions and limitations, which are:

1. The turbine shall not be erected on or attached to a building or other structure.
2. The total height of the turbines shall not exceed 20m.

3. The rotor diameter shall not exceed 8m.

4. The minimum clearance between the lower tip of the rotor and ground level shall not be less than 3m.

5. The supporting tower shall be a distance of not less than:

    (a) One and half times the total structure height (including the blade of the turbine at the highest point of its arc) plus 1m from any party boundary.

    (b) The total structure height (including the blade of the turbine at the highest point of its arc) plus:

       (i) 5m from any non-electrical overhead cables,

       (ii) 20m from any 38kV electricity distribution line,

       (iii) 30m from the centreline of any electricity transmission line of 110kV or more.

6. The turbine shall not be located within:

    (a) 100m of an existing wind turbine;

    (b) 5km of the nearest airport or aerodrome, or any communication, navigation and surveillance facilities designated by the Irish Aviation Authority, save with the consent in writing of the Authority and compliance with any condition relating to the provision of aviation obstacle warning lighting.

7. Noise levels must not exceed 43db(A) during normal operation, as measured from the nearest habitable house.

8. Not more than one turbine shall be erected within the agricultural holding.

9. All turbine and components shall have a matt, non-reflective finish and the blade shall be made of material that does not deflect telecommunication signals.

10. No sign, advertisement or object, not required for the functioning or safety of the turbine shall be attached to or exhibited on the wind turbine.

It should be noted that the restriction affecting wind turbines for industrial buildings, light industrial buildings and business premises, in the column 2 conditions and limitations no 11, provides that the wind turbine shall not be located within an architectural conservation area. That limitation does not apply to the construction, erection or placement of a wind turbine within an agricultural holding.

## *Solar panels within agricultural holdings*

**[2.463]** Column 1 of class 18(c) provides that the installation or erection on an agricultural structure or within the curtilage of an agricultural holding, of solar panels (thermal collector or photo-voltaic) is exempted development.

The column 2 conditions and limitations affecting 18(c) in relation to solar panels installed on an agricultural structure or within the curtilage of an agricultural holding are as follows:

1. The total aperture area of any such panel, taken together with any other such panel previously placed on or within the said holding, shall not exceed 50m² or 50% of the total roof area, whichever is the lesser.
2. The distance between the plane of the wall and the panel shall not exceed 15cm.
3. The distance between the plane of a pitched roof and the panel shall not exceed 50cm.
4. The distance between the plane of a flat roof and the panel shall not exceed 2m.
5. The solar panel shall be a minimum of 50cm from the edge of the wall or roof on which it is mounted or 2m in the case of a flat roof.
6. The total aperture area of any wall-mounted panel or free-standing solar array shall not exceed 25m²
7. Any equipment associated with the panels, including water tanks, shall be located within the roof space of the building.
8. The height of a free-standing solar array shall not exceed 2m, at its highest point, above ground level.
9. No sign, advertisement or other object, not required for the functioning or safety of the turbine shall be attached to or exhibited on the panels.

## Ground source heat pump systems within agricultural holdings

[2.464] Column 1 of class 18(d) provides that installation within an agricultural holding of a ground source heat pump system (horizontal and vertical) or air source heat pumps are exempted subject to the following column 2 restrictions and limitations:

1. The level of the ground shall not be altered by more than 1m above or below the level of the adjoining ground.
2. The total area of any air source heat pumps shall not exceed 10m².
3. The air source heat pump shall be a minimum of 50cm from the edge of the wall or roof on which it is mounted.
4. Noise levels must not exceed 43db(A) during normal operation, as measured from the nearest habitable house.
5. Distances from party boundaries and from the foundations of any structure or building shall be maintained in line with the Sustainable Energy Ireland Renewable Energy Information Office Procurement Guidelines on Heat Pump Systems for the time being in force.

## Biomass boilers as part of a heating system within agricultural holdings

[2.465] Column 1 of class 18(e) provides for the provision, as part of a heating system for an agricultural building, of a biomass boiler, including a boiler house, flues mounted on the boiler house, and an over ground fuel storage tank or structure as exempted development.

The column 2 conditions and limitations in relation to 18(e) are as follows:

1. The gross floor space of the boiler house shall not exceed 20m².

2. The capacity of the fuel storage tank or structure shall not exceed 75m³.
3. The height of a boiler house or fuel storage tank installed above ground level shall not exceed 3m.
4. The height of a flue mounted on a biomass unit shall not exceed 20m, measured from ground level.
5. No more than two flues shall be erected.
6. Not more than one such structure shall be erected within the agricultural holding.
7. The diameter of any flue shall not exceed 1m.
8. The boiler house shall not be located within:
    (a) 10m of any public road;
    (b) 100m of the nearest habitable house (other than the house of the person providing the structure) or other residential building or school, hospital, church or building used for public assembly, save with the consent in writing of the owner and, as may be appropriate, the occupier or person in charge thereof.
9. Noise levels must not exceed 43db(A) during normal operation, as measured from the site boundary.
10. The fuel shall not include products derived from wood containing dangerous substances.

## Class 19 exemptions

**[2.466]** PDR 2001–2008, Sch 2, Pt 3, class 19 (see PDR 2008 (SI 235/2008)) provides exemption for the erection of a mast for mapping meteorological conditions. The column 2 conditions and limitations on the column 1 description of development are as follows:

1. No such masts shall be erected for a period exceeding 15 months in any 24 month period.
2. The total mast height shall not exceed 80m.
3. The mast shall be a distance of not less than:
    (a) the total structure height plus;
        (i) 5m from any party boundary,
        (ii) 20m from any non-electrical overhead cables,
        (iii) 20m from any 38kV electricity distribution lines,
        (iv) 30m from the centrelines of any electricity transmission line of 110kV or more;
    (b) 5km from the nearest airport or aerodrome, or any communication, navigation and surveillance facilities designed by the Irish Aviation Authority, save with the consent in writing of the Authority and compliance with any conditions relating to the provision of aviation obstacle warning lighting.
4. Not more than one such mast shall be erected within the site.

5. All mast components shall have a matt, non-reflective finish and the blade shall be made of material that does not deflect telecommunication signals.
6. No sign, advertisement or object, not required for the functioning or safety of the mast shall be attached to or exhibited on the mast.

# Exempted developments under PDR 2001, arts 6–11

## PDR 2001, art 6

**[2.467]** Article 6 is the fundamental article which generally provides for exempted development specified in PDR 2001 (as amended) Sch 2, Pt 1 (general), Pt 2 (advertisement) and Pt 3 (rural development).

**[2.468]** PDR 2001, art 6 is the core article which provides for the exempted developments specified in Pts 1, 2 and 3 of Sch 2, subject, where applicable, to the limitations and conditions imposed upon such exempted development as set out in column 2 of Pts 1, 2 and 3 of Sch 2.

**[2.469]** PDR 2001, art 6 provides that, subject to art 7, development of a class specified in column 1 of Pt 1 of Sch 2 shall be exempted development for the purpose of the Act, provided that such development complies with the column 2 conditions and limitations of the said Pt 1 opposite the mention of that class in the said column 1.

**[2.470]** Article 6 should be read carefully, particularly art 6(2), which provides limitations on exempted development relating to advertising. PDR 2001, art 6(2)(a) provides that, subject to art 9, development consisting of the use of a structure or other land for the exhibition of advertisements of a class specified in column 1 of Pt 2 of Sch 2 shall be exempted development for the purposes of the Act provided that:

(i) such development complies with the conditions and limitations specified in column 2 of the said Part 2 opposite the mention of that class in the said column 1; and

(ii) the structure or other land shall not be used for the exhibition of any advertisement other than an advertisement of a class which is specified in column 1 of the said Part 2 and which complies with the conditions and limitations specified in column 2 of the said Part 2 opposite the mention of that class in the said column 1.

**[2.471]** PDR 2001, art 6(2)(b) provides that, subject to art 9, development consisting of the erection of any advertisement structure for the exhibition of an advertisement of any one of the classes specified in column 1 of Pt 2 of Sch 2 shall be exempted development for the purposes of the Act, provided that:

(i) the area of such advertisement structure which is used for the exhibition of an advertisement does not exceed the area, if any, specified in column 2 of the said Part 2 opposite the mention of that class in the said column 1;

(ii) the advertisement structure is not used for the exhibition of advertisements other than advertisements of the class to which the exemption relates;

(iii) further to s 57 of the Act, the advertisement structure is not erected on a protected structure or a proposed protected structure save an advertisement structure referred to in class 5, 9 or 15 of column 1 of Part 2 of Sch 2;

(iv) further to s 82 of the Act, the advertisement structure is not located on the exterior of a structure where the structure concerned is located within an architectural conservation area or an area specified as an architectural conservation area in a development plan for the area or, pending the variation of a development plan or the making of a new development plan, in the draft development plan, so as to materially affect the character of the area, save an advertisement structure referred to classes 5, 9 or 15 of column 1 of Part 2 of Sch 2; and

(v) where the advertisement structure is within a Gaeltacht area, any advertisement exhibited is:

(I) in Irish, or

(II) in Irish and other languages, with prominence give to the Irish text, and identical content in all versions of the text.

Article 6 deals with exempted development set out in Sch 2 of the Regulations under Pt 1 (general), Pt 2 (advertisements) and Pt 3 (rural development). It is clearly stated that any matter which is described in column 1 must, if it is to be exempted, fall within the conditions and limitations set out in column 2. If there is doubt as to whether or not the matter falls within the category of exempted development a declaration may be sought from the planning authority under s 5 of PDA 2000. PDA 2000, s 57 deals with works affecting the character of protected structures or proposed protected structures. PDA 2000, s 57 provides that, notwithstanding the provisions of s 4(1)(h), the carrying out of works to a protected structure or a proposed protected structure, shall be exempted development only if those works would not materially affect the character of:

(a) the structure; or

(b) any element of the structure which contributes to a special architectural, historical, archaeological, artist, cultural, scientific, social or technical interest.

In cases where it is not clear as to whether the works would be exempted development or not, s 57, as amended by PDA 2002, s 13(a), (b) and (c), allows the owner/occupier of a protected structure to seek a planning authority declaration as to what types of works would or would not materially affect the character of the structure or any element of the structure as set out in s 57(1)(a) and (b) above. The planning authority is given a period of 12 weeks in which to furnish the declaration and if a declaration is not acceptable to the owner/occupier it may be appealed to An Bord Pleanála within four weeks.

**[2.472]** The reference to classes 5, 9 or 15 of column 1 of Pt 2 of Sch 2 comprises the classes of advertisements to be placed in an architectural conservation area or on a protected structure. The advertisements covered by classes 5, 9 or 15 are dealt with at paras **2.255** to **2.291** above.

[2.473] PDR 2001, art 6(3) provides that, subject to art 9 and in areas other than a city, town or an area to which a local area plan has been made as specified in PDA 2000, s 19(1)(b) or the excluded area as defined in s 9 of the Local Government (Reorganisation) Act 1985, development of a class specified in column 1 of Pt 3 of Sch 2 of PDR 2001 shall be exempted development for the purposes of the Act, provided it complies with the conditions and limitations specified in column 2, Pt 3 of Sch 2 opposite the mention of the class in column 1. PDR 2001, Pt 3, Sch 2 deals with exempted development – rural.

[2.474] PDR 2001, art 6(4)(a) permits exempted development, subject to para (b), for the carrying out of such works as are necessary to secure compliance with the Building Regulations 1997, in the case of developments consisting of construction of a dwelling or dwellings in respect of which permission under Pt IV of the Act of 1963 was granted before 1 June 1992.

[2.475] PDR 2001, art 6(4)(b) provides that the exemption provided by para (a) shall not apply in the case of development consisting of the construction of a building designed for use as two or more separate dwellings.

## PDR 2001, art 7

[2.476] PDR 2001, art 7 exempts certain developments under other enactments:

(1) Any works consisting of or incidental to the carrying out of development referred to in s 84(4)(a) of the Environmental Protection Agency Act 1992, as amended, for the purpose of giving effect to a condition attached to a licence or revised licence granted by the EPA under Part IV of the said Act shall be exempted development.

(2) Works consisting of or incidental to the carrying out of development referred to in s 54(4)(a) of the Waste Management Act 1996 for the purpose of giving effect to a condition attached to a licence or revised licence granted by the EPA under Part V of the said Act shall be exempted development.

If an integrated pollution licence requires work to be carried out as a condition or if a waste licence requires work to be carried out as a condition, in either case where the work is not covered by any planning permission, those works are exempted by the provisions of PDR 2001, art 7.

## PDR 2001, art 8

[2.477] Article 8 deals with work specified in a drainage scheme. Works, which are specified in a drainage scheme confirmed by the Minister for Finance under Pt II of the Arterial Drainage Act 1945 or the Arterial Drainage (Amendment) Act 1995, carried out by, on behalf of, or in partnership with, the Commissioners of Public Works, with such additions, omissions, variations and deviations or other works incidental thereto, as may be found necessary by the Commissioners or their agents or partner in the course of the works, shall be exempted developments.

**[2.478]** The fact that the works envisaged by art 8 will amount to exempted development where the appropriate requirements are met does not imply that if EIA is required, same will have to be carried out and provided.

## PDR 2001, art 9

**[2.479]** Article 9 places important restrictions on exemption. Article 9 imposes specific restrictions on development of classes specified in Sch 2, Parts 1, 2 and 3, ie, developments to which art 6 relates, and, if the restrictions of art 9 apply, then the said development to which art 6 relates shall not be exempted development. This article de-exempts developments which come within a category of exempted developments set out in Pts 1, 2 and 3 of Sch 2 where certain conditions apply. The conditions are set out below. Development to which art 6 relates shall not be exempted development if the carrying out of such development would, under art 9(1)(a):

> (i) contravene a condition attached to a permission under the Act or be inconsistent with any use specified in a permission under the Act. If these circumstances apply the development will not be exempted.
>
> Note: PDA 2000[304] provides that where a permission is granted under this Part for a structure, the grant of permission may specify the purposes for which the structure may or may not be used, and in case the grant specifies use as a dwelling as a purpose for which the structure may be used, the permission may also be granted subject to a condition specifying that the use as a dwelling shall be restricted to use by persons of a particular class or description and that provision to that effect shall be embodied in an agreement under s 47. In effect, if an existing permission contains such condition the condition cannot be de-exempted. See *Dublin Corporation v Eircom plc, Eircell Limited and An Post*,[305] where the planning authority sought an injunction in respect of a telecom antenna structure situate at Whitehall. A local resident had complained to the planning authority that the structure was unauthorised whereas Eircom claimed that it was exempt under art 9 of the then Local Government (Planning and Development) Regulations 1994 and class 29(f) of Sch 2 to the 1994 Regulations. The development, however, breached a condition contained in an earlier planning permission granted in 1991 and as such the exemption was inapplicable. Although it is not clear what the situation is if an earlier planning permission has not been implemented it is probable that de-exemption would not apply. Similarly, if the life of the planning permission had expired (normally five years from the date of grant) de-exemption would not apply.[306]

---

304. PDA 2000, s 32(2).
305. *Dublin Corporation v Eircom plc, Eircell Limited and An Post* [2002] 3 IR 327.
306. Note however that in *Dublin Corporation v Eircom plc, Eircell Limited and An Post* [2002] 3 IR 327 the permission concerned was a 1991 permission and the case is a 2002 case.

(ii) consist of or comprise the formation, laying out or material widening of a means of access to a public road the surfaced carriageway of which exceeds 4m in width. If these circumstances apply the development will not be exempted.

Note: The development here deals with the development of a means of access to a public road. Thus, for example, class 6 (b)(ii) of Part 1 of Sch 2 de-exempts any works within the curtilage of a house for the provision to the front or side of the house of a hard surface for the parking of not more than two motor vehicles used for a purpose incidental to the enjoyment of the house as such. If it becomes necessary to carry out development which will connect the hard surface in which the car is parked to a public road which exceeds 4m in width. That development is not exempt development.

(iii) endanger public safety by reason of traffic hazard or obstruction of road users. If these circumstances apply the development will not be exempted.

Note: If exempted development is carried out it may not be exempted development if it creates a traffic hazard or obstruction of road users which will result in endangerment of public safety.

(iv) except in the case of a porch to which class 7 specified in column 1 of Part 1 of Sch 2 applies and which complies with the conditions and limitations specified in column 2 of the said Part 1 opposite the mention of that class in the said column 1, if the development to which art 6 relates comprises the construction, erection, extension or renewal of a building on any street so as to bring forward the building, or any part of the building, beyond the front wall of the building on either side thereof or beyond a line determined as the building line in a development plan for the area or, pending the variation of a development plan or the making of a new development plan, in the draft variation of the development plan or the draft development plan, it shall not be exempted development.

Note: The purpose of this restriction on exempted developments is to maintain either a building line which is prescribed in a development plan or alternatively to prevent add-ons (with the exception of porches to which class 7 applies, which protrude beyond the established and existing front wall of the building).

(v) consist of or comprise the carrying out under a public road of works other than a connection to a wired broadcast relay service, sewer, water main, gas main or electricity supply line or cable, or any works to which classes 25, 26 or 31(a) specified in column 1 of Part 1 of Sch 2 applies. If these circumstances apply the development will not be exempted.

Note: The purpose of this restriction is to protect public roadways against damage caused by carrying out development under the public roadway. The restriction is limited to the public roadway and therefore would not apply to land or ground other than a public road. There are extensive exceptions in PDA 2000, as amended.[307] A local authority may lay cables, wires and pipelines under a public road, and PDA 2000,[308] in certain circumstances, allows a statutory undertaker to place electricity transmission lines under a public road.

(vi) interfere with the character of the landscape, or a view or prospect of special amenity value or special interest, the preservation of which is an objective of a development plan for the area in which the development is proposed or, pending the variation of a development plan or the making of a new development plan, in the draft variation of the development plan or the draft development plan. In these circumstances development will not be exempted.

Note: Exempted development becomes de-exempted if the development would interfere with the character of a landscape or a view or prospect of special amenity value or special interest provided the landscape or view or prospect of special amenity is preserved as an objective of a development plan, a proposed development plan or a proposed variation of a development plan. The word 'interfere' is not statutorily defined and therefore what amounts to interference is primarily a subjective judgment. It might be 'interference' if a proposed development had the potential of detracting in some negative way from the existing character of the landscape or of a view or prospect of special amenity value or special interest.

(vii) consist of or comprise the excavation, alteration or demolition (other than peat extraction) of places, caves, sites, features or other objects of archaeological, geological, historical, scientific or ecological interest, the preservation of which is an objective of a development plan in which the development is proposed or, pending the variation of a development plan or the making of a new development plan, in the draft variation of the development plan or the draft development plan, save any excavation pursuant to and in accordance with a licence granted under s 26 of the National Monuments Act 1930. In these circumstances the development will not be exempted.

Note: For protection to apply here the listed features which will de-exempt excavation, alteration or demolition must be mentioned as an objective in the development plan or a proposed development or a proposed variation to the development plan. If a licence has been obtained under s 26 of the National Monuments Act 1930 the exemption stated of the excavation, etc, remains as exempted development.

(viii) consist of or comprise the extension, alteration, repair or renewal of an authorised structure or a structure, the use of which is unauthorised.

---

307. See PDA 2000, s 182 as extended by PD(SI)A 2006, s 4 and by PD(A)A 2010, ss 64, 65 and 66.
308. PD(SI)A 2006, s 4. The entire of this section, now contained in PDA 2000, ss 182 A–182E inclusive, should be read for the full understanding of this exemption.

Note: This restriction again illustrates the problems with non-conforming developments. An extension, alteration, repair or renewal may be exempt under the Regulations but if the use is an unauthorised use the exemption fails.

(ix) consist of the demolition or such alteration of a building or other structure as would preclude or restrict the continuance of an existing use of a building or other structure, where it is an objective of the planning authority to ensure that the building or other structure would remain available for such use and such objective has been specified in a development plan for the area or, pending the variation of a development plan or the making of a new development plan, in the draft variation of the development plan or the draft development plan. In these circumstances the development will not be exempted.

Note: It may be that a development plan has singled out a particular structure or building for a particular use. Several of the main theatres in Dublin, for example, are protected in the development plan and may only be used as theatres. If exempted development in the form of alteration or demolition of such a building will preclude or restrict the continuance of that building as, say, for example, a theatre the proposed demolition or alteration is de-exempted.

(x) consist of the fencing or enclosure of any land habitually open to or used by the public during 10 years preceding such fencing or enclosure for recreational purposes or as a means of access to any seashore, mountain, lakeshore, riverbank or other place of natural beauty or recreational utility. In these circumstances the development will not be exempt.

Note: Fencing or enclosing land is in some cases exempt development as, for example, the construction of a wooden fence within or bounding the curtilage of a house (class 5, Part 1). Any such fencing or enclosure of land which has been habitually used for the proceeding 10 years is de-exempted. There have been many examples of de-exempting fencing which had obstructed habitual right of ways or recreational use on the approaches to beaches and recreational use in the mountains.

(xi) obstruct any public right of way. If this is the case the development will not be exempt.

(xii) PDA 2000, s 82 deals with development in architectural conservation areas. In furtherance of the provisions of that section, any works consisting of or comprising the carrying out of works to the exterior of a structure, where the structure concerned is located within an architectural conservation area or an area specified as an architectural conservation area in a development plan for the area or, pending the variation of the development plan or the making of a new development plan, in the draft variation of the development plan or the draft development plan, are not exempt if they would materially affect the character of the area.

Development to which art 6 relates shall not be exempted development for the purpose of the Act if they are to take place in an area to which an SAAO applies.

**[2.480]** PDR 2001, art 9(1)(b) comprises a list of exempted developments where the developments (referred to in the list below) are located in an area to which an SAAO applies:

1. PDR 2001, art 9(1)(b)(i):

    (a) Class 1 which includes the extension of a house within the curtilage of the house.

    (b) Class 3 which includes tents, awnings, shades or other objects, greenhouses, garages, stores, sheds or other similar structure within the curtilage of a house.

    (c) Class 11 which includes fences and walls of brick, stone, blocks with decorative finish, other than, concrete blocks or mass concrete, other than within or bounding the curtilage of a house.

    (d) Class 16 which includes erections of structures, works, plant or machinery needed temporarily in connection with development during the period in which development pursuant to permission is being carried out.

    (e) Class 21 which includes development for industrial purposes of an industrial undertaker on its land used as a dock, harbour or quay for the purpose of any industrial undertaking comprising the provision, re-arrangement or replacement of private ways, private railways, sewers, mains, pipes, cables, structures, plant and machinery, etc.

    (f) Class 22 which includes storage within the curtilage of an industrial building in connection with industrial process of raw materials, products, packing materials or fuel, etc.

    (g) Class 27 which includes construction of overhead transmission lines by an electricity undertaker not exceeding 20kV.

    (h) Class 28 which includes a situation where an electricity undertaking is permitted to move overhead transmission lines by up to 40m from the position in respect of which permission was granted unless the permission contained a contrary requirement.

    (i) Class 29 which includes provision of sub-stations for distribution of electricity of voltage not exceeding 20kV by an electrical undertaker.

    (j) Class 31 which includes provision of telecommunication service comprising overhead telecommunications, telephone kiosks, equipment for transmitting and receiving signals from satellites provision of antennae in connection with telecommunications, etc.

    (k) Class 33(c) which includes development for athletics and sports (including golf or pitch and putt, or sports involving use of motor vehicles, aircraft or firearms) where no charge is made for admission.

    (l) Class 39 which includes lighthouses, beacons, buoys and other aids to navigation on water or in the air.

    (m) Class 44 which includes wells, pumps, boreholes, pump houses for domestic water supply or group water supply schemes, etc.

[2.480]

(n) Class 50(a) which includes demolition of a building other than a habitable house, building forming part of a terrace of buildings or building which abuts on another building in separate ownership.

2. PDR 2001, art 9(1)(b)(ii) comprises a list of exempted developments referred to in the list below which are located in an area to which an SAAO applies:

(a) Class 1 includes advertisements on business premises which refer to the business or other activity carried on or the goods or services provided on the premises.

(b) Class 4 includes advertisements on flags attached to a single flagstaff fixed upright on the roof of a business premises.

(c) Class 6 includes advertisements for religious, educational, cultural institution, guesthouse, club, hostel situated on the land in which the advertisement is exhibited.

(d) Class 11 includes advertisements relating to the carrying out of building or similar works on land on which they are exhibited, etc.

(e) Class 16 includes advertisements announcing local event of religious, cultural, educational, political, social, recreational or sporting character not for commercial purposes.

(f) Class 17 includes advertisements consisting of placards, posters or bills relating to visits of travelling circus, funfairs, carnivals, shows, musicians, etc.

3. PDR 2001, art 9(1)(b)(iii) again comprises a list of exempted development (rural) which is exempted development although situate within an area to which an SAAO applies:

(a) Class 3 includes works relating to gullies, drains, ponds, troughs, pits or culverts, widening or deepening of water courses, etc.

(b) Class 5 includes works of searching or prospecting for minerals and petroleum.

(c) Class 6 includes provision of roofed structures for housing of cattle, sheep, goats, donkeys, horses, deer or rabbits with floor area not exceeding 200m$^2$.

(d) Class 7 includes provision of roofed structures for housing of pigs, mink or poultry with floor area not exceeding 75m$^2$.

(e) Class 8 includes provision of roofless cubicles, open loose yards, self feeding silo or silage areas, feeding aprons, etc, in space not exceeding 200m$^2$.

(f) Class 9 includes stores, barns, sheds, glasshouses or other structures not exceeding 300m$^2$.

(g) Class 10 includes unroofed fenced area for exercising or training houses or ponies together with drainage bed, etc.

(h) Class 11 includes agricultural field drainage, land reclamation, removal of fences, improving of fences, improving of hill grazing and reclamation of estuarine, marsh lands, etc.

(i) Class 12 includes roofed structures for housing greyhounds not exceeding 50m².

(j) Class 13 includes works in connection with keeping of greyhounds of roofless hard surface yard or enclosed area not exceeding 100m².

4. PDR 2001, art 9(1)(b)(iv) provides that development to which art 6 relates shall not be exempted development for the purpose of the Act where the order made under PDA 2000, s 202[309] designating an area as an area of special amenity contains a restriction to the effect that such development shall be prevented or limited. Note: It is therefore important to look at the order made under PDA 2000, s 202 to see if any restrictions are contained which might limit any of the exemptions contained in any classes of Pts 1, 2 or 3 of Sch 2 limiting or preventing certain development.

5. PDR 2001, art 9(1)(c) provides that exempted development is excluded where an EIA is required. Part 10 of PDA 2000 deals with EIA and, specifically, s 172(1)–(5) provide the requirements for an EIS. PDR 2001, Sch 5, Pts 1 and 2 set out a list of development for which an EIS is mandatory or development for which an EIS is deemed necessary by reference to the criteria set out in Sch 7.[310]

6. PDR 2001, art 9(1)(d) provides that any development which consists of the provision of, or modifications to, an 'establishment', which could have significant repercussions on major accident hazards, are de-exempted. The Major Accident Directive is dealt with in Pt 11 of PDR 2001.

Development which consists of the provision of or modification to an establishment, which could have significant repercussions on major accident hazards, will not be exempted development, even if it otherwise fits within the categories of PDR 2001, Sch 2, Pts 1, 2 and 3.

7. PDR 2001, art 9(2) restricts art 6 exemptions, by providing that the restriction contained in sub-art (1)(a)(vi), which deals with interference with the character of a landscape or view or prospect of special amenity value or special interest, the preservation of which is an objective of a development plan, etc, shall not apply where the development consists of the construction by any electricity undertaking of an overhead line or cable not exceeding 100m in length or for the purpose of conducting electricity from a distribution or transmission line to any premises.

8. Article 9 of PDR 2001 is amended by the insertion after sub-art (2) of a new paragraph by virtue of Planning and Development (Amendment) Regulations 2008 (SI 256/2008) which provides a new art 9(3). This article provides that, for the avoidance of doubt, sub-art (1)(a)(vii) shall not apply to any operation

---

309. PDA 2000, Pt XIII under the heading 'amenities' contains ss 202–209 inclusive. Section 202 deals with areas of special amenity and provides for the making of a special amenity area order.
310. See **Ch 10**.

or activity in respect of which a Minister of the government has granted consent or approval in accordance with the requirements of reg 31 of the Habitats Regulations 1997, and where reg 31(5) does not apply.

[2.481] PDR 2001, art 10 deals with changes in use:

1. PDR 2001, art 10(1) provides that development which consists of the change of use within any one of the classes of use specified in Pt 4 of Sch 2 shall be exempted development for the purposes of the Act, provided that the development, if carried out would not:

   (a) involve the carrying out of any works other than works which are exempted development;

   (b) contravene a condition attached to a permission under the Act;

   (c) be inconsistent with any use specified or included in such a permission; or

   (d) be a development where the existing use is an unauthorised use, save where such change of use consists of the resumption of a use which is not unauthorised and which has not been abandoned.

   The article relates to a 'change in use' and it does not relate to the use itself. A breach of any one of the matters set out in paras (a) to (d) inclusive is sufficient to de-exempt an otherwise valid exemption. It is, of course, not necessary that all four matters mentioned in sub-para (a) to (d) inclusive are breached at one time for de-exemption to apply.

2. PDR 2001, art 10(2)(a) provides that a use, which is ordinarily incidental to any use specified in Pt 4 of Sch 2, is not excluded from that use as an incident thereto merely by reason of its being specified in the said Part of the said Schedule as a separate use.

3. PDR 2001, art 10(2)(b) provides that nothing in any class in Pt 4 of Sch 2 shall include any use:

   (i) as an amusement arcade;

   (ii) as a motor service station;

   (iii) for the sale or leasing, or display for sale or leasing, of motor vehicles;

   (iv) for a taxi or hackney business or for the hire of motor vehicles;

   (v) as a scrap yard, or a yard for the breaking of motor vehicles;

   (vi) for the storage or distribution of minerals;

   (vii) as a supermarket, the total net retail sale space of which exceeds €3,500m$^2$ in the Greater Dublin Area and 3,000m$^2$ in the remainder of the State;

   (vii) as a retail warehouse, the total gross retail sale space of which exceeds 6,000m$^2$ (including any ancillary garden centre); or

   (viii) as a shop, associated with a petrol station, the total net retail sale space of which exceeds 100m$^2$.

Article 10(2)(b) does (presumably by mistake) in fact contain two (vii)'s. The implication of limiting the floor space in the Greater Dublin Area of large food stores to 3,500m$^2$ and outside Dublin to 3,000m$^2$ is to discourage development of supermarkets in excess of those sizes, or indeed to permit the planning authority to refuse permission in respect of an application where the floor space areas are exceeded.

4   PDR 2001, art 10(3) provides that development consisting of the provision within a building occupied by, or under the control of, a State authority of a shop or restaurant for visiting members of the public shall be exempted development for the purposes of the Act.

PDA 2000[311] defines 'State Authority' as meaning: (a) a Minister of the government; or (b) the Commissioners (meaning the Commissioners of Public Works in Ireland).

5.   PDR 2001, art 10(4) provides that development consisting of the use of not more than four bedrooms in a house, where each bedroom is used for accommodation of not more than four persons as overnight guest accommodation, shall be exempted development for the purpose of the Act provided that such development would not contravene a condition attached to a permission under the Act or be inconsistent with any use specified or included in such permission.

The use of the words 'overnight guest accommodation' does not imply that the guests are required to pay for the accommodation. Up to four persons are allowed to sleep in a bedroom and there may not be more than four bedrooms in the house for use as overnight guest accommodation. The apparent purpose of this provision is to prevent a house from being used as a hostel without planning permission.

6.   PDR 2001, art 10(5) provides that development consisting of use of a house for childminding shall be exempted development for the purposes of the Act. PDR 2001, art 5(1) defines 'childminding' as the activity of minding no more than six children, including the children, if any, of the person minding, in the house of that person, for profit or gain.

## PDR 2001–2008, art 11

[2.482] Article 11 provides that development commenced prior to the coming into operation of this Part and which was exempted development for the purposes of the Act of 1963 or the 1994 Regulations shall, not withstanding the repeal of that Act, and the revocation of those Regulations, continue to be exempted development for the purposes of the Act. In effect, development which commenced prior to 21 January 2002 and exempted development under the 1963 Act or the 1994 Regulations continues to benefit from the exemption and the Regulations of 2001 are not retrospective to the extent that

---

311.   PDA 2000, s 2(1) as amended by PD(A)A 2010, s 4.

exempted development, after the passing of the new Regulations will no longer enjoy the status of being exempted.

**[2.483]** PDR 2001, art 7, as we have seen,[312] exempts the carrying out of certain development referred to in s 84(4)(a) of the Environmental Protection Agency Act 1992 and also exempts the carrying out of certain development referred to in s 54(4)(a) of the Waste Management Act 1996. Article 7 also exempts the Environmental Protection Agency (EPA) under Pt V of the Waste Management Act 1966.

## Exempted development under other enactments

**[2.484]** Examples of some of these are as follows:

### 1. Development in the Custom House Docks area

The Urban Renewal Act 1986, s 12(6) provides exemption for development carried out by the Custom House Dock Authority or in respect of development which is carried out by any person developing in that area who has been certified by the Authority, provided the development is consistent with a scheme prepared and approved under s 12. Although the exemption relates to planning permission it may still be subject to an EIA in relevant circumstances. It is hoped that this exemption will be withdrawn when its full potential has been reached if not sooner.

### 2. Development under the Roads Acts 1993–1998

The Roads Act 1993, s 19(6) exempts developments which involve any works carried out by or at the direction of the National Roads Authority relating to the construction or maintenance of roads.

### 3. Railway Development

The Transport (Dublin Light Rail) Act 1996, s 4 provides exemption for light railway works such as Luas tram-line construction.

### 4. Development in the Dublin Docklands area

The Dublin Docklands Development Authority Act 1997, s 25 provides exemption in an area in respect of which a planning scheme has been prepared and approved, provided the development is consistent with the said scheme. The development is exempted only if it is carried out by the planning authority or carried out by a person other than the planning authority where the development to be carried out by the other person as being certified by the planning authority has been consistent with the planning scheme. The exemption does apply in respect of planning permission but it will not exempt the requirement of having an EIA carried out.[313] An EIA planning scheme shall not include any development prescribed for the purpose of EIA other than industrial estate

---

312. See para **2.476**.
313. See the Dublin Docklands Development Authority Act 1997, s 26.

development projects, urban development projects and sea water marinas.[314] This is another renewal scheme which must be scrapped as soon as it reaches its full potential. Some commentators feel that it has already done so.[315]

## 5. Developments of derelict sites

The Derelict Sites Act 1990[316] exempts development which comprises works specified in a notice or amended notice served under s 11.

## 6. Development carried out under the Planning and Development (Strategic Infrastructure) Act 2006

This 2006 Act has added a new Sch 7 to PDA 2000 which sets out those classes of project for which a strategic consent procedure has been introduced. The purpose here is to provide a new streamlined consent procedure for strategic infrastructure developments. The application for development consisting of strategic infrastructure, is made directly to An Bord Pleanála. The Board must first determine that the project in question is of strategic importance and the application is then made to the Board.

[2.485] Part 1 of the new Sch 7 deals with energy infrastructure and covers such matter as onshore extraction of petroleum and natural gas, crude oil refineries, thermal power stations, production of electricity, steam or hot water systems, energy carrying systems for gas, steam or hot water, oil pipelines or terminals, surface storage of natural gas, underground storage of combustible gas, surface storage of oil or coal, installation of hydroelectric energy production, wind power, onshore terminals whether above or below ground for natural gas storage and terminals for liquefaction of natural gas either above or below ground.

[2.486] Part 2 of the new Sch 7 deals with transport infrastructure and includes intermodal transportation facilities, and intermodal terminals for passenger or goods, terminal buildings or installations associated with long distance railway, tramway, surface elevated or underground railway or railway supported by suspended lines or similar lines used for passenger transport, airports, to include runways, taxiways, piers, car parks, terminals, or other facilities or installation related to it (whether as regards passenger traffic or cargo traffic). Harbour or port installations:

(a) the area of additional area of water enclosed would be 20 hectares or more, or

(b) which would involve the reclamation of 5 hectares or more of land, or

(c) which would involve the construction of one or more quays which, or each of which, would exceed 100m in length, or

(d) which would enable a vessel of over 1,350 tonnes to enter within it.

---

314. See the Dublin Docklands Development Authority Act 1997, s 25.
315. The Custom House Docks Authority may have exceeded its mandate during the Celtic Tiger years by endeavouring to act as developers rather than as a development authority.
316. See Derelict Sites Act 1990, s 11(6).

**[2.487]** Part 3 of the new Sch 7 deals with environmental infrastructure and provides for development of waste disposal by incineration, chemical treatment or landfill of hazardous waste, waste disposal installation for incineration or chemical treatment of non-hazardous waste, waste recovery installations, ground water abstraction or artificial ground water recharge schemes, works for transfer of water recourses between rivers and basins, waste water treatment plant, sludge-deposition sites, canalisation or flood relief works, dams or other installations designed for the holding back or the permanent or long-term storage of water, installation of overground aquaducts and coastal works to combat erosion or maritime works capable of altering the coast through construction of, for example dikes, moulds, jetties and other sea defence works.

**[2.488]** The Act also provides for a specialised planning consent procedure for major electricity transmission lines and it amends the Railways (Infrastructure) Act 2001 to provide that An Bord Pleanála will approve railway orders.

**[2.489]** PD(SI)A 2006 is dealt with in more detail in **Ch 11**.

**[2.490]** PD(SI)A 2006, s 47 amends Pt XIX of PDA 2000 by inserting a new s 270A after s 270. The margin note reads:

> 'Exempted development not affected': PDA 2000, s 270A provides that for the avoidance of doubt, any category of exempted development by virtue of s 4 or regulations thereunder is not affected by the amendments of this Act made by the Planning and Development (Strategic Infrastructure) Act 2006.

## Further exempted development in PDA 2000

**[2.491]** PDA 2000, s 4(1)(h) exempts development consisting of the carrying out of works for the maintenance, improvement or other alterations of any structure, being works which affect the interior of the structure or which do not materially affect the external appearance of the structure so as to render the appearance inconsistent with the character of the structure or of neighbouring structures.

**[2.492]** PDA 2000, s 57[317] provides that, notwithstanding s 4(1)(a), (h), (i), (j), (k) or (l) and any regulations made under s 4(2), the carrying out of works to a protected structure, or a proposed protected structure, shall be exempted development only if those works do not materially affect the character of:

(a)  the structure; or

(b)  any element of the structure which contributes to its special architectural, historical, archaeological, artistic, cultural, scientific, social or technical interest.

---

317. As amended by PD(A)A 2010, s 34.

**[2.493]** PDA 2000, s 60(2) empowers a planning authority to serve a notice on each person who is the owner or occupier of a structure situated within its functional area, if:

(a) the structure is a protected structure and, in the opinion of the planning authority, the character of the structure or any of its elements ought to be restored; or

(b) the structure is in an architectural conservation area and, in the opinion of the planning authority, it is necessary, in order to preserve the character of the area, that the structure be restored. The notice will specify the works to be carried out and those works will not require planning permission.

**[2.494]** PDA 2000, s 68 provides that the carrying out of any work specified in a notice under s 59(1) or s 60(2) shall be exempted development. PDA 2000, s 59(1) deals with enforcement notices to require works to be carried out in relation to endangerment of protected structures. If a protected structure in the functional area of a planning authority becomes or continues to be endangered the authority shall serve each person who is the owner or occupier of the protected structure a notice:

(a) specifying the works which the planning authority considers necessary in order to prevent the protected structure from becoming or continuing to be endangered; and

(b) requiring the person on whom the notice is being served to carry out those works within a specified period of not less than eight weeks from the date the notice comes into effect under s 62. The works carried out pursuant to a PDA 2000, s 59 notice are exempted.

**[2.495]** PDA 2000, s 82[318] provides that, notwithstanding the exemption in s 4(1)(a), (h), (i), (j), (k) or (l) and any regulations made under s 4(2) (works which affect only the interior of the structure or which do not materially affect the external appearance of the structure), the carrying out of works to the exterior of the structural location within an architectural conservation area shall be exempted development only if those works do not materially affect the character of the area.

**[2.496]** PDA 2000, s 87[319] provides that, notwithstanding s 4(1)(a), (h), (i), (j), (k) or (l) and any regulations made under s 4(2), any development within an area of special planning control shall not be exempted development where it contravenes an approved scheme applying to that area, made under the provisions of PDA 2000, s 84.

**[2.497]** PDA 2000, s 90 provides that the court may compel compliance with a notice served under s 88.[320] Any work carried out pursuant to a PDA 2000, s 88 notice, is exempted development.

---

318. As amended by PD(A)A 2010, s 35.
319. PDA 2000, s 87 is amended by PD(A)A 2010, s 36.
320. PDA 2000, s 88 deals with service of notice relating to structures or other land in an area of special planning control.

**[2.498]** PDA 2000, s 92 provides that, notwithstanding Pt III, permission shall not be required in respect of a development required by notice under s 88 or an order under s 90. PDA 2000, s 88 provides for the service of notices relating to structures or other land in an area of special planning control. The notice will specify the measures to be undertaken for:

(2)(c) (i) the restoration, demolition, removal, alteration, replacement, maintenance, repair or cleaning of any structure, or

(ii) the discontinuance of any use or the continuance of any use subject to conditions.

**[2.499]** PDA 2000, s 154 makes provision for the enforcement notice and under the terms of that section the planning authority may require such steps as may be specified in the notice to be taken in a specified period including, where appropriate, the removal, demolition or alteration of any structure and the discontinuance of any use and, insofar as is practicable, the restoration of the land or its condition prior to the commencement of the development. Any works or discontinuance of use required in an enforcement notice prepared and served under the terms of PDA 2000, s 154 are exempted developments.

**[2.500]** PDA 2000, s 160[321] deals with injunctions in relation to unauthorised development. Any order made by the Circuit Court or the High Court requiring any person to do anything that the court considers necessary which comprises development, is exempted development.

**[2.501]** PDA 2000, s 163 provides that, notwithstanding Pt III, permission shall not be required in respect of development required by a notice under s 154 or an order under s 160 (disregarding development for which there is in fact a permission under Pt III).

**[2.502]** PDA 2000, s 178 provides that a local authority cannot undertake development within its functional area, which would otherwise be exempt development, if that development would be in material contravention of the development plan.

**[2.503]** PDA 2000, s 204 permits a planning authority, by order, to designate an area or place within the functional area of the authority as a landscape conservation area. Local authorities are obliged by s 10(2)(e) of PDA 2000 to include objectives for the preservation of the character of the landscape where, and to the extent that, in the opinion of the planning authority, the proper planning and sustainable development of the area requires it, including the preservation of views and prospects and the amenities of places and features of natural beauty or interest. PDA 2000, s 204(2)(a) permits the Minister, notwithstanding the exemption granted in s 4 or under any regulations made under that section, to prescribe development for the purposes of this section, which shall not be exempted development. PDA 2000, s 204(2)(b) provides that the Minister may impose conditions and restrictions on development prescribed under para (a) above.

---

321. PDA 2000, s 160 is dealt with in detail below and the amendments are highlighted.

**[2.504]** PDA 2000, s 254 provides that a person shall not erect, construct, place or maintain:

(a) a vending machine,

(b) a town or landscape map for indicating directions or places,

(c) a hoarding, fence or scaffold,

(d) an advertising structure,

(e) a cable, wire or pipeline,

(f) a telephone kiosk or pedestal, or

(g) any other appliance, apparatus or structure, which may be prescribed as requiring a licence under this section,

on, under, over or along a public road save in accordance with the licence granted by a planning authority under this section.

**[2.505]** The requirement to obtain a licence does not apply to the following:

(a) an appliance, apparatus or structure which is authorised in accordance with a planning permission granted under Part III;

(b) a temporary hoarding, fence or scaffold erected in accordance with a condition of a planning permission granted under Part III;

(c) the erection, construction, placing or maintenance under a public road of a cable, wire or pipeline by a statutory undertaker.

**[2.506]** PDA 2000, s 254(7) provides that development carried out in accordance with a licence under this section shall be exempted development for the purposes of this Act.

## DECLARATION AND REFERRAL ON DEVELOPMENT AND EXEMPTED DEVELOPMENT

**[2.507]** In spite of wordy statutory and regulatory provisions relating to the concepts of development and exempted development, ambiguities will arise and any doubts as to what constitutes development or exempted development may, in the first instance, be resolved by seeking a declaration from the planning authority or, secondly, by referral to An Bord Pleanála, where there is disagreement on the contents of the planning authority's declaration.

**[2.508]** The legislative provisions are contained in PDA 2000[322] and the purpose of the s 5 procedure is to decide as to whether or not an application for permission for development is or is not required. If the development proposed is exempted development no application for permission is necessary.

---

322. See PDA 2000, s 5.

**[2.509]** Another useful purpose of the s 5 procedure arises where an enforcement action is either threatened or initiated in relation to unauthorised development. Although it is not the purpose of s 5 to establish whether or not a particular development is authorised, if a development, in respect of which no permission has been granted, is not exempted development, it follows, inevitably, that it is an unauthorised development against which enforcement proceedings are justified.

**[2.510]** Prior to the passing of PDA 2000, a reference was initially made to An Bord Pleanála and the appeal was made to the High Court. Now the reference is made to the planning authority and the appeal is to the board.

**[2.511]** In the light of what has been said about using the s 5 procedure where enforcement proceedings are either threatened or initiated, an anomalous situation arises in cases where it is the planning authority which has threatened or initiated the enforcement proceeding.[323] In such cases, the degree of impartiality which is required by a planning authority in making a s 5 declaration might very well be questioned.

**[2.512]** PDA 2000, s 5(1) provides that if any question arises as to what, in any particular case, is or is not development or is or is not exempted development within the meaning of this Act, any person may, on payment of the prescribed fee, request in writing from the relevant planning authority a declaration on that question, and that person shall provide to the planning authority any information necessary to enable the authority to make its decision.

**[2.513]** PDA 2000, s 5(5) offers an escape clause to a planning authority where the planning authority is also the enforcer or has already made a decision as to whether or not a particular development is exempted development. Section 5(4) provides that, notwithstanding s 5(1), a planning authority may, on payment to the board of such fee as may be prescribed, refer any question as to what, in any particular case, is or is not development or is or is not exempted development to be decided by the board. PDA 2000, s 5(4) uses the word 'may' so that the planning authority's decision as to whether or not to refer the question as to whether the development is or is not exempted development to the board is purely discretionary. There must be a strong case for an amendment to s 5 which would provide that where a planning authority is conflicted at the date when it receives a request for a declaration, the planning authority should be compelled to forward the reference to the board immediately.

**[2.514]** The system which existed prior to 11 March 2002, when PDA 2000 became law, was that a party who disagreed with the planning authority's s 5 (as it then was also) declaration could refer the matter to the High Court. Most commentators respect the competence of An Bord Pleanála to determine issues which are purely planning issues.

---

323. The vast majority of enforcement cases are initiated by the planning authority, though some enforcement proceedings are initiated by individuals, organisations or limited companies, etc.

Garrett Simons SC feels that it is unfortunate that the statutory right of appeal to the High Court is lost:

> This will make it more difficult to obtain an authoritative ruling from the High Court in relation to the interpretation of the concepts of development and exempted development. In the absence of a statutory right of appeal, the only alternatives would seem to be, first, that an application be brought for a judicial review; and, secondly, that An Bord Pleanála refer the matter to the High Court pursuant to s 50(1). The difficulty with the former is that the High Court is generally reluctant to interfere with the substance of a decision on an application for judicial review; the difficulty with the latter is that An Bord Pleanála very rarely refers questions of law to the High Court.[324]

**[2.515]** The wording of PDA 2000, s 5 would seem to indicate that the responsibility for determining whether or not any particular activity is development or exempted development rests with a planning authority or with An Bord Pleanála. In enforcement cases, there is a trail of case law which has come before the courts, where the courts have decided that the interpretation as to whether or not a particular activity is development (requiring planning permission) or exempted development (not requiring planning permission) is self evidently an essential matter for the courts if they are to make a decision on enforcement. This view was accepted in *Stafford and Bates v Roadstone Limited*.[325] See also (i) *Dublin County Council v Tallaght Block Company Limited*,[326] (ii) *Carrick Hall Holdings v Dublin Corporation*,[327] and (iii) *Dublin Corporation v Regan Advertising Limited*.[328]

**[2.516]** In *Grianán an Aileach Interpretive Centre Ltd v Donegal County Council*,[329] the plaintiff argued before the High Court that a user clause contained in a planning permission was sufficiently wide to enable it to organise and carry out various functions of a social nature. In fact, the interpretive centre held the social functions and Donegal County Council, as the planning authority, threatened enforcement proceedings. Eventually, declaratory proceedings were submitted to the High Court seeking clarification on the meaning of the user clause. The relief sought by Donegal County Council was upheld in the High Court but the decision was appealed to the Supreme Court where the court was asked to consider what the correct procedure was. Should the plaintiff to seek a reference under PDA 2000, s 5 rather than appeal to the High Court? The Supreme Court allowed the appeal holding that to do otherwise would mean that the High Court was acting as a form of planning tribunal. The s 5 procedure effectively prevented the High Court interpreting the user clause in the planning permission. Effectively, PDA 2000, s 5 has barred any statutory appeal to the High Court against a

---

324. See Simons, *Planning and Development Law* (2nd edn, Thomson Round Hall, 2007) at p 484, para 10.04.
325. *Stafford and Bates v Roadstone Limited* [1980] ILRM 221.
326. *Dublin County Council v Tallaght Block Company Limited* [1982] ILRM 534.
327. *Carrick Hall Holdings v Dublin Corporation* [1983] ILRM 268.
328. *Dublin Corporation v Regan Advertising Limited* [1986] IR 171.
329. *Grianán an Aileach Interpretive Centre Ltd v Donegal County Council* [2004] 2 IR 265.

s 5 decision made by a planning authority or by An Bord Pleanála. The only court challenge which remains is a challenge by way of judicial review.

**[2.517]** Stephen Dodd[330] makes the point that although s 5 may preclude a court from interpreting development and exempted development or indeed the meaning of a user condition in a planning permission, the Supreme Court decision in the *Grianán* case may not go so far as to prevent:

1. Examination by the High Court in enforcement cases to determine whether there had been a material change of use or whether a development was sanctioned by a particular planning permission.

2. A Court being called upon to determine such questions where a commercial or conveyancing document, conditioning a particular term dealing with compliance with planning requirements, was the subject of litigation.

**[2.518]** As seen from the wording of PDA 2000, s 5(1) no particular guidelines are given as to how a request for a declaration should be drafted other than that the request should provide the planning authority with any information necessary to enable it to make its decision. In *Esat Digiphone Ltd v South Dublin County Council*,[331] the development involved attaching an antenna to an existing mast and the storage of telephone equipment in a building to the rear of the premises. The matter was referred to the board which concluded that the antenna and installation equipment were development which could not be considered to be exempted development. Arguments were presented at the hearing which had not been presented in the request for a declaration to the effect that 'works' and 'use' were two different concepts. The applicant argued that the placing of telecommunications equipment was a once-off operation which did not constitute 'works' as it was not ongoing. Kearns J refused the relief sought and held that the board was entitled to take into account any possible 'material change of use'. This development involved material change of use and that is what the board had correctly decided in relation to the reference submitted to it. The learned judge also held that since the essential purpose of a s 5 reference is to decide if the particular works or use constitute development or exempted development, either the planning authority or An Bord Pleanála is entitled to reformulate the question submitted by the applicant in order to clarify the issue. The Board should not be confined in some artificial way by the wording of the question referred to it. The planning authority and/or the board can alter the question asked of it in order to clarify the issue.

**[2.519]** PDA 2000, s 127 makes provision in relation to the making of appeals and referrals by providing that the request for a declaration or the request for a decision on a referral shall:

    (a) be made in writing,

    (b) state the name and address of the person making the referral and of the person, if any, acting on his or her behalf,

---

330. Dodd, *The Planning Acts 2000–2007 – Annotated and Consolidated* (Round Hall, 2008).
331. *Esat Digiphone Ltd v South Dublin County Council* [2002] 3 IR 585.

(c) state the subject matter of the referral,

(d) state in full the grounds of referral and the reasons, considerations and arguments on which they are based,

(e) in the case of an appeal under section 37 by a person who made submissions or observations in accordance with the permission regulations, be accompanied by the acknowledgment by the planning authority of receipt of the submissions or observations,

(f) be accompanied by such fee (if any) as may be payable in respect of such appeal or referral in accordance with section 144.[332]

[2.520] In *O'Reilly v Wicklow County Council*,[333] the request for a s 5 declaration was of poor quality in that it did not fully state the grounds of referral and the reasons, considerations and arguments on which they were based. Although Quirke J considered that the documentation submitted by Wicklow County Council in support of the reference was 'deplorable' nevertheless, the learned judge held that the reference was not invalid because:

> It was possible to discover the 'reasons considerations and arguments' on which the grounds of appeal were based within the documentation submitted by the Council.

Although the requirements of PDA 2000, s 127 are mandatory, the grounds do not have to be contained in a single document. The grounds could be contained within a series of documents submitted in an informal manner. Because the reasons, considerations and arguments on which the council's referral was based could, albeit, with some difficulty, be discovered within the documents submitted to the board, the reference was held not to be invalid.

[2.521] In *O'Connor v An Bord Pleanála*,[334] Finlay Geoghegan J held that the information (in this case the address of the appellant) can be contained within a series of documents and it may be submitted in an informal manner. It was not essential in that case that the appellant's address did not appear on the notice of appeal and it was sufficient that the said address could be ascertained from another document in the appeal file.

[2.522] PDA 2000, ss 5 and 127 do not contain any express provisions requiring notification to third parties nor do they require submissions by third parties. Nevertheless, there are circumstances where both natural and constitutional justice would require that a third party has a right to make submissions on referrals submitted to

---

332. PDA 2000, s 144 provides that the board may, subject to the approval of the Minister, determine fees in relation to appeals, referrals, etc. Fees are reviewed from time to time but at least every three years.
333. *O'Reilly v Wicklow County Council* [2006] IEHC 303, Quirke J.
334. *O'Connor v An Bord Pleanála* (unreported, 24 January 2009) HC, Finlay Geoghegan J.

the planning authority or to the board. Gareth Simons SC submits that the statutory procedure is deficient:

> The consequences of this are either that the planning authority must supplement the statutory procedure by reference to general concepts of fair procedure, or that the legal effect of a declaration must be severely curtailed. In particular, same cannot be binding as against third parties.[335]

**[2.523]** Clearly, if a referral is made to the planning authority in respect of a development not being carried out by the person making the referral, the actual developer should be informed of the referral and should be afforded an opportunity to make submissions. If the actual developer is not so informed and is not afforded an opportunity to make submissions, the likelihood is that the planning authority's decision would be quashed for want of fair procedure.

**[2.524]** The deficiency in the statutory procedures to which Simons correctly refers is somewhat mitigated by the provisions of PDA 2000, s 134. Section 134(1) provides that the board may, in its absolute discretion, hold an oral hearing of a referral under s 5. Section 134(2)(a) provides that a party to a referral under s 5 may request an oral hearing of the referral on application, as appropriate. The section allows the board an absolute discretion in determining whether an oral hearing of the referral will be allowed.

**[2.525]** In determining a s 5 referral An Bord Pleanála may rely on earlier decisions as precedents. The previous decisions of the board are a matter of public record which are available for inspection.

**[2.526]** PDA 2000, s 5(2)(a) provides that, subject to s 5(2)(b), a planning authority shall issue the declaration on request that has arisen and the main reasons and consideration on which its decision is based to the person who made the request under s 5(1), and, where appropriate, the owner and occupier of the land in question, within four weeks of the receipt of the request. The determination of a reference constitutes a quasi-judicial function which requires the person or persons making the determination to state reasons.

**[2.527]** PDA 2000, s 5(2)(b) provides that a planning authority may require any person who made a request under s 5(1) to submit further information with regard to the request in order to enable the authority to issue the declaration on the question and, where further information is received under this paragraph, the planning authority shall issue the declaration within three weeks of the date of receipt of the further information.

---

335. Simons, *Planning and Development Law* (2nd edn, Thomson Round Hall, 2007), para 10.13, p 487.

# Chapter 3
# CONTROL OF DEVELOPMENT

## CONTROL OF DEVELOPMENT

**[3.01]** Put simply, control of development refers to the determination of planning applications by a planning authority. In this sense the Planning and Development Act 2000 (PDA 2000), as amended, has the primary regulatory function of control of development. The planning legislation, on its own, cannot be said to be over active in supporting the concept of positive planning. Positive planning is more visibly demonstrated in the urban renewal and incentive legislation which has been sometimes effective in urban areas in restoring economic, cultural and social vitality. Without the combination of control of development and positive planning, it is the economic vitality which expands to the detriment of social vitality and ultimately to the detriment of cultural vitality. In some areas positive planning has been well worked and has proved successful but in others positive planning has given way to the pressures of poorly controlled development. In the case of social and affordable housing it can be readily observed that no satisfactory progress has been made towards the harmonious integration of communities. Planners have allowed developers to suffocate flood plains, and large sprawling developments have been given the green light with too little thought for social infrastructure and amenities to include such obvious necessities as schools, playing fields, parks, convenience stores, churches, community halls and an efficient transport feeder system. Zoning, too, has gone out of control as evidenced by disproportionate over-zoning which has been provided without a thought of the requirements, in terms of demand and in terms of projected population increases. However, the Planning and Development (Amendment) Act 2010 (PD(A)A 2010) has taken a step in the right direction by introducing the concept of a 'core strategy' for development plans and the Act also will result in much tighter control of environmental and zoning issues to ensure that sustainable standards will be maintained for the future.'

**[3.02]** As a means of exercising control of development, each planning authority draws up a development plan[1] for its area and its decision-making function is generally exercised in line with the core strategy and with other strategic policies expressed in that development plan and with the strategic policies of local area plans. Other instances of control of development include policies relating to density, car park space provision, site coverage, plot ratio, height restrictions and other design standards contained in the development plan. The aim and purpose of the control of the development (and the related and ever increasing environmental controls) is to facilitate the orderly creation of a pleasant, productive, healthy, habitable and sustainable environment.

---

1. See **Ch 1**.

## GENERAL OBLIGATION TO OBTAIN PLANNING PERMISSION

**[3.03]** In effect, the planning legislation contains the legal rules governing the use and development of land and the statutory provisions dealing with the control of development are contained in PDA 2000, Pt III (ss 32–50), as amended.[2]

**[3.04]** Section 32 reads:

> (1) Subject to the other provisions of this Act, permission shall be required under this Part—
>
> (a) in respect of any development of land not being exempted development, and
>
> (b) in the case of development which is unauthorised, for the retention of that unauthorised development.
>
> (2) A person shall not carry out any development in respect of which permission is required by subsection (1), except in accordance with a permission granted under this part.

PDA 2000, s 32 is the keystone section regarding permission for development. The section, however, makes no mention of development completed before 1 October 1964 which is the operative commencement date of the Local Government (Planning and Development) Act 1963. The 1963 Act was, effectively, the first statute which required permission for all development other than exempted development. The Local Government (Planning and Development) Act 1976 expressly exempted the requirement for permission in respect of development carried out prior to 1 October 1964. PDA 2000 has neglected to make similar provision.

**[3.05]** The provisions of s 39(4) are as follows:

> Notwithstanding anything in this Part, permission shall not be required under this Part, in the case of land which, on the 1st October 1964 was normally used for one purpose and was also used on occasions, whether as regular intervals or not, for any other purpose, for the use of the land for that other purpose on similar occasions after 1st October, 1964.

**[3.06]** Section 32(2):

> A person shall not carry out any development in respect of which permission is required by subsection (1) except under and in accordance with permission granted under this Part.[3]

**[3.07]** The meaning of 'development' and of 'exempted development' has been fully discussed in **Ch 2**. Unauthorised development, unauthorised use and unauthorised works are all dealt with and defined in **Ch 2**.

---

2. See, particularly, PD(A)A 2010, ss 23 to 32 inclusive.
3. PDA 2000, Pt III, s 32(1) and (2).

**[3.08]** The provisions of the PD(SI)A 2006 are dealt with in **Ch 11**. Part II, s 5 of PD(SI)A 2006 provides an additional schedule, namely Sch 7, for PDA 2000. The inserted Sch 7 lists infrastructure developments for the purposes of ss 37A and 37B where the application for planning permission is made to An Bord Pleanála in the first instance. This chapter deals only with applications for planning permission and related matters in respect of development other than Sch 7 development.

**[3.09]** PDA 2000, s 37A, as inserted by s 3 of PD(SI)A 2006 and as amended by s 25 of PD(A)A 2010, s 25, provides for a special planning procedure for development falling within any one of the categories specified in Sch 7. Schedule 7[4] specifies three categories of infrastructure development, namely:

1. energy;
2. transport infrastructure; and
3. environmental infrastructure.

Any person or body wishing to apply for development falling within the categories of Sch 7 must enter into consultation with the board under the provisions of PDA 2000, s 37B.

**[3.10]** PDA 2000, s 33 deals with regulations regarding applications for permission and the section enables the Minister by regulation to provide for such matters of procedural administration as appear to the Minister to be necessary or expedient in respect of applications for permission for development of land.[5] The section lists the matters in respect of which regulations may be made without prejudice to the generality of PDA 2000, s 33(1) and these are as follows:[6]

(a) requiring the submission of information in respect of applications for permission for development of land;

(b) requiring any applicants to publish any specified notices with respect to their applications;

(c) enabling persons to make submissions or observations on payment of the prescribed fee and within a prescribed period;

(d) requiring planning authorities to acknowledge in writing the receipt of submissions or observations;

(e) requiring any applicants to furnish to any specified persons any specified information with respect to their applications;

(f) requiring planning authorities to—

 (i) (I) notify prescribed authorities of such proposed development or classes of development as may be prescribed, or

 (II) consult with them in respect thereof, and

---

4. Schedule 7 is set out in full in **Ch 11**.
5. PDA 2000, s 33(1).
6. PDA 2000, s 33(2).

**[3.11]**

(ii) give to them such documents, particulars, plans or other information in respect thereof as may be prescribed:

(g) requiring any applicants to submit any further information with respect to their applications (including any information as to any estate or interest in or right over land) or information regarding any effect on the environment which the development may have;

(h) enabling planning authorities to invite an applicant to submit to them revised plans or other drawings modifying, or other particulars providing for the modification of, the development to which the application relates and, in case the plans, drawings or particulars are submitted to a planning authority in response to such invitation, enabling the authority in deciding the application to grant a permission for the relevant development as modified by all or any of the plans, drawings or particulars;

(i) requiring the production of any evidence to verify any particulars of information given by any applicants;

(j) requiring planning authorities to furnish to the Minister and to any other specified persons any specified information with respect to applications and the manner in which they have been dealt with;

(k) requiring planning authorities to publish or give notice of their decisions in respect of applications for permission, including giving of notice thereof to prescribed bodies and to persons who made submissions or observations in respect of such applications;

(l) requiring an applicant to submit specified information to the planning authority with respect to development, or any class of development carried out by a person to whom s 35(7) applies pursuant to a permission granted to the applicant or to any other person under this Part or under Part IV of the Act of 1963.

**[3.11]** PDA 2000, s 33(3) permits the Minister to make the following regulations also:

(a) Regulations under this section may, for the purposes of securing the attainment of an objective included in a development plan pursuant to s 10(2)(m), require any applicant for permission to provide the planning authority with such information, in respect of development (including development of a particular class) that the applicant purposes to carry out in a Gaeltacht area, as it may specify.

(b) A requirement to which paragraph (a) applies may relate to development belonging to a particular class.

(c) Before making regulations containing a requirement to which paragraph (a) applies the Minister shall consult with the Minister for Arts, Heritage, Gaeltacht and the Islands.[7]

PDA 2000, s 33(4) provides that regulations may be made by the Minister under this section to provide for additional or separate provisions in regard to applicants for outline permission within the meaning of s 36.[8]

---

7. PDA 2000, s 33(3)(a), (b) and (c).
8. PDA 2000, s 33(4).

## CONTROL OF DEVELOPMENT REGULATIONS

[3.12] Part 4 of PDR 2001[9] dealing with control of development has been entirely replaced by the insertion of a new and more substantial Pt 4 contained in PDR 2006 (SI 685/2006). PDR 2006 has been further amended by the Planning and Development (No 2) Regulations 2007 (SI 135/2007). Part 4 of PDR 2006 contains three chapters. Chapter 1[10] contains permission regulations dealing with planning applications and decisions to include such things as newspaper notices, site notices, restrictions and outline applications, content of planning applications generally to include requirements for plans, drawings, maps, etc, the procedure of the planning authority to be adopted on receipt of the planning application, weekly lists, notices to certain bodies, submissions or observations, minimum period for determination of an application and the planning decisions. Chapter 2[11] deals with the regulations of further information and other matters including revised plans, notice of further information, notice for material contravention, notice of withdrawal of a planning application, provision of forms and instructions and provisions of certain information to the Minister. Chapter 3[12] deals with regulations for extension of the duration of planning permission.

## TYPES OF PLANNING PERMISSION WHICH MAY BE OBTAINED ON APPLICATION

[3.13] Four types of planning permission exist and application must, in each case, relate to one of the four types of planning permission, namely:

(a) an application for a standard planning permission;

(b) an application for an outline permission;

(c) a subsequent application for permission made within the statutory time limits after the grant of an outline permission to enable the development to proceed;

(d) an application for retention permission of development.

## OUTLINE PLANNING PERMISSION

[3.14] The concept of outline permission was revised and improved by the provisions of PDA 2000.[13] Outline permission means permission granted in principle under s 34 for the development of lands subject to a subsequent detailed application for permission

---

9. SI 600/2001.
10. PDR 2006 (SI 685/2006), arts 16–32 as amended by Planning and Development (No 2) Regulations 2007 (SI 135/2007) ('PDR 2007').
11. PDR 2006, arts 33–39 as amended by PDR 2007.
12. PDR 2006, arts 40–47 as amended by PDR 2007.
13. PDA 2000, s 36. Prior to s 36, the legislation for outline permission was dealt with only in planning regulations.

under that section.[14] Prior to the commencement of PDA 2000, outline permission was no more than an agreement in principle between an applicant and a planning authority to carry out development. The planning legislation was silent on what exactly a developer was entitled to expect from an outline permission and the courts had, more or less, determined that outline permission could effectively be overturned at approval stage.

[3.15] Outline permission is now in a much more certain category since 11 March 2002.[15] An application for outline permission under PDA 2000 is made in accordance with the permission regulations[16] and where it is granted it does not authorise the carrying out of development to which the outline permission relates until a subsequent permission has been granted under PDA 2000.[17] The subsequent permission is now referred to as a planning permission and the word 'approval', which applied to outline permission under the Local Government (Planning and Development) Act 1963, is no longer used in connection with an outline permission. PDA 2000 provides that where a planning authority grants outline permission, the subsequent application for permission must be made not later than three years from the grant of outline permission.[18] The section continues by providing a discretion to the planning authority to extend the life of the outline permission from three years to a period not exceeding five years.[19] The outline permission shall cease to have effect after three years or such longer period, not exceeding five years, as the planning authorities shall specify.[20] Sections 40, 41 and 42 shall not apply to the grant of an outline permission.[21]

[3.16] PDA 2000 provides an important amendment which greatly strengthens the value of an outline permission by providing that a planning authority may not refuse permission when a subsequent application for permission is made, on the basis of a matter agreed by the planning authority when the outline permission was granted, provided that the authority is satisfied that the proposed development is within the terms of the outline permission.[22] Furthermore, no appeal may be brought to the board against a decision of a planning authority to grant permission consequent on the grant of outline permission in respect of any aspect of the proposed development which was decided in the grant of outline permission.[23] The appeal must be taken at the time of the grant of outline permission. An appeal can be taken against a decision to grant permission subsequent to a grant of outline permission if there are matters in the grant of permission which were not referred to or dealt with in the grant of outline permission.

---

14. PDA 2000, s 36(6).
15. Planning and Development Act 2000 (Commencement) (No 3) Order 2001 (SI 599/2001).
16. PDA 2000, s 36(1).
17. PDA 2000, s 36(2).
18. PDA 2000, s 36(3)(a).
19. PDA 2000, s 36(3)(b).
20. PDA 2000, s 36(3)(b).
21. PDA 2000, s 36(3)(c).
22. PDA 2000, s 36(4).
23. PDA 2000, s 36(5).

[3.17] There are two permissions. The first is the 'outline permission' being a permission granted in principle under PDA 2000, s 34 for the development of land. That permission is subject to a subsequent detailed application for permission under s 34[24] which, if granted, is a grant of permission. The outline permission which results from the first application has a life of three years which may be extended to five years at the discretion of the planning authority. When, however, an application is made for permission consequent upon an existing outline permission within the three year period (or for a period in excess of three years but not exceeding five years if extended at the discretion of the planning authority), the life of the second permission which issues will be determined, as appropriate, by the provisions of PDA 2000, s 40, 41 or 42 and, normally, the life of the second permission will be five years.

[3.18] The time limits or duration which relate to standard planning permissions are dealt with under PDA 2000, s 40. That section provides that the duration of a planning permission is limited, in general, to five years. Section 41 provides that a planning authority or the board may, having regard to the nature and extent of the development and any other material considerations, specify a period which is in excess of five years during which time the permission will be effective. Section 42[25] (as amended) provides that a planning authority may, in relation to an application, as regards a particular permission, extend the normal five year period by such additional period as the authority considers requisite to enable the development to which the permission relates to be completed, subject to certain requirements. The requirements are set out in s 28 of PD(A)A 2010, amending s 42, and they are as follows:

    (a)    either—
        (i)    the authority is satisfied that—
            (I)    the development to which the permission relates was commenced before the expiration of the appropriate period sought to be extended,
            (II)    substantial works were carried out pursuant to the permission during that period, and
            (III)    the development will be completed within a reasonable time,

        or
        (ii)    the authority is satisfied—
            (I)    that there were considerations of a commercial, economic or technical nature beyond the control of the applicant which substantially militated against either the commencement of development or the carrying out of substantial works pursuant to planning permission,
            (II)    that there have been no significant changes in the development objectives in the development plan or in regional development objectives in the regional planning guidelines for the area of the

---

24.    PDA 2000, s 36(6).
25.    PDA 2000, s 42 has been changed and there is now one opportunity only to apply for an extension. See PD(A)A 2010, s 28 which fully replaces the old s 42.

[3.19] Planning and Environmental Law in Ireland

planning authority since the date of the permission such that the development would no longer be consistent with the proper planning and sustainable development of the area,

(III) that the development would not be inconsistent with the proper planning and sustainable development of the area having regard to any guidelines issued by the Minister under section 28, notwithstanding that they were so issued after the date of the grant of permission in relation to which an application is made under this section, and

(IV) where the development has not commenced, that an environmental impact assessment or an appropriate assessment, or both of those assessments, if required, was or were carried out before the permission was granted.

(b) the application is in accordance with such regulations under this Act as applied to it,

(c) any requirements of or made under those regulations are complied with as regards the application, and

(d) the application is duly made prior to the end of the appropriate period.

If the planning authority decides to extend the life of a planning permission it may either require further security to be given for the satisfactory completion of the development or may add to or vary any condition already imposed under PDA 2000, s 34(4)(g) requiring the giving of adequate security for satisfactory completion of the proposed development.[26]

[3.19] Where the planning authority is considering whether or not to extend the life of a planning permission it will make the decision as expeditiously as possible and it shall be the objective of the planning authority to ensure that notice of its decision will be given within a period of eight weeks from the date of receipt of the application seeking extension or, where all of the regulations have not been complied with, the application is so notified from the date of compliance by the applicant with the regulation requirements. Once again the planning authority is not bound by s 28(3) of PD(A)A 2010 and either it makes its decision as expeditiously as possible or, in any event, within a period of eight weeks. The eight weeks is not an absolute period in that the section only requires them to have an objective to give notice of decision within the eight week period.

[3.20] If a decision to extend the period of permission is granted that will be the only extension given and no further extensions to the appropriate period are allowed.[27]

[3.21] The consequences of the legislative provisions mean that no appeal may be brought to the board under s 37 against a decision of a planning authority to grant permission consequent on the grant of outline permission in respect of any aspect of the proposed development which was decided in the grant of outline permission. It is

---

26. PD(A)A 2010, s 28 amending PDA 2000, s 42.
27. PD(A)A 2010, s 28 substituting PDA 2000, s 42(4).

important to remember that submissions and observations in relation to outline permission must be made by potential appellants within five weeks of the first application for outline permission being made to the planning authority by the applicant. If there is to be an appeal the appeal must be lodged with the board within four weeks of the date of the decision of the planning authority on the first application, which is the application for outline permission.

## OUTLINE PERMISSION REGULATIONS

[3.22] The regulations in respect of outline application are contained in PDR 2001, art 96.

[3.23] An outline application may not be made in respect of development which comes within the definition of PDR 2001, Sch 5. Schedule 5 lists classes of development for which environmental impact assessment (EIA) is mandatory for the purposes of Pt 10 of PDR 2001. Part 10 deals with EIA:[28]

> Where a planning authority receives an outline application, or the Board an appeal in respect of such application, in relation to sub-threshold development which would, in its opinion be likely to have significant effects on the environment, it shall, as soon as may be after receipt of the application or appeal, as appropriate, by notice in writing:
>
> (a) inform the applicant that an outline application may not be made in respect of the development,
>
> (b) indicate that the authority or the Board, as appropriate, considers that the development would be likely to have significant effects on the environment, and that an application for permission to the authority, accompanied by an EIS, would be required for such a development.[29]

Where a planning authority issues a notice under art 96(2), the outline application shall be regarded as having been withdrawn and the planning authority shall return the outline application and all particulars, plans, drawings and maps and any fee paid with the application to the applicant. The planning authority shall enter the relevant details on the register and, by notice in writing, inform any persons or body who made submissions or observations of the fact that the outline application has been withdrawn and indeed so shall return any fees paid in respect of such submissions or observations to the person or body who made them.[30]

Where the board, as opposed to the planning authority, issues a notice of withdrawal in relation to a sub-threshold development under sub-art (2), both the outline application and the appeal shall be regarded as having been withdrawn and no permission shall be granted by the planning authority on foot of any decision by the authority under PDA 2000, s 34 (as amended). The Board shall by notice in writing inform any party to the

---

28. PDR 2001, art 96(1).
29. PDR 2001, art 96(2).
30. PDR 2001, art 96(3).

appeal or any person or body who made submissions or observations under PDA 2000, s 130[31] of that fact.[32]

## RESTRICTION ON OUTLINE APPLICATION

(*Article 21*)

**[3.24]** PDR 2001, art 21 makes special provisions in relation to outline applications under PDA 2000, s 36. Application for outline permission cannot be made for (a) retention of development, (b) development consisting or comprising the carrying out of works to a protected structure or to a proposed protected structure, or (c) development which comprises or is for the purposes of an activity requiring an integrated pollution control licence or a waste licence.[33]

## RETENTION PERMISSION

**[3.25]** Retention permission[34] is no longer available in cases where an EIA should have been undertaken in the first instance, not in cases where an environmental impact statement (EIS) is lodged with the official for retention permission. That said, where EIA or EIS are not relevant, planning permission shall be required in the case of development which is unauthorised, for the retention of the unauthorised development. The Act imposes an obligation on a person to obtain retention permission in order to retain structures or to continue an unauthorised use where structures have been developed or a use has been established without permission or where there is non-compliance with a condition or with conditions in a planning permission. The obligation to obtain retention permission in those circumstances applies where unauthorised development has or is being carried out.[35]

**[3.26]** In *Weston v An Bord Pleanála*,[36] MacMenamin J held that the Act requires a planning authority to apply a heightened level of scrutiny where an application for retention permission is received relating to an unauthorised development. The

---

31. PDA 2000, s 130 makes provision for submissions or observations by persons other than parties to the appeal, ie, by any member of the public. Section 130(5) has been amended by PD(A)A 2010, s 42 and the subsection now reads: 'sub-ss (1)(b) and (4) shall not apply to submissions or observations made by a Member State of the European Communities (within the meaning of the European Communities Act, 1972) or another State which is a party to the Transboundary Convention, arising from consultation which is subject to the Environmental Impact Assessment Directive or Transboundary Convention, as the case may be in relation to the effects on the environment of development to which the appeal under s 37 relates'.
32. PDR 2001, art 96(4).
33. PDR 2001, art 31(a), (b)&(c).
34. PDA 2000, s 35 deals with the general obligation to obtain planning permission. It states the circumstances in which planning permission shall be required and includes, (b) in the case of development which is unauthorised, for the retention of that unauthorised development. Note that retention permission is fully dealt with in **Ch 2**.
35. PDA 2000, s 32(1)(b).
36. *Weston v An Bord Pleanála* [2008] IEHC 71 (14 March 2008) *per* MacMenamin J.

supervisory obligation of the planning authority is enhanced in cases where an application is received for retention permission.

**[3.27]** It is probably not possible to apply for planning permission for the retention of the demolition of a building.[37]

**[3.28]** The fees payable for retention of permission are set at a significantly higher level than in the case of an application for permission *ab initio*. PDA 2000, s 246 permits the Minister to make regulations providing for various matters including retention permission. Section 246(2) provides that the Minister may prescribe that a fee payable to the planning authority for an application for retention permission shall be an amount which shall be related to the estimated cost of the development or the unauthorised part thereof as the case may be. For example, the fee, at the time this book goes to press, for an application for provision of a house is €65. If retention permission is required for the provision of a house which was built without permission, the fee is €195 or €2.50 for each square metre of gross floor area space for which permission is sought, whichever is the greater. The maximum fee to a planning authority by an applicant in respect of an application for permission for retention of unauthorised development shall be €125,000.

**[3.29]** In respect of retention permission for unauthorised developments in cases where an EIA should have been undertaken in the first instance, the requirement now is that the application for retention permission, in appropriate cases, must be accompanied by EIA. This follows a judgment in the European Court of Justice (ECJ) dated 3 July 2008 where the court invalidated Irish law allowing planning authorities and the board to grant retention permission for developments which have failed to comply with the EIA Directive.[38]

**[3.30]** PDA 2000, s 34(12) has been replaced by a new provision in PD(A)A 2010, s 23(c)(12). The new section provides that the planning authority shall refuse to grant retention permission to retain unauthorised development where it decides that if an application had been made to it before the development commenced that application would have required one of the following to be carried out namely:

(a) an environmental impact assessment,

(b) a determination as to whether an environmental impact assessment is required, or

(c) an appropriate assessment.

**[3.31]** Three further subsections have been inserted by PD(A)A 2010, s 23, namely (12A), (12B), and (12c):

(12A) For the purposes of subsection (12) if an application for permission had been made in respect of the following development before it was commenced, the

---

37. See Simons, *Planning and Development Law* (2nd edn, Thomson Round Hall, 2007) at para 5.40.
38. *Commission of European Communities v Ireland* (Case C–215/06) (unreported, 3 July 2008) ECJ.

application shall be deemed not to have required a determination referred to at subsection (12)(b):

(a) development within the curtilage of a dwelling house, for any purpose incidental to the enjoyment of the dwelling house as a dwelling house;

(b) modifications to the exterior of a building.

(12B) Where a planning authority refuses to consider an application for permission under subsection (12) it shall return the application to the application together with any fee received from the applicant in respect of the application and shall give reasons for its decision to the applicant.

(12C) Subject to subsections (12) and (12A), an application for development of land in accordance with the permission regulations may be made for the retention of unauthorised development, and this section shall apply to such an application, subject to any necessary modifications.

## Substitute consent

**[3.32]** In exceptional circumstances, where developers find themselves in a situation where they cannot apply for retention permission because, for example, they failed to carry out EIA or appropriate assessment under the Habitats Directive, they may apply to An Bord Pleanála for leave to lodge an application for substitute consent in order to regularise the development. The conditions in relation to an application for leave to apply for substitute consent are onerous and there is no guarantee and no presumption in law that the application to the board will be successful.

**[3.33]** The most common operations which will be affected by the substitute consent procedure are quarries and they will only be entitled to avail of that consent in strictly regulated circumstances. Quarries which have not had permission since 31 October 1964 and which failed to regularise their operations under s 261 of PDA 2000 will be excluded from the possibility of seeking leave to apply for substitute consent. If a quarry has permission and did register under s 261 it still may be the case that the expansion which may have taken place during the so called 'Celtic tiger years' amounted to development within the meaning of the term 'intensification'. If development by intensification occurred without the necessity of the various environmental consents and assessments which apply then a final opportunity is offered to quarries to put their house in order under this strictly time limited 'sunset' provision which offers quarry owners and operators one last chance to regularise their activities. This is dealt with in more detail in **Ch 8**.

**[3.34]** Prior to the commencement of PD(A)A 2010, John Gormley TD, Minister for the Environment, Heritage and Local Government stated that he envisaged that legislation would be introduced which would revoke the current seven year time limit within which enforcement action may be taken in respect of all unauthorised developments, whether or not they would require a prior EIA under the EU rules. The mischief which would have resulted from the abolition of the seven year time limit would have been almost unimaginable. Planning warranties, where the planning search takes you back to 1 October 1964 should be reliable. However it is often possible, because of poor maintenance of the planning register and because people may no longer know what occurred in the 1960s, 1970s, 1980s, etc, that such warranties are, in many cases, unreliable. At least the seven year time limit gives some limited assistance. Although an unauthorised development, developed after 1 October 1964, will remain an unauthorised development, unless retention permission is obtained or unless it is demolished and taken away, the possibility of enforcement ends after seven years if no permission was obtained for the unauthorised development and after twelve years in circumstances where permission was granted but the development was not developed strictly in accordance with that planning permission. Happily, Minister Gormley changed his mind on this matter and the seven year rule still stands, albeit slightly modified. One way or another what is needed is a planning amnesty which, for example, would provide that after, say, a period of 15 years the development would be statutorily deemed to be a conforming development even though it was not one on the date before the 15-year period lapsed.[39]

## APPLICATIONS ACCOMPANIED BY EIS OR RELATING TO ESTABLISHMENTS TO WHICH MAJOR ACCIDENT REGULATIONS APPLY[40]

*(Article 16)*

**[3.35]** Articles 16 to 47 inclusive are contained in Pt 4 (Control of Development), Chs 1 to 3 inclusive of PDR 2001. The entire of Pt 4 of PDR 2001, Chs 1, 2 and 3 has been substituted by art 8 of PDR 2006.[41] In fact, the public notice requirements of PDR 2006 provide slight alterations only in the now redundant provisions of Pt 4, Chs 1, 2 and 3 of PDR 2001. If application is made in respect of development which requires an EIS then the applicant must comply with the general requirements for all planning applications and also with the EIS requirements.[42] The information to be contained in an EIS is set out in PDR 2001, Sch 6.[43] Where an EIS has been prepared, the court will not concern itself with the contents or with the qualitative nature of the EIS. All that is required is that an EIS has been prepared and lodged with the application. In *Kenny v An Bord Pleanála*,[44] McKechnie J stated:

> Once the statutory requirements have been satisfied I should not concern myself with the qualitative nature of the EIS or the debate on it had before the Inspector. These are not matters of concern to this Court.

---

39. This author made a submission to the Department of the Environment, Heritage and Local Government in much the same terms as outlined in the above paragraphs but whether or not this had any influence on the Minister cannot be determined. No substantive replies have been received since the correspondence began on 6 August 2008.
40. PDR 2001, art 16 as substituted by PDR 2006.
41. SI 685/2006.
42. PDR 2001, art 16(1) as substituted by PDR 2006.
43. PDR 2001, Sch 6.
44. *Kenny v An Bord Pleanála (No 1)* [2001] 1 IR 565.

Article 16 also provides that where any planning application for development is considered by the planning authority to be relevant to the risk or consequences of a major accident, in those circumstances the provisions of PDA 2000, Pt II must be complied with in the applicant's application which application must also comply with the general requirement to satisfy the planning application rules set out in PDR 2001, Pt 4 (as substituted by PDR 2006).

## NOTICE OF PLANNING APPLICATION

(*Article 17*)

[3.36] Applications for planning permission are generally made to the relevant planning authority except in the case of certain strategic infrastructure categories of development where the application is made, in the first instance, to An Bord Pleanála.[45] Within a period of two weeks before the making of a planning application, an applicant must give notice of intention to make an application in an approved newspaper and also by the erection or affixing of a site notice in the prescribed form on the land or structure to which the application relates. Where the last day of the two week period is a Saturday, Sunday, a public holiday or any other day on which the offices of the planning authority are closed, the application will be valid if it is received on the next following day on which the offices of the planning authority are open. The site notice requirement does not apply to a planning application for development comprising the construction or erection of an electricity undertaking of overhead transmission or distribution lines for conducting electricity, or development comprising construction or erection by a statutory undertaker authorised to provide a telecommunications service of overhead telecommunication lines.[46]

### Newspaper notices

(*Article 18*)

[3.37] The newspaper notice must be published in an approved newspaper within a period of two weeks before the making of the application. A planning authority now has an obligation to approve a list of newspapers, including national newspapers, which it considers to have sufficiently large circulation in its functional area. Different newspapers may be approved in respect of different parts of such functional areas. The approved list of newspapers must be reviewed by the planning authority at least once a year. The list of newspapers is then displayed at the office of the planning authority and may be displayed at other places, including the website, which the authorities consider appropriate. Copies of the approved list of newspapers may be obtained from the planning authority free of charge.[47] The newspaper notice must be headed with the name

---

45. PD(SI)A 2006, and see **Ch 11**.
46. PDR 2006, art 17(3).
47. PDR 2006, art 18(2)(a), (b) and (c) as substituted by PDR 2006.

of the planning authority to which the planning application will be made. The notice shall contain the following information:

(a) name of applicant,

(b) location, townland or postal address of the land or structure to which the application relates (as may be appropriate),

(c) whether the application is for permission for development, permission for retention of development, outline permission for development or permission consequent on the grant of the relevant outline permission (stating the relevant reference number of the outline permission),

(d) a brief description of the nature and extent of the development including—

  (i) where the application relates to development consisting of or comprising housing the notice must specify the number of houses to be provided,

  (ii) where the application relates to the retention of a structure, the notice must specify the nature of the proposed use and, if relevant, the period for which it is proposed to retain the structure,

  (iii) where the application relates to development which would consist of or comprise the carrying out of works to a protected structure or a proposed protected structure, an indication of that fact,

  (iv) where the application relates to a development which comprises or is for the purposes of an activity requiring an integrated pollution prevention and control licence or a waste licence, an indication of that fact, or

  (v) where a planning application relates to development in a strategic development zone, an indication of that fact, and

(e) the notice must state that the planning application may be inspected or purchased at a fee not exceeding the reasonable costs of making a copy, at the offices of the planning authority during its public opening hours and that a submission or observation in relation to the application may be made to the authority in writing on payment of the prescribed fee within the period of five weeks beginning on the date of receipt by the authority of the application.[48]

## Site notice

*(Article 19)*

**[3.38]** A site notice must be erected or fixed by the applicant giving notice of intention to make the application in accordance with art 19.[49] The form of a site notice is set out at Form No 1 of Sch 3, PDR 2001 as substituted by PDR 2006. The form of the notice must be in the form as set out in Sch 3 or a form substantially to the like effect (see **Appendix**).[50]

---

48. PDR 2001, art 18(1) as substituted by PDR 2006.
49. PDR 2001, art 17(1)(b) and also see below PDR 2001, art 19. Both arts 17(1)(b) and 19 have been substituted by PDR 2006.
50. PDR 2001, art 19(1)(a) as substituted by PDR 2006.

A site notice is in addition to and not instead of a newspaper notice and notice is required in all cases and not just in cases where an EIS is lodged.

**[3.39]** A site notice must be inscribed or printed in indelible ink on a white background affixed on rigid, durable material and secured against damage from bad weather or other causes.[51] If a planning application is made in respect of any land or structure, and a subsequent application is made within six months of the date of making the first application in respect of land substantially consisting of the site or part of the site to which the first application related, the site notice must be inscribed or printed in indelible ink on a yellow background and affixed in the same way.[52] In either case the notice must be secured against damage from bad weather.

**[3.40]** In the case of a notice with a yellow background, being a subsequent application which is made within six months from the date of making the first application, PDR 2006 has made it clear that the yellow site notice is only required where the earlier application is a valid application. In fact, the High Court, even prior to PDR 2006, had already decided that the necessity for a yellow background on the site notice only applied where the first notice was a valid notice.[53]

**[3.41]** Site notices must be securely erected or fixed in a conspicuous position on or near the main entrance to the land or structure concerned from a public road or where there are more than one entrance from public roads, on or near all such entrances, or any other part of the land or structure adjoining the public road, so as to be easily visible and legible by persons using the public road, and it must not be obscured or concealed at any time.[54] If the land or structure to which the planning application relates does not adjoin a public road the site notice must be erected or affixed in a conspicuous position on the land or structure so as to be easily visible and legible by persons outside the land or structure, and it must not be obscured or concealed at any time.[55]

**[3.42]** Where a planning authority considers that the erection or affixing of a single site notice is not sufficient to comply with the requirements of the regulations, or does not adequately inform the public, the authority may require the applicant to erect or affix such further site notice(s) in such manner and in such terms as it may specify. The applicant must submit to the authority such evidence as it may specify in relation to compliance with this requirement.[56]

**[3.43]** A site notice must be maintained in a position on the land of structure concerned for a period of five weeks from the date of receipt of the planning application by the planning authority, and it shall be renewed or replaced if it is removed or becomes defaced or illegible within that period. The site notice shall be removed by the applicant

---

51. PDR 2001, art 19(1)(b) as substituted by PDR 2006.
52. PDR 2001, art 19(4) as substituted by PDR 2006.
53. *Kelly v Roscommon County Council* [2006] IEHC 30 (20 June 2006), McGovern J.
54. PDR 2001, art 19(1)(c) as substituted by PDR 2006.
55. PDR 2001, art 19(2) as substituted by PDR 2006.
56. PDR 2001, art 19(3) as substituted by PDR 2006.

following the notification of the planning authority decision under art 31.[57] The five week period corresponds exactly with the period allowed for making submissions or observations. It must be assumed that a site notice must be renewed or replaced where it is defaced or becomes illegible within the period but, curiously, the regulations are silent on the question as to how quickly the notice must be replaced and no provision is made for extending the five week period if a site notice has been missing for a period of, say, one week. It may be anticipated that these regulations will be interpreted strictly and that the onus is on the applicant to ensure that the site notice is in good order throughout the period. An applicant should be advised to make a daily inspection of the site notice, during the five week period, to ensure that it is still compliant. As seen, the site notice may be erected within two weeks prior to the making of the planning application but the five week period only runs from the date the application is received by the planning authority so that, effectively, a site notice may be in position for seven weeks or more.

**[3.44]** *Marshall v Arklow Town Council*[58] is a High Court case heard before Peart J before PDR 2006 was commenced. It was alleged that no site notice had been put in place in accordance with the requirement of art 19 of PDR 2001 and the case was made by the applicants for judicial review that since there was no notice, they had not become aware of the application for planning permission until the decision had been made by the planning authority. The respondent stated that the site notice was in place during the prescribed period but from the evidence before the court, the learned judge held that he was not in a position to determine the factual issues with absolute certainty. Peart J held that the planning authority was obliged to inspect the land to which the application relates, within the five week period. The obligation must be an implied obligation because the planning Acts and the regulations are both silent in relation to the necessity of an inspection of the site the subject matter of an application within five weeks from the date of the lodgement of the application. The obligation which the court implied in this case is supported by the provisions of art 26(4) of PDR 2001 (as substituted by PDR 2006) which reads:

> Where, on inspection of the land to which the application relates, the planning authority considers that the requirements of art 17(1)(b) or 19 or 20 have not been met, or the information submitted in the planning application is substantially incorrect, or substantial information has been omitted, the planning application shall, notwithstanding the fact that an acknowledgment has been sent to an applicant in accordance with sub-art (2), be invalid.

As a consequence of Peart J's decision in *Marshall v Arklow Town Council*,[59] planning authorities frequently inspect the site and make particular inspection, during the five week period, of the site notice to see (a) that it is in position, and (b) that the form of the notice is compliant. Details of that inspection are now regularly entered in the planning register.

---

57. PDR 2001, art 20 as substituted by PDR 2006.
58. *Marshall v Arklow Town Council* [2004] 4 IR 92.
59. *Marshall v Arklow Town Council* [2004] 4 IR 92.

## CONSULTATIONS IN RELATION TO PROPOSED DEVELOPMENT

**[3.45]** PDA 2000, s 247 deals with pre-application consultations in relation to proposed planning applications for development.

**[3.46]** The section provides that a person who has an interest in land and who intends to make a planning application may, with the agreement of the planning authority concerned (which shall not be unreasonably withheld), enter into consultations with the planning authority in order to discuss any proposed development in relation to land and the planning authority may give advice to that person regarding the proposed application.[60] The ministerial guidelines published in November 2006 encourage applicants to avail of the s 247 pre-application consultation and, in that sense, the guidelines also encourage planning authorities to receive potential applicants for permission who are seeking the planning authority's advice before lodging their application. These consultations are particularly useful and necessary in cases where the applicant is required to comply with PDA 2000, Pt V (housing supply). Because Pt V conditions are mandatory and because they are inevitable in cases where Pt V applies, and since Pt V conditions are pre-conditions which must be fully agreed before development commences, it does make perfect sense that developers and planning authorities should use s 247 consultations to agree the conditions required by Pt V, where possible, before planning permission is granted.

**[3.47]** It will be seen that the obligation of the planning authority to give advice under PDA 2000, s 247(1) is discretionary. Planning authorities may agree to a consultation with an applicant and cannot unreasonably disagree to hold a consultation. In practice it may, on occasions, be difficult to arrange a s 247 consultation with a planning authority. Section 247(1) does not compel a planning authority to give advice concerning the application other than the specific advice set out in s 247(2).

**[3.48]** The advice which 'shall' be given at a s 247 consultation appears to be limited to the following:

> The procedures involved in considering a planning application, including any requirements of permission regulations, and, as far as possible, indicate the relevant objectives of the development plan which may have a bearing on the decision of the planning authority.[61]

The section continues by providing that the carrying out of consultations shall not prejudice the performance by the planning authority of any other of its functions under this Act, or any regulations made under this Act, and cannot be relied upon in the formal planning process or in legal proceedings.[62] Effectively, the matters discussed at a s 247 consultation are discussed entirely on a 'without prejudice' basis.

**[3.49]** The section adds to the statutory formality of these consultations, by providing that a planning authority may specify that consultations may be held at particular times

---

60. PDA 2000, s 247(1).
61. PDA 2000, s 247(2).
62. PDA 2000, s 247(3).

and at particular locations, and the authority shall not be obliged to enter into consultations, otherwise than as specified by it.[63] This provision has the potential of allowing a reluctant planning authority to provide a valid statutory excuse in order to frustrate the holding of these consultations. It is, however, clear that if a s 247 consultation is agreed between the applicant and the planning authority, it must be held before the application is lodged. If a s 247 consultation is held, the planning authority shall at least in each year publish notice of the times and locations at which consultations are held, in one or more newspaper circulating the area of authority.[64]

[3.50] Section 247 consultations received statutory recognition after 11 March 2002. Informal pre-application consultations were reasonably common place before that date, and some, at least, of those pre-PDA 2000 non-statutory consultations went astray and were, on occasions, abused, both on the part of some applicants and on the part of some planning authority officials. The PDA 2000 legislative provisions dealing with these consultations are heavily weighted in favour of the planning authority to such an extent that a genuine, potential benefit is often lost. If, for example, a development proposal either exceeds or comes close to exceeding the bounds as to what may or may not be permissible in a particular area it is of benefit to the planning process that an applicant is made fully aware by the planning authority of the development potential for the area. Guided by that information a potential developer can either modify or partly modify the proposal or alternatively he/she can make the application and take his/her chances with An Bord Pleanála. However, because it is at the discretion of the planning authority to give or not to give advice at a s 247 consultation guidance may or may not be given by the planning authority.

[3.51] The section also requires the planning authority to keep a record, in writing, of any consultations under this section and to include the names and addresses of those who participate in the consultations, and a copy of such record shall be placed and kept with the documents to which any planning application, in respect of the proposed development, relates.[65]

[3.52] Finally, the section also provides that a member or official of a planning authority is guilty of an offence if he or she takes or seeks any favour, benefit or payment, direct or indirect (on his or her own behalf or on behalf of any other person or body), in connection with any consultation entered into or any advice given under this section.[66]

## CONTENT OF PLANNING APPLICATIONS GENERALLY

(*Article 22*)

[3.53] The planning application form is set out in Form 2 of Sch 3 of PDR 2006. The form lists the documents which should accompany the application. The form contains

---

63. PDA 2000, s 247(4)(a).
64. PDA 2000, s 247(4)(b).
65. PDA 2000, s 247(5).
66. PDA 2000, s 247(6). The offence is a criminal offence and penalties may involve a fine and/or imprisonment.

**[3.54]** Planning and Environmental Law in Ireland

directions for completing the application. PDR 2001 did not offer a planning application form. The application form in PDR 2006 and the attendant directions are set out in the **Appendix**. The directions for completing the form are particularly helpful.

**[3.54]** Article 22 in PDR 2001 has be en substantially amended by Article 22 in PDR 2006.

**[3.55]** A planning application under s 34 of the Act shall be in the form as set out in Form No 2 of Sch 3 or a form substantially to the like effect:[67]

A planning application referred to in sub-article (1) shall be accompanied by—

(a) the relevant page of the newspaper or a copy of the relevant page, including the date and title of newspaper, in which notice of the application has been published and a copy of the site notice erected or affixed on the land or structure,

(b) 6 copies of a location map of sufficient size and containing details of features in the vicinity such as to permit the identification of the site to which the application relates, to a scale (which shall be identified thereon) of not less than 1:1000 in built up areas and 1:2500 in all other areas, or such other scale as may be agreed with the planning authority prior to the submission of the application. The map must be marked so as to identify clearly:

   (i) the land or structure to which the application relates and the boundaries thereof in red,

   (ii) any land which adjoins, abuts or is adjacent to the land to be developed and which is under the control of the applicant or the person who owns the land which is the subject of the application in blue,

   (iii) any wayleaves in yellow, and

   (iv) the position of the site notice or notices erected or affixed to the land or structure pursuant to Article 17(1)(b),

(c) where it is proposed to dispose of waste water from the proposed development other than to a public sewer, information on on-site treatment system proposed and evidence as to the suitability of the site for the system proposed,

(d) the documents, particulars and plans drawings and maps referred to in sub-article (4), – (below),

(e) in the case of an application for permission for the development of houses or of houses or other development, to which s 96 of the Act applies (Social and Affordable Housing), proposals as to how the applicant proposes to comply with the condition referred to in sub-s (2) of that section to which the permission, if granted, would be subject,

(f) where appropriate, a certificate issued by the planning authority in accordance with s 97 of the Act, or if such a certificate has been applied for but not issued, a copy of the application made in accordance with article 48,

---

67. See PDR 2006, art 22(1).

(g) where the applicant is not the legal owner of the land or structure concerned, the written consent of the owner to make the application, and

(h) the appropriate fee as set out in Sch 9.[68]

Where the planning authority consents to the making of a planning application wholly or partly in electronic form, an application or any part thereof may be made by the applicant in that form; where that occurs, one copy of the application or part thereof will be sufficient.[69]

**[3.56]** Subject to arts 24 and 25:

(a) a planning application in respect of any development consisting of or mainly consisting of the carrying out of works on, in, over or under land or for the retention of such works shall be accompanied by 6 copies of such plans (including a site or layout plan and drawings of floor plans, elevations and sections which comply with the requirement of article 23), and such other particulars, as are necessary to describe the works to which the application relates,

(b) a planning application for any development consisting of or mainly consisting of the making of any material change in the use of any structure or other land, or for retention of any such material change of use shall be accompanied by—

(i) a statement of the existing use and of the use proposed together with particulars of the nature and extent of any such proposed use,

(ii) where the development to which the application relates comprises the carrying out of works on, in, over or under the structure or other land, 6 copies of such plans (including a site or layout plan and drawings of floor plans, elevations and sections which comply with the requirements of article 23), and such other particulars, as are necessary to describe the works proposed, and

(iii) such plans and such other particulars as are necessary to identify the area to which the application relates.[70]

Notwithstanding paragraph (a) of sub-article (4), drawings of floor plans are not required to be submitted in respect of a structure, other than a protected structure or a proposed protected structure, that is proposed to be demolished.[71]

## SPECIFIED ADDITIONAL INFORMATION

*(Article 22A)*

**[3.57]** (1) In addition to the information required by article 22, the planning authority may require the applicant to submit with the planning application specified additional information.

---

68. PDR 2001, art 22(2) as substituted by PDR 2006. Note: Sch 9 in this sub-para (h) refers to Sch 9 in PDR 2001.
69. PDR 2001, art 22(3) as substituted by PDR 2006.
70. PDR 2001, art 22(4) as substituted by PDR 2006.
71. PDR 2001, art 22(4).

**[3.58]**

(2) No planning application shall be invalidated under article 26 for failure to submit with the application any information or particulars requested under sub-article (1).[72]

Although it is clear that failure to comply with art 22A shall not invalidate the application, it is equally clear that failure to comply with art 22 or with art 23 will, almost invariably, invalidate the permission.

## REQUIREMENTS FOR PARTICULARS TO ACCOMPANY AN APPLICATION UNDER ARTICLE 22

(*Article 23*)

**[3.58]** Article 23 requires that plans, drawings and maps be lodged in metric scale. It goes on to list other requirements in relation to maps, plans, elevations, layout plans, etc. The requirements of art 23 are matters which would normally be dealt with by an engineer or an architect. Article 23(5) does provide that in addition to the other requirements from art 23, a planning authority may request an applicant to provide a scale model of a proposed development including land and buildings in the vicinity, showing the elevations and perspective of the proposed development and any other photographs, plans, maps, drawings or other material or particulars required by the planning authority to assess an application.[73]

**[3.59]** Apart from the matters set out in the regulations relating to the content of planning applications generally and the particulars which must accompany the application under art 22, the planning application, itself as it appears in Sch 3, Form No 2, contains a caveat to the effect that failure to complete the form or to attach the necessary documentation, or submissions of incorrect information or omission of required information will lead to the invalidation of the application. The form also states that where additional information is sought in order to determine whether the application conforms to the development plan, failure to supply the supplementary information will not invalidate the planning application.[74] It warns, however, that if the planning authority is unable to reach a decision because information has not been supplied that may result in a refusal of permission. The form advises applicants to contact the relevant planning authority to determine what local policies and objectives will apply to the development proposed and whether additional information is required.

**[3.60]** The planning application form (Form 2, Sch 3) requires details of the location of the proposed development to include the postal address or townland or location as may best identify the land or structure in question. Where available it requires the ordinance survey map reference number and the grid reference in terms of the Irish Transverse

---

72. PDR 2001, art 22A as substituted by PDR 2006.
73. PDR 2001, art 23 as substituted by PDR 2006.
74. Presumably a planning authority will take the view that it is well capable of determining whether or not the application conforms to its own development plan.

Mercator. In *Crodaun Homes Ltd v Kildare County Council*,[75] the Supreme Court held that the then regulations required accurate identification, particularly for land not situate in an urban area. The land must be identified by the estate of which it forms part or the townland or the neighbouring village so as to be readily and reasonably identifiable. The Supreme Court held that an informal, local name was not a sufficient description.

**[3.61]** In *Dooley v Galway County Council*,[76] the notice published referred to a proposed development in a townland which had an identical name to at least eighteen other townlands in the same county. The court held that the use of the name and the townland only, in those circumstances, did not readily and reasonably identify the location of the land and the permission granted to the applicant was set aside.

**[3.62]** The planning application form requires a description of the type of permission sought. Four categories of permission are listed and the applicant is asked to tick the correct category. The categories are permission, permission for retention, outline permission or permission consequent on a grant of outline permission. Where the permission is consequent on a grant of outline permission, the applicant must furnish the register reference number of the outline permission and the date of grant of the outline permission.

**[3.63]** The applicant for permission must state his/her name, address, telephone number and his/her mobile, e-mail and fax address (if any). The applicant cannot apply in the name of an agent but para 7 of the planning application form allows a person to nominate an agent or an agent to sign para 7 on behalf of an applicant in cases where it is the applicant's wish that all correspondence be sent to the agent at the agent's address. It frequently happens that an architect or other professional adviser would complete box 7 and deal with correspondence relating to the application. In such cases, the planning authority will send all correspondence relating to the application to the agent's address.

**[3.64]** Where the applicant is a company (registered under the Companies Acts 1963–2009) the form of application requires that the names of the company directors are furnished together with the registered address of the company, the company registration number and the company's telephone number. If there are e-mail and fax numbers these also should be furnished. In disclosing the name of the applicant, whether it be a company or an individual, the true identity of the applicant must be furnished. In *State (NCE) v Dublin County Council*,[77] the Supreme Court held that an application made by a nominee company which was in fact a subsidiary of the true applicant for development of land which was in the ownership of the parent company, was not an application under the regulations. The applicant had no interest in the lands. In consequence, all subsequent steps taken by the applicant were held to be void.

**[3.65]** The courts however will tolerate some flexibility in dealing with companies. In *State (Toft) v Galway Corporation*,[78] the application was made in the name Spirits Rum

---

75. *Crodaun Homes Ltd v Kildare County Council* [1983] ILRM, SC.
76. *Dooley v Galway County Council* [1992] 2 IR 136.
77. *State (NCE) v Dublin County Council* [1979] ILRM 249.
78. *State (Toft) v Galway Corporation* [1981] ILRM 439.

Company Ltd instead of the actual name which was Rum Spirits Ltd. The evidence concluded that the plaintiff should have been aware of the true identity of the applicant company as the evidence had shown that the plaintiff's true purpose was to prevent a competitor from opening a business close by. In those circumstances the *de mimimus* rule was applied and the court refused to make an order of *certiorari* in favour of the plaintiff which would have quashed the planning permission. Also, in *Blessington and District Community Council Ltd v Wicklow County Council*[79] the High Court held that a notice was adequate in circumstances where the word 'Ltd' was omitted from the company's name. The omission was not an omission which had misled the plaintiffs.

**[3.66]** Henchy J in the Supreme Court indicated *obiter* that where the applicant was, in fact, an unincorporated company, the application for planning permission might fail: see *State (Finglas Industrial Estates) v Dublin County Council*.[80]

**[3.67]** The form of application requires that the person responsible for the preparation of the drawings and plans must furnish their name, address and telephone number and if available, mobile, e-mail and fax number. Where the plans have been drawn up by a firm/company the name of the person primarily responsible for the preparation of the drawings and plans, on behalf of that firm/company, must be given.

**[3.68]** The planning application form must give a description of the proposed development being a brief description of the nature and extent of the development, including reference to the number and height of buildings, protected structure, etc. In *Monaghan UDC v Alf-a-Bet Promotions Ltd*,[81] application was made for the change of user of premises at The Diamond, Monaghan. The nature and extent of the proposed development was described as 'alterations and improvement' at the applicant's premises at The Diamond, Monaghan. In fact the developers sought permission for conversion of a drapery shop to a betting office and amusement arcade. The published notice was held to be ineffective to the extent that it nullified the application.

> What the legislature has prescribed, or allowed to be prescribed in such circumstances as necessary should be treated by the Courts as nothing short of necessary, and any deviation from the requirement must, before it can be overlooked, be shown, by the person seeking to have it excused, be so trivial, so technical, or so peripheral, or otherwise so insubstantial that, on the principle that it is the spirit rather than the letter of the law that matters, the prescribed obligation has been substantially and therefore adequately complied with.[82]

## LEGAL INTEREST OF APPLICANT IN LAND OR STRUCTURE

**[3.69]** An applicant is compelled to say whether the application is made by the applicant as owner, occupier or other. Where the legal interest is 'other', full details of the precise ownership of the land must be stated. If the applicant is not the legal owner, the name

---

79. *Blessington and District Community Council Ltd v Wicklow County Council* [1997] IR 273.
80. *State (Finglas Industrial Estates) v Dublin County Council* (unreported, 17 March 1983) SC.
81. *Monaghan UDC v Alf-a-Bet Promotions Ltd* [1980] ILRM 64.
82. *Monaghan UDC v Alf-a-Bet Promotions Ltd* [1980] ILRM 249 *per* Henchy J.

and address of the legal owner together with a letter of consent to the making of the application, from the owner, must accompany the documentation. There is no general requirement in PDA 2000 which obliges an applicant for planning permission to have any estate interest or right over land which is the subject matter of his/her application. The word 'owner' is defined in PDA 2000, s 2 as, in relation to land, meaning a person, other than a mortgagee not in possession who, whether in his or her own right or as trustee or agent for another person, is entitled to receive the rack rent from the land or, where the land is not let at rack rent, would be so entitled if it were so let. The word 'applicant' is not defined anywhere.

**[3.70]** In *Frescati Estates Ltd v Walker*,[83] the Supreme Court was asked to determine what interest an applicant had to have in land in order to make an application for planning permission. The Supreme Court held that a person who has no interest of any kind in land and no prospect of acquiring such an interest could not make an application for permission to develop that land. However, if the applicant has the authority of the owner or the authority of a person who has a reasonable prospect of carrying out the development, even though the applicant has no legal estate in the land, the application for planning permission would be valid. In *McCabe v Harding Investments Ltd*,[84] O'Higgins CJ noted that what the planning authority required was a general idea of the applicant's interest in the land. The indication from that case is that if an applicant is a person who genuinely intended to develop the land that intention amounted to a sufficient interest in the land. One way or another, the principles involved appear to have moved on since the decision in the *Frescati* case. More recent decisions would seem to suggest that the courts would allow a flexible approach in deciding whether the applicant's legal interest in the land was sufficient to justify the application. In *Keane v An Bord Pleanála*,[85] the Supreme Court seemed doubtful as to whether an applicant for permission required to have an interest in the land or indeed the permission of someone who had such an interest. In the court's view, in that case, all that was necessary was to avoid unnecessary or vexatious applications.

**[3.71]** In *Arklow Holidays v An Bord Pleanála*,[86] it was claimed that Arklow Urban District Council did not have sufficient interest in the property, the subject matter of the application for planning permission. Arklow Urban District Council had a confirmed compulsory purchase order. The council had served notice to treat so that, at the very least, by *Frescati* standards, it had a 'sufficient interest'. Clarke J felt that he was precluded from deciding on the conflict between *Frescati* and the decision in *Keane v An Bord Pleanála*[87] which latter case had suggested that the true position was that in deciding on the question of sufficient interest, the court only needed to exclude cases where the applicant was engaged in a vexatious or spoiling exercise. Clarke J in the *Arklow Holidays* case was asked for leave to apply for judicial review and the learned

---

83. *Frescati Estates Ltd v Walker* [1975] IR 177.
84. *McCabe v Harding Investments Ltd* [1984] ILRM 763.
85. *Keane v An Bord Pleanála* [1998] 2 ILRM 241.
86. *Arklow Holidays v An Bord Pleanála (No 3)* [2006] IEHC 280.
87. *Keane v An Bord Pleanála* [1998] 2 ILRM 241.

judge granted it on the basis that the definition of 'sufficient interest' seemed to lie somewhere between *Frescati* and *Keane*.

> The position therefore remains that the precise extent of the exclusion is one which requires a definitive decision. It may, on the one hand, be that, as suggested in Keane, the true position is one which requires the Court to exclude only cases where the applicant for planning permission is engaged in a vexatious or spoiling exercise. It may, on the other hand, be that the clear wording of the judgement in Frescati will prevail. Between those poles there are a number of intermediate positions which might also find favour.[88]

## PLANS AND PARTICULARS TO ACCOMPANY AN APPLICATION FOR OUTLINE PERMISSION

*(Article 24)*

**[3.72]** Notwithstanding art 22(2)(d), an outline application shall, in addition to the requirements of art 22(2), be accompanied only by such plans and particulars as are necessary to enable the planning authority to make a decision in relation to the siting, layout or other proposals for development in respect of which a decision is sought.[89]

## PLANNING APPLICATION BY ELECTRICITY UNDERTAKING

*(Article 25)*

**[3.73]** Where development consists of the construction or erection by an electricity undertaking of overhead transmission or distribution lines for conduction of electricity the requirements set out in art 22(4) shall not apply. The documents required by art 22(2) must be lodged by an electricity undertaking in making an application for overhead transmission or distribution lines for conducting electricity together with six copies of such plans or drawings drawn to a scale of not less than 1:100, as are necessary to describe any form of structure or apparatus which will support, or form part of, the lines referred to the said sub-article. Article 23(1) shall not apply to an electricity undertaker in connection with an application for development of overhead cables and wires, with the exception of paras (g) and (h). Paragraph (g) requires that a map or plan which is based on an ordinance survey map shall indicate the relevant ordinance survey sheet number and (h) requires that the north point shall be indicated on all maps and plans other than drawings of elevations and sections and maps or plans referred to in para (g) in this sub-article.[90]

---

88. *Arklow Holidays v An Bord Pleanála (No 3)* [2006] IEHC 280 (8 September 2006), *per* Clarke J.
89. PDR 2001, art 24 as substituted by PDR 2006.
90. PDR 2001, art 25(1)(2) and (3) as substituted by PDR 2006.

## PROCEDURE OF PLANNING AUTHORITY ON RECEIPT OF PLANNING APPLICATION

*(Article 26)*

[3.74] Article 26(1) provides that when a planning authority receives a planning application it shall, in the first instance, consider whether the applicant has complied with the requirements of arts 18, 19(1)(a) and 22 and, as may be appropriate, has complied with the requirements of arts 24 and 25. Article 26(2) provides that if the planning authority considers that the application is compliant it shall stamp each document with the date of its receipt and send to the applicant an acknowledgment stating the date of receipt of the application.[91] Article 26(3) provides that where, after consideration of the application, the planning authority considers that any of the requirements of art 18, 19(1)(a) or 22 and, as may be appropriate of art 24 and 25, has not been complied with or where the notice in the newspaper or the site notice, because of its content or for any other reason, is misleading or inadequate for the information of the public, the planning application shall be invalid.[92] Article 26(4) provides that where, on inspection of the land to which the application relates, the planning authority considers that the requirements of art 17(1)(b), 19 or 20 have not been met, or the information submitted in the planning application is substantially incorrect or substantial information has been omitted, the planning application shall, notwithstanding the fact that an acknowledgement has been sent to the applicant, be invalid.[93]

[3.75] PDR 2001, art 26(5) provides that as soon as may be after the receipt of an invalid application, a planning authority is required to provide written notification to the applicant informing the applicant that the application is invalid and cannot be considered by the planning authority. The notice must also indicate which requirements of the permission regulations have not been complied with and must request the applicant to remove any site notices erected or fixed which relate to the application. The planning authority on receipt of an invalid application will also return the planning application, the application fee and all particulars, plans, drawings and maps to the applicant. Details of the invalid application must be entered in the planning register. Where a planning authority has advised an applicant that their application is invalid the planning authority shall by notice in writing inform any person or body who has made a submission or observation of the fact that the application was invalid and it must also return any fee paid in respect of such a submission or observation.[94] In the event of any invalid application being notified to the applicant, the planning authority must also advise any body to which notice was sent in accordance with art 28(2).[95]

---

91. PDR 2001, art 26(2) as substituted by PDR 2006.
92. See PDR 2001, art 26(3) as substituted by PDR 2006.
93. See PDR 2001, art 36(4) as substituted by PDR 2006.
94. See PDR 2001, art 26(5) as substituted by PDR 2006.
95. PDR 2001, art 26(1)–(8) inclusive, as substituted by PDR 2006.

[3.76] The procedure prescribed under art 26 of PDR 2001 (as substituted by PDR 2006) requires, in the first instance, the planning authority to consider whether the applicant has complied with the requirements of the regulations in terms of public notice of the contents of the planning applications. After that review has been undertaken the planning authority must decide whether to accept or to reject the application as invalid. If the planning authority accepts the planning application it is date-stamped and acknowledgment of the receipt of the application is sent to the applicant. If the planning authority concludes that there are shortcomings in relation to the content of the planning applications or the public notices or if they establish that the information submitted is either incorrect or deficient in some other respect then it is given a second opportunity, even though it has acknowledged receipt of the application, to reject the application as invalid. This is specifically stated in art 26(4) but if a site notice has been maliciously defaced or destroyed by any person other than the applicant, art 26(7) provides that if the planning authority is satisfied that the site notice terms were initially complied with but were later defaced or damaged, the application (on those grounds alone) would not be declared to be invalid. PDR 2001 (as substituted by the PDR 2006, art 26) expressly provides that a request for further information cannot require the submission of any further information in relation to notice in newspapers, site notices or in relation to the content of planning applications generally. Similarly, a defective public notice, either in a newspaper or site notice, cannot be remedied at the direction of the planning authority.

[3.77] The regulations require that notice of intention to make a planning application must be given by publication of the notice in a newspaper within the period of two weeks before lodging the planning application.[96] The regulations also require that, before making the planning application, notice of intention to make the application must be given within a period of two weeks, by the erection or fixing of a site notice.[97] The detailed provisions relating to the notice in the newspaper are contained in art 18 and the detailed provisions in relation to a site notice are contained in art 19. If there is non-compliance with those articles and regulations, the application will be invalid. Similarly, if the content of planning applications as detailed in art 22 is not complied with or if the plans and particulars required to be lodged for outline permission in art 24 are not complied with the application will be invalid. The specified additional information to be submitted with the application is a requirement which is in addition to art 22 and the planning authority may require the applicant to submit with the planning application specified additional information. No planning application shall be invalidated under art 26 for failure to submit with the application any information or particulars requested under art 22(1)(a).[98] Other regulations may also render a planning application invalid, and where the validity of an application is referred to the courts it is likely that the application may be declared invalid where the evidence indicates that the non-compliance with the regulations was likely to mislead the planning authority or potential objectors. Thus, an application was held to be invalid where the plans lodged with the

---

96. PDR 2001, art 17(1)(a) as substituted by PDR 2006.
97. PDR 2001, art 17(1)(b) as substituted by PDR 2006.
98. PDR 2001, art 21(1)(a).

application misstated the distance between the proposed development and an existing house in circumstances where occupiers of the existing house wished to object on the basis of overlooking and the proximity of the new dwelling house to their own dwelling house.[99] In *Dublin Co Co v Marron*,[100] the application for permission did not include floor plans, elevations or sections and the map did not include the north point. The name of the person who prepared the drawings was not stated. Although these failures did not mislead the planning authority, they might have misled members of the public. As such, the omissions were not *de minimus* and the application was set aside.

**[3.78]** No general rule has emerged from court decisions as to whether or not the effects of the regulations are mandatory or discretionary. Each case would seem to be dealt with on an individual basis. Thus, in *Monaghan UDC v Alf-a-Bet Promotions Ltd*[101] the court held that regulations regarding public notice were mandatory. Failure to comply with the public notice requirements would render the permission void. In *Molloy v Dublin County Council*,[102] the plans were lodged but failed to indicate the identity of the person who had prepared them. The court held that this omission did not render the application invalid.

**[3.79]** Since it is expressly provided that failure to comply with specific requirements of the regulations will result in the planning application being invalid, the planning authority is left with very little discretion in the matter. In each case, the courts are asked to decide whether any particular regulation, which required compliance, is discretionary or mandatory. From a reading of the regulations it is clear that the requirements are mandatory but this would not preclude overlooking some unimportant or trivial breaches, and in those cases the *de minimis* rule would still apply.

**[3.80]** Just as members of the public are bound by the regulations so too is the planning authority. This has been illustrated in a number of cases where the planning authority has purported to send out a request for further information. Normally, a genuine request for further information would have the effect of suspending the eight week time period but the courts, in cases of doubt, will look carefully at the request for further information to ensure that it is just that. In *O'Connor's Downtown Properties Ltd v Nenagh UDC*,[103] O'Hanlon J examined a request for further information from the Nenagh UDC which indicated that the council as planning authority was prepared to grant permission if the proposal received in the application was modified. The court held that this request was not a genuine request for further information but was a request seeking a revision of the application and as such it did not stop the eight week time period from running, and so a default permission followed. Similarly, in *State (Conlon Construction Ltd) v Cork County Council*[104] the applicant received a letter from Cork

---

99. *Seery v An Bord Pleanála* (unreported, 26 November 2003) HC.
100. *Dublin Co Co v Marron* [1985] ILRM 593.
101. *Monaghan UDC v Alf-a-Bet Promotions Ltd* [1980] ILRM 64 SC.
102. *Molloy v Dublin County Council* [1991] IR 90.
103. *O'Connor's Downtown Properties Ltd v Nenagh UDC* [1993] 1 IRHC.
104. *State (Conlon Construction Ltd) v Cork County Council* (unreported, 31 July 1975) HC.

County Council which advised the applicant that his application was unacceptable in relation to details of layout and in relation to proposals for the disposal of effluents. The letter also made some enquiries as to the title of the applicant. Butler J considered that those observations and enquiries did not amount to a genuine request for further information. The letter, on the contrary, only seemed to indicate the council's disapproval of the layout and of the plans for disposal of effluents. As the layout enquiry did not amount to a valid notice requiring the developer to give further information or to produce evidence in respect of the title it did not stop the period running, and in consequence a default permission issued.

[3.81] It is not open to a planning authority to seek to negotiate changes in the proposal laid out in the application. Where further information is sought by a planning authority the request must be a genuine request for further information which will enable the planning authority to grasp the full picture in the sense of having sufficient information necessary to make a decision in relation to the application which is before it. In *Illium Properties Ltd v Dublin City Council*,[105] the applicant for permission became entitled to planning permission by default where O'Leary J concluded that the real purpose of the request for further information was not to gain further understanding in relation to particular matters contained in the application but rather to gain more time to allow the planning authority to complete its examination and investigation of the application before making its decision.

## WEEKLY LIST OF PLANNING APPLICATIONS

(*Article 27*)

[3.82] PDR 2001, art 27(1) (as substituted by PDR 2006) provides that a planning authority shall, not later than the fifth working day following a particular week make available in accordance with art 27(2) a list of the planning applications received by the authority that week. The purpose of this disclosure is to extend the network of information which is available in respect of applications for planning permission. The weekly list provides information which is also available from the site notice and from the notice placed in the relevant newspaper.

[3.83] PDR 2001, art 27(2) (as substituted by PDR 2006) provides that a list referred to in art 27(1) shall have a banner heading stating that, under s 34 of the Act (as amended),[106] the applicants for permission may be granted permission, subject to or without conditions or permission may be refused; that it is the responsibility of any person wishing to use the personal data on planning applications and decisions lists for direct marketing purposes to be satisfied that they may do so legitimately under the requirements of the Data Protection Acts 1998 and 2003 taking account of preferences

---

105. *Illium Properties Ltd v Dublin City Council* [2004] IEHC 403, per O'Leary J.
106. See PD(A)A 2010, s 23.

outlined by the applicants in their application[107] and shall indicate in respect of each planning application received during the week to which the list relates:

(a) the name of the applicant [Note: it is no longer necessary to provide the address of the applicant],[108]

(b) whether the application is for permission, for development, permission, for retention of development, outline permission for development or permission consequent on the grant of outline permission (stating the reference number on the register of the relevant outline permission),

(c) the location, townland or postal address of the land or structure to which the application relates (as may be appropriate),

(d) the nature and extent of the development including—

    (i) where the application relates to development consisting of or comprising the provision of houses, the number of houses to be provided,

    (ii) where the application relates to the retention of a structure, the nature of the proposed use of the structure and where appropriate, the period for which it is proposed to be retained,

    (iii) where the development relates to a protected structure or a proposed protected structure, an indication of that fact,

    (iv) where the application relates to development which comprises or is for the purposes of an activity requiring an integrated pollution control licence or a waste licence, an indication of that fact,

    (v) where a planning application relates to development in a strategic development zone, an indication of that fact, and

(e) the date of receipt of the application.

The list required by art 27(1) and (2) (as amended) must be kept available for a period of not less than eight weeks beginning on the day on which the list is made available for inspection at the offices of the planning authority and in each public library or mobile library in the functional area of the authority, in a position convenient for inspection during office hours and at any other place or by any other means, including electronic form, that the authority considers appropriate. Copies of the list are to be made available to members of the public free of charge or for a fee not exceeding the reasonable cost of making a copy together with the cost of postage where applicable. This list shall also be made available to members of the planning authority in such a manner as they may, by resolution, direct.[109]

**[3.84]** PDR 2001, art 27(3) (as substituted by PDR 2006) provides that a list referred to in art 27(1) shall, in addition to the requirements of art 27(2), indicate any planning application in respect of which: (a) the planning authority has served a notice under art 26(5) (rejecting the application); (b) further information or evidence or revised plans,

---

107. The words in italics here had been inserted by PDR 2007 (SI 135/2007), art 11(2)(b) amending Regulations 2001-2007, art 32.
108. See amendment PDR 2007.
109. See PDR 2006, art 27(5)(a)(b) as amended by PDR 2007, arts 9(a) and (b).

drawings or particulars have been received by the planning authority pursuant to requirement, under arts 33 or 34.

**[3.85]** PDR 2001, art 27(4) (as substituted by PDR 2006) provides that a planning authority may include in a list any other information in respect of planning applications which the planning authority considers appropriate.

## NOTICE TO CERTAIN BODIES

(*Article 28*)

**[3.86]** Article 28 lists circumstances in which the planning authority is compelled to send notice to various bodies as soon as may be after receipt of the application. The notice party would include bodies such as An Chomhairle Ealaíon, Fáilte Ireland, An Taisce, the Heritage Council, the National Trust for Ireland, the appropriate Regional Fisheries Board, the Irish Aviation Authority, Coras Iompair Éireann, the Railway Procurement Agency, the National Roads Authority, the Dublin Transportation Office, the Environmental Protection Agency, the Minister for Community, Rural and Gaeltacht Affairs and Údarás Na Gaeltachta, the Minister for Justice, Equality and Law Reform, the Health Services Executive, the Ministers for Communications, Marine and Natural Resources, the Commission for Energy Regulation, the Railway Safety Commission and the Shannon Free Airport Development Company Ltd.[110]

**[3.87]** Notice must also be given to another local authority where it appears that that local authority might be affected by the development. Where the development would be inconsistent with and would materially contravene any regional planning guidelines of a regional authority, notice must be served on that regional authority.[111]

**[3.88]** In all cases, the notice must include a copy of the planning application and must state the date of receipt by the authority of the application. The notice must state that any submissions or observations made to the authority in relation to the application within a period of five weeks, beginning on the date of receipt by the authority of the application, will be taken into account by the planning authority in making its decision on the application.[112] Where the authority receives such submissions or observations it must acknowledge receipt thereof in writing.

## REVOCATION OR MODIFICATION OF PERMISSION

**[3.89]** A grant of planning permission is a vested right and for that reason PDA 2000, s 44 is careful to ensure that the provisions for revocation and modification of permission are limited. In *ESB v Cork Co Co*,[113] the respondent revoked a planning

---

110. See PDR 2001, art 28(1)(a)–(x) inclusive, as substituted by PDR 2006.
111. PDR 2001, art 28(1)(d) as substituted by PDR 2006.
112. PDR 2001, art 28(2) as substituted by PDR 2006.
113. *ESB v Cork County Council* [2001] IEHC 190, *per* Finnegan J.

permission for overhead electricity lines and the applicant challenged the planning authority's decision. It was held that the manufacture of steel pylons which would support the overhead cables constituted 'works' within the meaning of the Local Government (Planning and Development) Act 1963, s 30. Where the work had commenced, the planning authority could not revoke the permission. It was further held that the applicant was not afforded an opportunity to make any submissions concerning the revocation which omission, in the opinion of the court, amounted to a breach of natural justice.

[3.90] The Local Government (Planning and Development) Act 1963 did not provide for the making of submissions or observations in relation to a planning authority's proposal to revoke or modify a planning permission but, in spite of that omission, the revocation in this case was held to be a breach of natural justice. This principle was further supported and clarified in *Eircell Limited v Leitrim Co Co*,[114] where the planning authority revoked a planning permission to erect a radio/telephone transmission mast on the grounds that the proposed development would give rise to a health hazard resulting from the emissions of radiation. The court held that the change of circumstances was not such as to justify the planning authority's revocation of permission in that particular case. The court also held that the planning authority's decision to revoke is a quasi-judicial function and that, as such, the planning authority must act within the constraints of natural and constitutional justice.

[3.91] PDA 2000, s 44 provides that if the planning authority considers that it is expedient that any permission to develop land granted under that Part should be revoked or modified, it may serve a notice in accordance with s 44(3) on the applicant and on any other person who, in its opinion, will be materially affected by the revocation or modification. That seemingly wide power is immediately curtailed by s 44(2), which provides that a planning authority shall neither revoke nor modify a permission under the section unless the development to which the permission relates no longer conforms with the provisions of the development plan.[115]

[3.92] PDA 2000, s 44 sets up a notice procedure in the event of a planning authority seeking to revoke or modify a permission. The notice shall:

(a) refer to the permission concerned,

(b) specify the provisions of the development plan to which the permission no longer conforms, and

(c) invite persons served to make written submissions and observations to the planning authority within the periods specified in the notice (being not less than four weeks from the service of the notice) concerning the proposed revocation or modification.[116]

---

114. *Eircell Limited v Leitrim Co Co* [2000] 1 IR 479.
115. PDA 2000, s 44(1) and (2).
116. PDA 2000, s 44(3).

The planning authority shall then consider the submissions and observations received before making its decision.[117] Where a planning authority decides to revoke or modify the permission under s 44(4), it shall specify in the decision the provisions of the development plan to which the permission no longer conforms, and the main reasons and considerations on which its decision is based.[118] An appeal against a decision to revoke or modify may be taken to the board at any time within four weeks of the date of the decision.[119] Where an appeal is brought under this section against a decision, the board may confirm the decision with or without modifications, or annul the decision with or without modification, and, it shall specify the main reasons and considerations for its decision.[120]

[3.93] Revocation and/or modification of permission to develop can be exercised:

(a) where the permission relates to the carrying out of works, at any time before those works have commenced, or in the case of works which have been commenced and which, consequent on the making of a variation in the development plan, will contravene the plan, at any time before the works have been completed,

(b) where the permission relates to a change of use of any land, at any time before the change has taken place,

but the revocation or modification of permission for the carrying out of works shall not affect so much of the works as have been previously carried out.[121]

A planning authority may at any time, for stated reasons, by notice in writing, withdraw a notice of modification or revocation served under s 44.[122] Particulars of a decision made under this section shall be entered in the register.[123] The revocation or modification under this section of a permission shall be a reserved function.[124]

## SUBMISSIONS OR OBSERVATIONS IN RELATION TO A PLANNING APPLICATION

(*Article 29*)

[3.94] PDR 2001, art 29 (as substituted by PDR 2006) provides that any person or body, on payment of the prescribed fee, may make a submission or observation in writing to a planning authority in relation to a planning application within a period of five weeks beginning on the date of receipt by the planning authority of the application.[125]

---

117. PDA 2000, s 44(4).
118. PDA 2000. s 44(5).
119. PDA 2000, s 44(6).
120. PDA 2000, s 44(7).
121. PDA 2000, s 44(8)(a) and (b).
122. PDA 2000, s 44(9).
123. PDA 2000, s 44(10).
124. PDA 2000, s 44(11).
125. PDR 2001, art 29(1)(a) as substituted by PDR 2006 and amended by PDR 2007.

**[3.95]** Article 29(1)(b) was further amended by the Planning and Development (No 2) Regulations 2007 by the substitution of para (b) with the following:

    (b)   any submission or observation received shall—

        (i)   state the name of the person or body making the submission or observation, and

        (ii)   indicate the address to which any correspondence relating to the application should be sent.

Where a submission or observation, under this article, is received by the planning authority after the period of five weeks beginning on the date of receipt of the application, the planning authority shall return to the person or body concerned the submission or observation received and the fee and notify the person or body that their submission or observation cannot be considered by the planning authority.[126]

When a planning authority so consents, a submission or observation may be made in electronic form.[127]

**[3.96]** PDA 2000, s 34(3) gives statutory recognition to submissions or observations made to a planning authority on planning applications. In effect, the planning authority must take into account written submissions or observations made by third parties on a planning application. In addition to the planning application itself, the planning authority shall have regard to any information relating to the application furnished to it by the applicant in accordance with the permission regulations.

**[3.97]** Where a party wishes to appeal a decision to grant planning permission made by a planning authority, it is a precondition to that appeal that the submissions or observations must have been lodged by the appellant within five weeks from the date of the application. The five week time limit is absolute and if submissions or observations have not been received by the planning authority within that five week period the right to appeal is lost except in one instance. PDA 2000, s 37(6)(a)[128] provides an exception to the general rule restricting the right of appeal to persons who have made submissions or observations in writing in relation to a planning application. This subsection provides that a person, who has an interest in land adjoining land in respect of which a decision to grant permission has been made, may, within four weeks and on payment of the appropriate fee, apply to the board for leave to appeal against a decision of the planning authority under PDA 2000, s 34, as amended by PD(A)A 2010, s 23. The application must state the name and address of the applicant and the grounds upon which the application is made and it must give a description of the applicant's interest in the adjoining lands. If an applicant, in making an application to the board for leave to appeal under this section, shows that the development in respect of which a decision to grant permission is made will differ materially from the development as set out in the

---

126.   PDR 2001, art 29(3).
127.   PDR 2001, art 29(4) as substituted by PDR 2006.
128.   PDA 2000, s 37(6)(a) has been amended by PD(A)A 2002, s 10 by correcting an error which mistakenly referred to a grant of permission when what was intended was a reference to a decision to grant permission.

application for permission, by reason of conditions imposed by the planning authority, and that the imposition of such conditions will materially affect the applicant's enjoyment of the land or reduce the value of the land, the board shall grant the applicant leave to appeal within four weeks from the date of receipt of the application, even though the applicant has not made any submission or observation to the planning authority within five weeks of the date of the original application for planning permission. Within three days of making its decision either to grant or refuse an application for leave to appeal, the board shall notify the planning authority and the applicant, and if leave to appeal is granted, the applicant will have two weeks from the date of notification to bring the appeal. Once an application is made under this subsection the planning authority shall not make any grant of permission unless the application is refused.[129]

**[3.98]** Article 29(2)[130] provides that the planning authority shall acknowledge any submissions or observations as soon as may be after receipt in the form set out at Form No 3 of Sch 3 or a form substantially to like effect. PDA 2000, s 127(1)(e) provides that an appeal or referral shall, in the case of an appeal under s 37 by a person who made submissions or observations in accordance with the permission or regulations, be accompanied by the acknowledgement by the planning authority of receipt of the submissions or observations. The acknowledgement of receipt of submissions or observations on a planning application is an important document and without it the appeal will fail.

**[3.99]** Form No 3 of Sch 3 of PDR 2001 (as substituted by PDR 2006) is set out below. It advises that the document should be safely kept and will be required in the event of an appeal to An Bord Pleanála. In *Lynch v Dublin City Council*,[131] the planning authority failed to issue an acknowledgement of receipt of submissions or observations on the planning application. Furthermore, the planning authority failed to notify the objector that it had made a decision to grant permission. The objector had only learned of the decision after the four week period for making an appeal had expired. Ó Caoimh J held that the requirements to furnish a written acknowledgement were mandatory (as indeed it would appear to be), but that the failure to do so would not invalidate any subsequent decision to grant planning permission. In that instance the High Court was seen to accept the planning authority's planning decision even though it had not acknowledged receipt of the submissions or observations made by the objector. In effect, the planning authority had precluded the objector from lodging an appeal because the form of receipt is an essential document which must be lodged when the appeal is made. It may have been some consolation to the applicant, in those unhappy circumstances, that the High Court ordered the planning authority to pay the applicant's costs. The problem with the learned judge's decision in this case is that it could be used by a mischievous planning authority as a means of frustrating a genuine appeal (see **Appendix**).

---

129. See PDA 2000, s 37(6)(a)–(i) inclusive as amended by Planning and Development (Amendment) Act 2002, s 10.
130. See PDR 2006, art 29(2).
131. *Lynch v Dublin City Council* (unreported, 25 July 2003) HC, Ó Caoimh J.

## ALLOWANCE FOR PUBLIC HOLIDAYS, ETC

(*Article 29A*)[132]

[3.100] Where a requirement of these regulations requires submissions, observations or a request to be made, or documents, particulars or other information to be submitted to the planning authority within a specified period and the last day of that period is a public holiday (within the meaning of the Organisation of Working Time Act 1997) or any other day on which the offices of the planning authority are closed, the submissions, observations or request for documents, particulars or other information (as the case may be) shall be regarded as having been received before the expiration of that period if received by the authority on the next following day on which the office of the authority is open.

[3.101] In summary, an extra day or days may be added on to any time limit for submission, observations, lodgement of documents, etc, where there is a public holiday or where the offices of planning authority are closed during the time-limit period.

## MINIMUM PERIOD FOR DETERMINATION OF PLANNING APPLICATION

(*Article 30*)[133]

[3.102] A planning authority shall not determine an application for permission until after a period of five weeks, beginning on the date of receipt of an application, has elapsed. The five week period coincides with the five week period in which submissions and observations may be made by potential applicants.

## MAXIMUM PERIOD FOR DETERMINATION OF PLANNING APPLICATION

[3.103] PDA 2000, s 34(8)(a) provides that, subject to paras (b), (c), (d) and (e), where:

(i) an application is made to a planning authority in accordance with the permission regulations for permission under this section, and

(ii) any requirements of those regulations relating to the application are complied with, a planning authority shall make its decision on the application within a period of eight weeks beginning on the date of receipt by the planning authority of the application.

That is the general rule but the eight week period for making the decision can be altered in the following ways.

---

132. Inserted by PDA 2006 after PDR 2001, art 29 as substituted by PDR 2006.
133. PDR 2001, art 30 has not been altered.

**[3.104]** PDA 2000, s 34(8)(b)[134] provides that:

> where a planning authority, within 8 weeks of the receipt of the planning application, serves notice in accordance with the permission regulations requiring the applicant to give to the planning authority further information or to produce evidence in respect of the application, the authority shall make its decision on the application as follows:
> 
> (i) within 4 weeks of the notice been complied with, or
> 
> (ii) if in relation to further information given or evidence produced in compliance with the notice, the planning authority—
> 
> > (I) considers that it contains significant additional data which requires the publication of a notice by the applicant in accordance with the permission regulations, and
> > 
> > (II) gives notice accordingly to the applicant,
> 
> within 4 weeks beginning on the day in which notice of that publication is given by the applicant to the planning authority.

**[3.105]** PDA 2000, s 34(8)(c) provides that:

> where in the case of an application accompanied by an environmental impact statement, a planning authority serves a notice for further information or to produce evidence in respect of the application, the authority shall make its decision within 8 weeks of the notice being complied with.

**[3.106]** PDA 2000, s 34(8)(d) provides that:

> where a notice referred to in sub-s (6) is published in relation to the application [this refers to the invocation of material contravention procedures], the authority shall make its decision within a period of 8 weeks beginning on the day on which the notice is first published.

**[3.107]** PDA 2000, s 34(8)(e) provides that:

> where, in the case of an application for permission for development that—
> 
> (i) would be likely to increase the risk of a major accident, or
> 
> (ii) is of such a nature as to be likely, if a major accident were to occur, and, having regard to all the circumstances, to cause there to be serious consequences,
> 
> a planning authority consults, in a accordance with the permission regulations, with a prescribed authority for the purposes of obtaining technical advice regarding such risk or consequences, the authority shall make a decision in relation to the application within four weeks beginning on the day on which the technical advice is received.

---

134. PDA 2000, s 34(8)(b) and (c) as substituted by PD(A)A 2010, s 23(b)(i) and (ii).

# DEFAULT PLANNING PERMISSION

**[3.108]** PDA 2000, s 34(8)(f)[135] provides for a statutory default permission. For default permission to occur, the planning application must be a valid application made in accordance with the permission regulations and complying with any requirements of those regulations relating to the application. If the application is made in accordance with PDA 2000, s 34(8)(a), that subsection requires that the decision on the application must be made within a period of eight weeks beginning on the date of receipt by the planning authority of the application. The eight-week period may be extended in accordance with the provisions of PDA 2000, s 34(8)(b)–(e) inclusive.[136] The eight-week period or such other extended period specified in s 34(8)(b), (c), (d) and (e) within which a planning authority must make its decision on the application is, for the purposes of s 34(8)(f), as inserted by PD(A)A 2010, s 23, referred to as the 'first period'. Where a planning authority fails to make a decision within the first period the planning authority is given another 12 weeks after the first period to make its decision. This means that the period for making a decision can be 20 weeks – (eight weeks plus 12 weeks).

**[3.109]** The supposed purpose of default permission is to encourage planning authorities to make their decisions within the now 20-week period or such other period as may be extended. A planning permission imposed in this way through the default permission procedure without any conditions attached to it or without any consideration of the merits or demerits of the application by the planning authority is undesirable but it must also be said that the default permission will be a rare occurrence allowing for the minimum period of 20 weeks before it can happen. The worry is that the provision may encourage overburdened planning authorities to delay decisions for 20 weeks or more as appropriate, but if they fail to make the decision within the first period they are compelled to pay 'the appropriate sum' to the applicant. An appropriate sum means three times the amount paid by the applicant for the application or €10,000 whichever is the lesser amount. It remains to be seen whether this penalty will be a sufficient incentive to discourage planning authorities from delaying their decisions beyond the first period.[137]

**[3.110]** In *Molloy v Dublin County Council*,[138] Blayney J expressed judicial disapproval of the principle involved in obtaining permission by default:

> It is with considerable regret that I have arrived at this decision as it means that the plaintiffs are obtaining a planning permission which the defendant, for a number of reasons, considered should be refused. It does not seem reasonable that failure to give notice of a decision within two months should result in an application being automatically granted, but such is the law and I have to apply it. It is only the legislature can change it and I am strongly of the opinion that they should consider doing so.

---

135. PDA 2000, s 34(8)(f)(i)–(viii) is as inserted by PD(A)A 2010, s 23(b)(ii).
136. See paras **3.104** to **3.107**.
137. PDA 2000, s 34(8)(f)(ii) and (vii) as inserted by PD(A)A 2010, s 23.
138. *Molloy v Dublin County Council* [1990] 1 IR 90.

**[3.111]** In *Abbeydrive Developments v Kildare Co Co*,[139] lawyers representing An Taisce drew the court's attention to the ECJ decision in *Commission v Belgium*,[140] which held that any development which has an EIA requirement cannot be authorised by way of a tacit grant of planning permission. The amendments made in PD(A)A 2010, s 23 to PDA 2000, s 34 have addressed that situation, and where an application for permission is subject to the requirements of EIA or a determination as to whether an EIA or an appropriate assessment under the Habitats Directive is required, a default decision to grant permission cannot be obtained. In the same context, and as seen in relation to PDA 2000, s 34(6), a planning authority can no longer be compelled to issue a default permission where the development proposed would materially contravene a local area plan.

**[3.112]** The remainder of the substituted provisions of s 23(f), amending PDA 2000, s 34(8)(f), dealing with default permission, provide as follows:

(f) (iii) Where a planning authority fails to make a decision within a period of twelve weeks after the expiry of the 'first period' a decision (referred to in this paragraph as the 'deemed decision') of the planning authority to grant the permission shall be regarded as having been given on the last day of that period of twelve weeks.

(iv) Any person who has made submissions or observations in writing in relation to the planning application to the planning authority may at any time within the period of four weeks after the expiry of the period of twelve weeks referred to in subparagraph (3), appeal the deemed decision.

(v) Subparagraphs (i)–(iv) shall not apply where there is a requirement under Part X or Part XAB to carry out an environmental impact assessment, a determination whether an environmental impact assessment is required or an appropriate assessment in respect of the development relating to which the authority has failed to make a decision.

(vi) Where the planning authority has failed to make a decision in relation to development where an environmental impact assessment, a determination whether an environmental impact assessment is required, or an appropriate assessment is required within the first period and becomes aware, whether through notification by the applicant or otherwise that it has so failed—

(I) the authority shall proceed to make the decision notwithstanding the fact that the first period had expired,

(II) where a planning authority fails to make a decision within the first period, it shall pay the appropriate sum to the applicant,

(III) provided that no notice under paragraph (b) or (c) was served on the applicant prior to the expiry of the first period, where a planning authority proceeds to make a decision under clause (I) in

---

139. *Molloy v Dublin County Council* (unreported, 16 July 2005) HC, Macken J.
140. *Commission v Belgium* [2001] ECR 1–4605.

relation to an application, it may serve notice on the applicant requiring the applicant to give to the authority further information or to produce evidence in respect of the application under paragraph (b) or (c) and paragraph (b) or (c) shall apply to such notice subject to any necessary modifications,

(IV) subject to service of notice under paragraph (b) or (c) in accordance with clause (III), where a planning authority fails to make a decision before the expiry of the period of twelve weeks beginning on the day immediately after the day on which the first period expires, the authority shall, subject to clause (V), pay the appropriate sum to the applicant, and shall pay a further such sum to the applicant where it fails to make a decision before the expiry of each subsequent period of twelve weeks beginning immediately after the preceding twelve week period,

(V) not more than five payments of the appropriate sum shall be made by a planning authority to an applicant in respect of the failure by the authority to make a decision in relation to an application,

(VI) where a planning authority makes a decision in relation to an application more than one year after the expiration of the first period the authority, before making the decision—

(A) notwithstanding that notice has been previously published in relation to the application, shall require the applicant to publish additional such notice concerning the planning application in accordance with the permission regulations (and the planning authority shall refund the costs of so publishing to the applicant),

(B) notwithstanding that, notice of the application has previously been given to prescribed bodies, shall give additional such notice in accordance with the permission regulations, and

(C) notwithstanding anything contained in paragraph (b) or (c), or that the authority has previously been given further information or evidence under those paragraphs may require the applicant to give to the authority further information or to produce evidence in respect of the application as the authority requires and paragraph (b) or (c) as appropriate, shall apply to such additional requests subject to any necessary modifications,

and the planning authority shall consider any submissions made in accordance with the Regulations following on such additional notices, or additional further information or evidence produced under this clause.

(vii) Any payment or refund due to be paid under this paragraph shall be paid as soon as may be and in any event not later than four weeks after it becomes due.

(viii) In this paragraph, 'appropriate sum' means a sum which is equal to the lesser amount of the three times the prescribed fee paid by the applicant to the planning authority in respect of his or her application for permission or €10,000.

Where default permission arises from the failure of a planning authority to give notice to the applicant of its decision, that decision is still subject to the four week period in which third parties can lodge an appeal with the board, provided they have made submissions or observations on the planning application in question. If valid objections are lodged, the matter will go before the board in the usual way. The more common procedure, in such cases, requires that the applicant will apply to the High Court for an order of *mandamus* compelling the planning authority to issue a grant of permission. That application should be made before the development commences.

[3.113] There are a number of instances where an applicant is disqualified from receiving a default permission, including the following:

(a) if the documentation submitted by the applicant does not substantially comply with the regulations made under PDA 2000 dealing with planning applications, a default permission will not be deemed to have been so granted. In *Molloy & Walsh v Dublin County Council*,[141] it was argued that the application was invalid in that it had indicated that the applicant held a freehold estate when in fact the title to the estate was subject to a will and the executor had not yet assented to the devise. In that case, the court held that the application was valid as non-compliance was trivial, technical or insubstantial and it was excused by the principle *de minimis non curat lex* (the law does not concern itself with trifles);

(b) a default permission cannot issue where the decision is a material contravention of the development plan. In *State (Pine Valley Development Ltd) v Dublin County Council*,[142] Walsh J held that where a decision is a material contravention of the development plan, an order for *mandamus* 'cannot issue to compel the planning authority to consider an application to do something which would be illegal if done'. In effect, granting default permission where the decision is a material contravention of the planning authority's own development plan would be *ultra vires*. In order for a planning authority to grant a permission which is in material contravention of its development plan it must first go through the entire material contravention procedure by publishing its intention in at least one daily newspaper circulating in the planning authority's functional area indicating its intention to grant a permission in material contravention. Notice must also be given to the applicant and to anyone who has submitted submissions or observations in writing to the planning authority in relation to the development. The planning authority must first consider any submissions or observations which it receives. A resolution of the elected members approving the grant of a decision in material contravention must then be passed at a council meeting. Not less than three-

---

141. *Molloy & Walsh v Dublin County Council* [1990] ILRM 633.
142. *State (Pine Valley Development Ltd) v Dublin County Council* [1984] 1 IR 407.

quarters of the total number of the elected members of the planning authority must vote in favour of the resolution to grant permission in material contravention of the development plan. If the material contravention procedure is not carried out by the council and the council fails to make a decision within the prescribed time no default permission can issue.

(c) a default permission cannot issue where the permission contravenes a special amenity area order.

Where default permission issues it is a grant of planning permission without conditions. Simons has this to say of default permissions:

> The existence of this default mechanism is indefensible. There is nothing to be said in its favour: it is inherently unfair; unpopular with Judges; disproportionate to the mischief which it is intended to remedy; and inconsistent with other aspects of PDA 2000.[143]

It is difficult to find much argument against such a well-constructed statement. In circumstances where default permission issues under the current statutory provisions, it is suggested that a more effective manner of dealing with the situation would be to compel the planning authority to submit the application, together with the planning authority's file, to An Bord Pleanála who would make a decision either to grant permission with or without conditions or to refuse it within a period of, say, four weeks. Perhaps some form of sanction by means of fine or otherwise should be imposed on the defaulting planning authority.

# NOTIFICATION OF DECISION ON PLANNING APPLICATION

*(Article 31)*[144]

[3.114] Notification of a decision to grant planning permission by a planning authority in respect of a planning application shall be given to the applicant and to any person or body who made submissions or observations in accordance with arts 28 and 29, within three working days of the day of the decision, and shall specify:

(a) the reference number of the application in the register,

(b) the development to which the decision relates,

(c) the nature of the decision,

(d) the date of decision,

(e) in the case of a decision to grant a permission – any conditions attached thereto,

(f) the main reasons and considerations on which the decision is based, and, where conditions are imposed in relation to the grant of any permission, the main reasons for the imposition of any such conditions, provided that

---

143. See Simons, *Planning and Development Law* (2nd edn, Thomson Round Hall, 2007) at para 3.200.
144. See PDR 2001, art 31 as substituted by PDR 2006, art 31.

where a condition imposed is a condition described in s 34(4) of the Act,[145] a reference to the paragraph of sub-s (4) in which the condition is described shall be sufficient to meet the requirements of this sub-article,

(g) that in deciding a planning application the planning authority, in accordance with s 34(3) of the Act, has had regard to submissions or observations received in accordance with these Regulations,

(h) in the case of a decision to grant a permission for the construction, erection or making of a structure and to specify the purposes for which the structure may or may not be used – such purposes,

(i) in the case of a decision to grant a permission – any period specified by the planning authority pursuant to section 40 of the Act as the period during which the permission is to have effect,

(j) in the case of a decision to grant permission – that permission shall be issued as soon as may be, but not earlier than 3 working days after the expiration of the period for the making of an appeal if there is no appeal before the Board on the expiration of the said period,

(k) that an appeal against the decision may be made to the Board within the period of 4 weeks beginning on the date of the decision of the planning, and

(l) in the case of a decision to grant or refuse a permission where the decision by the planning authority is different, in relation to the granting or refusal of permission, from the recommendation in the report or reports on a planning application to the manager (or such other person delegated to make the decision), the main reasons for not accepting the recommendation in the report or reports to grant or refuse permission.

Clearly these notification requirements are mandatory rather than discretionary.

## NOTIFICATION OF GRANT OF PERMISSION

[3.115] A notification of decision to grant planning permission does not authorise an applicant to proceed with the development. The applicant must wait for the expiration of the four-week period in which third parties, who have made submissions and observations, are entitled to proceed by way of appeal provided they lodge with their appeal the planning authority's receipt of the submissions and observations made.

[3.116] PDA 2000, s 34(11)(a)(i) provides that where a planning authority decides to grant permission – and no appeal is taken – it shall make the grant as soon as may be after the expiration of the period for taking the appeal. PDA 2000, s 34(11)(a)(ii) provides that if an appeal is taken or appeals are taken against the decision the planning authority shall not make a grant unless:

(I) the appeal is withdrawn; or

---

145. PDA 2000, s 34(4) comprises a list of conditions which may be attached to a planning permission.

(II) the appeal is dismissed by the Board pursuant to section 133 or section 138; or

(III) in relation to it a direction is given to the authority by the Board pursuant to section 139, and, in the case of the withdrawal or dismissal of an appeal or of all such appeals, as may be appropriate, it shall make the grant as soon as may be after such withdrawal or dismissal and, in the case of such a direction, it shall make the grant, in accordance with the direction, as soon as may be after the giving by the Board of the direction.

## WEEKLY LIST OF PLANNING DECISIONS

(*Article 32*)

**[3.117]** Article 32(1) provides that a planning authority shall, not later than the fifth working day following a particular week, make available in accordance with art 32(2) a list of the planning applications in respect of which decisions were given by the authority during that week.

**[3.118]** Article 32(2) provides as follows:[146]

A list referred to in sub-article (1) shall have a banner heading stating – (a) that in deciding a planning application the planning authority, in accordance with s 34(3) of the Act, has had regard to submissions or observations received in accordance with these Regulations, (b) that it is the responsibility of any person wishing to use the personal data on planning applications and decisions lists for direct marketing purposes to be satisfied that they do so legitimately under the requirements of the Data Protection Acts 1998 and 2003 taking account of the preferences outlined by applicants in their applications, and shall indicate in addition to the matters specified in article 27(2) the nature of the decision of the planning authority in respect of the application.

**[3.119]** Article 32(3) provides that:

A planning authority may include, in a list referred to in sub-article (1), any other information on decisions in respect of planning applications which the authority considers appropriate.

**[3.120]** Article 32(4) provides that:

(a) The list referred to in sub-article (1) shall, for a period of not less than 8 weeks beginning on the day on which it is made available, be made available in or at the offices of the planning authority and in each public library and mobile library in the functional area of the authority, in a position convenient for inspection during office hours and at any other place or by any other means, including in electronic form, that the authority considers appropriate.

(b) Copies of the list referred to in sub-article (1) shall, for a period of not less than 8 weeks beginning on the day on which it is made available, be made

---

146. PDR 2001, art 32(2) has been amended by PDR 2007, art 11.

        available at the offices of the planning authority during office hours, free of charge, or for such fee as the authority may fix not exceeding the reasonable cost of making a copy, and shall be sent, on request to any person or body free of charge or for such fee, not exceeding the reasonable cost of making the copy and the cost of postage as the authority may fix.

  (c)    A list referred to in sub-article (1) shall be made available to members of the planning authority in such manner as they may by resolution direct.

## PERMISSION REGULATIONS – FURTHER INFORMATION AND OTHER MATTERS

**[3.121]** Chapter 2 contains arts 33–39 inclusive.

**[3.122]** Where a planning authority acknowledges receipt of a planning application in accordance with art 26 a planning authority can within 8 weeks of receipt of a valid application serve a notice requesting the applicant (a) to submit further information (including plans, maps, drawings or any other information as to any estate or interest in or right over land) which the authority considers necessary to enable it to deal with the application; or (b) to produce any evidence which the authority may reasonably require to verify any particulars or information given in or in relation to the application:[147]

        A planning authority shall not require an applicant who has complied with the requirement under sub-art (1) to submit any further information or evidence save:

  (a)    as may reasonably be necessary to clarify the matters dealt with in the applicant's response to a requirement to submit further information or evidence to enable them to be considered or assessed, or

  (b)    where a request for further information is made concerning the inadequacy of an EIS or the inadequacy of submissions made concerning lands, boundaries and environmental effects.[148]

The purpose of this sub-article is to compel a planning authority to request all further information and all the documents required, in their first request. A planning authority cannot send a further request for information or documents unless that request or those requests are within the limits set out in PDR 2006, art 33(2)(a) and/or (b).

**[3.123]** If a request for further information is ignored for a period in excess of six months from the date of requirement for further information, or such additional period, not exceeding three months, as may be agreed by the planning authority, the planning application shall be declared to be withdrawn, and the planning authority shall, as soon as may be, notify the applicant that the application has been declared to be withdrawn and it shall enter an indication that the application has been declared to be withdrawn in the register.[149]

---

147.    PDR 2001, art 33(1)(a)(b) as substituted by PDR 2006.
148.    PDR 2001, art 33(3) now corresponds with PDR 2006, art 33(2).
149.    See PDR 2001, art 33(4) as substituted by PDR 2006, art 33(3).

**[3.124]** PDA 2000, s 34(8)(b)[150] provides that:

> Where a planning authority, within eight weeks of receipt of a planning application, serves notice in accordance with the permission regulations requiring the applicant to give to the authority further information or to produce evidence in respect of the application, the authority shall make its decision on the application as follows—
>
> (i) within four weeks of the notice being complied with, or
>
> (ii) if in relation to further information given or evidence produced in compliance with the notice, the planning authority—
>
> > (I) considers that it contains significant additional data which requires the publication of a notice by the applicant in accordance with the permission regulations, and
> >
> > (II) gives notice accordingly to the applicant,
>
> within four weeks beginning on the day on which notice of that publication is given by the applicant to the planning authority.

Effectively, where a planning authority serves notice requesting further information or requesting the production of further evidence, the service of such notice stops the clock, that is to say, stops time running in respect of the eight week period which is given to the planning authority to make its decision. As soon as the request for information or for evidence has been complied with, the clock starts to run again. However, a planning authority cannot extend the period for making its decision on the planning application by serving a subsequent or further request for information outside the eight week period allowed for such applications. The eight week period starts to run from the date of receipt of the planning application.[151]

**[3.125]** The planning authority cannot use a request for further information as a means of requiring an applicant to rectify alleged planning breaches. See *Illium Properties Limited v Dublin City Council*[152] in which O'Leary J criticised the planning authority when it sought further information on conservation matters. A request for further information from a planning authority must be limited to planning matters which are relevant to the application. Also, the planning authority cannot use a request for further information to vary the planning application before it. O'Leary J defined the scope of art 33 as follows:

> The power of the planning authority to request further information under this Article is limited to matters which fall within Article 33. Article 33 requests should not (indeed cannot) be used to vary a planning application. Variation can only be done by agreement or by condition (and in these circumstances to a limited extent only in view of the public interest in planning applications) or by re-application. If a planning authority cannot get agreement or cannot apply suitable

---

150. PDA 2000, s 34(8)(b) as substituted by Planning and Development (Amendments) Act 2010, s 23(b)(i) and (ii).
151. PDA 2000, s 34(8)(b).
152. *Illium Properties Limited v Dublin City Council* [2004] IEHC 327, per O'Leary J.

## REVISED PLANS

(*Article 34*)[153]

**[3.126]**

(1) Where the planning authority, having considered a planning application, is disposed to grant a permission subject to any modification of the development, it may, within 8 weeks of receipt of the application, invite the applicant to submit to it revised plans or other drawings modifying, or other particulars providing for the modification of, the said development.

(2) Where the applicant wishes to avail of the opportunity to submit the revised plans, drawings or particulars referred to above, he shall, in writing and within such time limit as may be specified by the planning authority, not being later than 8 weeks from receipt of the application, indicate that he intends to submit such plans, drawings or particulars.

(3) Where the applicant indicates in writing under art 34(2) that he intends to submit the plans, drawings or particulars referred to in art 34(1), he shall, at the same time and in writing, consent under s 34(9)[154] of the Act to the extension of the period for making a decision under s 34(8) of the Act.

This section is fraught with danger. The planning process is, for the main part, an open and transparent process. Yet, art 34 has, at the very least, a potential to deny or prejudice the right of public participation in a relevant and significant part of the process. The section makes no attempt to control the level or degree of modification which a planning authority may require. The obvious danger is that without any control being placed on it, a modification requested by a planning authority may so alter the application as to render an application, which was possibly unobjectionable, into one which is objectionable. The word 'modification' is not defined in PDA 2000, s 2. The *Oxford Dictionary* definition of 'modification' includes the following:

> 'the bringing of a thing into a variety of form'; 'the action or act of making changes to something without altering its essential nature or character'.

That *Oxford Dictionary* definition might, in theory, set tight restraints to the changes which could be made but these of course are not statutory limitations. The changes are limited to what might be described as insubstantial changes rather than substantial changes. They are changes which will not alter the essential nature or character of the proposal. If it were otherwise, the 'modification' would attract the probability of a judicial review.

---

153. PDR 2001, art 34 has been substituted and amended by PDR 2006, art 34(1), (2) and (3).
154. PDA 2000, s 34(9) empowers an applicant to consent to the extension of the eight-week time-limit in which a decision under s 34(8) shall be made.

**[3.127]** In *State (Abenglen Properties Ltd) v An Bord Pleanála*,[155] the Supreme Court upheld what were, by any standards, substantial modifications to the proposed development. Butler J in *Irish Hardware Association v South Dublin County Council*[156] did much the same thing. In that case, a permission was granted to a developer for a modified development which, on the face of it, was utterly different from what was sought in the planning application. The applicant applied to the High Court for an order of *certiorari* on the basis that the public were not on notice of the substantial change in the development. Butler J refused to grant a *certiorari* order and held that a change from five retail warehousing units to one large unit did not amount to a materially different development requiring re-advertising.

**[3.128]** A helpful case on the topic is *Dietacaron Ltd v An Bord Pleanála*[157] in which An Bord Pleanála had invited revised plans (modifications) for development at the renowned Quarryvale site in County Dublin. The Board sensibly stated that it intended to circulate the revised plans to all parties to the appeal and to invite those parties to make further submissions or observations on the revised plans. A party to the appeal argued that the revised plans were of such a nature and extent that they radically revised what was envisaged by the initial application. In the applicant's submission a further or fresh planning permission was required. On the facts, Quirke J held that the decision of An Bord Pleanála to invite revisions of the type contemplated was not an unreasonable decision. The reasonableness or otherwise of the decision was certainly helped by the judge's decision to require publication of a further notice advertising the fact that significant modifications were proposed and inviting further submissions and observations, thus reopening the pubic consultation process.

**[3.129]** A number of court cases have made it clear that a planning authority cannot use PDR 2001 (as substituted by PDR 2006) as a means of either extending the statutory period for making a decision on the application or attempting to impose changes on the applicant's proposal as contained in the application for permission. There is no obligation on a planning authority to serve a request for further information or for further documents. It is always open to the planning authority to simply refuse permission. There is no obligation on a planning authority to offer an applicant for planning permission an opportunity to alter the application as submitted by requesting further information even though the planning authority considers that the details in the planning application are inadequate. Where insufficient or inadequate information is given by the applicant the proper course for the planning authority to take is to refuse the application. As will be seen below, PDR 2001, art 35(1) (as substituted by PDR 2006) provides that where information or documents are furnished by an applicant, pursuant to a request by a planning authority, which contain significant additional data, including information in relation to the effects on the environment, the planning authority will

---

155. *State (Abenglen Properties Ltd) v An Bord Pleanála* [1984] IR 381.
156. *Irish Hardware Association v South Dublin County Council* (unreported, 19 July 2000) HC, Butler J.
157. *Dietacaron Ltd v An Bord Pleanála* [2005] 2 ILRM 32, HC, Butler J.

require the applicant to give further public notice in an approved newspaper marked 'Further Information' or 'Revised Plans'.

**[3.130]** In *O'Connor's Downtown Properties Limited v Nenagh UDC*,[158] the planning authority served a notice indicating that the proposal as submitted would be disapproved but that the planning authority would consider a modified version. Ó Caoimh J held that the planning authority's request was not a valid request for further information and as such the two-month period (now eight weeks) was not extended by the notice. To be valid, a request for further information must require information, evidence or explanation which will assist the planning authority to decide on the merits of the application on planning grounds.

**[3.131]** In *State (Conlon Construction Ltd) v Cork County Council*,[159] where the applicants sought a default permission in the High Court, the planning authority relied on a letter, written by it to the applicant, within the two month period, which would, if held valid, have stopped the time running against the planning authority until a reply was received. Butler J held that the letter did not amount to a valid notice in that it did not require the applicant to provide further information or to produce evidence in respect of its application so as to stop the two-month period running. The planning authority did not require the information which it sought in order to properly adjudicate on the development proposal. The form of the planning authority's letter was, in fact, an indication of its dislike of the proposal as submitted and as such it was not a valid request for information which would have stopped the two-month period from running.

**[3.132]** In *State (NCE Ltd) v Dublin County Council*,[160] the planning authority wrote a letter to the applicant requesting that certain features of the proposed development be modified. The request was made on traffic safety grounds. It was, in effect, a request to the developer to alter his proposals in order to meet the planning authority's objections. As such, it was held that it was not a valid notice seeking further information and it was insufficient to extend the then two-month period allowed to the planning authority to make a decision on the application.

## NOTICE OF FURTHER INFORMATION ON REVISED PLANS

*(Article 35)*

**[3.133]** PDR 2001 (as substituted by PDR 2006)[161] provides that where a planning authority receives further information or evidence following a request or where it receives revised plans, drawings or particulars, following a request or otherwise receives further information, evidence, revised plans, drawings or particulars in relation to the application, and it considers that the information, evidence, revised plans, drawings or

---

158. *O'Connor's Downtown Properties Ltd v Nenagh UDC* [1993] 1 IR 1.
159. *State (Conlon Construction Ltd) v Cork County Council* (unreported, 31 July 1975) HC.
160. *State (NCE Ltd) v Dublin County Council* [1979] ILRM 249.
161. PDR 2001, art 35 is substantially substituted in PDR 2006, art 35(1)–(6) inclusive.

particulars received, as appropriate, contain significant additional data, including information in relation to the effects on the environment, the authority shall:

(a) require an applicant, within a specified period, to publish a notice in an approved newspaper containing as a heading the name of the planning authority, marked 'Further Information' or 'Revised Plans' as appropriate, and stating – (i) the name of the applicant, (ii) the location, townland or postal address of the land or structure to which the application relates (as may be appropriate), (iii) the reference number of the application on the register, (iv) that significant further information or revised plans, as appropriate in relation to the application has or have been furnished to the planning authority, and is or are available for inspection or purchase at a fee not exceeding the reasonable cost of making a copy, at the offices of the authority during its public opening hours, and (v) that submissions or observations in relation to the further information or revised plans may be made in writing to the planning authority on payment of the prescribed fee, not later than 2 weeks after the receipt of the newspaper notice and site notice by the planning authority under (a) and (b) of this sub-article or, in the case of a planning application accompanied by an EIS within 5 weeks of receipt of such notice by the planning authority, and to submit a copy of the notice to the planning authority.

(b) require the applicant, within the period specified in (a) of this sub-article for publication of the newspaper notice, to erect or fix a site notice on the land or structure to which the further information relates, in the form set out in Form No. 4 of Schedule 3 or a form substantially to the like effect and to submit a copy of the notice to the planning authority.[162]

(c) as soon as may be, send notice and a copy of the further information, evidence, revised plans, drawings or particulars, to any person or body specified under article 28, as appropriate, indicating that a submission or observation in relation to the further information or evidence or revised plans, drawings or particulars received may be made in writing to the authority not later than 2 weeks after receipt of the newspaper notice and site notice by the planning authority within the period specified in paragraph (a).

(d) as soon as may be, notify any person who made a submission or observation in relation to the planning application in accordance with article 29(1) indicating – (i) that significant further information or revised plans, as appropriate, in relation to the application has or have been furnished to the planning authority, and is or are available for inspection or purchase at a fee not exceeding the cost of making a copy, at the offices of the authority during its public opening hours, (ii) that a submission or observation in relation to the further information or evidence or revised plans, drawings or particulars received may be made in writing to the authority within the period specified in paragraph (a), (iii) that no fee or further fee shall be payable on condition that any submission or observation referred to in sub-paragraph (ii) is accompanied by a copy of

---

162. Form No 4 Sch 3 is reproduced in **Appendix**.

the acknowledgement by the authority of the receipt of a submission or observation referred to in article 29.[163]

(2) Where a planning authority considers that the notices published in accordance with sub-article (1)(a) and (b) do not adequately inform the public, the authority may require the applicant to give such further notices in such a manner and in such terms as the authority may specify.[164]

(3) Sub-articles (1)(b) and (c), (2) and (3) of article 19 shall apply to a site notice erected or fixed under sub-article (1)(b).[165]

(4)(a) The 4 week period referred to in s 34(8)(b) of the Act shall not, in a case where the planning authority considers that the further information, evidence, revised plans, drawings or particulars received contain significant additional data, commence until the planning authority has received the notices referred to in sub-article (1)(a) and (b).[166]

(5) The planning authority shall as soon as may be acknowledge receipt of any submissions or observations referred to in sub-article (1)(a)(v) in the form set out at Form No. 3 of Schedule 3, or a form substantially to the like effect.[167]

(6)(a) A planning authority may, with the consent of any person or body referred to in sub-article (1), send notice under that sub-article in electronic form.[168]

(b) where the planning authority so consents a submission or observation referred to in sub-article (1) may be made in electronic form.[13]

See **Appendix**.

**[3.134]** In summary, PDR 2001, art 35 (as substituted by PDR 2006) provides for notices for further information or revised plans. If the revised plans contain significant additional data this will give rise to further public participation in the planning process by way of further public consultation. If an objector or a potential objector had made submissions or observations during the five week period from the date of the lodgement of the application for planning permission he/she will be notified by the planning authority. If it is the case that significant additional data has been received, then he/she will be invited to make further submissions or observations. The right to make further submissions or observations is not, however, limited to objectors or potential objectors who had already made those submissions or observations.

Where the planning authority has received further information or evidence following a request or where it has received revised plans, drawings or particulars following a request or otherwise receives further information, evidence, revised plans, drawings or particulars in relation to the application and the planning authority considers that the information, evidence, revised plans, drawing or particulars received, as appropriate,

---

163. PDR 2006, art 35(1)(a)–(d) inclusive.
164. PDR 2001, art 35(2) as substituted by PDR 2006.
165. PDR 2006, art 35(3).
166. PDR 2006, art 35(4)(a)&(b).
167. PDR 2006, art 35(5).
168. PDR 2006, art 35(6)(a)&(b).

contain significant additional data, including information in relation to the effects on the environment, it is bound to send a copy of the additional material to any person or body specified in art 28 (as appropriate)[169] indicating that a submission or observation in relation thereto can be made in writing to the authority within a specified time period, and it must also notify any person who has made submissions or observations in relation to the planning application indicating that significant further information or revised plans, as appropriate, in relation to the application have been furnished and that they are available for purchase or inspection. The planning authority must also invite submissions or observations to be made in relation to such significant additional data and no fee is payable for the lodging of any further submissions or observations in respect of further information received by the planning authority.

**[3.135]** It is the planning authority which must decide whether additional material received contains 'significant additional data'. In *Donal Kinsella v Dundalk Town Council*,[170] it was held that the decision as to whether the material received contained significant additional data was a matter to be decided by the planning authority. In determining whether or not the submitted information does contain significant additional data the question to ask is whether some member of the public might reasonably wish to object to the planning application as modified. If the answer is yes then notice must be served on the parties affected and the planning authority may require the applicant to give such further notice in such a manner and in such terms as the planning authority may specify in order to ensure that members of the public will be adequately informed. The High Court will not interfere with the planning authority's interpretation of what is or what is not significant additional data unless it can be demonstrated that the planning authority's assessment is unreasonable or irrational.

*White v Dublin City Council & Others*[171] is a case which was dealt with under the Local Government (Planning and Development) Regulations 1994, art 35. The applicant applied for a planning permission which was refused. After further consultation with the local authority a subsequent application was lodged, which significantly modified the original proposal. Permission was ultimately granted. The Whites, who lived close by, were not notified of the modified application and no public notices were exhibited. By the time the Whites had learned what had happened, the two month period within which they had time to seek judicial review had expired. The Supreme Court endorsed the High Court's decision to grant leave outside the two-month time-limit (this has been remedied in PDA 2000) but on the substantive issue the Supreme Court, following the High Court decision, granted an order of *certiorari* setting aside the decision to grant planning permission on the grounds that the planners' reasoning and the planners' decision were unreasonable and irrational. The planning authority had not required publication of any new notices in spite of the fact that the modification involved substantial changes which went well beyond the meaning of 'modification', in its ordinary sense.

---

169. PDR 2001, art 28, as substituted by PDR 2006, art 28, lists certain bodies who must be notified in appropriate cases.
170. *Donal Kinsella v Dundalk Town Council* [2004] IEHC 373, Kelly J.
171. *Donal Kinsella v Dundalk Town Council* [2004] 1 IR 545.

## PROPER PLANNING AND SUSTAINABLE DEVELOPMENT OF AREA

**[3.136]** PDA 2000, s 34(1) provides that where an application is made to a planning authority in accordance with the permission regulations for permission for development of land and where all requirements of the regulations are complied with the authority may decide to grant permission subject to or without conditions or to refuse it. The planning authority, in making its decision on the planning application shall be restricted to considering the proper planning and sustainable development of the area with regard being had to a number of other prescribed matters. It is, however, the proper planning and sustainable development of the area which is the primary consideration which the planning authority must consider when making a decision in relation to an application. Similarly, An Bord Pleanála, in deciding appeals, is restricted to considering the proper planning and sustainable development of the area.[172] Apart from the proper planning and sustainable development of an area, both the planning authority and the board shall have regard to:

- (i) The provisions of the development plan;
- (ii) The provisions of any special amenity area order relating to the area;
- (iii) Any European site or other area prescribed for the purposes of s 10(2)(c) which provides for the conservation and protection of the environment including, in particular, the archaeological and natural heritage and the conservation and protection of European sites and any other sites which may be prescribed for the purposes of this paragraph;
- (iv) Where relevant, the policy of the Government, the Minister or any other Ministers of the Government;
- (v) The matters referred to in sub-s 4 which deal with a list of conditions which may be attached to a grant of planning permission; and
- (vi) Any other relevant provisions of this Act and any regulations made thereunder.[173]

In considering its decision a planning authority shall consult with any other planning authority where it considers that a particular decision to be made by it may have a significant effect on the area of that authority, and the authority shall have regard to the views of that other authority and, without prejudice to the foregoing, it shall have regard to the effect that a particular decision by it may have on any area outside its area (including areas outside the State).[174]

**[3.137]** Subject to s 99(f) of the Environmental Protection Agency Act 1992 and s 54 (as amended by s 257 of PDA 2000) of the Waste Management Act 1996, where an application under this section relates to development which comprises or is for the purposes of an activity for which an integrated pollution control licence or a waste license is required, a planning authority shall take into consideration that the control of

---

172. See PDA 2000, s 37(1)(b).
173. PDA 2000, s 34(2)(a)(i)–(vi) inclusive.
174. PDA 2000, s 34(2)(b).

emissions arising from the activity is a function of the Environmental Protection Agency.[175]

**[3.138]** The long title to PDA 2000 reads:

> An Act to revise and consolidate the law relating to planning and development by repealing and re-enacting with amendments the Local Government (Planning and Development) Acts 1963–1999; to provide, in the interests of the common good, for proper planning and sustainable development including the provision of housing; to provide for the licensing of events and control of funfairs; to amend the Environmental Protection Agency Act 1992, the Roads Act, 1993, the Waste Management Act 1996 and certain other enactments; and to provide for matters connected therewith.

It was thus, the concept of sustainable development appeared for the first time in an Irish Planning Act.

**[3.139]** There is no definition of 'proper planning and sustainable development' provided in PDA 2000. When PDA 2000 was first introduced as a Bill on 28 September 1999, the then Minister for the Environment, Noel Dempsey TD said as follows:

> On first glance it can be seen that the 'proper planning and development' of an area has been replaced as the Bill's touchstone by 'the proper planning and sustainable development', but it goes deeper than a change in terminology. For example, the development objectives to be contained in development plans reflect the environmental concerns of the modern age. Environmental assessment of regional planning guidelines, development plans and local area plans is provided for. The interface between pollution control, licensing and planning control has been revised to allow a more holistic approach to be adopted in considering development which requires IPC licences.

**[3.140]** PDA 2000 requires that a development plan shall set out an overall strategy for the proper planning and sustainable development of the area of the development plan and that it shall consist of a written statement and a plan or plans indicating the development objectives for the area in question.[176] PDA 2000, as amended, does not set out 'specific sustainability objectives' to be included in development plans. Instead, development plans should be infused with the sustainable development concerned, and to ensure that this occurs PD(A)A 2010 requires a 'core strategy'. A Green Party TD, Junior Minister Ciarán Cuffe, gave a brief but useful explanation of the meaning of 'core strategy' when he stated:

> The 'core strategy' requirement in the new legislation for all city and county plans will be a key tool in translating national and regional targets into these plans. The Department will work closely with regional and local authorities to introduce these 'core strategies' and restructure the national housing land bank, retaining those priority areas which infrastructure is ready available and reprioritising, or changing or removing, inappropriate zonings over and above the required levels ...

---

175. PDA 2000, s 34(2)(c).
176. PDA 2000, s 10(1).

Over zoning and bad planning played a fundamental role in creating the property bubble. The legislation aims to ensure these practices have become a thing of the past. Good planning laws will protect communities and protect Government investment. Planning authorities and communities they serve will significantly benefit from these new planning laws and they will enable more joined-up delivery of essential infrastructure and facilities such as public transport, schools, amenities in the areas prioritised for development.

This will be facilitated by ensuring that there is a consistent and coherent approach to the national, regional and city/county estimation and prioritisation of land requirements for future residential development in a way that enables Government to work more closely with local authorities in prioritising investment in the areas that are most likely and are most suited to be developed into the future.[177]

It is a matter for each local authority to ensure that the development plan addresses the whole area of the sustainability criteria. Local authorities and the board must give proper consideration to environmental issues in the course of carrying out their functions of providing for and controlling development. Local authorities and the board are required to implement strategies for planning and sustainable development of the area by taking account of environmental concerns and integrating these into all aspects of decision making so that future development is not made at the expense of environmental quality.

**[3.141]** Sustainable development is development which meets the needs of the present without compromising the ability of future generations to meet their own needs. It is achieved by ensuring that environmental concerns are taken into account in all aspects of the planning process to ensure that development progress shall not, as far as is possible, damage the environment. However, the concept of sustainable development is not limited to environmental concerns. It extends to economic sustainability (in the sense that development must encourage economic growth and development), to social sustainability (in the sense of discouraging the provision of substandard accommodation for the less well-off and encouraging social integration in well planned and thoughtfully developed residential units). There is also cultural sustainability (which, for example, would include the protection of the linguistic and cultural heritage of the Gaeltacht). Another developing area of sustainable development includes the necessity to provide crèches, schools and childcare facilities, community and recreational facilities.

**[3.142]** PDA 2000, for the main part, became law on 11 March 2002, but it is has taken developers, planners and planning authorities too long a time to comprehensively implement the concept of 'sustainable development'. It is a concept which rolls lightly off the tongues of politicians. That said, the progress in achieving the 'sustainability' aspirations of the Act have experienced a very slow start. Carbon emissions remain at unacceptably high levels. Every effort was made to protect Pt V of PDA 2000 (housing supply – social and affordable housing) when the Bill which preceded the Act was passed by both Houses of the Oireachtas and Pt V was referred to the Supreme Court pursuant to Art 26(2)(i) of the Constitution for determination as to whether or not its

---

177. From statement made by Minister for State Ciarán Cuffe TD on 2 August 2010.

provisions were unconstitutional. The Supreme Court,[178] in a judgment delivered by Keane CJ on 28 August 2000, decided that Pt V was not unconstitutional and as a consequence of that referral, none of the provisions of the Act dealing with social/affordable housing are open to constitutional challenge. The lofty principles which the Act had hoped to achieve in terms of social integration received a mortal blow when the PD(A)A 2002 became law. The cornerstone objective contained in Pt V of PDA 2000, which offered just three types of conditions, which a planning authority could impose by way of agreement between the authority and the developer, was altered and a further three options were put on the table bringing the total number of options to six. In some parts of Ireland there are waiting lists of up to three to four years for affordable housing while in other parts there is an oversupply. During a period of record development growth between 2002 and 2007 much was spoken about the concept of proper planning and sustainable development. The difference between cost of development and the sale price went unchecked and unheeded. Price in relation to cost spiralled out of control. The real meaning of 'sustainable development' was clearly either not understood or deliberately parked as development rushed across the floodplains and paid token heed to necessary infrastructural development such as schools, playing fields, open space and other social and recreational amenities which would have greatly assisted the progress towards an integrated society.

## 'PROPER PLANNING AND SUSTAINABLE DEVELOPMENT'

[3.143] To understand 'proper planning and sustainable development' some guidance is given in the following paragraphs.

## Alternative sites

[3.144] The consideration of the suitability and availability of alternative sites for the location of the proposed development may, in certain circumstances, be a valid planning consideration. For example, where a development proposal requires the submission of an EIS, some of the factors which must be included in an EIS are prescribed in PDR 2001, Sch 6, paras 1(a)–(d) inclusive: 1(a) requires a description of a proposed development comprising information on the site, design and size of the proposed development; 1(b) requires a description of the measures envisaged in order to avoid, reduce and, if possible, remedy significant adverse effects; 1(c) requests the data required to identify and assess the main effects which the proposed development is likely to have on the environment; and 1(d) requires an outline of the main alternatives studied by the developer and an indication of the main reasons for his/her choice, taking into account the effects on the environment.

---

178. *In re Article 26 and the Constitutionality of Pt V of the Planning and Development Bill 1999* [2001] ILRM 81.

Schedule 6, para 2 provides for further information to be contained in an EIS by way of explanation or amplification of the information referred to in para 1, on the following matters:

2(a)(i)   requires a description of the physical characteristics of the whole proposed development and the land/use requirements during the construction and operational phases;

2(a)(ii)  requires a description of the main characteristics of the production processes, for instance, the nature and quantity of the materials used;

2(a)(iii) requires an estimate, by type and quantity, of expected residues and emissions (including water, air and soil pollution, noise, vibration, light, heat and radiation) resulting from the operation of the proposed development;

2(b)   requires a description of the aspects of the environment likely to be significantly affected by the proposed development, including, in particular: human beings, fauna and flora; soil, water, air, climatic factors and the landscape; material assets including the architectural and archaeological heritage, and the cultural heritage; and the inter-relationship between the above factors;

2(c)   requires a description of the likely significant effects (including direct, indirect, secondary, cumulative, short, medium and long-term, permanent and temporary, positive and negative) of the proposed development on the environment resulting from: the existence of the proposed development; the use of natural resources; the emission of pollutants, the creation of nuisances and the elimination of waste; and a description of the forecasting methods used to assess the effects on the environment; and

2(d)   requires an indication of any difficulties (technical deficiency or lack of know-how) encountered by the developer in compiling the required information.

[3.145] The investigation of an alternative suitable site for location of a proposed development usually occurs where the proposed development will have adverse affects on the environment.

## Amenity

[3.146] Matters which affect the amenities of an area, including possible depreciation of value of property in the vicinity, are a valid planning consideration. In *Maher v An Bord Pleanála*,[179] the proposal was to develop a sow integrated pig rearing installation. An Bord Pleanála, on hearing an appeal, had taken into consideration the fact that lands in the vicinity of the pig rearing installation were likely to depreciate in value. It was a matter which An Bord Pleanála rightly 'had regard to'.

---

179. *Maher v An Bord Pleanála* [1993] 1 IR 439.

**[3.147]** Other examples of matters to which either the planning authority or the board should have regard to include such things as development which might cause air pollution, noise pollution, vibration, or water pollution. The contents of some of the schedules attached to PDA 2000 give other further examples of development which would interfere with the use and enjoyment of adjoining land in a serious way. These schedules deal with matters to which a planning authority must have regard. They include:

(i) PDA 2000, Sch 1 dealing with purposes for which objectives may be indicated in a development plan.

(ii) PDA 2000, Sch 3 dealing with developments in respect of which refusal of planning permissions will not attract compensation.

(iii) PDA 2000, Sch 4 dealing with reasons for the refusal of planning permission which exclude compensation.

(iv) PDA 2000, Sch 5 dealing with conditions which may be imposed on the granting of planning permission to develop land without compensation.

## Common good

**[3.148]** The planning authority is entitled, having regard to the provisions of the Constitution, to take the common good into account in making its decision. In *Keane v An Bord Pleanála*,[180] the Commissioners of Irish Lights (as agents for the government) sought permission to erect a Loran C Mast near Loop Head in County Clare. The purpose of the mast was to provide an alternative terrestrial system as a backup for the more comprehensive satellite navigation system which is entirely controlled by governments outside the EU. In the event that, for one reason or another, the US or Russian satellite systems were no longer available for use by members of the EU, the terrestrial Loran C system is available within the EU and beyond. The Supreme Court held that An Bord Pleanála, when it considers it appropriate, in considering proper planning and development, is entitled to have regard not just to the physical surrounding environment but also to the impact on people both inside and outside the State. The applicant in *Keane v An Bord Pleanála*[181] contended that the planning permission granted by the respondent was *ultra vires* because in arriving at its decision it took into consideration matters which it had no jurisdiction to consider, namely an international agreement that the mast, the subject of the application, would operate up to 500 miles off-shore outside the jurisdiction of Clare County Council, the board and the State itself. The court held that the development of a mast for the purpose of signals to assist marine navigation as part of the significant international network could properly be taken into account in determining the application.

---

180. *Keane v An Bord Pleanála* [1998] 2 ILRM 241, SC.
181. *Keane v An Bord Pleanála* [1998] 2 ILRM 241, SC.

## Compulsory purchase orders

**[3.149]** In *State (Sweeney) v Minister for the Environment*,[182] it was held that it is within the power of the planning authority to refuse outline permission on the basis that the subject site was affected by a compulsory purchase order (CPO). The planning authority was entitled to have regard to the reality of the situation which included the planning authority's own proposal, as housing authority, to acquire the lands and to use them for its own purposes. The refusal did not in any way prejudice the possibility of compensation in the event that the CPO was confirmed.

## Planning history of lands

**[3.150]** The previous planning history of the lands the subject of an application for development is a relevant consideration but that does not imply that planning authorities and the board are bound by precedent in the same way as the courts. PDA 2000[183] permits the board, in determining an appeal, to grant permission even if the proposed development materially contravenes the development plan relating to the area of the planning authority to whose decision the appeal relates. PDA 2000, s 37(2)(b)(iv) gives an example where the planning history of a development is a relevant consideration in referring to 'a pattern of development, and permissions granted in the area since the making of the development plan'.

**[3.151]** The courts have indicated that planning authorities do have a general power to have regard to previous decisions. *In State (Kenny and Hussey) v An Bord Pleanála and Meenan*,[184] McCarthy J expressed the view that it was difficult to see how a planning authority could come to a different view on how an application for planning permission should be determined in the absence of a change in circumstances of an area and how the concept of *res judicata* would apply to a decision of the planning authority. Also, in *Irish Hardware Association v South Dublin County Council*[185] Butler J held that a planning authority was entitled to have regard to its previous decisions in respect of the same planning unit.

## Permission in material contravention of development plan

**[3.152]** The Board's power to determine an appeal by granting permission which is in material contravention of the development plan is subject to a number of constraints which are set out in PDA 2000, s 37 as follows.

> (b) Where a planning authority has decided to refuse permission on the grounds that a proposed development materially contravenes the development plan, the Board may only grant permission in accordance with para (a) where it considers that—
>
> > (i) the proposed development is of strategic or national importance,

---

182. *State (Sweeney) v Minister for the Environment* [1979] ILRM 35.
183. PDA 2000, s 37(2)(a).
184. *State (Kenny and Hussey) v An Bord Pleanála and Meenan* (unreported, 20 December 1984) SC.
185. *Irish Hardware Association v South Dublin County Council* [2001] 2 ILRM 291.

(ii) there are conflicting objectives in the development plan or the objectives are not clearly stated, insofar as the proposed development is concerned, or

(iii) permission for the proposed development should be granted having regard to the regional planning guidelines for the area, guidelines under s 28, policy directives under s 29, the statutory obligations of any local authority in the area, and any relevant policy of the Government, the Minister, or any Minister of the Government, or

(iv) permission for the proposed development should be granted having regard to the pattern of development, and permissions granted, in the area since the making of the development plan.[186]

(c) Where the Board grants a permission in accordance with paragraph (b), the Board shall in addition to the requirements of s 34(10) indicate in its decision the main reasons and considerations for contravening materially the development plan.[187]

# Precedent

**[3.153]** A planning authority may have regard to a wish not to provide an undesirable precedent when deciding on a planning application because, inevitably, a grant of planning permission may set a precedent for other development. For example, PDA 2000, Sch 4, para 7, in listing reasons for the refusal of permission which exclude compensation, states that one such reason is where the proposed development, by itself or by the precedent which the grant of permission for it would set for other relevant developments, would adversely affect the use of a national road or other major road by traffic. Also see PDA 2000, Sch 4, para 11 which provides, as a reason for refusal of permission which excludes compensation, that the development would contravene materially a condition attached to an existing permission for development.

# Private interest

**[3.154]** The possibility of a development interfering with private interest by, for example, causing subsidence and consequent damage to a neighbouring house, is a proper planning consideration. In recent times, wind farm contractors have caused catastrophic landslides by their failure to carry out a proper site investigation, and in some cases these have damaged and in other cases have seriously threatened land and buildings in private ownership.

**[3.155]** At the same time, PDA 2000[188] provides that a person shall not be entitled, solely by reason of a permission under this section, to carry out any development. There may be legal impediments and, typically, a planning authority frequently will not concern itself with questions of rights of light or whether or not the proposed development will

---

186. PDA 2000, s 37(2)(b)(i)–(iv) inclusive.
187. PDA 2000, s 37(2)(c).
188. PDA 2000, s 34(13).

diminish a neighbours right of light. Any aggrieved neighbour is entitled to pursue private law remedies in such matters as rights of light, trespass, nuisance, etc, irrespective of what a grant of permission provides. Obtaining a planning permission means no more than that the applicant has complied with the planning law. Planning laws do not and will not ride rough shod over other laws including such things as obliterating established rights of way, interfering with the right of light or other rights or committing some other tort or unlawful damage affecting neighbouring property, including something which is commonly done, namely building on party walls. In *State (Boyd) v Cork County Council*,[189] Murphy J held that the possibility that a proposed development might damage a third party's property was, in the circumstances of that case, a proper planning consideration. In general, however, the private interest of an individual landowner is not usually relevant to the planning concerns unless there is some public element also involved. In view of the decision in *State (Boyd) v Cork County Council*,[190] there must be some uncertainty as to whether or not the fact that a development proposal might damage a third party's property is a proper planning consideration to be taken into account by the planning authority or by An Bord Pleanála on appeal.

## Public health and safety

**[3.156]** The generation of pollution and the creation of traffic hazards by proposed development are, generally, proper planning considerations. In *Keane v An Bord Pleanála*,[191] the Supreme Court accepted that the concept of proper planning and development is not confined to the consequences of development on the physical environment but also includes impact on people. Prior to PDA 2000, the legislation appeared to be determined to separate pollution control from the planning system. The Environmental Protection Agency Act 1992, s 98 and the Waste Management Act 1996, s 54 precluded both planning authorities and the board from taking environmental pollution considerations into account when adjudicating on planning applications.

**[3.157]** The Environmental Protection Agency Act 1992, as substituted by the Protection of the Environment Act 2003, covers 'environmental protection' to include:

(a) the prevention, limitation, elimination, abatement or reduction of environmental pollution, and

(b) the preservation of the quality of the environment.[192]

**[3.158]** 'Environmental pollution' is defined as meaning the direct or indirect introduction to an environmental medium, as a result of human activity, of substances, heat or noise which may be harmful to human health or the quality of the environment,

---

189. *State (Boyd) v Cork County Council* [1983] IEHC 8.
190. *State (Boyd) v Cork County Council* [1983] IEHC 8.
191. *Keane v An Bord Pleanála* [1998] 2 ILRM 401.
192. Environmental Protection Agency Act 1992 as amended by the Protection of the Environment Act 2003, s 4(1).

result in damage to material property, or impair or interfere with amenities and other legitimate uses of the environment, and includes:

  (a) 'air pollution' for the purposes of the Air Pollution Act 1987,
  (b) the condition of waters after the entry of polluting matter within the meaning of the Local Government (Water Pollution) Act 1997,
  (c) the disposal of waste in a manner which, to a significant extent, would endanger human health or harm the environment and in particular—
      (i) create a risk to the atmosphere, waters, land, plants or animals,
      (ii) create a nuisance through noise, odours, or litter, or
      (iii) adversely affect the countryside or places of special interest,
  (d) noise which is a nuisance or would endanger human health or damage property or harm the environment.[193]

**[3.159]** Clearly, land use and environmental considerations overlap and PDA 2000, s 34(2)(c) provides that the role of the Environmental Protection Agency Act 1992 in controlling environmental pollution emissions arising out of licensed activity, must be taken into account by the planning authority or the board. Professor Yvonne Scannell[194] gives another reason as to why planning authorities have an obligation to take account of pollution, public health and safety concerns:

> In *Keane v An Bord Pleanála*[195] the Supreme Court accepted that the concept of proper planning and development is not confined to the affects of the developments on the physical environment but also includes its impact on people. This must be truer under the 2000 Act where sustainable development, a concept that comprises the needs of current and future generations, is a proper planning consideration. Matters which affect public health and safety such as, for example, the generation of pollution, the creation of traffic hazard or the interference with safety of aircraft could be proper planning considerations in some cases, particularly when not regulated under other legislation. In particular, the transposition of Directive 96/82/EC, as amended, on the control of major accident hazards involving dangerous substances requires planning authorities to have regard to the requirements of that Directive. Planning authorities have some express and implied powers to have regard to the public health, safety and pollution implications of development because they are entitled to impose some types of environmental management conditions under s 34(4) and to refuse planning permission (without attracting an obligation to pay compensation) if the proposed development will cause 'serious' air, noise, vibration or water pollution etc, but they have been advised by circular letter (and reminded by Courts) not to duplicate controls with other regulatory authorities and they are obliged to have regard to the fact that the control of omissions from IPC/IPPC and waste facilities is the function of the EPA which is more expert in this respect. Various legislative texts provide that conditions in planning permissions relating to water and air

---

193. Environmental Protection Agency Act 1992 as amended by the Protection of the Environment Act 2003, s 4(2).
194. See Scannell, *Environmental and Land Use Law* (Thomson Round Hall, 2006), at p 164
195. *Keane v An Bord Pleanála* [1998] 2 ILRM 401.

pollution control lapse when air, water and IPC/IPPC licences are granted thus ensuring that there is no duplication of controls and that each regulatory authority will act within the limits of its particular expertise.

## *RES JUDICATA PRO VERITATE ACCIPITUR*

**[3.160]** This Latin phrase means that a thing adjudicated is received as the truth. Thus, the doctrine of *res judicata* may be relevant and may have to be considered by a planning authority or by the board on appeal in making planning decisions. The law in relation to outline permissions has been altered by PDA 2000, s 36. Today no appeal may be brought to the board under PDA 2000, s 37 against a decision of a planning authority to grant permission, consequent on the grant of outline permission in respect of any aspect of the proposed development which was decided in the grant of outline permission.

**[3.161]** *State (Tern Houses (Brennanstown) Ltd) v An Bord Pleanála*[196] is a case which dealt with an outline planning permission granted prior to PDA 2000. The question in *State (Tern Houses (Brennanstown) Ltd)* arose where a change in the proper planning and sustainable development of the area took place between the grant of outline permission and the application for approval. The Board's entitlement to refuse the approval or to refuse to revise conditions attached to the outline permission was upheld. The outline permission did not refer to traffic safety and no conditions were imposed dealing with traffic safety. Nevertheless, the board refused the application for approval on the grounds of traffic safety, because of a change in the law between the date of the grant of outline permission and the date of the final grant. Where there is a conflict between an outline permission and the proper planning and development of the area it is the latter that must prevail.

**[3.162]** In *Grealish v An Bord Pleanála*,[197] An Bord Pleanála had granted permission on two previous occasions for development comprising a tri-vision rotating advertising sign. Each grant of permission was a temporary grant and the purpose of the temporary grant was to allow an assessment of the effects or impact of the rotating advertising sign to take place. The applicant had made the case that the board had no power to refuse the application for approval in circumstances where outline permission had been granted in principle. The applicant contended that when a third application was made, the refusal of that third application was at odds with the conclusion in the first two applications. Leave to apply to challenge the subsequent refusal was denied and it was held that the determination of an approval does not depend on the conditions imposed at outline stage, but rather, it depends on the circumstances prevailing when the grant of approval is being decided upon. Although An Bord Pleanála was entitled to reach a different decision on a later application in respect of the same development, where the previous permission had expired, the board is obliged to state the reasons and considerations upon which the change of position was based. It might be concluded, on the balance of

---

196. *State (Tern Houses (Brennanstown) Ltd) v An Bord Pleanála* [1985] IR 725.
197. *Grealish v An Bord Pleanála* [2006] 1 ILRM 140.

probabilities, that a change in the development plan was the reason for the refusal of the third application. In this case, the board had not stated the reasons and considerations upon which the change of position was based. It was held that the failure to give an explanation for departing from the original conclusions arrived at in the first two instances, constituted substantial grounds. The reasons were not expressly stated and the requirement to state the main reasons and considerations to the change of position was not met.

**[3.163]** The doctrine of *res judicata* is, in practice, of little use in planning law in supporting the idea that something that has already been adjudicated on cannot be changed. The primary consideration of the planning authority and of the board in these cases is to give full consideration, in all cases, to the proper planning and sustainable development of the area. If there has been a change of circumstances within the area, that change will allow either the planning authority or the board to alter a previous decision. In summary, the planning authorities and the board are not bound by a precedent in the same way as the courts but there are circumstances where precedents will be taken into consideration.

## PLANNING GAIN

**[3.164]** Simons, in *Planning and Development Law*,[198] includes 'planning gain' under the heading of 'relevant considerations' while Scannell, in *Environmental and Land Use Law*,[199] includes 'planning gain' under the heading 'irrelevant considerations'. A 'planning gain' might occur where an applicant for permission offers a public benefit or some other benefit which might be helpful to the planning authority. A 'planning gain' is generally illegal unless it is a planning gain which is authorised by statute. Two examples of statutory planning gains include the provision of sites, completed houses or serviced sites to the local authority under Pt V of PDA 2000 (as amended) and the payment of development contribution in compliance with conditions lawfully imposed in a grant of permission. The planning gain which is authorised by statute is an 'irrelevant consideration'.

**[3.165]** In *Thomas McDonagh and Sons Ltd v Galway Corporation*,[200] the planning authority inserted a condition requiring the developer to provide car parking spaces in excess of the immediate needs of the development. Although the condition required the developer to provide car park spaces in excess of its own development needs the condition did not require the local authority to compensate the developer for the excess spaces provided. In fact, in this case, the site in respect of which the development proposal was made had been zoned for a public car park by the planning authority. Clearly if permission were granted for the development envisaged by the applicant the

---

198. Simons, *Planning and Development Law* (2nd edn, Thomson Round Hall, 2007), pp 178 and 179.
199. Scannell, *Environmental and Land Use Law* (Thomson Round Hall, 2006), at pp 169 and 174.
200. *Thomas McDonagh and Sons Ltd v Galway Corporation* [1995] 1 IR 191, SC.

car parking zoning objective in the development plan would have been frustrated. The developer's proposal only provided sufficient car park spaces for the development itself. By imposing the condition the planning authority wished to ensure that alternative public car parking would be made available. Scannell[201] sums up the situation as follows:

> in other words, the condition was imposed to overcome a problem created by the development and it is submitted that the condition requiring the development for this purpose is not necessarily ultra vires if proportionate.

In conclusion, it does seem that 'planning gain' falls somewhere between relevant and irrelevant considerations, depending on the circumstances. Clearly, if a planning gain is offered as a means of persuading a planning authority to grant permission to the applicant and the planning gain is in no way related to the proper planning and sustainable development of the area it must be an irrelevant consideration.

## REFUSALS FOR PAST FAILURES

[3.166] PDA 2000,[202] as amended by PD(A)A 2010, s 24, permits the planning authority to refuse a grant of planning permission for past failures to comply.

[3.167] In considering whether or not a planning authority will issue a refusal on the basis of past failures to comply the planning authority must have regard for the following:

(a) any information furnished pursuant to regulations made under s 33(2)(1),[203]

(b) any information available to the planning authority concerning development carried out by a person to whom this section applies pursuant to a permission (in this section referred to as a 'previous permission') granted to the applicant or to any other person under this Part or Part (IV) of the Act of 1963,

(c) any information otherwise available to the planning authority concerning a substantial unauthorised development, or

(d) any information concerning a conviction for an offence under this Act.

[3.168] If the planning authority is satisfied having had regard to the matters at (a), (b), (c) and (d) that a person or company to whom the section applies is not in compliance with the previous permission, or with a condition to which the previous permission is subject, the authority may form the opinion:

(i) that there is a real and substantial risk that the development in respect of which permission is sought would not be completed in accordance with

---

201. See Scannell, *Environmental and Land Use Law* (Thomson Round Hall, 2006), at p 170, para 2.315.
202. PDA 2000, s 35 as amended by Planning and Development (Amendment) Act 2010, s 24(a), (b) and (c).
203. PDA 2000, s 33 deals with the making of regulations regarding applications for permission.

such permission if granted, or with a condition to which such permission if granted would be subject, and

(ii) that accordingly planning permission should not be granted to the applicant concerned in respect of that development.

(2) In forming its opinion under sub-s (1), the planning authority shall only consider those failures to comply with any previous permission, or with any condition to which that permission is subject, that are of a substantial nature.[204]

(3) An opinion under this subsection shall not be a decision on an application for permission under this Part.[205]

(4) If the planning authority considers that there are good grounds for its being able to form an opinion under sub-s (1) in relation to an application for permission in respect of the development considered and, accordingly, to exercise the power under sub-s (5) to refuse that permission it shall serve notice in writing on the applicant to that effect and that notice shall:

(a) specify the failures to comply that the authority intends to take into consideration with regard to the proposed exercise of that power, and

(b) invite the applicant to make submissions to the authority, within a period specified in the notice, as to why the applicant considers that the authority should not exercise that power (whether because the applicant contends the views of the authority in relation to compliance by the applicant or any other person with any previous permission, or any condition to which it is subject, are incorrect or that there are not good grounds for forming the opinion under sub-s (1)).[206]

(5) If the planning authority, having considered any submission made to it in accordance with a notice under sub-s (4), proceeds to form the opinion under sub-s (1) in relation to the application concerned it shall decide to refuse to grant the permission concerned and notify the applicant accordingly.[207]

(6) The applicant may, within eight weeks from the receipt of that notification, notwithstanding s 50 and s 50A, apply by motion on notice to the planning authority, to the High Court for an order annulling the planning authority's decision and, on the hearing of such application, the High Court may, as it considers appropriate, confirm the decision of the authority, annul the decision and direct the authority to consider the applicant's application for planning permission without reference to the provisions of this section or, make any other order as it thinks fit.[208]

(6A) If, in pursuance of sub-s (6) the High Court directs the planning authority to consider the applicant's application for planning permission without reference to the provision of this section, the planning authority shall makes its decision on the application within a period of eight weeks from the date the order of the High

---

204. PDA 2000, s 35(2).
205. PDA 2000, s 35(3).
206. PDA 2000, s 35(4) as amended by the PD(SI)A 2006, s 9.
207. PDA 2000, s 35(5) as amended by the PD(SI)A 2006, s 9.
208. PDA 2000, s 35(6), as amended by PD(SI)A 2006, s 9.

Court in the matter is perfected but this section is subject to the provisions of s 34(8) as applied, to the foregoing case by sub-s (6)B.[209]

No appeal shall lie to the board from a decision of a planning authority to refuse to grant planning permission under s 35(5).[210]

## IRRELEVANT CONSIDERATIONS

**[3.169]** There are some considerations which are irrelevant and which must be disregarded by the planning authority. In *P&F Sharpe Ltd v Dublin City and County Manager*,[211] it was stated that the planning authority 'has a duty to disregard any irrelevant or illegitimate factors that might be advanced'. An irrelevant consideration will not always invalidate a decision to grant or to refuse to grant planning permission but an irrelevant or illegitimate consideration may invalidate a decision if the irrelevant consideration goes to the root of the decision and influences the outcome. Examples of irrelevant or illegitimate factors follow.

### Compensation

**[3.170]** Where as a result of refusal on appeal to grant planning permission to develop land or a grant of permission to develop subject to conditions, the value of an interest of any person existing in the land to which the decision relates at the time of the decision is reduced, that person shall, subject to other provisions in Pt XII, Ch II, be entitled to be paid by the planning authority by way of compensation.[212]

**[3.171]** Compensation shall not be payable in respect of the refusal of permission for any development (a) of a class or description set out in Sch 3 or, (b) if the reason or one of the reasons for the refusal is a reason set out in Sch 4.[213] The provision of Schs 3 and 4, respectively, are set out below in **Ch 7**.

**[3.172]** In *Grange Developments v Dublin County Council*[214] and in *Dublin County Council v Eighty-Five Developments Ltd*,[215] it was clearly stated that a planning authority cannot have regard to its desire to exclude a claim for compensation in adjudicating on a planning application and cannot grant permission merely to forestall a claim for compensation. Neither the planning authority nor the board can insert non-compensatory reasons into the statement of reasons for refusal other than reasons which are properly applicable as valid planning matters. The interests of proper planning and

---

209. See PDA 2000, s 35(6A), (6B) and (6C) as amended by PD(SI)A 2006, s 9.
210. See PDA 2000, s 35(6C) as amended by PD(SI)A 2006, s 9.
211. *P&F Sharpe Ltd v Dublin City and County Manager* [1989] ILRM 565, [1989] IR 701, HC and SC.
212. See PDA 2000, s 190, dealing with the right to compensation.
213. PDA 2000, s 191(1).
214. *Grange Developments v Dublin County Council* [1989] IR 296, HC.
215. *Dublin County Council v Eighty-Five Developments Ltd (No 2)* [1993] 2 IR 392.

sustainable development of the area must be the overriding concern of the planning authority or of the board.

## Licences or permission required as pre-condition under other legislation

**[3.173]** A person shall not be entitled solely by reason of permission under this section to carry out any development.[216] There are cases where licences or other permissions may have to be obtained but the absence of any licence or permission is not a relevant consideration because it is not open either to the planning authority or to the board to assume that a developer will act illegally on foot of a planning permission.

**[3.174]** In *Frank Dunne v Dublin County Council*,[217] two conditions were attached to a grant of permission which required developers to inform purchasers of the houses that aircraft noise would be significant in the area and to provide sound insulation in the houses against aircraft noise. These conditions were both held to be invalid as not being related to the proper planning and development of the area or the preservation of the amenities thereof. The reasons for invalidating those two conditions were valid at the time they were made but now PDA 2000, s 34(4)(c) provides for the making of conditions which require the taking of measures to reduce or prevent the intrusion of any noise or vibration which might give reasonable cause for annoyance to any person lawfully occupying any such structure or site.

**[3.175]** In *Cablelink v An Bord Pleanála*,[218] Carroll J refused to quash the decision of the board to grant planning permission for the erection of a television deflector system where Cablelink did not in fact possess the appropriate licence. The judge expressed the view that the board was entitled to proceed on the basis that enforcement of the Wireless Telegraphy Acts was a matter for Central Government and had nothing to do with planning considerations. The grant of planning permission to Cablelink did not authorise it to undertake an illegal activity on the land to which it referred. The necessity to obtain a licence was separate and distinct from the grant of planning permission.

**[3.176]** In *Kelly v An Bord Pleanála*,[219] an application was made to extend a building in a scrap yard. A condition in an earlier permission had clearly prohibited any further intensification in the building which would lead to an intensification of the activity within the scrap yard. Permission for the new application was refused on the precise grounds that if granted it would lead to an intensification of the scrap yard activity on the site. As the intensification would be contrary to an earlier condition which was legally binding on the applicant the decision to refuse permission was unlawful as being against plain reason and common sense. It was unreasonable to refuse permission because a building might be used for purposes that it could not lawfully be used for.

---

216. PDA 2000, s 34(13).
217. *Frank Dunne v Dublin County Council* [1974] IR 45.
218. *Cablelink v An Bord Pleanála* [1999] 1 IR 596, HC.
219. *Cablelink v An Bord Pleanála* (unreported, 19 November 1993) HC.

## Ownership of land

**[3.177]** Where permission to develop land or for the retention of development is granted, unless the contrary is stated in the permission or in conditions attached to the permission, the grant of permission shall enure for the benefit of the land and of all persons for the time being interested therein.[220] Permission is granted for the benefit of the land and may therefore be sold or passed on with the land. In general, ownership of land is not a relevant planning consideration.

**[3.178]** In *Furlong v McConnell*,[221] an application was made to the court to stop the use of lands as a caravan park. The existing use was not so different to its use on the appointed day as to affect the proper planning and development of the area. It is the use and not the particular occupier that is relevant. If, however, ownership is passed to a body such as a housing authority, to be used for objectives which impact on the proper planning and development of the area, such change of ownership is a proper planning consideration. If the owner has a bad track record in completing developments or in failing to comply with the terms of the planning permission, the planning authority is entitled to refuse permission under PDA 2000, s 35, as amended by PD(SI)A 2006, s 9.

## Personal circumstances

**[3.179]** Two views which appear to be contradictory have been expressed as to whether or not the consideration of personal circumstances of the applicant is an irrelevant consideration.

**[3.180]** In *Griffin v Galway City Council and County Manager*,[222] it was stated that the consideration of personal circumstances of the applicant is not within the scope of proper planning and development.

**[3.181]** Also, in *Flanagan v Galway City and County Manager*[223] the elected representatives of the planning authority passed a s 4 resolution directing the county manager to grant planning permission which materially contravened the development plan. An order of *mandamus* was sought from the High Court, but the High Court refused to make the order on the basis that the elected members had taken into account the personal circumstances of the applicant and in doing so had taken account of irrelevant considerations in coming to their decision. The court held that the elected members were confined to a consideration of the proper planning and development of their area and that they could not take account of the personal circumstances of the applicant. In contrast, Lord Scarman in *Great Portland Estates plc v Westminster City Council*[224] stated that 'it would be inhuman pedantry to exclude from the control of our

---

220. See PDA 2000, s 39(1).
221. *Furlong v AF and GW McConnell* [1990] IRLM 48.
222. *Griffin v Galway City Council and County Manager* (unreported, 31 October 1990) HC *per* Blayney J.
223. *Flanagan v Galway City and County Manager* [1990] 2 IR 66.
224. *Great Portland Estates plc v Westminster City Council* [1985] AC 661.

environment, the human factor'. In England, therefore, it seems that personal circumstances may be taken in account in exceptional and special situations.

## Other provisions limiting discretions of planning authorities
### *Special amenity area orders*

**[3.182]** In circumstances where a special amenity area order (SAAO) relates to the area, the planning authority must have regard to any provisions of that SAAO.[225] Areas of special amenity will predominantly relate to less developed areas outside towns, cities and villages. A large area of Howth Head is an area of special amenity and such areas are becoming more common. The concept first appeared in the Local Government (Planning and Development) Act 1963, ss 42 and 43 as amended by the Local Government (Planning and Development) Act 1976, s 40. Statutory provisions dealing with SAAOs are now contained in PDA 2000, s 202 as follows:

>(1) Where, in the opinion of a planning authority, by reason of—
>
>(a) Its outstanding natural beauty, or
>
>(b) Its special recreational value, and having regard to any benefits for nature conservation, an area should be declared under this section to be an area of special amenity, it may, by resolution, make an order to do so and the order may state the objective of the planning authority in relation to the preservation of the area or the enhancement of the character or special features of the area, including objectives for the prevention or limitation of development in the area.[226]

The Minster, where he or she is of the opinion that paras (a) and (b) apply, has the same powers to declare an area to be an SAAO.[227] The initiative for making an SAAO may be taken either by the local authority or by the Minster for the Environment, Heritage and Local Government.

**[3.183]** As soon as may be after the order has been made, the planning authority is required to publish a notice in one or more newspapers circulating the area advising of the fact that the order has been made and describing the area to which it relates. The planning authority is also required to disclose where the order may be inspected and the newspaper notice invites objections to be lodged within a specified period not being less than four weeks. The notice also specifies that the order requires confirmation by the board and where any objections are duly made to the order, which are not withdrawn, an oral hearing will be held and the objections will be considered before the order is confirmed.[228]

**[3.184]** When the period for making objections (being not less than four weeks) has expired, the planning authority may submit the order to the board for confirmation. If

---

225. PDA 2000, s 34(2)(a)(ii).
226. See PDA 2000, s 202(1)(a) and (b).
227. See PDA 2000, s 202(2)(a) and (b).
228. PDA 2000, s 203(1)(a), (b), (c) and (d).

there are any objections to the order, then the board must hold an oral hearing before deciding whether to confirm the order with or without modifications, or to refuse to confirm it.[229]

[3.185] When a planning authority is considering a planning application, it is required to have regard to the provisions of any SAAO. SAAOs may be revoked or varied by subsequent orders and the planning authority may, from time to time, review the order for the purpose of deciding whether it is desirable to revoke or amend the order[230] and if two planning authorities overlap, one planning authority, with the consent of the other, may make an SAAO over the functional area of the other planning authority.[231]

## European sites

[3.186] European sites are other areas that are prescribed for the purposes of PDA 2000, s 10(2)(c). If an application for permission is made to a planning authority within the area of a European site or other area prescribed for the purpose of conservation and protection of the environment regard must be had by the planning authority to that fact.[232]

## Policy of government or Minister

[3.187] In deciding a planning application, and where it is relevant, a planning authority must have regard to the policy of the government, the Minster for Environment, Heritage and Local Government or any other Ministers of government.[233]

## Statutory planning conditions under s 34(4)

[3.188] The planning authority or the board is also required to have regard to the list of conditions which are set out in s 34(4).[234]

## Other relevant provisions or requirements

[3.189] In considering an application for planning permission a planning authority, or An Bord Pleanála in considering an appeal, shall have regard to a number of matters specified in the Act and in the regulations made under the Act.[235]

[3.190] A planning authority or An Bord Pleanála must have regard to the provisions of any local area plan. A planning authority or the board may (and this is discretionary)

---

229. See PDA 2000, s 203(2), (3) and (4).
230. PDA 2000, see s 202(6) and (7).
231. See PDA 2000, s 202(5).
232. See PDA 2000, s 34(2)(a)(iii) which refers to any European site or other prescribed area for the purposes of PDA 2000, s 10(2)(c).
233. See PDA 2000, s 34(2)(a)(iv).
234. See PDA 2000, s 34(2)(a)(v) and PDA 2000, s 34(4)(a) to (q) inclusive.
235. See PDA 2000, s 34(2)(a)(vi).

have regard to any draft local area plan. They may have regard to an integrated area plan under the Urban Renewal Act 1998.[236]

## Protected structures

**[3.191]** PDA 2000, s 57 (as amended)[237] deals with works affecting the character of protected structures or proposed protected structures. In cases of applications or appeals, respectively, the planning authority and the board must have regard to the protected status of a structure and the protected status of a proposed protected structure. For the avoidance of doubt, it is declared that a planning authority or the board on appeal: (i) in considering any application for permission in relation to a protected structure, shall have regard to the protected status of the structure; or (ii) in considering any application for permission in relation to a proposed protected structure shall have regard to the fact that it is proposed to add the structure to a record of protected structures.

**[3.192]** A planning authority, or the board on appeal, shall not grant permission for the demolition of a protected structure or proposed protected structure, save in exceptional circumstances.[238]

**[3.193]** When considering an application for permission for development which (a) relates to the interior of a protected structure, and (b) is regularly used as a place of public worship, the planning authority and the board on appeal shall, in addition to any other requirements of the Act, respect liturgical requirements.[239]

## Architectural conservation area

**[3.194]** In considering an application for permission for development within architectural conservation areas a planning authority, or the board on appeal, shall take into account the material effect (if any) that the proposed development would be likely to have on the character of an architectural conservation area.[240]

## Application for development in SDZs

**[3.195]** PDA 2000, s 170:[241]

> (1) Where an application is made to a planning authority under section 34 for a development in an SDZ, that section and any permission regulations shall apply, subject to the other provisions of this section.

---

236. See PDA 2000, s 18 and specifically s 18(3)(a) and (b).
237. PDA 2000, s 57(1) as amended by PD(A)A 2010, s 34.
238. See PDA 2000, s 57(10)(a) and (b).
239. See PDA 2000, s 57(6).
240. See PDA 2000, s 82(2) as amended by PD(A)A 2010, s 35 but only in respect of s 82(1).
241. PDA 2000, s 170(1), (2), (3) and (4) as amended in relation to sub-s (2) only by PD(A)A 2010, s 52.

(2) Subject to the provisions of Part XA or Part XAB or both of those Parts, as appropriate, a planning authority shall grant permission in respect of an application for a development in an SDZ where it is satisfied that the development, where carried out in accordance with the application or subject to any conditions which the planning authority may attach to a permission, would be consistent with any planning scheme in force for the land in question, and no permission shall be granted for any development which would not be consistent with such a planning scheme.

(3) Notwithstanding section 37, no appeal shall lie to the board against a decision of a planning authority on an application for permission in respect of a development in an SDZ.

(4) Where a planning authority decides to grant permission for a development in an SDZ, the grant shall be deemed to be given on the date of the decision.

## Development in special planning control areas

[3.196] PDA 2000, s 87:[242]

(1) Notwithstanding s 4(1)(a), (h), (i), (j), (k) or (m), and any regulations made under section 4(2), any development within an area of special planning control shall not be exempted development where it contravenes an approved scheme applying to that area.

(2) When considering an application for permission in relation to land situated in an area of special planning control, a planning authority, or the board on appeal, shall, in addition to the matters set out in section 34, have regard to the provisions of an approved scheme.

(3) An owner or occupier of land situated in an area of special planning control may take a written request to the planning authority, within whose functional area the area of special planning control is situated, for a declaration as to:

(a) those developments or classes of development that it considers would be contrary or would not be contrary, as the case may be, to the approved scheme concerned,

(b) the objectives or provisions of the approved scheme that apply to the land, or

(c) the measures that will be required to be undertaken in respect of the land to ensure compliance with such objectives or provisions.

(4) Within 12 weeks of receipt by a planning authority of a request under sub-s (3), or within such other period as may be prescribed by regulations of the Minister, a planning authority shall issue a declaration under this section to the person who made the request.

(5) A planning authority may at any time rescind or vary a declaration under this section.

---

242. PDA 2000, s 87(1) to (8) inclusive as amended by PD(A)A 2010, s 36 but only in relation to sub-s (1).

(6) The rescission or variation of a declaration under sub-s (5) shall not affect any development commenced prior thereto in reliance on the declaration concerned and that the planning authority has indicated, in accordance with paragraph (a) of sub-s (3), would not be contrary to an approved scheme.

(7) A declaration under this section is without prejudice to the application of section 5.

(8) A planning authority shall cause—

(a) the particulars of any declaration issued to that authority under this section to be entered on the register kept by the authority under section 7, and

(b) a copy of the declaration to be made available for inspection by members of the public during office hours, at the principal office of the authority, following the issue of the declaration.

## Social and affordable housing

[3.197] For the avoidance of doubt, it is declared that in respect of any planning application or appeal, compliance with the housing strategy and any related objective in the development plan shall be a consideration material to the proper planning and sustainable development of the area.[243]

[3.198] Where an application for development of housing is affected by Pt V of PDA 2000 as amended by the PD(A)A 2002, the planning authority shall have regard to any proposals which specify the manner in which the application would propose to comply with a condition to be attached by the planning authority to any permission granted.[244]

## Environmental impact assessment

[3.199] In addition to the requirements of s 34(3), where an application in respect of which an EIS was submitted to the planning authority in accordance with s 172, the planning authority, and the board on appeal, shall have regard to the EIS, any supplementary information furnished relating to the statement and any submissions or observations furnished concerning the effects on the environment of the proposed development.[245]

## Board to have regard to certain policies and objectives

[3.200] The Board shall, in performing its functions, have regard to: (a) the policies and objectives, for the time being, of the government, a State authority, the Minister, planning authorities and any other body which is a public authority whose functions have, or may have, a bearing on the proper planning and sustainable development of cities, towns or other areas, whether urban or rural; (b) the national interest and any effect the performance of the board's functions may have on issues of strategic

---

243. See PDA 2000, s 93(4).
244. PDA 2000, s 96(4) as substituted by the PD(A)A 2002.
245. PDA 2000, s 173(1).

**[3.201]** economical or social importance to the State, and (c) the National Spatial Strategy and any regional planning guidelines for the time being in force.[246]

**[3.201]** In *Keane v An Bord Pleanála*,[247] the court held that An Bord Pleanála had to keep itself informed on the policies and objectives of the Minister, the planning authorities and the Commissioners as required by the Local Government (Planning and Development) Act 1976, s 5.

**[3.202]** Further, the requirement to do so would be entirely meaningless if the board was not entitled, and indeed obliged, to take such policies and objectives into account in discharging its own functions. The decision dealt with the provisions under the 1976 Act but it is equally applicable to the provisions of PDA 2000, s 143. The decision in *Keane v An Bord Pleanála*[248] also held that the board is entitled to take into account the common good and in that sense it is not restricted to looking at the harmful effects of the development only but may also have regard to the beneficial effects. The requirement of the board to take into account the policies and objectives of the government, State authorities, the Minister, planning authorities and other bodies also relates to the functions which should be transferred from the Minister to the board in relation to compulsory acquisition and that includes the transfer of certain ministerial functions under the Roads Acts 1993 and 1998 to the board[249] and the transfer of certain ministerial functions under the Gas Act 1976 to the board.[250]

**[3.203]** It should be noted that PDA 2000, s 256 was repealed by the Protection of the Environment Act 2003 indicating that the control and prevention of pollution and waste by licence is a matter for the EPA.

**[3.204]** Where permission is granted for a structure the grant of permission may specify the purpose for which the structure may or may not be used, and in case the grant specifies use as a dwelling house as a purpose for which the structure may be used, the permission may also be granted subject to a condition specifying that the use as a dwelling shall be restricted to use by persons of a particular class or description, and that provision to that effect shall be embodied in an agreement under PDA 2000, s 47.[251]

**[3.205]** The Development Management Guidelines for planning authorities published in June 2007 by the Department for Environment, Heritage and Local Government cautioned in relation to occupancy of buildings as follows:

> Planning permissions attach to the land, and not to the applicant. Section 39(2) of the Planning Act, enables a condition to be attached, specifying that the use of a structure as a dwelling shall be restricted to use by persons of a particular class or

---

246. PDA 2000, s 143(1) and (2) as substituted by PD(SI)A 2006, s 26.
247. *Keane v An Bord Pleanála* [1998] 2 IRLM 214, SC.
248. *Keane v An Bord Pleanála* [1998] 2 IRLM 214, SC.
249. PDA 2000, s 215(1) and (2): note that the functions of the Minister under the Roads Acts 1993–1998 are now transferred to the board.
250. PDA 2000, s 215A(1)–(3) inclusive, as inserted by PD(SI)A 2006, s 37.
251. PDA 2000, s 39(2).

description. Planning authorities should be sparing in their approach to such conditions, as they can limit the freedom of the owner to dispose of his or her property or to obtain a mortgage. However, the Sustainable Rural Housing Guidelines outline circumstances in which it would be reasonable to attach occupancy conditions, eg in rural areas under considerable development pressure where the applicant is a person with roots in or links to the area. Those guidelines also advise that the use of so-called 'sterilisation agreements' under s 47, that is, agreements for the purpose of restricting or regulating the development and use of land permanently or for a specified period, should be avoided apart from highly exceptionally cases, because of the inflexible nature of such agreements.

Also, the European Convention on Human Rights Act 2003 provides that it will be necessary to have regard to the personal circumstances of those affected by certain Acts and decisions, especially in the context of enforcement action.

[3.206] It seems likely that it may not be too long before personal circumstances will, in many instances, be a matter to be taken into account. The view of Lord Scarman reported as long ago as 1985 may have been correct after all.[252]

# CONDITIONS IN PLANNING PERMISSIONS

[3.207] PDA 2000, s 34(1) provides that a planning authority on receipt of a compliant application may decide to grant planning permission subject to or without conditions, or to refuse them. A planning authority and An Bord Pleanála may grant permission with conditions but PDA 2000, s 34(2)(a) provides that the planning authority shall be restricted to considering the proper planning and sustainable development of an area, regard being had to a number of matters as are set out in the subsection and in particulars to the matters referred to in s 34(4). Within the provisions of s 34(4) the planning authority is bound to consider whether or not conditions must be attached and the list of conditions, to which the planning authority must have regard, are set out in s 34(4). Simons makes a valuable comment in this context:

> The better view would be that this requirement extends to an obligation to consider whether or not conditions might be attached which would save an application which would otherwise have to be refused.[253]

PDA 2000, s 34, as amended by the PD(SI)A 2006 and by PD(A)A 2010, gives planning authorities both a general power to attach conditions and, without prejudice to that general power, express authorisation for certain enumerated conditions. The general power to impose conditions is subject to a number of limitations laid down in case law precedent.

---

252. *Great Portland Estates plc v Westminster City Council* [1985] AC 661: 'It would be inhuman pedantry to exclude from the control of our environment, the human factor'.
253. Simons, *Planning and Development Law* (2nd edn, Thomson Round Hall, 2007).

## General conditions

**[3.208]** PDA 2000, s 34(1) confers a general right to impose conditions in planning permissions. That is not to say that any condition may be imposed and it is still open to the courts to declare conditions to be *ultra vires*, invalid or void. There is a clear statement of the law on this point contained in the judgment of Lord Denning in *Pyx Granite v Minister for Housing and Local Government*:

> The principles to be applied are not, I think, in doubt. Although the planning authorities are given very wide powers to impose such conditions as they may see fit, nevertheless the law says that those conditions, to be valid, must fairly and reasonably relate to the permitted development. The planning authority are not at liberty to use their power for any ulterior object, however desirable that object may seem to them to be in the public interest. If they are mistaken or misuse their powers, however bona fide, the Court can intervene by declaration and injunction.[254]

Lord Denning cited with approval a ministerial decision to the effect that a condition contained in a grant of permission for a new factory, which provided that the applicant's existing factory on another site should cease work, was an *ultra vires* condition.

**[3.209]** In *Fawcett Properties v Buckingham County Council*,[255] it was said by Lord Denning that the local authority does not have an uncontrolled discretion to impose whatever conditions it likes. In exercising its discretion it must have regard to all relevant considerations and disregard all improper considerations and it must produce a result which does not offend against common sense. Planning guideline no 13 for planning authorities, entitled 'Development Management' and published in June 2007 by the Department of Environment, Heritage and Local Government, deals in ch 7 with the drafting of planning conditions. The introduction at para 7.1 reads:

> Conditions proposed to be attached to permissions, and the reasons for them, should be carefully drafted so that their purpose and meaning are clear. Conditions must always be precise and unambiguous, particularly since the effectiveness of subsequent enforcement action may depend on the wording. Moreover, adequate reasons should be given by planning authorities to justify conditions; it is not, for example, in the majority of cases, acceptable to give a reason 'in the interest of proper planning and sustainable development of the area' since this affords the applicant no indication of the particular object of the condition.

> The number of conditions should be kept to a minimum as the attempt to regulate detail to an excessive extent may defeat its own ends. Moreover, difficulties can arise for developers and land owners generally at conveyancing and other stages in attempting to provide evidence of compliance with numerous conditions especially those of a vague or general nature.[256]

---

254. *Pyx Granite v Minister for Housing and Local Government* [1958] 1 QB 554 at 573.
255. *Fawcett Properties v Buckingham County Council* [1960] 3 All ER 503.
256. This recommendation is frequently overlooked by local authority planners and the number of conditions grows each year but, in their defence, it must be said that as planning and environmental law becomes more complex an increase is inevitable. It is not the number but rather the relevance of the conditions imposed which would require a planner to ponder.

## Fair and reasonable

**[3.210]** The meaning of 'unreasonable' was discussed by Lord Green MR in *Associated Provincial Houses Ltd v Wednesbury Corporation*:[257]

> In planning matters it is clear that the condition must be fair and reasonable and must relate to the proposed development. If the Court is to interfere, a condition must be wholly unreasonable, that is, such as could find no justification in the minds of reasonable men.[258]

In that case, it was held that the planning authority had not acted unreasonably or *ultra vires* in imposing a condition providing that children under the age of 18 should not be admitted to any entertainment at the cinema on Sunday, whether accompanied by an adult or not. That decision was made in 1947 and it may have reflected the social and moral issues of the time but it was hardly a planning issue.

**[3.211]** In *Dunne (Frank Ltd) v Dublin County Council*,[259] Pringle J expressed the view that a condition which required a developer to provide sound insulation in houses constructed in the flight path to Dublin airport so as to protect against aircraft noise was *ultra vires*. That decision was made prior to PDA 2000, s 34(4)(c)(ii) which provides that conditions may be made in relation to the intrusion of noise and vibration which might give reasonable cause for annoyance to any person lawfully occupying any such structure or site. By today's standards it would have been a perfectly acceptable condition to impose.

**[3.212]** The Development Management Guidelines for Planning Authorities (June 2007) give examples of unreasonable conditions as follows:

> It would normally be lawful to impose a continuing restriction on the hours during which an industrial or other use can be carried out, if the use of the premises outside these hours would seriously injure the amenities of property in the vicinity, but it would be unreasonable to restrict the hours of operation to such an extent as to effectively nullify the permission. Again, it may be unreasonable to make a permission subject to a condition which has the affect of deferring the development for a very long period, by requiring, for example, that the permitted development should not be carried out until a sewerage scheme for the area – which may only be at the preliminary design stage – has been completed. If the development is genuinely premature, the application ought to be refused.

## Relevant to planning policy

**[3.213]** A condition must be imposed for genuine planning purposes relating to the proper planning and sustainable development of the area and not for any extraneous purpose or for any ulterior motive. Therefore, conditions requiring compliance with Building Regulations, Food and Hygiene Regulations, Public Health Acts, Fire Services

---

257. *Associated Provincial Houses Ltd v Wednesbury Corporation* [1947] 2 All ER 680.
258. It frequently occurs to this author that 'the minds of reasonable men' are in short supply and that the 'man on the Clapham omnibus' got off at his stop many years ago.
259. *Dunne (Frank Ltd) v Dublin County Council* [1974] IR 45.

Act, Industry Acts, Water Pollution Acts etc. should not be included in a grant of planning permission but there is nothing to prevent a planning authority, when notifying the grant of permission, from issuing clear warnings about the requirement of other codes.

## Applicant not required to carry out planning authority's duties

**[3.214]** In *R v Hillingdon LBC Exp Royco Homes Ltd (No 2)*,[260] the planning authority was held not to be entitled to impose a condition in a permission for a housing development requiring the houses to be occupied initially by persons on the local authority's waiting list and for the first 10 years of occupation by persons entitled to the protection of the relevant Rent Restrictions legislation. This was, in effect, obliging the applicant to discharge the duties of the authority as housing authority at the developer's own expense, and the condition was held to be *ultra vires*.

## Implementation not dependent on cooperation of third party

**[3.215]** In *Killiney and Ballybrack Development Association Ltd v Minister for Local Government and Templefinn Estates Ltd*,[261] permission included a condition which read:

> no house shall be constructed on that part of the site to the south of the culverted stream before the expiration of three years from the date of this order.

The appellants did not complain about the condition itself but about the reasons for the condition which read:

> to control and regulate the development so as to ensure that all sewage disposal facilities are satisfactory in relation to residential development on the site.

Three years had passed and the developer had not constructed a single house on the south side of the culverted stream but the appellants claimed that since no further sewage disposal facilities had been built during that three year period, the condition must be invalid because its supporting reasons were invalid as 'wanting in feasibility of purpose', *per* Henchy J. The Minister had argued that at the time he granted permission he was satisfied that adequate sewage disposal facilities existed but he had been advised by the local authority that a further sewage scheme would be carried out and his reason for imposing the three-year delay period was that there would be a further and better sewage disposal scheme available in three years time. Henchy J held that the condition simply expired by the effluxion of time after a period of three years and that the permission could be treated as if it did not contain this condition. In relation to the Minister's statement, the judge felt that he had been satisfied at the time of the grant that adequate disposable facilities were available but that further sewage facilities were imminent.

> I do not accept however that a development permission may be construed with the aid of extrinsic matters of this kind put forward as an elaboration of formal written

---

260. *R v Hillingdon LBC Exp Royco Homes Ltd (No 2)* [1974] 2 All ER 643.
261. *Killiney and Ballybrack Development Association Ltd v Minister for Local Government and Templefinn Estates Ltd* (unreported, 24 April 1978) SC.

reasons given for one of the conditions of a permission. The condition in question must stand or fall by its written terms or conditions. *Per* Henchy J.

## Depriving landowner of existing use rights or uses

[3.216] Clearly there are many cases where the proposed development cannot be carried out without destroying an existing use. For example, where permission is granted on a garage site for the erection of a new office block, the old use lapses.

[3.217] See *Allnatt London Properties Ltd v Middlesex County Council*.[262] In that case permission for the extension of an existing factory was granted subject to conditions, namely: (a) the new extension should be used only in conjunction with the main existing factory as one industrial unit so as to avoid multiplication of industrial uses; and (b) that until 1971 the site should be used only by a person or a firm occupying at the date of the permission, as a light or general industrial building in the county of Middlesex.

[3.218] In effect, these conditions potentially deprived the applicant of an existing use right in its main factory and it was held that the applicant had a right to continue its existing use right or that if it was to be withdrawn, it could only be done by payment of compensation.

[3.219] See also *Minister for Housing and Local Government v Hartnell*,[263] where Hartnell owned a five-acre field and kept six caravans on three-quarters of an acre. When it became necessary to apply for permission he applied for a licence to station 94 caravans on the entire five-acre site but the permission which issued contained a condition that not more than six caravans should be stationed on the land at any time. Hartnell's existing use right in respect of the three-quarters of an acre had not been limited to six caravans and it was held that he could, on the three-quarters of an acre area, bring such number of caravans as the site could take so as not to amount to a material change in use. It was held that Hartnell could not be deprived of his existing use right by the imposition of the condition.

[3.220] It is clear, however, that express conditions can validly revoke or modify existing use rights provided: (a) they reasonably relate to the permitted development; (b) they are not so unreasonable that no reasonable local authority would have imposed them; (c) they must be imposed for a planning purpose.

## Conditions imposed by subsequent permission

[3.221] *Lucas (F) & Sons Ltd v Dorking and Horley RDC*[264] held that a planning authority can impose a condition in a permission to the effect that the permission is not to be exercised in addition, or in combination, as to part, with an existing permission. If a planning authority does impose such a condition it must impose an express condition

---

262. *Allnatt London Properties Ltd v Middlesex County Council* [1994] 62 LGR 304.
263. *Minister for Housing and Local Government v Hartnell* [1965] 1 All ER 490.
264. *Lucas (F) & Sons Ltd v Dorking and Horley RDC* [1960] 59 LGR 132.

to this effect. In the *Lucas* case, there was no such express condition, so the first permission remained valid with the second permission. Contrast this decision with *Slough Estates Ltd v Slough Borough Council*[265] which case makes it clear that a new permission granted for one area of land nullifies and overrides a permission which may also be in existence for the same area of land. Clearly, several permissions can co-exist and this is common in housing estates where, for example, one permission allows for the development of town houses and another allows for the development of mews houses on an undeveloped part of the estate upon which the permission for town houses was already granted.

## Enforceability

[3.222] Since enforcement proceedings can be taken where a condition is breached, conditions must be enforceable. Fulfilment of a condition must be within the competence of the developer. For example, a condition requiring a developer to carry out works on land outside his control will be *ultra vires*. In *Drogheda Port Company v Louth County Council*,[266] Morris J held that for a condition to be enforceable it must be within the capacity of the developer. However, it appears that this difficulty can be overcome in certain cases by the imposition of a negative condition, which provides that no development is to commence until that condition has been complied with.[267]

[3.223] In *Irish Cement Limited v An Bord Pleanála*,[268] McCracken J seemed to entertain some doubt as to the validity of negative conditions which provide that no development is to commence until the condition has been complied with. In that case, a traffic management plan had been drawn up but although the plan was in existence, no application for permission for the traffic management plan had been made to the planning authority. On appeal, An Bord Pleanála did not impose a condition on the planning permission that the traffic management plan be implemented.

> Had it done so, it might well be said that the decision was premature as it postponed the implementation of the decision for an indefinite time, and it left the possibility or otherwise of the development being carried out in the hands of some other party. *Per* McCracken J.

[3.224] A negative condition, if attached to the planning permission in that case, directing that a grant of permission was subject to permission being obtained for the traffic management plan would have introduced an unacceptable degree of uncertainty in the grant of permission (if granted). A permission, when granted, should be capable of being implemented with certainty and at the earliest possible date. A permission is for a fixed time (normally five years). The further delay incurred in making the application for permission for the traffic management plan would use up a significant part of the time given by the grant of permission to complete the development.

---

265. *Slough Estates Ltd v Slough Borough Council* [1962] 2 All ER 988.
266. *Drogheda Port Company v Louth County Council* [1997] IEHC 61.
267. See *Grampian Regional Council v Aberdeen UDC* [1983] 47 P&CR 633.
268. *Irish Cement Limited v An Bord Pleanála* [1998] IEHC 30.

[3.225] The Development Management Guidelines for Planning Authorities issued in June 2007, in dealing with drafting planning conditions at para 7.33 states that conditions should be enforceable. The advice in that document is being given to the planning authorities and from the planning authorities' point of view a condition should not be imposed if it cannot be made effective. From a planning authority's point of view in drafting a condition, it must consider how the enforcement provisions of the Act could be operated in the event of non-compliance with a proposed condition. Conditions, therefore, should be framed in such a way as to require some specific act to be done at or before a specified time, or to prohibit some specific thing from being done in carrying out the development. The paragraph continues as follows:

> Conditions should be capable of being complied with. It is doubtful that a condition requiring the maintenance of sitelines by the removal or trimming of hedges or trees on a neighbour's property is within the applicant's power to fulfil; even where the neighbour has given consent, that consent may subsequently be withdrawn. The Law Society has advised that such conditions may create difficulty as to title and have advised that in such cases the applicant be required to obtain an easement over the neighbour's property thus obtaining the legal right to maintain the siteline.

A condition should be reasonable and in that sense it must not be unreasonable. Certainly, conditions should never seek to obtain an unauthorised 'planning gain' from the party to whom permission is granted.

## Precision

[3.226] The condition must be precise and certain and should be capable of interpretation without reference to extraneous documents. In *Dun Laoghaire Corporation v Frascati Estates Ltd*,[269] the condition imposed, which required the defendants to retain a house of historical value, was held to be too vague because it was impossible to know what the condition required. The necessity for precision in the wording of conditions is for the purpose of advising the applicant as to what he must do and what he must not do.

[3.227] The condition cannot be so vague as to be incapable of meaning. In the course of his judgment in *Fawcett Properties v Buckingham County Council*,[270] Lord Denning stated:

> For I am of the opinion that a planning permission is only void for uncertainty if it can be given no meaning or sensibly ascertainable meaning, and not merely because it is ambiguous or leads to absurd results. It is the daily task of the Courts to resolve ambiguities of language and choose between them and to construe words so as to avoid absurdities or to put up with them and this applies to conditions and planning permissions as well as other documents.

---

269. *Dun Laoghaire Corporation v Frascati Estate* [1982] ILRM 493.
270. *Fawcett Properties v Buckingham County Council* [1960] 3 All ER 505.

Under the heading 'conditions should be precise' at para 7.3.4 of the Development Management Guidelines for Planning Authorities (June 2007) the following advice is given:

> Every condition should be precise and clearly understandable. It must tell the developer from the outset exactly what he or she has to do, or must not do. A condition which requires the developer to take action if and when some other indefinite thing takes place, is unacceptable eg. to improve an access 'if the growth of traffic makes it desirable'. A condition that requires that the site 'shall be kept tidy at all times' is clearly of little value, as is a condition requiring that a permitted development 'shall not be used in any manner so as to cause nuisance to nearby residents'. In the one case, the condition is too vague, and in the other, the question of whether or not a particular use constitutes a nuisance is left open. Conditions that can only be expressed in such vague general terms will often be found to be unnecessary or unenforceable.

## No abdication of jurisdiction of planning body

[3.228] It is not unusual to see a condition which leaves the more detailed aspects of the development subject to a negotiation agreement between the planning authority and the developer. The principal objection to this practice is that it defeats the right of public participation, and in particular the right of appeal in relation to matters dealt with by the condition. In *Boland v An Bord Pleanala and Minister for Marine*,[271] the Supreme Court held that in imposing a condition making some detailed aspects of a development the subject of a negotiated agreement between the planning authority and the developer, the board is entitled to have regard to:

(a) the desirability of leaving to a developer who is hoping to engage in a complex enterprise, a certain limited degree of flexibility having regard to the nature of the enterprise,

(b) the desirability of leaving technical matters or matters of detail to be agreed between the developer and the planning authority, particularly when such matters or such details are within the responsibility of the planning authority and may require redesign in the light of practical experience,

(c) the impracticability of imposing detailed conditions, having regard to the nature of the development, and

(d) whether enforcement of a condition requires monitoring or supervision.

The Board may not generally abdicate its decision-making powers but it may do so depending on the nature of the matter left to be determined and in the particular circumstances of each individual application and development.

[3.229] The conditions which may be imposed under s 34(1) may provide that points of detail relating to a grant of permission may be agreed between the planning authority

---

271. *Boland v An Bord Pleanala and Minister for Marine* [1996] 3 IR 435, HC and SC.

and the person carrying out the development, if the planning authority and that person cannot agree on the matter, the matter may be referred to the board for determination.[272]

## Standard conditions

**[3.230]** The practice of using standard conditions in planning permissions is not uncommon with some planning authorities. Not only are the conditions standard but so too are the reasons provided on the right hand margin of the document drafted in standard form. The Development Management Guidelines for Planning Authorities (June 2007) gives the following warning:

> This practice is useful in the interests of consistency and can achieve time savings. Great care should be taken, however, to ensure that standard conditions are used only where they actually apply or that they are properly adapted to meet the needs of particular cases and that the availability of sets of standard conditions does not lead to the automatic inclusion of unnecessary conditions in particular cases, eg conditions which are irrelevant to the particular development, or which deal with matters best dealt with under other codes.

## Direct departure from application

**[3.231]** Again, the Development Management Guidelines for Planning Authorities (June 2007) draws attention to another type of condition which should be avoided:

> A condition that radically alters the nature of the development to which the application relates will usually be unacceptable. For example, a condition should not require the omission of a use which forms an essential part of a proposed development, or a complete re-design of a development. If there is a fundamental objection to a significant part of a development proposal, and this cannot fairly be dealt with in isolation from the rest of the proposal, the proper course is to refuse permission for the whole.

## Fire conditions

**[3.232]** Again reference is made to a useful paragraph in the Development Management Guidelines for Planning Authorities (June 2007) dealing with fire conditions:

> While it is appropriate that the Planning Acts should be used to the full to ensure that all developments meet adequate fire safety standards, it must be emphasised that when dealing with a planning application, fire safety can only be considered where it is relevant to the primary purpose of the Acts, namely the proper planning and sustainable development of the area. For example, fire safety considerations may arise in respect of:
> 
> - The location of proposed development in relation to existing industrial or other hazards;
> - The historic fabric and contents of protected structures;
> - Fire service access for proposed development;
> - Water supplies for fire fighting.

---

272. PDA 2000, s 34(5) as amended by PD(SI)A 2006, s 8(2).

Under no circumstances should a condition be included in a permission requiring that 'the developer shall consult with and comply with the requirements of the fire officer' (or other words to that effect), whether or not such requirements are known at the time the decision is made. This kind of condition is objectionable in principle, and probably invalid.

In some cases it may become apparent from the information provided in a planning application that a proposed development would also require a fire safety certificate under the Building Control Regulations and, where this is made known to the planning authority, it may be appropriate to inform the applicant (eg by means of a cover letter with the planning decision).

Similarly, the information provided as part of a planning application may indicate that aspects of a proposed development could give rise to difficulties for the developer in obtaining a fire safety certificate, and the planner may need to discuss with the applicant whether any design modifications should be made before a planning decision issues.

## Conditions requiring matters to be agreed

**[3.233]** Conditions sometimes require matters to be agreed or to be attended to 'prior to the commencement of the development'. Where such conditions are of a fundamental nature or where they are such that third parties could be affected they should be avoided. That recommendation is contained in the Development Management Guidelines of June 2007. At para 7.9 of the guidelines it is recommended that the use of such conditions should be minimised, in order to reduce the number of compliance submissions that have to be dealt with subsequently. Care needs to be taken in the wording of these conditions; for example, some minor details (eg, type of paving) will not need to be agreed before development commences, but could be negotiated during the construction phase.

**[3.234]** Planning permissions often include conditions requiring developers to carry out certain actions prior to or during the course of development. These are pre-conditions which must be fulfilled before any work commences on the development. They are frequently overlooked by developers and where they are so overlooked it opens up the possibility of an enforcement action being commenced by the planning authority against the developer. The use of s 247 pre-application consultations are to be encouraged so that an applicant is fully informed as to the information needed to be submitted with an application. Every effort should be made, at the pre-application stage, to ensure that full information is lodged with the application and that the requirement to seek further information or to impose compliance conditions is kept to a minimum. From a developer's point of view compliance conditions are likely to delay the commencement of works on the development after permission has been granted. Bearing in mind that the planning authority is not under any statutory constraint to reply within any particular given time, compliance conditions are not in a developer's interest.

[3.235] The Development and Management Guidelines for Planning Authorities (June 2007) in advising planning authorities in relation compliance conditions recommend the following:

> Accordingly, the number of compliance conditions should be kept to a minimum, to ease the burden of both developers and planning authorities.
>
> While as a general principle compliance conditions should be kept to a minimum, they can be of value in certain circumstances, such as:
>
> - Where they relate to matters of detail which could cause the applicant undue expense (eg detailed design of external facades) before the principle of development has been established through a grant of planning permission;
> - Where they relate to matters of detail which the planning authority may wish to have an input, such as the layout/landscaping of public open spaces;
> - Where they relate to the implementation or monitoring of mitigation measures proposed in a planning application or accompanying EIS.
>
> Conversely, there are situations where compliance conditions would not be appropriate, such as:
>
> - Where the details would be required by the planning authority or the Board in order to decide on the overall merits of the planning application, which situation would apply, for instance, in the case of proposals in connection with the restoration of a protected structure;
> - Where an inadequate EIS has been submitted, or the information supplied does not adequately address issues in relation to potential impact on a site of international importance for nature conservation (Natura 2000), eg where drainage outfalls might affect an environmentally sensitive site, or inadequate mitigation measures have been proposed;
> - Where compliance with the condition might affect the amenities of a third party, without that party having the right to comment on the compliance submission.
>
> In such cases, if the development is acceptable in principle, further information should be sought.

## STATUTORY PLANNING CONDITIONS ENUMERATED IN PDA 2000, S 34(4)

[3.236] PDA 2000, s 34(4) sets out the conditions which can be imposed in a planning permission by a planning authority. The list is not exclusive. It will be noted that conditions which deal with the provisions for financial contributions are not in this part of the section but are dealt with separately under PDA 2000, ss 48[273] and 49.[274] PDA

---

273. PDA 2000, s 48 as amended by PD(A)A 2010, s 30(a)–(c).
274. PDA 2000, s 49 as amended by PD(A)A 2010, s 31(a) and (b).

2000, s 34(4) gives planning authorities both the general power to attach conditions and, without prejudice to the general power, express authorisation for certain enumerated conditions, which later conditions are set out below. In all there are 17 types of statutory planning conditions.[275]

[3.237] (a) Conditions for regulating the development or use of any land which adjoins, abuts or is adjacent to the land to be developed and which is under the control of the applicant if the imposition of such conditions appears to the planning authority:

(i) to be expedient for the purposes of or in connection with the development authorised by the permission,

(ii) to be appropriate, where any aspect or feature of that adjoining, abutting or adjacent land constitutes an amenity for the public or a section of the public, for the purposes of conserving that amenity for the public or that section of the public (and the effect of the imposition of conditions for the purpose would not be to burden unduly the person in whose favour the permission operates).[276]

If a planning authority is aware that an applicant, who has applied for development on a piece of land, owns adjoining land which is not included in the application, the planning authority may require that the applicant's adjoining land or portion of it should be used for the benefit of or the advantage of the lands, the subject matter of the application. The imposition of a condition under this paragraph can only be imposed if it appears expedient or appropriate in relation to the lands the subject matter of the application. A condition may also be imposed where it appears to the planning authority that the adjoining land constitutes an amenity for the public or a section of the public. In those circumstances, for example, where the adjoining lands enjoy an amenity which would be appropriate to the application lands, a condition may be imposed conserving the benefit of that amenity for the application lands. PDA 2000, s 34(4)(a), in its amended form, permits a planning authority to impose additional conditions for the purpose of conserving an amenity for the public or a section of the public.

[3.238] In *Ashbourne Holdings v An Bord Pleanala*,[277] the planning authority was restricted to imposing conditions strictly within the terms of s 26 of the Local Government (Planning and Development) Act 1963 which gave a power to the planning authority to impose conditions in relation to any land which adjoins, abuts or is adjacent to the lands to be developed, so far as appears to the planning authority to be expedient for the purposes of or in connection with a development authorised by the permission. In that case, the planning authority granted permission which contained conditions allowing public access to the Kinsale Head lighthouse along cliff paths. It was held that such a condition would be outside the terms of the LG(PD)A 1963, s 36 and would in fact frustrate and render inoperable the use of the headland as a golf course. The condition was held to be manifestly unreasonable.

---

275. The 17 statutory planning conditions are dealt with at paras **[3.237] to [3.249]**.
276. PDA 2000, s 34(4)(a) as amended by PD(SI)A 2006, s 8(1).
277. *Ashbourne Holdings v An Bord Pleanala* [2003] 2 IR 114.

**[3.239]** In its new form, PDA 2000, s 34(4)(a) (as amended)[278] no longer requires that a condition imposed under the subsection is necessarily relevant to the permitted development nor does it require that it be of advantage or benefit to the permitted development.

**[3.240]** (b) Conditions requiring the carrying out of works (including the provisions of facilities) which the planning authority considers are required for the purposes of the development authorised by the permission.[279]

The purpose here is to ensure not only that the primary aims of the development are catered for but also that the secondary or ancillary aims are provided for so that, if the application is for a shopping centre, the planning authority must ensure that there are sufficient facilities available to serve the centre, its employees, customers and other visitors. The works to be carried out in accordance with conditions imposed under this subsection must relate to the permitted development.

**[3.241]** (c) Conditions for requiring the taking of measures to reduce or prevent:

(i) the emission or any noise or vibration from any structure or site comprised in the development authorised by the permission which might give reasonable cause for annoyance either to persons in any premises in the neighbourhood of the development or to persons lawfully using any public place in that neighbourhood, or

(ii) the intrusion of any noise or vibration which might give reasonable cause for annoyance to any person lawfully occupying any such structure or site.[280]

Noise pollution[281] is a matter which is subject to increasing regulation. The Department of the Environment, Heritage and Local Government issued a 'noise issues consultation paper' on 27 August 2008 which is a review initiated by the Minister for the Environment pertaining to noise and noise nuisance. The paper invited submissions from the public on the issue of noise and the aim of the Minister's consultation paper is to achieve the following goals:

- to make the procedures for dealing with noise issues more accessible and understandable for the citizen;
- to ensure that noise complaints can be dealt with in a timely manner;
- to address classes of noise problems not currently covered by legislation;
- to consolidate the various pieces of existing legislation where appropriate.

---

278. PDA 2000, s 34(4)(a) as amended by PD(SI)A 2006, s 8(1).
279. PDA 2000, s 34(4)(b).
280. PDA 2000, s 34(4)(c).
281. See the comprehensive chapter on 'noise' in Scannell, *Environmental and Land Use Law* (Thomson Round Hall, 2006) at ch 9, pp 881–901. This comprehensive investigation of noise sources and the legislation which is supposed to control it reminds us in the opening words that: 'the word noise evolved from the Latin *nausea* meaning sickness and undoubtedly noise is one of the worst kinds of pollution'.

In 2004, the Environmental Information Service (ENFO) issued an information paper on noise pollution drawing attention to the steps which are open to members of the public under the law where noise nuisance is experienced. They draw attention to the Environmental Protection Agency Act 1992 (Noise) Regulations 1994 (SI 179/1994). Those regulations provide redress in cases of general neighbourhood noise problems, such as continual noise from other houses, home workshops, local businesses, etc. The regulations are designed to permit access to the courts by individuals or groups concerned about excessive noise. Complaints about aircraft noise can be made to the Irish Aviation Authority in the first instance. Problems caused by barking dogs are covered by the Control of Dogs Acts 1986 and 1992. The paper advises:

> Whenever you consider a noise to be so loud, so continuous, so repeated, of such duration or pitch or occurring at such times that it gives you *reasonable cause for annoyance* you can initiate action to deal with it [emphasis added].

The paper recommends, in the first instance, a consultation between the complainant and the person or persons creating the noise. If that consultation process does not resolve the matter advice may be obtained from the relevant local authority or from the Environmental Protection Agency (EPA). Local authorities or the EPA would be naturally reluctant to become involved in disputes between neighbours but they may consider serving notice in respect of noise from industrial or commercial sources. If all else fails, the paper recommends that the final step to be taken is to make a formal complaint to the District Court seeking an order to deal with the nuisance. ENFO's noise pollution paper outlines the steps required to take the case to the District Court. Noise pollution cases are relatively uncommon and there are a number of 'good defence' conditions listed in the leaflet to include the following:

- that he/she took all reasonable care to prevent or limit the noise by using facilities, practices and methods of operation that are suitable for that purpose, or

- that the noise is in accordance with a licence issued under the Environmental Protection Agency Act 1992.

Ireland does not have a universal statutory noise standard to apply so each case must be judged individually. In spite of this, in cases where notice is served under s 107 of the Environmental Protection Agency Act 1992 a local authority will generally refer to the relevant international guidance and standards. The ENFO guide to noise regulation also gives the usual advice in relation to construction noise, faulty alarms, noise from pubs/discos and traffic-related noise. It is clear from the consultation paper issued by the Department of the Environment, Heritage and Local Government that new legislation will be introduced to deal with these noise issues and special mention is made of noise, violence and disruption arising from the exiting of clients from bars, nightclubs and discos or noise made by young people loitering and engaging in boisterous activities at 3am or 4am generating a considerable level of noise in residential areas.

**[3.242]** (d) Conditions for requiring the provision of open spaces.[282]

PDA 2000, s 45 deals with the acquisition of land for open spaces. In summary, if an owner of land has been requested to provide an open space but fails to do so the planning authority may seek to acquire the land by compulsory purchase in circumstances where very limited compensation only is payable. Where a condition of this nature is included in a grant of planning permission the planning authority will ensure that open space is properly sited and that the space is of a suitable and manageable size and shape. It will, insofar as possible, ensure that the open space is useable space and that it is not sited in some awkward or unusual part of the site. PDA 2000 makes provision for the compulsory acquisition and maintenance of open spaces within housing estates if required to do so by a majority of the residents living in the estate.[283]

**[3.243]** (e) Conditions for requiring the planting, maintenance and replacement of trees, shrubs or other plants or the landscaping of structures or other land.[284]

Where possible, a planning authority will always try to preserve mature trees even if this means re-siting or relocating structures. The visual breaks at the rear of houses, earth banks to sound proof parking areas for residential property, to baffle noise are familiar conditions. A tree preservation order may also be made under PDA 2000, s 205. Commonly, many planning authorities require 'native species' when imposing conditions for hedge planting.

**[3.244]** (f) Conditions for requiring the satisfactory completion within a specified period, not being less than 2 years from the commencement of any works, of the proposed development (including any roads, open spaces, car parks, sewers, water mains or drains or other public facilities) where the development includes the construction of 2 or more houses.[285]

The purpose of this condition is to encourage developers of housing estates to complete them within a 'specified period' which shall not be less than two years. In *Bord Na Mona v An Bord Pleanála*,[286] it was held that the date of the commencement of development should be at the election of the developer. Without such a condition the only obligation on a developer is that the development must be concluded within the lifespan of the planning permission or, if it is not, application for further permission must be obtained. In fact, in this case, the condition was held to be invalid because no provision was made for the repayment of the contribution in circumstances where the

---

282. PDA 2000, s 34(4)(d).
283. PDA 2000, s 180. Note: s 180(1) was amended by PD(A)A 2010, s 59(a); s 180(2)(a) was amended by PD(A)A 2010, s 59(b); s 180(2A) was inserted by PD(A)A 2010, s 59(c); s 180(3)(a) was amended by PD(A)A 2010, s 59(d); s 180(3)(b) was amended by PD(A)A 2010, s 59(e); s 180(4) was substituted by PD(A)A 2010, s 59(f); and s 180(6) was substituted by PD(A)A 2010, s 59(g).
284. PDA 2000, s 34(4)(e).
285. PDA 2000, s 34(4)(f).
286. *Bord Na Mona v An Bord Pleanála* [1985] IR 205, HC.

**[3.245] Planning and Environmental Law in Ireland**

works were not carried out. The condition offered by s 34(4)(f) has the potential of limiting the date on which the developer should commence development. The purpose of this condition is to prevent housing estates being left in a permanent state of turmoil due to continuing slow development. It is not a condition which has been too effective in recent times. At the same time, it could be seen as unfair that a developer should be compelled to finish an estate within a 'specified period' in a poor housing market where supply exceeds demand, but, perhaps interpretation of 'specified period' will relieve this type of situation.

**[3.245]** (g) Conditions for requiring the giving of adequate security for satisfactory completion of the proposed development.[287]

This is a standard provision and is particularly common in housing development permissions. The usual requirement is for payment of a bond or a lump sum payment to ensure that all the works specified in the grant of permission are completed and that the development is not left unfinished. PDA 2000, s 35 (as amended) empowers a planning authority to refuse permission for past failures to complete a development:

(h) Conditions for determining the sequence and timing in which and at the time at which works shall be carried out;[288]

(i) Conditions for the maintenance or management of the proposed development (including the establishment of a company or the appointment of a person or body of persons to carry out such maintenance or management);[289]

(j) Conditions for the maintenance, until taken in charge by the local authority concerned, of roads, open spaces, car parks, sewers, water mains or drains and other public facilities or where there is an agreement with the local authority in relation to such maintenance, conditions for maintenance in accordance with the agreement;[290]

(k) Conditions for requiring the provision of such facilities for the collection or storage of recyclable materials for the purposes of the proposed development;[291]

(l) Conditions for requiring construction and demolition waste to be recovered or disposed of in such a manner and to such extent as may be specified by the planning authority;[292]

(m) Conditions for requiring the provision of roads, including traffic calming measures, open spaces, car parks, sewers, watermains or drains, facilities for the collection or storage of recyclable materials and other public facilities in excess of the immediate needs of the proposed development, subject to the local authority paying for the cost of the additional works

---

287. PDA 2000, s 34(4)(g).
288. PDA 2000, s 34(4)(h).
289. PDA 2000, s 34(4)(i).
290. PDA 2000, s 34(4)(j).
291. PDA 2000, s 34(4)(k).
292. PDA 2000, s 34(4)(l).

and taking them in charge or otherwise entering into an agreement with the applicant with respect to the provision of those public facilities.[293]

This condition is in contrast to s 34(4)(b) which allows for conditions for the carrying out of works which the planning authority considers are required for the purposes of the development authorised by the permission. The conditions under s 34(4)(b), however, require that the works to be carried out must relate to works required for the purposes of the proposed development. Under this subsection the planning authority may impose a condition providing for the construction of public facilities which may not be relevant to the development, the subject matter of the application, but may be relevant for surrounding development. If, however, a developer is required to carry out construction of or to provide facilities which are in excess of the immediate needs of the development, which is the subject matter of the developer's application, the planning authority would be required to pay for the costs of any additional works in excess of the developer's own requirements. The purpose of condition (m) is to ensure that there is harmony between the developer's proposal in the context of the surrounding area. It does seem to be a sensible provision which enables a planning authority to require a developer to, for example, install a larger water main or foul sewer pipe than was required for the developer's actual development in order to facilitate potential future applications in the area. The planning authority may impose a condition providing for the construction of public facilities which may not be relevant to the development, the subject of the application, but may be relevant to the surrounding development. In those cases, the additional cost must be borne by the planning authority.

**[3.246]** (n) Conditions for requiring the removal of any structures authorised by the permission, or the discontinuance of any use of the land so authorised, at the expiration of a specified period, and the carrying out of any works required for the reinstatement of land at the expiration of that period.[294]

In effect, this clause empowers the planning authority to grant a temporary permission. In circumstances where the planning authority's intentions are long term, it might be considered unreasonable to deny the developer an opportunity to make some use of his/ her property until such time as the planning authority's objectives are to be implemented. The Development Management Guidelines for Planning Authorities (June 2007) give a useful insight into the Department's view of temporary permissions, and the recommendations which they make in advising planning authorities are as follows:

> In deciding whether a temporary permission, which can apply to a particular structure or use, is appropriate, three main factors should be taken into account. First, the grant of a temporary permission will rarely be justified where an applicant wishes to carry out development of a permanent nature that conforms with the provisions of the development plan. Secondly, it is undesirable to impose a condition involving the removal or demolition of a structure that is clearly intended to be permanent. Lastly, it must be remembered that the material considerations to which regard must be had in dealing with applications are not

---

293. PDA 2000, s 34(4)(m).
294. PDA 2000, s 34(4)(n).

limited or made different by a decision to make the permission a temporary one. Thus, the reason for a temporary permission can never be that a time limit is necessary because of the adverse affect of the development on the amenities of the area. If the amenities will certainly be affected by the development they can only be safeguarded by ensuring that it does not take place.

An application for a temporary permission may, however, raise different material considerations from an application for permanent permission. Permission could reasonably be granted on an application for the erection of a temporary building to last seven years on land that will be required for road improvements in eight or more years time, whereas permission would have to be refused on an application to erect a permanent building on the land. Similarly, an application for permission to erect an adverse structure in a run down area may warrant more favourable treatment if the structure is to be removed at the expiration of a specified period when re-development works are likely to be underway.

In the case of a use which may possibly be a 'bad neighbour' to uses already existing in the immediate vicinity, it may sometimes be appropriate to grant a temporary permission in order to enable the impact of the development to be assessed, provided that such provision would be reasonable having regard to the expenditure necessary to carry out the development. A second temporary permission should not normally be granted for that particular reason for it should have become clear by the expiration of the first permission whether permanent permission or a refusal is the right answer. In other circumstances, an application for a second temporary permission may be quite genuine and should be dealt with on its merits. For example, where a temporary permission has been granted for a structure which is inherently impermanent, an application for a permission for a further limited period could reasonably be made if the structure has been well maintained and there has been no other change in circumstances relating to the proper planning and sustainable development of the area concerned.

In all temporary permissions for structures, express provision should be made by condition requiring the removal of the structure and the carrying out of appropriate reinstatement works on the land at the expiration of the specified period. In addition, the condition should specify the period for which the permission is being granted by reference to some particular date and not by reference to the occurrence of some indefinite future event. Use of expressions such as 'such longer period as the planning authority may allow' or 'on three months notice' should be avoided.

**[3.247]** (o) Conditions requiring appropriate naming and numbering of and provision of appropriate signage for, the proposed development.[295]

This condition normally requires that the naming, numbering and signage within a development be agreed with the planning authority prior to work commencing.

**[3.248]** (p) Conditions for requiring, in any case in which the development authorised by the permission would remove or alter any protected structure or any element of a protected structure which contributes to its special

---

295. PDA 2000, s 34(4)(o).

architectural, historical, archaeological, artistic, cultural, scientific, social or technical interest:[296]

(i) the preservation by a written and visual record (either measured architectural drawings or colour photographs and/or audio-visual aids as considered appropriate) of that structure or element before the development authorised by the permission takes places, and

(ii) where appropriate, the architectural salvaging of any element, or the reinstatement of any element in a manner specified by the authority.

[3.249] (q) Conditions for regulating the hours and days during which a business premises may operate.[297]

## Points of detail to be agreed between authority and developer

[3.250] PDA 2000, s 34(5), as amended by s 8(2) of PD(SI)A 2006, provides that:

The conditions under sub-s (1) may provide that points of detail relating to a grant of permission may be agreed between the planning authority and the person carrying out the development; if the planning authority and that person cannot agree on the matter, the matter may be referred to the Board for determination.

[3.251] In *Boland v An Bord Pleanála*,[298] Hamilton CJ set out some useful principles dealing with conditions which require matters to be agreed between the planning authority or An Bord Pleanála and the developer. In that case, permission was granted to the Minister to carry out improvements at the ferry terminal at Dun Laoghaire. The permission contained a condition requiring the Minister to agree certain matters with the planning authority, namely:

(1) management of ferry traffic;

(2) monetary contribution for road works necessitated by the proposed development – the Board was to fix the amount if the parties failed to agree;

(3) assessment of, the possible contribution towards, further offsite road works – here, too, the Board was to fix the amount if the parties failed to agree; and

(4) design plans for road parking and pedestrian facilities.

[3.252] The applicant claimed that the board's decision should be quashed on the grounds that the condition attached constituted an improper abdication of the board's planning functions to the planning authority. In the High Court, Keane J upheld the planning authority's decision and the matter was appealed to the Supreme Court. In the Supreme Court, the appellant also argued that the rights of the members of the public to

---

296. PDA 2000, s 34(4)(p).
297. PDA 2000, s 34(4)(q).
298. *Boland v An Bord Pleanála* [1996] 3 IR 435, SC.

object to work being carried out under conditions was excluded. Hamilton CJ upheld the High Court decision and set out the following guidelines in relation to such conditions:

(1) the Board is entitled to grant permission subject to conditions,

(2) the Board is entitled, in certain circumstances, to impose a condition on the grant of planning permission in regard to a contribution or other matter and to provide that such contribution or other matter be agreed between the planning authority and the person to whom the permission or approval is granted;

(3) whether or not the imposition of such a provision of a condition imposed by the Board is an abdication of the decision-making powers of the Board depends upon the nature of the 'other matter' which is to be the subject matter of agreement, between the developer and the planning authority;

(4) the 'matter' which is permitted to be the subject matter of agreement between the developer and the planning authority must be resolved having regard to the nature and circumstances of each particular application and development;

(5) in imposing a condition, that a matter be left to be agreed between the developer and the planning authority the Board is entitled to have regard to:

 (a) the desirability of leaving to a developer who is hoping to engage in a complex enterprise a certain limited degree of flexibility having regard to the nature of the enterprise;

 (b) the desirability of leaving technical matters or matters of detail to be agreed between the developer and the planning authority, particularly when such matters or such details are within the responsibility of the planning authority and may require re-design in the light of practical experience;

 (c) the impracticability of imposing detailed conditions having regard to the nature of the development;

 (d) the functions and responsibilities of the planning authority;

 (e) whether the matters essentially are concerned with off-site problems and do not affect the subject lands;

 (f) whether the enforcement of such conditions requires monitoring or supervision.

(6) in imposing conditions of this nature, the Board is obliged to set forth the purpose of such details, the overall objective to be achieved by the matters which have been left for such agreement to the State, clearly the reasons therefore are to lay down criteria by which the developer and planning authority can reach agreement.

**[3.253]** Blayney J added a further criterion as follows:

Could any member of the public have reasonable grounds for objecting to the work to be carried out pursuant to a condition having regard to the precise nature of the instructions in regard to it laid down by the Board and having regard to the fact that the details of the work have to be agreed by the Planning Authority?

The decision of the Supreme Court held that the conditions imposed by the board were *intra vires* its power and accordingly the appeal was dismissed.

**[3.254]** The Supreme Court decision in *Boland v An Bord Pleanála*[299] was made before the provisions of PDA 2000, s 34(5), as amended by PD(SI)A 2006, s 8(2), gave express statutory authority providing for conditions requiring that points of detail may be agreed between the planning authority and the developer and if the planning authority and the developer cannot agree, the matter may be referred to the board for determination. In *Ryanair v An Bord Pleanála*,[300] the legality of the conditions provided for in s 34 were considered. It was held that PDA 2000, s 34(5) (as amended)[301] was worded in such a way that the express power to attach conditions leaving points of detail over for agreement was not confined to the planning authority. An Bord Pleanála could, on appeal, on its own initiative, leave points of detail to be agreed between the developer and the planning authority even though the wording of s 34(5) does not directly grant this power. Nevertheless, the court has held that it is an implied power.

## Social and affordable housing agreements

**[3.255]** Part V of PDA 2000 came into effect on 1 November 2000 bringing in the social/affordable housing provisions to provide for housing strategies to be prepared by planning authorities for inclusion as part of the development plan in order that planning authorities can ensure that adequate land is zoned for housing and that sufficient social and affordable housing is provided in their areas. The relevant sections are contained in PDA 2000, being ss 93–101. Part V of PDA 2000 has been amended by the PD(A)A 2002.[302] PDA 2000 offered three types of condition which the planning authority could impose by way of agreement between the authority and the developer. The amendment Act of 2002 offered additional options. PDA 2000, s 93(4) provides that for the avoidance of doubt it is hereby declared that, in respect of any planning application or appeal, compliance with the housing strategy and any related objective in the

---

299. *Boland v An Bord Pleanála* [1996] 3 IR 435, SC.
300. *Ryanair v An Bord Pleanála* [2004] 2 IR 334.
301. As amended by PD(SI)A 2006, s 8(2).
302. Other amendments have been made to Pt V also, namely as follows: (1) Section 93(1) – the term 'housing strategy' has been deleted by PD(A)A 2010, s 37; (2) Section 96 was substituted by PD(A)A 2002, s 3; (3) Section 96(3)(b)(vi)(a) was inserted by PD(A)A 2010, s 38(a)(i); (4) Section 96(3)(b)(viii) was amended by PD(A)A 2010, s 38(a)(ii); (5) Section 96(3)(da) was inserted by PD(A)A 2010, s 38(a)(iii); (6) Section 96(7)(a)(ii)(a) was inserted by PD(A)A 2010, s 38(b); (7) Section 96(8) was amended by PD(A)A 2010, s 38(c); (8) Section 96A was inserted by PD(A)A 2002, s 4; (9) Section 96B was inserted by PD(A)A 2002, s 4; (10) Section 97(3) was amended by substituting 0.1 hectares for 0.2 hectares by PD(A)A 2002, s 5; (11) Section 97(3) now provides that conditions requiring transfer of land under s 96(2) will not be imposed where development is for four houses or less or is on 0.2 hectares or less; (12) Section 97(12)(b)(2)(II) has been amended by substituting 0.2 hectares for 0.1 hectares by Local Government (No 2) Act 2003, s 5; (13) Section 99(3A) was inserted by the Housing (Miscellaneous Provisions) Act 2004, s 2; and (14) Section 99(3A)(c) was amended by Land and Conveyancing Law Reform Act 2009 s 8(1), Sch 1.

development plan shall be a consideration material to the proper planning and sustainable development of the area.

**[3.256]** PDA 2000, s 96(2) provided that a planning authority, or the board on appeal, may require as a condition of grant of permission that the applicant would enter into an agreement with the planning authority concerning the development of housing land to which a specific objective (eg, housing strategy or development plan) applies. The PD(A)A 2002 has removed any discretion which the planning authority had and provides that a planning authority must impose such condition in a relevant residential or mixed (including residential) planning permission. PDA 2000, s 96(2), as amended by the PD(A)A 2002, s 3, provides that a planning authority, or the board on appeal, shall require as a condition of a grant of permission that the applicant, or any other person with an interest in the land to which the application relates, must enter into an agreement under this section with the planning authority, provided, in accordance with this section, for the matters referred to in s 96(3)(a) or (b).

**[3.257]** In fact, PDA 2000, s 96(2) used the enabling word 'may'. Even before the Act was amended and the word 'may' substituted by the word 'must', grants of permission for residential development or mixed residential development, except those expressly excluded, were subject to a condition under the section. An applicant affected by the provisions of Pt V in making an application for planning permission must state how it is proposed, in the course of development, to comply with the condition to enter into an agreement (a 'Part V agreement') with the planning authority. A Part V agreement will, in its mandatory form, require the transfer of land in its undeveloped state to the planning authority.

**[3.258]** An applicant developer is, as a matter of right, entitled to require a condition of a transfer of undeveloped lands within the site in respect of which the application for permission is made to the planning authority which land shall not exceed a maximum of 20% of the total lands the subject matter of the planning application. PDA 2000, s 96(3)(c) (as substituted) provides that the planning authority in considering whether to enter into a housing agreement shall consider each of the following:

(i) whether such an agreement will contribute effectively and efficiently to the achievement of the objectives of the housing strategy;

(ii) whether such an agreement will constitute the best use of the resources available to it to ensure an adequate supply of housing and any financial implications of the agreement for its functions as a housing authority;

(iii) the need to counteract undue segregation in housing between persons of different social background in the area of the authority;

(iv) whether such an agreement is in accordance with the provisions of the development plan;

(v) the time within which housing referred to in s 94(4)(a) is likely to be provided as a consequence of the agreement.

**[3.259]** The agreement required by PDA 2000, s 96(2) is an agreement in principle. It does not go into specific detail but rather, the agreement requires a planning authority to enter into discussion and to finalise the details to include such matters as the location of the lands to be transferred, or the type of sites and services to be provided, or the type of houses to be built or, exceptionally, the amount of money to be paid. The nuts and bolts of the agreement are to be negotiated after the grant of planning permission but it is almost invariably a condition of that planning permission that no development is to commence on the site until the completed agreement has been signed off. Since the finalisation of the details of the agreement results from discussion between the applicant developer and the planning authority it follows that the process is not subject to public scrutiny and it is not open, when the terms of agreement are finalised, for a member of the public to appeal those terms to An Bord Pleanála.

### Transboundary environmental impacts

[3.260] PDA 2000, s 174(3), as amended by PD(SI)A 2006, s 33(c), provides that notwithstanding any other provisions of this Act, a planning authority or the board, as the case maybe, may, following the consideration of any submissions or observations received or any consultations entered into by a planning authority or the board, impose conditions on a grant of permission or approval in order to reduce or eliminate potential transboundary effects of any proposed development.

## CONDITIONS RESTRICTING USE OF PREMISES BY PERSONS OF A PARTICULAR CLASS OR DESCRIPTION

[3.261] PDA 2000[303] provides that where permission is granted under this Part for a structure, the grant of permission may specify the purposes for which the structure may or may not be used, and where the grant specifies use as a dwelling as a purpose for which the structure may be used, the permission may also be granted subject to a condition specifying that the use as a dwelling shall be restricted to use by persons of a particular class or description and provision to that effect shall be embodied in an agreement under s 47.

### Sterilisation/planning agreements

[3.262] PDA 2000, s 47 deals with agreements regulating development or use of land, commonly referred to as 'sterilisation agreements' or more properly now as agreements between an owner, a planning authority and a person interested in land in their area for the purpose of restricting or regulating the development or use of land.

[3.263] PDA 2000[304] provides that a planning authority may enter into an agreement with any person interested in land in their area, for the purpose of restricting or regulating the development or use of the land, either permanently or during such period as may be specified by the agreement, and any such agreement may contain such incidental and consequential provisions (including provisions of a financial character) as

---

303. PDA 2000, s 39(2).
304. PDA 2000, s 47(1)–(5) inclusive.

appear to the planning authority to be necessary or expedient for the purpose of the agreement.[305]

**[3.264]** A planning authority in entering into an agreement under this section may join with any body which is a prescribed authority for the purposes of s 11.[306] A body for the purposes of s 11 is one which is entitled to prepare a draft development plan.

**[3.265]** An agreement made under this section with any person interested in land may be enforced by the planning authority, or any body joined with it, against persons deriving title under that person in respect of that land as if the planning authority or body, as may be appropriate, were possessed of adjacent land, and as if the agreement had been expressed to be made for the benefit of that land.[307]

**[3.266]** A planning authority may join other parties to a s 47 agreement to include State authorities. It may enter into an agreement with a person interested in land in its area for the purpose of restricting or regulating the development or use of the land either permanently or for a specified period. The planning authority may also impose a condition compelling an applicant for development permission to enter into a s 47 planning agreement, restricting or regulating the use of lands or a portion of lands. The section is drafted in such a way that it is intended that these planning agreements may be enforced against successors in title. They are somewhat akin to a restrictive covenant but, as will be seen below, they may not have the same potential for longevity. Particulars of an agreement made under PDA 2000, s 47 shall be entered on the planning register.[308]

**[3.267]** The usual purpose of a planning agreement is to prohibit all development on the land affected by it. From time to time, citizens apply to the planning authority to have their land sterilised so as to prevent development upon it. Planning authorities have typically used planning agreements where a farmer seeks permission for a single house on his land to impose a condition in the planning permission requiring that the lands adjoining the house site be sterilised so that no future development could be carried out in the immediate area, and the existence of a single house could not be used as a precedent for the erection of additional houses. Such agreements have also been used in the context of urban development, where certain areas might be designated as open space. A sterilisation or planning agreement is entered into to prevent pressure for the subsequent development of that space.

**[3.268]** Residents' associations and other interested parties have encouraged planning authorities to impose planning agreements by way of a condition in planning permissions to preserve open areas. The problem is that it is often done in good faith in the belief that for all time the piece of ground which has been sterilised will remain undeveloped. That is not the case, and although the planning agreement cannot be

---

305. PDA 2000, s 47(1).
306. PDA 2000, s 47(2).
307. PDA 2000, s 47(3).
308. PDA 2000, s 47(5).

unilaterally withdrawn by the landowner or the person having an interest in the land, PDA 2000[309] provides that nothing in that section or in any agreement made thereunder, shall be construed as restricting the exercise, in relation to land which is the subject of any such agreement of any powers exercisable by the Minister, the board or the planning authority under the Act, so long as those powers are not exercised so as to contravene materially the provisions of the development plan, or as required in the exercise of any such powers so as to contravene materially those provisions. In plain language, the Minister, the board and the planning authority concerned may withdraw a planning agreement.

[3.269] In *Langarth Properties Ltd v Bray UDC*,[310] a landowner applied for permission to develop certain lands situate in Bray, Co Wicklow. The planning authority refused planning permission on the basis that there was a planning agreement in existence given by the applicant's predecessor in title in March 1974 which bound the applicant not to construct any further houses on the land. The applicant appealed the planning authority's decision to the board and permission was granted by the board for the development. The planning authority sought to enforce the planning agreement notwithstanding that the board had issued a planning permission. In the High Court, Morris P held that when considering applications for the future development of land, a planning authority is limited to considering the proper planning and development of the area. The Board had granted a planning permission authorising the development of the lands in direct conflict with a covenant contained in the planning agreement and that, on its own, was a clear indication that the proper planning of the area no longer required observance of the covenant. Morris P stated:

> To prevent or inhibit the development of lands for any such reason, other than the proper planning and development of the area, would be an unconstitutional interference with the rights of private ownership of land. It would follow that the limitations and restrictions imposed by a Deed of Covenant of this nature remain valid only for so long as the proper planning of the area requires that the restrictions be maintained. When the proper planning of an area no longer requires that the restriction be retained, the land must be freed of the impediment to develop.

From this decision it is now clear that if any existing planning agreements are in conflict with the zoning provisions for development in the local authority's development plan, the sterilisation agreements will be set aside if a subsequent permission is granted.

## OCCUPANCY CONDITIONS

[3.270] The validity of occupancy conditions have been carefully scrutinised by the Law Society's law reform committee. 'Discriminatory Planning Conditions: The case for reform', was published in February 2005. Its authors Oran Doyle BL and Alan Keating BL have undertaken a scholarly and comprehensive review of discriminatory planning

---

309. PDA 2000, s 47(4).
310. *Langarth Properties Ltd v Bray UDC* (unreported, 25 June 2001) HC.

conditions. The investigations made and the conclusions recorded by the authors are well worth reading. Regrettably they have, thus far, been ignored by the legislature.[311]

**[3.271]** The provisions of PDA 2000, s 39(2) indicate that occupancy conditions may be inserted in a grant of planning permission by planning authorities. There are, however, some limits to this and we have seen that a planning condition must have a planning purpose. The planning condition, in particular, must be relevant to the permitted development. Thus, the imposition of a condition which bears no relationship to the matters set out in an application for planning permission should be invalid.

**[3.272]** In the Law Society report, the authors highlight six examples of discriminatory conditions used to control occupancy. These conditions are as follows:

(i) Local residency conditions – discriminating between local residents and non-local residents.

(ii) Local employment conditions – discriminating between local employees and non-local employees.

(ii) Agricultural worker conditions – discriminating between agricultural workers and non-agricultural workers.

(iv) Language conditions – discriminating between Irish speakers and non-Irish speakers.

(v) Blood line conditions – discriminating between relatives of local residents and non-relatives of local residents.

(vi) Returning emigrant conditions.

The authors' principal conclusions, in their thoughtful paper, are as follows:

*Recommendation 1*

Planning authorities and An Bord Pleanála should never impose blood line conditions. Blood line conditions discriminate between relatives of local residents and non-relatives of local residents as regards who constitutes a legitimate occupant of a newly permitted dwelling.

*Reason*

Such conditions contravene the Constitution, the European Convention on Human Rights and EU law.

*Recommendation 2*

Planning authorities and An Bord Pleanála should never impose a local residency condition independently of a local employment condition. Local residency conditions discriminate between local residents and non-local residents as regards who constitutes a legitimate occupant of a newly permitted dwelling.

---

311. Doyle and Keating, *Discriminatory Planning Conditions: The case for reform* (Law Society, 2005).

*Reason*

Such conditions contravene EU law insofar as they preclude consideration of other circumstances pertaining to a prospective resident. Such free standing residency conditions also contravene the European Convention on Human Rights.

*Recommendation 3*

If planning authorities and An Bord Pleanála wish to restrict use of a dwelling to persons of a particular class or description with some local connection, they should do so by means of a condition restricting occupancy to local residents and local employees.

*Reason*

Such conditions would be compatible with the Constitution, the European Convention on Human Rights and EU law and would go some way towards meeting the objective of securing strong rural communities.

*Recommendation 4*

Planning authorities and An Bord Pleanála should impose language conditions where they consider that such conditions are required by the proper planning and sustainable development of the particular area, but should be slow to apply such conditions uniformly over a large area.

*Reason*

Such conditions are prima facie compatible with the Constitution, the European Convention on Human Rights and EU law. However, there is a risk that the uniform imposition of such conditions over a large area could be disproportionate interference with rights under the Convention.

*Recommendation 5*

Planning authorities and An Bord Pleanála should impose agricultural worker conditions where they consider that such conditions are required by the proper planning and sustainable development of the particular area, but should be slow to apply such conditions uniformly over a large area.

*Reason*

Such conditions are prima facie compatible with the Constitution, the European Convention on Human Rights and EU law. However, there is a risk that the uniform imposition of such conditions over a large area could be a disproportionate interference with rights under the Convention.

*Recommendation 6*

If planning authorities and An Bord Pleanála wish to discriminate in favour of persons who used to live in a particular area but left that area and now wish to return, they should do so in a very limited way. The expansive scope of such a discriminatory planning condition should thus be limited by requiring the person to have been resident, in the past, for a considerable period of time in the local area, demonstrating a substantial connection with the community.

**[3.273]**      Planning and Environmental Law in Ireland

*Reason*

Such conditions are probably incompatible with EU law and the European Convention on Human Rights. If they are to have any chance of surviving a legal challenge, they should be narrowly drafted.

Based on our reading of the case law, we believe that the Irish Courts, the European Court of Human Rights and the European Court of Justice would recognise the maintenance of a strong rural population, independent of the holiday sector, as a legitimate objective. For this reason we recommended that, if planning authorities wish to impose discriminatory planning conditions that in some way favour 'local people', they should do so through a combination of a local residency and a local employment condition. That is, they should restrict occupancy of the dwelling to those who are either already local resident or local employees, although we suggest a specific definition of 'employee' to render such conditions consistent with EU Laws on freedom of movement and establishment.[312]

**[3.273]** The Development Management Guidelines for Planning Authorities (June 2007), a portion of which has already been quoted above, is relatively cautious in its approach to the advice which it gives to planning authorities relating to the occupation of buildings. Clause 7.6 reads as follows:

Planning permissions are attached to the land, and not the applicant. Section 39(2) of the Planning Act, enables a condition to be attached, specifying that the use of a structure as a dwelling shall be restricted to use by persons of a particular class or description. Planning authorities should be sparing in their approach to such conditions, as they can limit the freedom of the owner to dispose of his or her property or to obtain a mortgage. However, the Sustainable Rural Housing Guidelines outline circumstances in which it would be reasonable to attach occupancy conditions, eg in rural areas under considerable development pressure where the applicant is a person with roots in or links to the area. Those guidelines also advise that the so called use of 'sterilisation agreements' under s 47, that is, agreements for the purposes of restricting or regulating the development and use of land permanently or for a specified period, should be avoided apart from highly exceptional cases, because of the inflexible nature of such agreements.

**[3.274]** Appendix 1 of the Sustainable Rural Housing Guidelines for Planning Authorities (April 2005) gives indicative occupancy conditions and these are set out below as follows:

(a) The proposed dwelling when completed shall be first occupied as the place of residence of the applicant, members of the applicant's immediate family or their heirs and shall remain so occupied for a period of seven years thereafter, unless consent is granted by the planning authority for its occupation by other persons who belong to the same category of housing need as the applicant.

---

312. Doyle and Keating, *Discriminatory Planning Conditions: The case for reform* (Law Society, 2005).

(b) Before development commences, the applicant shall enter into an agreement with the planning authority, pursuant to s 47 of PDA 2000 providing for the terms of this occupancy requirement.

(c) Within two months of the occupation of the proposed dwelling, the applicant shall submit, to the planning authority, a written statement of the confirmation of the first occupation of the dwelling in accordance with para (a) and the date of such occupation.

(d) This condition shall not affect the sale of the dwelling by the mortgagee in possession or by any person deriving title from such sale.

It will be noted that the Sustainable Rural Housing Guidelines (April 2005) recommend the use of a planning agreement while the Development Management Guidelines (June 2007) state firmly that the use of s 47 planning agreements should be avoided apart from highly exceptional cases, because of the inflexible nature of such agreements.

[3.275] In relation to the conveyancing aspects of these planning conditions, the guidelines recommend that solicitors should not certify compliance with discriminatory planning conditions, as they have no special expertise or knowledge to qualify them to do so. Instead, the guidelines suggest that a statutory declaration by the proposed occupant would be acceptable to the planning authorities.

[3.276] Dealing specifically with blood line conditions, para 3.40 of the Law Society report reads as follows:

> Blood line is equivalent to pedigree and is, if one adopts the Great Blasket Case reasoning, a presumptively prescribed ground of classification. We suggest that blood line conditions do not meet the heightened standard of review suggested in the Great Blasket Case. No substantial governmental objective is served by allowing people, many of whom may never have lived in the State let alone in the particular rural area in question, gain priority over other applicants for Planning Permission, simply on account of the blood line connection to a local resident.

In conclusion, para 3.43, Ch 3 of the Law Society report, which deals with constitutional and administrative law issues, reads as follows:

> We suggest that, owing to the constitutional protection of equality, Section 39(2) must be interpreted in such a way as to prohibit the imposition of blood line conditions. Any such conditions actually imposed are thus ultra vires the planning authority concerned. We suggest that there are no objections, either as a matter of statutory interpretation or constitutional law, to local residency, local employment, returning emigrant, and agricultural worker and language conditions.

## DEVELOPMENT CONTRIBUTION SCHEMES

[3.277] PDA 2000, s 48[313] deals with the provision for and the making of development contribution schemes. PDA 2000, s 49[314] deals with the provision for and the making of

---

313. PDA 2000, s 48 as amended by PD(A)A 2010, s 30(a)–(b).
314. PDA 2000, s 49 as amended by PD(A)A 2010, s 31(a) and (b).

supplementary development contributions schemes. The system of levying development contribution is operated by the use of a condition or conditions in a grant of planning permission. The contributions are paid by the developer in respect of public infrastructure and facilities which benefit or will benefit the developments which are provided by the local authority.

[3.278] PDA 2000 provides that a planning authority may, when granting permission under s 34, include conditions for requiring the payment of a contribution in respect of public infrastructure and facilities benefiting development in the area of the planning authority and that is provided, or that is intended will be provided by or on behalf of a local authority (regardless of other sources of funding from the infrastructure and facilities).[315]

[3.279] PDA 2000, s 48(2) provides:

(a) Subject to paragraph (c), the basis for the determination of a contribution under sub-s (1) shall be set out in a development contribution scheme made under this section and a planning authority may make one or more schemes in respect of different parts of its functional area.

(b) A scheme may make provision for payment of different contributions in respect of different classes or descriptions of development.

(c) A planning authority may, in addition to the terms of a scheme, require the payment of a special contribution in respect of particular development where specific exceptional costs not covered by a scheme are incurred by any local authority in respect of public infrastructure and facilities which benefit the proposed development.[316]

[3.280] The definition of 'public infrastructure and facilities'[317] as contained in PDA 2000 means:

(a) the acquisition of land,

(b) the provision of open spaces, recreational and community facilities and amenities and landscaping works,

(c) the provision of roads, car parks, car parking places, sewers, waste water and water treatment facilities, service connections, watermains and flood relief work,

(d) the provision of bus corridors and lanes, bus interchange facilities (including car parks for those facilities) infrastructure to facilitate public transport, cycle and pedestrian facilities and traffic calming measures,

(e) the refurbishment, upgrading, enlargement or replacement of roads, car parks, car parking spaces, sewers, waste water and water treatment facilities, service connections or watermains,

---

315. PDA 2000, s 48(1).
316. PDA 2000, s 48(2)(a)–(c) inclusive.
317. The phrase 'public infrastructure and facilities' as defined in PDA 2000, s 48(17) relates to development contribution schemes under s 48.

(f) the provision high-capacity, telecommunications, infrastructure, such as broadband,

(g) the provision of school sites, and

(h) any matters ancillary to paragraphs (a)–(g).[318]

**[3.281]** PDA 2000 defines the word 'scheme' as a development contribution scheme made under this section. It also defines 'special contribution' as a special contribution referred to in PDA 2000, s 48(2)(c).

**[3.282]** 'Public infrastructure and facilities' is distinguished from 'public infrastructure projects or services', which are defined in PDA 2000 as meaning:

(a) The provision of particular rail, light rail or other public transport infrastructure, including car parks and other ancillary development,

(b) The provision of particular new roads,

(c) The provision of particular new sewers, waste water and water treatment facilities, service connections or watermains and ancillary infrastructure.[319]

(d) The provision of new schools and ancillary infrastructure.[309]

**[3.283]** Development contribution conditions may only be attached to a grant of planning permission if they accord with the provisions of either s 48 or 49 of PDA 2000 (as amended). There are three categories of conditions under which the payment of financial contributions may be required, namely:

(i) Section 48 (general) schemes relating to the existing or proposed provision of public infrastructure and facilities benefiting development within the area of the planning authority and these are applied as a general levy on development.

(ii) Section 49 (supplementary) schemes relating to separately specified infrastructural service or projects such as roads, rail or other public transport infrastructure which benefit the proposed development.

(iii) Special contribution requirements in respect of a particular development may be imposed under s 48(2)(c) of PDA 2000 where a planning authority may, in addition to the terms of a general s 48 scheme, require the payment of a special contribution in respect of a particular development where specific exceptional costs not covered by a scheme are incurred by any local authority in respect of public infrastructure and facilities which benefit the proposed development. A planning condition in a grant of permission, requiring a special contribution,

---

318. PDA 2000, s 48(17) as amended by PD(A)A 2010, s 30(a)–(c). Note that s 17(e) and (f) substituted by (g) and (h) as inserted by PD(A)A 2010, s 30(c).

319. The phrase 'public infrastructure project or service' is defined in PDA 2000, s 49(7)(b) as amended by the PD(A)A 2002, s 11. The phrase relates to supplementary development contribution schemes under PDA 2000, s 49.

must be amenable to implementation under the terms of PDA 2000, s 48(12),[320] which sets out the provisions which apply to special contributions, namely:

(a) the condition shall specify the particular works carried out, or proposed to be carried out by any local authority to which the contribution relates,

(b) where the works in question—

   (i) Are not commenced within 5 years of the date of payment to the authority of the contribution, (or final instalment thereof, if paid by phased payment under subsection (15)(a))

   (ii) Have commenced, but have not been completed within 7 years of the date of payment to the authority of the contribution, (or final instalment thereof, if paid by phased payment under subsection 15(a)) or

   (iii) Where the local authority decides not to proceed with the proposed works or part thereof,

   the contribution shall, subject to paragraph (c) be refunded to the applicant together with any interest that may have accrued over the period while held by the local authority,

(c) where under sub-paragraphs (ii) or (iii) of paragraph (b), any local authority has incurred expenditure within the required period in respect of a portion of the works proposed to be carried out, any refund shall be in proportion to those proposed works which have not been carried out.

It is essential that, in relation to special contributions, the basis for the calculation of the contribution must be explained in the planning decision. The explanation must set out the nature and scope of the works, the expenditure involved and the basis of calculation, including how it is apportioned to the particular development. A special contribution will frequently be levied by the imposition of a special contribution condition in a grant of planning permission where the costs are or will be incurred directly by the local authority as a result of, or in order to facilitate, the development which is the subject matter of the application. If the costs are such as would spread beyond the development, the subject matter of the application, and if they will benefit other developments in the area, the planning authority concerned, should proceed by way of adopting a revised (general) scheme under s 48 rather than putting a special contribution scheme in place. Conditions imposing special contribution schemes may be appealed to An Bord Pleanála whereas conditions imposing general contribution schemes under s 48(1) or supplemental contribution schemes under s 49 (as amended) may not be appealed to An Bord Pleanála.

**[3.284]** PDA 2000, s 48 (as amended) is designed to provide transparency so that any developer proposing to carry out any development can, by inspecting the development contribution scheme, anticipate what the level of financial contribution would be. The development contribution scheme can relate not only to public infrastructure and facilities already provided, but also to such public infrastructure and facilities as are to

---

320. PDA 2000, s 48(12)(b)(i) and (ii) as substituted by Planning and Development (Amendment) Act 2010, s 30(a).

be provided by the local authority in the future. The schemes are drawn up having regard to the actual estimated cost of providing the public infrastructure and facilities and the schemes may provide for the payment of reduced contribution or no contribution in certain circumstances, eg, for voluntary groups and generally for other disadvantaged members of the community.[321]

[3.285] The commencement date in relation to schemes under s 48 was 11 March 2002. Each planning authority was given a two-year period in which to complete their development contribution scheme and any scheme which had not been completed by 11 March 2004 would have prohibited the planning authority concerned from requiring or collecting any contribution towards the cost of infrastructure and facilities benefiting the development. Suffice it to say that every planning authority in the Republic of Ireland did complete a development contribution scheme prior to 11 March 2004.

[3.286] The planning authority is required to draw up a development contribution scheme setting out the basis of the estimated cost of providing the relevant infrastructure and facilities, less any benefit which accrues to existing development.

## Formalities for drawing up a development contribution scheme

[3.287] Planning authorities are required to prepare a draft development contribution scheme and to give public notice of its proposal to make a development contribution scheme in one or more newspapers circulating in the area to which the scheme relates.[322]

[3.288] PDA 2000 provides that the notice proposing that a scheme is to be made will be published in one or more newspapers circulating in the area to which the scheme relates. The notice shall:

(a) state that the draft scheme has been prepared,

(b) give details of the proposed contributions under the draft scheme,

(c) indicate the times at which, the period (which shall be not less than 6 weeks) during which, and the place where, a copy of the draft scheme may be inspected and,

(d) state that submissions or observations may be made in writing to the planning authority in relation to the draft scheme, before the end of the period for inspection.

The Minister for the Environment, Heritage and Local Government is a notice party who is entitled to make recommendations to the planning authority regarding the terms of the draft scheme, within six weeks of being sent the scheme.[323] PDA 2000 does not contain any provisions to indicate what action the planning authority should take on the recommendations received from the Minister. In the absence of any such express conditions it may be assumed that the planning authority is not bound by the Minister's

---

321. See PDA 2000, s 48(3)(a) to (c) inclusive.
322. See PDA 2000, s 48(4)(a) to (d) inclusive.
323. PDA 2000, s 48(5)(a)&(b).

recommendations. In *Construction Industry Federation v Dublin City Council*,[324] the plaintiff argued that the council's development contribution scheme in respect of public infrastructure benefiting the development proposal did not specify the particular projects of that scheme which the contribution was intended to fund. The plaintiff also complained that the council had not held any further public consultation even though a material variation was made to the draft scheme. Gilligan J rejected both arguments on the grounds that PDA 2000, s 48 did not require the council to specify the individual projects in the scheme and it did not require the council to re-advertise the draft scheme where variations were made to it.

[3.289] Section 48 of PDA 2000 further provides that:

(6)(a) Not later than four weeks after the expiration of the period for making submissions or observations under subsection (4) the manager of a planning authority shall prepare a report on any submissions or observations received under that sub-section, and submit the report to the members of the authority for their consideration.

(b) A report under paragraph (a) shall—

(i) list the persons or bodies who made submissions or observations under the section,

(ii) summarise the issues raised by the persons or bodies in the submissions or observations, and

(iii) give the response of the manager to the issues raised, taking account of the proper planning and sustainable development of the area.[325]

(7) The members of the planning authority shall consider the draft scheme and the report of the manager under subsection (6) and shall have regard to any recommendations made by the Minister under subsection (5).[326]

(8). (a) Following the consideration of the manager's report, and having had regard to any recommendations made by the Minister, the planning authority shall make the scheme, unless it decides, by resolution, to vary or modify the scheme, otherwise then as recommended in the manager's report or otherwise decides not to make the scheme.

(b) A resolution under paragraph (a) must be passed not later than 6 weeks after receipt of the manager's report.

(9). (a) Where a planning authority makes a scheme in accordance with subsection (8), the authority shall publish notice of the making, or approving, of a scheme, as the case may be, in at least one newspaper circulating in its area.

(b) A notice under paragraph (a) shall—

(i) give the date of the decision of the planning authority in respect of the draft scheme,

---

324. *Construction Industry Federation v Dublin City Council* [2005] 2 IR 496.
325. PDA 2000, s 48(6)(a) and (b).
326. PDA 2000, s 48(7).

(ii) state the nature of the decision, and

(iii) contain such other information as may be prescribed.[327]

[3.290] Once a development contribution scheme has been made, there is no appeal to the board in relation to a financial condition in a planning permission imposed in accordance with the scheme[328] except for an appeal by the applicant for permission on the grounds that the terms of the scheme have not been properly applied.[329] Where such an appeal is lodged and there is no other appeal, the planning authority is required to grant permission when the appeal period has expired, provided the developer furnishes security for payment of the full amount of the contribution as required by the condition.[330]

[3.291] Where an appeal is brought to the board in respect of a refusal to grant permission under this Part, and where the board decides to grant permission, it shall, where appropriate, apply as a condition to the permission the provisions of the contribution scheme for the time being in force in the area of the proposed development.[331] The purpose here is to speed up the planning process so that applications will not be held up while the appeal goes through.

[3.292] In *Cork City Council v An Bord Pleanala*,[332] it was held by Kelly J that the board had misinterpreted the relevant development contribution scheme, misapplied its functions and was wrong in law where it had sought to reduce an amount to be paid by a developer to Cork City Council pursuant to a condition in the planning permission. The role of the board in relation to a condition requiring a contribution to be paid in accordance with the development contribution scheme made under PDA 2000, s 48(1) is a limited one. The Board has no entitlement to consider or review the merits of the scheme, only to consider whether or not the terms of the relevant scheme have been properly applied.

[3.293] If the local authority requires the payment of a 'special contribution' under PDA 2000, s 48(2)(c) special provisions shall apply as follows:

(a) The wording of the special condition must specify the particular works which have or will be carried out by the local authority to which the special contribution relates.[333]

(b) The special contribution will be refunded with interest by the local authority to the developer who has paid it where any of the following matters apply:

---

327. PDA 2000, s 48(9)(a) and (b).
328. PDA 2000, s 48(10)(a).
329. PDA 2000, s 48(10)(b).
330. PDA 2000, s 48(10)(c).
331. PDA 2000, s 48(11).
332. *Cork City Council v An Bord Pleanala* [2007] 1 IR 761.
333. PDA 2000, s 48(12)(a).

Where the works in question:

(i) are not commenced within five years of the date of payment to the authority of the contribution (or final instalment thereof, if paid by phased payment under section (15(a)),

(ii) have commenced, but have not been completed within seven years of the date of payment to the authority of the contribution (or the final instalment thereof, if paid by phased payment under sub-s (15)(a)), or[334]

(iii) where the local authority decides not to proceed with the proposed works or part thereof.

If any of the above factors numbered (i) to (iii) apply the contribution shall, subject to paragraph (c) below, be refunded to the applicant together with interest that may have accrued over the period while held by the local authority.

**[3.294]** PDA 2000, s 48(12)(c) reads:

(c) where under sub-paragraph (i) or (iii) of paragraph (b), any local authority has incurred expenditure within the required period in respect of a proportion of the works proposed to be carried out, any refund shall be in proportion to those proposed works which have not been carried out.

Any monies paid to the local authority by way of contribution to a development contribution scheme or as a special contribution must, in each case, be retained in a separate account and applied as capital for public infrastructure and facilities only.[335] Under s 50 of the Local Government Act 1991, a local authority must prepare a report containing details of the money paid to it under s 48 and indicating how such monies paid have been expended by the local authority.

**[3.295]** Provision is made for phased payments of contributions which is a repetition of a practice which predated PDA 2000. However, the local authority may require security for payment of phased or future contributions, and if a phased or future contribution is not paid in accordance with the terms laid down in the planning condition, then interest will be payable and both the phased amount payable and the interest may be recovered by the local authority as simple contract debt in a court of competent jurisdiction.[336]

## Supplementary development contribution schemes

**[3.296]** PDA 2000, s 49 (as amended)[337] provides that a planning authority may, when granting permission under s 34, include conditions requiring the payment of a contribution in respect of any public infrastructure service or project:

(a) specified in a scheme made by the planning authority (hereinafter in this section referred to as a 'supplementary development contribution scheme'),

---

334. PDA 2000, s 48(12)(b)(i) and (ii) is substituted by PD(A)A 2010, s 30(a).
335. PDA 2000, s 48(14)(a).
336. PDA 2000, s 48(15)(a),(b)&(c).
337. PDA 2000, s 49(1) as amended by Planning and Development (amendment) 2010, s 31 allows the planning authority to make a supplementary contribution scheme.

(b) provided or carried out, or proposed to be provided or carried out—

  (i) by a planning authority;

  (ii) where the provision of the infrastructure concerned is an objective in the development plan of a planning authority, or of a planning scheme of the Dublin Docklands Development Authority under s 25 of the Dublin Docklands Development Act 1997, by a public authority, or, pursuant to an agreement entered into by a public authority, any other person, by that person or

  (iii) pursuant to an agreement entered into by a local authority with any other person, by that person, and

(c) that will benefit the development to which the permission relates when carried out.[338]

(1A)[339] In this section 'public authority' means any body established by or under statute which is for the time being declared, by regulations made by the Minister, to be a public authority for the purposes of this section.

**[3.297]** Supplementary contribution schemes in dealing with a public infrastructure project or service relate to particular works which will facilitate particular developments while the general development contribution scheme dealing with public infrastructure and facilities relates to works which are of general benefit. Otherwise, the two schemes are similar and the procedure for preparing a development contribution scheme and the restrictions on appeal to the board apply equally to supplementary development contribution schemes. The elected representatives make the supplementary contribution scheme as required in ss 48 and 49.[340]

(3A)[341] Notwithstanding sub-s (3) and s 48(10), the Board shall consider an appeal brought to it by an applicant for permission under s 34, in relation to a condition requiring the payment of a contribution in respect of public infrastructure service or project specified in a supplementary development contribution scheme, where the applicant considers that the service or project will not benefit the development to which the permission relates and s 48(13) shall apply to such appeal.

**[3.298]** A planning authority may enter into an agreement with third parties regarding the provision of a public infrastructure project or service including arrangements regarding the financing of the project or service and the manner in which the contribution is paid or owing to a planning authority. The aim is to encourage participation by private enterprise in the provisions of necessary infrastructure and would, for example, permit a planning authority to agree with a developer or, with a number of developers, for the provision of a public road and the financing or part financing of the construction of that road by imposing financial conditions in planning permissions subsequently granted in respect of lands which would benefit from it.[342]

---

338. PDA 2000, s 49(1)(a), (b) and (c).
339. Subsection (1A) as inserted by PD(A)A 2010, s 31(1A).
340. PDA 2000, s 49(2) and (3).
341. Subsection (3A) as inserted by PD(A)A 2010, s 31(b).
342. PDA 2000, s 49(4).

**[3.299]** A planning authority shall not, pursuant to a condition under s 49(1), require the payment of the contribution in respect of a public infrastructure project or service where the person concerned has made a contribution under s 48 in respect of public infrastructure and facilities of which the said public infrastructure project or service constitute a part.[343] In effect, this is a prohibition against double charging.

**[3.300]** The guidelines issued by various local authorities dealing with their respective general and special development contribution schemes under PDA 2000, s 48 and the supplementary development contribution scheme under PDA 2000, s 49[344] are very similar. What follows below is taken from the Dublin City Council Development Contribution Scheme explanation paper, which carefully explains the provisions of ss 48 and 49 and demonstrates a local authority's approach to calculating the contribution and including conditions requiring payment of the contribution, by way of example:

### Basis for determination of contribution

6 The basis for determination of a contribution of a development contribution scheme ('the Scheme') is as follows:

A detailed study carried out by a senior Council staff and consultants established the following:- (a) The amount of the costs which are attributable, in the years to 2009 to the five classes of public infrastructure and facilities. These costs are given in Table A which is annexed to this scheme. (b) The aggregated floor areas in square meters of projected development, in the years to 2009, in each of the classes or descriptions of development, namely residential class and industrial/commercial class. These floor areas are given in Table B which is annexed to this Scheme. (c) The development contributions payable per unit of residential development and per square metre of industrial/commercial development are, respectively, determined by dividing the relevant costs by the number of units/relevant floor space. The results of carrying out the division exercises are given in the table in article 9 of the scheme below.

### Development contribution scheme

7. The Dublin City Council Development Contribution Scheme ('the Scheme') is made within the terms of s 48 of PDA 2000 ('the Act').

8. Under the Scheme, Dublin City Council will, when granting a planning permission under s 34 of the Act, include conditions for requiring the payment of a contribution (the amount of which is indicated below under the heading Level of Contribution) in respect of public infrastructure and facilities benefiting development in the city of Dublin and that is provided, or it is intended will be provided, by or on behalf of Dublin City Council, (regardless of other sources of funding for the infrastructure and facilities).

---

343. PDA 2000, s 49(5).
344. PDA 2000, s 49(7)(c) and (d) have been amended by the PD(A)A 2010, s 31(c).

**Level of Contribution**

9. Under the Scheme, the contributions to be paid, except where an Exemption applies, (see below) in respect of the different classes of public infrastructure and facilities are as follows:

| Class of public Infrastructural Development | € per residential unit | € per square metre of industrial/ commercial development |
|---|---|---|
| Class 1 Roads infrastructure and facilities | 2,588.65 | 24.76 |
| Class 2 Water and drainage infrastructure and facilities | 6,592.95 | 63.06 |
| Class 3 Parks facilities and amenities | 412.85 | 3.95 |
| Class 4 Community facilities and amenities | 771.65 | 7.38 |
| Class 5 Urban regeneration facilities and amenities | 1,133.90 | 10.85 |
| Total of Contributions Payable | €11,500.00 | €110 |

**Note 1:** These rates of contribution shall be updated effective from 1 January each year during the life of the Scheme in accordance with the Tender Price Index. (See art 12 of the Scheme below).

**Note 2:** The floor area of proposed development shall be calculated as the gross floor area. This means the gross floor area determined from the external dimensions of the proposed buildings, including the gross floor area of each floor including mezzanine floors.

**Exemptions**

10. The following categories of development will be exempted, or partly exempted, from the requirement to pay development contributions under the Scheme:

(a) development by or on behalf of a voluntary organisation which is designed or intended to be used for social, recreational, educational or religious purposes by the inhabitants of a locality, or by people of a particular group or religious denomination, and is not to be used mainly for profit or gain,

(b) is designed or intended to be used as a workshop, training facility, hostel or other accommodation for persons with disabilities and is not to be used mainly for profit or gain,

(c) social and affordable housing units, including those which are provided in accordance with an agreement made under Part V of the Act (as amended under the Planning and Development (Amendment) Act, 2002) or which are provided by a voluntary or co-operative housing body, which is recognised as such by the Council.

(d) development ancillary to development referred to in paragraphs (a), (b) or (c).

**Payment of contribution**

11. Conditions requiring payment of the contributions provided for in the Scheme will be imposed in all decisions to grant planning permissions made following the making of the Scheme by the Council.

12. The contributions under the Scheme shall be payable prior to commencement of development or as otherwise agreed by the Council. Contributions shall be payable at the index adjusted rate pertaining to the year in which implementation of the planning permission is commenced, as provided for in the Note I to the table at Article 9 above.

13. The Council may facilitate the phased payment of contributions payable under the Scheme, and the Council may require the giving of security to ensure payment of contributions.

**Appeal to An Bord Pleanála ('the Board')**

14. An appeal may be brought to the Board where the applicant for planning permission under Section 34 of the Act considers that the terms of the Scheme have not been properly applied in respect of any conditions laid down by the Council.

**Review of Scheme**

15. The Scheme may be reviewed from time to time by the Council having regard to circumstances prevailing at the time. After a review of the Scheme, a new Scheme may be made. The cut-off year for the Scheme (unless a new Scheme is made before then) is 2009. A new Scheme will be made by then at the latest.

**Special Development Contributions**

16. A special development contribution, in addition to the terms of the Scheme, may be imposed under Section 48 of the Act where exceptional costs not covered by the Dublin City Council Development Contribution Scheme are incurred by the Council in the provision of a specific public infrastructure or facility. (The particular works will be specified in the planning conditions when special development contributions are levied). Only developments that will benefit from the public infrastructure or facility in question will be liable to pay the special development contribution. Conditions imposing special contributions may be appealed to An Bord Pleanála.

**Table A – Costs attributable to the Lifetime of the Scheme**

| Class of Public Infrastructural Development | € |
|---|---|
| Class 1<br>Roads infrastructure and facilities | 55,373,000 |
| Class 2<br>Water and drainage infrastructure and facilities | 141,041,000 |
| Class 3<br>Parks facilities and amenities | 8,831,000 |

| Class of Public Infrastructural Development | € |
|---|---|
| Class 4 | 16,519,000 |
| Community facilities and amenities | |
| Class 5 | 24,256,000 |
| Urban regeneration facilities and amenities | |
| Total | €246,020,000 |

**Table B – Projected Development to year 2009**

| | |
|---|---|
| Residential Development | 18,189 |
| Projected Number of residential units | |
| Non-Residential | 335,000 m$^2$ |
| Floor areas in square metres of projected industrial/commercial development | |

# Chapter 4
# CHALLENGING PLANNING DECISIONS

## PART I: APPEALS AND REFERRALS TO AN BORD PLEANÁLA

**[4.01]** The decision of a planning authority either to grant permission with or without conditions or to refuse permission may be appealed to An Bord Pleanála by the applicant for permission and/or any person who has made a valid written submission or observation in relation to the application for planning permission, provided the appropriate fee is paid. Planning appeals are quite separate to judicial review. In the latter case application is made to the court to have a planning decision reviewed to test the legal validity of the decision. An appeal to the board requires An Bord Pleanála to examine and to review the minutiae of the decision of the local authority where that decision has been objected to on planning grounds. A judicial review asks the courts to examine the legal validity of the decision to see whether, for example, the planning authority or the board has acted within its powers and/or that the decision made by the planning authority or indeed by the board is not *ultra vires*.

### Jurisdiction of the Board to hear appeals

**[4.02]** In summary, An Bord Pleanála has jurisdiction to deal with the following matters:

(i) an appeal against a decision to grant planning permission subject to or without conditions or to refuse permission;[1]

[Note: No appeal can be taken against a decision of a planning authority to grant a permission following the grant of outline permission in respect of any aspect of the proposed development which was decided in the grant of outline permission. The procedure for lodging that appeal is by the making of submissions and observations within five weeks from the date of the application for outline permission, and making the appeal within four weeks of the granting of the outline permission.]

(ii) an appeal against a notice for the acquisition of land for open spaces;[2]

(iii) an appeal against the making of a draft planning scheme for a strategic development zone;[3]

---

1. PDA 2000, s 37(1)(a).
2. PDA 2000, s 45(3).
3. PDA 2000, s 169 re making of a planning scheme and, specifically, see s 169(6) dealing with appeals against a planning authority's decision to make an SDZ. Note that PDA 2000, s 169(4) and (7) have been amended by PD(A)A 2010, s 51.

**[4.03]**     Planning and Environmental Law in Ireland

(iv) an appeal against a decision to revoke or modify a planning permission;[4]

(v) an appeal against a notice requiring the removal or alteration of a structure or the discontinuance of a use;[5]

(vi) an appeal against a notice relating to structures or other land in an area of special planning control;[6]

(vii) an appeal against the decision of a landowner or occupier to withhold consent for the construction, laying or attaching of cable, wire or pipeline or ancillary apparatus;[7]

[Note: The appeal procedures prescribed by PDA 2000, Pt VI, Ch III do not apply to these appeals.]

(viii) an appeal against an order creating a public right of way over land;[8]

(ix) an appeal against a grant, refusal, withdrawal or continuation of a licence for the erection, construction, placing or maintaining of an appliance, apparatus or structure.[9]

## Jurisdiction of the Board to hear referrals

**[4.03]** An Bord Pleanála has jurisdiction to deal with referrals in the following circumstances:

(i) a referral of a question as to what is or is not an exempted development;[10]

(ii) a referral of a dispute as to whether an application for permission is for the same development or is for a development of the same description as an application for permission which is subject to an appeal;[11]

---

4. PDA 2000, s 44 concerning the making or modifying of a planning permission and, specifically, s 44(6) dealing with an appeal against a planning authority's decision to revoke or modify a planning permission.
5. PDA 2000, s 46 concerning the decision of a planning authority requiring removal or alteration of a structure or discontinuance of a use and, specifically, s 46(6) re appeal against planning authority's decision.
6. PDA 2000, s 88 concerning notices relating to structure or other land in an area of special planning control and, specifically, s 88(5) concerning the appeal to the board against such a decision. Note also PDA 2000, s 88(6) listing matters which the board must take into account when hearing an appeal under s 88(5).
7. PDA 2000, s 182(4)(b) which allows for an appeal to the board where the local authority considers that the landowner's authority has been unreasonably withheld.
8. PDA 2000, s 207(5).
9. PDA 2000, s 254(6). Note that where an appeal under this section is allowed the board will give directions to the planning authority with respect to withdrawing, granting or altering a licence. See PDA 2000, s 254(7).
10. PDA 2000, s 5.
11. PDA 2000, s 37(5)(c).

(iii) a referral for determination of certain disputes in relation to any matter which may be the subject of an agreement for the provision of social and affordable housing;[12]

(iv) a referral of a dispute or question as to whether a new structure would or does substantially replace a demolished or destroyed structure;[13]

(v) a referral to determine points of detail relating to a grant of planning permission in default of agreement between the planning authority and the developer.[14]

**[4.04]** In *Boland v An Bord Pleanála*,[15] a permission to develop was granted by An Bord Pleanála subject to a condition that traffic and traffic management were to be agreed between the Minister and the planning authority. The applicant for permission contended that such condition was *ultra vires* and that the board had avoided its responsibility to determine the issue. In the applicant's submission the condition was *ultra vires* because:

(i) Third parties where excluded from the decision-making process in circumstances where agreement was to be reached between the Minister and the planning authority;

(ii) The conditions imposed by the board did not set out any criteria or parameters by which agreement could be reached;

(iii) The Board neglected to reserve a right to itself to make a decision in relation to the condition in default of agreement between the parties.

**[4.05]** The Board contended that four tests could be used to determine whether conditions properly left matters to be agreed between the developer and the planning authority, namely:

(1) Are the matters the subject of the delegation essentially concerned with problems which are off site and which do not affect the subject lands?

(2) Does the effect of enforcement of the conditions require monitoring or supervision?

---

12. PDA 2000, s 96(5). Note that a reference can be made to the board in respect of all disputes concerning an agreement required by a condition imposed under PDA 2000, s 96(2) except for such matters which must be referred to the property arbitrator. Note that PDA 2000, s 96(3)(b) and (d) and s 96(7)(a) and (8) have been amended by PD(A)A 2010, s 38. Further note that PDA 2000, s 96 has been extended by the addition of ss 96A and 96B as inserted by PD(A)A 2010, s 4.
13. PDA 2000, s 193(2).
14. PDA 2000, s 34(5) as amended by PD(SI)A 2006, s 8(2).
15. *Boland v An Bord Pleanála* [1996] 3 IR 435 SC *per* Keane J.

(3) Is it reasonable to suppose that aspects of the proposed development may require redesign in the light of practical experience?

(4) In leaving matters to be agreed between the planning authority and the developer has the board laid down criteria by which the authority and the developer can reach agreement?

[4.06] Keane J concluded that whether or not the board had abdicated its responsibilities was a matter of degree and in this case the condition did not amount to an abdication of the board's responsibilities or of its statutory duties. In imposing these types of conditions the board may have regard to the need to allow for flexibility in a complex development, the desirability of leaving technical matters to be agreed, particularly where these matters are the responsibility of the local authority and whether any member of the public could reasonably object to the work carried out pursuant to such condition.

## Who may appeal?

[4.07] The legislation dealing with appeals to An Bord Pleanála is comprehensively dealt with in the Planning and Development Act 2000 (PDA 2000), s 37 (as amended)[16] as part of the section of the Principal Act (ie, PDA 2000) which is headed 'control of development'. Decisions of a planning authority involve a two tier process: First, the grant of permission under PDA 2000, s 34.[17] Second, the potential under PDA 2000, s 37(1) for an applicant and any person who has made submissions or observations in writing, in relation to the planning application, to the planning authority in accordance with the permission regulations and, on payment of the appropriate fee, at any time before the expiration of the appropriate period, to appeal to the board against the decision of the planning authority made under PDA 2000, s 34.

[4.08] Applicants do not have to make an appeal on any prescribed form because there is no statutorily prescribed form. An Bord Pleanála has produced a *'Planning Appeal Form / Check List'* which may be used as a cover page in an appeal. The cover page would be followed by the substantive grounds on which the appeal is made. The form may be drawn down from the An Bord Pleanála website at www.pleanala.ie. This is a useful document and the reverse side of the form gives good and clear advice to applicants.

---

16. PDA 2000, s 37 as amended by PD(SI)A 2006, s 10 and by PD(A)A 2010, s 25 by amendments to s 37A.
17. Section 34(2)(c) as amended by the Protection of the Environment Act 2003, s 61; s 34(4)(a) as substituted by PD(SI)A 2006, s 8(1); s 34(5) as amended by PD(SI)A 2006, s 8(2); s 34(6)(a) as amended by PD(A)A 2010, s 23(a)(i); s 34(6)(a)(ii) as substituted by PD(A)A 2010, s 23(a)(ii); s 34(6)(a)(iii) as amended by PD(A)A 2010, s 23(a)(iii); s 34(6)(a)(iii)(a) inserted by PD(A)A 2010, s 23(a)(iv); s 34(8)(b) and (c) as substituted by PD(A)A 2010, s 23(b)(i); s 34(8)(f) as substituted by PD(A)A 2010, s 23(b)(ii); and s 34(12) as substituted by s 34(12A), (12B) and (12C) inserted by PD(A)A 2010, s 23(c).

**[4.09]** The rules and procedures for making an appeal are set out in PDA 2000, Pt VI, Ch III, ss 125–146D inclusive as amended.[18]

**[4.10]** An applicant for permission and any person who makes submissions or observations in writing in relation to the planning application to the planning authority in accordance with the permission regulations and on payment of the appropriate fee, may, at any time before the expiration of the appropriate period, appeal to the board against a decision of a planning authority under s 34.[19] There are a number of exceptions to the general statement set out above and these are as follows.

## Exceptions

### A prescribed body that is not notified

**[4.11]** This is an exception to the general rule that only persons who have made submissions and observations in writing in relation to the planning application, may submit and appeal to the board. If a prescribed body should have been notified of the planning application under art 28 of Planning and Development Regulations 2006 (PDR 2006) and the planning authority failed to notify it, that authority or body will be entitled to appeal the decision to the board, without having to make submissions or observations, but the board has power to dismiss any appeal if it considers that the body concerned was not entitled to be sent notice of the planning application in accordance with the permission regulations.[20] A planning authority is compelled to serve notice on certain prescribed bodies as soon as may be after receipt of the application.[21]

**[4.12]** A summary of the circumstances where a notice must be served on prescribed bodies is listed below.[22]

  (a) where it appears to the authority that the land or structure is situated in an area of special amenity or that the development or retention of the structure might obstruct any view or prospect of special amenity, value or interest notice must be given to An Chomhairle Ealaíon, Fáilte Ireland, and An Taisce,

---

18. (a) Section 125 as substituted by PD(SI)A 2006, s 20; (b) s 128 as substituted by PD(SI)A 2006, s 21; (c) s 130(5) as amended by PD(A)A 2010, s 42; (d) s 134 as substituted and s 134(a) as inserted by PD(SI)A 2006, s 22; (e) s 135(2), (2AB)–(AE) and (2B)(dd) as inserted respectively by PD(A)A 2010, s 43(a)–(c) (note that s 135(1) to (3) were substituted by PD(SI)A 2006, s 23(a). Section 135(5)(a) as amended by PD(SI)A 2006, s 23(b)); (e) s 140(1) as substituted by PD(SI)A 2006, s 25(a); (f) s 140(2)(a) as amended by PD(SI)A 2006, s 25(b); (g) s 143 as substituted by PD(SI)A 2006, s 26; (h) s 144(1) as substituted by s 144(1A) and (1B) as inserted by PD(A)A 2010, s 44; (i) s 145(1)(b) as substituted by PD(SI)A 2006, s 28; (j) s 146 as amended by PD(SI)A 2006, s 29 with the substitution of s 29(3) and (4) and the insertion of s 29(5), (6) and (7). Note that Ch 4 of PDA 2000, comprising s 146A to 146D, was inserted in its entirety by PD(SI)A 2006, s 30.
19. PDA 2000, s 37(1)(a).
20. PDA 2000, s 37(4)(a)&(b).
21. PDR 2006, art 29(1)(a)–(u) inclusive.
22. PDR 2006, art 29(1)(a)–(u) inclusive.

(b) where it appears to the authority that the development might obstruct or detract from the value of any tourist amenity or tourist amenity works – to Fáilte Ireland,

(c) where it appears to the authority that the development:

    (i) would involve the carrying out of works to a protected structure or proposed protected structure, or to the exterior of a structure which is located within an architectural conservation area,

    (ii) might detract from the appearance of a structure referred to in sub-paragraph (i),

    (iii) might affect or be unduly close to:

        (I) a cave, site, feature or other object of archaeological, geological, scientific, ecological or historic interest,

        (II) a monument or place recorded under s 12 of the National Monuments (Amendment) Act 1994,

        (III) a historic monument or archaeological area entered in the Register of Historic Monuments under s 5 of the National Monuments (Amendment) Act 1987,

        (IV) a national monument in the ownership or guardianship of the Minister under the National Monuments Act 1930–2004, or

    (iv) might obstruct any scheme for improvement of the surroundings or, or any means of access to, any structure, place, feature or object referred to in sub-paragraph (iii), notice must be served on the Minister, the Heritage Council, and An Taisce and in the case of development of the type referred to in sub-paragraph (i) or (ii), notice to An Chomhairle Ealaíon and Fáilte Ireland,

(d) where it appears to the authority that the area of another local authority might be affected by the development notice must be given to that local authority,

(e) where it appears to the authority that the development would not be consistent with or would materially contravene any regional planning guidelines (or any objective thereof) of a regional authority notice should be given to that regional authority,

(f) where it appears to the authority that if permission were granted, a condition should be attached under s 34(4)(m) of the Act notice should be given to any local authority (other than a planning authority) which would be affected by such condition,[23]

---

23. PDA 2000, s 34(4)(m) reads: 'Conditions for requiring the provision of roads, including traffic calming measures, open spaces, car parks, sewers, water mains or drains, facilities for the collection or storage of recyclable materials and other public facilities in excess of the immediate needs of the proposed development, subject to the local authority paying for the cost of the additional works and taking them in charge or otherwise entering into an agreement with the applicant with respect to the provision of those public facilities'.

(g) where it appears to the authority that:
- (i) the development might cause the significant abstraction or addition of water either to or from surface or ground waters, whether naturally occurring or artificial,
- (ii) the development might give rise to significant discharges of polluting matters or other materials to such waters or be likely to cause serious water pollution or the danger of such pollution, or
- (iii) the development would involve the carrying out of works in, over, along or adjacent to the banks of such waters, or to any structure in, over or along the banks of such waters, which might materially affect the waters – notice to be given to the appropriate Regional Fisheries Board and, in any case where the waters concerned are listed in Pt 1 of Annex 1 of the Schedule to the British–Irish Agreement Act 1999, to Waterways Ireland,

(h) where it appears to the authority that the development might endanger or interfere with the safety of, or the safe and efficient navigation of aircraft – notice to be given to the Irish Aviation Authority,

(i) where it appears to the authority that the development might interfere with the operation and development of a licensed airport, whose annual traffic is not less than 1 million passenger movements – notice to be given to the airport operator,

(j) where the development may have an impact on bus or rail-based transport, notice to be given to Córas Iompair Éireann and the Railway Procurement Agency, as appropriate,

(k) where it appears to the authority that:
- (i) the development consists of or comprises the formation, laying out or materially widening of an access to a national road within the meaning of s 2 of the Roads Act 1993, not being a national road within a built-up area within the meaning of s 45 of the Road Traffic Act 1961, or
- (ii) the development might give rise to a significant increase in the volume of traffic using a national road – notice to be given to the National Roads Authority,

(l) where the development might significantly impact on surface transport in the Greater Dublin Area – notice to be given to the Dublin Transportation Office,

(m) where the development comprises or is for the purpose of an activity requiring an integrated pollution control licence or a waste licence – notice to be given to the Environmental Protection Agency,

(n) where it appears to the authority that the development might have significant effects in relation to nature conservation – notice to be given to the Heritage Council, the Minister and An Taisce,

(o) where the development is in a Gaeltacht area and it appears to the authority that it might materially affect the linguistic and cultural heritage of the Gaeltacht, including the promotion of Irish as the community language – notice to be given to the Minister for Community, Rural and Gaeltacht Affairs and Údarás na Gaeltachta,

(p) where the development is in the vicinity of an explosives factory, storage magazine or local authority explosives store – notice to be given to the Minister for Justice, Equality and Law Reform,

(q) where the application relates to development for the purposes of breeding or rearing of salmonid fish – to the Minister for Communications Marine and Natural Resources and the appropriate regional fisheries board,

(r) where the application relates to development for the purposes of initial afforestation or the replacement of broadleaf high forest by conifer species – notice to be given to the Minister for Agriculture and Food, the Heritage Council and An Taisce,

(s) where it appears to the authority that the development might have significant effects on public health – notice to be given to the Health Service Executive,

(t) where the application relates to extraction of minerals within the meaning of the Minerals Development Acts 1940–1955 – notice to be given to the Minister for Communications, Marine and Natural Resources,

(u) where it appears to the authority that the development might impact on the foreshore – notice to be given to the Minister for Communications, Marine and Natural Resources,

(v) where the application relates to the development of energy infrastructure, or may have an impact on energy infrastructure – notice to be given to the Commission for Energy Regulation,

(w) where the development might:

    (i) give rise to a significant increase in the volume or type of traffic (including construction traffic) passing under a height restricted railway bridge, or using a railway level crossing, or a bridge over a railway,

    (ii) because of its proximity to a railway, impact on the structural integrity of railway infrastructure during construction of the development, or

    (iii) endanger or interfere with the safe operation of a railway during or after construction – notice to be given to the railway operator, the Railway Safety Commission, and, in the case of development which might impact on a light railway or metro, the Railway Procurement Agency,

(x) where the application relates to:

    (i) the extraction of minerals, other than minerals within the meaning of the Minerals Development Acts 1941–1999, whether by surface or underground means,

    (ii) the development of or extensions to quarries, including sand or gravel pits, for the extraction of earth materials, or

(iii) a development which for other purposes, requires the excavation of earth materials greater than a total volume of 50,000m$^3$ or the excavation of earth materials on a site area greater than 1 hectare – notice to be given to the Minister for Communications, Marine and Natural Resources.

## Non-governmental organisations

[4.13] PD(SI)A 2006 has added another body or organisation which will be entitled to appeal within the prescribed time limit even though it has not made any submissions or observations.[24] A body or organisation (not being a State authority, a public authority or a governmental body or agency), where its aims or objectives relate to the promotion of environmental protection and which has, during the period of twelve months preceding the making of the appeal, pursued those aims or objectives and is a body which satisfies such additional requirements (if any) as may be prescribed by the Minister by way of additional requirements shall be entitled to appeal to the court against the decision by the planning authority on an application for development (being development in respect of which an environmental impact statement (EIS) was required to be submitted to the planning authority in accordance with s 172) before the expiration of the appropriate period within the meaning of that subsection.[25] This amendment was inserted to satisfy Ireland's obligations and requirements under Directive 2003/35/EC.

## Landowner of adjoining lands

[4.14] In certain circumstances a landowner whose land adjoins an applicant's lands will not have to make submissions or observations. Another exception to the general rule restricting the right of appeal to persons who have made submissions and observations in writing in relation to the planning application provides that a person who has an interest in land adjoining land in respect of which permission is being granted may, within four weeks and on payment of the appropriate fee, apply to the board for leave to appeal against a decision of a planning authority under PDA 2000, s 34. The application must state the name and address of the applicant and the grounds upon which the application is made and it must give a description of the applicant's interest in the adjoining lands. If an applicant, in making an application to the board for leave to appeal under this subsection, shows that the development for which permission is being granted will differ materially from the development as set out in the application for permission, by reason of conditions imposed by the planning authority and that the imposition of such conditions will materially affect the applicant's enjoyment of the land or reduce the value of the land, the board shall grant the applicant leave to appeal within four weeks from the date of receipt of the application, even though the applicant has not made any

---

24. See PD(SI)A 2006, s 10 now inserted into PDA 2000 as s 37(4)(c), (d), (e) and (f). These bodies are commonly referred to as non-governmental organisations (NGOs).
25. See PD(SI)A 2006, s 10 now inserted into PDA 2000 as s 37(4)(c),(d), (e) and (f). These bodies are commonly referred to as non-governmental organisations (NGOs).

submissions or observations to the planning authority within five weeks of the date of the original application for planning permission. Within three days of making its decision either to grant or to refuse an application for leave to appeal, the board will notify the planning authority and the applicant, and if leave to appeal is granted, the applicant will have two weeks from the date of notification to bring his appeal. Once an application is made under this subsection,[26] the planning authority shall not make any grant of permission unless the application is refused. Where leave to appeal is granted in these circumstances it shall be the duty and objective of the board, in relation to the appeal, to ensure that the appeal is determined within 14 weeks. (Note: The period prescribed in other forms of appeal is 18 weeks beginning on the date of receipt by the board of the appeal or such other period as the Minister may prescribe by regulations either generally or in respect of a particular class or classes of appeals.)[27 & 28]

## Time limits for lodging an appeal to An Bord Pleanála

**[4.15]** The 'appropriate period' referred to in s 37(1)(a)[29] within which the appeal must be lodged with the board, whether it is lodged by an applicant, by an objector who has made submissions and observations or by any other party who or which is entitled to appeal, is four weeks beginning on the day of the decision of that planning authority.[30] The day of the decision is the day that the notification of grant of planning permission issues. It is not the day that the notification of decision to grant planning permission issues. It is not necessarily the date on which the notification of grant of permission was notified to the applicant. Difficulties in relation to the four-week time limit can arise for prescribed bodies which have not made submissions or observations and which should have been notified but were not notified by the planning authority of the application for planning permission lodged with the authority. The statutory provisions make no concession whatsoever in terms of any potential extension of the time limit and while the courts have, from time to time, facilitated the prescribed body by imposing an extension of time 'by agreement of the parties' it is a questionable procedure. The more likely alternative is that the court will decline to quash the decision of the planning authority even though the consequence is that the potential objector is left without any remedy under the Planning Code. In *Lynch v Dublin City Council*,[31] Ó Caoimh J refused to quash a planning authority decision on discretionary grounds. If in doubt, An Bord Pleanála's website at www.pleanala.ie has a ready-reckoner to assist in calculating the last day for making an appeal.

Where a person is given leave to appeal, the appeal must be received by the board within two weeks of receiving the notification of that fact.

---

26. PDA 2000, s 37(6)(a).
27. PDA 2000, s 126(2)(a) and (b) also s 126(4).
28. PDA 2000, s 37(6)(a)–(i) inclusive.
29. PDA 2000, s 37(1)(a).
30. PDA 2000, s 37(1)(d).
31. *Lynch v Dublin City Council* (unreported, 25 July 2003) HC *per* Ó Caoimh J.

## Circumstances in which Board may direct a material contravention of plan

[4.16] In determining an appeal the board may grant permission even though the proposed development will be in material contravention of the development plan relating to the area of the planning authority to whose decision the appeal relates. Where the planning authority has decided to refuse permission because the proposed development is in material contravention of the development plan, the board may grant permission where it considers that:

(i) the proposed development is of strategic or national importance, or

(ii) there are conflicting objectives in the development plan or the objectives are not clearly stated, insofar as the proposed development is concerned, or

(iii) permission for the proposed development should be granted having regard to regional planning guidelines for the area, being ministerial guidelines and directives under PDA 2000, s 28, ministerial policy directives under PDA 2000, s 29, the statutory obligations of any local authority in the area, and any relevant policy of the government, the Minster or any Minister of government, or

(iv) permission for the proposed development should be granted having regard to the pattern of development, and permissions granted, in the area since the making of the development plan.[32]

In all cases where the board grants permission subsequent to a refusal by the planning authority on the basis of material contravention, the board must indicate in its decision the main reasons and considerations for contravening materially the development plan.[33]

[4.17] The circumstances in which the board can grant permission on appeal, which permission is in material contravention of the local authority's development plan, are limited to the circumstances as set out in sub-paras (i), (ii), (iii) and (iv).[34] These limitations are eminently fair and underline the importance of development plans and the fact that material contravention of a development plan is something which should only be permitted in very special circumstances. The elected members of a local authority are not constrained by these four limitations and this is a further reason why elected members, whose skills are mainly political and social in the broadest sense, rather than planning, should not be permitted to direct a manager of a local authority to grant a permission which is in material contravention of the development plan. This is something that should be remedied sooner rather than later and, where there is a proposal for material contravention of the development plan, the most the elected representatives should be entitled to do is to submit the matter to the board for its decision which decision should be made within the confines of sub-paras (i)–(iv) inclusive. An Bord Pleanála is only required to pay attention to these four restrictions

---

32. PDA 2000, s 37(2)(a) and (b).
33. PDA 2000, s 37(2)(c).
34. PDA 2000, s 37(2)(b).

where the planning authority had, in the first instance, decided to refuse permission on the grounds of material contravention.

## An Bord Pleanála must determine the appeal *de novo*

**[4.18]** Where an appeal is brought against a decision of a planning authority and the appeal is not withdrawn, the board shall determine the application as if it had been made to the board in the first instance. The decision of the board shall operate to annul the decision of the planning authority as and from the time that decision was given.[35] If, however, an appeal is lodged with the board but withdrawn before the board makes its decision, the planning authority's decision will stand. In *O'Keefe v An Bord Pleanála*,[36] Costello J considered the board's situation in circumstances where it was clear that the planning authority in making its decision did so in a manner which would have rendered its decision invalid. In the course of his judgment Costello J stated:

> This means that it is determining the matter de novo and without regard to anything that had transpired before the planning authority ... it would follow that I should construe this Statute as meaning that no defect in the proceedings before the planning authority should have any bearing or impose any legal constraints on the proceedings before the Board.

## Vexatious or frivolous appeals

**[4.19]** Board may dismiss appeals or referrals if vexatious, frivolous or without substance or foundation or where they are made for the purpose of delaying the development or securing payment of money.[37]

(1) The Board is given absolute discretion to dismiss an appeal or referral in the following circumstances:

(a) Where, having considered the grounds of appeal or referral or any other matter to which, by virtue of this Act, the board may have regard in dealing with or determining the appeal or referral, the board is of the opinion that the appeal or referral:

(i) is vexatious, frivolous or without substance or foundation, or

(ii) is made with the sole intention of delaying the development or the intention of securing the payment of money, gifts, consideration or other inducement by any person, or

(b) Where the board is satisfied that, in the particular circumstances, the appeal or referral should be further considered by it having regard to:

(i) the nature of the appeal (including any question which in the board's opinion is raised by the appeal or referral), or

(ii) any previous permission which in its opinion is relevant.

---

35. PDA 2000, s 37(1)(b).
36. *O'Keefe v An Bord Pleanála* [1993] 1 IR 39.
37. PDA 2000, s 138 as amended by PD(SI)A 2006, s 24 in relation to s 138(1)(a).

There are two further points worth noting in s 138, namely:

> (2) A decision made under this section shall state the main reasons and considerations on which the decision is based.[38]
>
> (3) The Board may, in its absolute discretion, hold an oral hearing under s 134 to determine whether an appeal or referral is made with the intention referred to in s 138(1)(a)(ii), namely, delaying the development or securing payment of money, etc.[39]

## Appeal against conditions only

[4.20] An appeal may be made specifically against a condition or conditions specified in a notification of grant of planning permission.[40] A planning authority may have granted a permission to an applicant in circumstances where the applicant was satisfied to obtain permission but unhappy with one or more of the conditions attached to that permission. In those circumstances, the applicant is entitled to appeal the condition or conditions which may in some way detract from the value of the permission granted. If the appeal against the condition or conditions fails the permission will still stand and if the appeal is successful the condition or conditions which were the subject matter of the appeal may be struck out or altered. In considering an appeal against a condition or conditions in a planning permission An Bord Pleanála, importantly, retains a discretion to re-open the entire decision. That is the risk which the appellant whose appeal is limited to an appeal against a condition or conditions only, must take. The Board has discretion either to re-open the entire planning application or it may decide to confine itself to considering the actual condition or conditions the subject matter of the appeal. If the board considers the condition or conditions only it may, in its absolute discretion, give the relevant planning authority such directions as it considers appropriate relating to the attachment, amendment or removal by that authority either of the condition or conditions to which the appeal relates or of other conditions.[41]

[4.21] Apart from considering the relevant condition or conditions which are the subject matter of the appeal the board is confined to considering the matters set out in s 34(2)(a), namely:

(i) The provisions of the development plan,

(ii) The provisions of any special amenity area order relating to the area,

(iii) Any European site or other area prescribed for the purposes of s 10(2)(c),

(iv) Where relevant, the policy of the government, the Minister or any other Minister of the government,

---

38. PDA 2000, s 138(2).
39. PDA 2000, s 138(3).
40. PDA 2000, s 139.
41. PDA 2000, 139(1)(c).

(v) The matters referred to in s 34(4), and

(vi) Any other relevant provisions or requirement of this Act, and any regulations made thereunder.

The Board is also confined to considering the terms of any previous permission considered by the board to be relevant.[42]

## Appeal against conditions requiring payment of a financial contribution

**[4.22]** There is a limited right of appeal to An Bord Pleanála in relation to a financial condition requiring a contribution to be paid in accordance with a scheme made under PDA 2000, s 48. An appeal in these circumstances can only be brought against a financial contribution condition where the grounds of appeal are based on the fact that the terms of the scheme have not been properly applied by the planning authority.[43] In *Cork City Council v An Bord Pleanála*,[44] it was held that the board in overturning a financial contribution condition had done so incorrectly by misinterpreting the development contribution scheme. The Board had misapplied its function and was wrong in law. The Board has no entitlement to consider or review the merits of a development contribution scheme. The Board's function is strictly limited to considering whether or not the terms of the development contribution scheme have been properly applied.

**[4.23]** Where an appeal is brought to challenge the terms of a development contribution scheme and no other appeal against the decision is brought by any other person, provided the person making the appeal furnishes security for payment of the full amount of the contribution as specified in the condition, then, so as not to delay the commencement of the development, the planning authority is bound to make the grant of permission as soon as may be after the expiration of the period for the taking of the appeal has expired.[45]

**[4.24]** The circumstances in which an appeal can be taken against a condition requiring a special contribution are even more limited in that An Bord Pleanála cannot treat an appeal against a special contribution as a full review entitling the board to look at the entire decision. In the case of an appeal against a special contribution, the board's considerations are limited strictly to the matters under appeal.[46] However, in the case of an appeal against a special contribution, provided there are no other appeals, if the appellant furnishes security for payment of the full amount of the special contribution as specified in the condition in the planning permission then the planning authority must grant planning permission in advance of the determination of the limited appeal.[47]

---

42. PDA 2000, s 139(2).
43. PDA 2000, s 48(10)(a) and (b).
44. *Cork City Council v An Bord Pleanála* [2007] 1 IR 761 *per* Kelly J.
45. PDA 2000, s 48(10)(c).
46. PDA 2000, s 48(13)(a).
47. PDA 2000, s 48(13)(b).

## Prohibition against further planning applications pending appeal

[4.25] No application for planning permission can be made by any person for the same development or for a development of the same description as a development proposal which is the subject matter of a pending appeal to An Bord Pleanála until:

(i) The Board has made its decision on the appeal,

(ii) The appeal is withdrawn, or

(iii) The appeal is dismissed by the board pursuant to s 133 or 138.[48]

The absolute prohibition provided for in this section leaves the planning authority with no discretion to deal with an application in circumstances where the matter is still pending before the board. PDA 2000, s 133 permits the board to determine the appeal or referral where notice has been served under s 131, 132 or 133.[49] The planning authority is compelled to return the application submitted under the terms of PDA 2000, s 37(5)(a) and any other information submitted together with any fee paid to the applicant.[50]

[4.26] In *Swords Cloghran Properties v Fingal County Council*,[51] the submission of a revised application was described as a 'revised development'. The planning authority had already refused permission for a commercial development. The developer appealed against the planning authority's refusal and it lodged the second, almost identical, application on the day before it lodged its appeal. The developer argued that it had not offended the section because, firstly, the application for the second development was not the same as the first application and, secondly, the second application was lodged at a time when there was no appeal to the board in existence for the reason that the appeal was lodged the day after the revised application was lodged. The developer argued that the planning authority had no right to return the second application and further that a default permission existed because the planning authority had not made any decision on the second application within the eight week period.

---

48. PDA 2000, s 37(5)(a).
49. PDA 2000, s 131 deals with the power of the board to request submissions or observations and allows an extended period of not less than two weeks or not more than four weeks to do so. If submissions and observations are not received within the period specified the board will proceed to determine the appeal or referral. PDA 2000, s 132 gives the board power to require the submission of documents, particulars or other information as may be necessary for the board to enable it to determine an appeal or referral and if documents, particulars or other information, etc, are not furnished within the time specified the board may without further notice dismiss the appeal or referral. PDA 2000, s 133 deals with powers of the board where notice is served under s 131 or 132. The Board may at any time after expiration of the period specified in the notice having considered submissions or observations or documents, particulars or other information submitted without further notice determine (or in the case of a s 132 notice) dismiss the appeal or referral.
50. PDA 2000, s 37(5)(b).
51. *Swords Cloghran Properties v Fingal County Council* (unreported, 29 June 2006) HC *per* Herbert J.

**[4.27]** Herbert J held that on the facts of the case the second revised application was not a development of the same description as the first application. For the second application to be the same as the first application it had to be, in every material respect, exactly the same as the first application. Herbert J rejected a claim for default permission on the grounds that returning the application constitutes a 'decision' being made within the eight week period. The section is designed to assert the primacy of the board's decision as the appellate body in order to prevent a situation arising whereby the same issues were being considered at the same time by the planning authority and by the board in circumstances which could give rise to differing conclusions. Herbert J held that the board was not acting *ultra vires* in refusing to consider the second application.

**[4.28]** The doctrine of *res judicata* may also be relevant in cases where the board has either made its decision, dismissed the appeal or, indeed, where the applicant withdraws the appeal from the board.[52] In *Athlone Woollen Mills Co Ltd v Athlone Urban District Council*,[53] the applicant's permission was granted by the planning authority in the first instance and subsequently by the Minister on appeal. The grant of permission contained some onerous conditions which would have allowed the applicant to make a claim for compensation. However, the applicant allowed the time limit for submission of its claim for compensation to expire. In an attempt to keep the matter alive the applicant sought to revive the permission by lodging an identical claim for planning permission. The second identical application was rejected both by the planning authority and by the Minister. Both had relied on the doctrine of *res judicata* and having already refused permission for the proposed development in the first application, the board and the Minister refused to accept the subsequent identical application in the absence of any change of circumstances. Gavin Duffy J summed the matter up as follows:

> In my opinion, the grant of a special permission (with or without conditions) by a planning authority, or its grant as passed by the Minister on appeal, involves the exercise of limited powers of a judicial nature, so that the decision is properly described as a judicial decision pronounced by a judicial tribunal, as those terms are understood in relation to the doctrine of res judicata. I am of the opinion that the doctrine of res judicata with the consequent estoppel applies.

This case may be distinguished from the judgment in *O'Dea v The Minister for Local Government and Dublin County Council*,[54] where Dixon J held that the doctrine of *res judicata* did not apply to the facts of that case in which the two planning applications were not identical, but were entirely of a different kind. The two applications were not merely the same applications in a different guise.

## Rules and procedures in relation to appeals and referrals

**[4.29]** Part IV, Ch III of PDA 2000 (as amended) sets out the rules and procedures for making an appeal. Chapter III applies to all appeals and referrals to the board[55] and, to

---

52. PDA 2000, s 37(5)(a).
53. *Athlone Woollen Mills Co Ltd v Athlone Urban District Council* [1950] 1 IR1.
54. *O'Dea v The Minister for Local Government and Dublin County Council* [1991] 91 ILTR 169.
55. PDA 2000, s 125(a) as substituted by PD(SI)A 2006, s 20.

the extent provided, to applications made to the board under s 37(e) and to any other matter with which the board may be concerned.[56] Chapter III does not apply where an appeal is taken by the local authority to the board in circumstances where an owner or occupier of land, not forming a public road or place, has unreasonably, in the view of the local authority, withheld consent to allow the local authority to place, construct or lay cables, wires or pipelines (including waterpipes, sewers or drains) and ancillary apparatus on, under or over land or where the said owner or occupier has refused to allow the local authority to inspect, repair, alter, renew or remove any such cables, wires or pipelines.[57]

## Time limits within which Board must make its decision

**[4.30]** It is the duty of the board to determine appeals and referrals as expeditiously as may be and to take all steps that are open to it to ensure, as far as is practicable, that there are no unavoidable delays at any stage.[58] It is the objective of the board to ensure that every appeal or referral is determined within a period of 18 weeks, beginning on the date of receipt by the board of the appeal or referral or, within such other period as the Minister may prescribe, either generally or in respect of a particular class or classes of appeals or referrals.[59]

**[4.31]** The reference to 18 weeks in s 126 is construed as a reference to 14 weeks where leave to appeal is granted to a person or persons who have an interest in land adjoining the land in respect of which the permission has been granted.[60]

**[4.32]** The statutory provisions say no more than it is the duty of the board to ensure that appeals and referrals are disposed of as expeditiously as may be and, for that purpose, to take all such steps as are open to it to ensure that, insofar as is practicable, there are no avoidable delays at any stage in the determination of appeals and referrals.[61] The provisions of s 126(1) are aspirational and when they are combined with s 126(2), which acknowledges the 18 week time limit for making decisions on appeals and referrals and states that if the decision is not made it may be made within such other period as the Minister may prescribe either generally or in respect of a particular class or classes of appeals or referrals, it can be seen that the concept of a time limit in which the board must make its decision on appeals is an elastic time limit which has a starting point but which is more or less without a finishing point.

## Notice of postponement

**[4.33]** The Board, on its own initiative, where it appears to it that it would not be possible or appropriate, because of particular circumstances of an appeal or referral or

---

56. PDA 2000, s 125(b) as substituted by PD(SI)A 2006, s 20.
57. PDA 2000, s 125(b) and PDA 2000, s 182(4)(b).
58. PDA 2000, s 126(1).
59. PDA 2000, s 126(2)(a)&(b).
60. PDA 2000, s 37(6)(h).
61. PDA 2000, s 126(1).

because of the number of appeals and referrals which have been submitted to the board, to determine the appeal or referral within the 18-week period or indeed within the period prescribed by regulation by the Minister, shall by notice in writing served upon the parties to the appeal or referral before the expiration of the 18 weeks, inform the parties of reasons why it would not be possible or appropriate to determine the appeal or referral and specify the day when the board intends that that appeal or referral will be determined. A notice of postponement is also served on persons who have made submissions or observations to the board but where the notice extending the 18-week period is served, the board shall take all necessary steps to ensure that the appeal or referral is determined before the date specified in its notice.[62]

## Minister's entitlement to vary the time limit

**[4.34]** The Minister is permitted to vary the 18-week period by regulations, either generally or in respect of particular classes of appeals or referrals where it appears to him to be necessary by virtue of exceptional circumstances to do so, and so long as such regulations are in force, the section shall be construed and shall have effect in accordance therewith. The regulations will replace the 18-week time limit for the period specified. Apart from the Minister's right to vary the 18-week time period by regulation in the circumstances set out above the Minister may also extend the 18-week time period by prescription. Since there was no provision for a default decision in the event of An Bord Pleanála failing to meet its time limit of 18 weeks and since the time can, in any case, be extended on notice to the parties, inevitably lengthy delays do occur from time to time. The Minister, where he considers it to be necessary to ensure expediency, in relation to appeals and referrals which deal with developments which are of strategic, economic or social importance to the State, may give a direction to the board to give priority to such class of developments.

## Provisions as to the making of appeals and referrals

**[4.35]** An appeal or referral shall:

(a) be made in writing,

(b) state the name and address of the appellant or person making the appeal or referral, and the person, if any, acting on this or her behalf,[63]

(c) state the subject matter of the appeal or referral,

(d) state in full the grounds of appeal or referral and the reasons, considerations and arguments upon which they are based,

---

62. PDA 2000, s 126(3)(a) and (b).
63. See *O'Connor v An Bord Pleanála* [2008] IEHC 13 (24 January 2008) *per* Finlay Geoghegan J where it was decided that the information, in this case the address, can be contained within a series of documents and it can be submitted in an informal manner. It does not have to appear on the notice of appeal provided it appears on some other document lodged with the board.

(e) in the case of an appeal under s 37 by a person who made submissions and observations in accordance with the permission regulations, be accompanied by the acknowledgement by the planning authority of receipt of the submission or observation made,

(f) be accompanied by such fee (if any) as may be payable in respect of such appeal or referral in accordance with s 144 (as amended) and s 37(6),[64]

(g) be made within the period specified for making the appeal or referral.[65]

[4.36] PDA 2000, s 144(1), as amended by PD(A)A 2010, s 44(1), 44(1A)(a) to (j) and 44(1B), which amendments allow the board to determine fees to be charged in relation to any of the matters set out in s 144(1A):

(1A) The matters in relation to which the Board may determine fees under subsection (1) are:

(a) an appeal or referral;

(b) an application to the Board for any strategic infrastructure development or an application for leave to appeal under section 37(6)(a);

(c) an application for a consultation under section 37B, 181C, or 182E or under section 47B of the Act of 2001;

(d) a request under section 146B;

(e) a request for a written opinion on the information to be contained in an environmental impact assessment under section 173(3), under section 39 of the Act of 2001 or under section 50 of the Roads Act 1993;

(f) an application for leave to apply for substitute consent or an application for substitute consent under Part XA;

(g) submission of an environmental impact statement in accordance with a request by the Board to furnish same;

(h) submission of a Natura impact statement in accordance with a request by the Board to furnish same;

(i) request for an oral hearing under section 134 or 177Q; and

(j) making a submission or observation under section 37E, 37F, 130, 135(2B)(e), 146B, 146C, 146D, 175, 181A, 182A, 182C, 217(B), or 226, section 51 of the Roads Act 1993, section 40 (other than by persons required to be served with a notice under section 40(1)(d)), section 41, or section 47D of the Act of 2001 or making an objection under section 48 of the Roads Act 1993 (other than by persons on whom notice is served under section 48(b)).

[4.37] Where a person, being a person who has an interest in land adjoining the land in respect of which permission is granted, applies to the board for leave to appeal a

---

64. PDA 2000, s 37(6), as amended by PD(A)A 2002, s 10, allows an adjoining landowner to appeal a decision even though he/she has not made any submissions or observations provided the appeal is lodged within four weeks of the decision and provided the appropriate fee is paid.

65. PDA 2000, s 127(1)(a)–(g).

**[4.38]** decision of the planning authority under the section, and where leave to appeal is granted by the board, the applicant must lodge his appeal within two weeks from the date of receipt of the decision to grant or refuse application to make the appeal.[66]

**[4.38]** If the appeal does not comply with the requirements above it will be invalid. The requirements (a)–(g) apply to persons making either an appeal or a referral and they apply whether or not there is a request for an oral hearing.[67]

**[4.39]** The decision in *O'Reilly Brothers (Wicklow) Limited v Wicklow County Council*[68] would seem to indicate that in some cases substantial compliance may be sufficient. In that case, it was held that although the quality of the documentation submitted was 'deplorable' it was possible to discover the reasons, considerations and arguments within this.

> That was so because the Board was prepared, patiently and conscientiously to carry out a diligence search of the 'rag-tag' bundle of documents submitted to it by the Council – *per* Quirke J.

An Bord Pleanála, very fairly, argued against the necessity to comply unreservedly with the provisions of s 127(1)(a)–(g) on the basis that public participation should not be discouraged in the referral process and allowance should be made for the fact that members of the public may not have expertise in providing technical documentation and dealing with technical terminology. Members of the public should be allowed to present their case in straightforward and sensible terms, as long as the reasons, considerations and arguments can be understood albeit with some difficulty.

**[4.40]** See also *Lennon v Limerick County Council*,[69] where it was held that the person named in the appeal or referral must be the person who is entitled to make the appeal or referral and not the agent. The named party, therefore, cannot be a planning consultant, engineer or architect though one of those may have prepared the documentation. The agent's principal must always be the named party and must be disclosed as such. Although it was argued in this case that the consulting engineers had a potential beneficial interest in the planning application because they prepared the documentation and were being paid a fee which was contingent on the planning permission being granted, Laffoy J held that the consulting engineer retained by the applicant to obtain planning permission could not attribute to himself the interests of the applicant for permission.

**[4.41]** PDA 2000, s 127(1)(b) reads as follows:

> State the name and address of the appellant or person making the referral and of the person, if any, acting on his or her behalf.

Both names must be given where there is an agent.

---

66. PDA 2000, s 37(6)(f).
67. PDA 2000, s 37(2)(a) and (b).
68. *O'Reilly Brothers (Wicklow) Ltd v Wicklow County Council* [2006] IEHC 363 *per* Quirke J.
69. *Lennon v Limerick County Council* [2006] IEHC 112 *per* Laffoy J.

**[4.42]** In *Kenney Construction v An Bord Pleanála*,[70] Finlay Geoghegan J held that the requirement that the address of the appellant must be stated in the appeal is mandatory and not discretionary. Nevertheless, the learned judge was satisfied that the requirement to state the address of the appellant was satisfied where, although the address was not stated in the letter of appeal, it was correctly stated in a letter from the board which acknowledged receipt of the appeal and as such amounted to compliance with s 127(1)(b).

**[4.43]** In *O'Connor v An Bord Pleanála*,[71] in considering the requirement for accuracy as to the name of the appellant or the person making the referral, O'Neill J held that the mis-description of a third party appellant by the omission of the word 'limited' did not render the appeal invalid.

**[4.44]** The planning authority is required to acknowledge receipt in writing of submissions or observations as soon as may be.[72]

**[4.45]** In *Murphy v Cobh Town Council and Anor*,[73] the planning authority's letter acknowledging receipt of submissions and observations was not in fact lodged with the appeal. The appellant mistakenly lodged another letter of similar layout which letter indicated unequivocally that submissions and observations had been made. It was held by MacMenamin J that no prejudice arose as a result of this save of a technical or trivial nature. The judge ruled that the *de minimus* rule should apply and the second letter should be accepted as it could be readily inferred that submissions or observations had been made.

**[4.46]** An appellant will not generally be entitled to elaborate in writing or make further submissions in writing in relation to the grounds of appeal or to submit further grounds of appeal and the appellant is given one chance and one chance only to comply with the provisions of PDA 2000, s 127(1) and to submit documents, particulars or other information relating to the appeal or referral as the applicant may consider necessary. Any documents or particulars so submitted must be submitted within the time limit (usually four weeks), and if submitted outside the time limit, they will not be considered.[74]

**[4.47]** The appeal or referral must be sent to the board by prepaid post or left with an employee of the board at the offices of the board during office hours or by such other means as may be prescribed. If appeal or referral documents are sent by post they must reach the offices of the board before expiration of the four week time limit and if delivered, it is necessary that they be left with an employee of the board personally. It is not sufficient that any employee may subsequently come into possession of the appeal

---

70. *Kenney Construction v An Bord Pleanála* [2005] IEHC 30 (10 February 2005).
71. *O'Connor v An Bord Pleanála* [2008] IEHC 13 (24 January 2008).
72. PDR 2001, art 29(2) and, in particular, see PDR 2001, Sch 3, Form 3 as amended by PDR 2006 which is the prescribed form of acknowledgment of receipt of submissions and observations.
73. *Murphy v Cobh Town Council and Anor* [2006] IEHC 324, *per* McMenamin J.
74. PDA 2000, s 37(3) and (4).

documents.[75] The requirement contained in PDA 2000, s 127(1)(g) to make an appeal or referral within the relevant period is usually strictly construed. Posting an appeal or referral to An Bord Pleanála towards the end of the four week period for appeal can be risky even if it is sent by registered or recorded post. The appeal must be received by the board within the appropriate time limit. It is not sufficient to say, for example, that the appeal was sent by registered post to An Bord Pleanála one week before the expiration of the period. If the appeal is not received within the appropriate period the appeal will be declared invalid.

**[4.48]** In *Graves v An Bord Pleanála*,[76] the appropriate period by which the appeal was to be lodged by the appellant was 18 December 1996. The appeal was delivered to the board on 18 December 1996 which was a Saturday. The offices were closed and no employees were present. It was held that the appeal was not made in time and this decision illustrates the importance of strict compliance with the provisions relating to the making of appeals which provisions are mandatory and not discretionary in nature. In *Graves*, because the appeal had not been left with an employee of An Bord Pleanála within office hours, it had not been validly made within the appropriate period.

## Submission of documents, etc by planning authorities[77]

**[4.49]** In the case of an appeal under PDA 2000, s 37,[78] the planning authority must within two weeks, commencing the day on which a copy of the appeal or referral is sent to it, submit to the board the following documents:

(i) A copy of the planning application concerned and any drawings, maps, particulars, evidence, environmental impact statement, other written study or further information received or obtained by it from the applicant in accordance with regulations made under the Act;

(ii) A copy of any submission or observation made in accordance with regulations under the Act in respect of the planning application;

(iii) A copy of any report prepared by or for the planning authority in relation to the planning application; and

(iv) A copy of the decision of the planning authority in respect of the planning application and a copy of the notification of the decision given to the applicant.

The documents listed at (i)–(iv) are the documents which must be submitted by the planning authority to the board in the case of an appeal under s 37. In any other appeal or referral, any information or documents in the planning authority's possession relevant to the matter must be submitted by the planning authority to the board.[79]

---

75. PDA 2000, s 127(5).
76. *Graves v An Bord Pleanála* [1997] 2 IR 2005.
77. PDA 2000, s 128(1)&(2) as amended by PD(SI)A 2006, s 21.
78. Note PDA 2000, s 37(1), (4)(c)–(f) inclusive as inserted by PD(SI)A 2006, s 10, also PDA 2000, s 37(6)(a) as amended by PD(A)A 2002, s 10 and PDA 2000, s 37(6)(d)(i) as amended by PD(A)A 2010, s 10.
79. PDA 2000, s 128(1) as amended by PD(SI)A 2006, s 21.

**[4.50]** The requirements of PDA 2000, s 128 are mandatory. In *McAnenley v An Bord Pleanála and Monaghan County Council*,[80] Kelly J held, on the facts of the case, that there had been substantial non-compliance with the requirement that the planning authority must submit all documents to the board. In fact, a copy of the notification of decision to grant planning permission had been forwarded to the board but the copy of the decision of the planning authority to grant planning permission was not forwarded to the board. Kelly J directed that the decision of the board be quashed and that the matter be remitted to the board to be dealt with afresh.

**[4.51]** Where a copy of an appeal or referral is sent to a planning authority by the board, the planning authority, as soon as may be after receipt of the copy of the appeal, is required to notify any person who made a submission or observation in accordance with the regulations in relation to the planning application in respect of which an appeal has been made.[81]

**[4.52]** The notice shall:

(a) Specify the reference number of the board in respect of the appeal;

(b) Specify the date on which the appeal was received by the board;

(c) Specify that a copy of the appeal is available for inspection or purchase for a fee not exceeding the reasonable cost of making a copy during office hours at the offices of the planning authority; and

(d) State that submissions and observations in relation to the appeal may be made in writing to the board within the appropriate period and on payment of the appropriate fee.[82]

A planning authority must include, in its weekly list, a list of appeals sent to it by the board. The list must be available not later than the third working day following a particular week.[83]

**[4.53]** The Board is required, not later than the third working day following the particular week, to make available a list of:

(a) The appeals and referrals received by the board;

(b) The appeals and referrals determined, dismissed or withdrawn or in relation to which a direction is given by the board pursuant to s 139 of the Act;

(c) The applications for approval under ss 175(3) and 215 of the Act received by the board; and

---

80. *McAnenley v An Bord Pleanála and Monaghan County Council* [2002] 2 IR 763.
81. PDR 2001, art 69(1).
82. PDR 2001, art 69(2).
83. PDR 2001, art 72.

(d) The applications for approval under ss 175(3) and 215 of the Act determined or otherwise disposed of by the board during that week.[84]

Where a planning authority is notified by the board of an appeal the planning authority shall, as soon as may be, notify the applicant for permission[85] and any person who made a submission or observation on the appeal.[86]

## Availability of documents relating to appeals and referrals

[4.54] The planning authority is required to make available documents relating to an appeal/referral for inspection or purchase at a fee not exceeding the reasonable cost of making a copy during office hours at its offices until the matter has been disposed of.[87]

## Submissions or observations by other parties

[4.55] The Board is required to give a copy of an appeal or referral to each other party.[88] Each other party can make submissions or observations in writing to the board in relation to the appeal or referral within a period of four weeks commencing on the day on which a copy of the appeal or referral was sent to that party by the board, and any submission or observation received by the board after the expiration of the four-week period shall not be considered.[89] If no submissions or observations have been received from a party within the four-week period under the terms of s 129, the board may determine the appeal or referral without further notice to that party.[90] Any submission or observations submitted under s 129 cannot be elaborated upon outside the four-week period.[91] A comprehensive definition of 'party to an appeal or referral' is set out below:[92]

(a) the appellant,

(b) the applicant for any permission in relation to which an appeal is made by another person (other than a person acting on behalf of the appellant),

(c) in the case of a referral under s 5, the person making the referral, and any other person notified under sub-s (2) of that section,

(d) in the case of a referral under s 34(5), the applicant for the permission which was granted,

---

84. PDR 2001, art 70. Note: art 72 has been substantially amended by provisions of art 14 and a sizeable volume of information must be contained in the board's weekly list as a means of keeping the public informed. For further details see PDR 2006, art 14(1)–(10) inclusive.
85. PDR 2001, art 71.
86. PDR 2001, art 69.
87. PDR 2001, art 68 as amended by PDR 2006, art 13.
88. PDA 2000, s 129(1).
89. PDA 2000, s 129(2)(a) and (b).
90. PDA 2000, s 129(3).
91. PDA 2000, s 129(4).
92. PDA 2000, interpretation s 2(1) as amended by the PD(A)A 2002, s 6(a).

(e) in the case of a referral under s 37(5), the person who made the application for permission which was returned by the planning authority,

(f) any person served or issued by a planning authority with a notice or order, or copy thereof, under ss 44, 45, 46, 88 and 207,

(ff) in the case of a referral under s 57(8), the person making the referral,

(g) in the case of a referral under s 96(5), a prospective party to an agreement under s 96(2),

(h) in the case of an appeal under s 169, the development agency,

(i) in the case of a referral under s 193, the person by whom the application for permission for erection of a new structure was made,

(j) the applicant for a licence under s 254 in relation to which an appeal is made by another person (other than a person acting on behalf of the appellant),

And 'party' shall be construed accordingly.

## Submissions or observations other than by parties to appeals or referrals

[4.56] Submissions and observations can be made by persons other than parties to the appeal.[93] Such parties are referred to as 'observers' and observers may make submissions and observations in writing within a period of four weeks. The submissions or observations must state the name and address of the person making them and the name and address of any person acting on his or her behalf. It must also state the subject matter of the submission or observation and furnish full reasons, considerations and agreements on which the submission or observation is based. The submission or observations must be accompanied by a fee (if any) as may be payable in accordance with s 144.

[4.57] Submissions and observations which do not comply with the above requirements shall be deemed to be invalid.[94]

[4.58] The four-week period runs from different starting points as follows:

(a) Where a notice of receipt of an environmental impact statement is published in accordance with regulations under PDA 2000, s 172(5) the period of four weeks begins on the day of publication of any notice required under those regulations;

(b) Where a notice is required by the board to be given under PDA 2000, s 142(4), the period of four weeks begins on the day of publication of the required notice;[95]

---

93. PDA 2000, s 130(1)–(5) inclusive. Note: PDA 2000, s 130(5) is amended by PD(A)A 2010, s 42.
94. PDA 2000, s 130(1)(c) and (2).
95. PDA 2000, s 142(4) provides that the board may require a party to an appeal or referral to give public notice as the board may specify and, in particular, may require notice to be given at the site or by publication in a newspaper circulating in the district in which the land or structure to which the appeal or referral relates is situate.

(c) In any other appeal under PDA 2000, the period of four weeks begins on the day of receipt of the appeal by the board, or, where there is more than one appeal against the decision of the planning authority on the day on which the board last receives an appeal; or

(d) In the case of a referral, the period of four weeks begins on the day of receipt by the board of the referral.[96]

[4.59] Observers who make submissions or observations to the board under s 130 are not entitled to elaborate in writing upon the submissions or observations or make further submissions or observations in writing in relation to the appeal or other matter and any such elaboration, submissions or observations that are received by the board shall not be considered by it.[97] The prohibitions relating to receiving submissions or observations within certain time limits and the prohibition against making further submissions or observations outside those time limits do not apply to submissions or observations made by a Member State of the European Communities or other State which is a party to the Transboundary Convention, arising from consultation which is subject to the EIA Directive[98] or Transboundary Convention, as the case may be, in relation to the effects on the environment of the development to which the appeal under PDA 2000, s 37 relates.[99]

[4.60] The time limits are prescribed by PDA 2000, s 130(3), and failure to comply with any of the conditions imposed by PDA 2000, s 130 will render the submissions invalid, subject, however, to circumstances where the board requests further submissions[100] or requests a document or information[101] or where an oral hearing is held.[102]

## Power of Board to request submissions or observations

[4.61] The Board may, in the case of an appeal or referral, where it is appropriate in the interests of justice, request (a) a party to an appeal or referral; or (b) any person who has made submissions or observations to the board in relation to the appeal or referral; or (c) any other person or body, to make submissions in relation to any matter which has arisen in relation to the appeal.[103] If such a request is made, notice must be served on the person requested to submit to the board submissions or observations in relation to the matter in question within a period of not less than two weeks and not more than four weeks from the date of service of the notice. If no further submissions or observations are received after the four-week period, the board may proceed to determine the appeal or referral.

---

96. PDA 2000, s 130(3)(a), (b), (c) and (d).
97. PDA 2000, s 129(4).
98. EIA Directive, 85/337/EEC.
99. PDA 2000, s 130(5) as amended by PD(A)A 2010, s 42.
100. PDA 2000, s 131.
101. PDA 2000, s 132.
102. PDA 2000, s 134 as substituted by PD(SI)A 2006, s 22.
103. PDA 2000, s 131.

There have been occasions when parties have been given less than two weeks to furnish their submissions and observations and these have received judicial attention.

**[4.62]** In *Ryanair v An Bord Pleanála*,[104] the applicant was requested to make submissions within 11 days from the date of receipt of the notice. The applicant did make the submissions within the 11-day period but later challenged the board's decision on the basis that a minimum of two weeks and a maximum of four weeks should have been offered. Ó Caoimh J refused the plaintiff's application for leave to appeal because it was clear from the facts that this non-compliance did not preclude the plaintiff from making the required submissions within the 11-day time limit.

**[4.63]** In *Hickey v An Bord Pleanála*,[105] Smyth J refused leave although the plaintiff had been given 13 and not 14 days in which to make her submissions and observations. In refusing leave to appeal, Smyth J ruled that there had been substantial compliance. The effect of s 131 is far-reaching in the sense that it allows submissions and observations to be sought from a party who is not a party to the appeal but who has already made submissions or from any person or body irrespective of whether or not they have made submissions. The section requires the board to be of the opinion that in the particular circumstances of an appeal or referral it is appropriate in the interests of justice to request submissions and observations.

**[4.64]** In *State (Havarty) v An Bord Pleanála*,[106] Murphy J noted that there could be exceptional circumstances where '... further communications from the developer extended the original submissions so radically as to constitute a different or additional case and in that event natural justice may well require An Bord Pleanála to postpone its decision until it had afforded interested parties an opportunity of commenting upon the revised submission'. The application in this case was an attempt to have the board's decision quashed because it had failed to provide the appellants with all of the submissions of the developer. In the circumstances, Murphy J rejected the application on the grounds that the requirements of fairness of procedure had been satisfied and the submissions in question had not radically altered the nature of the proposal.

## Power of Board to require submission of documents, etc

**[4.65]** The Board is permitted by PDA 2000, s 132 to request documents, particulars or other information as may be necessary for the purpose of enabling it to determine an appeal or referral and to serve notice requiring the submission of documents, etc, in much the same terms as apply in PDA 2000, s 131. The section also provides that nothing in the section will be construed as affecting any other power conferred on the board under the Act to require submission of further or additional information or documents. The section is clear in emphasising that any request for further documents, etc, is entirely at the board's 'absolute discretion'.

---

104. *Ryanair v An Bord Pleanála* [2004] 2 IR 334.
105. *Hickey v An Bord Pleanála* (unreported, 10 June 2004) HC *per* Smyth J.
106. *State (Havarty) v An Bord Pleanála* [1987] IR 485 *per* Murphy J.

## Power of Board where notice is served under ss 131 and 132

[4.66] Where a notice has been served under s 131 or 132, the board, at any time after the expiration of the period specified in the notice, may, having considered any submissions, observations, document, particulars or other information submitted by the person on whom the notice has been served, without further notice to that person determine or, in the case of a notice served under s 132, dismiss the appeal or referral.[107]

## Oral hearings of appeals and referrals and applications

[4.67] A party to an appeal or referral or any person who makes a submission or observation on appeal (but this does not include an observer unless that observer makes his request within the time limit for making submissions and observations) may request an oral hearing on payment of a fee.[108] The Board has 'absolute discretion' as to whether or not to hold such an oral hearing. The wording of the section is so clear that it is almost certain that no refusal of the board to have an oral hearing could be challenged. Furthermore, in refusing an oral hearing the board is not required to state reasons as to why it may have decided not to hold an oral hearing. The Local Government (Planning and Development) Act 1963 provided that a person bringing a planning appeal had a right to an oral hearing. That right was cancelled by the Local Government (Planning and Development) Act 1976 and the change was constitutionally challenged in *Finnegan v An Bord Pleanála*.[109] O'Higgins CJ had this to say:

> As to section 16 the Plaintiff contends that giving the discretion to the Board as to whether an appeal should be heard orally or otherwise is an unconstitutional interference with certain constitutional rights of citizens which he did not clearly specify. His complaint appears to have been that as such a citizen bringing a planning appeal under the 1963 Act had an absolute right to an oral hearing and this change in the law was an unconstitutional deprivation of a right. In the opinion of the Court this submission is fallacious. It is open to the Oireachtas in providing for this type of appeal to alter the law in the manner provided in the section.

PDA 2000, s 134 has been substituted and s 134A inserted by s 22 of the PD(SI)A 2006 and the main change is the inclusion of references to strategic infrastructure applications. Section 134A(1) reads:

> The Board may in its absolute discretion, hold an oral hearing of an appeal, a referral under s 5 or an application under s 37E.

Section 134A(1) makes it quite clear that the board's absolute discretion in deciding whether or not to hold oral hearings is extended to strategic infrastructure projects. The right to make a request for an oral hearing remains but the request must be accompanied by the appropriate fee and if not so accompanied the request will not be considered by

---

107. PDA 2000, s 133.
108. PDA 2000, s 134 as substituted by PD(SI)A 2006, s 22 and PDA 2000, s 135 as amended by PD(SI)A 2006, s 23(a) and (b).
109. *Finnegan v An Bord Pleanála* [1979] ILRM 134.

the board.[110] The fee payable, as this book goes to press, is €75.[111] The Board's fees are currently set out in SI 525/2001. It is a useful instrument as it provides a note of all planning fees payable.

[4.68] A request for an oral hearing by an appellant must be made within four weeks from the date of the decision, that is to say, the date of the notification of grant of permission as opposed to the notification of decision to grant permission. A request for an oral hearing by a party who is not the appellant must be made within the four-week period from when the board sent a copy of the appeal or referral to persons entitled to make submissions under PDA 2000, s 129(2)(a). There is no requirement to make the request for an oral hearing at the same time as the appeal. Both applications can be made separately but clearly the appeal must pre-empt any application for oral hearing. Once the appeal is lodged within the four-week period the application for oral hearing may be lodged with the appeal or at any time from the date of the lodgement of the appeal up to the last day of the four weeks from the date of grant of permission.

[4.69] If the board refuses a request to hold an oral hearing it will serve notice of that decision on:

(a) the person who requested the hearing and on each other party to the appeal or referral as appropriate to include, where appropriate, the applicant under s 37E; and

(b) each person who has made submissions or observations to the board in relation to the appeal, referral or application (not being the person who was the requester).[112]

This section does not provide a time limit in which the board is required to make any decision as to whether or not to hold an oral hearing. A request for an oral hearing may be withdrawn at any time and if withdrawn notice is served by the relevant parties on the board.[113] The Board may hold an oral hearing, in its absolute discretion, if it considers it necessary or expedient for the purpose of making a determination in respect of any of its functions under the Act and if the board decides to hold an oral hearing it will consider the report and any recommendations of the person holding the oral hearing before making its determination.[114]

## *Supplemental provisions relating to oral hearings*[115]

[4.70] The Board or an employee of the board duly authorised by the board, may assign a person to conduct an oral hearing of an appeal or referral on behalf of the board. The

---

110. PDA 2000, s 134(2)(a) and (b).
111. PDA 2000, s 144 which allows the board to determine fees that may be charged subject to the approval of the Minister. Section 144(1) has been substituted by s 144(1)(a) and (b) inserted by PD(A)A 2010, s 44.
112. PDA 2000, s 134(3)(a) and (b).
113. PDA 2000, s 134(4)(a) and (b).
114. PDA 2000, s 134A(1)(2) and (3) as inserted by PD(SI)A 2006, s 22.
115. PDA 2000, s 135(1)–(8) inclusive as substituted by PD(SI)A 2006, s 23.

conduct of the hearing is left to the discretion of the person conducting the oral hearing. The oral hearing shall be conducted as expeditiously as possible and without undue formality. However, the board may give a direction to the person conducting the oral hearing that he or she shall require persons intending to appear at the hearing to submit to him or her, in writing and in advance of the hearing, the points or a summary of the arguments they propose to make at the hearing; where such a direction is given that person shall comply with it.[116]

[4.71] Additional directions which may be given by the board and the manner in which they may be given by the board and recorded are dealt with in PDA 2000, s 135AB–135AD inclusive as inserted by PD(A)A 2010, s 43(b). The inserted sections read as follows:

> (2AB) The Board may in its absolute discretion, following a recommendation in relation to the matter from a person assigned under section 146, give a direction to a person assigned to the conduct of an oral hearing that he or she shall only allow points or arguments in relation to specified matters during the oral hearing.
>
> (2AC) Where a direction is given by the Board under subsection (2AB), the person to whom it is given shall comply with it (and accordingly, is enabled to make such a requirement) unless that person forms the opinion that it is necessary, in the interests of observing fair procedures, to allow a point or an argument to be made during the oral hearing in relation to matters not specified in the direction.
>
> (2AD) The Board shall give a notice of its direction under subsection (2AB) to –
>
> (i) each party, in the case of an appeal or referral,
>
> (ii) the applicant and planning authority, or in the case of an application under this Act for a railway order under the Act of 2001, or for approval under section 51 of the Roads Act 1993, and
>
> (iii) each person who has made objections, submissions or observations so the Board in the case of an appeal, referral or application.

(2AE) provides:

> The points or summary of the arguments that a person intending to appear at the oral hearing shall submit to the person conducting the hearing, where a direction has been given under subsections (2A) and (2AB), shall be limited to points or arguments in relation to matters specified in the direction under subsection (2AB).[117]

[4.72] The person conducting the hearing (known as an 'inspector'):

(a) shall decide the order of appearance of persons at the hearing,

(b) shall permit any person to appear in person or to be represented by another person,

---

116. PDA 2000, s 135(2A).
117. Section 135(2AE) as inserted by PD(A)A 2010, s 43(b).

(c) may limit the time within which each person may make points or arguments (including arguments in refutation or arguments made by others at the hearing) or question the evidence of others, at the hearing,

(d) may refuse to allow the making of a point or an argument if:

    (i) the point or summary of the argument has not been submitted in advance to the person in accordance with the requirement made pursuant to a direction given under sub-s (2A),

    (ii) the point or argument is not relevant to the subject matter of the hearing, or

    (iii) it is considered necessary so as to avoid undue repetition of the same point of argument,

may refuse to allow the making of a point or an argument in relation to the matter where

(dd) may refuse to allow the making of a point or an argument in relation to any matter where:

    (i) a direction has been given under sub-s (2AB) and the matter is not specified in the direction, and

    (ii) he or she has not formed the opinion referred to in sub-s (2AC).[118]

(e) may hear a person other than a person who has made submissions or observations to the board in relation to the subject matter of the hearing if it is considered appropriate in the interests of justice to allow the person to be heard.

If a person conducting an oral hearing requires an officer of a planning authority or a local authority to give information in relation to the appeal application or referral which is reasonably required it shall be the duty of the local authority/planning authority officer to comply with that requirement.[119]

**[4.73]** A person conducting an oral hearing would need to take care in exercising the imposition of time limits or refusal to make certain arguments to ensure that the ordinary rules of constitutional justice, natural justice and fair procedures have not been infringed. Clearly, where legal issues arise at an oral hearing and if a witness or a person presenting a case is prevented from elaborating on submissions or making legal points they should register an objection as failure to do so could prejudice a subsequent judicial review application on the basis that the applicant might not be able to establish that there were substantial grounds.

**[4.74]** The person conducting the oral hearing may take evidence on oath or affirmation and a person giving evidence at any such hearing shall be entitled to the same immunities and privileges as if he or she were a witness before the High Court.[120]

---

118. Section 135(2B)(dd) has been inserted by PD(A)A 2010, s 43(c).
119. PDA 2000, s 135(3). Note also that PDA 2000, s 135(1)–(3) were substituted by PD(SI)A 2006, s 23(a).
120. PDA 2000, s 135(4).

**[4.75]** The Board in relation to oral hearings may, by giving notice in that behalf in writing to any person, require that person to do either or both of the following:

(i) To attend at such time and place as is specified in the notice to give evidence in relation to any matter in question at the hearing;

(ii) To produce any books, deeds, contracts, accounts, vouchers, maps, plans, documents or other information in his or her possession, custody or control which relate to any such matter.[121]

This power to compel attendance by summons to a witness requires that the board shall pay or tender to any person whose attendance is required such reasonable subsistence for travelling expenses to be determined by the board in accordance with standard rates applicable to senior planning authority officials. Expenses of attendance may also be claimed by a witness and in default of their being paid are recoverable as a simple contract debt in any court of competent jurisdiction.[122]

**[4.76]** Any person who is summonsed but who refuses or wilfully neglects to attend or who wilfully alters, suppresses, conceals or destroys any document or other information to which the notice relates or who, having so attended, refuses to give evidence or refuses or wilfully fails to produce any document or other information to which the notice relates shall be guilty of an offence.[123] Furthermore, where any person (a) wilfully gives evidence which is material to the oral hearing and which he or she knows to be false or does not believe to be true, (b) by act or omission, obstructs or hinders the person conducting the oral hearing in the performance of his or her functions, (c) refuses to take an oath or to make an affirmation when legally required to do so by a person holding the oral hearing, (d) refuses to answer any question to which the person conducting an oral hearing may legally require an answer, (e) does or omits to do anything which if the inquiry had been by the High Court, would have been contempt of that court, that person shall be guilty of an offence.[124]

**[4.77]** An oral hearing may be heard either through the medium of English or Irish. Where an oral hearing relates to a development within the Gaeltacht, the hearing shall be conducted in Irish unless the parties agree that it should be conducted in English. If the oral hearing relates to a development outside the Gaeltacht, the hearing will be conducted in English unless the parties agree that it should be conducted in Irish.[125]

**[4.78]** The requirement that an oral hearing must be conducted in Irish, unless the parties agree otherwise, is a bad example of misusing legislation in an arbitrary manner to promote cultural and political aspirations as opposed to strict principles of planning. If, for example, the parties in a Gaeltacht area do not agree to conduct the hearing in

---

121. PDA 2000, s 135(5).
122. PDA 2000, s 135(5)(b).
123. PDA 2000, s 135(6) – see PDA 2000, s 156 as amended PD(A)A 2010, s 46 for specific penalties for infringement.
124. PDA 2000, s 135(7) – see PDA 2000, s 156 as amended PD(A)A 2010, s 46 for specific penalties for infringement.
125. PDA 2000, s 135(8).

English, the presumption is that the oral hearing will be conducted through the medium of Irish. Allowing for the fact that a survey conducted in 2002 concluded that only 9% of areas nominated as 'Gaeltacht' areas in fact qualify as Gaeltacht areas, this provision could produce unjust results. The provision should provide that if there is a dispute as to which language should be used in a Gaeltacht area, the oral hearing shall be conducted in both English and in Irish with interpreting services provided for and paid for by the State, assuming the State wishes to continue to enforce PDA 2000, s 135(8)(a)–(c).

[4.79] The 2007 annual report of An Bord Pleanála contained criticisms made by the chairman of the board, Mr John O'Connor, where he indicated that some lawyers in participating in oral hearings in planning cases were engaging in 'courtroom histrionics'. The chairman's comments in the board's 2007 annual report may be summarised by saying that it was the chairman's view that lawyers participating in oral hearings should concentrate on the substantive planning and environmental arguments for and against the development proposed. The chairman's comments are not wholly without merit.

[4.80] Commenting on chairman O'Connor's written remarks contained in the board's annual report Simons had this to say:

> There is, in my opinion, a danger that an over emphasis of avoiding 'undue formality' at oral hearings might detract attention from the fact that decisions of An Bord Pleanála can and do radically affect the rights of individuals. It is entirely legitimate, therefore, that lawyers should remind the person conducting the oral hearing of An Bord Pleanála's legal responsibilities, and to cite relevant legislation and case law. Moreover, the Courts have consistently indicated that an objector is required to raise before An Bord Pleanála any legal objection which he or she may subsequently wish to rely upon in judicial review proceedings. This, by definition, necessitates the making of detailed legal submissions at an oral hearing. Such submissions should not be regarded as a distraction from the substantive planning and environmental arguments for or against the development proposed, but should be seen as setting the context for the board's decision. An Bord Pleanála is an emanation of the State, and is thus required as a matter of EC law to give effect to the requirements of EC Directives, even if this necessitates dis-applying conflicting national legislation.
>
> Finally, the legal requirement for fair procedures will often necessitate the cross-examination of witnesses. This is especially so in the context of EIA development. In circumstances where the EIS documentation is prepared by experts engaged by the developer, it must be permissible to test the independence and robustness of the views expressed by those experts by way of cross-examination.[126]

---

126. *Per* Garrett Simons SC speaking at seminar on planning law organised by the School of Law, Trinity College, Dublin in December 2008. Mr Simons's points are entirely meritorious but on balance they do not address the 'courtroom histrionics' point made by Chairman O'Connor, which undeniably occur from time to time and are generally much lower down on the scale than citing case law, indulging in robust cross-examination or taking the necessary steps at the tribunal in order to lay the grounds for a possible subsequent judicial review.

**[4.81]** An appellant is prohibited from elaborating in writing upon his/her submissions or observations or from making further submissions or observations in writing to the board in relation to the appeal.[127] It should also be noted that, in general practice, parties to an appeal frequently submit written submissions in order to expedite the hearing. Frequently or, indeed, usually these written submissions tend to elaborate on the parties' grounds of appeal at an oral hearing. In practice, inspectors at an appeal tend to allow some latitude in elaboration contained in written submissions at an oral hearing. The question which must be asked is to what extent the appellant may elaborate on the grounds of appeal at an oral hearing. The matter has not been determined judicially, but it is likely that if an issue is raised that goes to the root of the board's jurisdiction the point must be entertained, notwithstanding that the issue was raised for the first time at the oral hearing.

**[4.82]** In *Keane v An Bord Pleanála*,[128] the applicants sought to amend their grounds of appeal in relation to planning matters. It was held that they could not add new grounds after the expiry of the appropriate period, namely, two months from the date on which the notification of grant of permission issued. If it were otherwise, it would allow the applicants to bring an amended case outside the period specified which, at the time that *Keane v An Bord Pleanála* was heard, was specified in the Local Government (Planning and Development) Act 1963. The prohibition against amending grounds applied only to planning matters but it did not apply to non-planning grounds which could be added as these were not caught by the planning statute. *Keane v An Bord Pleanála*[129] also correctly recognised that the inspector has discretion to abbreviate excessive arguments or submissions in the interests of justice. Oral hearings, though far less frequent now, have always been a productive source of litigation. It is probably the case that where legal issues arise at the oral hearing which require to be challenged, that challenge should be made before any decision is made by the board as failure to do so could imply that the plaintiff had waived his rights or that he was in some way acquiescent.

**[4.83]** In *Lancefort Ltd v An Bord Pleanála*,[130] the clear implication from that case is that an objector is bound to raise all legal issues at the oral hearing if he is not to prejudice any subsequent judicial review proceedings. In the *Lancefort* case, the applicant served proceedings on some of the mandatory parties after 5pm on the last day of the two-month period at a time when most offices and business were closed. The evidence showed that Lancefort Ltd was not in existence at the date when the decision to grant permission was made by An Bord Pleanála. The court held that while the two-month time limit must be strictly construed, nevertheless the legislation referred only to two months and, relying on the Interpretation Act 1937, s 11(h) the court held that the two-month limitation period must include the whole day since no contrary intention appears in the section. Lancefort had served the proceedings in the last seven hours of the two month period. Reference was made to comments of Murray CJ by Finlay

---

127. PDA 2000, s 130(4).
128. *Keane v An Bord Pleanála* (unreported, 23 May 2005) HC *per* Laffoy J.
129. *Keane v An Bord Pleanála* (unreported, 23 May 2005) HC *per* Laffoy J.
130. *Lancefort Ltd v An Bord Pleanála* [1998] 2 ILRM 401.

Geoghegan J in *Linehan v Cork County Council*[131] to the effect that the present legislation implies that an applicant cannot await the outcome of the decision of the board but if an applicant wishes to proceed with judicial review and if the applicant did not wish to prejudice his position by failing to act he should act immediately. Another case which supports the view that it may not be advisable to await the board's decision when considering a challenge by judicial review of something which occurred during the course of the oral hearing is *Sloan v An Bord Pleanála, Louth County Council and National Roads Authority*.[132] The applicant sought leave to judicially review a decision of the board to approve a road construction scheme. The application was made under s 50 of PDA 2000. The court, among other matters, decided to refuse relief because of delay. The applicant's complaint was less concerned with the decision of the board to confirm the road scheme, but rather with the refusal of the inspector to broaden the terms of the public inquiry during the course of same to allow for consideration of alternative routes. The court found that time had begun to run at the time the inspector announced his refusal and not when the scheme was confirmed by the board. As a subsidiary issue the court also found that where a major infrastructural project is the subject matter of a judicial review the application should be brought as soon as possible so as not to delay the works.

**[4.84]** In *Max Developments v An Bord Pleanála*,[133] the inspector in the course of the oral hearing agreed to adjourn the hearing to enable the applicant to apply to the High Court. The inspector disagreed with the applicant's argument that the development project exceeded the relevant threshold but he was happy to allow the matter go forward to the High Court. The applicant decided not to bring the application to the High Court at that time and, accordingly, the inspector continued the oral hearing. The oral hearing concluded and later a decision was made by An Bord Pleanála granting permission for the development of the roadway. That decision was then challenged by judicial review and Flood J refused leave to appeal in the circumstances where the applicant had continued the oral hearing and failed to challenge the procedure at the time of the oral hearing.

**[4.85]** From the forgoing it can be seen that there is strong judicial support for the view that the application for leave to appeal should be made as soon as possible after the event which gives rise to the application for judicial review has occurred. In *Huntstown Air Park Ltd v An Bord Pleanála*,[134] a developer claimed that an observer held certain documents which were 'necessary and relevant' to an oral hearing by way of appeal. At the oral hearing, the inspector also requested the observer to produce the documents but the observer refused to do so and claimed that the documents could not be produced on the grounds of commercial confidentiality. The inspector seemed to accept the objector's reasons for not producing the documentation and declined to make any further

---

131. *Linehan v Cork County Council* [2008] IEHC 76 *per* Finlay Geoghehan J.
132. *Sloan v An Bord Pleanála, Louth County Council and National Roads Authority* [2003] 2 ILRM 61.
133. *Max Developments v An Bord Pleanála* [1994] 2 IR 121.
134. *Huntstown Air Park Ltd v An Bord Pleanála* [1999] 1 ILRM 281, HC *per* Geoghegan J.

direction. The oral hearing proceeded and an application for judicial review was brought before the High Court. As part of the order granting leave to apply for judicial review, the High Court granted a stay on the oral hearing. Ultimately, the application for judicial review was dismissed and it was held that the fact that a document might be relevant to the determination of an appeal does not make it necessary for the purpose of enabling the board to determine the appeal. Furthermore, since the board has the power to request such documents at any time before it determines the appeal, the application at the oral hearing stage was premature. Simons[135] makes a compelling argument against bringing a challenge directed to the oral hearing on the grounds that the challenge is inappropriate and premature. Simons's analysis of the concept of prematurity is summarised as follows:

> First, the challenge may be one not properly directed at the oral hearing at all. For example, the objection raised may be one which the members of An Bord Pleanála, as opposed to the person conducting the oral hearing, are in a position to remedy.

That was the very point made in *Huntstown Air Park Ltd v An Bord Pleanála*,[136] where the application for judicial review (for failure to produce certain documents), which was taken during the oral hearing, was deemed premature, where the board could have ordered production of those documents at any time prior to the determination. Simons illustrates his first point further as follows:

> Indeed, it is arguable that the point raised in *Max Developments Ltd v An Bord Pleanála* [[1994] 2 IR 121], namely, whether or not to require an Environmental Impact Statement, was not a matter for the inspector conducting the oral hearing at all, in circumstances where the power to call for an Environmental Impact Statement would appear to have resided with the members of An Bord Pleanála.[137]

In continuing his analysis of the concept of prematurity, Simons's second point is clearly stated in the following terms:

> It is trite law that judicial review is not concerned with the substance or merits of a decision but rather with its legality. One consequence of this seems to be that, generally speaking, the High Court will not determine any facts but will, instead, merely review the findings of fact of the decision-maker depending on the nature of the objection raised it may be crucial that the High Court have before it findings of fact of the decision-maker on the relevant point. To use again the example of Environmental Impact Assessment, an argument may arise as to whether or not an Environmental Impact Assessment should have been required in respect of a proposed development. This might require a consideration of matters such as whether or not the nature and extent of the proposed development would be such as to bring it above the specified threshold, or, more generally, as to whether the proposed development would or would not be likely to have significant effects on the environment. These are matters which might well not be fully elucidated until after the oral hearing.[138]

---

135. Simons, *Planning and Development Law* (2nd edn, Thomson Round Hall, 2007) at 9.91–9.100.
136. *Huntstown Air Park Ltd v An Bord Pleanála* [1999] 1 ILRM 281, HC.
137. Simons, *Planning and Development Law* (2nd edn, Thomson Round Hall, 2007) at 9.92, p 477.
138. Simons, *Planning and Development Law* (2nd edn, Thomson Round Hall, 2007) at 9.94, p 477.

**[4.86]** Simons's third point in his analysis of the concept of prematurity is as follows:

> The third, and broadest sense in which prematurity might be understood is that of the application for judicial review being premature on account of the fact that the ultimate decision on the substantive appeal might be to the satisfaction of the objector. To put the matter another way, it might be thought unnecessary to embark on a possible lengthy judicial review hearing in circumstances where An Bord Pleanála might have decided, on the planning merits of the appeal, to refuse planning permission (or to modify the development so as to remove the aspects objected to). For this pragmatic reason then it might be thought that a 'wait and see' attitude should be adopted and that it would only be in the event that the decision of the substance of the appeal went against the objector that he or she should be required to institute judicial review proceedings.[139]

## Matters other than those raised by parties

**[4.87]** The Board may take into account matters other than those raised by parties or by observers.[140] If the board does take such matters into account it must afford an opportunity to the parties and the observers to make submissions on those matters, either in writing or at an oral hearing. If the oral hearing of the appeal or referral has been concluded, and the board considers it expedient to reopen the hearing, submissions may be made to the inspector at the re-opened hearing. Where there is no oral hearing or where the oral hearing has been concluded and the board does not consider it expedient to re-open it, the board is compelled to notify in writing each of the parties or persons who have made submissions or observations in relation to the appeal or referral and to invite their further submissions or observations within a period of not less than two weeks or not more than four weeks beginning on the date of service of the notice.

**[4.88]** Where the board has given notice that it proposes to hold an oral hearing or where an oral hearing has been concluded to re-open the oral hearing, the parties and any other person who is given notice shall be permitted, if present at the oral hearing, to make submissions to the board in relation to matters which are the subject of the notice or which, in the opinion of the person conducting the hearing, are of relevance to the appeal or referral.

**[4.89]** Submissions and observations that are received by the board after a period of not less than two weeks or more than four weeks referred to can be considered by the board. Once the submissions and observations are made to the board and accepted by it the party making the submissions and observations shall not be entitled to elaborate in writing upon those submissions and observations or to make further submissions and observations in writing in relation to the matters referred to and any such elaboration, submissions or observations received by the board shall not be considered by it. In effect, s 137 allows the board to consider matters not raised in submissions by the parties.

---

139. Simons, *Planning and Development Law* (2nd edn, Thomson Round Hall, 2007) at 9.95, p 477.
140. PDA 2000, s 137(1)–(4) inclusive.

**[4.90]** In *Stack v An Bord Pleanála, Kerry County Council and Michael McKiernan*,[141] the applicant claimed that the board had based its decision to refuse planning permission on an earlier decision to refuse planning permission and that, consequently, this new refusal was not, in reality, a new matter. It was noted that the earlier decision was a matter of public record and further that the board was entitled to be mindful of the earlier decision and mindful of the fact that it could not advance the same reasons for refusal on the basis of a consistency of approach. The matters which the board may raise must be within the parameters set out in the Act and so they must relate to proper planning and sustainable development of the area. The earlier decision, as a matter of public record, was not something that would have come as a surprise to the applicant. It was held that the board is entitled to refer to earlier decisions made by it without the necessity of canvassing all of these with the parties to the appeal.

**[4.91]** *Stack v An Bord Pleanála*[142] may be contrasted with *Ferryhouse Club v An Bord Pleanála*,[143] where it was held that fair procedures were deemed to have been breached. The case concerned an appeal on a s 5 referral which had been determined by An Bord Pleanála on a reference. In the circumstances, it was held that the board had not accorded the applicant a fair hearing and had not complied with fair procedures when the board concluded that insufficient evidence had been adduced to show that the development was other than of recent origin and was unauthorised, notwithstanding the willingness of the applicant to provide such evidence. This was especially the case when the import of the ultimate decision tended to impugn the applicant's honesty.

## Withdrawal of appeals, applications and referrals

**[4.92]** PDA 2000, s 140 (as amended)[144] is the section which deals with withdrawal of appeals, applications and referrals which are before An Bord Pleanála. There is also a new reference in s 140(1)(iv), which provides that:

> A person who has made an application for permission or approval (as may be appropriate) in respect of a strategic infrastructure development, may withdraw, in writing, the appeal, application or referral at any time before that appeal, application or referral is determined by the Board.

**[4.93]** Not only is an applicant entitled to withdraw appeals, referrals or applications in respect of strategic infrastructure development but he is also entitled to withdraw a planning application to which the appeal relates. Once the notice of withdrawal is received by An Bord Pleanála it will, as soon as may be, notify all parties who have made submissions or observations.

---

141. *Stack v An Bord Pleanála, Kerry County Council and Michael McKiernan* (unreported, 7 March 2003) HC *per* O'Caoimh J.
142. *Stack v An Bord Pleanála* [2000] IEHC 155 *per* O'Neill J.
143. *Ferryhouse Club v An Bord Pleanála* [1997] 1 IR 497.
144. PDA 2000, s 140(1) as substituted by PD(SI)A 2006, s 25(a), s 141(2) as amended by PD(SI)A 2006, s 25(b).

**[4.94]** If a person withdraws a planning application to which an appeal relates, or if the board declares that an application is to be regarded as having been withdrawn, the following provisions shall apply as regards the application:

(a) any appeal in relation to the application shall be regarded as having been withdrawn and accordingly shall not be determined by the board; and

(b) notwithstanding any previous decision under s 34 by a planning authority as regards the application, no permission shall be granted under that section by the authority on foot of the application.[145]

## Time for decisions on lodging appeals, etc[146]

**[4.95]** The purpose of this section is to regulate the situation when the last day for determining the appeal falls on a public holiday, a Sunday or outside office hours, where appropriate. Where the planning authority or the board is required to give a decision and the last date for giving that decision is a public holiday (within the meaning of the Organisation of Working Time Act 1997) or any other day on which the offices of the planning authority or the board are closed, the decision shall be valid if given on the next day on which the offices of the planning authority or the board, as the case may be, are open.[147] In relation to an appeal or referral, where the end of the relevant period falls on a Sunday, holidays or outside office hours an appeal or referral shall be valid as having been made in time if it is received by the board on the next day on which the offices of the board are open.[148]

**[4.96]** Where the Act requires that submissions, observations or a request to be made or documents, particulars or other information are to be submitted to the board within a specified period and the last day of that period is a public holiday or any other day on which the offices of the board are closed, the submissions, observations or requests for documents, particulars or other information (as the case may be) shall be regarded as having been received before the expiration of that period if received by the board on the next day on which the offices of the board are open.[149]

## The making of Regulations regarding appeals and referrals

**[4.97]** The Minister may make regulations for additional, incidental, consequential or supplemental matters in respect of appeals as appears to the Minister to be necessary and expedient.[150] The Minister may make similar regulations with reference to referrals as appears to the Minister to be necessary and expedient.

---

145. PDA 2000, s 140(3)(a) and (b).
146. PDA 2000, s 141(1)–(3) as amended by LGA 2001 s 247(d).
147. PDA 2000, s 141(1) as amended by LGA 2001, s 247(d).
148. PDA 2000, s 141(2) as amended by LGA 2001, s 247(d).
149. PDA 2000, s 141(3) as amended by LGA 2001, s 247(d).
150. PDA 2000, s 142(1)–(4).

**[4.98]** Where the board is determining an appeal, it may invite an applicant to submit to it revised plans or other drawings modifying or other particulars providing for the modification of, the development to which the appeal relates.[151] If plans and drawings or particulars are submitted to the board under the regulations the board may, in determining the appeal, grant permission for the relevant development as modified. It is significant that the word used is 'modified' and not 'revised'.[152] In *White v Dublin Corporation*,[153] Ó Caoimh J dealt with the term 'modifying' and suggested that that term implied changes of a limited nature only. The changes which the word 'modify' implies will be slight or partial.

**[4.99]** Section 141 does make provision for circumstances in which the board may require any party to an appeal or referral to give further public notice in the manner specified by the board and this additional public notice will be given where the board considers that the modification was perhaps more than 'slight or partial'. The Board can direct further public notice either on the site, in a newspaper circulating in the area or site and newspaper notices.[154]

## Board to have regard to certain policies and objectives

**[4.100]** In performing its function, the Board is bound to have regard to certain policies and objectives of government,[155] a State authority, the Minister, planning authorities and any other body which is a public authority whose functions have, or may have, a bearing on the proper planning and sustainable development of cities, towns or other areas whether urban or rural. The Board shall also have regard to the national interest and any effect the performance of its functions may have on issues of strategic economic or social importance to the State and the board shall have regard to the National Spatial Strategy and any regional planning guidelines for the time being in force. The Board will have regard to a planning authority's 'core strategy' which is a specific part of the planning authority's development plan.

**[4.101]** Quirke J in *McEvoy and Smith v Meath County Council*[156] stated that the requirement to 'have regard to' is less onerous than a requirement to 'take into account'. *McEvoy and Smith v Meath County Council*[157] involved a councillor and the chairman of An Taisce challenging a decision to make the development plan. It was the applicants' case that the planning authority had not had proper regard to the statutory regional planning guidelines. In the course of his judgment, Quirke J stated candidly that he was uneasy and concerned about the extent of the consideration given by the elected members to the regional planning guidelines but he was satisfied from the evidence that

---

151. PDA 2000, s 142(2).
152. PDA 2000, s 142(3).
153. *White v Dublin Corporation* [2002] IEHC 68 *per* O'Caoimh J.
154. PDA 2000, s 142(4).
155. PDA 2000, s 143(1) and (2) as substituted by PD(SI)A 2006, s 26.
156. *McEvoy and Smith v Meath County Council* [2003] 1 IR 208 *per* Quirke J.
157. *McEvoy and Smith v Meath County Council* [2003] 1 IR 208 *per* Quirke J.

the planning authority had not failed to 'have regard to' the regional planning guidelines. Nevertheless, to 'have regard to' is probably a step up from the provision in the Local Government (Planning and Development) Act 1976, s 5 which required the board to 'keep itself informed' on certain policies and objectives of the Minister, planning authorities and any other body which is a public body whose functions have, or may have a bearing on the proper planning and sustainable development of cities, towns and other areas whether urban or rural.

### Fees payable to the Board

**[4.102]** Section 144 enables the board, with the approval of the Minister, to determine fees[158] in relation to appeals, referrals, the making of an application under s 37(5) or in respect of a strategic infrastructure development (including application under s 146(B) or submission of an environmental impact statement under s 146(C)), the making of submissions or observations to the board under s 130 and requests for oral hearings under s 134. The section enables the board to provide for the payment of different fees in relation to different classes or descriptions of appeals, referrals and applications for exemption from payment of fees in specified circumstances and for waiver, remission or refund in whole or in part of fees in specified circumstances.[159]

**[4.103]** Such fees may be altered by the board without the Minister's approval, only when the alterations are in line with the consumer price index. If the alterations are not in line with the movement of the consumer price index, the Minister must approve any change. If any changes are made, the board must give notice of the new fees in at least one newspaper circulating in the State not less than eight weeks before the fees come into effect. The section also allows the board to specify fees for making copies of documents available to the public or to other parties which costs should not exceed the cost of making the copies. It is not clear whether that is the costs incurred in using a photocopier or whether some contribution also is made towards the wages of the person or persons engaged in making the photocopies.

### Expenses of appeals and referrals

**[4.104]** Section 145 allows the board, if it so thinks proper and irrespective of the result of the appeal or referral, to direct the planning authority to pay the appellant or the person making the referral compensation for expenses[160] incurred by the appellant or the person making the referral. The amount of the compensation or whether any compensation is made at all is entirely at the discretion of the board. What is clear from the section is that what is offered by the board is compensation for expenses. Costs incurred by an appellant or a person making a referral are not contemplated by the section. The Board may in certain circumstances make a payment of costs even though

---

158. PDA 2000, s 144(1)–(6). Section 144(1) is substituted by s 144(1A) and (1B) inserted by PD(A)A 2010, s 44.
159. Local Government (Planning and Development) (Fees) Regulations 2001 (SI 2001/525) lists the board's fees payable in all circumstances.
160. PDA 2000, s 145(1) and (2) as amended by PD(SI)A 2006, s 28.

the appeal or referral may have been unsuccessful and again that is entirely at the discretion of the board. An appellant may be directed to make a payment where the appeal or referral was not acceded to in substance by the board. The Board may also compel an appellant to pay the planning authority in circumstances where the board considers that the appeal or referral was made with the intention of delaying the development or securing monitory gain by a third party.

## Reports and documents of the Board

**[4.105]** PDA 2000, s 146 permits the board or an employee of the board duly authorised to assign a person to report on any matter on behalf of the board in connection with the performance of the board's functions.[161] A person assigned shall make a written report on the matter to the board, which shall include a recommendation, and the board shall consider the report and recommendation before determining the matter. If the board is required to supply any person with documents, maps, particulars or other information in relation to the matter or if the board considers that it is appropriate, in the exercise of its discretion, to supply any person with such documents, maps, particulars or information, then, in exercising that discretion, the board will make available for inspection all relevant material or information at the offices of the board or any other place or by electronic means and the board will also notify the person concerned that the relevant material or information is so available for inspection.

**[4.106]** Within three days of making the decision, any matter calling to be decided by it in performance of a function under or transferred by this Act[162] or under any other enactment, the documents relating to the matter shall be made available by the board for inspection at its offices, by members of the public and shall be made available by the board for such inspection at any other place or by electronic means as the board considers appropriate. Subsequent to the inspection, if any person wishes to purchase those documents they may do so for a fee not exceeding the reasonable costs of making a copy. The section requires that the documents should remain available for a period of at least five years beginning on the third day following the making by the board of the decision on the matter concerned. Under the provisions of PDA 2000, s 146, as amended by PD(SI)A 2006, s 29, the person assigned makes a written report to the board and that report includes a recommendation but it does not include a decision. The Board considers the report and the recommendation before making a determination on the matter. The inspector assigned to the task of making the report is also authorised by art 75 of PDR 2001 to carry out a site inspection. In *Geraghty v Minister for Local Government*,[163] five guiding principles were set out by Walsh J, with Budd J concurring, relevant to reports under s 146.

> There are certain fundamental matters or principles which are unalterable. The *first* is that the Minister is the deciding authority. He cannot in any way be treated simply as an authority whose function is to review the recommendations or

---

161. PDA 2000, s 146(1)–(7) as amended by PD(SI)A 2006, s 29.
162. PDA 2000, s 146 as amended by PD(SI)A 2006, s 29.
163. *Geraghty v Minister for Local Government* [1976] IR 153, SC.

opinions, if any such are made or offered, of the person holding or conducting the inquiry. The *second* is that the Minister is acting ultra vires if he comes to a conclusion or makes a decision which is not supportable upon the evidence or the materials properly before him. *Thirdly*, neither the Minister nor the person holding or conducting the inquiry can come to a conclusion of fact unless there is evidence upon which such a conclusion could be formed. *Fourthly*, if the person holding or conducting the inquiry should come to a conclusion of fact and should express it, the Minister is not bound to come to the same conclusion of fact and is quite free to form a contrary conclusion if there is evidence and materials properly before him from which he could come to such a conclusion. *Fifthly*, to enable the Minister to come to any decision, the person holding or conducting the inquiry must transmit to the Minister a report which fairly and accurately informs the Minister of the substance of the evidence and the arguments for and against the issues raised at the inquiry by those represented at the inquiry.[164]

The facts in *Geraghty v Minister for Local Government*[165] were that the inspector prepared and presented his report but before the report reached the Minister it was altered by the inspector's superiors within the Department of Local Government. A decision to refuse planning permission for a housing development was quashed because of the interference by the inspector's superiors. The decision was held to be *ultra vires* and void.

[4.107] In *Killiney and Ballybrack Development Association Ltd v Minister for Local Government (No 2)*,[166] Henchy J in the Supreme Court set aside a decision which recognised a condition in a grant of planning permission for a housing development which provided that no houses could be built for three years because of an inadequate sewage system. Henchy J stated that where the reason given for the imposition of the condition cannot fairly and reasonably be held to be capable of justifying the condition then the condition cannot be said to be a valid exercise of the statutory power. The inspector's report in *Killiney and Ballybrack (No 2)*[167] contained matters which could not validly be included and it was likely that the Minister acted on this evidence in reaching his decision. If evidence, which is not disclosed at a public hearing, is sent to the board as part of the inspector's report this may offer grounds for challenging the board's decision. In *Killiney and Ballybrack Development Association Ltd v Minister for Local Government and Templefinn Estates Ltd (No 1) (1978)*,[168] it was noted that following an oral hearing the report prepared by the inspector for the Minister contained references to

---

164. Note: the function of the Minister in deciding planning appeals is now transferred to An Bord Pleanála.
165. *Geraghty v Minister for Local Government* [1976] IR 153, SC.
166. *Killiney and Ballybrack Development Association Ltd v Minister for Local Government (No 2)* [1978] ILRM 78.
167. *Killiney and Ballybrack Development Association Ltd v Minister for Local Government (No 2)* [1978] ILRM 78.
168. *Killiney and Ballybrack Development Association Ltd v Minister for Local Government and Templefinn Estates Ltd (No 1)* [1978] 112 ILTR 69.

facts and evidence which were not presented at the oral hearing. The presumption must be that the decision was based on materials other than those disclosed at the oral hearing and as such it rendered the decision invalid. The decision was set aside.

**[4.108]** In *Lancefort Ltd v An Bord Pleanála*,[169] it was the applicant's case that the inspector should have provided a separate site inspection report for the board or should at least have included material from such inspection of the site with the report submitted to the board. The applicant's contention was held to be incorrect as no such obligation arises from the statutory provisions. The Board has a general discretion to carry out or indeed not to carry out a site inspection. The Board may also appoint persons to carry out inspections generally, or appoint persons to carry out inspections for a specific matter or for a specific class of matters, including inspections in a particular local authority. The article does not impose any specific obligation on the board to carry out inspections in any particular case.[170] Where a decision by a planning authority or by the board to grant or refuse permission is different, in relation to the granting or refusal of permission, from the recommendation in:

(i) the report on a planning application to the manager (or such other person delegated to make the decision) in the case of a planning authority; or

(ii) a report of a person assigned to report on an appeal on behalf of the board (namely an inspector),

that decision shall indicate the main reasons for not accepting the recommendations in the report or reports to grant or refuse permission. Where the board agrees with the inspector's report and with the reasons contained in that report that agreement can be assumed although it is not expressed. The assumption can be made on the basis that the decision will not contain any statement of the main reasons and considerations for not accepting the recommendation in the report.

**[4.109]** In *Mulholland and Kinsella v An Bord Pleanála (No 2)*,[171] it was held that where the board departs from the inspector's recommendations, its reasons given for either granting or refusing permission apply equally to the reasons when not accepting the recommendation of the board's inspector. These reasons must be sufficient to enable the courts to review the decision in order to satisfy the applicant that the board directed its mind adequately to the issues before it. The Board's reasons for not accepting the inspector's recommendations must be clear and cogent.

**[4.110]** In all cases where an inspector is assigned and where he/she prepares a report, the report merely contains recommendations. It does not contain decisions. The responsibility for making the decision rests with the board. It seems reasonably clear from this that an inspector's report is not open to judicial review. The work required of

---

169. *Lancefort Ltd v An Bord Pleanála* [1998] 2 IR 511.
170. PDR 2001, art 75.
171. *Mulholland and Kinsella v An Bord Pleanála (No 2)* [2005] 1 ILRM 287.

an inspector in preparing his report was summarised by O'Neill J in *Kenney Construction Ltd v An Bord Pleanála*[172] as follows:

> In essence, therefore, what is involved in giving to the Board a fair and accurate report is one which fairly sets out and fully sets out for the benefit of the Board the relative contentions in regard to whatever the issues are in the planning application, but bearing in mind that the Board already have a variety of material before them, and it would be superfluous for any report to recite material which was clearly available and highlighted in other documentation. But the essence of it is that the report must present to the Board a fair and accurate picture of the proposal and of the reasons for it and of the reasons against as made by the objectors and as made by the applicant in the planning permission.

**[4.111]** As seen the provisions under PDA 2000, s 146(5) (as amended by the PD(SI)A 2006, s 29) requires that within three days of the making of a decision on any matter falling to be decided by the board in performance of a function under or transferred by the Act or under any other enactment, the documents relating to the matter:

(a) shall be made available by the board for inspection at the offices of the board by members of the public; and

(b) may be made available by the board for such inspection:

    (i) at any other place, or

    (ii) by electronic means,

    as the board considers appropriate.

This obligation only arises after the decision has been made and the board is not required to make available any material in its possession before the decision is made. Accordingly, an application for discovery of documents in the possession of the board may be refused where no decision has been made. The case of *Arklow Holidays Ltd v An Bord Pleanála*[173] is perhaps relevant in this context. Clarke J withheld making an order for discovery on an application for leave in judicial review proceedings. The learned judge indicated that he was not prepared to rule that the High Court did not have jurisdiction to make an order for discovery at the leave stage but he conceded that availability of discovery in judicial review proceedings is significantly more limited than in ordinary plenary proceedings. Clarke J stated that, in particular, it would be necessary for the applicant to demonstrate that the documents concerned were required for the proper resolution of the issues that would arise at the leave stage. PDA 2000, s 132 gives power to the board to require submission of documents where the board is of the opinion that any document, particulars or other information may be necessary for the purpose of enabling it to determine the appeal or referral. In those circumstances the board may, in its absolute discretion, serve any party or any person who has made submissions or observations to the board requiring submission of specified documents

---

172. *Kenney Construction Ltd v An Bord Pleanála* [2005] IEHC 306 (10 February 2005) *per* O'Neill J.
173. *Arklow Holidays Ltd v An Bord Pleanála* [2005] IEHC 303, *per* Clarke J.

or other information as is specified in the notice to the board within two weeks. If s 132 proves to be ineffective, the board can always rely on the provisions of PDA 2000, s 135(5)(a)(ii) to ensure that any books, deeds, contracts, accounts, vouchers, maps, plans, documents or other information are produced to it summarily.

## Documents to be made available to the public

**[4.112]** PDA 2000, s 38 (as amended)[174] requires that certain documents relating to planning applications must be made available to the public but only after the planning authority has given its decision in respect of a planning application. The documents, as listed below, must be made available to the public within three working days of the authority's decision, to be inspected and, if required, purchased by members of the public during office hours at the offices of the authority. The section also provides that the documents listed below may also be made available by the authority by placing the documents on the authority's website or otherwise in electronic form. The following are the documents referred to:

(a) a copy of the planning application and of any particulars, evidence, environmental impact statement, other written study or further information received or obtained by the authority from the applicant in accordance with regulations made under this Act;

(b) a copy of any submission or observation in relation to the planning application which has been received by the authority;

(c) a copy of any report prepared by or for the authority in relation to the planning application;

(d) a copy of the decision of the authority in respect of the planning application and a copy of the notification of the decision given to the applicant; and

(e) a copy of any documents relating to a contribution or other matter referred to in s 34(5).[175]

**[4.113]** A new provision has been added by PD(A)A 2010, s 27(b), as follows:

(1A) Details of any telephone numbers of the applicant or addresses for communication with the applicant in electronic form provided by or on behalf of the applicant shall be taken not to be part of the planning application and shall not be made available by a planning authority to members of the public.[176]

The documents referred to in 1A above must be kept available for a period of not less than seven years after the making of a decision by the authority. This provision is without prejudice to the Freedom of Information Act 1997 and the European Communities Act 1972 (Access to Information on the Environment) Regulations 1998

---

174. PDA 2000, s 38(1)–(7) as amended by PD(A)A 2010, s 27.
175. PDA 2000, s 38(1)(a)–(e) as amended by PD(A)A 2010, s 27(a).
176. PD(A)A 2010, s 27(b) inserted s 38(1A).

(SI 125/1998), and any regulations amending those regulations and the Data Protection Acts 1988 and 2003.[177]

**[4.114]** The documents which should be made available are referred to in paras (a) and (b) of s 38(1) (as amended) (set out above), and shall be made available for inspection and purchase by members of the public during office hours of the authority from as soon as may be after the receipt of the document until a decision is made on the application and may also be made available by the authority by placing the documents on the authority's website or otherwise in electronic form.[178] The fee charged for copies shall be a fee not exceeding the reasonable cost of making such copies.[179] At the end of the seven-year period, the planning authority shall retain at least one original copy of those documents in the local archive as per s 65 Local Government Act 1994.[180]

**[4.115]** The Minister may prescribe additional requirements in relation to availability for inspection by members of the public of documents relating to planning applications.[181] Section 38 will apply to any applications made to the planning authority after the commencement of the section, ie, 11 March 2002.[182]

**[4.116]** It should be noted that although maps and drawings prepared by architects, engineers and other designers may be inspected at the planning office, they may not be copied without the consent of the copyright owner. Planning officials will always refuse to make and hand over copies of such maps or drawings. As Costello P stated in *Gormley v EMI Records (Ireland) Ltd*: 'By copyright legislation, Parliament intended to reward the skills involved in producing works'.[183] The provisions of PDA 2000, s 38 (as amended) attempt to ensure that documents are made available for a period of not less than seven years after the making of the decision by the authority. The legislation does not, however, impose any obligation on the planning authority to control, supervise or maintain its archive to ensure that documents are not stolen, lost or kept in legible condition and sadly this is something which occasionally happens.

## Planning Regulations dealing with appeals and referrals[184]

**[4.117]** Appeals accompanied by an EIS must satisfy the requirements of PDA 2000, Pt 10 and PDR 2001, Pt 7. Appeals or referrals which relate to 'establishment' to which the Major Accident Directive regulations apply where the planning authority received from the National Authority for Occupational Safety and Health under art 138 must satisfy the requirements of PDA 2000, Pt II.

---

177. PDA 2000, s 38(2) has been amended by the PD(SI)A 2006, s 11.
178. PDA 2000, s 38(3) has been amended by the PD(A)A 2010, s 27(c).
179. PDA 2000, s 38(4).
180. PDA 2000, s 38(5).
181. PDA 2000, s 38(6).
182. PDA 2000, s 38(7).
183. *Gormley v EMI Records (Ireland) Ltd* [1997] IEHC 221 *per* Costello P.
184. PDR 2001, Pt 7, Ch 2 (arts 66–78) as amended by PDR 2006, arts 12–16.

PRD 2001, art 66(1) reads:

> Where an appeal is required to be accompanied by an EIS in accordance with s 172 of the Act or these Regulations the requirements of Pt 10 shall be complied with in addition to the requirements of this Part.

**[4.118]** PDA 2000, s 172[185] provides for the basic requirements for planning applications to be accompanied by an EIS where the application relates to development requiring EIA. The Board may grant exemption from the requirements to carry out an EIA in exceptional circumstances. The regulations which deal specifically with EIA are contained in PDR 2001, Pt 10 and these regulations have been amended by PDR 2006 and by PDR 2008. Part 10 of PDR 2001 (as amended) contains arts 92 to 132 inclusive.

**[4.119]** PDR 2001, art 66(2) reads:

> Any appeal or referral under s 5 of the Act relating to development of a type referred to in art 138 shall be subject to the requirements of Pt 11 in addition to the requirements of this Part.

**[4.120]** PDA 2000, s 5 provides that a person may seek a declaration from a planning authority on whether or not a particular development is or is not exempted development. PDR 2001, art 138 deals with advice to be obtained from the Health and Safety Authority (formerly the National Authority for Occupational Safety and Health), such advice to be sought by the planning authority or by the board as the case may be. Any appeal or referral under PDA 2000, s 5 relating to a development of a type referred to in PDR 2001, art 138 shall be subject to the requirements of PDR 2001, Pt 11 (arts 133–155), as amended by PDR 2006, arts 33–37. PDR 2001, Pt 11 (as amended) deals with the regulations on the Major Accidents Directive.

**[4.121]** PDR 2001, art 67 (as amended by PDR 2006) contains a number of interpretations, as follows.

**[4.122]** 'Appeal' does not include appeals under PDA 2000, s 182(4)(b).

PDA 2000, s 182 deals with cables, wires and pipelines and permits the relevant authority with the consent of the owner and occupier of any land not forming part of the public roadways to place, to construct or lay cables, wires or pipelines on, under or over the land and further that local authorities may, with the consent of an owner or occupier of the structure, attach to that structure any bracket or other fixture required for the carrying or support of any cables, wires or pipelines. Also, local authorities may erect and maintain notices indicating the position of cables, wires or pipelines placed, erected or constructed under PDA 2000, s 182 and may, with the consent of the owner or occupier of any structure affix such notices on the structure. If a local authority considers that a consent has been unreasonably withheld, it may appeal to the board.

**[4.123]** 'Oral hearing' means an oral hearing within the meaning of PDA 2000, ss 134, 203 and 218.

PDA 2000, s 134 has been substituted by PD(SI)A 2006, s 22. The section provides that the board may in its absolute discretion hold an oral hearing of an appeal, a referral

---

185. PDA 2000, s 172: note that s 172(1) and (1A) have been substituted by PD(A)A 2010, s 54(a).

under s 5 or an application under s 37E.[186] The power is entirely discretionary. A party to an appeal or referral or any person who makes or submits an observation may request an oral hearing on payment of the necessary fee.

PDA 2000, s 203 deals with the confirmation of an order for an area of special amenity. The power of confirmation was transferred from the Minister to the board by the provisions of PDA 2000.

PDA 2000, s 218 has been amended by PD(SI)A 2006, s 39(b). The section deals with oral hearings in relation to compulsory acquisition of land. Where the board, as a result of the transfer of functions, would otherwise be required to hold a local inquiry, public local inquiry or oral hearing, that requirement shall not apply to the board but the board may, at its absolute discretion, hold an oral hearing in relation to the matter the subject of the function transferred. The holding of the oral hearing in relation to CPOs, road schemes, etc, is entirely at the board's discretion and the board may decide to dispense with the necessity for an oral hearing where it considers that a hearing would not be likely to aid its understanding of the issues involved.

**[4.124]** Relevant persons'[187] means:

(a) In the case of an oral hearing under s 134(1) of the Act, the parties to the appeal or referral or any applicant for permission for a strategic infrastructure development, and any persons who have made submissions or observations to the board in relation to the application, appeal or referral in accordance with the provisions of the Act or these regulations.

(b) In the case of an oral hearing under PDA 2000, s 134(5), the planning or local authority and, as appropriate, the person who is seeking the determination or any person who made a submission, observation or objection in accordance with PDA 2000, PDR 2001 or the applicable enactment, and, in the case of any development in respect of which an EIS is submitted, any person who made a submission or observation in respect of the effects on the environment of the proposed development.[188]

(c) In the case of an oral hearing under s 203,[189] the planning authority and any person who made an objection to an order under that section. PDA 2000, s 203 deals with the confirmation of an SAAO.

---

186. An application under s 37(e) is an application to the board, in the first instance, for strategic infrastructure. Also, PDA 2000, s 134(A), as inserted by PD(SI)A 2006, s 22, is the section which allows the board to hold an oral hearing when it considers it necessary in order to properly carry out its functions.
187. PDR 2001, art 67, where it defines 'relevant persons' has been amended by the substitution of a new paragraph at (a) which is quoted above at para **4.124**. See PDR 2006, art 12.
188. The reference in this paragraph to PDA 2000, s 134(5) is more than a little confusing since there is not now and never was a sub-s (5) in PDA 2000, s 134, as amended, to the date of this publication. Presumably the reference to sub-s (5) should be deleted.
189. PDA 2000, s 203 deals with the confirmation of an SAAO (special amenity area order).

(d) In the case of an oral hearing under s 218[190] of the Act, the local authority and any person who made an objection in accordance with the enactments referred to in s 214[191] or 215[192] of the Act.

**[4.125]** PDR 2001, art 68 provides that:

a copy of any appeal or referral sent to the Board shall be passed to the planning authority and the planning authority shall make copies of the said appeal or referral available for inspection or purchase at a fee not exceeding the reasonable cost of making a copy at its offices until the appeal or referral is either withdrawn, dismissed or determined by the Board or, in the case of an appeal referred to in s 139[193] of the Act, a direction is given to the authority in relation to that appeal.[194]

**[4.126]** PDR 2001, art 69(1) and (2) provide that:

(1) subject to sub-art (2), where a copy of an appeal under s 37 of the Act is sent to a planning authority by the Board in accordance with s 128 of the Act, the planning authority, as soon as may be after receipt of the copy of the appeal, shall notify in writing any person who made a submission or observation in accordance with these Regulations in relation to the planning application in respect of which an appeal has been made.

(2) a notice under sub-article (1) shall:

(a) specify the reference number of the Board in respect of the appeal,

(b) specify the date on which the appeal was received by the Board,

(c) state that a copy of the appeal is available for inspection or purchase for a fee not exceeding the reasonable cost of making a copy during office hours at the offices of the planning authority, and

(d) state that submissions or observations in relation to the appeal may be made in writing to the Board within the appropriate period and on payment of the appropriate fee.

**[4.127]** PDR 2001, art 70 provides that any appeal of planning permission shall be published in the planning authority's weekly list.

**[4.128]** PDR 2001, art 71 provides that where the board notifies the planning authority that an appeal has been received, the authority shall, as soon as may be, notify the applicant for the permission that the board has received an application for leave to appeal the decision of the planning authority. The notice shall specify the reference

---

190. PDA 2000, s 218 allows the board to hold an oral hearing on CPOs, road schemes, etc, but it need not do so if it considers that such hearing would not be likely to aid its understanding of the issues.
191. PDA 2000, s 214 transferred the compulsory acquisition approval functions of the Minister to the board, bearing in mind that it is only a compulsory acquisition of land by local authorities which is affected.
192. PDA 2000, s 215 transferred the Minister's functions for approving road schemes including motorway schemes, the subject of an EIA, to the board.
193. PDA 2000, s 139 deals with appeals against conditions in a grant of permission.
194. PDR 2001, art 68 has been amended by PDR 2006, art 13.

number of the board, the name and address of the applicant for leave to appeal and it will state that the planning authority will not make the grant of permission unless the application for leave to appeal is refused.

**[4.129]** PDR 2001, art 72(1)[195] deals with the requirement of the board to publish a weekly list not later than the third working day following a particular week which list shall include: (a) the appeals and referrals received by the board; (b) the appeals and referrals determined, dismissed or withdrawn or in relation to which a direction is given by the board pursuant to s 139 of the Act;[196] (c) the applications for approval under ss 175(3)[197] and 215[198] of the Act received by the board; and (d) the application for approval under ss 175(3) and 215 of the Act determined or otherwise disposed of by the board during that week.[199] The contents of the various notices to appear in the list are detailed in the sub-articles of PDR 2001, art 72 as substituted by art 14 of PDR 2006, sub-paras (2)–(10) inclusive.

PDR 2001, art 72(2) provides that a list referred to in art 72(1) shall indicate, in respect of appeals under s 37 of the Act received by the board during the week to which the list relates that, under s 34 of the Act, the applications may be granted permission, subject to or without conditions, or refused and shall also indicate in respect of each appeal:

(a) the name of the appellant,

(b) the date on which the appeal was received by the board,

(c) the reference number of the appeal,

(d) the nature and location of the development to which the appeal relates,

(e) the name of the planning authority and the reference number of the planning application concerned in the register of the authority,

(f) the name of the person by or on behalf of whom the planning application was made.[200]

PDR 2001, art 72(3) provides that a list referred to in art 72(1) shall indicate, in respect of appeals under s 37 of the Act determined, dismissed or withdrawn or in relation to which a direction is given by the board pursuant to s 139 of the Act during the week to

---

195. PDR 2001, art 72 has been substituted by PDR 2006, art 14. The substituted article appears here and it deals with the requirement of the board to publish a weekly list.
196. PDA 2000, s 139 deals with appeals against a condition or conditions in a planning permission and the section empowers the board, in its absolute discretion, to give such directions to the relevant planning authority as it considers appropriate relating to the attachment, amendment or removal by that authority either of the conditions or conditions to which the appeal relates or of other conditions.
197. PDA 2000, s 175(3) provides that where an EIS has been prepared, the local authority shall apply to the board for approval.
198. PDA 2000, s 215 deals with the transfer of ministerial functions under the Roads Acts 1993 and 1998 to An Bord Pleanála.
199. Note that the Roads Acts 1993 and 1998 have been amended by the Roads Act 2007.
200. PDR 2001, art 72 has been substituted by PDR 2006, art 14. The substituted article of the 2006 Regulations is included in this paragraph.

which the list relates, that in accordance with s 34(3) of the Act, the board in making decisions on appeal under s 37 has regard to submissions or observations received and shall also indicate in respect of each appeal:

(a) the reference number of the appeal,

(b) the nature and location of the development to which the appeal relates,

(c) the name of the planning authority and the reference number of the planning application concerned in the register of the planning authority,

(d) the name of the person by or on behalf of whom the planning application was made,

(e) in the case of an appeal determined by the board, the nature of the decision of the board and the date of the order of the board in relation to the appeal,

(f) in the case of an appeal dismissed by the board, an indication of that fact and the date of the order of the board in relation to the appeal,

(g) in the case of an appeal which has been withdrawn, an indication of that fact and the date on which it was withdrawn,

(h) in the case of an appeal in relation to which a direction has been given by the board pursuant to s 139 of the Act, an indication of that fact and the date of the order of the board in relation to the appeal.

PDR 2001, art 72(4) provides that a list referred to in art 72(1) shall indicate in respect of each of the appeals (other than appeals under s 37 of the Act) and referrals received by the board during the week to which the list relates:

(a) the name of the appellant or person making the referral as appropriate,

(b) the reference number of the appeal or referral,

(c) the nature of the appeal or referral, and

(d) the date on which the appeal or referral was received by the board.

PDR 2001, art 72(5) provides that a list referred to in art 72(1) shall indicate, in respect of each appeal (other than an appeal under s 37 of the Act) or referral determined, dismissed or withdrawn during the week to which the list relates:

(a) the nature of the appeal or referral,

(b) in the case of an appeal or referral determined by the board, the nature of the decision of the board and the date of the order of the board in relation to the appeal or referral,

(c) in the case of an appeal or referral dismissed by the board, an indication of that fact and the date of the order of the board in relation to the appeal or referral, or

(d) in the case of an appeal or referral which is withdrawn, an indication of that fact and the date on which it was withdrawn.

PDR 2001, art 72(6) provides that a list referred to in art 72(1)(c) shall include, in respect of applications for approval under ss 175(3) and 215 of the Act received by the board during the week to which the list relates, that the board may approve the applications subject to or without conditions, or refuse the applications and shall also indicate in respect of each application,

(a) the reference number of the application for approval,

(b) the name of the local authority or road authority,

(c) the nature and location of the development, and

(d) that the application for approval is accompanied by an EIS.

PDR 2001, art 72(7) provides that a list referred to in art 72(1) shall indicate, in respect of applications for approval under ss 175(3) and 215 of the Act determined by the board during the week to which the list relates, that the board in determining applications for approval has regard to submissions or observations received and shall also indicate in respect of each application for approval:

(a) the reference number of the application for approval,

(b) the name the local authority or road authority,

(c) the nature and location of the development, and

(d) the nature of the decision of the board and the date of the order of the board in relation to the application for approval.

PDR 2001, art 72(8) provides that the board may include in a list referred to in art 72(1) any information which the board considers appropriate in relation to matters before, or to be determined for, or to be determined by, the board under the Act or any other enactment.

PDR 2001, art 72(9) provides that a list referred to in art 72(1) shall, for a period of not less than four weeks beginning on the day on which it is made available, be displayed in or at the offices of the board in a position convenient for inspection during office hours or by any other means, including in electronic form, that the board considers appropriate.

PDR 2001, art 72(10)(a) provides that copies of a list referred to in art 72(1) shall, during the period of four weeks referred to in art 72(7), be made available at the offices of the board during office hours, free of charge or for such fee as the board may fix not exceeding the reasonable cost of making a copy.

PDR 2001, art 72(10)(b) provides that a copy of the list referred to in art 72(1) shall, during the period of four weeks as aforesaid, be sent (including by electronic means) on request, to any person or body, free of charge or for such fee not exceeding the reasonable cost of making a copy and the cost of postage, as the board may fix.

**[4.130]** PDR 2001, art 73 empowers the board, when considering an appeal under PDA 2000, s 37, to invite the applicant for permission concerned to submit revised plans or other drawings modifying or other particulars providing for the modification of the development to which the appeal relates and such applicant so invited may submit to the board such number of plans, drawings or particulars as the board may specify.

PDR 2001, art 73 invites revised plans or other drawings modifying or other particulars providing for the modification of the development. In *White v Dublin Corporation*,[201] O'Caoimh J suggested that the terms 'modify' or 'modifying' would suggest changes of a limited nature and that any such changes would be slight or partial. But this was looked at in a different way in *Dietacaron Limited v An Bord Pleanála*.[202] Quirke J took a broader view of the meaning of 'modify' or 'modification' indicating that the words would allow the board a general discretion to invite modifications and further that the court would only interfere if the modifications to be put into place were somehow irrational.

**[4.131]** PDR 2001, art 74 deals with notification by the board of decisions on appeals or referrals. The Board is required, as soon as may be, following the making of a decision, to notify any party to the appeal or referral and any person who made submissions or observations in relation to the appeal or referral. The contents of the various notices to be served are dealt with in art 74(2)[203] and (3).

**[4.132]** PDR 2001, art 75 permits the board to arrange for the carrying out of inspections in relation to appeals or referrals or other matters determined by the board under PDR 2000 (as amended) by persons appointed for that purpose by the board, generally or for a particular appeal, referral or matter or for appeals, referrals or matters of a particular class, including appeals, referrals or matters relating to land in the area of a particular planning authority.

**[4.133]** PDR 2001, art 76 is substituted by PDR 2006, art 16. The substituted article provides that where the board decides to hold an oral hearing, it shall inform the 'relevant persons'[204] and any other persons and bodies which it considers appropriate giving not less than five working days notice of the time and place of the opening of the oral hearing or such shorter notice as may be accepted by all such persons or bodies. The Board will also make available at its offices and at the offices of the local authority or planning authority a copy of any correspondence, documents, particulars or other information received from any relevant person for a period of not less than seven days before the commencement of the oral hearing and ending on the last day of the oral hearing. Where making available of models or other information or particulars would

---

201. *White v Dublin Corporation* (unreported, 21 June 2002) HC *per* O'Caoimh J.
202. *Dietacaron Ltd v An Bord Pleanála* [2005] 2 ILRM 32 *per* Quirke J.
203. Note that PDR 2001, art 74(2) has been substituted by PDR 2006, art 15.
204. See definition of 'relevant persons', set out at para **4.124**: PDR 2001, art 67(a) as amended by PDR 2006, art 12.

lead to undue administrative or technical difficulties the board will not be required to make such available.

**[4.134]** PDR 2001, art 77 deals with the adjournment or re-opening of oral hearings and permits the board or other persons conducting an oral hearing to adjourn or reopen any hearing notwithstanding that any relevant person has failed to attend a hearing. The Board shall give notice of a time and place for the opening of an oral hearing or resumption of an oral hearing that has been adjourned indefinitely to each relevant person and all other persons previously informed. PDR 2001, art 77(3) provides that an oral hearing under PDA 2000, s 218, or a report which has been submitted to the board, shall not be re-opened unless the board considers it expedient to do so and so directs. PDA 2000, s 218[205] provides that where, as a result of the transfer of functions under PDA 2000, ss 214, 215, 215(a) or 215(b), the board would otherwise be required to hold a local enquiry, public local inquiry or oral hearing, that requirement shall not apply to the board and the board may now, at its absolute discretion, hold an oral hearing in relation to the matter, the subject of the function transferred. The effect of this section is to provide for oral hearings instead of public local inquiries in relation to CPOs, road schemes, etc.

**[4.135]** PDR 2001, art 78 provides that, if, for any reason, a person appointed to conduct an oral hearing is unable or fails to conduct the oral hearing, the board may appoint another person to conduct the oral hearing. Also, if a person appointed to conduct an oral hearing is unable to complete the conduct of the oral hearing or is unable or fails to furnish a report of an oral hearing to the board, the board may appoint another person to conduct a new oral hearing.

### Referrals to An Bord Pleanála

**[4.136]** 'Referral' is defined in PDA 2000, s 2, as amended by PD(A)A 2002, s 6(b), as meaning a referral to the board under ss 5, 34(5), 37(5), 57,[206] 96(5) or 193(2).

### *PDA 2000, s 5*

**[4.137]** If any question arises as to what is or is not development or is or is not exempted development within the meaning of this Act, any person may, on payment of the prescribed fee, request a declaration from the planning authority on that question. The person seeking the declaration must furnish to the planning authority any information which is necessary to enable the authority to make its decision.[207] The planning authority is required to issue a declaration on the questions raised and to give reasoned decisions in the declaration within a time limit of four weeks from the date of the receipt of the request. The planning authority's declaration is given to the person who made the request and, where appropriate, to the owner and occupier of the land in question. If, however, the planning authority considers that it does not have sufficient information to

---

205. Note that PDA 2000, s 218 has been amended by PD(SI)A 2006, s 39(a).
206. PDA 2000, s 57(1) as amended by PD(A)A 2010, s 34 and by PD(A)A 2002, s 13.
207. PDA 2000, s 5(1).

prepare its declaration it may require the person making the request to submit further information and where that further information is received by the planning authority the planning authority will make its declaration within three weeks of the date of receipt of the further information. A planning authority may request persons other than the person making the request to submit information in order to enable it to issue a declaration.[208]

**[4.138]** PDA 2000, s 5(3) provides that any person issued with a declaration may, on payment of the prescribed fees, refer the declaration for review by the board within four weeks of the date of issue of the declaration. In the event that no declaration is issued by the planning authority, any person who requested the declaration may, on payment of the prescribed fee, refer the question for decision to the board within four weeks of the date when the declaration was due to issue (namely four weeks after the request was submitted to the planning authority).[209]

**[4.139]** PDA 2000, s 5(4) provides that a planning authority may itself, on payment of the prescribed fees, refer any question as to what is or is not exempted development to the board by way of referral.

**[4.140]** PDA 2000, s 5(5) provides that details of any declarations issued by the planning authority or details of the decision of the board on referral shall be entered in the planning authority's planning register.

**[4.141]** PDA 2000, s 5(6) requires the board to keep a record of any decision made by it on referral, to include the main reasons and considerations on which its decision is based, and these shall be made available for purchase and inspection. The Board may charge a fee not exceeding the cost of making a copy for the purchase of a copy of the record kept by the board. At least once a year, the board is compelled to forward a copy of the record kept by the board of the decisions made by it on referrals to each planning authority. Members of planning authorities are entitled to a copy of the board's record of referrals, the record to be given to the member by the manager of the planning authority concerned.[210]

**[4.142]** The main purpose of the s 5 procedure is to provide a service so that members of the public and, in some circumstances, planning authorities may obtain a decision as to whether any particular development is or is not exempted development. There are frequent occasions in the course of development when the decision as to whether the development is or is not an exempted development is unclear. The section has a second purpose. It may also be used by members of the public when they are threatened with an enforcement action because a particular development is, in the opinion of the planning authority, an unauthorised development. In order to determine the matter, members of the public may submit a referral and if, for example, that referral determines that the development is not authorised under a planning permission and is not exempted development then, it follows, that it is unauthorised development. The referral

---

208. PDA 2000, s 5(2)(a), (b) and (c).
209. PDA 2000, s 5(3)(a) and (b).
210. PDA 2000, s 5(6)(a)–(d).

procedures effectively permit any person who submits a referral to determine whether a development falls within the scope of an existing planning permission. PDA 2000, s 5 has removed the statutory right of appeal to the High Court. It is now outside the jurisdiction of the High Court to decide, as a question of law, whether or not a development is or was a development requiring planning permission or is a development which does not require permission because it is exempted development.

**[4.143]** In *Grianán an Aileach Interpretive Centre Co Ltd v Donegal County Council*,[211] the plaintiff obtained permission to develop a visitor centre and the user clause was defined in the grant of permission as being for the 'erection of a visitor centre with history exhibition space, nature exhibition space, audio visual theatre, craft shop, centre of intercultural activity, waiting area and associated facilities as well as an outdoor pond and sewage treatment system at Speenoge, Burt, Co Donegal.' The plaintiff's case was that his interpretation of the user clause was to the effect that he could operate a full restaurant at the centre and hold evening functions such as concerts, banquets, music and dancing celebrations. Donegal County Council relied strictly upon the wording of the user clause and the plaintiff sought a declaration that the planning authority had misinterpreted the condition. In the High Court, Kelly J granted the declaration sought on the basis that the permission clearly contemplated the provision of food and drink as ancillary functions on the premises and evening functions which cover music, poetry, song and dance, etc, also involved cultural and intercultural activities. The High Court held that there was no material change of use for which a new planning permission was required. The Supreme Court reversed the High Court decision. Keane CJ held that the appeal of the local authority should be allowed. The Chief Justice relied on the position as set out in *O'Keefe v An Bord Pleanála*,[212] which made it perfectly clear that the legislature has unequivocally and firmly placed questions of planning, questions of the balance between development and the environment and the proper convenience and amenities of an area within the jurisdiction of the planning authority and the board. The Supreme Court held that the court is not vested with that jurisdiction nor is it expected to nor can it exercise discretion with regard to planning matters. In allowing the appeal, the Supreme Court held that to do otherwise would mean that the High Court was acting, in effect, as a form of planning tribunal.

> The reasoning adopted in both *McMahon v Dublin Corporation*[213] and *Palmerlane Ltd v An Bord Pleanála*[214] which, I am satisfied, is correct in law would indicate that, in such circumstances, a question as to whether the proposed uses constitute a 'development' which is not authorised by the planning permission is one which may be determined under the 2000 Act either by the planning authority or by An Bord Pleanála.[215]

---

211. *Grianán an Aileach Interpretive Centre Co Ltd v Donegal County Council* [2004] 2 IR 625, SC.
212. *O'Keefe v An Bord Pleanála* [1993] 1 IR 39.
213. *McMahon v Dublin Corporation* [1997] 1 ILRM 227.
214. *Palmerlane Ltd v An Bord Pleanála* [1999] 2 ILRM 514, HC.
215. *Grianán an Aileach Interpretive Centre Co Ltd v Donegal County Council* [2004] 2 IR 625 *per* Keane J.

In *Palmerlane Ltd v An Bord Pleanála*,[216] the developer contended that his retail premises could be used for the sale of hot food and this was disputed by the planning authority. The matter was submitted by referral to the board but the board refused to deal with it because in the board's view the matter as to use was, at least in part, governed by a grant of planning permission. The Board claimed it had no jurisdiction to decide whether or not a particular development was carried out in accordance with a particular permission. The High Court, applying the judgment in *McMahon v Dublin Corporation*,[217] held that the board had jurisdiction in these circumstances and further the court held that to say otherwise would have created the anomalous position that some of the chain of the applicant's shops which were governed by planning permission would have such issues determined in prosecutions brought by the planning authority whereas other shops which had a pre-1963 use would have these matters determined before the board. The court made an order of *certiorari* quashing the board's decision to refuse to consider the reference.

**[4.144]** Section 5 referrals are not confined to existing development; these referrals can also relate to future development. The effect of this is that a person who is contemplating development may submit a referral by submitting plans for the proposed development to the planning authority seeking a determination as to whether or not a particular development is exempted development or development which requires planning permission. No appeal can be taken to the High Court against the determination of a referral to either the planning authority or An Bord Pleanála. If any proceedings are contemplated in the High Court these must be limited to a judicial review to examine the steps taken in making the determination on the basis of the restricted judicial review procedure in PDA 2000, s 50 (as substituted by the PD(SI)A 2006, s 13).[218]

**[4.145]** If the board misinterprets a statutory provision in applying it to particular circumstances, the court is at liberty to set aside the board's decision on the basis that it erred in law.[219] There are still some incidents where an appeal to the High Court may be possible. In *Roadstone Provinces Ltd v An Bord Pleanála*,[220] Finlay Geoghegan J in the High Court set aside a referral determination made by An Bord Pleanála due to the absence of any factual finding. The Board had made a s 5 declaration stating that since different planning considerations applied to the further extension of a quarry, this meant that the development was not exempt from the requirement of the planning permission. In coming to that conclusion the board did not take into account as to whether or not there had been a material change in use from the pre-1964 use of the quarry. Whether or

---

216. *Palmerlane Ltd v An Bord Pleanála* [1999] 2 ILRM 514, HC.
217. *McMahon v Dublin Corporation* [1997] 1 ILRM 227.
218. The margin note for PDA 2000, s 50 as substituted by PD(SI)A 2006, s 13 reads 'Judicial review of applications, appeals, referrals and other matters'.
219. See *Coras Iompair Éireann v An Bord Pleanála* (unreported, 19 June 2008) HC *per* Clark J.
220. *Roadstone Provinces Ltd v An Bord Pleanála* [2008] IEHC 210 (4 July 2008) *per* Finlay Geoghegan J.

not there was a material change of use was a question of fact to be determined independently from planning considerations. The court approved the decision in *Galway County Council v Lackagh Rock Ltd* where Barron J was quoted as follows:

> To test whether or not the uses are materially different, it seems to me, that what should be looked at are the matters which the planning authority would take into account in the event of a planning application being made either for the use on the appointed day or for the present use. [221]

Finlay Geoghegan J set aside the board's s 5 declaration holding that the board would have to determine that there had been a change in use before looking at planning considerations such as, as was the situation in this case, the impact which the extension works would have on the proposed natural heritage area.

[4.146] In *Meath County Council v Patrick Shiels*,[222] Hedigan J gave a clear endorsement of the test set out in the *Roadstone* case.[223] The defendant operated a pre-1964 quarry and the evidence showed that there had been a greatly increased activity in the amount of stone extracted from the quarry since 2006. In the course of the evidence it had also been shown that the defendant had forged a registration form and in doing so had greatly understated the activity in the quarry at the time that the form was filed. Hedigan J held that, in applying the test in *Roadstone*, there had been a change of use since 2006. Firstly, there was a substantial increase in output estimated at three times the volume compared with pre-2006 volumes. Secondly, there had been a significant change in production methods with a consequent increase in noise and dust. Thirdly, there had been an increase in the area of operation within the quarry. Having determined that there was a change of use the next question was whether or not that change was a material change in use. The learned judge determined that it was material and that, in consequence, the development was unauthorised. It is clear from these cases that a court will not be precluded from determining whether a matter is development in an enforcement action such as under PDA 2000, s 160.[224]

## *PDA 2000, s 34(5) referrals*

[4.147] A referral under PDA 2000, s 34(5),[225] as amended, must be considered in the context of the entirety of s 34 which, in effect, provides that a planning authority may decide to grant permission under this section (as amended) where it has received an

---

221. *Galway County Council v Lackagh Rock Ltd* [1985] IR 120 *per* Barron J.
222. *Meath County Council v Shiels* [2008] IEHC 355.
223. *Roadstone Provinces Ltd v An Bord Pleanála* [2008] IEHC 210 (4 July 2008) *per* Finlay Geoghegan J.
224. PDA 2000, s 160 deals specifically with injunctions in relation to unauthorised development. The section has been amended in s 160(6) by excluding the operation of a quarry and the extraction of peat from the provision which excludes enforcement proceedings from being taken against an unauthorised development which has been in existence for more than seven years.
225. PDA 2000, s 34(5) has been amended by PD(SI)A 2006, s 8(2). The above paragraph contains the amended version.

application in accordance with permission regulations and all requirements of those regulations have been complied with. The planning authority's decision to grant permission may be made subject to or without conditions. On occasions, conditions in planning permissions often provide that there may be matters which are outstanding and which must be agreed between the planning authority and the person carrying out the development. Examples of this would include a condition which provides for a scheme of tree planting. If the scheme cannot be agreed between the planning authority and the person carrying out the development then the matter may be submitted to the board for determination by way of referral.

**[4.148]** Under the provisions of PDA 2000,[226] where points of detail relating to a grant of permission could not be agreed between the planning authority and the person carrying out the development, such points of detail were submitted to the board by either party by way of referral. The PD(SI)A 2006 provides that agreement on points of detail should be reached between the planning authority and the person carrying out the development (as opposed to the person who was granted permission). In the event of disagreement it is the planning authority or the person carrying out the development, or both, who will submit the referral to An Bord Pleanála for decision.[227]

## *PDA 2000, s 37(5) referrals*

**[4.149]** PDA 2000, s 37(5) deals with appeals to the board and, in that context, prevents any further application for permission being made for the same development, or for a development of the same description as an application for permission for development which is the subject of an appeal before the board, unless:

(i) The Board has made its decision on the appeal;

(ii) The appeal is withdrawn; or

(iii) The appeal is dismissed by the board in circumstances where either certain documents have not been produced to the board when required by it[228] or where the board has dismissed the appeal because it is vexatious, frivolous or made with the sole intention of delaying the development or securing payment of money, gifts, consideration or other inducements.[229]

If a dispute arises as to whether the application for permission is for the same development or is for a development of the same description as an application for permission which is subject to an appeal, that dispute may be sent by referral to the board for determination by referral.[230]

---

226. PDA 2000, s 34(5) as amended by PD(SI)A 2006, s 8(2).
227. See also **Ch 3** re conditions in planning permissions.
228. PDA 2000, s 133.
229. PDA 2000, s 138. Note: s 138(1)(a) was substituted by PD(SI)A 2006, s 24.
230. PDA 2000, s 37(5)(a), (b) and (c).

## PDA 2000, s 57(2), (3) and (4) referrals[231]

**[4.150]** PDA 2000, Pt IV deals with protected structures. PDA 2000, s 57 (as amended)[232] permits an owner or occupier of a protected structure or of a proposed protected structure to make a written request to a planning authority within whose functional area the structure is situated, to issue a declaration as to the type of works which it considers would or would not materially affect the character of a structure or any element of the structure which contributes to a special architectural, historical, archaeological, artistic, cultural, scientific, social or technical interest.[233] The planning authority shall issue a declaration within 12 weeks after receiving a request having regard to guidelines issued by the Minister for Arts, Heritage, Gaeltacht and the Islands and having regard to any recommendations to the planning authorities concerning specific structures made by that Minister in writing to that planning authority.[234] Any person who has had a declaration from a planning authority or had a declaration reviewed by a planning authority may on payment of the prescribed fee to the board refer the declaration for review by the board within four weeks from the date of the issuing of the declaration, or the declaration as reviewed as the case may be.[235] A declaration issued under PDA 2000, s 57 may be reviewed by a planning authority at any time but any review will not affect any works carried out in reliance on the declaration prior to the review.[236]

## PDA 2000, s 96(5) referrals[237]

**[4.151]** PDA 2000, s 96 as amended by PD(A)A 2002, s 3 is a part of the provisions of Pt V dealing with housing supply. PDA 2000, Pt V provides for housing strategies to be prepared by planning authorities for inclusion as part of the development plan in order that planning authorities can ensure that adequate land is available for housing and sufficient social and affordable housing is provided in their areas. PDA 2000, s 96 has been substituted by s 3 of PD(A)A 2002, which came into effect on 24 December 2002. The purpose of s 96 is to ensure that applicants for planning permission for the development of dwelling houses on land are compelled to enter into an agreement with the planning authority to transfer part of the land or enter into some other agreement such as building other houses or paying a sum of money to satisfy the social and affordable requirement specified in the housing strategy. The principal change in the

---

231. PDA 2000, s 57 has been amended by PD(A)A 2002; s 57(4)(a) is amended by PD(A)A 2002 s 13(a); s 57(4)(b) is amended by PD(A)A 2002, s 13(b); and s 57(8) and (9) amended by PD(A)A 2002, s 13(c).
232. *Meath County Council v Patrick Shiels* [2008] IEHC 355.
233. PDA 2000, s 57(1) and (2). Note: PDA 2000, s 57(1) has been amended by PD(A)A 2010, s 34.
234. PDA 2000, s 57(2), (3), (4) and (5) as amended by PD(A)A 2002, s 13(a) and (b). Note that two separate ministerial positions now exist in place of one, namely (i) Minister for the Environment, Heritage and Local Government (ii) Minister for Community, Rural and Gaeltacht Affairs.
235. PDA 2000, s 57(8) as inserted by PD(A)A 2002, s 13(c).
236. PDA 2000, s 57(7).
237. PDA 2000, s 96(5) has been substituted by a new sub-s (5). See PD(A)A 2002, s 3.

**[4.152]** *Planning and Environmental Law in Ireland*

new s 96 is that a greater range of options were provided in relation to the types of agreement which could be entered into.

**[4.152]** PDA 2000, s 96(5) as substituted provides that:

> In the case of a dispute in relation to any matter which may be the subject of an agreement under this section, other than a dispute relating to a matter that falls within sub-section (7), the matter may be referred by the planning authority or any other prospective party to the agreement to the Board for determination.

**[4.153]** The original s 96 of PDA 2000 contained restrictions which precluded certain disputes from being forwarded to the board for resolution by referral namely:

(a) a dispute on the question of transferring land to the planning authority under the agreement or transferring such number of fully or partially serviced sites as the agreement may specify,

(b) a dispute as to the amount of compensation payable,

(c) a dispute as to the sum payable to the planning authority where, for some reasons of size, shape or other attribute of a site, either the planning authority or the board consider that an agreement is not practical, the planning authority or the board may, as a condition of grant of permission, require payment to the planning authority.

These restrictions have been removed and in consequence any dispute in relation to a matter the subject of an s 96 agreement may be sent by way of referral to the board for determination except those matters which must be referred to the property arbitrator.

## *PDA 2000, s 193(2) referrals*

**[4.154]** PDA 2000, s 193 provides that compensation shall be payable where a permission is refused for the erection of a new structure which substantially replaces a structure which has been demolished or destroyed by fire or otherwise than by an unlawful act of the owner or occupier within the two years preceding the date of application for permission or, if a condition has been imposed in consequence of which the structure may not be used for the purpose for which the demolished or destroyed structure was last used or where a condition has been imposed in consequence of which the new structure or the front of the new structure or the front of an existing structure (other than an unauthorised structure) which has been taken down in order to be re-erected or altered, is set back or forward, in any of those circumstances where a dispute arises as to whether a new structure would or does replace substantially a demolished or destroyed structure such dispute may be referred to the board for determination by way of referral.[238]

---

238. PDA 2000, s 193(1) and (2).

# PART II: STATUTORY JUDICIAL REVIEW

## Article 10(a) of the EIA Directive – Judicial Review in Ireland

[4.155] Scannell defines environmental impact assessment (EIA) as

> an integrated process designed to assess the environmental impact of new and sometimes modified developments before they are carried out in order to mitigate the adverse environmental impacts of the proposed development to the point where the project becomes environmentally acceptable.[239]

EC law has increasingly started to impact on Irish land use planning and development principally through Directive 85/337/EEC, as amended by Directive 97/11/EC on Environmental Impact Assessment. There are numerous other examples where EU Environmental Directives have impacted with good effect on planning and development law in Ireland including, by way of example: (a) Directive 79/409/EEC on wild birds; (b) Directive 91/271/EEC dealing with urban waste water treatment; (c) Directive 91/676/EEC dealing with protection of waters against pollution from nitrates and other agricultural fertilisers; (d) Directive 92/43/EEC on conservation of natural habitats and of wild flora and fauna;[240] and (e) Directive 96/82/EC on control of major accident hazards involving dangerous substances (as amended).

[4.156] In contrast to the Directives listed at (a)–(e) inclusive above, Directive 85/337/EEC is a Directive which affects procedural aspects of land use management and regulation and which specifically deals with EIA.

[4.157] Directive 2003/35/EC is dated 26 May 2003 and provides for public participation in respect of the drawing up of certain plans; it provides programmes relating to the environment and amendments with regard to public participation and access to justice. Directive 2003/35/EC provides two definitions as follows:

> 'the public' means: one or more natural or legal persons and, in accordance with national legislation or practice, their associations, organisations or groups;[241]

> 'the public concerned' means: the public affected or likely to be affected by or having an interest in, the environmental decision-making procedures referred to in art 2(2);[242]

For the purposes of this definition, non-governmental organisations (NGOs) promoting environmental protection and meeting any requirement under national law shall be deemed to have an interest.

---

239. See Scannell, *Environmental and Land Use Law* (Thomson Round Hall, 2006) at para 5-01, p 377.
240. The Habitats Directive (Council Directive 92/43/EEC on the Conservation of Natural Habitats and of Wild Flora and Fauna Directive has probably had the most influence on land use policies in Ireland).
241. Directive 2003/35/EC, arts 2(1) and 3(1).
242. Directive 2003/35/EC, art 3(1).

**[4.158]** Article 2(2) referred to above provides that Member States shall ensure that the public is given early and effective opportunities to participate in the preparation and modification or review of the plans or programmes required to be drawn up under the provisions listed in Annex 1 and to that end Member States shall ensure that the public is informed, whether by public notice or other appropriate means such as electronic media where available, about any proposals for such plans or programmes or for their modification or review and that relevant information about such proposals is made available to the public including, *inter alia*, information about the right to participate in decision making and about the competent authority to which comments or questions may be submitted. Member states will also ensure that the public is entitled to express comments and opinions when all options are open and before decisions on the plans and programmes are made. Also, when Member States make those decisions, due account shall be taken of the results of the public participation. Member states will also ensure that having examined the comments and opinions expressed by the public, the competent authority makes reasonable efforts to inform the public about the decisions taken and the reasons and considerations upon which those decisions are based, including information about the public participation process.

**[4.159]** Member States shall identify the public entitled to participate for the purposes of para 2, including relevant NGOs meeting any requirements imposed under national law, such as those promoting environmental protection. The detailed arrangements for public participation under the article shall be determined by the Member States so as to enable the public to prepare and participate effectively. Reasonable time-frames shall be provided allowing sufficient time for each of the different stages of public participation required by art 2(2). The article shall not apply to plans and programmes designed for the sole purpose of serving national defence or to actions taken in cases of civil emergencies. The article shall not apply to plans and programmes set out in Annex A for which a public participation procedure is carried out under Directive 2001/42/EC of the European Parliament and of the Council of 27 June 2001 on the assessment of the affects of certain plans and programmes on the environment or under Directive 2000/60/EC of the European Parliament and of the Council of 23 October 2000 establishing a framework for Community action in the field of water policy.[243]

**[4.160]** In relation to Irish judicial review procedures, as amended, art 10(a) has been introduced to the EIA Directive and Member States are now required to ensure that, in accordance with the relevant national legal system members of the public concerned are protected by certain guidelines and guarantees. EIA Directive 85/337/EEC was amended with the insertion of art 10(a) of the Public Participation Directive 2003/35/EC. Art 10(a) provides as follows:

> Member States shall ensure that, in accordance with the relevant national legal system, members of the public concerned:
>
> (a)   having a sufficient interest, or alternatively,

---

243. See Directive 2003/35/EC, art 2 (1)–(5).

(b) maintaining the impairment of a right, where administrative procedural law of a Member State requires this as a pre-condition,

(c) have access to a review procedure before a court of law or another independent and impartial body established by law to challenge the substantive or procedural legality of decisions, acts or omissions subject to the public participation provisions of this Directive,

(d) Member States shall determine at what stage the decisions, acts or omissions may be challenged,

(e) what constitutes a sufficient interest and impairment of a right shall be determined by the Member States, consistently with the objective of giving the public concerned wide access to justice. To this end, the interest of any non governmental organisation meeting the requirements referred to in art 1(2), shall be deemed sufficient for the purpose of sub-paragraph (a) of this Article. Such organisations shall also be deemed to have rights capable of being impaired for the purpose of sub-paragraph (b) of this Article,

(f) the provisions of this Article shall not exclude the possibility of a preliminary review procedure before an administrative authority and shall not affect the requirement of exhaustion of administrative review procedure prior to recourse to judicial review procedures, where such a requirement exists under national law,

(g) any such procedure shall be fair, equitable, timely and not prohibitively expensive,

(h) in order to further the effectiveness of the provisions of this article, Member States shall ensure that practical information is made available to the public on access to administrative and judicial review procedures.

The 'Participation Directive' 2003/35/EC was, effectively, spawned from the deliberations which took place at the Aarhus Convention. The purpose of that Convention, signed at Aarhus in Denmark on 25 June 1998, was to provide articles allowing for access to information, public participation in decision making and access to justice in environmental matters. The purpose of art 9(4) of the Aarhus Convention is to allow members of the public to assert personal rights in environmental matters before a tribunal or court where the procedures, as laid down by the Member States, are fair, equitable, timely and not prohibitively expensive. Directive 2003/35/EC requires Member States to provide a review procedure which will allow challenges to the substantive or procedural legality of decisions and of acts or omissions subject to public participation provided by the Directive. Member States had until 25 June 2005, at latest, to comply with Directive 2003/35/EC.

**[4.161]** In summary, the aim of Directive 2003/35/EC is to ensure that certain provisions of the Aarhus Convention dealing with such matters as public participation in decision making, access to justice in environmental matters and access to information are reflected fairly in the legislation of Member States.

## Commission v Ireland Case C–427/07

[4.162] In *Commission of the European Communities v Ireland*,[244] Ireland was challenged for failure to fulfil obligations imposed on 14 September 2007. The Commission made two separate complaints against Ireland:

1. That Council Directive 85/337/EEC of 27 June 1985 on the assessment of the effects of certain public and private projects on the environment as amended by Council Directive 97/11/EC of 3 March 1997 ('the EIA Directive') has not been transferred by Ireland in relation to private roads.

2. Ireland had not fully transposed Directive 2003/35/EC dated 26 May 2003 providing for public participation in respect of the drawing up of certain plans and programmes relating to the environment and amending with regard to public participation and access to justice, Council Directive 85/337/EEC and 96/61/EC; and Ireland did not inform the Commission regarding such transpositions.

[4.163] A clear statement was made by Advocate General Kokott on 15 January 2009 which reads as follows:

> Access to justice under Irish planning law is the focal point of the action. In this context it is necessary in particular to deal with a contradiction in the Commission's submissions: on the one hand, it insists that it is complaining only about the lack of implementing measures and not about the quality of such measures while, on the other, it discusses assiduously the quality of Irish measures, that is to say whether certain Irish measures satisfy the requirements of Directive 2003/35.

In fact, Advocate General Kokott was quite correct to highlight this 'contradiction' and this was picked up at para 49 of the judgment in *Commission v Ireland* C–427/07:

> The second complaint, considered in its various parts, as pleaded in essence by the Commission, thus relates exclusively – as the Commission, moreover, confirmed at the hearing – to the failure to transpose certain provisions of Directive 2003/35, without any criticism of the quality of transposition, and, consequently, no such criticism may properly be raised by the Commission in the context of this case.[245]

[4.164] Questions as to the quality or effectiveness of the implementing measures will, in all probability, be looked at again by the Commission if they should decide to challenge, as a separate issue, the quality of transposition. The Commission's first complaint against Ireland in Case C–472/07 to the European Courts of Justice (ECJ) was registered in 2001 and it concerned damage to a coastal wet land at Commogue Marsh, Kinsale, Co Cork caused by the construction of a private road project. The Commogue Marsh is served by a private road and the Commission made the case that

---

244. *Commission of the European Communities v Ireland* (Case C–427/07) judgment of the Court (Second Chamber) delivered 16 July 2009.
245. *Commission of the European Communities v Ireland* (Case C–427/07) judgment of the Court (Second Chamber) delivered 16 July 2009, para 49.

Ireland had not undertaken any EIA in relation to the development of the private road to establish whether or not that development would have an adverse impact on the Commogue Marsh. The Commission contended that the area where the roadway was built was a sensitive area and that the road had been built contrary to the requirements of Directive 85/337/EEC as amended by Directive 97/11/EC. It was also the Commission's case that the construction of a private road constitutes an infrastructure project and that Ireland is bound to ensure that before consent (planning permission) was given an EIA must be carried out to assess the effects on the environment of the construction of the road. Ireland agreed that private road development falls within Directive 85/337/EEC, as amended by Directive 97/11/EC, but Ireland's case was that development of private roads is almost invariably an integral part of other developments which do require EIA. Furthermore, Ireland accepted that Directive 85/337/EEC, as amended by Directive 97/11/EC, does not make the distinction between public and private road projects. Ireland stated that it intended to amend its legislation so as to include road development as a stand-alone category subject to an EIA if the road development (whether public or private) is likely to have significant effects on the environment. The Commission was satisfied that any road construction development carried out in isolation in Ireland could, as the legislation then existed, avoid an EIA even if the development was likely to have significant effects on the environment. The ECJ concluded that the complaint in relation to the private road was well founded. The court stated the following:

> In that regard, by subjecting private road construction development to an environmental impact assessment only if that development formed part of other developments coming within the scope of Directive 85/337 as amended by Directive 97/11 and themselves subject to the assessment obligation, the Irish legislation, as applicable when the time-limit set in the reasoned opinion expired meant that any private road construction development carried out in isolation could avoid an environmental impact assessment, even if the development was likely to have significant affects on the environment.[246]

The second complaint has a number of component parts all of which result from the fact that Ireland has not transposed a number of articles from Directive 2003/5/EC but that complaint is made in relation to the failure to transpose and is made without any criticism of the quality of transposition. Various parts of the second complaint include the following.

## *Transposition of the term 'the public concerned'*

[4.165] The Commission required Ireland to adopt measures to ensure that domestic legislation does not treat concepts of 'the public' and 'the public concerned' more narrowly than Directive 2003/35/EC. Directive 2003/35/EC does accord the public concerned with certain rights but the Commission submitted that, in particular, the rights of NGOs are not adequately safe-guarded in Ireland. Ireland replied that there is already a general obligation to interpret national law in accordance with the provisions

---

246. *Commission of the European Communities v Ireland* (Case C–427/07) Judgement of the Court (Second Chamber) delivered 16 July 2009 at para 44.

of Community law and that that obligation is adhered to by the courts in Ireland. It was Ireland's case that no separate legislative definitions of 'the public' and 'the public concerned' were necessary in order to give full effect to those definitions. The newly created rights are already guaranteed to all the public and in those circumstances there is no necessity for any specific definition of 'the public concerned'. Ireland has introduced a specific provision which makes it clear that NGOs promoting the environment are exempt from the requirement to demonstrate that they have a substantial interest.[247] This complaint, insofar as it concerns the transposition of art 3(1) of Directive 2003/35/EC, was held by the ECJ to be unfounded.

**[4.166]** The Commission also complained that arts 3(3)–(6) and art 4(2) and (3) have not been fully transposed and that in relation to art 4(2) and (3), Ireland recognised that it still had to adopt and notify certain measures in relation to full transposition of those provisions when the time limit prescribed in the reasoned opinion furnished by the Commission had elapsed. The ECJ found that the complaints in relation to art 3(3)–(6) and art 4(2) and (3) were well founded.

## *Access to justice*

**[4.167]** The Commission made two complaints in relation to the transposition of art 10(a) of the EIA Directive (2003/35/EC) and in relation to art 15(a) of Directive 96/61/EC. The Commission claimed that art 10(a) has not been transposed into Irish law and that the requirements of art 15(a) of Directive 96/61, which requires Ireland to communicate all measures taken for the purposes of transposition, had not been complied with.

**[4.168]** The Commission looked at five separate headings in relation to the failure to transpose art 10(a) of the EIA Directive and art 15(a) of Directive 96/61/EC and the failure to communicate all measures taken for the purposes of transposition. These five complaints by the Commission are dealt with at paras (a)–(e) below.

    *(a) Sufficient interest*

    An immediate difference arises here in that the first paragraph of art 10(a) of the EIA Directive and sub-para (a) of the first paragraph of art 15 of Directive 96/61/EC allow the Member States to make access to justice conditional upon the applicant having a 'sufficient interest'. The Commission objected to the fact that under Irish law provision for judicial review can only be sought by an applicant having a 'substantial interest'.[248] It was the Commission's case that the concept of 'sufficient interest' is not the same as the concept of 'substantial interest'. The two standards required by the Commission and by Ireland respectively do not correspond and the Irish requirement of a 'substantial interest' is stricter than the phrase used in art 10(a), namely, 'sufficient interest'. The Commission argued that that difference amounted to non-

---

247. PDA 2000, s 50A(3)(b)(ii) as substituted by PD(SI)A 2006, s 13.
248. PDA 2000, s 50A(3)(b)(i) as inserted by PD(SI)A 2006, s 13.

transposition of the requirements laid down in Directive 2003/35/EC. In support of its case, the Commission referred to the two judgments of the Irish High Court in *Friends of Curragh Environment Ltd* as demonstrating that the system of judicial review in Ireland cannot be regarded as implementing Directive 2003/35/EC since, in that case, the High Court stated, in relation to the assessment of 'substantial interest', that that Directive had not yet been implemented in Irish law.[249]

One of the arguments which the Commission relied upon in support of its case was based on a statement made by Kelly J in *Friends of the Curragh Environment Ltd v An Bord Pleanála*.[250] In that case, Kelly J concluded that art 10(a) of Directive 85/337/EEC, as inserted by Directive 2003/35/EC, though not given effect by the State within the time permitted, cannot be considered to have direct effect.

Ireland disagreed with the Commission stating that the judgment handed down by the High Court in *Sweetman v An Bord Pleanála*[251] established, on the contrary, that the above mentioned provisions of that Directive were implemented by the judicial review procedure, supplemented by specific procedural rules laid down in certain legislation, in particular, s 50 of PDA 2000. In *Sweetman*,[252] Clarke J held that the requirement to meet a higher 'substantial interest' rather than the former 'sufficient interest' does not breach the 'sufficient interest' test set out in art 10(a). The words used in art 10(a) are that *'what constitutes a sufficient interest and impairment of right shall be determined by the Member State'*. Clarke J held that the terms 'substantial interest' and 'sufficient interest' have particular meaning in Irish judicial review law. Clarke J stated:

> If it should prove to be necessary, on the facts of any individual case, to give a more generous interpretation of the requirement of 'substantial interest' so as to meet the 'wide access to justice' criteria set out in art 10(a) then there would be no difficulty in construing the term 'substantial interest' in an appropriate manner. It seems to me that it follows, therefore, that the term needs to be construed having regard to the required that art 10(a) (in the case to which it applies, such as this) and having regard to the requirement that there be wide access to justice.

Article 10(a) was also considered by Kearns J in *Harding v Cork County Council and Another*,[253] where the learned judge, in agreeing with an argument submitted to him that what constitutes a sufficient interest and impairment of a

---

249. See *Friends of the Curragh Environment Ltd v An Bord Pleanála and Others* [2006] IEHC 390.
250. *Friends of the Curragh Environment Ltd v An Bord Pleanála* (unreported, 14 July 2006) HC, Kelly J.
251. *Sweetman v An Bord Pleanála and Others* [2007] IEHC 361 (26 April 2007).
252. *Sweetman v An Bord Pleanála and Others* [2007] IEHC 361 (26 April 2007).
253. *Harding v Cork County Council and Another* [2008] IESC 27.

right are expressly reserved by art 10(a) to the individual Member States, felt that it was not necessary to decide the point in that case but went on to say:

> Accepting that the Act falls to be interpreted in the light of the terms and objectives of the Directive in question it is also an established principle that such an interpretive approach does not mean that the Act be interpreted contra legem.

Advocate General Kokott had this to say:

> Ireland has decided that only a substantial interest is 'sufficient' for the purposes of the Directive. The Act explicitly makes it clear that a substantial interest is not limited to an interest in land or other financial interest. According to a judgement delivered quite recently by the Irish Supreme Court, the applicant must prove a peculiar and personal interest of significant weight which is affected by or connected with the development in question. The Commission puts forward no argument as to why this standard should be incompatible with the Directive.
>
> It could at most be wondered whether the restriction on rights of action is compatible with the express objective of granting wide access to justice. The earlier more generous rules regarding the necessary interest show that wider access to the Courts is in principle possible under the Irish legal system.
>
> However, in order to determine what constitutes sufficient interest to bring an action, a balance must necessarily be struck. Effective enforcement of the law militates in favour of wide access to the Courts. On the other hand, it is possible that many Court actions are unnecessary because the law has not been infringed. Unnecessary actions not only burden the Courts, but also in some cases adversely affect projects, whose, implementation can be delayed. Factors such as an increasing amount of legislation or a growing litigiousness of citizens, but also a change in environmental conditions, can affect the outcome of that balancing exercise. Accordingly, it cannot be automatically inferred from more generous access to the Courts than was previously available that a more restrictive approach would be incompatible with the objective of wide access.[254]

As regards the argument in relation to sufficient interest, the ECJ found that the argument was unfounded.

(b) *The scope of review before Irish Courts*

In relation to the possible scope of judicial review, the ECJ found that the Commission did not raise any specific objections and since there was no complaint alleging incorrect transposition of those provisions the Court ruled that the argument was unfounded.

(c) *The timely conduct of judicial proceedings*

This complaint is in relation to art 10(a) of the EIA Directive and art 15(a) of Directive 96/61/EC and concerns the duration of proceedings. Both articles, in

---

254. See opinion of Advocate General Kokott in *Commission of European Communities v Ireland* (Case C–427/07) delivered 15 January 2009.

their fifth paragraph, require that the conduct of proceedings must be timely. In this instance also the Court relied on the second judgment in *Friends of the Curragh Environment Ltd v An Bord Pleanála and others*,[255] where Kelly J stated that the Directive had not been transposed. The Court made reference to para 49 in its judgment, which is relevant to 'the timely conduct of judicial proceedings', where it states that since the Commission's complaints relate exclusively to the failure to transpose certain provisions of Directive 2003/35/EC that was the only matter to be considered and the Court felt that it should make that consideration without making any criticism of the quality of transposition. Consequently, no such criticism could properly be raised by the Commission in the context of the case. Ireland also referred to the provisions of PDA 2000, s 50(10)(a) and (11)(b), as amended by the Planning & Development (Strategic Infrastructure) Act 2006, which requires that applications must be determined as expeditiously as possible consistent with the administration of justice. The ECJ held that the argument in relation to this complaint was unfounded.

*(d) Legal costs*

The fifth paragraph of both art 10(a) of the EIA Directive and art 15(a) of Directive 96/61/EC provides that the procedures in question are not to be prohibitively expensive. The Commission made the point that there was no applicable ceiling as regards the amount that an unsuccessful applicant would have to pay and there is no legislative provision to state that the procedure will not be prohibitively expensive.

One of the arguments which the Commission relied upon was based on a statement of Kelly J in *Friends of the Curragh Environment Ltd v An Bord Pleanála*.[256] In that case, Kelly J held that the provisions of art 10(a) were not sufficiently clear, precise and unconditional as to have direct effect in considering the meaning of the words 'prohibitively expensive' which are used in art 10(a). The learned judge felt that it was not clear whether that term referred to court fees, which are chargeable by the State, or to the legal costs, which are not. The judge concluded that since the court fees are modest, if the Directive is dealing only with court fees it has no application whatsoever in the case of a pre-emptive or protective costs order (PCO).[257] In *Friends of the*

---

255. *Friends of the Curragh Environment Ltd v An Bord Pleanála and others* [2006] IEHC 390.
256. *Friends of the Curragh Environment Ltd v An Bord Pleanála* (unreported, 16 July 2006) HC, Kelly J.
257. Kelly J's conclusion was clearly wrong and, indeed, obtuse. PD(A)A 2010 in recognition of art 10(a) provides that costs in judicial review dealing with environmental matters shall be paid on the basis of each party bearing its own costs but adjustments can be made: (1) if the claim or counterclaim is frivolous or vexatious; (2) because of the manner in which the party conducted the proceedings; or (3) where the party is in contempt of court.

*Curragh Environment Ltd v An Bord Pleanála*,[258] the applicant company, as an NGO, applied for a PCO the effect of which, if granted, would offer immunity from any liability for the legal costs of the other parties to the application. The applicant also, in applying for the PCO, sought immunity from having to furnish security for costs or to provide undertakings as to damages. Kelly J ruled that the applicant company was not entitled under national law to a PCO. The learned judge then went on to rule that art 10(a) does not have direct effect.

It was Ireland's case that existing procedures are fair, equitable and not prohibitively expensive. The Commission was aware that the costs of unsuccessful parties can be very high in Ireland, stating that costs of hundreds of thousands of euro are possible. It was the Commission's case that there was insufficient protection against prohibitive costs. The ECJ had no difficulty in ruling that costs of procedures extends to all legal costs incurred by the parties involved and not merely to court fees. Advocate General Kokott, at paras 97 and 98 of her opinion delivered on 15 January 2009, said the following:

> 97. As the Commission acknowledges and Ireland emphasises, Irish Courts can though, in the exercise of their discretion, refrain from awarding costs against the unsuccessful party and even order the successful party to pay his costs. Therefore, a possibility of limiting the risk of prohibitive costs exists.
>
> 98. This possibility of limiting the risk of costs is, in my view, sufficient to prove that implementing measures exist. The Commission's action is therefore unfounded in relation to this point too.

In para 99 of her opinion, Ms Kokott stated:

> I wish to make the supplementary observation that the Commission's wider objection that Irish law does not oblige Irish Courts to comply with the requirements of the Directive when exercising their discretion as to costs is correct. In accordance with settled case-law, discretion which may be exercised in accordance with a Directive is not sufficient to implement provisions of a Directive since such a practice can be changed at any time. However, this objection already concerns the quality of the implementing measure and is therefore inadmissible.

In spite of that fairly firm opinion from the Advocate General, the ECJ, recognising that the Irish courts could decline to order an unsuccessful party to pay costs and could, in addition, order expenditure incurred by an unsuccessful party to be borne by the other party, noted that it was, nevertheless, a discretionary practice on the part of the courts. The ECJ concluded that since it was a discretionary practice it could not, by definition, be certain and the Irish practice could not be regarded as valid implementation of the obligations arising from art 10(a) of Directive 85/337/EEC, inserted by art 3(7) of Directive 2003/35/EC, and art 15(a) of Directive 96/61/EC, inserted by art 4(4) of Directive 2003/35/EC.

---

258. *Friends of the Curragh Environment Ltd v An Bord Pleanála* (unreported, 16 July 2006) HC, Kelly J.

The argument in relation to costs was held by the ECJ to be well founded.

*(e) Informing the public*

The final complaint made by the Commission in relation to art 10(a) of the EIA Directive and art 15(a) of Directive 96/61/EC dealt with the alleged failure on the part of Ireland to inform members of the public of their rights under the Directive. Member States have an obligation to provide practical information to the public dealing with the steps to be taken to access administrative and judicial review procedures. Once again, the Commission relied on both of the decisions in *Friends of the Curragh Environment Ltd v An Bord Pleanála and Others*.[259] In each case, Ireland neglected to disseminate practical information concerning access to justice. It was held that merely publishing legislation is not sufficient to meet the standards required in informing the public. The information that Member States are obliged to supply to the Commission must be clear and precise and must indicate unequivocally the laws, regulations and administrative provisions by which the Member State considers that it has satisfied the various requirements imposed by the Directive. It was held that the complaint against Ireland for failing to inform the public was well founded.

The ECJ found for and against Ireland in relation to the preliminary issue as to whether or not Ireland had put in place implementing measures. Those implementing measures are in place since PD(A)A 2010[260] became law but it remains to be seen if the Commission will pursue a second case against Ireland dealing with the quality or effectiveness of the implementing measures. Paragraph 49 of the judgment, which has been referred to, reads as follows:

> The second complaint, considered in its various parts, as pleaded in essence by the Commission, thus relates exclusively, as the Commission, moreover, confirmed at the hearing – to the failure to transpose certain provisions of Directive 2003/35, without any criticism of the quality of transposition, and, consequently, no such criticism may properly be raised by the Commission in the context of this case.

## Conclusion

**[4.169]** Statutory and conventional judicial review are both necessary and valuable processes in helping to keep all parties involved in the planning business on the straight and narrow path. The significance of the ECJ's findings against Ireland on the question of costs may not be fully recognised. To say anything about the costs of judicial review other than that they were 'prohibitively expensive' is, in reality, a matter of some difficulty. With respect to Kelly J's reasoning that the provisions of art 10(a) were not

---

259. First case *Friends of the Curragh Environment Ltd v An Bord Pleanála and Others* (unreported, 14 July 2006) HC, Finlay Geoghegan J and second case [2006] IEHC 390, Kelly J.
260. PD(A)A 2010, ss 32 and 33, which insert s 50B into PDA 2000, s 50. The amendment which will have the greatest effect is the requirement that each party (as a general rule) will bear their own costs but even that amendment may still discourage impecunious applicants from seeking judicial review.

sufficiently clear, precise and unconditional as to have direct effect because the learned judge could not decide from the wording whether the article referred to court fees or to the legal charges of practitioners, it is perfectly obvious that no complaint could be made against the court fees charged by the State which are modest and reasonable. The complaint is clearly related to legal charges charged by solicitors and by barristers in the course of this work. In defence of the lawyers it may be said that the level of their fees reflect the tortuous complexity of the judicial review process in planning matters. It is to be hoped that the amendments made in PD(A)A 2010 will be affective in assisting the process and in making it fairer.

[4.170] If judicial review is to work in a fair and equal way the process must be rationalised so that all citizens may embrace it. As it stands it is, like the doors of the Ritz Hotel, open to all comers. A large majority of the citizens cannot afford the prices on the menu. This is a serious complaint because it emphatically means that justice is denied to a great number of people. Many lawyers will have experienced the situation where they are forced to tell their clients that, although the case is stateable, the costs of bringing it to judicial review are 'prohibitive' in the sense that they are set so high as to debar a great number of people who might wish to use the process. The prohibitive expense of judicial review results in a stark and telling inequality in Irish society. It is one of a number of potential remedies which must be re-worked so that all comers may appear before the Courts of Ireland without having to put a second mortgage on the house.[261]

## What is statutory judicial review?

[4.171] Statutory judicial review may be distinguished from appeals and referrals to An Bord Pleanála in that statutory judicial review is neither an appeal against a decision nor a request for a ruling on a particular planning issue. It is a review of the decision-making process to establish whether or not mistakes have been made in the course of that process.[262] Statutory judicial review may also be distinguished from conventional judicial review procedures by the following characteristics, which relate only to statutory judicial review, namely:

(a) Proceedings must generally be issued and served within an eight-week period but that eight-week period can be extended by the High Court in certain limited circumstances.[263]

---

261. PD(A)A 2010, ss 32 and 33, which insert s 50B into PDA 2000, s 50. The amendment which will have the greatest effect is the requirement that each party (as a general rule) will bear their own costs but even that amendment may still discourage impecunious applicants from seeking judicial review.
262. *Chief Constable of North Wales Police v Evans* [1982] 1 WLR 1155.
263. PDA 2000, s 50(6), (7) and (8) as substituted by PD(SI)A 2006, s 13. The High Court can extend the eight-week period if it is satisfied (a) that there is good and sufficient reason for doing so, and (b) that the circumstances which resulted in the failure to make the application for leave within the period so provided were outside the control of the applicant for the extension.

(b) The application to the court for leave to appeal is made by motion *ex parte* grounded in the manner specified in the order in respect of an *ex parte* motion for leave.[264]

(c) The court, in considering an *ex parte* application for leave to appeal, will require an applicant to establish 'substantial grounds' for making the application and it will require the applicant to demonstrate that he has a 'substantial interest' in the subject matter of the application.[265]

(d) Any appeal, which the applicant may wish to take against a High Court decision to the Supreme Court in statutory judicial review cases, is restricted in that leave to appeal must be certified by the High Court.[266]

**[4.172]** Judicial review does not involve an appeal from a decision but rather it requires an applicant to make the case that there was some procedural error in the manner in which that decision was made. Judicial review does go beyond that. The review may also examine the procedures followed by the planning authority, the local authority or An Bord Pleanála to establish whether or not the decision made might have been in breach of fair procedures. In judicial review the courts may also examine the substantive merits of the decision in terms of administrative unreasonableness in order to establish whether or not the decision-maker has disregarded the principles of natural justice in the context of fundamental reason and common sense. Not all decisions or acts of a planning authority or of An Bord Pleanála are suitable for review under PDA 2000, s 50 as amended.[267]

**[4.173]** For example, judicial review is specifically excluded as a means of testing the validity of development plans that are not completed within the two year time limit provided.[268]

Where certain decisions are not suitable for statutory judicial review they may be dealt with by conventional judicial review procedures.

**[4.174]** PDA 2000, s 50 (as amended) provides as follows:

(1) Where a question of law arises on any matter with which the Board is concerned, the Board may refer the question to the High Court for decision.

(2) A person shall not question the validity of any decision made or other act done by:

(a) a planning authority, a local authority or the Board in the performance or purported performance of a function under this Act,

(b) the Board in the performance or purported performance of a function transferred under Part XIV,[269] or

---

264. PDA 2000, s 50A(2) as inserted by PD(SI)A 2006, s 13 and substituted by PD(A)A 2010, s 32.
265. PDA 2000, s 50A(3)(a) and (b), (4) and (5) as inserted by PD(SI)A 2006, s 13.
266. PDA 2000, s 50A(7) and (8) as inserted by PD(SI)A 2006, s 13.
267. PDA 2000, s 50 as amended by PD(SI)A 2006, s 13.
268. PDA 2000, s 12(16) as amended by PD(A)A 2002, s 7.
269. PDA 2000, Pt XIV, as amended deals with acquisition of land, etc, amending s 212.

(c) a local authority in the performance or purported performance of a function conferred by an enactment specified in s 214 relating to the compulsory acquisition of land.[270]

otherwise than by way of an application for judicial review under Order 84 of the Rules of the Superior Courts (SI No 15 of 1986) (the 'Order').

(3) Sub-section (2)(a) does not apply to approval or consent referred to in Chapter I or II of Part VI.[271]

Section 50(2) and (3) of PDA 2000 (as amended) deal with judicial review whereas s 50(1) permits the board to refer a question of law to the High Court in respect of any matter with which the board is concerned.

**[4.175]** In comparing the new statutory judicial review procedure subsequent to the amendments made by PD(SI)A 2006 with the provisions of PDA 2000, s 50 it is clear that, in some respects at least, the scope of statutory judicial review has been expanded in that it is no longer restricted to certain defined categories of decision and it now applies to any decision or act to which s 50(2) applies. For planning authorities or for the board that includes any decision or other acts done in performance or purported performance of a function under PDA 2000 (as amended). Furthermore, the amendments made to PDA 2000, s 50 by PD(SI)A 2006 remove a previous provision which required that the applicant had to show that he had prior participation in the process before making the application. Another distinction introduced by PD(SI)A 2006, s 13 is that the eight-week period in which the judicial review proceedings must be brought can be extended in limited circumstances only, namely:

(a) that the High Court is satisfied that there is good and sufficient reason for doing so; and

(b) that the circumstances that resulted in the failure to make the application for leave within the eight-week period were outside the control of the applicant for the extension.[272]

The courts have always made it perfectly clear that they are reluctant to interfere with the decisions of administrative bodies which work to make decisions as specialists or as experts in a particular field. To do otherwise would have wholly undermined the purpose for which such bodies were constituted. However, where planning authorities, the board or the EPA make decisions which are either unconstitutional or where such bodies stray from the legislative path provided by the relevant governing statute, the courts, if requested, are bound to examine the matter. The functions of the court may not permit it to question the merits of a decision of an administrative tribunal for

---

270. PDA 2000, s 214 deals with transfer of Minister's functions, in relation to compulsory acquisition of land, to the board. Section 214(2)(f) has been amended by LG Act 2001, s 247.
271. PDA 2000, Pt VI deals with An Bord Pleanála. Chapter 1, between ss 102 and 108, deals with the establishment and constitution of An Bord Pleanála. Chapter 2, between ss 109 and 124, deals with organisation, staffing, etc, in relation to An Bord Pleanála.
272. PDA 2000, s 50(3) as amended by PD(SI)A 2006, s 13(8).

unreasonableness or irrationality other than in very exceptional circumstances where the unreasonableness or the irrationality is outstanding.

**[4.176]** The decision in *O'Keefe v An Bord Pleanála*[273] is important in the planning law context and in the administrative law context. The decision greatly strengthens the hand of all administrative tribunals (not just planning tribunals) and the proposition is clearly stated that the court will not intervene on the basis of 'irrationality' unless the test laid down in *The State (Keegan) v Stardust Compensation Tribunal*[274] is met, namely that the decision can only be challenged for unreasonableness or irrationality where:

(a) it is fundamentally at variance with reason and common sense;

(b) it is indefensible for flying in the face of plain reason and common sense;

(c) the court is satisfied that the decision-maker has reached his decision by flagrantly rejecting or disregarding fundamental reason or common sense.

**[4.177]** The main points established by *O'Keefe v An Bord Pleanála*[275] are as follows:

1. The court will not intervene on the basis of irrationality or unreasonableness unless the tests laid down above are met (see *State (Keegan) v Stardust Compensation Tribunal*).[276]

2. The onus of proof is on the plaintiff to establish all relevant material, in the case of challenging for unreasonableness or irrationality, which was put before the board. This may involve affidavits of discovery, interrogatories, etc, which will produce the documentation, but those documents, on their own, will not necessarily prove precisely what material was before the board.

3. In *O'Keefe v An Bord Pleanála*,[277] it was contended that the board's order was bad for want of adequate reasoning, but this contention was not upheld by the Supreme Court on the basis that the board must rely not only upon the stated reasons given for granting permission, but also upon the conditions attached to the grant which were accompanied by the reasons.

4. The alleged failure to keep a minute book did not invalidate the decision. It was held that there was a sufficient minute but, even if it was not sufficient, the onus was on the plaintiff to request the minute or the minute book and any insufficiency could be made good subsequently in the context of a challenge, by responding to such a request.

In *O'Keefe v An Bord Pleanála*,[278] Finlay CJ stated that planning authorities and the board are expected to have special skills, competence and experience in planning

---

273. *O'Keefe v An Bord Pleanála* [1993] 1 IR 39.
274. *The State (Keegan) v Stardust Compensation Tribunal* [1986] IR 642.
275. *O'Keefe v An Bord Pleanála* [1993] 1 IR 39.
276. *The State (Keegan) v Stardust Compensation Tribunal* [1986] IR 642.
277. *O'Keefe v An Bord Pleanála* [1993] 1 IR 39.
278. *O'Keefe v An Bord Pleanála* [1993] 1 IR 39.

questions. Therefore, the courts are very reluctant to interfere with their decisions and will only find their decision to be 'unreasonable' in rare circumstances, where it is so manifestly unreasonable, in the sense of flying in the face of fundamental reason and common sense, that no reasonable planning authority could come to such a decision. This is a very difficult standard for an applicant to reach because the *O'Keefe* decision held that, in order to succeed the applicant must satisfy the court that there was no relevant material before the planning authority which would support its decision. Indeed, it can be seen from *O'Keefe* that the standard set is so high that it is almost impossible to satisfy. It is only rarely that the courts will set aside an administrative tribunal's decision on grounds of unreasonableness.

[4.178] In dealing with the *O'Keefe* standards, O'Sullivan J spoke out boldly in *Aer Rianta CPT v Commissioners for Aviation Regulation* when he stated that for the court to set aside a decision of an administrative tribunal:

> It is not sufficient that the decision-maker goes wrong or even hopelessly and fundamentally wrong. He must have gone completely and inexplicably mad, taken leave of his senses and come to an absurd conclusion.[279]

*O'Keefe* has overshadowed the Irish judicial review system since 1993. Recent judicial views and decisions indicate that a more flexible approach may emerge. It may not be too long before *O'Keefe* is taken off the pitch and placed on the sideline.

## Leave to apply must be sought by *ex parte motion*

[4.179] At the *ex parte* application for leave the applicant must show that he has 'substantial grounds'. An applicant must also show that he has a 'substantial interest'. The former procedure, where application for leave was made by way of motion on notice, produced a difficulty and the leave application could last as long or almost as long as the hearing of the application for statutory judicial review resulting in inevitable duplications and significant additional costs and delays. The underlying purpose of the former 'leave application' by way of motion on notice was supposed to streamline and fast-track the procedure by eliminating unsustainable and worthless judicial review cases but on many occasions it had the opposite effect. The new procedure, allowing application for leave *ex parte*, should result in a faster and cheaper procedure for judicial review but an applicant in the new *ex parte* application is still obliged to establish 'substantial grounds'.

[4.180] Simons advocated the abolition of the leave to apply stage altogether and the point which he makes has much to recommend it:

> The Judge hearing the leave application is in an invidious position. There will ordinarily be sufficient material before the High Court at the stage of the leave application to allow the court to decide the substance of the case. The logic of ss 50 and 50A, however, of course precludes such an outcome. Thus, a Judge having heard the full argument must resist the temptation to decide the case, but

---

279. *Aer Rianta cpt v Commissioners for Aviation Regulation* [2003] IEHC 12 *per* O'Sullivan J.

instead grant leave in the knowledge that the case may well be unsuccessful ultimately, with further delays being suffered in the interim.[280]

It is significant that the PD(SI) Bill of 2006 omitted the 'application for leave to apply' stage in judicial review. It is perhaps regrettable that the requirement was re-established as the Bill passed through the Houses of the Oireachtas.[281]

[4.181] The commercial court list of the High Court, even before PD(A)A 2010 became law, had adopted a practice of listing planning judicial review cases on the basis of a 'telescoped' hearing where the leave application and the substantive application were heard together; a farseeing initiative, frequently put in place by Kelly J. Section 50A of PD(A)A 2010 provides that an application for leave will ordinarily be made *ex parte*. The court now has a discretion to treat the application for leave as if it were the hearing of the application for judicial review and if it is necessary for the court to do so it may adjourn the full hearing of the judicial review upon such terms as the court may direct.

[4.182] Since 12 January 2004, it was possible to have judicial review proceedings commenced in the Commercial Court.[282] The judge in charge of the commercial list has discretion as to whether or not to hear a judicial review case and it can never be assumed that any particular case will be admitted for hearing in the Commercial Court. The advantages, in terms of an expeditious hearing and determination of judicial review before the Commercial Court, are obvious especially since it is the practice of that court to combine the 'leave application' with the 'substantive hearing' so that both are heard at the same time. Commenting on Order 63A, r 1(g) and dealing generally with the wide discretion which the order provides to the judge in deciding whether or not to admit an appropriate judicial review case to the Commercial Court Kelly J observed as follows:

> It would be unwise to set out hard and fast rules as to the business which can qualify for admission to the list under (Order 63A), r 1(g) particularly since the rules committee itself gave such a wide discretion to a judge in charge of the list. It would seem to me however, that any case involving a statutory appeal or judicial review of the type described in Order 63A, r 1(g) should be capable of admission to the list if it can be demonstrated that a commercial development or process or substantial sums of money, whether by way of profit, investment, loan or interest are likely to be jeopardised if the case is not given a speedy hearing or is denied the case management procedures which are available in the Commercial Court. This is so where one or more of the parties to the suit are involved in commerce, giving a broad meaning to that term. Such parties will include entities involved in

---

280. See Simons, *Planning and Development Law* (2nd edn, Thomson Round Hall, 2007) at para 11–11, p 520.
281. Significantly recent trends indicate that in some statutory judicial review cases a judge may hear an application for leave, and where it is successful they will continue with the hearing of the substantive issue.
282. See RSC, O 63(a). Specifically, O 63A, r 1(g) defines 'commercial proceedings' so as to include appeals from or judicial review of, a decision given by a person or body authorised by statute to make such decision where the judge in charge of the commercial list considers it appropriate for entry in the list having regard to the commercial or any other aspect thereof.

commercial activities, whether they be individuals, corporate bodies, semi-State bodies, State bodies or indeed the State itself in an appropriate case.[283]

**[4.183]** Article 7 of Council Directive 2003/35/EC,[284] inserting art 10a to Directive 85/337/EEC of the European Parliament and Council Directive 96/61/EC,[285] provides for public participation in respect of drawing up certain plans and programmes relating to the environment. Article 10(a) also requires that the review procedure must not be 'prohibitively expensive'. PDA 2000, s 50B, as inserted by PD(A)A 2010, s 3, in complying with the ECJ ruling in *Commission v Ireland* Case C–427/07[286] provides that each party will pay their own costs in judicial review cases which concern environmental matters unless (a) the court considers the claim or the counterclaim to be frivolous or vexatious; (b) the manner in which the party has conducted the proceedings decrees otherwise; (c) the party is in contempt of court.

**[4.184]** PD(A)A 2010, ss 32 and 33 respectively provide for the new telescoped procedure and provide that costs in environmental matters will generally be borne by each party to the proceedings. These two sections are fundamentally important to the new statutory judicial review procedure and, without apology, both sections are set out below.

> 32. Section 50A of the Principal Act [ie, PDA 2000] is amended by the substitution of the following sub-section for sub-section (2):
>
> (2)(a) An application for Section 50 leave shall be made by motion and *ex parte* and shall be grounded in the manner specified in the Order in respect of an *ex parte* motion for leave.
>
> (b) The Court hearing the *ex parte* application for leave may decide, having regard to the issues arising, the likely impact of the proceedings on the respondent or another party, or for good and sufficient reason, that the application for leave should be conducted on an *inter parties* basis and may adjourn the application on such terms as it may direct in order that a notice may be served on that person.
>
> (c) If the Court directs that the leave hearing is to be conducted on an *inter partes* basis it shall be by motion on notice (grounded in the manner specified in the Order in respect of an *ex parte* motion for leave) –
>
> > (i) If the application relates to a decision made or other act done by a planning authority or local authority in the performance or purported performance of a function under this Act, to the authority concerned and, in the case of a decision made or other act done by a planning authority on the application for permission, to the applicant for permission where he or she is not the applicant for leave,

---

283. Per Kelly J in *Mulholland and Kinsella v An Bord Pleanála (No 1)* [2005] IEHC 188.
284. Directive 2003/35/EC is commonly referred to as the Public Participation Directive.
285. These Directives are part of the outcome and the result of the Aarhus Convention (held in Aarhus, Denmark) which completed its business when it delivered its report in October 1998.
286. *Commission of the European Communities v Ireland* (Case C–427/07), Judgment of the Court (Second Chamber) delivered 16 July 2009.

(ii) If the application relates to a decision made or other act done by the Board on an appeal or referral, to the Board and each party or each other party, as the case may be, to the appeal or referral,

(iii) If the application relates to a decision made or other act done by the Board on an application for permission or approval, to the Board and to the applicant for permission or approval where he or she is not the applicant for leave,

(iv) If the application relates to a decision made or other act done by the Board or a local authority in the performance or purported performance of a function referred to in Section 50(2)(b) or (c), to the Board or the local authority concerned, and

(v) To any other person specified for that purpose by the order of the High Court.

(d) The Court may –

(i) On the consent of all parties, or

(ii) Where there is good and sufficient reason for so doing and it is just and equitable in all the circumstances,

treat the application for leave as if it were the hearing of the application for judicial review and may for that purpose adjourn the hearing on such terms as it may direct'.

33. The Principal Act is amended by the insertion of the following new section after s 50A:

'50B. (1) This section applies to proceedings of the following kinds

(a) Proceedings in the High Court by way of judicial review, or seeking leave to apply for judicial review, of –

(i) any decision or purported decision made or purportedly made,

(ii) any action taken or purportedly taken, or

(iii) any failure to take any action,

pursuant to the law of the State that gives effect to –

(I) a provision of Council Directive 85/337/EEC of 27th June 1985 to which Article 10(a) (inserted by Directive 2003/35/EC of the European Parliament and of the Council of 26th May 2003 providing for public participation in respect of the drawing up of certain plans and programmes relating to the environment and amending with regard to public participation and access to justice Council Directive 85/337/EEC and 96/61/EC) of that Council Directive applies.

(II) Directive 2001/42/EC of the European Parliament and of the Council 27th June 2001 on the assessment of the effects of certain plans and programmes on the environment or

(III) A provision of Directive 2008/1/EC of the European Parliament and of the Council of 15th 2008 concerning integrated pollution prevention and control to which Article 16 of that Directive applies; or

(b) An appeal (including an appeal by way of case stated) to the Supreme Court from a decision of the High Court in a proceeding referred to in paragraph (a);

(c) Proceedings in the High Court or the Supreme Court for interim or interlocutory relief in relation to a proceeding referred to in paragraph (a) or (b).

(2) Notwithstanding anything contained in Order 99 of the Rules of the Superior Courts and subject to sub-section (3) and (4), in proceedings to which this section applies, each party (including any notice party) shall bear its own costs.

(3) The Court may award costs against the party in proceedings to which this section applies if the Court considers it appropriate to do so –

(a) because the Court considers that a claim or counterclaim by the party is frivolous or vexatious,

(b) because of the manner in which the party has conducted the proceedings, or

(c) where the party is in contempt of Court.

(4) Sub-section (2) does not affect the Court's entitlement to award costs in favour of a party in a matter of exceptional public importance and where in the special circumstances of the case it is in the interests of justice to do so.

(5) In this section a reference to 'the Court' shall be construed as, in relation to particular proceedings to which this section applies, a reference to the High Court or the Supreme Court, as may be appropriate.'

[4.185] The general rule in Ireland, in relation to costs, is that costs are at the discretion of the High Court judge and, usually, the successful party will be awarded costs. Generally costs are said to 'follow the event'. In the case of an application for leave to proceed with a judicial review, costs (other than costs in environmental matters) are normally reserved and determined later after the full hearing of the action. Although there has been a certain amount of unevenness in relation to the award of costs in 'public interest' cases, a distinct trend has emerged to the effect that, in many cases, in a 'public interest' case, costs should not be awarded against the applicant. Clarke J has considered the question of costs in a number of cases.[287] In *Usk and District Residents Association v Environmental Protection Agency*,[288] Clarke J upheld the position that costs should normally follow the event and:

> where that successful party is a defendant, respondent, or indeed, a notice party who opposes an application, then that position should be departed from only where the Court is satisfied that there are good grounds for taking the view that

---

287. See *Sweetman v An Bord Pleanála (No 1)* [2007] 2 ILRM 328, *Kenny v An Bord Pleanála* [2008] IEHC 320 and also *Veolia Water UK plc and Others v Fingal County Council* [2006] IEHC 137.

288. *Usk and District Residents Association v Environmental Protection Agency* [2007] IEHC 30 *per* Clarke J.

the costs of the proceedings as a whole (including any appropriate interlocutory applications) have been clearly increased by reason of an unreasonable position adopted by that successful party in respect of some issue which has not already been the subject of a costs orders reflecting the relevant unreasonableness.

**[4.186]** In *Sweetman v An Bord Pleanála (No 1)*,[289] Clarke J departed from the normal practice which dictated that costs should follow the event. The judge made reference to art 10(a)[290] and to the fact that the review procedure should not be 'prohibitively expensive'. Article 10(a), however, in no way precludes the court from imposing 'reasonable' legal costs on an unsuccessful party. In *Sweetman*, no order for costs was made against the applicant but the State as respondent was required to pay 50% of the applicant's costs. In special circumstances, the court did award costs or a portion of the costs to an unsuccessful applicant where both of the following factors were present, namely:

(a) that the plaintiff was acting in the public interest in a matter which involved no personal advantage; and

(b) the issues raised by the proceedings were of sufficient general public importance to warrant an order for costs being made in his favour.

**[4.187]** In *McEvoy and Smith v Meath County Council*,[291] an application for leave to proceed with judicial review of the local authority's decision to adopt its development plan, in circumstances where parts of the plan were contrary to strategic planning guidelines, was refused. In determining the question as to costs Quirke J ordered Meath County Council to pay 100% of the costs in relation to the transcript and 50% of the applicant's costs. The judge noted that the applicant would derive no personal benefit from the outcome of the proceedings and that the case was one of genuine 'public interest'. The council had failed in a number of its arguments and that failure led directly or indirectly to delay of the proceedings. In that sense, the award of costs against the council was punitive.

**[4.188]** It is probable that NGOs and other public interest bodies would have been happier with the old system in relation to costs, and that the provisions of s 50B, which primarily state that each party is liable for its own costs save in exceptional circumstances, will work to their disadvantage. Section 50B does apply to any proceedings pursuant to a law of the State that gives effect to the EIA Directive, the SEA Directive or the IPPC Directive, subject to the court's discretion, as outlined above. Simons, commenting on the newly inserted s 50B, wrote as follows:

> A potential difficulty arises from the use of the word 'and' as opposed to 'or' in section 50B(4). Although the wording is somewhat inelegant, it is the writer's opinion that the two criteria ('exceptional public importance' and 'special circumstances') are disjunctive, not cumulative. In other words the High Court

---

289. *Sweetman v An Bord Pleanála (No 1)* [2007] 2 ILRM 328 *per* Clarke J.
290. Directive 2003/35/EC, art 10(a) amending, with regard to public participation and access to justice, Council Directives 85/337/EEC and 96/61/EC.
291. *McEvoy and Smith v Meath County Council* [2003] 1 IR 208.

**[4.189]** would always have discretion to make a cost order where in the special circumstances of a case it is in the interests of justice to do so, and it is not necessary that an additional separate criteria of 'exceptional public importance' be met. The significance of this, of course, is that the threshold or test established elsewhere under the planning legislation for a point of law of exceptional public importance is extremely high. More specifically, in the context of leave to appeal to the Supreme Court, it is necessary for a putative appellant to demonstrate that the decision of the High Court gives rise to a point of law of exceptional public importance. This requirement has been interpreted very narrowly by the courts in a number of judgments. Where this criteria to govern all applications for costs under s 50B(4) it is likely that the subsection would rarely be invoked. In my view, what s 50B(4) endeavours to do is to identify to distinct circumstances in which it would be appropriate to make a cost order. Though subsection thus identifies that the court would have an 'entitlement' to award costs in two scenarios. As I say, I do not think that these requirements are cumulative. Finally, an interesting issue arises as to whether an applicant who is a developer, as opposed to an objector, is entitled to reply on the special cost regime under s 50B. Strictly speaking, the requirements of Article 10(a) of the EIA Directive are directed to challenges by members of the public concerned: a 'developer' is defined separately under art 1 of the EIA Directive and would thus appear to be excluded.[292]

**[4.189]** In *KSK Enterprises Ltd v An Bord Pleanála*, Finlay CJ had this to say:

> It is clear that the intention of the legislature was greatly to confine the opportunity of persons to impugn by way of judicial review decisions made by the planning authorities and in particular one must assume that it was intended that a person who has obtained a planning permission should, at a very short interval after the date of such decision, in the absence of judicial review, be entirely legally protected against subsequent challenge to the decision that was made and therefore presumably left in a position to act with safety upon the basis of that decision.[293]

However, the scope of statutory judicial review under PDA 2000, ss 50 and 50A (as amended)[294] has been significantly enlarged by the new provisions. Under the previous planning legislation the scope of statutory judicial review was confined to the 'decisions' of the board, the planning authority or the local authority.

**[4.190]** In addition to allowing judicial review of 'decisions' of An Bord Pleanála, a planning authority or a local authority, PDA 2000, ss 50 and 50A, as amended,[295] have extended judicial review beyond 'decisions' to include 'acts done' by An Bord Pleanála, a planning authority or a local authority within the decision-making process.

**[4.191]** The legislative provisions have always required that the statutory judicial review must be taken quickly. The application for leave must be made within eight weeks

---

292. See Simons 'An Overview of the PD(A)A 2010' (2010) 17(4) PELJ.
293. *KSK Enterprises Ltd v An Bord Pleanála* [1994] 2 IR 128 *per* Finlay CJ.
294. PDA 2000, ss 50 and 50A as amended by PD(SI)A 2006, s 13.
295. PDA 2000, s 50(2) as amended by PD(SI)A 2006, s 13.

commencing on the date of the decision or the act of An Bord Pleanála, the planning authority or the local authority.

**[4.192]** In the High Court hearing of *Harding v Cork County Council*,[296] Clarke J held that an appeal such as an appeal to An Bord Pleanála will be accepted as an adequate remedy in a two-stage statutory or administrative process unless either:

(a) The matters complained of in respect of the first stage of the process are such that they can taint the second stage of the process or affect the overall jurisdiction; or

(b) The process at the first stage is so flawed that it can reasonably be said that the person concerned had not been afforded their entitlement to a proper first stage of the process in any meaningful sense. *Harding v Cork County Council* came before the Supreme Court where Kearns J commented:

> It is impossible to conceive of these legislative provisions as being intended for any purpose other than to restrict the entitlement to bring court proceedings to challenge decisions of planning authorities. There is an obvious public policy consideration driving this restrictive statutory code. Where court proceedings are permitted to be brought, they may have amongst their outcomes not merely the quashing or upholding of decisions of planning authorities but also the undesirable consequences of expense and delay for all concerned in the development project as the court process works its way to resolution. The Act of 2000 may thus be seen as expressly underscoring the public and community interest in having duly authorised development projects completed as expeditiously as possible.[297]

**[4.193]** Dodd[298] provides a useful summary of acts or decisions which do now but did not fall within the scope of the former provisions of s 50 and these include:

(a) decisions of the planning authority in relation to the making and varying of the development plans or local area plans under Pt II of the Act;

(b) decisions under Pt III (Control of Development) other than on applications for permission such as, *inter alia*, on points of detail in relation to planning conditions under s 34(5), extension of the life of a permission under s 42, revocation of a permission under s 44, and development contribution schemes under ss 48 and 49;[299]

(c) decisions on the making of a CPO under Pt XIV and decisions in the context of Pt IV (Architectural Heritage) such as a proposal to add to a protected structure or issuing endangerment or restoration notices, Pt VIII (Enforcement) including the service of enforcement notices;

(d) Pt IX (strategic development zones);

---

296. *Harding v Cork County Council* [2006] IEHC 295 *per* Clarke J.
297. *Harding v Cork County Council* [2008] IESC 27.
298. Dodd, *Planning and Development Acts, 2000–2007 Annotated and Consolidated* (Thomson Reuters, 2008) at 210.
299. PDA 2000, ss 48 and 49 are amended by PD(A)A 2010, ss 30 and 31 respectively.

[4.194]

(e) Pt XII (Compensation);

(f) Pt XIII (Amenities) such as making tree preservation orders;

(g) Pt XVI (Events and Funfairs) including the granting of licences thereunder;

(h) PDA 2000, s 50(2)(c) provides for judicial review of the making of a CPO by a local authority in the performance or purported performance of a function conferred by an enactment specified in s 214 relating to the compulsory acquisition of land. Prior to this being introduced, under PD(SI)A 2006, s 13, the only decision was of a planning authority in the context of a CPO process which fell within s 50, namely the confirmation of its own CPO in the limited circumstances under s 216. It may be noted that s 78(4) of the Housing Act 1966 provides that 'Subject to the provision of subsection (2) of this section, a person shall not question a compulsory purchase order by prohibition or certiorari or in any legal proceedings whatsoever'. Section 78(2) allows a person aggrieved to challenge the confirmation of a CPO by the Minister (the function is now transferred to the board) by making an application to the court within three weeks on specified grounds. Although not explicitly repealed, s 78(2) appears to be superseded by s 50, as amended, insofar as it provides that a person may not question the validity of the enlisted acts or decisions otherwise than by way of application for judicial review under O 84.

(i) PDA 2000, s 50(3) provides that the restricted form of judicial review does not apply to an approval or consent under Ch 1 or 2 of Pt VI, which relates to the establishment and constitution of An Bord Pleanála (Ch 1) and the organisation and staffing, etc, of An Bord Pleanála (Ch 2).

[4.194] The courts' role in judicial review is predominantly limited to considering procedural errors which may have occurred in the decision-making process. By way of useful illustration, Simons has listed five examples of procedural errors which have resulted in successful challenges, namely, as follows:[300]

(i) failure to provide a proper statement of the main reasons and considerations for a decision;

(ii) failure to afford an affected party a right to make submissions in relation to revised plans or in relation to a response to a request for further information;

(iii) the taking into account of irrelevant considerations;

(iv) the imposition of unreasonable planning conditions;

(v) unlawful delegation of decision-making functions.

Another potential ground for judicial review is where there is 'prejudgment or objective bias'. In *North Wall Quay Property Holdings Co Ltd v Dublin Docklands Development*

---

300. See Simons, 'Challenging Planning Decisions: Judicial Review and Appeals' (Intensive Course on Planning Law, School of Law, TCD, 8/9 December 2008).

*Authority*,[301] it was recognised that the DDDA can effectively grant a permission by certifying under s 25 of the Dublin Docklands Development Authority Act 1997 that a proposed development is consistent with a planning scheme. If the DDDA so certify under s 25, the development referred to in the certificate is exempt from the requirement to obtain planning permission. In spite of the lack of direction in the 1997 Act, Finlay Geoghegan J, in a carefully reasoned judgment, held that adjacent landowners should be given an opportunity to make submissions. The learned judge felt that the DDDA should not issue a s 25 certificate in secret but that it should maintain a public register listing all s 25 certificates so that adjoining landowners can inspect the register and see what certificates have issued. Adjoining landowners should be given an opportunity to make submissions within a reasonably short period of time. Finlay Geoghegan J held that such steps are necessary if the DDDA is to free itself not merely from actual bias but from the apprehension of bias in the minds of reasonable people. In this case, the judge found that the DDDA had acted *ultra vires* because executive staff in the DDDA had recommended that the board should issue a s 25 certificate in circumstances where, if the development proceeded, the developer would cede the land to the Docklands Authority free of charge, thus conferring a benefit on the decision-maker (DDDA) which might raise the apprehension of bias in the minds of reasonable people.

**[4.195]** More recently, in *Usk and District Residents Association Ltd v An Bord Pleanála, Ireland and the Attorney General*,[302] Greenstar first received permission for a landfill development at Usk, County Kildare from An Bord Pleanála in July 2006 having been initially refused by Kildare County Council. The Board's inspector recommended against granting the permission. The Board's permission was challenged by the residents. As a result of admissions made by the board (a) that it had not maintained satisfactory records leading to the decision, and (b) that it had not properly monitored the public planning file (the file, contrary to law, was not available to the public for inspection at various times), Kelly J in the High Court in March 2007 quashed the decision of the board and remitted the case back to the board for further consideration. In doing so, Kelly J suggested that it would be prudent that reconsideration of the case would be undertaken by members of the board who had not been involved in the granting of the permission. The learned judge made that recommendation to the board in order to avoid any possible suggestion of bias. On 30 July 2008, An Bord Pleanála again granted permission to Greenstar for the development and operation of an engineered residential landfill intended to receive 200,000 tonnes of waste. Once again, the board, in making this decision, disagreed with the inspector's recommendation as it is entitled to do. Significantly, however, in spite of Kelly J's suggestion, four members of the board, who were involved in the 2006 decision, were also involved in the 2008 decision. The Board's decision to grant permission on 30 July 2008 was unanimous. The Usk and District Residents challenged the 2008 decision to

---

301. *North Wall Quay Property Holdings Co Ltd v Dublin Docklands Development Authority* [2008] IEHC 305.
302. *Usk and District Residents Association Ltd v An Bord Pleanála, Ireland and the Attorney General* [2009] IEHC 346 *per* McMenamin J.

grant permission and joined the State as respondents for allegedly failing to implement certain EU Directives. The grounds of challenge were:

(a) Objective bias or want of fair procedures;

(b) Failure to address the non-implementation of a previous order of the court requiring restoration of the site before any development took place. Greenstar in fact accepted that the site had to be restored to prime condition before the landfill construction and operation commenced. No restorative work had taken place up to the time of the hearing of the resident's challenge before MacMenamin J in the High Court;

(c) That the board should have imposed conditions regarding mitigation of dust and noise and conditions to ensure that the water on the Usk marshes did not become contaminated.

During the High Court hearing it was established that there were alternative Board members available to deal with the case and in commenting on this the learned judge had this to say:

> The logic of the Board's reasoning here is unfathomable.

In the course of the hearing, the State changed its position and argued that in fact the board should have left the assessment of all environmental matters to the EPA.

**[4.196]** The Board also made the case that the permission granted in 2006 was not identical to the permission granted in 2008. McMenamin J compared the two permissions of 2006 and 2008 respectively and came to the conclusion that:

> An objective observer would have little difficulty in seeing the symbiotic relationship between the two. I am constrained to conclude that the 2006 permission was used as a template for that made in 2008.

The judge granted the applicant an order of *certiorari* quashing the board's decision on the following grounds:

1. Objective bias on the part of the four Board members who had participated in both decisions.

2. Failure to implement the restoration order made in 2004 to restore the site, as far as possible, to agricultural use.

3. Failure on the part of the board, to implement noise and dust control conditions. It was conceded that the issues were dealt with by the EPA in issuing a 'waste licence' but control of noise and dust are relevant planning issues which should have been addressed by the board specifically in respect of the impact on nearby houses.

4. Failure to deal with the potential for environmental pollution arising from the construction of the 'liner' which was the board's responsibility as opposed to the subsequent potential for environmental pollution arising from the operation of the landfill development subsequent to its contract. Any environmental

pollution which was a result of the performance and/or operation of the landfill, as opposed to the construction of the landfill development, was a matter for the EPA to be controlled by it in the licence which it would issue.

After the judgment was delivered, An Bord Pleanála indicated that it would not appeal this High Court decision.

## Applications to stay proceedings

**[4.197]** Local authorities or An Bord Pleanála may apply to the High Court to stay judicial review proceedings in circumstances where the decision of the planning authority or of the board has not been made.[303]

**[4.198]** PDA 2000, s 50(4) reads:

> A planning authority, a local authority or the Board may, at any time after the bringing of an application for leave to apply for judicial review of any decision or other act to which sub-s (2) applies and which relates to a matter for the time being before the authority or the Board as the case may be, apply to the High Court to stay the proceedings pending the making of a decision by the authority or the Board in relation to the matter concerned.

**[4.199]** PDA 2000, s 50(5) reads:

> On the making of such an application, the High Court may, where it considers that the matter before the authority or the Board is within the jurisdiction of the authority or the Board, make an order staying the proceedings concerned on such terms as it thinks fit.

**[4.200]** PDA 2000, s 50(4) and (5) have enlarged the application for stay process by including a 'planning authority' and a 'local authority'. Previously, an application to stay judicial proceedings could only be made in relation to appeals or referrals pending before the board. This amended legislation extends the possibility of an application to stay judicial review proceedings questioning the validity of any decision made or other act done by a planning authority, a local authority or the board in the performance or purported performance of a function under PDA 2000, as amended. An application to stay judicial review proceedings will also apply to An Bord Pleanála in the performance or purported performance of a function transferred to it under Pt XIV[304] or to a local authority in the performance or purported performance of a function conferred on it by an enactment specified in s 214 relating to compulsory acquisition of land.

**[4.201]** These provisions will only allow the planning authority, a local authority or the board to make application for stay of judicial review proceedings whereas prior to the PD(SI)A 2006 any party to an appeal could also make application for leave to stay

---

303. PDA 2000, s 50(4)&(5) as amended by PD(SI)A 2006, s 13.
304. PDA 2000, Pt XIV deals with the acquisition of land.

judicial review proceedings. The application for a stay can only be brought after the application for leave has been completed.

## Time limits

**[4.202]** The strict eight-week time limit placed on the statutory judicial review process during which time an application for leave must be made, implies with some degree of certainty that applicants for leave are obliged to apply for leave to move for judicial review during the planning process and even before the outcome is known. In order to avoid having an application for leave declared statute-barred as being outside the eight-week period for challenging decisions made or other acts done by a planning authority, by a local authority or by the board,[305] an applicant may have to challenge a decision or acts as they occur rather than waiting for the final decision at the end of the process.[306] In *Goonery v Meath County Council*,[307] a notice of appeal was lodged with the Supreme Court which complained of a decision made and other acts done by An Bord Pleanála. Shortly after the appeal was lodged An Bord Pleanála in fact granted the permission sought by the applicant and, thereafter, all parties agreed that there was no point in proceeding with the full hearing before the Supreme Court. The only matter left for the Supreme Court to decide was the question of an order for costs made against the applicant by the High Court and, in the event, the High Court order for costs was upheld in the Supreme Court.

**[4.203]** The requirement for short time limits in all cases where the validity of a planning decision or other act done by a planning authority, the local authority or the board as appropriate has been correctly recognised in the planning legislation. It has been strongly supported and enforced by the courts.

**[4.204]** PDA 2000, s 50(6) reads:

> Subject to subsection (8), an application for leave to apply for judicial review under the Order in respect of a decision or other act to which subsection 2(a) applies shall be made within a period of eight weeks beginning on the date of the decision or, as the case may be, the date of the doing of the act by the planning authority, the local authority or the Board, as appropriate.[308]

PDA 2000, s 50(7) reads:

> Subject to subsection (8), an application for leave to apply for judicial review under the Order in respect of a decision or other act to which subsection (2)(b) or (c) applies shall be made within the period of eight weeks beginning on the date

---

305. See PDA 2000, s 50(2) as amended by PD(SI)A 2006, s 13.
306. See *Linehan v Cork County Council* [2008] IEHC 76 *per* Finlay J which proposes that acts or decisions may have to be challenged as they occur rather than await the final decision.
307. *Goonery v Meath County Council* (unreported, 1 July 2002) SC.
308. PDA 2000, s 50(6) as amended by PD(SI)A 2006, s 13. Note: PDA 2000, s 50(8) is dealt with below and PDA 2000, s 50(2)(a) provides that a person shall not question the validity of any decision made or other act done by a planning authority, a local authority or the board in the performance or purported performance of a function under this Act.

on which notice of the decision or act was first sent (or as the case may be the requirement under the relevant enactment, functions under which are transferred under Pt XIV or which is specified in Section 214, was first published).[309]

PDA 2000, s 50(8) reads:

> The High Court may extend the period provided for in sub-s (6) or (7) within which an application for leave referred to in that sub-section may be made but shall only do so if it is satisfied that –
>
> (a) there is good and sufficient reason for doing so, and
>
> (b) the circumstances that resulted in the failure to make the application for leave within the period so provided were outside the control of the applicant for the extension.[310]

**[4.205]** In the case of a decision of the local authority, the planning authority or An Bord Pleanála, the time limit starts to run from the date of the decision to grant permission as opposed to the date of grant of permission or the date of notification to the applicant for planning permission, and judicial review proceedings must be commenced within eight weeks. There is, however, an exception to that general rule which applies to decisions or acts of An Bord Pleanála relating to the compulsory acquisition functions under Pt XIV or by a local authority in respect of transferred functions under s 214. In both of those cases, the period commences not on the date of the decision but on the date when the notice of the decision is sent or published, as the case may be. The words in PDA 2000, s 50(7) (as amended) have been carefully drafted and where it is stated that the period runs from the date when the notice was first sent that clearly means what it says. It does not mean the date when the notice was first received. Since there is no statutory obligation imposed by the Act to send a notice to an applicant, this infers the time will run, where no notice is sent, from the date of publication and that will be the case even though publication of the decision may have occurred sometime after the board sent the notice to the applicant.

**[4.206]** In *McCann v An Bord Pleanála*,[311] the court held that the first day of the eight-week period (in that case it was a month at the time) should be included and the last day excluded. In *Hynes v Wicklow County Council and Arklow UDC*,[312] an application was granted for leave to seek judicial review of a decision by Wicklow County Council to grant permission to Arklow UDC for water treatment works. In making the application, the applicants neglected to include a claim for illegal bias in relation to the dual role of

---

309. PDA 2000, s 50(7) as amended by PD(SI)A 2006, s 13. Note that PDA 2000, s 50(2)(b) and (c) read: (b) a person shall not question the validity of any decision made or other act done by the board in performance or purported performance of a function transferred under Part XIV or (c) a local authority in the performance or purported performance of a function conferred by an enactment specified in s 214 relating to the compulsory acquisition of land, or otherwise than by way of any application for judicial review under the Rules of the Superior Courts (SI 15/1986), O 84.
310. PDA 2000, s 50(8) as amended by PD(SI)A 2006, s 13.
311. *McCann v An Bord Pleanála* [1997] 1 ILRM 264.
312. *Hynes v Wicklow County Council and Arklow UDC* [2003] 3 IR 66 *per* Murphy J.

the assistant county manager in promoting the works on behalf of Arklow UDC and in granting permission on behalf of Wicklow County Council. At the hearing of the case the applicant sought leave to amend the pleadings to include a claim for illegal bias. The court held that the time limits as laid down in O 84 (of the Rules of the Superior Courts 1986, as amended (RSC)) may be extended for 'good reason' and the court held that similar requirements could be applied when considering applications to amend a statement of grounds. In the circumstances of the case, however, the applicants had failed to give 'good reasons' for the delay between February 2002 and 15 May 2003 when the claim for illegal bias was first put forward. The application to amend was refused. In *Keelgrove Properties Ltd v An Bord Pleanála*,[313] Quirke J held that the 28-day period (as it was then) started from the date stated in the planning authority's decision and not when the document was received by interested parties as was contended by the applicant.

**[4.207]** RSC, O 84, r 21 requires that an applicant must move promptly. In *Harrington v An Bord Pleanála (No 1)*,[314] Macken J stated *obiter* that, if it had been necessary to do so, she would have held that the applicant did not comply with the O 84 requirement to move promptly even though, the applicant had filed his papers on the last day of the eight-week period. On the one hand, O 84 requires that an applicant should move promptly while on the other hand PDA 2000, s 50(6), (7) and (8) specifies an eight-week period starting on the first day and finishing at midnight, seven weeks and six days later.

**[4.208]** Peart J, in *Marshall v Arklow Town Council*,[315] held that even though an application is brought within the statutory eight-week period it was not open to the court to refuse an application for leave on the grounds that, within that eight-week period, the applicant had not moved 'promptly'. With respect to the learned judge, this statement may have to be treated with some caution, tempting as it is, in the interest of fairness, to accept Peart J's reasoning.

**[4.209]** Perhaps the safe view is to recognise that both the time limit and the requirement to move promptly co-exist and that a court may, within the eight-week period, look to see if application for leave should or could have been brought earlier. Merely because the statutory provision provides an eight-week period in which to make the application for leave does not necessarily mean that, the 'promptness' principle is to be overlooked. If, within the eight-week period, there is clear evidence that the applicant did not move promptly, the requirement to move promptly may survive. Until the matter is settled more certainly the clear advice must be that an applicant should move promptly and if that means lodging the application within a period of less than eight weeks then that is the safe course to take. In *Harding v Cork County Council* Murray CJ had this to say:

> I would add in passing that a person who complains of a complete denial of a statutory right vested personally in him or her by law (such as the right to make

---

313. *Keelgrove Properties Ltd v An Bord Pleanála* [2000] I IR 47 Quirke J.
314. *Harrington v An Bord Pleanála (No 1)* [2005] IEHC 388.
315. *Marshall v Arklow Town Council* [2004] 4 IR 92.

further submissions in respect of further significant information as envisaged by Article 35 of the Regulations) should not always just sit back and leave the process proceed at length until it reaches its final conclusion and then seek to impugn the final decision where it would have been properly open to such a person to seek a remedy at an earlier stage, such as by way of mandamus, requiring the authority to observe the statutory right in question. That is something which a Court would fully take into account when deciding whether or not to grant leave to bring judicial review. It may be otherwise where, for example, the decision was taken before the breach of the legal right could reasonably have been known or before there was an opportunity to seek any other properly available remedy.[316]

As seen in *Harding*, there are instances where perhaps the outcome of the 'decision' or the full facts and nature of the 'acts done' may not be known or may not become apparent to a party with full rights of public participation in the relevant process, and in such cases the court has discretion to extend the time beyond the eight-week period where there are 'good and sufficient reasons' and where it is shown that the failure to bring the application within the eight-week period was 'outside the control of the applicant'.

**[4.210]** In *Jerry Beades Construction Ltd v The Right Honourable Lord Mayor Aldermen and Burgesses of the City of Dublin and Others*,[317] An Bord Pleanála issued a decision refusing planning permission. The applicant challenged the board's decision on the grounds that there had been serious irregularities in the way in which the application had been processed by the planning officials in Dublin Corporation. The proceedings issued by the applicant were issued some 11 months after the board's decision to refuse permission. At the time the proceedings were issued by the applicant the Supreme Court had ruled in *White v Dublin City Council*[318] (in circumstances where the Local Government (Planning and Development) Act 1976 provided for a two-month time limit without any power for the High Court to extend that period in appropriate circumstances) that the unqualified two-month time limit was unconstitutional. As a consequence of that decision the only time limit was the time limit contained in RSC, O 84 which required that the application had to be made 'promptly'. In deciding for Jerry Beades Construction Ltd, McKechnie J held that the applicant company was justified in delaying its application for judicial review because it took that time for the company to learn of the irregular manner in which the planning application had been dealt with by Dublin City Council's planning department. In the course of his decision, McKechnie J found that the planning application had not been fairly or impartially considered by the planners in Dublin City Council. The learned judge ruled that an extension of time beyond what O 84 required in terms of 'promptness' was essential to protect justice.

---

316. *Harding v Cork County Council* (unreported, 2 May 2008) SC *per* Murray CJ.
317. *Jerry Beades Construction Ltd v The Right Honourable Lord Mayor Aldermen and Burgesses of the City of Dublin and Others* [2005] IEHC 406, McKechnie J.
318. *White v Dublin City Council* [2004] 1 IR 545.

## Extension of time

**[4.211]** PDA 2000, s 50(8) deals with extension of time as seen at para **4.204**.

The insertion of PDA 2000, s 50(8) was the direct result of a decision in *White v Dublin City Council*.[319] The Supreme Court endorsed the High Court's decision to grant leave to apply for judicial review on the basis that the two-month time limit was unconstitutional because no provision whatsoever was made for the possibility of an extension of time. Denham J in the Supreme Court held that the provisions of the LG(PD)A 1963, s 82(3)(B)(a)(i) constituted an injustice to such an extent that in exercising its discretion to exclude any power to extend time for cases such as the present, the legislature undermined or compromised a substantive right guaranteed by the Constitution, namely, the right of access to the courts. The applicants, through no fault of their own, but through an unlawful act of the decision-maker were deprived of any genuine opportunity to challenge the legality of the decision within the permitted time.

**[4.212]** As will be seen from the provisions of s 50(8), the decision as to whether or not to extend time is entirely at the discretion of a court.

**[4.213]** The use of the words 'good and sufficient reason for doing so' means that there are good and sufficient reasons for extending the time. It does not mean that there were good and sufficient reasons which delayed the application. Also, the circumstances giving rise to the delay must be 'outside the control of the applicant for the extension'.

**[4.214]** In *O'Shea v Kerry County Council*,[320] the High Court held that the applicant could not show good and sufficient reason to extend the time where the substance of her case was that she had failed to see the site notice because it had been placed in an obscure location. In applications for extension of time the court will examine the length of delay and the reasons for it. In *Kelly v County Council of Leitrim and An Bord Pleanála*,[321] Clarke J outlined the relevant factors to be taken into account as follows:

(a) The length of time specified in the relevant statute within which the application must be made;

(b) The question of whether third party rights may be affected;

(c) Notwithstanding (b) above there is nonetheless a clear legislative policy involved in all such measures which requires that, irrespective of the involvement of the rights of third parties, determinations of particular types should be rendered certain within a short period of time as part of an overall process of conferring certainty on certain categories of administrative or quasi-judicial decisions. Therefore, while it may well be legitimate to take into account the fact that no third party rights are involved, that should not be regarded as conferring a wide or extensive jurisdiction to extend time in cases where such rights may be affected. The

---

319. *White v Dublin City Council* [2004] 1 IR 545.
320. *O'Shea v Kerry County Council* [2003] 4 IR 143.
321. *Kelly v County Council of Leitrim and An Bord Pleanála* [2005] 2 IR 404, [2005] IEHC 11.

(d) Blameworthiness;
(e) The nature of the issues involved;
(f) The merits of the case.

**[4.215]** In *Marshall v Arklow Town Council*,[322] Peart J held that PDR 2001, art 19 requires that an inspection must be made by the planning authority within the period of five weeks from receipt of the planning application to ascertain that the site notice had been erected and maintained in accordance with the article. As a consequence of that decision site notices are inspected by the planning authority within the five-week period and the status of the notice is recorded. In *Marshall*,[323] the applicant sought an extension of time in s 50 judicial review proceedings to quash a grant of planning permission on the basis that the developer had not erected a site notice as required by the regulations. Peart J granted the extension of time on the basis that the developer had not erected a site notice and the applicant had not seen a notice and was not aware of the fact that time was running against him. When the applicant realised that an application for permission had been lodged with the planning authority he acted as speedily as could be expected in the circumstances. The question might be asked as to why the applicant bothered to go to the site to look for the site notice in the first place. If the answer to that question was that the applicant went to the site to look for the site notice because he was aware that an application for permission had been lodged with the planning authority, that knowledge may be reason enough to refuse to extend the time. Thus, in *Openneer v Donegal County Council*,[324] the court would not accept that the applicant had only become aware of the position on receipt of a letter immediately prior to the issue of proceedings. The application for leave was refused. Also, in *Kenny v Dublin City Council*,[325] where the applicant had previously sought to quash a grant of planning permission in relation to a development but the subsequent application seeking to quash a compliance order in relation to the same development made within the six-month time limit (as it applied then) was held not to be sufficiently expeditious and that the applicant's knowledge of the events must be related back to the previous applications.

**[4.216]** In *Casey v An Bord Pleanála*,[326] an application for judicial review was refused on the grounds that the applicant did not participate in the process before An Bord Pleanála. The applicant had not been an objector at the planning stage, and the court, in considering the conduct of the applicant, was not satisfied that the reasons given for the delay were sufficient to extend the relevant time limit. In that case, the court also confirmed that where there is delay on the part of the applicant's solicitor then that delay is attributable to the applicant as the principal. Clearly, however, there may be cases

---

322. *Marshall v Arklow Town Council* [2004] 4 IR 92.
323. *Marshall v Arklow Town Council* [2004] 4 IR 92.
324. *Openneer v Donegal County Council* [2006] 1 ILRM 150.
325. *Kenny v Dublin City Council* [2004] IEHC 381, Murphy J.
326. *Casey v An Bord Pleanála* [2004] 2 IR 296.

**[4.217]** where the delay on the part of solicitors or barristers may not be attributable to the applicant as principal.

**[4.217]** It is almost inevitable that applications for judicial review under ss 50 and 50A will prejudice the respondent (usually the developer) by delaying his development plans. Just as the absence of prejudice cannot automatically prevent a good and sufficient reason for extending time so too the presence of prejudice in ss 50 and 50A judicial review applications will not in all cases result in a decision not to extend time. In *Hogan v Waterford County Manager*,[327] the applicant sought leave to judicially review a decision by the local authority to carry out site investigations and environmental impact assessment of a potential waste facility. The applicant had been aware of the grounds of complaint since June 2000 and only applied for leave to seek judicial review in December 2000. Although the applicant was just within the time limit for seeking an order for *certiorari* by way of judicial review (six months), Herbert J concluded as follows:

> In the circumstances, I find that no 'good reason' has been established by the applicant as to why the Court should exercise its discretion to extend the time to enable the applicant to seek an Order of Prohibition, an Order of Mandamus, a Declaration or an Injunction by way of judicial review. I find that this application for leave to seek judicial review was not made promptly even though the application for an Order of Certiorari by way of judicial review was made eight days prior to the expiration of the period of six months provided by Order 84 Rule 21(1) of the Rules of the Superior Courts 1986. I find that Waterford County Council has suffered substantial prejudice by reason of the delay. Relief by way of judicial review is a discretionary remedy in the Court. On this application the Court will decline to exercise its discretion in favour of the applicant. The application is therefore refused.[328]

It will be readily seen that prejudice to a third party developer may be a significant factor in refusing relief.

**[4.218]** In *Lynch v Dublin City Council*,[329] Ms Lynch had made a written objection to the application for permission but Dublin City Council neglected to issue the requisite receipt. When Dublin City Council made its decision it failed to notify Ms Lynch of the making of a decision to grant permission. The applicant, Ms Lynch, did not learn of the making of the decision until the four-week period for making an appeal had expired. Ms Lynch, as objector, was not in a position to make an appeal to the board because in making an appeal it is a mandatory requirement that the receipt of the objection issued by Dublin City Council must be lodged. By the time Ms Lynch learnt of Dublin City Council's decision she was, in any case, out of time. O'Caoimh J acknowledged that the requirement to furnish the planning authority's receipt of the objection is mandatory but

---

327. *Hogan v Waterford County Manager* (unreported, 30 April 2003) HC, Herbert J.
328. *Hogan v Waterford County Manager* (unreported, 30 April 2003) HC, Herbert J.
329. *Lynch v Dublin City Council* (unreported, 25 July 2003) HC, O'Caoimh J.

the learned judge was not prepared to make any decision as to whether the planning authority is required to notify its decision to objectors.[330] O'Caoimh stated:

> I am conscious of the fact that I have indicated that the requirement in question was mandatory, but at the same time I am not inclined to hold that the failure to comply with that requirement necessarily results in an invalidity in the decision process itself.
>
> In the instant case, as I have already indicated, the passage of time has resulted in the construction of the extension to property owned by the notice party. While some suggestion has been made that the notice party may have proceeded with works somewhat prematurely, in the light of the decision that had been made, it is quite clear that any works that have been effected were effected in circumstances where a decision had been made to grant planning permission. No application was made to this Court at any time to restrain the development in question pending the outcome of the proceedings.

O'Caoimh J refused to set aside the permission granted but he did require that the planning authority should pay the applicant's costs. The applicant was made liable for the notice parties' costs with an order over as against the planning authority.[331]

## Application for leave to apply

[4.219] 'Section 50 leave' means leave to apply for judicial review under the order in respect of a decision or other act to which s 50(2) applies.[332] The application for leave to apply is made by motion *ex parte* (grounded in the manner specified in the order in respect of an *ex parte* motion for leave) as follows:

> (b) The Court hearing an ex parte application for leave may decide having regard to the issues arising, the likely impact of the proceedings on the respondent or another party, or for other good and sufficient reason, that the application for leave should be conducted on an inter partes basis and may adjourn the application of such terms as it may direct in order that a notice may be served on that person.

---

330. PDR 2001, art 31 requires that the decision and certain other information must be notified to prescribed parties. See also PDR 2006, art 31 which requires that notification of a decision by a planning authority in respect of a planning application shall be given to the applicant and any other person or body who has made submission or observations in accordance with art 28 or 29 within three working days of the day of the decision. The section continues to give a list of matters which must be specified. See also PDA 2000, s 249(2) as substituted by LGA 2001, s 247. That section provides for dispensation for the requirement to give notice to persons who have made representations, submissions or observations to a planning authority where there are large numbers provided that the authority or the board use some other means of giving notice to the public in a manner which would draw attention of the public to that notice.

331. This seems to be a harsh decision in the light of the planning authority's statutory failures in failing to issue a receipt for Ms Lynch's written objection, compounded further by failing to notify her of the decision to grant permission. The learned judge may have balanced those factors against a situation where the person who received the permission was a completely innocent party.

332. PDA 2000, s 50A(1) as inserted by PD(SI)A 2006, s 13.

(c) If the Court directs that the leave hearing is to be conducted on an inter partes basis it shall be by motion on notice (grounded in the manner specified in the Order in respect of an ex parte motion for leave):

    (i) if the application relates to a decision made or other act done by a planning authority or local authority in the performance or purported performance of a function under this Act, to the authority concerned and, in the case of a decision made or other act done by a planning authority on an application for permission, to the application for the permission where he or she is not the applicant for leave,

    (ii) if the application relates to a decision made or other act done by the Board on an appeal or referral, to the Board and each party or each other party, as the case may be, to the appeal or referral,

    (iv) if the application relates to a decision made or other act done by the board on an application for permission or approval, to the Board and to the applicant for the permission or approval where he or she is not the applicant for leave,

    (v) if the application relates to a decision made or other act done by the Board or a local authority in the performance or purported performance of a function referred to in s 50(2)(b) or (c), to the Board or the local authority concerned, and

    (vi) to any other person specified for that purpose by order of the High Court.

(d) The Court may:

    (i) on the consent of all the parties, or

    (ii) where there is good and sufficient reason for so doing and it is just and equitable in all the circumstances,

treat the application for leave as if it were the hearing of the application for judicial review and may for that purpose adjourn the hearing on such terms as it may direct.[333]

All parties mentioned in paras (b) to (d) inclusive must be served with proceedings as appropriate and they must also be served with all necessary papers.

**[4.220]** In *Monopower v Monaghan County Council*,[334] two separate applications were made by separate parties who wished to join the judicial review proceedings. The first application was made by a number of local residents. The case concerned an application to the court claiming that the applicant was entitled to a default planning permission. Herbert J held that the local residents might be indirectly affected in the event that the default planning permission issued and the development proceeded, but that they were not directly affected at the time of the application. The second application was made by the Minister for the Environment, Heritage and Local Government who wished to be joined in the proceedings because he considered that an article in the planning

---

[333]. PDA 2000, s 50(2)(a)–(d) inclusive as inserted by PD(SI)A 2006, s 13 and substituted by PD(A)A 2010, s 32.

[334]. *Monopower v Monaghan County Council* [2006] IEHC 253 *per* Herbert J.

regulations was being challenged. Herbert J, perhaps surprisingly, held that the Minister was not 'directly affected'. In holding that the first and second applicants were not 'directly affected', Herbert J ruled that the only parties who were directly affected were the planning authority and the applicant for planning permission. Clearly, the local residents may have been able to make a significant contribution to the proceedings and it was somewhat surprising that the Minister was not considered to be a person directly affected. RSC, O 84, r 26 provides that a person who desires to be heard in opposition on the motion or summons and appears to the court to be a proper person to be heard shall be heard notwithstanding that he has not been served with a notice of motion or summonses. Order 84, r 26 gives the trial judge discretion and if the trial judge considers that such witnesses should be heard they will be heard if the trial judge considers this to be necessary in the interest of justice.

[4.221] In *O'Keefe v An Bord Pleanála*,[335] although notified of the proceedings by the applicants, Radio Tara decided that it would not appear. By order of the Supreme Court, Radio Tara was joined as a party because it was clearly 'directly affected'.

[4.222] In hearing an application for leave to apply under PDA 2000, s 50A the court must, before the application is granted, be satisfied that:

(a) there are substantial grounds for contending that the decision or act concerned is invalid or ought to be quashed and[336]

(b) (i) the applicant has a substantial interest in the matter which is the subject of the application, or

(ii) where the decision or act concerned relates to a development identified in or under regulations made under s 176, for the time being in force, as being development which may have significant effects on the environment, the applicant–

(I) is a body or organisation (other than a state authority, a public authority or governmental body or agency) the aims or objectives of which relate to the promotion of environmental protection,

(II) has, during the period of 12 months proceeding the date of the application, pursued those aims or objectives, and

(III) satisfies such requirements (if any) as a body or organisation, if it were to make an appeal under s 37(4)(c), would have to satisfy by virtue of s 37(4)(d)(iii) (and, for this purpose, any requirement prescribed under s 37(4)(e)(iv) shall apply as if the reference in it to the class of matter into which the decision, the subject of the appeal, falls were a reference to the class of matter into which the decision or act, the subject of the application for s 50 leave, falls).[337]

---

335. *O'Keefe v An Bord Pleanála* [1993] 1 IR 39.
336. PDA 2000, s 50A(3)(a) as inserted by PD(SI)A 2006, s 13.
337. PDA 2000, s 50A(3)(b)(i) and (ii) as inserted by PD(SI)A 2006, s 13.

## Substantial interest

**[4.223]** An applicant is required to have a 'substantial interest' in the subject matter of the judicial review application. There is no substantive definition of 'substantial interest' in the Act, other than PDA 2000, s 50A(4),[338] which provides that:

> a substantial interest for the purposes of sub-section 3(b)(i) is not limited to an interest in land or other financial interest.

In effect, 'substantial interest' is the *locus standi* statutory threshold which must be met by an applicant in statutory judicial review proceedings. The standard of 'substantial interest' may be compared with the standard of 'sufficient interest' which is the threshold required in conventional judicial review. The threshold of demonstrating 'substantial interest' is considerably higher than the threshold required in conventional judicial review of 'sufficient interest'. An application for leave under PDA 2000, s 50, as amended, will not be granted by the court unless the court is satisfied that the applicant has a 'substantial interest' in the matter which is the subject of the application. As already noted, a 'substantial interest' is not limited to an interest in land or other legal or financial interest.[339]

**[4.224]** Prior to the amendment introduced by PD(SI)A 2006, there was a general obligation placed on an applicant for leave to demonstrate that he had engaged in the planning process. That requirement has been omitted from the current legislative provisions and, in consequence, the case law which pre-dates PD(SI)A 2006 and which indicated that prior participation was a pre-condition, will have to be re-examined. In *Harding v Cork County Council*,[340] the appellant sought to bring judicial review proceedings to set aside a Cork County Council decision to grant permission for a golf and leisure resort at Ballymacus Head, Kinsale. The applicant lived two to three kilometres from the development and the meaning of 'substantial interest' was considered on appeal in some depth by Murray CJ in the Supreme Court. Murray CJ noted that the Oireachtas had given members of the public a full opportunity to make submissions or observations. Nevertheless, Clarke J's judgment was approved in the Supreme Court and it is now clear that 'substantial interest' and 'substantial grounds' are separate requirements of PDA 2000, s 50 (as amended) creating, as they do, two fences, not one. The applicant who fails to establish substantial interest has no entitlement to obtain leave even though the grounds of his application may be substantial.

**[4.225]** If the court concludes that the applicant does not have a 'substantial interest' it should go no further.

---

338. PDA 2000, s 50A(4) as inserted by PD(SI)A 2006, s 13.
339. PDA 2000, s 50A(4) as inserted by PD(SI)A 2006, s 13.
340. *Harding v Cork County Council* [2006] IEHC 295 (12 October 2006), Clarke J and *Harding v Cork County Council* [2008] IESC 27 (2 May 2008).

[4.226] In *Harding v Cork County Council*, Clarke J, in the High Court, held that once the interest was identified the next step was to identify whether or not the interest was a substantial interest by reference to the following criteria:

(a) The scale of the project and the extent to which the project might be said to give rise to a significant alteration in the amenity of the area concerned. The greater the scale and the more significant the alteration in the area then the wider the range of persons who may legitimately be able to establish a substantial interest;

(b) The extent of the connection of the applicant concerned to the effects of the project by particular reference to the basis of the challenge which he puts forward to the planning permission and the planning process;

(c) Such other factors as may arise on the facts of an individual case.[341]

[4.227] In the Supreme Court, Murray CJ had this to say in relation to 'substantial interest':

> Although the criteria as laid down by the Oireachtas in the Act of 'Substantial Interest' is vague some clear delineations can be made.
>
> It is clearly intended to raise the threshold so to speak which applicants for leave to bring judicial review proceedings must cross. As a very first step it may mean that an applicant should have a direct interest of some material substance in the development, or its effects, with which the decision to grant planning permission is concerned.
>
> If the applicant does not have a 'substantial interest' related to the development, or its effects, as such, a person who has exercised a statutory right to participate in the planning process may potentially have a 'substantial interest' related to the exercise of that right. This case involves an applicant who claims to have a 'substantial interest' in the development as such by reason of its effect on the local environment as well as a 'substantial interest' in the vindication of his right to participate in the planning process ... I would categorise these two grounds on which he claims to have a 'substantial interest' in the matter the subject of the applicant, within the meaning of s 50, as the applicant's environmental interest in the statutory process.[342]

In the event, the learned judge concluded that the appellant's grounds of complaint did not amount to the 'substantial interest' required and the appeal was dismissed by the Supreme Court.

[4.228] The question is asked as to whether 'substantial interest' requires an applicant to have had a substantial interest in the decision-making process. The Supreme Court was divided in its opinion in the *Harding* case[343] with Kearns J holding that the applicant must always have a substantial interest in the development project itself. Murray CJ put

---

341. *Harding v Cork County Council* [2006] IEHC 295 (12 October 2006).
342. *Harding v Cork County Council* [2008] IESC 27 (2 May 2008).
343. *Harding v Cork County Council* [2006] IEHC 295, Clarke J and *Harding v Cork County Council* [2008] IESC 27 (2 May 2008).

the matter differently by holding that even if the applicant does not have a substantial interest related to the actual development, if the applicant had made submissions or observations during the planning process, in exercising that statutory right the applicant may, in limited circumstances, be deemed to have a 'substantial interest'.

**[4.229]** An applicant no longer has to show that he had participated in the planning process. In *Harding v Cork County Council*,[344] the Supreme Court held that to have a substantial interest within the meaning of PDA 2000, s 50 (as amended), it is necessary for an applicant to establish:

(a) That he has an interest in the development the subject of the proceedings which is 'peculiar and personal' to him;

(b) That the nature and level of his interest is significant or weighty;

(c) That his interest is affected by or connected with the proposed development.[345]

**[4.230]** RSC, O 84, r 20(4) provides that:

> The Court shall not grant leave unless it considers that the applicant has a sufficient interest in the matter to which the application relates.

**[4.231]** In *O'Shea v Kerry County Council*,[346] the applicant was a nearby landowner. Because she failed to show how she would be personally affected and because it was held that a general interest, to ensure that the law must be complied with, did not amount to a 'substantial interest', the applicant was refused leave to apply.

**[4.232]** In *Harding*, Kearns J examined the meaning of the words 'substantial interest in the matter'. The learned judge had this to say:

> The words 'substantial interest in the matter which is subject of the application' receives no further definition in the Act. However, it is clear from a reading of the section as a whole that the word 'application' means the application for leave to apply for judicial review. The 'matter' must, it seems to me, by reference to the wording contained in s 50(4)(d)[347] be taken as meaning the development project itself and the outcome of the planning process in relation to it. It cannot mean the legal proceedings themselves, not only because of the way in which 'substantial interest' is contextualised by s 50(4)(d), but also because it would be a trite and superfluous use of a statutory provision to make it a requirement that a litigant have a substantial interest in their own litigation when this is so obviously the fact in every case.[348]

---

344. *Harding v Cork County Council* [2008] IESC 27 (2 May 2008).
345. Per Kearns J in *Harding v Cork County Council* [2008] IESC 27 (2 May 2008).
346. *O'Shea v Kerry County Council* [2003] 4 IR 143.
347. PDA 2000, s 50A(3)(b) as inserted by PD(A)A 2010, s 13.
348. *Harding v Cork County Council* [2006] IEHC 295, Clarke J and *Harding v Cork County Council* [2008] IESC 27 (2 May 2008).

**[4.233]** In the event Murray CJ concluded that Mr Harding's interests were:

> Too general and remote to be considered substantial.[349]

**[4.234]** In spite of the Supreme Court's strict interpretation of 'substantial interest', which may, in part, be a result of an unspecified wish on the part of the judiciary to avoid any encouragement of what may be described as 'crank litigation', genuine public interest cases have proceeded forward from an application for leave to apply for judicial review, particularly where environmental issues are involved. For example, in *Murphy v Wicklow County Council*,[350] where 'eco-warriors' sought to challenge Wicklow County Council's decision to build a dual-carriageway through a notoriously scenic area with wildlife habitats, known as the Glen of the Downs, Kearns J held that the applicant had 'sufficient interest' to proceed with the challenge against the local authority. The learned judge held that the applicant had a genuine interest in the area and that he was in a position to present expert evidence on a whole range of issues all of which were pertinent to the huge stake that the public had with regard to the proper and lawful management of the woodland. The Glen of the Downs site was recognised in both Irish and European legislation as an area of environmental importance. The court recognised that the dual-carriageway development would have significant consequences for the Glen of the Downs and it granted *locus standi* to the applicant. A subsequent appeal to the Supreme Court failed and as many readers who travel that way will know, the eco-warriors have come down from the tree-tops and the dual-carriageway has been fully operational for many years undoubtedly with a mix of good and not so good consequences.

**[4.235]** In *Salafia v The Minister for the Environment, Heritage and Local Government*,[351] a challenge was made by the applicant against the proximity of the M3 motorway to one of Ireland's best known and historic sites, the Hill of Tara. The route of the M3 had been decided by An Bord Pleanála some three years previously and considerable funds had been invested in laying out the route and in acquiring land over which the roadway, with its attendant flood plains, drains and other services, would travel. The applicant had not participated in the planning process and was not a resident in the area. Smyth J held that the applicant did not, in the circumstances, even meet the 'sufficient interest' threshold, which is the standard required for conventional judicial review. The learned judge also held that although the challenge was made against the ministerial directions it was, in fact, a challenge against the selection of the route by the board. The applicant knew of the board's decision made some three years earlier but neglected to challenge it at that time. Smyth J held that the challenge should have been made at the time of the board's decision and not three years later when a course of action had been embarked upon at public expense.

---

349. *Harding v Cork County Council* [2006] IEHC 295, Clarke J and *Harding v Cork County Council* [2008] IESC 27 (2 May 2008).
350. *Murphy v Wicklow County Council* [1999] IEHC 225 *per* Kearns J.
351. *Salafia v The Minister for the Environment, Heritage and Local Government* (unreported, 1 March 2006) HC *per* Smyth J.

**[4.236]** The learned judge's decision in those circumstances is beyond reproach but it may be difficult to remain completely detached in relation to the entire process of road planning and of road building. In the Glen of the Downs it is undeniable that a part of a notable woodland was destroyed with consequent damage to wildlife habitats in the area. The M3 motorway undoubtedly impacts on one of Ireland's most historic sites, namely, the Hill of Tara. The significant levels of frustration, which many thousands of motorists experience as a result of inadequate roadways, are pitched against the entirely reasonable and desirable aspirations of EIA. In reality, the conflict may often be decided by, but not remedied by, a spoonful of expedience ladled out at some cost to the principles which EIA endeavours to protect and maintain.

**[4.237]** In *Lancefort Ltd v An Bord Pleanála*,[352] the applicant company was a company limited by guarantee with no assets which had been incorporated after the decision of An Bord Pleanála to grant permission for an extensive development of a hotel, bank and other facilities in the centre of Dublin. The High Court ruled that the applicant had *locus standi* but that decision was reversed by the Supreme Court. Lynch J agreed with the judgment of Keane J, but Denham J in a minority judgment indicated that she would affirm the order of the High Court to the effect that Lancefort Ltd had *locus standi*.

**[4.238]** The judgment of Keane J in *Lancefort* gives an interesting insight into the principles involved in making a decision as to whether or not an applicant has *locus standi*. The judgment also deals with the status of companies limited by guarantee, with no assets. The following extracts from Keane J's judgment are relevant and they offer a good appreciation of the principles involved:

> In the light of the affidavits filed, I would accept, as did Morris J and McGuinness J in the High Court, that it should be assumed in their favour that the persons concerned in the formation of the company are genuinely concerned to ensure that good planning decisions are made in Dublin and elsewhere and that they incorporated the appellants wishes with that objective in mind. At the same time, it can hardly be disputed that, since the appellants were not even in existence at the time the decision which is challenged was made, their interest in the subject matter of the proceedings is somewhat tenuous, if indeed it can be said to exist at all.
> 
> The claim that the permission was invalid rests solely on the alleged failure on the Board to consider whether an EIS was required in the circumstances of the present case. Such an EIS, it should be stressed, could have been required by the Board at any stage up to the granting of permission. Although Mr Smith attended the hearing on behalf of An Taisce, as did junior counsel, they at no stage put forward the objection that an EIS had not been required by the planning authority or An Bord Pleanála. Nor was that suggestion made at any stage by any of the reputable conservation groups which attended the hearing or by any of the architects, planning consultants or other experts who were present. It must be assumed that some at least of those present were aware, at least in a general sense, of the circumstances in which an EIS and EIA were required. In the particular case of Mr Smith and junior counsel representing An Taisce, no explanation was given at any

---

352. *Lancefort Ltd v An Bord Pleanála* [1999] 2 IR 270, SC.

stage of these proceedings as to why the objection was not taken until the application was made for leave to issue the present proceedings.

It is clear as was held by this Court in *Chambers v An Bord Pleanála*[353] that the fact that a person affected by a proposed development did not participate in the appeals procedure is not of itself a reason for refusing locus standi. It may even be that a company which came into being after the decision which it sought to challenge may, in particular circumstances, be in a position to assert locus standi as held by Comyn J in the case to which I have already referred. But it would, in my opinion, be a significant injustice to a party in the position of the Notice Party to be asked to defend proceedings on the grounds of an alleged irregularity which could have been brought to the attention of all concerned at any time prior to the granting of permission, but which was not relied on until the application was made for leave to bring the proceedings.

An examination of the merits of the case, accordingly, leads me to the conclusion that, if there has been any irregularity in the manner in which the Board discharged their functions, it could not possibly be regarded as constituting an abuse of power or a default in procedure sufficiently grave to justify affording locus standi to a body such as the appellants. Not only were they not in existence at the relevant time and hence are in serious difficulties in contending that they had an interest in the subject matter: the procedural irregularity, if such it was, was of so little weight that neither Mr Smith, the persons who took the leading part in the formation of the appellants, nor counsel appearing on behalf of An Taisce nor any of the experts who participated in the procedure leading to the decision considered it worthy even of mention.

I do not arrive at the conclusion that the appellants lacked standing solely because of the fact that they are a company limited by guarantee owning no property affected by the permission. I would accept, as a general proposition, that such bodies may be entitled to locus standi in proceedings of this nature although they cannot point to any property or economic interests being affected by the relevant decision. In *Blessington Heritage Trust v County Council of the County of Wicklow, Minister for the Environment and Roadstone (Dublin) Ltd* (unreported HC 21 January 1998) McGuinness J said of companies such as the Appellant:

'"Blank" refusal of locus standi to all such companies may tip the balance too far in favour of the large scale and well resourced development.'

I would agree with that approach, although not with its application by the Learned High Court Judges in the present case. It is, understandably, a matter of concern that companies of this nature can be formed simply to afford residents' associations and other objectors immunity against the costs of legal challenges to the granting of planning permissions. Our law, however, recognises the right of persons associating together for non-profit making or charitable activities to incorporate themselves as limited companies and the fact that they have chosen so to do should not of itself deprive them in every case of locus standi. While shielding the members against an order for costs in the event of the company becoming involved in litigation may well be a consequence of limited liability, it is not necessarily the only reason why citizens concerned with issues as to the

---

353. *Chambers v An Bord Pleanála* [1992] 1 IR 134.

environment may decide to incorporate themselves as a company. It must also be remembered that, in the case of such a company, the High Court may order security for costs to be provided under s 390 of the Companies Act 1963, as indeed happened in this case.

I cannot agree, however, with the submission advanced on behalf of the appellants that the fact that there were substantial grounds for contending that the decision was invalid necessarily leads to the conclusion that they had locus standi ...

... it is clear that this was not a case in which the Appellant should have been recognised as having locus standi to mount a challenge.[354]

**[4.239]** The courts have often adopted a favourable approach in leave to apply cases based on the fact that it is in the public interest that the rule of law shall be upheld. The public interest factor is of particular significance where the development concerned requires an EIS and the 'substantial interest' threshold may be interpreted in a more flexible way in those cases. In *Lancefort Ltd v An Bord Pleanála*, Denham J, dissenting, had this to say:

> While not every person who declares a public interest may be considered to be acting in and for the public interest such aspiration must be analysed also in the circumstances of each case. I am satisfied in this case on the facts Lancefort has expressed a valid public interest in the environment. The issue of the environment presents unique problems, not only in the Court s In much litigation on eg. personal injuries or as to individual constitutional rights, the party is obvious. In litigation on the environment, however, there are unique considerations in that often the issues affect the whole community as a community rather than as an individual per se. This affects the concept of locus standi also. The 'sufficient interest' required by the Rules and Statutes should be interpreted accordingly.[355]

**[4.240]** In *O'Brien v Dun Laoghaire/Rathdown County Council*,[356] the applicant lived 78 metres from the proposed development. O'Neill J held that to have a 'substantial interest' an applicant must have an interest in the outcome of the application for planning permission. In *O'Brien*, it was shown that the proposal for development did not have any significant detrimental effects on the applicant's visual amenity and as such she had no 'substantial interest'. O'Neill J also held that the fact that the applicant was a member of An Taisce did not imply a substantial interest. An Taisce is a prescribed body but that does not mean that members of An Taisce can derive a 'substantial interest' because of their membership.

**[4.241]** As the law moves forward, and, in particular, with reference to the provisions of PDA 2000, s 50A(3)(b)(ii),[357] which excuses NGOs from the necessity of proving 'substantial interest' in an application for leave to seek judicial review subject to certain requirements listed in the section, access to the court in judicial review cases is becoming more readily available in genuine cases.

---

354. *Lancefort Ltd v An Bord Pleanála* [1999] 2 IR 270, SC.
355. *Lancefort Ltd v An Bord Pleanála* [1999] 2 IR 270, SC.
356. *O'Brien v Dun Laoghaire/Rathdown County Council* [2006] IEHC 177 *per* O'Neill J.
357. As inserted by PD(SI)A 2006, s 13.

## Substantial grounds

**[4.242]** An applicant for leave to apply for judicial review must satisfy the High Court that there are 'substantial grounds' for contending that the decision or the act concerned of a planning authority, a local authority or the board is invalid or ought to be quashed.[358] The threshold requirement in a conventional application for judicial review requires an applicant to satisfy the court that there are *'prima facie* grounds'.

**[4.243]** Finlay CJ, in dealing with *'prima facie* grounds' in a conventional judicial review, had this to say:

> An applicant must satisfy the court in a prima facie manner by the facts set out in his affidavit and submissions made in support of his application of the following matters:
>
> (a) that he has a sufficient interest in the matter to which the application relates to comply with Rule 20(4), (b) that the facts averred in the affidavit should be sufficient if proved to support a stateable ground for the form of relief sought by way of judicial review, (c) that on those facts an arguable case in law can be made that the applicant is entitled to the relief which he seeks, (d) that the application has been made promptly and in any event within the 3 months and 6 months time limits provided for in O 84, r 21(1) or that the court is satisfied that there is good reason for extending the time limit. The Court, in my view, in considering this particular aspect of an application for liberty to institute proceedings by way of judicial review should, if possible, on the ex-parte application, satisfy itself as to whether the requirement of promptness and of the time limit have been complied with, and if they have not been complied with, unless it is satisfied that it should extend the time, should refuse the application. If, however, an order for refusing the application would not be appropriate unless the facts relied on to prove compliance with r 21(1) were subsequently not established, the court should grant liberty to institute the proceedings if all other conditions are complied with, but should leave as a specific issue to the hearing, upon notice to the respondent, the question of compliance with the requirements of promptness and of the time limits, (e) that the only effective remedy, on the facts established by the applicant, which the applicant could obtain would be an order by way of judicial review or, if there be an alternative remedy, that the application by way of judicial review is, on all the facts of the case, a more appropriate method of procedure. These conditions or proofs are not intended to be exclusive and the court has a general discretion, since judicial review in many instances is an entirely discretionary remedy which may well include, amongst other things, consideration of whether the matter concerned is one of importance or of triviality and also as to whether the applicant has shown good faith in the making of an ex parte application.[359]

---

358. PDA 2000, s 50A(3)(a) as inserted by PD(SI)A 2006, s 13.
359. *G v Director of Public Prosecutions* [1994] 1 IR 374.

**[4.244]** The definition of 'substantial grounds' in the context of an application for leave in a s 50 judicial review most commonly quoted is that of Carroll J in *McNamara v An Bord Pleanála*:

> What I have to consider is whether any of the grounds advanced by the appellant are substantial grounds for contending that the Board's decision was invalid. In order for a ground to be substantial, it must be reasonable, it must be arguable, it must be weighty. It must not be trivial or tenuous, however, I am not concerned in trying to ascertain what the eventual result would be. I believe that I should go no further than satisfy myself that the grounds are 'substantial'. A ground does not stand any chance of being sustained (for example, where the point has already been decided in another case) could not be said to be substantial. I draw a distinction between the grounds and the various arguments put forward in support of those grounds. I do not think I should evaluate each argument and say whether it is sound or not. If I consider the ground as such to be substantial, I do not also have to say that the applicant is confined in his arguments at the next stage to those which I believe may have some merit.[360]

**[4.245]** A sample of the grounds which were held to be 'substantial' by Carroll J is set out below to illustrate what the learned judge meant by grounds which are reasonable, arguable and weighty not trivial or tenuous:

(a) The EIS accompanying the application for planning permission is defective and fails to comply with the statutory requirements.

(b) The newspaper advertisement as published and on foot of which Dublin County Council advertised its intention to make application for planning permission, is defective and fails to comply with the statutory requirements.

(c) The purported decision of the respondent under reference PL09.091910 Planning Register No 92/942 insofar as it purports to impose conditions *inter alia* Conditions No 3, 13, 17, 18, 20 and 22 (9 and 19 having been dropped) and which are directed to be matters for agreement as between Dublin County Council, the applicant for planning permission, and Kildare County Council as the planning authority are such as to constitute an abdication of responsibility of the respondent, in consequence of which no valid or proper determination has been made by the respondent on foot of the appeal and such decision as purports to have issued is null and void and of no effect.

(d) The respondent acted *ultra vires* in reaching a conclusion that no reasonable planning authority applying appropriate standards of reason and common sense and having due regard for proper planning and development considerations would reach and insofar as the respondent has reached the decision to grant permission under reference No PL09.091910, the respondent has acted contrary to the weight of the evidence as adduced and such decision is manifestly unreasonable and without justification.

---

360. *McNamara v An Bord Pleanála* [1995] 2 ILRM 125.

The test in *McNamara* was endorsed by the Supreme Court in *Re Article 26 and the Illegal Immigrants (Trafficking) Bill, 1999*.[361]

**[4.246]** Apart from the popularity of Carroll J's definition among textbook writers on the subject of judicial review the definition has been approved in a substantial number of cases.[362]

**[4.247]** In commenting on Carroll J's definition that for a ground to be 'substantial', 'it must be reasonable, it must be arguable, it must weighty. It must not be trivial or tenuous ...' Geoghegan J in *Jackson Way Properties Ltd v Minister for the Environment*[363] expressed the view that there also had to be 'real substance in the argument and not merely that it is just about open to argument'.

**[4.248]** In further considering Carroll J's definition of 'substantial grounds', McKechnie J in *Kenny v An Bord Pleanála (No 1)* stated:

> Indeed in a consideration of these words, one can think of grounds which could be both reasonable and arguable and yet fall significantly short of meeting the threshold of being substantial. The words 'trivial or tenuous' are undoubtedly helpful but probably more so as words of elimination rather than qualification. The description of being 'weighty' and of 'real substance' are in my view of considerable importance in the interpretation of this threshold phrase. However, it must also be remembered that, from a base say, opposite substantial, namely insubstantial, an applicant must navigate the considerable distance in between, and in addition, must arrive at and meet the threshold while still afloat and on course. In truth I feel, whilst many attempts have been made to explain or convey 'the equivalent of its meaning' I am not certain that one can better the original phrase itself.[364]

McKechnie J has brought Carroll J's definition of 'substantial grounds' back to square one.

**[4.249]** McCracken J in *Irish Cement Ltd v An Bord Pleanála*[365] also adopted the definition of 'substantial grounds' given by Carroll J in the *McNamara* case. McCracken J pointed out that in such applications for leave to apply the court is not trying to ascertain what the eventual result will be but rather the court is going no further than to ascertain whether the grounds are substantial. The learned judge felt that the judgment of Carroll J could be criticised as it uses language such as 'arguable' or 'trivial' and those words as applied to statutory judicial review do not offer any

---

361. *Re Article 26 and the Illegal Immigrants (Trafficking) Bill, 1999* [2000] 2 IR 360.
362. Other cases which have approved Carroll J's definition of 'substantial grounds' include *Keane v An Bord Pleanála* (unreported, 20 June 1995) HC *per* Murphy J; *Mulhall v An Bord Pleanála* (unreported, 10 June 1996) HC *per* McCracken J; *Blessington Community and District Council v Wicklow County Council* [1997] 1 IR 273 *per* Kelly J; *Maire DeFaoite v An Bord Pleanála* [2000] IEHC 154 *per* Laffoy J and *Mulholland v An Bord Pleanála (No 2)* [2006] 1 IR 453.
363. *Jackson Way Properties Ltd v Minister for the Environment* [1999] 4 IR 608, *per* Geoghegan J.
364. *Kenny v An Bord Pleanála (No 1)* [2001] 1 IR 565.
365. *Irish Cement Ltd v An Bord Pleanála* [1998] IEHC 30 *per* McCracken J.

distinction from the threshold required in conventional judicial review where all that is required are *'prima facie* grounds'.

**[4.250]** Another often quoted definition of 'substantial grounds' is that of Egan J speaking for the Supreme Court in *Scott v An Bord Pleanála*:

> What meaning should I give to the word 'substantial'? ... I fall back on a word which is so often used as a test in legal matters. It is the word 'reasonable' and I suggest, therefore, that the words 'substantial grounds' require that the grounds must be reasonable.[366]

**[4.251]** In *DeFaoite v An Bord Pleanála*,[367] judicial review was sought in respect of a Board decision to grant planning permission for a housing development. The applicant argued that the field on which the development was to take place should have been retained as a sports ground but Laffoy J held that the applicant had failed to establish substantial grounds and she refused leave to apply for judicial review.

**[4.252]** In the case of conventional judicial review, the function of the High Court is merely to establish at the leave stage that the grounds are arguable and stateable. The court will not make any attempt to express the view as to whether the case is strong or weak.[368]

**[4.253]** In *De Faoite v An Bord Pleanála*, Laffoy J acknowledged that both the board and the developer unreservedly recognised the *bona fides* of both the applicant and of the club. In relation to the specific grounds advanced by the applicant the learned judge had this to say:

> (a) It is clear that there was evidence before the Board that the development site at Mount St. Joseph's is and has been private property. Neither the Board nor this court has any jurisdiction to require, either directly or indirectly, that privately owned land be dedicated to a public or community purpose unconnected with the development under consideration. The first ground is wholly unsustainable.
>
> (b) The existence or otherwise of a private contractual arrangement between the Developer and the Club, as alleged, is not a matter which can be canvassed on an application for judicial review. It is a matter of private law and I understand that civil proceedings have been initiated by the Applicant against the Developer in relation to this aspect of the matter. As a ground for seeking leave, it is wholly unsustainable.
>
> (c) On the basis of the evidence before me, I must conclude that, applying the principles which I must apply on the basis of the decision of the Supreme Court in the O'Keefe case, it is not the case that there was no relevant material before it which would support the Board's determination that the

---

366. *Scott v An Bord Pleanála* [1995] 1 ILRM 424 *per* Egan J.
367. *DeFaoite v An Bord Pleanála* [2000] IEHC 154 *per* Laffoy J.
368. See *O'Reilly v Cassidy* [1995] 1 ILRM 306 which deals with the requirements of an arguable case. Also see extract of judgement *per* Finlay CJ in *G v Director of Public Prosecutions* [1994] 1 IR 374 at para **4.243**.

proposed development would not seriously injure the amenities of the area or of property in the vicinity and would be in accordance with the proper planning and development of the area, whether in relation to density, scale or otherwise.

Accordingly, there being no arguable ground, let alone a substantial ground, for challenging the Board's decision, there will be an Order refusing leave and dismissing the application.[369]

**[4.254]** It is likely but not certain that an application for leave to apply in a conventional judicial review will be a relatively short hearing involving a relatively short perusal of the documents available at the time. The leave to apply stage under ss 50 and 50A is a more serious and a more searching affair.

**[4.255]** In *P v Minister for Justice Equality and Law Reform*,[370] Smyth J indicated that at the leave to apply for judicial review stage it was appropriate to consider whether or not the case had any prospects of success. The learned judge indicated that the court should only grant leave if it is satisfied that the applicant's case is not merely arguable but strong and likely to succeed.

**[4.256]** In *Village Residents Association v An Bord Pleanála*,[371] an issue of facts arose at the leave stage which were disputed. The case concerned an application by McDonalds Restaurant in Kilkenny for permission for a restaurant and take-away. The first application was refused by the planning authority on the grounds that the inclusion of a take-away facility was contrary to the planning authority's own development plan. The matter came before the board on appeal and the board also refused the application for permission. The applicant argued that the board's decision was irrational and that the board had an additional duty to give reasons in circumstances where planning permission was granted in material contravention of the development plan. Geoghegan J in granting leave for judicial review did not seek to determine those factual issues at the leave stage. Factual issues should not generally be sought to be resolved at the leave stage but in *Kenny v An Bord Pleanála (No 1)*[372] it was noted that while the court should not resolve conflicts of fact on an application for leave, nonetheless within the existing limitations an evaluation of the factual matrix should be made.[373]

**[4.257]** In *Arklow Holidays Ltd v An Bord Pleanála and Wicklow County Council*,[374] where arguments arose between the parties at the application for leave stage as to whether there had been a proper assessment of all aspects of the project outside of the

---

369. *DeFaoite v An Bord Pleanála* [2000] IEHC 154.
370. *P v Minister for Justice Equality and Law Reform* [2002] I ILRM 16 *per* Smyth J. Note: Smyth J's standard in this case appears to be in conflict with the view expressed in *O'Reilly v Cassidy* [1995] 1 ILRM 306, where it was stated that the court will not express the view as to whether a case is strong or weak.
371. *Village Residents Association v An Bord Pleanála* [2000] 1 IR 65, HC.
372. *Kenny v An Bord Pleanála (No 1)* [2001] 1 IR 565.
373. Note that with the potential of telescoping the application for leave and the full hearing now available these divisions will merge.
374. *Arklow Holidays Ltd v An Bord Pleanála and Wicklow County Council* [2006] IEHC 15, Clarke J.

waste water treatment plant itself in terms of EIA, Clarke J held that the court should not express any opinion on the relative strengths or weaknesses of those conflicting arguments at the leave stage.[375]

**[4.258]** In *Linehan v Cork County Council*,[376] a dispute as to facts arose in the course of the leave application and Finlay Geoghegan J said that she would not exclude the possibility of a court considering it appropriate, in a particular case, to determine that dispute as part of the leave application if the disputed facts were so central to the existence or absence of substantial grounds that it would be considered appropriate, even at the leave stage, to determine the disputed facts by cross-examination or otherwise. Generally, however, it is not appropriate for the court to make a final determination of fact for the very reason that the parties are still only at the leave stage. Where there are direct disputes between the averments of sworn affidavits as to relevant facts an assumption should be made in favour of the applicants for the purpose of the leave application.[377]

## Alternative remedies in judicial review cases

**[4.259]** Leave to apply may not be granted if there is an alternative remedy especially if the alternative remedy is more appropriate. This is no longer a statutory provision but it is well established in case law. Under the Local Government (Planning and Development) Act 1963[378] an applicant had the right to proceed by way of judicial review even though the right of appeal to An Bord Pleanála was available also. The provision of the 1963 Act which allowed that right of appeal to An Bord Pleanála was not a bar to judicial review. In the past, once it was established that a tribunal had jurisdiction the courts did not interfere even in cases where it was shown that the tribunal had made an error in fact or in law.[379]

**[4.260]** It soon became clear that a distinction needed to be drawn between a review of judicial decision-making and a review of administrative decision-making. In *State (Abenglen Properties Ltd) v Dublin Corporation*, when the applicant pursued a line of authority derived from a review of judicial decisions, Henchy J had this to say:

> Where an inferior Court or a Tribunal errs within jurisdiction without recording that error on the face of the record, certiorari does not lie. In such cases, it is only when there is the extra flaw that the Court or Tribunal acted in disregard of the requirements of natural justice that certiorari will issue. In the present case, there is no suggestion that the Respondents, in dealing with Abenglen's application, acted in disregard of any of the requirements of natural justice. They went wrong in law, if at all, in answering legal questions within their jurisdiction, and they did not reproduce any such legal error on the face of the record of their decision.

---

375. Note that with the potential of telescoping the application for leave and the full hearing now available these divisions will merge.
376. *Linehan v Cork County Council* [2008] IEHC 76 *per* Finlay Geoghegan J.
377. *Linehan v Cork County Council* [2008] IEHC 76 *per* Finlay Geoghegan J.
378. LG(PD)A 1963 s 82(3)A and 3(B) as substituted by LG(PD)A 1992, s 19(3).
379. See *State (Davidson) v Farrell* [1960] IR 438.

Consequently, in my view, they did not leave themselves open to certiorari in respect of their decision.[380]

**[4.261]** The *Abenglen* case dealt with a challenge to grant planning permission which claimed to be in conflict with the relevant development plan. Counsel for Abenglen admitted that the only purpose for seeking *certiorari* was to enable Abenglen to claim a default permission on the grounds that the corporation, not having dealt within its jurisdiction with the application, had not made a decision to grant planning permission. Henchy J disagreed and held that the corporation's decision, even if it had been made in excess of jurisdiction, nevertheless remained a decision to grant permission for the purposes of the planning code and, in consequence, even if *certiorari* had been granted there were no legal grounds which would have entitled Abenglen to default permission. Henchy J went on to say:

> The present case does not seem to me to exhibit the exceptional circumstances for which the intervention of the Courts was intended. On the contrary, certiorari proceedings would appear to be singularly inapt for the resolution of the questions raised by Abenglen. Certiorari proceedings, based as they are on affidavit evidence can result only in a stark and comparatively unilluminating decision to quash or not to quash; whereas an appeal to the Board would have allowed all relevant matters to be explored (if necessary), in an oral hearing, with the aid of experts in the field of planning, thus allowing an authorative practice and procedure, aided, if necessary, by reference to the High Court of a question of law.[381]

The learned judge refused *certiorari* and indicated that Abenglen should have availed of its alternative remedy by way of appeal to An Bord Pleanála. Adequacy of appeal to the board or adequacy of any alternative remedy should be considered prior to considering whether or not there are substantial grounds for challenging a s 50 judicial review.

**[4.262]** The *Abenglen* case was heard in 1984 but another case, *P&F Sharpe Ltd and Grove Developments v Dublin City and County Manager*,[382] confirmed the right of an objector to have a decision of a planning authority quashed for want of validity and it was held that the applicants could have the decision quashed although the applicants had sought an appeal to An Bord Pleanála. In that case, the firm advice of the county engineer and of other technical officers of Dublin City Council was that if a decision were granted to allow access from a housing development onto a dual carriageway that would be a material contravention of the local authority's development plan. The county manager accepted the technical advice as being correct and accurate and acknowledged that the proposed development would constitute a significant road hazard. In general, the provisions of the development plan provide for absolute priority of traffic safety in the planning authority's approach to development. Once a development proposal constitutes a material contravention there can be no question of the planning authority

---

380. *State (Abenglen Properties Ltd) v Dublin Corporation* [1984] IR 381.
381. *State (Abenglen Properties Ltd) v Dublin Corporation* [1984] IR 381.
382. *P&F Sharpe Ltd and Grove Developments v Dublin City and County Manager* [1989] ILRM 565, [1989] IR 701.

being deemed to have decided to grant permission by reason of the fact that no decision was made by the planning authority within the time limits prescribed. The manager was correct in refusing to obey a direction from the council members to grant planning permission for the purposed development and it was held that because there is no power vested in a planning authority to grant permission in those circumstances no permission by default can arise.

**[4.263]** In *Kinsella v Dundalk Town Council*,[383] it was said that, compared with ordinary judicial review, the requirement that an applicant demonstrate that judicial review is the only or remedy a more appropriate remedy than any other available remedy, applies with at least equal force and probably more force in a judicial review under s 50. Kelly J held that a right of appeal to An Bord Pleanála was an adequate alternative remedy in circumstances where it was submitted that significant further information and additional data, including the exhibition of a further public notice under art 35 of PDR 2001 was required. At the time the applicant commenced the judicial review proceedings he had already appealed to An Bord Pleanála and in those circumstances the court refused leave for judicial review. The adequacy of an appeal to An Bord Pleanála or the adequacy of any other alternative remedy should be considered prior to considering whether there are substantial grounds for the challenge in a s 50 judicial review. In *Harding v Cork County Council (No 2)*,[384] Clarke J suggested that the adequacy of an appeal to An Bord Pleanála should be considered before the determination is made at the application for leave stage as to whether or not there are substantial grounds unless there are a multiplicity of grounds or unless the court is persuaded by the parties that an appeal to the board would be an adequate remedy. In relation to circumstances where a multiplicity of grounds are raised Clarke J had this to say in the *Harding* case:

> Where, however, as here, a multiplicity of grounds are relied upon, and where it is at least possible that the Court may be satisfied that substantial grounds might be found to exist in respect of some but not all of those grounds, it may be that the Court might have to adopt a somewhat different approach.
>
> In such circumstances it seems to me that it is likely that the Court will first have to consider whether, on the assumption that all of the grounds put forward are valid, such a finding would give rise to circumstances where an appeal would nonetheless be an adequate remedy. If that be the case then there is no point in going on to consider whether substantial grounds exist for the contentions of the applicant concerned.
>
> If, however, the Court takes the view that it is at least possible that the cumulative effect of all of the issues complained of by the applicant might render the process before the planning authority so flawed that it would justify reaching a conclusion that an appeal would not be an adequate remedy, then it may be necessary for the Court to consider each of the grounds put forward to ascertain whether there are substantial grounds for the applicant's contention. In the event that the applicant succeeds in persuading the Court in respect of some, but not all, of the grounds relied on, then it may be necessary to revisit the question of the adequacy or

---

383. *Kinsella v Dundalk Town Council* [2004] IEHC 373, Kelly J.
384. *Harding v Cork County Council (No 2)* [2006] IEHC 295, Clarke J.

otherwise of an appeal to the Board based upon a review of those grounds in respect of which it has been successfully established that the applicant has substantial grounds for challenge.[385]

This approach was approved by Murray CJ on appeal before the Supreme Court.[386]

## Case law examples of statutory judicial review

**[4.264]** Set out below, by way of example, are a number of cases where it was found that the procedural requirements were not always met by the relevant administrative tribunal:

1. In *Law v Minister for Local Government and Another*,[387] a decision to grant planning permission was set aside because it was, to a large degree, based upon a soil soakage report requested by the inspector at the hearing and that report was never furnished to the plaintiff. The plaintiff's right to fair procedures was infringed and, in consequence, the decision of the Minister was quashed.

2. In *Geraghty v Minister for Local Government*,[388] the inspector's report, prepared after the oral hearing, was modified and amended by civil servants in the Department for Local Government. It was held that extraneous material had been introduced for consideration by the Minister and in consequence the Minister's decision to refuse permission was quashed.

3. In *Simonovich v An Bord Pleanála*,[389] a decision of the board was based on a report completed by the Inspector who had conducted the oral hearing, into a proposed quarry development. The report was not a fair or accurate record of what had occurred at the oral hearing and, consequently, the board's decision was based on inaccurate information. In consequence of that deficiency in the report, the board's determination was held to be invalid.

4. In *McGoldrick v An Bord Pleanála*,[390] a reference to An Bord Pleanála under the LG(PD)A 1963 (now PDA 2000, s 5) was decided by the board on an issue that had never been advised to the applicant, despite his offer to furnish additional evidence. The Board's decision was quashed on the grounds that it violated the applicant's rights to a fair hearing thus offending the long established principle of a*udi alteram partem*. Barron J stated:

> It is not just a question whether an alternative remedy exists or whether the applicant has taken steps to pursue such remedies. The true question is which is the more appropriate remedy considered in the context of common sense, the ability to deal with the questions raised and the

---

385. *Harding v Cork County Council (No 2)* [2006] IEHC 295, Clarke J.
386. See *Harding v Cork County Council and An Bord Pleanála* [2008] IESC 27.
387. *Law v Minister for Local Government and Another* (unreported, 30 May 1974) HC, Deale J.
388. *Geraghty v Minister for Local Government* [1976] IR 153.
389. *Simonovich v An Bord Pleanála* (unreported, 23 April 1993) HC.
390. *McGoldrick v An Bord Pleanála* [1997] IR 497.

principles of fairness; provided, of course, that the applicant has not gone too far down one road to be estopped from changing his or her mind.[391]

5. In *Killiney and Ballybreack Development Association v Minister for Local Government (No 2)*,[392] the Inspector's report to the board contained statements and evidence which had not been presented at the oral hearing. Because the decision of the board was based on materials which had not been presented the decision was held to be invalid and was set aside.

6. In *Ardoyne House Management Co Ltd v Dublin Corporation*,[393] the respondent served notice on the applicant stating that both the site notice and the newspaper notice were inadequate in that they did not comply with art 17 of the 1994 Regulations. Dublin Corporation required a re-publication of both notices. The applicant for planning permission, Legis Ltd, replied to the corporation and complained that it disagreed with the corporation. Legis Ltd stated that the notices were validly published and that they would not re-publish them. The corporation accepted that response and issued, subsequently, a notice of decision to grant planning permission. The applicant for judicial review argued that once the corporation had issued the notice of complaint about the site notice and about the newspaper notice it could not proceed to determine the application until the notice requiring amendment of the site notices had been complied with. The High Court agreed and quashed the grant of planning permission.

7. In *Dunne and McKenzie v An Bord Pleanála*,[394] there were technical errors in that the fee lodged with the application for planning permission was €5 short of the correct amount. The court held that the applicant had not been prejudiced by this €5 shortfall and the court refused an order for *certiorari* in those circumstances.

8. In *McAnenley v An Bord Pleanála and Monaghan County Council*,[395] it was noted that PDA 2000, s 128[396] provides that where an appeal or referral is made to the board the planning authority concerned shall submit all documents as required by the section to the board. Kelly J noted that there had been substantial non-compliance with s 128 by the local authority and in consequence quashed the decision of the board but directed that the appeal, with full complement of documents, should be remitted to the board and heard afresh.

---

391. *McGoldrick v An Bord Pleanála* [1997] IR 497.
392. *Killiney and Ballybreack Development Association v Minister for Local Government (No 2)* [1978] 112 ILTR 69.
393. *Ardoyne House Management Co Ltd v Dublin Corporation* [1998] 2 IR 147.
394. *Dunne and McKenzie v An Bord Pleanála* [2006] IEHC 400, McGovern J.
395. *McAnenley v An Bord Pleanála and Monaghan County Council* [2002] 2 IR 763.
396. PDA 2000, s 128(1)(a)(b) as amended by PD(SI)A 2006, s 21. Note that specific documents are listed in sub-s (1)(a) as amended.

## Undertaking as to damages

**[4.265]** PDA 2000, s 50 (as amended)[397] provides that the court may, as a condition of granting leave under s 50, require an applicant for leave to give an undertaking as to damages. The unamended s 50 procedure did not provide a statutory discretion enabling a judge to require an undertaking as to damages but RSC allowed for that possibility in O 84, r 20(b).

**[4.266]** In *Seery v An Bord Pleanála*,[398] Finnegan J granted leave to the applicant to apply for judicial review. The learned judge then had to consider an application seeking an undertaking as to damages to be given by the applicant and, in doing so, he referred to the statement of Laffoy J in *Broadnet Ireland Ltd v Offices of the Director of Telecommunications Regulations and Eircom plc* in the following terms:

> In considering whether or not to exercise the discretion under sub-rule (6) to require an undertaking as to damages as a condition of the grant, or the continuance, of leave to apply for judicial review, the essential test is whether such requirement is necessary in the interest of justice or, put another way, whether it is necessary to mitigate injustice to parties directly affected by the existence of the pending (judicial review) application. If in substance the existence of the application has an effect similar to the effect of an interlocutory injunction in private litigation – that activity which would otherwise be engaged in is put 'on hold' pending final determination of the controversy, with resulting loss and damage – in my view, it is appropriate for the Court to adopt the approach traditionally adopted in private law litigation in determining whether an interlocutory injunction should be granted or not. The High Court should require an applicant to give an undertaking to make good that loss and damage if it is ultimately found that the applicant's case is unsustainable, provided there is no countervailing factor arising from the public nature of the jurisdiction it exercises under Order 84 which precludes it from adopting that approach.[399]

Finnegan J, in ordering an undertaking for damages from the applicant, said that the granting of leave had the same effect upon the notice party developers, in terms of delaying the development, as an interlocutory injunction would have and the judge recognised that it would be 'commercial folly to embark upon the development envisaged by the planning permission sought to be impugned while these proceedings are pending.' Finnegan J recognised that the court should not seek an undertaking for damages in cases where the nature of the application for judicial review raises issues of public interest. In *Seery*,[400] there were no such public issues and the applicants were ordered to provide an undertaking as to damages.

**[4.267]** In many of these cases an applicant may not hesitate to give an undertaking as to damages in the knowledge that the undertaking might be worthless. Nevertheless, in

---

397. PDA 2000, s 50A(6) as inserted by PD(SI)A 2006, s 13.
398. *Seery v An Bord Pleanála* [2001] 2 ILRM 151.
399. *Broadnet Ireland Ltd v Offices of the Director of Telecommunications Regulations and Eircom plc* [2000] 2 ILRM 241.
400. *Seery v An Bord Pleanála* [2001] 2 ILRM 151.

*Coll v Donegal County Council (No 2)*[401] the application for leave to apply concerned a public law issue, namely, the extinguishment of a right of way. Dunne J declined to grant an order requiring an undertaking as to damages.

**[4.268]** It is only in rare cases that the court will require security from an applicant in relation to an undertaking to pay damages. Undertakings are often given by applicants in circumstances where the applicant would be unlikely to be able to meet the amount of damages in the event of the undertaking being relied upon on some date in the future.

**[4.269]** In *O'Connell v Environmental Protection Agency*,[402] Herbert J acknowledged that a 'fortified undertaking to pay damages' must be very rare. The development here concerned the provision of a gas turbine electricity generating plant and the learned judge made an order in the case requiring an undertaking as to damages from the applicant, Collette O'Connell. In the course of his judgment Herbert J said:

> The fact that the potential loss to Dungarvan Energy Ltd might exceed her ability to make good that loss is no basis for regarding her undertaking as worthless and an abuse of the process of the Court. I therefore refuse the application that the undertaking to pay damages which the Court requires to be given by Collette O'Connell should be supported in any way whatever by the giving of security or the payment of money into Court or otherwise. Counsel informed the Court that he had carefully advised Collette O'Connell as to the possible consequences of this undertaking and that he is satisfied that she fully understood them and was prepared to give the undertaking if sought by the Court.[403]

## Appeals to the Supreme Court

**[4.270]** PDA 2000, s 50A(7)[404] provides that the court's determination of an application for s 50 leave or the determination of an application for leave for judicial review shall be final and in either case no appeal shall lie from the court's decision to the Supreme Court save with leave of the court which leave shall only be granted where the court certifies that its decision involves a point of law of exceptional public importance and that it is desirable in the public interest that an appeal shall be taken to the Supreme Court. In conventional judicial review cases there is no requirement for the High Court to grant leave to appeal in the case of an appeal to the Supreme Court. PDA 2000, s 50A(7)[405] requires that two conditions must be satisfied before leave to appeal can be granted, namely:

(i) The High Court must certify that its decision involves a point of law of exceptional public importance.

(ii) That it is desirable in the public interest that an appeal should be taken to the Supreme Court.

---

401. *Coll v Donegal County Council (No 2)* (unreported, 29 March 2007) HC, Dunne J.
402. *O'Connell v Environmental Protection Agency* [2002] 1 ILRM 1, Herbert J.
403. *O'Connell v Environmental Protection Agency* [2002] 1 ILRM 1, Herbert J.
404. PDA 2000, s 50A(7) as inserted by PD(SI)A 2006, s 13.
405. *Ardoyne House Management Co Ltd v Dublin Corporation* [1998] 2 IR 147.

Both of those conditions must be fully satisfied before the Supreme Court is entitled to hear the appeal. The leave to appeal restriction in relation to appeals from the High Court to the Supreme Court relates only to s 50 judicial reviews. The obligation to obtain leave to appeal does not, however, apply to a determination of the court insofar as it involves a question as to the validity of any law having regard to the provisions of the Constitution.[406] In *Jackson Way Properties Ltd v Minister for the Environment*,[407] the High Court refused to grant leave to apply for judicial review but certified a point of law of exceptional public importance and allowed an appeal to the Supreme Court on this point of law. Nevertheless, a distinction was made in that case between the parts of the case which involved a question as to the validity of any law having regard to the provisions of the Constitution and other non-constitutional grounds of appeal. A certificate was required in respect of the non-constitutional grounds of appeal.

[4.271] Further restrictions are imposed on the Supreme Court in that the Supreme Court shall have jurisdiction to determine only the point of law certified by the court under s 50(7) (and to make only such order in the proceedings as follows from such determination).[408] The restrictive provisions of s 50(11)(a) have reversed the Supreme Court decision in *Clinton v An Bord Pleanála*[409] where it was held that an applicant was not confined in an appeal to a single ground of appeal arising from a point of law the subject of the High Court certificate. In *Clinton*, it was held that an appellant, once a certificate had been granted, could argue any additional grounds of appeal and that the appellant was not confined to the certified point or points. The case went further to decide that certified points may be abandoned. The appellant may fail on a certified point and succeed on an uncertified point. The Supreme Court held that the granting of a certificate gives the right to appeal but that certificate does not limit the scope of the appeal. *Clinton v An Bord Pleanála*[410] had reaffirmed *Scott v An Bord Pleanála*.[411]

[4.272] There is a specific exception to the certificate required by PDA 2000, s 50(A)(7) (as inserted by PD(SI)A 2006) which arises in cases where there are constitutional grounds of appeal. The requirement to obtain leave to appeal to the Supreme Court which requires the High Court to certify that its decision involves a point of law of exceptional public importance and that it is desirable in the public interest that an appeal should be taken to the Supreme Court does not apply to a determination of the court insofar as it involves a question as to the validity of any law having regard to the provisions of the Constitution.[412] In *Jackson Way Properties Ltd v Minister for the Environment and Local Government*,[413] a road scheme was approved by the Minister under the Road Traffic Act 1993 which divided the applicant's land in two. The

---

406. PDA 2000, s 50A(8) as inserted by PD(SI)A 2006, s 13.
407. *Jackson Way Properties Ltd v Minister for the Environment* [1999] 4 IR 608.
408. PDA 2000, s 50A(11)(a) as inserted by PD(SI)A 2006, s 13.
409. *Clinton v An Bord Pleanála* [2007] 1 IR 272.
410. *Clinton v An Bord Pleanála* [2007] 1 IR 272.
411. *Scott v An Bord Pleanála* [1995] 1 ILRM 424, SC.
412. PDA 2000, s 50A(8) as inserted PD(SI)A 2006, s 13.
413. *Jackson Way Properties Ltd v Minister for the Environment* [1999] 4 IR 608.

applicant's challenge was a constitutional challenge in relation to the provisions of the Roads Act 1993 and as such no certificate was required from the High Court in respect of that constitutional challenge. There were, however, other grounds of appeal and it was held that a certificate would be required in respect of any non-constitutional grounds.

**[4.273]** The phrase 'involves a point of law of exceptional public importance and that it is desirable in the public interest that such an appeal be taken' has been analysed in many cases. To amount to a point of law of exceptional public importance, the point of law must transcend the interests and considerations of the case itself and of the parties before the court.

**[4.274]** In *Neville v An Bord Pleanála (No 2)*,[414] O'Caoimh J had refused application for leave to seek judicial review on 31 July 2001. The applicant sought leave to appeal to the Supreme Court on the grounds that it was a point of exceptional public importance. It was the applicant's case that the court should not look at the merits of the argument which resulted in the decision, but instead should look at the decision itself, and if the decision was one of exceptional public importance then leave to appeal should be granted. In the event, O'Caoimh J refused leave to appeal to the Supreme Court because in the learned judge's opinion the issues were essentially questions of fact and were not issues of exceptional public importance.

**[4.275]** In circumstances where a court may certify that its decision to allow an appeal to the Supreme Court involves a point of law of exceptional public importance and that it is desirable in the public interest that the appeal should be taken to the Supreme Court, McMenamin J, having examined a considerable body of case law, set out the following principles in his judgment in *Glancré Teo v An Bord Pleanála*:[415]

> I am satisfied that a consideration of these authorities demonstrates that the following principles are applicable in the consideration of the issues herein:
>
> 1. The requirement goes substantially further than that a point of law emerges in or from the case. It must be one of exceptional importance being a clear and significant additional requirement.
>
> 2. The jurisdiction to certify such a case must be exercised sparingly.
>
> 3. The law in question stands in a state of uncertainty. It is for the common good that such law be clarified so as to enable the Courts to administer that law not only in the instant, but, in future such cases.
>
> 4. Where leave is refused in an application for judicial review ie in circumstances where substantial grounds have not been established a question may arise as to whether, logically, the same material can constitute a point of law of exceptional public importance so as to justify certification for an appeal to the Supreme Court.
>
> 5. The point of law must arise out of the decision of the High Court and not from discussion or consideration of a point of law during a hearing.

---

414. *Neville v An Bord Pleanála (No 2)* [2001] IEHC 145, O'Caoimh J.
415. *Glancré Teo v An Bord Pleanála* [2006] IEHC 205.

6. The requirements regarding 'exceptional public importance' and 'desirable in the public interest' are cumulative requirements which although they may overlap, to some extent, require separate consideration by the Court.

7. The appropriate test is not simply whether the point of law transcends the individual facts of the case since such an interpretation would not take into account the use of the word 'exceptional'.

8. Normal statutory rules of construction apply which mean, inter alia, that 'exceptional' must be given its normal meaning.

9. 'Uncertainty' cannot be 'imputed' to the law by an applicant simply by raising a question as to the point of law. Rather the authorities appear to indicate that the uncertainty must arise over and above this, for example, in the daily operation of the law in question.

10. Some affirmative public benefit from an appeal must be identified. This would suggest a requirement that a point to be certified be such that it is likely to resolve other cases.

Looking at point 4 in McMenamin J's list in the *Glancré Teoranta* case what emerges is that a situation may arise where an applicant establishes 'substantial grounds' at the application for leave stage but this does not necessarily mean that the case will automatically be treated as one which involves a point of law of exceptional public importance. Again, it may also happen that at the leave to apply for judicial review stage leave is refused. The applicant is entitled to appeal that refusal but in order to proceed with the appeal he will require a certificate from the High Court which will effectively state that the High Court's decision involves a point of law of exceptional public importance and that it is in the public interest that an appeal should be taken to the Supreme Court even though the High Court has already decided that the grounds of challenge by way of judicial review are insubstantial.

[4.276] In *Keane v An Bord Pleanála*,[416] a decision of the High Court to refuse leave on the basis of 'insubstantial grounds' was appealed to the Supreme Court after the High Court judge had certified the appeal to the Supreme Court indicating that there was a point of law of exceptional public importance and that it was in the public interest that the appeal should be taken to the Supreme Court. The Supreme Court, in an *ex tempore* judgment, held that if the issue was such as to raise a point of such importance then there were substantial grounds for the purpose of the Act and an order granting leave to apply for judicial review was made. The case was returned to the High Court to be litigated there.

[4.277] With reference to point 5 of McMenamin J's list, it is clear that regard must be had to the decision itself rather than to the merits of the arguments. The point of law must arise from the decision and not merely from discussions which took place during the course of the case.[417]

---

416. *Keane v An Bord Pleanála* [1997] 1 IR 184.
417. See *Lancefort Ltd v An Bord Pleanála* (unreported, 23 July 1997) HC, Morris J.

**[4.278]** With reference to point 6 of McMenamin J's list, it should be noted that the fact that a point of law is of 'exceptional public importance' is, of itself, insufficient and, if an appeal is to be justified it must also be shown that 'it is desirable in the public interest that an appeal should be taken'. The requirements are cumulative and both points must be accepted by the High Court if an appeal to the Supreme Court is to be justified.[418] So, apart from the court's certificate that its decision involves a point of law of exceptional public interest, the court must also certify that it is desirable in the public interest that an appeal should be taken to the Supreme Court. PDA 2000, s 50A(7) has two distinct matters which must be certified by the High Court before an appeal will be sent forward for hearing to the Supreme Court. In *Arklow Holdings v An Bord Pleanála*,[419] Clarke J was satisfied that the evidence showed that a point of law of exceptional public importance was involved but the learned judge still refused to certify leave to appeal because he considered that it was not in the public interest to do so.

**[4.279]** Case law on the subject of 'public interest' shows that there are two distinct interests which must be demonstrated. In the first place, public interest is the interest expressed by members of the public in planning and environmental matters. Secondly, interest shown by the public is an interest in checking to see that the various legal procedures which applied to the making of administrative decisions are properly followed.

**[4.280]** In *Irish Hardware Association v South Dublin County Council*,[420] the applicant appealed against the High Court judge's refusal to grant a certificate allowing an appeal to the Supreme Court on the basis that the High Court decision involved a point of law of exceptional public importance. The Supreme Court held that no appeal lies from a decision to refuse a certificate of appeal. The Supreme Court followed its decision in *Irish Asphalt v An Bord Pleanála*,[421] where it had clearly stated it had no jurisdiction to entertain an appeal against Costello J's refusal to certify that the issue raised constituted a point of law of exceptional public importance. That decision was for the High Court alone. Only the High Court could decide whether or not to grant a certificate for leave to appeal.

**[4.281]** No time limit is prescribed for the making of an application for leave to appeal, although, in practice, a time limit is often indicated by the court at the time of giving its judgment. In *Ní Ghruagain v An Bord Pleanála, Applebridge Developments Ltd, Fingal County Council and Friends of the Irish Environment*,[422] the applicant made an application for leave to seek judicial review involving a point of law of exceptional public importance and, at the time of the application, the applicant was not legally represented. Making due allowances for the fact that the applicant was not legally represented the court nevertheless found that there were no substantial grounds and

---

418. See *Raiu v Refugee Appeals Tribunal* [2003] 2 IR 63, Finlay Geoghegan J.
419. *Arklow Holdings v An Bord Pleanála* [2007] 4 IR 112, Clarke J.
420. *Irish Hardware Association v South Dublin County Council* [2001] 2 ILRM 291, SC.
421. *Irish Asphalt v An Bord Pleanála* [1996] 1 ILRM 81.
422. *Ní Ghruagain v An Bord Pleanálat* (unreported, 19 June 2003) HC, Murphy J.

accordingly the application was dismissed. An application for leave to appeal was made three months after the judgment refusing application for leave. The court, recognising that there was no time limit, nevertheless held that parties should be aware of the importance of acting promptly and, in this case, they had failed to do so. The application for leave to appeal was again refused.

[4.282] Arklow Holidays Limited was a most persistent applicant, which appeared before the High Court in at least six different cases. At the time of writing there is still an appeal to the Supreme Court pending. Two of these *Arklow Holiday* cases are particularly relevant to the principles involved in statutory judicial review.

[4.283] In the first of the *Arklow Holidays Limited v An Bord Pleanála*[423] cases, the applicant sought leave to apply for judicial review of a decision of An Bord Pleanála to permit Arklow Urban District Council to build a waste water management treatment plant in order to increase the water supply in the Arklow area. Clarke J, who heard this case, had previously granted the applicant leave to apply for judicial review and, in doing so, the learned judge approved of some but not all of the grounds advanced. All of the grounds which Arklow Holidays Limited relied upon were grounds which could have been raised as a challenge to the original planning decision. Clarke J, in dealing with the rule in *Henderson v Henderson*,[424] had this to say:

1. The jurisprudence in this area stems from *Henderson v Henderson*. The so-called rule in that case was considered by the Supreme Court in *AA v The Medical Council*[425] where Hardiman J (speaking for the Supreme Court) noted the principle to the effect that a party to previous litigation is bound not only by matters actually raised but by matters which ought properly to have been raised but were not. It is clear, however, that Hardiman J also determined that a rule or principle so described could not, in its nature, be applied in an automatic or unconsidered fashion and that the public interest in the efficient conduct of litigation did not render the raising of an issue in later proceedings necessarily abusive where, in all the circumstances, the party concerned was not misusing or abusing the process of the Court.

2. It is clear, therefore, that a plaintiff or applicant is at risk of being prohibited from raising, in a second set of proceedings, an issue which, it can properly be said, could and should have been raised in an earlier set of proceedings relating generally to the subject matter.

3. There is, however, an overriding discretion in the court to consider whether the raising of the issue in the second set of proceedings truly amounts to an abuse of process and, if it does not, then the party may be permitted to proceed.'[426]

---

423. *Arklow Holidays Limited v An Bord Pleanála* [2007] IEHC 327.
424. *Henderson v Henderson* (1843) 3 Hare 100.
425. *AA v The Medical Council* [2003] 4 IR 302.
426. *Arklow Holidays Limited v An Bord Pleanála* [2007] IEHC 327.

**[4.284]**

In conclusion, Clarke J held that Arklow Holidays Limited was precluded by the rule in *Henderson v Henderson*[427] from arguing any of the issues in respect of which leave was granted. Since Arklow Holidays was not entitled to any of the reliefs in respect of which leave was granted it followed that the application for judicial review had to be refused.

**[4.284]** In the second of the *Arklow Holiday Limited v An Bord Pleanála*[428] cases, the applicant sought a certificate for leave to appeal Clarke J's decision in the first case.[429] The key issue in the second case was whether or not the application of the rule in *Henderson v Henderson* in planning matters is a point of law which falls within the criteria laid down in PDA 2000, s 50 (as amended), that is to say whether or not it is a point of law of exceptional public importance and that it is desirable in the public interest that an appeal should be taken to the Supreme Court on that point.

**[4.285]** Clarke J referred to and agreed with two paragraphs in Simons on *Planning and Development Law*,[430] being paras 11–360 and 11–361, which read as follows:

11–360:

> Leave to appeal shall only be granted where the High Court certifies that its decision involves a point of law of exceptional public importance. Two consequences appear to flow from this. First, in determining whether or not to grant leave to appeal, regard must be had to the decision itself and not to the merits of the arguments which resulted in that decision.[431] This would appear to suggest that the High Court should not attempt to predict what the outcome of the appeal might be; instead, it should take the appellants case at its height and consider whether or not the point of law is of exceptional public importance.

11–361:

> Secondly, it is the decision of the High Court which must give rise to the point of law. Thus if the decision of the High Court was based on narrow grounds (in particular, on factual grounds), it may be that no point of law can properly be isolated.[432] To put the matter another way, it is not permissible to allow an appeal on a moot, or on theoretical points of law which might have arisen for discussion

---

427. *Henderson v Henderson* (1843) 3 Hare 100.
428. *Arklow Holiday Limited v An Bord Pleanála and Others* [2008] IEHC 2.
429. Note that a certificate granting leave to appeal is required under PDA 2000, s 50A(7) as inserted by PD(SI)A 2006, s 13.
430. Simons, *Planning and Development Law* (2nd edn, Thomson Round Hall, 2007) pp 641 and 642, paras 11–360 and 11–361.
431. Simons's footnote reads: *Lancefort Ltd v An Bord Pleanála* (unreported, 23 July 1997) HC Morris J, at 3–4; and *Raiu v Refugee Appeals Tribunal* [2003] 2 IR 63, Finlay Geoghegan J.
432. Simons's footnote reads: See *Lancefort Ltd v An Bord Pleanála* (unreported, 31 March 1998) HC, McGuinness J: 'Many of the questions seem to me to be closely connected either with the facts of the instant case or with the specific arguments made by Counsel for the applicant during the hearing before me.' The requirement that the point of law have immediacy also occurs in the analogous situation of security for costs or pre-emptive costs. For example, in *Village Residents Association Limited (No 2)* [2000] 4 IR 321, [2001] 2 ILRM 22, Laffoy J found that before the point of law relied upon in that case could actually be isolated, several controversies had to be disposed of, and the issue of general importance was not sufficiently immediate. See also *Begley v An Bord Pleanála* (unreported, 23 May 2003) HC Ó Caoimh J.

or consideration during the hearing, but which did not go to the actual determination or decision of the High Court.[433] The point of law must be 'of' or in some way contained 'in' the decision or determination in the first instance, and must at the same time transcend the case itself to meet the requirements of exceptional public importance and public interest.[434]

[4.286] The learned judge went on to say that if he was wrong in applying the rule in *Henderson v Henderson*[435] that error would open up a detailed scrutiny of significant aspects of the project which might or might not have had the affect of persuading the planning authority not to grant planning permission. Clarke J concluded that:

> I have considerable sympathy not only for Arklow County Council but also for the population whose needs are to be serviced by the proposed project. There have been protracted delays which have been encountered in the planning process and its associated legal challenges. I have already commented (as have a number of colleagues) on the fact that in many cases (and this seems to be one of them) the so called 'tightening up' of the provisions concerning leave and certification for appeal introduced for the purposes of expedition have, in fact, had the opposite effect. Notwithstanding that unfortunate state of affairs it seems to me that the point raised is one of exceptional public importance and that it is in the public interest that it be certified and I propose to do so.[436]

## Remittal

[4.287] The High Court has a discretion to remit a matter to a decision-maker and to direct that decision-maker to reconsider its decision and to reach a decision in accordance with the findings of the High Court.[437] The remittal to the decision-maker can only occur where the High Court is satisfied that there are grounds for quashing the decision.

[4.288] The matter of remittal was considered in the High Court in *Usk and District Residents Association Ltd v An Bord Pleanála*.[438] In this case, the inspector made a recommendation that planning permission should be refused but An Bord Pleanála was unable to produce any evidence that conditions drafted by the inspector were ever approved at a formal board meeting. The Board, as it was entitled to do, granted planning permission. The inspector was then requested to draft a grant of permission with conditions as determined by the board. The records did not disclose that any

---

433. Simons's footnote reads: *Ashbourne Holdings Ltd v An Bord Pleanála (No 3)* (unreported, 19 June 2001) HC, Kearns J.
434. Simons's footnote reads: *Harding v Cork County Council (No 3)* (unreported, 30 November 2006) HC, Clarke J. See also *Harrington v An Bord Pleanála (No 2)* (unreported, 16 March 2006) HC, Macken J, where it is suggested that as the question of delay is always something to be considered, in the context of a particular application, it was difficult to see how a point of exceptional public importance could arise in the absence of a finding of general application.
435. *Henderson v Henderson* (1843) 3 Hare 100.
436. *Arklow Holiday Limited v An Bord Pleanála and Others* [2008] IEHC 280 (unreported, 8 September 2006) Clarke J.
437. Order 84, r 6(4).
438. *Usk and District Residents Association Ltd v An Bord Pleanála* [2007] 2 ILRM 378, Kelly J.

meeting had taken place approving the inspector's draft conditions and the board conceded that the decision should be quashed. Kelly J, in the High Court, was faced with the decision either to confirm that the planning permission had been quashed leaving an opportunity for the developer to reapply for planning permission or to remit the decision back to the board for further consideration. Kelly J decided upon the latter course and in doing so the learned judge included a firm suggestion that it would be prudent for the board, in re-opening the oral hearing, to ensure that none of the personnel who had dealt with the original appeal would sit for the hearing of the remitted appeal. The Board ignored the judge's suggestion and proceeded with the oral hearing which was attended by some of the members who had been present at the first hearing. The inspector's report again recommended refusal but An Bord Pleanála decided to grant planning permission for an engineered landfill. The residents sought and obtained a judicial review of the decision and in the High Court, McMenamin J held that the decision of An Bord Pleanála to grant permission would, in the circumstances, give rise to a reasonable apprehension that there had not been an impartial decision-making process and he granted an order of *certiorari* quashing the board's decision.

## The quashing of part of a decision or act

[4.289] A review may be made in respect of part only of a decision or act to which it applies and PDA 2000, s 50A(9),[439] provides for severance of a decision which is challenged. If a court finds that part only of a decision which is challenged is invalid the court may declare that part to be invalid and leave the remainder of the decision intact.

[4.290] PDA 2000, s 50A(9) reads:

> If an application is made for judicial review under the Order in respect of part only of a decision or other act to which s 50(2) applies, the Court may, if it thinks fit, declare to be invalid or quash the part concerned or any provision thereof without declaring invalid or quashing the remainder of the decision or other act or part of the decision or other act, and if the Court does so, it may make any consequential amendments to the remainder of the decision or other act or part thereof that it considers appropriate.

In reviewing part only of a decision or act the court may declare the part concerned to be invalid while the remainder of the decision will be unaffected. But if consequential amendments are required to the remainder of the decision, the section empowers the court to amend the remainder as it considers appropriate.

## Expeditious determination

[4.291] PDA 2000, s 50A(10)[440] provides:

> The Court shall, in determining an application for s 50 leave or an application for judicial review on foot of such leave, act as expeditiously as possible consistent with the administration of justice.

---

439. PDA 2000, s 50A(9) as inserted by PD(SI)A 2006, s 13.
440. PDA 2000, s 50A(10) and (11) as inserted by PD(SI)A 2006, s 13.

In spite of the good intentions of s 50A(10), statutory judicial review can sometimes be a torturously complicated and slow process involving, as it was in *Arklow Holidays Limited v An Bord Pleanála and Others*,[441] many years of litigation which greatly delayed the installation of a much needed additional water supply scheme.

**[4.292]** PDA 2000, s 50A(11) (as amended) provides:

> On appeal from a determination of the Court in respect of an application referred to in sub-s (10), the Supreme Court shall:
>
> (a) Have jurisdiction to determine only the point of law certified by the Court under sub-s (7) (and to make only such order in the proceedings as follows from such determination), and
>
> (b) In determining the appeal, act as expeditiously as possible consistent with the administration of justice.

The explanation for s 50A(11)(a) is that before the law was changed by the 2006 Act,[442] it was held in *Talbot v An Bord Pleanála*[443] that in the case of a successful appeal from a refusal to grant leave to apply for judicial review the Supreme Court had the choice of either granting leave itself or making an order remitting the entire matter to the High Court for further consideration. The change introduced in s 50A(11) of PD(SI)A 2006 provides that, on hearing the appeal, the Supreme Court's jurisdiction is limited to a determination only of the point of law certified by the court and to make such orders as may result from that determination.

**[4.293]** PDA 2000, s 50A(12) (as inserted)[444] makes provision for statutory judicial review proceedings, under PDA 2000, s 50, to be heard in the Commercial Court. The section reads:

> Rules of the court may make provision for the expeditious hearing of applications for s 50 leave and applications for judicial review on foot of such leave.[445]

---

441. *Arklow Holidays Limited v An Bord Pleanála and Others* [2006] IEHC 280, Clarke J.
442. PD(SI)A 2006.
443. *Talbot v An Bord Pleanála* [2009] 1 ILRM 356.
444. PDA 2000, s 50A(12) as inserted by PD(SI)A 2006, s 13.
445. PDA 2000, s 50 judicial review applications for leave and application for judicial review itself are generally heard at the same time in the Commercial Court thus giving effective meaning to the words 'provision for the expeditious hearing ... etc'.

# Chapter 5
# ENFORCEMENT AND PLANNING INJUNCTIONS

## PART I: ENFORCEMENT

**[5.01]** PDA 2000, Pt VIII comprises ss 151–164 inclusive.[1] Part VIII deals with enforcement, and the Act provides a number of different types of enforcement procedures some of which are civil remedies and others which are criminal. Enforcement is the keystone to a successful planning regime and although Ireland measures up reasonably well there have been occasions where social or political intervention has interfered in an unwelcome and destructive manner.

### Offence

**[5.02]** The first section, namely, s 151 of Part VIII of PDA 2000 creates a general offence in respect of the carrying out of unauthorised development:

> Any person who has carried out or is carrying out unauthorised development shall be guilty of an offence.[2]

Although not statutorily defined, unauthorised development comprises the carrying out of unauthorised work or the making of any unauthorised use. It includes development which is not carried out in accordance with the planning permission or in accordance with a condition in the planning permission. Neither the carrying out of works nor the use of land is unauthorised in any of the following circumstances:

(a) where the development is being carried out either in the case of works or in the case of a change of use, pursuant to the terms and conditions of a valid grant of planning permission; or

(b) where there is a pre-1 October 1964 development in existence; or

(c) where the development, whether it comprises the carrying out of work or a change in use, is exempted development; or

(d) where the development is an immaterial change from an authorised use.

PDA 2000, s 32(1) provides that permission is required for any development of land, not being exempted development and that in the case of unauthorised development,

---

1. PDA 2000, s 153(1) is amended by PD(A)A 2010, s 45(a), s 153(6) and (7) as inserted by PD(A)A 2010. PDA 2000, s 156(1)(b), (2)(b), (3)(b), (4) and (5) are amended by PD(A)A s 46(a) to (e) inclusive. PDA 2000, s 157 has been amended by the insertion of sub-s (4)(aa) and by the amendment of s 157(4)(b) by PD(A)A 2010, s 47(a) and s 47(b) respectively. PDA 2000, s 160 has been amended by the insertion of sub-s (6)(aa) by PD(A)A 2010, s 48. PDA 2000, s 162(3) is amended by PD(A)A 2010, s 49.
2. PDA 2000, s 151. Section 156 deals with penalties for offences as amended by PD(A)A 2010, s 46.

retention permission is required.[3] PDA 2000, s 32(2) requires that a person shall not carry out development in respect of which permission is required under sub-s (1) except in accordance with the permission granted under Pt III of the Act.

## Development carried out pursuant to a planning condition

**[5.03]** Usually, notification of a decision to grant planning permission will contain a list of conditions which must be complied with in the course of the development. A question as to the validity of a permission may arise where a condition requires development which was not contemplated by the applicant in making the application for permission. Thus, the inclusion of conditions in a grant of permission may give rise to new issues in respect of which third parties may not have been given an opportunity to express their views in relation to the development envisaged by the conditions. This matter was considered in *Mason and McCarthy v KTK Sand and Gravel Ltd*,[4] where Smyth J wisely held that a condition in a planning permission requiring works to be carried out could, in principle, authorise the carrying out of those works but that the authorisation would only apply in a case where the works required by the condition come within the scope of the permission. The scope of the permission is a matter of construction and as such it is subject to the principle that the permission itself cannot go beyond the scope of the application or the scope of matters reasonably incidental thereto. By way of example, a condition, which requires a contractor to remove all builder's rubble from the site when the building works are completed, would come within the scope of the application. It is, after all, a condition which a third party objector might reasonably anticipate. However, a condition requiring a contractor to construct public shower and toilet facilities on a central green or park of a housing development might well be considered to be outside the scope of the application to develop a housing scheme. Smyth J's decision in the *Mason and McCarthy* case is more circumspect than the English authorities which appear to support the proposition that no planning permission is needed for development required by a planning condition attached to a planning permission.[5]

**[5.04]** Where the works envisaged by the condition do come within the scope of the permission and within the scope of the application for permission, if those works are not attended to it may be readily appreciated that enforcement proceedings (whether criminal or civil) may be taken by a planning authority or by any third party for failure to comply with the works required by the planning condition.

## Retention permission in relation to enforcement proceedings

**[5.05]** PDA 2000, s 162(2) provides that it shall not be a defence to a prosecution under Pt VIII if the defendant proves that an application for retention permission has been

---

3. Note that the status of retention permission has undergone change as is dealt with below.
4. *Mason and McCarthy v KTK Sand and Gravel Ltd* [2004] IEHC 183, Smyth J.
5. See *R v Derbyshire County Council ex parte North East Derbyshire District Council* [1997] 77 LGR 389.

made or that a retention permission has been granted, if either the application or the grant has occurred:

(a) since the initiation of proceedings under this part;

(b) since the date of sending a warning letter under s 152;[6] or

(c) since the date of service of an enforcement notice in a case of urgency in accordance with s 155.[7]

**[5.06]** PDA 2000, s 162(3) provides that no enforcement action under Part VIII (including an application under s 160)[8] shall be stayed or withdrawn by reason of an application for permission for retention of unauthorised development under s 34(12C) or the grant of that permission.[9]

**[5.07]** Before PDA 2000 became law it was common practice for a respondent to apply for and generally obtain an adjournment if an application for retention permission had been made. The adjournment granted would be an adjournment until a determination on the application had been made by the planning authority or by An Bord Pleanála as the case may be. Clearly, if the applicant obtained retention permission the enforcement proceedings would usually go no further but if the applicant's application was refused the enforcement case would proceed.

**[5.08]** The prohibition contained in PDA 2000, s 162(3) (as amended)[10] does not imply that a planning authority may not consent to an adjournment in a prosecution or consent to an adjournment in a planning injunction case, where the decision of an applicant for retention permission is still pending. A planning authority or the board may use its discretion in consenting to an adjournment but it is a discretion which is seldom availed of in a manner which might be wholly favourable to the applicant.

**[5.09]** PDA 2000, s 162(3)[11] does remove all discretion from the court in this context and the court may not stay proceedings before it in a situation where the application for retention permission has not been determined. A court may, however, at its discretion, place a stay on any order granting an injunction in accordance with PDA 2000, s 160, to enable a respondent to apply for retention permission in respect of unauthorised development, provided the unauthorised development does not require environmental impact assessment (EIA) and provided also that there are 'exceptional circumstances'. If a court does grant a stay on an order made in s 160 injunction proceedings it will usually impose a time limit on the respondent to ensure that the application is lodged by the respondent within a specified time. In the event of a subsequent refusal of retention

---

6. PDA 2000, s 152(1)–(4) provides for 'warning letters'.
7. See PDA 2000, s 162(2)(a), (b) and (c).
8. PDA 2000, s 160 deals with injunctions in relation to unauthorised developments.
9. PDA 2000, s 162(3) as amended by LGA 2001, s 247 and by PD(A)A 2010, s 49.
10. PDA 2000, s 162(3) is amended by PD(A)A 2010, s 49 by the substitution of s 34(12C) for s 34(12).
11. PDA 2000, s 162(3) is amended by PD(A)A 2010, s 49 by the substitution of s 34(12C) for s 34(12).

permission the stay will lapse immediately. In *Dublin Corporation v Kevans*,[12] the planning authority was granted an injunction restraining the continued use of a building as offices. The use had been in existence for eight years and although Finlay P found that Dublin Corporation had not acquiesced in the unauthorised use the learned judge allowed the respondent a substantial time to make alternative arrangements.

**[5.10]** PDA 2000, s 162(3) (as amended)[13] clearly requires that even if a retention permission has been granted between the date that the enforcement proceedings were issued and the date of the court hearing, the enforcement case must proceed. This requirement gives rise to a contradictory situation in that the planning authority is compelled to press on with enforcement against a respondent who has obtained planning permission (probably subject to conditions). It is often the case that the enforcement proceedings would seek either to have the development removed or the use discontinued, when all that is required, once the permission has been granted, is to sanction the developer for proceeding to develop without planning permission.

**[5.11]** In *Dublin County Council v Tallaght Block Company Ltd*,[14] the Supreme Court held that once an applicant has lodged an application for retention permission, he is precluded from subsequently claiming that the development did not require planning permission because the development was exempted development. That irrational proposition was overruled (albeit *obiter*) in *Fingal County Council v William P Keeling & Sons Ltd*,[15] where it was held that a developer cannot be estopped from making a claim that a development is an exempted development, by reason only of having made an application for permission for retention of that development. To allow such an estoppel would deprive a developer of a right at law simply because he had exercised a different right.

**[5.12]** In enforcement matters both the planning authorities and the courts have discretion in making a decision as to whether or not enforcement proceedings should be taken. The discretion is, however, lost to both the planning authority and to the courts where the development is one which requires an EIA.

**[5.13]** The European Court of Justice (ECJ) has examined the Irish system in relation to retention permission and in the case *Commission v Ireland*,[16] the ECJ has ruled that the Irish provisions for retention permission made under PDA 2000[17] are inconsistent with the requirements of the EIA Directive.[18] In attempting to put this ruling into effect in the

---

12. *Dublin Corporation v Kevans* (unreported, 14 July 1980) HC, Finlay P.
13. PDA 2000, s 162(3) is amended by PD(A)A 2010, s 49 by the substitution of s 34(12C) for s 34(12).
14. *Dublin County Council v Tallaght Block Company Co Ltd* [1982] ILRM 534.
15. *Fingal County Council v William P Keeling & Sons Ltd* [2005] 2 IR 108.
16. *Commission v Ireland* (Case C–215/06).
17. PDA 2000, s 34(12).
18. Directive 85/337/EEC of 27 June 1985 re the assessment of the effects of certain public and private projects on the environment, as amended by Directive by 97/11/EC of 3 March 1997, which permits the granting of retention permission only in cases where 'exceptional circumstances are proved'.

short term the Department of the Environment, Heritage and Local Government issued a circular in October 2008 advising all planning authorities and An Bord Pleanála that any application for retention permission in respect of development which requires an EIA, is invalid. The circular has now been superseded by PD(A)A 2010, s 23(12) which abolishes retention permission for EIA projects. The 2010 Act offers in place of retention permission for EIA projects a new 'substitute consent' procedure which only becomes available in 'exceptional circumstances'. The restrictions on the granting of retention permission extend to all sub-threshold projects.[19]

[5.14] Substitute consent is a new concept which may be obtained in exceptional circumstances where developers find themselves in a situation where they cannot apply for retention permission because, for example, they failed to carry out EIA or appropriate assessment under the Habitats Directive.[20] They may apply to An Bord Pleanála for leave to lodge an application for substitute consent in order to regularise the development. The conditions in relation to an application for leave to apply for substitute consent are onerous and there is no guarantee or presumption in law that the application to the board will be successful.

[5.15] The most common operations which will be affected by the 'substitute consent' procedure are quarries. Quarries will only be entitled to avail of substitute consent in strictly regulated circumstances. Excluded from the possibility of seeking leave to apply to An Bord Pleanála for a substitute consent are quarries which have never had planning permission since 31 October 1964 and which failed to register under s 261 of PDA 2000. If a quarry has permission and did register under s 261 it still may be the case that expansion which may have taken place during the 'Celtic Tiger' years may amount to development within the meaning of 'intensification', and if that expansion was carried out without the benefit of the necessary environmental consents and assessments which apply a final opportunity is offered to such quarries in order to regularise their situation by means of applying for and, with luck, obtaining a substitute consent. The substitute consent is strictly a time-limited 'sunset' provision to give quarry operators one last chance to regularise their activities and it is dealt with in more detail in **Ch 8**.

[5.16] The case which prompted the ECJ ruling in *Commission v Ireland*[21] was *Derrybrien Cooperative Society Limited v Saorgus Energy Limited*.[22] In that case, the applicant was precluded from making a complaint in relation to the EIA Directive. The case involved the development of a wind farm at Derrybrien, Co Galway. The planning authority, in granting permission for the development, failed to require an assessment from the developer dealing with the environmental effects of the windmills in the area.

[5.17] There were 23 wind turbines required in the first and second phase and permission was granted for those 23 windmills on 12 March 1998. An application was made on 5 October 2000 for the third phase comprising a further 25 turbines and service

---

19. See **Ch 3** for further detail on retention permissions.
20. Habitats Directive 92/43/EEC.
21. *Commission of European Communities v Ireland* (Case C–215/06) [2008] ECR I–4911.
22. *Derrybrien Cooperative Society Limited v Saorgus Energy Limited* [2005] IEHC 485, Dunne J.

**[5.18]**         **Planning and Environmental Law in Ireland**

roadways. Permission was granted on 15 November 2001 (presumably after requests for further information were satisfied). On 20 June 2002, the developer applied for consent to alter the first two phases and those changes were authorised on 30 July 2002. In October 2003, the original phase 1 and phase 2 permission had expired and an extension was granted by the planning authority in November 2003. At that time, the Derrybrien wind farm was the largest terrestrial wind-energy development ever planned in Ireland and one of the largest in Europe. The construction of the wind farm required the destruction of large areas of coniferous forest amounting to 263 hectares of woodland, but no EIA was carried out for the operation of felling that forest which was contrary to the requirements both of the Irish legislation and of Directive 85/337/EEC. A catastrophic landslide occurred on 16 October 2003 with a consequent ecological disaster when a peat mass in the area of development became dislodged and rolled down the hill to pollute the Owendalulleegh River causing the death of some 500,000 fish and causing lasting damage to the fish spawning beds. What occurred during the course of this development at Derrybrien ably demonstrated the necessity for thorough and comprehensive EIA prior to development and, of course, prior to the granting of planning permission. The case also dramatically illustrated the importance of compliance with the EIA Directive. In its judgment the ECJ stated:

> The purpose of carrying out an environmental impact assessment in conformity with requirements of Directive 85/337 is to identify, describe and assess in an appropriate manner the direct and indirect effects of a project on factors such as fauna and flora, soil and water and the interaction of those factors. In the present case, the Environmental Impact Statements supplied by the developer had certain deficiencies and did not examine, in particular, the question of soil stability, although that is a fundamental when excavation is intended.[23]

**[5.18]** Part of the summary of the judgment in *Commission of European Communities v Ireland*[24] makes specific reference to the harm which Ireland's retention permission regime can do in cases where EIA is required. The paragraph reads:

> A system of after–the event regularisation [ie, retention permission][25] may have the effect of encouraging developers to forego ascertaining whether intended projects satisfy the criteria of art 2(1) of that directive, and consequently, not to undertake the action required for identification of the effects of those projects on the environment and for their prior assessment. The first recital of the preamble to Directive 85/337, however, states that it is necessary for the competent authority to take effects on the environment into account at the earliest possible stage in all the technical planning and decision-making processes, the objective being to prevent the creation of pollution or nuisances at source rather than subsequently trying to counteract their effects.[26]

---

23. See *Commission of European Communities v Ireland* (Case C–215/06) [2008] ECR I–4911 at para 104.
24. *Commission of European Communities v Ireland* (Case C–215/06) [2008] ECR I–4911.
25. Words in brackets added.
26. *Commission of European Communities v Ireland* (Case C–215/06) [2008] ECR I–4911.

**[5.19]** Ireland was held to have failed to fulfil its obligations under arts 2, 4 and 5–10 of Directive 85/337/EEC as amended by Directive 97/11/EC and Ireland was ordered to pay the costs. In order to understand the relevant parts of Directive 85/337/EEC, as amended,[27] the following extract is reproduced from the summary of the judgment in *Commission of the European Communities v Ireland*[28] as follows:

Article 2(1) and (2) and the first subparagraph of Article 2(3) of Directive 85/337 as amended provide:

1. Member States shall adopt all measures necessary to ensure that, before consent is given, projects likely to have significant effects on the environment by virtue, inter alia, of their nature, size or location are made subject to an assessment with regard to their effects. The projects are defined in Article 4.

2. The environmental impact assessment may be integrated into the existing procedures for consent to projects in the Member States, or, failing this, into other procedures or into procedures to be established to comply with the aims of this Directive.

3. Without prejudice to Article 7 Member States may, in exceptional cases, exempt a specific project in whole or in part from the provisions laid down in this Directive.

Article 3 of Directive 85/337 as amended provides:

The environmental impact assessment shall identify, describe and assess in an appropriate manner, in the light of each individual case and in accordance with Articles 4 to 11, the direct and indirect effects of a project on the following factors:

- human beings, fauna and flora,
- soil, water, air, climate and the landscape,
- material assets and the cultural heritage,
- the inter-action between the factors mentioned in the first, second and third incidents.

Article 4 of Directive 85/337 as amended provides:

1. Subject to Article 2(3), projects of the classes listed in Annex I shall be made subject to an assessment in accordance with Articles 5 to 10.

2. Subject to Article 2(3) for projects listed in Annex II the Member States shall determine through:

    (a) a case-by-case examination, or

    (b) thresholds or criteria set by the Member State,

---

27. Reference is only made to the amendments of Directive 85/337/EEC which have direct relevance to the failure by Ireland to fulfil its obligations. Reference is not made to the amendments introduced by Directive 97/11/EC to arts 5–10 of Directive 85/337/EEC since those amendments had no bearing on the determination of the case against Ireland before the ECJ.
28. *Commission of the European Communities v Ireland* (Case C–215/06) [2008] ECR I–4911.

**[5.20]** Planning and Environmental Law in Ireland

whether the project shall be made subject to an assessment in accordance with Articles 5 to 10. Member States may decide to apply both procedures referred to in (a) and (b).

3. When a case-by-case examination is carried out or thresholds or criteria are set for the purpose of paragraph 2, the relevant selection criteria set out in Annex III shall be taken into account.

4. Member States shall ensure that the determination made by the competent authorities under paragraph 2 is made available to the public.

Point 3(i) of Annex II to Directive 85/337 as amended specifies installations for the harnessing of wind power for energy production (wind farms).

By virtue of point 13 of Annex II, any change or extension of projects listed in Annex I or Annex II, already authorised, executed or in the process of being executed, which may have significant adverse effects on the environment (being a change or extension not listed in Annex I) must be regarded as a project within the scope of art 4(2) of Directive 85/337 as amended.

Annex III to Directive 85/337 as amended, relating to the selection criteria referred to in art 4(3) of that directive, provides that the characteristics of projects must be considered in relation, inter alia, to pollution and nuisances, and to the risk of accidents having regard in particular to technologies used. That annex also indicates that the environmental sensitivity of geographical areas likely to be affected by projects must be considered having regard, inter alia, to the absorption capacity of the natural environment, paying particular attention to certain areas, including mountain and forest areas.[29]

**[5.20]** Earlier in it's judgment, the court stated, having regard to the criteria in art 4(3), that Member States may, *inter alia*, specify certain types of projects as being subject to an assessment or may establish the criteria and/or thresholds necessary to determine which of the projects of the classes listed in Annex II are to be subject to an assessment in accordance with arts 5 to 10 (prior to the amendments introduced by Directive 97/11/EC).

**[5.21]** Article 5 of Directive 85/337/EEC states:

1. In the case of projects which, pursuant to Article 4, must be subjected to an environmental impact assessment in accordance with Articles 5 to 10, Member States shall adopt the necessary measures to ensure that the developer supplies in an appropriate form the information specified in Annex III inasmuch as:

   (a) the Member States consider that the information is relevant to a given stage of the consent procedure and to the specific characteristics of a particular project or type of project and of the environmental features likely to be affected;

---

29. Extracted from judgment of the court (second chamber) 3 July 2008 from pp 5 to 9 inclusive *Commission of European Communities v Ireland* (Case C–215/06) [2008] ECR I–4911.

(b) the Member States consider that a developer may reasonably be required to compile this information having regard inter alia to current knowledge and methods of assessment.

2. The information to be provided by the developer in accordance with paragraph 1 shall include at least:

– a description of the project comprising information on the site, design and size of the project,

– a description of the measures envisaged in order to avoid, reduce and, if possible, remedy significant adverse effects,

– the data required to identify and assess the main effects which the project is likely to have on the environment,

– a non-technical summary of the information mentioned in indents 1 to 3.

3. Where they consider it necessary, Member States shall ensure that any authorities with relevant information in their possession make this information available to the developer.

**[5.22]** Article 6 of Directive 85/337/EEC reads as follows:

1. Member States shall take the measures necessary to ensure that the authorities likely to be concerned by the project by reason of their specific environmental responsibilities are given an opportunity to express their opinion on the request for development consent. Member States shall designate the authorities to be consulted for this purpose in general terms or in each case when the request for consent is made. The information gathered pursuant to Article 5 shall be forwarded to these authorities. Detailed arrangements for consultation shall be laid down by the Member States.

2. Member States shall ensure that:

– any request for development consent and any information gathered pursuant to Article 5 are made available to the public,

– the public concerned is given the opportunity to express an opinion before the project is initiated.

**[5.23]** Article 7 of Directive 85/337/EEC provides that:

Where a Member State is aware that a project is likely to have significant effects on the environment in another Member State or where a Member State likely to be significantly affected so requests, the Member State in whose territory the project is intended to be carried out shall forward the information gathered pursuant to Article 5 to the other Member State at the same time as it makes it available to its own nationals. Such information shall serve as a basis for any consultations necessary in the framework of the bilateral relations between two Member States on a reciprocal and equivalent basis.

**[5.24]** Article 8 of Directive 85/337/EEC provides that:

Information gathered pursuant to Articles 5, 6 and 7 must be taken into consideration in the development consent procedure.

**[5.25]** Article 9 of the Directive provides that:

> When a decision has been taken, the competent authority or authorities shall inform the public concerned of:
> 
> – the content of the decision and any conditions attached thereto,
> 
> – the reasons and considerations on which the decision is based where the Member States' legislation so provides.
> 
> The detailed arrangements for such information shall be determined by the Member States.
> 
> If another Member State has been informed pursuant to Article 7, it will also be informed of the decision in question.

**[5.26]** Article 10 of the Directive provides that:

> The provisions of this Directive shall not affect the obligation on the competent authorities to respect the limitations imposed by national regulations and administrative provisions and accepted legal practices with regard to industrial and commercial secrecy and the safeguarding of the public interest.
> 
> Where Article 7 applies, the transmission of information to another Member State and the reception of information by another Member State shall be subject to the limitations in force in the Member State in which the project is proposed.

Annex II to Directive 85/337 lists projects subject to art 4(2) of that directive, namely those for which an environmental impact assessment is necessary only where the Member States consider that their characteristics so require. Projects referred to in that annex include, in point 2(a), extraction of peat, and in point 2(c), extraction of minerals other than metalliferous and energy-producing minerals, such as marble, sand, gravel, shale, salt, phosphates and potash.

Projects listed in point 10(d) of Annex II include the construction of roads.

**[5.27]** Article 3 of Directive 97/11/EC provides that:

> 1. Member States shall bring into force the laws, regulations and administrative provisions necessary to comply with this Directive by 14 March 1999 at the latest. They shall forthwith inform the Commission thereof.
> 
> 2. If a request for development consent is submitted to a competent authority before the end of the time-limit laid down in paragraph 1, the provisions of Directive 85/337/EEC prior to these amendments shall continue to apply.

**[5.28]** The main thrust of the judgment in *Commission of the European Communities v Ireland*[30] indicated that retention permission should not be available if its availability encourages or facilitates developers to avoid making an application for permission in advance of the commencement of development works.

---

30. *Commission of the European Communities v Ireland* (Case C–215/06) [2008] ECR I–4911.

[5.29] In England, in *Ardagh Glass Ltd v Chester City Council*[31] Judge Mole QC[32] examined the ECJ decision in *Case C–215/06*. The learned judge indicated that he did not consider that the decision of the ECJ meant that retrospective planning permission would never be lawfully granted. The learned judge was correct and as long as the competent authorities (the planning authority and An Bord Pleanála) paid careful attention to the need to protect the objectives of the Directive retention permission will still be possible. Dealing with the decision of the ECJ, Judge Mole QC had this to say:

> I read the decision as focusing upon the possibility of circumvention and the danger that it will be encouraged. The court feared that if retention permission were given in anything other than exceptional circumstances, the Directive would be got round and was concerned that the use of retention of permission in Ireland was 'common in planning matters lacking any exceptional circumstances'. The Court did not say whether it was referring to retention permission in general or retention permission for EIA consent only. (I have no reason to think that the grant of retrospective planning permission where an EIA is required is common in England, although the grant of retrospective permission in other cases certainly is). Easy regularisation would encourage developers to ignore the criteria of art 2(1) of the Directive.
>
> The proper concern is at the heart of the Court's decision. It may be met by making a claim that a developer will gain no advantage by pre-emptive development and that such development will be permitted only in exceptional circumstances. Such an approach, it seems to me, could preserve and protect the objectives of the Directive.[33]

## Warning letter procedure

[5.30] Although only one type of enforcement notice can be served PDA 2000 provides for a four step process:

(i) the issue of a warning letter;

(ii) the making of a decision as to whether or not to take enforcement action;

(iii) service of an enforcement notice;

(iv) the taking of steps to compel compliance with the enforcement notice (if necessary).

[5.31] In relation to the warning letter, PDA 2000, s 152(1) provides:

(1) Where –

(a) A representation in writing is made to a planning authority by any person that unauthorised development may have been, is being or may be carried out, and it appears to the planning authority that the representation is not vexatious, frivolous or without substance or foundation, or

---

31. *Ardagh Glass Ltd v Chester City Council* [2009] EWHC 745.
32. Judge Mole was sitting as a default High Court Judge.
33. *Ardagh Glass Ltd v Chester City Council* [2009] EWHC 745.

(b) It otherwise appears to the authority that unauthorised development may have been, is being or may be carried out,

The authority shall issue a warning letter to the owner, the occupier or any other person carrying out the development and may give a copy, at that time or thereafter, to any other person who in its opinion may be concerned with the matters to which the letter relates.

The purpose of PDA 2000, s 152(1) is to encourage public participation in the planning process by enabling members of the public to submit well founded representations drawing the planning authority's attention to unauthorised development which has taken place or which is taking place, or where the planning authority becomes aware that unauthorised development may be carried out, the authority shall issue a warning letter to the owner, the occupier or other person carrying out or proposing to carry out the development. The obligation imposed on the planning authority here is mandatory though it is the experience of many planning practitioners that there are many cases where requests to a planning authority to issue a warning letter have been ignored.

**[5.32]** Nevertheless, the planning authority is left with some discretion and it shall not be compelled to serve a warning letter if it considers that the representation is vexatious, frivolous or without substance or foundation.[34] If the planning authority concludes that the development in question is of a trivial or minor nature it may decide not to issue a warning letter.[35]

**[5.33]** The trouble with the use of the words 'vexatious, frivolous', or without substance or foundation' is that they are not defined. Also, it is not precisely clear what is meant by a development which is 'of a trivial or minor nature'. The lack of definition makes it difficult, in borderline cases, for a party who has made a request to the planning authority to serve a warning letter which request has been ignored. If a planning authority ignores a request to serve a warning letter it does leave itself open to a challenge by way of seeking an order for *mandamus* or by way of judicial review but an applicant would have to be confident that the local authority could not justify its exercise of discretion not to issue a warning letter on the basis of the fact that the representation was vexatious, frivolous or without substance or that the development in question was of trivial or minor nature.

**[5.34]** The obligation on the planning authority to serve a warning letter is obligatory unless circumstances exist which enable it to use its discretion not to serve such a warning letter. The words used in the section in relation to unauthorised development are, 'which may have been, is being or may be carried out', and that means that the warning letter may be issued with respect to unauthorised development in the past, present or future.[36] Also, it should be noted that the warning letter may be initiated by a representation in writing by any person or alternatively it may be issued on the initiative of the planning authority.

---

34. PDA 2000, s 152(1)(a).
35. PDA 2000, s 152(2).
36. PDA 2000, s 152(1)(a)(b).

**[5.35]** Where a representation in writing is received, the warning letter must be issued as soon as may be and not later than six weeks after receipt of the representation.[37] The warning letter is issued to the owner or occupier or any person carrying out the development, such as a contractor, within the six-week time limit. If a planning authority fails to issue a warning letter under PDA 2000, s 152, that failure will not prejudice the issue of a subsequent enforcement notice or any other decision to take enforcement action[38] including an application for an injunction.

**[5.36]** Although the wording of PDA 2000, s 152(1) requires the planning authority to issue a warning letter to the owner, the occupier or any other person carrying out the development, it is regrettable, in the interests of transparency and openness, that the planning authority is only required to give a copy of the warning letter, at the time or thereafter, to any person who, in its opinion, may be concerned with the matters to which the letters relate. PDA 2000, s 152 does not compel or require the planning authority to send a copy of the warning letter to the person or persons who have made the representation in the first instance. The planning authority's only obligation is to notify a person who made the representation of its decision not to serve an enforcement notice within two weeks after the expiration of the six week period.[39] The planning authority must also notify any other person who made representations of the decision in writing within two weeks of making that decision. There is no obligation on the planning authority to inform members of the public who may have made representations and/or observations, of the steps taken or to be taken by the planning authority in relation to enforcement procedures. It is only when a planning authority decides whether or not to issue an enforcement notice that it must notify any person who has made representations or observations under PDA 2000, s 152(1). Also, if a planning authority decides not to issue a warning letter there is, at least, an implied obligation on the planning authority to notify any person who has made a representation under PDA 2000, s 152. Many local authorities issue an enforcement complaint form with attendant notes attached. An example of such an enforcement complaint form as issued by Cork City Council and the explanatory memorandum is both helpful and informative. For a sample of Cork City Council's Enforcement Complaint Form and notes accompanying the planning complaint form[40] see the **Appendix**.

**[5.37]** This implied obligation to notify the complainant as to whether or not a warning letter will be issued has been recognised by a number of planning authorities who include in their enforcement complaint forms (on which s 152 representations are requested to be made) an undertaking to notify the party making the s 152 representation as to whether a warning letter has issued or if it has been decided by the planning authority that a warning letter is not warranted.

---

37. PDA 2000, s 152(3).
38. PDA 2000, s 153(5).
39. PDA 2000, s 154(2).
40. Reproduced by kind permission of Cork City Council.

[5.38] The issuing of a warning letter and the service of same on a developer does not impose any obligation or liability on the developer. Nevertheless, the fact that a warning letter has been issued by a planning authority must be recorded in the planning authority's planning register specifying the date of issue of the letter and the fact of its withdrawal, if that is appropriate.[41] If property and/or development is affected by a warning letter this fact will appear on a planning search made prior to exchange of contract and the existence of the warning letter in the register would undoubtedly require explanation and would have some potentially negative effect on the likelihood of the parties proceeding to exchange contracts.

[5.39] It is obvious that if a warning letter is discovered by a planning search from the planning authority's register, and if the contents of the warning letter have not been attended to, a vendor will be in difficulties in providing a satisfactory architect's certificate of compliance to the effect that the development has been carried out in compliance with the planning permission and the conditions therein. The warning letter is a first step and although there is no sanction or consequence arising from the warning letter on its own, nevertheless, the fact that a warning letter has issued may indicate that an enforcement notice is likely to follow.

[5.40] Any requests made to a planning authority by a complainant seeking to have a warning letter issued against a party who has not complied with the relevant planning permission should stress the urgency of the complaint as a means of ensuring that the planning authority will respond promptly. It would also be advisable for the complainant, in seeking a warning letter, to request the planning authority to state (if it is the case) its reasons in the event that the decision is made not to issue a warning letter. The complainant should also ask for a copy of any other warning letters which may have been served because, in consequence of an absurd omission in the Act, the planning authority has no obligation to serve such copy on the complainant. The drafting of a warning letter requires a lot of thought because if the planning authority takes no action or takes inadequate action the only step left to a complainant is judicial review.

## Contents of a warning letter

[5.41] PDA 2000, s 152(4) states that the warning letter shall refer to the land concerned. The subsection provides a list of the contents of the warning letter as follows:

> (4) A warning letter shall refer to the land concerned and shall –
> 
> (a) State that it has come to the attention of the authority that unauthorised development may have been, is being or may be carried out,
> 
> (b) State that any person served with the letter may make submissions or observations in writing to the planning authority regarding the purported

---

41. PDA 2000, s 7(2)(r) which provides that particulars of any warning letter issued under s 152, including the date of issue of the letter and the fact of its withdrawal, if appropriate, shall be entered in the register.

offence not later than four weeks from the date of service of the warning letter,

(c) State that when a planning authority considers that unauthorised development has been, is being or may be carried out, an enforcement notice may be issued,

(d) State that officials of the planning authority may at all reasonable times enter on the land for the purposes of inspection,

(e) Explain the possible penalties involved where there is an offence, and

(f) Explain that any costs reasonably incurred by the planning authority in relation to enforcement proceedings may be recovered from a person on whom an enforcement notice is served or where court action is taken.

**[5.42]** Although PDA 2000 does make it clear that a *bona fide* request from a member of the public requesting the planning authority to serve a warning letter on a person, persons, company, etc, carrying out unauthorised development, which request is not frivolous, vexatious, etc, should be acted upon by the planning authority, the question must be asked as to what would happen if the planning authority fails to serve a warning letter within the six-week time limit prescribed and fails to notify the party who requested the service of the warning letter of any reasons as to why the warning letter was not served. This has occurred, all too frequently, but the point does not appear to have been tested in the courts. PDA 2000, s 152 leaves the planning authority with a defined discretion to refuse the serving of a warning letter. The planning authority would have to make the case that the representation is vexatious, frivolous or without substance or foundation or that the development in question is of a trivial or minor nature. The problem is that the warning letter *per se* is of very limited effect. The service of the warning letter does not stop the time from running in relation to enforcement proceedings. Therefore, if application were made to the High Court by way of judicial review (which is a most costly procedure) the most that the High Court could do would be to order the local authority to issue a warning letter if it had not done so within the period of six weeks from the date of receipt of the request and if it had not, within two further weeks after the six weeks, notified the person or persons making the request that the request would be denied because it was vexatious, frivolous, etc The planning authority's discretion as to service of the warning letter may be limited, and prior to the passing of PD(A)A 2010 it enjoyed almost complete discretion in relation to service of an enforcement notice. Under PDA 2000 it was most unlikely that a High Court would direct the planning authority to serve an enforcement notice. However, PDA 2000, s 153 has been amended by PD(A)A 2010, to provide, firstly, that as soon as may be after the issue of a warning letter the planning authority shall make such investigations as it considers necessary to make a decision as to whether to issue an enforcement notice or to make an application for an injunction under PDA 2000, s 160 (as amended).[42] A planning authority has a duty to ensure that a decision on whether or not to issue an enforcement notice must be taken as expeditiously as possible. It shall be the objective of the planning authority to make that decision within 12 weeks of the date of issuing a

---

42. The reference to 'making an application under s 160' has been added by PD(A)A 2010, s 45(a).

warning letter. In making its decision the planning authority shall consider any representations made to it, to include any submissions or observations made to it, and any other material considerations. Failure to issue a warning letter shall not prejudice the issue of an enforcement notice or any other proceedings. Note also the new provision inserted into PDA 2000, s 157 (which deals with the prosecution of offences). Section 157(4)(aa) has been inserted by the PD(A)A 2010, s 47(a) and it reads:

> (aa) Where the development was carried out not more than seven years prior to the date on which this section comes into operation and notwithstanding paragraph (a), a warning letter or enforcement notice may issue or proceedings may be commenced, at any time in respect of the following development:
>
> (i) Operation of a quarry;
>
> (ii) Extraction of peat.

**[5.43]** PDA 2000, s 157(4)(b) has also been amended by PD(A)A 2010, s 47(b) and it now reads:

> (b) Notwithstanding paragraph (a) a warning letter or enforcement notice may issue, proceedings may be commenced at any time in respect of any condition concerning the use of land to which the permission is subject.

**[5.44]** There has been no alteration in PDA 2000, s 152 which deals with the warning letter. In relation to the warning letter it seems that, if a planning authority simply ignores a request to serve one, although it may be in breach of the conditions of PDA 2000, the very most that can be achieved (and the point does not appear to have been decided) would be an order to compel the service of a warning letter. There is no provision in the Act to say that the service of a warning letter operates to stop the clock running in relation to time when the transgressor will obtain immunity from enforcement proceedings or criminal prosecution.[43] Furthermore, because of delays inherent in judicial review proceedings, the case itself might not come on for full hearing for some six to twelve months. That further loss of time might prove fatal in that the developer who has transgressed may obtain immunity within that period. It is probable that a planning authority would be perfectly entitled to decline to serve a warning letter in circumstances where the limitation period has expired, but in cases of intensification or creeping intensification, it may be open to argument as to the date on which the seven-year immunity period is to start. Nevertheless, it would seem that the limitation period provides a third circumstance in which the planning authority can

---

43. PDA 2000, s 157(4) provides that there is a seven-year time limit to issue a warning letter which runs from the date of the commencement of the unauthorised development or from the beginning of the expiration of the life of the planning permission (as appropriate). If the warning letter is not served within seven years from the date of commencement of development, where no planning permission was obtained, it cannot be served outside the seven-year time limit. If a warning letter has not been served within the combined period of the life of the planning permission (normally five years) plus seven years (the time begins at the expiration of the life of the planning permission (normally five years) and runs for seven years after that date) then no warning letter can be served.

decline to serve a warning letter. PDA 2000 does require a planning authority to notify the person, persons or body making the request, within two weeks after the expiration of six weeks from the date of request, of a decision not to serve an enforcement notice.

[5.45] There is one tangible benefit in seeking an order against a planning authority which has failed to serve a warning letter and, where the court is satisfied that the authority has disregarded the request, without giving reasons. If the courts are disposed to make an order requiring the planning authority to serve a warning letter the planning authority must, as soon as may be, take the next step, namely to make such investigation as it considers necessary to enable it to make a decision on whether or not to issue an enforcement notice. The legislation dealing with warning letters has missed a genuine opportunity to give some positive impact to the genuine warning letter. As the legislation stands, there seems little point in providing that the local authority must issue a warning letter save in certain limited circumstances, on the basis that few people would be encouraged to consider judicial review or an application for an order for *mandamus* as a prudent option where the planning authority ignores their request to issue a warning letter. The enforcement process, as a whole, would certainly have been greatly improved if a genuine warning letter served under PDA 2000, s 152 had the effect of stopping the clock in relation to the time limit for obtaining immunity against enforcement or prosecution, at least until such time as a planning authority has made its decision (which is discretionary) either to issue or not to issue an enforcement notice or to take such other steps, or not to take such other steps as are available to it, to include prosecution, under PDA 2000.

[5.46] It should be noted that the date of issue of a warning letter is relevant in the context of an application for retention planning permission and if the application is made after the issue of a warning letter that fact will not amount to a defence in a subsequent prosecution.[44] Furthermore, it is not a defence to a prosecution under PDA 2000 if the defendant proves that he has applied for or has been granted planning permission under s 34(12):

(a) since the initiation of proceedings under this part;

(b) since the date of the sending of a Warning Letter under s 152; or

(c) since the date of service of an enforcement notice in a case of urgency in accordance with s 155.[45]

## Decision on enforcement

[5.47] PDA 2000 provides for one type of enforcement notice for all types of unauthorised development. The procedures for issuing an enforcement notice, as set out in PDA 2000, ss 153 (as amended),[46] 154 and 155 are designed both to ensure early prevention of unauthorised development and to ensure that third party complainants are kept fully informed of decisions. The enforcement system is primarily about trying to

---

44. PDA 2000, s 162(2) as amended by LGA 2001 s 247.
45. PDA 2000, s 162(2)(a), (b) and (c).
46. PD(A)A 2010, s 45(a) and (b).

**[5.48]** PDA 2000, s 153(1) provides:

> As soon as may be after the issue of a warning letter under s 152, the planning authority may make such investigation as it considers necessary to enable it to make a decision on whether to issue an enforcement notice or make an application under s 160.[47]

The use of the phrase 'as soon as may be' is unfortunate. It is another example of giving favourable time limits to officials when none are available to members of the public. If, as has been stated, it was the genuine intention of the policy-makers to streamline enforcement procedures, a time limit should have been put in place between the issue of the warning letter and the completion of the investigations which the planning authority considers necessary in order for it to decide whether or not to issue an enforcement notice.

**[5.49]** PDA 2000, s 153(2)(a) provides:

> (a) It shall be the duty of the planning authority to ensure that decisions on whether to issue an enforcement notice are taken as expeditiously as possible.

Admittedly, PDA 2000, s 153(2)(a) does provide that the decision on whether to issue an enforcement notice must be taken 'as expeditiously as possible' but that phrase also stretches the time limit too far.

**[5.50]** The phrase 'as expeditiously as possible' undoubtedly encourages a sense of urgency but it does not impose any time limit and, when the two phrases, 'as soon as may be' and 'as expeditiously as possible' are read together they have the potential of allowing for considerable delay. The danger of any form of delay is that each day has the potential of bringing a planning transgressor one day closer to obtaining immunity from prosecution or from enforcement.

**[5.51]** PDA 2000, s 153(2)(b) provides:

> Without prejudice to the generality of para (a), it shall be the objective of a planning authority to ensure that the decision on whether to issue an enforcement decision shall be taken within twelve weeks of the issue of a warning letter.

Again no time limit is imposed by this subsection. The paragraph is little more than an aspiration and, in practice, the 12-week period is frequently exceeded.

The 'investigation'[48] to be made by a planning authority in coming to a decision as to whether or not to issue an enforcement notice would include an inspection of the development in respect of which a warning letter is issued by an inspector who does not have to give notice to the owner or occupier of the site to be inspected before he enters

---

47. PDA 2000, s 153 as amended by PD(A)A 2010, s 45.
48. PDA 2000, s 153(1).

the land. PDA 2000, Pt VIII does not offer any guidance as to the 'considerations' which are necessary to enable the planning authority to make a decision on whether or not to issue an enforcement notice. Simons[49] suggests that the absence of any guidelines or suggestions as to how a decision as to whether or not to serve an enforcement notice may very well be unconstitutional:

> There is a very real question mark over the constitutionality of the enforcement notice procedure. It is a well established principle of administrative law that statutory powers are to be exercised only in a manner that would be in conformity with the Constitution and within the limitations of the power as they are to be gathered from the statutory scheme or design. Yet, the failure under Pt VIII of the PDA 2000 to state principles and policies renders a decision whether or not to take enforcement action unreviewable.[50]

It was clear from the words used throughout PDA 2000, s 153 that a planning authority had an absolute discretion as to whether or not to issue an enforcement notice but the provisions of the PD(A)A 2010, s 45(a) and (b), amending PDA 2000, s 153, have altered and improved the situation slightly.

**[5.52]** PDA 2000, s 153(2) does not mean that a planning authority has a period of 12 weeks, from the issue of a warning letter, to take a decision as to whether or not to issue an enforcement notice. The language in the subsection is far from clear and if it was intended that a 12-week time limit would apply, there would have been no use or reason for the inclusion of PDA 2000, s 153(2)(a). What is expressed in this subsection is no more than an aspiration that the planning authority should, if it decides to do so, issue an enforcement notice within 12 weeks of issuing a warning letter. The case cannot be put further and there would appear to be a total absence of any sanctions to be invoked in the event that the planning authority takes a considerably longer period before issuing an enforcement notice. The reason as to why no strict time limit is given in this section is to allow the planning authority to pursue enforcement action, even where it fails, for whatever reason, to make a decision to serve an enforcement notice within the 12-week period.

**[5.53]** PDA 2000, s 153(3) provides:

> A planning authority, in deciding whether to issue an enforcement notice shall consider any representations made to it under s 152(1)(a) or submissions or observations made under s 152(4)(b) and any other material considerations.

PDA 2000 does not offer any definition of the words 'other material considerations'.

PDA 2000, s 153(4) provides:

> The decision made by the planning authority under sub-s (1) including the reasons for it shall be entered by the authority in the register.

---

49. See Simons, *Planning and Development Law* (2nd edn, Thomson Roundhall, 2007) at pp 301 and 302, para 7–91.
50. Simons's footnote refers to *State (Lynch) v Cooney* [1982] IR 337 at 380.

PDA 2000, s 153(5) provides:

> Its failure to issue a Warning Letter under s 152 shall not prejudice the issue of an enforcement notice or any proceedings that may be initiated by the planning authority.

**[5.54]** The decision in *Dublin Corporation v O'Callaghan*[51] was made before PDA 2000 became law. Nevertheless, Herbert J's finding is relevant insofar as it held that the planning authority must make a formal decision to serve an enforcement notice and must record same and it must record the basis on which the decision was made. Herbert J also held that the formal record must have come into existence prior to the enforcement notice being signed or served on the relevant owner or occupier. The enforcement notice itself cannot constitute a record of the decision. A planning authority is obliged to follow the procedural steps set out in s 153(1), (2), (3) and (4). But while it must follow those steps, the planning authority nevertheless has absolute discretion as to whether or not to issue an enforcement notice. As things stand, any challenge by way of judicial review of a decision not to serve an enforcement notice would be judged by the high standards laid down in *O'Keefe v An Bord Pleanála*.[52] Another avenue is open to a party who wishes to challenge a planning authority's decision not to serve an enforcement notice and that is that a party on his or her own initiative may institute planning injunction proceedings under PDA 2000, s 160.

**[5.55]** In summary, the case would seem to be that a planning authority cannot be compelled by a judicial review to issue an enforcement notice unless its decision and the reasons for that decision are so unreasonable and so irrational that they come within the principles laid down in the *O'Keefe* case. Then again, because of the existence of the 'alternative remedy', which is open to all comers, judicial review, as a remedy, may not be available.

**[5.56]** If a planning authority fails to carry out its statutory obligation to make a decision as to whether or not to issue an enforcement notice after a warning letter has been issued it is likely that an order of *mandamus* would be available, and in those circumstances the court would make an order directing the planning authority to take a decision one way or the other. The court would not, however, go so far as to dictate the form of that decision.

**[5.57]** In looking again at the undefined phrase 'other material considerations', it is suggested that the development plan could be deemed to be 'a material consideration'. Also, under the EIA Directive, Member States are bound to take all the general or particular measures necessary to ensure that projects which are likely to have significant effects on the environment are subject to consent procedure. As seen, in *Commission v Ireland*[53] it was held that Ireland had breached the EIA Directive by allowing an application for retention permission in respect of a development which required an EIS. Ireland was also held to be in breach of the EIA Directive for its failure to take

---

51. *Dublin Corporation v O'Callaghan* [2001] IEHC 22, Herbert J.
52. *O'Keefe v An Bord Pleanála* [1993] 1 IR 39.
53. *Commission of European Communities v Ireland* (Case C–215/06) [2008] ECR I–4911.

enforcement action in those circumstances. From this decision it is clear that if a development requires an EIA but no such assessment is undertaken, that may be an 'other material consideration' which might require but should certainly encourage a planning authority to issue enforcement proceedings.

[5.58] In *Dublin Corporation v McGrath*,[54] the general rule that estoppel cannot operate so as to validate an invalid exercise of statutory power was applied. In that case a building contractor erected a building without planning permission and when complaints were made a planning inspector from the planning authority called to Mr McGrath's site and assured him that he could proceed with the building and that he, the inspector, would look after things with the planning authority. Mr McGrath, relying on the planning inspector's representations, proceeded with the development and completed the building. Later the planning inspector was suspended and subsequently dismissed. It was held that the planning inspector's representations made to Mr McGrath to the effect that the building was an exempted structure were not binding on the planning authority. The decision as to whether or not to issue an enforcement notice is a decision taken by the manager of the planning authority and, accordingly, any statement issued by a planning inspector was held to be *ultra vires*.

[5.59] In *Greendale Building Co v Dublin County Council*,[55] Henchy J had this to say:

> The general rule is that a plea of estoppel of any kind cannot prevail as an answer to a well-founded claim that something done by a public body in breach of a statutory duty or limitation of function is ultra vires.' (The learned judge then cited a number of English decisions to support that statement and concluded by saying.) ...'The reason I believe is that it is incompatible with parliamentary democracy for the Court under the guise of estoppel or waiver or any other document to set aside the will of Parliament as constitutionally embodied in a Statute.

[5.60] PDA 2000, s 153(6) provides:

> The planning authority instead of issuing an enforcement notice under this section, may decide to make an application under s 160.[56]

The provisions of PDA 2000, s 153 increased public participation in initiating enforcement procedures. The provisions of PDA 2000 encourage a planning authority to make an expeditious decision as to whether or not to issue an enforcement notice but they do not compel the planning authority to do so with any threat of sanction. It is unfortunate that this is the case. The planning authority is both watchdog and enforcer in respect of planning transgressions and, as such, it is now compelled to enforce but it should be compelled to enforce expeditiously. While the planning authority did retain an absolute discretion as to whether or not to pursue enforcement action under PDA 2000 this has been altered and a planning authority is now compelled to take enforcement action in certain circumstances.

---

54. *Dublin Corporation v McGrath* [1978] ILRM 208.
55. *Greendale Building Co v Dublin County Council* [1977] 1 IR 256.
56. PDA 2000, s 153(6) as inserted by PD(A)A 2010, s 45(b).

PDA 2000, s 153(7) provides:

> Where a planning authority establishes, following an investigation under this section that unauthorised development (other than development that is of a trivial or minor nature) has been or is being carried out and the person who has carried out or is carrying out the development has not proceeded to remedy the position, then the authority shall issue an enforcement notice under this section or make an application pursuant to section 160 unless there are compelling reasons for not doing so.[57]

## Enforcement notice

**[5.61]** PDA 2000, s 154(1) provides:

(a) Where a decision to enforce is made under s 153, or where urgent action is required under s 155, the planning authority shall, as soon as may be, serve an enforcement notice under this section.

(b) Where an enforcement notice is served under this section, the planning authority shall notify any person who made representations under s 152(1)(a) and any other person, who in the opinion of the planning authority may be concerned with the matter to which the notice concerned relates, not being a person on whom the enforcement notice was served, of the service of the enforcement notice.

**[5.62]** PDA 2000, s 154(1)(a) uses the words 'as soon as may be' in relation to the time available to the planning authority to serve the enforcement notice. This unfortunate phrase does not indicate any sense of urgency nor does it impose any definite time limit and, in consequence, it gives rise to slow process and to uncertainty. In *Harding v Cork County Council*,[58] Murray CJ expressed some support for the phrase 'as soon as may be'. Although the Chief Justice dealt with the phrase in a different context he concluded that:

> ... concerning the 'as soon as may be' requirement it has to be borne in mind first of all that this is an administrative procedure and requirements as to time must be interpreted having regard to the ordinary burdens of administration in any organisation or body. It is not as if the matter in question was the only such matter which the planning authority in question had to deal with.

With respect to the Chief Justice's view the reality is that enforcement is the keystone to a successful planning regime. If the planning regime is to be successful in Ireland, planning authorities must be compelled to take enforcement action against planning transgressions within a reasonable time and irrespective of other matters which they may have to deal with. The reasonable time should be defined in terms of a fixed and specified number of weeks. Legislative favouritism which benefits officials should be abolished and both officials and members of the public should be dealt with in an equal manner by statutory provisions. Both should equally be compelled to comply with the statutory provisions in the Planning Acts but within defined time limits.

---

57. PDA 2000, s 153(7) is inserted by the PD(A)A 2010, s 45(b).
58. *Harding v Cork County Council* [2008] IESC 27.

**[5.63]** Where a planning authority decides to issue an enforcement notice, the enforcement notice must be served on the transgressor. The planning authority must notify the person or persons who made representations that unauthorised development may have been or is being carried out and it must also notify any other persons who, in the opinion of the planning authority, are concerned and who are not the person or persons on whom the enforcement notice was served.[59]

**[5.64]** If a planning authority decides not to issue an enforcement notice it shall notify any persons to whom the warning letter under PDA 2000, s 152 was copied, and any other persons who made representations under that section, of the decision in writing within two weeks of making that decision.[60]

**[5.65]** An enforcement notice must be served on the person carrying out the development and, where the planning authority considers it necessary, on the owner or occupier of the land or on any other person who, in the opinion of the planning authority, may be concerned with the matters to which the notice relates. If, subsequent to the service of an enforcement notice, the planning authority becomes aware that any other person may be carrying out development or is an owner or occupier of the land, or may be affected by the notice, the notice may be served on them also.[61]

The enforcement notice takes effect on the date of the service thereof.[62]

*Contents of an enforcement notice*

**[5.66]** PDA 2000, s 154(5) deals with the contents of an enforcement notice and may be summarised as follows.

The enforcement notice must:

(a) Identify the land concerned and it must also indicate the type of breach involved. If it is the case where the development has no planning permission, the notice must indicate that the development must cease or that it must not commence, as appropriate. If the development is a development for which permission has been granted but where the development is or may not be in compliance with the permission or with a condition of the permission granted, the notice must require that the development will proceed in conformity with the permission and in conformity with any conditions to which the permission is subject.[63]

(b) The enforcement notice must identify the steps to be taken, as indicated in the warning notice, within the time limit specified in the warning notice, by a person in order to comply with a notice. The steps could include, for example, requiring the development to cease or not to commence, requiring a person to

---

59. PDA 2000, s 154(1)(b).
60. PDA 2000, s 154(2).
61. PDA 2000, s 153(3)(a)&(b).
62. PDA 2000, s 154(4).
63. PDA 2000, s 154(5)(a)(i)(ii).

proceed in conformity with the permission or with the conditions in a permission, or require the removal, demolition or alteration of any structure and the discontinuance of any use.[64]

(c) The enforcement notice must warn the person served with the enforcement notice that if the steps are not taken within the period specified in the notice, or at the latest within six months or such other period as may be allowed, the planning authority may enter the land and take such steps, including the removal, demolition or alteration of any structure and may recover any expenses reasonably incurred by them or on their behalf.[65]

(d) The enforcement notice shall require the person served with the notice to refund the planning authority the costs which the authority incurred in investigating the breach and issuing the notice, including, for example, salary and expenses of employees, consultants and advisors.[66] The planning authority cannot, however, recover costs and expenses if it merely issues a warning letter, but if it proceeds to make a decision to serve an enforcement notice the planning authority may recover costs and expenses reasonably incurred in relation to the investigation, detection and service of the enforcement notice concerned and any warning letter issued including costs incurred in respect of the remuneration and other expenses of employees, consultants and advisors. Those costs and expenses could, potentially, be substantial and should act as a deterrent to developers from, as is sometimes the case, sitting back and waiting for the enforcement notice to be served before taking any steps.

(e) The enforcement notice will warn that if specified steps are not taken within the period specified in the notice or such extended period, not being more than six months, the person or persons served with the notice may be guilty of an offence.[67]

[5.67] The wording used in PDA 2000, s 154(5) was put under the magnifying glass in *Dundalk Town Council v Lawlor*[68] heard before O'Neill J with judgment delivered on 18 March 2005. Dundalk Town Council served an enforcement notice on Bill Lawlor in respect of alleged unauthorised development carried out at Soldiers Point, Lower Point Road, Dundalk. Mr Lawlor owned a site at Soldiers Point and carried out excavation clearance works on the site without permission. Dundalk Town Council required Mr Lawlor to return the site to its previous condition. The site was an old shipyard which had, for some years, been overgrown and was a habitat for wild birds. The excavation had been carried out by Mr Lawlor and top soil had been stripped. Debris had been removed from the site. Dundalk Town Council served an enforcement notice

---

64. PDA 2000, s 154(5)(b).
65. PDA 2000, s 154(5)(c).
66. PDA 2000, s 154(d).
67. PDA 2000, s 154(5)(e). See PDA 2000, s 156 as amended PD(A)A 2010, s 46 for specific penalties for infringement.
68. *Dundalk Town Council v Lawlor* [2005] 2 ILRM 106.

pursuant to PDA 2000, s 154 requiring the accused Mr Lawlor to cease unauthorised development on the site and to return the site to its previous condition. Mr Lawlor wrote to Dundalk County Council on 26 October 2003 requesting clarification and that letter was not replied to. Dundalk Town Council issued a summons against Mr Lawlor and the matter came before the District Court on 10 March 2004 where District Justice Flann Brennan submitted a case stated to the High Court in which he posed two questions:

1. Whether the District Justice was correct in law in determining that the period of time set out on the enforcement notice satisfied the requirement of s 154 of the Planning and Development Act 2000.

2. Whether the District Justice was correct in law in determining that the requirement in the said enforcement notice to 'return the site to its previous condition' satisfied the requirement of s 154 of the Planning and Development Act 2000.

Undoubtedly, the enforcement procedure provided by PDA 2000, s 154 is more prescriptive than the provisions in previous planning statutes. Failure to comply with an enforcement notice is a criminal offence and O'Neill J went to considerable lengths in his judgment to stress that 'criminal offences must be defined with clarity and precision so that a person can know whether his conduct is or is not a commission of an offence. This means that in construing any notice which issues pursuant to s 154, a strict construction is required'.

**[5.68]** The contents of an enforcement notice shall, under PDA 2000, s 154(5)(b):

Require such steps as may be specified in the notice to be taken within a specified period, including where appropriate, the removal, demolition or alteration of any structure and the discontinuance of any use and, insofar as is practicable, the restoration of the lands to its condition prior to the commencement of the development.

**[5.69]** In considering the meaning of 'within a specified period', O'Neill J held that in construing any enforcement notice issued pursuant to PDA 2000, s 154, a strict construction is required. The subsection in question and any enforcement notice must be construed in accordance with the natural and ordinary meaning of the words used and there is no scope for any kind of purposive or teleological approach, because failure to comply with the enforcement notice is a criminal offence and the person accused of a criminal offence must be put in a position so that he can know whether his conduct is or is not the commission of an offence. O'Neill J held that a 'specified period' must be capable of having a beginning and an end and the beginning and the end must be clearly ascertained. In this enforcement notice the word used was 'immediately' and while that word may provide a beginning it does not indicate when the period would end. The notice did not create a period but rather it gave a starting point, with no ending, from which work had to commence in order to give effect to the enforcement notice. The notice served entirely failed to describe or limit a time within which the work was to be accomplished. O'Neill J held that the subsection requires that the period must be given a date on which the works commence and a date by which they must be completed and,

**[5.70]** Planning and Environmental Law in Ireland

accordingly, he held that the enforcement notice as served by Dundalk Town Council was ineffective and invalid.

**[5.70]** Dealing with the second question submitted by District Justice Brennan as to whether the use of the words 'return the site to its previous condition' satisfied the requirement under PDA 2000, s 154, O'Neill J stated that as failure to comply with an enforcement notice is a criminal offence any enforcement notice issued pursuant to PDA 2000, s 154(5)(b) must 'with clarity and precision set out the steps that are required to be taken in the specified period'. O'Neill J was satisfied that the enforcement notice served in this case did not set out with sufficient clarity or precision the steps required having regard to the fact that failure to comply with the notice was a criminal offence. In drafting the enforcement notice, Dundalk Town Council had simply borrowed the words from s 154(5)(b). That subsection refers to 'the restoration of the land to its condition prior to commencement of the development'. The words used in this enforcement notice by Dundalk Town Council were 'return the site to its previous condition'. Subsection (5)(b) also used the phrase 'and insofar as is practicable'. It was O'Neill J's view that this would not relieve Dundalk Town Council from carefully setting out the precise steps required by the Council as to work which was required to comply with the enforcement notice. O'Neill J held that Bill Lawlor did not have the necessary information to know precisely what work he had to carry out in order to retain the status of compliance required by the enforcement notice. For example, on this site, there was a considerable volume of debris strewn about the site which had been removed by Mr Lawlor. In the absence of precision and clarity in the enforcement notice O'Neill J posed the question as to whether the notice in fact required that debris be brought back and strewn across the site as it had been before it was cleared. It was also not clear as to whether the notice actually required the top soil to be replaced on the site or whether, for example, it was only necessary for Mr Lawlor to re-seed the site at the level which it was at after the removal of the top soil. O'Neill J held that for an enforcement notice to be effective it must:

> Be specific, by giving a commencement date and a finishing date. It must define a reasonable time period in which the works are to be carried out. Therefore the enforcement notice should say that within (say for example) four days from the date of service of the enforcement notice, work should be commenced to carry out the works necessary to comply with the enforcement notice and that those works should be completed by, (say for example) a date of five weeks from the date of commencement of the works. The notice could say, if it was reasonable so to state, that (for example) the works should commence on the 5th June and should be completed by the 30th June. In all cases the time specified must clearly be adequate to allow the accused to undertake and complete the works required. If a reasonable time, in the ordinary sense of reasonableness, is not allowed for the completion of the compliance works then it is likely that the notice would be declared invalid.[69]

---

69. *Dundalk Town Council v Lawlor* [2005] 2 ILRM 106.

**[5.71]** O'Neill J's decision in this case also required the local authority to carefully and with precision and detail, set out the works that were required to be carried out to arrive at a situation where the development was put back to such condition that it was no longer 'unauthorised development'. Mr Lawlor was entitled to receive direction from Dundalk Town Council which he could fully understand, as to the work which he had to do in order to rectify the situation he had created by carrying out unauthorised development. Examples of things which might have been specified, in order to achieve compliance in that case, might be as follows:

1. To replace all top soil removed from the site in such volume and quantity as to ensure that the site is restored to the same level as it was prior to the carrying out of unauthorised development.

2. After replacing the top soil to re-seed the ground with grass.

3. To remove from the site permanently all items of debris which might have been on the site prior to the unauthorised work being carrying out. However, it might be argued that the removal of debris which was on site before the unauthorised development was carried out would go further than the statute intended. PDA 2000, s 154(5)(b) requires the restoration of the lands to its condition prior to the commencement of development which might, somewhat illogically, imply that the debris should be returned.

## Service of an enforcement notice

**[5.72]** PDA 2000[70] deals with the methods of service of notices at s 250.[71] Any notice or copy of an order must be served in one of the following ways:

(a) Where it is addressed to him or her by name, by delivering it to him or her;

(b) By leaving it at the address at which he or she ordinarily resides or, in a case in which an address for service has been furnished, at that address;

(c) By sending it by post in a prepaid registered letter addressed to him or her at the address at which he or she ordinarily resides or, in a case in which an address for service has been furnished, at that address;

(d) Where the address at which he or she ordinarily resides cannot be ascertained by reasonable enquiry and the notice or copy is so required or authorised to be given or served in respect of any land or premises, by delivering it to some person over the age of 16 years resident or employed on the land or premises or by affixing it in a conspicuous place on or near the land or premises;

(e) In addition to the methods of service provided in paragraphs (a), (b), (c) and (d), by delivering it (in the case of an enforcement notice) to some person over the age of 16 years who is employed, or otherwise engaged, in

---

70. Read PDA 2000, s 250 for a complete understanding of the requirements in relation to service of notices. What appears above is contained in PDA 2000, s 250(1) which effectively restates LG(PD)A 1963, s 7.

71. See *Dublin Corporation v McGrath* [1978] ILRM 208.

connection with the carrying out of the development to which the notice relates, or by affixing it in a conspicuous place on the land or premises concerned.

PDA 2000, s 250(2) allows notice or copy order or any order or regulation to be served on or given to the owner or occupier of the land or premises to be addressed to the 'the owner' or 'the occupier' as the case may require without naming him or her in circumstances where the names cannot be ascertained by reasonable enquiry.

For the avoidance of doubt PDA 2000, s 250(9) provides that 'notice' in this section includes a warning letter.

*The effect of non-compliance with an enforcement notice*

[5.73] PDA 2000, s 154(6) and (7) provide that if a notice is not complied with within the time specified in the notice or such extended time not being more than six months, the planning authority may enter upon the land and carry out the works itself with the costs of such works recoverable as a simple contract debt from the persons served with the notice. The planning authority may also secure the costs recoverable by:

(i) Charging the land under the Registration of Title Act 1964, or

(ii) Where the person on whom the enforcement notice was served is the owner of the land, an instrument vesting the ownership of the land in the authority subject to a right of redemption by the owner within five years.[72]

PDA 2000, s 154(8) provides that any person served with an enforcement notice who fails to comply with the requirements of the notice (other than a notice which has either been withdrawn or which has ceased to have affect) within the time specified in the notice or within such extended time as may be allowed, not exceeding six months, shall be guilty of an offence. PDA 2000, s 154(9) provides that any person who knowingly assists or permits the failure by another to comply with an enforcement notice shall be guilty of an offence. PDA 2000, s 154(10) provides that particulars of any enforcement notice shall be entered in the planning authority's planning register.

*Withdrawal of an enforcement notice*

[5.74] PDA 2000, s 154(11) provides that a planning authority may, for stated reasons, by notice in writing, withdraw an enforcement notice by serving a notice of withdrawal on the appropriate persons and where an enforcement notice is withdrawn or where the planning authority is satisfied that the enforcement notice has been complied with, the fact that the enforcement notice was withdrawn and the reasons for its withdrawal or the fact that it was complied with shall be recorded in the planning register.

*Enforcement notice no longer effective after 10 years*

[5.75] PDA 2000, s 154(12) is an important provision which states that an enforcement notice shall no longer be effective 10 years from the date of service of the enforcement

---

72. PDA 2000, s 154(7)(b).

notice in accordance with the provisions of PDA 2000, s 154(1). If the notice is served under PDA 2000, s 154(3)(b), the 10 years runs from the date of service of that notice under that subsection. PDA 2000, s 154(3)(b) provides that if, subsequent to the service of the enforcement notice, the planning authority becomes aware that any other person may be carrying out development or is an owner or occupier of the land or may be affected by the notice, the notice may be served on that person in the period specified for compliance with the notice which period shall be extended as necessary to a maximum of six months, and the other person or persons on whom the notice had previously been served shall be informed in writing. In summary, PDA 2000, s 154(12) provides that an enforcement notice withers 10 years from the date of service of the notice under sub-s (1) or, if a notice is served under sub-s (3)(b), 10 years from the date of service of the notice under that subsection.

[5.76] PDA 2000, s 154(13) provides that the validity of an enforcement notice cannot be questioned by reason only that the person or other persons, not being the person served with the enforcement notice, was not notified of the service of the enforcement notice. Prior to the introduction of this subsection it was always possible to have a notice set aside or to evade conviction where it could be shown to the satisfaction of the court that notice had not been served on every owner or occupier.

[5.77] PDA 2000, s 154(14) provides that a s 50 report of a local authority shall contain details of the number of enforcement notices issued under this section, warning notices issued under s 153, prosecutions brought under s 157 and injunctions sought under s 160 by the authority.[73]

## *Issue of enforcement notice in cases of emergency*

[5.78] The procedures for issuing an enforcement notice in normal circumstances when a complaint is made to the planning authority about unauthorised development are outlined above. Reference is also made to urgent cases under PDA 2000, s 155. The normal procedure for service of an enforcement notice is detailed and elaborate because the aspiration of the policy-makers is to ensure that if a problem exists, it can be dealt with at an early stage so that the complainant is kept fully aware of all decisions being made. In certain circumstances the planning authority may become aware of a serious problem that necessitates urgent action. PDA 2000, s 155 permits a planning authority to issue an enforcement notice immediately without sending a warning letter if it is of the opinion that due to the nature of the unauthorised development and to any other material considerations, it is necessary to take urgent action with regard to unauthorised development. PDA 2000, s 155 allows a planning authority to serve an enforcement notice where there is an urgency and in doing so the planning authority will not have to complete the procedures set out in ss 152 and 153 dealing with the issue of warning letters and inviting submissions from the person served. As already seen, the Act provides that failure to issue a warning letter will not prejudice the issue of an

---

73. See Local Government Act 1991, s 50.

enforcement notice.[74] Clearly, if a planning authority wishes to avail of the benefit of s 155 it will have to demonstrate that it expressly considered that urgent action was required. The term 'urgent action' is not defined, but, if the planning authority has any doubt as to the acceptability of their contention that urgent action was required, the authority need only refrain from serving the enforcement notice under the terms of s 155 and may issue it, in any case, without service of a warning letter in accordance with the provisions of s 153(5).

## Penalties for offences

[5.79] PDA 2000, s 156 provides the penalties for offences under the Act and these offences are listed in s 156(1) by reference to particular sections in the Act, namely as follows:

- s 58(4) – causing damage to a protected structure;
- s 63 – failing to comply with a notice for works on the structure;
- s 135(7)[75] – giving false evidence, obstructing, etc, an oral hearing before the board;
- s 151 – carrying out unauthorised development;
- s 154(8) – failing to comply with an enforcement notice;
- s 154(9) – knowingly assisting in the breach of an enforcement notice;
- s 205 – breaching a tree protection order;
- s 230(3) – organising an event other than in accordance with the licence;
- s 239 – failure to comply with a notice requiring compliance with the rules regarding funfairs;
- s 247[76] – seeking a favour or benefit in connection with a pre planning consultation.

A person found guilty shall be liable:

On conviction on indictment to a fine that shall not exceed €12,697,381[77] or to imprisonment for a term not exceeding two years or to both.

On summary conviction to a fine not exceeding €5,000[78] or to imprisonment for a term not exceeding six months or to both.

---

74. PDA 2000, s 153(5).
75. As inserted by PD(SI)A 2006, s 31.
76. See LGA 2001 s 247.
77. See Council Regulation (EC) 974/98.
78. PD(A)A 2010, s 46(a) to (e).

**[5.80]** PDA 2000, s 156(2) provides that a further offence is committed on every day on which the contravention continues and a person guilty of continuing offences shall be liable as follows for each such offence (meaning each day the offence continues):

(a) On conviction on indictment to a fine not exceeding €12,697[79] *per* day as the offence continues or to imprisonment not exceeding two years or to both provided that the term of years for the imprisonment shall not exceed two years or to both irrespective of the length of the continuing offence.

(b) On summary conviction to a fine not exceeding €1,500[80] for each day on which the offence continues or to a term of imprisonment not exceeding six months or to both provided that the total term shall not exceed six months.

**[5.81]** A minimum fine is created by PDA 2000, s 156(3) involving the construction of an unauthorised structure. The minimum fine payable on conviction on indictment is either the cost of the construction of the structure or €12,697, whichever is the less;[81] on summary conviction the estimated cost of construction of the structure or €5,000, whichever is the less[82] except where the person convicted can show to the court's satisfaction that he or she does not have the necessary financial means to pay the minimum fine.

**[5.82]** PDA 2000, s 156(4) provides for a fine not exceeding €5,000 or, at the discretion of the court, imprisonment for a term not exceeding six months or both[83] in respect of any person found guilty of an offence under this Act other than an offence referred to in s 156(1) or (2).

**[5.83]** PDA 2000, s 156(5) creates a further offence on every day which the contravention continues after conviction for offences concerning failure to comply with the notice requiring removal or alteration of a structure which fine shall not exceed €1,500.[84]

**[5.84]** PDA 2000, s 156(6) provides that in prosecuting an offence of carrying out unauthorised development and in prosecuting an offence of failing to carry out the requirements of an enforcement notice it is not necessary for the prosecution to show, and it will be assumed until the contrary is shown by the defendant, that the subject matter of the prosecution was development and not exempted development.

**[5.85]** PDA 2000, s 156(7) provides that where an enforcement notice has been served it shall be a defence to a prosecution against a person who has carried out or is carrying out unauthorised development or against a person who refuses to comply with the

---

79. See LGA 2001, s 247.
80. PD(A)A 2010, s 46(a) to (e).
81. See Council Regulation No 974/98/EC.
82. See Council Regulation No 974/98/EC.
83. See Council Regulation No 974/98/EC.
84. See Council Regulation No 974/98/EC.

directions in an enforcement notice if the defendant proves that he or she took all reasonable steps to secure compliance with the enforcement notice.

**[5.86]** PDA 2000, s 156(8) provides that if a person is convicted for failing to carry out directions in an enforcement notice under PDA 2000, s 154 the court may, in addition to imposing penalties specified in s 154(1) and (2), as the case may be, order the person convicted to take all or any of the steps specified in the enforcement order within such period as the court considers appropriate.[85]

**[5.87]** PDA 2000, s 156(9)[86] provides that where a person is convicted on indictment of an offence concerning an oral hearing the court may order that the convicted person or other body who consented to or connived at the offence to pay the board or persons who appeared at the hearing an amount equal to additional costs incurred as a result of the offence. For this subsection to apply the court must be satisfied that the offence delayed the conduct of the oral hearing.

## Other provisions relating to enforcement

**[5.88]** PDA 2000, s 157(4)(a) provides that no warning letter or enforcement notice shall issue and that no proceedings for an offence under this Part shall commence:

(i) In respect of a development where no permission has been granted after seven years from the date of the commencement of the development.

(ii) In respect of a development for which permission has been granted under Pt III, after seven years beginning on the expiration, as respects the permission authorising the development, of the appropriate period within the meaning of s 40 or, as the case may be, of the period as extended under s 42.

**[5.89]** Most importantly a new clause has been added to PDA 2000, s 157 as inserted by PD(A)A 2010, s 47(a) being s 157(4)(aa) which reads as follows:

(aa) Where the development was carried out not more than seven years prior to the date on which this section comes into operation, and notwithstanding paragraph (a), a warning letter or enforcement notice may issue, or proceedings may be commenced, at anytime in respect of the following development:

(i) Operation of a quarry;

(ii) Extraction of peat.

**[5.90]** PDA 2000, s 157(4)(b) reads:

(b) Notwithstanding paragraph (a) a warning letter or enforcement notice may issue, proceedings may be commenced at anytime in respect of any condition or concerning the use of land to which the permission is subject.[87]

---

85. PDA 2000, s 156(8) as substituted by PD(A)A 2010, s 46(f).
86. This subsection has been inserted by PD(SI)A 2006, s 31.
87. As amended by PD(A)A 2010, s 47(b).

Where the offence concerns a condition in a planning permission which relates to the use of land (for example, to be used as a seafront café for a two year period only pending a comprehensive re-development of the area), that condition can be enforced at any time after the expiration of the two-year period, where the use continues.

[5.91] PDA 2000, s 157(4)(c) provides that it will be presumed that proceedings were commenced within the appropriate period unless the contrary is proved.

[5.92] PDA 2000, s 157(5) provides that all other offences under PDA 2000 shall not be initiated later than seven years from the date in which the offence concerned was alleged to have been committed.

[5.93] PDA 2000, s 158 provides for the prosecution of directors or other officers of corporate bodies where a corporate body nominally commits the offence.

[5.94] PDA 2000, s 159 provides that where a court imposes a fine or affirms a fine or varies a fine imposed by another court the payment for the amount of the fine is made to the planning authority. The planning authority can enforce payment of the fine due to it on foot of the decree or order in the same manner in which it would enforce a decree or order made in civil proceedings.

[5.95] PDA 2000, s 160 (as amended) deals with the planning injunction and this is comprehensively dealt with in **Part II** of this chapter.

[5.96] PDA 2000, s 161 deals with the costs of prosecutions and applications for injunctions and provides that the court shall, unless it is satisfied that there are special and substantial reasons not to do so, order a person convicted of an offence under the Act to pay the costs of the planning authority in investigating the offence. In the case of a planning injunction, the costs will be payable to either the planning authority or to a person who made the application.

[5.97] PDA 2000, s 162 provides that the burden of proof concerning the existence of a relevant planning permission rests on the person charged with the offence. The shifting of the burden of proof in this instance is perhaps unfortunate. The onus of proof should, as in normal criminal cases, rest with the prosecution to prove the non-existence of a relevant planning permission. The section also provides that it is not a defence to a prosecution to show that retention permission has been applied for or granted since the enforcement proceedings began and furthermore no enforcement action may be stayed or withdrawn because retention permission has been applied for and granted. The section intends that the persons will still have to apply for permission but that their application will not act to prevent enforcement being taken against them for an offence which they have already committed.[88]

[5.98] PDA 2000, s 163 provides that planning permission shall not be required for development carried out pursuant to the requirements of an enforcement notice served under PDA 2000, s 154. Nor will permission be required in respect of development

---

88. See LGA 2001, s 247.

carried out pursuant to an order of the court in a planning injunction case under PDA 2000, s 160 (disregarding development for which there is in fact permission under Pt III).

## Challenging enforcement notices

**[5.99]** Specifically, the legislation does not offer any right of appeal in respect of the service of an enforcement notice. A reference under s 5 is a possibility[89] but the outcome of a s 5 reference results in the making of a declaration which does not in any sense seek to set aside an enforcement notice or to stay enforcement proceedings. The only effective remedy in enforcement notice matters is judicial review. In *O'Connor v Kerry County Council*,[90] an applicant issued *certiorari* proceedings where enforcement proceedings had been taken and the grounds for the enforcement proceedings were contested by the plaintiff on the basis that the development carried out was in fact exempt development. In that case, the court exercised discretion and refused *certiorari* pointing out that the proper procedure for the determination of that issue was by way of reference to An Bord Pleanála under s 5.

**[5.100]** Clearly, to proceed with judicial review where an enforcement notice has been served, it is the decision to serve the enforcement notice which must be challenged on the basis that the reasons for issuing the enforcement notice are somehow incorrect. For example, the enforcement notice may be taken outside the seven-year period, the development may be 'exempt development', or perhaps the enforcement proceedings may be disproportionate in relation to some trivial or minor breach. If an applicant for judicial review is successful in highlighting some defect in the enforcement notice, the court may set aside the enforcement notice on the grounds that it has been issued *ultra vires* the planning authority's powers.

**[5.101]** Simons[91] suggests that the enforcement procedures may not be compliant with the European Convention on Human Rights and that it may offend the provisions of the Irish Constitution.

**[5.102]** In relation to the European Convention on Human Rights Act 2003, Simons writes:

> There must be a very real doubt as to whether the enforcement notice procedure is compliant with the European Convention on Human Rights. The effect of the service of an enforcement notice is to authorise a planning authority – following the expiration of a specified period – to enter onto land and to take such steps as are specified in the notice. This may involve the demolition of structures and the restoration of land. Thus, a planning authority is afforded draconian powers, without there being any necessity for court approval. It is only if the planning authority wishes to pursue criminal prosecution for failure to comply with the

---

89. PDA 2000, s 5.
90. *Dundalk Town Council v Lawlor* [1988] ILRM 660.
91. Simons, *Planning and Development Law* (2nd edn, Thomson Roundhall, 2007). at paras 7.80–7.83 and 7.91, pp 299–302

notice that it is necessary to bring the matter before the court: the power to enter onto land and carry out works is self executing.[92]

Simons goes on to point out that the absence of any right of appeal would appear to breach art 6(1). Also, since the planning authority is author of the development plan and, at the same time, makes the decision to serve enforcement notices which involve a 'determination' of the affected landowner's rights, the requirements of independence and impartiality required by art 6(1) are not met.[93]

**[5.103]** In addition to the offences created in PDA 2000, Pt VIII there are other specific offences in PDA 2000, namely as follows:

(a) failure to comply with a notice from the planning authority requiring that a structure should be demolished, removed, altered or replaced or a use should be discontinued which allows the planning authority to serve notice on the owner or occupier of the structure or land concerned and on any persons who, in the opinion of the planning authority, will be affected by the notice;[94]

(b) owners or occupiers of protected structures or proposed protected structures have a duty to protect those structures from endangerment and if a planning authority concludes that the owner or occupier is in breach of that duty a notice may be served;[95]

(c) any person who causes damage to a protected structure or proposed protected structure without lawful authority shall be guilty of an offence;[96]

(d) failure to comply with a notice requiring works to be carried out in order to prevent a protected structure from becoming or continuing to be in danger will enable a planning authority to serve notice;[97]

(e) failure to obtain a licence for the holding of an 'event' (as defined in PDA 2000, s 229)[98] is an offence;

(f) failure to comply with a notice issued pursuant to s 239(8)(a) calling for the immediate cessation of any activity or preparations being made in relation to a funfair or the cessation of the use of any fairground equipment without a valid certificate of safety or the removal of any fairground equipment, temporary buildings or structures, plant, machinery or other equipment which the authority believes is intended to be used in relation to funfair and/or calling for

---

92. Simons, *Planning and Development Law* (2nd edn, Thomson Roundhall, 2007) at para 7.80, p 299.
93. See particularly paras 7.81–7.83 of Simons, *Planning and Development Law* (2nd edn, Thomson Round Hall, 2007) at pp 299 and 300.
94. PDA 2000, s 46(1).
95. PDA 2000, s 58(1) and (2).
96. PDA 2000, s 58(4).
97. PDA 2000, s 59(1) and PDA 2000, s 63. Section 63 creates an offence for failing to comply with a notice under s 59(1).
98. PDA 2000, s 230(3).

the restoration of the land to its prior condition within a specified time is an offence;[99]

(g) an organiser of a funfair or owner of fairground equipment who makes available for use any funfair equipment by members of the public without a valid safety certificate shall be guilty of an offence;[100]

(h) damage or obstruction of a public right of way or the hindrance or interference with the exercise of a public right of way is an offence;[101]

(i) PDA 2000, s 247 deals with consultations in relation to proposed developments with members of the planning authority staff and any member or official who seeks any favour, benefit or payment direct or indirect in connection with any such consultation or any advice given under a section shall be guilty of an offence;[102]

(j) PDA 2000, s 252 provides a power for authorised persons to enter onto land for the purpose of carrying out surveys, making inspections, plans, taking photographs, making excavations, etc. If such authorised persons are obstructed in the lawful exercise of the powers conferred upon them to enter the land the person obstructing the authorised person shall be guilty of an offence.[103]

See **Appendix** for Enforcement Complaint Form.

## PART II: THE PLANNING INJUNCTIONS

### Enforcement by injunction in relation to unauthorised development

**[5.104]** PDA 2000, s 160(1) reads:

Where an unauthorised development has been, is being or is likely to be carried out or continued, the High Court or the Circuit Court may, on the application of a planning authority or any other person, whether or not the person has an interest in the land, by order require any person to do or not to do, or to cease to do, as the case may be, anything that the Court considers necessary and specifies in order to ensure, as appropriate, the following:

(a) that the unauthorised development is not carried out or continued;

(b) in so far as is practicable that any land is restored to its condition prior to the commencement of any unauthorised development;

(c) that any development is carried out in conformity with the permission pertaining to that development or any condition to which the permission is subject.

---

99. PDA 2000, s 239(8)(c).
100. PDA 2000, s 239(4)(b).
101. PDA 2000, s 208(2)(b).
102. PDA 2000, s 247(6).
103. PDA 2000, s 252(9).

PDA 2000, s 160 provides the statutory grounds which permit an application to be made either to the High Court or to the Circuit Court for a planning injunction in respect of unauthorised development which 'has been, is being or is likely to be carried out or continued'. The court has considerable discretion in drafting the orders which it can make under s 160 and the use of the words 'anything that the court considers necessary' enhances that discretion.

Section 160 of PDA 2000 has reversed the decision in *Mahon v Irish Rugby Football Union*,[104] and an injunction may now be obtained in respect of unauthorised development which has not yet occurred but, 'which it is likely to be carried out or continued'.[105] *Quia timet* or anticipatory relief is now available but it will only be granted where there is a proven and substantial risk and a real likelihood that the development will be unauthorised.

**[5.105]** In *Birmingham v Birr Urban District Council*,[106] the applicant claimed that the respondent's proposal to carry out a development of a halting site was a material contravention of the local authority's development plan and, as such, it was *ultra vires*. The respondent argued that an injunction prohibiting the works would cause financial hardship to the council and to its contractor. Notwithstanding the council's submission, the court granted the *quia timet* relief sought on the basis that the applicant had established a fair question to be tried and the balance of convenience favoured the granting of an injunction. In *Westport UDC v Golden*,[107] the respondent changed the use of part of his building from a sit-in restaurant with waiter service and some take-away facilities, to a Supermac fast food outlet. The applicant objected to the change in use anticipating that it would have undesirable consequences in terms of additional noise, traffic and litter in the area. The court granted the *quia timet* injunctive relief sought by the applicant.

**[5.106]** PDA 2000, s 160(1) provides for the possibility of making an application either to the High Court or the Circuit Court. To proceed within the jurisdiction of the High Court the rateable valuation of the land[108] must be in excess of IR£200 (€253.95). The Circuit Court is the appropriate venue for cases where the rateable valuation of the land is less than IR£200 (€253.95).

**[5.107]** It is proposed that the provision of the Civil Liability and Courts Act 2004, s 53(2) which sets the rateable valuation at €253.95 in distinguishing whether the

---

104. *Mahon v Irish Rugby Football Union* [1997] ILRM SC 446; see judgment of Denham J.
105. In *Mahon v Butler* [1997] 3 IR 369, the applicants wished to prevent a proposed concert at Lansdowne Road. At that time the Local Government (Planning and Development) Act 1976, s 27 (as amended) only referred to development which 'has been carried out or is being carried out'. However, Costello P decided that the court is empowered, unless expressly prohibited from doing so, to exercise its equitable jurisdiction to prohibit the anticipated commission of wrongful acts.
106. *Birmingham v Birr Urban District Council* [1998] IEHC 190.
107. *Westport UDC v Golden* [2002] 1 ILRM 439 HC, Morris P.
108. Note that PDA 2000, s 2 defines land 'as including any structure and any land covered with water (whether in land or coastal)'.

application is made to the High Court or to the Circuit Court should be replaced by a 'market value' figure. The figure proposed to replace the rateable valuation figure of €253.95, is €3,000,000. As at the date of going to press, s 53 of the Civil Liability and Courts Act 2004 has not yet been commenced although it is perfectly obvious that a market value threshold is much more relevant today than a rateable valuation threshold in circumstances where all dwelling houses are exempt from rates and the valuations have not been revised in the case of established housing stock or struck in the case of new houses, for very many years. Also, agricultural land is rates exempt. In spite of the obvious improvement which the market value threshold would have over the old rateable valuation threshold, the government has not troubled to commence s 53.[109]

**[5.108]** The jurisdiction of the Circuit Court is without prejudice to the jurisdiction of the High Court. This means that an applicant may, even though the rateable valuation is less than €253.95, proceed in the High Court but if he does so he may be at risk in relation to costs.

**[5.109]** PDA 2000, s 160(2) provides that in making an order under s 160(1) the court may specify that certain types of work must be carried out including the restoration, restructuring, removal, demolition or alteration of a structure or other feature. The wording of s 160(2) provides that 'the court may order the carrying out of any works' which phrase also makes it quite clear that the court has full power to make mandatory orders.

## Discretion of the court

**[5.110]** An application for an injunction under PDA 2000, s 160 may be made by the planning authority, or by any person whether or not that person has an interest in the land. There is no *locus standi* requirement. The entitlement to make the application for an injunction is afforded in the widest possible sense to members of the public to ensure the prevention of any breach of the planning laws. The role which the members of the public are entitled to play in a s 160 application is often referred to as 'the watch-dog role'. The 'watch-dog' role implies that a private citizen is not applying to the court in order to enforce a private right. The role of the 'watch-dog' is directed towards enforcing laws relating to public interest, in seeking compliance with the planning code. In spite of the 'citizen's watch-dog role' it remains the case that the court retains a wide discretion as to whether or not to grant the injunction sought and this wide discretion

---

109. The Department of Environment, Heritage and Local Government has produced an unofficial consolidation of the Planning and Development Acts 2000–2006; the publication is extremely useful and it does contain a disclaimer to the effect that while every effort has been made to ensure the accuracy of the contents, no responsibility is accepted for any errors or omissions. They request that any errors or omissions are notified to planning@environ.ie. The author made such a notification in relation to PDA 2000, s 60(5)(b), (c), (d), and (e) which, as published, refers to the market valuation of €3,000,000 being the amendment provided by the Civil Liability and Courts Act 2004, s 53(2)(a) and (b). It is a point that should be checked because it must be a certainty that the s 53 amendment will be commenced shortly. Undoubtedly the market value is a much safer measure than the rateable valuation threshold.

permits the court to restrain the antics of vexatious litigants. The weight which the court will attach to any particular factor will vary with the circumstances of each individual case. The court is engaged in a balancing process where it will attempt to balance the rights and interests of each of the three parties to the planning process, namely the developer, the planning authority and the public.

[5.111] Under the provisions of s 27 of the Local Government (Planning and Development Act) 1976 the courts enjoyed a very wide discretion in the matter of planning injunctions and they continue to do so in dealing with the planning injunction under PDA 2000, s 160.

[5.112] The court's wide discretion to grant or to withhold an order in s 160 cases was highlighted in *Avenue Properties Limited v Farrell Homes Limited*,[110] where Barrington J made the point that it was essential that the court should enjoy a wide discretion as to whether it should or should not grant a s 160 injunction (or s 27 as it was then) because of the absence of any restrictions on *locus standi* granted to members of the public.

[5.113] In *Stafford and Bates v Roadstone Limited*, Barrington J had this to say:

> In the normal case a Court of Equity, in deciding whether or not to issue an injunction, would be primarily concerned with the position as between the parties to the litigation. But it appears to me that if a private citizen comes forward under s 27 as a watch-dog of the public that the Court in exercising its discretion is entitled to look not only at the convenience of the parties but at the convenience of the public. Again, it appears to me that the Oireachtas could hardly have intended that the High Court would be obliged on the application of a private citizen with no interest in the lands automatically to close down, eg an important factory because of some technical breach of the planning law irrespective of the convenience to the workers and to the public generally.[111]

In that case, although Barrington J held that the quarrying operations of the respondents were unauthorised, that fact did not require the court to issue a prohibiting injunction. Similarly, in *White v McInerney Construction Limited*[112] Blaney J in the Supreme Court highlighted the extent of the discretion which the court has either to grant or to refuse to grant an injunction and that in exercising its discretion the court should be influenced in some measure by the same factors which would influence a Court of Equity in deciding to grant or refuse to grant an injunction. In that case, a planning permission contained a condition requiring the applicant's neighbour, McInerney Construction Limited, to agree screening details in writing with the planning authority prior to the commencement of the development. McInerney sought permission to develop 56 houses and Mr White, in the first instance, obtained an order prohibiting McInerney from interfering with or moving existing screening between the two properties. Mr White then sought to restrain McInerney from carrying out any further development on the site. McInerney undertook not to remove any screening pending the hearing of the action and, based on that

---

110. *Avenue Properties Limited v Farrell Homes Limited* [1982] ILRM 21, Barrington J.
111. *Stafford v Roadstone Ltd* [1980] ILRM 1, Barrington J.
112. *White v McInerney Construction Limited* [1995] ILRM 374, Blaney J.

undertaking, the court refused to restrain McInerney from continuing with the development of the site. Blaney J had this to say:

> The Court has a very wide discretion under section 27. It is admirably expressed by Barrington J in his Judgment in *Avenue Properties Limited v Farrell Homes Limited* at page 26. Counsel for the appellant contended that the Court was bound to exercise its discretion in a particular way, namely, in order to ensure compliance with the Planning Acts and accordingly an injunction ought to have been granted stopping the development until all conditions which were to be performed before development commenced had been complied with. Counsel did not, however, refer the Court to any authority which supported this restriction on the exercise of the Court's discretion and I am satisfied that it would be wholly inconsistent with the wider discretion given to the Court under s 27.[113]

Blaney J refused an injunction in spite of the fact that the development was not being carried out strictly in accordance with the planning permission granted.

[5.114] In *Dublin City Council v Liffey Beat Limited*,[114] the planning authority inserted a condition in a grant of permission to permit use of premises for public entertainment with restrictions against use as a nightclub. Quirke J observed that the condition had been poorly drafted and that a meaningful interpretation of it proved to be very difficult. When the premises were found by the planning authority, being used as a nightclub, the planning authority sought an injunction against such use. In refusing to grant an injunction, Quirke J held that it was not the function of the court to intervene in the planning process by attempting to interpret what is the meaning of any particular condition contained in a grant of permission. Furthermore, the learned judge held that the planning authority has an obligation to draft its conditions in such a way that they are reasonably comprehensible to interested persons. The planning authority has a duty to provide clarification of conditions where clarification is sought. Quirke J refused the applicant's request for an injunction against the use of the respondent's premises as a nightclub because the planning authority had refused to provide evidence by way of clarification as to what was intended by this poorly drafted condition.

[5.115] It is possible to identify a number of factors which would influence the exercise of the court's discretion, and the following is a guideline to the balancing process which the court will engage in to ensure that the rights and interests of the parties are properly recognised.

*Technical or trivial breach*

[5.116] A court may be willing to exercise its discretion not to grant an order where the breach of the planning code complained of is merely technical or trivial or otherwise insignificant in planning terms. In *Leech v Reilly*,[115] Mr Reilly built a workshop without obtaining planning permission. The applicant applied for an injunction and at the

---

113. *White v McInerney Construction Limited* [1995] ILRM 374, Blaney J.
114. *Dublin City Council v Liffey Beat Limited* [2005] IR 478, Quirke J.
115. *Leech v Reilly* [1983] IEHC 65, O'Hanlon J.

hearing of the interlocutory application Mr Reilly undertook not to carry out any further development. Mr Reilly then applied for retention and retention permission was granted by An Bord Pleanála. The Board's decision required modification to the building and Mr Reilly proceeded to comply with the terms of the permission granted. A further injunction was applied for and while the court accepted that the works carried out by Mr Reilly were in breach of the court order, nevertheless those works represented a *bona fide* attempt to eliminate possible nuisances and to comply with the conditions laid down by An Bord Pleanála. As such those works were upheld.

**[5.117]** In *Marry v Connaughton*,[116] the case was made by the applicant that a permission did not authorise the development as the plans submitted did not precisely correspond with the actual location of the houses. The claim was dismissed on the basis that the dwellings were in substantial compliance with those shown on the plans and any deviation was *de minimus*.

**[5.118]** In *O'Connell v Dungarvan Energy*,[117] the court upheld its discretion to grant injunctive relief but stated that it was not necessary to grant relief where a variation of the planning permission was not a material variation. The circumstances in that case were that a steel structure was replaced by a building of similar but stronger structure. The court held that the variation was a permissible variation of the planning permission because it was of a trivial nature and because the planning authority had consented to it. It was also noted that the variation would have no impact on residents and that in any case the variation was required to comply with the condition inserted in an integrated pollution control (IPC) licence.

**[5.119]** In *Cork County Council v Cliftonhall Limited*,[118] a developer had constructed a residential development in conformity with the plans and particulars submitted with the planning application. Finnegan J did not grant relief to Cork County Council in respect of matters which he considered to be trivial and immaterial including, for example, an increased ridge height of 0.5m on one of the blocks.

**[5.120]** In *Mountbrook Homes Limited v Oldcourt Developments Limited*,[119] the grant of permission contained 'prior to commencement' conditions. Peart J held that where the failure to comply with planning conditions is trivial in nature and does not in any way prejudice the applicant, no obligation was placed on the court to punish the respondent by way of an order under s 160 for delay in complying with the precondition. In this case, the respondent had failed to submit revised drawings prior to the commencement of the development but the respondent, albeit belatedly, had, in fact, effectively complied with the precondition. The application for an injunction was refused and no order as to costs was made. Peart J, in exercising his discretion in this case, agreed that 'the exercise of discretion must be informed by the individual circumstances of each case coming before the Court'.

---

116. *Marry v Connaughton* [1984] IEHC 74, O'Hanlon J.
117. *O'Connell v Dungarvan Energy* (unreported, 27 February 2000) HC, Finnegan J.
118. *Cork County Council v Cliftonhall Limited* [2001] IEHC 85, Finnegan J.
119. *Mountbrook Homes Limited v Oldcourt Developments Limited* [2005] IEHC 171, Peart J.

## Hardship to the developer

**[5.121]** A court may refuse an order in circumstances where if the order were granted it would result in a gross or disproportionate hardship to the developer, as was the case in *Avenue Properties Limited v Farrell Homes Limited*,[120] where the applicant sought injunctive relief although he had not suffered any damage peculiar to himself. Farrell Homes was in the course of constructing an office block other than in accordance with the permission but the court refused to make an order against it as the applicant was not in any way affected by the deviations shown.

**[5.122]** However, such hardship will not be taken into account where the hardship is a direct result of the developer's deliberate disregard of the planning laws. In *Morris v Garvey*[121] the developer constructed a flat complex which was not in accordance with the permission granted. An order for the demolition of the flat complex was made against the developer because of his deliberate disregard for the planning laws. It was stated in that case that it would take 'exceptional circumstances' such as mistake, acquiescence over a long period, trivial infraction or gross and disproportionate hardship before a court would refrain from making an order.

**[5.123]** See also *Curley v Galway Corporation*.[122] Where Galway Corporation obtained a planning permission on appeal from An Bord Pleanála to operate a refuse dump in Co Galway, it was held to be guilty of a 'conscious and deliberate violation' of the terms of its planning permission in relation to the operation of the dump. The history of the dump was such that the matter was before the High Court on three separate occasions. In an earlier decision, Kelly J had this to say:

> ..., it is said to me that an order made today will give rise to very considerable difficulties for the corporation in complying with its statutory obligations under, for example, the waste management legislation. In my view the Corporation has nobody but itself to blame if such difficulties are created. I cannot conceive of a situation where the Court can, in order to enable Galway Corporation to comply with its statutory obligations under one piece of legislation, permit it to breach obligations imposed on it by another piece of legislation. In particular, the Court cannot permit the fulfilment of a statutory obligation, for example, under the Waste Management Act by the commission of criminal offences under the planning legislation.[123]

The corporation received a fine of IR£50,000 and an independent engineer was appointed to report on the steps to be taken by Galway Corporation to ensure that future operation of the dump was in compliance with the terms of the permission granted by its neighbouring planning authority, Galway County Council.

---

120. *Avenue Properties Limited v Farrell Homes Limited* [1982] ILRM 21, HC.
121. *Morris v Garvey* [1983] IR 319.
122. *Curley v Galway Corporation* [2001] IEHC 53, Kelly J.
123. *Curley v Galway Corporation* [1998] IEHC 231, Kelly J.

**[5.124]** In *Grimes v Punchestown Developments Company Limited*[124] the applicant sought but failed to obtain an injunction. The facts of the case related to an application to injunct the holding of a pop concert. The concert had been widely publicised for a long time but the applicant did not institute proceedings until very shortly before the concert was to take place. In the course of his judgment, Herbert J had this to say:

> I think I have to look at the evidence of the enormous financial outlay which the second named respondent, at least, has incurred in this case and has acted neither rashly nor imprudently.

In refusing to grant the injunction, the learned judge accepted that the gross and disproportionate hardship to the respondent may be a reason for refusing relief. Costs were awarded against the applicant and an appeal against the award of costs was grounded on the principle that members of the public had a 'watch dog' responsibility to uphold. The Supreme Court found that the High Court had exercised its discretion in determining the issue of costs in accordance with the law and, in effect, costs followed the event.[125]

**[5.125]** At the time that *Grimes v Punchestown Developments Company Limited*[126] was heard it was notorious for another reason. It was a primary finding in this case that transient concert events of this nature do not require planning permission. The matter is now specifically dealt with in PDA 2000, s 240 which does provide that the holding of an event shall not be construed as 'development' within the meaning of the Act[127] but a license is now required.

## Laches and acquiescence

**[5.126]** Under the doctrine of laches, an applicant's entitlement to relief may be lost where he delays unduly in seeking it. An applicant may also be disentitled to relief where he has acquiesced in the wrong complained of over a long period of time. In *Dublin Corporation v Mulligan*,[128] it was held that the fact that the limitation period had expired without enforcement action having been taken, does not have the effect of making the unauthorised development a lawful development. In *Dublin Corporation v Kevans*,[129] because the applicants did not pursue their enforcement action with any sense of urgency, the learned President placed a lengthy stay on the order made therein.

**[5.127]** Time limits for commencing applications for an injunction were first introduced in 1992. PDA 2000, s 160(6)(a)(i) provides a seven-year time limit which runs from the date of the commencement of the development in cases where no planning permission

---

124. *Grimes v Punchestown Developments Company Limited* [2002] 1IRLM 409.
125. *Grimes v Punchestown Developments Company Limited* (unreported, 20 December 2002) SC; see the judgment of Denham J.
126. *Grimes v Punchestown Developments Company Limited* [2002] 1IRLM 409.
127. See PDA 2000, ss 230–239 which set out certain regulations effecting both events and funfairs and require that events and funfairs must be licensed.
128. *Dublin Corporation v Mulligan* (unreported, 6 May 1980) HC, Finlay P.
129. *Dublin Corporation v Kevans* (unreported, 14 July 1980) HC, Finlay P.

exists. Where planning permission does exist PDA 2000, s 160(6)(a)(ii) provides a seven-year time limit which begins on the date of the expiration of the life of the planning permission granted for the development. The life of a planning permission is generally five years. The question as to whether or not delay can arise before the expiration of the respective statutory time limits was considered in *Dublin Corporation v Lowe*,[130] where Morris P held that notwithstanding the statutory outer time limit in which the application for an injunction must be made, unreasonable delay on the part of an applicant could amount to acquiescence, although it did not do so on the facts of that particular case.[131]

## Conduct of applicant

**[5.128]** A court may exercise its discretion not to grant an injunction where the applicant has not acted in a *bona fide* manner or where he has not come before the court with clean hands such as where he has withheld material facts from the court. In *Scarrif v Commissioners of Public Works*,[132] the applicant sought to have buildings removed which had been erected by the OPW and which the applicants alleged were obstructing an existing right of way. The court in coming to its decision applied the general test applicable to ordinary injunctions and asked whether a fair question had been raised by the applicant. The court also asked where the balance of convenience lay. On the facts it was held that the applicants had not raised a fair question as to the existence of the rights alleged and that, in consequence, they were not entitled to the relief sought.

**[5.129]** The applicant has a duty to place before the court all facts known to him which are relevant to the exercise of the court's discretion. In *Dublin Corporation v McGowan*,[133] the respondent purchased 134 Leinster Road in 1988 as a residence with seven residential units. Although the respondent caused a planning search to be made the results of that search failed to discover that a permission for a garden mews had been obtained in 1978 with a condition requiring that the premises at 134 Leinster Road be maintained as three residential units. The respondent sought an injunction under s 27 of LG(PD)A 1976 claiming unauthorised use and breach of a condition in an earlier planning permission. The mews house was built and the applicant made no complaint of that. In complete defiance of the planning permission the main house was converted from three units to seven units without permission but no evidence of that conversion was presented to the learned judge who could not therefore determine whether or not that conversion had taken place before or after 1 October 1964.[134] Keane J was satisfied

---

130. *Dublin Corporation v Lowe* (unreported, 4 February 2000) HC, Morris P, and [2004] 4 IR 259, SC.
131. Further information on time limits in this context is available at paras **[5.165] to [5.173]**.
132. *Scarrif v Commissioners of Public Works* (unreported, 15 March 1995) HC, Flood J.
133. *Dublin Corporation v McGowan* [1993] 1 IR 405, Keane J.
134. 1 October 1964 was the date on which the LG(P D)A 1963 became law and all developments which had been completed prior to that date do not require planning permission.

that the respondent had acted in good faith throughout and the learned judge had this to say:

> ... I will consider it unjust and inequitable that an order should be made in circumstances such as the present where, if anybody is to blame, it is the person whom has misled the planning authority at the stage of the application for planning permission or who thereafter simply converted the house into seven units in defiance of the planning permission. It is not necessary to express any view as to what happened in relation to that matter and I have no evidence in relation to it. In any event, the then owner of the premises and the applicant for planning permission is not a party to these proceedings. It would be manifestly unjust to have the draconian machinery of this section brought into force against a person who behaved in good faith throughout.
>
> In refusing the application, the Court is not conferring any benediction on the present use of the premises. The extent to which the use of the premises conforms with the planning law is a matter for the respondents to consider. I conclude on this application that the planning authority have not satisfied me that it is a case in which a Court should make the order sought under section 27(2) of the Act of 1976. On that basis alone I am refusing the present application.

**[5.130]** In *O'Connor v Frank Hetherington Limited*,[135] the relief sought was refused to the applicant because he had failed to disclose the fact that his proceedings were financed by a competitor of the respondent. The decision in *Cairnduff v O'Connell*[136] is a good indication that a self interest is not necessarily a bar to injunctive relief. In that case, the respondent converted a premises adjoining the plaintiff's premises from a premises with multiple bed sitting room lettings to a residence with two flats. The respondent did not apply for planning permission for that conversion but in carrying out the conversion he made some exterior alterations to the rear of the premises comprising a window in the side wall and the construction on the rear of the balcony was facilitated by taking out a window and replacing it with a door. The applicants sought injunctive relief claiming that the proximity of the balcony resulted in their rear garden patio and downstairs rooms being overlooked. It was the applicants' case that the alterations seriously interfered with the privacy of the patio and downstairs rooms. The Supreme Court held that the works were exempted development. Finlay CJ had this to say:

> Having regard to these conclusions, it is not necessary for the purpose of deciding this appeal to deal with the further submissions made on behalf of the Defendant that the Plaintiffs purpose of seeking to preserve their privacy of their premises disentited them to an injunction. I would, however, share with Barrington J the sympathy he expressed for the position of the Plaintiffs, the privacy of the patio and downstairs rooms has been, by reason of the carrying out of this work, seriously interfered with. Had the work, in my opinion of the interpretation of the Act, constituted an unauthorised development I would have no hesitation in granting the appropriate injunction.

---

135. *O'Connor v Frank Hetherington Limited* (unreported, 28 May 1987) HC, Barr J.
136. *Cairnduff v O'Connell* [1986] IR 73, SC

## Conduct of the developer

**[5.131]** If a developer is not acting in a *bona fide* manner on the basis of a genuine mistake, this may influence the court. In *Dublin Corporation v McGowan*,[137] the respondent made a planning search which incorrectly failed to disclose that a planning permission had been granted which affected the lands. The court upheld that the developer/respondent had acted in a *bona fide* manner and refused to make an order granting the injunction sought.

**[5.132]** In *Dublin County Council v Sellwood Quarries Limited*,[138] the respondent, in the *bona fide* belief that planning permission was not required, began blasting for rock extraction without any separate permission. Heretofore the quarry had been used for the extraction of sand and gravel only. Gannon J refused the applicant's request for injunctive relief to prevent the respondent from extracting by blasting on the site which had previously only been used for extracting sand and gravel. This was a case where the respondent developer had acted *bona fide* on the basis of a genuine mistake and it was in those circumstances that the learned judge refused the order. In making its decision the court had regard to the damaging consequences that such an order would have for the respondent, its employees and those to whom it was bound by contracts. The court also took into account the fact that the failure on the part of the respondent to apply for permission to blast rock was due to a *bona fide* belief that such permission was not required.

**[5.133]** Conversely, if a developer deliberately engages in unauthorised development or otherwise demonstrates bad faith, this will weigh heavily against him. In *Dublin Corporation v O'Dwyer Brothers (Mount St) Limited*,[139] the respondents changed the façade of the building and erected new signs. They also changed the use of the building from a restaurant to a nightclub (which was to be called 'Howl at the Moon'). The respondents argued that the signs simply replaced earlier signs but the court considered that the new signs materially affected the external appearance of the building such as to render it inconsistent with the adjoining buildings and as such it was not exempt. It was argued on behalf of O'Dwyer Brothers (Mount St) Limited that no change of use had occurred from the existing use as a bar/restaurant to a nightclub but the respondents did not specifically deny that the premises was used as a nightclub. While no specific evidence was given as to the use of the premises as a nightclub the court made an order to restrain the unauthorised use and further refused a stay which was applied for to enable the respondents to make an application by way of retention. The refusal to grant a stay to allow the respondents to apply for retention permission was subsequently upheld in the Supreme Court on appeal.

**[5.134]** The relevance of the conduct of a developer was recognised in the decision in *Curley v Galway Corporation*,[140] where an application was brought by the applicants

---

137. *Dublin Corporation v McGowan* [1993] 1 IR 405, Keane J.
138. *Dublin County Council v Sellwood Quarries Limited* [1981] ILRM 23, Gannon J.
139. *Dublin Corporation v O'Dwyer Brothers* (Mount St) Ltd [1997] IEHC 77, Kelly J.
140. *Curley v Galway Corporation* [2001] IEHC 53, Kelly J.

against the respondent because of its failure to comply with conditions imposed upon it on foot of a planning permission granted by An Bord Pleanála for a dump. Kelly J laid considerable emphasis on the flagrant breaches by the respondent of the permission granted to it and of the planning laws, which breaches were exacerbated by its status as a planning authority with responsibility for planning enforcement in its own functional area. In the course of his judgement Kelly J had this to say:

> The unauthorised developments at this premises have, I am satisfied, been carried out with a view to enhancing its commercial development and the profit which it makes for its owners. Notwithstanding these clear breaches of the Planning Acts I am nonetheless asked to permit the Respondent to continue to profit from its wrong doing by placing a stay upon my injunction so as to enable it to commence another procedure with a view to regularising its position. It has already in effect, obtained a stay on any action against it since December 1995. By carefully ignoring the correspondence from the applicant, by contesting these proceedings right up to the very last moment necessitating their adjournment from December 1996 until April 1997 and by avoiding filing its final Affidavits until the day upon which the Court had the matter listed for hearing, it has succeeded in delaying matters until now. At any time during that period it could have made the necessary applications for retention but it did not do so and, indeed, to date it has not done so. There is nothing in the attitude and behaviour of the Respondent in relation to this litigation which would permit of the Court's discretion being exercised in its favour. I am not prepared to assist the Respondent's continuation of these unauthorised developments any longer. If the Respondent is put to cost and expense, it has only itself to blame in this regard.

Although urged to do so, Kelly J refused to withhold an order because of the difficulties encountered by Galway Corporation in complying with the terms of the planning permission or the problems which would be created for the corporation and for the people of Galway. The learned judge was satisfied that the endeavours of the corporation to comply with the permission were both too little and too late and the hardship which would be caused to it was of little weight where it was brought about by the conscious behaviour of the respondent. Kelly J concluded:

> The Court has an obligation to ensure that the planning code is enforced and it must do so. The planning laws apply to everybody, including planning authorities where they act as the developer of land under the Planning Acts. In my view it would be entirely wrong for the Court to withhold an Order in this case, particularly when one considers that the Respondent, which is a Planning Authority itself, is in gross breach of its obligations.

There was a second case in *Curley v Galway Corporation*[141] which arose in contempt proceedings against Galway Corporation which had continued the waste disposal business at the same site in County Galway subsequent to Kelly J's order forbidding it. The corporation's case was that it was not dumping waste. The material which the corporation was disposing of at the dump was marl which is a soil consisting of clay mixed with calcium carbonate and often used as a fertiliser. It was the corporation's case

---

141. *Curley v Galway Corporation* [1998] IEHC 231, Kelly J.

that it was using the marl for the purpose of landscaping the dump. In the course of that hearing, Kelly J learned that the marl was being supplied free-of-charge by a company which had no use for it. In those circumstances, Kelly J held that the marl was waste and that the corporation was in breach of the previous order made by the learned judge.

**[5.135]** In *Cavan County Council v Eircell*,[142] Geoghegan J granted an interlocutory injunction and refused to adjourn an applicant's application for an injunction where the adjournment was opposed by the applicant planning authority and the learned judge was satisfied that the respondent had been aware that it was carrying out unauthorised development. The respondent in this case was a major commercial company in competition with another major commercial company in the telephone business. The respondent claimed that the erection of a telecommunications transmitter or relay mast was exempt development. Cavan County Council sought a restraining injunction when the work commenced on the mast. Geoghegan J refused an application for an adjournment and granted an interlocutory injunction on the grounds that it was inconceivable that a commercial company of the size of the respondent would not have taken legal advice. The company would have been fully advised as to the planning implications required for erecting a telecommunications transmitter mast. The learned judge was satisfied that Eircell was aware that it was carrying out an unauthorised development or that if it was not so aware it was behaving in a reckless manner.

*Public interest*

**[5.136]** The Courts will take the public interest into account in adjudicating on applications for planning injunctions. In *Leen v Aer Rianta*,[143] it was common case that the development of a passenger terminal facility at Shannon Airport was carried out without complying with a condition precedent which required resolution in relation to the treatment of effluent discharge. McKechnie J, in the course of his judgment, distinguished between the public interest and the commercial interest of the airport. The court had regard to the public interest only in ensuring that this international airport at Shannon was not closed down.

*Attitude of the planning authority*

**[5.137]** The attitude of the planning authority may also be a relevant consideration as seen in *Grimes v Punchestown Developments Company Limited and MCD Promotions Limited*.[144] In that case, an injunction was not granted to prevent the respondents from holding a concert at Punchestown Racecourse. In the High Court, Herbert J, in exercising his discretion to refuse an injunction, had regard to the fact that the planning authority as *'official watchdog'* was fully aware of what was happening but had not considered to take enforcement action. Herbert J's decision to refuse an injunction was

---

142. *Cavan County Council v Eircell* [1999] IEHC 125, Geoghegan J.
143. *Leen v Aer Rianta* [2003] 4 IR 394, McKechnie J.
144. *Grimes v Punchestown Developments Company Limited and MCD Promotions Limited* [2002] 1 ILRM 409, Herbert J.

appealed to the Supreme Court.[145] In the Supreme Court, Mr Grimes argued that significance should be placed on the public watchdog nature of s 27 (as it then was) which enabled a member of the public to take action. As that point had not been raised in the High Court the Supreme Court decided that if a matter had not been argued in the High Court it could not be canvassed in the Supreme Court. Costs had been awarded against Mr Grimes in the High Court and that matter was appealed also but the Supreme Court held that the normal rule that costs following an event applied in this case.

## Procedure for application for injunction under PDA 2000, s 160

[5.138] The procedure under PDA 2000, s 160 is summary procedure commenced by notice of motion grounded upon affidavit. The procedure involved in s 160 injunctions was described by Gannon J as 'a fire brigade section'. PDA 2000, s 160(3) provides:

(a) an application to the High Court or the Circuit Court for an order under this section shall be by motion and the Court when considering the matter may take such interim or interlocutory order (if any) as it considers appropriate;

(b) subject to s 161, the order by which an application under this section is determined may contain such terms and conditions (if any) as to the payment of costs as the Court considers appropriate.

[5.139] PDA 2000, s 160(4) provides:

(a) rules of the court may provide for an order under this section to be made against a person whose identity is unknown;

(b) any relevant rules of court made in respect of s 27 (inserted by s 19 of the Act of 1992) of the Act of 1976 shall apply to this section and shall be construed to that effect.

[5.140] In *Dublin County Council v Kirby*,[146] the pleadings, if they may be called such, consisted of the originating notice of motion. In a way the absence of any exchange of pleadings between the parties renders this summary procedure inappropriate to resolve complex issues of fact and of law.

Such issues are more appropriate for a full plenary hearing. When complex issues of law and/or of fact arise the court has, in any case, a complete discretion to make directions as to pleadings and to order any mode of trial as may be appropriate as indicated by the Supreme Court in *Mahon v Butler*.[147] In *Waterford County Council v John A Woods*,[148] Murphy J stated that the summary nature of the proceedings in s 27[149] cases was unsuitable where the subject matter of the hearing involved novel questions of law and complex questions of fact.

---

145. *Grimes v Punchestown Developments Company Limited and MCD Promotions Limited* [2002] IESC 79.
146. *Dublin County Council v Kirby* [1985] ILRM 325 HC, Gannon J.
147. *Mahon v Butler* [1997] 3 IR 369.
148. *Waterford County Council v John A Wood* [1999] 1 IR 556, Murphy J.
149. LG(PD)A 1976, s 27.

**[5.141]** In *Dublin County Council v Kirby*,[150] Gannon J had this to say:

> The distinction between the extent of the intervention by the High Court which may be invoked in a summary manner under s 27(1) as compared with sub-section (2) of the section is clearly evident from the wording of the two sub-sections, is very significant, and is in accordance with procedures founded upon principles of justice. There cannot be any doubt but that such distinction was intentional on the part of the legislature. It leaves no room for inferring that the High Court may in such summary proceedings be moved to make orders of a mandatory nature which are made only after full and fair investigation in the course of proceedings instituted in the ordinary way.

Although the general view is that s 160 applications for injunctions should proceed summarily with evidence presented on affidavit only, the reality is that the injunction procedure has been so extended that it is no longer an exclusively summary procedure. If a defence is put forward on affidavit in circumstances where the issues raised are complex, to such an extent that a party cannot properly sustain a comprehensive defence without oral evidence, the court may allow oral evidence. In appropriate circumstances, the court may also allow pleadings and discovery. The court may also permit an applicant to have the matter heard on oral evidence and, if such an application is to be made, it should be made at the interlocutory stage.

**[5.142]** A party is entitled to serve notice to cross-examine a deponent on the contents of an affidavit. Where an affidavit makes an assertion which is not contradicted that assertion shall be deemed to have been established on the balance of probabilities. On the other hand, if an assertion is contradicted the onus of proof in respect of that assertion shall be deemed not to have been satisfied.

**[5.143]** In *Limerick County v Joseph Tobin t/a Harry Tobin Sand and Gravel*,[151] Peart J held that the matters to be considered in an application for a s 160 injunction at interlocutory stage include:

(a) whether there is a fair issue to be tried;

(b) whether irreparable harm will be suffered if an injunction is not granted;

(c) the adequacy of damages as a possible remedy;

(d) the balance of convenience.

The test is equivalent to the test to be met in applications for interlocutory injunctive relief laid down by the Supreme Court in *Campus Oil Limited v Minister for Industry and Commerce*.[152] The *Campus Oil* principles have also been held to govern applications for interlocutory injunctions in conventional judicial review subject to some

---

150. *Dublin County Council v Kirby* [1985] ILRM 325, HC, Gannon J.
151. *Limerick County v Joseph Tobin t/a Harry Tobin Sand and Gravel* [2005] IEHC 281 (unreported, 15 August 2005), Peart J. Judgment delivered on 15 August 2005.
152. *Campus Oil Limited v Minister for Industry and Commerce* [1983] IR 88.

modifications relating to the other requirements of ss 50 and 50A.[153] In summary, the *Campus Oil* principles firstly ask as to whether a fair *bona fide* question has been raised by the person seeking the relief. If it is established that a fair question has been raised the next matters to be considered are as follows:

(i) whether or not the applicant has established a serious issue to be tried;

(ii) the adequacy of damages as a remedy;

(iii) the balance of convenience.

Paragraph (b) above in asking whether irreparable harm will be suffered if an injunction is not granted was included by Peart J and that principle, could, of course, only be relevant to s 160 applications for injunctions. Looking at para (c), which refers to the adequacy of damages, as a possible remedy, it might well be asked how relevant damages are in a s 160 application?

**[5.144]** In *Glencar Explorations plc v Mayo County Council*,[154] it was clearly stated that for the court to award damages an applicant must demonstrate that there is a damages entitlement over and above the mere fact that the conduct complained of was unlawful. Merely because, for example, An Bord Pleanála acts *ultra vires* in making a decision does not by itself entitle an applicant to damages. Although Herbert J in *Grimes v Punchestown Development*[155] indicated, *obiter*, that circumstances may arise where an undertaking as to damages may be required, there is no express requirement which would compel an applicant to give such an undertaking.

**[5.145]** In *Limerick County Council v Tobin (No 1)*,[156] Peart J had this to say in relation to the giving of directions as to the exchange of pleadings, in appropriate circumstances:

> Of course even in plenary proceedings relief by way of interim injunction is available, and at short notice, but in planning matters the legislature has specifically provided the procedure under s 160 and it is reasonable that the Planning Authority in such circumstances would avail of that in the first instance. If, upon the interlocutory hearing, it appears that a defence put forward by the Respondent is one where oral evidence, and even pleadings or discovery are necessary or desirable, there does not seem to be any reason why the Court cannot order such directions as to pleadings and mode of trial as may be appropriate, and certainly there could in my view be no question that the Planning Authority could not be non-suited as it were, having commenced its application by the method provided for in s 160, merely because the Respondent raises a matter by way of defence which for its determination requires either pleadings or oral evidence.

---

153. See PDA 2000, s 50 as amended by PD(SI)A 2006, s 13 and see also PDA 2000, s 50A.
154. *Glencar Explorations plc v Mayo County Council* [2002] 1 ILRM 481.
155. *Grimes v Punchestown Developments Company Limited and MCD Promotions Limited* [2002] IESC 79.
156. *Limerick County v Joseph Tobin t/a Harry Tobin Sand and Gravel* [2005] IEHC 281 (unreported, 15 August 2005), Peart J.

**[5.146]**

There is a degree of confusion as to whether or not s 50 applications for injunctive relief are exclusively a summary procedure. Simons argues that Peart J's judgment in the *Tobin* case[157] should be treated with some caution:

> The Judgement was delivered in the context of an interlocutory application and appears difficult to reconcile with the earlier Supreme Court Judgements.[158]

## Discretionary remedies – *Wicklow County Council v Forest Fencing Ltd*

**[5.146]** The matter of the court's discretion was highlighted more recently by Charleton J in *Wicklow County Council v Forest Fencing Limited t/a Abwood Homes and Anor*.[159] The respondent claimed that it had obtained permission by default to develop a substantial development close to the N11 Motorway. Injunctive relief had been granted in the Circuit Court in 2004 but the order was stayed by reason of the appeal to the High Court. The evidence disclosed that no default permission existed and that the development which had taken place on the site was substantially different, in a material way, from the plans originally submitted to the planning authority. The learned judge had to exercise his discretion in deciding whether or not to order the demolition of the substantial structures which had been erected in these circumstances. Charleton J had this to say:

> Here I find that no default permission ever existed in favour of the Respondents/Appellants. The Court must approach this matter in a balanced way. It should look to how the parties have approached the planning process, and if there are errors, whether these are deliberate or accidental, material or unimportant, explicable or evidence of bad faith. The balance of authority is in favour of the Court exercising its discretion to make a declaration that planning permission has been granted where the Court has found as a fact that there is a default planning permission in favour of the Developer. The Court is there to uphold the Law. Its discretion should not be used to change the Law or to its operation. A similar principle to that outlined in the separate Judgements of O'Leary J and Clarke J should apply in the opposite circumstances, such as here, where the Court has found that there is no default permission: where the developer has, on the contrary, developed the site entirely in accordance with his own wishes and with little or no reference even to the plans in respect of which he once sought permission. The discretion of the Court, in this context, is very limited. The balancing of that discretion must start with the duty of the Court to uphold the principle of proper planning for developments under clear statutory rules. Then, the Court should ask what might allow the consideration of the exercise of its discretion in favour of not granting injunctive relief. To fail to grant injunctive relief in these circumstances, on these facts, would be to cause a situation to occur where the Court is effectively taking the place of the Planning Authority. The Court should not do that. This is a major

---

157. *Limerick County v Joseph Tobin t/a Harry Tobin Sand and Gravel* [2005] IEHC 281 (unreported, 15 August 2005), Peart J.
158. See Simons, *Planning and Development Law* (2nd edn, Thomson Round Hall, 2007) at paras 7–119 and 7–120, pp 309 and 310.
159. *Wicklow County Council v Forest Fencing Limited t/a Abwood Homes and Anor* [2007] IEHC 242, Charleton J.

development for which there is no planning permission. It is a material contravention of the County Wicklow Development Plan. It is built entirely to suit the Developer and with almost no reference to legal constraint. I am obliged to decide in favour of injunctive relief.

## Onus of proof

[5.147] There is no express statutory provision made in the case of a planning injunction establishing where the onus of proof lies in proceedings taken under s 160. Bearing in mind that the proceedings taken under s 160 are very civil proceedings, there is no overall statutory provision allocating the burden of proving a particular matter to one party or another and the presumptions under s 162[160] and s 157(4)(c) do not apply.[161] Generally, a respondent against whom injunctive relief is sought will not be entitled to give any evidence which is additional to the points of defence set out in the respondent's affidavit. In *South Dublin County Council v Balfe*,[162] a defence was raised enclosing submissions to the effect that the alleged unauthorised use had been commenced more than five years before the issue of proceedings and as such the proceedings were statute-barred under the provisions of the legislation then in force. The points, which had not been mentioned in the respondent's affidavit, could not be relied upon by the respondent. Also, dealing with that disallowed submission, Costello P had this to say;

> ... when a wrongful continuous act (such as an unauthorised user of land) has been discontinued and abandoned then the wrong has ceased. When it has recommenced a new wrongful act occurs and it is from that date of recommencement that the time limit in the Section begins to run in respect of this new unauthorised use.

[5.148] In *South Dublin County Council v Fallowvale Limited*,[163] a dispute arose as to whether or not a particular development was exempted development. Although it was agreed that the onus of proof was on the applicant and that the provisions of PDA 2000, s 162 were irrelevant in civil proceedings because that section applied only to criminal cases, McKechnie J ruled that the onus of proof in establishing that a development was exempt development rests with the person making the assertion, namely the respondent/developer.

[5.149] In *Ryan v Roadstone*,[164] O'Donovan J held that the applicant must establish facts from which the court can raise the probable inference that what the applicant asserts is true. However, in *Dillon v Irish Cement Limited*[165] Finlay CJ took the view that exempt

---

160. PDA 2000, s 162(1) reads: 'In any proceedings for an offence under this Act the onus of proving the existence of any permission under Pt III shall be on the defendant'.
161. PDA 2000, s 157(4)(c) reads: 'It shall be presumed until the contrary is proved that proceedings were commenced within the appropriate period'.
162. *South Dublin County Council v Balfe* (unreported, 3 November 1995) HC, Costello P.
163. *South Dublin County Council v Fallowvale Ltd* [2005] IEHC 408, McKechnie J.
164. *Ryan v Roadstone* [2006] IEHC 53.
165. *Dillon v Irish Cement Ltd* (unreported, 26 November 1984) SC, Finlay CJ (Griffin and McCarthy JJ concurring).

development provisions placed developers in a 'privileged category' in allowing exempted development to proceed without being subject to the views or possible objections of other interested parties. The suggestion, in that case, was that the respondent/developer had an obligation of proving that the development is exempt development. Many commentators take the view that in the absence of express statutory provisions it is the applicant, in making the application for an injunction under s 160, who bears the onus of proving that the matter complained of constitutes development and, further, that it is not exempted development.

**[5.150]** There do not appear to be any hard and fast rules for all circumstances as to whether it is the applicant or the respondent who bears the onus of proof, and there are a compelling number of cases which disagree with the High Court decision in *South Dublin County Council v Fallowvale Limited*[166] and with the Supreme Court decision in *Dillon v Irish Cement Limited*.[167]

**[5.151]** In *Dublin Corporation v O'Sullivan*,[168] Finlay P had this to say:

> I am satisfied, since the Applicants come seeking relief which would affect the ordinary property rights of the Respondents and which potentially could cause him loss that in the absence of some express provision to the contrary that does not exist either in Section 27 of the 1976 Act or otherwise in the planning code that the general position must be that it is upon the Applicants there rests the onus of proving the case which they are making.

**[5.152]** In *Westport UDC v Golden*,[169] Morris P indicated that the onus of proof rested with the applicant. In *Peter Sweetman v Shell E & P Ireland Limited and Others*, Smyth J[170] stated:

> It is settled law that the onus of proof is on the Applicant to make out his case and satisfy the Court that an Order under S 160 should be made.

Smyth J refused to grant the relief sought by Peter Sweetman on the grounds that he was not satisfied, on the evidence, that the terms of the planning permission had been breached. The learned judge concluded:

> If I am incorrect in that regard, there has been no deliberate disregard by Shell of the requirements, or any attempt to avoid the obligations imposed on them.

**[5.153]** In *Molumby v Kearns*,[171] O'Sullivan J held that the applicants had failed to discharge the onus of proof to satisfy the court that the respondents were in breach of a condition in a planning permission. In *Fingal County Council v RFS Limited*,[172] Morris

---

166. *South Dublin County Council v Fallowvale Limited* [2005] IEHC 408, McKechnie J.
167. *Dillon v Irish Cement Limited* (unreported, 26 November 1984) SC, Finlay CJ (Griffin J and McCarthy JJ concurring).
168. *Dublin Corporation v O'Sullivan* (unreported, 21 December 1984) HC, Finlay P.
169. *Westport UDC v Golden* [2002] 1 IRLM 439, Morris P.
170. *Peter Sweetman v Shell E & P Ireland Limited and Others* [2006] IEHC 85, Smyth J.
171. *Molumby v Kearns* (unreported, 19 January 1999) HC, O'Sullivan J.
172. *Fingal County Council v RFS Limited* [2000] IEHC 163, Morris P.

P had no doubt that the onus of proof rested with the applicant, Fingal County Council, to prove a variety of issues of a factual nature which remained to be resolved in relation to a pre-October 1964 use.

**[5.154]** In *Altara Developments v Ventola Limited*,[173] the court exercised its discretion in refusing an injunction under PDA 2000, s 160 where the respondent was found to be in breach of a planning permission in circumstances where he had acted on advice and in accordance with an agreement reached with the planning authority.

**[5.155]** In *Curley v Galway Corporation*,[174] permission was granted by An Bord Pleanála enabling the corporation to operate a dump in County Galway. In the course of the case, Kelly J found that the corporation was in breach of several of the conditions attached to the permission and in particular to a condition relating to rehabilitation. Galway Corporation, in urging the court to refuse the reliefs sought, submitted that complying with its statutory obligations under the Waste Management Acts would give very considerable trouble to the corporation which would result in inconvenience to the citizens of County Galway in the disposal of their waste. In the event, Kelly J found that Galway Corporation was in deliberate and conscious violation of the terms of the planning permission which could not be described as trivial or technical in nature. Kelly J held that he could not and would not permit the fulfilment of one statutory obligation by the commission of criminal offences under the planning legislation. The learned judge stated:

> I cannot conceive of a situation where the court can, in order to enable Galway Corporation to comply with its statutory obligations under one piece of legislation, permit the breach of obligations imposed upon it by another piece of legislation. In particular the court cannot permit the fulfilment of a statutory obligation, for example, under the Waste Management Act by the commission of offences under the planning legislation.

**[5.156]** PDA 2000, s 162(1) and (2) provide as follows:

> (1) In any proceedings for an offence under this Act, the onus of proving the existence of any permission granted under Part (III) shall be on the defendant.
>
> (2) Notwithstanding subsection (1) of this section, it shall not be a defence to the prosecution under the Part if the defendant proves that he or she has applied for or has been granted permission under section 34(12) –
>
> (a) since the initiation of proceedings under this Part,
>
> (b) since the date of the sending of a warning letter under section 152, or
>
> (c) since the date of service of the enforcement notice in the case of urgency in accordance with section 155.

---

173. *Altara Developments v Ventola Limited* [2005] IEHC 312, O'Sullivan J.
174. *Curley v Galway Corporation* [1998] IEHC 231, Kelly J.

[5.157] PDA 2000, s 162(3), as amended by s 247 of LGA 2001, reads as follows:

> No enforcement action under this Part (including an application under s 160) shall be stayed or withdrawn by reason of an application for permission for retention of unauthorised development under s 34(12C) or the grant of that permission.[175]

A useful means of producing evidence in court of intensification or change of use, especially in quarry cases, is by producing Ordinance Survey Office photographs taken at different dates. These photographs may sometimes be helpful when the build date of the development is in dispute or to refute a claim that a development was *in situ* on a particular date. The service offered by the Ordinance Survey Office is impressive, speedy and polite. See *Callan v Boyle*,[176] where photographs were taken before 2004 and again in 2006 which showed significant topographical change to the quarry site.

## Hearsay

[5.158] No hearsay evidence can be admitted in support of an application for an injunction under s 60. In *Dublin Corporation v Sullivan*,[177] Dublin Corporation sought an order against the respondent seeking to prohibit the unauthorised use of the premises, 70 Beachwood Avenue, as a multiple dwelling or in any manner other than as a single unit, and that the use of the premises should be restricted to the use that was regularly in operation on or before the 1 October 1964. Although the respondents admitted that a change of use from single dwelling to a multiple dwelling unit had taken place it was their contention that the applicants had failed to discharge the onus of proof and that the burden of proving that the change had taken place after 1 October 1964 (the appointed day) rested with the applicants. The applicants (Dublin Corporation) argued that the onus lay on the respondents to show that the change had taken place on or before 1 October 1964. Finlay P held:

(1) That the burden of proving the case that they were making lay on the applicants to establish facts in which the court could raise a probable inference that the premises had been used at and immediately before 1 October 1964 as a single dwelling and that there had been a change of use to multiple dwelling after 1 October 1964 which was still continuing;

(2) As the application was for a permanent injunction hearsay evidence could not be submitted in support of the case. Having read the declarations submitted the learned judge was satisfied that the applicants had not discharged the onus of establishing the

---

175. PDA 2000, s 162(3) as amended by PD(A)A 2010, s 49. Note that s 34(12C) deals with permission for development and, in particular, with retention permission; that is no longer available under PDA 2000 (as amended) if the application would have required: (a) EIA, (b) a determination as to whether EIA is required or (c) an appropriate assessment – but that retention permission is otherwise available.
176. *Callan v Boyle* [2007] IEHC 91, Murphy J.
177. *Dublin Corporation v Sullivan* (unreported, 21 December 1984) HC, Finlay P.

change of use after 1 October 1964 which is the operative date in the Act. In quoting from an affidavit of Kathy Brennan submitted by the applicants as follows:

> I say that I am concerned that the said premises should have this intense increase in occupation as increases in the number of residents in the area generally lower the character of the neighbourhood which I have known for considerable time and diminish the value of the property in the area.

Finlay P said the following:

> This statement of opinion or belief is in my view not a sufficient discharge by the applicants of the onus of proof which is upon them of establishing that the conversion or alteration of these premises from a premises containing two separate flats which on the accommodation described in the Letting Agreements could well have contained a family of four people or even five people into five separate units is such an intensification of user as would constitute a change of use within the meaning of the Planning Acts. I am, therefore, satisfied that this application for an Order under s 27 must be dismissed.

An exception was made by Costello P in *South Dublin County Council v Balfe*.[178] In that case, the special condition was held to be admissible as evidence of the fact that certain structures had not been erected prior to 1 October 1964.

## Undertakings as to damages

**[5.159]** Whereas the giving of undertakings as to damages is common in cases where an application is made for an equitable or non-statutory injunction, there is no requirement for an applicant to give an undertaking for damages where an application is being made under PDA 2000, s 160. There is no express statutory provision which requires an applicant to give an undertaking as to damages in s 160 applications although Herbert J (*obiter*) in *Grimes v Punchestown Developments Co Limited and MCD Promotions Limited*[179] suggested that an undertaking in s 160 applications might be required in certain circumstances.

**[5.160]** Normally, the question of an undertaking as to damages will not arise in a s 160 application for the reason that, unlike the situation which arises in a non-statutory plenary proceeding, the court will not have to make interlocutory orders. The court will have made its final determination on the issues before making its order. In those circumstances there should be no requirement for an undertaking as to damages.

**[5.161]** There may, however, be a necessity for an undertaking as to damages in non-statutory applications for injunctions in circumstances where preliminary findings only are made by the court at the interlocutory hearing but the final decision is postponed to await the full hearing. In a s 160 application, the final decision is made on the basis of the notice of motion and grounding affidavit, and there is generally no plenary hearing

---

178. *South Dublin County Council v Balfe* (unreported, 3 November 1995) HC, Costello P.
179. *Grimes v Punchestown Developments Co Limited and MCD Promotions Limited* [2002] 1 ILRM 409, Herbert J.

**[5.162]**

to follow. Bearing in mind that PDA 2000, s 160(3) allows the court, when considering an application to it by motion and grounding affidavit, to make such interim or interlocutory orders as it considers appropriate before the proceedings are fully determined, it might be expedient for the court to seek an undertaking as to damages from the applicant and this concept is supported by Peart J's judgment in *Limerick County Council v Tobin*.[180] As there can be no obvious reason why a planning authority should be treated any differently from any other applicant, the assumption must be that it too must give an undertaking as to damages if required to do so by the court.

**[5.162]** Following the Supreme Court decision in *Mahon v Irish Rugby Football Union*,[181] unless the matter is further clarified, some degree of caution is necessary before either requesting or accepting an order of the court requiring an undertaking for damages. PDA 2000, s 160 makes no provisions for it. The 'conclusion' of Denham J in the *Mahon* case reads as follows:

> The High Court has no jurisdiction to make a section 27 order in favour of the residents in relation to an anticipated breach of the planning code nor did it have the jurisdiction to extend the statutory jurisdiction by way of general equitable jurisdiction of the High Court. The appeal should be allowed.

This 'conclusion' may suggest that the courts have no jurisdiction to require an undertaking for damages from an applicant in a s 160 application for the very reason that PDA 2000 provides no authority for it and the courts cannot extend the statutory jurisdiction.

## No damages payable in respect of s 160 application

**[5.163]** It is clear that neither s 27 of the Local Government (Planning and Development) Act 1976 nor s 160 of PDA 2000 was ever intended to include or permit a claim for damages. In *Ellis v Nolan and Bray Developments Limited (in Liquidation)*,[182] McWilliam J in the final paragraph of his judgment said the following:

> Finally, it would appear to me that s 27(2) although very wide in its terms, was not intended to include a claim in damages, which is the essence of the alternative claim on this application, and I will confine myself to making an order directing compliance with the planning permission and approval although, in view of the liquidation, I will hear further arguments as to the form of the Order.

**[5.164]** In *Drogheda Corporation v Gantley*,[183] Gannon J refused to order payment of a fine under a bond made between an insurance company, the applicant and the respondent. In that case also the corporation had sought to recover damages arising after

---

180. *Limerick County Council v Tobin* (unreported, 15 August 2005) HC, Peart J.
181. *Mahon v Irish Rugby Football Union* [1997] ILRM 446, SC.
182. *Ellis v Nolan and Bray Developments Limited (in Liquidation)* 1983] IEHC 38, McWilliam J.
183. *Drogheda Corporation v Gantley* [1983] IEHC 35, Gannon J.

the sale where a loss was incurred because of the vendor's failure to comply with conditions contained in the planning permission for the development of the property.

## Time limits

**[5.165]** PDA 2000, s 160(6)(a) provides:

> An application to the High Court or Circuit Court for an order under this section shall not be made:
>
> (i) In respect of a development where no permission has been granted, after the expiration of a period of seven years from the date of the commencement of the development, or
>
> (ii) In respect of a development for which permission has been granted under Part III, after the expiration of a period of 7 years beginning on the expiration, as respects the permission authorising the development, of the appropriate period (within the meaning of s 40)[184] or as the case may be, of the appropriate period as extended under s 42.[185]

PDA 2000 extended the time limits referred to in s 160(6)(a)(i) and (ii) from five years to seven years.

**[5.166]** PDA 2000, s 160(6)(aa) provides:

> Where the development was carried out not more than seven years prior to the date on which this section comes into operation, and notwithstanding paragraph (a) an application for an order under this section may be made at any time in respect of the following development:
>
> (i) operation of a quarry;
>
> (ii) extraction of peat;[186]

**[5.167]** PDA 2000, s 160(6)(b) provides:

> Notwithstanding paragraph (a) an application for an order under this section may be made at any time in respect of any condition to which the development is subject concerning the ongoing use of the land.

**[5.168]** PDA 2000, s 160(7) provides:

> Where an order has been sought under this section, any enforcement action under this Part may be commenced or continued.

---

184. PDA 2000, s 40 provides that the general 'life' of a grant of permission is five years beginning on the date of the grant. The planning authority or the board may specify a longer time in excess of five years having regard to the nature and extent of the development and any other material considerations (see PDA 2000, s 41).
185. PDA 2000, s 42 enables the planning authority, on application, to extend the period specified in the grant of planning permission (normally five years) in cases where substantial works have already taken place but pursuant to the permission granted and it is clear that the development would be completed within a reasonable time.
186. PDA 2000, s 160(6)(aa) was inserted by PD(A)A 2010, s 48.

**[5.169]**

**[5.169]** If development has taken place in respect of which no permission was granted, no application can be made to the court under s 160 if a period of seven years has elapsed. Time in relation to the seven-year period starts to run from the date of commencement of the development.

**[5.170]** No application shall be made to the court under s 160 if a development has been completed with the benefit of planning permission once the life of the planning permission (normally five years) plus seven years has expired (generally 12 years). These time limits, which exclude an application to the court once they have expired, do not apply where the permission is made subject to a condition concerning the ongoing use of the land. In *Lanigan t/a Tullamaine Castle Stud v Michael Barry t/a Tipperary Recovery and Tipperary County Council*,[187] the respondents obtained permission for a motor racing track in South Tipperary. The use contemplated by the permission was three hours of racing on a Saturday or a Sunday from April to October, with some practice hours in the other months. The evidence showed that the use had been increased, without permission, by a multiple of 10 or more. The use had caused significant noise and nuisance which adversely affected an adjoining stud farm business. Charleton J had this to say:

> There is nothing in the Planning and Development Act 2000 or its predecessor, which authorises the Court to ignore, by virtue of the passage of time, a completely new user of a site, or an intensification of a use in respect of which some form of planning permission has been granted and which had been entirely altered by the illegal use thereof. I am satisfied that as a matter of law, the Defendants have had the choice of using this racetrack in accordance with the planning permission of 1981, or of ignoring it. They have chosen the latter course. Instead of having one race on each weekend over a seven month period with occasional supervised practice or use during the week, they have operated the racetrack on a week-to-week basis during the entire year in a manner which is utterly at odds with the terms of the planning permission granted to their predecessor in 1981.

And further, Charleton J continued:

> Unfortunately, this is a clear case where I must act to restrain major breaches of the planning code which have flaunted the legal rights of a community in favour of an unrestrained action that has seriously impacted on the character of a quiet area and the reasonable use by neighbours of their farms and dwellings.

The learned judge injuncted the defendants to comply strictly with the terms of the planning permission going forward and compelled the defendants to give adequate notice of the holding of races. What is clear from this and other cases is that there is no time limit prescribed in relation to a condition concerning the ongoing use of land. This exemption from time limits only applies to a condition concerning 'ongoing use of land'. All other conditions are within the seven-year rule.

---

187. *Lanigan t/a Tullamaine Castle Stud v Michael Barry t/a Tipperary Recovery and Tipperary County Council* [2008] IEHC 29, Charleton J.

**[5.171]** Where there is intensification of use and the intensification is such as to amount to a material change in use, the time limit will run from the date of such intensification.

**[5.172]** Where a use commences but is either abandoned or interrupted a new seven-year limitation period will only start to run from the date of the recommencement of such use. In *South Dublin County Council v Balfe*,[188] the planning authority sought to restrain the use of lands for certain business activity. The respondent claimed that the proceedings were statute-barred on the grounds that the unauthorised use had commenced in excess of five years from the date of institution of the proceedings.[189] The evidence showed that the use of the lands had materially changed within the five-year period. The lands had originally been used as a plant hire business and subsequently they were used for the storage of chemical containers and for the repair and storage of forklift trucks. The time limit only started to run from the date that the new use commenced.

**[5.173]** Although unauthorised developments are immune from general enforcement proceedings to include injunctions after seven years where there is no planning permission or after the expiration of the life of a planning permission plus seven years where there is planning permission, those unauthorised developments remain unauthorised developments and suffer from a number of disadvantages as non-conforming developments.

## Costs of prosecutions and applications for injunctions

**[5.174]** PDA 2000, s 161 comprises two subsections which read as follows:

> (1) The Court shall, unless it is satisfied that there are special and substantial reasons for not doing so, order the person to pay –
>
> (a) Where a person is convicted of an offence under this Part to the planning authority, or
>
> (b) Where the person is the subject of an order under section 160, to the planning authority or to any other person as appropriate, the costs and expenses of the action, measured by the court.
>
> (2) Where costs or expenses are to be paid to the authority, they shall include any such costs or expenses reasonably incurred by the authority in relation to the investigation, detection and prosecution of the offence or order, as appropriate including costs incurred in respect of the remuneration and other expenses of employees, consultants and advisers.

In the case of prosecution, a convicted person will be ordered to pay the cost to the planning authority or in the case of a s 160 order being made against another party, that party will have to pay the applicant's costs and expenses unless, in either case, 'special and substantial reasons' exist. In effect, in the awarding of costs the costs will follow the event unless there are 'special and substantial reasons'.

---

188. *South Dublin County Council v Balfe* (unreported, 3 November 1995) HC, Costello P.
189. This case was taken under the LG(PD)A 1976 when the time limit was five years.

**[5.175]** There is no case law definition of 'special and substantial reasons'. The key words here are 'special', which implies that it must be different from what is normal, and 'substantial', which implies that the difference must be significant and that the difference must be what is often referred to in judicial parlance as 'weighty'. It is probable that this interpretation may alter the general discretion of the court in awarding costs on the basis that costs should follow the event. Clearly, a higher onus is placed on the respondent to demonstrate why costs should not follow the event.

**[5.176]** The conduct of the applicant may deprive the applicant of costs, as seen in *Donegal County Council v O'Donnell*,[190] where Donegal County Council made an error in the designation of a site which subsequently proved to be totally inappropriate. In that case, because of the unsatisfactory manner in which the planning authority had dealt with the application, O'Hanlon J made no order as to costs.

**[5.177]** In *Curley v Galway County Council*,[191] Kelly J concluded that the developer (Galway Corporation) was guilty of a 'conscious and deliberate violation' of the terms of its planning permission relative to the operation of a dump. The learned judge imposed a fine of IR£50,000 on Galway Corporation and the applicant was awarded costs on a solicitor and client basis.

**[5.178]** See also *Dublin Corporation v Bentham*,[192] where the court held that the replacement of original timber windows by aluminium windows on a listed building in Kenilworth Square was not exempted development because the new windows materially affected the external appearance and rendered that appearance inconsistent with the character of the structure. This was so even though neighbouring premises had already carried out a similar replacement with aluminium windows. Morris J did not order the respondent to replace the aluminium windows with wooden windows. On the second point Morris J held that since the premises had been used on 1 October 1964 (the appointed day) as a bed-sitter or flat and that use had been changed to use as a guesthouse, the guesthouse was an unauthorised use. Morris J clearly considered that the circumstances of the case gave rise to 'special and substantial reasons' and the learned judge had this to say:

> With regard to costs I take the view that the respondents have succeeded in defeating what was stated by the Corporation to have been a test case and notwithstanding the fact that the Corporation has succeeded on the second leg of their claim I am of the opinion that the respondents are entitled to their costs. I believe that the Corporation may well have derived benefit from the hearing.

**[5.179]** In *Cork County Council v Cliftonhall Limited*,[193] Finnegan J awarded the applicant's costs against the respondent when Cork County Council sought to restrain the respondent from making deviations in the height of the development which deviations did not conform with the plans submitted with the application. Finnegan J

---

190. *Donegal County Council v O'Donnell* [1982] IEHC 12, O'Hanlon J.
191. *Curley v Galway County Council* [2001] IEHC 53, Kelly J.
192. *Dublin Corporation v Bentham* [1993] 2 IR 58, Morris J.
193. *Cork County Council v Cliftonhall Limited* [2001] IEHC 85, Finnegan J.

was satisfied that conditions in the original permission had not been complied with and awarded the costs of the applicant against the respondent. In *Fingal County Council v RFS Limited*,[194] the exceptional circumstances comprised the fact that the respondent had allowed the case to go to the first day of hearing and only then made concessions. In those circumstances, Finnegan J awarded Fingal County Council's costs and expenses against the respondent.

**[5.180]** In *Marray v Connaughton*,[195] the respondent was ordered to pay the applicant's costs where the respondent sought to rely on a subsequent grant of retention permission.

**[5.181]** Although PDA 2000, s 162(3) removes any discretion from the court to stay or withdraw any enforcement action, including an application under s 160, if an application for permission or retention permission has been granted, nevertheless the section does not prevent the court, at its discretion, from placing a stay on any order granting an injunction under s 160 to enable the respondent to apply for retention permission in respect of unauthorised development. Also, the subsection does not prevent a planning authority from consenting to adjourn a prosecution or planning injunction proceedings to facilitate the making of an application for retention permission or to await the outcome of a retention permission application already made. In this context it should be noted that in the decision in *Fingal County Council v William P Keeling & Sons*[196] the Supreme Court held that a developer is not estopped from claiming that a development is in fact an exempt development by reason only of his having made an application for planning permission for retention of that development. This decision reversed the stated position in *Dublin County Council v Tallaght Block Company Limited*[197] on the grounds that to allow estoppel would deprive a developer of a right at law simply because he exercised a different right. As already seen, in the decision in *Commission v Ireland*[198] the ECJ held that retention permission is no longer available for development which requires an EIA (see PDA 2000, s 34(12)).[199]

**[5.182]** PDA 2000, s 160(7) provides that where an application is made for a planning injunction under s 160 this will not preclude either the commencement or the continuation of any other enforcement action under Pt VIII of the Act.

## Proceedings against company directors

**[5.183]** On the application of a planning authority the High Court and Circuit Court are empowered by the provisions of PDA 2000, s 160(1) to require any person to do or not to do, or to cease to do, as the case may be, anything that the court considers necessary and specifies in the order to ensure, that unauthorised development is not carried out or continued, and that any development being carried out is carried out in conformity with the permission pertaining to that development or any condition to which the permission

---

194. *Fingal County Council v RFS Limited* (unreported, 6 February 2000) HC, Morris P.
195. *Marray v Connaughton* (unreported, 25 January 1984) HC, O'Hanlon J.
196. *Fingal County Council v William P Keeling & Sons* [2005] 2 IR 108, SC.
197. *Dublin County Council v Tallaght Block Co Ltd* (unreported, 17 May 1983) SC.
198. *Commission of European Communities v Ireland* (Case C–215/06) [2008] ECR I–4911.
199. Subsection (12) substituted and (12A), (12B) and (12C) inserted by PD(A)A 2010, s 23(c).

**[5.184]**

is subject. The court may also require any person, insofar as is practicable, to restore any land to its condition prior to the commencement of any unauthorised developments. The use of the words 'require any person' may include the making of orders against directors of companies. PDA 2000, s 158(1) reads as follows:

> Where an offence under this Act is committed by body corporate or by a person acting on behalf of a body corporate and is proved to have been so committed with the consent, connivance or approval of, or to have been facilitated by any neglect on the part of a person being a director, manager, secretary or other officer of the body or a person who was purporting to act in any such capacity, that person shall also be guilty of an offence and shall be liable to be proceeded against and punished as if he or she were guilty of the first-mentioned offence.

**[5.184]** In *Dublin County Council v Elton Homes Limited*,[200] a respondent limited liability company obtained permission to develop a number of dwelling houses. Elton Homes Limited failed to complete the development for which it had permission and the company went into liquidation. The effect of this was that the people who had purchased the houses were living in a partially completed housing development with incomplete roadways and no public lighting. Dublin County Council sought an order pursuant to s 27 of the 1976 Act and Barrington J cited two incidences where it may be appropriate to make an order against the directors of a company namely:

(1) where it is shown that the directors are guilty of fraud;

(2) where it is shown that the directors have withdrawn large sums of money from the company so as to leave it without funds and unable to meet its commitments.

Barrington J had this to say:

> If the case were one of fraud, or if the directors had siphoned off large sums of money out of the Company, so as to leave it unable to fulfil its obligations, the Court might be justified in lifting the veil of incorporation and fixing the directors with personal responsibility. But that is not the case ... the worst that can be imputed against them is mismanagement ... I am aware that the result is an unfortunate one for the planning authority and the local residents. Perhaps the moral is that the planning authority before granting permission, should be very careful ... to ensure that the security demanded by it of a developer for completion of the proposed works is realistic.[201]

**[5.185]** In *Dublin County Council v O'Riordan*,[202] Murphy J, concurring with the views expressed by Barrington J, confirmed that s 27 of the 1976 Act is deliberately expressed by the legislature in the widest possible terms. Murphy J said the following:

> I would respectfully agree with the views expressed by Mr Justice McWilliam [in *Ellis v Nolan, Brady Developments Limited (in Liquidation)*].[203] Section 27 of the 1976 Act is a valuable summary remedy available to a wide range of interested

---

200. *Dublin County Council v Elton Homes Limited* [1984] ILRM 297, Barrington J.
201. *Dublin County Council v Elton Homes Limited* [1984] ILRM 297, Barrington J.
202. *Dublin County Council v O'Riordan* [1985] IR 159, Murphy J.
203. *Ellis v Nolan, Brady Developments Limited (in Liquidation)* (unreported, 6 May 1983) HC, McWilliam J.

parties to ensure compliance with the terms on which planning permissions are granted. This is a very desirable goal but justice certainly requires that if and in so far as it is to be alleged that the party against whom such an order is sought has been guilty of fraud or the misapplication of monies that some form of plenary proceedings should be instituted in which the party charged with such misconduct would have the opportunities which the legal system provides for knowing the full extent of the case be made against him and to have a proper opportunity to defend themselves against it. Similarly, where the application turns upon the relationship between a director or shareholder and the company in which he is interested I will anticipate that in most case it would be necessary that the relationship would be investigated in the first instance by a liquidator in accordance with procedures provided in the Companies Act for that purpose rather than seeking to establish all of the relevant facts on proceedings designed to be heard on Affidavit.

In that case it was clear that Mr O'Riordan was not the beneficiary of monies siphoned off from the company which, by reason of its reduced financial position, had not been able to complete the estate. Murphy J held that an order was not appropriate in that case.

**[5.186]** In *Dublin County Council v O'Riordan*,[204] it was shown that the company had failed to comply with the provisions of the Companies Act and had not filed accounts or made returns for tax purposes. The company had not held proper directors meetings but those matters may not of themselves be sufficient to justify the making of an order against a director.

**[5.187]** In *Meath County Council v Beachmount Homes and Thomas McCluskey*,[205] an order was made against the director despite the absence of any evidence of fraud or siphoning off of monies in circumstances where there was almost a complete lack of compliance with the Companies Act in relation to holding of meetings, the filing of annual returns and the keeping of proper accounts. Again, in *Dun Laoghaire Corporation v Parkhill Development*[206] Hamilton P refused to make an order against the directors of the company which had left a housing estate uncompleted in circumstances where there was no evidence of fraud or misappropriation of the company's finances.

**[5.188]** In *Johnston and Staunton Limited v Esso (Ireland) Limited*,[207] it was noted that the court will take into account an allegation of the substantial risk that a development would be in breach of the Public Safety Code. In such cases, the court will halt the development regardless of the balance of convenience.

## Permission not required for any works required under this Part

**[5.189]** PDA 2000, s 163 provides that no permission is required in respect of development required by a notice under s 164 or an order under s 160 (disregarding development for which there is in fact permission under Pt III).

---

204. *Dublin County Council v O'Riordan* [1985] IR 159, Murphy J.
205. *Meath County Council v Beachmount Homes and Thomas McCluskey* (unreported, 11 May 1987) HC.
206. *Dun Laoghaire Corporation v Parkhill Development* [1989] IR 447, Hamilton P.
207. *Johnson and Staunton Limited v Esso (Ireland) Limited* [1990] 1 IR 289.

# Chapter 6
# HOUSING SUPPLY – SOCIAL AND AFFORDABLE HOUSING

## INTRODUCTION

[6.01] The purpose of Pt V of the Planning and Development Act 2000 (PDA 2000) (as amended) is to address land shortages for social and affordable housing. In an open market economy, the cost of purchasing a site or indeed a developed house is beyond the means of a very large number of residents in Ireland. The legislation has introduced a mechanism whereby developers of residential developments are required to cede land at its existing use value to the planning authority. As a matter of social policy, a planning authority is required under the Act to take into account the need to counteract undue segregation in housing between persons of different social backgrounds. More particularly, the planning authority must also take into account the needs of elderly persons and persons with disabilities in preparing a housing strategy.

[6.02] Part V is there to encourage residential integration. That is a process which does and will produce its own problems but the initiative, if implemented now, will be well worthwhile. Part V proposes to integrate communities in a manner which will demolish and replace ghettos and poorly developed, underspecified residential areas, where an unspoken anxiety often damages both the social and physical fabric of the lives of the residents and the dwelling units which they inhabit. The aspirations of the policy-makers who presented Pt V in November 2000 have not been achieved. The problems of unsustainable development and the problems of the homeless have increased in Ireland since 1980 in spite of the good intentions of the legislators. Sr Stanislaus Kennedy, the founder of Focus Ireland, had this to say in late 2008 on the occasion of the 23rd anniversary of the founding of her organisation in 1985:

> It is shocking to see the level of shortfall in the delivery of social housing during the boom years. This is largely a direct result of a conscious decision by successive governments to, in effect, cut back on provisions of social housing while the level of need was rising year on year.
>
> In the 1970s and 1980s social housing as a percentage of total housing output in the country ranged from 20–33 per cent. There was a shift in 1987 when it dropped to 16 per cent and in subsequent years it dropped as low as 4 per cent.
>
> The shift of State policy continued during the 1990s as general housing output rose significantly but social housing output did not follow suit. In 1993, social housing was 9.8% of total housing output, in 1999 it was 7.5 per cent and in 2004 it fell as low as 6.6 per cent. These figures support the view that year on year, the State was turning away from its commitment to provide social housing for people in need.
>
> I believe that this was a conscious decision by the State to transfer the responsibility for meeting social needs, namely housing, to the private sector and

**[6.03]** Planning and Environmental Law in Ireland

massively subsidising them in this role. This tragedy has backfired spectacularly
...

The housing shortfall must be addressed as a home is the very foundation stone of any attempt to create a more equal society.

By failing to take steps to deal with homelessness and with undue segregation, Ireland is merely creating a larger and a more costly social problem which is well reflected in the number of sub-standard building estates, the number of people who are forced to sleep on the street and the bulging numbers incarcerated in our prisons at the time that this book goes to press.

**[6.03]** Planning law has an important role to play in dealing with these problems but, unless it is enforced with a firm hand by planning authorities and by government, the problem will continue to grow.

**[6.04]** Some planning authorities, notably Dun Laoghaire-Rathdown, have started to take up the challenge by refusing to issue letters of compliance and by initiating s 160 injunction proceedings where development work is started without a legal or binding agreement under Pt V. Dun Laoghaire-Rathdown County Council has also initiated a policy of refusing to grant permission unless an outline agreement is in place, in relation to Pt V, prior to the submission of the planning application. Planning authorities must, however, go further than this. They must ensure that all housing, including social and affordable housing, is built to the standard required by the Building Regulations and insulated to an extent which will enable completed dwelling units within this category to achieve a rating of nothing less than a high C on BER.[1] Most of all, planning authorities must ensure that the dwelling units and the area where they are developed are sustainable in terms of the facilities and transport connections which the area offers to its residents. The disproportionate sums of money paid for land during the boom years and the overprovision of housing in some areas has done untold damage to the Irish economy and to housing development in Ireland. The prices paid were such as to exclude any real possibility of providing sustainable facilities for residents to include such things as schools, open spaces, playing fields, churches, community halls, swimming pools, facilities for cyclists, sheltered residences for the disabled, accommodation and facilities for the elderly and the disabled, and amenity shopping within the local area, etc. These are an important part of the planning system and sustainable development must be applied evenly to all development as it occurs.

**[6.05]** In supplying dwelling units, developers and planners alike must make some effort to estimate demand so as to ensure that there will be no oversupply.[2] The Department of the Environment cannot be blamed for failing to advocate the need for sustainable

---

1. BER stands for Building Energy Rating. It is now compulsory to have buildings assessed both for renting and for sale. A lessee or purchaser is entitled to know what the Building Energy Rating of the premises is before entering into a lease or before signing a contract to purchase. Energy efficiency is professionally measured within the premises on a scale between A and G.
2. On 27 January 2010 the *Irish Times* reported that there were '621 ghost estates built across the State.' (contd .../)

development at every level. Its publications would fill several book shelves but to be effective those guidelines must be read by and implemented by planning authorities. It is the Department of the Environment, Heritage and Local Government and the government, collectively, who must take control of land prices. Building land is far too scarce a resource to be left to the dim uncertainty of market conditions. The market may work when supply and demand are roughly equal forces but it is easily manipulated and distorted by developers who will buy at any cost as a means of obtaining control. That is what happened in Ireland and it is another reason why Ireland's housing strategy has failed. It has been the case that once the field is sold and the price has been paid, there is nothing left in the kitty to deal with essential sustainable issues. Developers need to know that they are no longer just developing a house, an apartment block, an office block, a warehouse or a factory that earns money for them on the sale or lease of the premises. They must be encouraged or, if necessary, compelled to develop the sustainable facilities which serve those developments and which will give them their integrity.

[6.06] The day to day operation of planning law in Ireland, since 1 October 1963, at least, has too often been reflected in the mirror of money and of power without much thought being given to issues of sustainability in its widest sense. Errors have occurred. No real effort has been made to tackle social integration. Dwellings and other buildings have been developed on obvious flood plains which must suggest, at the very least, that planning authorities took their eye off the ball and that the planners within the system, in some instances, gave in to pressure from elected members and others to develop unsuitable sites and to overlook sustainable issues by granting permission to develop populated areas with little or insufficient provision for facilities which would sustain the community which might live there.

[6.07] It is increasingly clear that democratic input in planning matters at local authority level needs to be controlled so that the engine which drives sustainable planning is not exclusively fuelled by the prospect of making a profit. Although it is not necessarily so in all cases, in Ireland it seems that profitability and sustainability are forces which frequently contradict each other and which may cause chaos if a sound balance between the two is not achieved. Sustainability profits the community while profitability sustains the developer. For the moment the developer receives seven out of ten and the remaining three fall into the hands of the local authority planners. This imbalance needs to be addressed.

[6.08] As the water levels rise, development land and fertile alluvial farmland will be in increasingly short supply. We have seen the hardship that the level of flooding caused in the winter of 2009/2010.

---

2. (contd) The National Institute of Regional and Spatial Analysis (Nirsa) claimed that more than 300,000 new homes are empty. Between 2006 and 2009, based on population growth, Leitrim would have needed approximately 588 new houses, yet there were actually 2945 houses built. The Minister for Housing, Michael Finneran estimated that there were between 100 and 140 houses lying empty while the construction industry claimed that the true figure was 40,000.

**[6.09]** It is likely that the water levels, which did so much damage and caused so much distress in 2009/2010, will increase progressively to such an extent that all low lying development, etc, in our cities, towns, villages and countryside will have to find somewhere else to go. Although this is not offered as an expert view it is possible that, even in the short term, the 'somewhere else to go' may have to be a minimum of 5 to 10 metres above spring tide high water sea level, and it may, as time passes, become worse than that. The obvious and the cheaper solution is, in the first instance, to rule out all development on low lying areas. The next step is more difficult, but if the world's land ice does not stop melting and if the oceans do not stop expanding as they are warmed by rising temperatures there will be a significant rise in sea water levels which will result in a necessity to relocate existing development which is, even now, consistently flooded after periods of heavy rainfall. This is a matter which needs to be addressed today. The alternative to relocation is to construct a dam in progressive stages (perhaps step by step to 30 metres) around low lying coastal areas, along the river banks and those lakeshores of Ireland which lie close to the flood plain. There is a proposal to build a new road across Dublin Bay from Howth to Dun Laoghaire which, apart from relieving traffic in the city, would also act as a tide-gate to deal with rising sea levels. As a tidal barrage stretching across Dublin Bay it will not work effectively to keep the water out unless other measures are taken. As water will, always, find its own level, it is never enough to shut the front door unless you also shut all of the back doors. Ordered and progressive redevelopment and relocation is clearly the better alternative, but, one way or another, some form of price control of development land is probably a requirement for today and it is definitely a requirement for the future. Plans for taking action and, in some cases, taking that action are both matters of immediate concern if we are to avoid the errors which we have made in the past and which were so thoroughly demonstrated by the relatively small amount of flooding which occurred in the winter of 2009/2010.

**[6.10]** Part V of the Planning and Development Act of 2000 came into effect on 1 November 2000. It introduced the social and affordable housing provisions which are designed to provide for housing strategies to be prepared by planning authorities for inclusion as part of the development plan in order that planning authorities can ensure that adequate land is zoned for housing and sufficient social and affordable housing is provided in their areas. The relevant sections in PDA 2000, as amended,[3] are ss 93 to 101. PDA 2000, Pt V has been amended by the PD(A)A 2002. Whereas the Act of 2000 offered three types of condition which the planning authority can impose by way of agreement between the authority and the developer, the Amendment Act of 2002 offered additional options which are dealt with below. The Act of 2002 also abolished 'withering permissions' and replaced them with a levy which is also dealt with below.

**[6.11]** The integration of housing (previously dealt with in separate legislation) within the planning system was achieved by the incorporation of a housing strategy policy within the local authorities' Development Plans. Planning permissions granted by the local authorities for development of housing (with some exceptions which are dealt with below) contain conditions which require that a specified percentage of land or of houses

---

3. See PD(A)A 2002.

or of developed sites is reserved for social and affordable housing. In certain circumstances (dealt with below), the reservation of land, or sites or of houses may, in special circumstances, be replaced by the payment of a monetary sum or by a combination of all three elements.

[6.12] When the Bill which preceded PDA 2000 was passed by both houses of the Oireachtas, Pt V was referred to the Supreme Court pursuant to Art 26.2.1° of the Constitution for determination as to whether or not these provisions were unconstitutional. The Supreme Court, in *Re Article 26 and the constitutionality of Pt V of the Planning and Development Bill 1999*,[4] gave its judgment on 28 of August 1999 deciding that the terms of the Bill were not unconstitutional. As a consequence of that referral none of the provisions of the Act dealing with social and affordable housing are open to constitutional challenge. In the course of that judgment Keane CJ had this to say:

> In the present case, as a condition of obtaining a planning permission for the development of lands for residential purposes, the owner may be required to cede some part of the enhanced value of the land deriving both from its zoning for residential purposes and the grant of planning permission in order to meet what is considered by the Oireachtas to be a desirable social objective, namely the provision of affordable housing and housing for persons in special categories and of integrated housing. Applying the tests proposed by Costello J in *Heaney v Ireland*[5] and subsequently endorsed by this court, the court in the case of the present Bill is satisfied that the scheme passes those tests. They are rationally connected to an objective of sufficient importance to warrant interference with a constitutionally protected right and, given the serious social problems which they are designed to meet, they undoubtedly relate to concerns, which, in a free and democratic society, should be regarded as pressing and substantial.
>
> At the same time the court is satisfied that they impair those rights as little as possible and their effects on those rights are proportionate to the objectives sought to be obtained.[6]

## DEFINITIONS OF SOCIAL AND AFFORDABLE HOUSING

[6.13] Social and affordable housing are two separate concepts which should not be confused with each other. The distinction between social housing and affordable housing was dealt with by Clarke J in *Cork County Council v Shackleton/Dun Laoghaire Rathdown County Council v Glenkerrin Homes* which highlighted the difference between social housing and affordable housing as follows:

> Social housing stems from the obligation of the local authority to provide rented accommodation to persons in need of housing in accordance with its statutory

---

4. *Re Article 26 and the Constitutionality of Part V of the Planning and Development Bill 1999* [2000] 2 IR 321, Keane CJ.
5. *Heaney v Ireland* [1994] 3 IR 593, Costello J.
6. *Re article 26 and the constitutionality of Part V of the Planning and Development Bill 1999* [2000] 2 IR 321, Keane CJ.

obligations. On the other hand affordable housing is a mechanism whereby qualifying persons may become entitled to purchase property at a reduced price.[7]

**[6.14]** PDA 2000, s 93(1) (as amended)[8] sets out interpretations relevant to the other sections in Pt V including the criteria for the determination of a person's eligibility for social and affordable housing. The definitions are crucial to an understanding of the concept of the housing supply provisions.

**[6.15]** PDA 2000, s 93(1) provides the following definitions:

> 'accommodation needs' means the size of accommodation required by an eligible person determined in accordance with the regulations made by the Minister under s 100(1)(a) of PDA 2000;

**[6.16]** Those regulations SI 90/2003, reg 4 are as follows:

(a) for one person, a house with one bedroom and gross floor area of 38$m^2$ (increased from 35$m^2$ to 38$m^2$);

(b) for two persons, a house with one bedroom and a gross floor area of 42$m^2$ (increased from 40$m^2$ to 42$m^2$);

(c) for three persons, a house with two bedrooms and a gross floor area of 52$m^2$ (increased from 50$m^2$ to 52$m^2$);

(d) for four persons, a house with two bedrooms and a gross floor area of 62 $m^2$ (increased from 60$m^2$ to 62$m^2$);

(e) for five persons, a house with three bedrooms and a gross floor area of 74 $m^2$ (this read five or six persons and referred to an area of 72$m^2$. It now refers to five persons and a gross floor area of 74$m^2$);

(f) for six persons, a house with three bedrooms and a gross floor area of 78 $m^2$ (this is new and deals with six persons and provides for an area of 78$m^2$); or

(g) for seven or more persons, a house with four bedrooms and a gross floor area of 92$m^2$ (this reduces the area for seven persons from 100$m^2$ to 92$m^2$).[9]

> 'affordable housing' means housing or land made available, in accordance with s 96(9) or (10) for eligible persons;

> 'eligible person'[10] means, subject to sub-s (3) and to the regulations, if any, made by the Minister under s 100(1)(b), a person who is in need of accommodation and whose income would not be adequate to meet the payments on a mortgage for the purchase of a house to meet his or her accommodation needs because the

---

7. *Cork County Council v Shackleton and Murphy Construction (Carrigtwohill) Ltd/Dun Laoghaire Rathdown County Council v Glenkerrin Homes* [2007] IEHC 241 (unreported, 19 July 2007), Clarke J.
8. Note that is PDA 2000, s 93(1) is amended by the deletion of the definition of 'housing strategy' by PD(A)A 2010, s 37.
9. These sizes referred to in this interpretation section are the sizes as amended by the PD(A)A 2002.
10. 'Eligible person' includes not only persons who are entitled to social housing under the Housing Acts but also persons in need of accommodation where mortgage repayments to meet those needs would exceed 35% of their annual income.

payments calculated over the course of a year would exceed 35 percent of that persons' annual income net of income tax and pay related social insurance;

'market value' in relation to a house means the price which the unencumbered fee simple of the house would fetch if sold on the open market.

'mortgage' means a loan for the purchase of a house secured by mortgage in an amount not exceeding 90 percent of the price of the house;

'house' means:

(a) a building or part of a building which has been built for use as a dwelling, and;

(b) in the case of a block of apartments of other building or part of a building comprising two or more dwellings, each of those dwellings.[11]

'relevant house' means a house, permission for which would have ceased to have effect or expired but for s 4 of the Planning and Development (Amendment) Act 2002.[12]

PDA 2000, s 93(2) reads:

For the purposes of this Part, the accommodation needs of an eligible person includes the accommodation needs of any other person who might reasonably be expected to reside with the eligible person.

The meaning of the phrase 'who might reasonably be expected to reside' with an 'eligible person' is not defined in the Act but it may be supposed that it would include immediate family such as husband, wife, partner, son or daughter, etc. It is not clear if the phrase would extend beyond the immediate family but it probably would apply to close relatives including father, mother, sister, brother, etc.

**[6.17]** Section 93(3) provides that when a planning authority is deciding whether or not someone is eligible for the purposes of Pt V it must take the following into account:

(a) half the annual income, net of income tax and pay related social insurance, of any other person who might reasonably be expected to reside with the eligible person and contribute to the mortgage payments, and

---

11. This is a new definition inserted by the Planning and Development (Amendment) Act, 2002, s 4 now Planning and Development Acts 2000–2010, s 96B.
12. Note: There has been some discussion on the wording of this definition and some commentators feel that the reference to PD(A)A 2002, s 4 should in fact be a reference to PD(A)A 2002, s 3. Section 3 got rid of the special type of withering permission which withered on 31 December 2002 or two years from the date of grant of permission, whichever was the later, if permission had been applied for after the 25 August, 1999. Strictly speaking s 4 does not cause a social and affordable housing permission 'to cease to have effect or expire.' Section 4 restores PDA 2000, ss 40, 41 and 42 time limits to Social and Affordable withering permissions and it imposes a levy where a Social and Affordable withering permission would have withered but for the provisions of the Amendment Act 2002. It is doubtful if this potential error will affect the provisions of the Amendment Act 2002. The definition of 'housing strategy' in sub-s (1) has been simply deleted. See PDA (Amendment) Act 2010, s 37. Housing strategies are comprehensively dealt with in PDA 2000, s 94 and they were first prepared prior to 1 August 2001 and are renewed in each development plan. 'Housing strategy' must provide not more than 20% of residential land (so zoned) such land to be reserved for social and affordable housing.

(b) any other financial circumstances of the eligible person and any other person who might reasonably be expected to reside with the eligible person and contribute to the mortgage payments.

It follows, therefore, that two persons whose annual net income is insufficient to purchase a house or apartment of 40m² with one bedroom in that area, will be eligible.

**[6.18]** PDA 2000, s 93(4) is an important provision which provides:

> For the avoidance of doubt, it is hereby declared that, in respect of any planning application or appeal, compliance with the 'Housing Strategy' and any related objective in the development plan shall be a consideration material to the proper planning and sustainable development of the area.

This is an important consideration in relation to any planning application made to a planning authority or any appeal before An Bord Pleanála.

**[6.19]** In the broadest possible sense, the concept of social and affordable housing is consistent with the concept of sustainable development which first made its appearance in PDA 2000. Although there may be some exceptions, when developments which include social and/or affordable housing are examined it is clear that insufficient effort has been made to achieve sustainable integration and that far too little effort has been made to provide the facilities which permit a development and its community to live in a residential area which is genuinely 'sustainable.' Artificially high land prices have gobbled up any potential of achieving sustainability where a developer has an option to build and sell housing units to purchasers who will borrow a high percentage of the price from a lending institution. The temptation must be to build a better house for purchasers who are borrowers than a house, within the same development, which the developer is compelled to make available as either social housing or affordable housing. For as long as those distinctions are in existence it is difficult to see how, if at all, equal standards will be applied.

**[6.20]** There is no definition of 'social housing' in PDA 2000 and indeed, the expression is not used in the Act. Reference is made to s 9(2) of the Housing Act 1988 which refers to the need for 'social housing' of persons who:

(i) Are homeless;

(ii) Are persons to whom s 13 applies (s 13 deals with the provision of sites for Travellers);

(iii) Are living in accommodation that is unfit for human habitation or is materially unsuitable for their adequate housing;

(iv) Are living in overcrowded accommodation;

(v) Are sharing accommodation with another person or persons and who, in the opinion of the Housing Authority, have a reasonable requirement for separate accommodation;

(vi) Are young persons leaving institutional care or without family accommodation;

(vii) Are in need of accommodation for medical or compassionate reasons;

(viii) Are elderly;

(ix) Are disabled or handicapped; or

(x) Are, in the opinion of the Housing Authority, not reasonably able to meet the cost of the accommodation which they are occupying or to obtain suitable alternative accommodation.

## HOUSING STRATEGIES

**[6.21]** Local authorities were given a period of nine months from the commencement of PDA 2000, s 94 to prepare a housing strategy for the area administered by the planning authority in its development plan. Those housing strategies have long since been incorporated into the various planning authorities' development plans. As new development plans are prepared by Local authorities those new plans must also incorporate a housing strategy.

**[6.22]** A housing strategy is a strategy for the purpose of ensuring that the proper planning and sustainable development of the area of the development plan provides for the housing of the existing and future population of the area in the manner set out in the housing strategy. A housing strategy relates to housing in general but the power to require a Pt V agreement relates specifically to social and affordable housing. In accordance with the provisions of PDA 2000, s 94(1)(a) a housing strategy shall be for the period of the development plan or the remaining life of the existing plan, as the case may be. Housing strategies can be prepared jointly by two or more planning authorities in respect of the combined areas of their development plans.[13] A direction may be issued by the Minister requiring the housing strategy to be prepared jointly. PDA 2000, s 15(1) provides that:

> It shall be the duty of the planning authority to take such steps within its powers as may be necessary for securing the objectives of the development plan.

**[6.23]** PDA 2000, s 178(1)(3) prohibits local authority development which is in material contravention of the local authorities' own development plan. This prohibition covers both development sanctioned by the local authority and development carried out by the local authority itself.

**[6.24]** In *Attorney General (McGarry) v Sligo County Council*,[14] McCarthy J considered that a development plan amounted to an environmental contract between the planning authority and members of the public. A local authority cannot escape by simply excluding substantial development from its development plan. The local authorities are compelled to include all of their objectives in their development plans. If this were not the case, a local authority could materially contravene its own development plan by carrying out development which was not mentioned in the development plan.

---

13. See PDA 2000, s 94(1)(a)–(e) inclusive.
14. *Attorney General (McGarry) v Sligo County Council* [1991] 1 IR 99, McCarthy J.

**[6.25]** In *Keogh v Galway Corporation*,[15] the question was whether or not a local authority has a duty to disclose. In that case, the corporation had included a number of specified sites within its administrative area which were proposed to be developed as halting sites. The corporation then decided to develop a halting site which was not included on this list of sites. Carney J held that the proposal, if it were to proceed, would be in material contravention of the corporation's own development plan because it had not given notice of its proposal in its development plan.[16]

**[6.26]** In *Roughan v Clare County Council*,[17] Barron J held firmly to the line that all of the local authority's objectives must be announced in its development plan. If it were not so and if a local authority could proceed with development not disclosed in its development plan the detailed consultative process which precedes the making of the development plan could be ignored.

**[6.27]** PDA 2000, s 94(2) provides:

> In preparing a Housing Strategy, a planning authority shall have regard to the most recent assessment or assessments made under s 9 of the Housing Act 1988 that relate to the area of the development plan.

**[6.28]** PDA 2000, s 94(3) provides that a housing strategy must take the following matters into account:

(a) The existing need and the likely future need for housing to which sub-s (4)(a) applies.

(b) The need to ensure that housing is available for persons who are at different levels of income.

(c) The need to ensure that a mixture of house types and sizes is developed to reasonably match the requirements of different categories of households, as may be determined by the planning authority, and including the special requirements of elderly persons and persons with disability.

(d) The need to counteract undue segregation in housing between persons of different social backgrounds.

---

15. *Keogh v Galway Corporation* [1995] 3 IR 457, Carney J.
16. See PDA 2000, s 10(1)–(8) inclusive, which section deals with the contents of a development plan. This section has been radically amended by PD(A)A 2010, s 7: (i) to make provision for the concept of 'core strategy', (ii) connecting article 10 of the Habitats Directive to the development plan in encouraging management features of landscape and in stressing the importance of ecological coherence of the Natura 2000 network, (iii) by promoting compliance with environmental standards and objectives in relation to the quality of surface water and ground water, (iv) by promoting the provision of community services such as schools and crèches, (v) by the protection of the linguistic and cultural heritage of the Gaeltacht, (vi) by promotion of sustainable settlement and transportation strategies, (vii) by reducing energy demand and greenhouse gas omissions, (viii) by adapting to climate change, (ix) by promoting and protecting public rights of way, and (x) by promoting and managing landscapes.
17. *Roughan v Clare County Council* (unreported, 18 December 1996) HC, Barron J. See also *Wicklow Heritage Trust Ltd v Wicklow County Council* (unreported, 5 February 1998) HC, McGuiness J.

Very little effort has been made to ensure compliance with PDA 2000, s 94(3)(d) which legislates for the avoidance of undue social segregation. The purpose of the statutory provision is to avoid placing groups of people from the same social background in the same areas. Different areas should have a mix of people from different social, cultural, and ethnic backgrounds. Of course, there is social resistance to the idea of mixing people from different backgrounds. It is, however, an objective which must be tackled head on and although it may produce teething problems to start with one generation or perhaps even a half a generation will cure those problems.

[6.29] The housing strategy must include an estimate of the amount of social and affordable housing required during the period of the development plan, and may exclude people who qualify as 'eligible persons'[18] but who own or have previously owned a house. Persons who own or who have previously owned a house may be excluded for the purposes of estimating affordable housing. In most cases, but not in all instances, the presumption is that persons who have previously owned a house, will be able to afford another.[19]

[6.30] A housing strategy must provide that a specified percentage, not exceeding 20%, of land zoned for residential use or for a mixture of residential and other uses, shall be reserved for social and affordable housing. Nothing in the provision, however, will prevent any person (including a local authority) from using more than 20% of land zoned for residential use, or a mix of residential and other uses, for the provision of social and affordable housing. See s 94(4)(d), which paragraph ensures that, in any period, more than 20% of all residentially zoned land may be developed for social and affordable housing where the additional land developed is provided by means other than under Pt V, eg, land owned by voluntary organisations, local authority owned lands, etc. The 20% stated in this Part is not an overall limit on how much land may be developed for social and affordable housing.

[6.31] The wording of PDA 2000, s 94(4)(a)–(d) is important in understanding the elements which make up a housing strategy and for ease of reference the subsection is set out below.

[6.32] PDA 2000, s 94(4)(a)–(d) provides:

    (a)    A housing strategy should include an estimate of the amount of –

        (i)    Housing for persons referred to in s 9(2) of the Housing Act 1988, and

        (ii)    Affordable housing,

    required in the area of the development plan during the period of the development plan and the estimate may state the different requirements for different areas within the area of the development plan.

---

18. See definition of social housing in the Housing Act 1988, s 9(2).
19. For further details see PDA 2000, s 94(4).

(b) For the purpose of making an estimate under paragraph (a)(ii) a planning authority may exclude eligible persons who own or who have previously owned a house.

(c) Subject to paragraph (d) a housing strategy shall provide that as a general policy a specified percentage, not being more than 20 per cent, of the land zoned for residential use, or for a mixture of residential use and other uses, shall be reserved under this Part for the provision of housing for the purposes of either or both subparagraphs (i) and (ii) of paragraph (a).

(d) Paragraph (c) shall not operate to prevent any person (including a local authority) from using more than 20 percent of land zoned for residential use, or for a mixture of residential and other uses, for the provision of housing for which paragraph (a) applies.

**[6.33]** PDA 2000, s 94(5)(a) provides that when a local authority is making its estimate of the amount of social and affordable housing required, it must have regard to:

(i) The supply of and demand for housing generally, or houses of a particular class or classes, in the whole or part of the area of the development plan;

(ii) The price of houses generally or houses of a particular class (or classes), in the whole or part of the area;

(iii) The income of persons generally or of a particular class (or classes) of person, who require houses in the area of the development plan;

(iv) The rates of interest on mortgages for house purchase;

(v) The relationship between the price of housing under sub-s (ii), incomes under sub-s (iii) and rates of interest under sub-s (iv) for the purpose of establishing the affordability of houses in the area of the development plan;

(vi) Such other matters as the planning authority considers appropriate or as may be prescribed for the purposes of this subsection.

Any regulations made after a development plan has come into force or after a housing strategy is in place will not affect the development plan or the housing strategy, respectively.[20]

**[6.34]** In taking the matters listed in PDA 2000, s 94(5)(a)(i)–(vi) into account, the local authority will have to remember that the life of the housing strategy is the same as the life of the development plan, namely six years, and that thereafter it will be replaced by a new housing strategy.

## HOUSING STRATEGIES AND DEVELOPMENT PLANS

**[6.35]** Section 95 requires that the development plan for an area must address the housing needs of the population, which has been identified in the housing strategy through 'zoning'. Planning authorities are required to ensure that sufficient and suitable land is zoned for residential use, or for a mixture of residential and other uses, to meet

---

20. PDA 2000, s 94(4)(5)(b).

the requirements of its housing strategy and to ensure that a scarcity of such land does not occur at any time during the period of the development plan. In deciding on the amount of land to be zoned for the six year period, the planning authority should select an area greater than that calculated to accommodate the required number of houses. This is necessary to ensure that there is no undue shortage of zoned and serviced lands at any stage during the planned period. There is a need for a careful balance between providing for this additional element and avoiding a wasteful over provision, which would require excessive advanced funding on services.[21]

[6.36] The Guidelines for Planning Authorities – Pt V of PDA 2000 – Housing Supplement at para 2.6 reads as follows:

> As the Housing Strategy will inform the whole development plan, work on the collection of data to input into the strategy should be one of the first tasks undertaken in preparing the draft development plan as a whole. Procedures and time-scales for the review of the existing Housing Strategy and the preparation of a new draft strategy must accord with those for drafting the development plan itself as set out in subsections (11) and (12) of the Act. As stated, the first time the Housing Strategy is prepared, it is likely that it will be incorporated into the development plan by means of a variation of the plan. A consultation process along the lines laid out in Section 11 of the Act (including public meetings, written and oral submissions) with the general public, interested bodies and relevant housing and infrastructure providers should be pursued by the planning authority in the preparation of the strategy having regard to the time-scale set out at Section 94 of the Act ie that the strategy must be prepared within nine months of the 1st of November 2000. However the procedures to apply in relation to publication and making of the strategy will be those of Section 13 rather than those of Section 12 of the Act.
>
> It is essential that the elected representatives and management cooperate fully during the course of preparing the housing strategy so as to ensure its smooth passage through the prescribed procedures.[22]

The development plan must include objectives to secure the implementation of the housing strategy (including the provision of housing for people with different levels of income and social integration) and require that a specified percentage of land zoned for residential use, or a mixture of residential and other uses, is made available for social and affordable housing. Different specific objectives may be laid down for different areas and different percentages of social and/or affordable houses can apply in respect of different areas (and indeed in some cases it may be that there is no requirement for social and affordable housing). In all cases the percentage to be reserved is that identified in the housing strategy.[23]

---

21. See PDA 2000, s 95(1)(a).
22. The reference to the time limit of nine months from 1 November 2000 was the time limit provided in the Act and if any local authority had not prepared its housing strategy prior to 1 November 2000 it could not insert Part V conditions in any grant of permission. In fact, every local authority in Ireland did have their housing strategy in place before 1 November 2000.
23. See PDA 2000, s 95(1)(b) and (c).

**[6.37]** It is important to note that in order to counteract social segregation an authority may decide that there is no requirement for social and affordable housing in that area or that a lower percentage than that specified in the development plan will apply. This should be used where a particular area already has a high level of social housing, and affordable or market housing is, in the opinion of the authority, required to encourage social integration.[24]

**[6.38]** PDA 2000, s 15(2) provides that a manager is required to prepare a progress report for elected members within two years of the development plan being made, to set out the progress made in implementing the housing strategy. Where a manager identifies new or revised housing needs, he or she may recommend an adjustment or variation to the housing strategy and the development plan will be varied accordingly.[25]

**[6.39]** Furthermore, where a manager of a planning authority considers that, at any time during the lifetime of the development plan, there has been a change:

(a) In the housing market, or

(b) In the regulations made by the Minister under s 100, that significantly affects the Housing Strategy, the manager may prepare a report for the elected members. In this report, the manager may recommend that the Housing Strategy be adjusted and that the development plan be varied accordingly.[26]

In deciding on the amount of land to be zoned for the six year period of the plan the guidelines recommend that the authority should select an area greater than that calculated to accommodate the required number of houses so as to ensure that there is no undue shortage of zoned and service land at any stage during the planned period. The guidelines also provide at para 8.2:

> The amount of land to be zoned and serviced for residential development during the period of the plan should have regard to the proper planning and sustainable development of the area, taking account of factors such as existing or proposed shopping and community facilities, public transport routes, utility services, adjoining uses including amenities, existing commitments, land demand for other uses and land availability.[27]

The plea made here for sustainable development has fallen on deaf ears in too many cases.

## SOCIAL AND AFFORDABLE HOUSING CONDITIONS AND AGREEMENTS

**[6.40]** The changes made to PDA 2000, s 96 by PD(A)A 2002, s 3 are the most important changes made and the purpose of the revised section is to require applicants

---

24. See PDA 2000, s 95(1)(d).
25. PDA 2000, s 95(3)(a).
26. PDA 2000, s 95(3)(b).
27. Guidelines for Planning Authorities re Part V of the Planning and Development Act 2000 – Housing Supply, para 8.2.

for planning permission to develop houses on lands to enter into an agreement with the planning authority to transfer part of the land or to enter into some other arrangement in order to satisfy the social and affordable housing requirement specified in the housing strategy. The amended s 96 provides the developer with a greater range of options. Section 96 makes it clear that the social and affordable housing provisions will apply to an application for permission for the development of houses and land. The provisions shall also apply where the application relates to a mixed development. In the case of a mixed development the social and affordable housing conditions will apply only to the part of the application which relates to the development of houses on such land.[28]

**[6.41]** Before Pt V conditions can be attached to a grant of permission, there are a number of pre-conditions which must be in place in relation to the development proposal. Before a developer is required to enter into an agreement with the planning authority, it must be clear that the application is for the 'development of houses' or for a 'mixed development' with some residential content. The land to be developed must, at the time that the application for planning permission is made, be zoned for residential use, or, where appropriate for a mixed use with residential content. Also, the land must be referred to in the planning authority's development plan, as land which is regarded as an objective of the development plan to be developed for residential use or, where appropriate, for a mixed use with residential content. The development plan must have specified what percentage of such land (not exceeding 20%) is set aside for development of social and affordable housing.

**[6.42]** PDA 2000, s 2 defines a 'house' as follows:

> 'house' means a building or part of a building which is being or has been occupied as a dwelling or was provided for use as a dwelling but has not been occupied, and where appropriate, includes a building which was designed for use as two or more dwellings or a flat, an apartment or other dwelling within such building;

That definition is generally accepted by planning authorities as including holiday homes. In *Kerry County Council v Kerins*,[29] a development of holiday chalets were held to be 'houses' by the Supreme Court but that case related to rates valuations and it predated PDA 2000. The matter is hotly disputed as between developers and planning authorities and there does not seem to be any conclusive answer. It is a matter which should be resolved in a clear and unambiguous manner, one way or the other, by statutory provisions in future legislation. The definition of a 'house' would seem to be stretched to its limit if an application for golfing lodges for renting on a short term basis required a developer to sign up to a Pt V agreement before commencing development. For the moment, a decision as to whether or not holiday homes are a house seems to rest with the discretion of the planning authorities which have sometimes but not always acted reasonably in these cases.

---

28. PDA 2000, s 96 as substituted by PD(A)A 2002, s 3.
29. *Kerry County Council v Kerins* [1996] 3 IR 493.

**[6.43]** Where an application for planning permission seeks a mixed development of residential units and non-residential units, the requirements of PDA 2000, s 96 (as amended)[30] will apply only to residential units.

**[6.44]** For a Pt V agreement to be a necessary condition in a grant of planning permission, the land on which the housing development is to take place must be subject to a zoning objective for social and affordable housing. If there is no zoning objective for social and affordable housing, the applicant for permission should expressly state that fact in his application.

**[6.45]** One way or another, the relevant zoning should be carefully checked because PDA 2000, s 95(1)(c) reads:

> Specific objectives as referred to in paragraph (b) may be indicated in respect of each area zoned for residential use, or for a mixture of residential use and other uses, and, where required by local circumstances relating to the amount of housing required as estimated in the housing strategy under section 94(4)(a), different specific objectives may be indicated in respect of different areas subject to the specified percentage referred to in section 94(4)(c) not being exceeded.

The requirements in respect of social and affordable housing are, as seen, specifically connected to the zoning objectives in a planning authority's development plan and, so it follows, inevitably, that if a proposed development represents a material contravention of the development plan there can be no social and affordable housing condition. The likelihood is that the material contravention will prevent the entire proposal for a housing development from going ahead.

**[6.46]** A housing strategy shall provide that as a general policy a specified percentage not exceeding 20% of the lands zoned for residential use or for a mixture of residential and other uses shall be reserved for the provision of either social or affordable housing.[31]

**[6.47]** In many cases, planning authorities have specified 20% for the entire of their administrative areas. There is nothing to prevent a planning authority from specifying nil percent if it is of the view that a particular area within its administrative area already has a sufficient number of social and/or affordable houses.

**[6.48]** PDA 2000, s 96(2) provided that a planning authority, or the board on appeal, may require as a condition of grant of permission that the applicant would enter into an agreement with the planning authority concerning the development of housing land to which a specific objective (eg, housing strategy or development plan) applies. The PD(A)A 2002 has removed any discretion which the planning authority might have had and provides that a planning authority must impose such condition in a relevant residential or mixed (including residential) planning permission.[32]

---

30. Amended by PD(A)A 2002, s 38(a)(i), (a)(ii), (a)(iii), (b) and (c).
31. PDA 2000, s 94(4)(c).
32. Although a planning authority may have had discretion the record shows that no planning authority ever exercised the discretion which it might have had by failing to impose social and affordable housing conditions in any grants of permission for residential development or mixed residential development unless those areas were expressly excluded.

**[6.49]** Effectively, a grant of permission which is affected by Pt V must be subject to either a condition under s 96(2) requiring an agreement to be entered into regarding the reservation of land, houses or sites, or, exceptionally, a condition requiring the payment of money in lieu of the reservation of land, houses or sites.

**[6.50]** PDA 2000 offered and still offers three types of conditions which the planning authority may impose by way of agreement between the authority and the developer, namely:

(A) The transfer of ownership of land which is subject to an application for permission to develop residential property specified in the agreement from the developer to the planning authority for the provision of social and affordable housing.[33]

(B) Instead of transferring land, the developer may build and transfer completed houses to the authority or to persons nominated by the authority. The number and description of the houses will be specified in the agreement and they will be transferred at a price determined on the basis of site cost of the houses, calculated at the existing use value and the building and development costs, including profit as agreed between both parties. The houses to be transferred must be located on the developer's site in respect of which an application for permission has been made.[34]

(C) Alternatively, the developer may transfer fully or partially serviced sites to the local authority or its nominee. The number of sites will be specified in the agreement and the developer is entitled, 'to be paid attributable development costs as agreed between the Authority and the Developer to include the site costs calculated at existing use value and the development costs, including profit, as agreed between both parties.' The sites to be transferred must be located on the developer's site in respect of which an application for permission has been made.

The PD(A)A 2002 does not in any way undermine the principle of a housing strategy and the purpose of the PD(A)A 2002 is to ensure the delivery of social and affordable housing in a less bureaucratic way by providing new options for developers as to how they can comply with social and affordable housing conditions.

**[6.51]** The existing options listed at (A), (B) and (C) above were not altered. The PD(A)A of 2002, s 3(3)(a) makes it absolutely clear that the planning authority may still enter into an agreement with an applicant for housing permission to reserve land within the proposed development for the local authority or to provide houses or sites within that development. The percentages to be transferred depend on the housing strategy of the local authority. 20% is a common figure which cannot be exceeded but, in Fingal County Council, for example, some areas are zoned for 14%, others for 7% and others may not be zoned for any percentage. The PD(A)A 2002 preserves the right of an

---

33. PDA 2000, s 96(2) and (3) as substituted by PD(A)A 2002, s 3.
34. PDA 2000, s 96(2) and (3) as substituted by PD(A)A 2002, s 3.

applicant to enter into an agreement under sub-para 3(a) as a matter of right, namely the transfer of land within the site only, and no applicant can be forced to adopt the alternatives which are offered by the PD(A)A of 2002. The probability is that it would be in the interests of the developer to use the new alternatives in finalising an agreement with the planning authority.

**[6.52]** The PD(A)A 2002 offers additional options to the options listed at (A), (B) and (C) above, namely as follows:

(i) the building or transfer, on completion, to the ownership of the planning authority, or to the ownership of persons nominated by the authority in accordance with this Part, of houses on the land which is subject to the application for permission of such number and description as may be specified in the agreement,[35]

(ii) the transfer of such number of fully or partially serviced sites on the land which is subject to the application for permission as the agreement may specify to the ownership of the planning authority, or to the ownership or persons nominated by the planning authority in accordance with this Part,[36]

(iii) the transfer to the planning authority of the ownership of any other land within the functional area of the planning authority,[37]

(iv) the building and transfer, on completion, to the ownership of the planning authority, or to the ownership of persons nominated by the authority in accordance with this Part, of houses on land to which sub-paragraph (iii) applies of such number and description as may be specified in the agreement.

(v) the transfer of such number of fully or partially serviced sites on land to which sub-paragraph (iii) applies as the agreement may specify to the ownership of the planning authority, or to the ownership of persons nominated by the authority in accordance with this part,

(vi) a payment of such an amount as specified in the agreement to the planning authority,[38]

(via) One of the following –

(I) The entry into a rental accommodation availability agreement (which term shall, in this section, have the meaning given to it by s 2 of the Housing (Miscellaneous Provisions) Act 2009 with the planning authority under Part 2 of that Act, in respect of, or

(II) A grant of a lease to the planning authority of,

houses on the land which is subject to the application for permission, or other land within the functional area of the planning authority or such number and description as may be specified.[39]

---

35. PDA 2000, s 96(3)(b)(i) as amended by PD(A)A 2002, s 3.
36. PDA 2000, s 96(3)(b)(ii) as amended by PD(A)A 2002, s 3.
37. PDA 2000, s 96(3)(b)(iii) as amended by PD(A)A 2002, s 3.
38. PDA 2000, s 96(3)(b)(vi) as amended by PD(A)A2002, s 3.
39. Subsection (3)(b)(vi)(a) is inserted by PD(A)A 2010, s 38(a)(i).

(vii) a combination of a transfer of land referred to in paragraph (a) (but involving a lesser amount of such land if the agreement solely provided for a transfer under that paragraph) and the doing of one or more of the things referred to the preceding paragraphs,[40]

(viii) a combination of the doing of two or more of the things referred to in sub-paragraphs (i) to (vi)(a)

but, subject, in every case, to the provision that is made under this paragraph resulting in the aggregate monetary value of the property or amounts or both, as the case may be, transferred or paid by virtue of the agreement being equivalent to the monetary value of the land that the planning authority would receive if the agreement solely provided for the transfer of land under paragraph (a),[41]

In effect, this means that if any of these alternative options are used, the value of the property or amounts of money paid under the agreement must be equivalent and never greater than the value of the land that the planning authority would have received if the agreement solely provided for a transfer of land within the site, the subject matter of the planning permission, and it must be equivalent to the percentage specified in the relevant local authority's housing strategy.[42]

**[6.53]** If one of these new alternative agreements is finalised, as envisaged by PD(A)A 2002, there are a number of considerations which must be addressed by the local authority before completing the agreement, to include the following:

(i) Does the proposed agreement contribute effectively and efficiently to the achievement of the objectives of the housing strategy?

(ii) Will the agreement constitute the best use of the resources available to the local authority to ensure an adequate supply of housing and what are the financial implications of the agreement for the local authority's functions as a housing authority?

(iii) Will the agreement address the need to counteract the undue segregation of housing between persons of different social backgrounds in the area of the authority?

(iv) The terms of the agreement must be in accordance with the provisions of the local authority development plan.

(v) The timing of delivery of the social and/or affordable housing.[43]

**[6.54]** PDA 2000, s 96(2), as amended,[44] uses the word 'condition' which implies that a grant of permission will be subject to a planning condition. Although it is described as a 'condition' it is not a planning condition in the same sense of a planning condition

---

40. PDA 2000, s 96(3)(b)(vii) as amended by PD(A)A 2002, s 3.
41. PDA 2000, s 96(3)(b)(viii) as amended by PD(A)A 2002, s 3.
42. PDA 2000, s 96(3)(b).
43. See PDA 2000, s 96(3)(c)(i) to (v) inclusive as amended by PD(A)A 2002, s 3.
44. See PD(A)A 2002, s 3 which came into force on 24 December 2002.

imposed under the provisions of PDA 2000, s 34(1) or 34(14). The amended subsection provides that a planning authority 'shall,' as opposed to 'may,' require a condition that the applicant for permission shall enter into an agreement for the provision of social and/or affordable housing. The obligation on the planning authority is mandatory and the planning authority must include a condition to be imposed on the applicant requiring the applicant to enter into an agreement for social and affordable housing where the application is a residential application. If the planning authority does not do so the permission granted would be invalid.[45] The condition compelling the applicant to enter into an agreement is mandatory but the agreement itself is just that and as such there is always scope for disagreement. Those disagreements may be referred to An Bord Pleanála (dealing with disputes as to the terms of the housing strategy and disputes concerning the nature of the applicant's proposals), to the property arbitrator (dealing with matters related to valuation) or to the courts by way of judicial review, depending on the nature of the disagreement between the planning authority and the applicant.

**[6.55]** Pre-planning consultations under the provisions of PDA 2000, s 247 are strongly recommended and appendix A of the publication entitled *'Planning Applications and Part V of the Planning and Development Act 2000–2006 Implementation Issues'* published by the Department of the Environment, Heritage and Local Government advises as follows:

> 1. The purpose of engaging in pre-planning consultation[46] is to improve the quality of a planning application and any subsequent application, to avoid the necessity for seeking additional information where possible and in some cases, to spare the costs of what is likely to prove an abortive application.
> 
> While the pre-planning phase is not a statutory requirement for applicants, applicants and planning authorities are strongly advised to engage in pre-planning consultation. The extent of the pre-planning stage consultation will vary depending on:
> 
> - Size and complexity of the development;
> - Location of the development;
> - Staff resources available to the planning authority and the applicant.
> 
> The local authority's planning and housing functions should be represented at pre-planning meetings with applicants for planning permission which are subject to Part V. There may be a need for further meetings with housing staff to ascertain more detailed requirements and to ensure that the Part V proposal is appropriate in terms of the authority's housing strategy.

An agreement in principle should normally be reached prior to the submission of a planning application.[47] on the measures necessary to comply with Part V.

---

45. This point does not appear to have been decided by the courts but it is difficult to see how a court could avoid declaring a permission invalid in those circumstances.
46. See PDA 2000, s 247.
47. Regulatory function of planning authority in relation to consideration of the planning application is not affected by this agreement.

## Housing Supply – Social and Affordable Housing [6.55]

The Department's circular[48] in advising that details of the applicant's Part V proposal should be submitted with the planning application.[49] The Department's recommendation is as follows:

2. When submitting a planning application for the development of homes on lands subject to Part V, an applicant must specify the manner in which they intend to comply with the Part V condition. This requires the applicant to indicate which of the options set out in Section 96(3)(a) or Section 96(3)(b) it is proposed to use to achieve compliance with Part V. Submission of the agreement in principle reached, if any, and provided it clearly specifies the manner of compliance with Part V will be sufficient to comply with this requirement.

If the applicant has not specified how they intend to comply with Part V the planning application should be considered invalid and the applicant notified accordingly.

Where the option proposed is land on-site or off-site, this should be clearly identified on an accompanying separate map. Where units or sites are proposed on-site or off-site, the applicant must indicate in writing either the number of units, including types and sizes, to be transferred, or the number of sites. In all instances the applicant must indicate the location within the application lands or off-site lands as appropriate.

In selecting an option the applicant shall have regard to the planning authority's requirement to consider the proposal under Section 96(3)(c) and, in that context, to have regard to its Housing Strategy and other matters.

3. Assessment of Part V Proposals

As soon as a planning application which is subject to Part V has been validated by the Planning Department, a copy should be sent to the Housing Department for assessment of the Part V proposal as set out in Section 96(3)(a)/S 96(3)(b)/ S 96(3)(c).

Planning Authorities should establish internal procedures for ensuring the planning applications affected by Part V are circulated to the Housing Section as soon as possible in order to ensure that its assessment of the proposal is available in writing to the Planning Department in time for the relevant planner to address the issue in his/her report. If clarification on some points is required, the Housing Department should liaise directly with the developer on these points or spell out in its assessment precisely what further information is required so that this may be sought under Article 33 of the Planning and Development Regulations 2001.

4. Proposals to transfer land on-site (Section 96(3)(a) and Section 96(3)(g))

Satisfactory Proposal – Planning Condition.

Where a proposal is made for the transfer of land within the application site, the Housing Department should assess the proposal as to whether it is in accordance with the agreement in principle reached prior to the submission of the planning

---

48. See Planning Applications and Part V of the Planning and Development Acts 2000–2006 Implementation Issues (Appendix A).
49. See PDA 2000, s 96(4) as amended by PD(A)A 2002, s 3.

application. In those cases where no such agreement has been reached the planning authority must assess whether it meets the requirements of the housing strategy and is suitable for appropriate residential development. Where the proposal meets these requirements, the authority must accept this option and cannot compel the applicant to provide an alternative option. In this case, the Housing Department must submit an assessment to the Planning Department stating that the proposal is acceptable in terms of the housing strategy and is suitable for appropriate residential development. It should also set out the terms of the proposed agreement as precisely as possible, eg transfer of specific plot(s) at specific location(s), bearing in mind that there will probably be further negotiation necessary between the Housing Department and the developers to agree on the precise terms eg price.

The assessment from the Housing Department should form an integral part of matters to be considered by the relevant planner in making a recommendation on the planning application. Where it is decided to grant planning permission in such a case the relevant condition, as required under Section 96(2) should be worded to include the specific method of compliance and should require, that prior to the commencement of construction, the developer must enter into a written agreement with the authority, on the terms set out by the Housing Department, to transfer the specific land in question to the authority. A specific condition will ensure that there is clarity for the applicant and, any future owner of the site, regarding the manner of compliance with Part V.

The requirements of this sub-paragraph are also applicable to the alternative options set out in paragraph 6 below.

5. Consideration of Alternative Options – s 96(3)(b) and s 96(3)(c)

Where an alternative to the transfer of land on-site is proposed ie transfer of units (see also paragraph 10 below) sites, off-site provision, financial payment, etc, the planning authority must consider whether the proposal would:

- contribute effectively and efficiently to achieving the objectives of the housing strategy;
- represent the best uses of its resources;
- counteract undue segregation in housing between persons of different social backgrounds in the area of the authority;
- be in accordance with the provisions of the Development Plan; and
- deliver the social and affordable housing in a timely manner.

The Housing Department should speedily assess the proposal having regard to the above criteria.

6. Alternative options: Satisfactory Proposal.

> If the proposal is acceptable, the Housing Department's assessment back to the Planning Department must set out how the proposal meets the five criteria in Section 96(3)(c) and must set out the terms of the proposed agreement as precisely as possible (eg transfer of x no. specified units), again bearing in mind that there will probably be further consultation on specific terms, eg unit price.

## 7. Proposals to transfer land on-site: Unsatisfactory Proposal

Where the Housing Department consider that the proposed land transfer does not meet the requirements of the housing strategy and/or is not suitable for appropriate residential development, it should consult with the Planning Department as to how to proceed. There are a number of options available.

(a) Invite the submission of revised plans under Article 34 of the Planning and Development Regulations 2001, which identify the land it is proposed to transfer, subject, where necessary, to extending the period for taking a decision on the application, or

(b) Seek further information from the applicant under Article 33 of the Planning and Development Regulations 2001 how it is proposed to meet the requirements; the applicant should consult with the applicant with the Housing Department in that regard.

It should be noted that revised plans or further information may need to be re-publicised under Article 35 of the Planning and Development Regulations 2001 should they contain significant additional information.

Where further information is requested and not submitted within the statutory time limit, the application is deemed withdrawn, in accordance with the provisions of the Planning and Development Regulations 2001.

Where an acceptable Pt V proposal is received by way of revised plans or further information (having been assessed in accordance with paragraphs 3 and 5 above) the appropriate condition should be attached to the planning permission as set out in paragraphs 4 or 6 above.

(c) Condition compliance with Part V by means of the default proposal in Section 96(3)(a), namely the transfer of up to 20% of the application land as required in accordance with the housing strategy. The precise location of the land to be transferred should be identified in the planning decision.

## 8. Alternative Proposals: Unsatisfactory proposal

Where the Housing Department consider that the proposed Part V option does not meet all five criteria as set out in Section 96(3)(c) it should consult immediately with the Planning Department as to how to proceed. As in the case of paragraph 7 above the following options are available:

(a) Invite the submission of revised plans.

(b) Seek further information from the applicant under Article 33 on how it is proposed to meet the five criteria set out in Section 96(3). The applicant should consult with the Housing Department regarding the criteria to be met and to discuss/supply details on land to be transferred to the authority in the event that the transfer of land is ultimately conditioned, due to the applicant being unable to satisfy the authority as to compliance with Section 96(3)(c).

The comments made under paragraph 7 above about re-publication of significant further information and withdrawal of the planning application where further information is not received within the statutory deadline also apply here.

Again, where an acceptable Part V proposal is received by way of revised plans or further information (having been assessed in accordance with paragraphs 3 and 5 above) the appropriate condition should be attached to the planning permission as set out in paragraphs 4 or 6 above.

(c) Condition compliance with Part V by means of the default proposal in Section 93(3) (a), namely the transfer of up to 20% of the application land as required in accordance with the Housing Strategy. The precise location of the land to be transferred should be identified in the planning decision.

9. Reaching Agreement

Section 96(2) requires that the applicant enter into an agreement in relation to Part V. The purpose of the agreement is to set out and finalise in a formal manner details of the option that has been conditioned by the planning permission.

As in the case of compliance submissions, the planning authority should ensure that details of the Part V agreement are dealt with in a prompt manner.

An assessment of the proposal under Section 96(3)(h) should be undertaken by the planning authority at the time the agreement is being entered into and it shall consider:

- The proper planning and sustainable development of the area;
- The Housing Strategy and the relevant Development Plan specific objectives;
- The overall coherence of the development; and
- The views of the applicant in relation to the impact of the agreement on the development

This assessment should be carried out irrespective of the option agreed. The manager's order approving the agreement being entered into should record the fact that the planning authority has considered these matters. The agreement should be written and signed by both parties.

10. Part V Agreements – Transfer of Units

Where an alternative option other than land on-site is proposed to satisfy a Part V agreement, eg transfer of units, the planning authority is obliged to consider the applicant's proposal in accordance with Section 96(3)(c). In addition, the alternative option proposed must achieve equivalent monetary value, the requirements of which are set out in Section 96(3)(b).

The requirements in relation to achieving equivalent monetary value provide some flexibility to ensure that practical and timely agreements can be reached in the context of the various criteria set out in Section 96(3)(c). Irrespective of the methodology used for compliance with Part V, the ultimate objective must be to ensure that a reasonable practical agreement is reached.

Equivalent monetary value can be achieved through acceptance of a percentage of the total units on-site based on the percentage unit requirement in the relevant housing strategy. In addition, the appropriate size of the units should be such as would reflect typical social homes or affordable homes in terms of starter home sizes.

Where transfer of units is proposed by a developer for compliance with Part V as outlined above, it is strongly recommended that planning authorities accept the unit's basis for compliance, wherever possible.

11. Calculation of Price for Units Transferred On-Site

Where units are transferred on-site in accordance with an agreement under Section 96(3)(b), the unit price must be calculated as set out in Section 96(3)(d). This is determined on the basis of the site cost (at existing use value) plus construction and attributable costs as agreed between the applicant and the planning authority, including profit on costs.

The local authority's housing strategy specifies an estimate of the amount of social and affordable housing required in an area of the development plan during the period of that development plan and the estimates may state the different requirements for different areas within the area of the development plan. The agreement, in order to comply with the estimate provided in the housing strategy, must ensure that the actual estimate of the amount of social and affordable housing required for the area during that period of the development plan will, in fact, be achieved as a consequence of the agreement.

[6.56] It is clear that the decision as to whether or not to allow the new options offered by the Amendment Act 2002 to developers is to be made entirely at the discretion of the local authority because new options can only be incorporated in an agreement with the developer where the planning authority is satisfied that items (i) to (v)[50] above have been complied with. At the time when the 2002 Amendment Act was passed the then Minister for Environment, Martin Cullen TD stated:

> Alternatively the Developer could make a payment to the Local Authority which will be used for the provision of Social and Affordable Housing. However, I intend to convey to the Local Authorities my view that financial compensation to Authorities, while an option, is the final option. All other aspects will have to be exhausted.

[6.57] In *Glenkerrin Homes v Dun Laoghaire Rathdown County Council*,[51] Clarke J noted that the housing strategy could specify a preference for certain types of agreement. Commenting on this Clarke J stated:

> that policy appears to have been in favour of obtaining units rather than land or money. The stated reason for that policy, which appears to me to be entirely reasonable, was that having regard to the needs of Dun Laoghaire Rathdown in respect of both social and affordable housing and having regard to the limited developable land available, those needs and obligations were more readily met by purchasing (at the beneficial price provided for in the legislation) units in each development.[52]

---

50. Items (i) to (v) are listed at para **6.53**.
51. *Glenkerrin Homes v Dun Laoghaire Rathdown County Council* (unreported, 26 April 2007) HC, Clarke J.
52. *Glenkerrin Homes v Dun Laoghaire Rathdown County Council* (unreported, 26 April 2007) HC, Clarke J.

An agreement entered into pursuant to a social and affordable housing Pt V condition cannot be separately enforced. Such agreement can only be enforced if enforcement proceedings are taken in relation to a breach of condition in the planning permission. The effect of this is that if a developer does not proceed with the development committed by the planning permission the Pt V agreement cannot be implemented separately. If a developer proceeds with his development without an agreement with the local authority in accordance with the Pt V condition an enforcement action may be taken against him by the planning authority in the same way as an enforcement action can be taken for breach of any planning condition.

**[6.58]** There are occasions when the parties (developer and planning authority) drift apart in their negotiations to finalise a Pt V agreement but even though a planning authority may drag its feet in a negotiation to conclude an agreement this does not entitle the developer to commence the development.

**[6.59]** PDA 2000, s 96(3)(d), as amended,[53] reads:

> (d) Where houses or sites are to be transferred to the planning authority in accordance with an agreement under paragraph (b), the price of such houses or sites shall be determined on the basis of –
>
> > (i) The site cost of the houses or the cost of the sites (calculated in accordance with subsection (6)), and
> >
> > (ii) The building and attributable development costs as agreed between the authority and the developer, including profit on the costs.

In commenting on the provisions of s 93(3)(d) Fintan Valentine BL[54] makes the following observation:

> If one accepts that a 'price' is indeed to be paid by a planning authority for houses or serviced sites transferred on foot of a Part V agreement, a further ambiguity arises as to how that price is to be calculated. Section 96(3)(d) states that the 'price' shall be determined on the basis of
>
> > (i) The site cost of the houses or the cost of sites (calculated in accordance with subsection (6) and
> >
> > (ii) The building and attributable development costs as agreed between the authority and the developer, including profit on costs.
>
> The cross reference to subsection (6) is potentially problematic as s 96(6)(b) requires the cost of the house or site to be calculated by 'reference to its existing use on the date of the transfer of ownership.' In the case of built houses, the development will, by definition, have already taken place on the date of transfer and, on the basis of the wording of s 96(6)(b), this existing development will have to be taken into account in assessing the cost. In effect, this would mean that the planning authority pays open market value for the transferred house and achieves

---

53. See PD(Amendment) Act 2002, s 3.
54. Fintan Valentine BL speaking at intensive course on planning law 8/9 December 2008.

no planning gain. Whether such a result was intended by the legislature is extremely doubtful.

A new sub-clause has been inserted in PDA 2000, s 96(3) which reads as follows:

>  (da) Where a planning authority proposes to enter into a rental accommodation availability agreement or to take a lease in accordance with an agreement under paragraph (b), then, to the extent as may be appropriate the payment to be made, or the rent payable by the planning authority as the case may be shall not be reduced (without prejudice to any other relevant discount or allowance) but such amount as may be agreed or in default of agreement as may be prescribed by the Minister as takes account of the obligations imposed by this section and in particular the attribution to the site cost of the houses of a value calculated in accordance with subsection (6).[55]

**[6.60]** PDA 2000, s 96(3)(e) reads:

> Where an agreement provides for the transfer of land, houses or sites, the houses or sites or land, whether in one or more part shall be identified in the agreement.

**[6.61]** PDA 2000, s 96(3)(f) reads:

> (f) In so far as it is known at the time of the agreement, the planning authority shall indicate to the applicant its intention in relation to the provision of housing, including a description of the proposed houses, on the land or sites to be transferred in accordance with paragraph (a) or (b).

**[6.62]** PDA 2000, s 96(3)(g) reads:

> (g) Nothing in this subsection shall be construed as requiring the applicant or any other person (other than the planning authority) to enter into an agreement under paragraph (b) instead of an agreement under paragraph (a).

This provision makes it clear that the transfer of undeveloped land is the only one of the options that a developer can be compelled to accept. If a developer insists on the transfer of land option the local authority must accept that option. The remaining options, to include transfer of built houses or transfer of service sites, must be negotiated if they are to be agreed. The transfer of undeveloped land is the default option.

**[6.63]** The provisions of PDA 2000, s 96(3)(h)(i) to (iv) inclusive read as follows:

> (h) for the purposes of an agreement under this section, the planning authority shall consider–
>
> > (i) the proper planning and sustainable development of the area to which the application relates,
> >
> > (ii) the housing strategy and the specific objectives of the development plan which relate to the implementation of the strategy,
> >
> > (iii) the need to ensure the overall coherence of the development to which the application relates, where appropriate and

---

55. Subsection (3)(da) as inserted by PD(A)A 2010, s 38(a)(iii).

**[6.64]**   *Planning and Environmental Law in Ireland*

(iv) the views of the applicant in relation to the impact of the agreement on the development.

**[6.64]** PDA 2000, s 96(3)(i) reads as follows:

(i) Government guidelines on public procurement shall not apply to an agreement made under paragraph (a) or (b) except in the case of an agreement which is subject to the requirement of Council Directive No 93/37/EEC on the co-ordination of procedures relating to the award of Public Works Contracts and any directive amending or replacing that directive.

**[6.65]** PDA 2000, s 96(3)(g) is referred to as 'the default provision'. In *Glenkerrin Homes v Dun Laoghaire Rathdown County Council*,[56] the developer had completed the development of the entire site without ever having agreed an option with the planning authority as to how it would comply with Pt V. In effect, the default option was no longer possible and in those circumstances Clarke J ruled that since the default option of the transfer of undeveloped land was no longer available the local authority could impose another option. Glenkerrin Homes had, by its own actions, placed itself in a position where its only means of complying with its Pt V obligations was to provide developed units or cash. In the event, Glenkerrin Homes was required to transfer built houses to the planning authority to satisfy its Pt V obligations.

**[6.66]** Before having that option imposed upon it, Glenkerrin Homes had applied to the local authority, seeking letters of compliance which the planning authority, not unnaturally, refused to issue on the basis that Glenkerrin had not satisfied its social and affordable housing obligations. The developer's argument was that it could not be bound to comply with any decision directing one of the alternative means to be used. Glenkerrin made the case that it was entitled to a condition containing the default option even though that option could not be fulfilled. As author of its own misfortune, Glenkerrin had gone out on a limb and Clarke J ruled that the company could be forced to accept whatever alternative option remained to meet its Pt V obligations. The learned judge accepted that the local authority was within its rights to withhold issuing letters of compliance for the relevant percentage of the completed units when no agreement had been reached.

**[6.67]** Where the default provision is insisted upon and an agreement is entered into between the developer and the local authority, the transaction is relatively straightforward in that the relevant percentage of land in its undeveloped condition is transferred to the planning authority. In that case, PDA 2000, s 96(6)(b) (as amended) provides that the compensation payable by the local authority for the transfer of the land is calculated on the basis of a sum equal to the value of the land by reference to its existing use on the date of the transfer of ownership of the land to the planning authority concerned, without taking into account any development potential or benefit of planning permission granted in relation to the land other than exempted development. It goes without saying that existing use value of the land would be a fraction of the open market value of the land.

---

56. *Cork County Council v Shackleton and Murphy Construction (Carrigtwohill) Ltd/Dun Laoghaire Rathdown County Council v Glenkerrin Homes* [2007] IEHC 241, Clarke J.

**[6.68]** In *Cork County Council v Shackleton/Dun Laoghaire Rathdown County Council v Glenkerrin Homes*,[57] Clarke J dealt with the interpretation of an 'equivalent monetary value' in Pt V. The interpretation of 'equivalent monetary value' in Pt V was the main issue in both the *Cork* and *Dun Laoghaire* cases. The learned judge's judgment was delivered in both cases on the same date. In both cases it was agreed that the appropriate means for each developer to meet its Pt V obligations was by the provision of completed housing units. In the *Cork* case, Clarke J rejected the method of calculation put forward by Glenkerrin Homes. Glenkerrin Homes said that the correct approach was to calculate the planning gain which is the difference between the development value of 20% of the land less existing use value and to divide that figure by the sum of the average planning gain *per* site plus site costs and construction costs. If the developer had been successful in that argument it would have meant that a small number of units (between 6% and 7%) would be transferred to the local authority free of charge or almost free of charge. In each case the local authorities argued that the number of units to be transferred should be 20% of the total in return for a monetary payment. The monetary payment is made up of the site costs of the unit and the building and development costs including an element of profit on those costs. Clarke J had this to say:

> The only means by which the local authority can obtain an equivalent monetary benefit (as required by the proviso) is if the total value of the sites attributable to the built housing units transferred, represents 20% of the planning gain. The reason why this is so stems from the fact that the payment of what I have described as the building costs is neutral. The price at which built housing units must be transferred is required, by subsection 3(d), to be as defined in that subsection.[58]

Noreen Gilheany, solicitor,[59] summarises Clarke J's main findings as follows:

> 1. If any of the alternative arrangements were agreed to be used, then the benefit of such agreements must be equal to the relevant percentage of the planning gain. Justice Clarke explained that a planning gain refers to the open market value of the sites less the existing use value (the pre-development value of the site as though the planning permission had not been granted.)
>
> 2. The approach favoured by Mr Justice Clarke essentially involves calculating the net planning gain per site and then calculating the total number of units to be transferred (for which the Local Authority makes a payment to the developer) by dividing the total planning gain of the development by the net planning gain per site.
>
> 3. The building cost element should be neutral as the general intention of the legislation is that the outcome of any alternative agreement should be the same as if the Local Authority had taken the land under the default provisions and then built the units themselves.

---

57. *Cork County Council v Shackleton and Murphy Construction (Carrigtwohill) Ltd/Dun Laoghaire Rathdown County Council v Glenkerrin Homes* [2007] IEHC 241, Clarke J.
58. *Cork County Council v Shackleton and in Dun Laoghaire Rathdown County Council v Glenkerrin Homes* [2007] IEHC 241 (unreported, 19 July 2007), Clarke J.
59. Ms Gilheany is a solicitor with McCann Fitzgerald Solicitors, Commercial Property Department and the extract quoted is taken, with her kind permission, from an article appearing in Housing Times Volume 12 Issue 1 Spring 2008.

**[6.69]** **Planning and Environmental Law in Ireland**

    4. The relevant dates for valuing the built units is the date that they are to be transferred to the Local Authority with the site being valued as though the development had not yet taken place.

    5. Justice Clarke acknowledged that this approach does not remove all difficulties:

       5.1    The first complication arises where the sites upon which the housing units are built are not identical. The planning gain to be derived from the sites into which the development as a whole is divided may not be the same in each case. In such case the total number of units transferred must be such that the aggregate planning gain attributable to the total of the sites concerned is equal to 20% of the planning gain of the whole development.

       5.2    Where sites are not homogenous, Justice Clarke advised that the property arbitrator must do the best he can (having regard to the type of units required by the Local Authority) to identify a set of housing units for transfer where the aggregate of the planning gain attributable to the site upon which each of those units have been built approximates to 20% of the total planning gain of the development as a whole subject only to a balancing payment.

       5.3    Justice Clarke acknowledged that the legislative reference to a site value in the context of apartments is particularly problematic as obviously a number of apartments may be said to occupy the same site. Justice Clarke felt that the best approach is to divide the entirety of the site occupied by a block of apartments, by a number of apartments in that block, weighted to the size of such apartments. One interesting point to note in this regard is that Justice Clarke felt that this calculation should be carried out not by reference to the value of the units but by reference to the size of the sites upon which such units are built. It would seem therefore that there is nothing preventing a developer of a development containing some standard units and some hi-spec luxury units (with a much higher open market value), from reaching an agreement to transfer the relevant number of standard units to the authority with no right for the local authority to insist on receiving the hi-spec units. While Justice Clarke had rejected Dun Laoghaire/Rathdown's approach of a floor space calculation, it is obvious that floor space is still relevant in the case of apartments.

In summary, Clarke J's judgment in relation to the number of units to be transferred in response to a developer's Pt V obligations to the planning authority can be achieved by transferring 20% of the total units or sites to the planning authority for the purposes of social and affordable housing.

**[6.69]** When making a planning application, the applicant must specify the manner in which he or she proposes to comply with social and affordable housing conditions if they are to be imposed. Should the planning authority grant permission for the development, it must have regard to any such proposal.[60]

**[6.70]** In order to prevent delay in the granting of planning permission, it is important for an applicant to ensure that a full proposal, as to how he or she would comply with a

---

60.    PDA 2000, s 96(4) as amended by PD(A)A 2002, s 3.

condition requiring the transfer of land for social and affordable housing, is dealt with in a comprehensive manner.

**[6.71]** If any dispute arises as to any aspect of the agreement it may be referred by any party to the agreement (including the planning authority) to An Bord Pleanála,[61] but this does not apply to:

(a) A dispute regarding an agreement for the construction of housing units for the local authority and the transfer of sites with completed houses nor to the transfer of fully or partially serviced sites to the local authority. (The dispute must relate to an agreement to transfer the ownership of land.)

(b) A dispute as to the level of compensation payable.

(c) A dispute as to the sum payable to the authority paid under s 96(12) which provides, in exceptional circumstances, for a payment to the planning authority of an amount equivalent in value to the value of the land which was to be transferred.

The disputes referred to at (a), (b) and (c) are matters to be resolved by the property arbitrator.[62]

**[6.72]** Although the payment of a cash sum is the least preferred option from the point of view of a planning authority it is nevertheless an option which may, in certain circumstances, be the best option for both parties. In effect, the cash sum must be equivalent to the monetary value of 20% of the land which the planning authority would have received under the default provision. In *Cork County Council v John Shackleton & Murphy Construction (Carrigtwohill) Limited*,[63] Clarke J gave this example by way of illustrating the calculation:[64]

> 6.6 'Consider two separate cases, where in one case, the land under development already has a reasonably beneficial existing use, so that its existing use value is €250,000 per acre. In the alternative case the existing

---

61. PDA 2000, s 96(5) as amended by PD(A)A 2002, s 3.
62. The property arbitrator is appointed under the Property Values (Arbitration and Appeals) Act 1960, s 2. In default of agreement the property arbitrator shall fix the following:
    (a) the number and price of houses (including site costs and building and development costs) to be transferred;
    (b) the number and price of sites (including site costs and development costs) to be transferred;
    (c) the number of houses and the amount to be paid, or rent payable therefor under a rental accommodation availability agreement or a lease under sub-s (3)(b)(VIa);
    (d) the sum payable to the planning authority under PDA 2000, s 96(12) where, in exceptional circumstances, a payment is required in lieu of transfer of land;
    (e) the allowance to be made in respect of the clawback of the profit by the seller of an affordable house.
63. *Cork County Council v Shackleton and Murphy Construction (Carrigtwohill) Ltd/Dun Laoghaire Rathdown County Council v Glenkerrin Homes* [2007] IEHC 241 (unreported, 19 July 2007), Clarke J.
64. From the judgment of Clarke J in *Cork County Council v Shackleton/Dun Laoghaire Rathdown County Council v Glenkerrin Homes* [2007] IEHC 241 (unreported, 19 July 2007) at paras 6.6, 6.8. 6.9 and 6.10.

use value might be based on agricultural use or the like and might, as in the Cork case, be put at €25,000 per acre. I will also assume that, in both cases, the open market value of the land at the relevant date (of which more later) was €1 million per acre. In the first case, therefore, the planning gain is €750,000 per acre while in the second case it is €975,000 per acre. If I further assume that both developments are of five acres, then 20% of the planning gain will, in fact, be the planning gain from one acre and will thus be, respectively, €750,000 or €975,000. If the term 'monetary value' as applied to the land that the planning authority would receive under the default provision, is to be taken as the gross value of the land converted into money then it would, of course, be €1 million in both cases. If an alternative agreement for the payment of cash was to be applied, then a cash sum of €1 million would need, on that basis, to be paid. Apart from the fact that this would give the local authority, in either case, more cash than the value which they would obtain by receiving €1 million worth of land for either €25,000 or €250,000, it would also create an unjustifiable distinction between the two cases. The developer who held land with an existing use value of €250,000 would have to pay €250,000 more than the planning gain as a cash payment while the other developer, with an identically beneficial planning permission, would only have to pay €25,000 more than the planning gain.

6.7 This is not a construction which should find favour unless the clear wording of the Act compelled only such view to be taken. In my view the term monetary value is ambiguous as to whether it represents a gross value or a net value.

6.8 For the reasons which I have just set out it seems to me that to interpret monetary value as representing gross value would give rise to significant inequalities and absurdities in the construction of the section and, for those reasons, it seems to me that I should prefer the construction which defines monetary value as being the net benefit, converted into money where necessary, to be obtained by the local authority.

6.9 Having taken that view of the phrase 'monetary value' it seems to me that it would be wholly irrational to assume that the term 'aggregate monetary value' as used earlier in the same proviso could have a different meaning. It follows therefore, it seems to me, that both the terms 'aggregate monetary value' and 'monetary value' represents the net benefit, converted where appropriate into money, to the local authority concerned.

6.10 Viewed in that way the proviso simply requires that the net benefit of an alternative agreement should be the same as the net benefit of the default agreement. As the net benefit of the default agreement is the so called planning gain, then the proviso simply requires that the net benefit of any alternative agreement must be the same, in money or money terms, as the planning gain.'

## Compensation for land transferred to local authority

[6.73] PDA 2000, s 96(6), as amended, sets out the level of compensation payable where the ownership of land is transferred to the planning authority by the owner to be applied to social or affordable housing. If, instead of land transfer, houses or sites are transferred, the equivalent sites costs must also be calculated.

[6.74] The amount of the consideration which the planning authority must pay for land acquired pursuant to the social/affordable housing conditions depends on a number of circumstances.

[6.75] PDA 2000, s 96(6)(a)(i), as amended, provides that:

(I) land purchased by the applicant before 25 August 1999.

Where land was purchased by the applicant for permission before 25 August 1999 (the date on which the Planning and Development Bill was first published), or

(II) land purchased by the applicant pursuant to a legally enforceable agreement entered into before 25 August 1999, or in exercise of an option in writing to purchase the land granted or acquired before that date,

the price paid for the land, or the price agreed to be paid for the land pursuant to the agreement or option, together with such sum in respect of interest thereof (including, in circumstances where there is a mortgage on the land, interest paid in respect of the mortgage) as may be determined by the property arbitrator.

PDA 2000, s 96(6)(a)(ii), as amended, provides:

(ii) In the case of land the ownership of which was acquired by the applicant by way of a gift or inheritance taken (within the meaning of the Capital Acquisitions Tax Act 1976) before 25 August 1999, a sum equal to the market value of the land on the valuation date (within the meaning of that Act) estimated in accordance with s 15 of that Act,

PDA 2000, s 96(6)(a)(iii), as amended, provides that in the case of:

(I) land purchased before 25 August 1999, or

(II) land purchased pursuant to a legally enforceable agreement to purchase the land entered into before that date, or in exercise of an option, in writing, to purchase the land granted or acquired before that date, (where the applicant for permission is a mortgagee in possession of the land) the price paid for the land, or the price agreed to be paid for the land pursuant to the agreement or option, together with such sum in respect of interest thereon calculated from that date (including any interest accruing and not paid in respect of the mortgage) as may be determined by the property arbitrator.

Or

PDA 2000, s 96(6)(b) reads:

(b) the value of the land calculated by reference to its existing use on the date of the transfer of ownership of the land to the planning authority concerned on the basis that on that date it would have been, and would thereafter have continued to be unlawful to carry out any development in relation to that land other than exempted development,

whichever is the greater.

**[6.76]** The statutory provisions under s 96 are somewhat indigestible. What follows is an attempt to explain the statutory provisions in a more understandable way.

(a) *Land purchased by applicant prior to 25 August 1999*

Where the land was purchased by the applicant for permission before 25 August 1999 (the date on which the Planning and Development Bill was first published), or land was purchased pursuant to a legally enforceable agreement entered into before 25 August 1999 or having exercised an option to purchase in writing made before that date then, the compensation to be paid by the local authority is the price which the applicant paid for the land or, in the case of an option to purchase, the price which the purchaser agreed to pay for the land together with a sum in respect of interest (including interest on any mortgage on the land) as may be determined by the property arbitrator. Where there is a mortgage on the land the calculation of interest includes an amount in respect of interest actually paid by the applicant on that mortgage. No account is taken of any improvements which may have been carried out, or costs of insurance, maintenance of security or any other expenses incurred by the applicant during their period of ownership. It is, however, certain that a higher level of compensation will be payable in pre-25 August 1999 cases than in other cases where the compensation is calculated with regard to 'existing use value'.

(b) *Gifts and inheritances*

Where an applicant acquired land by gift or inheritance before 25 August 1999 the planning authority is required to pay the applicant a sum which is the equivalent to the market value of the land on the valuation date as estimated for the purposes of capital acquisitions tax under the Capital Acquisitions Tax Act 1976, s 25.

Section 15(1) of the Capital Acquisitions Tax Act 1976 provides:

> that the market value of any property for the purposes of this Act shall be estimated to be the price which, in the opinion of the Commissioners, such property would fetch if sold in the open market on the date on which the property is to be valued, in such manner and subject to such conditions as might reasonably be calculated to obtain for the vendor the best price for the property.

The date on which the property is to be valued as a taxable gift is the date of the gift, and the valuation date of a taxable inheritance is the date of death of the deceased person.

(c) *Mortgagee in possession*

Where a mortgagee in possession applies for planning permission in respect of land purchased before 25 August 1999 (or purchased pursuant to a legally enforceable contract entered into before that date, or in exercise of an option in writing to purchase the land, granted before that date), then the price paid for the land together with such sum in respect of interest thereon (including any interest accruing and not paid in respect of the mortgage), calculated from 25 August 1999 will be the amount of the consideration to be paid.

(d) *In any other case – existing use value*

The compensation to be paid to the owner of land must be calculated on the basis of the land's existing (ie, current use) value at the date the ownership was transferred to the planning authority. In calculating existing use value it must be assumed that no development can be lawfully carried out on the land, now or in the future, other than exempted development. Clearly the words used are intended to remove any argument which might include 'hope value' in the calculation. In many cases of residential development the existing use value would have been agricultural and that would therefore be the basis on which the value is assessed. Where the value, calculated in accordance with para (d), is greater than that calculated pursuant to (a), (b) and (c), then the applicant is entitled to the larger amount. That would be most unusual.

In effect the provisions dealing with the consideration to be paid by the planning authority to the developer have not been altered and the developer is entitled to the existing use value of the land or, if it was purchased (or if a contract or option was entered into) before 25 August 1999 the developer is entitled to the price paid for the land with interest thereon, whichever is the greater. A developer is still entitled to recover the building and attributable development costs in relation to full or partially serviced sites or for the provision of houses, whether provided on or off site together with an element of profit.

[6.77] PDA 2000, s 96(16) defines 'an owner' as:

(a) a person other than a mortgagee not in possession who is for the time being entitled to dispose (whether in possession or reversion) of the fee simple of the land, and

(b) a person who, under a lease, or agreement the unexpired term of which exceeds five years holds or is entitled to the rents or profits of the land.

[6.78] PDA 2000, s 96(7)(a), as amended,[65] provides that in default of agreement (and subject to PDA 2000, s 96(7)(b) below) a property arbitrator shall, in default of agreement, fix the following where appropriate:

(i) The number and price of houses (including site cost and building and development costs) to be transferred.

(ii) The number and price of sites (including site cost and development costs) to be transferred.

(iia) The number of houses, and the amount to be paid or rent payable therefore under a rental accommodation availability agreement or a lease under sub-s (3)(b)(via).[66]

(iii) The compensation payable by the authority to the owner of the land as specified under PDA 2000, s 96(6).

---

65. PDA 2000, s 96(7)(a)(iia) was inserted by PD(A)A 2010, s 38(b).
66. Subsection (7)(a)(iia) inserted by PD(A)A 2010, s 38(b).

(iv) The payment of an amount to the planning authority under s 96(3)(b)(vi), (vii) or (viii); and

(v) The allowance to be made under s 99(3)(d)(i).

**[6.79]** Section 99(3)(d) refers to the fact that due allowance shall be made for any material improvements made by the person to whom the house or land was sold.[67]

**[6.80]** PDA 2000, s 96(7)(b) deals with the payment of money in lieu of lands, sites or houses and reads as follows:

> For the purposes of paragraph (a), s 2(2) of the Acquisition of Land (Assessment of Compensation) Act 1919 shall not apply and the value of the land shall be calculated on the assumption that it was at that time and would remain unlawful to carry out any development in relation to the land other than exempted development.

**[6.81]** The property arbitrator is appointed under the Property Values (Arbitration and Appeals) Act 1960, s 2. Compensation is fixed in accordance with the Acquisition of Land (Assessment of Compensation) Act 1919 which provides that compensation is awarded on the basis of open market value. This, however, does not apply to compensation to be paid for land which is valued on the basis of its existing use value as at the date when the ownership where such land is transferred to the local authority. It will also be remembered that 'existing use' in this context assumes that no development can be lawfully carried out on the land now or in the future other than exempted development so that 'hope value' is ruled out.

**[6.82]** PDA 2000, s 96(7)(c) provides that s 187[68] shall apply to compensation payable under PDA 2000, s 96(6), and when compensation has been determined it may be recovered from the planning authority as a simple contract debt in any court of competent jurisdiction and all costs and expenses of the parties to the arbitration to determine the amount of compensation shall, insofar as costs and expenses are payable by the planning authority, be recoverable from the authority as a simple contract debt in any court of competent jurisdiction.

**[6.83]** PDA 2000, s 96(8) (as amended)[69] provides that where there is a dispute as to the terms of any agreement to be entered into under a social and/or affordable housing condition, which dispute is not resolved within eight weeks from the grant of permission, the planning authority, applicant or any other person with an interest in the land to which the application relates may:

(a) if the dispute relates to a matter falling within sub-s (5) refer the dispute under that subsection to the Board, or

---

67. This is the allowance to be made in respect of the clawback of profit by the seller of an affordable house.
68. PDA 2000, s 187 deals with recovery of compensation from the planning authority once it is ascertained by agreement or determined by arbitration in accordance with PDA 2000, Pt XII.
69. PDA 2000, s 96(8) is amended as shown in bold print by PD(A)A 2010, s 38(c).

(b) if the dispute relates to a matter falling within sub-s (7) refer the dispute under that subsection to the Property Arbitrator,

and the Board or the Property Arbitrator, as may be appropriate, shall determine the matter as soon as practicable.

**[6.84]** In *Glenkerrin Homes v DunLaoghaire Rathdown County Council*,[70] a dispute arose between the developer and the planning authority as to whether An Bord Pleanála or the property arbitrator had jurisdiction to determine which units were to be transferred by the developer to the planning authority. The planning authority and the developer could not agree on this point but the developer made the case that the dispute fell within the jurisdiction of the property arbitrator. The developer referred that matter to the property arbitrator. The planning authority's case was that An Bord Pleanála was the appropriate authority to identify which particular units were to be transferred to the planning authority.

**[6.85]** Clarke J held that the property arbitrator did have jurisdiction to identify which units should be transferred. Clarke J in the *Glenkerrin Homes* case finally determined the division of functions as between An Bord Pleanála and the property arbitrator.

**[6.86]** Garrett Simons SC spoke on the division of functions between An Bord Pleanála and the property arbitrator as follows:[71]

> The property arbitrator has jurisdiction over matters which entail valuation, ie the number and price of houses to be transferred; the number and price of sites to be transferred; or the amount of any monetary payment to be made. In cases where the method of compliance has been settled on as involving the transfer of built units, the property arbitrator also has an implicit jurisdiction to identify which particular units are to be transferred. An Bord Pleanála has jurisdiction over all other disputes, which will generally require the Board to exercise judgement on matters of planning policy.
>
> In at least some cases, it will be necessary to make a reference to each of An Bord Pleanála and the property arbitrator in turn. First, it will be necessary to make a reference to An Bord Pleanála in order that the principle of the agreement may be determined: for example, whether the developer is to transfer built houses to the planning authority. Thereafter, it may be necessary to make a subsequent reference to the property arbitrator in order that the details – for example in terms of the number and prices of built houses, can-be determined.
>
> An Bord Pleanála will determine disputes by reference principally to matters such as the terms of the housing strategy and the nature of the proposals submitted at the time of the application for planning permission.

Arbitrators are no longer able to refer questions of law to the courts even if requested to do so by one of the parties to the arbitration.

---

70. *Glenkerrin Homes v DunLaoghaire Rathdown County Council* [2007] IEHC 298.
71. Garrett Simons SC, Planning and Environmental Conference – November 2007.

**[6.87]** An arbitrator's award is subject to judicial review (other than s 50 judicial review).

**[6.88]** Arbitrators are now bound to give reasoned awards and the only way of obtaining recourse against an award is dealt with in Ch VII, art 34 of the UNCITRAL Model Law on International Commercial Arbitration which has been adopted almost worldwide and in particular by Ireland in Sch 1 of the Arbitration Act 2010. Chapter VII deals with recourse against award and art 34 sets out the ground rules for applications for setting aside as exclusive reports against arbitral award namely as follows:

> (1) Recourse to a court against an arbitral award may be made only by application for setting aside in accordance with paras (2) and (3) of this Article.
>
> (2) An arbitral award may be set aside by the court specified in art 6 only if:
>
>     (a) The party making the application furnishes proof that –
>
>         (i) A party to the arbitration agreement referred to in art 7 was under some incapacity; or the said agreement is not valid under the law to which the parties have subjected it or failing any indication thereon, under the law of this State; or
>
>         (ii) The party making the application was not given proper notice of the appointment of an arbitrator or of the arbitral proceedings or was otherwise unable to present his case; or
>
>         (iii) The award deals with a dispute not contemplated by or not falling within the terms of the submission to arbitration, or contains decisions on matters beyond the scope of the submission to arbitration, provided that, if the decisions on matters submitted to arbitration can be separated from those not so submitted, only that part of the award which contains decisions on matters not submitted to arbitration may be set aside; or
>
>     (b) The court finds that:
>
>         (i) The subject-matter of the dispute is not capable of settlement by arbitration under the law of this State; or
>
>         (ii) The award is in conflict with the public policy of this State;
>
>         (iii) An application for setting aside may not be made after three months have elapsed from the date on which the party making that application had received the award or, if a request had been made under art 33, from the date on which that request had been disposed of by the arbitral tribunal.
>
> (3) The court, when asked to set aside an award, may, where appropriate and so requested by a party, suspend the setting aside proceedings for a period of time determined by it in order to give the arbitral tribunal an opportunity to resume the arbitral proceedings or to take such other action as, in the arbitral tribunal's opinion will eliminate the grounds for setting aside.[72]

The courts are slow to usurp the functions of an arbitrator or indeed any other tribunal.

---

72. See Arbitration Act 2010, Ch VII, art 34.

[6.89] The options of the planning authority in relation to lands or sites transferred to it are provided for by PDA 2000, s 96(9). PDA 2000, s 96(9)(a) provides that where a planning authority acquires land or sites under a social and/or affordable housing condition it may:

(a) (i) provide, or arrange for the provision of houses on the land or sites for persons referred to in s 94(4)(a),

(ii) make land or sites available to those persons for the development of houses by them for their own occupation, or

(iii) make land or sites available to a body approved for the purposes of s 6 of the Housing (Miscellaneous Provisions) Act, 1992 for the provision of houses on the land for persons referred to in s 94(4)(a).

(b) Pending the provision of houses or sites in accordance with paragraph (a)(i), or the making available of land or sites in accordance with paragraph (a)(ii) or (iii), the planning authority shall maintain the land or sites in a manner which does not detract, and is not likely to detract, to a material degree from the amenity, character or appearance of land or houses in the neighbourhood of the land or sites.

[6.90] PDA 2000, s 96(10)(a) makes provision to enable houses or sites to be transferred directly by the developer to any nominee of the planning authority.

[6.91] PDA 2000, s 96(11) provides that if a planning authority is satisfied that any land, house or site transferred to it is no longer required for the provision of social or affordable housing it may:

(a) use the land, house or site for another purpose connected with its functions; or

(b) sell it for the best price reasonably obtainable,

and in either case it shall pay an amount equal to the market value of the land, site or house or the proceeds of their sale, as the case may be, into a separate account referred to in sub-s (12).

[6.92] PDA 2000, s 96(12) provides that if either option (a) or (b) above is used, the planning authority must pay an amount equal to the market value of the land, house or site or the proceeds of sale, as the case may be, into a separate account and any monies lodged to that account can only be used as capital funding for the purposes of PDA 2000, Pt V or for the performance by the authority of its functions in relation to provision of housing under the Housing Acts 1966–2002.

[6.93] Even though PDA 2000, s 96(12) requires a planning authority to lodge the proceeds of sale to a special account to be used only as capital funding for the purposes of PDA 2000, Pt V, or for provision of housing under the Housing Acts, it is both absurd and unjust that a planning authority can, without restraint, profit in this manner from the sale of land, houses or sites which are no longer required for the provision of social or affordable housing. When one contrasts the advantages which the planning authority has over individuals who are saddled with claw back payments on the sale of social and affordable housing it seems difficult to understand how this provision survived the scrutiny of the Supreme Court when PDA 2000, Pt V was submitted to it under Art 26.2.1° of the Constitution. The record of planning authorities in making over-provision in zoning, particularly in the provision of housing and of hotels in recent times, is catastrophic. To allow more than 300,000 dwelling units to be constructed, for which there are no purchasers, demonstrates how poorly local authority planners understand the need to assess market conditions before granting these types of approvals. PDA 2000, s 96(11) provides planning authorities with an opportunity to acquire the maximum amount of social and/or affordable housing irrespective of market conditions.

**[6.94]** PDA 2000, s 211 empowers a local authority to sell, lease or exchange, subject to such conditions as it considers necessary, any land acquired for the purposes of or appropriated under this Act or any other Act provided the local authority no longer requires the land for any of its functions or in order to secure:

- (a) the best use of that or other land, and any structures or works which have been, or are to be, constructed, erected, made or carried out on, in or under that or other land, or
- (b) the construction, erection, making or carrying out of any structures or works appearing to it to be needed for the proper planning and sustainable development of its functional area.

**[6.95]** In PDA 2000 (as amended),[73] s 96(15) 'owner' means:

- (a) a person other than a mortgagee not in possession, who is for the time being entitled to dispose (whether in possession or reversion) of the fee simple of the land, and
- (b) a person who, under a lease or agreement the unexpired term of which exceeds five years, holds or is entitled to the rents or profits of the land.

Compensation is payable to the 'owner' of the land under s 96(6).

## Withering permissions

**[6.96]** Section 3 of the PD(A)A 2002 abolished the special type of withering permission which withered on 31 December, 2002 or two years from the date of grant of a permission, whichever was the later, if permission had been applied for after 25 August 1999, in relation to the development of land for housing. Section 4 of PD(A)A 2002 restores ss 40, 41 and 42 time limits to social and affordable withering permissions and it imposes a levy where social and affordable withering permission would have withered but for the provision of the Amendment Act of 2002. It is, therefore, important that the old provisions of s 96(15), before amendment, are fully understood even though they no longer cause the permission to wither. Nevertheless, if the permission would have withered under the Act of 2000, the levy provided for in the Amendment Act of 2002 will be payable.

---

73. PDA 2000, s 96(16) defined 'owner'. The definition has not been changed but it appears as PDA 2000, s 96(16).

**[6.97]** The original PDA 2000, s 96(15) was drafted with the express purpose of catching developers who obtained permission before local authorities adopted the housing supply provisions/housing strategy into their development plans.

It provided that where a planning permission has been granted:

(a) Pursuant to an application made after 25 August 1999 but before the development plan for that area had been varied to include the Housing Strategy and;

(b) Where the provisions of Pt V would have applied had the application for permission been made following the variation/amendment of the development plan to include the Housing Strategy (that is, the application is for residential development or mixed residential development on land to which a specific objective reserving land for Social and Affordable Housing applies), then the permission would have ceased to have effect but for the provisions of the Amendment Act of 2002, on 31 December 2002 or two years from the date of the granting of the permission, whichever was to be the later.

**[6.98]** The ordinary five-year life span of a planning permission provided for under s 40 or such extended life span as may be provided for under ss 41 and 42 of the Act of 2000 did not apply to withering permissions under Pt V of PDA 2000. It was felt that that type of withering permission was likely to cause incredible confusion in that the permission would lapse in respect of any portion of the development authorised by the permission consisting of buildings, the external walls of which had not been completed. If no part of the development had been started, the entire permission would have failed. If the development was partially completed, the permission only ceased in relation to those buildings for which external development had not been completed. If a permission withered, the developer would have to apply for a new permission and the new permission, if granted, would undoubtedly have contained a social and affordable housing condition.

**[6.99]** As stated, that type of withering permission has been replaced by a levy.

**[6.100]** It should be said that the concept of withering permission has existed for many years, and the normal life of a planning permission is five years or such other period as may be specified in the permission or as may be allowed by way of extension during the course of a development (see PDA 2000, ss 40, 41 and 42). Once the time limit provided expires, the permission is said to wither. With the abolition of this special category of social and affordable withering permissions, the time limit set out in PDA 2000, ss 40, 41 and 42 now applies to all grants of permission.[74] Section 4 of PD(A)A 2002 provides that all houses built on foot of a permission which would otherwise have withered but for the provisions of the 2002 Act, will be subject to a levy of 1% of the sale price if equal to or in excess of €270,000 or 0.5% of the sale price if less than that amount.[75] That section takes considerable trouble to ensure that the levy is not passed on to the

---

74. PDA 2000, s 96A as inserted by PD(A)A 2002, s 4.
75. See PDA 2000, s 96B as inserted by PD(A)A 2002, s 4.

purchaser and the planning authority is required to issue a receipt similar to a receipt for a financial contribution as soon as the levy has been paid. This is a receipt which a purchaser's solicitors will have to look for in addition to the receipts for financial contributions contained in the planning permission. Once the receipt has been issued by the local authority that receipt shall be *prima facie* evidence that the liability for the payment of the amount to which it relates has been discharged. The Act specifically provides that any of the following:

(a) a provision of a contract of a sale of a house,

(b) a provision of a contract for the building for a person of a house for his or her occupation,

(c) a covenant or other provision of a conveyance of an interest in a house,

(d) a covenant or other provision of a lease or tenancy agreement in respect of a house,

(e) a provision of any other agreement (whether oral or in writing) which purports to require the purchaser, the person referred to in paragraph (b), the grantee of the interest or the grantee of the lease or tenancy, as the case may be, to pay the amount referred to in sub-s (2) or to indemnify another in respect of that others paying or liability to pay that amount, shall be void.[76]

In practice, it might be very difficult indeed to prevent a builder from anticipating the levy and putting it in as part of the purchase price in an indirect or general way.

**[6.101]** Where houses are not sold, the levy is determined by the market value of the house at the time of its completion, so that if the market value equals or exceeds €270,000 the levy is 1% and if it is less than that sum the levy again is 0.5%. Another change is that the section providing for the levy will not apply to permissions for development consisting of the provision of four or less houses or for a house on land of 0.1 hectares or less. It should be noted that the amount of ground specified in the Act of 2000 was 0.2 hectares and this has now been reduced, *overall*, to 0.1 hectares for exemption purposes.[77]

**[6.102]** PDA 2000, s 96B, as inserted,[78] does not provide any definite time for the payment of the levy but merely states that the levy shall be paid at such time as the planning authority specifies (and the time that is so specified may be before the date on which the disposal concerned of the relevant house is effective). Any amount paid to the planning authority in accordance with this section shall be accounted for in a separate account and shall only be applied as capital for its functions under this Part by a housing authority or for its function in relation to the provisions under the Housing Acts 1996 to 2002.

---

76. See PDA 2000, s 96B(8) as inserted by PD(A)A 2002, s 4.
77. See PDA 2000, s 96B(4)–(10) inclusive as inserted by PD(A)A 2002, s 4.
78. See PDA 2000, s 96B, specifically sub-s (5), as inserted by PD(A)A 2002, s 4.

**[6.103]** The situation as to whether a levy is or is not payable may be summarised as follows:

(i) There is no levy payable in respect of a house built on foot of a planning permission, application for which was lodged prior to 25 August 1999.

(ii) Where a planning permission was granted on foot of an application lodged after 25 August 1999, and before the relevant planning authority incorporated its housing strategy in its development plan (a 'qualifying permission') no levy is payable if either the entire house has been completed before 31 December 2002 or within two years of the date of grant of planning permission, whichever shall be the later.

(iii) No levy will be payable in respect of a house or houses or an apartment or apartments (not exceeding four units) built on land which is 0.1 hectares or less even if built under a qualifying permission.

(iv) A housing levy is payable in circumstances where either the house built under a qualifying permission has not been built or the external walls have not been completed prior to 31 December 2002 or within two years of the date of the grant of permission, whichever shall be the later.

(v) In the case of a building estate, those houses built under a qualifying permission which would have been fully built or the external walls of which have been completed prior to 31 December 2002 or within two years from the date of the grant of planning permission, whichever shall be the later, are exempt from the levy but any houses which have not been fully completed or in respect of which the external walls have not been completed prior to 31 December 2002 or within two years of the date of grant of planning permission, whichever shall be the later, will be liable to pay the levy.

(vi) Any house built on foot of a planning permission, application for which was lodged after the local authority incorporated its housing strategy into its development plan is not liable for a levy but the social and affordable housing conditions will apply.

## Exemption from social and affordable housing conditions

**[6.104]** PDA 2000, s 96(13) exempts the following types of planning applications from the provisions of this part, namely:

(a) development consisting of the provision of houses by a body standing approved for the purposes of s 6 of the Housing (Miscellaneous Provisions) Act 1992, for the provision of housing for persons referred to in s 9(2) of the Housing Act 1988, where such houses are to be made available for letting or sale,

(b) the conversion of an existing building or the reconstruction of a building to create one or more dwellings, provided that 50% or more of the existing external fabric of the building is retained,

**[6.105]**

(c) the carrying out of works to an existing house, or

(d) development of houses pursuant to an agreement under this section.

**[6.105]** PDA 2000, s 97, as amended,[79] provides generally for certain small housing developments (being four houses or less) which are also excluded from the social and affordable housing provisions of Pt V. The provision has been amended by the Planning and Development (Amendment) Act of 2002 in that the 2000 Act referred to housing on land of 0.2 hectares or less and the 0.2 has now been reduced, *overall*, to 0.1 hectares. A person intending to apply for permission for one of these developments must apply to the planning authority for a certificate stating that the requirements of this Part do not apply to the grant of permission, with a right of appeal to the courts where the application for a certificate is turned down. Planning permission will still be required for a development even where a certificate has been granted. The proposed developments for which a certificate may be sought are:

(a) the provision of four or fewer houses, or

(b) housing on land of 0.1 hectares or less (approximately half an acre or less).[80]

The application for a certificate under s 97 in respect of a proposed development should be made prior to the submission of an application for permission for development. Unless a certificate is granted, the Social and Affordable provisions of s 97 *will* apply. Without an exemption certificate granted by the appropriate planning authority development of the type envisaged by paras (a) and (b) above cannot take place. Whereas types of planning applications listed in PDA 2000, s 96(13) are recognised as exceptions from Social and Affordable conditions, in contrast PDA 2000, s 97 allows the planning authority some discretion as to whether it will or will not grant a certificate of exemption. The guidelines which were issued in December 2000 dealing with the anti-avoidance provisions of Pt V (s 97) state as follows in paras 12(2) and 12(3):

> (2) the building of up to 4 houses or development of housing on land of 0.2 hectares[81] or less will be exempt from the requirement to transfer land to the local authority for social or affordable housing. To avail of this exemption a person who wishes to obtain permission for the building of up to 4 houses or for housing development on land of 0.2 hectares or less where either is zoned with a social and affordable housing condition, will have to obtain an exemption certificate in advance by applying to the planning authority. When applying for this certificate, the person will have to swear a statutory declaration stating certain facts, such as the history of the ownership of the land, and whether they have interests in land in the immediate vicinity to allow the authority to take a view as to whether this is a genuine application.
>
> (3) the planning authority can refuse to grant a person a certificate if, based on the information provided by the person and any other knowledge it has, it believes that

---

79. PD(A)A 2002, s 5 amending PDA 2000, s 97(3) & (12)(b)(ii), Local Government (No 2) Act 2003, s 5 amending PDA 2000, s 97.
80. See PDA 2000, s 97(3) as amended by PD(A)A 2002, s 5.
81. Note the 0.2 hectares has now been reduced to 0.1 hectares.

a person is trying to avoid the application of a social and affordable housing condition. If the certificate is refused, the applicant may appeal that decision to the Circuit Court and the Court will decide whether the authority has the right to do so.

The legislation has gone to considerable trouble to ensure that persons do not try to avoid social and affordable housing supply conditions by making multiple applications for small scale residential developments.

**[6.106]** There are two relevant definitions contained in PDA 2000, s 97(1), as follows:

> 'Applicant' includes a person on whose behalf a person applies for a certificate. If application for a certificate is made by a person acting on behalf of a landowner in a professional capacity, information on the landowner must be included.

> 'The Court' (except in relation to sub-ss (19) & (21)),[82] means the Circuit Court for the Circuit in which all or part of the development to which the application for a certificate relates, is situate. An appeal against a refusal to issue a certificate may be made to the Circuit Court.

**[6.107]** PDA 2000, s 97(2)(a) provides that two persons shall be deemed to be acting in concert if, pursuant to an agreement, arrangement or understanding between them, one of them makes or causes to be made an application for a certificate. Any such agreement, etc, may be oral or written and need not be in the form of a formal contract.

**[6.108]** PDA 2000, s 97(2)(b) provides that land which is more than 400 metres from a particular piece of land will not be considered to be in the vicinity of that other land. This provision is of importance in determining the information that must be supplied by an applicant for a certificate and in deciding whether a certificate should be refused.

**[6.109]** PDA 2000, s 97(3), as amended,[83] provides that before applying for a planning permission

    (a) for a development comprising four or fewer houses; or

    (b) for housing situate on land of 0.1 hectares or less;

application should be made for a certificate stating that the provisions of s 96 (being the provisions for social and affordable housing) shall not apply to grant of permission.

**[6.110]** These 'exemption certificates' are applied for in respect of a development consisting of four houses or less, or for housing on land of 0.1 hectares or less. The application for the certificate is an application to the planning authority to certify that social and affordable housing conditions should not apply. The planning authority may, subject to PDA 2000, s 97(6) and (12) and subject to compliance by the applicant with PDA 2000, s 96(8), grant the certificate to the applicant. However, the provisions of s 96(6)(a) and (b) are relevant.

---

82. PDA 2000, s 97(19) and (21) deal with convictions for offences under PDA 2000, s 97.
83. LG(No 2)Act 2003, s 5 substituted 0.2 hectares for 0.1 hectares.

**[6.111]** PDA 2000, s 97(6)(a) and (b) reads:

(a) A planning authority may require an applicant for a certificate to provide it with such further information or documentation as it is reasonably necessary to enable it to perform its functions under this section.

(b) Where an applicant refuses to comply with a requirement under paragraph (a), or fails, within a period of eight weeks from the date of the making of the requirement, to so comply, the planning authority concerned shall refuse to grant the applicant a certificate.

**[6.112]** PDA 2000, s 96(7) allows the planning authority, for the purpose of performing its functions under s 96, to make such further enquiries as it considers appropriate. Further, it is the duty of the applicant making an application for a certificate to provide the planning authority concerned with such information as it may reasonably require to enable it to perform its functions under this section.[84]

**[6.113]** A default position arises under the provisions of s 96(10), which gives the planning authority a period of four weeks from the date of application or four weeks from the date when the planning authority required further information to grant a certificate, and if such certificate is not granted within that four-week period the planning authority shall be deemed to have granted a certificate to the applicant concerned.

**[6.114]** All particulars of certificates granted are entered in the planning authority's planning register.[85]

**[6.115]** PDA 2000, s 97(5) requires the applicant for a certificate to provide a statutory declaration dealing with the following matters:

(a) giving, in respect of the period of five years preceding the application, such particulars of the legal and beneficial ownership of the land, on which it is proposed to carry out the development to which the application relates, as are within the applicant's knowledge or procurement,

(b) identifying any person with whom the applicant is acting in concert,

(c) giving particulars of –

  (i) any interest that the applicant has, or had at any time during the said period, in any land in the immediate vicinity of the land on which it is proposed to carry out such development, and

  (ii) any interest that any person with whom the applicant is acting in concert has, or had at any time during the said period, in any land in the said immediate vicinity, of which the applicant has knowledge,

(d) stating that the applicant is not aware of any facts or circumstances that would constitute grounds under sub-s (12) for the refusal by the planning authority to grant a certificate,

(e) giving such other information as may be prescribed.

---

84. PDA 2000, s 97(7).
85. PDA 2000, s 97(11).

## REFUSAL OF CERTIFICATE UNDER PDA 2000, S 97

[6.116] This is dealt with in s 97(12).[86] A certificate shall be refused by a planning authority where the applicant or person with whom it is acting in concert:

(a) Has been granted a certificate in respect of a development in the proceeding five years which remains in force at the time of the application, or

(b) Has carried out or has been granted permission to carry out a development of the type referred to in sub-s (3), as amended[87] namely the provision of four or fewer houses or housing on land of 0.1 hectares or less:

   (i) Five years before the date of applying for the certificate; and

   (ii) After 1 November 2001 (One year from the date of commencement of s 97),

on the land for which the person is now seeking a certificate or land within that immediate vicinity unless:

   (I) The aggregate of the development for which a certificate is being sought and the development to which this paragraph (a) or (b) relates would not exceed four houses or;

   (II) Where the proposed development would exceed four houses, and the land on which it is proposed to be carried out is less than 0.1 hectares.

Effectively, a person is entitled to one certificate in a five-year period or is entitled to carry out one development of up to four houses, or develop a house(s) on 0.1 hectares on a particular land. However, an additional certificate may be granted in respect of that land or land in the immediate vicinity, where some of the development carried out, either pursuant to a previous certificate or under a planning permission, was not carried out by the person who applied for the certificate in respect of that permission, and the proposal in the application for the certificate applied for does not exceed four houses. Where the total number would exceed four houses, but the total land involved would be less than 0.1 acres, a certificate may also be granted.

[6.117] Any decision to refuse a certificate must be a reasoned decision.[88] A refusal to grant a certificate may be appealed to the Circuit Court within three weeks of receiving notification of a refusal, seeking an order directing that the certificate be granted. The court may also permit the applicant an extension of the three-week period. The Circuit Court may either dismiss the appeal and uphold the refusal by the authority or allow the

---

86. PDA 2000, s 97(12)(b)(ii) has been amended by the Local Government (No 2) Act 2003, s 5.
87. PDA 2000, s 97(3), as amended by PD(A)A 2002, s 5, provides that a certificate is required before making application for planning permission for development of four houses or for development for housing on land of 0.1 hectares or less if social and/or affordable housing conditions are to be avoided.
88. PDA 2000, s 97(13).

**[6.118]** *Planning and Environmental Law in Ireland*

appeal and direct the authority to grant the certificate.[89] The planning authority is obliged to comply with any court direction made under PDA 2000, s 97(14).[90]

**[6.118]** PDA 2000, s 97(13) provides that if a planning authority refuses to grant a certificate under this section it must notify the applicant in writing of the reasons for making that decision to refuse to grant a certificate.[91]

**[6.119]** PDA 2000, s 97(16) provides that if an owner of land, or if a person acting with his or her permission, applies to have a certificate relating to that land revoked, the planning authority must comply with that request unless permission has already been granted for the development to which the certificate relates.

## OFFENCES FOR NON-COMPLIANCE WITH THE PROVISIONS OF PDA 2000, s 97

**[6.120]** It is an offence to knowingly or recklessly make a false or misleading statutory declaration or to provide false or misleading material applying for a certificate.[92]

**[6.121]** On summary conviction a fine of up to €1,905[93] or a term of imprisonment not exceeding six months may be applied. On conviction on indictment a fine of up to €634,869 or imprisonment for a term not exceeding five years may be imposed.[94] In addition, the court can order that the person convicted shall pay into court an amount equal to the gain accruing to that person by reason of a false declaration or false information or document.[95] Such additional amounts will be paid to the planning authority to be lodged to a special account.[96] Anyone who forges a certificate or purports that a certificate has been granted where no such certificate exists or anyone who alters a certificate with intent to deceive or anyone who has in his possession, without lawful authority or other reasonable excuse, a forged certificate shall be guilty of an offence and shall be liable on summary conviction to a fine not exceeding €1,905 or imprisonment not exceeding six months or both and on conviction on indictment to a fine not exceeding €634,869 or not more than five years imprisonment or both.

**[6.122]** Provision is also made that where a person is convicted of an offence under s 97(17) the court may revoke any certificate granted on foot of a false declaration, etc, on application by the planning authority.[97]

---

89. PDA 2000, s 97(14).
90. PDA 2000, s 97(15).
91. PDA 2000, s 97(13).
92. PDA 2000, s 97(17).
93. Council Regulation EC No 974/98 which deleted the previous fine of IR£1,500.
94. Council Regulation EC No 974/98 which deleted the previous fine of IR£500,000.
95. PDA 2000, s 97(19).
96. PDA 2000, s 97(20).
97. PDA 2000, s 97(21).

**[6.123]** PDA 2000, s 97(22) makes it clear that a person who has received a certificate is not automatically entitled to planning permission. Once the certificate is received, an application for planning permission will have to be made.

## ALLOCATION OF AFFORDABLE HOUSING

**[6.124]** Section 98 provides that a local authority must allocate affordable housing in accordance with a scheme to be determined by the elected members. The scheme sets out a number of considerations which must be taken into account by the authority when prioritising eligible persons for allocation of affordable housing. The key terms in this section are 'accommodation needs', 'affordable housing' and 'eligible person'.

**[6.125]** Planning and Development Regulations 2001, art 50 deals with accommodation needs. This article has also been amended by Planning and Development Regulations 2003 (SI 90/2003). What appears below is the amended version.

> The minimum size of accommodation required by eligible persons for the purpose of s 100(1)(a) of the Act shall be:
>
> (a) for one person, a house with 1 bedroom and gross floor area of 38 square metres;
>
> (b) for two persons, a house with 1 bedroom and gross floor area of 42 square metres;
>
> (c) for three persons, a house with 2 bedrooms and a gross floor area of 52 square metres;
>
> (d) for four persons, a house with 2 bedrooms and a gross floor area of 62 square metres;
>
> (e) for five persons, a house with 3 bedrooms and a gross floor area of 74 square metres;
>
> (f) for six persons, a house with 3 bedrooms and a gross floor area of 78 square metres;
>
> (g) for seven or more persons, a house with 4 bedrooms and a gross floor area of 92 square metres.
>
> 'Affordable Housing' means the land or housing made available to the local authority for accommodating eligible persons pursuant to Pt V of the Act.[98]
>
> 'Eligible Person' means a person in need of accommodation but whose income is insufficient to meet the payments on a mortgage large enough to pay for a house which would meet their accommodation needs as defined above. A person's income is insufficient where the annual Mortgage payments will exceed 35% of their annual net income (after tax and PPS deductions).[99]

**[6.126]** Section 93(3) provides that a local authority must take into account half the annual income, net of income tax and PPS or any other person who might reasonably be

---

98. PDA 2000, s 93(1) to (4) inclusive.
99. PDA 2000, s 98(7).

expected to reside with the eligible person and contribute to the mortgage payment, and any other financial circumstances of the eligible person and that other person or persons.

**[6.127]** Affordable housing may be sold or leased only to eligible persons who qualify in accordance with the scheme established by the local authority.[100]

**[6.128]** 'Leased' means a shared ownership lease within the meaning of s 2 of the Housing (Miscellaneous Provisions) Act 1992.[101]

**[6.129]** A local authority is required by s 98(2) to establish this scheme to determine the order of priority of eligible persons for the allocation of housing. In establishing the scheme, the local authority must take the following matters into account:

(a) the accommodation needs of eligible persons particularly those who have not purchased or built a house for their own occupation or for any other purpose;

(b) the current housing circumstances of the eligible persons;

(c) the incomes or other financial circumstances of the eligible persons (and priority may be accorded to eligible persons whose income level is lower than that of other eligible persons);

(d) the period for which eligible persons have resided in the area of the development plan;

(e) whether eligible persons own houses or land in the area of the development plan or elsewhere;

(f) the distance of affordable housing from places of employment of eligible persons;

(g) any other matters which the authority considers appropriate or as may be prescribed for the purposes of this section.[102]

When making or reviewing a development plan the planning authority is required to review its affordable housing scheme, and it may review that scheme at any other time. The making of such a scheme is a reserved function to be adopted by resolution of the council.[103]

**[6.130]** For the purposes of allocating affordable housing a planning authority may, from time to time, set aside a specified number or proportion of affordable houses for eligible persons or for classes of eligible persons as it considers appropriate.[104]

## Controls on subsequent sale or resale of certain houses

**[6.131]** In summary, this section provides for conditions on the resale of houses or sites sold or leased to eligible persons. Where these houses are subsequently sold by a person,

---

100. PDA 2000, s 98(7).
101. PDA 2000, s 98(7).
102. PDA 2000, s 98(3)(a) to (g) inclusive.
103. PDA 2000, s 98(4) and (5).
104. PDA 2000, s 98(6).

there is requirement for a payment to the authority of part of the profit on such sale. The conditions may also include the basis on which each property may be occupied and a requirement to notify the planning authority of the resale of the house or site.

## Section 99(3) clawback

**[6.132]** Section 99(3)(a) provides that (subject to the provisions of paras (b) and (c) of this subsection), where a person sells land or a house within 20 years, the person must pay a percentage of the proceeds of sale to the local authority. The percentage of the sale proceeds is equal to the percentage by which the market value of the property on the date of sale exceeded the price actually paid by the purchaser. The Act sets out a formula to be applied in calculating that percentage. The formula is:

$$\frac{Y \times 100}{Z}$$

Where:

Y = the market value of the house or land when it was sold to the person less the price actually paid, and

Z = the market value of the house at the time of sale to the person.

An example of this calculation is as follows. If an eligible person paid €160,000 for a house at a time when the open market value was €200,000 the difference is €40,000. Using the formula above and applying these figures, the calculation is made as follows:

$$(40,000 \times 100) \div 200,000 = 20\%$$

Accordingly, 20% of the sale proceeds must be repaid to the planning authority on sale within 20 years. This applies when the house is sold at any time within 20 years of its original acquisition by the eligible person.

Note that s 99(3)(b) provides that the amount payable, using the formula above, must be reduced by 10% in respect of each full year after the tenth year during which the person has been in occupation of the house as their normal place of residence.

Applying the example, in the first 10 years if the house is sold at the same market value as the market value when it was bought, namely €200,000, then the 20% to be repaid to the planning authority amounts to €40,000. If, within that 10-year period, the value of the house has increased to €220,000 then the 20% repaid amounts to €44,000.

If sold after 15 years of occupation at a price of €300,000 then the calculation is:

$$(€300,000 \times 20) \div 100 = €60,000$$

This is reduced by 50% for five years occupation between 10 and 15 years so that the total amount repaid out of the proceeds amounts to €30,000.

**[6.133]** PDA 2000, s 99(3)(c) provides that if the application of the formula would reduce the proceeds of sale (disregarding solicitor's and estate agent's fees and costs) below the price actually paid, then the amount payable to the planning authority must be reduced to the extent necessary to avoid that result.

## PDA 2000, s 99 controls on resale of certain houses – clawback

**[6.134]** PDA 2000, s 99(3)(d) provides that due allowance must be made for any material improvements made by the owner. Material improvements include extending and enlarging, preparing and converting the house, but not decoration or any improvements on the land, including the construction of the house.

**[6.135]** All monies received by the planning authority must be lodged to the separate account already referred to (see s 96(13)).

**[6.136]** Set out below is an example which illustrates how s 99 provisions work, taking account of inflation. This example was prepared by Ronan Hession[105] of the Department of the Environment and in the example the annual inflation figures are taken as 5% for the first 10 years and 3% for the 10 years after that.

| Year | % Increase Per Annum | Market Value | Y/Z x100 (%) | Amount Payable to local authority | Profit on Sale to Owner |
|---|---|---|---|---|---|
|  |  | Y €20,000 |  |  |  |
|  |  | Z €100,000 |  |  |  |
| 0 | Sale Price (0%) | €80,000 |  |  |  |
| 1 | 5.00% | 105,000 | 20.00% | 21,000 | 4,000 |
| 2 |  | 110,250 | 20.00% | 22,050 | 8,200 |
| 3 |  | 115,763 | 20.00% | 23,153 | 12,610 |
| 4 |  | 121,551 | 20.00% | 24,310 | 17,241 |
| 5 |  | 127,628 | 20.00% | 25,526 | 22,103 |
| 6 |  | 134,010 | 20.00% | 26,802 | 27,208 |
| 7 |  | 140,710 | 20.00% | 28,142 | 32,568 |
| 8 |  | 147,746 | 20.00% | 29,549 | 38,196 |
| 9 |  | 155,133 | 20.00% | 31,027 | 44,106 |
| 10 |  | 162,889 | 20.00% | 32,578 | 50,312 |
| 11 | 3% | 167,776 | 20.00% | 30,200 | 57,576 |
| 12 |  | 172,809 | 20.00% | 27,650 | 65,160 |
| 13 |  | 177,994 | 20.00% | 24,919 | 73,075 |
| 14 |  | 183,334 | 20.00% | 22,000 | 81,334 |
| 15 |  | 194,499 | 20.00% | 18,883 | 89,950 |
| 16 |  | 200,333 | 20.00% | 15,560 | 98,939 |
| 17 |  | 206,343 | 20.00% | 12,020 | 108,313 |
| 18 |  | 212,534 | 20.00% | 8,254 | 118,090 |
| 19 |  | 212,534 | 20.00% | 4,251 | 128,283 |
| 20 |  | 218,910 | 20.00% | 0 | 138,910 |

Y = Market Value at date of initial sale – Sale Price to person (€100,000–€80,000);
Z = Market Value at date of initial sale (€100,000).

---

105. Republished here with the kind permission of Ronan Hession.

The clawback provisions may have significant importance for a solicitor who may give undertakings regarding the proceeds of sale of properties. If the local authority is entitled to a large portion of the house sale proceeds, solicitors will need to be careful that any undertaking that they give in respect of the proceeds of sale does not inadvertently include proceeds which are payable to the local authority.

**[6.137]** Local authorities may protect their position by registering mortgages, in respect of such payments, on the title.

## PART 5 OF THE HOUSING (MISCELLANEOUS PROVISIONS) ACT 2009

**[6.138]** At the time of going to press new provisions replacing the time limited clawback repayment system for affordable housing have not been introduced. The status of Pt 5 (ss 78 to 96) of the Housing (Miscellaneous Provisions) Act 2009 should be checked because its introduction must be imminent.

**[6.139]** The purpose of Pt 5 is to replace the 'clawback' provisions with an equity based approach for recovery discounts granted to purchasers on the re-sale of 'affordable dwellings'. In summary, a legal charge will be placed on 'affordable dwellings' the value of which will be equivalent to the amount of the subsidy paid by the housing authority to a purchaser of an affordable dwelling. Taking the figures used in the example above, where the market value was €200,000 but the eligible person paid a contribution of €160,000, the difference between the two figures is €40,000. The housing authority will, when the legislation comes into force, charge the repayment of €40,000 on the affordable dwelling. The purchaser is entitled to pay off the charge on the affordable dwelling during the charge period but either the entire charge or what remains unpaid of the charge must be paid off either at the expiration of the charge period or on the re-sale of the affordable dwelling, whichever happens first. The pay-off of whatever is owing to the local authority at the date the payment becomes due is calculated at *current market value*, which, as has been forcibly demonstrated recently, may go up or may go down.

**[6.140]** Part 5 of the Housing (Miscellaneous Provisions) Act 2009 is headed:

AFFORDABLE DWELLING PURCHASE ARRANGEMENTS.

Section 78 of Pt 5 provides definitions which are essential to an understanding of the provisions of this part.

'Affordable dwelling' has the meaning given to it by s 82.

Section 82 of Pt 5 provides that this part of the Act applies to affordable dwellings which are defined as:

(a) dwellings made available by a housing authority under s 79;

(b) dwellings to which a Pt V agreement applies including dwellings made available for sale under such an agreement but not yet sold before the coming into operation of this Part;

> (c) dwellings made available for sale in accordance with Pt 2 of the Act of 2002 but not yet sold before the coming into operation of this Part and s 7 (insofar as it applies to the said Act).

'Affordable dwelling fund' has a meaning given to it in s 94 of Pt 5.

**[6.141]** Section 94(1) provides:

> There shall stand established, on the coming into operation of this Part a fund to be known in this Act referred to as the Affordable Dwellings Fund (in this section referred to as 'Fund').

**[6.142]** The remainder of s 94 deals with the sources from which monies are paid into the fund, the management and control of the fund by the housing finance agency, the preparation of the accounts of the fund and other details.

**[6.143]** 'Affordable dwelling purchase arrangement' is defined in s 83 of Pt 5 which section permits a housing authority to enter into an arrangement ('an affordable dwelling purchase arrangement') for the sale of an affordable dwelling to an eligible household in accordance with a scheme of priority. The different types of arrangement are provided for in s 83(2), but in all cases the funds provided by the housing authority to the purchaser will be secured by a charge over the property which charge shall be repaid where the purchaser sells the dwelling during the charge period by payment of an amount calculated in accordance with s 90 which is dealt with below. During the charged period, s 83 provides that the charged property must be the normal place of residence of the purchaser or of a member of the purchaser's household unless prior written consent is obtained. It further provides that the dwelling may not be let or sub-let and the premises are subject to the usual conditions in the charge relating to the payments required and the consequences for the purchaser of failure to make those payments.

**[6.144]** The terms 'charging order' and 'charged period' have the meaning given to them in s 86 which is dealt with below.

**[6.145]** The term 'direct sales agreement' has the meaning given to it in s 80. The Housing (Miscellaneous Provisions) Act 2009, s 80(2) provides that a housing authority pursuant to s 79 or a planning authority pursuant to its functions under Pt V of the P&D Act 2000 may enter into a direct sales agreement with a person to whom the section applies for the direct sale, in accordance with this Part, of the dwellings specified in the agreement to eligible households nominated by the housing authority in accordance with the scheme of priority. The direct sales agreement allows for the necessary transactions in relation to the direct sale in accordance with this Part of dwellings to eligible households subject to certain terms and conditions, to include the following:

> (i) that the sale price for each dwelling specified in the agreement shall be the purchase money;
>
> (ii) that the dwelling specified in the agreement shall be sold directly to eligible households nominated by the housing authority in accordance with a scheme of priority;

(iii) terms and conditions relating to –
- (i) arrangements for the completion of sales,
- (ii) notification of sales to the housing authority,
- (iii) any other matters relating to the sale of dwellings specified in the agreement, to eligible households,

and

(b) may include such other terms and conditions relating to the transactions referred to in subsection (3) as may be prescribed for the purposes of affordable dwelling purchase arrangements

**[6.146]** Section 84 of the Housing (Miscellaneous Provisions) Act 2009 deals with the assessment of eligibility of households for affordable dwelling purchase arrangements. Any reference to a household is read to include two or more persons who, in the opinion of the housing authority, have a reasonable requirement to live together. That definition must be conceded as a bald and tolerant definition. Once the household is identified, where the household applies to a housing authority to purchase an affordable dwelling an assessment of the household's eligibility is carried out, taking account of the following,

**[6.147]** Section 84(2):

(a) the accommodation needs of the household, having regard to but not necessarily limited to the following –
- (i) the current housing circumstances of the household,
- (ii) the distance of such preferred location or locations as the household may indicate in its application from the place of employment of any member of the household and
- (iii) whether any members of the household are attending any university, college, school or other educational establishment in the administrative area concerned;

(b) subject to subsection (3) whether the income of the household is adequate to meet the repayments on a mortgage for the purchase of a dwelling to meet the accommodation needs of the household because the payments calculated over the course of the year would exceed 35% of the annual income of the household net of income tax and pay related social insurance;

(c) subject to subsection (4) & (5), whether the household or any household member has previously purchased or built a dwelling for his or her occupation or for any other purpose in the State;

(d) subject to subsections (4) & (5), whether the householder or any household member either owns, or is beneficially entitled to, an interest in any dwelling or land in the State, or elsewhere.

**[6.148]** Section 84(3) provides that if the household has any other assets which could be used towards providing part of the costs of accommodation, those assets will be taken into account.

**[6.149]** 'Eligible household' refers to a household assessed by the housing authority to be eligible for an affordable dwelling purchase arrangement. Reference is made to s 84 and, in particular, to the method of making an assessment in relation to a person who was espoused to a marriage subject to a deed of separation, a decree of judicial separation, a decree of divorce or a decree of nullity provided he/she has not retained an interest in the previous family home and does not have an interest in any other premises other than the said family home. Also, if a household requires to relocate, the fact that it previously had a dwelling under an affordable dwelling purchase arrangement or had purchased a dwelling to which a Pt 5 agreement applies or a dwelling made available for sale in accordance with Pt 2 of the Act of 2002 but in either case said dwelling had not been sold before the coming into operation of Pt 5 of this Act, it will not be ineligible for an affordable home purchase arrangement.

**[6.150]** 'Market value,' in relation to an affordable dwelling, means the price for which the dwelling might reasonably be expected to be sold on the open market.

**[6.151]** 'Net market value' is the market value reduced by an allowance equal to the amount of the market value attributable to material improvements.

**[6.152]** 'Open market value' has the meaning given to it by s 81 of this Part. Section 81 defines an 'open market dwelling' as a dwelling for purchase available in the State of a class of dwelling prescribed under s 95(1)(a) for the purpose of this section. The household will not be precluded from purchasing an open market dwelling even though the housing authority might have provided financial assistance to an eligible household under s 81.

**[6.153]** 'Part V agreement' is an agreement under s 96(2) of Pt V of PDA 2000 for the provision of dwellings referred to in s 94(4)(a) of that Act and referred to in Pt V of the Housing (Miscellaneous Provisions) Act 2009 as a 'Part V agreement'.

**[6.154]** 'Purchase money' in relation to an affordable dwelling, means the monetary value of the proportion of the purchase price of the dwelling fixed by the housing authority as the proportion that is required to be paid by an eligible household to purchase the dwelling under an affordable dwelling purchase arrangement.

**[6.155]** 'Purchaser' means a person who purchases an affordable dwelling under an affordable dwelling purchase arrangement and includes a person in whom subsequently becomes vested (other than for valuable consideration) the interest of the purchaser or his or her successors in title and all personal representatives of that person or successors in title.

**[6.156]** 'Scheme of priority' is a scheme of priority for affordable dwelling purchase arrangements in accordance with s 85 of the Act.

**[6.157]** The purpose of s 79 of the Housing (Miscellaneous Provisions) Act 2009 is to make provision for dwellings to be made available to eligible households under affordable dwelling purchase arrangements.

**[6.158]** Section 79(2) permits a housing authority, for the purpose of making affordable dwellings available to eligible households, to enter into:

(a) arrangements with an approved body; or

(b) public private partnership arrangements.

**[6.159]** Section 79(3) enables the Minister to make grants towards the costs of affordable dwellings and those grants will be paid out to the housing authority in respect of dwellings which are provided by the housing authority itself or in respect of dwellings provided by approved bodies or other persons on behalf of the housing authority. Grants will also be made available to the Affordable Homes Partnership, which was established by the Affordable Homes Partnership (Establishment) Order 2005 (SI 383/2005), ring-fenced in respect of affordable dwellings acquired or provided by the Partnership on behalf of housing authorities. Monies may also be made available by the Minister to other statutory prescribed bodies providing services to the housing authorities for the acquisition of dwellings. Importantly, s 79(4) in relation to the provision of dwellings requires that the housing authority shall have regard to its housing services plan and the need to:

(a) counteract undue segregation in housing between persons of different social backgrounds,[106] and

(b) ensure that a mixture of dwelling types and sizes is provided to reasonably match the requirements of eligible households.

**[6.160]** Section 80 deals with direct sales agreements. A housing authority may enter into a 'direct sales agreement' for the sale of affordable housing to eligible households with the persons defined in s 80, namely:

(a) a person with whom the housing authority has contracted for the provision of dwellings for the purposes of s 79, and

(b) a public private partnership with whom the housing authority has entered into an arrangement under s 79(2)(b) for the provision of dwellings for the purposes of that section, and

(c) a person with whom the planning authority has entered into an agreement under s 96(2) of Pt V of the Planning and Development Act 2000 for the provision of dwellings referred to in s 94(4)(a) of that Act ('Part V Agreement').

Once the direct sales agreement has been concluded the party who has entered the agreement with the housing authority is authorised to sell affordable dwellings at stipulated prices and under agreed terms, direct to the eligible households concerned. The eligible households are nominated by the housing authority in accordance with the housing authority's scheme of priority.

---

106. Housing (Miscellaneous Provisions) Act 2009, s 99(4). This section has been spectacularly ineffective to date possibly because at the date this book went to press the section has not been commenced.

**[6.161]** Where a Pt V agreement has been entered into under this Act if the amount payable under the direct sales agreement is less than the amount due under a Pt V agreement the difference shall be paid by the housing authority to the person with whom the housing authority has signed the direct sales agreement.

**[6.162]** Section 81 of the Housing (Miscellaneous Provisions) Act 2009 provides enabling powers for an open market component of the scheme to be introduced at a later stage to replace the shared ownership scheme when market conditions are suitable. Section 81 will permit a housing authority to grant financial assistance to a household which is eligible for affordable housing, to enable it to purchase an open market dwelling in the State of a type prescribed by the Minister. The amount of financial assistance being offered from the housing authority will be the difference between the market value of a dwelling and the amount of the assistance which the housing authority will require the eligible household to pay in order to purchase the affordable dwelling. The maximum amount of financial assistance which a housing authority may provide under this section may be limited by the Minister by regulation.

## PDA 2000, S 100: REGULATIONS UNDER Part V – HOUSING SUPPLY

**[6.163]** PDA 2000, s 100, 'Regulations under Pt V – Housing Supply' are contained in PDR 2001, arts 48–50 inclusive as amended.[107] Regulation 48 of PDR 2001 deals with applications for certificates under s 97 of PDA 2000. The application should state the name, address and telephone number together with the e-mail address (if any) of the applicant or person acting on the applicant's behalf. If the applicant is a company the name of the company director and the address and registration number of the company must be furnished. The application must state the location, townland or postal address (as may be appropriate) of the land in respect of which it is attempted to apply for permission. It must indicate the number of houses for which it is intended to apply for permission and indicate the area of the land in respect of which it is intended to apply for permission. The application must be accompanied by a location map of sufficient size and containing details of features in the vicinity such as to permit the identification of the land to which the application relates to a scale of not less than 1:1,000 in built up areas and 1:1,250 in all other areas. The scale must be identified on the map and the map must be marked or coloured to identify clearly the land to which the application relates and the boundaries thereof.

**[6.164]** Article 49 refers to the content of the declaration required by s 97(5) of PDA 2000. The applicant is required to state in the declaration:

    (a)    whether the applicant, or any person with whom the applicant is acting in concert, has been granted, within the period of five years prior to the date of making of the application, a certificate under s 97 of the Act which at the time of the application remains in force, and,

---

107. See Planning and Development Regulations 2003 (SI 90/2003), arts 3, 4 and 5.

(b) whether the applicant or any person with whom the applicant is acting in concert, has carried out or has been granted permission to carry out, a development consisting of the provision of four or fewer houses or of housing on land of 0.1 hectares or less, within the period of five years prior to the date of making of the application for a certificate, on land in respect of which the certificate is being sought or land in its immediate vicinity (save that any such development carried out, or permission granted, before 1 November 2001 may be disregarded).

**[6.165]** Article 5 of the Planning and Development Regulations 2003 (SI 90/2003) provides that:

> A receipt issued as evidence of the making of a payment under s 96(b) of the Planning and Development Act 2000 (as inserted by s 4 of the Planning and Development (Amendment) Act 2002) shall be in the form set out in the Schedule to these regulations or a form substantially to the like effect.

The Minister is given power to make regulations specifying the criteria to determine the size of the accommodation required by eligible persons, including minimum and maximum size requirements, having regard to guidelines under the Housing Acts 1966 to 1998. Regulations may be made governing the determination of income of eligible persons, how the planning authority should estimate the requirement for affordable housing, and conditions under which the planning authority should sell or lease social and/or affordable houses.

**[6.166]** PDA 2000, s 101 deals with housing authority and planning authority functions.

This section provides that where a planning authority, performing its function under Pt V, is not the housing authority for the functional area, then the planning authority must consult with the relevant housing authority.

# Chapter 7
# COMPENSATION AND COMPULSORY ACQUISITION

## PART I: COMPENSATION

### Introduction

**[7.01]** PDA 2000, Pt XII deals with compensation. Part XII is divided into three sections. Chapter I comprises ss 183–189[1] and deals with compensation generally. Chapter II comprises ss 190–195[2] dealing with compensation in relation to decisions under Pt III (Control of Development). Chapter III comprises ss 196–201 dealing with compensation in relation to s 46 (Requiring removal or alteration of a structure or discontinuance of use), s 85 (Special planning control scheme), s 88 (Service of notice relating to structures or other land in an area of special planning control), s 182 (Cables, wires and pipelines), s 207 (Compulsory powers for creation of a right of way) and s 252 (Power of authorised person to enter land).

**[7.02]** The Irish Constitution[3] provides express protection for the property rights of landowners but those rights are not absolute and they have been restricted in circumstances where the property rights of the individual come into conflict with the interests of the general public and where those interests are deemed to be for the common good.[4] A citizen has a general and *prima facie* entitlement to compensation where a planning permission is refused on appeal by the board. A person must pursue the planning process to its full extent before any claim for compensation can be made. The general or *prima facie* case for compensation is restricted by the provisions of PDA 2000, Third Schedule, Fourth Schedule and Fifth Schedule.[5]

**[7.03]** The Constitution also provides that citizens are entitled to procedural rights. In *MacPharthalain v Commissioners of Public Works*,[6] lands were designated as an area of scientific interest. The designation affected the rights of certain landowners and the designation was held to be *ultra vires* because in designating the site the OPW had not adopted the procedures required by natural and constitutional justice. The OPW gave the affected parties no notice of their intention to make the designation and afforded them no opportunity of being heard or of making objections or representations on the issue, on either a formal or informal basis. The value of the lands of the affected parties was

---

1. These sections have not been amended by PD(A)A 2010.
2. As will be noted PDA 2000, s 191(2) has been amended by PD(A)A 2010, s 67 but PDA 2000, s 190 and ss 192 to 195 inclusive have not been amended by PD(A)A 2010.
3. Constitution of Ireland, Arts 40(3) and 43.
4. Constitution of Ireland, Art 43.
5. These three schedules are guided by PDA 2000, s 191 as amended by PD(A)A 2010, s 67.
6. *MacPharthalain v Commissioners of Public Works* [1992] 1 IR 111, HC; on appeal [1994] 3 IR 353, SC.

reduced and, specifically, in that case, grants which had been applied for a sheep station were refused. The designation of the area as an area of scientific interest was quashed by the High Court.

**[7.04]** Provision is made for notifying parties in most of the planning legislation provisions as in cases where land is to be compulsory acquired or where buildings are to be recorded as protected structures under a development plan. There are also cases where no notice is required, for example PDA 2000, Sch 4 which specifically excludes compensation where a development proposal would interfere with a view of natural interest or beauty which it was felt necessary to preserve. In that case, no notice is given to the landowner in the sense that there is no requirement to identify a view of natural interest or beauty in the development plan.[7]

**[7.05]** Prior to the passing of LG(PD)A 1963, the common law position was that the landowner was entitled to use and develop his land as he wished, provided he did not interfere with the rights of others. The 1963 Act introduced considerable limitations on this common law position and the constitutionality of these restrictions was upheld in *Central Dublin Development Association v Attorney General*,[8] where the plaintiffs challenged development plans, enforcement notices, s 5 references, planning permission decisions and appeals. Kenny J, in recognising the obvious tension between community interests and private interests, especially where environmental planning is concerned, observed as follows:

> Town and regional planning is an attempt to reconcile the exercise of property rights with the demands of the common good and Part IV (of the 1963 Act) defends and vindicates as far as practicable the rights of citizens and it is not an unjust attack on their rights.

**[7.06]** LG(PD)A 1990 followed recommendations in the 1988 Report of the Irish Planning Institute Sub-Committee on Planning and Compensation, which refers to the compensation provisions under the planning code as an attempt to:

> provide a balance between the need to plan for the benefit of the community, particularly as identified in the Development Plan and the rights of an individual who has suffered loss as a result of a planning decision.

**[7.07]** The LG(PD)A 1990 limited compensation by extending the list of circumstances in which compensation is not payable and all of these matters are now dealt with in PDA 2000, specifically in the Third, Fourth and Fifth Schedules. Although compensation is now something of a rarity in planning law it does still survive. For example, PDA 2000, s 71 deals with the power to acquire a protected structure and enables a planning authority to acquire a protected structure by agreement or compulsorily within its functional area. The section can only be used where the planning authority considers

---

7. PDA 2000, Sch 4, para 8.
8. *Central Dublin Development Association v Attorney General* (1975) 109 ILTR 69.

that it is necessary to protect the structure and the structure is not occupied as a dwelling other than by a caretaker. However, where premises are acquired compensation will be payable under PDA 2000, s 71.

**[7.08]** In *Central Dublin Development Association v Attorney General*,[9] Kenny J undertook an analysis of the text of the Constitution and of the decisions on it. The learned judge's analysis led to the following conclusions:

(1) The right of private property is a personal right;

(2) In virtue of his rational being, man has a natural right to individual or private ownership of worldly wealth;

(3) This constitutional right consists of a bundle of rights most of which are founded in contract;

(4) The State cannot pass any law which abolishes all the bundle of rights which we call ownership or the general right to transfer, bequeath and inherit property;

(5) The exercise of these rights ought to be regulated by the principles of social justice and the State accordingly may by law restrict their exercise with a view to reconciling this with the demands of the common good;

(6) The Courts have jurisdiction to inquire whether the restriction is in accordance with the principles of social justice and whether the legislation is necessary to reconcile this exercise with the demands of the common good.

(7) If any of the rights which together constitute our conception of ownership are abolished or restricted (as distinct from the abolition of all the rights), the absence of compensation for this restriction or abolition will make the Act which does this, invalid if it is an unjust attack on property rights.[10]

## Compensation claims – time limits

**[7.09]** A compensation claim under PDA 2000, Pt XII must be made not later than six months after:[11]

(a) in the case of a claim under s 190,[12] the date of the decision of the board;

(b) in the case of a claim under s 195,[13] the date of the decision of the planning authority or the board, as the case may be;

---

9. *Central Dublin Development Association v Attorney General* (1975) 109 ILTR 69.
10. *Central Dublin Development Association v Attorney General* (1975) 109 ILTR 69.
11. PDA 2000, s 183 (1)(a)–(h).
12. PDA 2000, s 190 allows for payment of compensation after a refusal of permission or grant of permission subject to conditions where the refusal results in a reduction in value of the person's interest in land. The refusal must be a consequence of a decision on appeal to An Bord Pleanála.
13. PDA 2000, s 195 allows for payment of compensation where a permission is revoked or modified.

(c) in the case of a claim under s 196,[14] the removal or alteration of the structure;

(d) in the case of a claim under s 197,[15] the discontinuance or compliance;

(e) in the case of a claim referred to under s 198,[16] the date of approval of a scheme under s 85 or the date of complying with a notice under s 88, as the case may be;

(f) in the case of a claim under s 199,[17] the date on which the action of the planning authority occurred;

(g) in the case of a claim under s 200,[18] the date on which the order creating the public right of way commences to have effect; and

(h) in the case of a claim under s 201,[19] the date on which the damage is suffered.[20]

PDA 2000, s 183(2) permits the High Court, where it considers that the interests of justice so require, to extend the six-month period allowed for commencing a claim for compensation under this Part if an application is made to it in that behalf.

## Determination of compensation claim[21]

**[7.10]** PDA 2000, s 184 provides that in the absence of agreement between the parties compensation is determined by arbitration under the Acquisition of Land (Assessment of Compensation) Act 1919, subject to the rules for assessing compensation in PDA 2000, Sch 2.[22] The determination is also subject to the proviso that the arbitrator has jurisdiction to make a nil award.[23] Obviously, where agreement is reached between the parties as to the amount of compensation payable there is no need to proceed to arbitration.

**[7.11]** A claim for compensation under Chapter 1, to be determined by arbitration in default of agreement, as provided in s 184 is also subject to:

(c) the application of the Second Schedule to a claim for compensation under Chapter III of this Part for a reduction in the value of an interest as if a reference to 'the relevant decision under Part III' or to 'the decision' was, in relation to each of the sections in that Chapter set out in column A of

---

14. PDA 2000, s 196 allows for payment of compensation regarding the removal or alteration of a structure.
15. PDA 2000, s 197 allows for payment of compensation regarding discontinuance of a use.
16. PDA 2000, s 198 allows for payment of compensation relating to an area of special planning control.
17. PDA 2000, s 199 allows for payment of compensation regarding cables, wires and pipelines.
18. PDA 2000, s 200 allows for payment of compensation regarding creation of public rights of way.
19. PDA 2000, s 201 allows for payment of compensation regarding entry on land.
20. Note that PDA 2000, ss 190, 195, 196, 197, 198, 199, 200 and 201 are dealt with below in this chapter.
21. See PDA 2000, s 184.
22. See pp 937–940 below. See also PDA 2000, s 184(a).
23. PDA 2000, s 184(b).

the Table to this section, a reference to the matter set out in column B of that Table opposite the reference in column A to that section.[24]

Table

| A Section | B |
|---|---|
| 196 | the removal or alteration of a structure consequent upon a notice under section 46 |
| 197 | the discontinuance with, or the compliance with conditions on the continuance, of the use of land consequent upon a notice under section 46 |
| 198 | the approval of a scheme under section 85 or the compliance with a notice under section 88 |
| 199 | the action by the planning authority under section 182 |
| 200 | the making by the planning authority of an order under section 207 |

The provisions of PDA 2000, s 184(c) are difficult to follow but an excellent statement of what it means is provided by Stephen Dodd as follows:

> sub-s (c) provides that in so far as Sch 2 calculates the reduction in value by reference to Pt III (a decision on an application for planning permission), the rules stated therein shall be read as also applying to claims for compensation under the sections set out in Tables A and B.[25]

The arbitrator appointed under PDA 2000, s 184 having heard the evidence presented determines the amount of compensation payable but that determination is subject to the rules of determination of the amount of compensation as set out in Sch 2.[26]

## Arbitrator cases and the High Court

**[7.12]** Section 6 of the Acquisition of Land (Assessment of Compensation) Act 1919 permits an arbitrator to state a case to the High Court in the following circumstances:

1. The decision of an official arbitrator upon any question of fact, shall be final and binding on the parties, and the persons claiming under them respectively, but the official arbitrator may, and shall, if the High Court so directs, state at any stage of the proceedings, in the form of a special case for opinion of the High Court, any question of law arising in the course of the proceedings, and may state his award as to the whole or part thereof in the form of a special case for the opinion of the High Court.

2. The decision of the High Court upon any case so stated shall be final and conclusive, and shall not be subject to appeal to any other court.[27]

---

24. PDA 2000, s 184(c).
25. See Dodd, *The Planning Acts 2000–2007 Annotated and Consolidated* (Roundhall-Thomson Reuters, 2008) at pp 502 and 503.
26. See paras **7.43** to **7.47**.
27. See the Acquisition of Land (Assessment of Compensation) Act 1919, s 6. Most commonly, questions of law submitted by arbitrators arose from the provisions of Schs 2–5 inclusive.

**[7.13]** The Arbitration Act 2010 has abolished the case stated procedure in many instances but it appears that the case stated procedure under s 6 of the Acquisition of Land (Assessment of Compensation) Act 1919 remains in place. The Act is not referred to in the Arbitration Act 2010. Article 1(5) of UNCITRAL Model Law on International Commercial Arbitration, Arbitration Act 2010, Sch 1 states that:

> This Law shall not affect any other law of this State by virtue of which certain disputes may not be submitted to arbitration or may be submitted to arbitration only according to provisions other than those of this Law.

**[7.14]** Section 29(1) of the Arbitration Act 2010 states that:

> This Act, other than the excluded provisions, shall apply to every arbitration under any other Act as if the arbitration were pursuant to an arbitration agreement and as if that other Act were an arbitration agreement, except insofar as this Act is inconsistent with that other Act or with any rules or procedure authorised or recognised under that Act.

Taking art 5(1) and s 29(1) together it does appear that the case stated procedure in s 6 of the Acquisition of Land (Assessment of Compensation) Act 1919 will remain in place although it is possible that it could become the subject of a challenge in the courts.

**[7.15]** A number of High Court judgments indicate a reluctance on the part of the High Court to intervene.

**[7.16]** In *Hogan v St Kevin's Company and Purcell*,[28] Murphy J indicated a reluctance on the part of the courts to interfere with arbitration awards where it was indicated that the conclusions of either fact or of law in the case was wrong or unsustainable. Murphy J had this to say:

> ... where parties refer disputes between them to the decision of an arbitrator chosen by them perhaps for his particular qualifications in comprehending technical issues involved in the dispute or perhaps for reasons relating to expedition, privacy or costs, it is obviously and manifestly their intention that the issue between them should be decided, and decided finally, by the person selected by them to adjudicate upon the matter ...[29]

**[7.17]** In *Power Securities Ltd v Daly*,[30] Murphy J, in dealing with compensation awards, stated:

> The Court should be slow to usurp the functions of the chosen tribunal by intervening, whether by way of setting aside an award and remitting an award or directing a case to be stated.[31]

**[7.18]** In *Dublin Corporation v Flan McGinley and Shackleton*,[32] Murphy J upheld the arbitrator's decision to refuse an application on the basis that the arbitrator did not

---

28. *Hogan v St Kevin's Company and Purcell* [1986] IR 80, Murphy J.
29. *Hogan v St Kevin's Company and Purcell* [1986] IR 80 *per* Murphy J.
30. *Power Securities Ltd v Daly* [1984] IEHC 88.
31. *Power Securities Ltd v Daly* [1984] IEHC 88.
32. *Dublin Corporation v Flan McGinley and Shackleton* (unreported, 22 January 1996) HC, Murphy J.

require any further guidance from the court on the point of law at issue. Murphy J had this to say:

> The property arbitrator rejected the Corporation's argument and refused to state a case for the Court on the basis that no further guidance was required by him in relation to the point of law which arose ... In the present case the property arbitrator refused to state a case on the basis that he did not require further guidance of the Courts and in my view he was correct in taking that view.[33]

[7.19] In *Dublin County Council v Healy and Shackleton*,[34] the applicant sought orders from the court to require the property arbitrator to state a case on a point of law and to hear additional evidence after the close of the hearing. Again, in this case the arbitrator had decided that he did not require the assistance of the court on the point of law issue and Barrington J upheld the arbitrator's decision stating that it was a proper exercise of the arbitrator's discretion. Barrington J had this to say:

> The decision not to accept new evidence was a responsible decision made by him (the arbitrator) in the exercise of his discretion. The decision appears to me to have been the right decision. But even if I thought the decision was erroneous I do not think it would be proper for me to interfere by way of mandamus, in the circumstances of this case, with the exercise by the arbitrator of his discretion as to the proper conduct at the arbitration proceedings.[35]

## Regulations in relation to compensation

[7.20] PDA 2000, s 185 allows the Minister to make regulations in respect of making a claim for compensation being regulations for the following matters:

(a) the form in which claims for compensation are to be made;

(b) the provision by a claimant of evidence in support of his or her claim, an information as to his or her interest in the land to which the claim relates;

(c) a statement by a claimant of the names and addresses of all other persons (so far as they are known to him or her) having an interest in the land to which the claim relates and, unless the claim is withdrawn, the notification by the planning authority or the claimant of every other person (if any) appearing to it or him or her to have an interest in the land.[36]

[7.21] PDR 2001, art 174 is contained in Pt 13 of the PDR 2001, which provides that a compensation claim shall be made to the planning authority in writing and shall include:

(a) the name and address of the claimant and a statement of his or her interest in the land to which the claim relates,

---

33. *Dublin Corporation v Flan McGinley and Shackleton* (unreported, 22 January 1996) HC *per* Murphy J.
34. *Dublin County Council v Healy and Shackleton* (unreported, 3 March 1984) HC, Barrington J.
35. *Dublin County Council v Healy and Shackleton* (unreported, 3 March 1984) HC *per* Barrington J.
36. PDA 2000, s 185.

**[7.22]** Planning and Environmental Law in Ireland

> (b) a statement of the matter in respect of which the claim is made, the provision of the Act under which it is made, the amount of compensation claimed and the basis on which that amount has been calculated, and
>
> (c) the names and addresses of all other persons (so far as they are known to the claimant) having an interest in the land to which the claim relates, or, where the claimant does not know of any such persons, a statement to that effect.

**[7.22]** PDR 2001, s 174(2) provides:

> (2) where a planning authority receives a compensation claim which fails to comply with a requirement of sub-article (1), the authority shall, by notice in writing, require the claimant to comply with such requirement and defer consideration of the claim until the claimant has complied with such requirement.[37]

The provisions of art 174(2), which allow the planning authority to serve notice in writing requiring the claimant to comply with any defects in the compensation claim served on the authority, will not extend the time limit for making the claim. PDA 2000, s 183 requires that a claim for compensation be made within six months from the date of the relevant decision but provision is made which allows the High Court to grant an extension of time under PDA 2000, s 183(2).[38] If a corrected claim is not served by the claimant within the six-month time period then the claim will be rejected by the planning authority unless the High Court has granted an extension of time.

**[7.23]** In *Abbeydrive Developments Limited v Kildare County Council*,[39] the claimant did set out his name and address and a statement of his interests in the land and also stated that he knew of no other persons having any legal interest in the lands. The planning authority requested certified copies of the conveyance 'so as to enable the Council to comply with its statutory requirements'. Macken J held that art 174 did not place an obligation on the applicant to disclose the precise legal nature of his interest and further that where a planning authority alleges non-compliance with the formalities, it must call on the claimant to comply with the specific requirement that has not been met

**[7.24]** PDR 2001, art 175 provides that within four weeks of the receipt of a compensation claim or within four weeks of compliance with a requirement under art 174, the planning authority must notify every person appearing to them to have an interest in the land to which the claim relates.

**[7.25]** PDR 2001, art 176 states that the planning authority may require a claimant to provide full details of his title or interest in the land but, as seen in *Abbeydrive*

---

37. PDR 2001, art 174(1)(a), (b), (c) and (2).
38. See PDA 2000, s 183(1)(a)–(b) setting out the full text of the various 'relevant decisions'.
39. *Abbeydrive Developments Limited v Kildare County Council* [2005] IEHC 209, Murphy J.

*Developments Limited v Kildare County Council*,[40] if it requires those details it must specify that such details are required.

## Prohibition of double compensation

**[7.26]** PDA 2000, s 186 disentitles a claimant from claiming more than once for compensation. For example, compensation may also be obtainable under some other enactment and if that is the case the claimant must elect which Act he wishes to claim the compensation under but he cannot claim under two enactments. Also, the claimant cannot claim more compensation under PDA 2000 than he would be entitled to under any other enactment.

## Recovery of compensation from planning authority

**[7.27]** PDA 2000, s 187 provides that when the amount of compensation has been determined that amount is recoverable together with costs from the planning authority and may be enforced in a court as a simple contract debt. The section applies both to court awards of compensation and to compensation awards made by an arbitrator in the course of an arbitration.

## Registration of compensation

**[7.28]** PDA 2000, s 188 obliges a planning authority to keep a record of all compensation amounts payable which exceed €635.[41] The record shall specify the amount of the award and also the refusal of permission or the grant of permission subject to conditions or the revocation or modification of the permission. The land to which the claim for compensation relates must also be recorded. The statement prepared by the planning authority shall be entered into its Register; such entries will be made within two weeks beginning on the day of the preparation of the statement.[42]

## Recovery by planning authority of compensation on subsequent developments

**[7.29]** PDA 2000, s 189 provides that where a sum of compensation has been paid in respect of land (for which a compensation statement has been registered) further development on that land is precluded unless the compensation paid is repaid to the planning authority.

**[7.30]** PDA 2000, s 189(2) provides that the section applies to any development of the kind specified in PDA 2000, s 192(2) and that it does not apply to exempted developments.

---

40. *Abbeydrive Developments Limited v Kildare County Council* [2005] IEHC 209.
41. See Council Regulation (EC) No 974/98 which deleted £500.
42. PDA 2000, s 188(1) and (2)(a) and (b).

**[7.31]** PDA 2000, s 192(2) defines what it describes as 'other development' for the purposes of PDA 2000, s 192(1) as:

> Development of a residential, commercial or industrial character consisting or mainly of the construction of houses, shops or office premises, hotels, garages and petrol filling stations, theatres or structures for the purpose of entertainment or, industrial buildings (including warehouses), or any combination thereof.

**[7.32]** Apart from exempted developments to which the recovery of compensation provisions under PDA 2000, s 189(2) do not apply, s 189 also does not apply to:

(a) any development by virtue of a permission to develop land under Pt III referred to in s 192(5) where the permission was granted subject to conditions other than conditions of a class or description set out in the Fifth Schedule; and

(b) in a case where the compensation specified in the statement became payable in respect of the imposition of conditions on the granting of permission to develop land, this section shall not apply to the development for which that permission was granted.[43]

If compensation is paid and a subsequent development is carried out which covers the full area for which the compensation was granted then the full amount of the compensation must be repaid. If the compensation paid relates to part of the land only which is to be redeveloped then repayment of the compensation shall be apportioned rateably to effect the division between the land to be developed in respect of which compensation was paid as opposed to other land in respect of which no compensation was paid.[44]

**[7.33]** PDA 2000, s 189(5) is a complex piece of draughtsmanship. It is hard to rephrase it and it may take more than one reading before its meaning becomes clear. The section reads:

> Where, in connection with the development of any land, an amount becomes recoverable under this section in respect of the compensation specified in a compensation statement, then no amount shall be recoverable, insofar as it is attributable to that land, in connection with any subsequent development thereof.

Put another way, compensation will not be payable again for each subsequent development of the same land.

**[7.34]** PDA 2000, s 189(6) provides that the repayment of compensation may be by a single capital payment or as a series of instalments of capital and interest, or as a series of other annual or periodical payments, payable at such times as the planning authority may direct after taking into account any representations made by the person by whom the development is to be carried out. In other words, the planning authority has complete discretion in making its decision to pay compensation either by way of a single payment or by making a series of instalment payments or by paying a series of annual payments.

---

43. PDA 2000, s 189(2)(a) and (b).
44. PDA 2000, s 189(3)(a), (b) and (4)(a)–(d) inclusive.

Where the repayments are payable by instalments such repayments shall be secured by mortgage, covenant or otherwise as the planning authority may direct.[45]

**[7.35]** PDA 2000, s 189(7) provides that if a person initiates development to which s 189(1) applies without repaying any compensation or without repaying the full amount of the compensation the planning authority may serve a notice requiring payment within a period to be specified by the planning authority being not less than 12 weeks after the date of service of the notice. If no payment is received by the planning authority within the time specified in the notice the planning authority may recover the amount due to it as a simple contract debt in any court of competent jurisdiction.

## Right to compensation

**[7.36]** PDA 2000, Pt XII, Ch 2 comprises ss 190–195 dealing with compensation in relation to decisions under Pt III.

**[7.37]** PDA 2000 Pt III deals with control of development which relates to the making of applications for planning permissions, decisions on those applications and related matters. PDA 2000, s 32 is the central provision of the planning code in providing for the necessity to obtain planning permission for development when that development is not exempted under the provisions of the Act or under the provisions of the Regulations, and, if it happens that a person has carried out unauthorised development they are required by the Act to seek retention permission for it, provided retention permission is available in the circumstances.[46]

**[7.38]** PDA 2000, s 190 makes provision for the basic principle of planning compensation first established by the Town and Regional Planning Act 1934, whereby a person is entitled to be paid compensation if the value of interest in land is reduced by a planning decision. It will be seen, however, that since the 1934 Act the list of circumstances for which compensation was available has been greatly reduced. PDA 2000, ss 191 and 192 have significantly qualified the entitlement to compensation in circumstances where an application for planning permission has been refused or where conditions have been imposed. PDA 2000, s 190 is an important section dealing with the right to compensation and it reads as follows:

> If, on a claim made to the planning authority, it is shown that, as a result of a decision on an appeal under Pt III involving a refusal of permission to develop land or a grant of permission to develop land subject to conditions, the value of an interest of any person existing in the land to which the decision relates at the time of the decision is reduced, that person shall, subject to the other provisions of this chapter, be entitled to be paid by the planning authority by way of compensation:
> 
> (a) such amount, representing the reduction in value, as may be agreed,

---

45. PDA 2000, s 189(6)(a) and (b).
46. Retention permission is no longer available in cases where an EIA should have been undertaken in the first instance or in cases where an EIS is lodged with the application for retention permission.

(b) in the absence of agreement, the amount of such reduction in value, determined in accordance with the Second Schedule, and

(c) in the case of the occupier of the land, the damage (if any) to his or her trade, business or profession carried out on the land.

Prior to 1990 and the introduction of LG(PD)A 1990, claims for compensation were every day events. Since the passing of the 1990 Act, compensation claims are about as rare as the white owl. The reason for this rarity is set out in PDA 2000, s 191 which is dealt with below.

**[7.39]** Any person claiming compensation from a refusal to grant permission, or from the grant of permission subject to conditions, must show that they have or had an interest in the lands at the time when the decision either to refuse to grant permission or to impose conditions in the grant of permission was made. In *Dublin Corporation v Smithwick*,[47] it was held that an application for compensation could be made although the claimants had sold their interest in the property since the date of the application. The applicants were the owners of the property at the time the permission was refused. Also, in *Grange Developments Limited v Dublin County Council*[48] the claimant did not have a sufficient interest in one plot on the site but this did not preclude him from making an application for compensation in respect of the balance of the land. Furthermore, the claimant was held to have a sufficient compensatable interest although the monies for the purchase of the lands had been provided through another company which had made a declaration of trust in favour of the claimant.

**[7.40]** It is acknowledge that Art 43 of the Constitution seeks to protect the institution of private property. Furthermore, Art 40(3) seeks to protect an individual who wishes to exercise his property rights. Nevertheless, restrictions are justified in the interest of the common good. The general rule that a citizen whose land is being compulsorily acquired is generally entitled to the market value of the land is not an absolute rule. In *Re Article 26 and Part V of the Planning and Development Bill 1999*,[49] the Supreme Court held that a grant of permission does enhance the 'essential value' of the land for which the permission has been granted. In consequence, the planning authority should be entitled to reclaim, for the benefit of the public, a portion of that enhanced value. In normal circumstances, compensation is calculated with reference to 'existing use' value, that is to say, a value which is based on the proposition that it would be unlawful to carry out any development in relation to the land other than exempted development. The limitation on the compensation which the Oireachtas proposed in Pt V of the Planning and Development Bill 1999 ruled out 'hope value' and that interference with property rights was held by the Supreme Court to be fair and reasonable in the context of achieving desirable social objectives, namely an increase in the supply of social and affordable housing.

---

47. *Dublin Corporation v Smithwick* [1976–1977] 1 ILRM 280, Finlay P.
48. *Grange Developments Ltd v Dublin County Council* (No 2) [1989] IR 296.
49. *Re Article 26 and Part V of the Planning and Development Bill 1999* [2000] 2 IR 321.

**[7.41]** Apart from the Constitution, art 1 of the First Protocol of the European Convention on Human Rights and the European Court of Human Rights have each indicated that the taking of property in the public interest, which is without payment of compensation reasonably related to its value, is justified, albeit in exceptional circumstances. The requirement for proportionality applies similarly to the regulation of or restrictions on the use of land as it does the compulsory acquisition of it.

**[7.42]** As we have seen, the right to compensation under the provisions of PDA 2000, s 190 allows a claimant a payment of compensation by the planning authority equal to the amount of the reduction in value of the lands as may be agreed and in the absence of agreement the amount of the reduction in value is determined by an arbitrator in accordance with the provisions of the Second Schedule.

## Determination of compensation in relation to decisions under PDA 2000, Part III

**[7.43]** Where there is no agreement between the local authority and the claimant, the amount of compensation is determined by the rules set out in PDA 2000, Sch 2 which are as follows:

Rule 1:

> The reduction in value shall, subject to the other provisions of this Schedule, be determined by reference to the difference between the antecedent and subsequent values of the land, where –
> 
> (a) the antecedent value of the land is the amount which the land, if sold in the open market by a willing seller immediately prior to the relevant decision under Part III (and assuming that the relevant application for permission had not been made), might have been expected to realise, and
> 
> (b) the subsequent value of the land is the amount which the land, if sold in the open market by a willing seller immediately after that decision, might be expected to realise.

The antecedent value of the land in para (a) is equivalent to the price which it would have obtained if it had been sold on the open market by a willing vendor immediately prior to the relevant decision being made. The subsequent value of the land in para (b) is equivalent to the price which would have been obtained if it were sold on the open market by a willing vendor immediately after that decision was made. If the parties cannot agree then the matter is referred to arbitration under PDA 2000, s 184 and the arbitrator is guided by the basic principle of seeking to value the 'reduction in value' resulting from the refusal to grant planning permission or from the imposition of conditions.

**[7.44]** Rule 2:

> In determining the antecedent value and subsequent value of the land for the purposes of paragraph 1 –
> 
> (a) Regard shall be had to –
> 
> > (i) any contribution which a planning authority might have required or might require as a condition precedent to the development of the land,

> (ii) any restriction on the development of the land which, without conferring a right to compensation, could have been or could be imposed under any Act or under any order, regulations, rule or bye-law made under any Act,
>
> (iii) the fact that exempted development might have been or may be carried out on the land, and
>
> (iv) the open market value of comparable land, if any, in the vicinity of the land whose values are being determined;

The matters to which 'regard' shall be had in determining antecedent value and subsequent value are mandatory matters, not discretionary matters, but this will not preclude an arbitrator from using his/her discretion and expertise in deciding upon their relevance.

> (b) no account shall be taken of –
>
> (i) any part of the value of the land attributable to subsidies or grants available from public monies, or to any tax or rating allowances in respect of development, from which development of the land might benefit,
>
> (ii) the special suitability or adaptability of the land for any purpose if that purpose is a purpose to which it could be applied only in pursuance of statutory powers, or for which there is no market apart from the special needs of a particular purchaser or the requirements of any statutory body as defined in paragraph 5:
>
> Provided that any bona fide offer for the purchase of the land which may be brought to the notice of the arbitrator shall be taken into consideration,
>
> (iii) any increase in the value of land attributable to the use thereof or of any structure thereon in a manner which could be restrained by any court, or is contrary to law, or detrimental to the health of the inmates of the structure, or to public health or safety, or to the environment,
>
> (iv) any depreciation or increase in value attributable to the land, or any land in the vicinity, being reserved for a particular purpose in a development plan,
>
> (v) any value attributable to any unauthorised structure or unauthorised use,
>
> (vi) the existence of proposals for development of the land or any other land by a statutory body, or
>
> (vii) the possibility or probability of the land or other land becoming subject to a scheme of development undertaken by a statutory body; and

Paragraph 2(b) of Rule 2 lists the matters in respect of which no account whatsoever will be taken in determining the value. The items listed at paras (i) to (vii) are self explanatory. In the case of para (iii) any increase in the value which results from the unlawful use of the land or any structure upon it shall *not* be taken into account.

**Compensaton and Compulsory Acquisition** [7.46]

(c) all returns and assessments of capital value for taxation made or acquiesced in by the claimant may be considered.

**[7.45]** Rule 5:

(1) In paragraph 2, 'statutory body' means:[50]

(a) a Minster of the Government;

(b) the Commissioners – (meaning the Commissioners of Public Works in Ireland);

(c) a local authority within the meaning of the Local Government Act, 1941;

(d) a harbour authority within the meaning of the Harbours Act, 1946;

(e) a health board established under the Health Act, 1970;

(f) a vocational education committee within the meaning of the Vocational Education Act, 1930;

(g) a board or other body established by or under statute;

(h) a company in which all the shares are held by, or on behalf of, or by directors appointed by, a Minister of the Government, or

(i) a company in which all the shares are held by a board, company, or other body referred to in subparagraph (g) or (h).

The exception is wide-ranging in that it refers both to unauthorised use and to unauthorised works. Because unauthorised use and unauthorised works still remain 'unauthorised', even though they may escape enforcement because the relevant time limits have expired, they will be taken into account even though they have obtained immunity from enforcement.[51]

Rule 5:

(2) In clauses (h) and (i) of sub-paragraph (1), 'company' means a company within the meaning of section 2(g) of the Companies Act, 1963.

The restrictions on compensation included in para 2(b) are wide-ranging and devastating from the point of view of the person who is seeking payment of compensation. From an examination of 2(b)(vi) it will be appreciated that the full extent of the restriction will only become clear when the definition of 'statutory body' is taken into account.

**[7.46]** PDA 2000, Sch 2, Rule 3 provides that only the possibilities for developing land must be considered in determining the antecedent value of the land. Rule 3(2) goes on to list 'material considerations' which must be considered in determining the antecedent value.

Rule 3:

(1) In assessing the possibilities, if any, for developing the land, for the purposes of determining its antecedent value, regard shall be had only to such reasonable

---

50. PDA 2000, Sch 2, para 5(1).
51. *Dublin Corporation v Mulligan* (unreported, 6 May 1980) HC, Finlay P.

possibilities as, having regard to all material considerations, could be judged to have existed immediately prior to the relevant decision under Part III.

(2) Material considerations for the purposes of subparagraph (1) shall, without prejudice to the generality thereof, include –

1. the nature and location of the land,
2. the likelihood or unlikelihood, as the case may be, of obtaining permission or further permission, to develop the land in the light of the provisions of the development plan,
3. the assumption that, if any permission to develop the land were to be granted, any conditions which might reasonably be imposed in relation to matters referred to in the Fifth Schedule (but no other conditions) would be imposed, and
4. any permission to develop the land, not being permission for the development of a kind specified in section 192(2), already existing at the time of the relevant decision under Part III.

It should be noted that PDA 2000, s 192 provides that a planning authority may avoid liability for compensation where that would arise, by serving a notice on the claimants stating that, in its opinion, the land in question is capable of other development for which planning permission ought to be granted. PDA 2000, s 192(2) defines 'other development' in relation to sub-s (1) as being a:

> ... development of a residential, commercial or industrial character consisting wholly or mainly of the construction of houses, shops or office premises, hotels, garages and petrol filling stations, theatres or structures for the purposes of entertainment, or industrial buildings (including warehouses), or any combination thereof.

**[7.47]** Rule 4 of the Second Schedule deals with the method of determining the subsequent value of land where there has been a refusal to grant permission:

(1) In determining the subsequent value of the land in a case in which there has been a refusal of permission –

(a) it shall be assumed, subject to subparagraph (2), that, after the refusal, permission under Part III would not be granted for any development of a kind specified in section 192(2),

(b) regard shall be had to any conditions in relation to matters referred to in the Fifth Schedule (but no other conditions) which might reasonably be imposed in the grant of permission to develop the land.

(2) In a case in which there has been a refusal of permission in relation to land in respect of which there is in force an undertaking under Part VI of the Act 1963, it shall be assumed in determining the subsequent value of the land that, after the refusal, permission under Part III of this Act would not be granted for any development other than development to which the undertaking relates.

## Restriction of compensation

**[7.48]** PDA 2000, s 191 provides that:

> Compensation under s 190, shall not be payable in respect of the refusal of permission for any development –
> 
> (a) of a class or description set out in the Third Schedule, or
> 
> (b) if the reason or one of the reasons for the refusal is a reason set out in the Fourth Schedule.

## *PDA 2000, Third Schedule*

**[7.49]** The eight classes of development (including 'use') described in the Third Schedule are self-explanatory.

1. Any development that consists of or includes the making of any material change in the use of any structures or other land.

2. The demolition of a habitable house.

3. Any development which would materially affect a protected structure or proposed protected structure.

4. The erection of any advertisement structure.

5. The use of land for the exhibition of any advertisement.

6. Development in an area to which a special amenity area order relates.

7. Any development on land with respect to which there is available (notwithstanding the refusal of permission) a grant of permission under Pt III for any development of a residential, commercial or industrial character, if the development consists wholly or mainly of the construction of houses, shops or office premises, hotels, garages and petrol filling stations, theatres or structures for the purpose of entertainment, or industrial buildings (including warehouses), or any combination thereof, subject to no conditions other than conditions of the kind referred to in the Fifth Schedule.

8. Any development on land with respect to which compensation has already been paid under s 190, s 11 of the Act of 1990 or under s 55 of the Act of 1963, by reference to a previous decision under Pt III of this Act or under Pt IV of the Act of 1963 involving a refusal of permission.

**[7.50]** In dealing with compensation generally, the courts hold the view that any rules restricting the payment of compensation must be interpreted strictly. Thus, in *Dublin Corporation v Smithwick*[52] dealing with the interpretation of the statute, Finlay P stated:

> I should not put by implication a restriction or condition on a right to compensation unless I am forced to do so.

---

52. *Dublin Corporation v Smithwick* [1976–1977] ILRM 280, Finlay P.

**[7.51]** In *Hoburn Homes Limited and Gortalough Holding Limited v An Bord Pleanála*,[53] Denham J held that the development could not be premature by reference to the order of priority in the development plan because the plan had indicated no development in the relevant area. To base a decision on that ground was *ultra vires* the power of the board. Denham J stated:

> In coming to this conclusion I am also influenced in construction by the fact that compensation is a statutory right, and it should only be removed in clear precise cases.

**[7.52]** From time to time attempts were made by planning authorities to try and avoid paying compensation by deliberately inserting non-compensatable reasons in refusals to grant permission. In *Eighty-Five Developments Ltd v Dublin County Council (No 1)*[54] and *Dublin County Council v Eighty Five Developments Ltd (No 2)*,[55] it was held in the High Court and subsequently in the Supreme Court that a planning authority cannot have regard to its desire to exclude a claim from compensation in adjudicating on a planning application and cannot grant planning permission merely to forestall a claim for compensation.

**[7.53]** Eighty Five Developments Limited wished to develop 196 houses, a filling station, shopping centre and a primary school at Seapark, Portrane, Co Dublin. The land to which the application related was zoned for agricultural use. On appeal, the application was refused by An Bord Pleanála on two grounds:

1. It was considered that the proposed development would be contrary to proper planning and development of the area because the site was located in an area zoned B in the Dublin County Development Plan 1983 with the objective *'to protect and provide for the development of agriculture'* and that the proposal would materially contravene this objective which is considered to be reasonable.

2. The proposed development was to be located on the main Donabate Road which is substandard in width and alignment and would give rise to traffic hazard by reason of the additional traffic turning movements which it would generate.

**[7.54]** The prevailing legislation was the LG(PD)A 1963 and, in particular, ss 55 and 56 of that Act. The question posed by Carroll J in the High Court was as to whether the measure of compensation in the case of refusals was to be the value of land assuming that permission for the development had not been granted on the one hand and/or, on the other hand, the value of the land following the refusal, or was it merely the market value of the land prior to the making of the application less the market value of the land after the refusal. Carroll J held in the High Court that the meaning of s 55 was that in

---

53. *Hoburn Homes Limited and Gortalough Holding Ltd v An Bord Pleanála* [1993] 1 ILRM 368, HC, Denham J.
54. *Eighty-Five Developments Ltd v Dublin County Council (No 1)* [1993] 2 IR 378, Carroll J.
55. *Dublin County Council v Eighty-Five Developments Ltd (No 2)* [1993] 2 IR 392, SC.

determining reduction in value the calculation had to be made as if the permission had been granted. The learned judge stated that she could see no way of interpreting the section other than by holding that in determining the reduction value the calculation had to be made as if the permission had been granted. An Bord Pleanála did not state in its decision that the roadway, which was substandard in width and alignment and by reason of additional turning movements, amounted to a traffic hazard.

**[7.55]** The High Court decision was appealed to the Supreme Court. Referring to the matter of zoning, McCarthy J concluded that although the proposal was for housing and other mixed development and the zoning was agricultural, s 56 of LG(PD)A 1963 did not exclude the zoning issue as a matter which would disallow the payment of compensation. Judgments were handed down by Finlay CJ (Hederman and O'Flaherty JJ concurring) and McCarthy J.

**[7.56]** Section 56 did provide that:

> (1) Compensation under s 55 of this Act shall not be payable –
>
> ...
>
> (e) in respect of the refusal of permission for development if the reason or one of the reason for the refusal is that the proposed development would endanger public safety by reasons of traffic hazard or obstruction of road users or otherwise ...

It was the respondent's case that unless the precise wording in s 56 is used in the reasons stated for refusal, the exclusion from compensation does not apply. The Supreme Court did not accept this argument and the court concluded that an analysis of condition 2 clearly highlighted 'traffic hazard'. McCarthy J excused An Bord Pleanála's reticence in failing to use the precise wording of s 56 as follows:

> It may be that the Board is reluctant to use the precise wording of the relevant portion of the section for the very reason that it might be thought that the reason was being advanced in order to defeat a claim for compensation, in effect, an allegation of bad faith. One must look to the wording used and determine whether or not it is a reason which, if construed in its ordinary meaning, would be understood by members of the public without legal training, as well as by developers and their agents, as being within the relevant exclusion. In the instant case, the reason must be looked at against the background of the nature of the development, to which I have referred, its stated location on a road which is substandard in width and alignment, and the nature of the immediate cause of the alleged traffic hazard – by reason of the additional traffic turning movements which it would generate. In my opinion, on an ordinary reading of this stated reason, one must conclude that it means that the proposed development would endanger public safety by reason of traffic hazard.[56]

The Supreme Court allowed the appeal.

---

56. *Per* McCarthy J in *Dublin City Council v Eighty Five Development Ltd (No 2)* [1993] 2 IR 392 at 402.

**[7.57]** *Planning and Environmental Law in Ireland*

## PDA 2000, Fourth Schedule

**[7.57]** The Fourth Schedule[57] excludes compensation where the development proposed is premature by reason of the absence of adequate services or roads, etc, or where the development is premature by reference to the order of priority specified in the development plan.

**[7.58]** Apart from the eight conditions excluding compensation in the Third Schedule a further 26[58] conditions are listed in the Fourth Schedule which also exclude compensation. The Fourth Schedule reasons for the exclusion of payment of compensation include such matters as the development being premature by reason of the lack of facilities or awaiting a road layout plan; public safety reasons and protecting development of amenities in case of material change of use; and danger of causing pollution.

> 1. Development of the kind proposed on the land would be premature by reference to any one or combination of the following constraints and the period within which the constraints involved may reasonably be expected to cease –
>
> (a) an existing deficiency in the provision of water supplies or sewerage facilities,
>
> (b) the capacity of existing or prospective water supplies or sewerage facilities being required for prospective development as regards which a grant of a permission under Part III of this Act, an undertaking under Part VI of the Act of 1963 or a notice under s 13 of the Act of 1990 or section 192 of this Act exists,
>
> (c) the capacity of existing or prospective water supplies or sewerage facilities being required for the prospective development of another part of the functional area of the planning authority, as indicated in the development plan,
>
> (d) the capacity of existing or prospective water supplies or sewerage facilities being required for any other prospective development or for any development objective, as indicated in the development plan,
>
> (e) any existing deficiency in the road network servicing the area of the proposed development, including considerations of capacity, width, alignment, or the surface or structural condition of the pavement, which would render that network, or any part of it, unsuitable to carry the increased road traffic likely to result from the development,

---

57. PDA 2000, s 191 – (note s 191(2) as amended by PD(A)A 2010, s 67).
58. In setting out reasons for the refusal of permission which exclude payment of compensation, the Fourth Schedule list has been extended by the addition of six additional reasons for refusal of payment of compensation making a total of 26 conditions by including the insertion of sub-s (20A) inserted by LGA 2001, 247(m) and sub-s (20B) inserted by Dublin Transport Authority Act 2008, s 94.

(f) any prospective deficiency (including the considerations specified in subparagraph (e)) in the road network serving the area of the proposed development which –

    (i) would arise because of the increased road traffic likely to result from that development and from prospective development as regards which a grant of permission under Part III, an undertaking under Part VI of the Act of 1963 or a notice under section 13 of the Act of 1990 or section 192 exists, or

    (ii) would arise because of the increased road traffic likely to result from that development and from any other prospective development or from any development objective, as indicated in the development plan, and

would render that road network, or any part of it, unsuitable to carry the increased road traffic likely to result from the proposed development.

2. Development of the kind proposed would be premature pending the determination by the planning authority or the road authority of a road layout for the area or any part thereof.

3. Development of the kind proposed would be premature by reference to the order of priority, if any, for development indicated in the development plan or pending the adoption of a local area plan in accordance with the development plan.

4. The proposed development would endanger public safety by reason of traffic hazard or obstruction of road users or otherwise.

5. The proposed development –

(a) could, due to the risk of a major accident or if a major accident were to occur, lead to serious danger to human health or the environment, or

(b) is in an area where it is necessary to limit the risk of there being any serious danger to human health or the environment.

6. The proposed development is in an area which is at risk of flooding.

7. The proposed development by itself, or by the precedent which the grant of permission for it would set for other relevant development, would adversely affect the use of a national road or other major road by traffic.

8. The proposed development would interfere with the character of the landscape or with a view or prospect of special amenity value or natural interest or beauty, any of which it is necessary to preserve.

9. The proposed development would cause serious air pollution, water pollution, noise pollution or vibration or pollution connected with the disposal of waste.

10. In the case of development including any structure or any addition to or extension of a structure, the structure, addition or extension would –

(a) infringe an existing building line or, where none exists, a building line determined by the planning authority or by the Board,

(b) be under a public road,

(c) seriously injure the amenities, or depreciate the value, of property in the vicinity,

- (d) tend to create any serious traffic congestion,
- (e) endanger or interfere with the safety of aircraft or the safe and efficient navigation thereof,
- (f) endanger the health or safety of persons occupying or employed in the structure of any adjoining structure, or
- (g) be prejudicial to public health.

11. The development would contravene materially a condition attached to an existing permission for development.

12. The proposed development would injure or interfere with a historic monument which stands registered in the Register of Historic Monuments under section 5 of the National Monuments (Amendment) Act, 1987, or which is situated in an archaeological area so registered.

13. The proposed development would adversely affect an architectural conservation area.

14. The proposed development would adversely affect the linguistic or cultural heritage of the Gaeltacht.

15. The proposed development would materially contravene an objective indicated in a local area plan for the area.

16. The proposed development would be contrary to any Ministerial guidelines issued to the planning authorities under section 28 or any Ministerial policy directive issued to the planning authorities under section 29.

17. The proposed development would adversely affect a landscape conservation area.

18. In accordance with section 35, the planning authority considers that there is a real and substantial risk that the development in respect of which permission is sought would not be completed in accordance with any permission or any condition to which such permission would be subject.

19. The proposed development –

- (a) would contravene materially a development objective indicated in the development plan for the conservation and preservation of a European site insofar as the proposed development would adversely affect one or more specific –
  - (i)
    - (I) natural habitat types in Annex I of the Habitats Directive, or
    - (II) species in Annex II of the Habitats Directive which the site hosts,
    
    and which have been selected by the Minister for Arts, Heritage, Gaeltacht and the Islands in accordance with Annex III (Stage 1) of that Directive,
  - (ii) species of bird or their habitat or other habitat specified in Article 4 of the Birds Directive, which formed the basis of the classification of that site, or
- (b) would have a significant adverse affect on any other areas prescribed for the purpose of section 10(2)(c).

20. The development would contravene materially a development objective indicated in the development plan for the zoning of land for the use solely or primarily of particular areas for particular purposes (whether residential, commercial, industrial, agricultural or recreational) as open space or otherwise or a mixture of such uses.

20A. The proposed development would not be consistent with the planning scheme in force in respect of a strategic development zone.[59]

20B. The proposed development would not be consistent with the transport strategy of the Dublin Transport Authority.[60]

21.(a) Subject to paragraph 22, paragraphs 19 and 20, shall not apply in a case where a development objective for the use specified in paragraph 20 applied to the land at any time during the period of a development plan and the development objective of which was changed as a result of a variation of the plan during such period prior to the date on which the relevant application for permission was made to develop the land, and the development would not have contravened materially that development objective.

(b) Paragraph 20, shall not apply in a case where, as a result of a direction by the Minister under section 31(2)[61] given within one year of the making of a development plan, a planning authority amends or revokes a development objective referred to in paragraph 19 but without prejudice to any right of compensation which may otherwise arise in respect of any refusal of permission under Part III in respect of an application made before such direction was issued by the Minister.

22. Paragraph 21 shall not apply in a case where a person required his or her interest in the land –

(a) after the objective referred to in paragraph 19 or 20 has come into operation, or

(b) after notice has been published,

(i) In accordance with section 12 or 13, of a proposed new development plan or of proposed variations of a development plan, as the case may be, or

(ii) in accordance with section 12, of a material alteration of the draft concerned,

indicating in draft the development objective referred to in paragraph 19 or 20, or

---

59. See LGA 2001, s 247(m) inserting PDA 2000, Sch 4, para 20A.
60. See the Dublin Transport Authority Act 2008, s 94 inserting PDA 2000, Sch 4, para 20B.
61. PDA 2000, s 31(2) deals with Ministerial directions regarding a development plan where the Minister feels that any development plan fails to set out an overall strategy for the proper planning and sustainable development of the area, or the planning authority otherwise significantly fails to comply with PDA 2000.

(c) in the case of paragraph 19, after notice has been published by the Minister for Arts, Heritage, Gaeltacht and the Islands of his or her intention to propose that the land be selected as a European site.[62]

23. For the purpose of paragraph 22, the onus shall be on a person to prove all relevant facts relating to his or her interest in the land to the satisfaction of the planning authority.

24. In this Schedule, 'road authority' and 'national road' have the meanings assigned to them in the Roads Act, 1993.

If a planning authority wishes to avoid paying compensation in the first instance, the reasons for the refusal must be genuine and not merely inserted for the purpose of avoiding payment of compensation. In the case of Fourth Schedule reasons for refusal of permission, which exclude compensation, the Supreme Court has ruled that if the compensation is to be excluded the wording of the reasons for exclusion should, as closely as possible, follow the wording of the provision of the Fourth Schedule. In *Dublin County Council v Eighty Five Developments Limited (No 2)*,[63] the Supreme Court ruled that although the wording of a reason for refusal should follow the wording of the legislation as closely as possible, nevertheless if the precise words were not used the court would undertake a common sense appraisal and provided the meaning is otherwise clear it is not necessary to follow the exact wording. By way of example, see also *J Wood & Co Limited v Wicklow County Council*,[64] where the words 'visually sensitive location' appeared in one of the conditions justifying the refusal of grant of permission. The court held that the description was sufficiently unclear to exclude the refusal from the necessity to pay compensation. The words used in para 8 of the Fourth Schedule are:

> the proposed development would interfere with the character of the landscape or with a view or prospect of special amenity value or natural interest or beauty, any of which it is necessary to preserve.

**[7.59]** In *Hoburn Homes v An Bord Pleanála*,[65] a condition was imposed which read: 'To slow down the growth in the "west harbour"'. That condition did not exclude the payment of compensation. The plaintiff's development proposal was not 'premature by reference to the order of priority' in the development plan for the very reason that the development plan indicated 'no development' in the relevant area. In making this judgment, Denham J stated that: 'Compensation is a statutory right and shall only be removed in clear precise cases'.

**[7.60]** Again it must be stressed that in no circumstances will compensation be payable in respect of a refusal for permission or a grant subject to onerous conditions issued by a

---

62. PDA 2000, s 10(2)(c), in dealing with the context of a development plan, provides that such plan shall include objectives for the conservation and protection of European sites and other sites which may be prescribed for the purposes of this paragraph.
63. *Dublin County Council v Eighty Five Developments Limited (No 2)* [1993] 2 IR 392, SC.
64. *J Wood & Co Limited v Wicklow County Council* [1995] ILRM 51, Costello P.
65. *Hoburn Homes v An Bord Pleanála* [1993] ILRM 368, HC, Denham J.

planning authority. In order to qualify for compensation the affected landowner must have received the refusal or the onerous condition by decision on appeal of An Bord Pleanála.

[7.61] Compensation is not payable in respect of a refusal of permission resulting from a change of the zoning of any land in consequence of the making of a new development plan. In *O'Connor v Clare County Council*,[66] it was noted that the Clare County Development Plan was adopted in 1998 and subsequently was amended by the Cliffs of Moher Development Plan in respect of the area set aside for visitors at the Cliffs of Moher. The area marked off as the visitors' area was designated as an environmental zone for agricultural use which zoning prohibited development of buildings. Specific provision was made within that zoning for an integrated visitor facility to be contained in a single building. The applicant's lands lay within the small zoned area for the single building and when they made application for planning permission to construct a shop and storage unit the application was refused because the plans specifically permitted a single building which would act as an integrated visitor facility only. The applicant subsequently claimed compensation and the arbitrator submitted a special case to the High Court. Murphy J held that the applicant's proposal was a material contravention and that in consequence compensation was excluded by virtue of reason 11 of the Third Schedule. The Clare County Plan, in its development objectives, specified that the visitors' area at the Cliffs of Moher be developed as an integrated visitor facility and any other development or use of the site or part of the site as a stand-alone shop with storage units would materially contravene that development objective.

[7.62] In the course of his judgment, Murphy J defined 'zoning' as follows:

> The limited area designated for development could hardly be described as being 'zoned' in the sense in which that is ordinarily understood. That term is generally used to describe a wider area where activities or developments having some measure of uniformity may be undertaken by a considerable number of owners or occupiers. However, there does not appear to be anything in reason 11 aforesaid which would prevent a planning authority from indicating a specific development objective in relation to a limited area with a view to or as a consequence of formulating a development objective in relation to an adjoining larger area. As clearly as words and plans can so provide the Clare County Council have indicated their development objective that the area specified as one for 'development' is to be used for the particular purpose of an integrated visitor facility which is described in detail in the 1991 Plan. It seems to me that any other development or use of that site, or any part of it, as a shop and storage unit or otherwise than in the context of an integrated visitor facility would contravene materially this development objective.[67]

[7.63] See also *Ebonwood Limited v Meath County Council*,[68] where Peart J held that a reason for refusal of planning permission will not exclude payment of compensation if it

---

66. *O'Connor v Clare County Council* (unreported, 11 February 1994) HC, Murphy J.
67. *O'Connor v Clare County Council* (unreported, 11 February 1994) HC *per* Murphy J.
68. *Ebonwood Ltd v Meath County Council* [2004] 3 IR 34, Peart J.

refers to an objective of a draft development plan. The learned judge held that it was beyond doubt that any reference in the Act to a development plan is a reference only to the development plan currently in force and not to any draft development plan. Peart J cited *Chawke Caravans Limited v Limerick Corporation*,[69] where Flood J had held that in determining whether a development was a material contravention of a development plan, the development plan is the development plan is in force at that time. The fact that there was a draft plan on display in Limerick City Corporation's offices was utterly irrelevant. PDA 2000, s 191(2)[70] specifically provides that compensation under s 190 shall not be payable in respect of a refusal of permission for any development based on any change of the zoning of any land as a result of the making of a new development plan under s 12 or the preparing, making, amending or revoking of a local area plan under s 18 or s 20.

## PDA 2000, Fifth Schedule

**[7.64]** PDA 2000, s 191(3) provides that compensation shall not be payable where the grant of permission is subject to any of the 34 conditions set out in the Fifth Schedule:

1. A condition, under paragraph (g) and (j) of section 34(4), requiring the giving of security for satisfactory completion of the proposed development (including maintenance until taken in charge by the local authority concerned of roads, open spaces, carparks, sewers, watermains or drains).

2. A condition, included in a grant of permission pursuant to section 48 or 49, requiring the payment of a contribution for public infrastructure benefiting the development.

3. A condition under paragraph (n) of section 34(4), requiring the removal of an advertisement structure.

4. Any condition under paragraph (n) of section 34(4) in a case in which the relevant application for permission relates to a temporary structure.

5. Any condition relating to the reservation or allocation of any particular land, or all land in any particular area, for development of a specified class or classes, or the prohibition or restriction either permanently or temporarily, of development on any specified land.

6. Any condition relating to the preservation of the quality and character of urban or rural areas.

7. Any condition relating to the regulation, restriction and control of development of coastal areas or development in the vicinity of inland waterways.

8. Any provision relating to the protection of the linguistic or cultural heritage of the Gaeltacht.

---

69. *Chawke Caravans Ltd v Limerick Corporation* (unreported, February 1991) HC, Flood J.
70. PDA 2000, s 191(2) has been amended by PD(A)A 2007, s 67 and the amended version appears here.

9. Any condition relating to reducing the risk or limiting the consequences of a major accident, or limiting the risk of there being any serious danger to human health or the environment.

10. Any condition regulating, restricting or controlling development in areas at risk of flooding.

11. Any condition relating to –

(a) the regulation and control of the layout of areas and structures, including density, spacing, grouping and orientation of structures in relation to roads, open spaces and other structures,

(b) the regulation and control of the design, colour and materials of structures and groups of structures,

(c) the promotion of design in structures for the purposes of flexible and sustainable use, including conservation of energy and resources.

12. Any condition limiting the number of structures or the number of structures of a specified class which may be constructed, erected or made on, in or under any area.

13. Any condition regulating and controlling all or any of the following matters –

(a) the size, height, floor area and character of structures;

(b) building lines, coverage and the space about houses and other structures;

(c) the extent of parking places required in, on or under structures of a particular class or size or services or facilities for the parking, loading, unloading or fuelling of vehicles;

(d) the objects which may be affixed to structures;

(e) the purposes for and the manner in which structures may be used or occupied, including, in this case of dwellings, the letting thereof in separate units.

14. Any condition relating to the alteration or removal of unauthorised structures.

15. Any condition relating to the provision and siting of sanitary services and waste facilities, recreational facilities and open spaces.

16. Any condition relating to the protection and conservation of the environment including the prevention of environmental pollution and the protection of waters, groundwater, the seashore and the atmosphere.

17. Any condition relating to measures to reduce or prevent the emission or the intrusion of noise or vibration.

18. Any condition prohibiting, regulating or controlling the deposit or disposal of waste materials and refuse, the disposal of sewage and the pollution of rivers, lakes, ponds, gullies and the seashore.

19. Any condition relating to the protection of features of the landscape which are of major importance for wild fauna and flora.

20. Any condition relating to the preservation and protection of trees, shrubs, plants and flowers.

21. Any condition relating to the preservation (either *in situ* or by record) of places, caves, sites, features or other objects of archaeological, geological, historical, scientific or ecological interest.

22. Any condition relating to the conservation and preservation of –

   (a) one or more specific –

       (i)      (I)     natural habitat types in Annex I of the Habitats Directive, or

              (II)    species in Annex II of the Habitats Directive which the site hosts,

             contained in a European site selected by the Minister for Arts, Heritage, Gaeltacht and the Islands in accordance with Annex III (Stage 1) of that Directive,

       (ii)    species of bird or their habitat or other habitat contained in a European site specified in Article 4 of the Birds Directive, which formed the basis of the classification of that site,

   or

   (b) any other area prescribed for the purpose of section 10(2)(c).[71]

23. Any condition relating to the preservation of the landscape in general, or a landscape conservation order in particular, including views and prospects and amenities of places and features of natural beauty or interest.

24. Any condition for preserving any existing public right of way.

25. Any condition reserving, as a public park, public garden or public recreation space, land normally used as such.

26. Any condition prohibiting, restricting or controlling, either generally or within a specified distance of the centre line of any specified road, the erection of all or any particular forms of advertisement structure or the exhibition of all or any particular forms of advertisement.

27. Any condition preventing, remedying or removing injury to amenities arising from the ruinous or neglected condition of any structure, or from the objectionable or neglected condition of any land attached to a structure or abutting on a public road or situate in a residential area.

28. Any condition relating to a matter in respect of which a requirement could have been imposed under any other Act, or under any order, regulation,

---

71. PDA 2000, s 10(2)(c) reads: 'The conservation and protection of the environment including, in particular, the archaeological and natural heritage and the conservation and protection of European sites and any other sites which may be prescribed for the purposes of this paragraph.' PDA 2000, s 10(2)(c) has been extended by the addition of (ca) and (cb) inserted by PD(A)A 2010, s 7(b)(i). (ca) reads: 'The encouragement, pursuant to art 10 of the Habitats Directive, of the management of features of the landscape, such as to additional field boundaries, important for the ecological coherence of the Natura 2000 network and essential for the migration, dispersal and genetic exchange of wild species; (cb) reads: 'the promotion of compliance with environmental standards and objectives established – (i) for bodies of surface water, by the European Communities (Surface Waters) Regulations 2009; (ii) for groundwater, by the European Communities (Groundwater) Regulations 2010; which standards and objectives are included in river basin management plans (within the meaning of the European Communities (Water Policy) Regulations 2003, reg 13).

rule or bye-law made under any other Act, without liability for compensation.

29. Any condition prohibiting the demolition of a habitable house.
30. Any condition relating to the filling of land.
31. Any condition in the interest of ensuring the safety of aircraft or the safe and efficient navigation thereof.
32. Any condition determining the sequence in which works shall be carried out or specifying a period within which works shall be completed.
33. Any condition restricting the occupation of any structure included in a development until the completion of other works included in the development or until any other specified condition is complied with or until the planning authority consents to such occupation.
34. Any conditions relating to the protection of a protected structure or a proposed protected structure.

Again, most of the 34 conditions are self explanatory. Compensation will not be payable in respect of conditions requiring security for the completion of development nor shall it be paid in respect of conditions requiring contribution for a public infrastructure which will benefit the development. Many of the conditions which are excluded from compensation relate to environmental protection and to conditions dealing with the control of accidents. In *Cooper v Cork County Council*,[72] Murphy J held that the phrase used in PDA 2000, s 191(3) namely 'any condition of a class or description set out in PDA 2000, Fifth Schedule is broader than the phrase used in PDA 2000, s 191(1) namely 'reasons for refusal set out in PDA 2000, Fourth Schedule'. Murphy J considered that a more purposive approach shall be taken in interpreting the Fifth Schedule. In the *Cooper* case, Murphy J examined a condition which prohibited development of a particular part of the site the subject matter of the application, and the condition required that the area be retained in its natural stage. The learned judge held that the 'preservation of trees, shrubs, plants and flowers' was a condition which excluded compensation.

[7.65] The notice generally continues in force for a period of five years unless planning permission is, in fact, refused for 'other development' specified in the notice, in which case a claim for compensation should succeed.[73]

[7.66] Significantly, PDA 2000, s 191(4) provides that compensation shall not be payable in respect of a refusal of permission or in respect of the imposition of conditions on the granting of permission, for retention on land of any unauthorised structures.

## Notice preventing compensation

[7.67] Where a planning authority has refused a particular planning application it may legally avoid the payment of compensation by serving a notice under PDA 2000, s 192,

---

72. *Cooper v Cork County Council* [2006] IEHC 353 (8 November 2006), Murphy J.
73. PDA 2000, Sch 5, para 20.

specifying that in the opinion of the planning authority the land is capable of other development for which permission ought to be granted. Having granted a refusal in respect of an application for permission a planning authority may indicate to the applicant that planning permission will be available for other development. If a planning authority refuses permission but serves a notice under s 192 indicating that permission would, in principle, be available for a different type of development the notice must be served not later than 12 weeks after the claim for compensation has been received in respect of the original application. The relevant part of s 192 uses the following wording:

> ... notwithstanding the refusal of permission to develop land or the grant of permission to develop land subject to conditions, the land in question is in its opinion capable of other development for which permission under Part III ought to be granted.[74]

The notice generally continues in force for a period of five years unless planning permission is, in fact, refused for other development specified in the notice in which case a claim for compensation should succeed.[75] A claim for compensation which follows refusal for the alternative permission indicated by the planning authority is compensatable based on the original refusal for permission.

**[7.68]** In *Arthur v Kerry County Council*,[76] Kerry County Council granted the applicant's application for planning permission on two separate occasions. Third party objections were made and an appeal was lodged with An Bord Pleanála in respect of each of the permissions granted by Kerry County Council and two separate refusals were issued by An Bord Pleanála. The applicant claimed compensation under s 11 of LG(PD)A 1996 in respect of both refusals. Kerry County Council, in respect of both notices, served, what was then, a s 13 notice on the applicant refusing compensation but indicating that permission should be granted specifically in respect of the second s 13 notice, if the applicant ensured that all of the board's objections were complied with. The applicant then sought an order for *certiorari* seeking to quash the second s 13 notice and an order for *mandamus* requiring that his compensation claim be dealt with. The High Court granted the order of *certiorari* but refused the order of *mandamus* stating that such an order was unnecessary because Kerry County Council would, in any case, deal with the issue of compensation. It was also held in this case that statutory provisions regarding compensation should be given strict interpretation in favour of the parties seeking the compensation.

**[7.69]** A s 192 notice preventing compensation and indicating that permission might be available for an alternative development is not, of course, a grant of permission. In *Byrne v Dublin County Council*,[77] Gannon J, in dealing with the provisions of s 57 of the LG(PD)A 1963, held that the only sensible construction of that section is that it

---

74. PDA 2000, s 192(1).
75. PDA 2000, s 192(3).
76. *Arthur v Kerry County Council* [2000] 3 IR 407, McGuinness J.
77. *Byrne v Dublin County Council* [1983] ILRM 213, Gannon J.

precludes an award of compensation in a case where an undertaking has been given that an alternative form of development will be permitted, but the undertaking to grant permission does not equate to a grant of permission. See also *Grange Developments Limited v Dublin County Council*,[78] where an undertaking was given to grant permission for industrial buildings, a hotel and structures for the purpose of entertainment on land zoned for agricultural use. The undertaking was given by Dublin County Council in order to avoid payment of compensation. The undertaking was held to be invalid on the grounds that if the applicant's development proposal was permitted it would constitute a material contravention of the Council's own development plan. The planning authority was entitled to avail of the material contravention procedure. The case also held that if the claimant received a subsequent refusal of permission in the terms of the undertaking given by the planning authority or by the board, the claimant would be entitled to the credit deducted from the compensation by the arbitrator, together with interest on that amount.

[7.70] As seen in *Arthur v Kerry County Council*,[79] the planning authority refused permission in the first instance but served a s 192 notice. A second application was made for permission. If that second application was refused in respect of the development specified in the notice, then the original claim for compensation would revive. What this means is that the planning authority will not normally be permitted to serve a second s 192 notice because a s 192 notice must be served within 12 weeks of the date of receipt of the claim for compensation. A second notice cannot be served as the 12-week period from the date of the original claim for compensation would, almost invariably, have long since expired. PDA 2000, s 192(4) provides that where a claimant fails to apply for planning permission of the type specified in the s 192 notice, within the five-year life time of the notice, the claim for compensation becomes permanently barred.

[7.71] Article 177 of PDR 2001 provides precise details of the contents of the notice to be served by a planning authority under s 191 of the Act. The wording of the article is useful in understanding the procedures involved in preparing a s 192 notice. Article 177 requires that the nature and extent of the development proposed must be indicated in outline. Article 177 of PDR 2001 provides as follows:

[7.72] A notice under section 192 of the Act served on a person by whom or on behalf of whom a compensation claim under section 190 of the Act has been made shall:

    (a)    indicate the land to which the notice relates,

    (b)    state that, notwithstanding the refusal of permission to develop the land or the grant of such permission subject to conditions (as the case may be), the land in question is, in the opinion of the planning authority, capable of other development for which permission under Part III of the Act ought to be granted,

---

78.   *Grange Developments Limited v Dublin County Council* [1989] IR 296, SC.
79.   *Arthur v Kerry County Council* [2000] 3 IR 407.

- (c) indicate in outline the nature and extent of the other development (being other development within the meaning of section 192 of the Act) of which, in the opinion of the planning authority, the land is capable,
- (d) state that the notice shall continue in force for a period of five years commencing on the day of service of the notice unless, before the expiration of that period:
    - (i) the notice is withdrawn by the planning authority,
    - (ii) a permission is granted under Part III of the Act to develop the land to which the notice relates in a manner consistent with other development specified in the notice, subject to no conditions or to conditions of a class or description set out in the Fifth Schedule of the Act, or
    - (iii) the notice is annulled by virtue of section 192(5)[80] of the Act, and
- (e) state that compensation shall not be payable on the claim in respect of the land in question where:
    - (i) the notice is in force,
    - (ii) an application for permission under Part III of the Act to develop the land to which the notice relates in a manner consistent with the other development specified in the notice has not been made before the expiry of the notice, or
    - (iii) permission is granted under Part III of the Act to develop the land to which the notice relates in a manner consistent with the other development specified in the notice, subject to no conditions or to conditions of a class or description set out in the Fifth Schedule of the Act.

The purpose of art 177 in the planning regulations is to regulate the contents of a s 192 notice which enables the planning authority to refuse payment of compensation in respect of a refusal of permission or in respect of the imposition of conditions where it has stated that in its opinion the land is capable of 'other development' for which permission ought to be granted.

**[7.73]** PDA 2000, s 192(2) defines 'other developments' for the purposes of s 192(1) and for the purposes of the application notice as meaning:

... development of a residential, commercial or industrial character, consisting wholly or mainly of the construction of houses, shops or office premises, hotels, garages and petrol filling stations, theatres or structures for the purpose of entertainment or industrial buildings (including warehouses), or any combination thereof.

**[7.74]** Simons[81] draws attention to a peculiar effect of s 192 as follows:

One of the curious features of section 192 is that there is no suggestion that the scale of the development indicated in the notice be similar to that for which

---

80. PDA 2000, s 192(5).
81. See Simons, *Planning and Development Law* (2nd edn, Thomson Round Hall, 2007) at para 6–87, p 268.

planning permission has been refused. Rather, it seems that the claim for compensation can be deferred by serving a notice indicating that land is capable of development of a type indicated above at para 6–85,[82] even on a small scale. This might give rise to unfairness in certain cases. For example, it would seem unjust were a claim in respect of the refusal of planning permission for, say, one hundred houses to be met with a section 192 notice specifying development of ten houses.

[7.75] In dealing with the content of development plans, PDA 2000, s 10(2) provides that a development plan shall include various zoning objectives whereby land is zoned for use solely or primarily for particular purposes (whether residential, commercial, industrial, agricultural, recreational, as open space or otherwise, or a mixture of those uses). PDA 2000, s 192(2) makes it clear that a planning authority in using the phrase 'other development' is required to define the 'other development' precisely. If the 'other development' referred to in a s 192 notice is not precisely defined the ambiguity which results might lead to a refusal of the application submitted. Article 177(c) requires that the s 192 notice should 'indicate in outline the nature and extent of the other development (being other development within the meaning of s 192 of the Act) of which, in the opinion of the planning authority, the land is capable'.

[7.76] The outline nature and extent of the development should be described in detail. It appears that a s 192 notice can be served by a planning authority even in circumstances where the 'other development' specified in the notice would constitute a material contravention of the development plan. In *Browne v Cashel UDC*,[83] Geoghegan J held that 'other development' must not be a material contravention of the development plan. However, that decision was overruled in the Supreme Court in *Ballymac Designer Village Limited v Louth County Council*,[84] where the court held that a notice under LG(PD)A 1990, s 13 was not invalidated by reason of the fact that the planning permission proposed therein involved a material contravention of the development plan and that it could be granted, but only after the successful conclusion of the material contravention procedure.

[7.77] So it is now clear that a s 192 notice can be served by a planning authority even where the 'other development' specified in the notice would constitute a material contravention of the development plan. As the Supreme Court noted, the planning authority can invoke the material contravention procedure to set aside the material contravention provisions.

[7.78] PDA 2000, s 192(3) gives a s 192 notice a five-year lifespan commencing on the date of service of the notice unless before the expiration of that period:

(a) the notice is withdrawn by the planning authority,

(b) a permission is granted under Part III to develop the land to which the notice relates in a manner consistent with the other development specified

---

82. Paragraph 6–85 deals with notices excluding compensation under PDA 2000, s 192.
83. *Browne v Cashel UDC* (unreported, 26 March 1993) HC, Geoghegan J.
84. *Ballymac Designer Village Limited v Louth County Council* [2002] 3 IR 247.

in the notice, subject to no conditions or to conditions of a class or description set out in the Fifth Schedule, or

(c) the notices annulled by virtue of subsection (5).[85]

**[7.79]** PDA 2000, s 192(5) provides that:

A notice under subsection section (1) shall be annulled where, upon an application for permission under Part III to develop the land to which the notice relates in a manner consistent with the other development specified in the notice, the permission is refused or is granted subject to conditions other than conditions of a class or description set out in the Fifth Schedule.

No claim for compensation can be made where a s 192 notice has been annulled.[86]

## Structures substantially replacing structures demolished or destroyed by fire

**[7.80]** It is recognised that permission will be granted to erect a new structure which substantially replaces a structure which was demolished or destroyed by fire. It is recognised that a permission is not required if the user of the new replacement structure is the same as the user prior to the destruction of a premises by fire.

**[7.81]** PDA 2000, s 193(1) provides that compensation will be payable where there has been a refusal of permission concerning the erection of a new structure which substantially replaces the structure which was demolished or destroyed by fire or where a condition was imposed whereby the new structure cannot be used for the purpose of the demolished or destroyed structure. The subsection provides a two-year time limit and an application for compensation must be made within two years preceding the date of application for permission. It also follows that if the structure which was demolished by fire was, itself, an unauthorised structure no compensation will be payable. No compensation will be paid if the structure was demolished or destroyed as a result of an unlawful act of the owner or of the occupier with the consent of the owner. Where, as a result of an imposed condition or imposed conditions, the new structure or the part of such structure or the front of an existing structure which has been taken down, has been set back or set forward, compensation may also be payable.

**[7.82]** PDA 2000, s 193(2) provides that any dispute on the question as to whether or not the replacement structure is substantially the same as the structure destroyed by fire is referred to An Bord Pleanála for determination. It is clear, however, that the replacement structure need not be precisely identical to the structure which was in existence prior to the fire but it must 'substantially' replace such structure.

---

85. See PDA 2000, s 192(3)(a), (b) and (c).
86. See PDA 2000, s 192(6).

## Restriction on assignment of compensation under s 190

**[7.83]** PDA 2000, s 194 prohibits the assignment of all or part of any prospective compensation to another party and it provides that any promise to assign or any purported assignment, either express or implied, of the compensation is void. The section renders an assignment or promise to assign compensation void but it does not render the assignment of the land void. See *Dublin Corporation v Smithwick*,[87] where Finlay P stated:

> ... as to the principle of interpretation of this Statute, that I should not by implication, put a restriction or condition on a right to compensation unless I am forced to do so.

## Compensation where permission is revoked or modified

**[7.84]** PDA 2000, s 195(1)(a) and (b) provides that compensation will be payable to any persons interested in the land in respect of any expenditure incurred or in respect of any contract entered into for work which was subsequently rendered useless because of notice served by the planning authority under PDA 2000, s 44 to revoke or modify a planning permission already issued because it is no longer in accordance with the development plan. For the purposes of payment of compensation under this section revocation of permission is dealt with in the same way as a refusal of permission and modification is dealt with in the same way as if the permission was granted subject to conditions.

**[7.85]** PDA 2000, s 195(2) allows for compensation in respect of expenditure reasonably incurred in the preparation of plans for the purpose of any works or other proprietary matters but no compensation will be payable for any expenditure or loss incurred on works carried out prior to the grant of the planning permission which has been revoked or modified, or in respect of any other loss or damage arising out of anything done or omitted to be done before the grant of planning permission.

## Compensation regarding removal or alteration of a structure

**[7.86]** PDA 2000, s 46 enables a planning authority to serve notice requiring:

 (i) the demolition or alteration of a structure;
 (ii) the discontinuance of a use; or
 (iii) the imposition of conditions on a use.

While s 46 gives the planning authority discretion to take the steps listed at (i), (ii) and (iii), the power may only be exercised in exceptional circumstances. If it is exercised in accordance with the terms of PDA 2000, s 46, compensation is payable to a person or persons who have an interest in the structure and is calculated by reference to a reduction in the value of the structure or damage as a result of being disturbed in the enjoyment of the structure.

---

87. *Dublin Corporation v Smithwick* [1976–1977] 1 ILRM 280, Finlay P.

**[7.87]** PDA 2000, s 46(2) provides that notice under s 46(1) may not be served in respect of unauthorised development unless such notice is served after the expiration of seven years from the commencement of the authorised development.

## Compensation regarding discontinuance of use

**[7.88]** PDA 2000, s 197 also refers to circumstances arising from the service of a notice under PDA 2000, s 46. Compensation will be paid to a person having an interest in the land in respect of which there is a reduction in value of the land. Compensation will also be paid to a person where damage was suffered as a result of being disturbed in the enjoyment of the land. The payment of compensation is not certain in all cases. The person having an interest in the land must demonstrate either that the value of the interest in the land existing at the time of the imposition of the condition is reduced, or that any person having an interest in the land at that time has suffered damage by being disturbed in his or her enjoyment of the land.

**[7.89]** Compensation is excluded by s 197(2) where a condition is imposed in order to avoid serious water pollution or danger of such pollution.

**[7.90]** Section 197(3) excludes compensation where the use of the land is for the exhibition of advertising unless at the time of discontinuance or compliance the land has been so used for less than five years whether the use was continuous or intermittent or whether or not, while the land was being so used, advertising was exhibited at the same place on the land.

## Compensation claim relating to area of special planning control

**[7.91]** PDA 2000, s 198 makes a special case for the payment of compensation in relation to land within a special area of planning control adopted under PDA 2000, s 85, where it can be shown that the value of an interest of any person in land in an area of special planning control has been reduced. Under PDA 2000, s 88 a planning authority may serve a notice in pursuance of a special planning control scheme requiring an occupier to take certain steps in relation to taking measures for restoration, demolition, removal, alteration, replacement, maintenance, repair or cleaning of any structure or the discontinuance of any use or the continuance of any use subject to conditions. Compensation may be payable where, as a result of complying with a s 88 notice, the value of the land has been reduced or such person has suffered damage by being disturbed in the enjoyment of the land. Separately, PDA 2000, s 88(2)(g) and (h) require that a s 88 notice shall:

> (g) state that the planning authority shall pay any expenses that are reasonably incurred by that person in carrying out the steps specified in the notice, other than expenses that relate to unauthorised development carried out not more than seven years prior to the service of the notice, and

(h) state that that the planning authority shall, by way of compensation, pay, to any person who shows that as a result of complying with the notice –

　　(i) the value of an interest he or she has in the land or part thereof existing at the time of the notice has been reduced, or

　　(ii) he or she, having an interest in the land at that time, has suffered damage by being disturbed in his or her enjoyment of the structure or other land,

a sum equal to the amount of such reduction in value or a sum in respect of the damages suffered.

## Compensation regarding cables, wires and pipelines

**[7.92]** PDA 2000, s 182(1)–(5) permits a local authority with the consent of the owner/occupier of any land or structure to lay cables, wires or pipelines (including water pipes, sewers or drains) and any ancillary apparatus on or over the land. With the consent of the owner/occupier of any structure it may attach brackets or other fixtures required for carrying or supporting any cable, wire or pipeline and the local authority can maintain notices indicating the position of cables, wires or pipelines. In the event of a dispute arising between the local authority and the occupier of lands or premises, as to whether the consent was or was not unreasonably withheld, that matter is to be determined by An Bord Pleanála.

**[7.93]** Under PDA 2000, s 199 compensation is payable by the local authority, where it has used its power under s 182, based on the reduction in value of the structure/land or damage resulting from being disturbed in the enjoyment of the structure/land.

## Compensation regarding creation of public rights of way

**[7.94]** PDA 2000, s 207 gives compulsory powers to a planning authority for the creation of public rights of way. There are detailed procedures set out in this section dealing with the implementation of the creation of public rights of way by a planning authority. Supplemental provisions dealing with public rights of way are contained in PDA 2000, s 208. PDA 2000, s 200 provides for compensation where the local authority has used its power under s 207 for compulsory creation of public rights of way over land. The compensation payable is in respect of a reduction in the value of the land or damage as a result of being disturbed in the enjoyment of the land.

## Compensation regarding entry on land

**[7.95]** PDA 2000, s 252 gives power to an authorised person to enter land between the hours of 9am and 6pm or during business hours in respect of premises which are normally open outside those hours for any purpose connected with the Act. The authorised person on entering the land may do all things reasonably necessary, including surveys, inspections, taking photographs, taking levels, making excavations and examining depth and nature of subsoil. Entry is usually gained by consent but if no consent is forthcoming notices must be served on the owner/occupier not less than 14 days prior to entry. If an owner/occupier, served with a 14-day notice, objects to the proposed entry he may apply by a notice to the judge of the District Court having jurisdiction within the area for an order prohibiting entry. The judge may either wholly prohibit entry or allow entry on certain conditions. PDA 2000, s 253 deals with power of entry in relation to enforcement. An authorised person under s 253 may enter lands or premises at any time if he or she has reasonable grounds for believing that unauthorised development has been, is being, or is likely to be, carried out. The authorised person may be accompanied by others including a member of An Garda Siochána and the authorised officer may bring whatever equipment is necessary for the purposes of the entry.

[7.96] Under PDA 2000, s 201, if a claim is made to the planning authority and if it is shown that a person has suffered damage by reason of anything done under s 252 and s 253, the planning authority shall pay compensation equivalent to the value of the amount of damage done.

## PART II: COMPULSORY ACQUISITION

### Appropriation of land for local authority purposes

[7.97] Compulsory acquisition of land by a planning authority is provided for by the provisions of PDA 2000, Pt XIV. Powers of acquisition were extended by the provisions of PDA 2000, Pt XIV and since 31 January 2001, jurisdiction in relation to compulsory acquisition has been transferred from the Minister to An Bord Pleanála.[88]

[7.98] PDA 2000, s 210(1) provides that where the land is vested in a local authority for the purposes of its functions under this or any other enactment, the local authority, if it is satisfied that the land is vested in it for those functions, may appropriate the land for those purposes. The functions are not limited to the planning functions of a local authority. The functions extend to all functions as set out and provided for in LGA 2001.

[7.99] PDA 2000, s 210(2) provides that once a local authority has decided to appropriate the land for its own functions, no claim for compensation or for additional compensation can be made. The time for making a claim for compensation only arises at the time of the confirmation of the original compulsory purchase order (CPO). In effect, the appropriation of land under PDA 2000, s 210 cannot be challenged once the local authority is satisfied that the land should be made available for the purposes of its functions under this Act or under any other enactment.[89]

[7.100] The local authority must be properly satisfied that the land should be made available for its functions. Thus, acquisition for the provision of social and affordable housing or for the regeneration of obsolete areas would justify acquisition of land by a

---

88. PDA 2000, s 210(1) and (2).
89. PDA 2000, s 210(1) and (2).

local authority. Also, acquisition of land for purposes of public safety, such as for the improvement of a dangerous bend in a roadway, would be a justifiable acquisition.

**[7.101]** In *Central Dublin Development Association v Attorney General*,[90] interference with property rights resulting from various provisions in the LG(PD)A 1963 was held not to be unconstitutional where a genuine case was made that such interference was for the 'common good'. In *Liddy v Minister for Public Enterprise, Irish Aviation Authority, Aer Rianta Teoranta Ireland and the Attorney General*,[91] Clare County Council had refused permission for the development of a housing estate within a red safety zone adjoining Shannon Airport. That refusal was challenged before An Bord Pleanála. Schedule 8 of the LG(PD)R 1994 (now PDA 2000, Sch 4) eliminates the payment of compensation where it is claimed that the development would interfere with air traffic. If the Irish Aviation Authority had objected under the provisions of s 14 of the Air Navigation and Transport Act 1950 that objection, if successful, would enable compensation to be paid to affected landowners. Because the Irish Aviation Authority had made its objections under the planning legislation the affected landowners were denied payment of any compensation. The court held that although the option to take proceedings was available to the Irish Aviation Authority under both the Air Navigation and Transport Act 1950 and the planning legislation there was no basis in law which would prevent them from electing to proceed under the planning legislation and consequently there was no unjust discrimination under Art 40.1 of the Constitution.

**[7.102]** The judgment of Keane CJ In *Re Article 26 of the Constitution and Part V of the Planning and Development Bill 1999*[92] contains useful information which is helpful in understanding the principles involved in paying compensation to a landowner who is deprived of his land. It offers a good insight into the structure of compensation payments in social and affordable housing schemes. Keane CJ quoted an extract from Costello P's judgment in *Heaney v Ireland*[93] dealing with the approach which, in general, should be taken by the courts in considering whether a constitutional right has been validly abridged, as follows:

> In considering whether a restriction on the exercise of rights is permitted by the Constitution, the courts in this country and elsewhere have found it helpful to apply the test of proportionality, a test which contains the notions of minimal restraint on the exercise of protected rights, and the exigencies of the common good in a democratic society. This is a test frequently adopted by the European Court of Human Rights (see, for example, *Times Newspapers Limited v United Kingdom*)[94] and has recently been formulated by the Supreme Court in Canada in the following terms. The objective of the impugned provision must be of sufficient importance to warrant overriding a constitutionally protected right. It must relate

---

90. *Central Dublin Development Association v Attorney General* (1975) 109 ILTR 68, HC, Kenny J.
91. *Liddy v Minister for Public Enterprise, Irish Aviation Authority, Aer Rianta Teoranta Ireland and the Attorney General* [2004] 1 ILRM 9, Finnegan P.
92. *Re Article 26 and Part V of the Planning and Development Bill 1999* [2000] 2 IR 321.
93. *Heaney v Ireland* [1994] 3 IR 593 at 607 *per* Costello P.
94. *Times Newspapers Limited v United Kingdom* (1979) 2 EHRR 245.

to concerns pressing and substantial in a free and democratic society. The means chosen must pass a proportionality test. They must:

(a) be rationally connected to the objective and not be arbitrary, unfair or based on irrational considerations;

(b) impair the right as little as possible; and

(c) be such that their effect on rights are proportional to the objective; See *Chaulk v R* [1990] 3 SCR 1303, at pages 1335 and 1336.[95]

Costello P applied those principles to private property rights in *Daly v Revenue Commissioners*[96] as did Keane J in *Iarnród Éireann v Ireland*[97] where the learned judge had this to say:

> If the State elects to invade the property rights of the individual citizen, it can do so only to the extent that this is required by the exigencies of the common good. If the means used are disproportionate to the end sought, the invasion will constitute an 'unjust attack' within the meaning of Art 40, s 3, sub-s (2).[98]

PDA 2000, s 210 is not limited to the acquisition of land by a local authority for purposes of its functions as a planning authority. The section extends to any functions of local authorities as set out in LGA 2001. The significant amendments made in PDA 2000, Pt XIV go so far as to allow the acquisition of land by a local authority for, almost, any purpose.

## Disposal of land by local authority

**[7.103]** PDA 2000, s 211 allows a local authority to sell, lease or exchange any land acquired for the purpose of, or appropriated under the Act or any other Act or acquired otherwise by a local authority, subject to such conditions as it may consider necessary, where it no longer requires the land for any of its functions, or in order to secure:

(a) the best use of that or other land, and any structures or works which have been, or are to be, constructed, erected, made or carried out on, in or under that or other land, or

(b) the construction, erection, making or carrying out of any structures or works appearing to it to be needed for the proper planning and sustainable development of its functional area.[99]

If the land is being disposed of under (a) or (b) above, the local authority is not restricted to selling only land for which it has no use or requirement for any of its functions.

**[7.104]** The procedure, before land can be disposed of by a local authority, is provided for in LGA 2001, s 183. The local authority must first send notice of its intention to sell,

---

95. *Re Article 26 and the Constitutionality of Part V of the Planning and Development Bill 1999* [2000] 2 IR 321 at 349.
96. *Daly v Revenue Commissioners* [1995] 3 IR 1, Costello P.
97. *Iarnród Éireann v Ireland* [1996] 3 IR 312, Keane J.
98. *Iarnród Éireann v Ireland* [1996] 3 IR 312 at 361 *per* Keane J.
99. PDA 2000, s 211(1)(a) and (b).

lease or exchange land to the elected members of the Council and the notice to be sent or delivered to the members of the local authority must give the following particulars:

(a) (i) the land,
 (ii) the name of the person from whom such land was acquired, if this can be ascertained by reasonable inquiries,
 (iii) the person to whom the land is to be disposed of,
 (iv) the consideration proposed in respect of the disposal,
 (v) any covenants, conditions or agreements to have effect in connection with the disposal.[100]
(b) at the first meeting of the local authority held after the expiration of 10 days after the day on which such notices are sent or delivered, the local authority may resolve that the disposal shall not be carried out or that it shall be carried out in accordance with terms specified in the resolution;[101]

[7.105] PDA 2000, s 211 does beg the question as to whether a local authority could use its powers of compulsory acquisition by completing an acquisition of land from a private individual while demonstrably acting in the public interest and then disposing of it the next day to a commercial developer.

[7.106] Unless the Minister has made regulations dispensing with the necessity to obtain the Minister's consent to disposal in certain circumstances, the consent of the Minister is required for any sale, lease or exchange where the price or matter obtained in exchange 'is not the best reasonably obtainable'. If the sale, lease or exchange is for the best price, matter or exchange reasonably obtainable, the consent of the Minister is not required.[102]

[7.107] Regulations have been made by the Minister under PDA 2000, s 211(3) and these are now comprised in art 206 of PDR 2001 under the heading 'Disposal of land without consent of Minister under s 211 of Act'.

[7.108] The consent of the Minister is not required where a local authority is of the opinion that, for economic or social reasons, it is reasonable that the disposal of land be carried out in accordance with terms specified by the local authority in the notice which is to be given to members of the authority under s 183 of LGA 2001.[103] If it is the case that no consent of the Minister is to be obtained, the following procedure must be followed.

PDR 2001, art 206(2):

The following conditions shall apply in relation to a disposal of land referred to in sub-art (1):

(a) the manager shall prepare a report setting out the economic or social reasons which apply in relation to the disposal of land;

---

100. See LGA 2001, s 183(1).
101. See LGA 2001, s 18(1)(b).
102. PDA 2000, s 211(2) and (3).
103. See PDR 2001, art 206(1).

**[7.109]** Planning and Environmental Law in Ireland

(b) the report shall be incorporated in or accompany the notice referred to in sub-art (1); and

(c) the notice referred to in sub-art (1) and the report referred to in paragraph (a) shall be made available for public inspection at the offices of the local authority during office hours for a period of one year.[104]

**[7.109]** PDR 2001, art 206(3) provides:

A disposal of land under this Article shall be carried out in accordance with the terms of the notice referred to in sub-art (1).

**[7.110]** PDA 2000, s 211(4) provides that:

Capital money arising from the disposal of land under sub-s (1) shall be applied for a capital purpose for which capital money may be properly applied, or for such purposes as may be approved by the Minister whether generally or in relation to specified cases or circumstances.[105]

**[7.111]** PDA 2000, s 211(5)(a) provides that where a local authority acquires land sometime before it has use for it, it may make a short term letting to fill the time gap between acquisition and development. PDA 2000, s 211(5)(b) provides that the Landlord and Tenants Acts 1967–1994 shall not apply to such a letting, and that provision deliberately excludes the possibility of any statutory right of renewal.[106]

## Development by planning authority

**[7.112]** PDA 2000, s 212, as amended by PD(A)A 2010, s 68(a), (b) and (c), empowers a planning authority to develop or secure or facilitate the development of land and, in particular, s 212(1)(a)–(g) (as amended) allows for development as follows:

(a) secure, facilitate and control the improvement of the frontage of any public road by widening, opening, enlarging or otherwise improving;

(b) develop any land in the vicinity of any road or public transport facility which it is proposed to improve or construct;

(c) provide areas with roads, infrastructure facilitating public transport and such services and works as may be needed for development;

(d) provide, secure or facilitate the provision of areas of convenient shape and size for development;

(e) secure, facilitate or carry out the development and renewal of areas in need of physical, social or economic regeneration and provide open spaces and other public amenities;

(f) secure the preservation of any view or prospect, any protected structure or other structure, any architectural conservation area or natural physical feature, any trees or woodlands or any site of archaeological, geological or historical interest.[107]

---

104. See LGA 2001, s 183(1)(a) and (b).
105. PDA 2000, s 211(4) has been amended by LGA 2001, s 247.
106. PDA 2000, s 211(5)(a) and (b).
107. Paragraph (f) has been amended by PD(A)A 2010.

(g) secure the creation, management, restoration or preservation of any site of scientific or ecological interest, including any Nature Conservation Site.[108]

It will be seen that PDA 2000, s 212(1) (as amended) is broadly concerned with providing the local authority with a general power to 'develop or secure or facilitate the development of land'. Section 212(2), which is set out below, provides a specific list of matters which a local authority may either provide itself or arrange to have provided by third parties.

[7.113] PDA 2000, s 212(2) provides:

(2) A planning authority may provide or arrange for the provision of –

(a) sites for the establishment or relocation of industries, businesses (including hotels, motels and guesthouses), houses, offices, shops, schools, churches, leisure facilities and other community facilities and of such buildings, premises, houses, parks and structures as are referred to in paragraph (b),

(b) factory buildings, office premises, shop premises, houses, amusement parks and structures for the purpose of entertainment, caravan parks, buildings for the purposes of providing accommodation, meals and refreshments, buildings for the purpose of providing trade and professional services and advertisement structures,

(c) transport facilities, including public and air transport facilities, and

(d) any services which it considers ancillary to anything which is referred to in paragraphs (a), (b) or (c), and may maintain and manage any such site, building, premises, house, park, structure or service and may make any charges which it considers reasonable in relation to the provision, maintenance or management thereof.

[7.114] While PDA 2000, s 212(1) (as amended) and (2) empower a local authority to carry out certain activities or to have certain activities carried out by third parties, that section does not attempt to confer upon a local authority a statutory right to compulsorily acquire lands or buildings. Arguably, PDA 2000, s 213(2) and (4) may provide local authorities with the power of compulsory acquisition in relation to matters dealt with in Pt XIV of the Act. However, Simons[109] makes the following observation:

In considering the provisions of Pt XIV, it is important to distinguish between those provisions which empower a planning authority to carry on particular activities, and those other provisions which might actually confer a statutory right to compulsorily acquire lands. The former are found mainly in s 212.[110] Insofar as

---

108. Paragraph (g) has been inserted by PD(A)A 2010.
109. See Simons, *Planning and Development Law* (2nd edn, Thomson Round Hall, 2007) at p 436, para 8–399. Note that Simons's section on Compulsory Acquisition of Lands, paras 1–9, at pp 435–449 provides a thoroughly enlightening insight into the diverse principles, philosophy and ethos of compulsory acquisition of lands in Ireland. A reading of those paragraphs should not be missed.
110. Note that PDA 2000, s 212 has been amended by the insertion of a new s 212(5) which defines a 'Nature Conservation Site'.

the actual power to acquire land compulsorily is concerned, it is not at all clear that Pt. XIV of PDA 2000 actually confers such a power. On one view, Pt XIV merely supplements existing powers of compulsory purchase, and it is, therefore, necessary to identify the source of the power to compulsorily acquire in some other piece of legislation. This was the interpretation adopted by the Supreme Court in *Clinton v An Bord Pleanála*.[111] Geoghegan J suggested that all powers of compulsory acquisition by a local authority for any one or more of its many statutory functions derived in the first place from s 10 of the Local Government (Ireland) Act 1898 (as amended).[112]

**[7.115]** PDA 2000, s 212(3) enables local authorities to carry out arrangements and enter into agreements with any persons or bodies for the development or management of land. Local authorities are authorised to incorporate a company for that purpose.

**[7.116]** PDA 2000, s 212(4) permits a local authority to use its powers under any enactments including its compulsory purchase powers to acquire land for the purposes of this section. Particularly, local authorities may use those powers to facilitate the assembly of sites for the purposes of orderly development of land.

**[7.117]** PDA 2000, s 212(5) is a new provision inserted by PD(A)A 2010, s 68(c), which defines a nature conservation site, referred to in PDA 2000, s 212(1)(g),[113] as follows:

> (5) In this section 'Nature Conservation Site' means –
> 
> (a)  A European site,
> 
> (b)  An area proposed as a natural heritage area and the subject of a notice made under section 16(1) of the Wildlife (Amendment) Act 2000,
> 
> (c)  An area designated as a natural heritage area by a natural heritage area order made under section 18 of the Wildlife (Amendment) Act 2000,
> 
> (d)  A nature reserve established under an establishment order made under section 15 (amended by section 26 of the Wildlife (Amendment) Act 2000) of the Wildlife Act 1976,
> 
> (e)  A nature reserve recognised under a recognition order made under section 16 (amended by section 27 of the Wildlife (Amendment) Act 2000) of the Wildlife Act 1976, or
> 
> (f)  A refuge for fauna or flora designated under a designation order made under section 17 (amended by section 28 of the Wildlife (Amendment) Act 2000) of the Wildlife Act 1976.

## Making the compulsory purchase order

**[7.118]** PDA 2000, s 213 does not amend the provisions governing the CPO powers of local authorities but rather the section provides that the scope of the pre-existing statutory compulsory acquisition powers must now be interpreted within the context of

---

111. *Clinton v An Bord Pleanála* [2007] 4 IR 701.
112. Local Government (Ireland) Act 1898, s 10 has been amended on a number of occasions but particularly by the Local Government (No 2) Act 1960, s 11.
113. PDA 2000, s 212(1)(g) was inserted by PD(A)A 2010, s 68(b).

the provisions of s 213. PDA 2000, s 213 is the 'core' provision dealing with compulsory acquisition. In effect, if a local authority already has power to acquire land under any legislation already in existence, the provisions of PDA 2000, s 213 will apply to those powers. In summary, PDA 2000, s 213 gives a local authority power to acquire land temporarily or permanently and by agreement or compulsorily for the purposes of fulfilling its functions including giving effect to facilitating the implementation of its development plan or its housing strategy. A local authority, under s 213, is also empowered to acquire any easements, wayleaves or other rights. The section also empowers a local authority to restrict or curtail or temporarily or permanently, and either by agreement or compulsorily, any existing easements, wayleaves or other rights whether or not the land in question is within or outside the functional area of the local authority and whether or not the land is immediately required.

**[7.119]** The section has been the subject of scrutiny by the courts. In *Clinton v An Bord Pleanála*,[114] the Supreme Court held that Pt XIV of PDA 2000 does not in fact confer a statutory right to acquire land but rather Pt XIV enables compulsory acquisition which already exists under various other statutory provisions, to be used, or operated by local authorities for the purpose of carrying out the activities which are listed in PDA 2000, s 212, as amended.[115]

**[7.120]** PDA 2000, s 213(1) provides that:

> (1) The power conferred on a local authority under any enactment to acquire land shall be construed in accordance with this section.

The effect of s 213(1) above quoted would clearly seem to be supported by the Supreme Court decision in *Clinton v An Bord Pleanála*.[116] However, PDA 2000, s 213(2) appears to confuse the matter by stating expressly that a local authority may acquire land compulsorily. Section 213(2) provides:

> (a) A local authority may, for the purposes of performing any of its functions (whether conferred by or under this Act, or any other enactment passed before or after the passing of this Act), including giving effect to or facilitating the implementation of its development plan or its housing strategy under section 94, do all or any of the following:
>
> > (i) acquire land, permanently or temporarily, by agreement or compulsorily,
> >
> > (ii) acquire, permanently or temporarily, by agreement or compulsorily, any easement, way-leave, water-right or other right over or in respect of any land or water or any substratum of land,
> >
> > (iii) restrict or otherwise interfere with, permanently or temporarily, by agreement or compulsorily, any easement, way-leave, water-right

---

114. *Clinton v An Bord Pleanála* [2005] IEHC 84, Finnegan P; affirmed in the Supreme Court [2007] 4 IR 701.
115. See PD(A)A 2010, s 68.
116. *Clinton v An Bord Pleanála* [2007] 4 IR 701.

or other right over or in respect of any land or water or any substratum of land,

and the performance of all or any of the functions referred to sub-paragraphs (i), (ii) and (iii) are referred to in this Act as an 'acquisition of land'.

(b) A reference in paragraph (a) to acquisition by agreement shall include acquisition by way of purchase, lease, exchange or otherwise.

(c) The functions conferred on a local authority by paragraph (a) may be performed in relation to –

(i) land, or

(ii) any easement, way-leave, water-right or other right to which that paragraphs applies,

whether situated or exercisable, as the case may be, inside or outside the functional area of the local authority concerned.

The term 'acquisition of lands' includes the permanent or temporary acquisition of land or the permanent or temporary restriction or interference with easements, wayleaves, water rights or other rights over or in land or water. It also includes the acquisition of any substratum of land. Express power is given to the local authority to acquire land, by agreement or compulsorily, outside the functional area of the local authority concerned. Furthermore, the local authority's power of compulsory acquisition under PDA 2000 would seem to be re-affirmed by the provision of PDA 2000, s 213(4) which provides:

> A local authority may be authorised by compulsory purchase order to acquire land for any of the purposes referred to in sub-s (2) of this section and s 10 (as amended by s 86 of the Housing Act 1966) of the Local Government (No 2) Act 1960, shall be construed so as to apply accordingly and the reference to 'purposes' in s 10(1)(a) of that Act shall be construed as including purposes referred to in sub-section (2) of this section.

**[7.121]** Taking PDA 2000, s 213(1), (2) and (4) together it seems that s 213(1) empowers local authorities to acquire land under other enactments but that the provision is to be construed in accordance with the provisions of s 213.[117]

**[7.122]** PDA 2000, s 213(2) is drafted in broad terms and the last paragraph provides that the term 'acquisition of land' includes the performance of all or any of the functions referred to in paragraphs (i), (ii) and (iii).

**[7.123]** PDA 2000, s 213(4) provides that a local authority may be authorised to acquire land by CPO for any of the purposes listed in s 213(2). The Supreme Court ruling in *Clinton v An Bord Pleanála*[118] affirms that the power to compulsorily acquire land under any enactment by a local authority is to be construed in accordance with s 213. In spite

---

117. As is noted, PDA 2000, s 213(4) empowers the local authority to acquire lands under any of the Acts listed in PDA 2000, s 214(1). Also note that the term 'local authority' and not 'planning authority' is used throughout PDA 2000, s 213. Section 213 applies to a local authority acting in its varied capacities as housing authority, sanitary authority, etc.

118. *Clinton v An Bord Pleanála* [2007] 4 IR 701.

of the *Clinton* decision there is at least an argument that the wording of PDA 2000, s 213(2) does, on its own, confer a power of compulsory acquisition for local authorities.

**[7.124]** PDA 2000, s 213(3) provides that:

(a) The acquisition may be affected by agreement or compulsorily in respect of land not immediately required for a particular purpose if, in the opinion of the local authority, the land will be required by the authority for that purpose in the future.

(b) The acquisition may be affected by agreement in respect of any land which, in the opinion of the local authority, it will require in the future for the purposes of any of its functions notwithstanding that the authority has not determined the manner in which or the purpose for which it will use the land.

(c) Paragraphs (a) and (b) shall apply and have effect in relation to any power to acquire land conferred on a local authority by virtue of this Act or any other enactment further enacted before or after this Act.

PDA 2000, s 213(3) allows a local authority to acquire land for which it has no use at present but which it will have use for in the future. In order to acquire land compulsorily the local authority must have decided the purpose for which the land to be acquired will be used either immediately or in the future. If, for example, a local authority decides on the step by step purchase of a land bank for future use, and at the time of the purchase or at the times of the purchases, the local authority has not determined the particular purpose for which the land will be used, in those circumstances the purchase can only be concluded between the local authority and the landowner by agreement. In those circumstances the local authority cannot acquire the land compulsorily.

**[7.125]** A compulsory acquisition of land which has been made for one stated purpose by a local authority cannot be used for another purpose or for any additional purpose.

**[7.126]** In *Crosbie v Custom House Dock Development Authority*,[119] a compulsory purchase order was made in respect of part of the plaintiff's lands by the defendant pursuant to its powers under s 5 of the Urban Renewal (Amendment) Act 1987. The wording of the order included the following:

> ... the authority is hereby authorised to acquire compulsorily for the purposes of the Urban Renewal Acts 1986 and 1987 and, in particular, for the purposes of s 9 of the Urban Renewal Act 1986, the land described in the schedule hereto.

Whereas s 5 of the 1987 Act is a provision to enable compulsory acquisition of land within the defined area of the Custom House Docks, the purpose of s 9 of the 1986 Act is to secure re-development of the Custom House Docks area. The particular purpose put forward by the authority at the public inquiry was to build what was described as a National Sports Centre. No mention was made of that purpose in the order and, in any case, it was later agreed by the government that the site was unsuitable and that the construction of the National Sports Centre would not proceed on that site. It transpired

---

119. *Crosbie v Custom House Dock Development Authority* [1996] 2 IR 531, Costello P.

later that the site, having been acquired from the plaintiff, was to be sold on to be developed as a commercial office without public user. Costello J held that the compulsory purchase order had been made for the purposes of the Urban Renewal Acts 1986 and 1987, and, in particular, for the purposes of s 9 of the Urban Renewal Act 1986; accordingly, the compulsory acquisition could be lawfully confirmed. Costello P stated:

> The issue as to what the purpose for which the lands were required by the Authority is a question of fact. The purpose for which a statutory authority performs an act may be ascertained from the resolutions it adopts, official documents emanating from it and statements made on its behalf. In this case the evidence establishes that the authority decided to make the compulsory purchase order for 'the purpose of the Urban Renewal Acts, 1986 and 1987, and, in particular, for the purpose of s 9 of the Urban Renewal Act, 1986'. The purpose was clearly stated in the compulsory purchase order it issued, and by Council and by its witnesses at the public inquiry. At the time the compulsory purchase order was made the evidence establishes that the Authority intended that the means by which it would carry out this purpose was by building a National Sports Centre and this intention was publicly declared. I can find no justification for concluding that the Authority's purpose was other than its stated purpose. The Authority did not choose to limit the purpose of the acquisition to a particular proposed development. It had good reasons (as events eloquently proved) for not doing so and it was not required by statute so to do. Planning schemes may be amended, and proposals for development made before a planning scheme is adopted may be changed and so the Authority's decision was that it would acquire the lands for its general statutory purposes and not for the particular development which at that time was the means by which it intended to carry out its statutory obligations.[120]

**[7.127]** In *Clinton v An Bord Pleanála*,[121] the Supreme Court also held that there was no requirement on a planning authority to put forward specific development proposals where the lands to be acquired are in need of regeneration and where that need had been established in the order made for the acquisition of the land by reference to s 9 of the Urban Renewal Act 1986. A very much earlier decision than the decision in *Clinton v An Bord Pleanála*[122] and the decision in *Crosbie v Custom House Dock Development Authority*[123] was made in *Bradshaw and Faulkner v Bray UDC*.[124] In that case, the court held that an acquiring authority is not compelled to use lands which it has compulsorily acquired for the exact purposes enunciated at the time of acquisition of the lands and that it is sufficient if the lands are used generally for the purpose for which they were acquired.

**[7.128]** In *Clinton v An Bord Pleanála*,[125] Geoghegan J, in the Supreme Court, dealt with the powers of a planning authority as outlined in PDA 2000, s 212(1)–(4) enabling a

---

120. *Crosbie v Custom House Dock Development Authority* [1996] 2 IR 531 *per* Costello J..
121. *Clinton v An Bord Pleanála* [2007] 4 IR 701.
122. *Clinton v An Bord Pleanála* [2007] 4 IR 701.
123. *Crosbie v Custom House Dock Development Authority* [1996] 2 IR 531.
124. *Bradshaw and Faulkner v Bray UDC* [1906] 1 IR 560.
125. *Clinton v An Bord Pleanála* [2007] 4 IR 701.

planning authority to develop or secure or facilitate the development of land in general for the purposes of regeneration of an area. The learned judge had this to say:

> The regeneration purpose, which the Council had in mind when deciding to make the Compulsory Purchase Order, was expressly permitted by the Oireachtas. It cannot have been envisaged that the Council would have to have a specific plan as to how the regeneration was to be carried out and would have to specify that in the CPO because, as in this case, the whole process would usually involve private developers in some form at least and plans as yet unknown which they would propose and envisage and which would eventually require planning permission. This is quite different from the property required for the purposes of Council offices or a public swimming pool for instance.
>
> It was at all times perfectly clear that the property was being acquired for regeneration of O'Connell Street. In my view, it was only necessary for the Council to demonstrate that a CPO was desirable in the public interest to achieve that purpose. It was not necessary to prove how exactly it would be carried out. Quite apart from the necessity to obtain planning permission into the future, such a requirement would defeat the purpose of the power conferred by the section.

[7.129] The debate as to whether the regeneration of an area is, on its own, sufficient to permit a local authority to make a CPO may not be over. Simons, in commenting on Geoghegan J's view that the regeneration purpose was a *'particular purpose'* within the meaning of PDA 2000, s 231, wrote as follows:

> It has to be said, however, that the limited role ascribed in *Clinton* to the confirming authority undermines greatly the ability of an affected landowner to demonstrate – whether before the confirming authority or before the courts – that the competing rights of the public and the landowner had been properly balanced. In particular, the finding that it is sufficient that the acquiring authority identify as the 'particular purpose', for which the compulsory acquisition is required, one of the statutory purposes under s 212, ie urban regeneration, tends to undermine the credibility of the entire process. Further, the failure to insist that An Bord Pleanála, as confirming authority, provide other than the most perfunctory statement of reasons is also regrettable.[126]

Compulsory acquisition of land by a local authority increasingly involves more complex issues in an evolving society which is no longer concerned only with the development of roads, railways and parks. Compulsory acquisition was spawned on the acquisition of land for the development of transport infrastructure but it has developed into more delicate areas of social justice and it will, undoubtedly, continue to develop. Examples of new areas where compulsory acquisition is relied upon include regeneration of derelict areas, social and affordable housing, public safety issues and environmental protection.

[7.130] In all cases where compulsory acquisition is utilised it can only be utilised where it is in the public interest/common good to do so. Powers of compulsory

---

126. Simons, *Planning and Development Law* (2nd edn, Thomson Round Hall, 2007) at p 446, para 8–432.

acquisition are an interference with constitutionally protected property rights, as noted by Costello J in *Crosbie v Custom House Dock Development Authority*.[127] Reference has been made to the statement of Costello J in *Heaney v Ireland*[128] in considering whether a constitutional right has been validly abridged.[129]

**[7.131]** In *Clinton v An Bord Pleanála*,[130] Geoghegan J said the following:

> I think it appropriate to make the following further observation. It is axiomatic that the making and confirming of a Compulsory Purchase Order (CPO) to acquire a person's land entails an invasion of his constitutionally protected property rights. The power conferred on an administrative body such as a local authority or on An Bord Pleanála to compulsorily acquire land must be exercised in accordance with the requirements of the Constitution, including respecting the property rights of the affected landowner (*East Donegal Co-Operative v Attorney General* [1970] IR 317). Any decision of such bodies are subject to judicial review. It would insufficiently protect constitutional rights if the court, hearing the judicial review application, merely had to be satisfied that the decision was not irrational or was not contrary to fundamental reason and common sense.

It is clear that the Supreme Court accepts that a more exacting standard of judicial review applies in a case of the judicial review of compulsory acquisition of land.

**[7.132]** There have been many examples of local authorities using the powers of compulsory acquisition to acquire private land for the purpose of transferring that land to a private developer although the majority of these transfers have occurred in areas which were in need of regeneration. It has yet to be determined whether or not courts will sanction a transfer of private land acquired by a local authority to a commercial developer which is not in a regeneration or obsolete area. It remains to be seen if such a transaction could ever be held to amount to an objective of sufficient importance to warrant interference with a constitutionally protected right. If all the good is taken out of the democratic process and the legislative protection which that process requires, the march towards absolutism will be unstoppable. In the view of Justice O'Connor, speaking in the US Supreme Court, all property in the United States is already susceptible to compulsory acquisition. A striking part of Justice O'Connor's powerful dissent, as quoted by Costello P in the *Crosbie* case, reads as follows:

> Any property may now be taken for the benefit of another private party, but the fallout from this decision will not be random. The beneficiaries are likely to be those citizens with disproportionate influence and power in the political process, including large corporations and development firms. As for the victims, the government now has licence to transfer property from those with fewer resources to those with more. The Founders cannot have intended this perverse result.[131]

---

127. *Crosbie v Custom House Dock Development Authority* [1996] 2 IR 531.
128. *Heaney v Ireland* [1994] 3 IR 593.
129. See judgment of Costello J in *Heaney v Ireland* [1994] 3 IR 593.
130. *Clinton v An Bord Pleanála* [2007] 4 IR 701.
131. *Kelo v City of New London* 545 US 469 (2005); Justice O'Connor's judgment was a dissenting judgment in the US Supreme Court.

## Transfer of Minister's functions to the Board

**[7.133]** PDA 2000, s 214 transferred the functions formerly conferred on the Minister in relation to compulsory acquisition to An Bord Pleanála. Any reference in any relevant provision of the Acts listed below to the Minister shall be deemed to be a reference to the board except that any powers under the enactments to make regulations or to prescribe any matter shall remain with the Minister.[132]

**[7.134]** The list of enactments referred to in PDA 2000, s 214(1) are as follows:

- (a) Public Health (Ireland) Act 1878; (see s 203).
- (b) Local Government (Ireland) Act 1898; (see s 10).
- (c) Local Government Act 1925; (see s 68 and the Sixth Schedule).
- (d) Water Supplies Act 1942; (see ss 4, 8, 9, 10 and the Schedule).
- (e) Local Government (No 2) Act 1960; (see s 10 as amended by s 86 of the Housing Act 1966).
- (f) Local Government (Sanitary Services) Act 1964; (see ss 7, 8, 9 & 16).
- (g) Housing Act 1966; (see ss 76, 77, 78, 80 and the Third Schedule).
- (h) Derelict Sites Act 1990; (see s 16 and 17).
- (i) Roads Acts 1993 and 1998; (see ss 47 to 52 of the Roads Act 1993).
- (j) Dublin Docklands Development Authority Act 1997; (see s 27(1)).[133]

The Board now has responsibility for confirming the making of a CPO, if the order is to be confirmed after the holding of an oral hearing.

**[7.135]** PDA 2000, s 214(3) provides that:

> The transfer of the Minister's functions to the Board in relation to the compulsory purchase of land in accordance with subsection (1) shall include the transfer of all necessary ancillary powers in relation to substrata, easements, rights over land (including public rights of way), rights of access to land, the revocation or modification of planning permissions or such other functions as may be necessary in order to ensure that the Board can fully carry out its functions in relation to the enactments referred to in subsection (1).

**[7.136]** PDA 2000, s 214(4) provides that in ss 215 and 216 any reference to 'local authority' includes the Dublin Docklands Development Authority.

---

132. PDA 2000, s 214(1), (2) and (3), as amended by the Roads Acts 1998 and 2007, set out procedures for acquiring land for the purposes of: (a) a motorway scheme, (b) a bus way scheme, (c) a protected road scheme, (d) a protected road scheme amending a protected road scheme approved under PDA 2000, s 49, or (e) certain prescribed road developments such as bridges.
133. As amended by the Roads Acts 1998 and 2007 setting out procedures for acquiring land for the purposes of: (a) a motorway scheme, (b) a bus way scheme, (c) a protected road scheme, (d) a protected road scheme amending a protected road scheme approved under PDA 2000, s 49, or (e) certain prescribed road developments such as bridges.

[7.137] In the context of An Bord Pleanála's role in confirming an order for compulsory acquisition, Simons correctly observes:

> One of the greatest mysteries of compulsory purchase law is as to what precisely it is that An Bord Pleanála must be satisfied of before it confirms a compulsory purchase order. In particular, there is little guidance as to the nature and extent of the considerations which An Bord Pleanála is to take into account in reaching its decision.[134]

[7.138] In *Crosbie v Custom House Development Authority*,[135] Costello P proposed that in making a confirmation of a compulsory purchase order the Minister (now the board) had to be satisfied only that the acquisition was necessary in order to give effect to a particular statutory purpose such as, for example, regeneration or renewal of a particular area. It appears that no consideration is required as to whether the development proposal is desirable or necessary in planning terms. Whatever about a particular Minister's qualifications to adjudicate on the planning merits of a particular proposal, it might be thought that one of the reasons why the board replaced the Minister is because it does have the skills necessary to judge the merits, or otherwise, of the planning proposal.

## Judicial review in relation to PDA 2000, Pt XIV

[7.139] PDA 2000, s 50(1) provides that the board may refer a question of law arising on any matter with which the board is concerned, to the High Court. Section 50(2) provides that:

> A person shall not question the validity of any decision made or other act done by–
>
> (a) A planning authority, a local authority or the Board in the performance or purported performance of a function under this Act,
>
> (b) The Board in the performance or purported performance of a function transferred under Pt XIV, or
>
> (c) A local authority in the performance or purported performance of a function conferred by an enactment specified in s 214 relating to the compulsory acquisition of land,
>
> otherwise than by way of an application for judicial review under Order 84 of the Rules of the Superior Courts (SI No 15 of 1986) (the 'Order').

The Supreme Court judgment in *Clinton v An Bord Pleanála*[136] indicates that a more exacting standard of judicial review will be required by the court where compulsory acquisition of land is the subject matter of the review, as seen in the quoted extract from Geoghegan J's judgment.[137]

---

134. Simons, *Planning and Development Law* (2nd edn, Thomson Round Hall, 2007) at p 441, para 8–419.
135. *Crosbie v Custom House Dock Development Authority* [1996] 2 IR 531.
136. *Clinton v An Bord Pleanála* [2007] 4 IR 701.
137. See quotation of Geoghegan J at para **7.131**.

**[7.140]** Geoghegan J also referred to statements made in the English courts, in the absence of constitutional protection, by Denning MR and by Watkins LJ in *Prest v Secretary of State for Wales*:[138]

> It is clear that no Minister or public authority can acquire land compulsorily except the power to do so be given by Parliament: and Parliament only grants it, or should only grant it, when it is considered necessary in the public interest ... I regard it as a principle of our Constitutional law that no citizen is to be deprived of his land by any public authority against his will, unless it is expressly authorised by Parliament and the public interest decisively so demands; and then only on the condition that proper compensation is paid. – *Per* Denning MR.

> The taking of a persons, land against his will is a serious invasion of his property rights. The use of statutory authority for the destruction of those rights requires to be most carefully scrutinised. The Courts must be vigilant to see that the authority is not abused. – *Per* Watkins LJ.

Geoghegan J, commenting on those two statements, said:

> In my view, the procedures at a compulsory purchase hearing must ensure that these principles are observed. The acquiring authority must be satisfied that the acquisition of the property is clearly justified by the exigencies of the common good.[139]

## Transfer of certain ministerial functions

**[7.141]** Certain ministerial functions were transferred under the Roads Acts 1993 and 1998 (as amended by the Roads Act 2007) and under the Gas Act 1976 and the Air Navigation and Transport (Amendment) Act 1998. PDA 2000, s 215, 215(A),[140] 215(B), 119 and 215(C)[141] are the relevant sections.

**[7.142]** PDA 2000, s 215 transfers the functions of the Minister under the Roads Acts 1993 and 1998 to the board. Specifically, the functions transferred to the Minister relate to a scheme or proposed development under ss 49, 50 and 51 of the Roads Act 1993 and those functions are now vested in An Bord Pleanála with the exception that any powers under those sections to make regulations or to prescribe any matter shall remain with the Minister.

**[7.143]** As already seen, it would be a reasonable assumption that once the confirming function to the making of a CPO under these Acts had been transferred from the Minister to An Bord Pleanála, the board, in making its confirmation, would give some consideration to the planning merits of the proposal. Costello P in *Crosbie v Custom House Development Authority*[142] discouraged any notion that it was the board's function

---

138. *Prest v Secretary of State for Wales* (1982) 81 LGR 193 at 211 and 212 *per* Denning MR.
139. *Clinton v An Bord Pleanála* [2007] 4 IR 701.
140. PDA 2000, s 215A and 215B have been added by PD(SI)A 2006, s 37.
141. Certain functions under the Harbours Act 1996 are to be transferred to An Bord Pleanála from the Minister for Transport.
142. *Crosbie v Custom House Dock Development Authority* [1996] 2 IR 531.

to consider the planning merits of the proposal to confirm a CPO. In contrast, McMenamin J in *Kildare County Council v An Bord Pleanála*[143] indicated that the concepts of proper planning and sustainable development are incorporated into s 51 of the Roads Act 1993 (as amended by the Roads Act 2007) which amendments expressly refer to An Bord Pleanála and, in particular, to the power of the board to approve a proposed road development and the accompanying EIA, where applicable. The implication of this decision in relation to s 51 of the Roads Act 1993 is that the transfer of the power to make a confirmation of the CPO process from the Minister to the board means that the board's decision must include a consideration of proper planning and sustainable development.

**[7.144]** PDA 2000, s 215(A) (as inserted by PD(SI)A 2006, s 37) transfers certain functions, including acquisition of land, prescribed by the Gas Act 1976 in respect of strategic gas infrastructure from the Minister for Communications, other Minister or the Commission for Gas Energy Regulation, to the board.

**[7.145]** PDA 2000, s 215(B) transfers certain functions, including acquisition of land, prescribed by the Air Navigation and Transport (Amendment) Act 1998 from the Minister for Transport, in respect of the approval of compulsory acquisition of land by Aer Rianta, to An Bord Pleanála.

**[7.146]** PDA 2000, s 215(C) deals with certain functions under the Harbours Act 1996 which are to be transferred from the Minister of Transport to An Bord Pleanála pursuant to the Harbours (Amendment) Act 2009, but this has not yet been commenced.

**[7.147]** PDA 2000, s 215(C) reads as follows:

> (1) The functions of the Minister for Transport under section 16 of, and the Fourth Schedule to, the Harbours Act 1996, as amended, in relation to compulsory acquisition of land for the purposes set out in that section are transferred to, and vested in, the Board, and subject to section 7(3) of the Harbours (Amendment) Act 2009, relevant references in that Act to the Minister for Transport shall be construed as references to the Board and any connected references shall be construed accordingly.
>
> (2) The transfer of the functions of the Minster for Transport in relation to the compulsory acquisition of land in accordance with sub-section (1) shall include the transfer of all necessary ancillary powers necessary in relation to substrata of land, easements, rights over land (including wayleaves and public rights of way), rights over land or water or other such functions as may be necessary in order to ensure that the Board can fully carry out its functions in relation to the enactments referred to in sub-section (1).

## Confirmation of compulsory purchase order where there are no objections

**[7.148]** PDA 2000, s 216(1) provides that once a CPO is made by a local authority and no objections are received by either the board or the local authority, or if objections are

---

143. *Kildare County Council v An Bord Pleanála* [2006] IEHC 73, McMenamin J.

received they are withdrawn, or if the board concludes that objections received can be dealt with by the property arbitrator, the board shall, where appropriate, inform the local authority and proceed as soon as may be to confirm the order with or without modification or to refuse to confirm the order.

**[7.149]** Special procedures apply to the requirement to obtain approval for a scheme under s 47 of the Roads Act 1933. The scheme must be advertised to the general public permitting members of the public to inspect the scheme. Submissions from the public must be invited and the public must be advised that objections in writing must be submitted to An Bord Pleanála within a period of not less than two weeks from the conclusion of the public inspection period. The public inspection period must be advertised to members of the public and the period must not be less than one month. The procedure under PDA 2000, s 216(1) shall not prejudice any requirement to obtain approval for a scheme in accordance with the provisions of the Roads Act 1993[144] of for proposed development under PDA 2000, s 175.[145]

## Time limits in respect of compulsory purchase of land

**[7.150]** These time limits are specified in PDA 2000, s 217(1) to (7). They concern the compulsory acquisition process after objections have been lodged or notice of the CPO has been given and the different types of acquisitions under the various Acts together with the relevant time limits are summarised in the following paragraphs.

**[7.151]** PDA 2000, s 217(1) to (4) permit the local authority a time limit of six weeks, from the date of receipt of the objections, to apply to the board for confirmation or approval of the CPO.

**[7.152]** PDA 2000, s 217(1) deals with an objection under s 6 of the Water Supplies Act 1942. Section 6 deals with objections to taking of a water supply from a water source.

**[7.153]** PDA 2000, s 217(2) deals with an objection under s 8 of the Local Government (Sanitary) Services Act 1964 and s 8 deals with the compulsory acquisition of land by a sanitary authority.

**[7.154]** PDA 2000, s 217(3) deals with an objection under para 4 of the Third Schedule to the Housing Act 1966. The Third Schedule to the Housing Act 1966 deals with compulsory acquisition of land under the Housing Act 1966.

**[7.155]** PDA 2000, s 217(4) deals with an objection under s 48 of the Roads Act 1993. Section 48 of the Roads Act 1993 deals with the provision of a road scheme.

**[7.156]** PDA 2000, s 217(5) permits the local authority a time limit of 12 weeks to furnish or serve a notice making a confirmation order in accordance with s 78(1) of the

---

144. PDA 2000, s 216(2) and the Roads Act 1993, s 47, 49 and 51.
145. PDA 2000, s 175 deals with EIA of certain development (including roads) by or on behalf of a local authority.

Housing Act 1966. The 12-week period starts to run from the date of the making of the confirmation order.

**[7.157]** PDA 2000, s 217(6) allows the local authority a period of 18 months from the date of the confirmation of the CPO becoming operative (this used to be three years) to serve a notice to treat. Service of a notice to treat is an essential step in the CPO process if a local authority is acquiring land. Where a local authority fails to serve a notice to treat, within the 18-month period specified in this section the confirmation of the CPO lapses and the process is ended. Service of a notice to treat allows a local authority to enter upon the lands to be acquired. If the compensation has not been paid by the local authority to the landowner, interest will be payable at a fixed rate on the outstanding date from the date of notice to treat. Section 217(6) applies notwithstanding s 123 of the Lands Clauses Consolidation Act 1845.[146]

**[7.158]** PDA 2000, s 217(6A) was inserted by PD(A)A 2010, s 69 and it reads as follows:

> (6A) (a) Notwithstanding subsection (6) where legal proceedings are in being either—
> 
> > (i) challenging the validity of the compulsory purchase order or provisional order concerned, or
> > 
> > (ii) challenging the validity of permissions, consents or authorisations granted by or under this Act or by or under any other enactment relating to the project in respect of, or purpose for which, the land concerned is being acquired,
> 
> and a notice to treat is not served within the period of 18 months (in this subsection referred to as the 'first period'), the first period shall be extended for a further period (in this subsection referred to as the 'second period') beginning on the day immediately after the day on which the first period expires and expiring on the earlier of—
> 
> > (I) 30 days after the day on which the legal proceedings are concluded, or
> > 
> > (II) 18 months after the day on which the first period expires.
> 
> (b) Where proceedings referred to in paragraph (a) have not been concluded during the second period, on an application to the High Court by the Local Authority not later than four weeks after the expiry of the second period, the Court considers that in the particular circumstances there is good and sufficient reason for doing so, the Court may extend the second period by such further period as it believes necessary in the circumstances provided that it is just and equitable to do so having regard to all of the circumstances.

**[7.159]** PDA 2000, s 217(7)(a) provides that a decision of the board to confirm a CPO will become operative three weeks from the date on which the notice of decision was first published.

---

146. PDA 2000, s 217 has been amended by the insertion of s 217(6A) by PD(A)A 2010, s 69.

**[7.160]** PDA 2000, s 217(7)(b) provides that s 52(8) and (9) of the Roads Act 1993 (as inserted by s 5 of the Roads (Amendment) Act 1998) and s 78(2) to (4) of the Housing Act 1966 shall not apply in relation to decisions of the board under this Part.

## Transferred functions: supplemental provisions

**[7.161]** PDA 2000, ss 217A, 217B and 217C were inserted by s 38 of PD(SI)A 2006.

**[7.162]** PDA 2000, s 217A(1)–(3) provide that the board may, before making a decision either to confirm or otherwise any compulsory acquisition, and entirely at the board's own discretion, (a) request further submissions or observations from any person who, in the opinion of the board, may have information relevant to its decision, or (b) hold meetings with the local authority, or in the case of s 215A with persons who applied for the acquisition order, or with any other person for the purpose of making a decision confirming or otherwise the compulsory acquisition or for the purpose of resolving any issue or disagreement with the local authority or with the applicant or any other person, including resolving an issue or disagreement in advance of the oral hearing. Subsection (2) requires that a written record must be kept of any such meeting which is held and the record must be made available for inspection.

**[7.163]** Section 217A(3) provides that:

> The Board, or an employee of the Board duly authorised by the Board, may appoint any person to hold a meeting referred to in subsection (1)(b).

This wording may not produce the result which was intended by the subsection. It is *not* stated that a *Board employee* may be appointed to hold such meeting. The subsection only allows *'any person'* once appointed to hold such meeting. The appointment of 'any person' is made by the board or by an employee of the board duly authorised by the board. The same comment applies to PDA 2000, s 217B(3).

## Section 217B: supplemental provisions

**[7.164]** PDA 2000, s 217B is another supplemental provision similar to s 217A but dealing specifically with the making of a decision on a scheme or a proposed road development under PDA 2000, s 215. The Board cannot be compelled to take any steps under this section and, as in s 217A, it is left entirely to the board 'at its absolute discretion'. Again, submissions may be invited and a meeting may be held to assist the board in deciding whether or not to confirm the compulsory acquisition or to resolve issues or disagreements between the local authority and the applicant or other person.

**[7.165]** Section 217B(4) does contain a requirement which is additional to the requirements set out in s 217A. Section 217B(4) allows the board to request further information from the local authority in relation to:

> (i) the effects on the environment of the proposed scheme or road development, or

(ii) the consequences for proper planning and sustainable development in the area or area in which it is proposed to situate the said scheme or road development of such scheme or road development as the Board may specify ...

If it is provisionally the view of the board that the scheme or development should be approved if altered, the board will invite the local authority to alter the proposed development or scheme and submit the alteration for approval together with a revised EIS if such is required. If the alterations to the proposed development or scheme are significant in terms of the likely effects on the environment and the likely consequences for proper planning and sustainable development of the area, the board will require the local authority to publish further notice inviting submissions, etc. What is interesting about s 217B(4) is that the subsection does provide a statutory obligation on the board to examine environmental considerations and the consequences of the proposal from the perspective of proper planning and sustainable development in the area. In this single instance the statutory provision offers a choice to the board to take into consideration the environmental and planning issues before confirming the order and in doing so it provides an exception to Costello P's view as held in *Crosbie v Custom House Development Authority*[147] where the learned judge indicated that there was no need for any consideration of the planning merits of the proposal to be undertaken by the board in confirming compulsory acquisition provided the acquisition of land was for general statutory purposes such as regeneration and not for a particular development. PDA 2000, s 217B(4) (as inserted) specifically offers a choice to the board either to investigate or not to investigate planning issues such as environmental impact and the consequences for proper and planning and sustainable development in the area where the proposed scheme or road development is to take place. The Board is also given powers by the section to deal with environmental effects or unacceptable consequences of the development in relation to proper planning and sustainable development. The provisions are, however, specifically related to road schemes and/or road developments. The provision could be taken as lending support to Costello P's view in *Crosbie v Custom House Development Authority*[148] to the effect that no consideration of the planning merits of a proposal is required in cases of confirmation of compulsory acquisition save in the case of road schemes, and in that sense PDA 2000, s 217B(4) is an exception to the general rule.

**[7.166]** PDA 2000, s 217B(5) (as inserted) provides:

If a road authority makes the alterations to the terms of the scheme or proposed road development specified in a notification given to it under subsection (4), the terms of the scheme or road development as so altered shall be deemed to be the scheme or proposed road development for the purposes of sections 49, 50 and 51 of the Roads Act 1993.

---

147. *Crosbie v Custom House Dock Development Authority* [1996] 2 IR 531.
148. *Crosbie v Custom House Dock Development Authority* [1996] 2 IR 531.

**[7.167]** PDA 2000, s 217B(6) provides:

The Board shall –

(a) where it considers that any further information received pursuant to a requirement made under subsection (4)(a) contains significant additional data relating to –

(i) the likely effects on the environment of the scheme or proposed road development, and

(ii) the likely consequences for proper planning and sustainable development in the area or areas in which it is proposed to situate the said scheme or road development of such scheme or road development, or

(b) where the road authority has made the alterations to the terms of the proposed development specified in a notification given to it under subsection (4)(b),

require the authority to do the things referred to in subsection (7).

**[7.168]** PDA 2000, s 217B(7) provides:

The things which a road authority shall be required to do as aforesaid are –

(a) to publish in one or more newspapers circulating in the area or areas in which the development to which the scheme relates or, as the case may be, the proposed road development would be situate a notice stating that, as appropriate –

(i) further information in relation to the scheme or proposed road development has been furnished to the Board, or

(ii) the road authority has, pursuant to an invitation of the Board, made alterations to the terms of the scheme or proposed road development (and the nature of those alterations shall be indicated) and, if it be the case, that information in relation to the terms of the scheme or road development as so altered or a revised environmental impact statement in respect of the scheme or development has been furnished to the Board,

indicating the times at which, the period (which shall not be less than 3 weeks) during which and the place, or places, where a copy of the information or the environmental impact statement referred to in sub-paragraph (i) or (ii) may be inspected free of charge or purchased on payments of a specified fee (which fee shall not exceed the reasonable cost of making such copy) and that submissions or observations in relation to that information or statement may be made to the Board before the expiration of the indicated period, and

(b) to send to each body or prescribed authority to which a notice was given pursuant to section 51(3)(b) or (c) of the Roads Act 1993 –

(i) a notice of the furnishing to the Board of, as appropriate, the further information referred to in paragraph (a)(i) or the information or statement referred to in paragraph (a)(ii), and

(ii) a copy of that further information, information or statement, and to indicate to the body or authority that submissions or observations in relation to that further information, information or statement may be made to the Board before the expiration of a period (which shall be not less than 3 weeks) beginning on the day on which the notice is sent to the prescribed authority by the road authority.

**[7.169]** PDA 2000, s 217B(8) provides:

> The Board shall, in making its decision in respect of a scheme or proposed development, have regard to any information submitted on foot of a notice under subsection (4), including any revised environmental impact statement or any submissions or observations made on foot of a request under subsection (1) or a notice under subsection (7).[149]

## Board to make decision on transferred functions

**[7.170]** PDA 2000, s 217C deals with the board's powers to make decisions on transferred functions. The purpose of this section is to dispel any doubts which may exist in relation to or in respect of functions transferred to the board which were exercised under previous enactments. The section enables the board, notwithstanding any provisions of any enactments referred to in s 214, 215 or 215A, to confirm a compulsory acquisition or any part thereof with or without modifications, or to annul any acquisition or any part thereof.[150] The Board is also enabled to make a similar decision in relation to a scheme or proposed road development or part thereof with or without conditions or modifications.[151]

**[7.171]** Section 217C(3) allows the board to attach to any approval of a scheme or proposed road development under the Roads Act 1993 a condition requiring:

(a) the construction or the financing, in whole or in part, of the construction of a facility, or

(b) the provision or the financing, in whole or in part, of the provision of a service,

in the area in which the proposed development would be situated, being a facility or service that, in the opinion of the Board, would constitute a substantial gain to the community.

**[7.172]** In effect, s 217C(3) permits the board to impose a condition which would offer a significant planning gain to the community. The planning gain for the local community conditions can only be imposed in cases of approval of a road scheme or of a proposed road development and similar planning gain conditions could be added to a confirmation of a general CPO. The planning gain on offer under this section can be either the construction of a facility or the provision of a service. Also, the planning gain must be for the benefit of the entire community and not just a section or part of the community. The planning gain conditions inevitably serve another function, namely to

---

149. The entire of PDA 2000, s 217B(1)–(8) has been inserted by PD(SI)A 2006, s 38.
150. PDA 2000, s 217C(1).
151. PDA 2000, s 217C(2).

control or tame, to some extent at least, any local opposition to the proposal. A limitation is placed on the planning gain condition in s 217C(4) which provides as follows:

> (4) A condition attached pursuant to subsection (3) shall not require such an amount of financial resources to be committed for the purposes of the condition being complied with as would substantially deprive the person in whose favour the approval operates of the benefits likely to accrue from the grant of the approval.

Similar incentives or planning gains are available in PDA 2000, s 175(9) and in PDA 2000, s 181B(7). Section 175 deals with EIA of certain development carried out by or on behalf of local authorities and s 175(9)(b)(i) and (ii) provide as follows:

> (b) Without prejudice to the generality of the foregoing power to attach conditions, the Board may attach to such an approval, under paragraph (a)(i), (ii) or (iii) a condition requiring –
>
> (i) the construction of or the financing, in whole or in part, of the construction of a facility, or
>
> (ii) the provision or the financing, in whole or in part, of the provision of a service,
>
> in the area in which the proposed development would be situated, being a facility or service that, in the opinion of the Board, would constitute a substantial gain to the community.[152]

Similar wording is used in PDA 2000, s 181B(7).[153]

## Oral hearings

**[7.173]** PDA 2000 replaced the requirement for a public inquiry by an oral hearing in compulsory acquisition of land procedure. PDA 2000, s 218(1), as amended by s 39(a) of PD(SI)A 2006, provides as follows:

> (1) where, as a result of the transfer of functions under sections 214, 215, 215A or 215B, the Board would otherwise be required to hold a local inquiry, public local inquiry or oral hearing, that requirement shall not apply to the Board but the Board may, at its absolute discretion, hold an oral hearing in relation to the matter, the subject of the function transferred.

**[7.174]** It should be noted that the amended s 218(1) does not require the board to hold an oral hearing and the decision as to whether or not to hold such an oral hearing is entirely at the discretion of the board. Although the section uses the phrase 'absolute discretion', the decision as to whether or not to hold an oral hearing must be made bearing in mind the requirements of natural and constitutional justice and also the right of fair procedures required by art 6 of the European Convention of Human Rights.

---

152. As amended by PD(SI)A 2006, s 34(c).
153. As inserted by PD(SI)A 2006, s 36.

**[7.175]** PDA 2000, ss 135,[154] 143 and 146 deal with oral hearings of planning appeals and PDA 2000, s 218(4) applies the provisions of those sections to oral hearings in relation to compulsory acquisition of land in the confirming of an order for compulsory acquisition of land.

## Supplemental provisions relating to oral hearings[155]

**[7.176]** This is an important section and it is set out in the amended version as follows:

> (1) The Board or an employee of the Board duly authorised by the Board may assign a person to conduct an oral hearing of an appeal, referral or application on behalf of the Board.
>
> (2) The person conducting an oral hearing of an appeal, referral or application shall have discretion as to the conduct of the hearing and shall conduct the hearing expeditiously and without undue formality (but subject to any directions given by the Board under sub-s (2A) or sub-s (2B)).
>
> (2A) The Board may give a direction to the person conducting an oral hearing that he or she shall require persons intending to appear at the hearing to submit to him or her, in writing and in advance of the hearing, the points or a summary of the arguments they propose to make at the hearing; where such direction is given that person shall comply with it (and, accordingly, is unable to make such a requirement).
>
> (2AB) The Board may in its absolutely discretion, following a recommendation in relation to the matter from a person assigned under s 146, give a direction to a person assigned to conduct an oral hearing that he or she shall only points or arguments in relation to specified matters during the oral hearing.
>
> (2AC) Where a direction is given by the Board under sub-s (2AB), the person to whom it is given shall comply with it (and accordingly, is unable to make such a requirement) unless that person forms the opinion that it is necessary, in the interests of observing fair procedures, to allow a point or an argument to be made during the oral hearing in relation to matters not specified in the direction.
>
> (2AD) The Board shall give a notice of its direction under sub-s (2AB) to –
>
> (i) each party, in the case of an appeal or referral,
>
> (ii) the applicant and planning authority, in the case of an application under this Act, for a railway order under the Act of 2001, or for approval under s 51 of the Roads Act 1993, and

---

154. PDA 2000, s 135 is amended as follows: Section 135(2) amended by PD(A)A 2010, s 43(a); s 135(2AB) to (2AE) inserted by PD(A)A 2010, s 43(b); s 135(2B)(dd) inserted by PD(A)A 2010, s 43(c). PDA 2000, s 134(1) to (3) were substituted by PD(SI)A 2006, s 22. PDA 2000, s 135(5)(a) is amended by PD(SI)A 2006, s 23(b).
155. PDA 2000, s 135 is amended as follows: Section 135(2) amended by PD(A)A 2010, s 43(a); s 135(2AB) to (2AE) inserted by PD(A)A 2010, s 43(b); s 135(2B)(dd) inserted by PD(A)A 2010, s 43(c). PDA 2000, s 134(1) to (3) were substituted by PD(SI)A 2006 s 22. PDA 2000, s 135(5)(a) is amended by PD(SI)A 2006, s 23(b).

(iii) each person who has made objections, submissions or observations to the Board in the case of an appeal, referral or application.

(2AE) The points or summary of the arguments that a person intending to appear at the oral hearing shall submit to the persons conducting the hearing, where a direction has been given under sub-s (2A) and sub-s (2AB), shall be limited to points or arguments in relation to matters specified in the direction under sub-s (2AB).

(2B) Subject to the foregoing provisions, the person conducting the oral hearing –

(a) shall decide the order of appearance of persons at the hearing.

(b) shall permit any person to appear in person or to be represented by another person,

(c) may limit the time limit within which each person may make points or arguments (including arguments in reputation of arguments made by others at the hearing), or question the evidence of others, at the hearing,

(d) may refuse to allow the making of a point or an argument if–

(i) the point or a summary of the argument has not been submitted in advance to the person in accordance with a requirement made pursuant to a direction given under sub-s (2A),

(ii) the point or argument is not relevant to the subject matter of the hearing, or

(iii) is considered necessary so as to avoid undue repetition of the same point or argument.

(dd) may refuse to allow the making of a point or argument in relation to any matter where –

(i) a direction has been given under sub-s (2AB) and the matter is not specified in the direction, and

(ii) he or she has not formed the opinion referred to in sub-s (2AC)

(e) may hear a person other than a person who has made submissions or observations to the Board in relation to the subject matter of hearing if it is considered appropriate in the interests of justice to allow a person to be heard.

(3) A person conducting an oral hearing of an appeal, application or referral may require any officer of a planning authority or a local authority to give to him or her any information in relation to the appeal, application or referral which he or she reasonably requires for the purposes of the appeal, application or referral, and it shall be the duty of the officer to comply with the requirement.

(4) A person conducting an oral hearing of any appeal, referral or application may take evidence on oath or affirmation and for that purpose may administer oaths or affirmations, and a person giving evidence at any such hearing shall be entitled to the same immunities and privileges as if he or she were a witness before the High Court.

(5)(a) Subject to paragraph (b), the Board in relation to an oral hearing of any appeal, referral or application may, by giving notice in that behalf in writing to any person, require that person to do either or both of the following:

    (i)    to attend at such time and place as is specified in the notice to give evidence in relation to any matter in question at the hearing;

    (ii)    to produce any books, deeds, contracts, accounts, vouchers, maps, plans, documents or other information in his or her possession, custody or control which relate to any such matter.

(b) Where a person is given a notice under paragraph (a):

    (i)    the Board shall pay or tender to any person whose attendance is required such reasonable subsistence and travelling expenses to be determined by the Board in accordance with the rates for the time being applicable to senior planning authority officials;

    (ii)    any person who in compliance with a notice has attended at any place shall, save insofar as the reasonable and necessary expenses of the attendants have already been paid to him or her, be paid those expenses by the Board, and those expenses shall, in default of being so paid, be recoverable as a simple contract debt in any court of competent jurisdiction.

(6) Every person to whom a notice under sub-s (5) has been given who refuses or willfully neglects to attend in accordance with the notice or who willfully alters, suppresses, conceals or destroys any documents or other information to which the notice relates or who, or who, having so attended, refuses to give evidence or refuses or willfully fails to produce any document or other information to which the notice relates shall be guilty of an offence.

(7) Where any person –

(a) willfully gives evidence which is material to the oral hearing and which he or she knows to be false or does not believe to be true,

(b) by act or omission, obstructs or hinders the person conducting the oral hearing in the performance of his or her functions,

(c) refuses to take an oath or make an affirmation when legally required to do so by a person holding the oral hearing.

(d) refuses to answer any questions to which the person conducting the oral hearing may legally require an answer, or

(e) does or omits to do any other thing which, if the enquiry had been by the High Court, would have been contempt of that court,

the person shall be guilt of an offence.

(8)(a) An oral hearing may be conducted through the medium of Irish or the English language.

(b) Where an oral hearing relates to development within the Gaeltacht, the hearing shall be conducted through the medium of the Irish language, unless the parties to the appeal, referral or application to which the hearing relates agree that the hearing shall be conducted in English.

(c) Where an oral hearing relates to development outside the Gaeltacht, the hearing shall be conducted through the medium of the English, unless the parties to the appeal, referral or application to which the hearing relates agree that the hearing shall be conducted in the Irish language.[156]

**[7.177]** The person conducting the oral hearing shall have discretion as to the conduct of the hearing and shall conduct the hearing expeditiously and without undue formality. The person holding the oral hearing may decide the order of appearance of persons at the hearing and may permit a person to be represented by another person. The person conducting the oral hearing may impose time limits on witnesses making statements or giving evidence or on persons questioning other persons. The person holding the hearing has discretion to hear persons who have not made submissions or observations to the board where it is considered appropriate in the interest of justice to allow such persons to be heard. The person hearing the oral hearing may require any officer of the planning authority or of a local authority to give information which is reasonably required for the purposes of the hearing. Evidence may be taken on oath or affirmation and witnesses before the oral hearing are entitled to immunity and privileges as if they were before the High Court. The person hearing the oral hearing can give notice in writing to any person requiring them to attend and to give evidence and/or to produce any books, deeds, contracts, maps, plans, documents or other information provided that the board shall pay reasonable subsistence and travel expenses. If a person refuses to attend or to produce documents or if a person destroys any documents required by the person conducting the oral hearing he/she shall be guilty of an offence.

**[7.178]** The inspector is encouraged by the statutory provisions to conduct an oral hearing in an efficient and orderly manner by the creation of the following offences by PDA 2000, s 135(7):

(7) Where any person –

(a) willfully gives evidence which is material to the oral hearing and which he or she knows to be false or does not believe to be true,

(b) by act or omission, obstruct or hinders the person conducting the oral hearing in the performance of his or her functions,

(c) refuses to take an oath or to make an affirmation when legally required to do so by a person holding the oral hearing,

(d) refuses to answer any questions to which the person conducting an oral hearing may legally require an answer, or

(e) does or omits to do any other thing which, if the enquiry had been by the High Court, would have been contempt of that court,

the person shall be guilty of an offence.

The structure of an oral hearing presided over by a person appointed is such that the hearing convened is an expert body discharging functions of a quasi-judicial nature. If

---

156. PDA 2000, s 135 is amended as follows: Section 135(2) amended by PD(A)A 2010, s 43(a); s 135(2AB) to (2AE) inserted by PD(A)A 2010, s 43(b); s 135(2B)(dd) inserted by PD(A)A 2010, s 43(c). PDA 2000, s 134(1) to (3) were substituted by PD(SI)A 2006 s 22. PDA 2000, s 135(5)(a) is amended by PD(SI)A 2006, s 23(b).

the substance of the decision made by the person conducting the oral hearing is to be challenged by judicial review, the *O'Keefe*[157] principles will apply and unless the person conducting the hearing is held to have acted unreasonably and irrationally in the *O'Keefe*[158] sense judicial review is unlikely to succeed. In *Kildare County Council v An Bord Pleanála*,[159] McMenamin J held as follows:

> Under the statutory regime the respondent is entrusted with considering the adequacy of an EIS. It is the exercise of the statutory discretion which the applicants now seek to challenge. A challenge can only be mounted on contention that the decision of the Board was unreasonable, or irrational and that the well established principles laid down in *O'Keefe v An Bord Pleanála*[160] therefore apply.

**[7.179]** PDA 2000, s 143 (as substituted by PD(SI)A 2006, s 26) deals with matters which the board shall have 'regard to' and it covers certain policies and objectives which are relevant to the board in the performance of its functions. The particular policies and objectives are set out in PDA 2000, s 143(1)(a), (b) and (c) as follows:

(a) the policies and objectives for the time being of the Government, a State authority, the Minister, planning authorities and any other body which is a public authority whose functions have, or may have, a bearing on the proper planning and sustainable development of cities, towns or other areas, whether urban or rural,

(b) the national interest and any effect the performance of the Board's functions may have on issues of strategic economic or social importance to the State, and

(c) the National Spatial Strategy and any regional planning guidelines for the time being in force.

**[7.180]** PDA 2000, s 143(2) provides that a 'public authority' means any body established by or under statute which is for the time being declared, by regulations made by the Minister, to be a public authority for the purposes of this section.[161] Although the board is bound to 'have regard' to certain policies and objectives this does not mean that it is bound, without thought or alternative, to comply with the policies and objectives of the government, the Minister or any other Minister of government. In *McEvoy and Smith v Meath County Council*,[162] Quirke J held that to have regard to any regional planning guidelines when drafting a county development plan was permissive rather than mandatory. While Quirke J believed that the planning authority should seek to accommodate objectives and policies contained in relevant regional planning guidelines it was not bound to do so and it could depart from those guidelines as long as there were genuine reasons to do so particularly if those reasons were consistent with proper

---

157. *O'Keefe v An Bord Pleanála* [1993] 1 IR 39.
158. *O'Keefe v An Bord Pleanála* [1993] 1 IR 39.
159. *Kildare County Council v An Bord Pleanála* [2006] IEHC 73, McMenamin J.
160. *O'Keefe v An Bord Pleanála* [1993] 1 IR 39.
161. PDA 2000, s 143(2) as substituted by PD(SI)A 2006, s 26.
162. *McEvoy and Smith v Meath County Council* [2003] 1 IR 208, Quirke J.

planning and development of an area for which the planning authority had responsibility. Quirke J's reasoning on this point is almost certainly altered by the requirement compelling planning authorities to prepare a 'core strategy' to be submitted with the development plan.

**[7.181]** PDA 2000, s 146 enables the board to assign a person to report on any matter on behalf of the board. The Board is permitted to appoint an inspector or inspectors to report on matters on which a decision must be made. Any person assigned shall make a written report on the matter to the board which shall include a recommendation, and the board shall consider the report and the recommendation before determining the matter.

## Power to direct payment of certain costs

**[7.182]** PDA 2000, s 219, dealing with the power of the board to require payment of costs arising from an oral hearing, where such costs are to be paid by the local authority and/or the applicant, has been substituted by s 40 of PD(SI)A 2006. The significant change in the section is the recognition of the fact that the applicant for compulsory acquisition may be a person or body other than the local authority. The award of costs related to an oral hearing where the board has made a decision in performance of any function transferred under s 214, 215, 215A or 215B is entirely at the board's 'absolute discretion'. The Board may direct payment of such costs as it considers reasonable by the local authority concerned or, in the case of s 215A or 215B, payment may be ordered against the person who applied for the acquisition order (namely the appellant), to allow the board to direct payment of costs by such persons as well as by the local authority. The section provides a breakdown of the costs of the board which it may make the local authority pay, as follows:

(a) to the Board towards the cost and expenses incurred by the Board in determining the matter, including –

(i) the costs of holding any oral hearing in relation to the matter,

(ii) the fees of any consultants or advisers engaged in the matter, and

(iii) an amount equal to such portion of the remuneration and any allowances for expenses paid to the members and employees of the Board as the Board determines to be attributable to the performance of duties by the members and employees in relation to the matter,

and

(b) to any person appearing at an oral hearing held in relation to the matter as a contribution towards the costs, other than costs referred to in section 135, incurred by that person of appearing at that hearing,

and the local authority or applicant, as appropriate, shall pay the sum.[163]

---

163. PDA 2000, s 219(1)(a)(b).

All costs are construed as a reference to such costs as the board, in its absolute discretion, considers to be reasonable costs.[164]

**[7.183]** If a local authority and/or an applicant do not pay the costs directed by the board these costs may be recovered as a simple contract debt in a court of competent jurisdiction.[165]

## Certain procedures to run in parallel

**[7.184]** PDA 2000, s 220 recognised that some, if not many, of the compulsory acquisition confirmation applicants who come before the board will require that an EIA will be carried out by or on behalf of the local authority in accordance with the provisions of PDA 2000, s 175.

**[7.185]** PDA 2000, s 220 permits the person holding the oral hearing in relation to compulsory acquisition of land to hear evidence in relation to the compulsory acquisition at the same time as evidence concerning the approval of an EIS is given. Once an EIS has been prepared the local authority must seek approval for it from An Bord Pleanála and then both approvals (the confirmation of the compulsory acquisition and the approval of the EIS) must be sought at the same time and the board is obliged to arrive at its decision in relation to both approvals at the same time.[166]

## Objective of the Board in relation to transferred functions

**[7.186]** PDA 2000, s 221 attempts to provide time limits in which an oral hearing must be completed and time limits for other functions in connection with confirming a CPO. Section 221(1), (2)(a), (5) and (7) have been amended by s 41 of PD(SI)A 2006. PDA 2000, s 221(9) has been added to the section by s 247(k) of LGA 2001. Section 221 is not dissimilar to PDA 2000, s 126 which deals generally with the duty and objectives of the board to ensure that all appeals and referrals are dealt with as expeditiously as possible so as to ensure that, insofar as is practicable, there are no avoidable delays at any stage in the determination of appeals and referrals. Some practitioners, at least, will have a fairly jaundiced view as to the effectiveness of s 126.

**[7.187]** Section 221(1) provides:

> (1) It shall be the duty of the Board to ensure that any matters submitted in accordance with the functions transferred to it under section 214, 215, 215A and 215B are disposed of as expeditiously as may be and, for that purpose, to take all such steps as are open to it to ensure that, in so far as is practicable, there are no avoidable delays at any stage in the determination of those matters.[167]

---

164. PDA 2000, s 219(2).
165. PDA 2000, s 219(3).
166. PDA 2000, s 220(1) and (2).
167. As amended by PD(SI)A 2006, s 41.

**[7.188]** A number of more specific objectives with qualifications and escape clauses are provided in s 221(2). Section 221(2) is 'without prejudice' to the generality of sub-s (1) and is subject to sub-ss (3), (4), (5) and (6). PDA 2000, s 221(2) provides:

> Without prejudice to the generality of subsection (1) and subject to subsections (3), (4), (5) and (6) it shall be the objective of the Board to ensure that –
>
> (a) the matter is determined within a period of 18 weeks beginning on the last day for making objections, observations or submissions, as the case may be, in accordance with the relevant enactment referred to in sections 214, 215, 215A or 215B, or
>
> (b) the matter is determined within such other period as the Minister may prescribe in relation to paragraph (a), either generally or in respect of a particular class or classes of matter.[168]

There is, of course, no 'default' decision where either the time limit, or the 'duty' implied by this section is not adhered to. The planning system in Ireland generally is afflicted by delays on the part of planning authorities and on the part of the board. Without any real sanctions or time limits to worry them it is hardly surprising that time is seldom, if ever, of the essence. The system would be greatly improved if the mandatory time limits and sanctions which apply to members of the public were fairly extended to planning authorities and to the board. If that is not done the present situation will continue and things will be done 'as soon as may be'. Legislators and their draftsmen will continue to favour their own kind.

**[7.189]** PDA 2000, s 221(3)(a) provides that 'where it appears to the board that it would not be possible or appropriate, because of the particular circumstances of the matter with which the board is concerned, to determine the matter' ... within 18 weeks or such longer time as determined by the Minister, the board will notify the local authority and the other persons concerned, in writing, stating the reason why it would not be possible or appropriate to determine the matter within the prescribed period. The notice will also indicate a date by which the matter will be determined. PDA 2000, s 221(3)(b) follows with the announcement that the board 'shall take all such steps as are open to it to ensure that the matter is determined before the date specified in the notice'. The subsection is almost devoid of meaning and it must be perfectly clear, even to the casual reader, that the 'matter' to be 'compulsorily acquired' is not a level playing pitch when it comes to comparing statutory time limits as applied to the State with statutory time limits which members of the public endure and which they are compelled to abide by if they are to avoid firm penalties.

**[7.190]** PDA 2000, s 221(5) provides that if matters come before the board under ss 214, 215, 215A or 215B which are of special strategic, economic or social importance to the State, the Minister may direct the board to deal with such matters as expeditiously as

---

168. The 'qualifications' are detailed in the introduction to PDA 2000, s 221(1) and the 'escape clause' is clearly stated at PDA 2000, s 221(2)(b). 'Sean Citizen' and the State do not balance the see-saw when each is standing at either end of the board. Sean is well up in the air but the State has its feet firmly on the ground! Note that PDA 2000, s 221(2) has been amended by PD(SI)A 2006, s 41.

**[7.191]** possible, consistent with proper planning and sustainable development and the board shall comply with such direction.[169]

**[7.191]** PDA 2000, s 221(7) provides:

> For the purposes of meeting its duty under this section, the chairperson may, or shall when so directed by the Minister, assign the functions transferred to the Board under sections 214, 215, 215A and 215B to a particular division of the Board in accordance with section 112.[170]

**[7.192]** PDA 2000, s 221(8) deals with the annual report made by the board to the Minister which, in practice, is delivered before 30 June each year. The report must include a statement of the number of matters which the board has determined stating, in each case, the period taken and relating that period to the relevant subsection of s 221 and such other information as to the time taken to determine such matters as the Minister may direct.

**[7.193]** PDA 2000, s 221(9) allows the Minister to make regulations to provide for additional, incidental, consequential or supplemental matters concerning procedure in respect of the functions transferred from the Minister to the board as may be necessary or expedient.[171]

## Amendment of s 10 of Local Government (No 2) Act 1960

**[7.194]** The amendment made in PDA 2000, s 222 deletes s 10(2) of the Local Government (No 2) Act 1960. Section 10(2) of the 1960 Act did provide:

> Where –
> 
> (a) a local authority consider that any land, whether situate within or outside their functional area, would, if required by them, be suitable for the provision of halls, buildings and offices, for the local authority, and
> 
> (b) the local authority consider that it would be convenient to effect the acquisition under the Housing of Working Classes Acts 1890–1958,
> 
> the local authority may decide so to effect the acquisition.

It appears that the provision was duplicated in s 10 of the 1960 Act. The substituted provision makes an addition to the 1960 Act and s 10(4)(d) of the Local Government (No 2) Act 1960 provides:

> (d) Where –
> 
> (i) an order is made by virtue of this section, and

---

169. PDA 2000, s 221(5) has been amended by PD(SI)A 2006, s 41.
170. PDA 2000, s 112 deals with divisions of the board. The Board can set up internal divisions 'for the speedy dispatch of the business of the Board'. Any division shall have at least three members, and any matters referred to a division by the chairperson of the board shall have all the functions of the board. Also note that PDA 2000, s 221(7) has been amended by PD(SI)A 2006, s 41.
171. This section has been inserted by LGA 2001, s 247(k).

(ii) there is a public right of way over the land to which the order relates or any part thereof or over land adjacent to or associated with the land or any part thereof,

the order may authorise the local authority, by order made by them after they have acquired such land or part, to extinguish the right of way.[172]

## References to transferred functions in regulations, etc

[7.195] PDA 2000, s 223(1) is the last section in Pt XIV and it is a 'catch all' provision to ensure that any references made to the Minister, any other Minister or the Commission for Energy Regulation in any regulation, prescribed forms or other instruments, made under all of the legislation referred to in PDA 2000, ss 214, 215, 215A or 215B, and which relate to the functions transferred to An Bord Pleanála under the section, shall be deemed to refer to the board.

[7.196] PDA 2000, s 223(2) provides that any references in similar documents referred to in s 223(1) to local inquiries or to public inquiries and which relate to functions transferred to the board under those sections shall be deemed to be references to oral hearings by the board.

[7.197] PDA 2000, s 223 has been amended by s 42 of PD(SI)A 2006 to take account of any newly inserted provisions.

## Part IX, Ch 5 of the National Asset Management Agency Act 2009

[7.198] The National Assets Management Agency Act 2009 makes separate provision for the compulsory acquisition of land in Pt IX, Ch 5, ss 157–171. The circumstances of a compulsory acquisition by the National Assets Management Agency (NAMA) are limited by the provisions of s 158 of the NAMA Act 2009. If the only purpose of compulsory acquisition by NAMA was an economic purpose it would be difficult to see how that acquisition would be in the public interest. Public interest is a fundamental ingredient in drawing the fine line between the property rights of individuals and the public benefits of compulsory acquisition. In general, compulsory acquisition is confirmed by An Bord Pleanála. Compulsory acquisition under the NAMA Act 2009 can only be operated within the limits of s 158, which deals with NAMA's power to acquire land compulsorily, and confirmation of the NAMA compulsory acquisition must be confirmed by the High Court.[173] Undoubtedly, this is an inconvenient step for NAMA but for the long run it may prevent a volume of legal challenges on the basis that the High Court will insist that the Supreme Court principles established in *Clinton v An Bord Pleanála (No 2)*[174] are fully respected, in that, any NAMA compulsory acquisition of land will be justified by the exigencies of the common good and further that the requirements of the Constitution, which respect the property rights of the landowner whose lands are to be acquired, will be taken into account.[175]

---

172. PDA 2000, s 222(d)(i) and (ii).
173. See NAMA Act 2009, s 159(1) and (2).
174. *Clinton v An Bord Pleanála* [2007] 4 IR 701.

**[7.199]** NAMA's powers to acquire land compulsorily are set out in the NAMA Act 2009, s 158 as follows:

> (1) NAMA may compulsorily acquire land if in its opinion it is necessary to do so –
>
> > (a) to enable NAMA to perform the functions referred to section 10(1)(b) and (c),
> >
> > (b) to enable a building constructed on charged land to be used or enjoyed for the purpose for which it was developed, or
> >
> > (c) to enable NAMA or a NAMA group entity to vest in a prudent and experienced purchaser good and marketable title to charged land but only if the land sought to be acquired is only of material benefit to the owner in so far as it affects the use or development of charged land.
>
> (2) In addition, NAMA may compulsorily acquire land where –
>
> > (a) the land is owned by a person who is a debtor, associated debtor, guarantor or surety in relation to an acquired bank asset, and that person is in material default of his or her obligations to NAMA or a NAMA group entity and the default has caused, or is likely to cause, NAMA or the NAMA group entity substantial loss,
> >
> > (b) the land was intended to form part of a security in relation to a credit facility provided by a participating institution but was not included in the security through an error or omission, or
> >
> > (c) a debtor, associated debtor, guarantor or surety in relation to an acquired bank asset is using or intends to use his or her ownership of the land to materially impede the disposition, at a fair and reasonable price, of land by NAMA or a NAMA group entity.
>
> (3) NAMA may compulsorily acquire land only if it has first made a reasonable attempt to acquire the land by agreement.

**[7.200]** Section 10(a), (b) and (c) reads as follows:

> (1) NAMA's purposes shall be to contribute to the achievement of the purposes specified in section 2 by –
>
> > (a) the acquisition from participating institutions of such eligible bank assets as is appropriate,
> >
> > (b) dealing expeditiously with the assets acquired by it, and
> >
> > (c) protecting or otherwise enhancing the value of those assets, in the interests of the State.

---

175. That does not mean that none of the NAMA CPO procedures are open to constitutional challenge.

**[7.201]** Section 2 of the NAMA Act 2009 deals with the purposes of the Act which are as follows:

(a) to address the serious threat to the economy and the stability of credit institutions in the State generally and the need for the maintenance and stabilisation of the financial system in the State, and

(b) to address the compelling need –

(i) to facilitate the availability of credit in the economy of the State,

(ii) to resolve the problems created by the financial crisis in an expeditious and efficient manner and achieve a recovery in the economy,

(iii) to protect the State's interest in respect of the guarantees issued by the State pursuant to the Credit Institutions (Financial Support) Act 2008 and to underpin the steps taken by the Government in that regard,

(iv) to protect the interests of tax payers,

(v) to facilitate restructuring of credit institutions of systemic importance to the economy,

(vi) to remove uncertainty about the valuation and location of certain assets of credit institutions of systemic importance to the economy,

(vii) to restore confidence in the banking sector and to underpin the affect of Government support measures in relation to that sector, and

(viii) to contribute to the social and economic development of the State.

The NAMA Act 2009 is there to address the problems which have arisen as a result of a financial crisis. The Act makes no mention of bad planning decisions which flew in the face of planning legislation and bad rezoning decisions which were made without a thought for sustainable planning development. The planning issues are matters to be addressed separately and the presumption is that they are to be addressed in the PD(A)A 2010.

**[7.202]** Garrett Simons SC[176] summarised the circumstances in which NAMA can seek to acquire land compulsorily, under five separate headings, as follows:

1. Where the acquisition of land is necessary to protect or enhance assets required by NAMA.[177]

    In relation to 1, which deals with the necessity to protect and enhance assets, the NAMA website has dealt with the intent of the legislation in seeking to protect and enhance assets as follows:

    > This provision is primarily directed at resolving difficulties which would arise due to the creation or retention of so called 'ransom strips'. This

---

176. Garrett Simons SC – paper delivered at a NAMA conference held at the Westbury Hotel, Dublin chaired by the Hon Mr Justice Frank Clarke, 6 March 2010.
177. See NAMA Act 2009, s 10(1)(b) and (c).

involved strips of land or rights essential to the development of the property being carved out from the main property. Examples could include essential rights of way or strips of land cutting off access to roads or infrastructure.[178]

2. Where the acquisition of other land is necessary to enable a building which is constructed on the 'charged land' to be used or enjoyed for the purpose for which it was developed.[179]

In relation to 2, this might arise where a building has been constructed on 'charged land' but cannot be used because, for example, the right of access to it is owned by a third party and the building is landlocked. In those circumstances, NAMA can acquire the other land comprising the right of way in order to solve the problem.

3. Where the land sought to be acquired compulsorily has no practical value to its owner, other than its nuisance value.[180]

In relation to 3, this deals with land which has no practical value to its owner other than nuisance value and if land adjoining 'charged land' has no material benefit to its owner other than the possibility of obtaining an artificially high price for 'nuisance value', NAMA can compulsorily acquire that land in order to provide a purchaser of the 'charged land' with marketable title.

4. Where circumstances justify compulsory acquisition of other land owned by a debtor.[181]

In relation to 4, this arises due to the conduct of a debtor who may, for example, be in default of his obligations to NAMA and that default is likely to cause NAMA substantial loss. In those circumstances, NAMA can compulsorily acquire the debtor's lands.

5. Where land has not been properly included as part of the security for a credit facility by error or omission.[182]

In relation to 5, this arises where land was intended to form a part of the security but due to an error or omission it was not included in that security. In those circumstances, NAMA can use its power of compulsory acquisition to acquire those lands.

---

178. The author's attention was drawn to this piece of information on the NAMA website (http://www.nama.ie/ (accessed 10 May 2011)) which was given in response to a FAQ. See paper prepared by Garrett Simons SC for a NAMA conference held on 6 March 2010 at the Westbury Hotel, Dublin and chaired by the Hon Mr Justice Frank Clarke.
179. See NAMA Act 2009, s 158(1)(b).
180. See NAMA Act 2009, s 158(1)(c).
181. See NAMA Act 2009, s 158(2)(a).
182. See NAMA Act 2009, s 158(2)(b).

## Acquisition of land for open spaces

**[7.203]** PDA 2000, s 45 deals with acquisition of land for open spaces. In effect, s 45 is an enforcement mechanism which can be used against a developer for failure to comply with a condition in a planning permission to provide or to maintain open space. If a condition in a planning permission requires the provision of open space, and this is often expressed in terms of a percentage of open space in relation to the total size of the area submitted for development, and the developer fails to comply with that condition, the planning authority may seek enforcement under Pt VIII of PDA 2000 or, alternatively, it may serve an acquisition notice and complete the procedure to acquire the open space as set out in s 45.

**[7.204]** PDA 2000, s 45 has three separate elements:

1. The first element is contained in PDA 2000, s 45(1) and (2). Section 45 enables a planning authority to acquire land for the provision of open spaces and when the planning permission which issues in respect of the development applied for contains a condition that open space is to be provided by the developer, or if it is either explicit or implicit in the application for permission, that land is to be provided or maintained for such space, then the planning authority will serve notice on the owner in writing requesting the developer, within a time period of not less than eight weeks, to provide, level, plant or otherwise adapt or maintain the land in a manner which, in the opinion of the planning authority, would make it suitable for the purposes for which the open space is to be provided. If the owner fails to comply or to secure compliance with the request, within the period specified in the request, being a period of not less than eight weeks, the planning authority may publish a notice in a newspaper circulating in the district, called 'an acquisition notice', of its intention to acquire the land by order under s 45. The acquisition notice will specify a period, being a period of not less than four weeks commencing on the date on which the notice was published, within which an appeal may be made under the section. When the planning authority publishes an acquisition notice, it will serve a copy on the owner of the land to which the notice relates not less than 10 days after the date of publication.

2. The second element of PDA 2000, s 45 deals with appeals to the board against the decision to acquire and it is contained in s 45(4), (5), (6) and (7). These subsections also deal with the situation where the planning authority publishes an acquisition notice and no appeal is made. An acquisition notice is subject to a right of appeal to An Bord Pleanála and, where an appeal is made, the board may either annul the acquisition notice or confirm the acquisition notice with or without modifications in respect of all or any such part of the relevant land. If a planning authority publishes an acquisition notice and the period for appealing the notice expires, or no appeal is taken, or an appeal has been taken and withdrawn, or the notice has been confirmed whether conditionally or subject to modification, the planning authority may make an order which will operate to vest the land in it. When the order is made, the local authority will obtain the

same rights and title which the landowner had, together with any rights or liabilities which the owner had enjoyed or incurred in connection with the land and subject also to an obligation to comply with the planning authority's own request to level, plant or otherwise adapt or maintain the land in a manner specified in the written request above referred to. When the order is made, the order is sent to the Land Registry for registration under the Registration of Title Act 1964.

3. The third element of the s 45 acquisition procedure entitles a landowner to a limited right of compensation. The relevant provisions relating to compensation in relation to an acquisition notice are dealt with in PDA 2000, s 45(8), (9) and (10).

**[7.205]** If compensation cannot be agreed under this section it is referred to arbitration under the Acquisition of Land (Assessment of Compensation) Act 1919 in the same way as a compulsory purchase order but subject to the proviso that the arbitrator has jurisdiction to make a nil award and also to the following provisions:

(a) the arbitrator shall make a nil award, unless it is shown by or on behalf of the owner that an amount equal to the value of the land to which the relevant permission under s 34 relates, being that value at the time when the application for the permission was made, as a result of the development has not been recovered and as a further such result will not in the future be recoverable by disposing of the land which is land to which the permission relates and which is not land to which the order relates, and

(b) in the assessment of the value of the land to which the order relates, no regard shall be had to its value for use other than as open space and a deduction shall be made in respect of the cost of carrying out such works as may be necessary to comply with the request made pursuant to subsection (1)(c).[183]

If an acquisition notice is made, details of same must be entered in the register giving full particulars of the acquisition notice, the date and effect of any decision on appeal in relation to this notice and particulars of any order made under PDA 2000, s 45, such entry to be made within a period of seven days commencing on the date of publication, receipt of notification of the decision or the making of the order, as may be appropriate.

**[7.206]** PDA 2000, s 45 applies to any form of open space (whether referred to as open space or by any other description in the relevant application for permission or in a condition attached to the relevant permission), being land which is not described in the application or condition either as private open space or in terms of indicating that it is not intended that members of the public are to have resort thereto without restriction.

**[7.207]** It will be seen that the circumstances in which compensation will be payable for the acquisition of land for open spaces is very limited indeed. It will also be noted that, in this instance, the entry relating to the acquisition notice, any appeal or an order made

---

183. PDA 2000, s 45(8)(a) and (b).

under PDA 2000, s 45 must be entered within seven days in the planning register. This is a sound provision and certainly an improvement on the normal provision for making entries in the planning register which require that the entry should be made 'as soon as may be'. The phrase 'as soon as may be' may encourage a sense of urgency but it does not compel it.

**[7.208]** The term 'open space' is not defined in Irish statute law but the definition appears in s 20 of the English Open Spaces Act 1906 as 'any land, whether enclosed or not, on which there are no buildings of which not more than one-twentieth part is covered with buildings, and the whole or the remainder of which is laid out as a garden or is used for purposes of recreation, or lies waste and unoccupied'.

**[7.209]** The provision requiring acquisition of land for open spaces was first introduced by s 25 of LG(PD)A 1976 and since the provisions of the Act are not retrospective they cannot be applied to development carried out before the 1976 Act became law.

# Chapter 8

# ADDITIONAL PLANNING CONTROLS ON LAND AND ON BUILDINGS[1]

## ADVERTISEMENTS

[8.01] The Planning and Development Act 2000 (PDA 2000), s 2 defines 'advertisement' as meaning:

> [A]ny word, letter, model, balloon, inflatable structure, kite, poster, notice, device or representation employed for the purpose of advertisement, announcement or direction;
>
> 'advertisement structure' means any structure which is a hoarding, scaffold, framework, pole, standard, device or sign (whether illuminated or not) and which is used or intended for use for exhibiting advertisements or any attachment to a building or structure used for advertising purposes;
>
> 'exhibit', in relation to an advertisement, includes affix, inscribe, print, paint, illuminate and otherwise delineate.

[8.02] PDA 2000, s 3 defines 'development' and the definition is relevant to advertisements in s 3(2)(a), which reads:

> For the purposes of subsection (1)[2] and without prejudice to the generality of that subsection –
>
> (a) Where any structure or other land or any tree or other objection on land becomes used for the exhibition of advertisements ...
>
> the use of the land shall be taken as having been materially changed.

[8.03] Advertisements also receive attention in PDA 2000, s 209(1)–(3) which is headed: Repair and tidying of advertisement structures and advertisements.

A planning authority may serve a notice requiring the repair, tidying or removal of an advertisement under the section where it appears to the planning authority, having regard to the interest of public safety or amenity, an advertisement structure or an advertisement in its area should be repaired or tidied. The notice is served on the person having control of the structure or advertisement and it requires that person to repair or tidy the advertisement structure within the period specified in the notice.

[8.04] Similar provisions apply if it appears to a planning authority that any advertisement structure or advertisement is derelict and a notice may be served on the

---

1. This chapter should be read in conjunction with **Ch 1**.
2. PDA 2000, s 3(1) reads: In this Act '"development" means, except where the context otherwise requires, the carrying out of any works on, in, over or under land or the making of any material change in the use of any structure or other land'.

739

person having control of the structure or advertisement requiring the removal of the advertising structure or advertisement within the period specified in the notice.

**[8.05]** If the action required by a notice is not taken within the period specified in a notice under s 209 the planning authority is authorised by this section to enter the land and carry out the steps required by the notice. The expenses of taking this action may be recovered against the person served with the notice.

**[8.06]** PDA 2000, s 191 (as amended by the PD(A)A 2010, s 67) provides for certain restrictions on compensation. Section 191(2) (as amended) provides that:

> Compensation under section 190 shall not be payable in respect of the refusal of permission for any development based on any change of the zoning of any land as a result of the making of a new development plan under section 12 or the preparing, making, amending or revoking of a local area plan under section 18 or 20.

The restriction on payment of compensation for refusal to grant permission for advertising or for the imposition of conditions in such grant is contained in PDA 2000, Sch 3 and that list includes:

> The erection of any advertisement structure.
>
> The use of land for the exhibition of any advertisement.

**[8.07]** Article 6 of Pt 2 of the Planning and Development Regulations 2001 (PDR 2001) deals with categories of exempted development for advertisements. Exempted developments in relation to advertisements are set out in PDR 2001, Pt 2, art 6 classes 1–18, inclusive.[3]

**[8.08]** An examination of art 6 of Pt 2 makes it clear that the word 'advertisement' does not cover all the categories listed in art 6 of Pt 2 of PDR 2001. The categories in art 6 of Pt 2 include what are commonly called 'signs' or 'notices' some of which may not include any promotional activity which would be the hallmark of an advertisement.

**[8.09]** Just because an advertising hoarding has been erected on a site does not mean that the hoarding can be used for all purposes of exhibition. In *Dublin Corporation v Regan Advertising*,[4] Blayney J held that where an advertisement on the façade of a business premises, which had advertised the business being carried on in the premises, was altered to an advertisement for goods and services of another party who had no connection with the business premises, a material change of use had occurred for which planning permission was required. Blayney J expressed the view that:

> ... an enormous number of things can constitute an advertisement. The difference between them can in my opinion be so great that a change from using a site for an advertisement of one kind to using it for an advertisement of a different kind can readily constitute a material change of use.

---

3. See PDR 2001, Pt 2, art 6; **Ch 2** under heading Exempted Developments – Advertisements, paras **[2.385] to [2.422]**.
4. *Dublin Corporation v Regan Advertising* [1989] IR 61, HC, Blayney J.

Blayney J's decision was upheld in the Supreme Court.[5]

**[8.10]** In *Dublin Corporation v Lowe and Signways Holdings Limited*,[6] the Supreme Court treated an advertisement as 'works' and, as such, 'works' is 'development' or it might also be a 'material change in use'.[7] Morris P in the High Court made an order:

> ... directing the Respondents and each or either of them to forthwith discontinue the unauthorised use of the exterior flank wall (Chancery Place) elevation (at first and second floor level of the premises situate at and known as Number 3, Inns Quay, Dublin 7, for advertisement purposes).[8]

The plaintiffs had sought a second order which Morris P refused to grant. The second order sought by the plaintiffs was an order:

> ... directing the Respondents and each or either of them, to forthwith remove the advertisement hoarding (including all fixtures and fittings) erected on the exterior flank wall (Chancery Place elevation) of the premises situate and known as Number 3, Inns Quay, Dublin 7, by the Respondents and each and either of them, without the benefit of planning permission.

**[8.11]** The facts of the case were that David Allen Holdings Ltd had erected an advertising hoarding in the early part of the 1950s on the gable wall of Number 3, Inns Quay, facing into Chancery Place. When the licence expired the hoarding was removed by David Allen Holdings Ltd and the removal took place on 15 December 1995. The respondents, Signway Holdings Ltd, signed a new licence with Mr Lowe and erected a new hoarding on 19 December 1995. Dublin Corporation claimed that the erection of the new notice constituted 'development' and that planning permission should have been obtained.

The LG(PD)A 1963, s 3 defined 'development' as follows:

> The carrying out of any works on, in or under land or the making of any material change in the use of any structures or other land.

And s 2 defined 'works' as follows:

> 'Works' includes any act or operation of construction, excavation, demolition, extension, alterations, repair or renewal and, in relation to an protected structure or proposed protected structure, including any act or operation involving the application or removal of plaster, paint, wallpapers, tiles or other material to or from the surfaces of the interior or exterior of a structure.[9]

---

5. On appeal, *Dublin Corporation v Regan Advertising* [1989] IR 61.
6. *Dublin Corporation v Lowe and Signways Holdings Limited* [2004] 4 IR 259, SC.
7. PDA 2000, s 3(1).
8. The HC reference is *Dublin Corporation v Lowe and Signways Holdings Limited* [2000] IEHC 161, Morris P.
9. The definitions of 'development' and of 'works' as appeared in LG(PD)A 1963 have not been altered by PDA 2000, s 3.

The relevant portion of LG(PD)A 1963, s 2 defined 'unauthorised structure' as a structure other than a structure in existence on the commencement on the appointed day.[10]

**[8.12]** It was not part of the evidence in the case that the hoarding which was erected prior to 1 October 1964 was materially different from the hoarding erected by Signways Holdings Ltd on 19 December 1995. In fact, the new hoarding was exactly the same in its dimensions but not in its content as the hoarding which was removed on 15 December 1995.

**[8.13]** The LG(PD)A 1963, in s 4(1)(g), provided as follows:

> (1) The following shall be exempted development for the purposes of this Act ...
>
> > (g) development consisting of the carrying out of works for the maintenance, improvement or other alteration of any structure, being works which affect only the interior of the structure or which do not materially affect the external appearance of the structure so as to render such appearance inconsistent with the character of the structure or of neighbouring structures.

The respondents accepted that what occurred between 15 and 19 December 1995 was not maintenance or improvement. The respondents argued that what occurred was an 'alteration'. Section 2 of the 1963 Act defined 'alteration' as follows:

> ... includes any plastering or painting which materially alters the external appearance of a structure so as to render such appearance inconsistent with the character of the structure or of neighbouring structures.

Clause 4(1)(g) of the 1963 Act, by referring to 'other alteration', clearly implies that there can be alterations which do not materially affect the external appearance of the structure or render such appearance inconsistent with the character of the structure or of neighbouring structures.

**[8.14]** In dismissing the appeal in the Supreme Court, McCracken J had this to say:

> For reasons I have already stated, I am of the view that the word 'alteration' must apply to something wider than a mere visual alteration. I think the learned trial judge was correct in treating the gable wall with the hoarding affixed to it as a unit or structure within the meaning of the planning legislation, and that removing the hoarding and replacing it with a new hoarding altered the structure. Indeed, it could at least be argued that the removal of the hoarding could itself be an alteration to the gable wall which would not come within the exemption provided by s 4(1)(g), insofar as it might materially affect the external appearance of the structure.
>
> I think it is unreal to look at a hoarding of this nature as a structure in isolation from the rest of the building. I also think it is unreal to suggest, as seems to be implicit in the Appellant's case, that it would be lawful to replace all the

---

10. The appointed day in this context is 1 October 1964.

constituent parts of the hoarding provided the parts were replaced separately, while it is unlawful to replace the entire hoarding at the same time.

The Appellant also submits that in any event the advertisement hoarding did materially affect the external appearance of the premises so as to render its appearance inconsistent with the character of the premises itself or that of neighbouring structures. It is, of course, true that the building itself is an old Georgian building, and no doubt advertising hoardings such as the present one would not have been present or in contemplation of the owners of the original building in Georgian times. However, what this Court is concerned with is the alteration of the hoarding by the substitution of a new hoarding, and that in itself in my view cannot possibly be said to have materially affected the external appearance of the premises.[11]

## ARCHAEOLOGICAL OBJECTS

[8.15] Special controls in relation to archaeological objects have been in place since the commencement of the National Monuments (Amendment) Act 1994. An 'archaeological object' is defined in s 2 of the National Monuments Act 1930, as amended by s 14 of the National Monuments (Amendment) Act 1994, as follows:

> 'Archaeological object' means any chattel whether in a manufactured or partly manufactured or in an unmanufactured state which by reason of the archaeological interest attaching thereto or of its association with any Irish historical event or person has a value substantially greater than its intrinsic value (including artistic), and the said expression includes ancient human, animal or plant remains.[12]

[8.16] Section 26 of the National Monuments Act 1930, as amended by s 21 of the National Monuments (Amendment) Act 1994, provides that it is an offence to dig or to excavate any land[13] for the purpose of searching for archaeological objects in general or for the purpose of examining any particular structure or thing of archaeological interest known or believed to be in or under land[14] other than in accordance with an excavation licence.[15] The penalty for offences under the National Monuments (Amendment) Act 1994 is £1,000 on summary conviction and/or a term of imprisonment not exceeding 12 months or £50,000 on conviction on indictment or a term of imprisonment not exceeding five years or both.

[8.17] The prohibition against excavation for archaeological purposes does not apply to digging or excavation in the course of any agricultural or industrial operation.

---

11. *Dublin Corporation v Lowe and Signways Holdings Limited* [2004] 4 IR 259 *per* McCarthy J.
12. This definition appeared in the National Monuments Act 1930, s 2 as amended by the National Monuments (Amendment) Act 1994, s 14. Interestingly, the National Monuments Act 1930, s 26(3) provided for a fine not exceeding £25 on summary conviction for excavating without a licence, which was presumably a sufficient deterrent at that time.
13. Land includes land both above and below water.
14. See National Monuments Act 1930, s 26.
15. See the National Monuments Act 1930, s 25 as amended by the National Monuments (Amendment) Act 1994, s 26.

**[8.18]** Every archaeological object which is found must be reported within 14 days to a member of An Garda Síochána in the district or to the keeper of Irish Antiquities in the National Museum and the report must state the name and address of the finder, the nature of the object and the time, place and circumstances in which it was found. If authorised digging for agricultural or industrial purposes is undertaken and if such digging reveals an archaeological object the object shall not be removed or otherwise interfered with unless the finder reasonably believes that its removal is necessary for the preservation or for the safe keeping of the object.[16]

**[8.19]** Any excavations undertaken for the purpose of securing the safety of a national monument may be undertaken without an excavation licence.

**[8.20]** All archaeological objects discovered since the commencement of the National Monuments (Amendment) Act 1994 are the property of the State and it is an offence for any person to retain possession of such object other than in accordance with the discovery and reporting procedures outlined in ss 4 and 5 of the National Monuments (Amendment) Act 1994.

**[8.21]** Section 10 of the National Monuments (Amendment) Act 1994 gives the director of the National Museum of Ireland discretion, following consultation with the Minister for Arts, Culture and the Gaeltacht and with the Minister for Finance, to pay the finder, the owner of the land and/or the occupier of the land a reward where the object found is retained by the director on behalf of the State. Section 10(2) aforesaid clearly states that the payment of any reward under s 10(1) does not confer any rights in respect of the archaeological object on the person who has found the object or on the owner or occupier of the land where the object was discovered. Section 10(4) specifically states:

> Nothing in this section shall impose an obligation on the Director to pay a reward unless he is satisfied that it is in the public interest to do so.

Section 10(5) provides that the section will not apply to the finder of any archaeological object which is located while digging or excavating pursuant to a licence issued under s 26 of the National Monuments Act 1930.

**[8.22]** The fact that the payment of a reward is not a 'right' but merely a 'discretion' has been so held by the Supreme Court in *Webb v Ireland*.[17]

**[8.23]** 'An archaeological area' is defined as:

> An area which the Commissioners consider to be of archaeological importance but does not include the area of a historic monument standing entered in the register.[18]

'An archaeological area' may be entered separately into the Register of Historic Monuments maintained by the Minister for the Environment, Heritage and Local

---

16. See the National Monuments Act 1930, s 23 as amended by the National Monuments (Amendment) Act 1994, s 19.
17. *Webb v Ireland* [1988] IR 353.
18. National Monuments (Amendment) Act 1987, s 2.

Government.[19] The Register records places where there are believed to be monuments and all additions, amendments and deletions of entries for archaeological areas in the Register must be notified in writing to the owner and must be published in Iris Oifigiúil. Significantly, neither prior to nor subsequent to the entry of an archaeological area in the Register of Historic Monuments, is a right provided to the owner or occupier of the lands to make representations. The absence of the right to make representation boldly ignores the normal procedural rights under the Irish Constitution and under the European Convention on Human Rights and the omission in this instance may yet be the subject of a constitutional challenge which has a serious chance of succeeding.

[8.24] If an archaeological area is listed in the Register, the owner of the lands affected cannot carry out any works to a monument within the area without giving two months notice to the Minister for the Environment, Heritage and Local Government. If, however, urgent works are required they may be carried out without the Minister's consent.

[8.25] The National Monument Acts fail to provide compensation for owners the use of whose property is curtailed by the provisions of this legislation. The matter was examined in the Supreme Court in *O'Callaghan v Commissioners of Public Works*,[20] where the plaintiff was prohibited from ploughing a portion of his lands containing a pre-historic ring fort. Since the National Monuments Acts contain no provision for compensation it was the plaintiff's case that the prohibition was an unjust infringement of his constitutional rights. O'Higgins J, in rejecting the plaintiff's claim for compensation, had this to say:

> The absence of such a provision for the payment of compensation to him in respect of a limitation of use of which he was substantially on notice before his purchase and which was a requirement of what should be regarded as the common duty of all citizens – to preserve a national monument – can be no ground for suggesting that the prohibition or limitation is an unjust attack on his property rights. In short, by the impugned statute as the occasion requires, the State, through s 8 delimits by law, not the right of private ownership or the general right to transfer etc. but the exercise of those rights – in this instance the user of the land – so that that user will be reconciled with the exigencies of the common good – here, the national aspirations as set out in the preamble and Article 1 of the Constitution.[21]

This decision may not be the definitive judgment on the rights of landowners to compensation for restrictions placed on their property by the National Monuments Acts because there were special features in the facts of the case that may distinguish it from other cases. Mr O'Callaghan was aware of the 'heritage obligation' prior to purchasing the land. The ring fort mound had never been ploughed before and Mr O'Callaghan's situation had not been dis-improved to any greater extent than his predecessors. Mr O'Callaghan could still enjoy the 'existing' beneficial use of his land.

---

19. National Monuments (Amendment) Act 1994, s 12(1).
20. *O'Callaghan v Commissioners of Public Works* [1995] ILRM 364, SC.
21. *O'Callaghan v Commissioners of Public Works* [1995] ILRM 364, SC per O'Higgins J.

## CONTROL OF QUARRIES

[8.26] The operation of quarries has given rise to much litigation, particularly in the area of intensification of use. Undeniably, quarries have been troublesome both in relation to planning issues and also in relation to the impact which the operation of quarries has on the surrounding areas and on the population living in those surrounding areas, including such things as noise, dust, dirt on roadways, potholes, damage to structures caused by explosions, etc. Since the passing of the Local Government (Planning and Development) Act 1963, Ireland has been in a hurry to catch up with its European neighbours in developing its economy. Undoubtedly there have been some 'troughs of disillusionment' but in times of high activity shortcuts were taken in the business of quarrying stone. Efforts have been made to rein in quarry operators and although the legislation offered some hope, enforcement was uneven.

[8.27] Planning legislation in general and PDA 2000 in particular has failed to provide effective regulation and control of quarrying operations and of quarry operators. The provisions of PDA 2000 failed to recognise the unique features of quarrying which require to be controlled. Quarrying operations are frequently spread over long periods of time and they are sometimes stop/go operations which are influenced by market conditions. Abandonment, intensification, material alteration and development interact in a special way in endeavouring to control quarrying operations. There are a significant number of quarries which have been in operation (though not always continuously) since prior to 1 October 1964 and these were regarded as having existing use rights but that did not imply 'unlimited' existing use rights. The Supreme Court in *Kildare County Council v Goode*[22] held that pre-existing use rights (pre-1 October 1964) did not imply that a quarry operator could continue without restriction until the last stone was removed from the quarry. The quarry operation is limited to completing such quarrying operation as would have been reasonably contemplated at the time operations commenced prior to 1 October 1964. Once the quarrying operations went beyond what was reasonably contemplated at their commencement prior to 1964 it was necessary after 1 October 1964 to obtain planning permission. It is, of course, difficult to gauge what was reasonably contemplated at the time operations commenced prior to 1 October 1964. The measure was, in practice, somewhat elastic and many pre-64 quarrying operations stretched so far that the extent of the quarrying simply could not have been contemplated when the pre-64 operations were commenced. In many cases, the extensions were of such a scale as to come into conflict with the EIA Directive[23] which requires that 'development consent' is required where the extension of the surface area of the site is significant.

[8.28] PDA 2000, s 261 was first commenced on 28 April 2004. Section 261 has 13 subsections and the aim of the section is to control quarries. There is compelling

---

22. *Kildare County Council v Goode* [1999] 2 IR 495, SC.
23. Council Directive 85/337/EEC as amended by Directive 97/11/EC.

evidence that s 261 has not succeeded in controlling quarries. Scannell refers to s 261 as:

> '... a very badly drafted s 261 of the Act introduces a new statutory regime for the regulation of:
>
> (a) Quarries granted planning permission under the Local Government (Planning & Development) Act 1963 before April 28, 1999; and
>
> (b) Any other quarry in operation on April 22, 1999 for which no planning permission was granted under the 1963 Act. This includes pre-64 quarries.'[24]

The quarries described at para (a) above are quarries which have an established use by virtue of having been in operation prior to 1 October 1964. Such quarries did not require planning permission under LG(PD)A 1963 provided they continued to operate on a fairly consistent basis since 1 October 1964 where the operation of the quarry was not abandoned or intensified to such an extent that the intensification amounted to a 'development' which required planning permission.

**[8.29]** In *Waterford County Council v John A Woods Ltd*,[25] s 24(f) of LG(PD)A 1963 was examined by Murphy J who said as follows:

> It seems to me to be clear that the purpose of s 24 was to permit (among other things) a developer to continue works which he had commenced before the appointed day without the necessity of seeking a planning permission which might not be forthcoming and the application for which would at the very least involve significant delay.
>
> On the other hand it is, in my view, equally clear that the right to continue works commenced before the appointed day does not give the developer an unrestricted right to engage in activities of the nature commenced before the relevant date. The exclusion from the operation of s 24 could not be invoked so as to confer on the particular development a licence to carry on generally the trade or occupation in which he was engaged. The section merely permits the continuation to completion of the particular works commenced before the appointed day at an identified location.

Quarrying had started at this quarry in 1952 and it was subsequently purchased by John A Woods Limited. The question was whether quarrying operations, which had been commenced before 1 October 1964, could be continued without permission after that date. If, for example, operations at the quarry were to intensify to such an extent that the increased operation amounted to a material change in use, planning permission would be required. The extent to which such works may be continued requires an examination of all the established facts in order to ascertain what was or might reasonably have been anticipated at the relevant date as having been involved in the works then taking place. Also, the 'use' for a quarry would be deemed to be abandoned where the work stops for

---

24. See Scannell, *Environmental and Land Use Law* (Thomson Round Hall, 2006) at 216, para 2.7426.
25. *Waterford County Council v John A Woods Ltd* [1999] 1 IR 556, SC.

a considerable time and where there is no evinced intention to resume the use of the quarry.[26] Murphy J held that in the particular circumstances of the case the works could not be described as a continuation of the original quarrying operations which had been carried out prior to 1 October 1964 and that, consequently, planning permission was required for the new operation undertaken by John A Woods Ltd at the quarry.

**[8.30]** In *Lee v O'Riordan*,[27] a sand and gravel pit operated until 1980 drawing between 30,000 and 60,000 tonnes *per annum*. It was sold in 1992 but no excavation had taken place for 12 years. The price paid for the quarry at the time of sale in 1992 was consistent with the value of a worked out gravel pit. The new operator began to draw limestone at a rate of approximately 650,000 tonnes in the first eight months. Although there was no blasting or stone crushing on site, cracks started to appear in nearby housing. O'Hanlon J held that for all intents and purposes the quarry had been abandoned between 1980 and 1992 and the resumed operation of limestone extraction was a material change in use, evidenced by substantial intensification. A further permission was required.

**[8.31]** In *Stafford and Bates v Roadstone Limited*,[28] the quarry had operated prior to 1 October 1964. It continued to operate thereafter. The extent of the operation changed materially in that the size of the site was greatly increased and the activity on the site was intensified. A very much higher tonnage was being extracted annually by modern means and new machinery. Although Barrington J held that the operation then under consideration amounted to a material change in the use of the lands the learned judge also held that it was not mandatory on the court to issue an injunction solely because unauthorised development had been proven. Barrington J had this to say:

> ... it appears to me that if a private citizen comes forward under s 27 as a watchdog of the public that the Court, in exercising its discretion, is entitled to look not only at the convenience of the parties but at the convenience of the public. Again, it appears to me that the Oireachtas could hardly have intended the High Court would be obliged on the application of a private citizen with no interest in the lands automatically to close down, eg an important factory, because of some technical breach of the planning law irrespective of the inconvenience to workers and the public generally.
>
> In the present case, I am satisfied, on the evidence ... that the development of the quarry at Carrickfoyle is of importance, not only to the defendants but also to the people of Wexford generally. I am also conscious of the interests of the workers employed by the defendants who might lose their jobs in the event of the quarry being closed or the defendants finding it impracticable to continue it in operation. As previously noted those witnesses who complained of the way in which the quarry is presently been operated asked, not that it be closed, but that it be placed subject to conditions.[29]

---

26. See **Ch 2**, paras **[2.26]** to **[2.38]** re abandonment, **Ch 2**, paras **[2.56]** to **[2.73]** on intensification and **Ch 2**, paras **[2.09]** to **[2.20]** on material change in use.
27. *Lee v O'Riordan* (unreported, 10 February 1995) HC, O'Hanlon J.
28. *Stafford and Bates v Roadstone Limited* [1980] ILRM 1, Barrington J.
29. *Stafford and Bates v Roadstone Limited* [1980] ILRM 1 *per* Barrington J.

The learned judge refused to issue an injunction but accepted an undertaking from the respondents to apply to the local authority for planning permission for a change in use and for retention of structures built without planning permission and to make such application as expeditiously as practicable. This was a generous judgment but it is one which may not survive in the light of the ever developing environmental issues which are responsibly accommodated within the provisions of PD(A)A 2010. The 2010 Act has fundamentally altered s 261 of PDA 2000 by the addition to it of s 261(A), which contains some far reaching environmental and administrative provisions all of which are dealt with below.

[8.32] In *McGrath Limestone Works Ltd v Galway County Council*,[30] permission was granted to a mushroom grower for a mushroom growing facility on an area of a limestone quarry which did not exceed 5% of the entire quarry. The mushroom growing operation continued for a period of two years and then closed down. During that two-year period, McGrath Limestone continued to extract limestone from the quarry. Galway County Council claimed that the existing use rights of the quarry as a limestone quarry had been abandoned when permission was granted for mushroom growing. Egan J, taking into consideration the small area of the site actually used for mushroom growing and the short duration of the project, rightly held that the existing quarrying rights had not been abandoned.

[8.33] PDA 2000, s 261(1) imposed an obligation on all owners or operators of quarries to register specified information concerning their quarry, within one year of the coming into operation of the section. Commencement of s 261 occurred on 28 April 2004. The time for providing the specified information to be entered in the planning authority's planning register was 28 April 2005. The obligation imposed by s 261 to provide specified information to the appropriate planning authority by 25 April 2005 applied to all quarries. Effectively, all quarries, other than fully and finally abandoned quarries, had to register s 261 information. The requirement included both quarries which were operating with the benefit of a full planning permission and all quarries which had been operating prior to 1 October 1964. Most of the pre-64 quarries had continued to operate without planning permission, subject to the limitation that pre-64 quarries could only extract from an area which was anticipated or contemplated in the pre-1 October 1964 period, as being an area to be worked to completion. It would not, for example, include additional land purchased subsequent to 1 October 1964. The test in *Waterford County Council v John A Wood Ltd*[31] must be applied and all the established facts must be ascertained in order to establish what was or might reasonably have been anticipated at the relevant date as being involved in the works then taking place. In cases where planning permission exists, the extent of the area of extraction would be determined by the planning permission usually by reference to an area measured in acres in the earlier cases and later in hectares. In all other cases, a planning authority should refuse to register a larger area than that which was contemplated at the time operations began.

---

30. *McGrath Limestone Works Ltd v Galway County Council* [1989] ILRM 602.
31. *Waterford County Council v John A Woods Ltd* [1999] 1 IR 556.

**[8.34]** In spite of the ambivalence created by lax standards of enforcement against quarry owners and operators by planning authorities in dealing with pre-1964 quarrying cases,[32] and in spite of the failure of s 261 to solve quarrying problems by requiring quarry owners and operators to obtain planning permission for quarries or parts of quarries which had no permission, all quarries which are likely to have significant effects on the environment must undertake environmental impact assessment (EIA).[33]

**[8.35]** Under the provisions of PDA 2000, s 261(2) the information to be provided must specify the following:

(a) the area of the quarry, including the extracted area delineated on a map,

(b) the material being extracted and processed (if at all),

(c) the date when quarrying operations commenced on the land (where known),

(d) the hours of the day during which the quarry is in operation,

(e) the traffic generated by the operation of the quarry including the type and frequency of vehicles entering and leaving the quarry,

(f) the levels of noise and dust generated by the operations in the quarry,

(g) any material changes in the particulars referred to in paragraphs (a) to (f) during the period commencing on the commencement of this section and the date on which the information is provided,

(h) whether –

   (i) planning permission under Pt IV of the Act of 1963 was granted in respect of the quarry and if so, the conditions, if any, to which the permission is subject, or

   (ii) the operation of the quarry commenced before 1 October 1964, and

   (iii) such other matters in relation to the operations of the quarry as may be prescribed.

**[8.36]** PDA 2000, s 261(3) provides that a planning authority, which has received information, may seek further information from the quarry owner and/or operator within such period as the planning authority shall specify relating to the operation of the quarry concerned. Any such further information received will also be entered in the planning authority's planning register.

**[8.37]** PDA 2000, s 261(4) provides that within six months from the registration of the quarry, the planning authority would publish a notice of registration in one or more newspapers circulating in the area in which the quarry is situate and the notice would specify:

(i) that the quarry has been registered in accordance with this section,

(ii) where planning permission has been granted in respect of the quarry, that it has been so granted and whether the planning

---

32. The fact that local authorities were, in many cases, important customers of quarry owners and operators, may have contributed to this situation.
33. See below re PDA 2000, s 261(7) at para **8.56**.

authority is considering restating, modifying or adding to conditions attached to the planning permission in accordance with subsection (6)(a)(ii), or

(iii) where planning permission has not been granted in respect of the quarry, that it is not been so granted and whether the planning authority is considering –

  I. imposing conditions on the operation of the quarry in accordance with subsection (6)(a)(i), or

  II. requiring the making of a planning application and the preparation of an environmental impact statement in respect of the quarry in accordance with subsection (7),

(iv) the place or places and times at which the register may be inspected,

(v) that submissions or observations regarding the operation of the quarry may be made to the planning authority within four weeks from the date of publication of the notice,

(c) a notice under this subsection may relate to one or more quarries registered in accordance with this section.

**[8.38]** PDA 2000, s 261(5) provides that where a planning authority intends to impose, restate, modify or add to conditions on the operation of a quarry or where the planning authority requires a planning application to be made and an environmental impact statement (EIS) to be submitted in respect of the quarry, the planning authority shall as soon as possible, after the expiration of the period for making observations or submissions, serve notice of that proposal on the owner or operator of the quarry. The notice must give reasons for the proposal and it must also invite submissions and observations on the proposal by the owner or operator of the quarry to be made within a period specified which period shall not be less than six weeks from the service of the notice.

**[8.39]** PDA 2000, s 261(6) deals with renewed controls by way of conditions and makes a distinction between quarries which were established with a pre-1964 use and quarries in respect of which permission has/had been granted under the LG(PD)A 1963 more than five years before s 261 was commenced on 28 April 2004, namely prior to 28 April 1999. These permissions are commonly referred to as 'old planning permissions'.

**[8.40]** Dealing firstly with the established pre-1964 use, a planning authority could impose conditions on the operation of a quarry. In effect, these planning conditions could be imposed without any planning application but the planning authority must notify the owner or operator of the quarry in writing as soon as may be. If a planning authority is to impose conditions it must have regard to the proper planning and sustainable development of the area, the development plan, and any submissions or observation received.

**[8.41]** Secondly, in relation to a quarry in respect of which planning permission was granted under Pt IV of the LG(PD)A 1963, which issued before 28 April 1999, a planning authority could restate, modify or add to conditions imposed on the operation of a quarry and the owner or operator of the quarry concerned shall as soon as may be thereafter be notified in writing thereof. Again, this action had to be taken by the planning authority not later than two years from the registration of the quarry and again the planning authority must have regard to the proper planning and sustainable development of the area, the development plan and any submissions or observations received from members of the public.

**[8.42]** PDA 2000, s 261(6), as amended by PD(A)A 2010, s 74, allows for the imposition of conditions on the operation of a quarry and it reads:

- (a) Not later than 2 years from the registration of a quarry under this section, a planning authority may, in the interests of proper planning and sustainable development, and having regard to the development plan and submissions and observations (if any) made pursuant to a notice under subsection (4) or (5) –
    - (i) in relation to a quarry which commenced operation before 1 October 1964, impose conditions on the operation of that quarry, or
    - (ii) in relation to a quarry in respect of which planning permission was granted under Part IV of the Act of 1963 restate, modify or add to conditions imposed on the operation of that quarry

    and the owner and operator of the quarry concerned shall as soon as may be thereafter be notified in writing thereof.

- (aa) Notwithstanding any other provisions of this Act, the operation of a quarry in respect of which the owner or operator fails to comply with conditions imposed under paragraph (a)(i) shall be unauthorised development,[34] and

- (b) Where, in relation to a grant of planning permission conditions have been restated, modified or added in accordance with paragraph (a), the planning permission shall be deemed, for the purposes of this Act, to have been granted under section 34, on the date the conditions were restated, modified or added, and any condition so restated, modified or added shall have affect as if imposed under section 34.[35]

- (c) Notwithstanding paragraph (a), where an integrated pollution control licence has been granted in relation to a quarry, a planning authority, or the Board on appeal shall not restate, modify, add to or impose conditions under this subsection relating to –
    - (i) the control (including the prevention, limitation, elimination, abatement or a reduction) of omissions from the quarry or
    - (ii) the control of omissions related to or following the cessation of the operation of the quarry.

**[8.43]** In plain language, PDA 2000, s 261, as amended by PD(A)A 2010, s 74, and PDA 2000, s 261A, as inserted by PD(A)A 2010, s 75, are another attempt to regulate quarries primarily by insuring that conditions imposed on quarry operations under

---

34. PD(A)A 2010, s 74(a)(i).
35. PD(A)A 2010, s 74(a)(ii).

s 261(6) are enforceable. Section 261(6)(aa) makes it completely clear that any quarry owner or operator who fails to comply with the conditions imposed upon the quarry operation will be the owner or operator of an unauthorised development. Note also the provisions of PDA 2000, s 261(6)(b) and (c), set out above.

[8.44] PDA 2000, s 261A, as inserted by PD(A)A 2010, s 75 and which is dealt with in greater detail below, is intended to catch quarries which should have undertaken EIA but did not do so. The failure to carry out screening at any stage is what will put the provisions of s 261A into action, and this is so even where the screening decision establishes that the operations of the quarry were not likely to have any significant effects on the environment and that in consequence no EIA would have been necessary.

[8.45] Each quarry will be thoroughly inspected and examined by the planning authority in whose area the quarry is located and these inspections and examinations must be carried out within nine months from the date of the commencement of s 261A. Any quarries which should have carried out EIA, screening for EIA or an appropriate assessment for the purposes of art 6 of the Habitats Directive, but which did not do so, will be identified by the relevant planning authority. The planning authority's examination will also establish in the case of each quarry within its administrative area whether the quarry operations were authorised in the sense that they either had obtained planning permission or were in operation prior to 1 October 1964 and had continued the operation of the quarry since that time without abandonment. The planning authority's examination and investigation would also establish whether the quarry was a registered quarry in accordance with the provisions of PDA 2000, s 261.

[8.46] If a quarry was carrying out unauthorised operations and if it was not registered under PDA 2000, s 261 the planning authority is bound to issue enforcement proceedings with a view to closing down the quarry.

[8.47] If a quarry has complied with the statutory planning requirements and registration requirements, its continued operation can be secured by making an application for 'substitute consent'. Quarries which commenced operations before 1 October 1964 and which did not abandon those operations, may, provided they are registered, apply for substitute consent.

[8.48] Quarries which commenced operations after 1 October 1964 without planning permission and without PDA 2000, s 261 registration will not even be entitled to apply for substitute consent and without any consent they will either have to close down voluntarily or be forced to close down by the planning authority.

[8.49] Quarries which do not avail of the regularisation process within the nine-month period (provided they can do so) will also have to close down voluntarily or they will be shut down by the relevant planning authority.

[8.50] Another type of quarry operation which will be forced to close its gates is a quarry which commenced its operations either with or without planning permission after 3 July 2008. The significance of that date is that it is the date when the European

Court of Justice (ECJ) gave its judgment in *Commission v Ireland* C–215/06 (the *Derrybrien Windfarm* case).[36] This type of quarry (if any such exists) will receive enforcement notice from its planning authority if it continues its operations. Furthermore, this type of quarry is not entitled to make any application for substitute consent.

**[8.51]** For the quarries that are entitled to apply for substitute consent the application is made to An Bord Pleanála for permission or leave to make an application for substitute consent. To succeed, an applicant must satisfy the board that there are 'exceptional circumstances' which is an exacting task. The matters to which the board shall have to have regard in considering whether or not 'exceptional circumstances' exist are dealt with in detail in **Ch 9**.[37]

**[8.52]** In effect, the amendment contained in the PD(A)A 2010, s 74(a)(i) means that if conditions imposed are not complied with the entire operation of the quarry may be closed down.

**[8.53]** It should be noted that if an integrated pollution control (IPC) licence has been granted in relation to a quarry then neither the planning authority nor the board should impose any conditions or additional conditions relating to the licence as the imposition of such conditions is exclusively a matter for the Environmental Protection Agency (EPA).

**[8.54]** PDR 2001, Sch 5, Pt 1, art 19 provides that quarries and open-cast mining, where the surface area of the site exceeds 25 hectares, require an EIS if development is to occur on that site. Schedule 5, Pt 2, para 2 of PDR 2001, sub-paras 2(b) and (d) provide for a mandatory EIA in circumstances where:

> (b) Extraction of stone, gravel, sand or clay, where the area of extraction would be greater than 5 hectares.
>
> (d) Extraction of stone, gravel, sand or clay by marine dredging (other than maintenance dredging), where the area involved would be greater than 5 hectares or, in the case of fluvial dredging (other than maintenance dredging), where the length of the river involved would be greater than 500 metres.

**[8.55]** Schedule 2, Pt 2, para 13 requires a mandatory EIS where:

> (a) any change or extension of development[38] which would:
>
> > (i) result in the development being a class listed in Pt 1 or paragraphs 1–12 of Pt 2 of this Schedule, and
> >
> > (ii) result in an increase in size greater than –
> >
> > > – 25 per cent, or
> > >
> > > – An amount equal to 50 per cent of the appropriate threshold, whichever is the greater.[39]

---

36. *Commission of European Communities v Ireland* (Case C–215/06) [2008] ECR I–4911.
37. See **Ch 9** generally for further detail.
38. Not being a change or extension referred to in Pt 1.
39. For further information and detail on EIA and EIS see **Ch 10**.

**[8.56]** PDA 2000, s 261(7), as amended by PD(A)A 2010, s 74(b), provides that there is a requirement to carry out an EIA in respect of certain quarries. This subsection applies to quarries which were commenced prior to 1 October 1964 and where the continued operation of such quarry would be likely to have significant effects on the environment. In such cases, the planning authority must, not later than one year after the registration, require, by notice in writing, the owner or occupier to apply for planning permission and to submit an EIS not later than six months from the service of the notice or within such other agreed period. For s 261(7) to have applied, the following conditions would also apply.

PDA 2000, s 261(7)(a) reads:

Where the continued operation of a quarry –

(a) (i) (I) the extracted area of which is greater than 5 hectares, or

(II) that it is situated on a European site or any other area prescribed for the purpose of s 10(2)(c),[40] or land to which an order under s 15, 16 or 17 of the Wildlife Act 1976 applies,

and

(ii) that commenced operation before 1st October 1964, and would be likely to have significant effects on the environment (having regard to any selection criteria prescribed by the Minister under s 176(2)(e), a planning authority shall not impose conditions on operation of a quarry under subsection (6), but shall not later than one year after the date of registration of the quarry, require, by notice in writing, the owner or operator of a quarry to apply for planning permission and to submit an environmental impact statement to the planning authority not later than 6 months from the date of service of the notice or such other period as may be agreed with the planning authority.

PDA 2000, s 261(7)(b) provides that s 172(1),[41] concerning the requirement for an EIS, will not apply to development to which application is made pursuant to a requirement under s 261(7)(a).

**[8.57]** The provisions of PDA 2000, s 261(7) require an application for what is, effectively, retention permission. The development referred to is pre-1964 development continuing after the 1st October 1964. PDA 2000, s 261(7)(c) provides:

(c) a planning authority, or the Board on appeal, shall, in considering an application for planning permission made pursuant to requirement under paragraph (a) have regard to the existing use of the land as a quarry.

---

40. PDA 2000, s 10(2)(c) deals with the objectives of a development plan and, in particular, this subsection refers to the conservation and protection of the environment, including, in particular, the archaeological and natural heritage and the conservation and protection of European Sites and any other sites which may be prescribed for the purpose of this paragraph.
41. PDA 2000, s 172, as amended by PD(A)A 2010, s 54, sets out the circumstances where there is a requirement for an environmental impact assessment.

**[8.58]** P&D (Amendment) Act 2010, s 74(b) has clarified the standards required by the insertion of paras (d), (e) and (f) respectively after PDA 2000, s 261(7)(c), namely:

    (d) Notwithstanding any other provision of this Act, the continued operation of a quarry in respect of which notification under paragraph (a) applies, unless a planning application in respect of the quarry is submitted to the planning authority within the period referred to in that paragraph, shall be unauthorised development.

    (e) Notwithstanding any other provision of this Act, the continued operation of a quarry in respect of which the owner or operator has been refused permission in respect of an application for permission made on foot of a notification under paragraph (a) shall be unauthorised development.

    (f) Notwithstanding any other provision of this Act, the continued operation of a quarry in respect of which the owner or operator fails to comply with conditions attached to a permission granted in respect of an application for permission made on foot of a notification under paragraph (a) shall be unauthorised development.

**[8.59]** PDA 2000, s 261(8), as extended by PD(A)A 2010, s 74(c), provides that if a quarry has obtained permission under LG(PD)A 1963 and the planning authority adds or modifies conditions which conditions are more restrictive than the existing conditions, the owner or operator of the quarry may claim compensation under PDA 2000, s 197, but no claim can be made for compensation in respect of a condition relating to a matter specified in PDA 2000, s 34(4)(a), (b) or (c), or in respect of a condition relating to preventing, limiting or controlling emissions from the quarry, or the reinstatement of land on which the quarry is situated.

**[8.60]** PDA 2000, s 34(4) provides a list of conditions (a)–(q) which may be imposed in a planning permission.[42]

**[8.61]** PDA 2000, s 34(4)(a) deals with conditions regulating the development or use of adjoining or adjacent land under the control of the applicant if the imposition of such conditions appears to the planning authority:

    (i) To be expedient for the purposes of or in connection with the development authorised by the permission, or

    (ii) To be appropriate, where any aspect or feature of the adjoining, abutting or adjacent land constitutes an amenity for the public or a section of the public, for the purposes of conserving that amenity for the public or that section of the public (and the affect of the imposition of conditions for that purpose would not be to burden unduly the person in whose favour the permission operates).[43]

**[8.62]** PDA 2000, s 34(4)(b) deals with conditions requiring the carrying out of works (including the provision of facilities) which the planning authority considers are required for the purpose of development.

---

42. See paras **[3.236]** to **[3.249]**.
43. As substituted by PD(SI)A 2006, s 8(1).

**[8.63]** PDA 2000, s 34(4)(c) deals with conditions the taking of measures to reduce or prevent:

    (i) the emission of noise or vibration from any structure or site comprised in the development authorised by the permission which might give reasonable cause for annoyance either to persons in any premises in the neighbourhood of the development or to persons lawfully using any public place in that neighbourhood, or

    (ii) the intrusion of any noise or vibration which might give reasonable cause for annoyance to any person lawfully occupying any such structure or site.

Where a quarry owner or an operator is compelled to apply for permission and submit an EIS under PDA 2000, s 261(7) and a planning authority, or the board on appeal, refuses permission for development or grants permission subject to conditions on the operation of the quarry, the owner or operator of the quarry shall be entitled to a claim for compensation under PDA 2000, s 197. However, no such claim shall be made in respect of any condition relating to matters specified in PDA 2000, s 34(4)(a), (b) or (c), nor shall any claim for compensation be made in respect of a condition relating to the prevention, limitation or control of emissions from the quarry, or the reinstatement of land on which the quarry is situated.

**[8.64]** The effect of PDA 2000, s 261(8)(b) is to allow compensation, subject to the stated exceptions, where a planning authority either imposes additional conditions or modifies conditions in a way which is more restrictive than the existing conditions or where a planning authority or the board refuses permission or grants permission subject to conditions on the operation of a quarry.

**[8.65]** PD(A)A 2010, s 74(c) provides the following insertion after PDA 2000, s 261(8)(a)&(b), namely:

    (c) Where in relation to a quarry which commenced operation before 1st October 1964 a planning authority imposes conditions under sub-section (6)(a)(i) on the operation of the quarry, the owner of operator of the quarry may claim compensation under section 197 and references in that section to compliance with conditions or the continuance of any use of land consequent upon a notice under section 46 shall be construed as including references to compliance with conditions so added or modified, save that no such claim may be made in respect of any condition relating to a matter specified in paragraph (a), (b) or (c) of section 34(4), or in respect of a condition relating to the prevention, limitation or control of emissions from the quarry, or the reinstatement of land on which the quarry is situated.

The provisions of the PD(A)A 2010, s 74 are forceful in that they require compliance with the provisions of PDA 2000, s 261(6), (7), (8). In the event of non-compliance, the owner or operator runs the risk of having his operation declared to be an unauthorised development.

**[8.66]** PDA 2000, s 261(9)(a) and (b) provide that where a quarry owner or operator has provided information which has been entered on the local authority's planning register in accordance with this section and, subsequently, the planning authority imposes, restates, adds to or modifies the conditions, an appeal to the board lies against those conditions provided it is taken within four weeks from the date of notification of the condition. In making its determination on appeal the board may confirm the decision of the planning authority either with our without modifications or it may annul that decision.

**[8.67]** PDA 2000, s 261(10)(a) and (b) have been substituted by PD(A)A 2010, s 74(d) and the revised s 261(10) now reads:

> (10) Notwithstanding any other provisions of this Act, a quarry to which this section applies in respect of which the owner or operator fails to provide information in relation to the operation of the quarry in accordance with subsection (1) or in accordance with the requirement under subsection (3) shall be unauthorised development.

The section does not, however, deal with how the normal seven-year time limit for the taking of enforcement action is to apply to a quarry which is deemed to be an unauthorised development. The so called 'seven-year rule' runs for a period of seven years from the date when the unauthorised development commenced where no application for planning permission was made or obtained. If a planning permission was granted, the seven-year rule only starts to run from the date when the life of the planning permission expired. If a planning permission does not contain any conditions as to the length of its life it will mean that the life of the permission is five years from the date of notification of grant of permission. On the other hand, if a planning permission contains a condition, because of the scale of the development or for other reasons, to the effect that the life of the permission shall be longer than five years, the seven-year time limit only starts to run on the expiration of that extended and stated period. Thus, if a development is held to be unauthorised under s 261(10) does this mean that there could be no enforcement if, as would normally be the case, the seven-year rule applied? Although there is no decided case on the point it is clear that the provisions of PDA 2000, s 261(10) would be utterly pointless if the penalty for failing to comply could not be imposed because of the seven-year rule. One possibility is that a court could make a ruling that the seven-year rule would only start to run as and from the date that the planning authority deemed the development to be an unauthorised development.

**[8.68]** In discussing the seven-year time limit in the context of a development which requires EIA, Simons has this to say:

> It is arguable that a planning authority is required to disapply the national law time-limit in circumstances where the extension of the quarry is likely to have a significant effect on the environment. As flagged earlier, a planning authority as an emanation of the State, is required to give effect to the EIA Directive. If the only thing preventing proper implementation of the Directive is a conflicting provision of national law, then there is a strong argument to be made that the national law must be dis-applied.[44]

---

44. See Simons, *Planning and Development Law* (2nd edn, Thomson Round Hall, 2007) at p 387, para 8.175.

**[8.69]** PDA 2000, s 261(11) states that PDA 2000, s 261 applies to:

    (a) a quarry in respect of which planning permission under Pt IV of the Act of 1963 was granted more than five years before the coming into operation of this section, and

    (b) any other quarry in operation on or after the coming into operation of this section, being a quarry in respect of which planning permission was not granted under that Part.

In effect, this means that PDA 2000, s 261 (as amended by PD(A)A 2010) shall apply to a quarry which has obtained a planning permission under LG(PD)A 1963 more than five years from 28 April 2004 (the commencement date of s 261) or to any other quarry in operation on or after 28 April 2004 carrying out quarrying operations without planning permission.

**[8.70]** PDA 2000, s 261(12) permits the Minister to issue guidelines to planning authorities regarding the performance of their functions under PDA 2000, s 261 and a planning authority shall have regard to such guidelines. Ministerial guidelines entitled *Guidelines for Planning Authorities on Quarries and Ancillary Activities* have issued. It is a useful document dealing with the purpose of the registration system and, as it states, it is there 'to give a snapshot of the current use of land for quarrying'.[45]

**[8.71]** PDA 2000, s 261(13) is an interpretation section containing the following definitions:

    'emission' means –

        (a) an emission into the atmosphere of a pollutant within the meaning of the Air Pollution Act 1987,

        (b) a discharge of polluting matter, sewage, effluent or trade effluent within the meaning of the Local Government (Water Pollution) Act, 1977, to waters or sewers within the meaning of that Act,

        (c) a disposal of waste, or

        (d) noise;

The definitions of 'operator' and of 'quarry', which appeared in PDA 2000, s 261(10), have been deleted by PD(A)A 2010, s 74(e).

**[8.72]** The Mines and Quarries Act 1965, s 3(2) defines 'quarry' as:

    An excavation or system of excavations made for the purpose of, or in connection with, the getting of minerals (whether in their natural state or in solution or suspension) or products of minerals, being neither a mine or merely a well or bore-hole or a well and/or hole combined.

**[8.73]** The clear intent of PDA 2000, s 261 was to introduce a level of control to be exercised over quarrying operations. The section required quarry operators to register

---

45. Note: the *Guidelines for Planning Authorities on Quarries and Ancillary Activities* issued prior to the commencement of PD(A)A 2010.

those quarries with the relevant planning authority and after some considerable delay registration was finally achieved. After registration, the continued operation of quarries could be controlled by conditions imposed by the planning authority and, where it is relevant, the planning authorities could require EIA of quarries in the context of an application for planning permission. One of the main controls of s 261 is to ensure compliance with the requirements of the EIA Directive. Section 261 provided clear time limits within which a planning authority was required to give notice of its intention to impose conditions on the continued operation of a quarry or indeed to require a new application for planning permission, accompanied where relevant by an EIS. Those time limits were not met by a considerable number of planning authorities. PDA 2000, s 261 aspired to provide planning control in respect of the operations of established quarries, with a view to ensuring proper planning and sustainable development within the quarry operations but a second and certainly more important purpose of s 261 was to ensure that the requirements of the EIA Directive were complied with. The importance of compliance with the EIA Directive cannot be understated and Ireland, as are all other EU countries, is bound to amend or discard any national legislation which prevents EU law from being purposefully implemented. In practice, the introduction of PDA 2000, s 261 and the delayed but finally completed introduction of the registration procedures clearly did not cure the s 261 deficiencies in relation to control of quarries in the interest of proper planning and sustainable development and, most particularly, in relation to ensuring compliance with the EIA Directive.

[8.74] In contrast to most development, quarry development is continuous over a number of years or even decades. Development of, for example, an office block, a housing estate or a factory has a beginning and an end which is generally ascertainable at the time the application for permission is made. The normal planning permission has a lifespan of five years. Quarrying has a beginning but the end is usually difficult to determine being dependent, as it is, on varying market conditions and a not very precise determination of how much material can be excavated or extracted over any particular period. There are many examples of quarries which have operated for periods of between 50 and 100 years or more which continue to operate today. If operations commenced prior to 1 October 1964 and have more or less continued since that time, the quarry was deemed to have an existing use right for which no permission is required provided the operator is still in the course of completing quarrying operations which could have been contemplated in October 1964. It is a difficult assessment to measure as to what was or was not 'contemplated' in 1964. It is an assessment which may have some divergent and some predictable opinions depending on which party is interpreting the principle. One way or another, the inevitable result is that if any quarrying operation has fallen foul of the EIA Directive it will have a condition imposed on it to make it comply with the Directive. PDA 2000, s 261 made provision for the registration of quarries and registration was finally achieved, albeit some nine years later.

[8.75] The registration of quarries under PDA 2000, s 261, in permitting the planning authorities to impose conditions on the continued operation of the quarries, inevitably meant that the planning authorities, in following and recording quarrying operations, were playing 'catch-up' with quarry owners and operators. The licensing system did not permit the planning authority, where circumstances allowed for it, to require EIA of the quarrying operations in the context of a planning application.

[8.76] The need for further reform of s 261 was highlighted in a number of High Court decisions.

[8.77] *Pearce v Westmeath County Council*[46] was unusual in that it was a local resident who wished to have the planning authority's decision to require registration of a quarry judicially reviewed. The plaintiff also sought judicial review of the planning authority's decision to impose a condition requiring the quarry operator to apply for planning permission with an accompanying EIS. Hanna J agreed that the planning authority's requirement to have the quarry registered with the express condition was judicially reviewable but that, in the event, the planning authority had sufficient information before it to enable it, within the principles applied in the *O'Keefe v An Bord Pleanála*[47] decision, to require registration subject to conditions. The learned judge dismissed the application for judicial review.

[8.78] PDA 2000, s 261 provided a two-year time limit for giving notice of intention to impose conditions on the continuing operation of a quarry. It provided a one-year time limit to require a quarry owner/operator to make application for planning permission, accompanied by an EIS. In many cases, the planning authority failed to give notice and time limits passed by with no action being taken by the planning authority. The question arose as to whether the time limits were mandatory, in the sense that failure to take action within the prescribed time limits rendered such action invalid. The matter was considered in *Browne v Kerry County Council*[48] by Hedigan J who held that the time limits were mandatory and not discretionary. In the learned judge's opinion, failure to comply within the time limits specified was fatal because the legislation offered no alternatives. There was no power in the Act to extend time and the Act was silent as to what should happen if the time limits were exceeded. Hedigan J also made reference, in the course of his judgment, to the constitutional right of applicants under Art 43 to quiet enjoyment of their property.

[8.79] Hedigan J's decision in the *Browne* case is well reasoned but the finding that time limits are mandatory would appear to go against the general thrust in planning legislation where time limits are rigorously enforced against the citizen but less rigorously enforced against officialdom, to include the Minister and the planning authorities. On occasions, there may be good reason as to why the time limit playing field is tilted against the citizen. An examination of the purpose of PDA 2000, s 261 indicates that the section was introduced in an attempt to control the operations of established quarries. Control of quarries was required in the public interest and it was also required in the interest of promoting proper planning and sustainable development. Section 261 attempted to compel applicants to comply with the provisions of the EIA

---

46. *Pearce v Westmeath County Council* (unreported, 19 December 2008) HC, Hanna J.
47. *O'Keefe v An Bord Pleanála* [1993] 1 IR 39, SC.
48. *Browne v Kerry County Council* [2009] IEHC 552, Hedigan J.

Directive. Unfortunately, however, PDA 2000, s 261 was not effective in achieving its aims.

**[8.80]** It is undeniable that control of quarries is very much in the public interest and it is also in the public interest that comprehensive EIA is undertaken in appropriate cases. Indeed, most quarry cases are 'appropriate'.

**[8.81]** In *Browne v Kerry County Council*,[49] Hedigan J also considered the effect of PDA 2000, s 251. PDA 2000, s 251 (as amended) provides that any time limit referred to in the Act shall disregard the period between 24 December and 1 January (both days inclusive). Section 251(2) of PDA 2000 provided that the exclusion of such time does not apply in the context of Pt II of PDA 2000, which concerns development plans, local area plans and regional planning guidelines.[50] It was argued by counsel for the applicant that the exclusion of days in calculating a one or two-year time limit was absurd. Hedigan J considered whether nine days should be added in respect of each year giving rise to a total extension of one year and eighteen days. The learned judge held that the provisions of s 251 are plain and unambiguous and he did not accept the applicant's argument that the extension provisions could only be logically applied to time limits of less than one year.

**[8.82]** Hedigan J considered that:

> The provision is undoubtedly capable of effecting a quite serious extension of mauling the time limits, such extension will no doubt be of significance in many cases such as the present one. The effect could be described as curious, and its merit might well be open to debate but it cannot in my view be construed as 'absurd' within the meaning of the 2000 Act.[51]

The High Court also considered the extent of the conditions which may be imposed under the provisions of PDA 2000, s 261(6) in *MF Quirke and Ors v An Bord Pleanála*,[52] where it was argued on behalf of the quarry operator that the power to impose additional conditions under PDA 2000, s 261(6) was limited to the imposition of conditions which applied to the continuing operation of the quarry. It was argued that any quarry which had operated prior to October 1964 had established use rights which would preclude conditions being imposed under s 261(6) and would preclude any necessity to make application for fresh planning permission subject to EIA as required by s 261(7). The plaintiffs made the case that the section did not permit a condition which would, effectively, shut down the quarrying operations either by limiting the area of quarrying operations, whether vertically or horizontally, or require the operation within the quarry to cease until planning permission had been obtained.

**[8.83]** PDA 2000, s 261(6) allows a planning authority to impose conditions on the operation of a quarry which would have operated prior to 1 October 1964. It also

---

49. *Browne v Kerry County Council* [2009] IEHC 552.
50. PDA 2000, s 251 has been amended by PD(A)A 2010 s 72 by the deletion of sub-s (2).
51. *Browne v Kerry County Council* [2009] IEHC 552 per Hedigan J.
52. *MF Quirke and Ors v An Bord Pleanála* [2009] IEHC 429, O'Neill J.

permits a planning authority to restate, modify or add to conditions imposed in a planning permission under the LG(PD)A 1963.

**[8.84]** PDA 2000, s 261(7) provides a requirement to carry out EIA mainly in circumstances where the continued operation of a quarry would be likely to have significant effects on the environment. Section 261(7) only applied to pre-1964 quarries.

**[8.85]** In *MF Quirke and Ors v An Bord Pleanála*,[53] counsel on behalf of the quarry owners/operators further argued that in the absence of provisions for compensation and because existing use rights had been thoroughly established in respect of the operation of quarries which had been working continuously since before 1 October 1964, s 261(6) could not be used to require closure of the quarry operation and s 261(7) could not be used to require an EIS.

**[8.86]** O'Neill J disagreed with the quarry operators and held that the provisions of s 261 were 'a fresh regulatory scheme' which could be imposed on quarry operations in the public interest and in the interests of proper planning and sustainable development. Merely because a quarry was operated in a certain manner for sometime before 1 October 1964 did not mean that it should continue to operate in the same way for all time. O'Neill J stated:

> It could never be said that there was an unrestricted right to use property for any activity, including quarrying, regardless of the effects that activity had on the enjoyment of other persons of their lives, health and properties. Many activities are regulated and restricted in a variety of statutory codes in the interest of the common good. I see no difference in principle or in substance between these statutory regulatory regimes and the type of regulation provided for in section 261(6). In all cases the activity restricted by Statute should have been unregulated or unrestricted before the enactment of that type of legislation.[54]

O'Neill J continued:

> In the absence of a description of the types of conditions to be imposed in section 261(6) and in the light of the wide criteria under which conditions may be imposed (ie 'in the interest of proper planning and sustainable development') I am satisfied that the conditions that can be imposed on the operations of quarries can encompass the wide spectrum of the various normal planning concerns as these are or are likely to be affected by the works carried on at a given quarry in its particular location. To suggest that a condition which required the obtaining of planning permission at some stage in the future was per se ultra vires s 261(6) is, in my judgment, to impermissibly restrict the scope of s 261(6), in effect, adding to the language of the subsection words of restriction which are clearly not there, and, therefore, not intended to be there by the Oireachtas. In my view, whether one adopts a literal approach or a purposive approach to the interpretation of s 261(6), the result will be the same.[55]

---

53. *MF Quirke and Ors v An Bord Pleanála* [2009] IEHC 429.
54. *MF Quirke and Ors v An Bord Pleanála* [2009] IEHC 429 *per* O'Neill J.
55. *MF Quirke and Ors v An Bord Pleanála* [2009] IEHC 429 *per* O'Neill J.

[8.87] Garrett Simons SC, in the context of O'Neill J's judgment in *MF Quirke & Others v An Bord Pleanála*,[56] lists the type of conditions which would be allowed under PDA 2000, s 261(6) as follows:

> It follows from the judgment that conditions of the following type are allowed under s 261(6).
>
> - Conditions regulating blasting activities;
> - Conditions restricting the area, whether horizontal or vertical, within which quarrying activities can be carried out; and
> - Conditions requiring that quarrying activities cease within a specified period unless planning permission has been obtained in the interim.[57]

The following additional conditions (and the list is not intended to be conclusive) might be appropriately included in a list of conditions permitted under s 261(6):

- Conditions regulating the times during which the quarry can operate – (eg, 08.00 hrs to 18.00 hrs Monday – Friday and 08.00 hrs to 13.00 hrs Saturday);
- Conditions dealing with control of dust and the provision of a wheel wash for all vehicles entering or leaving the site;
- Conditions dealing with safe traffic circulation within the site, etc.

In *MF Quirke & Sons v Maher*,[58] the High Court held that any planning permission granted must take account of the contents of an EIS lodged with the planning application. In *MF Quirke & Sons v Maher*,[59] the decision to grant planning permission made reference to the 'plans and particulars' lodged with the application and Herbert J held that the 'plans and particulars' most certainly include the EIS.

[8.88] A third attempt (and it looks as if this one will succeed) to control quarries has been introduced by s 75 of the PD(A)A 2010 and the marginal note for this section which provides the s 261A insertion, to follow s 261, reads: Further matters in relation to control of quarries.

[8.89] The amendment by the additional of s 261A to s 261, as inserted by s 75 of the PD(A)A 2010, has all the appearance of a piece of legislation which will finally control quarry operations both in planning and in environmental terms with a view to ensuring proper planning and sustainable development in quarry operations in the future. Section 261A has 15 subsections and the new section uses 11 pages of PD(A)A 2010. It is to be expected that the new section will provide a sound basis for the future planning and environmental control of quarrying operations.[60]

---

56. *MF Quirke & Sons v Maher* [2008] IEHC 428.
57. See Garrett Simons at Round Hall Planning & Environmental Law Conference 2010 speaking on the Planning & Development (Amendment) Bill 2009 at p 20 of his paper.
58. *MF Quirke & Sons v Maher* [2008] IEHC 428, Herbert J.
59. *MF Quirke & Sons v Maher* [2008] IEHC 428.
60. PDA 2000, s 261(A) as inserted by PD(A)A 2010, s 75 which section is dealt with fully below at **paras 8.96 to 8.120.**

## Additional Planning Controls on Land and on Buildings [8.93]

[8.90] The prime purpose of PDA 2000, s 261A is to bring in all quarries which should have been subject to EIA but which avoided that assessment. A failure on the part of a quarry owner/operator to carry out a screening exercise is sufficient to allow a planning authority to insist on immediate EIA and this applies also to sub-threshold quarrying operations which will have to carry out EIA even if screening would have established or, indeed, will establish that the development was not likely to have significant effects on the environment. The screening will apply in respect of any development which was carried out after 1 February 1990 in the case of an assessment under the EIA Directive and the screening will apply to any development which was carried out after 26 February 1997 in the case of an assessment under the Habitats Directive.

[8.91] PDA 2000, s 261A(1)[61] provides that each planning authority must publish a notice in one or more newspapers circulating in the area within four weeks of the commencement of the PD(A)A 2010.[62] The published notice must also be displayed on the authority's website.

[8.92] The newspaper notice and the notice displayed on the authority's website advised the public (to include quarry owners and operators) that the planning authority will examine every quarry in its area to determine, having regard to the EIA Directive, and having regard to the Habitats Directive, whether or not one or more of the following was required but not carried out:

(i) an environmental impact assessment;

(ii) a determination as to whether an environmental impact assessment is required;

(iii) an appropriate assessment.[63]

[8.93] Section 261A(1)(b), as inserted by PD(A)A 2010, s 75, provides that:

(b) Where the planning authority determines in relation to a quarry that an environmental impact assessment, a determination as to whether environmental impact assessment was required, or an appropriate assessment, was required but was not carried out and the planning authority also decides that –

(i) the quarry commenced operation prior to 1st October 1964, or permission was granted in respect of the quarry under Part III of the Planning & Development Act 2000 or Part IV of the Local Government (Planning & Development) Act 1963,

and

---

61. As inserted by PD(A)A 2010, s 75.
62. See SI 504/2010, SI 451/2010, SI 477/2010 and SI 132/2011, all of which relate to commencement dates of PD(A)A 2010.
63. See PD(A)A 2010, s 75 which inserts a new s 261A after PDA 2000, s 261. The terms 'appropriate assessment' and 'substitute consent' are deal with in detail in **Ch 9**.

(ii) if applicable, the requirements in relation to registration under section 261 of the Planning and Development Act were fulfilled,

the planning authority will issue a notice to owner or operator requiring him or her to submit an application to the Board for substitute consent, such application to be accompanied by a remedial environmental impact statement or a remedial Natura impact statement or both of those statements, as appropriate.

If a planning authority decides in relation to any particular quarry that no EIA of any kind has been carried out or that there was no determination as to whether EIA was required, or that an appropriate assessment was required but was not carried out and the planning authority decides that the quarry commenced operation on or after 1 October 1964 without planning permission and/or without finalising registration under the provisions of PDA 2000, s 261, the planning authority will issue a notice to the owner or operator of the quarry stating its intention to issue an enforcement notice under s 154 requiring all operations at the quarry to cease and requiring the taking of such steps as the planning authority considers appropriate.[64] If the planning authority determines that the operation of any particular quarry required EIA or a determination as to whether an EIA was required or other appropriate assessment was required but same was not carried out, then, if the planning authority is satisfied that development occurred after 3 July 2008, which should have had EIA, the planning authority will issue a s 154 notice advising that enforcement proceedings will be taken requiring all operations in the quarry to cease and requiring the taking of such other steps as the planning authority considers appropriate.[65] The quarry operator or owner or other relevant person may, within six weeks after the date of publication of the planning authority's notice advising of its intention to issue enforcement proceedings, lodge any submissions or observations in writing to the planning authority. No fee is payable for the lodgement of submissions or observations and those submissions or observations are to be considered by the planning authority.[66]

[8.94] A copy of the notice served by the planning authority on the quarry owner or operator directing him or her to apply to An Bord Pleanála for a substitute consent and informing him or her that s 154 enforcement proceedings will issue, shall be given to any person making submissions or observations within the six-week time limit.[67]

[8.95] An owner or operator of a quarry served with a notice threatening enforcement proceedings and any person to whom copy of a notice is given may apply to the board for a review of a determination or of a decision or of both, being a determination or decision of the planning authority referred to in the notice, and no fee shall be paid in relation to the application for the review sought.[68]

---

64. See PD(A)A 2010, s 261A(1)(c).
65. See PD(A)A 2010, s 261A(1)(d).
66. PD(A)A 2010, s 261A(1)(e).
67. PD(A)A 2010, s 261A(1)(f).
68. PD(A)A 2010, s 261A(1)(g).

**[8.96]** Each planning authority is given a period of nine months after the coming into operation of s 261A to examine every quarry within its administrative area for the purpose of making a determination as to whether:

> (i) development was carried out after 1st February 1990 which is not authorised by permission granted under Part IV of the Act of 1963, prior to the 1st February 1990, which development would have required, having regard to the Environmental Impact Assessment Directive, an environmental impact assessment or a determination as to whether an environmental impact assessment was required, but that such an assessment or determination was not carried out, or
>
> (ii) development was carried out after the 26th February 1997, which was not authorised by a permission granted under Part IV of the Act of 1963 prior to the 26th February 1997, which development would have required, having regard to the Habitats Directive, as appropriate assessment, but that such an assessment was not carried out.[69]

Matters to which the planning authority shall have regard in making its determination under this subsection shall include (i) any submissions or observations received by the authority not later than six weeks from the date of publication of the notice, (ii) any information submitted to the authority in relation to registration of the quarry under PDA 2000, s 261 (if any), (iii) any relevant information on the planning register, (iv) any relevant information obtained by the planning authority in any enforcement action in relation to the quarry and any other relevant information.[70]

**[8.97]** PDA 2000, s 261A(3), (4) and (5)[71] deal with the circumstances which arise when the planning authority makes a determination under PDA 2000, s 261A(2)(a).

**[8.98]** PDA 2000, s 261A(3)(a)[72] provides that where the planning authority makes the determination under s 261A(2)(a), sub-para (i) or (ii) or both, if applicable, apply in relation to the quarry (called in this section 'a determination under sub-s (2)(a)'), and also decides (i) that either the quarry commenced operations before 1st October 1964 or permission was granted in respect of the quarry under Part III of this Act or Part IV of the Act of 1963, and (ii) if applicable, that the registration requirements were fulfilled pursuant to PDA 2000, s 261, the planning authority shall issue a notice in writing to the quarry owner/operator not later than nine months from the coming into operation of this section.

**[8.99]** Section 261A(3):

> (b) In making a decision under paragraph (a), a planning authority shall consider all relevant information available to it including any submissions or observations received by the authority not later than six weeks after the date of publication of the notice under subsection (1)(a).

---

69. PDA 2000, s 261A(2)(a).
70. PDA 2000, s 261A(2)(b)(i) to (v) inclusive as amended by PD(A)A 2010, s 75.
71. As amended by PD(A)A 2010, s 75.
72. PD(A)A 2010, s 261A(1)(g).

**[8.100]** PDA 2000, s 261A(3)(c) provides that the written notice served under s 261A(3)(a) shall inform the person to whom it is issued of the following matters:

    (i) the determination under subsection (2)(a) and the reasons therefor;

    (ii) the decision of the planning authority under paragraph (a) and the reasons therefor;

    (iii) that the person is directed to apply to the Board for substitute consent in respect of the quarry under section 177E, not later than twelve weeks after the date of the notice, or such further period as the Board may allow;

    (iv) that the person may apply to the Board not later than 21 days after the date of the notice, for a review of the determination of the planning authority under subsection (2)(a) or the decision of the planning authority under paragraph (a) and that no fee in relation to either application for a review shall be payable.[73]

Any notice in writing by the planning authority given to the owner/operator of a quarry shall also be given to any person who has made submissions or observations to the authority in relation to the quarry within six weeks of the date of publication of the notice. Persons who have made submissions or observations to the planning authority in relation to the quarry and who have been given a copy of the notice must be informed that they have 21 days from the date of the notice to apply to the board for a review of the determination under s 261A(2)(a) or a determination of the decision of the authority under para (a) and that no fee in relation to either application for review is payable.[74]

    (iii) forward a copy of the notice to the Board.[75]

**[8.101]** Section 261A(4)(a)[76] applies where a planning authority makes a determination under s 261A(2)(a) and the authority also decides that:

    (i) the quarry commenced operation *on or after* 1 October 1964 and no permission was granted in respect of the quarry either under Part III of PDA 2000 or under Part IV of LG(PD)A 1963; or

    (ii) if applicable, the requirements in relation to registration under s 261 were not fulfilled,

the planning authority will also in these circumstances issue a notice within nine months from the date of the commencement of PD(A)A 2010.

**[8.102]** Section 261A(4)(b), (c)(i), (ii) and (iv) are precisely the same as paras (3)(b), (c)(i), (ii) and (iv). Note that sub-s (iii) differs in that the reference is to n enforcement notice under s 154. PDA 2000, s 261A(4)(c)(iii), as amended, reads as follows:

    (iii) that the planning authority intends to issue an enforcement notice in relation to the quarry under section 154 requiring the cessation of the

---

73. PDA 2000, s 261A(3)(c)(i) to (iv) as inserted by PD(A)A 2010, s 75.
74. PDA 2000, s 261A(3)(d)(i) to (iii) as inserted by PD(A)A 2010, s 75.
75. PDA 2000, s 261A(3)(d)(iii) as inserted by PD(A)A 2010, s 75.
76. PDA 2000, s 261A(4)(a) to (d) as inserted by PD(A)A 2010, s 75.

operation of the quarry and the taking of such steps as the authority consider appropriate;

**[8.103]** Paragraph 4(d)(i) and (ii) is precisely the same as para 3(d)(i) and (ii) but para 4(d) does not require that a copy of the notice is sent to the board.

**[8.104]** PDA 2000, s 261A(5)(a)[77] provides that, notwithstanding anything contained in sub-s (3) or sub-s (4), where a sub-s (2)(a) determination is made by the planning authority and the planning authority further determines that the development the subject of a sub-s (2)(a) determination took place after 3 July 2008, the authority shall also decide whether:

(i) the quarry commenced operation before October 1964 or that permission was granted under the provisions of either PDA 2000 or LG(PD)A 1963; and

(ii) if applicable, the requirements in relation to registration under s 261 were fulfilled,

the planning authority shall issue a notice in writing to the quarry owner/operator not later than nine months from the commencement date of the 2010 Act.

**[8.105]** Section 261A(5)(b) is identical to sub-s (3)(b) and sub-s (4)(b). Section 261A(5)(c) provides as follows:

A notice referred to in paragraph (a) shall be in writing and shall inform the person to whom it is issued on the following matters:

(i) the determination of the planning authority under subsection (2)(a) and the reasons therefor;

(ii) the determination of the planning authority under paragraph (a) that the development the subject of the determination under subsection (2)(a) took place after 3 July 2008 and the reasons therefor;

(iii) the decision of the planning authority under paragraph (a) and the reasons therefore;

(iv) that the planning authority intends to issue an enforcement notice in relation to the quarry under section 154 requiring the cessation of the operation of the quarry and the taking of such steps as the authority considers appropriate;

(v) that a person may apply to the Board, not later than twenty-one days after the date of the notice, for a review of the determination of the planning authority under subsection (2)(a), the determination of the planning authority under paragraph (a), or the decision of the planning authority under paragraph (a), and that no fee in relation to any application for a review shall be payable.

---

77. PDA 2000, s 261A(5)(a) to (d) as inserted by PD(A)A 2010, s 75.

**[8.106]** Section 261A(5)(d) provides as follows:

> (d) At the same time that the planning authority issues the notice to an owner or operator of a quarry, the authority shall –
>
> > (i) give a copy of the notice to any person who made submissions or observations to the authority in relation to the quarry not later than 6 weeks after the date of the publication of the notice under subsection (1)(a), and
> >
> > (ii) inform that person that he or she must, not later than twenty-one days after the date of the notice, apply to the Board for a review of the determination under subsection 2(a), the determination of the planning authority under paragraph (a) that the development the subject of the determination under subsection (2)(a) took place after 3 July 2008 or the decision of the planning authority under paragraph (a), and that no fee in relation to any application for a review shall be payable,

requiring the person served to apply in writing to the board for a substitute consent in respect of the quarry under PDA 2000, Pt XA, as inserted by PD(A)A 2010, which deals with substitute consent.[78] The person served must make an application for substitute consent not later than 12 weeks from the date of the notice or such further period as the board may allow. If the application for substitute consent is complex and more time for its preparation is required, an appropriate application may be made to the board for an extension. The section is silent in relation to the manner in which the board will decide whether or not to grant an extension and in the absence of any direction both the applicant in making an application for an extension and the board in making a decision on the application must act reasonably.

**[8.107]** Another option is available to the quarry owner/operator which is an inevitable result of the detailed steps to be taken by the planning authority as set out in the section. The quarry owner/operator may also apply to the board within 21 days of the date of the notice for a review of the determination of the planning authority under s 261A(2)(a) or a review of the decision of the planning authority under s 261A(1). No fee is payable in respect of either application.

**[8.108]** If the quarry owner/operator is of the opinion that the planning authority has not followed the steps provided by statute an application for judicial review is another option, albeit a potentially expensive option. The statutory provisions carefully lay out the procedure in a step by step way. It is likely that all actions taken by a planning authority will be carefully scrutinised to ensure that they do not offer the quarry owner/operator an opportunity to apply for judicial review.

**[8.109]** Apart from issuing the notice to the quarry owner/operator, the planning authority must give a copy of the notice to any person who has made submissions and

---

78. Pt XA has been added to PDA 2000. Pt XA deals with environmental impact assessment (see **Ch 10**). Pt XA and Pt XAB deal respectively with 'substitute consent' and with 'appropriate assessment' (See **Ch 9**).

observations to the planning authority in relation to the quarry within six weeks from the date of the publication of the notice. A person so served must be informed by the planning authority that he or she has 21 days from the date of the notice to apply to the board for a review of the determination under s 261A(2)(a) or for review of the decision of the planning authority under para (a). The planning authority must inform any person who has made submissions or observations that no fee is payable in respect of either application for review.

[8.110] Bearing in mind the determination which a planning authority must make within nine months of the commencement date of the PD(A)A 2010 under s 261A(2)(a) referred to in the Act 'as a sub-s (2)(a) determination', it is important to examine and identify the persons who are entitled to review a notice under s 261A(3)(a), (4)(a) and (5)(a), and under s 261A(3)(d), (4)(d) and 5(d). The subsection is poorly drafted and potentially confusing and the division between after 1 February 1990 and prior to 1 February 1990 in s 261A(2)(a)(ii) is not completely clear.

[8.111] PDA 2000, s 261A(6)(a)[79] provides that any person issued with a notice under this section or anyone who has been handed a copy of such notice has 21 days from the date of the notice to apply to An Bord Pleanála for one or more of the following:

(i) the determination under subsection (2)(a);

(ii) the decision of the planning authority under subsection 3(a);

(iii) a decision of the planning authority under subsection (4)(a);

(iv) a determination of the planning authority under subsection (5)(a) that the development the subject of the determination under subsection (2)(a) took place after the 3rd July 2008;

(v) a decision of the planning authority under subsection (5)(a).

[8.112] Section 261A(6)(b) to (h) inclusive deal with consequential matters resulting from the provisions of sub-s (6)(a). These subsequent paragraphs are summarised as follows:

(b) where a review is sought under para (a), submissions and observations may be made to the board by any person within 21 days of the issuing of the notice;

(c) where a review is sought under para (a), the board notifies the planning authority and requests the planning authority to furnish such information as the board specifies, the information to be furnished by the planning authority within the time limit specified by the board in its request;

(d) in making its decision, the board shall consider any documents or evidence submitted to the applicant for review, any submission or observation received under sub-s (6)(b) and any information furnished by the planning authority under sub-s (6)(c);

---

79. As inserted by PD(A)A 2010, s 75.

(e) the board's decision shall be made 'as soon as may be'[80] to confirm or set aside the determination or decision of the planning authority to which the application for review refers;

(f) 'as soon as may be' after the board has made its decision it shall be notified to the persons who sought the review and to the planning authority concerned. Once the decision is ratified, the review shall be deemed to be disposed of by the board;

(g) an application for review by the board under para (a) has the effect of suspending any direction contained in a notice issued under sub-s (3)(a) until that review has been disposed of;

(h) if the board sets aside the determination made under sub-s (2)(a), any direction to apply for substitute consent contained in the notice issued under sub-s (3)(a) shall cease to have affect.

**[8.113]** PDA 2000, 261A(7)(a) and (b)[81] provides that where, in relation to a quarry in respect of which a notice has been issued under s 261A(3)(a) and the planning authority decides that:

(a) either no application has been made to the Board for a review of a determination under subsection (2)(a) or the Board in making a decision in relation to such a review has confirmed the decision of the planning authority, and

(b) either no application has been made to the Board for a review of a decision of the planning authority under subsection (3)(a) or the Board in making a decision in relation to such review has confirmed the decision of the planning authority,

the person to whom the notice was issued under subsection (3)(a) shall apply to the Board for substitute consent under section 177E within 12 weeks from the date of the giving of the notice of its decision under section 261A(6)(f) by the Board or such further period as the Board may allow, save that where no application for review was made to the Board the person to whom the notice was issued under subsection (3)(a) shall apply to the Board for substitute consent within the period specified in the notice.

**[8.114]** PDA 2000, s 261A(8)[82] provides that if a notice is served on a quarry pursuant to s 261A(3)(a) and no application has been made to the board for a review of a determination under s 261A(2)(a) or the board's decision confirms the determination of the planning authority, and the board's decision in reviewing a decision of the planning authority under s 261A(3)(a) has set aside the planning authority's decision, the

---

80. This phrase is too commonly used in planning legislation. It is an indeterminate time the benefit of which is conferred statutorily on the Minister, the board and the planning authorities while members of the public are compelled to comply with a fixed time limited and they are frequently sanctioned if they do not do so. The playing pitch is anything but level.
81. As inserted by PD(A)A 2010, s 75.
82. As inserted by PD(A)A 2010, s 75.

**Additional Planning Controls on Land and on Buildings** [8.117]

direction which has issued requiring the person to whom the notice was issued to apply to the board for substitute consent shall cease to have effect and the board shall, as soon as may be, issue an enforcement notice under PDA 2000, s 154 to stop quarrying operations and to take such steps as the planning authority considers appropriate.

[8.115] PDA 2000, s 261A(9)[83] deals with quarries which have neither planning permission nor registration of the quarry under s 261.

[8.116] If a s 261A (4)(a) notice has issued and either application for a review of a s 261A(2)(a) determination has been made to the board or if the board's decision on such review confirms the determination of the planning authority and no application has been made to the board for a review of the planning authority's decision under s 261A(4)(a) or if the planning authority shall, or if the board's decision on such review has confirmed the decision of the planning authority shall, as soon as may be, after the expiration of the period for applying for a review or the date of the giving of the notice of its decision by the board under s 261A(6)(f) as the case may be, issue an enforcement notice under PDA 2000, s 154 to stop quarrying operations and to take such steps as the planning authority considers appropriate.

[8.117] PDA 2000, s 261A(10)[84] is another provision to deal with a situation where a s 261A(4)(a) notice has issued. The subsection provides for four consecutive conditions where the planning authority shall, as soon as may be, after the date of the giving of the notice of its decision by the board under s 261A(6)(f), issue a notice to the owner/operator of the quarry directing him or her to apply to the board for a substitute consent under s 177(e) within 12 weeks of the date of issue of the notice by the planning authority or such further period as the board may allow. The four separate conditions are as follows:

    (a) either no application has been made to the Board for a review of a determination under sub-s (2)(a) or the Board in making a decision in relation to such review has confirmed the determination of the planning authority, and

    (b) the Board in making a decision in relation to a review of a decision under sub-s (4)(a) has set aside the decision of the planning authority, and

    (c) either no application has been made to the Board for a review of a decision of the planning authority under sub-s (4)(a)(i) that the quarry commenced operation prior to 1 October 1964, or permission was granted in respect of the quarry under Part III of this Act or Part IV of the Act of 1963, or the Board in a review of such a decision has decided that the quarry commenced operation before 1 October 1964 or permission was granted in respect of the quarry under Part III of this Act or Part IV of the Act of 1963, and

    (d) either no application has been made to the Board for a review of a decision of the planning authority under sub-s (4)(a)(ii) that, if applicable, the s 261 registration requirements were fulfilled or the Board, in review, of such

---

83. As inserted by PD(A)A 2010, s 75.
84. As inserted by PD(A)A 2010, s 75.

decision has decided that, if applicable, the requirements in relation to the s 261 registration were fulfilled,

the planning authority shall, as soon as may be after the date of the giving of the notice of its decision by the board under s 261A(6)(f), issue a notice to the owner or operator of a quarry directing him or her to apply to the board for substitute consent under s 177E not later than 12 weeks after the date of the notice issued by the planning authority under this subsection or such further period as the board may allow.

[8.118] PDA 2000, s 261A(11)[85] provides that a s 261A(5)(a) notice is a notice which must issue within nine months of the commencement of PD(A)A 2010 and it arises where a planning authority makes a determination under s 261A(2)(a) and the planning authority further determines that the development the subject of the determination under s 261A(2)(a) took place after 3 July 2008. The authority shall also decide whether:

(i) the quarry commenced operation before 1st October 1964 or permission was granted in respect of the quarry under Part III of this Act or Part IV of the Act of 1963, and

(ii) if applicable, the requirements in relation to registration under s 261 were fulfilled.

[8.119] A s 261A(2)(a) determination is a determination to be made by each planning authority not later than six months after the coming into operation of PD(A)A 2010 in respect of every quarry within its administrative area as to whether:

(i) development as carried out after the 1st February 1990 which was not authorised by a permission granted under Part IV of the Act of 1963, prior to the 1st February 1990, which development would have required, having regard to the Environmental Impact Assessment Directive, an environmental impact assessment or a determination as to whether an environmental impact assessment was required but that such an assessment or determination was not carried out or made, or

(ii) development was carried out after 26th February 1997 which was not authorised by a permission granted under Part IV of the Act of 1963 prior to the 26th February 1997, which development would have required, having regard to the Habitats Directive an appropriate assessment, but that such an assessment was not carried out.

Both s 261A(5)(a) and (2)(a) are relevant to understanding PDA 2000, s 261A(11),[86] which provides that where a s 261A(5)(a) notice has been served in relation to quarry and no application has been made to the board for a review of a determination under s 261A(2)(a) or where the board in making its decision in relation to such a review has confirmed the determination already made by the planning authority, and either no application has been made to the board for a review of a determination of the planning authority under s 261A(5)(a) that the development the subject of a determination under s 261A(2)(a) took place after 3 July 2008 or the board has confirmed such a determination of the planning authority under s 261A(5)(a) then the planning authority

---

85. As inserted by PD(A)A 2010, s 75.
86. As inserted by PD(A)A 2010, s 75.

## Additional Planning Controls on Land and on Buildings [8.122]

as soon as may be after the expiration of the period for applying for a review or the date of giving of notice of its decision by the board under s 261A(6)(f) as the case may be issue an enforcement notice under PDA 2000, s 154 requiring immediate cessation of the quarry operation and taking such other steps as the planning authority considers appropriate.

[8.120] PDA 2000, s 261A(12)[87] also deals with the quarry where a notice under s 261A(5)(a) has issued and:

(a) either no application has been made to the board for a review of the determination under s 261A(2)(a) or the board in making a decision in relation to such a review has confirmed the determination of the planning authority, and

(b) the board, in making a decision in relation to a review of such notice has set aside the determination of the planning authority under s 261A(5)(a) that the development the subject of the determination under s 261A(2)(a) took place after 3 July 2008, and

(c) either no application has been made to the board for a review of a decision of the planning authority under s 261A(5)(a)(i) that the quarry commenced operation prior to 1 October 1964, or permission was granted in respect of the quarry under Part III of this Act or Part IV of the Act of 1963, or the board in a review of such decision has decided that the quarry commenced operation before 1 October 1964 or permission was granted in respect of the quarry under Part III of this Act or Part IV of the Act of 1963, and

(d) either no application has been made to the board for a review of a decision of the planning authority under s 261A(5)(a)(ii) that, if applicable, the requirements in relation to registration under s 261 were fulfilled or the board in a review of such decision has decided that, if applicable, the requirements in relation to registration under s 261 were fulfilled,

the planning authority shall as soon as may be after the date of giving of notice of its decision by the board under s 261A(6)(f), issue a notice to the owner or operator of the quarry directing him or her to apply to the board for substitute consent under s 177(e) not later than 12 weeks after the date of the notice issued by the planning authority under this subsection, or such further period as the board may allow.

[8.121] PDA 2000, s 261A(13)[88] deals with another case in relation to a quarry where notice has issued under s 261A(5)(a), and s 261A(13)(a) and (b) are precisely the same as s 261A(12)(a) and (b).

[8.122] Section 261A(13)(c) reads:

either—

(i) no application has been made to the Board for a review of a decision of the planning authority under subsection (5)(a)(i) that the quarry commenced

---

87. As inserted by PD(A)A 2010, s 75.
88. As inserted by PD(A)A 2010, s 75.

operation on or after 1st October 1964 and no permission was granted in respect of the quarry under Part III of this Act or Part IV of the Act of 1963, or the Board in review of such decision has decided that the quarry commenced operation on or after the 1st October 1964 and no permission was granted in respect of the quarry under Part III of this Act or Part IV of the Act of 1963, or

(ii) no application has been made to the Board for a review of a decision of the planning authority under subsection (5)(a)(ii) that if applicable, the requirements in relation to registration under section 261 were not fulfilled, or the Board in a review of such decision has decided that, if applicable, the requirements in relation to registration under section 261 were not fulfilled,

the planning authority shall as soon as may be after the date of the giving of the notice of its decision by the Board under subsection (6)(f), issue an enforcement notice under section 154 requiring the cessation of the operation of the quarry and the taking of such steps as the planning authority considers appropriate.

**[8.123]** PDA 2000, s 261A(14)[89] provides that any application for substitute consent should be made in relation to the development in respect of which the planning authority has made a determination under s 261A(2)(a).

**[8.124]** PDA 2000, s 261A(15)[90] states that the provisions of Part XA apply as appropriate to any application for substituted consent made in accordance with a direction under s 261A(3), (10) or (12).

## DERELICT SITES/DERELICT LAND

**[8.125]** Derelict sites and derelict land are regulated by the provisions of the Derelict Sites Act 1990. This Act was introduced specifically to deal with abandoned and neglected sites and the Act applies throughout a local authority's functional area. It is not confined to urban areas.

**[8.126]** At the time that the Derelict Sites Act 1990 became law there were very many more abandoned and neglected sites than there are today[91] which is a measure of the success of this particular piece of legislation. As each decade passes, more derelict sites appear, including some which are protected structures,[92] and so it seems that the work of the Derelict Sites Act will never be done.

---

89. As inserted by PD(A)A 2010, s 75.
90. As inserted by PD(A)A 2010, s 75.
91. Although perhaps since the demise of the Celtic Tiger we are starting to catch up again.
92. A notable example of a site which is visually derelict and statutorily protected may be seen on King Street at the north end of Smithfield Market in Dublin. These buildings are propped up with timber supports. They are an example of an unacceptable planning contradiction created by statute and implemented by Dublin City Council.

**[8.127]** Section 3 of the Derelict Sites Act 1990 defines a 'derelict site' as meaning:

> ... any land (in this section referred to as 'the land in question') which detracts, or is likely to detract, to a material degree from the amenity, character or appearance of the land in the neighbourhood of the land in question because of –
>
> (a) the existence on the land in question of structures which are in a ruinous derelict or dangerous condition, or
>
> (b) the neglected or objectionable condition of the land or any structures on the land in question, or
>
> (c) the presence, deposit or collection on the land in question of any litter, rubbish, debris or waste, except where the presence, deposit or collection of such litter, rubbish, debris or waste results from the exercise of a right conferred (by) statute or by common law.[93]

**[8.128]** Section 8 of the Derelict Sites Act 1990 requires local authorities to maintain a register of all derelict sites in its area. The derelict sites register is separate and distinct from the local authority's planning register and local authorities are obliged to enter a record of all derelict sites in their area in the register. Before the local authority makes an entry in the register it shall give notice of its intention to do so to any owner or occupier who may be ascertained by reasonable enquiry. The local authority shall also consider any representations of any owner or occupier made in writing within such period as is specified in the notice and having received the representations the local authority shall decide whether or not to enter the site as a derelict site in the register. Section 8(3) allows a local authority to remove an entry from the register where it considers that the entry is no longer appropriate. Section 8(4), however, requires a local authority to remove an entry from the register in relation to a derelict site where:

(a) a notice under section 11 has been complied with, or

(b) steps have been taken under section 11(5) to give effect to the terms of the notice under section 11,[94] or

(c) the land has otherwise ceased to be a derelict site.

**[8.129]** The register is open for inspection at the local authority offices by members of the public.[95] A copy of any document in the register, which is certified by an officer of the local authority as a true copy, is admissible without further proof to be received in evidence in any legal proceedings and it shall be deemed to be a true copy until the contrary is proved. Also, evidence of an entry in the register may be given by production

---

93. Derelict Sites Act 1990, s 3 omits the word 'by' before the word 'statute'.
94. Derelict Sites Act 1990, s 11(5) provides that if a person served with a s 11 notice fails, within the period specified in the notice, to comply with the requirements of the notice, the local authority who served the notice may enter the land and take such steps as they consider necessary to give effect to the terms of the notice. The local authority may recover the costs and expenses in taking this action from the person served with the notice and the costs are recoverable as a simple contract debt in any court of competent jurisdiction.
95. See the Derelict Sites Act 1990, s 8(5).

of a certified copy and it shall not be necessary to produce the register itself.[96] Where a site ceases to be a derelict site it must be removed from the register.

**[8.130]** Section 9 of the Derelict Sites Act 1990 obliges every owner and occupier (including State authorities[97] and statutory bodies[98]) to take all reasonable steps to ensure that land does not become a derelict site or does not continue to be a derelict site.

**[8.131]** Section 10 of the Derelict Sites Act 1990 provides that local authorities are bound to take all reasonable steps to ensure that any land within its functional area does not become or continue to become a derelict site. Local authorities are obliged to use their statutory powers to prevent dereliction within their functional area.

**[8.132]** Section 11 of the Derelict Sites Act 1990 enables a local authority to serve a notice on a person who appears to be the owner or occupier of a derelict site. The notice lists the works which the local authority considers necessary to prevent the land or site from continuing to be derelict. The notice will also provide a time period for the completion of the required works, which must not be less than one month, and it will advise the owner or occupier of their right to make written representations to the local authority with regard to a notice served within 14 days from the receipt of the notice. Any works required by the notice are exempt from the requirement to obtain planning permission under PDA 2000.[99]

**[8.133]** The Derelict Sites Act 1990, s 28(1) provides that a person who contravenes s 6(4), 11(4), 29(2), 29(3), 30(4) or 32(3) shall be guilty of an offence and liable, on summary conviction, to a fine not exceeding €1,249.74 (together with, in the case of a continuing offence, a fine not exceeding €126.97 for every day on which the offence is continued provided the total amount of the fine payment shall not exceed €1,249.74 when added to any other fine under this subsection) and/or imprisonment for a term not exceeding six months.

**[8.134]** The Derelict Sites Act 1990, s 28(2) provides that a person who contravenes s 11(4) shall be liable on conviction on indictment to a fine not exceeding €31,743.45 with continuing daily fines for each day that non-compliance continues of up to €2,539.47 or to imprisonment for a term not exceeding two years, or at the discretion of the court, to both such fine and such imprisonment.

**[8.135]** Part III of the Derelict Sites Act 1990 is a compelling incentive to persons whose names have been entered in the register to take the steps required by the notice in order to have the site removed from the register. Part III of the Act introduced a levy on derelict sites and that piece of legislation has had a positive effect on owners who have

---

96. See Derelict Sites Act 1990, s 8(8) and (9).
97. A State authority means a Minister of the government or the Commissioners – as defined in PDA 2000, s 2.
98. Statutory bodies include local authorities, harbour authorities, health boards, boards or bodies established under statute and companies owned by, or whose directors are appointed by, a Minister together with its subsidiaries.
99. See specifically the Derelict Sites Act 1990, s 11(6).

been served with a derelict site notice. The market value of the derelict site is determined by the provisions of s 22 of the Derelict Sites Act 1990. An obligation is placed on the local authority to determine the market value of the derelict site as soon as may be after it has been entered on the register but at least once every five years thereafter. The price is calculated on the basis of unencumbered fee simple offered for sale on the open market assuming best market price on the date of the valuation. Once determined, the market price is entered into the register and if the market price is revised, the owner or occupier of the land will be notified and may appeal to the Valuation Tribunal established under s 2 of the Valuation Act 1988. The determination of the Valuation Tribunal is final subject only to an appeal to the High Court on a question of law, which would, of course, include judicial review.

[8.136] The derelict sites levy is payable by the owner of the derelict property to the local authority in whose functional area the said land is situated.[100] Section 23 of the Derelict Sites Act 1990 deals with the calculation of the derelict sites levy, and s 23(3) provides as follows:

> The amount of the derelict sites levy shall be –
>
> (a) in respect of the local financial year which is prescribed in accordance with subsection (1), three per cent of the market value of urban land concerned, and
>
> (b) in respect of any subsequent such year such amount not exceeding ten per cent as may stand prescribed for each urban area or if there is no such amount prescribed three per cent of the said market value.

While the minimum derelict site levy is three per cent of the market value of the derelict site payable annually, the maximum permissible levy is 10 per cent of the market value of the derelict site payable annually. If an owner or occupier of a derelict site on whom the notice is served does not pay the levy, the levy will become a charge on the land as provided by the Derelict Sites Act 1990, s 24.

[8.137] The notice served under the Derelict Sites Act 1990 does not contain an express power to compel the owner or occupier of a derelict site to comply with a notice but failure on the part of the owner or occupier to comply with the notice will allow a local authority to take all reasonable necessary steps to give effect to its notice and to recover the cost of doing so from the person on whom the notice was served.

[8.138] Derelict Sites may be acquired by compulsory purchase by a local authority under the provisions of ss 14, 15 and 16 of the Derelict Sites Act 1990.

[8.139] Notice must be served on the owner or on any lessee[101] describing the area to be acquired, giving details of the procedure and prescribing a time limit for making representations which must be at least one month. The notice must also give the address of the public office where the map detailing the lands to be acquired may be inspected.

---

100. See Derelict Sites Act 1990, s 23(1)&(2).
101. Except as provided under of the Derelict Sites Act 1990, s 15(1)(b) which excludes tenants on a lease of one month or less.

The details to be given in the notice in writing served on the owner and on any lessees must also be published in at least one newspaper circulating in the locality. If any objections are made during the representation period the compulsory acquisition can only proceed with the consent of An Bord Pleanála. On the expiration of the representation period (which must be at least one month), the local authority may apply to the board for approval to proceed with the acquisition. If, however, any objections have been received, the board will furnish a copy of the local authority's comments to the objector and the objector then has 21 days in which to make any representations. Decision on the objector's representations will be made by the board, which may confirm the compulsory purchase order in respect of all or part of the site or refuse the compulsory purchase order in respect of all or part of the site.[102]

**[8.140]** Section 12 of the Derelict Sites Act 1990 permits the Minister for Environment, Heritage and Local Government to require a local authority to issue a s 11 notice and to take such steps as are necessary to give effect to that notice in order to prevent land owned by the local authority in question from being, becoming or continuing to be a derelict site.

## LICENSING OF EVENTS AND FUNFAIRS

**[8.141]** PDA 2000, Pt XVI deals with the licensing of events and funfairs in ss 229 to 241 inclusive. In *Mount Charles (Earl of) v Meath County Council*,[103] Meath County Council served a warning notice on the plaintiff in respect of a planned rock concert to be held on the grounds of Slane Castle for which no planning permission had been sought or obtained. The plaintiff argued that the notice was time barred as he had held pop concerts each year for a period in excess of five years. Kelly J consulted the *Concise Oxford Dictionary* which defines 'normal use' as 'open conforming to a standard; regular, usual, typical.' In the learned judge's view:

> ... the question of normal use should be approached without giving to that term any unusual or esoteric meaning. I have already accepted the notion that the normal use of land may involve more than one activity being carried on and it may be used for two purposes. However, it appears to me that before each activity can be regarded as part of the normal use of land, each would have to be recurrent and would have to account for a substantial part of the total amount of activity taking place on the land during the appropriate period. It is necessary to decide whether a particular activity is carried on to a sufficient extent and with sufficient regularity to constitute part of the normal use.[104]

Kelly J noted that in the preceding 15 years the land had only been used on nine occasions for the holding of concerts and in the learned judge's view had not become part of the normal use of the land. Kelly J held that the use of the land for such purposes

---

102. Derelict Sites Act 1990, s 16.
103. *Mount Charles (Earl of) v Meath County Council* [1996] 3 IR 417, HC, Kelly J.
104. *Mount Charles (Earl of) v Meath County Council* [1996] 3 IR 417, HC *per* Kelly J.

constituted a material change in use and that the proceedings were not time barred. He allowed the warning notice to stand.

**[8.142]** In *Mahon v Butler*,[105] the applicant sought an order prohibiting a U2 concert at the Lansdowne Road stadium. Costello P in the High Court came to much the same conclusion as Kelly J in the *Slane Castle* case and held that the proposed concerts would constitute a material change in use necessitating planning permission. The real point of interest in this case was the fact that the learned judge rejected the defendant's submission that the court had no power to grant an order under s 27 of LG(PD)A 1976 because the breach of the planning law had not yet occurred.

**[8.143]** The IRFU appealed Costello P's decision to the Supreme Court where Denham J, delivering a unanimous decision of the court, found in favour of the IRFU. Denham J took the view that s 27 only refers to events occurring in the present or events which have occurred in the past. The section makes no specific reference to future events. Denham J concluded that s 27 is written in clear and plain language and that it is not the function of the court to legislate in order to rectify possible gaps in the legislation. The provisions of PDA 2000, Pt XVI have altered the situation and it can now be stated that an 'event' does not amount to 'development' within the meaning of PDA 2000, s 168.

**[8.144]** PDA 2000, s 240 deals with the exclusion of events and funfairs from planning control.

> (1) Subject to subsection (2) the holding of an event to which this Part applies and works directly or solely relating to the holding of such an event shall not be construed as 'development' within the meaning of this Act.
>
> (2)(a) Notwithstanding s 230 or 239, the provisions of this part shall not affect the validity of any planning permission granted under Pt IV of the 1963 Act for the holding of an event or events for a funfair.
>
> (b) Where a planning permission referred to in paragraph (a) has been granted for the holding of an event or events in respect of land, a licence under this part shall be required for the holding of any additional event on the land concerned.

**[8.145]** Section 240 appears to indicate that funfairs and events are to be regulated other than by way of planning permission but although the margin note refers to exclusion of events and funfairs from planning control, s 240(1) and (2)(a) and (b) have neglected to use the word 'funfair'.[106] Simons SC noted this lacuna and writes:

> Although there is reference in the side note of s 240 to the exclusion of both events and funfairs from planning control, there is no reference to funfairs in the actual

---

105. *Mahon v Butler* [1997] 3 IR 369, HC and [1998] 1 ILRM 284, SC.
106. This omission was brought to the attention of the Minister for the Environment, Heritage and Local Government, John Gormley TD, by this author in a letter dated 21 April 2010. An acknowledgement was received on 21 April 2010 from the Minister's secretary stating that 'a further letter on this matter will issue to you as soon as possible'. No further communication on this topic was received from the Department and PDA 2000, s 240 remains unamended.

**[8.146]** Planning and Environmental Law in Ireland

text of the section. Thus it would seem that s 240 is not competent to exclude funfairs from the ordinary requirement to obtain planning permission. It should be noted that a limited exemption is provided under the Planning and Development Regulations 2001 for funfair use not exceeding 15 days continuously or 30 days in aggregate in a year.[107]

**[8.146]** Given the inherently transient nature of these types of event, and the types of control that are required when music concerts and other outdoor events are held, it is clear that the planning system is not the best system to regulate them. Funfairs also raise issues of regulation which are best dealt with by more specialised persons with a comprehensive knowledge of engineering and health and safety regulations relating to funfair equipment. It is for this reason that PDA 2000, Pt XVI merely provides for the licensing of certain outdoor events and funfairs by a local authority. These events will not be subject to planning control and they are outside the planning system. It has been recognised for some time that the regulation of these activities, through the formal planning permission process, is not a particularly efficient or wieldy process with which to regulate an increasingly important and ever expanding area.

**[8.147]** PDA 2000, s 229 is an interpretation section and an understanding of the words defined is crucial to an understanding of Pt XVI:

'event' means:

(a) a public performance which takes place wholly or mainly in the open air or in a structure with no roof or a partial, temporary or retractable roof, a tent or similar temporary structure and which is comprised of music, dancing, displays of public entertainment or any activity of a like kind, and

(b) any other event as prescribed by the Minister under s 241;

Note that 'outdoor events' are not intended to include sporting fixtures or sporting events.

**[8.148]** PDA 2000, s 241 is an enabling section which allows the Minister to make regulations providing that any activity or class of activity to which the public has access and which takes place wholly or mainly in the open air or in a structure with no roof, or a partial, temporary or retractable roof, a tent or other similar structure, is to be an event for the purposes of PDA 2000, Pt XVI.

**[8.149]** 'Funfair' is defined in PDA 2000, s 229 by reference to PDA 2000, s 239 as an entertainment where fairground equipment is used.

**[8.150]** 'Fairground equipment' is defined in PDA 2000, s 239 to include:

any fairground ride or any similar equipment which is designated to be in motion for entertainment purposes with members of the public on or inside it, any equipment which is designed to be used by members of the public for entertainment purposes either as a slide or for bouncing upon, and any swings,

---

107. See Simons, *Planning and Development Law* (2nd edn, Thomson Round Hall, 2007) at p 412, paras 8.289 to 8.291.

dodgems and other equipment which is designed to be in motion wholly or partly under the control of, or to be put in motion by a member of the public or any equipment which may be prescribed, in the interests of public safety, for the purposes of this section;

**[8.151]** 'Licence' is defined by PDA 2000, s 229 as meaning a licence granted by the local authority under PDA 2000, s 231. PDA 2000, s 231 is a comprehensive section allowing the Minister to make regulations providing for procedural matters in relation to the applications for and the granting of licences for events. Where an application for a licence is made in accordance with the regulations under this section, the local authority may decide to grant the licence subject to such conditions as it considers appropriate, or to refuse the licence.

**[8.152]** PDA 2000, s 229 defines the 'local authority' as meaning:

(a) in the case of a county, the county council of the county, and

(b) in the case of a county borough, the corporation of the borough.[108]

**[8.153]** PDA 2000, s 230 sets out the obligation on persons who plan to hold an event covered by PDA 2000, Pt XVI to obtain a licence. It is an offence to hold an event without a licence or to be in control of land where an unlicensed event is held. PDR 2001, art 183 provides that an event at which the audience comprises 5,000 or more people shall be an event prescribed for the purposes of s 230 of the Act.

**[8.154]** 'Audience' means:

Persons attending at an event on a particular day, other than persons working or performing at the event, and shall include persons attending by invitation and, where an event comprises more than one performance at one or more locations at the venue on a particular day, the audience shall mean the total number of persons attending all such performances.[109]

**[8.155]** The procedure for making an application for a licence is set out in Pt XVI in PDR 2001, arts 184–199. The principle points in relation to the application are summarised below.

## Pre-application consultation

**[8.156]** The Local Government and Environment Guidelines on the 2001 Regulations states that, 'This consultation is a necessary part of ensuring that these large events are properly planned and forms an integral part of the procedures set out under the Act.'

**[8.157]** The articles require the local authorities to consult with the prescribed bodies.[110] PDR 2001, art 182 defines the 'prescribed bodies' as:

(a) the relevant Chief Superintendant of An Garda Síochána,

---

108. These are now called City Councils.
109. PDR 2001, art 182.
110. PDR 2001, art 189.

(b) the relevant Health Board, or

(c) any county council, county borough, corporation, borough corporation or urban district council (other than the local authority to whom application is made), the area of which will be affected by the event.

**[8.158]** The purpose of the pre-application consultation is to enable the applicant to provide information to the authorities as to the type of event which is being planned and how it is planned to manage the event. There is no obligation on the local authority or on prescribed bodies to enter into these consultations and they are not compelled to offer advice.

**[8.159]** PDR 2001, art 185 requires the applicant for a licence to publish a notice of its intention to apply for a licence in one local paper and one national newspaper. Full details of the event must be listed, as provided in art 185(2), to include the name of the applicant, the type of the event proposed to be held and the venue thereof, the date of holding it, the estimated size of the audience who will attend and the fact that the application can be examined during office hours for a period of five weeks and further notifying members of the public that they are entitled to make submissions or observations to the local authority within five weeks of the date of receipt of the application.

**[8.160]** PDR 2001, art 186 provides that an application must be made at least 16 weeks prior to the holding of the event and PDR 2001, art 187 gives explicit details of the form and content of the application. PDR 2001, art 186(2) provides:

(2) As soon as may be after receipt of the application, the local authority shall consider whether the requirements of these Regulations have been complied with, and –

(a) acknowledge receipt of the application in writing, or

(b) inform the applicant that the application is invalid, by reason of the fee submitted being inadequate or for any other reason, and cannot be considered by the authority, indicating which requirement of these Regulations has not been complied with.

If, in submitting a document making an application for a licence, the document is not compliant with the regulations governing the application, that application is automatically invalid.

**[8.161]** The form and content of the application are set out in PDR 2001, art 187 as follows:

(1) An application shall –

(i) state the name, contact address (including e-mail address where appropriate) and telephone number of the applicant,

(ii) where the applicant is not the promoter of the event, state the name, contact address (including e-mail address where appropriate) and telephone number of the promoter,

(iii) state the anticipated number of the audience at the proposed event,

(iv) state the proposed date on which the event is to be held and the proposed duration of the event, including the times at which the event is proposed to commence and conclude,

(v) be accompanied by a copy of the relevant page of each newspaper containing the notice required to be published under art 185,

(vi) where the applicant is not the owner or occupier of the venue, be accompanied by confirmation in writing from such owner or occupier of his or her consent to the holding of the event,

(vii) be accompanied by a draft plan for the management or the event prepared in accordance with the appropriate code or codes of practice and including–

    (i) the names and responsibilities of the event controller, the event safety officer and their deputies,

    (ii) a draft site emergency plan,

    (iii) a draft traffic management plan,

    (iv) a draft safety strategic statement,

    (v) a draft environment monitoring programme for before, during and after the proposed event, and

    (vi) provision for the removal of structures and the carrying out of any works for the reinstatement of the venue subsequent to the event, for the full clean-up of the surrounding area, and any remedial works arising from any damage caused to public property, facilities or amenities associated with the event,

(viii) be accompanied by a location map of sufficient size and containing details of related sites and features in the vicinity of the venue, to a scale of not less than 1:1000 in built up areas and 1:2500 in all other areas and marked clearly to show such related sites or features and drawings to an appropriate scale of the venue, including a site layout plan and a viewing accommodation plan.

(2) Six copies of the application and accompany documents, maps and drawings shall be submitted to the local authority.

(3) Where an event is proposed to be held on a public road or on any other land under the control of the local authority, sub-article 1(f) shall not apply.

## Availability of documents

[8.162] PDR 2001, art 188 provides that the local authority shall make the application and any accompanying documents, maps and drawings and any submissions or observations made in relation to it available for inspection during office hours at the local authority offices or such other nominated places for a period of five weeks from the date of receipt of the application. The article also provides that the local authority will make copies of any documents requested by members of the public on payment of the fee not exceeding the reasonable sum of making such copy.

## Consultation with prescribed bodies

**[8.163]** PDR 2001, art 189 requires the local authority to consult with prescribed bodies by sending a copy of the application and seeking submissions and observations on it within a period of five weeks from the date that the application was made. The article also provides that the local authority can agree to an extension of time if it is of the opinion that the prescribed body needs further time to consider the matters submitted to it. A local authority may also consult with any other body, not being a prescribed body, in relation to the application where it considers that that is appropriate.

**[8.164]** When sending a copy of the application to the prescribed bodies the local authority will seek submissions or observations to be made to it in respect of the application within five weeks of the date of which the application was received by the prescribed authority.

PDR 2001, art 190 requires that any person making a submission or observation in writing to the local authority must do so within five weeks of receipt of the application by the local authority.

## Making of submissions or observations by any other person

**[8.165]** PDR 2001, art 190 allows any member of the public to make submissions or observations and the local authority may at its discretion invite other persons to make submissions or observations in relation to the application provided such submissions or observations are made within five weeks of the date of receipt of the application by the local authority. A specific fee is prescribed for the making of submissions or observations.

**[8.166]** Any person is entitled to make submissions or observations and the local authority may at its discretion invite other persons to make submissions and observations in relation to the application.

## Further information

**[8.167]** PDR 2001, art 191 permits the local authority to request further information from the applicant, from prescribed bodies or from persons who have made submissions, to enable it to reach its decision. The section allows the local authority to take whatever measures it considers necessary, including convening of meetings and taking oral submissions, in order to seek the views of any person with regard to the application but neither the applicant nor any other person has a right to demand an oral hearing and the decision as to whether or not an oral hearing will take place is a matter left entirely to the discretion of the local authority.

## Decision on application

**[8.168]** PDR 2001, art 192 provides that the local authority may decide to grant the licence, to grant the licence subject to conditions as it considers appropriate or to refuse the licence.

## Grant of licence

**[8.169]** In considering an application for a licence the local authority shall have regard to the matters set out in PDA 2000, s 231(3)(b), namely:[111]

- (i) any information relating to the application furnished to it by the applicant in accordance with subsections (2)(d) or (g),[112]
- (ii) any consultations under subsection (2)(e),[113]
- (iii) any submissions or observations made to it in accordance with subsection(2)(f).[114]
- (iv) whether events have previously been held on the land concerned,
- (v) the matters referred to subsection (4),[115] and
- (vi) any guidelines or codes of practice issued by the Minister or by any other Minister of the Government.

**[8.170]** PDA 2000, s 231(4) provides that without prejudice to the generality of sub-s (3)(a), a condition subject to which a licence is granted may relate to all or any of the following:

- (a) compliance with any guidelines or codes of practice issued by the Minister or any other Minister of the Government, or with any provisions of those guidelines or codes of practice;
- (b) securing the safety of persons at the place in connection with the event;
- (c) the provision of adequate facilities for the health and welfare of persons at the place in connection with the event, including the provision of sanitary facilities;
- (d) the protection of the environment in which the event is to be held, including the control of litter;
- (e) the maintenance of public order;
- (f) the avoidance or minimisation of disruption to the neighbourhood in which the event is to take place;
- (g) ensuring the provision of adequate means of transport to and from the place in which the event is to be held;
- (h) the number of events which are permitted at a venue with a specified period not exceeding one year;

---

111. PDA 2000, s 231(3)(b) lists matters to which the local authority shall have regard to in considering an application for a licence.
112. PDA 2000, s 231(2)(d) refers to regulations concerning the provision of plans, documents and information to be submitted with an application for a licence. PDA 2000, s 231(2)(g) refers to regulations requiring the applicant to submit any further information with respect to their applicant.
113. PDA 2000, s 232(2)(e) refers to regulations concerning the persons and bodies which must be consulted in relation to a licence.
114. PDA 2000, s 231(2)(f) refers to regulations enabling persons to make submissions or observations within a prescribed time.
115. This subsection is dealt within the next paragraph below (para **8.170**).

(i) the payment of a financial contribution to the authority of a specified amount or an amount calculated on a specified basis towards the estimated costs to the local authority of measures taken by the authority in connection with the event;

(j) the payment of financial contribution to a person or body consulted in accordance with subsection (2)(e) of a specified amount or an amount calculated on a specified basis towards the estimated cost to that person or body of measures taken by the person or body in connection with the event;

(k) maintaining public liability insurance;

(l) the display of notice for persons attending the event as to their obligations and conduct at the event.

(5) conditions under subsection (4)(i) or (j) requiring the payment of a financial contribution may only relate to an event which is held wholly or mainly for profit.

(6) a person shall not be entitled solely by reason of a licence under this section to hold an event.

## Codes of practice in relation to events

[8.171] PDA 2000, s 232 provides that the Minister or any Minister of government may draw up and issue codes of practice for the purpose of providing practical guidance with respect to the requirements of any of the relevant provisions under this part. Provision is made that the Minister or any Minister shall, before issuing a code of practice, consult with any other Minister of government or other person or body as appears to the Minister to be appropriate. Amendments or revocations of any code of practice may be made by the Minister or any government Minister following consultation with any other government Minister or any person or body that appears to the Minister to be appropriate.

## Service of notice in relation to events

[8.172] PDA 2000, s 233 entitles a local authority to serve a notice in relation to events if it has reason to believe that an event is likely to occur without licence or in contravention of the terms of the licence. The notice will require, as appropriate:

(a) the immediate cessation of any event or the discontinuance or alteration of any preparations which are being made in relation to an event,

(b) the removal of any temporary buildings, structures, plant, machinery or the like from land which the authority believes is intended to be used as the location of an event, and

(c) the restoration of the land to its prior condition.[116]

---

116. Paragraphs (a), (b) and (c) are from PDA 2000, s 223(2).

Under PDA 2000, s 233 any person who fails to comply with the requirement for the notice served shall be guilty of an offence.[117]

## General obligations with regard to safety at events

**[8.173]** PDA 2000, s 234 imposes general obligations with regard to safety at events and requires that a person to whom a licence is granted will take such care as is reasonable in all the circumstances having regard to the care which a person attending the event may reasonably be expected to take for his/her own safety and if the person at the event is in the company of another person, the extent of the supervision and control the latter person may be expected to exercise over the former person's activities, to ensure that persons on the land in connection with the event do not suffer any injury or damage by reason of any danger arising out of the licensed event or associated activities. Every person being on land in connection with the event has a duty to conduct himself or herself in such a way so as to ensure, as far as reasonably practicable, that any person is not exposed to danger as a consequence of any act or omission of his or hers.

## Powers of inspection in connection with events

**[8.174]** Powers of inspection by an authorised person or member of the gardaí are provided for in PDA 2000, s 235. Inspections may take place of structures on the land or equipment used in connection with the event and any person who refuses to allow an inspection or impedes an inspection or willfully or recklessly gives information which is false or misleading shall be guilty of an offence.

**[8.175]** As seen under the provisions of PDA 2000, s 230(4), a local authority is not required to hold a licence for an event held by the local authority. However, PDA 2000, s 238 requires a local authority to undertake formal public consultation in respect of an event organised by a local authority details of which are set out in the section.

## Control of funfairs

**[8.176]** Pt 16 of PDR 2001 introduced the licensing system for events. The licensing system in force takes these events outside the scope of planning control and, as seen, PDA 2000, s 240 excludes events, and the marginal note purports to exclude funfairs, from planning control.

As seen, the regulations are dealt with in PDR 2001, arts 183–199.

**[8.177]** PDA 2000, s 239 deals with the control of funfairs. Section 239(1) deals with the definition of 'fairground equipment' and of 'funfair':

> 'fairground equipment' includes any fairground ride or any similar equipment which is designed to be in motion for entertainment purposes with members of the public on or inside it, any equipment which is designed to be used by members of the public for entertainment purposes either as a slide or for bouncing upon, and any swings, dodgems and other equipment which is designed to be in motion

---

117. PDA 2000, s 233(3).

wholly or partly under the control of, or to be put in motion by, a member of the public or any equipment which may be prescribed, in the interests of public safety, for the purposes of this section;

'funfair' means an entertainment where fairground equipment is used.[118]

An obligation is imposed:

> on the organisers of a funfair and the owner of the fairground equipment used at a funfair to take such care as is reasonable in the circumstances, having regard to the care which a person attending the funfair may reasonably be expected to take for his or her own safety, and, if the person is at the event in the company of another person, the extent of the supervision and control the latter person may be expected to exercise over the former person's activity to ensure that persons on land in connection with the funfair do not suffer any injury or damage by reason of any danger arising out of the funfair or associated activities.[119]

> It shall be the duty of every person being on land in connection with a funfair to which this section applies shall conduct himself or herself in such a way as to ensure that as far as is reasonably practicable any person on the land is not exposed to danger as a consequence of any act or omission of his or hers.[120]

These subsections are similar to the terms in s 234(1) and (2) dealing with events. They outline the duty of care owed by an organiser to persons attending the funfair.

**[8.178]** Dodd sums up this duty of care as follows:

> The standard of care owed by organisers is defined by reference to the regard which a person may have for their own safety and the extent of supervision and control of a person may be expected to have over persons in their company, which would include children. Every person must conduct themselves to ensure, as far as reasonably practicable, that no person is exposed to danger. The provision covers both organisers and members of the public, in terms of the duty and the persons protected. The duty also applies to their own safety.[121]

**[8.179]** PDA 2000, s 239(4) provides that any fairground equipment which is used by the public must have obtained a valid certificate of safety which certificate must be in date unless the equipment being used is exempt from the provisions of this section. Where a certificate is required but the certificate is either not in date or not available the person organising the funfair or the owner of the fairground equipment shall be guilty of an offence.

**[8.180]** PDA 2000, s 239(5) permits the Minister to make regulations dealing with procedure, administration and control as may be necessary in relation to applications for and grants of certificates of safety for fairground equipment.

---

118. PDA 2000, s 239(1).
119. PDA 2000, s 239(2).
120. PDA 2000, s 239(3).
121. See Dodd, *Planning and Development Acts 2000–2007 Annotated and Consolidated* (Round Hall, 2008) at p 577, para 1–282.

**[8.181]** The Planning Regulations 2001 provided that advertisements consisting of placards, posters or bills relating to the visit of any travelling circus, funfair, carnival, show, musicians or other travelling entertainment are exempt provided:

1. They are not larger than 1.2m$^2$.

2. They are not exhibited higher than 2.5m above ground level and they must be affixed to an advertising structure.

3. They are not left in place for more than seven days after the last performance or closing of the entertainment.

**[8.182]** PDA 2000, s 239(6) deals with the specific type of regulations which the Minister may make under this section to include (a) the persons who are entitled to grant certificates of safety, (b) the matters to be taken into account in determining applications for safety certificates, (c) fees payable for such certificates, (d) the validity period for such certificates, and (e) the Minister may use his/her discretion to exempt certain class of fairground equipment from the necessity to obtain certificate of safety.

**[8.183]** Detailed regulations are contained in the Planning and Development Act 2000 (Certification of Fairground Equipment) Regulations 2003 (SI 449/2003) dealing specifically with 'funfair guidance documents' – safety certificates and specific exemptions from the provisions of PDA 2000, s 239 dealing with control of funfairs. In effect, the article exempts playground equipment provided by a local authority from the need to satisfy the requirements of s 239 of PDA 2000, as amended.

**[8.184]** An additional subsection, namely s 239(6A), has been inserted by the Planning & Development (Amendment) Act 2002 (s 14), which reads as follows:

> (6A) Regulations under this section may be made to any extent by reference to a document published by or on behalf of the Minister.

**[8.185]** PDA 2000, s 239(7)(a) and (b) provides:

> (a) A person who intends to hold or organise a funfair, other than at a place where the operation of the funfair equipment has been authorised by a permission under Part III of this Act or Part IV of the Act of 1963 or is not otherwise an authorised use shall give 2 weeks notice (or such other period of notice as may be prescribed) in writing to the local authority in whose functional area the funfair is to be held.
>
> (b) The notice referred to in paragraph (a) shall be accompanied by a valid certificate of safety for the fairground equipment to be used at the funfair and shall give details of the names of the organiser of the funfair, the owner or owners of the fairground equipment to be used at the funfair and the location and dates on which the funfair is to be held.

**[8.186]** PDA 2000, s 239(8) deals with enforcement against funfairs. If a local authority has reason to believe that a funfair is or is likely to take place which is not compliant with the requirement to hold a valid safety certificate or has not given the two weeks notice required, the local authority may serve a notice on the person involved in the organisation of the funfair requiring:

(i) the immediate cessation of any activity or any preparations which are being made in relation to the funfair within a specified time;

(ii) the immediate cessation of the use of any fairground equipment without a valid safety certificate;

(iii) the removal, within a specified time, of any fairground equipment, temporary buildings or structures, plant machinery or similar equipment which the authority believes is intended to be used in relation to the funfair; and

(iv) the restoration of the land to its prior condition within a specified time.

Any person who fails to comply with a notice so served shall be guilty of an offence.[122] The section also provides that the local authority may enter onto the lands concerned if a person ignores the notice served in order to give effect to the terms of the notice and it may recover the costs of doing so.

## MAJOR ACCIDENT HAZARD DIRECTIVE – SEVESO II DIRECTIVE

**[8.187]** The Major Accident Hazard Directive is Council Directive 96/82/EC dated 9 December 1996 which deals with the control of major accidents involving dangerous substances. The Directive has been transposed into Irish law principally through the European Communities (Control of Major Accident Hazards Involving Dangerous Substances) Regulations 2006. The Directive is also partly implemented under the provisions of PDA 2000.

**[8.188]** The Major Accidents Directive 96/82/EC of 9 December 1996 has been amended principally by Directive 2003/105/EC of the European Parliament and of the Council on 16 December 2003 and the purpose of the Directives is to identify major accident hazards of certain industrial activities. The Directives are concerned with the prevention of major accidents which might result from certain industrial activities. The Directives also seek to limit the consequences of major accidents for humans and for the environment. Some tragic consequences have been demonstrated by the hazard which arises when dangerous sites and dwelling houses are placed close together. The Directives have an affect both on land use and on the construction of buildings as they endeavour to ensure that hazardous industrial operations are properly managed and contained and that they are, insofar as possible, not sited in densely populated areas where they may put human life at risk of injury or death or both. The amending Directive 2003/105/EC issued on 16 December 2003. That Directive has been transposed into Irish law by the European Communities (Control of Major Accident Hazards Involving Dangerous Substances) Regulations 2006. Implementation of the Directive has been partly implemented by PDA 2000. Thus, PDA 2000, s 10 in dealing

---

122. PDA 2000, s 239(8)(c) and (e).

Additional Planning Controls on Land and on Buildings [8.189]

with the content of a development plan provides that a development plan shall include objectives for:

(1)(k) the control, having regard to the provisions of the major accident's directive and any regulations, under any enactment, giving effect to that directive, of –

(i) siting of new establishments,

(ii) modification of existing establishments and,

(iii) development in the vicinity of such establishments, for the purpose of reducing the risk or limiting the consequences of a major accident;[123]

[8.189] PDR 2001, art 145 deals with local authority prescribed development and provides:

> Development (excluding development referred to in Chapter 3 of this Part) which relates to the provision of, or modifications to, an establishment and which could have significant repercussions on major accident hazards, shall be prescribed for the purposes of section 179 of the Act and the provisions of Part 8 shall apply.

In effect, any local authority development which does not require an EIS but which relates to the provision of, or modification to, an establishment and which could have significant repercussions on major accident hazards must comply with the public consultation procedure set out in PDA 2000, s 179. That section sets out a public consultation procedure which must be followed, even though local authorities' own development is exempt from the necessity to obtain planning permission. The provisions of PDA 2000, s 179 do apply to local authority development which comes within the Major Accident Hazards Directive, as amended. Part 8 of the Regulations deals with requirements in respect of specified development by, on behalf, or in partnership with local authorities and particularly with development which relates to the establishment to which the Major Accident Regulations apply. PDA 2000, s 179, which deals with local authority own development, has been amended by PD(A)A 2010, s 58(a) and (b). PDA 2000 s 179(6) (as amended) provides that s 179 shall not apply to proposed development which:

(a) consists of works of maintenance or repair other than works to a protected structure, or a proposed protected structure, which would materially affect the character of –

(i) the structure, or

(ii) any element of the structure which contributes to its special architectural, historical, archaeological, artist, cultural, scientific, social or technical interest,[124]

buy the substitution of the following paragraph

(b) is necessary for dealing urgently with any situation which the manager considers is an emergency situation calling for immediate action,

---

123. PDA 2000, s 10(2)(k). This subsection has not been altered by PD(A)A 2010.
124. PDA 2000, s 176(6)(a) substituted by PD(A)A 2010, s 58(a).

(c) consists of works which a local authority is required to undertake –
  (i) by or under any enactment,
  (ii) by or under the law of the European Union, or a provision of any act adopted by an institution of the European Union, or
  (iii) by order of a court.[125]

The Major Accidents Hazards Directive is commonly referred to as the Seveso or Seveso II Directive. Seveso is a town located 15 km outside Milan in the Lombardy region of Italy. An industrial accident occurred there at 12.37pm on 10 July 1976 in a small chemical manufacturing plant which resulted in the highest known exposure to 2, 3, 7, 8–tetrachlorodibenzo–P–dioxin (TCDD) in any residential population. The accident at Seveso resulted in numerous scientific studies which were responsible for the introduction of industrial safety regulations known as the Seveso II Directive.

[8.190] At Seveso, the safety operations which were under the control of the company's directors were badly handled in that it took a week before the accident was disclosed and another week before evacuation of the surrounding area was commenced.

[8.191] Another notable example of a major accident hazard occurred at Bhopal in the state of Madhya Pradesh in India at a pesticide plant owned by Union Carbide as a result of a catastrophic gas leak in 1986 which killed more than 20,000 people. The Bhopal disaster remains one of the world's worst industrial disasters. Pathetically small awards were made to survivors and persons affected by this disaster in 2010, a mere 24 years after the event.

[8.192] The Chinso company in Japan at Minamata Bay dumped mercury compound into the sea over a period of 37 years from 1932 to 1968. Over 3,000 people suffered various deformities, severe mercury poisoning symptoms or death from what was known as 'Minamata' disease.

[8.193] The Texas City refinery disaster of 1947 was another notable industrial accident where a berthed cargo vessel exploded. A quantity of 3,206 tonnes of ammonium nitrate exploded. The result was the death of some 578 people and the injury of an estimated 3,500 people. Windows were shattered more than 40 km away.

[8.194] More recently the Enschede fireworks disaster was a fireworks explosion at the SE Fireworks Depot on 13 May 2000 in Holland. Twenty-three people died in the explosion and 947 people were injured. The company imported fireworks from China and was a supplier to pop concerts and other major festivals in Holland. Prior to the explosion it had a good safety record and met all safety audits.

[8.195] The Chernobyl disaster occurred on 26 April 1986 at 01.23 hrs. Reactor number 4 in the Chernobyl nuclear plant had a meltdown, the consequences of which were particularly devastating for the city of Pripyat in the Ukraine. The explosion caused 56 direct and immediate deaths and over 4,000 cancer deaths. The explosion sent a nuclear plume over the Soviet Union, Eastern, Western and Northern Europe and over large areas of the Ukraine, Belarus and Russia, resulting in the evacuation of 336,000 people.

---

125. PDA 2000, s 179(6)(c) substituted by PD(A)A 2010, s 58(b).

Over 60,000 people were highly exposed. Grazing reindeer in northern Sweden were exposed to serious nuclear contamination.

**[8.196]** These are just a small, and in many cases, a familiar list of industrial accidents which are set out to illustrate the extent of the potential problems which are associated with 'dangerous substances'. In planning terms they require to be addressed both in terms of planning conditions and in terms of a requirement for regular safety audits. The Major Accident Hazards Directives are there also to ensure, as far as is possible, that establishments where dangerous substances are present, must be sited away from residential and other densely populated areas and away from areas of natural interest or sensitivity. In relation to establishments which are and have been located for sometime in densely populated areas, the land use policy must ensure that all possible safety measures are implemented to control the dangerous substances during the course of industrial process so as to avoid a major accident.

**[8.197]** An 'establishment' is defined in the European Communities (Control of Major Accidents Hazards Involving Dangerous Substances) Regulations 2006 as meaning the whole area under the control of an operator where 'dangerous substances' are present in one or more installations, including common or related infrastructures or activities. The definition includes new, existing and other establishments.

**[8.198]** Where there are circumstances to which the Major Accidents Directive applies, Member States have an additional duty beyond the need to implement environmental protection. Member States shall also share and provide environmental information in accordance with the provisions of the European Convention on Human Rights.

**[8.199]** PDR 2001, Pt 11 provides regulations dealing with the Major Accidents Directive. In all there are six chapters in Pt 11 and some of these provisions have been amended by arts 32–37 of PDR 2006.

**[8.200]** Article 32 of PDR 2006 amends Pt 11 of the 2001 Regulations by the substitution of 'Health and Safety Authority' for 'National Authority for Occupational Safety and Health' in each place where it occurs.

## PDR 2001 (as amended), Part 11

*Chapter 1: planning applications (arts 133–137)*

**[8.201]** PDR 2000, art 133 notes that PDR 2001, art 18 deals with requirements for a newspaper notice in relation to planning applications. PDR 2001, art 133 provides that where the planning application relates to the provision of or modifications to an establishment, a notice under art 17(1) shall indicate that fact.[126]

---

126. PDR 2001, art 17 is the requirement that two weeks notice must be given of intention to make application for planning permission in a newspaper in accordance with PDR 2001, art 18 and also notice by erecting or affixing a site notice in accordance with PDR 2001, art 19.

**[8.202]** PDR 2001, art 134 provides that an application for outline permission may not be made in respect of the provision of or modification to an 'establishment'.

**[8.203]** PDR 2001, art 135 notes that PDR 2001, art 22 deals generally with contents of planning applications and if a planning application relates to the provision or modification of an 'establishment', four copies of additional information must be furnished as specified in the Major Accident Regulations, Sch 3.

**[8.204]** PDR 2001, art 136 provides that where a planning application relates to the provision of, or modification to an establishment, the list made under PDR 2001, art 27 shall indicate that fact. PDR 2001, art 27 provides that the planning authority shall, not later than the third working day following a particular week, make available a list of the planning applications received by the planning authority during that week.

**[8.205]** PDR 2001, art 137 (as amended)[127] provides that in addition to the requirements of PDR 2001, art 28 (dealing with the necessity to serve notice on certain bodies), if a planning authority receives an application relating to the provision of or modifications to an 'establishment' and if, in the authority's opinion, the development would be relevant to the risk or consequences of a major accident and where the Health and Safety Authority has not offered technical advice on the risk or consequences of a major accident, the planning authority shall notify the Health and Safety Authority. Any notice sent by the planning authority to the Health and Safety Authority shall, according to PDR 2001, art 137(3):

    (a) Issue within 3 weeks of receipt of the planning application,

    (b) Include a copy of the relevant planning application,

    (c) Where the planning application relates to development referred to in sub-article (1)(b) or (c), identify the relevant establishment or establishments,

    (d) Where an EIS has been submitted with the planning application, include a copy of the statement,

    (e) Where the planning application relates to development which comprises or is for the purposes of an activity requiring an integrated pollution control licence or a waste licence, indicate that fact,[128]

    (f) Request a determination as to whether the Major Accidents Regulations apply to the propose development, and

    (g) Request that, where the Authority determines under (f) above that the Major Accidents Regulations apply to the proposed development, technical advice on the effects of the proposed development on the risk of consequences of a major accident be provided to the Board.

---

127. PDR 2006, art 33 which amends PDR 2001, art 137(1)(b)(2).
128. PDR 2001, art 137(3) has been amended by substitution of a new paragraph in paras 138(3)(e), (f). An additional sub-clause (g) has been added.

**[8.206]** PDR 2001, art 137(2) requires the planning authority to notify the Health and Safety Authority that it is of the opinion that an application for development might entail the risk or consequences of a major accident. As seen, art 137(1) sets out in sub-articles (1)(a), (b) and (c) three incidences where the planning authority is obliged to notify the Health and Safety Authority. If a planning authority receives the planning application relating to development which would be of a category listed in PDR 2001, Sch 8, Table 1, and/or would be located within the distance listed in PDR 2001, Sch 8, Table 2, Column 1, or be located within such distance from a particular establishment as has been specified by the Health and Safety Authority in technical advice, and the Health and Safety Authority has not previously provided, either in relation to the development to which the application relates, or on a generic basis, relevant technical advice on the risk or consequences of a major accident, the planning authority shall notify the Health and Safety Authority.

**[8.207]** Reference to PDR 2001, Sch 8, Table 1 and PDR 2001, Sch 8, Table 2, columns 1 and 2 should be noted. PDR 2001, Sch 8 deals with tables for the purposes of PDR 2001, Pt 11. Table 1 is headed 'Development Categories'. These development categories as provided in Sch 8 are listed below.

### Schedule 8
### Tables For the Purposes of Part II

### TABLE 1
### Development Categories

1. Provisions of hotel, hostel or holiday accommodation or housing.
2. Provision of schools, crèches or other educational or childcare facilities, training centres, hospitals, convalescent homes, homes for the elderly or sheltered accommodation.
3. Retail developments greater than 250 sq. mts. in gross floor area.
4. Structures for community and leisure facilities, greater than 100 sq. mts. in gross floor space.
5. Provision of facilities or use of land for activities likely to attract more than 1000 people at any one time.
6. Commercial or industrial development designed to accommodate 20 or more employees.
7. Provision of parking facilities for more than 200 motor vehicles.
8. Transport links, including public roads.
9. Any development adjoining, or separated only by a road from, an establishment and which poses a risk of fire or explosion.
10. Modifications to categories 2, 3, 4, 6 or 7 which would give rise to an increase in size or capacity of 20% or more.

Table 2 deals with distances from establishments. Column 1 deals with the type of establishment and column 2 deals with the distances from establishment perimeters (metres). Table 2 is set out below.

### TABLE 2

### Distances from Establishments

| Column 1<br>Type of Establishment | Column 2<br>Distance from Establishment perimeter (metres) |
| --- | --- |
| Establishment where pressurised flammable substances (including liquefied petroleum gas) are stored in bulk: | |
| - above ground | |
| - mounded/underground | 600 |
| [not less or equal to] 100 tonnes | 100 |
| - > 100 tonnes | 200 |
| Establishments where pressurised or refrigerated toxic substances (inc. ammonia) are present: | |
| - in bulk storage | 2,000 |
| - in cylinder or drum storage | 700 |
| Establishment consisting of or comprising a warehouse where chemicals are present. | 700 |
| Establishment were non-pressurised flammable substances are stored in bulk. | 300 |
| Establishment where chemical processing involving flammable or toxic substances takes place. | 1,000 |
| Establishment where chemical processing, which involves a risk of dust explosion, takes place. | 300 |
| Establishment where explosives are manufactured. | 1,000[a] |

a. In providing distances from establishments it is significant that Table 2 makes no reference to nuclear establishments.

## Chapter 2: planning appeals (arts 138–141)

**[8.208]** PDR 2001, art 138 provides that where an appeal relates to development in respect of which the planning authority received technical advice from the Health and Safety Authority that technical advice must be submitted to the board with the appeal documents.

**[8.209]** PDR 2001, art 139 provides that where a notice is required under PDR 2001, art 133 and where an appeal relates to the provision of, or modification to an 'establishment', the notice shall indicate that fact. PDR 2001, art 133 deals with the right of the board to require notice of further information where an appeal involves an EIS.[129]

**[8.210]** PDR 2001, art 140 provides that if an appeal relates to development consisting of the provision or modification to an 'establishment', this must be published in the board's weekly list.

**[8.211]** PDR 2001, art 141[130] provides that the board may, if it is of the opinion that the development to be considered by it would be relevant to the risk or consequences of a major accident, and where the planning authority has not already sent notice under art 137, notify the Health and Safety Authority. If the board receives an appeal relating to a development which in its opinion would be of a category listed in Table 1 of Sch 8 and if the development would be located within a distance listed in column 2 of Table 2 of Sch 8 from an establishment of the corresponding type listed in column 1 of Table 2 or where an establishment is located within such distance from the development which is proposed as has been specified by the Health and Safety Authority in technical advice provided under art 39 of the Major Accident Regulations, the board shall notify the Health and Safety Authority. Any such notice sent by the board to the Health and Safety Authority must issue within two weeks of receipt from the planning authority of the documentation referred to in s 128 of the Act.[131] If the appeal relates to an 'establishment', the establishment or establishments must be identified. If the appeal relates to a development which is for the purpose of an activity which requires an integrated pollution control licence or a waste licence, an indication of that fact must also be furnished. PDR 2001, art 137(3)) has now been substituted by the following paragraphs as *per* PDR 2006, art 34(2)(b):

(e) where the appeal relates to development which comprises or is for the purposes of an activity requiring an integrated pollution control licence or waste licence, indicate that fact;

(f) request a determination as to whether the major accidents regulations apply to the proposed development, and

(g) request that, where the Authority determines under (f) above that the Major Accidents Regulations apply to the proposed development, technical advice on the effects of the proposed development on the risk or consequences of a major accident be provided to the planning authority.

---

129. It is clear that the vast majority of industrial activities which are controlled by Directive 96/82/EC, as amended by Directive 2003/105/EC, would require EIA/EIS at the time of making an application for planning permission.
130. PDR 2001, art 141 has been amended by PDR 2006, art 34(1) and (2). Note further that PDR 2006, art 34(2) has been amended by PDR (2) 2007, art 4.
131. PDA 2000, s 128, as substituted by the PD(SI)A 2006 s 21, lists the documents which must be sent by the planning authority to the board in event of appeal, to include a copy of the planning application and all drawings, maps, particulars, evidence, EIS and other written studies or further information received or obtained and a copy of any submissions or observations made in accordance with the regulations together with a copy of any report prepared for the planning authority in relation to the application and a copy of the decision of the planning authority together with any other documents in its possession which are relevant to the matter.

## Chapter 3: local authority development requiring EIA (arts 142–144)

**[8.212]** PDR 2001, art 142 provides that where an application for approval under PDA 2000, s 175 relates to the provision or modification to an establishment, the notice required to be published under PDA 2000, s 157(4) shall indicate that fact.[132]

**[8.213]** PDR 2001, art 143[133] provides that where the local authority's proposed development does require EIA, apart from having to notify the parties referred to in PDR 2001, art 121, the local authority must also notify the Health and Safety Authority, in circumstances where that authority has not given technical advice on the risk or consequence of a major accident. The circumstances in which the notice must be given to the Health and Safety Authority are similar to the circumstances outlined in Ch 1, Pt 11 where notice of planning applications must be given to the authority in certain circumstances.

**[8.214]** PDR 2001, art 144 provides that an application for approval under PDA 2000, s 175 shall include a copy of any relevant technical advice provided by the Health and Safety Authority.

## Chapter 4: local authority development not requiring EIA (arts 145–149)

**[8.215]** PDR 2001, art 145 provides that local authority development not requiring an EIA but which relates to the provision of or modification to an establishment which could have significant repercussions on major accident hazards shall be prescribed for the purposes of PDA 2000, s 179 and the provisions of Pt 8 of the PDR 2001 shall apply.[134]

**[8.216]** PDR 2001, art 146 provides that under PDR 2001, Pt 8, the local authority must publish a newspaper notice and must affix a site notice to the site giving details of the

---

132. PDA 2000, s 175(4) requires a local authority to publish a newspaper notice prior to making an application for approval of proposed local authority development which requires an EIS. The requirement applies where the local authority development proposal includes dangerous substances at or above the levels specified in SI 476/2000.
133. PDA 2000, s 175 provides that EIA may be necessary in the case of development carried out by local authorities in their own functional areas. Regulations under sections dealing with the necessity for EIS in certain local authority developments are contained in PDR 2001, Pt 10, Ch 4, as amended. The local authority's proposed development must be approved by the Minister under PDA 2000, s 175. PDR 2001, art 143(1)(b)(2) is amended by the substitution of 'art 27' for 'art 29' by PDR 2006, art 35.
134. PDA 2000, s 179 provides for public notification of local authority development which does not require EIA under PDA 2000, s 175. PDR 2001, Pt 8 requires submission of a planning report to local authority members on a proposed development, similar to a planning application report. The report must be considered by the elected members who will then vote either to accept, vary or modify or not to proceed with the proposal. If the members fail to make any decision upon the matter, the development may proceed.

## Additional Planning Controls on Land and on Buildings [8.220]

proposed development and, if it is a development to which PDR 2001, Pt 11, Ch 4 applies such notice must indicate that fact.[135]

**[8.217]** PDR 2001, art 147[136] provides that any report prepared by the management of a local authority under the provisions of PDA 2000, s 179(3) shall contain any technical advice received from the Health and Safety Authority.[137]

**[8.218]** PDR 2001, art 148 provides that any report prepared by the manager of a local authority under the provisions of PDA 2000, s 179(3) shall contain any technical advice received from the Health and Safety Authority.

**[8.219]** PDR 2001, art 149 provides that a notice referred to in PDR 2001, art 84 in respect of proposed development referred to in PDR 2001, art 147(1) shall also be sent to the Health and Safety Authority. A notice under PDR 2001, art 84 is a notice served on a body prescribed by PDR 2001, art 82 and on any other persons or bodies who made submissions or observations in respect of the proposed development. An art 84 notice is a notice to be issued at the end of the public consultation process as to whether the local authority will carry out the proposed development or carry out the proposed development with variations or modifications or that it will not proceed with the proposed development. The notice must be served as soon as may be after, as appropriate:

(a) the making of a resolution under PDA 2000, s 179(4)(b); or

(b) the expiry of a period of six weeks after the receipt of the manager's report referred to in PDA 2000, s 179(4).

## Chapter 5: State authority development (art 150)[138]

**[8.220]** The opening sentence of art 150(1) now reads 'In addition to the requirements of art 87 and s 181A(3) of the Act, where –' and art 150(1)(a)(ii) is amended by the substitution of 'art 27' and 'art 29' PDR 2006 (SI 685/2006) which deal, respectively with 'weekly lists of planning applications' and with submissions or observations in relation to planning applications. PDR 2001, art 151 provides, in summary, that notice of proposed State authority development must be given to the Health and Safety Authority where the proposed development would be of a category listed in PDR 2001, Sch 8, Table 1 and is located within the distances listed in PDR 2001, Sch 8, Table 2, column 2 from an establishment of the corresponding type listed in PDR 2001, Sch 8,

---

135. As already seen PDR 2001, Pt 11, Ch 4 deals with local authority development not requiring EIA.
136. As amended by PDR 2006, art 36.
137. PDA 2000, s 179(3), in dealing with local authority own development, provides that at the end of the period for submissions the manager must prepare a written report stating the nature and extent of the development and stating whether or not it is consistent with proper planning and development. It must list the persons who made submissions and must also list issues raised and also recommend whether the development should advance as proposed or whether it should be varied, modified or refused. For full details see s 179(3). The requirements of the report to be prepared by the manager are extensive.
138. PDR 2001, art 150(1)(a)(ii) has been amended by PDR 2006, art 37.

Table 2, column 1 or is located within such distance from a particular establishment as has been specified by the Health and Safety Authority in technical advice given. The regulations and conditions in which notices of proposed State authority development must be given to the Health and Safety Authority are similar to those already dealt with above relating to similar notices in the case of planning applications.

## Chapter 6: declaration and referral under PDA 2000, s 5 (arts 151–155)

[8.221] PDA 2000, s 5 permits an applicant for permission to seek a declaration from the planning authority, and if the applicant disagrees with the contents of that declaration furnished by the planning authority or the planning authority does not furnish a declaration within the prescribed time of four weeks, the applicant may make a referral to An Bord Pleanála for a decision as to whether or not the proposed development is or is not exempted development within the meaning of PDA 2000. A PDA 2000, s 5 declaration in this context, concerns development which relates to the provision or modification to an 'establishment' within the meaning of the Major Accidents Regulations.

[8.222] PDR 2001, art 151 provides that where a planning authority receives a request for a declaration under PDA 2000, s 5 relating to the provisions of or modification to an 'establishment' and, in the opinion of the authority, the development could have significant repercussions on major accident hazards, a copy must be sent to the Health and Safety Authority, as soon as may be, following the request and seeking technical advice on the effects of the proposed development and on the risk or consequences of a major accident.

[8.223] PDR 2001, art 152 provides that in addition to the documents specified in PDA 2000, s 128 a planning authority must also include a copy of any relevant technical advice received from the Health and Safety Authority.[139]

[8.224] PDR 2001, art 153 provides that where the board receives a referral under PDA 2000, s 5 which relates to the provisions of or modifications to an 'establishment' and which, in the board's opinion, could have significant repercussions on major accident hazards, and the planning authority has not already done so, the board shall give notice of the referral to the Health and Safety Authority as soon as may be after receipt of the referral and request technical advice on the affects of the proposed development on the risk or consequences of a major accident.

[8.225] PDR 2001, art 154 notes that the board is required to keep and publish weekly lists of all appeals and referrals received and of all appeals and referrals determined under art 72. Article 154 requires that the board must specifically indicate s 5 referrals which relate to the provision of or modification to an establishment.

---

139. PDA 2000, s 128 sets out the documents to be submitted by a planning authority to the board within two weeks, beginning on the day on which the copy of the appeal or referral is sent to it by the board.

**[8.226]** PDR 2001, art 155 provides that where notice is published under PDA 2000, s 142(4) and the development includes the provision of or modification to an 'establishment', which development could have significant repercussions on major accident hazards, the notice required under PDA 2000, s 142(4) must indicate that fact.[140]

**[8.227]** The aim of Directive 96/82/EC, as amended,[141] is, as far as possible, to prevent major accidents involving dangerous substances and the limitation of their consequences for people and the environment, with a view to ensuring high levels of protection throughout the Community in a consistent and effective manner. Directive 96/82/EC is known as the Seveso II Directive. The Directive, in art 4, has some notable if not surprising exclusions to include the following:

(a) Military establishments, installations or storage facilities;

(b) Hazards created by ionizing radiation;

(c) The transport of dangerous substances and intermediate temporary storage by road, rail, internal waterways, sea or air, outside the establishments covered by this directive, including loading and unloading and transport to and from another means of transport at docks, wharves or marketing yards;

(d) The transport of dangerous substances in pipelines, including pumping stations, outside establishments covered by this directive;

(e) The activities of extractive industries concerned with exploration for, and exploration of minerals in mines and quarries by means of boreholes;

(f) Waste land-fill sites.[142]

**[8.228]** The Seveso II Directive was amended by Directive 2003/105/EC dated 16 December 2003 and recital 2 of that Directive reads:

> In the light of recent industrial accidents and studies on carcinogens and substances, dangerous for the environment carried out by the Commission at the Council's request, the scope of Directive 96/82/EC should be extended.

Reference is made in the recitals of the 2003 Directive to a cyanide spill that polluted the Danube following an accident at Baia Mare in Romania in January 2000. The 2003 Directive also cited the Enschede fireworks accident in May 2000 and the Toulouse explosion of a fertiliser plant in September 2001. Article 1 of the 2003 Directive lists 12 amendments of the Seveso II Directive. Examples of these amendments follows.

**[8.229]** Article 4 of Seveso II dealing with exclusions is amended by para 1 of art 1 of Directive 2003/105/EC. The exclusion relating to the activities of the extractive

---

140. PDA 2000, s 142(4) provides that the board may require any party to an appeal or referral to give public notice in relation to such appeal or referral as the board may specify and it may also require that a notice be placed on the site and/or that the notice be published in a newspaper circulating in the area.

141. See Directive 2003/105/EC.

142. Looked at objectively, not a single matter listed between (a) and (f) should be excluded from the Accidents Hazards Directive. In each case, the exclusion is the result of political expedience which should have no part or influence in such matters.

industries concerned with exploitation for and the extraction of minerals, mines and quarries by means of boreholes was amended and now reads:

> The exploitation (exploration, extraction and processing) of minerals in mines, quarries or by means of boreholes, with the exception of chemical and thermal processing operations and storage related to those operations which involve dangerous substances, as defined in Annex I.[143]

The following addition was made in relation to the exclusion concerning waste landfill sites. The new para (g) of art 4 of Seveso II now reads:

> Waste land-fill sites, with the exception of operational tailings disposal facilities, including tailing ponds or dams, containing dangerous substances as defined in Annex I, in particular when used in connection with chemical and thermal processing of minerals.[144]

[8.230] Article 7 of the Seveso II Directive deals with major accident prevention policy and requires Member States to obtain major accident prevention policy statements from operators of establishments. The obligation to ensure that those policies are properly implemented rests with the Member States. The operators' prevention policy in relation to major accidents is to be designed in such a way as to guarantee a high level of protection for people and the environment by appropriate means, structures and management systems, subject, of course, to the not insignificant list of exceptions, which each have a realistic potential of causing major accidents.

[8.231] Article 8 of the Seveso II Directive deals with what is referred to as 'domino effect'. The purpose of the article is to require Member States to identify establishments or groups of establishments where the likelihood and the possibility of a major accident may be increased because of the location and the proximity of such establishments and because of their inventories of dangerous substances.

[8.232] Article 9 of the Seveso II Directive, as amended by the Directive of 2003, deals with safety reports. Member States are required to ensure that operators produce a safety report. Article 9 sets out the purpose of the safety report as follows:

> (a) Demonstrating that a major-accident prevention policy and a safety management system for implementing it had been put into effect in accordance with the information set out in Annex III;[145]

---

143. Annex I deals with the application of the Seveso Directive (as amended) in relation to the presence of dangerous substances at an establishment listing the substances or mixtures of substances and the qualifying quantities which would bring the establishment within the terms of the Seveso II Directive.
144. One of these caught fire in Kildare in February 2011 and some people in the area were forced to vacate their homes because they were correctly anxious about noxious fumes entering their homesteads.
145. Seveso II Directive, art 7 deals with major accident prevention policy and Seveso II Directive, art 9 deals with the safety management system operated in the establishment. Seveso II Directive, Annex III sets out the principles referred to in art 7 and the information referred to in art 9 on the management system and organisation of the establishment with a view to prevention of major accidents.

(b) Demonstrating that major-accident hazards have been identified and that the necessary measures have been taken to prevent such accidents and to limit their consequences for man and the environment;

(c) Demonstrating that adequate safety and reliability have been incorporated into the design, construction, operation and maintenance of any installation, storage facility, equipment and infrastructure connected with its operation which are linked to major-accident hazards inside the establishment;

(d) Demonstrating that internal emergency plans have been drawn up and supplying information to enable the external plan to be drawn up in order to take the necessary measures in the event of a major accident;

(e) Providing sufficient information to the competent authorities to enable decisions to be made in terms of citing of new activities or developments around existing establishments.

**[8.233]** Pt 2 of art 9 (as amended) provides the following:

(2) The safety report shall contain at least the data and information listed in Annex II.[146] It shall name the relevant organisations involved in the drawing up of the report. It shall also contain an updated inventory of the dangerous substances present in the establishment.

**[8.234]** Article 10 of the Seveso II Directive deals with modification of an installation, an establishment or a storage facility and, in the event of the modification which could have significant repercussions on major accident hazards, Member States must ensure that the operator reviews and where necessary revises the major accident prevention policy and the management systems and procedures referred to in arts 7 and 9. A Member State must also ensure, in the event of modification under art 10, that a review is carried out where necessary of the safety report and that the competent authorities are informed of the details of any revision prior to the modification or revision being carried out.

**[8.235]** Article 11 requires that Member States ensure that operators of establishments draw up an internal emergency plan for the measures to be taken in the event of a major accident.

**[8.236]** The emergency plans must be established with the objectives of:

– containing and controlling incidents so as to minimise the effects, and to limit damage to man, the environment and property,

– implementing the measures necessary to protect man and the environment from the effects of major accidents,

---

146. Seveso II Directive, Annex II lists the minimum data and information to be considered in the safety report required under Seveso II Directive, art 9. The headings include the following: Information on the Management System and Organisation of the Establishment with a view to Major Accident Prevention; Presentation of the Environment of the Establishment; Description of the Installation; Identification and Accidental Risks Analysis and Prevention Methods; Measures of Protection and Intervention to limit the consequences of an Accident.

- communicating the necessary information to the public and to the services or authorities concerned in the area,
- providing for the restoration and clean-up of the environment following a major accident.

Emergency plans shall contain the information set out in Annex IV.[147]

**[8.237]** Article 12 of the Seveso II Directive, as amended by art 1(7) of Directive 96/82/EC, requires Member States to ensure that the objectives of preventing major accidents and limiting the consequences of such accidents are taken into account in their land use policies to ensure that appropriate distances are maintained between establishments covered by the Directive and residential areas, buildings and areas of public use, major transport routes, recreational areas and areas of particular natural sensitivity or interest and, in the case of existing establishments, that account will be taken in land use policies of the need for additional technical measures in accordance with art 5 so as not to increase the risk to people.

**[8.238]** Article 13 of the Seveso II Directive, as amended, requires that Member States will ensure that information on safety measures and on the requisite behaviour in the event of an accident is supplied regularly, and in the most appropriate form, to all persons and establishments serving the public (such as schools and hospitals) liable to be affected by the major accident originating in an establishment covered by art 9. The information on safety measures and on the requisite behaviour in the event of an accident is to be supplied whether or not it is requested, and the information should be reviewed every three years and updated. The information must be made permanently available to the public. The information on safety measures shall contain as a minimum the information listed in Annex V. Annex V requires the following disclosures to be made to the public in furnishing information safety measures under art 13 namely:

1. Name of operator and address of the establishment.

2. Identification, by position held, of the person giving the information.

3. Confirmation that the establishment is subject to the regulations and/or administrative provisions implementing this Directive and that the notification referred to in art 6(3), or the safety report referred to in art 9(1) has been submitted to the competent authority.

4. An explanation in simple terms of the activity or activities undertaken at the establishment.

5. The common names or, in the case of dangerous substances covered by Part 2 of Annex I, the generic names or the general danger classification of the substances and preparations involved at the establishment which could give rise to a major accident, with an indication of their principal dangerous characteristics.

---

147. See Seveso II Directive, art 11 as amended by Directive 2003/105/EC, art 1(6). Seveso II Directive, Annex IV lists the information which is to be included in the emergency plan specified under art 11.

## Additional Planning Controls on Land and on Buildings [8.244]

6. General information relating to the nature of the major-accident hazards, including their potential effects on the population and the environment.

7. Adequate information on how the population concerned will be warned and kept informed in the event of a major accident.

8. Adequate information on the actions the population concerned should take, and on the behaviour they should adopt, in the event of a major accident.

9. Confirmation that the operator is required to make adequate arrangements on site, in particular, liaison with the emergency services, to deal with major accidents and to minimise their effects.

10. A reference to the external emergency plan drawn up to cope with any off-site effects from an accident. This should include advice to co-operate with any instructions or requests from the emergency services at the time of an accident.

11. Details of where further relevant information can be obtained, subject to the requirements of confidentiality laid down in national legislation.

**[8.239]** Article 14 requires an operator to furnish information following a major accident by informing the competent authorities and providing them with information on the circumstance of the accident, the dangerous substances involved, the data available for assessing the effects of the accident on people and the environment, and the emergency measures taken.

**[8.240]** Article 15 requires Member States to inform the Commission, as soon as practicable, of any major accidents meeting the criteria of Annex VI which have occurred within their territory. Annex VI sets out the criteria for notification of an accident to the Commission.

**[8.241]** Article 16 requires Member States to appoint a competent authority or authorities responsible for carrying out the duties laid down in this Directive.

**[8.242]** Article 17 provides that Member States are entitled to issue a prohibition order against establishments or installations or storage facilities where inadequate steps have been taken by the operator for the prevention and mitigation of major accidents and where those provisions for prevention and mitigation are seriously deficient. Member States may also prohibit the use or the bringing into use of any establishment, installation or storage facility where the operator has not submitted the notification, reports or other information required by the Directive. In the event of a prohibition of use order issuing, Member States shall ensure that the operators are entitled to appeal to an appropriate body determined by national law and procedures.

**[8.243]** Article 18 requires Member States to ensure that competent authorities organise a system of inspections of establishments and detailed criteria are set out in the article as to the method of inspection.

**[8.244]** Article 19 requires that Member States and the Commission exchange information on experiences acquired with regard to prevention of major accidents and the limitation of their consequences. The Commission is required to set up and keep at the disposal of Member States a register and information system containing, in particular, details of the major accidents which have occurred within the territory of the Member States. For establishments covered by the Directive, Member States shall supply the Commission with at least the following information:

(a) the name or trade name of the operator and the full address of the establishment concerned;

(b) the activity or activities of the establishment.[148]

## MINERAL DEVELOPMENT

[8.245] Mineral development is another activity which may frustrate an owner of property from normal enjoyment of his lands or premises. Exploration and extraction are the fundamental aspects of mineral development which are under government control. There are two principal groups of legislation which cover mineral development in Ireland, namely:

1. the Minerals Development Acts 1960–1995 dealing with valuable minerals generally;

2. the Petroleum and Other Minerals Development Acts 1960–1995 dealing specifically with mineral oils and hydrocarbons including gas.

All extraction of minerals under these two Acts, with the exception of the extraction of offshore gas more than 10km offshore, requires EIA.

[8.246] The mineral development legislation did stop short of transferring the ownership of all minerals to the State. Effectively, however, the State has a stranglehold on minerals in that it enjoys exclusive rights to extract and exploit minerals and that exclusive right does not differentiate between minerals on or under public property or on or under private property.

[8.247] Persons deprived of their extraction and exploitation rights by the provisions of the Mineral Development Act 1979 are entitled to be compensated. Compensation is calculated by reference to the net profit made from the extraction of the relevant minerals before any account is taken of any added value achieved by exploitation. If there is no agreement between the Minister and the landowner, the determination of the value of the compensation will be fixed by the Mining Board established under the Minerals Development Act 1979 subject to a right of appeal by either party to the High Court.

---

148. The purpose of **Pt 6 of Ch 8** herein dealing with the Major Accident Hazards Directive is to introduce the reader to the main principles and to the manner in which the accident hazard legislation operates. For a full understanding it will be necessary to read fully Directive 96/82/EC. Another essential document which should be studied is the European Communities (Control of Major Accident Hazards involving dangerous substances) Regulations 2006 (SI 74/2006) which regulations bring the Seveso II provisions, as amended, into Irish law.

**[8.248]** Prospecting licences which, by their very nature, may interfere with the development rights of a landowner, are issued by the Minister for Communications, Marine & Natural Resources. Prospecting licences are strictly limited to the prospector. The licences do not imply any right to sell or dispose of the mineral or minerals which are subject to the prospecting licence.

**[8.249]** Extraction licences will interfere more dramatically than prospecting licences with a landowner's development rights. Extraction licences are issued by the Minister for Communications, Marine and Natural Resources subject to such conditions as the Minister considers to be appropriate.

**[8.250]** A less formal extraction licence may be issued for small scale extractions and this is called a 'State mining permission'. The procedures for obtaining this licence are less arduous than the procedures for an extraction licence.

**[8.251]** Owners of buildings, the stability of which may be affected by licensed mining operations, can apply for a 'preservation of support order' but the conditions for obtaining such an order are especially stringent.[149] The following conditions must be satisfied by the applicant:

(1) that the mining operation is in progress, or is reasonably apprehended to occur, under or adjacent to the land where the building stands or is intended to stand;

(2) that the applicant has satisfied the Attorney General that he is not entitled in law to such a right of support as would enable him to obtain relief in the courts; and

(3) that it is not reasonably practicable for the applicant to reach a private agreement for a right of support which would effectively preserve the stability of the building.

If those three conditions apply and the Minister is satisfied that there is a *prima facie* case for granting a preservation of support order, the Minister will refer the matter to the Mining Board. The Mining Board, having considered the matter, will report back to the Minister and it is at that point that the Minister will decide whether or not to grant the order.[150]

**[8.252]** The provisions of the Petroleum and Other Minerals Development Acts 1960–1995 are distinct from the Mineral Development Acts in that the mineral oil, and all relevant hydrocarbons and natural gases[151] are the property of the Minister for Communications, Marine and Natural Resources. Compensation is payable to affected landowners and the amount payable is one-third of the royalty rent payable under the terms of the petroleum lease.[152] Compensation is only payable when the petroleum is brought to the surface, which might imply long periods of disruption without payment of compensation.

---

149. See the Mineral Development Act 1940, ss 44–47.
150. See the Mineral Development Act 1940, ss 44–47.
151. See Petroleum and Other Minerals Development Act 1960, s 2.
152. See Petroleum and Other Minerals Development Act 1960, ss 5 and 36.

**[8.253]** A petroleum and other hydrocarbons exploration licence does not grant any right of entry or access to or over the land the subject matter of the licence. Entry/access permission must be obtained by separate negotiation with the relevant landowners/ occupiers. A petroleum prospecting licence may be distinguished from an exploration licence in that it does not entitle the licensee to enter the land and carry out all actions consistent with the petroleum prospecting.[153] All petroleum prospecting licences must contain a condition that the licensee will not interfere unnecessary with the amenities of the area the subject matter of the licence.

## PROTECTED/PROPOSED PROTECTED STRUCTURES

### Introduction

**[8.254]** It is beyond argument that there is a necessity to preserve outstanding structures of historic architectural design and to protect streetscapes which are part of an historical town or a city. Owning and/or living in a protected structure gives great pleasure in that our ancestors, in most cases, had a far more generous sense of proportion in providing large rooms with high ceilings. Usually, each room was given a separate purpose. Many older houses were designed 'for living in' while today's houses are designed to be practical, maintainable by a family without outside help, and are often built in large numbers with an eye to profitability on the part of the developer. The living area in modern houses is substantially decreased and it is not unusual to see a kitchen, dining room and living room all in the one space, without walled divisions. Some of our ancestors also believed in providing a generous amount of garden and amenity space around the house and, for many people, the old designs do create a more pleasant and harmonious living space. In many cases, the generous garden space provided was not just ornamental. It was also a practical necessity for growing fruit and vegetables which were not, at that time, readily available on the supermarket shelf.

**[8.255]** There are many examples where structures have been protected because local groups, including An Taisce, make a subjective decision in a local area to persuade the local authority to protect a usually worthy but a sometimes unworthy structure. That is not to say that groups such as An Taisce have not, frequently, assisted the protection process to great advantage, but the decision as to whether a structure should be protected is, in some cases at least, haphazard. In view of the very considerable and onerous responsibilities which are imposed on the owner or occupier of a protected structure, which are dealt with below, there is a compelling argument in favour of setting up a division within An Bord Pleanála to which an application to have a structure/ structures protected could be made by local authorities either on their own initiative or when prompted by Dúchas, An Taisce or other national and local groups. Such a division within An Bord Pleanála would need to be controlled by strict guidelines to ensure uniformity and fairness in making its decisions. Such a body would eventually build up experience and precedent which would go some way towards ruling out the

---

153. See the Petroleum and Minerals Development Act 1960, s 8(2)&(3).

protection of unworthy structures. It would take account of the necessity, which is a very real necessity, to allow architects working in the 21st century to reflect the standards of our time and to put their own mark on the design of structures in cities, towns and in rural areas as, indeed, they have done in many places.

[8.256] There are some very strange buildings and structures which have found their way into the list of protected structures, including some undistinguished old buildings which are seriously derelict and which have long since passed their 'sell by date'. Such structures, among many others, are clearly visible in our principal towns and cities and there is a notable example at the north end of Smithfield in Dublin where the buildings are both utterly derelict and protected. That is an unacceptable contradiction which has produced a stalemate situation. It has existed for some 25 years or more. A time must inevitably come when the life of a building has reached its limits and this is something which should be clearly stated in the legislation and in the guidelines. Provision is made in the Act to add or delete from its records of protected structures, either a structure or a specified part of a structure, or a specified feature on the attendant grounds of a structure, when it considers that either the addition or deletion is desirable. Nevertheless, the decision to either add or delete is a reserved function, which must be made by the elected members of a planning authority. From the point of view of proper planning, it would be preferable if this decision was made by An Bord Pleanála as there is no evidence to suggest that the elected representatives have any particular, specialist planning or conservation expertise.

[8.257] PDA 2000, Pt IV is headed 'architectural heritage'. Chapter 6, ss 51–80 deal with protected structures and Ch 2 deals with architectural conservation areas and areas of special planning control.

## Definitions

[8.258] PDA 2000, s 2 provides definitions of three words and three phrases all of which are essential to an understanding of architectural heritage:

> 'Protection' in relation to a structure or part of a structure, includes conservation, preservation and improvement compatible with maintaining the character and interest of the structure or part;
> 
> 'Structure' means any building, structure, excavation, or other thing constructed or made on, in or under any land, or any part of a structure so defined, and –
> 
> > (a) Where the context so admits, includes the land on, in or under which the structure is situate, and
> > 
> > (b) In relation to a protected structure or a proposed protected structure, includes –
> > 
> > > (i) the interior of a structure,
> > > 
> > > (ii) the land lying within the curtilage or the structure,
> > > 
> > > (iii) any other structures lying within that curtilage and there interiors, and

(iv) all fixtures and features which form part of the interior or exterior of any structure or structures referred to in sub-paragraph (i) or (iii);

'Works' includes any act or operation of construction, excavation, demolition, extension, alteration, repair or renewal and, in relation to a protected structure or proposed protected structure, includes any act or operation involving the application or removal of plaster, paint, wallpaper, tiles or other material to or from the surfaces of the interior or exterior of a structure;

'Proposed protected structure' means a structure in respect of which a notice is issued under section 12(3) or under section 55 proposing to add the structure, or a specified part of it, to a record of protected structures, and, where that notice so indicates, includes any specified feature which is within the attendant grounds of the structure and which would not otherwise be included in this definition;

'Protected structure' means –

(a) a structure, or
(b) a specified part of a structure, which is included in a record of protected structures, and, where that record so indicates, includes any specified feature which is within the attendant grounds of the structure and which would not otherwise be included in this definition.

'Attendant grounds', in relation to a structure, includes land lying outside the curtilage of the structure.

**[8.259]** PDA 2000, s 51 provides that all planning authorities are required to keep a record of protected structures as part of their development plan for their area in order to protect structures which form part of the architectural heritage and which are of special architectural, historical, archaeological, artistic, cultural, scientific, social or technical interest.

**[8.260]** PDR 2001, art 51 provides details which are to be included in the record of protected structures. In preparing a record of protected structures planning authorities should have regard to the *Guidelines for Planning Authorities on Architectural Heritage Protection* which were first published on 23 February 2005. PDR 2001, art 51 requires a record of protected structures to record the following:

(1) (a) In respect of each protected structure –
  (i) An identifying number,
  (ii) An address,
(b) One or more maps showing the location of each protected structure to a scale that enables a clear identification of such structures, and
(c) Any other information that the planning authority considers necessary.

(2) A map referred to in sub-article 1(b) may, in addition to the information referred to in that sub-article, contain other information.

The 2005 Guidelines require that the planning authority should list each protected structure within its functional area by reference to a single numbered list, ordered alphabetically by postal address. Each protected structure must be separately identified so that if, for example, a terrace of houses has been protected each separate house in the terrace must have a separate entry in the record of protected structures. In rural areas, the most important identifying reference is the townland in which the protected structure is situate and where there are several townlands of the same name within the functional area of the planning authority then the townland should be accompanied by the electoral ward, or the name of the nearest postal town should be furnished.

**[8.261]** PDR 2001, art 51 requires emphatically that the location of each protected structure is marked on as large a scale map as practicable.

**[8.262]** Where a structure is designated a protected structure or a proposed protected structure the area of protection includes the curtilage of such structure. Unhappily, the word 'curtilage' has not been statutorily defined.

**[8.263]** Subject to any additions or deletions made to the record, either under this Part or in the course of a review of the development plan under Part II, a record of protected structures shall continue to be part of that development plan or any variation or replacement of the development plan. The map on which the area of a protected structure or a proposed protected structure is marked should be carefully drawn by the planning authority and the curtilage should be clearly outlined. The Architectural Heritage Guidelines 2004 define curtilage as 'a parcel of land immediately associated with the protected structure and which was or is in use for the purposes of the structure'. Curtilage should not be confused with the term 'attendant grounds' of structures. PDA 2000, s 2 defines 'attendant grounds' as 'in relation to a structure, includes lands lying outside the curtilage of a structure'.

**[8.264]** The meaning of 'curtilage' is defined in the *Oxford English Dictionary* as 'a small court, yard, garth or piece of ground attached to a dwelling house and forming one enclosure with it or so regarded by the law; the area attached to and containing a dwelling house and its outbuildings'. The curtilage of a house is ground which serves or served the purpose of the house or building in some necessary or reasonably useful way. It does not have to be physically enclosed. The use of any structure or other land within the curtilage of a house must be or have been for a purpose incidental to the enjoyment of the house as such. It seems from case law that the yardstick is always one of reasonableness. It has been held, for example, that the storage of a replica spitfire aeroplane in a garden of a dwelling house was not incidental to the enjoyment of a dwelling house as such. Using a flat patch in a garden as a helipad for flying to and from the house by helicopter might or might not be a use of land within the curtilage of a house which is incidental to the enjoyment of the house as such. There have, however, been several citations which ask the question:

> What is the nature and scale of the activity which was said to be incidental to the enjoyment of the dwelling house as such?

The more dominant the activity, the less likely it is to be described as incidental. The indulgence of a hobby was more likely to qualify than some commercial activity. Perhaps helicopter flying is a hobby and undoubtedly the owner of a dwelling house would consider it as such but his neighbours might consider that the noise and intrusion of helicopters flying in and out of a residential garden in a reasonably built up area was not a reasonable use and that it could not, in the ordinary sense, be described as being incidental to the enjoyment of the house as such. These are the type of questions which are difficult to answer but by way of a general statement it is clear that the ordinary user of a dwelling house in general does not require planning permission.

**[8.265]** A definition of curtilage appeared in the English case of *Sinclair Lockhart's Trustees v Central Land Board*[154] as:

> Ground which is used for the comfortable enjoyment of a house ... and thereby as an integral part of the same, although it has not been marked off or enclosed in any way. It is enough that it serves the purposes of the house ... in some necessary or reasonably useful way.

The matter was considered in Ireland in *Begley and Clarke v An Bord Pleanála, South Dublin County Council*.[155] An application for permission for the development of apartments and ancillary works in the curtilage of Riversdale House, Rathfarnham, a protected structure, was refused by An Bord Pleanála. Ó Caoimh J held against the applicant and the applicant subsequently made an application for leave to appeal to the Supreme Court.[156] Ó Caoimh J refused leave to appeal and set out his findings more precisely than at the original hearing. It was the applicant's case that the record of protected structures included the dwelling, Riversdale House, Rathfarnham, the original gates, piers and arched bridge, at the old entrance on Ballyboden Road. The gates, piers and arched bridge were specified features within the attendant grounds of Riversdale House, the protected structure. Thus, the planning authority had included only specified parts of the structure in the record of protected structures namely, Riversdale House itself, the original gates, and the bridge over a stream but it did not include the grounds forming part of the curtilage. Ó Caoimh J disagreed with that construction and held that having regard to the definition of 'structure' in the LG(PD)A 1990, s 1(1) (now PDA 2000, s 1) the protection extended to the curtilage of Riversdale House and consequently the applicant's proposal to build apartments was a proposal to build apartments within the curtilage of Riversdale House and, as such, the curtilage could not be excluded from the 'protected structure'.

**[8.266]** The court of appeal in England in *Methuen-Campbell v Walters*[157] decided that whether land fell within the curtilage of a house was a question of fact. Buckley LJ had this to say:

> What then is meant by the curtilage of property? In my judgment it is not sufficient to constitute two pieces of land parts of one and the same curtilage that

---

154. *Sinclair Lockhart's Trustees v Central Land Board* [1950] 1 P&CR 195, (1951) SC 258.
155. *Begley and Clarke v An Bord Pleanála, South Dublin County Council* (unreported, 14 January 2003) HC.
156. *Begley and Clarke v An Bord Pleanála, South Dublin County Council* (unreported, 23 May 2003) HC.
157. *Methuen-Campbell v Walters* [1979] 1 All ER 606.

they should have been conveyed or demised together, for a single conveyance or lease can comprise more than one parcel of land, neither of which need be in any sense an appurtenance of the other or within the curtilage of the other ... in my judgment, for one corporeal hereditament to fall within the curtilage of another, the former must be so intimately associated with the latter as to lead to the conclusion that the former in truth forms part and parcel of the latter. There can be very few houses indeed that do not have associated with them at least some few square yards of land, constituting a yard or a basement area or passageway or something of the kind, owned and enjoyed with the house, which on a reasonable view could only be regarded as part of the messuage and such small pieces of land would be held to fall within the curtilage of the messuage. This may extend to ancillary buildings, structures, areas such as outhouses, a garage, a driveway, a garden and so forth. How far it is appropriate to regard this identity as parts of one messuage or parcel of land as extending must depend on the character and circumstances of items under consideration. To the extent that it is reasonable to regard them as constituting one messuage or parcel of land, they will be properly regarded as all falling within one curtilage; they constitute one integral whole.[158]

Although some assistance is given in PDA 2000, s 51 as to the basis upon which a planning authority will make a decision to include a structure in its record of protected structures, the guidance given is minimal. A structure to be included must be of special interest in terms of architectural, historical, archaeological, artistic, cultural, scientific, technical and/or social interest. Also PDA 2000, s 10(2)(f), in dealing with the contents of development plans, provides that a development plan shall include objectives for *'the protection of structures or parts of structures, which are of special architectural, historical, archaeological, artistic, cultural, scientific, technical and/or social interest.'*

**[8.267]** In effect, it can be seen that PDA 2000, s 10(2)(f) does not really take the matter any further than the provisions of PDA 2000, s 51(1).

**[8.268]** In seeking assistance as to what should or should not be included in the record of protected structures the next step is to examine the ministerial guidelines issued by the Department of Environment, Heritage and Local Government. These guidelines have been issued pursuant to a mandatory requirement imposed by s 52(1) which provides that the Minister for Arts, Heritage, Gaeltacht and the Islands shall, after consulting with the Minister for Environment, Heritage and Local Government issue guidelines to planning authorities to assist the planning authority in making its decision as to what type of structures or parts of structures should be included in the register of protected structures. However, the heritage functions of the Minister for Arts, Gaeltacht and the Islands were transferred to what is now the Minister for the Environment, Heritage and Local Government[159] so that effectively under PDA 2000, s 52(1) and (2) the Minister is required to consult with himself.

---

158. *Methuen-Campbell v Walters* [1979] 1 All ER 606 *per* Buckley LJ.
159. This transfer was affected by the Heritage (Transfer of Departmental and Ministerial Functions) Order 2002 (SI 356/2002).

**[8.269]** Simons observes as follows:

> The fact that separate functions of issuing the guidelines and consultation now reside in one person, namely the Minister for the Environment, Heritage and Local Government, might be thought to offend against the principal confirmed in *Mulcreevy v Minister for the Environment, Heritage and Local Government*[160] that procedural safeguards provided for under primary legislation cannot be amended by way of secondary or delegated legislation. The safeguard of a requirement that there be consultation with a separate Minister before guidelines be issued has, in effect, been removed as a result of secondary legislation transferring Ministerial functions.[161]

**[8.270]** PDA 2000, s 52(2) provides that specific ministerial guidelines may be issued by the Minister for Arts, Heritage, Gaeltacht and the Islands after consulting with the authorities of any religious denominations which he or she considers necessary being guidelines concerning:

(a) The issue of declarations under section 57 in respect of protected structures which are regularly used as places of public worship and

(b) The consideration by planning authorities of applications for development affecting the interior of such structures.

**[8.271]** The Department of the Environment published *Guidelines for Planning Authorities on Architectural Heritage Protection for Places of Public Worship* (November 2003). As guidelines they are just that and while PDA 2000, s 52(3) requires that in considering development objectives a planning authority shall have regard to the guidelines, they are not bound by them. In *Sherwin v An Bord Pleanála*,[162] Edwards J had this to say:

> Finally, I should say something about the guidance material relied upon by An Bord Pleanála. Nobody is suggesting for a second that An Bord Pleanála were not entitled to have regard to the guidance material in question. However, they ought to have borne in mind that guidance cannot alter or displace substantive and established law. Legislation cannot be altered by guidance. The guidance must be with respect to how to proceed in a particular legal context. The guidance cannot itself alter and seek to alter that particular legal context. In other words a Minister cannot amend or add to existing legislation in the course of issuing guidance.

In the course of his judgment in *Sherwin v An Bord Pleanála*,[163] Edwards J held that if particular works are found to materially alter the interior of a protected structure then the normal exemption which applies to the interior of structures will not apply even if the alteration is required by the liturgical requirements of the religion.

---

160. *Mulcreevy v Minister for the Environment, Heritage and Local Government* [2004] 1 IR 72, SC.
161. See Simons, *Planning and Development Law* (2nd edn, Thomson Round Hall, 2007) at p 346, para 8-09.
162. *Sherwin v An Bord Pleanála* [2007] IEHC 227, Edwards J.
163. *Sherwin v An Bord Pleanála* [2007] IEHC 227, Edwards J.

**[8.272]** The meaning of 'have regard to' was considered in *McEvoy & Smith v Meath County Council*.[164] The provision of PDA 2000, s 27(1) requiring a planning authority to have regard to any regional planning guidelines in force for its area when making and adopting a development plan were considered by Quirke J who held that the obligation in s 27(1) to have regard to strategic planning guidelines when drafting the county development plan was permissive rather than mandatory. A planning authority is obliged by s 27(1) to inform itself fully and to give reasonable consideration to the guidelines with a view to accommodating the objectives and policies contained therein. However, planning authorities are not bound to comply with the guidelines and they may depart from them for *bona fide* reasons consistent with proper planning and development of the area.

**[8.273]** The marginal note to PDA 2000, s 57 reads: 'Words affecting character of protected structures or proposed protected structures'. PDA 2000, s 57(1), as amended by PD(A)A 2010, s 34, specifically provides that:

> Notwithstanding section 4(1)(a), (h), (i), (j), (k) or (l) and any regulations made under section 4(2) the carrying out of works to a protected structure, or a proposed protected structure shall be exempted development only if those works would not materially affect the character of –
> 
> (a) the structure, or
> 
> (b) any element of the structure which contributes to its special architectural, historical, archaeological, artistic, cultural, scientific, social or technical interest.

**[8.274]** PDA 2000, s 4(1) lists specific developments which are exempted developments for the purposes of the Act. PDA 2000, s 4(1) includes:

> (a) development consisting of the use of any land for the purpose of agriculture and development consisting of the use for that purpose of any building occupied together with the lands so used;
> 
> (h) development consisting of the carrying out of works for the maintenance, improvement or other alteration of any structure, being works which affect only the interior of the structure or which do not materially affect the external appearance of the structure so as to render the appearance inconsistent with the character of the structure or of neighbouring structures;
> 
> (i) development consisting of the thinning, felling or replanting of trees, forests or woodlands or works ancillary to that development, but not including the replacement of broadleaf high forest by conifer species;[165]
> 
> (ia) development (other than where the development consists of provision of access to a public road) consisting of the construction, maintenance or improvement of a road (other than a public road) or works ancillary to such road development, where the road serves forests and woodlands.[166]

---

164. *McEvoy & Smith v Meath County Council* [2003] 1 IR 208, HC, Quirke J.
165. PDA 2000, s 4(1)(i) has been amended by the PD(A)A 2010, s 5A(1)(ii) and the amendments are as outlined above.
166. PDA 2000, s 4(1)(ia) as amended by PD(A)A 2010, s 5(a)(ii).

(I) Development consisting of the carrying out of any of the works referred to in the Land Reclamation Act 1949, not being works comprised in the fencing or enclosure of land which has been open to or used by the public within ten years preceding the date on which the works are commenced or works consisting of land reclamation or reclamation of estuarine marshland and of callows, referred to in section 2 of that Act.[167]

[8.275] It should also be noted that s 4(4)(a) and (b) of PDA 2000 has been amended and now reads as follows:

(a) Notwithstanding subsections (1)(a)(i), or (l) and any regulations made under subsection 2, development commenced on or after the coming into operation of this section shall not be exempted development if an environmental impact assessment of the development is required.

(b) The Minister may, for the purposes of giving further effect to the Habitats Directive and requirements of efficiency and effectiveness in the control of proper planning and sustainable development, prescribe development or classes of development (whether or not by reference to an area or a class of areas in which the development is carried out) which, notwithstanding subsections (1)(a), and (h) to (j), and any regulations made under subsection (2) shall not be exempted development.[168]

In effect, PDA 2000, s 57(1) provides that the carrying out of works to a protected structure will require planning permission even if those works would normally be exempt under s 4, where the works would affect the character of a protected structure or of a proposed protected structure or any element of those structures.

[8.276] Owners and occupiers of protected structures sometimes overlook the prohibition against carrying out a development to the interior of a structure. The interior is part of the protected structure and the general exemption which excuses the necessity for planning permission for interior alterations does not, in most cases, apply to protected structures. Also, when one examines the definition of 'structure' it can be seen that it includes other structures lying within the curtilage of a protected structure. In effect, a line may be drawn around the house and gardens of a protected structure and anything within that line will be protected so that even if a modern glass house was added to the structure, just before it became a protected structure that glass house is also protected even though it may have no architectural merit. In such a case it might be fairly said that some of the provisions relating to protected structures contained in PDA 2000 have been drafted in a lazy and indiscriminate manner, which does little to help serious conservationists win the respect of the general public for their cause.

## Consequences of designation

[8.277] PDA 2000, s 57(1) had referred specifically to de-exemption of categories of work referred to in PDA 2000, s 4(1)(h). The Act before the amendment had restricted de-exemption to works on the interior of a premises. In *Córas Iompair Éireann v An*

---

167. PDA 2000, s 4(1) as amended by PD(A)A 2010, s 5(a)(iii) by insertion of the works in heavy type.
168. PD(A)A 2010, s 5(b), (4)(a)and(b).

*Bord Pleanála*,[169] Clarke J held that the literal interpretation of s 57(1) in making specific reference only to PDA 2000, s 4(1)(h) produced an absurd result and the learned judge ruled that the proper interpretation of the section would include exempted development categories under the 2001 Regulations. The drafting error has now been cured by the provisions of s 34 of PD(A)A 2010. In consequence, all exempted development defined in PDA 2000, s 4(1), (2), (3) and (4) and all exempted development listed in PDR 2001 (as amended) are de-exempted where the carrying out of works is to a protected structure where the works would affect the character of the structure or of the protected structure or of the proposed protected structure or any element of that structure. This, of course, does not mean that all works carried out to a protected structure are prohibited but it does mean that such works will require an application for and a grant of planning permission. It should also be noted that the words used in sub-s (1) apply to 'works' and do not apply to 'uses' of the protected structure. Therefore the exemption referable to use, where it is applicable, can still be claimed in respect of the changes of use of a protected structure.

[8.278] The meaning of the 'character' of the structure was discussed in *McCabe v Córas Iompair Éireann*.[170] In that case, CIE renewed and reconstructed parts of a railway bridge. The work did not amount to a total or substantial replacement or renewal or reconstruction but the question which arose was whether the works had changed the character of the bridge to such an extent that it could not reasonably be said that the bridge was the same bridge after the alterations and improvements had been completed. Herbert J in discussing whether the works carried out did or did not materially affect the character, design and external appearance of the bridge stated that:

> The court must assess the character of the structure by looking objectively at the entity as a whole and while one observer might consider that the character of the bridge lay in its environmental context and overall dimensions, its locus height, width, length and dimensions of the road opening; another might see its character in the type, cut, colour, size and placement of its structure, materials and ornamental work; while yet another might see the semi-circular voussoir arches and spandrels as entirely determining its character. I found that it is all of these features taken together and all other features to which I have adverted and their interaction with each other which gives a structure such as this its character.[171]

In that case, Herbert J concluded that the appearance of the bridge after the works had been carried out was not inconsistent with the character of the bridge and accordingly found that the development in question was exempted development under PDA 2000, s 4(1)(h).

[8.279] Section 57 provides for declarations seeking clarification from the planning authority as to whether proposed works would or would not affect the character of a protected structure or of a proposed protected structure or any element of the structure, etc.

---

169. *CIÉ v An Bord Pleanála* (unreported, 19 June 2008) HC, Clarke J.
170. *McCabe v CIÉ* [2007] 2 IR 392, Herbert J.
171. *McCabe v CIÉ* [2007] 2 IR 392 *per* Herbert J.

**[8.280]** PDA 2000, s 57(2) permits an owner of occupier of a protected structure to seek a declaration from the planning authority as to what works the local authority would consider as not materially affecting the character of the structure or any element of the structure which contributes to its architectural, historical, archaeological, artistic, cultural, scientific, social or technical interest. Any request for a declaration must be submitted in writing to the planning authority. The planning authority has 12 weeks in which to furnish the declaration.[172] In preparing the declaration the planning authority must have regard to any guidelines issued under s 52 and to any recommendations made to the authority under s 53. Any declaration which relates to a protected structure that is regularly used as a place of public worship requires that the planning authority or the board in addition to having regard to the relevant guidelines shall also respect liturgical requirements which requirements are ascertained by having regard to the guidelines concerning consultations or if there are no guidelines by consulting with such person or body as the planning authority considers appropriate.[173] When considering an application made to the planning authority or an appeal to the board the planning authority and the board respectively shall respect liturgical requirements where the application/appeal relates to the interior of a protected structure which is regularly used as a place of public worship.[174]

**[8.281]** A declaration which is issued may at any time be reviewed by a planning authority but the review will not affect any works carried out in reliance of the declaration prior to the review.[175]

**[8.282]** The details of any s 57 declaration issued by a planning authority or details of a decision of the board on a referral must be entered in the planning register and, in consequence, should be revealed by a planning search which is made on the register. Also, a copy of the planning authority's declaration or the board's decision, as appropriate, must be made available for inspection by members of the public during office hours at the offices of the authority.[176]

**[8.283]** PDA 2000, s 57(10)(a) provides that for the avoidance of doubt a planning authority or the board on appeal:

(i) In considering any application for permission in relation to protected structure, shall have regard to the protected status of the structure, or

(ii) In considering any application for permission in relation to a proposed protected structure, shall have regard to the fact that it is proposed to add the structure to a record of protected structures.

---

172. PDA 2000, s 57(3).
173. PDA 2000, s 57(5)(a) and (b)(i) and (ii) as amended by the PD(A)A 2002 s 13(b).
174. PDA 2000, s 57(6).
175. PDA 2000, s 57(7) as amended by the PD(A)A 2002, s 13(c).
176. PDA 2000, s 57(9) as amended by PD(A)A 2002, s 13(c).

Also s 57(10)(b) provides that neither the planning authority nor An Bord Pleanála shall grant planning permission for demolition of a protected structure or a proposed protected structure save in exceptional circumstances.[177]

## Duty of owners and occupiers to protect structures from endangerment

**[8.284]** Although the word 'endangerment' is not defined in PDA 2000, s 2 the word, 'endangered' is defined in s 2 as meaning:

> Exposed to harm, decay or damage, whether immediately or over a period of time, through neglect or through direct or indirect means;

PDA 2000, s 58(1) imposes on each owner and on each occupier of a protected structure or of a proposed protected structure a duty of care to protect that structure from endangerment either through direct action of the person involved or by their neglect of the building. Section 58(1) reads:

> Each owner and each occupier shall, to the extent consistent with the rights and obligations arising out of their respective interests in a protected structure or a proposed protected structure, ensure that the structure, or any element of it which contributes to its special architectural, historical, archaeological, artistic, cultural, scientific, social or technical interest, is not endangered.

This duty of care arises as soon as the owner of occupier is notified that the structure is proposed for inclusion in the record of protected structures.[178] PDA 2000, s 58 imposes both a positive and an onerous duty upon owners and occupiers of protected structures or of proposed protected structures and that duty will apply not just to freeholders but also to leaseholders. An owner can fail in their duty to prevent endangerment by omitting to take the necessary steps to prevent endangerment. Specifically there are two instances which are considered not to be a breach of duty, namely:

(a) Development in respect of which permission under section 34 has been granted;

(b) Development consisting only of works of a type which, in a declaration issued under section 57(3) to that owner or occupier, a planning authority has declared would not materially affect the character of the protected structure or any element, referred to in subsection (1) of this section, of that structure.[179]

**[8.285]** Any person who without lawful authority causes damage to a protected structure or a proposed protected structure shall be guilty of an offence.[180] However, there are a number of defences which may be raised in a prosecution against a person accused of causing damage to a protected structure if the person accused can prove that the damage to the structure resulted from works which were:

(a) Urgently required in order to secure the preservation of the structure or any part of it,

---

177. PDA 2000, s 57(10)(a) and (b).
178. PDA 2000, s 58(2).
179. PDA 2000, s 58(3)(a)&(b).
180. PDA 2000, s 58(4).

(b) Undertaken in good faith solely for the purpose of temporarily safeguarding the structure, and

(c) Unlikely to permanently alter the structure or any element of it referred to in subsection (1).[181]

## Notice to require works in relation to endangerment of protected structures

[8.286] PDA 2000, s 59 should be distinguished from PDA 2000, s 60. These sections provide two distinct types of notice. A s 59 notice requires works to be carried out in relation to endangerment of protected structures whereas a s 60 notice requires restoration of the character of protected structures and other places. These notices are also referred to as 'endangerment' notices and they are served on the owner/occupier of a protected structure. Apart from specifying the works, the notice will also specify a period of not less than eight weeks from the date of the notice to take effect for the completion of the works. The works to be carried out must be clearly specified in such a manner that the owner/occupier clearly understands what works are required.[182] In contrast to a restoration notice under s 60 an endangerment notice under s 59 allows a planning authority a discretion to provide assistance in any form it considers appropriate including advice, financial aid, materials, equipment and the services of the authority staff. In the case of a s 60 restoration notice, the planning authority shall pay any expenses that are reasonably incurred in carrying out the works other than works which relate to an unauthorised structure which has been constructed, erected or made seven years or less prior to the service of the notice.

[8.287] PDA 2000, s 59(3) provides that a person on whom an endangerment notice has been served may within four weeks make representations to the planning authority concerning the terms of the notice, the provision of assistance under s 59(2) and any other material considerations. Having considered the representations the planning authority may confirm, amend or revoke the notice and shall notify the owner/occupier accordingly. Particulars of the notice served must be entered in the register.

## Notice to require restoration of character of protected structures

[8.288] PDA 2000, s 60 permits a planning authority to serve a restoration notice on the owner/occupier of a protected structure requiring restoration works to be carried out. The Act does not define the word 'restoration' but para 7.21 of the *Architectural Heritage Protection Guidelines for Planning Authorities* describes conservation as 'the process of caring for buildings and places and of managing change to them in such a way as to retain their character and special interest'.

---

181. PDA 2000, s 58(5).
182. See, by analogy, *Dundalk UDC v Lawlor* [2005] 2 ILRM 106 *per* O'Neill J, where the learned judge in dealing with an enforcement notice held that because breach of a notice constitutes a criminal offence, a strict approach must be adopted so as to ensure the person knows precisely when compliance is required and what steps are necessary to achieve it.

[8.289] The duty to protect structures imposed by PDA 2000, ss 58 and 59 is imposed on each owner and each occupier of a protected structure or of a proposed protected structure who will have a duty of care to protect that structure from endangerment arising from either direct action of the person involved or arising from their neglect to the building. The duty of care arises as soon as the owner or occupier has been notified that the structure is proposed for inclusion in the record of protected structures. Each owner and each occupier of a protected structure or a proposed protected structure is required to ensure that the structure, or any element of it, which contributes to its special architectural, historical, archaeological, artistic, structural, scientific, social or technical interest is not endangered.

[8.290] The Act imposes both a positive and an onerous duty on owners or occupiers of protected structures or proposed protected structures and the onus distinguishes protected structures from other houses, offices or structures. The duty does not apply to the owner alone but also to the occupier and, for example, it will apply to a relatively short term tenant in the building, although that obligation is only imposed to 'the extent consistent with the rights and obligations arising out of their respective interest in the protected structure'. That sentence leaves the 'obligation' somewhat up in the air and its precise meaning is far from clear. Clearly, however, any development for which planning permission has been granted or development consisting of works in respect of which the planning authority has granted a declaration to say that the works to be carried out would not materially affect the character of a protected structure and, as such, do not require planning permission, is not in breach of this obligation.

[8.291] Persons advertising for tenants who propose to take a lease of a protected structure or of a proposed protected structure should carefully notify the tenant of the potential obligations which may arise outside the terms of the lease. This is something which is often overlooked and, again, where there is even the slightest suspicion that the premises may be protected, it is advisable to make a planning search.

## Damage

[8.292] Any person who, without lawful authority, causes damage to a protected structure or to a proposed protected structure is guilty of an offence under the Act and is liable to a fine on indictment of up to €12,697,380 and to imprisonment for a term not exceeding two years or both. The cause of damage to a protected structure without lawful authority includes damage through neglect. There are many houses in cities and towns and in rural Ireland which are protected but where damage continuously occurs, mainly due to lack of maintenance funds to preserve the structures. It is not uncommon for old stables and outhouses to collapse in circumstances where they may not have been used for many years, for example, for the reason that the design of the outbuildings may no longer be compatible with modern farming methods. The collapse, in many cases, would be attributed to neglect and neglect would be attributed to lack of funds.[183] It is to

---

183. In recent years, funds are available for the maintenance of and restoration of old/traditional farmyards.

be hoped that the courts would deal sympathetically with an impecunious owner of a protected structure but the Act allows for the imposition of fines on any person who does, without lawful authority, cause damage or allows damage to occur, through neglect of a protected structure or of a proposed protected structure. As seen, this is achieved by notice served on the owner or occupier and the notice is entered in the planning register. The recipient of such a notice has four weeks from its service to make representations to the planning authority and a recipient may seek assistance from the planning authority. Planning authorities may but are not obliged to assist in the carrying out of any works required and may provide assistance, financial aid, materials, equipment and services of the local authority staff. At the present time (2011), because of financial constraints, the amount of money available for such assistance is so inadequate as to be useless. Again, it must be stressed that the giving of financial and other assistance is discretionary but the obligation on the owner or occupier to maintain and to ensure that no damage is caused to a protected structure is absolute.

## Appeals against notices served on owner

[8.293] PDA 2000, s 61 deals with appeals against notices and provides that any person having been notified under s 59(4) or 60(6) of the confirmation of amendment of a notice has two weeks to appeal against the notice to the District Court on any one or more of the following grounds:

    (a) that the person is not the owner of occupier of the structure in respect of which the notice has been served;

    (b) that, in the case of a notice under s 59(1),[184] compliance with the requirements of the notice would involve unreasonable expense, and that the person had stated in representations made to the planning authority under s 59(3)[185] that he or she did not have the means to pay;

    (c) that the person has already taken all reasonable steps to –

        (i) in the case of a notice under s 59(1), prevent the structure from becoming or continue to be endangered,

        (ii) in the case of a notice under s 60(2)[186] in relation to a protected structure, restore the character of the structure or the element or,

---

184. PDA 2000, s 59(1) provides for notice to require works to be carried out to prevent a protected structure situated within the planning authority's functional area from becoming or continuing to be endangered.
185. A person who serves a notice under PDA 2000, s 59(1) may, under the terms of PDA 2000, s 59(3)(i), within four weeks of the date of the service of notice make a written representation to the planning authority concerning (a) the terms of the notice, (b) the provisions of assistance under sub-s (2), and (c) any other material considerations.
186. PDA 2000, s 60(2) permits a planning authority to serve notice on an owner or occupier of a structure situated within its functional area if (a) the structure is a protected structure and in the opinion of the authority the character of the structure or any of its elements ought to be restored or (b) the structure is in an architectural conservation area and, in the opinion of the planning authority, it is necessary, in order to preserve the character of the area, that the structure be restored.

### Additional Planning Controls on Land and on Buildings [8.295]

(iii) in the case of a notice under s 60(2) in relation to a structure that forms part of a place, area, group of structures or townscape referred to in paragraph (b) of that sub-section, assist in restoring the character of that place, area, group of structures or townscape as the case may be;

(d) that the time for complying with the notice is unreasonably short.[187]

**[8.294]** Provision is also made in the Act, where a person has complied with an endangerment notice by carrying out the works specified, allowing that person to apply to the court for an order directing that all or part of the cost of the works should be borne by another person who has an interest in the structure. This is an unfair provision because it means that the person served with the endangerment notice must carry out the works and incur the expense before they can make application to the court seeking contribution from the other person who may have an interest in the structure. PDA 2000, s 55 does provide that if a person served with a notice to carry out works to protect or restore a structure cannot carry out such works without the consent of a third party, and that third party refuses to consent, they may apply to the District Court which has the power to deem that consent has been given. These provisions are of particular relevance in a landlord and tenant relationship. It is suggested that the vast majority of owners or occupiers of protected structures are not aware of these and other potentially onerous obligations. There is a strong case to be made in favour of the publication of an explanatory booklet to be given to each owner and occupier of a protected structure or of a proposed protected structure explaining the respective obligations which are both statutory and mandatory. Each time a structure is entered in the planning authority's register as a protected structure or as a proposed protected structure the owner/occupier should receive a copy of the explanatory booklet. Such a proposal is well in line with ECJ 'thinking' on such matters.

## Notice to require restoration of character of protected structures and other places

**[8.295]** PDA 2000, s 60 gives even wider powers to the planning authority, which may serve notice on the owner or occupier of a protected structure requiring restoration works to include the removal, alteration or replacement of any specified part of a structure or element including the removal or alteration of any advertisement structure, if it is of the opinion that the character of the structure or any of its elements ought to be restored. The provisions of s 60 do not apply to a proposed protected structure. Any notice requiring restoration of works must be entered in the planning register, 'as soon as may be'. PDA 2000, s 60(2) specifically provides that a planning authority can serve notice on each person who is an owner or occupier of a structure situated within its functional area, if:

(a) The structure is a protected structure and, in the opinion of the planning authority, the character of the structure or any of its elements ought to be restored, or

---

187. PDA 2000, s 61(1)(a)–(d).

(b) The structure is an architectural conservation area and, in the opinion of the planning authority, it is necessary, in order to preserve the character of the area that the structure be restored.

**[8.296]** PDA 2000, s 62 provides for the effective date of notices. A notice requiring the restoration of the character of a protected structure including removal, alterations or replacements of any specified part of the structure or element of s 60(1) shall have effect on the expiration of four weeks from the date of service of the notice subject to the following three exceptions:

(a) If any representations have been made under s 59 or 60 in relation to the notice and no appeal has been taken within the period allowed under s 61(1), the notice has effect on the expiry of the appeal period;

(b) If an appeal is taken under s 61(1) and the notice is confirmed, the notice has effect on the date on which the decision of the district court is pronounced or the date in which the decision of the District Court is pronounced or the date on which that order is expressed to take effect, whichever is the later.

(c) If an application is made to the District Court under s 65(1) and an order is made under s 65(2)(a), the notice has effect on the date on which the decision of the court was pronounced, or the date in which that order is expressed to take effect, whichever is the later.[188]

## Restoration notices and endangerment notices

**[8.297]** A restoration notice shall specify the works required to be carried out for the purpose of restoring the structure and shall give the recipient not less than eight weeks to make representations to the planning authority and to invite the persons to enter into discussions with the planning authority concerning the provision of assistance and the period for carrying out the works. The notice must also state that the planning authority will pay any expenses incurred in carrying out the works under the notice other than works which relate to an unauthorised structure which has been constructed, erected or made less than seven years prior to the service of the notice. This implies that if the structure is an unauthorised structure or one which has been constructed in excess of seven years from the date of service of the notice, then the planning authority must pay any expenses reasonably incurred in carrying out the restoration work. There is some fairness in this provision but the only liability placed on the planning authority is to pay the expenses for the works, and there is no obligation to pay an owner or occupier compensation for any loss. If, for example, an owner or occupier was required by a restoration notice to demolish an extension, the planning authority is only liable for the expense of the demolition and the removal but is not liable for any loss of value to the owner.[189]

**[8.298]** In coming to the decision to serve a restoration notice a planning authority shall have regard to the guidelines (if any) issued under s 52 and to the recommendations (if

---

188. PDA 2000, s 62.
189. PDA 2000, s 60(3)(a), (b), (c), (d) and (e).

## Additional Planning Controls on Land and on Buildings [8.301]

any) issued under s 53.[190] If a person served with a restoration notice accepts the planning authority's invitation to enter into discussions within a period of eight weeks from the date of service of the notice the planning authority must facilitate the holding of those discussions.[191]

[8.299] Having considered representations and the discussions (if any) held under PDA 2000, s 60 the planning authority may confirm, amend or revoke the notice and the person or persons who made the representation shall be notified of the planning authority's decision.[192]

[8.300] Particulars of any restoration notice served under s 60 must be entered in the planning register.[193]

[8.301] PDA 2000, s 61 permits an appeal against confirmation or amendment of either an endangerment notice or a restoration notice. The appeal is to the District Court and must be taken within two weeks of the date of confirmation or amendment of the notice. In order to qualify as an appellant, a person must have made representations or observations in relation to the endangerment notice or to the restoration notice when it was served. The right to appeal under s 61 is restricted to four specific grounds which are set out in s 61(1)(a), (b), (c) and (d) as follows:

- (a) that the person is not the owner or occupier of the structure in respect of which the notice has been served;

- (b) that, in the case of a notice under s 59(1), compliance with the requirements of the notice would involve unreasonable expense, and that the person had stated in representations made to the planning authority under s 59(3) that he or she did not have the means to pay;

- (c) that the person has already taken all reasonable steps to –

    - (i) in the case of a notice under s 59(1), prevent the structure from becoming or continuing to be endangered,

    - (ii) in the case of a notice under s 60(2) in relation to a protected structure, restore the character of a structure or the element, or

    - (iii) in the case of a notice under s 60(2) in relation to a structure that forms part of a place, area, group of structures or townscape referred to in paragraph (b) of that subsection, assist in restoring the character of that place, area, group of structures or townscape, as the case may be;

- (d) that the time for complying with the notice is unreasonably short.

---

190. PDA 2000, s 60(4). PDA 2000, s 52 makes provisions for guidelines to be issued by the Minister to the planning authority concerning protected structures. Section 53 allows the Minister to make recommendations to the planning authority concerning particular structures, parts of particular structures or specific features within the attendant grounds of particular structures.
191. PDA 2000, s 60(5).
192. PDA 2000, s 60(6).
193. PDA 2000, s 60(7).

**[8.302]** An endangerment notice or a restoration notice takes effect four weeks after the date of service of the notice but some exceptions are provided. Where representations are made but no appeal is taken, the notice will be effective two weeks from the confirmation or amendment of the notice. Where an appeal is taken the notice will become effective either from the date of decision of the court or such other date as the court may direct. If an application is made to the District Court under PDA 2000, s 65 in circumstances where the person served cannot carry out the works without the consent of another person, the notice takes effect from the date of the court's decision or such other date as the court directs.[194]

**[8.303]** If a person fails to comply with an endangerment notice he or she will be guilty of a criminal offence.[195] Any person served with an endangerment notice or with a restoration notice is entitled to enter the land or structure to carry out the works. Presumably, the purpose of this section is to allow the owner of property or structure which has been leased to enter the leased land or structure for the purpose of carrying out works.[196]

**[8.304]** If a person served with an endangerment notice or a restoration notice requires the consent of some third party to carry out the works and that consent is not forthcoming the District Court may, entirely at its own discretion, (a) deem the consent has been given, and (b) if the consent is deemed to have been given the person making the application shall be entitled to carry out the works, and in those circumstances, the court order would be a defence to any action for trespass by other parties.[197]

**[8.305]** A person who has carried out works required under an endangerment notice served upon him is entitled to apply to a court of competent jurisdiction for an order directing all or part of the costs incurred to be paid by some other person who has an interest in the structure.[198]

**[8.306]** Significantly, any works carried out pursuant to an endangerment notice or a restoration notice will not require planning permission as it is exempted development.[199]

**[8.307]** If a person served with an endangerment notice or a restoration notice does not carry out the works directed by the notice, the planning authority is entitled to enter upon the land and carry out or arrange to have carried out the works specified in the notice. Any right of entry must be exercised in accordance with the provisions and conditions set out in PDA 2000, s 252.[200] If works to protect or restore a protected structure are carried out by the planning authority, the planning authority may recover

---

194. PDA 2000, s 62(a), (b) and (c).
195. PDA 2000, s 63.
196. PDA 2000, s 64.
197. PDA 2000, s 65.
198. PDA 2000, s 67(1) and (2).
199. PDA 2000, s 68.
200. PDA 2000, s 69; see also PDA 2000, s 252 which sets out the ground rules which apply to an authorised person entering any land.

the amount as an ordinary simple contract debt in a court of competent jurisdiction and, further, the planning authority may register a burden in the Land Registry or a mortgage in the Registry of Deeds in respect of the amount owing to it for such expenses as it may have incurred.[201]

## Compulsory acquisition of protected structures and related matters

[8.308] PDA 2000, ss 71–80 deal with compulsory acquisition of protected structures and related matters. A planning authority may compulsorily acquire any protected structure and its attendant grounds situate within its functional area if it considers it necessary to do so for the protection of that structure, provided the structure is not lawfully occupied as a dwelling house (other than by a caretaker). Reference to a protected structure in this context includes reference to any land which forms part of the attendant ground of the structure or is, in the planning authority's opinion, necessary to secure the protection of the structure whether or not the land lies within the curtilage of the structure or is specified as a feature in the record of protected structures. Unfortunately, the Act does not provide that the notice of intention to acquire a protected structure shall be registered in the Planning Register,[202] which, in conveyancing terms, is a serious omission.

[8.309] Notice of intention to acquire a protected structure must be served on any owner, lessee or occupier (except tenants for a period of one month or less) and the notice must also be published in a newspaper circulating in the area. The notice must specify a time, being not less than four weeks, during which objections may be made to the planning authority. An owner for the purposes of this section, in relation to a protected structure, means a person other than a mortgagee not in possession who is, for the time being, entitled to dispose of the freehold. An owner includes a person under a lease or agreement which has more than five years to run and who holds or is entitled to the rents or profits of the protected structure.[203]

[8.310] An owner, occupier or lessee may object to the proposed compulsory acquisition within the time and within the manner specified in the notice. It is specifically provided that a planning authority shall not compulsorily acquire a protected structure without the consent of An Bord Pleanála. An application for the board's consent shall be made by the planning authority within four weeks after the expiry of the time allowed for submitting an objection to that acquisition and in seeking the consent of An Bord Pleanála, the planning authority will submit the application together with its comments. An Bord Pleanála will allow an objector to make observations on the planning authority's comments. An Bord Pleanála may, as it thinks fit, grant or refuse to grant consent for compulsory acquisition of all or part of the protected structure referred to in the newspaper notice.[204]

---

201. PDA 2000, s 70(a) and (b).
202. PDA 2000, s 71(1) and (2).
203. PDA 2000, s 72(1) and (2).
204. PDA 2000, s 73.

## CPO vesting orders

**[8.311]** If a planning authority is permitted to compulsorily acquire the property then PDA 2000 sets out the procedure for the making of a vesting order which will vest the protected structure in the planning authority in fee simple, free from encumbrances and free from all other estates, rights, title and interest of whatever kind. The form of vesting order is contained in the planning regulations. The vesting order must then be sent to the Land Registry which will register the planning authority as owner of the land.[205] Some doubt must arise in relation to the high-handed assertion in PDA 2000, s 75(2) that a vesting order shall be expressed and shall operate to vest the protected structure to which it relates in the planning authority in fee simple, free from all encumbrances and all estates, rights, titles and interest of whatsoever kind. Could this mean, for example, that a bank or building society mortgage might disappear when the vesting order is made? PDA 2000, s 75 makes no compromise but PDA 2000, s 77 does allow for compensation for interests in protected structures. Presumably, a mortgage document is a valid contract between mortgagor and mortgagee but it is perhaps more than a little unsettling that the statutory provisions in the Act do not require the local authority to offer anything other than compensation to the mortgagee. Compensation may or may not include all of the elements which the mortgagee could recover by foreclosure. For example, would compensation include a possible loss of profit on a mortgage in circumstances where the term of the mortgage is greatly reduced? These are matters to be determined by the property arbitrator. To add insult to injury, the rights of the Minister for Agriculture, etc, and of the Revenue Commissioners are preserved in relation to any annual charges payable to them.[206] The question might also be asked if a long standing right of way over part of the attendant grounds of the protected structure, which favoured residents by allowing them to pass over the attendant ground for the purpose of obtaining access to their own premises, could suddenly be extinguished by this crude mechanism. If such a right of way is extinguishable by virtue of the vesting order made for protected structures it can hardly be said that compensation would be a satisfactory resolution for an adjoining owner suddenly losing, for example, a right of entrance to a private residence.

**[8.312]** Any person having an interest in land is entitled to apply to the local authority for compensation within one year of the making of the vesting order, or such other periods the High Court shall allow. The amount of compensation payable shall equal the value of that person's estate, interest or right in the land. A planning authority shall pay to the applicant, by way of compensation, an amount equal to the value (if any) of the estate, interest or right of the applicant. If any sum, including a sum for costs which remains due for payment to the planning authority by any person, under an order of the court (whether under PDA 2000 or under any other Act, or whether remaining due after deducting expenses recently incurred by the planning authority under PDA 2000 in relation to the structure) the amount of compensation payable to that person shall be reduced by the amount owing to the authority. The compensation which a planning

---

205. For full details see PDA 2000, ss 74, 75 and 76.
206. PDA 2000, s 75(3).

authority must pay shall be agreed but in default of agreement shall be determined by arbitration under the Acquisition of Lands (Assessment of Compensation) Act 1919.[207]

**[8.313]** Once a planning authority acquires the protected structure by vesting order, the planning authority may use that structure for any purpose connected with its functions. It may sell, let, transfer or exchange all or any part of the protected structure but, in doing so, the planning authority must have regard to the protected status of the structure. If, for example, a planning authority were to allow a use in the structure which was incompatible with its protected status, this would amount to a material contravention of the development plan.[208]

**[8.314]** A sanitary authority must consider the protected status of a structure in circumstances where it decides to issue a dangerous building notice under the terms of s 3(1) of the Local Government (Sanitary Services) Act 1964 which requires that works be undertaken to prevent the continuation of a danger to the public (including demolition). Apart from considering the protected status of a structure, the sanitary authority shall also consider whether it might be more appropriate, instead of serving a dangerous building notice under s 3(1), to serve an endangerment notice or a notice under s 59(1) or s 11 of the Derelict Sites Act 1990.

**[8.315]** After the service of a notice under s 3(1), a sanitary authority shall inform the Minister of Community, Rural and Gaeltacht Affairs of the particulars of the notice, if that Minister had recommended that the structure be protected. A sanitary authority which carries out works on a protected structure or on a proposed protected structure under s 3(1) shall, as far as possible, preserve as much as possible of the protected structure where it would not be dangerous to do so.[209]

**[8.316]** PDA 2000, s 80 permits the Minister for Finance to grant money to planning authorities for any monies spent in assisting persons carrying out works required under either an endangerment notice or a restoration notice and also in assisting persons carrying out other works to protected structures resulting from conditions specified by the planning authority.

**[8.317]** To give a local authority such a wide and subjective power is questionable even though it must first seek and obtain approval from An Bord Pleanála. To take an extreme example, if Dublin City Council served an endangerment notice or a restoration notice on a house in Fitzwilliam Square which is used as offices and in circumstances where the old stables at the rear had fallen into disrepair and were in need of restoration, then, because the stables are within the attendant grounds, if the local authority is of the opinion that compulsory acquisition is necessary for the protection of the structure it may (theoretically at least) acquire the entire protected structure. Admittedly, compensation will be paid to the owner or other person having any right or estate in the structure, but the Act may have gone too far in providing a mechanism for compulsory

---

207. For full details see PDA 2000, s 77(1)–(5).
208. PDA 2000, s 78.
209. PDA 2000, s 79(1)–(4).

acquisition which positively discriminates against owners or occupiers of protected structures. Considering the other penalties which may be imposed under the Act, it is suggested that the operation of compulsory acquisition under PDA 2000 in relation to protected structures should be more measured and balanced to avoid placing owners and occupiers of protected structures at a disadvantage, apart altogether from risking the possibility of infringing an owner's or an occupier's constitutional rights.

## REFUSAL OF PLANNING PERMISSION FOR PAST FAILURES TO COMPLY

[8.318] PDA 2000, s 35 introduced a new provision in planning legislation which permitted a planning authority to refuse to grant permission to an applicant who had, in the past, failed to comply with the terms of his planning permission.

[8.319] Dodd makes the following valid observation in relation to s 35 procedure in saying that:

> It is unique that the refusal is not based on planning considerations relating to the development itself but rather on the person who is seeking to carry out the development. The refusal is not based simply on the planning history of specific lands but on the history of the applicant himself. Under the previous legislation, such a reason would appear not to amount to a consideration based on proper planning and development and so would be ultra vires.[210]

[8.320] The s 35 procedures were rarely used by planning authorities but the procedures were placed on a more solid footing by the amendments provided in PD(SI)A 2006. Under the provisions of the unamended PDA 2000, s 35, if a planning authority formed an opinion that there was a real and substantial risk of non-compliance, based on the previous history of non-compliance of an applicant, it was required to apply to the High Court for an authorisation to refuse permission to that applicant. Under the revised procedure provided by the amendment made by s 9 of PD(SI)A 2006, the planning authority is no longer required to apply to the High Court for authorisation. PDA 2000, s 35(1) has been further amended by s 24 of the PD(A)A 2010 by the substitution of the following section for sub-s (1):

> (1) Where having regard to –
> 
> (a) any information furnished pursuant to regulations made under section 33(2)(l),
> 
> (b) any information available to the planning authority concerning development carried out by a person to whom this section applies pursuant to a permission (in this section referred to as a 'previous permission') granted to the applicant or to any other person under this Part or Part IV of the of 1963,

---

210. See Dodd, *Planning and Development Acts, 2000–2007 Annotated and Consolidated* published (Round Hall Thomson Reuters, 2008) at para 1.45, p 144.

(c) any information otherwise available to the planning authority concerning the substantial unauthorised development, or

(d) any information concerning a conviction for an offence under this Act,

the planning authority is satisfied that a person to whom this section applies is not in compliance with a previous permission or with a condition to which the previous permission is subject, has carried out a substantial unauthorised development, or has been convicted of an offence under this Act, the authority may form the opinion –

(i) that there is a real and substantial risk that the development in respect of which permission is sought would not be completed in accordance with such permission if granted, or with a condition to which such permission if granted would be subject, and

(ii) that planning permission should not be granted to the applicant concerned in respect of that development.

Looking at the amendment of PDA 2000, s 35 there is a strong possibility that this section will be used more frequently in the future.

**[8.321]** Since the passing of PD(SI)A 2006 a planning authority is no longer required to apply to the High Court for authorisation to implement s 35.

**[8.322]** It does seem that PDA 2000, s 35(1) requires that the past failure must still be in existence at the time that the planning authority forms its opinion. Presumably, if the past failure to comply is remedied before the planning authority forms its opinion, that is an end of the potential refusal procedure but, the fact that the seven-year period has elapsed rendering enforcement impossible will not mean that the planning authority cannot continue and conclude its procedure to refuse permission under the section. In forming its opinion under the new provisions a planning authority may take into account any information concerning a conviction for an offence under the Act.

**[8.323]** Apart from a breach of permission and/or a breach of a condition in the permission, in forming its opinion, a planning authority can also take account of the fact that the development in respect of which planning permission is sought would not be completed in accordance with such permission if granted or would not be completed in compliance with a condition or conditions to which such permission if granted would be subject.

**[8.324]** PDA 2000, s 35(2) has not been altered and the planning authority will only consider failures to comply with any previous permission or with the condition to which that permission was subject that are of a substantial nature.

**[8.325]** PDA 2000, s 35(3) has not been altered and provides that:

An opinion under this sub-section shall not be a decision on an application for permission for the purposes of this Part.

**[8.326]** PDA 2000, s 35(4) had been amended by PD(SI)A 2006, s 9. Section 35(4) has been substituted by a new subsection published in PD(A)A 2010, s 24(b) and now reads as follows:

> If the planning authority considers that there are good grounds for its being able to form the opinion under sub-section (1) in relation to an application for permission in respect of the development concerned and, accordingly, to exercise the power under sub-section (5) to refuse that permission, it shall serve a notice in writing on the applicant to that effect and that notice shall –
>
> > (a) specify the non compliance with a previous permission or condition of a previous permission, substantial unauthorised development, or conviction of an offence under this Act, as the case may be, that the authority intends to take into consideration with regard to the proposed exercise of that power, and
> >
> > (b) invite the applicant to make submissions to the authority within a period specified in the notice as to why the applicant considers that the authority should not exercise that power (whether because the applicant contends that the views of the authority in relation to the failure to comply by the applicant or any other person to whom this section applies with any previous permission, or any condition to which it is subject, the carrying out of substantial unauthorised development or conviction for an offence under this Act, as the case may be, or incorrect or that there are not good grounds for forming the opinion under subsection (1)).

Before serving notice in writing under the section on the applicant, a planning authority must have come to the conclusion that there are good grounds to enable it to form an opinion in accordance with the provisions of PDA 2000, s 35 (1)(i) and (ii) (as amended).

**[8.327]** The planning authority must consider any submissions made to it before making a decision to refuse the permission. Only then shall it form the opinion required by s 35(1). If the opinion is formed, in relation to the application concerned, the planning authority shall decide to refuse to grant planning permission and shall notify the applicant accordingly.[211] The planning authority's decision cannot be appealed to An Bord Pleanála[212] but it can be challenged by way of judicial review in the High Court provided the challenge is made within eight weeks from the date of the planning authority's notice of refusal to grant planning permission. The High Court may, as it considers appropriate, confirm or annul the planning authority's decision. If the planning authority's decision is annulled the High Court can direct the planning authority to consider the applicant's planning application without reference to the provisions of PDA 2000, s 35 (as amended) or make such other order as it thinks fit.[213] If the High Court annuls the decision and directs the planning authority to reconsider the application without regard to PDA 2000, s 35 (as amended) the planning authority has

---

211. PDA 2000, s 35(5) as substituted by PD(SI)A 2006, s 9.
212. PDA 2000, s 35(6)(c) as substituted by PD(SI)A 2006, s 9.
213. PDA 2000, s 35(6) as substituted by PD(SI)A 2006, s 9.

eight weeks from the date that the order is perfected in which to make its decision. If no decision is made within that time a default permission under s 34(8) will issue.[214]

**[8.328]** PDA 2000, s 35(7), as amended by PD(A)A 2001, defines 'a person to whom his section applies' as meaning:

    (a) the applicant for permission concerned,

    (b) a partnership of which the applicant is or was a member and which, during the membership of that applicant, carried out a development pursuant to a previous permission, carried out a substantial unauthorised development or has been convicted of an offence under this Act,[215]

    (c) in the case where the applicant for permission is a company –

        (i) the company concerned is related to a company (within the meaning of section 140(5) of the Companies Act, 1990) which carried out a development pursuant to a previous permission, carried out a substantial unauthorised development or has been convicted of an offence under this Act.[216]

        (ii) the company concerned is under the same control as a company which carried out a development referred to in sub-section (1)(b), where 'control' has the same meaning as in section 26(3) of the Companies Act, 1990,

    or

    (d) a company which carried out a development pursuant to a previous permission, carried out a substantial unauthorised development or has been convicted of an offence under this Act, which company is controlled by the applicant –

        (i) where 'control' has the same meaning as in section 26(3) of the Companies Act, 1990, or

        (ii) as a shadow director within the meaning of section 27(1) of the Companies Act, 1990.[217]

**[8.329]** It will be seen that s 35 is not a punitive section and neither can it be classed as an enforcement section. The planning authority may, in forming its opinion, come under a burdensome degree of scrutiny before the courts in subsequent judicial review proceedings. The planning authority will take great care in forming its opinion and most planning authorities will be too well aware of the level of proof which must be openly satisfied before it makes its determination. A planning authority must, if challenged, be able to demonstrate that there is a 'real and substantial risk' that the development will not be completed in accordance with the permission granted and/or that it will not be completed in accordance with a condition in the permission granted. The past failure must be of a 'substantial nature'.

---

214. PDA 2000, s 35(6A) as substituted by PD(SI)A 2006, s 9.
215. PDA 2000, s 35(7)(b) by PD(A)A 2010, s 20(4)(c)(1).
216. PDA 2000, s .35(7)(c)(i)&(ii) as amended by PD(A)A 2010, s 20(4)(c)(ii).
217. PDA 2000, s 35(7)(d) is amended by PD(A)A 2010, s 20(4)(c)(iii).

[8.330] In the light of development experience since 1 October 1964 it is, perhaps, time to have another look at PDA 2000, s 35 (even with all of its amendments) and to alter it to such an extent that the principal aim of the section is to provide planning authorities with a stronger procedure for issuing refusals for planning permission where there is evidence of meaningful and substantial non-compliance with past permissions granted or non-compliance with significant conditions in past permissions granted. There are instances of substandard and poorly finished developments in Ireland and perhaps this is a problem which needs to be addressed firmly. The new procedure introduced by PDA 2000 was a definite improvement on the systems provided by the 1963 Act but it remains a procedure which is inadequately used by planning authorities. Perhaps these new amendments in s 24 of PD(A)A 2010 will give it a new lease of life. Some developers need to learn that the terms of a permission, the conditions in a permission and the building regulations have a purpose which must be complied with to the letter. They need to understand 'sustainable development' and they need to put it into practice. Section 35 could be improved by concentrating more on considerations of proper planning and sustainable development and less on the subjective and often difficult decision as to whether or not there is a real and substantial risk that development, the subject matter of a new application, may not be completed. There is no reason why s 35 should not be a punitive section particularly when some of the so-called 'Celtic Tiger' developments are put to the test.

[8.331] Failure to comply with permissions, conditions in permissions and building regulations is unacceptable, and developers who fall short of the standards required by the planning process may be pursued by the enforcement process or by the imposition of other specific penalties under the Act. There is a case for giving planning authorities an unfettered option to refuse permission for past failures and to allow an appeal to An Bord Pleanála and/or judicial review against the planning authority's decision if a developer has good grounds to dispute it. The fact is that, as it stands at present, s 35 is ineffective. It is likely to remain ineffective in spite of the amendments. The section needs to be made effective to ensure that developers will not take short cuts or that if they do they will run the risk of a career change in the immediate future.

# REMOVAL OR ALTERATION OF A STRUCTURE

[8.332] PDA 2000, s 46 deals with removal or alterations of a structure and, at first sight, this section might appear to trespass beyond the bounds of reason. The section is calmed by the use of phrases such as 'in exceptional circumstances' and 'appeal to the board', etc.

[8.333] Essentially, PDA 2000, s 46(1) empowers a local authority, if it decides to do so, in exceptional circumstances, to serve a notice requiring that:

    (a) any structure should be demolished, removed, altered or replaced,

    (b) any use should be discontinued, or

    (c) any conditions should be imposed on the continuance of a use,

## Additional Planning Controls on Land and on Buildings [8.339]

The planning authority may serve notice on the owner and on the occupier of the structure or land concerned and on any other person who, in its opinion, will be affected by the notice.

[8.334] The decision to serve a s 46 notice may be taken by a local authority even where the land, structure or other use concerned is not an unauthorised development or an unauthorised use. Clearly, there is an obligation on the part of the local authority to demonstrate beyond reasonable doubt that exceptional circumstances do exist which justify the demolition or alteration of a structure, the discontinuance of a use or the imposition of conditions on a use. The section permits an interference with vested property rights and, as such, the exceptional circumstances must be strictly construed.

[8.335] PDA 2000, s 46 cannot be used to enforce or achieve something that is enforceable or achievable by means of other statutory provisions and, by way of example, s 46 would be an inappropriate method to require demolition of a dangerous building for the very reason that there is other legislation to deal with that situation. Specifically, PDA 2000, s 46(2) provides that a s 46 notice cannot be served in relation to an unauthorised development unless it is served seven years after the commencement of the unauthorised development. During the seven-year period it would be appropriate to use the normal enforcement proceedings under Pt VIII of the Act.

[8.336] PDA 2000, s 46(6) sets out the contents of the notice to be served. The notice specifies the location of the land or structure and the steps which will be required to be taken for the demolition, alteration, replacement or discontinuance of use as appropriate and the time period in which the required steps must be taken. The notice invites written submissions or observations from the person served to be made not less than four weeks from the date of service of the notice.

[8.337] PDA 2000, s 46(4) states boldly that a planning authority, having regard to any submissions or obligations made, may decide to confirm the notice with or without modifications, or not to confirm the notice. No time limit is specified even though the unfortunate party served with the notice must react within specified time limits provided in the section. This is an unfair and unwanted imbalance which is a common reoccurrence throughout the provisions of PDA 2000 (as amended).

[8.338] PDA 2000, s 46(5) requires a planning authority, in making its decision under this section, to consider:
    (a) The proper planning and sustainable development of the area,
    (b) The provisions of the development plan,
    (c) The provisions of any special amenity area order, any European site or other area designated for the purposes of section 10(2)(c) relating to the area, and
    (d) Any other relevant provision of this Act and any regulations made thereunder.

[8.339] PDA 2000, s 46(7) provides that where an appeal is made to An Bord Pleanála, the board can annul or confirm the notice with or without modifications. In the case of an appeal to the board, confirmation of the s 46 notice occurs on the date that the board confirms the notice. If an appeal is withdrawn confirmation occurs on the date of the withdrawal.

**[8.340]** PDA 2000, s 46(8) provides that any notice under this section other than one which is annulled shall take effect:

    (a) in case no appeal against it is taken, on the expiration of the period for taking an appeal, or

    (b) in case an appeal or appeals are taken against it and not withdrawn, when the appeal or appeals have been either withdrawn or decided.

**[8.341]** PDA 2000, s 46(9) provides that if a notice to remove or alter a structure or to discontinue use has not been complied with within the period specified in the notice or within such extended time as may be allowed by the planning authority, the planning authority may enter the structure an carry out the work required by the notice.

**[8.342]** PDA 2000, s 46(10) allows a person who has complied with a s 46 notice to obtain reasonable expenses for the work carried out.

**[8.343]** PDA 2000, s 46(11) provides that it is an offence to fail to comply with a s 46 notice or to cause or permit failure to comply with a s 46 notice.

**[8.344]** PDA 2000, s 46(12) provides that particulars of a s 46 notice shall be entered in the planning register of the local authority. No time limit is prescribed for entering these details in the register although, unusually, the often used but meaningless phrase, 'as soon as may be' has been omitted from the subsection.

**[8.345]** PDA 2000, s 46(13) provides that a planning authority may withdraw a s 46 notice but if it does so it must (a) give stated reasons for doing so and (b) record the withdrawal in the planning authority's planning register.

**[8.346]** PDA 2000, s 196 (Pt XII, Ch 1) provides for compensation in respect of a s 46 notice. Compensation is payable regarding removal or alteration of a structure or on the basis of reduction in value of a structure or disturbance in the enjoyment of a structure.

**[8.347]** PDA 2000, s 197 provides for compensation where a notice for discontinuance (or continuance subject to conditions) of land use under s 46 has been served. If it is shown that as a result of the discontinuance or the compliance with a condition imposed on the continuance of any use of land in consequence of the service of a s 46 notice, the value of an owner's or occupier's interest in land has been reduced or if the person served with a notice can show that he has suffered damage by being disturbed in his enjoyment of the land, compensation will be payable.

## STATUTORY PLANNING AGREEMENTS

**[8.348]** These agreements were formerly referred to as sterilisation agreements but the scope of such agreements has been broadened by PDA 2000, s 47 and they are now referred to as statutory planning agreements. The purpose of the statutory planning agreement is to allow a planning authority to enter into an agreement with persons having an interest in land in order to restrict its use or development.

[8.349] PDA 2000, s 47(1) sets out the terms of this special form of control as follows:

> A planning authority may enter into an agreement with any person interested in land in their area, for the purpose of restricting or regulating the development or use of land, either permanently or during such period as may be specified by the agreement, and any such agreement may contain such incidental and consequential provisions (including provisions of a financial character) as appear to the planning authority to be necessary or expedient for the purposes of the agreement.

The section clearly includes sterilisation agreements when land is restricted from development either permanently or for a specified period but it goes further than that. The section includes agreements entered into prior to the commencement of development provided such agreements relate, as the section says, to the development or to the restriction or regulation of the development or use of land.

[8.350] A s 47 agreement can be completed in respect of land for which no permission has been granted or indeed for land in respect of which there is no development proposal whatsoever. In *Charles McHugh v Kildare County Council*,[218] the applicant had agreed, during the review of a development plan, to complete a written agreement agreeing to dedicate 20% of his lands to Kildare County Council in return for having the rest of his land rezoned. The question to be determined by Gilligan J was whether the agreement to transfer a portion of his land for use by Kildare County Council for its statutory purposes met the requirement of s 47(1) in terms of being an agreement for the purpose of restricting or regulating the development or use of the land. The learned judge held that there had been good consideration and that the agreement was for the purposes of restricting or regulating the use of land. In this case, Mr McHugh, once his lands had been rezoned, felt that he was entitled to have the 20% of his lands freed from the dedication which he had made in his agreement on the basis that Kildare County Council had sought to gain an advantage merely for carrying out its statutory obligation to ensure proper planning and development of the area. Gilligan J held that the purpose of the agreement was to allow the local authority to develop lands for small industry independently of the adjoining private industrial development and that purpose was a purpose for restricting or regulating the development or use of land. Gilligan J's decision was overturned on appeal in the Supreme Court.[219]

[8.351] In *JA Pye (Oxford) Limited v South Gloucestershire DC and Ors*,[220] it was held that a statutory planning agreement need not relate to any ascertained or proposed

---

218. *Charles McHugh v Kildare County Council* (unreported, 24 February 2009) HC, Gilligan J.
219. *Charles McHugh v Kildare County Council* [2009] IESC 16 where Hardiman J considered that the agreement was *ultra vires* because, as it was then, LG(PD)A 1963, s 38 did not contemplate an agreement for the transfer of land.
220. *JA Pye (Oxford) Limited v South Gloucestershire DC and Ors* [2001] EWCA Civ 450.

development. It must, however, be entered into for the purposes of restricting or regulating the development or use of land. A planning agreement need not be related to a specific or to any development plan so long as the subject matter of the agreement is related to a proper planning condition. Under PDA 2000, s 47(2), a planning authority may enter into a s 47 agreement jointly with a prescribed authority for the purposes of PDA 2000, s 11[221] which deals with the preparation of a development plan. Article 13 of PDR 2001 prescribes 27 different prescribed bodies which may be joined in a planning agreement.

[8.352] The very nature of a statutory planning agreement indicates that it cannot be imposed by a planning authority unilaterally. The essence of PDA 2000, s 47, which is an agreement regulating the development or use of the land, is that it must be consensual. A planning authority cannot unilaterally extract a planning gain and it cannot impose, unilaterally, an imposition on a third party where neither the planning gain nor the condition to be imposed has a connection with the development. However, 'occupancy' conditions are an exception to the general rule that statutory agreements under s 47 must be consensual. PDA 2000, s 39, dealing with supplemental provisions to the granting of planning permission, specifically provides in sub-s (2) that a 'restrictive use condition' may be imposed by condition in a grant of planning permission for a structure and if the structure is a dwelling the permission may be granted subject to a condition specifying that the occupancy may be restricted to persons of a particular class or description and that a provision or provisions to that effect shall be embodied in an agreement under s 47. An example of this type of condition would be a condition restricting the occupancy of a dwelling in a Gaeltacht area to persons who are proficient in the Irish language. That type of condition can be the subject matter of a s 47 statutory agreement. Such a condition may be used to restrict occupancy to persons who have lived in the area for a certain length of time. Unquestionably, there must be some doubt as to whether these type of restrictive occupancy conditions would survive a detailed scrutiny either in terms of the provisions of the Constitution or in terms of the European Convention on Human Rights. That said, in the English decision in *JA Pye (Oxford) Limited v South Gloucestershire DC and Ors*,[222] a developer argued that an agreement similar to a s 47 agreement was not connected to the permitted development for the reason that in drafting the planning agreement the planning authority had taken into account irrelevant or immaterial considerations in determining an application for planning permission. The Court of Appeal, in examining the planning agreement, held that the restrictions placed on the developer in relation to proposed road development, which would clearly be of benefit for the locality, did not render the planning agreement invalid.

[8.353] A statutory planning agreement will survive the life of the parties entering into it. A s 47 agreement runs with the land and binds subsequent owners in much the same way as restrictive covenants survive and pass from owner to owner. PDA 2000, s 47(3) expressly provides that these agreements survive as if the agreement had been expressly

---

221. PDA 2000, s 11 has been amended by PD(A)A 2010, s 8.
222. *JA Pye (Oxford) Limited v South Gloucestershire DC and Ors* [2001] EWCA Civ 450.

made for the benefit of the land. Statutory agreements have something in common with planning permissions in that both attach to the land and not just to the parties. The statutory planning agreements also might run forever for the reason that there is no mechanism contained in s 47 setting out any circumstances in which such statutory agreement might come to an end.

**[8.354]** In *Langarth Properties Ltd v Bray Urban District Council*,[223] it was noted that an applicant's predecessor in title had entered into a statutory agreement in March 1974 which agreement precluded the construction of any further houses on the land. On 2 November 2000, a decision was made by An Bord Pleanála authorising the applicant to develop the same lands which were situate in Bray, County Wicklow and clearly that grant of permission was in conflict with the statutory agreement concluded in March 1974. Morris P held that the fact that An Bord Pleanála had granted a permission authorising the development of the lands, in spite of the earlier restriction in the statutory agreement, was, in itself, a clear indication that the proper planning of the area no longer required to be inhibited by the restriction contained in the planning agreement and that to prevent or inhibit the development of lands other than by reason of proper planning and sustainable development of the area would be an unconstitutional interference with the rights of private ownership. Morris P held that it was not open to the planning authority to rely solely upon the fact that there was a statutory agreement in existence. The decision, however, does not mean that a planning permission granted by An Bord Pleanála can effectively negate a pre-existing agreement. Indeed, the very existence of a planning agreement which attaches to the land ought to be a proper planning consideration. The provisions of PDA 2000, s 34(13) provide that a person shall not be entitled solely by reason of a permission under the section to carry out a development. From this provision it may be seen that although a grant of planning permission may be in existence it does not follow that the development can proceed in all circumstances.

**[8.355]** PDA 2000, s 47(4) provides that a statutory agreement shall not bind the Minister, the board or a planning authority so long as any powers exercised by them in relation to statutory agreements shall not materially contravene the provisions of the development plan or so long as the section shall not require the exercise of any such powers so as to contravene materially those powers. The powers to amend or indeed to end a statutory agreement under PDA 2000 do not extend in any manner to members of the public who, at first glance, may be seen to be stuck with a statutory agreement forever unless the Minister, the board or the planning authority comes to their rescue. However, a statutory agreement under s 47 cannot prevent the board or a planning authority from taking account of the proper planning and sustainable development of the area when it is considering a planning application. If a statutory planning agreement stands in the way of the proper planning and sustainable development of the area the board and/or the planning authority can sweep it aside. That was the rationale in Morris P's decision in *Langarth Properties Ltd v Bray Urban District Council*[224] where the

---

223. *Langarth Properties Ltd v Bray Urban District Council* (unreported, 25 June 2001) HC, Morris P.
224. *Langarth Properties Ltd v Bray Urban District Council* (unreported, 25 June 2001) HC, Morris P.

learned judge overturned the local authority's decision on the grounds that a planning authority could not rely on a planning agreement to inhibit the proper planning and sustainable development of the area. In effect, where the proper planning and sustainable development of an area is in conflict with the provisions of a statutory planning agreement the latter may be set aside. Nevertheless, the extent of the learned President's decision in *Langarth Properties* is not a green light which will allow a planning authority to ignore all statutory agreements. Planning authorities can only do so in limited circumstances. In a sense, PDA 2000, s 34(13) takes account of statutory agreements in a non-specific manner by providing that a person shall not be entitled solely by reason of a permission under this section to carry out any development. For example, licences or other permissions may still be required and, indeed, the permission cannot allow development which manifestly infringes the conditions of a statutory agreement save for those conditions which are, or have since become, in conflict with the proper planning and sustainable development of the area.

**[8.356]** PDA 2000, s 47(5) requires that all statutory agreements made under this section shall be entered in the planning register of the planning authority. The requirement to make the entry in the planning authority's planning register is that it should be made 'as soon as may be'. That phrase offers little more than an indefinite time period provided, however, that the entry is finally made. To take an extreme example, if a planning authority were challenged for failing to make an entry in its register some 10 years after the event, it is at least open to it to say that it will make the entry the day after tomorrow assuming, of course, that that is not a Saturday, Sunday or Bank Holiday.

## STRATEGIC DEVELOPMENT ZONES[225]

**[8.357]** Part IX of the Planning and Development Acts 2000–2010 permits the government to designate certain sites as SDZs in order to facilitate specified development which is of economic or social importance to the State.[226] Although an SDZ order is made by the government, the proposal to make the order is initiated by the Minister who consults with development agencies as set out in PDA 2000, s 165 or with the relevant planning authority. PDA 2000, s 165 defines 'development agency':

> 'development agency' means the Industrial Development Agency (Ireland), Enterprise Ireland, the Shannon Free Airport Development Company Limited, Údarás na Gaeltachta, the National Building Agency Limited, the Grangegorman Development Agency, a local authority or other such person as may be prescribed by the Minister for the purposes of this part.

---

225. Strategic development zones are dealt with in Pt IX of PDA 2000, s 165–s 171 inclusive. Within Pt IX, s 168 has been amended by s 50 of PD(A)A 2010 which amends sub-s (1). Subsection (3) of PDA 2000, s 168 has been amended by the European Communities (Environmental Assessment of Certain Plans and Programmes) Regulations 2004. The topic has been dealt with in **Ch 1**. PDA 2000, s 169 has been amended by s 51 of PD(A)A 2010. PDA 2000, s 170 has been amended by s 52 of PD(A)A 2010.
226. PDA 2000, s 166.

**[8.358]** PDA 2000, s 165 also defines 'strategic development zone':

> 'strategic development zone' means a site or sites to which a planning scheme made under s 169 applies.

**[8.359]** PDA 2000, s 166 provides for the designation of sites for SDZs. The section provides that the government may designate a site or sites for the making of an SDZ and specify the types of development for which the zone will be established. The designation of sites for strategic development is the responsibility of the government. PDA 2000, s 166(1) enables the government, on foot of a proposal by the Minister for the Environment and Local Government, to designate a particular site or sites for the establishment of an SDZ. This designation may be done to facilitate development which is, in the opinion of the government, of economic or social importance to the State. The designation may also facilitate development which is of strategic importance to the national economy. The types of development for which an SDZ may be established include industrial, residential, commercial or amenity development which is of importance in the national context.

**[8.360]** PDA 2000, s 166(2) requires the Minister, in advance of putting a proposal to the government to designate a site, to consult with any relevant development agency or local authority. In practice, it is likely that the proposal to designate a site will come from an agency or authority, perhaps, at the request of the Minister.

**[8.361]** PDA 2000, s 166(3) sets out the content of the government order. The order must specify:

    (a) the development agency or development agencies for the purposes of section 168,

    (b) the type or types of development that may be established in the Strategic Development Zone, and

    (c) the order shall state the reasons for specifying the development and for designating the site or sites.

**[8.362]** PDA 2000, s 166(4) provides that the Minister must put forward a copy of the government order to the relevant development agency, the planning authority and the regional authority for the area and to the board.

**[8.363]** PDA 2000, s 166(5) states that any development which is specified in an order under the section shall be deemed to include development that is ancillary to, or required for, the purposes of development so specified and may include any necessary infrastructural and community facilities and services. The section implies that a number of activities may be excluded from the requirement to obtain planning permission.

**[8.364]** PDA 2000, s 166(6) provides that the government may revoke or amend any order made under this section.

**[8.365]** PDA 2000, s 167 deals with the acquisition of a site for an SDZ. A planning authority may use any of its powers to acquire land that are available to it under any enactment to include powers of compulsory acquisition of land. Those powers can be used before the making of a planning scheme and the planning authority is empowered to negotiate with an owner of land in order to facilitate the relevant development of an SDZ. Any agreement entered into with the landowner is enforceable not just against the landowner but also it will bind that landowner's successors in title.

**[8.366]** PDA 2000, s 168(1), as amended by PD(A)A 2010, s 50(1), (1A) and (3A), now reads as follows:

> (1) Subject to subsection (1A), as soon as may be after the making of an order designating a site under section 166 –
>
> > (a) the relevant development agency (other than a local authority) or, where an agreement referred to in section 167 has been made, the relevant development agency (other than a local authority) and any person who is party to the agreement shall prepare a draft planning scheme in respect of all or any part of the site and submit it to the relevant planning authority,
> >
> > (b) the local authority, where it is the development agency, or where an agreement referred to in section 167 has been made, the local authority and any person who is a party to the agreement shall prepare a draft planning scheme in respect of all or any part of the site.
>
> (1A) The first draft planning scheme under subsection (1) in respect of all or any part of the site designated under section 166, shall be prepared not later than two years after the making of the order so designating the site.

The scheme must be prepared within two years of the making of the order. The main benefit from the point of view of strategic development of an SDZ is that special planning permission rules apply.

**[8.367]** Section 168(2) of PDA 2000 has been substituted as follows:

> A draft planning scheme under this section shall consist of a written statement and the plan indicating the manner in which it is intended that the site or part of the site designated under section 166 to which the scheme relates is to be developed ...[227]

**[8.368]** Section 168(2)(a) to (g) sets out the parameters for a draft planning scheme in the following terms:

> (a) the type or types of development which may be permitted to establish on the site (subject to the order of the government under section 166),
>
> (b) the extent of any such proposed development,
>
> (c) proposals in relation to the overall design of the proposed development, including the maximum heights, the external finishes of structures and the general appearance and design,
>
> (d) proposals relating to transportation, including public transportation, the roads layout, the provision of parking spaces and traffic management,

---

[227]. PDA 2000, s 168(2) has been substituted by the provision outlined above. See PD(A)A 2000, s 168(1)(b).

(e) proposals relating to the provision of services on the site, including the provision of waste and sewerage facilities and water, electricity and telecommunications services, oil and gas pipelines, including storage facilities for oil and gas,

(f) proposals relating to minimising any adverse affects on the environment, including the natural and built environment, and on the amenities of the area, and

(g) where the scheme provides for residential development, proposals relating to the provision of amenities, facilities and services for the community, including schools, crèches and other education and childcare services.

Subsection (3A) has been added by PD(A)A 2010, s 50(c) and it reads as follows:

An appropriate assessment of a draft planning scheme shall be carried out in accordance with Pt XAB.

**[8.369]** PDA 2000, s 169, as amended by PD(A)As 2010, s 51, deals with the adoption of a planning scheme following the preparation of and submission to the planning authority of a draft planning scheme. The section sets out the procedure by which the draft planning scheme is adopted. As soon as the draft planning scheme has been prepared and submitted to the planning authority copies are sent to the Minister, to the board and to prescribed authorities. Also, a notice confirming the preparation of the draft scheme is published in one or more newspapers circulating in the area.[228] The notice circulated in newspapers advises that members of the public may inspect the draft scheme stating the places and times of inspection and that the availability of inspection lasts for a period of six weeks from the date of the newspaper notice. The newspaper notice also invites written submissions or observations with respect to the draft scheme to be submitted within the period stated in the notice for consideration by the planning authority.[229]

**[8.370]** Within 12 weeks of giving notice in the newspapers a report is prepared by the manager of the planning authority listing the persons or bodies who made submissions or observations, summarising the issues raised by them and giving the manager's response to the issues raised taking into account the proper planning and sustainable development of the area, the statutory obligations of any local authority in the area and any other relevant policies or objectives for the time being of the government or of any Minister of government.[230]

**[8.371]** The members of the planning authority then consider the draft planning scheme and the manager's report. There is a substantial amendment to PDA 2000, s 169(4)(b)[231] as summarised below.

---

228. PDA 2000, s 169(1)(a) and (b).
229. PDA 2000, s 169(2)(a) and (b).
230. PDA 2000, s 169(3)(a) and (b).
231. See PD(A)A 2010, s 51(a), (ba), (bb), (bc), (bd) and (be).

**[8.372]** The planning scheme will be deemed to have been made six weeks after the submission of that draft planning scheme and the manager's report to the members of the planning authority unless the planning authority decides by resolution to make the draft scheme subject to variations and modifications or alternatively not to make the draft planning scheme. If such resolution is passed, the planning authority will determine if a strategic environmental assessment or other appropriate assessment or both should be carried out in respect of one or more of the proposed variations or modifications that would, if made, be a material alteration of the draft planning scheme. A new time limit is then set and a notice is published in the newspaper circulating in the area giving details of the proposed material alteration and stating that the proposed material alteration may be inspected stating the place and times of inspection. The notice also invites written submissions or observations from members of the public in relation to the proposed material alteration and/or to the proposed strategic environmental assessment or other assessment which the planning authority intends to carry out.

**[8.373]** Following the making of a decision under sub-s (4) by the planning authority the authority shall, as soon as may be and in any case not later than six working days of the making of that decision, give notice of the decision to the Minister, the board, the prescribed authorities and to any persons who made written submissions or observations on the draft scheme. A notice will also be published in one or more newspapers circulating in the area giving details of the decision.[232]

**[8.374]** Once notice has been given the development agency or any persons who made submissions or observations in respect of the draft planning scheme may, for stated reasons, appeal the decision of the planning authority to the board within four weeks of the date of the planning authority's decision.[233]

**[8.375]** PDA 2000, s 169(7)(a) has been substituted by the provisions of PD(A)A 2010, s 51(b) and sub-s (7) now reads as follows:

(a) The Board may, following the consideration of an appeal made under this section, approve the making of the planning scheme, with or without any modifications (and paragraph (a) shall apply in relation to any modifications) or it may refuse to approve it.

(aa) A modification made by the Board on appeal may be made where it is minor in nature and therefore not likely to have significant affects on the environment or adversely effect the integrity of a European site.

(b) Where the Board approves the making of a planning scheme in accordance with paragraph (a) and (aa) the planning authority shall as soon as practicable, publish notice of approval of the scheme in at least one newspaper circulating in its area, and shall state that a copy of the planning scheme is available for inspection at a stated place or places (and a copy shall be kept available for inspection accordingly).

---

232. For the full text please see PDA 2000, s 169(5)(a) and (b).
233. For the full text please see PDA 2000, s 169(6).

**[8.376]** PDA 2000, s 169(8) provides that both the planning authority and the board in considering a draft planning scheme shall bear in mind the proper planning and sustainable development of the area and the provisions of the development plan, the provisions of the housing strategy, the provisions of any special amenity area order or the conservation and preservation of any European site. Where appropriate it will also consider:

   (a) the effect the scheme would have on any neighbouring land to the land concerned,

   (b) the effect the scheme would have on any place which is outside the area of the planning authority and

   (c) any other consideration relating to development outside the area of the planning authority, including any area outside the State.[234]

Once the planning scheme has been adopted it will form part of the development plan in force for the area until the scheme is revoked and the planning scheme will overrule any contrary provisions of the development plan.

**[8.377]** PDA 2000, s 170 deals with the application for development in SDZs. The normal provisions of s 34 are modified somewhat by special rules set out in s 170, as amended by PD(A)A 2010, s 52. Subject to the provision of Pt XA or Pt XAB or both of those parts as appropriate:

   A planning authority shall subject to the provisions of Pt XA and Pt XAB or both of those parts, as appropriate, grant permission in respect of an application for a development in a strategic development zone where it is satisfied that the development, where carried out in accordance with the application or subject to any conditions which the planning authority may attach to a permission, would be consistent with any planning scheme in force for the land in question, and no permission shall be granted for any development which would not be consistent with such a planning scheme.[235]

**[8.378]** PDA 2000, s 170(3) provides:

   Notwithstanding s 37, no appeal shall lie to the Board against the decision of the planning authority on application for permission in respect of a development in a strategic development zone.

**[8.379]** PDA 2000, s 170(4) provides:

   Where a planning authority decides to grant permission for a development in a strategic development zone, the grant shall be deemed to be given on the date of the decision.

**[8.380]** It will be noted that the right of appeal to An Bord Pleanála has been removed in respect of a decision on an application for permission within the SDZ. Also, under s 170(4) there is no notification of decision to grant planning permission with notification of grant of permission following four weeks later. Once the planning

---

234. PDA 2000, s 169(8).
235. PDA 2000, s 170(2) as amended by PD(A)A 2010, s 52.

authority makes its decision to grant planning permission the grant is effective as and from that date.

**[8.381]** PDA 2000, s 171 deals with the revocation of a planning scheme and allows the planning authority to either amend or revoke a planning scheme with the consent of the relevant development agency. The decision to revoke a planning scheme is a reserved function passed by resolution of the elected members of the local authority.

**[8.382]** Section 171(5) provides that if there is no revocation of a planning scheme the life of the planning scheme is five years and PDA 2000, ss 42 and 42A apply in respect of any potential extensions.

**[8.383]** It should be appreciated how strategic development within SDZs can affect normal land use rules within the planning code.

## TAKING ESTATES IN CHARGE

**[8.384]** PDA 2000, s 180 has been substantially amended by PD(A)A 2010 and for the sake of understanding the section the fully amended section is set out below and commented upon. PDA 2000, s 180(1) (as amended) provides:[236]

> Where a development for which permission is granted under s 34 or under Pt IV of the Act of 1963 includes the construction of 2 or more houses and the provision of new roads, open spaces, car parks, sewers, water mains service connections within the meaning of the Water Services Act 2007[237] or drains, and the development has been completed to the satisfaction of the planning authority in accordance with the permission and any conditions to which the permission is subject, the authority shall, where requested by the person carrying out the development, or, subject to subsection (3), by the majority of the owners of the houses involved,[238] as soon as may be, initiate the procedures under s 11 of the Roads Act 1993.

**[8.385]** It will be noted that s 180(1) only requires the planning authority to initiate the procedures under s 11 of the Roads Act 1993. The subsection does not in fact say that the planning authority is obliged to take estates in charge. As a taking in charge is the inevitable outcome of initiating proceedings under s 11 of the Roads Traffic Act 1993 it is probable that the planning authority does not have any discretion in the matter. Prior to the amendment by s 59 of PD(A)A 2010 the request to the planning authority had to be made by a majority of qualified electors who owned or occupied the houses. Now this request is made by the majority of the owners of the houses involved.

---

236. PD(A)A 2010, s 59.
237. As inserted by Water Services Act 2007.
238. The phrase 'by the majority of the owners of the houses involved' is an amendment inserted by PD(A)A 2010, s 59(a).

**[8.386]** PDA 2000, s 180(2)(a) provides:

> Notwithstanding subsection (1), where the development referred to in subsection (1) has not been completed to the satisfaction of the planning authority and either enforcement proceedings have not been commenced by the planning authority within seven years beginning on the expiration, as respects the permission authorising the development, of the appropriate period, within the meaning of section 40 or the period as extended under section 42, as the case may be, the authority shall, where requested by the majority of owners of the houses involved comply with section 11 of the Roads Act 1993 except that subsection (1)(b)(ii) of that section shall be disregarded.[239]

The obligation imposed on a planning authority under s 180(2) is mandatory and the planning authority can be compelled by *mandamus* to initiate procedures under s 11 of the Roads Act 1993.

**[8.387]** PDA 2000, s 180(2)(b) provides:

> In complying with paragraph (a), the authority may apply any security given under section 34(4)(g) for the satisfactory completion of the development in question.

**[8.388]** PDA 2000, s 180(2) deals with a situation where the development has not been completed to the satisfaction of the planning authority and where enforcement proceedings have not been commenced within the seven years of the expiration of the life of the planning permission granted for the development or such other extended time as may have been allowed.[240]

**[8.389]** PD(A)A 2010, s 59(c) has inserted a new subsection to follow s 180(2)(a) and (b), which reads as follows:

> Notwithstanding subsections (1) or (2), where a development referred to in subsection (1) has not been completed to the satisfaction of the planning authority and either –
>
> (i) enforcement proceedings have been commenced by the planning authority within seven years beginning on the expiration as respects the permission authorising the development, of the appropriate period, or

---

239. This section is also slightly amended by PD(A)A 2010, s 59(b) and the amended version appears in this text.
240. Life of a planning permission is, unless otherwise stated in the permission, five years from the date of grant; see PDA 2000, s 40, unless (i) a longer period is specified in the grant for, say, a large development which could not realistically be completed in five years or (ii) where the period is specifically extended before the expiration of the provision of PDA 2000, s 41 to allow completion of the development. Clearly, time limits do not apply to 'use permission' unless a time is specifically included as a condition of the permission. PDA 2000 has been amended by PD(A)A, s 28 to allow extension of the life of a planning permission where the planning authority is satisfied that there were considerations of a commercial, economic or technical nature beyond the control of the applicant which substantially mitigated against either the commencement of development or the carrying out of substantial works pursuant to the planning permission. The maximum period of extension is five years and one extension only is allowed.

(ii) the planning authority considers that enforcement proceedings will not result in the satisfactory completion of the development by the developer,

the authority may in its absolute discretion, at any time after the expiration as respects the permission authorising the development of the appropriate period, where requested by a majority of the owners of the houses in question, initiate the procedures under section 11 of the Roads Act 1993.

(b) In exercising its discretion and initiating procedures under section 11 of the Roads Act 1993, the authority may apply any security given under section 34(4)(g) for the satisfactory completion of the development in question.

**[8.390]** PDA 2000, s 180(3) provides:

(a) The planning authority may hold a plebiscite to ascertain the wishes of the owners of the houses.[241]

(b) The Minister may make or apply any regulations prescribing the procedure to be followed by the planning authority in ascertaining the wishes of the owners of the houses.[242]

**[8.391]** PDA 2000, s 180(4) provides:

(a) Where an order is made under section 11(1) of the Roads Act, 1993 in compliance with subsection (1) or (2), the planning authority may, in addition to the provisions of that section, take in charge –

(i) (subject to paragraph (c)), any sewers, watermains or service connections within attendant grounds of the development and

(ii) public open space or public car parks within the attendant grounds of the development.[243]

(b) Where an order is made under section 11(1) of the Roads Act, 1993 in compliance with subsection (2A), the planning authority may, in addition to the provisions of that section, take in charge –

(i) (subject to paragraph (c)), some or all of the sewers, watermains or service connections within the attendant grounds of the development, and

(ii) some or all of the public open spaces or public car parks within the attendant grounds of the development,

and may undertake,

(I) any works which, in the opinion of the authority are necessary for the completion of such sewers, watermains or service connections, public open spaces or public car parks within the attendant grounds of the development, or

(II) any works as in the opinion of the authority, are necessary to make the development safe;

---

241. PDA 2000, s 180(3)(a) as amended by PD(A)A 2010, s 59(d).
242. PDA 2000, s 180(3)(b) as amended by PD(A)A 2010, s 59(e).
243. PDA 2000, s 180(4) as amended by PD(A)A 2010, s 59(f).

and may recover the costs of works referred to in clause (I) or (II) from the developer as a simple contract debt in a court of competent jurisdiction.

(c) A planning authority that is not a water services authority within the meaning of section 2 of the Act of 2007 shall not take in charge any sewers, watermains or service connections under paragraph (a)(i) or (b)(i), but shall request the relevant water services authority to do so.

(d) In paragraph (a)(ii), 'public open spaces' or 'public car parks' means open spaces or car parks to which the public have access whether as of right or by permission.

(e) In this subsection, 'public open spaces' means open spaces or car parks to which the public have access as of right or by permission.

[8.392] The 'Act of 2007' refers to the Water Services Act 2007 and s 95 deals with the taking in charge or acquisition by agreement of waterworks by a water services authority where not fewer than two-thirds of those persons entitled to dispose of it agree it such a transfer.

PDA 2000, s 180(4) provides:

(d) In subsection (4) 'public open spaces' or 'public car parks' means open spaces or car parks to which the public have access whether as of right or by permission,

PDA 2000, s 180(2A)(a) provides:

(5) Where a planning authority acts in compliance with this section references in section 11 of the Roads Act 1993, to a road authority shall be deemed to include references to a planning authority.

[8.393] If effect, a local authority is obliged to take in charge the internal roads services together with car parks, sewers, water mains or drains in a housing estate subject to certain conditions having been complied with. For PDA 2000, s 180, as amended by PD(A)A 2010, s 59, to operate there must be a development for which planning permission was granted under PDA 2000, s 34 or under Pt IV of the LG(PD)A 1963 for the construction of two or more houses and for the provision of open spaces, car parks, sewers, water mains or drains. Most importantly, before the section can operate the development must have been completed to the satisfaction of the planning authority in accordance with the permission granted and the conditions imposed in that permission.

[8.394] The manner in which the roads, footpaths, open spaces, car parks and services are taken in charge is by the making of an order under s 11 of the Roads Act 1993. The Roads Act 1993 covers not only roads but also footpaths, open spaces and services within the attendant grounds of the development. The planning authority is not required to initiate the s 180 procedure on its own imitative but rather it can only be initiated on the request of persons carrying out the development or on the request of the majority of the owners of the houses. In order to determine the wishes of the owners of the houses a planning authority may hold a plebiscite and the Minister may make or apply regulations prescribing the procedure to be followed by the planning authority in ascertaining the wishes of the owners of the houses. Prior to the amendment made by PD(A)A 2010 the persons to be consulted by plebiscite were 'qualified electors' living in the estate. A 'qualified elector' is every person who in relation to the area of the dwelling house in question is registered as a local government elector in the register of local government electors for the time being in force. Furthermore, the planning authority must initiate the procedure to have the roads, footpaths, open spaces, services, etc, taken in charge 'as soon as may be'.[244] PDA 2000, s 34(4)(m) provides:

> Conditions for requiring the provision of roads, including traffic calming measures, open spaces, car parks, sewers, water mains or drains, facilities for collection or storage or recyclable materials and other public facilities in excess of the immediate needs of the proposed development, subject to the local authority paying for the cost of additional works and taking them in charge or otherwise entering into an agreement with the application with respect to the provision of those facilities.

That provision does require the taking in charge of roads, open spaces and services which are in excess of the needs of the proposed development.

**[8.395]** In these circumstances, a planning authority is obliged to initiate the procedures under s 11 of the Road Act 1993 if requested to do so by a majority of the owners of the houses in question. The seven-year period referred to in PDA 2000, s 180(2) coincides with the period of seven years from the expiration of the life of a planning permission after which enforcement action cannot be commenced except in the case of a use permission imposed by condition or granted permission, which will have no time limit for enforcement. The seven-year time limit referred to in PDA 2000, s 180(2) is usually, therefore, a 12-year time limit being five years plus seven years – unless the period is extended.

**[8.396]** Finally, PDA 2000, s 180(6) has been substituted by PD(A)A 2010, s 59(g) so that the subsection now reads:

> In this section 'appropriate period' has the meaning given to the term in section 40, as extended under section 42 or 42(a) as the case may be.

## TREE PRESERVATION ORDERS

**[8.397]** PDA 2000, s 205 provides for the making of a tree preservation order (TPO) which provision, once a TPO is made, over-rules the exempted development provisions provided by PDA 2000, s 4(1)(i) which permit the thinning, felling and replanting of trees, forest and woodlands, bearing in mind that certain of these exempted

---

244. In *Harding v Cork County Council* (unreported, 2 May 2008) SC, Murray CJ examined the meaning of those often used and mischievous words 'as soon as may be': 'As regards the latter point concerning the "as soon as may be" requirement it has to be borne in mind first of all that this is an administrative procedure and requirements as to time must be interpreted having regard to the ordinary burdens of administration in any organisation or body. It is not as if the matter in question was the only such matter with which the planning authority in question had to deal with. In particular the requirement in such a regulation should not be interpreted strictly as might be the case in criminal procedure where the personal rights of individuals in the administration of justice are directly an issue'.

developments may come within the scope of requiring an EIS.[245] A planning authority may make a provision for the preservation of any tree, trees or group of trees or woodlands if it appears to it that it is expedient, in the interests of amenity or of the environment to make a TPO for stated reasons.[246] The statutory provisions take a serious view of TPOs and of proposed TPOs by making the contravention of such an order by any person a criminal offence.[247]

[8.398] The consequence of making a TPO is to prohibit the cutting down, topping, lopping or willful destruction of trees but the orders may be made subject to conditions.[248] The order will require the owner of the land concerned to enter into an agreement with the planning authority to ensure proper management of any trees, group of trees or woodlands (including the replanting of trees). The obligation imposed on the landowner by agreement is, however, subject to the planning authority providing assistance, including financial assistance, towards the management as may be agreed.[249]

[8.399] Particulars of any TPO made by a planning authority shall be entered in the planning register and should be discoverable there by making a planning search.[250]

[8.400] A TPO will not apply to the cutting down, topping or lopping of trees which are dying or dead or which have become dangerous, or the cutting down, topping or lopping, of any trees in compliance with any obligation imposed by or under any enactment or, so far as may be necessary, for the abatement of any nuisance or hazard.[251]

[8.401] Significantly, a common source of friction which may occur between neighbouring properties is not covered separately by this subsection. Where a neighbour's branches travel across a boundary the common law position is that the branches may be cut down and stacked on the offending neighbour's side of the fence. If the trees to which the branches belong are protected by a TPO they cannot be cut down in that way unless (1) they are dying or dead, (2) they have become dangerous, (3) cutting or lopping them would be in compliance with an obligation imposed by or under any enactment, (4) cutting or lopping trespassing branches is necessary for the prevention or abatement of nuisance or hazard, or (5) a successful application is made to the planning authority amending or revoking a TPO at least to the extent that trespassing branches may be cut.[252]

---

245. PDA 2000, s 4(1)(i) has been amended by PD(A)A 2010, s 5(1)(a) by excluding from the section as 'exempted development', 'the construction, maintenance and improvement of non-public roads serving forests and woodlands and works ancillary to that development'.
246. PDA 2000, s 205(1)(b).
247. PDA 2000, s 205(4)(c).
248. PDA 2000, s 205(2)(a).
249. PDA 2000, s 205(2)(b).
250. PDA 2000, s 205(12).
251. PDA 2000, s 205(11).
252. LG(PD)Act 1963, s 45 permitted the cutting and lopping of trees with the consent of the planning authority. It is perhaps regrettable that this section, or even a limited version of it, was not repeated in PDA 2000 to deal specifically with trespassing trees. It is significant that whereas s 45 of the 1963 Act provided a right of appeal to An Bord Pleanála, a TPO made by a planning authority under PDA 2000, s 205 offers no such right of appeal.

**[8.402]** PDA 2000, s 205(3)–(9) sets out the statutory procedures for the making of a TPO.

**[8.403]** A planning authority must serve notice containing a map indicating the tree, trees, group of trees or woodlands and the map must be served on the owner or occupier advising of the planning authority's intention to make a TPO. Public notice of the planning authority's intention to make a TPO must be published in one or more newspapers circulating in the area.[253]

**[8.404]** The notice must state that the planning authority proposes to make a TPO and it must invite submissions or observations to be lodged with the planning authority within six weeks of the date of the notice. Particularly, the notice must state that any submissions or observations lodged will be taken into consideration by the planning authority. Once the notice has been served and advertised it becomes effective as a proposed TPO and any acts in contravention of it amount to a criminal offence.[254] The planning authority, having considered any submissions or observations, may, by resolution, make a TPO with or without modification and with or without conditions or it may refuse to make such an order. Any person served with a notice of intention to make a TPO will be notified of the TPO when it is made.[255]

**[8.405]** Where a planning authority intends to either amend or revoke a TPO, it must follow the same notice and other procedures as are required for the initial making of a TPO.[256]

**[8.406]** Provision for payment of compensation in certain circumstances was available under the provisions of LG(PD)A 1990, s 21 where consent for cutting down, topping and/or lopping trees was refused. Also, compensation was payable under s 45 of LG(PD)A 1990 for the making of a TPO in certain circumstances. However, no compensation in respect of a TPO or a proposed TPO is payable under the provisions of PDA 2000, s 205.

**[8.407]** In *O'Callaghan v Commissioners of Public Works in Ireland*,[257] an agreement for compensation based on the proposition that the constitutional property rights of a property owner had been unlawfully attacked when the use of the land was restricted without payment of compensation when the owner was bound to protect and preserve a national monument, was unsuccessful. Dealing with the situation where s 205 does not provide any compensation for the various actions taken under the TPO provisions, Simons makes the following observation:

> The omission of provision for the payment of compensation is all the more worrying in circumstances where the right of appeal against the making of a Tree

---

253. PDA 2000, s 205(3)(a) and (b).
254. PDA 2000, s 205(4)(a),(b) and (c).
255. PDA 2000, s 205(5).
256. PDA 2000, s 205(6), (7)(a) and (b), (8)(a) and (b) and (9).
257. *O'Callaghan v Commissioners of Public Works in Ireland* [1993] ILRM 391, HC; on appeal [1995] ILRM 364, SC.

Preservation Order which had existed under the previous legislation has been omitted from s 205. To this extent, the owner or occupier of land is thrown at the mercy of a planning authority.[258]

It certainly does appear to be unusual that no right of appeal is allowed to An Bord Pleanála in respect of a TPO and the matter is left without possibility of challenging the potential whim and personal prejudice of a planner working in a local authority office who, in these circumstances, is accountable to nobody. A TPO could be judicially reviewed if the grounds for making it were wholly irrational or wholly unreasonable.

---

258. See Simons, *Planning and Development Law* (2nd edn, Thomson Round Hall, 2007) at para 8–115, p 371.

# Chapter 9
# SUBSTITUTE CONSENT AND APPROPRIATE ASSESSMENT

## ABOLITION OF RETENTION PERMISSION WHERE EIA IS REQUIRED[1]

[9.01] The possibility of obtaining retention permission was dealt with in s 27 of the Local Government (Planning and Development) Act 1963 (LG(PD)A 1963) and by s 34(12) of the Planning and Deveopment Act 2000 (PDA 2000). Those provisions permitted an application for retention of unauthorised development. In determining a retention application the planning authority and the board are both precluded from having regard to the fact that the development is in place and that if the application for retention permission is refused, the development structure may have to be removed.

[9.02] In *State (Fitzgerald) v An Bord Pleanála*,[2] the developer developed a structure which was not in accordance with the permission granted. An Bord Pleanála granted retention permission on the grounds that the differences between the developed structure and the structure envisaged by the planning permission were not so great as to justify an order requiring the removal of the structure. The Supreme Court held that in making a determination the High Court had relied on an irrelevant consideration and that the developer should not be entitled to benefit from his own wrong doing. Equally, neither the board nor the planning authority, in considering an application for retention permission, should take any account of the hardship which would be caused to the developer if his application for retention permission were refused.[3]

[9.03] PDA 2000, s 34(12) has been substituted by four new subsections in s 23 of the PD(A)A 2010 being sub-ss (12), (12A), (12B) and (12C). In effect, application for retention permission can no longer be applied for if the development is one which would require environmental impact assessment (EIA). The amendment is a direct result of the European Court of Justice (ECJ) decision in the *Derrybrien landslide* case[4] where the court held that Ireland was in breach of EU law in permitting retention permission to be granted for projects which require an EIA. Subsequent to that ECJ decision, the Minister issued a circular to all planning authorities and to An Bord Pleanála directing them not to grant retention permission for developments which require EIA. The amendments give statutory effect to the ministerial direction.

---

1. This topic has been dealt with extensively in preceding chapters (see index) and particularly [2.94] to [2.106]. What appears here is a brief explanation of the amended retention permission given as an introduction to the meaning of 'substitute consent'.
2. *State (Fitzgerald) v An Bord Pleanála* [1985] ILRM 117.
3. See also *Village Residents Association Limited v An Bord Pleanála* [2000] 1 IR 65, HC, Geoghegan J.
4. *Commission of European Communities v Ireland* (Case C–215/06) [2008] ECR I–4911.

**[9.04]** PDA 2000, s 34(12), as amended by s 23(12) of the PD(A)A 2010, now provides as follows:

> (12) A planning authority shall refuse to consider an application to retain unauthorised development of land where the authority decides that if an application for permission had been made in respect of the development concerned before it was commenced the application would have required that one or more than one of the following was carried out –
>
> > (a) an environmental impact assessment,
> >
> > (b) a determination as to whether an environmental impact assessment is required, or
> >
> > (c) an appropriate assessment.
>
> (12A) for the purposes of subsection (12), if an application for permission had been made in respect of the following development before it was commenced, the application shall be deemed not to have required a determination referred to at subsection (12B):
>
> > (a) development within the curtilage of a dwellinghouse, for any purpose incidental to the enjoyment of the dwellinghouse as a dwellinghouse;
> >
> > (b) modifications to the exterior of a building.
>
> (12B) where a planning authority refuses to consider an application for permission under subsection (12) it shall return the application to the applicant together with any fee received from the applicant in respect of the application, and shall give reasons for its decision to the applicant.
>
> (12C) subject to subsections (12) and (12A), an application for development of land in accordance with the permission regulations may be made for the retention of unauthorised development, and this section shall apply to such an application, subject to any necessary modifications.

## SUBSTITUTE CONSENT

**[9.05]** In taking steps to comply with its obligations under Directive 85/337/EEC, Ireland has abolished entitlement to obtain development permission for development requiring EIA where no such assessment has occurred and in doing so it has formed a new 'consent' procedure namely the 'substitute consent', which is legislated for in 17 detailed subsections of PD(A)A 2001, Pt XA and further supplemented by 14 additional subsections in Pt XAB dealing with 'appropriate assessment'. The purpose of the substitute consent procedure is to assist developers who can no longer apply for retention permission because the development which they completed was one which required EIA. The newly inserted 'substitute consent' procedure is aimed at regularising any developments which should have been subject to EIA but which were not so subject. The substitute consent procedure applies to all development which is prescribed for the purposes of either Annex I or Annex II of the EIA Directive. Its application is not limited to cases where an assessment was required but was not carried out. Its application also applies to sub-threshold cases where there was a failure to carry out 'screening', that is to say, without either the planning authority or the board determining whether or not the development was likely to have significant effects on the environment.[5] If there was no screening and even if the development proposal is sub-threshold it is, nevertheless, subject to the substitute consent procedure. An application for leave to apply for substitute consent must also be made if the development has neglected to or failed to carry out an 'appropriate assessment' for the purposes of art 6.3 of the Habitats Directive.

[9.06] One other matter which is now beyond argument is the fact that any development which requires EIA cannot, in any circumstances, be exempted development.[6]

[9.07] The application for substitute consent is made to An Bord Pleanála. An application for substitute consent arises in three separate circumstances namely as follows:

1. In cases where an existing planning permission is held to be defective, invalid or otherwise in breach of the law by a final judgment of a court of competent jurisdiction in the State or by the European Court of Justice. Where this occurs a planning authority must serve notice on the developer/developers and/or on the person(s) occupying the land as appropriate, stating that an application for substitute consent must be made.

2. A second instance where a proprietor applicant can apply for substitute consent may arise where the developer/occupier of land, as appropriate, is of the opinion that the permission which he/she has received may be in breach of the law, invalid or otherwise defective. In those circumstances the developer/occupier can lodge an application for substitute consent in order to regularise his/her position. Such an application for substitute consent may be made to An Bord Pleanála even if the time limit for taking judicial review proceedings has expired. In these circumstances also, the developer/occupier is relieved of the necessity to establish 'exceptional circumstances' on the grounds that the applicant who holds a permission which he considers to be invalid has, at least, taken the trouble to highlight that situation voluntarily and has made an application for substitute consent at a time when development has not commenced.

3. The third instance of an application for substitute consent may arise in a case where there are 'exceptional circumstances'. At the application for leave stage the board must be satisfied that there are 'exceptional circumstances' to enable an application for substitute consent to be considered. In considering whether or not there are such 'exceptional circumstances' the board shall have regard to the following matters:
    (a) whether regularisation of the development concerned would circumvent the purpose and objectives of the Environmental Impact Assessment Directive or the Habitats Directive;
    (b) whether the applicant had or could reasonably have had a belief that the development was not authorised;

---

5. See PDR 2001, Sch 7 (as amended).
6. PDR 2001, art 9(1)(c).

(c) whether the ability to carry out an assessment of the Environmental Impacts of the development for the purpose of an Environmental Impact Assessment or an appropriate assessment and to provide for public participation in such an assessment has been substantially impaired;

(d) the actual or likely significant effects on the environment or adverse effects on the integrity of a European site resulting from the carrying out or continuation of the development;

(e) the extent to which significant effects on the environment or adverse effects on the integrity of a European site can be remediated;

(f) whether the applicant has complied with previous planning permissions granted or has previously carried out an unauthorised development;

(g) such other matters as the Board considers relevant.[7]

[9.08] The largest category of development which may require an application for substitute consent is quarry development. Quarrying activity reflects the state of the economy and, not unlike the economy quarrying operations, is a stop/go affair. We have seen that quarries have been given a two-year period from the date on which notice is served upon the owner or operator of the quarry requiring an application to An Bord Pleanála for substitute consent which application must be accompanied by a remedial environmental impact statement (EIS) or a remedial Natura impact statement or both such statements, as appropriate. Within that two-year period quarry owners/operators will be compelled to put their affairs in order. Once the time limit has expired all quarries which are non-compliant with planning and with environmental legislative requirements will be deemed to be carrying out unauthorised development if they should continue to operate. The enforcement regime has been improved by the provisions of the PD(A)A 2010. Non-compliant quarries will be forced to cease operations.

## Natura 2000 sites and Natura impact statements

[9.09] Frequent mention is made in Pt XA and in Pt XAB to Natura 2000 sites and to Natura impact statements. The Natura 2000 network is the network of important ecological sites across the European Union made up of Special Protection Areas (SPAs) and of special areas of conservation (SACs). The purpose of designating areas as SPAs or SACs is to ensure that they are environmentally sustainable and that activities both of humans and of nature will be controlled, as far as possible, so as not to affect the integrity of the area or its habitats and that it will not adversely affect the EU objective of protected species conservation and biodiversity of species.[8]

---

7. PDA 2000, s 177D(2)(a) to (g) as inserted by PD(A)A 2010, s 57.
8. An Taisce – the National Trust for Ireland explains biodiversity with the following example: 'In Ireland 95 bird species are threatened or in serious decline. 120 plant species are in danger. Ireland's longest living animal, the freshwater pearl mussel, is facing extinction throughout its range in Irish rivers. Many types of fish are now scarce and population viability poor. Such reduction of biodiversity in Ireland have serious economic and social consequences'.

**[9.10]** Natura 2000 sites in Ireland, comprising both SACs and SPAs cover 10% of Ireland's land mass. Specifically, SACs are wildlife conservation areas which are considered to be important on an Irish as well as on a European scale. Mostly they are located in the countryside but a few are to be found close to town or city landscapes, including, for example, Dublin Bay and Cork Harbour. Irish habitats include raised bogs, active blanket bogs, turloughs,[9] sand dunes, machairs (flat sandy plains mainly located on the north and west coast), heaths, lakes, rivers, woodland estuaries and sea inlets. The 25 species which must be afforded protection in Ireland include, salmon, otter, freshwater pearl mussels, bottle-nosed dolphins and the Killarney fern. Ireland has contributed some 420 SACs to the Natura network and these sites have been adopted as Sites of Community Importance.

**[9.11]** SPAs protect special areas where wild birds breed, feed, roost and which are used by birds as wintering areas. The Birds Directive, which also caters specifically for the protection of long distance migratory birds, covers the protection, management, control and exploitation of wild birds throughout the European Union. Member States are required to take the necessary steps to maintain wild bird populations at levels determined by ecological, scientific and cultural needs. It is the Birds Directive 79/409/EEC which has for more than 30 years required the designation of SPAs to protect listed and vulnerable species such as the whopper swan, the Greenland white-fronted goose, the peregrine falcon, the corncrake, terns and perhaps the extremely rare and elusive morning dove. SPAs are also provided to encourage and to protect migratory species such as ducks, geese and waders and to ensure that wetlands of international importance, which attract large numbers of migratory birds each year, are preserved. The terms 'internationally important' means that 1% of the population of a species uses the site or that more than 20,000 birds use the site regularly. Familiar examples of SPAs include Wexford Nature Reserve, Bull Island, Skelligs, Rockabill, Baldoyle Estuary, Tralee Bay, Old Head of Kinsale, Broadmeadow/Swords Estuary, Galway Inner, Killarney National Park, the Shannon/Fergus Estuary, Loop Head and Rathlin O'Beirne. These examples are just some of the 132 SPAs in Ireland.

**[9.12]** A Natura impact statement was previously known as a statement for appropriate assessment. It is a statement prepared by ecological specialists who undertake surveys, research and analysis with input from other experts (such as hydrologists or engineers) dealing with SACs and/or SPAs. Where development is contemplated which might possibly have an adverse affect on the integrity of a Natura 2000 site or on the conservation objectives of a Natura 2000 site, a Natura impact statement must be prepared for submission to the planning authority or to the board, as appropriate. If the planning authority or the board, as appropriate, having examined the Natura impact statement are satisfied that the statement is complete and objective, it will carry out an 'appropriate assessment' on the basis of the Natura impact statement and any other necessary information which is available to it. Where the planning authority or the board

---

9. The word turlough meaning dry (tur) lake (lough) is peculiar to Ireland. It is a low lying area on limestone which becomes flooded in wet weather through the welling up of ground water through the rock.

concludes, subsequent to carrying out an appropriate assessment, that there will be no adverse effects on a Natura 2000 site, the plan or project can proceed to authorisation where the normal planning or other requirements will apply in reaching a decision to approve or refuse the application. However, if adverse effects are likely or if such adverse effects cannot be ruled out then 'appropriate assessment' will not be carried out unless the obligation imposed by art 6(4) of the Habitats Directive[10] applies.

**[9.13]** Article 6(4) of the Habitats Directive reads as follows:

> If, in spite of a negative assessment of the implications for the site and in the absence of alternative solutions, a plan or project must nevertheless be carried out for the imperative reasons of overriding public interest, including those of a social or economic nature, the Member State shall take all compensatory measures necessary to ensure that the overall coherence of Natura 2000 is protected. It shall inform the Commission of the compensatory measures adopted.

Where the site concerned hosts a priority natural habitat type and/or a priority species, the only considerations which may be raised are those relating to (a) human health or public safety, (b) beneficial consequences of primary importance for the environment, (c) further to an opinion from the Commission, (d) other imperative reasons of overriding public interest.

**[9.14]** Recourse to derogation to allow a plan or project to proceed should only be pursued in 'exceptional circumstances' and the Minister must be informed, at an early stage, of any possible 'imperative reasons' for overriding public interest (IROPI) requiring a project to proceed. 'Exceptional circumstances' also require that there are no less damaging alternative solutions and that compensatory measures have been identified and can be put in place.

**[9.15]** PDA 2000[11] contains an interpretation section at s 177A. The interpretation of the phrases used throughout Pt XA are specified and these are dealt with below in ss 177D(2), 177F, 177G and 177K.

**[9.16]** Subsection (2) of PDA 2000, s 177A (as inserted)[12] reads:

> Subject to this Part, a word or expression that is used in the Part and that is also used in the Birds Directive or the Habitats Directive has, unless the context otherwise requires, the same meaning in this Part as it has in the Birds Directive or the Habitats Directive.

## Application for substitute consent where notice served by the planning authority

**[9.17]** These applications are dealt with in PDA 2000, s 177B as inserted by PD(A)A s 57.

---

10. Habitats Directive 92/43/EEC, art 6(4).
11. This section was inserted by PD(A)A 2010, s 57.
12. This section was inserted by PD(A)A 2010, s 57.

**[9.18]** A planning authority which becomes aware that development in respect of which permission was granted in circumstances where:

(a) An environmental impact assessment,

(b) A determination in relation to whether an environmental impact assessment is required, or

(c) An appropriate assessment,[13]

was or is required, that a final judgment of a court of competent jurisdiction in the State or the Court of Justice of the EU[14] has been made to the effect that the permission was in breach of law, invalid or otherwise defective in a material respect because of:

(i) A matter contained in or omitted from the application, including omission of an EIS or of a Natura impact statement or the omission of both. Also, if an EIS or a Natura impact statement are inadequate,

(ii) An error of fact or law or a procedural error (no matter how trivial).[15]

If any of the above circumstances apply the planning authority shall give notice in writing to the developer. The notice in writing given to the developer will inform the developer of the proceedings and findings. It will also direct the recipient of the notice to apply for substitute consent within 12 weeks from the date of the notice and that the application must be accompanied by an EIS or a remedial Natura impact statement or both, if appropriate. The notice served will also advise the recipient that he or she may make submissions or observations to the planning authority within four weeks from the date of the notice. Within a period of eight weeks from the date of giving notice, the planning authority shall confirm the notice if no submissions or observations are made to it. Alternatively, if submissions or observations have been made to the planning authority it has the option either to confirm or to withdraw the notice. A planning authority will only withdraw a notice if it has been shown to it that no final judgment has been made by a court of competent jurisdiction in the State or by the Court of Justice of the European Union ruling that the permission granted was in breach of law, invalid or otherwise defective in a material respect regarding the adequacy of the EIS submitted or regarding appropriate assessment.[16] Details of the confirmation or withdrawal of the notice must be entered in the planning register.[17]

## Application for substitute consent where notice not served by planning authority

**[9.19]** PDA 2000, s 177C, as inserted by PD(A)A 2010, s 57, provides the ground rules for and the circumstances in which making an application for leave to apply for a

---

13. The meaning of 'appropriate assessment' is fully dealt with below in the explanations of PD(A)A 2001, Pt XAB; see paras **[9.78]** to **[9.88]**.
14. See *Derrybrien landslide* case: *Commission of European Communities v Ireland* (Case C–215/06) [2008] ECR I–4911.
15. See PD(A)A 2010, Pt XA, s 177B(1).
16. PDA 2000, s 177B(2), (3) and (4) as inserted by PD(A)A 2010, s 57.
17. PDA 2000, s 177B(8) as inserted by PD(A)A 2010, s 57.

substitute consent can be made where a notice has not been served by the planning authority. For the purpose of s 177C development in relation to which an applicant may make an application for leave to apply for substitute consent is a development which has been carried out where:

1. An EIA; or
2. A determination as to whether an EIA is required; or
3. An appropriate assessment, was or is required in respect of which assessment the applicant either:

   (a) the applicant for leave to apply for substitute consent considers that a permission granted by the planning authority or the board may be in breach of law, invalid or otherwise defective in a material respect, whether pursuant to a final judgment of a court of competent jurisdiction in the State or of the Court of Justice of the European Union or otherwise, by reason of:

   any matter contained in or omitted from an application for permission including omission of an environmental impact statement or a Natura impact statement or both of those statements, as the case may be, or inadequacy of an environmental impact statement or a Natura impact statement or both of those statements, as the case may be or by reason of any error of fact or law or a procedural error;

   or

   (b) the applicant is of the opinion that exceptional circumstances exist such that it may be appropriate to permit the regularisation of the development by permitting an application for substitute consent.[18]

A person who has carried out such a development as set out above and as referred to in s 177C(2)(a) and (b), or the owner or occupier of land, as appropriate, who has not received a notice from the planning authority under the provisions of s 177B may apply to the board for leave to apply for substitute consent in respect of the development.[19]

**[9.20]** In summary, s 177B deals with the circumstances in which a person served with a notice by the planning authority may seek leave to apply to the board to make an application for substitute consent, whereas s 177C deals with the circumstances in which a person may make application to the board for leave to apply for a substitute consent where no notice has been served by the planning authority.

**[9.21]** An applicant for leave to apply to the board for substitute consent under s 177C(1) must furnish to the board all documents which he or she, as applicant, considers to be relevant together with any additional information or documentation requested by the board.[20]

---

18. PD(A)A 2010, s 177C(2)(a) and (b).
19. PD(A)A 2010, s 177C(1).
20. PD(A)A 2010, s 177C(3)(a) and (b).

**[9.22]** The Board's request for additional information will contain a deadline for the furnishing of such additional information and if the deadline is not met or if any other time limit as the board may allow is not met, the application for leave shall be deemed to be withdrawn.[21]

**[9.23]** Broad powers are given to the board to require information and documents from the planning authority concerned and such documents and information must be furnished to the board within six weeks of the date that the information and/or documents were sought.[22]

**[9.24]** PDA 2000, s 177D, as inserted by PD(A)A 2010, s 57, deals with the circumstances which will allow the board to grant leave to apply for substitute consent. For the board to allow such an application for leave to apply, primarily the board must be satisfied that an EIA, a determination that an EIA is required, or an appropriate assessment is required. Furthermore, the board must be satisfied either:

> (a) that a permission granted for development by a planning authority or the Board is in breach of law, invalid or otherwise defective in a material respect whether by reason of a final judgment of a court of competent jurisdiction in the State or the Court of Justice of the European Union, or otherwise, by reason of –
>
>> (i) any matter contained in or omitted from the application for the permission including omission of an environmental impact statement or a Natura impact statement or both of those statements as the case may be, or inadequacy of an environmental impact statement or a Natura statement or both of those statements, as the case may be, or
>>
>> (ii) any error of fact or law or procedural error,
>
> or
>
> (b) that exceptional circumstance exist such that the Board consider it appropriate to permit the opportunity for regularisation of the development by permitting an application for substitute consent.[23]

In considering 'exceptional circumstances' as referred to in PDA 2000, s 177D(1)(b) the board is required to have regard to seven matters which are set out below, namely:

> (a) whether regularisation of the development concerned would circumvent the purpose and objectives of the Environmental Impact Assessment Directive or the Habitats Directive;
>
> (b) whether the applicant had or could reasonably have had a belief that the development was not unauthorised;
>
> (c) whether the ability to carry out an assessment of the environmental impacts of the development for the purpose of an Environmental Impact

---

21. PD(A)A 2010, s 177C(4).
22. PD(A)A 2010, s 177C(5).
23. PD(A)A 2010, s 177D(1)(a) and (b).

**[9.25]**                                  *Planning and Environmental Law in Ireland*

Assessment or an appropriate assessment and to provide for public participation in such an assessment has been substantially impaired;

(d)    the actual or likely significant effects on the environment or adverse effects on the environment or adverse effects on the integrity of a European site resulting from the carrying out or continuation of the development;

(e)    the extent to which significant effects on the environment or adverse effects on the integrity of a European site can be remediated;

(f)    whether the applicant has complied with previous planning permissions granted or has previously carried out an unauthorised development;

(g)    such other matters as the Board considers relevant.

By virtue of art 2(3) of the EIA Directive, which deals with the assessment of effects on certain public and private projects on the environment, a Member State may, in exceptional cases, exempt specific projects from the whole of or part of the EIA Directive. The difficulty is that the EIA Directive makes no attempt to state the circumstances in which the 'exceptional cases' exemption applies. Article 2(3) provides that specific projects may be exempted from the Directive in exceptional cases. There are no definitions and no examples provided of the kind of cases which might be exceptional cases and as such would avoid the assessment required under art 2(1), which deals with projects likely to have significant effects on the environment by virtue, *inter alia*, of their nature, size or location.

**[9.25]** The EIA Directive of 1985 has been amended three times as follows:

- Directive 97/11/EC widened the scope of the EIA Directive by increasing the types of projects covered, and the number of projects requiring mandatory environmental impact assessment (Annex I). The 97 amendments also provided for new screening arrangements, including new screening criteria at Annex III for Annex II projects, and established minimum information requirements. Finally the 97 Directive brought the EIA Directive into line with the UN ECE Espoo Convention on EIA in a Transboundary context.

- Directive 2003/35/EC sought to align the provisions on public participation with the Aarhus Convention on public participation in decision-making and access to justice in environmental matters.

- Directive 2009/31/EC amended Annexes I and II of the EIA Directive by the addition of projects related to transport and capture and storage of carbon dioxide.

Prior to carrying out EIA, a prospective developer can seek assistance from the competent authority and can request details of precisely what should be covered by the EIA information to be provided. That procedure is referred to as 'scoping'.

**[9.26]** Next the developer must furnish information which deals with the likely environmental impact which will occur if the development proceeds. That stage is referred to as the EIA report – Annex IV.

**[9.27]** Pursuant to the principles laid down at the Aarhus Convention, members of the public must be informed as indeed must Member States who may be affected by the development proposal and where necessary both members of the public and affected Member States must be consulted. Before making its decision the competent authority is required to take into consideration the result of the consultations. Once the decision is made the public are informed of that decision and thereafter are entitled to challenge the decision before the courts where there are grounds for doing so.

**[9.28]** In making a decision as to whether or not to grant leave to apply for substitute consent the board shall have regard both to the information furnished by the applicant and to the information furnished by the planning authority.[24] The Board may decide to grant or to refuse leave to apply but in either case the decision must be made within six weeks after the receipt of:

(a) an application;

(b) additional information from the applicant;

(c) information from the planning authority;

whichever is the later.[25]

The Board's decision shall be in writing and it shall be a reasoned decision.[26]

**[9.29]** Any leave for application to apply for substitute consent shall be granted by the board on the following terms:

(a) that the application for substitute consent shall be made within 12 weeks of the board's notice.

(b) that the application will be accompanied by a remedial impact statement or a remedial Natura impact statement or by both if the board considers that appropriate.[27]

**[9.30]** The Board's decision and direction shall be given to the planning authority in whose area the subject development is located and same shall be entered in the planning authority's planning register.[28]

## Application for substitute consent

**[9.31]** PD(A)A 2010, s 177E(1)–(5) deals with the actual application for a substitute consent as opposed to the application for leave to apply for substitute consent. The leave to apply procedure is, of course, a precondition to the application for substitute consent. Clearly, in the application for substitute consent the name of the applicant must be stated

---

24. PD(A)A 2010, s 177C(3) and (5).
25. PD(A)A 2010, s 177D(5).
26. PD(A)A 2010, s 177D(6).
27. PD(A)A 2010, s 177D(7).
28. PD(A)A 2010, s 177D(8).

and as required by s 177B(2) the application must be accompanied by either a remedial EIS and/or a remedial Natura impact statement.[29]

**[9.32]** The exact details required for an application for substitute consent are as follows:

Section 177E:

(2) An application to the Board for substitute consent shall –

- (a) be made pursuant to a notice given under section 177B or 261A or a decision to grant leave to apply for substitute consent under section 177D,
- (b) state the name of the person making the application,
- (c) in accordance with a direction of the planning authority under section 177B(2), shall be accompanied by a remedial environmental impact statement or a remedial Natura impact statement or both of those statements, as the case may be,
- (d) in accordance with a direction of the Board under section 177D(7), shall be accompanied by a remedial environmental impact statement or remedial Natura impact statement or both of those statements, as the case may be,
- (e) be accompanied by a fee payable in accordance with section 177M,
- (f) comply with any requirements prescribed under section 177N, and
- (g) be received by the Board within the period specified in section 177B, 177D or 261A, as appropriate.

The application must also be made in accordance with the regulations made by the Minister under the provisions of PD(A)A 2010, s 177N.[30]

**[9.33]** An application for a substitute consent which has not complied with the requirements of s 177E(2) shall be invalid.[31]

**[9.34]** The Board may, entirely at its own discretion, extend the time limit for making an application for leave to apply by such further period as it considers appropriate.[32]

**[9.35]** Having received an application for a substitute consent which is not invalid, the board must send a copy of the application and all associated documents, including any remedial EIS and/or the remedial Natura impact statement, to the planning authority for the area where the development is to take place and such documentation shall be placed on the planning authority's planning register. Interestingly, the provisions of PD(A)A 2010, s 177E(5) do not compel the planning authority to place the documentation on the register 'as soon as may be'; no time limit is prescribed by the subsection.

---

29. PD(A)A 2010, s 177B(2) and 177D(7).
30. The regulations concerned are Planning and Development Regulations 2010.
31. PD(A)A 2010, s 177E(3).
32. PD(A)A 2010, s 177E(4).

**[9.36]** The required contents for a remedial EIS are set out in s 177F(1). A remedial impact statement shall contain the following:

(a) a statement of the significant effects, if any, on the environment, which have occurred or which are occurring or which can reasonably be expected to occur because the development the subject of the application for substitute consent was carried out;

(b) details of –

  (i) any appropriate remedial measures undertaken or proposed to be undertaken by the applicant for substitute consent to remedy any significant adverse effects on the environment;

  (ii) the period of time within which any proposed remedial measures shall be carried out by or on behalf of the applicant;

(c) such information as may be prescribed under section 177N.[33]

An applicant may, before applying to the board for substitute consent, apply to the board for an opinion in writing setting out what information should be contained in a remedial EIS. The Board is only obliged to comply with that request 'as soon as may be' which is a phrase which, from past experience, does not appear to indicate any urgency at all.[34]

**[9.37]** The subsection continues by providing that in applying for the board's opinion the applicant must furnish sufficient information to enable the board to deal with the request and, further, that if the board seeks additional information the applicant shall forward it to the board. No time limit is provided in the section to say within what period the additional information should be given to the board by the applicant and that too is a weakness in the provision.

**[9.38]** The final provision in this subsection provides that any opinion provided to the applicant by the board shall not prejudice the performance by the board of any of its functions under the Act and that any opinion provided cannot be relied upon in the application for a substitute consent and cannot be relied upon in any legal proceedings. One might be tempted to ask what value, if any, does the subsection provide?[35] There would appear to be little point in obtaining an opinion of the board which cannot be relied upon.

**[9.39]** The required contents of a remedial Natura impact statement are set out in s 177G. The requirements are similar to the requirements for a remedial EIS except that they relate to the significant effects, if any, on the relevant European site. The statement to be provided shall also contain details of remedial or mitigation measures undertaken or proposed to be undertaken. The details of appropriate remedial measures and the period of time in which those measures should be taken are the same as the provisions

---

33. PD(A)A 2010, s 177N is an enabling section permitting the Minister to make Regulations.
34. It would be helpful to planning requirements in general if the Minister were to introduce a section defining the phrase 'as soon as may be' as meaning not less than, say, 'five weeks'. Even 10 weeks would, in most cases, be an improvement on 'as soon as may be'.
35. PD(A)A 2010, s 177F(2)(a), (b) and (c).

for remedial EIS. Additionally, in the case of a Natura impact statement the applicant, where relevant, and where he or she may wish to rely upon same may append:

(i) A statement of imperative reasons of overriding public interests;

(ii) Any compensatory measures being proposed by the applicant.[36]

**[9.40]** Section 177H deals with submissions or observations made by persons other than the applicant for substitute consent or a planning authority. The section provides that any person other than the applicant or a planning authority can make submissions or observations in writing to the board in relation to an application for substitute consent provided the person or persons making the application complies with the regulations made under s 177N. Compliance with the regulations is not a requirement where submissions or observations are made by a Member State or another state which is a party to the Transboundary Convention arising from consultation in accordance with the EIA Directive or the Transboundary Convention as the case may be, in relation to the effects on the environment of the development to which an application for substitute consent relates.

**[9.41]** Section 177I(1) and (2) provides that within 10 weeks of receiving a copy of the application and all associated documentation as provided by s 177E, the planning authority shall submit a report to the board and the board shall consider the report. The report prepared by the planning authority shall include the following:

(a) information relating to development (including development other than the development which is the subject of the application for consent) carried out on the site where the development, the subject of the application for consent is situated, and any application for permission made in relation to the site and the outcome of the application;

(b) information relating to any warning letter, enforcement notice or proceedings relating to offences under this Act that relate to the applicant for substitute consent;

(c) information regarding the relevant provisions of the development plan and any local area plan as they affect the area of the site and the type of development concerned;

(d) any information that the authority may have concerning –

    (i) current, anticipated or previous significant effects on the environment, or on a European site associated with the development or the site where the development took place and, if relevant, the area surrounding or near the development of site, or

    (ii) any remedial measures recommend or undertaken;

(e) the opinion, including reasons therefore, of the manager as to –

    (i) whether or not substitute consent should be granted for the development, and

    (ii) the conditions, if any, that should be attached to any grant of substitute consent.

---

36. PD(A)A 2010, s 177G(1)(d).

## Substitute Consent and Appropriate Assessment [9.44]

**[9.42]** Section 177J(1) provides that where the board has received and is considering an application for substitute consent it may issue a draft declaration in writing to the applicant requiring that all or part of his or her activity or operation on the site shall cease. Such direction can only be given when the board forms the opinion that the continuation of all or part of the activity or operations on the site is likely to cause significant adverse effects on the environment or on the integrity of a European site. The draft declaration requiring cessation of all activity or operations on site must inform the applicant of the board's reasons for its opinion that further activity or operations would be likely to cause significant adverse effects on the environment or would be likely to have adverse effects on the integrity of a European site. The person who receives the draft declaration may make submissions or observations to the board in relation to the contents of the draft declaration within two weeks of receiving it. The Board, having considered any submissions or observations received, may do one of the following:

(a) give a direction to the applicant for substitute consent confirming the draft direction;

(b) give a direction to the applicant varying the draft declaration;

(c) withdraw the draft declaration.

Whichever direction is made under (a), (b) or (c) must be sent to the planning authority.

**[9.43]** Failure to comply with a direction from the board under this section is an offence liable to a fine of €5,000 or to imprisonment for a term not exceeding six months or both on summary conviction or liable to a fine not exceeding €12,600 or to imprisonment for a term not exceeding two years or to both on indictment. If after conviction the offence is continued, a fine of €500 *per* day may be imposed on summary conviction or a term of imprisonment not exceeding six months or both provided that if a person is convicted, in the same proceedings, of two or more further offences the aggregate term of imprisonment shall not exceed six months. If the conviction is on indictment the fine is €12,600 for each day the offence is continued and/or a term not exceeding two years but again, if a person is convicted in the same proceedings of two or more further offences, the aggregate term of imprisonment shall not exceed two years.

**[9.44]** Section 177K deals with the decision of the board which decision may grant substitute consent, subject to or without conditions or to refuse to grant substitute consent. When the board makes a decision in relation to substitute consent it must consider the proper planning and sustainable development of the area and have regard to the following matters:

(a) the provisions of the development plan and any local area plan for the area;

(b) the provision of any special amenity area order relating to the area;

(c) the remedial environmental impact statement, or remedial Natura impact statement, or both of those statements, as the case may be, submitted with the application;

(d) the significant effects on the environment, or on a European site, which have occurred which are occurring or could reasonably be expected to occur because the development concerned was carried out;

(e) the report and the opinion of the planning authority under section 177I;

(f) any submissions or observations made in accordance with regulations made under section 177N;

(g) any report or recommendation prepared in relation to the application by or on behalf of the Board, including the report of the person conducting any oral hearing on behalf of the Board;

(h) if the area or part of the area is a European site or an area prescribed for the purposes of section 10(2)(c), that fact;

(i) conditions that may be imposed in relation to a grant of permission under section 34(4);

(j) the matters referred to in section 143;[37]

(k) the views of a Member State where the Member State is notified in accordance with the regulations under this Act;

(l) any relevant provisions of this Act and regulations made thereunder.[38]

**[9.45]** Conditions may be imposed in any decision of the board which conditions may include:

(a) one or more than one condition referred to in section 34(4),

(b) a condition or conditions relating to remediation of all or part of the site on which the development the subject of the grant of substitute consent is situated,

(c) a condition or conditions requiring financial contributions in accordance with section 48, or

(d) a condition or conditions requiring a financial contribution in accordance with a supplementary development contribution scheme under section 49.[39]

**[9.46]** The decision of the board shall be a reasoned decision and when made shall be sent to the applicant. The imposition of any conditions in a decision of the board shall be reasoned and in either case the decision shall set out the reasons for the decision and for the imposition of conditions. A copy of the decision is sent to the planning authority in whose area the development is situate and copies of the decision are also sent to any persons who have made submissions or observations in relation to the application.

---

37. PDA 2000, s 143 requires the board to have regard to certain policies and objectives (a) of the government, a State authority, the Minister, planning authorities and any other body which is a public authority whose functions have or may have a bearing on the proper planning and sustainable development of cities, towns or areas whether urban or rural, (b) the national interest and any effect the performance a Board's functions may have on issues of strategic, economic or social importance to the State, and (c) the National Spatial Strategy and any regional planning guidelines for the time being in force.
38. PD(A)A 2010, s 177K(2).
39. PD(A)A 2010, s 177K(3).

**[9.47]** Section 177K(6) specifically denies a right to compensation in respect to any of the following:

(a) a decision by the Board under section 177D to refuse to grant leave to apply for substitute consent;

(b) a direction of the Board to cease all or part of an activity or operation under section 177J;

(c) a decision of the Board under this section to refuse an application for substitute consent under this section;

(d) a decision of the Board under this section to grant substitute consent subject to one or more than one condition;

(e) a direction of the Board to cease activity or operations or to take remedial measures under section 177L.

**[9.48]** Section 177L deals with the situation where the board refuses an application for leave to apply for substitute consent or refuses to grant substitute consent and, in either case, it may give the applicant a draft direction requiring him or her to cease, within a period stated in the direction, all or parts of the activity carried on where the board forms the opinion that the continuation of all or part of the activity is likely to cause significant adverse effects on the environment or adverse effects on the integrity of a European site. Alternatively, the board may require that such remedial measures are taken as are necessary for either or both of the following:

(i) to restore the site on or at which the development referred to in the application is situated, to a safe and environmentally sustainable condition;

(ii) to avoid, in a European site the deterioration of natural habitats and the habitats of species or the disturbance of the species for which the site has been designated, insofar as such disturbance could be significant in relation to the objectives of the Habitats Directive.[40]

The draft direction must be a reasoned direction and the board must also advise the applicant that he or she can make submissions or observations to the board within four weeks from the date of the notice. A copy of the notice is also to be given by the board to the planning authority inviting submissions or observations within four weeks from the date of the notice.[41]

**[9.49]** If the board's direction requires specified remedial measures the direction will require the person to whom it is given:

(a) to take the remedial measures specified in the draft direction,

(b) to keep records of the remedial measures being carried out in accordance with the draft direction;

(c) to carry out the remedial measures in such order, specified in the draft direction, as the Board considers appropriate,

---

40. PD(A)A 2010, s 177L(1)(b).
41. PD(A)A 2010, s 177L(2) and (3).

(d) to comply with any requirements relating to monitoring and inspection, by the relevant planning authority of the remedial measures specified in the draft direction,

(e) to carry out the remedial measures within the period of time specified in the draft direction.[42]

Any submissions or observations received by the board shall be considered by it and the board will, as soon as may be, confirm, vary or withdraw the draft direction and the decision made by the board must be advised to the planning authority.[43]

[9.50] A person who fails to comply with a direction within the time prescribed shall be guilty of an offence and shall be liable, on summary conviction, to a fine not exceeding €5,000 or to imprisonment for a term not exceeding two years or to both. On conviction on indictment the fine shall not exceed €12,600 and the term of imprisonment shall not exceed two years. Whether it is a summary conviction or a conviction on indictment the fine is either specified or the term of imprisonment is specified but not both.[44]

[9.51] Further offences are committed on every day in which the contravention continues and on summary conviction the fine shall not exceed €500 *per* day and/or imprisonment not exceeding six months provided, that a person convicted in the same proceedings of two or more further offences shall not be imprisoned for a term exceeding six months. On conviction on indictment for a continuing offence the fine shall not exceed €12,600 *per* day and/or in the case of a term of imprisonment not exceeding two years provided that a person convicted in the same proceedings of two or more further offence, the term of imprisonment shall not exceed two years.[45]

[9.52] If a direction issues regarding the taking of remedial measures in respect of a development which comprises either the operation of a quarry or the extraction of peat, those remedial measures may only be required in relation to development which was carried out within the last seven years of the date when s 177 was commenced.[46]

## Enforcement

[9.53] Section 177O deals with enforcement in the context of substitute consent and sub-s (1) provides that substitute consent will be treated in the same way as a grant of permission made under s 34. Where the development is in compliance with the substitute consent or with the conditions in a substitute consent it will be deemed to be authorised development. Conversely, when a substitute consent or the conditions in a substitute consent are not complied with it shall, notwithstanding any other provision in this Act, be unauthorised development.[47]

---

42. PD(A)A 2010, s 177L(4)(a)–(e).
43. PD(A)A 2010, s 177L(5).
44. PD(A)A 2010, s 177L(6).
45. PD(A)A 2010, s 177L(7).
46. PD(A)A 2010, s 177L(8).
47. PD(A)A 2010, s 177O(1) and (2).

**[9.54]** If a person is required to obtain planning permission under the substitute consent provisions of s 177B, namely where notice is served by the planning authority requiring a substitute consent application or if notice was served under s 261A on a quarry owner/operator requiring an application for substitute consent and such person either fails to make the application or otherwise fails to furnish additional information as required, the board shall inform the planning authority of that fact and the development, notwithstanding any other provisions in this Act, shall be unauthorised development. Where a planning authority is so informed by the board it shall, as soon as may be, issue an enforcement notice under s 154 requiring cessation of the activity and the taking of such other steps as the planning authority shall require.[48]

**[9.55]** The awful phrase 'as soon as may be' appears here again. It does not convey the degree of urgency which should be applied by a planning authority in enforcement cases.

**[9.56]** Where the decision of the board is to refuse to grant permission under s 177K pursuant to an application for substitute consent or where the board issues a direction to cease activity or operations and to take remedial measures under s 177L an enforcement notice will also be issued by the planning authority under s 154.

## SUPPLEMENTARY PROVISIONS RELATING TO AN APPLICATION FOR SUBSTITUTE CONSENT

**[9.57]** Section 177P makes provision for supplementary provisions relating to an application for substitute consent.

**[9.58]** Section 177P(1) provides that the general duty imposed by s 126 on the board to act expeditiously in disposing of appeals or referrals shall also apply to substitute consent. In addition to that general duty is the objective of the board that determination is reached within 18 weeks from the date of receipt of the appeal or referral, or as the case may be, the date of receipt of the application for leave to apply or the application for substitute consent. Default permission does not occur if the board makes its decision outside the 18-week period and the use of the word 'objective' makes it clear that this is not a mandatory provision. Section 126 provides, however, that if the board is to depart from the 18-week rule or to extend the time beyond the time allowed by the Minister the board must have formed the view that it was not possible or appropriate to determine the matter in such time and it must give notice to the parties of its view. In giving notice, the board will also specify a date by which it will make its determination.[49]

**[9.59]** Section 177P(2) provides that s 130 shall apply in relation to making of submissions or observations by any person other than the applicant for substitute consent or the relevant planning authority. Section 130 concerns submissions or observations by an observer, that is to say, a person or persons other than parties to the

---

48. PD(A)A 2010, s 177O(3) and (4).
49. PD(A)A 2010, s 177P(1).

**[9.60]** Planning and Environmental Law in Ireland

appeal. Thus, any member of the public can make submissions in relation to an appeal or referral or in this context in relation to a substitute consent and those submissions or observations are made to the board. In the context of substitute consent s 130(3)(c) or (d) is excluded. The application of s 130 is also subject to the following and any other necessary modifications:

(a) references in that section to a party shall be construed as references to the applicant for substitute consent or the relevant planning authority, and

(b) references in that section to an environmental impact assessment shall be construed as references to a remedial environmental impact statement or a remedial Natura impact statement, or both such statements as the case may be.[50]

**[9.60]** PDA 2000, s 130 deals with submissions and observations by persons other than parties. Section 130(5) provides that sub-s (1)(b) and sub-s (4) shall not apply to any submissions or observations made by a Member State of the European Communities (within the meaning of the European Communities Act 1972) or other state which is subject to the EIA Directive or to the Transboundary Convention,[51] arising from consultation in accordance with the Council Directive or the Transboundary Convention, as the case may be, in relation to the effects on the environment of the development to which the appeal under s 37 relates. This subsection has been amended by s 42 of PD(A)A 2010. Section 42 reads:

> Section 130(5) of the Principal Act is amended by the substitution of 'which subject to Environmental Impact Assessment Directive or Transboundary Convention' for 'which is subject to the Council Directive or Transboundary Convention'.

Strangely the words 'which is subject to the Council Directive or Transboundary Convention' do not appear in the unamended version of s 130(5).

**[9.61]** Section 177P(3) provides that s 131 (which deals with the power of the board to request submissions and observations) shall apply in relation to an application for substitute consent subject to the following and other necessary modifications:

(a) references in that section to party to the appeal or referral shall be construed as references to applicant for substitute consent or the relevant planning authority, and

(b) references in that section to an appeal or referral shall be construed as references to an application for substitute consent.

**[9.62]** Section 177P(4) provides that s 132, which deals with the power of the board to require submission of documents, particulars or other information as may be necessary, shall apply in relation to the board requiring documents, particulars or other information

---

50. PD(A)/A 2010, s 177P(2).
51. PD(A)A 2010, s 42. The amendment as it stands may be defective. See remainder of this paragraph.

which it considers necessary to enable it to determine an application for substitute consent subject to the following and any other necessary modifications:

    (a)    reference in that section to party shall be construed as references to applicant for substitute consent or the relevant planning authority, and

    (b)    reference in that section to an appeal or referral shall be construed as references to an application for substitute consent.

**[9.63]** Section 177P(5) applies to s 133 in relation to the board determining or dismissing an application for substitute consent. Section 133 deals with the power of the board where a notice has been served under s 131 or s 132 and the section enables the board after the expiration of the period specified in the notice and having considered submissions or observations, documents, particulars or other information submitted, without further notice to determine or, in the case of a notice under s 132, dismiss, in this instance, the application for substitute consent subject to the following and any other necessary modifications:

    (a)    references in that section to party shall be construed as references to applicant for substitute consent or the relevant planning authority, and

    (b)    references in that section to an appeal or referral which shall be construed as references to an application for substitute consent.

Where submissions or information are supplied under s 131 or 132 outside the time given for a response to the request the board, having considered the submissions or information supplied, may, without notice to the parties, dismiss the referral or application for substitute consent.

**[9.64]** Section 177P(6) refers to a situation where an oral hearing is arranged in relation to an application for substitute consent. Section 135 shall apply in relation to the holding of the oral hearing. Section 135 enables the board to appoint a person to conduct an oral hearing of an appeal or referral and that is extended to an oral hearing in respect of a substitute consent. All the procedures set out in s 135 apply in relation to an oral hearing on an application for substitute consent.

**[9.65]** Section 177Q allows the board, entirely at its own discretion, for the purpose of making a determination in respect of an application for substitute consent, to hold an oral hearing. The section allows the board to consider the report and any recommendations of the person holding the oral hearing before making its determination. An applicant for substitute consent, a planning authority or a person who has made submissions or observations in relation to the application for substitute consent may request an oral hearing. The request shall be in writing to the board accompanied by the fee payable under s 144. Such request will not be considered if it is not accompanied by the payment of the fee. The application shall be made in accordance with the regulations made under s 177N.

**[9.66]** The Board having been requested to hold an oral hearing, and since the decision is entirely at the board's discretion, may refuse to do so and where the board decides to determine the application without an oral hearing after it received a request for oral hearing it will serve notices on the person requesting the oral hearing, on the relevant planning authority and on all persons who have made submissions or observations to the board stating that it has refused the request for an oral hearing.

**[9.67]** A request for an oral hearing can be withdrawn at any time and if withdrawn the board will give notice to the applicant for substitute consent, the planning authority and to each person who made submissions or observations.[52]

## WHAT IS APPROPRIATE ASSESSMENT?

**[9.68]** The Birds Directive was introduced in 1979 and the Habitats Directive in 1992 with the express purpose of counteracting the progressive destruction of habitats and of threatened species caused by both modern development techniques and by the intensification of development in land use projects.

**[9.69]** In Ireland, the Natura 2000 network of European sites consists of Special Areas of conservation (SACs, including candidate SACs) and special protection areas (SPAs and proposed SPAs). SACs are selected to conserve vulnerable habitats and threatened species which use or occupy the habitats (other than birds). SPAs are specifically for the protection of threatened bird species, including migratory birds, and for the protection of their habitats.

**[9.70]** PDA 2000, s 177V, as inserted by PD(A)A 2010, s 37, defines 'appropriate assessment' as follows:

> (1) An appropriate assessment carried out under this Part shall include a determination by the competent authority under Article 6.3 of the Habitats Directive as to whether or not a draft Land use plan or proposed development would adversely affect the integrity of a European site and the assessment shall be carried out by the competent authority before –
>
> (a) the draft Land use plan is made including, where appropriate, before a decision on appeal in relation to a draft strategic development zone is made, or
>
> (b) consent is given for the propose development.
>
> (2) In carrying out an appropriate assessment under sub-section (1) the competent authority shall take into account each of the following matters:
>
> (a) the Natura impact report or Natura impact statement, as appropriate;
>
> (b) any supplemental information furnished in relation to any such report or statement;
>
> (c) if appropriate, any additional information sought by the authority and furnished by the applicant in relation to a Natura impact statement;
>
> (d) any additional information furnished to the competent authority at its request in relation to a Natura impact report;
>
> (e) any information or advice obtained by the competent authority;

---

52. PDA 2000, s 177Q(3) and (4).

(f) if appropriate, any written submissions or observations made to the competent authority in relation to the application for consent for proposed development;

(g) any other relevant information.

(3) Notwithstanding any other provision of this Act, or, as appropriate, the Act of 2001, or the Roads Acts 1993 to 2007, a competent authority shall make a Land use plan or give consent for proposed development only after having determined that the Land use plan or proposed development shall not adversely affect the integrity of a European site.

(4) Subject to the other provisions of this Act, consent for proposed development may be given in relation to a proposed development where a competent authority has made modifications or attached conditions to the consent where the authority is satisfied to do so having determined that the proposed development would not adversely affect the integrity of a European site if it is carried out in accordance with the consent and the modifications or conditions attaching thereto.

(5) A competent authority shall give notice of its determination in relation to a proposed development under subsection (3) or (4), to the applicant for consent for the proposed development, giving reasons for the determination.

(6) A competent authority shall make available for inspection –

(a) any determination that it makes in relation to a Land use plan under subsection (3) and provide reasons for that determination, and

(b) any notice given by the authority under subsection (5),

as soon as may be after the making of the determination or giving the notice, as appropriate, by members of the public during office hours of the offices of the authority and shall also make the determination or notice available in electronic form including by placing the documents on the authority's website.

**[9.71]** The PD(A)A 2010 provides the statutory protection required in prescribing for compulsory appropriate assessment which, in effect, is a statutory requirement to examine and consider the possible nature conservation implications which any development project or which any land use scheme might have on a Natura 2000 site. Such examination and consideration must take place before the consent or planning permission is given enabling the project to proceed.

**[9.72]** Appropriate assessment does not just apply to new development projects or new land use schemes as stand-alone projects or schemes, but it applies also to the cumulative effect which the addition of one more development project or land use scheme may have on a Natura 2000 site when taken together with other development projects and land use schemes which were already up and running at the date that the appropriate assessment was taking place in the offices of the competent authority.

**[9.73]** The obligation to undertake appropriate assessment stems from the provisions of art 6(3) of the Habitats Directive which requires that any site which is likely to have significant effects on a Natura 2000 site either individually or in combination with other plans or projects shall be subject to assessment. Article 6(3) is followed by art 6(4) of the Habitats Directive which allows for derogation from the strict protection required by art 6(3) in certain prescribed but limited circumstances, that is to say, where there are 'imperative reasons of overriding public interest' (IROPI) including those of a social or of an economic nature. If a Member State does choose to override the appropriate assessment procedure it is bound to take compensatory measures to ensure that the overall coherence of Natura 2000 is protected. The competent authority is also bound to inform the Commission of any compensatory measures adopted.

**[9.74]** Appropriate assessment should not be seen as a prohibition on new development nor should it be seen as a prohibition against land use schemes of development but it does require a screening to be carried out by the competent authority during which process the competent authority is entitled to seek further information. The screening is a case-by-case examination of the principles which offer to protect a Natura 2000 site and the implication which the development proposals or the land use site proposals will have on the habitat site or sites. If significant effects cannot be ruled out at the screening stage it is almost certain that a full appropriate assessment will have to be carried out. The *ex situ* effects must also be taken into consideration. In some cases, the Natura site may not adjoin or even be near the location of the proposed development site or the proposed land use site. If the development site or the land use site is located beside a river the operations of the development site or the land use site could still have a significant effect on a Natura 2000 site many miles downstream.

**[9.75]** As the appropriate assessment procedure is a strict and detailed assessment of the likely effects which a development project or a land use project, taken together with existing projects in operation within an area of influence in relation to the location of the Natura 2000 site, where a development project is likely to have an effect on the integrity of the Natura 2000 site concerned, the legislation requires that the applicant must produce a Natura impact statement and, in doing so, ecological and other experts will be required to undertake surveys, research and analysis as necessary in the preparation of a comprehensive statement. It is only when the competent authority is satisfied that it has all the information which it requires and that the quality of the information is to an acceptably high standard that the appropriate assessment procedure will commence. If, after an examination of the Natura impact statement and an examination of all other information submitted by the applicant either on request or voluntarily, the competent authority concludes that there will be no adverse affects on the integrity of Natura site then, subject to other normal planning requirements being satisfied, it is likely that the decision on the appropriate assessment will be positive and it will allow the applicant to proceed with the development.

**[9.76]** If the derogation steps are to be applied in accordance with art 6(4) of the Habitats Directive, the competent authority must be satisfied that there are IROPI. The competent authority must also be satisfied that there are no less damaging solutions available as an alternative. If a less damaging alternative is available and if that alternative appears to be acceptable, as an alternative, the competent authority, in giving the go ahead, may impose such conditions as are necessary to achieve the less damaging alternative. For the derogation to be used it is clear that the IROPI must be just that. For example, it is unlikely that derogation would be granted in the case of a private project unless it related to infrastructural development of vital public interest.

**[9.77]** Two excellent documents have been produced on the subject of appropriate assessment of plans and projects which are essential reading for those who become seriously involved with the procedure. The first is a document produced by the Department of Environment, Heritage and Local Government and the title of it is 'Appropriate Assessment of Plans and Projects in Ireland – Guidance for Planning Authorities'. That document was published on 10 December 2009. The second document is headed 'For the attention of the County/City Manager'. The second document also comes from the Department of the Environment, Heritage and Local Government. It is dated 11 March 2010 and prepared by Peter Carvill of the Legislation Unit (National Parks and Wildlife).

**[9.78]** The Guidance for Planning Authorities provide a glossary which provides a brief dictionary of the principle words or phrases used in Part XAB and this is reproduced below as follows:

> **Annex I habitat:** A habitat in Annex I of the Habitats Directive.
>
> **Appropriate Assessment:** An assessment carried out under art 6(3) of the Habitats Directive of the implications of a plan or project, either individually or in combination with other plans and projects, on a Natura 2000 site in view of the site's conservation objectives.
>
> **Appropriate Assessment Conclusion Statement:** The statement of a competent authority of its decision on an appropriate assessment, and the reasons for its decision.
>
> **Biodiversity:** The variability among living organisms from all sources including, inter alia, terrestrial, marine and other aquatic ecosystems and the ecological complexes of which they are part; this includes diversity within species, between species and of ecosystems (UN Convention on Biological Diversity 1992).
>
> **Birds Directive:** Council Directive 79/409/EEC on the conservation of wild birds.
>
> **European Commission:** The Commission of the European Communities.
>
> **Ecology:** The study of the inter-relationships between living organisms and their environment.
>
> **Ex situ:** Outside – usually in the context of *ex situ* effects (or outside effects) on a Natura 2000 site. For example, abstraction of water from a river upstream of a Natura 2000 site located on the river could have an *ex situ* effect on the site.
>
> **Habitat:** A place in which a particular plant or animal lives. Often used in a wider sense, referring to major assemblages of plants and animals found together such as woodlands or grassland.
>
> **Habitats Directive:** Council Directive 92/43/EEC on the conservation of natural habitats and of wild fauna and flora (EC Habitats Directive).

[9.79]     Planning and Environmental Law in Ireland

**In situ:** Inside or within – usually in the context of *in situ* effects (or effects within) on a Natura 2000 site. For example, constructing a marina on the lakeshore in a Natura 2000 site could have an *in situ* effect.

**Natura 2000:** Network of Special Areas of Conservation and Special Protection Areas. For the purposes of this guidance, it includes candidate SACs and notified SPAs.

**Precautionary principle:** A principle underlying the concept of sustainable development which implies that prudent action be taken to protect the environment even in the absence of scientific certainty.

**Priority habitat:** Natural habitat types on Annex I of the Habitats Directive, and indicated by an asterisk (*), which are in danger of disappearance, and for which the Community has particular responsibility in view of the proportion of their natural range which falls within the territory.

**Priority species:** Species for the conservation of which the Community has particular responsibility in view of the proportion of their natural range which falls within the territory, these priority species are indicated by an asterisk (*) in Annex II of the Council Directive 92/43/EEC of 21 May 1992 on the conservation of natural habitats and of wild fauna and flora. At present, Ireland does not have any priority species.

**Screening for appropriate assessment:** the screening of a plan or project to establish if an appropriate assessment of the plan or project is required. unless the screening assessment can establish that there is no likelihood of any significant effect on a Natura 2000 site, then an AA must be carried out.

**Special Areas of Conservation (SACs):** are sites designated under European Communities Directive 92/43/EEC known as the 'Habitats Directive'. This requires the conservation of important, rate or threatened habitats and species (not birds, which are protected by Special Protection Areas) across Europe.

**Special Protection Areas (SPAs):** are sites designated under the European Communities Directive 79/409/EEC, known as the 'Birds Directive', to conserve the habitats of certain migratory or rare birds.

**Statement for Appropriate Assessment:** The report of a scientific examination of a plan or project and the relevant Natura 2000 sites, to identify and characterise any possible implications for the site in view of the site's conservation objectives.

## Appropriate assessment

[9.79] 'Appropriate assessment' is construed in accordance with s 177V. The main purpose of carrying out an appropriate assessment is to ensure that any proposed development or any draft land use plan will not adversely affect the integrity of a European site. The assessment on this point is made by a 'competent authority' which is commonly, but not always, a planning authority. Depending on the type of development being carried out it may be the planning authority, the board or the regional authority.[53]

---

53. The role of the planning authority, the board and the regional authority will become clear when the definition of 'competent authority' is read below; see para **9.100-9.101**.

The criteria for making a determination, as contained in art 6.3 of the Habitats Directive, reads as follows:

> Any plan or project not directly connected with or necessary to the management of a site but likely to have a significant effect thereon, either individually or in combination with other plans or projects, shall be subject to appropriate assessment of its implications for the site in view of the site's conservation objectives. In the light of the conclusions of the assessment of the implications for the site and subject to the provisions of para 4, the competent national authorities shall agree to the plan or project only having ascertained that it will not adversely affect the integrity of the site concerned and, if appropriate, after having obtained the opinion of the general public.

**[9.80]** Appropriate assessment screening is the first test to be carried out to determine whether or not appropriate assessment should be carried out. Screening will determine, by way of preliminary assessment and objective criteria whether a plan or project either alone or in combination with other plans or projects might have significant effects on a Natura 2000 site bearing in mind the conservation objectives of that site. The 'precautionary principle' in making decisions on screening of appropriate assessment must be applied. What this means is that if at the screening stage significant effects are either likely, uncertain or unknown, appropriate assessment will have to be undertaken.

**[9.81]** The assessment must be carried out before the draft land use plan is made including, where appropriate, before a decision on appeal in relation to a draft strategic development zone is made, or before planning consent is given for the proposed development.[54]

**[9.82]** There is no set formula for undertaking appropriate assessment. A statement for appropriate assessment must be prepared on the best scientific evidence and methods in order to determine and measure precisely what effects the development proposed will have on the integrity of a Natura 2000 site. Input will be required from ecological specialists and possibly also from hydrologists and from engineers in the preparation of the statement for appropriate assessment. Once completed the statement for appropriate assessment is submitted to the competent authority which will carry out the appropriate assessment of that statement to see whether or not a conclusion can be reached to the effect that there will not be significant adverse effects on the integrity of the Natura 2000 site.

**[9.83]** If adverse effects are certain, the application will be refused. If adverse effects are likely or if there is doubt, the derogation steps provided by art 6(4) will apply but only in circumstances where there are IROPI requiring the project to proceed and that can only occur:

(1) if there are no less damaging alternative solutions;

(2) where compensatory measures which can be put in place have been identified.

---

54. PD(A)A 2010, s 177V(1)(a)&(b).

[9.84] **Planning and Environmental Law in Ireland**

A stricter assessment will apply to any adverse effects identified which may affect the Annex I priority sites as opposed to the ordinary Annex I sites. Priority sites include the following:

Coastal lagoons, fixed coastal dunes with herbaceous vegetation (grey dunes), decalcified fixed dunes with *Empetrum nigrum*, Atlantic decalcified fixed dunes, *Callulo-Ulicetea Machairs* (these are flat low lying coastal strips of arable or grass land found mainly in Ireland and Scotland), turloughs (dry loughs with limestone beneath the surface which flood in heavy rainfall found in Ireland), species-rich *Nardus* grasslands on siliceous substrates in mountain areas (and sub mountain areas in Continental Europe), active raised bogs, *Calcareous* fens with *Cladium mariscus* and species of the Carision Davallianae, petrifying springs of the tufa formation (*Crationeurion*), limestone pavements, bog woodland, alluvial forest with *Alnus glutinosa* and *Fraxinus excelsior* (*Alno-padion, Alnoin incanae, Salicion Albae*) and *Taxus baccatas* woods of the British Isles.

[9.84] If compensatory measures are required the Habitats Directive requires Member States to advise the Commission of them. The Commission may then review the compensatory measures and if they are inadequate the Commission will take steps against the Member State up to and including litigation in the European Court of Justice.

[9.85] If derogation is made under art 6(4) of the Habitats Directive on grounds of IROPI, and derogation can only be sought in exceptional circumstances, the Minister must be informed at an early stage.

[9.86] Both the Birds and Habitats Directives are actively monitored by the European Commission and if the protection offered to Natura 2000 sites is inadequate or if there are breaches of the requirements of the Directive those responsible will be pursued actively by the Commission by letter of formal notice, by reasoned opinion and ultimately by referral of a case to the European Court of Justice. Persistent offending members will suffer substantial financial penalties to include significant daily finds until the infringement is rectified. Fines amounting to tens of millions of euro are aimed to ensure that Member States comply with both the Birds Directive and the Habitats Directive.

[9.87] Section 177V(2) lists the matters which must be taken into account when carrying out an appropriate assessment, namely:

(a) the Natura impact report or Natura impact statement, as appropriate;

(b) any supplemental information furnished in relation to any such report or statement;

(c) if appropriate, any additional information sought by the authority and finished by the applicant in relation to a Natura impact statement;

(d) any additional information furnished to the competent authority at its request in relation to a Natura impact report;

(e) any information or advice obtained by the competent authority;

(f) if appropriate, any written submissions or observations made to the competent authority in relation to the application for consent for proposed development;

(g) any other relevant information.[55]

Even though the Transport (Railway Infrastructure) Act 2001 or the Roads Acts 1993–2007 may provide otherwise, a competent authority can only make a land use plan and can only give consent for proposed development after it has determined that the land use plan or the proposed development shall not adversely affect the integrity of a European site.[56]

**[9.88]** Where a competent authority is satisfied that it can control a development by making modifications and/or attaching conditions to such an extent that the modified and conditioned consent would not adversely affect the integrity of a European site those modifications and conditions can be made and imposed in the consent which is granted to the developer.[57] As soon as the competent authority has made a determination, notice of that determination shall be given to the applicant for consent of the proposed development and the determination shall be a reasoned determination. Also the competent authority will make the determination that it makes in relation to a land use plan together with the reasons for that determination and copy of the notice given by the competent authority available to the applicant for consent as soon as may be after the making of the determination or giving of the notice, as appropriate. Members of the public will be notified that they may inspect the determination during office hours and the determination will also be made available in electronic form on the authority's website.[58]

## 'Candidate site of community importance'

**[9.89]** Article 4(1) of the Habitats Directive reads as follows:

> On the basis of the criteria set out in Annex III (Stage 1) and relevant scientific information, each Member State shall propose a list of sites indicating which natural habitat types in Annex I and which species in Annex II that are native to its territory the sites host. For animal species ranging over wide areas these sites shall correspond to the places within the natural range of such species which present the physical or biological factors essential to their life and reproduction. For aquatic species which range over wide areas, such sites will be proposed only where there is a clearly identifiable area representing the physical and biological factors

---

55. PD(A)A 2010, s 177V(2)(a) to (g).
56. PD(A)A 2010, s 177V(3).
57. PD(A)A 2010, s 177V(4).
58. See PD(A)A 2010, s 177V(5) and (6).

essential to their life and reproduction. Where appropriate, Member States shall propose adoption of the list in the light of the results of the surveillance referred to in Article 11.[59]

The list shall be transmitted to the Commission, within three years of the notification of this Directive, together with information on each site. That information shall include a map of the site, its name, location, extent and the data resulting from application of the criteria specified in Annex III (Stage 1) provided in a format established by the Commission in accordance with the procedure laid down in art 21.

**[9.90]** Where the Minister for Environment, Heritage and Local Government gives notice under the European Communities Act 1972 that a site that he/she considers might be eligible for identification as a site of community importance pursuant to art 4.1 of the Habitats Directive, and where the notice is included in a list transmitted to the Commission in accordance with art 4.1 of the Habitats Directive or is added, in accordance with art 5 of the Habitats Directive, to the list transmitted to the European Commission under art 4.1, that site becomes a 'candidate site of community importance' but only until the adoption of the site by a decision of the European Commission under art 21 of the Habitats Directive.

**[9.91]** Article 5.1 of the Habitats Directive reads as follows:

> In exceptional cases where the Commission finds that a national list as referred to in Article 4.1 fails to mention a site hosting a priority natural habitat type or priority species which, on the basis of relevant and reliable scientific information, it considers to be essential for the maintenance of that priority natural habitat type or for the survival of that priority species, a bilateral consultation procedure shall be initiated between that Member State and the Commission for the purpose of comparing the scientific data used by each.

**[9.92]** Article 5.2 reads as follows:

> If, on expiry of consultation period not exceeding six months, the dispute remains unresolved, the Commission shall forward to the Council a proposal relating to the selection of the site as a site of Community importance.

**[9.93]** Article 5.3 reads as follows:

> The Council, acting unanimously, shall take a decision within three months of the date of referral.

**[9.94]** Article 5.4 reads as follows:

> During the consultation period and pending a Council decision, the site concerned shall be subject to art 6.2.

---

59. The Habitats Directive, art 11 reads: Member States shall undertake surveillance of the conservation status of the natural habitats and species referred to in art 2 with particular regard to priority natural habitat types and priority species.

**[9.95]** Article 6.2 reads as follows:

> Member States shall take appropriate steps to avoid, in the special areas of conservation, the deterioration of natural habitats and the habitats of species as well as disturbance of species for which the areas have been designated, insofar as such disturbance could be significant in relation to the objectives of this directive.

Once the consultation procedure of art 5.1 has commenced and during the period in which a Council decision is pending in accordance with art 5.3 of the Habitats Directive the site becomes a 'candidate site of community importance'.

## 'Candidate special protection area'

**[9.96]** A 'candidate special protection area' is a site where the Minister has given notice that the site may be eligible for identification as a site of Community importance pursuant to art 4, para 1 of the Habitats Directive and it remains a candidate special protection area until the Minister decides either to classify or not to classify the site as a special protection area pursuant to art 4 of the Birds Directive, which directive provides protection and requires special conservation measures concerning the habitats of birds listed in Annex I to ensure their survival and reproduction in their area of distribution.

**[9.97]** Annex I of the Birds Directive is not for the faint hearted. It comprises a list of 242 different species of birds all identified by their Latin names and as such it is utterly incomprehensible to the layman. There must be a strong case for inserting a common English name for this species in brackets beside the Latin name. The purpose of Annex I of the Birds Directive is to identify the different species of birds to the layman. In that, Annex I has failed spectacularly.

## Compensatory measures

**[9.98]** 'Compensatory measures' shall be construed in accordance with s 177W(7) in relation to land use plans and in accordance with s 177AA(8) in relation to granting permission for proposed development. 'Compensatory measures', for the purposes of s 177W, 177X or 177Y, are measures proposed or considered by a competent authority in the first instance and by the Minister for the purpose of ensuring that overall coherence of Natura 2000 is protected and may include provision for a compensatory habitats.

**[9.99]** Section 177AA(8) states that 'compensatory measures' in ss 177AA, 177AB and 177AC are measures proposed, in the first instance, by the applicant and then by a competent authority or the Minister for the purpose of ensuring that the overall coherence of Natura 2000 is protected. These measures may include provision of compensatory habitat.[60]

---

60. In effect 'compensatory measures' are little more than 'robbing Peter to pay Paul'.

## Competent authority

**[9.100]** 'Competent authority' is defined by reference to s 177S. Section 177S(1) gives, as it were, the job description of a competent authority while s 177S(2) defines which authority acts in differing circumstances as a competent authority. The job description requires a competent authority to take appropriate steps to avoid deterioration of natural habitats and the habitats of species as well as the disturbance of species in a European site, insofar as such disturbance could be significant in relation to the objectives of the Habitats Directive.[61] The purpose of the competent authority is to ensure avoidance, in special areas of conservation, of deterioration of natural habitats and the habitats species as well as disturbance of species for which the areas have been designated. Bearing that purpose in mind, the competent authority will examine any plan or project which is likely to have significant effects on the special areas of conservation and those projects shall be subject to appropriate assessment of its implications for the conservation site. Consent will only be given for such a project where the competent authority is satisfied that the development will not adversely affect the integrity of the site concerned and, generally, the competent authority will seek the opinion of the public.

**[9.101]** Section 177S(2) defines 'competent authority' for the purposes of this part of the Act and for the purposes of arts 6 and 7 of the Habitats Directive as follows:

(a) in relation to draft regional planning guidelines, the regional authority for whose area the guidelines are made.

(b) in relation to a draft planning scheme in respect of all or any part of a strategic development zone, the planning authority (which term shall be construed in accordance with section 168(5)) in whose area the strategic development zone is situate, or, on appeal the Board, as the case may be.

(c) in relation to a draft development plan the planning authority for whose area the development plan is made.

(d) in relation to a proposed variation of a development plan, the planning authority for whose area the variation of the development plan is made.

(e) in relation to a draft local area plan, the planning authority in whose area the local area plan concerned is situate.

(f) in relation to a proposed development (other than development referred to in paragraph (g) or (h)), the planning authority to whom an application for permission is made or on appeal the Board, as the case may be.

(g) in relation to proposed development that is strategic infrastructure development, the Board or

(h) in relation to proposed local authority or State authority development, the Board, other than in relation to screening for appropriate assessment, in relation to which the competent authority shall be the planning authority in whose area the proposed development is to be carried out.

---

61. PD(A)A 2010, s 177S(1).

## Consent for a proposed development

**[9.102]** 'Consent for a proposed development' is construed in accordance with s 177U(8). Subsection (8) lists the various types of 'consent for proposed development' as follows:

- (a) a grant of permission,
- (b) a decision of the Board to grant permission on application or on appeal,
- (c) consent for development under Part IX,[62]
- (d) consent for development by local authority or a State authority under Part XI,[63]
- (e) consent for development on the foreshore under Part XV,[64]
- (f) consent for development under section 43 of the Act 2001,[65]
- (g) consent for development under section 51 of the Roads Act 1993, or
- (h) a substitute consent under Part XA.

## European site

**[9.103]** 'European site'[66] means:

- (a) a candidate site of community importance,
- (b) a site of community importance,
- (c) a special area of conservation,
- (d) a candidate special protection area,
- (e) a special protection area.

## Land use plan

**[9.104]** 'Land use plan' means:

- (a) regional planning guidelines,
- (b) a planning scheme in respect of all or any part of a strategic development zone,
- (c) a development plan,
- (d) a variation of a development plan or
- (e) a local area plan.

---

62. PDA 2000, Pt IX, ss 165–171 deal with strategic development zones and, in particular, the designation of certain sites as strategic development zones. It should be noted that PDA 2000, ss 168, 169 and 170 have been amended respectively by PD(A)A 2010, ss 50, 51 and 52.
63. PDA 2000, Pt XI deals with development by local and State authorities, etc. It comprises PDA 2000, ss 178–182 and these sections have been substantially added to and amended by PD(SI)A 2006, and specifically PDA 2000, ss 179, 180, 181A–181C and s 182A–182D have been amended by PD(A)A 2010, ss 58–66 respectively.
64. PDA 2000, Pt XV deals with development of the foreshore: PDA 2000, ss 224–228 as amended by PD(SI)A 2006.
65. Act of 2001 means the Transport (Railway Infrastructure) Act 2001.
66. PDA 2000, s 177R(1) as inserted by PD(A)A 2010, s 57.

## Natura 2000 network

**[9.105]** 'Natura 2000 network' is defined by reference to art 3 para 1 of the Habitats Directive which reads:

> A coherent European ecological network of special areas of conservation shall be set up under the title Natura 2000. This network, composed of sites hosting the natural habitat types listed in Annex I and habitats of species listed in Annex II, shall enable the natural habitat types and species' habitats concerned to be maintained or, where appropriate, restored at a favourable conservation status in their natural range.

The Natura 2000 network shall include the special protection areas classified by the Member States pursuant to Directive 79/409/EEC.

## 'Natura impact report' and 'Natura impact statement'

**[9.106]** The terms 'Natura impact report' and 'Natura impact statement' are both construed in accordance with s 177T.

**[9.107]** A Natura impact report is a statement for the purposes of art 6 of the Habitats Directive highlighting implications of a proposed land use plan either on its own or in combination with other projects dealing with the effects of either one or more Natura 2000 sites bearing in mind the conservation objectives of the site or sites.

**[9.108]** A Natura impact statement is a statement for the purposes of art 6 of the Habitats Directive highlighting the implications of a proposed development either on its own or in combination with other development projects affecting one or more Natura 2000 sites. The statement takes account of the conservation objectives of the Natura site or sites.

**[9.109]** Article 6 of the Habitats Directive deals with the conservation, management and administrative or contractual measures to be taken in relation to areas of conservation with a view to protecting the deterioration of natural habitats and the habitats of species and avoiding disturbance of species in designated areas. Any plan or project which may have significant effects on the special areas of conservation must be subject to appropriate assessment and the aim of that assessment is to ensure that no consent to proceed will issue unless it is ascertained that the integrity of the site will not be adversely affected. If, after the appropriate assessment has been carried out, there is a negative assessment of the implications for the site that plan or project may nevertheless proceed only if there are imperative reasons for overriding public interest (IROPI), including those of a social or economic nature, and the Member State will take compensatory measures to ensure that the overall coherence of Natura 2000 is protected. The compensatory measures must be advised to the Commission. If the site is one which hosts priority natural habitat type or species, it must, as a pre-condition, be shown in the appropriate assessment that there are human health or public safety issues.

**[9.110]** A Natura impact report or Natura impact statement must also include a scientific examination of evidence and examination of data to be carried out by competent persons who will both identify and classify any implications for one or more Natura sites in view of the conservation objectives.[67] A Natura impact report in relation to a draft land use plan will be prepared by:

(a) The regional authority in respect of drafting regional planning guidelines.

(b) The planning authority in relation to the preparation of the draft planning scheme in respect of any part of a strategic development zone.

(c) A planning authority in the case of preparation of a draft development plan or a draft variation to a development plan, and

(d) A planning authority in relation to the preparation of a draft local area plan.[68]

An applicant for consent for proposed development or an applicant directed by the competent authority to do so after the application for consent has been lodged shall furnish a Natura impact statement to the competent authority in relation to the proposed development. If an applicant is directed after the application has been made to lodge a Natura impact statement that statement must be lodged within the time specified in the notice. If an applicant for permission fails to furnish a Natura impact statement within the period specified in the notice, unless the competent authority otherwise directs, the application shall be deemed to be withdrawn.[69]

**[9.111]** Section 177T(7) deals with the contents of a Natura impact report or a Natura impact statement which, without prejudice to sub-s (1), includes information prescribed by regulations under s 177AD.[70]

**[9.112]** A Natura impact report or a Natura impact statement will also contain any other information which the competent authority considers necessary to enable it to ascertain if the draft land use plan or the proposed development will not affect the integrity of the site. If it is appropriate, the report and statement respectively will also provide alternative solutions that have been considered together with a statement as to the reasons why they were not adopted. If applicable, the report and statement respectively will also include the imperative reasons for overriding public interest where there are such and reasons as to why either the land use plan or the proposed development should proceed even though it may have an effect on the integrity of a European site. Finally, if it is applicable, the statement and report should also include details of any compensatory measures which are being offered.

---

67. PDA 2000, s 177T(2) inserted by PD(A)A 2010, s 57.
68. PDA 2000, s 177T(3).
69. PDA 2000, s 177(4), (5) and (6).
70. These regulations have not been introduced at the date of this publication.

## Proposed development

**[9.113]** 'Proposed development' is a proposal to carry out one or the following types of development, namely:

(i) Development to which Part III applies.[71]

(ii) Development that may be carried out under Part IX.[72]

(iii) Development by a local authority or a State authority under Part XI.[73]

(iv) Development on the foreshore under Part XV which part, in the principal Act, deals with development on the foreshore between s 224–s 228. This part has been amended by the Planning & Development (Strategic Infrastructure) Act 2006.

(v) Development under section 43 of the Act 2001.[74]

## Screening for appropriate assessment

**[9.114]** 'Screening for appropriate assessment' is construed in accordance with s 177U. The purpose of the screening is to establish whether or not a land use plan or a proposed development is likely to have significant effect on a European site. The screening process of the draft land use plan or the proposed development is carried out by the competent authority and the assessment is made before either a land use plan is made or before consent for a proposed development is given. The competent authority, in carrying out the screening, may request information from an applicant and may consult with such other persons as it considers appropriate. It is a matter for the competent authority to determine that an appropriate assessment of a draft land use plan or a proposed development is required. It would not be required if it was clear from objective information that neither the draft land use plan nor the proposed development (as applicable) would individually or, indeed, in combination with each other have any significant effect on the European site, in which case there would be no requirement for the screening of an appropriate assessment. If, however, a competent authority makes a determination that an appropriate assessment is required, the competent authority shall give a reasoned determination and shall notify the applicant, any persons who made

---

71. PDA 2000, Pt III deals with control of development and imposes the general obligation to obtain planning permission. It comprises PDA 2000, ss 32–50 and has been amended by LGA 2001, the PD(A)A 2002, the PD(SI)A 2006 and specifically PDA 2000, ss 34, 35, 37A, 37H, 38, 42A, 48, 49 and 50A have been amended respectively by PD(A)A 2010, ss 23–32.
72. PDA 2000, Pt IX deals with strategic development zones in PDA 2000, ss 165–171. PDA 2000, ss 172, 174 and 176 have been amended respectively by PD(A)A 2010, ss 54, 55 and 56.
73. PDA 2000, Pt XI deals with development by local and State authorities, etc, and places restrictions on development by certain local authorities. PDA 2000, Pt XI comprises PDA 2000, ss 178–182 and it has been amended by the PD(SI)A 2006, and specifically PDA 2000, ss 179, 180, 181A–181C, 182A–182D by PD(A)A 2010, ss 58–66 inc.
74. The Act refers to the Transport (Railway Infrastructure) Act 2001 (a) development under the Roads Act 1993, s 51 and (b) notwithstanding that the development is being carried out, development in relation to which an application for substitute consent is required under Part SA.

submissions or observations in relation to the application to the competent authority or any party to an appeal or referral of the contents of the reasoned determination made by the competent authority.

**[9.115]** The competent authority will make available for inspection any determination made together with the reasons for that determination in relation to a draft land use plan and it will make available for inspection any determination that it makes in relation to a proposed development as soon as may be after the making of the determination. Members of the public may inspect the respective determinations made at the offices of the competent authority during normal hours of business. The determination will also be made available for inspection on the authority's website.

## Site of community importance

**[9.116]** The Commission in Europe has adopted a list of 'sites of community importance' and the authority for adoption of these sites by the Commission is to be found in art 21 of the Habitats Directive which reads as follows:

> 1. The representative of the Commission shall submit to the Committee a draft of the measures to be taken. The Committee shall deliver its opinion on the draft within a time limited which the Chairman may lay down according to the urgency of the matter. The opinion shall be delivered by the majority laid down in Article 148(2) of the Treaty in the case of decisions which the council is required to adopt on a proposal from the Commission. The votes of the representatives of the Member States within the Committee shall be weighted in the manner set out in that Article. The Chairman shall not vote.
>
> 2. The Commission shall adopt the measures envisaged if they are in accordance with the opinion of the Committee. If the measures envisaged are not in accordance with the opinion of the Committee, or if no opinion is delivered, the Commission shall, without delay, submit to the Council a proposal relating to the measures to be taken. The Council shall act by a qualified majority. If, on the expiry of three months from the date of referral to the Council, the Council has not acted, the proposed measures shall be adopted by the Commission.

## Special area of conservation

**[9.117]** 'Special area of conservation' means a site that has been designated by the Minister as a special area of conservation pursuant to art 4, para 4 of the Habitats Directive which reads:

> Once a site of Community importance has been adopted in accordance with the procedure laid down in paragraph 2, the Member State concerned shall designate that site as a special area of conservation as soon as possible and within six years at most, establishing priorities in the light of the importance of the sites for the maintenance or restoration, at a favourable conservation status, of a natural habitat type in Annex I or a species in Annex II and for the coherence of Natura 2000, and in the light of the threats of degradation or destruction to which those sites are exposed.

## Wildlife site

**[9.118]** 'Wildlife site' means:

(a) an area proposed as a natural heritage area and the subject of a notice made under section 16(1) of the Wildlife (Amendment) Act 2000,

(b) an area designated as or proposed to be designated as a natural heritage area by a natural heritage area order made under section 18 of the Wildlife (Amendment) Act 2000,

(c) a nature reserve established or proposed to be established under an establishment order made under section 15 (amended by section 26 of the Wildlife (Amendment) Act 2000) of the Wildlife Act 1976,

(d) a nature reserve recognised or proposed to be recognised under a recognition order made under section 16 (amended by section 27 of the Wildlife (Amendment) Act 2000) of the Wildlife Act 1976, or

(e) a refuse for fauna or flora designated or proposed to be designated under a designation order made under section 17 (amended by section 28 of the Wildlife (Amendment) Act 2000) of the Wildlife Act 1976.[75]

## Draft land use plans and imperative reasons of overriding public interest

**[9.119]** Section 177W deals with a situation where the competent authority has decided that the draft land use plan or part thereof will have adverse affects on a European site. If, in those circumstances, the competent authority cannot see that there are any alternative solutions but, instead of providing a negative assessment it considers that the land use plan should be made for IROPI, then the competent authority must take the following steps:

(a) determine if there are imperative reasons of overriding public interest that necessitate the making of the Land use plan,

(b) propose the compensatory measures that are necessary to ensure that the overall coherence of the Natura 2000 network is protected,

(c) prepare a statement of case that imperative reasons of overriding public interest exist and of the compensatory measures that are required, and

(d) forward the said statement of case together with the draft Land use plan and Natura impact report to the Minister.[76]

The statement of case to be prepared by the competent authority shall state the following:

(a) the consideration that led to the assessment by the competent authority that the draft Land use plan would adversely affect the integrity of a European site,

(b) the reasons for the forming of the view by the competent authority that there are no alternative solutions (including the option of not proceeding with the draft Land use plan or part thereof),

---

75. See definition in PDA 2000, s 177R.
76. PDA 2000, s 177W.

(c) the reasons for the forming of the view by the competent authority that the imperative reasons of overriding public interest apply to the draft Land use plan, and

(d) the compensatory measures that are being proposed as necessary to ensure the overall coherence of Natura 2000 including, if appropriate, the provision of compensatory habitat.[77]

If the European site to be affected by the land use proposal is one which does not host a priority natural habitat type or priority species, the IROPI may include reasons of a social or economic nature.[78] If, on the other hand, the European site does host a priority natural habitat type or priority species, in those circumstances the IROPI are limited to:

(a) human health,

(b) public safety,

(c) beneficial consequences of primary importance to the environment, or

(d) subject to subsection (5) and having obtained an opinion from the European Commission, other imperative reasons of overriding public interest.[79]

Where the competent authority is invoking IROPI and is seeking an opinion from the European Commission it will advise the Minister as to why he or she should be satisfied to request such an opinion.[80]

[9.120] When prepared, the statement of case will be made available for public inspection after it has been forwarded to the Minister and it will also be made available on the competent authority's website.[81]

[9.121] 'Compensatory measures' for the purposes of s 177W, 177X or 177Y are measures proposed by the competent authority in the first instance and by the Minister as the case may be for the purpose of ensuring that the overall coherence of Natura 2000 is protected. 'Compensatory measures' may include the provision of compensatory habitats.[82]

## European site that does not host priority habitat or species and draft land use plan

[9.122] Section 177X provides that when the Minister receives a statement of case which discloses that the European site does not host either a priority type or priority species the Minister, having considered the statement will form an opinion:

(a) whether imperative reasons for overriding public interest apply,

(b) whether the compensatory measures proposed are sufficient to ensure that the overall coherence of Natura 2000 is protected.[83]

---

77. PDA 2000, s 177W(2).
78. PDA 2000, s 177(3).
79. PDA 2000, s 177W(4).
80. PDA 2000, s 177W(5).
81. PDA 2000, s 177W(6).
82. PDA 2000, s 177W(7).
83. PDA 2000, s 177X(1).

If the Minister concludes that IROPI do not apply or that the compensatory measures suggested to ensure that the overall coherence of Natura 2000 is protected, are not sufficient he/she will, subject to s 177Z, notify the competent authority not to make a land use plan or, if applicable, not to make part of the land use plan that has an adverse effect on the integrity of a European site.[84]

**[9.123]** When the Minister has informed the competent authority of his opinion, and subject to sub-s (2), the relevant provisions of this Act concerning the making of the land use plan and s 177Z, having considered the Minister's opinion the competent authority may either make a land use plan or part of a land use plan, make the land use plan or part thereof with modifications or not make the land use plan. If the competent authority either makes the land use plan or part of it or makes the land use plan or part of it with modifications it will notify the Minister and furnish the Minister with a statement of the following:

(a) the considerations that led to the assessment by the competent authority that the Land use plan would adversely affect the integrity of a European site;

(b) the reasons for the forming of the view by the competent authority that there are no alternative solutions (including the option of not proceeding with the Land use plan or part thereof);

(c) the reasons for the forming of the view by the competent authority that the imperative reasons of overriding public interest apply to the Land use plan;

(d) the compensatory measures that are being adopted as necessary to ensure the overall coherence of Natura 2000, including if appropriate, the provision of compensatory habitat.[85]

The Minister, on receipt of the competent authority's notice, shall inform the Commission of the contents of the notice. The notice given to the Minister will be made available for public inspection at the competent authority's public offices during stated office hours and it shall also be made available in electronic form on the authority's website.[86]

## European site that hosts priority habitat type or species and draft land use plan

**[9.124]** Section 177Y requires that the Minister, having received a statement of the case relating to a European site that does host a priority habitat type or species, shall consider the statement and then form an opinion:

(a) whether imperative reasons of overriding public interest apply,

(b) whether the compensatory measures proposed are sufficient to ensure that the overall coherence of Natura 2000 is protected, or

---

84. PDA 2000, s 117X(2)(a) and (b).
85. PDA 2000, s 177X (4).
86. PDA 2000, s 177X(5) and (6).

(c) where relevant, if he or she should seek an opinion from the Commission that imperative reasons of overriding public interest referred to in section 177W(4)(d) apply.[87]

If the Minister seeks an opinion from the Commission he shall give notice thereof to the competent authority and no decision will be made until the opinion of the Commission has been received and the Minister has given notice of it to the competent authority.[88]

**[9.125]** If the Minister concludes that the IROPI do not apply or that compensatory measures offered by the competent authority are insufficient in relation to the overall coherence protection for the Natura 2000 site, he will notify the competent authority, subject to s 177Z, not to make a land use plan or part of a land use plan where that part has adverse effects on the integrity of a European site.[89]

**[9.126]** Having received the Commission's opinion, the Minister shall inform the competent authority of both his opinion and the opinion of the Commission. The competent authority, having considered the opinion of the Minister and of the Commission, subject to sub-s (3), the relevant provisions of this Act concerning the making of the land use plan and s 177Z, may decide either to make the land use plan or part thereof or to make the land use plan or part thereof with modifications or not to make the land use plan. If the competent authority decides to make the land use plan or make part of the land use plan it will furnish a statement to the Minister setting out the following:

(a) the considerations that led to the assessment by the competent authority that the Land use plan would adversely affect the integrity of a European site;

(b) the reasons for the forming of the view by the competent authority that there are no alternative solutions (including the option of not proceeding with the Land use plan or part thereof);

(c) the reasons for forming the view by the competent authority that the imperative reasons of overriding public interest apply to the Land use plan;

(d) the compensatory measures that are being adopted as necessary to ensure the overall coherence of Natura 2000, including if appropriate, the provision of compensatory habitat.[90]

The Minister will inform the Commission of the contents of the notice given to him by the competent authority under sub-s (5) and the competent authority will make its notice available for public inspection by members of the public during ordinary office hours at its offices and will also make it available in electronic form on the authority's website.

---

87. PDA 2000, s 177Y(1).
88. PDA 2000, s 177Y(2).
89. PDA 2000, s 177Y(3).
90. PDA 2000, s 177Y.

## Making land use plans

[9.127] Section 177Z draws attention to certain pre-requisites before a competent authority can be satisfied that a land use plan[91] can be made.

[9.128] Firstly, the competent authority must consider the opinion of the Minister in relation to a European site that does not host a priority habitat type or a priority species under s 177X(3) and it must also consider the opinion of the Minister and, if applicable, notification of the opinion of the Commission under s 177Y(4). Secondly, the competent authority must be satisfied that a draft land use plan may be made excluding part of the land within the draft land use plan in respect of which the Minister and, if applicable, the Commission has or have formed an opinion that imperative reasons of overriding political interest do not exist or that compensatory measures are insufficient. Then, the competent authority can make a draft land use plan by amending or excluding any part of the area in relation to which the Minister, and if applicable, the Commission, has or have formed that opinion.[92]

[9.129] If the competent authority has submitted a statement of case to the Minister demonstrating that imperative reasons of overriding public interest exist and that compensation measures are required,[93] it may nevertheless proceed to make a land use plan which will only apply to lands outside the area referred to in the competent authority's statement of case.[94]

[9.130] Clearly the legislators expect that the process of making a land use plan, with all its accompanying bells and whistles will be a long, drawn out affair and s 177Z(4) provides that any delay in making a land use plan or part thereof arising from compliance with this part shall not invalidate the plan or part thereof.

## Proposed development and IROPI

[9.131] Section 177AA provides that where a competent authority, in the absence of alternative solutions, considers that a consent should be given for development in circumstances where it is agreed that the development will adversely affect a European site but because there are imperative reasons of overriding public interest then, the competent authority must address a number of factors before proceeding to grant the consent, namely the authority shall:

    (a)    determine if there are imperative reasons of overriding public interest that necessitate the giving of consent for the proposed development,

    (b)    propose the compensatory measures that are necessary to ensure that the overall coherence of the Natura 2000 network is protected,

---

91.    As seen, a land use plan means (a) regional planning guidelines, (b) a planning scheme in respect of all or any part of a strategic development zone, (c) a development plan, (d) a variation of a development plan or (e) a local area plan.
92.    PDA 2000, s 177Z(1).
93.    PDA 2000, s 177W(1).
94.    PDA 2000, s 177Z(3).

(c) prepare a statement of case that imperative reasons of overriding public interest exist and of the compensatory measures that are required,

(d) forward the said statement to the Minister together with a copy of the planning application and the Natura impact statement.[95]

The section continues by providing that certain matters must be specified in a statement of case which is to be forwarded to the Minister together with a copy of the planning application and the Natura impact statement under s 177AA(1)(d). A statement of case must specify the following:

(a) the considerations that led to the assessment by the competent authority that the proposed development would adversely affect the integrity of a European site,

(b) the reasons for the forming of the view by the competent authority that there are no alternative solutions (including the option of not giving consent for the proposed development),

(c) the reasons for the forming of the view by the competent authority that the imperative reasons of overriding public interest apply to the proposed development,

(d) compensatory measures that are being proposed as necessary to ensure the overall coherence of Natura 2000 including, if appropriate, the provisions of compensatory habitat and the conditions to which any consent for proposed development shall be subject requiring that the compensatory measures are carried out.[96]

Section 177AA then repeats in sub-s (3), (4) and (6) the same provisions as have already been dealt with in s 177B(3), (4) and (6).[97] A copy of the statement of case shall be furnished by a competent authority to the applicant for consent for proposed development.[98]

**[9.132]** In invoking imperative reasons for overriding public interest, the competent authority shall advise the Minister why he should be satisfied to request an opinion from the European Commission.[99]

**[9.133]** 'Compensatory measures' for the purpose of ss 177AA, 177AB and 177AC are measures which are proposed in the first instance by the applicant and then by a competent authority or by the Minister as the case may be for the purpose of ensuring that the overall coherence of Natura 2000 is protected. As has already been seen, compensatory measures may include the provision for a compensatory habitat in another place.[100]

---

95. PDA 2000, s 177AA(1).
96. PDA 2000, s 177AA(2).
97. These provisions are set out at para **9.17–9.20** hereof.
98. PDA 2000, s 177A(5).
99. PDA 2000, s 177AA(7).
100. PDA 2000, s 177AC(8).

[9.134] A competent authority may oppose conditions in any grant of assessment for the purpose of development relating to compensatory measures in ss 177AA, 177AB and 177AC. The authority or the Minister may, by condition, require a financial contribution from the applicant for the purpose of financing the provision of a compensatory habitat in another place.

## European site that does not host priority habitat type or priority species

[9.135] Section 177AB provides that where the Minister receives a statement of case which identifies a European site that does not host a priority habitat type or priority species the Minister shall consider the statement of case and form an opinion as to whether the compensatory measures and conditions proposed and imposed respectively are sufficient to ensure that the overall coherence of Natura 2000 is protected.[101]

[9.136] If the Minister forms the opinion that the compensatory measures are insufficient to ensure that the overall coherence of Natura 2000 is protected, notice will be given to the competent authority and the competent authority shall not grant consent to the proposed development.[102]

[9.137] The Minister shall inform the competent authority of his opinion and having considered that opinion, although the determination will adversely affect the integrity of a European site, the competent authority may grant permission for the development, grant permission for the development subject to conditions or refuse to grant permission for the development.[103]

[9.138] If the competent authority either grants permission for the development or grants permission subject to conditions it shall give notice of its decision to the Minister including a statement exactly similar to the matters set out in s 177AA(2)(a), (b) and (c).

[9.139] Section 177AA(2)(d) provides as follows:

> the compensatory measures that are being adopted as necessary to ensure the overall coherence of Natura 2000 including, if appropriate, the provision of a compensatory habitat.[104]

The Commission shall be informed by the Minister of the contents of the notice furnished by the competent authority to the Minister under s 177AB(4). The applicant, and, if appropriate, any person who made submissions or observations in relation to the application or, if appropriate, any party to an appeal or referral shall be furnished with copies of the following notices by the competent authority, namely:

    (a)    copy of the notice served by the Minister on the competent authority under section 177AB(2),

---

101. PDA 2000, s 177AB(1).
102. PDA 2000, s 177AB(2).
103. PDA 2000, s 177AB(3).
104. PDA 2000, s 177AB(4)(a)–(d).

(b) copy of the determination of the competent authority together with the reasons therefore made under section 177AB(3),

(c) copy of the notice of the competent authority's determination and statements setting out the matters provided for in section 177AB(4).

Copies of the above mentioned notices will also be made available for inspection at the office of the competent authority during office hours and on the competent authority's website.

## European site that hosts priority habitat or priority species

**[9.140]** Section 177AC provides for the situation where the Minister receives a statement of case relating to a European site that hosts a priority habitat type or priority species.[105] On receipt of a statement of case in these circumstances the Minister, having considered the statement, must form an opinion on two matters, namely:

(a) whether the compensatory measures and conditions referred to in section 177AA(2)(d) are sufficient to ensure the overall coherence of Natura 2000 is protected,

(b) where relevant, if he or she should seek an opinion from the Commission that other imperative reasons of overriding public interest referred to in section 177AA(4)(d) apply.[106]

If the Minister does seek an opinion of the Commission he will notify the competent authority of same and no decision shall be made in relation to the proposed development until the opinion of the Commission has been received by the Minister and the Minister has given notice of the Commission's opinion to the competent authority.

**[9.141]** The same procedure is followed in s 77AC(3), (4), (5), (6), (7) and (8) as the procedure specified in s 177AB(2), (3), (4), (5), (6) and (7).

## REGULATIONS

**[9.142]** Section 177AD(1)–(3) empowers the Minister to make regulations for procedural and administrative matters as appear necessary or expedient for any matter referred to in Pt XAB of PD(A)A 2010.

## Certain development carried out by or on behalf of local authorities

**[9.143]** Section 177AE(1) requires a local authority that is a planning authority, or where some other person either on behalf of the local authority or acting jointly or in partnership with the local authority pursuant to a contract entered into by that local authority, to prepare or cause to be prepared a Natura impact statement in respect of any proposed development to be carried out by it or by some person on its behalf or jointly with the local authority within the functional area of the local authority concerned.

---

105. PDA 2000, s 177AA(1).
106. PDA 2000, s 177AC(1).

**[9.144]** Where appropriate assessment is required in respect of a proposed development, no such development shall be carried out unless the board has approved it with or without modifications. As soon as the Natura impact statement has been prepared, the local authority is required to apply to the board for approval and all of the provisions of Pt XAB shall apply to the carrying out of the 'appropriate assessment'.[107]

**[9.145]** Section 177AE does not apply to road development within the meaning of the Roads Acts 1993–2007 carried out by or on behalf of the road authority.[108]

**[9.146]** The procedures to be followed by the local authority in making an application for approval to the board are set out in s 177AE(4).

**[9.147]** The obligations of the board in relation to making its decision are set out in s 177AE(5), (6), (8), (9), (10) and (12).

**[9.148]** Section 177AE(7) deals with the obligations of the person conducting an oral hearing in relation to compulsory purchase of land which relates wholly or partly to a proposed development under this section in respect of which a local authority has applied for approval.

**[9.149]** Specifically, s 177AE(10)(a), (b), (c), (d) and (e) deals with the situation where an integrated pollution control licence or a waste licence is required. The subsection permits the board to decide to refuse permission for the proposed development where it considers that development, notwithstanding the licensing of the activity, is unacceptable on environmental grounds having regard to the proper planning and sustainable development of the area in which the development is or will be situate or is unacceptable on habitats grounds having regard to the provisions of Pt XAB. Before making such a decision the board may request the Environmental Protection Agency (EPA) to make observations within a period of not less than three weeks from the date of the request as may be specified by the board in relation to the proposed development. The Board shall have regard to the EPA's observations.

**[9.150]** Section 177AE(11) permits the Minister to make regulations providing for procedural and administrative matters as appear necessary or expedient in respect of applications for approval under this section, such regulations to be made by the Minister.

**[9.151]** Section 177AE(13) provides that a person who contravenes a condition imposed by the board under this section shall be guilty of an offence.

## CONCLUSION

**[9.152]** The number of procedural steps required to apply for an appropriate assessment coupled with the number of steps the competent authority must take before issuing an appropriate assessment are such that it is likely to be a fruitful area for judicial review.

---

107. PDA 2000, s 177AB(1), (2) and (3).
108. PDA 2000, s 177AE(14).

# Chapter 10
# THE EIA DIRECTIVE

## INTRODUCTION

**[10.01]** PDA 2000, Pt X, ss 172–177 provide the statutory ground rules for environmental impact assessment (EIA).[1] Pt X also deals with environmental impact statements (EIS). Part X of PDA 2000 has been amended by PD(A)A 2010, s 57 and by the addition of Pt XA (substitute consent) and Pt XAB (appropriate assessment).

**[10.02]** EIA is an interactive process carried out by the decision-maker as a means of assessing the environmental impact of development before consent to development is granted. EIA is carried out in order to ensure that a development proposal is environmentally acceptable. EIA is defined as a process for anticipating the effects on the environment caused by development. It is an assessment which is required in certain public and private projects and the process has been incorporated into Irish law.

**[10.03]** The relevant European Community Directives on the assessment of the effects of certain public and private projects on the environment are provided in Council Directive 85/337/EEC,[2] as amended by Council Directive 97/11/EC,[3] by Directive 2003/35/EC[4] which latter Directive increases the extent of public participation in the EIA process,[5] and by Directive 2009/31/EC[6] dealing with the storage of carbon dioxide. Apart from assessing harmful effects which a development may have on the environment, EIA may also be required where a particular development may have positive effects on the environment. Furthermore, the adverse or beneficial effects which a development may have on the environment are not confined to adverse effects within the Republic of Ireland. The trans-frontier effects of a development must also be taken into account. For example, the nuclear reprocessing plant at Sellafield/Windscale in Cumbria is believed by many to pose a very real threat in terms of a health hazard not just in Cumbria and its surrounding areas but also to part, at least, of the east coast of Ireland. Representations have been made concerning trans-frontier effects of Sellafield/

---
1. PDA 2000, ss 172, 174 and 176 and Pt X of the Act have been amended by PD(A)A 2010, ss 54, 55, 56 and 57.
2. [1985] OJ L175/40.
3. [1997] OJ L73/5.
4. [2003] OJ L156/17.
5. Environmental impact assessment is dealt with comprehensively by Yvonne Scannell in her work *Environmental and Land Use Law* (Thomson Round Hall, 2006) Ch 5 paras 5-01 to 5–211, pp 377–474. Readers are strongly recommended and encouraged to read Professor Scannell's scholarly work on this topic.
6. [2009] OJ L140/5.

**[10.04]**      **Planning and Environmental Law in Ireland**

Windscale for many years by Ireland to the British government albeit that the Irish representations have, for the most part, been persistently ignored.

**[10.04]** Where Seveso sites are either in existence or are to be developed, planning authorities are bound to consider the potential trans-frontier implications. In *Keane v An Bord Pleanála*,[7] the board had regard to the consequences of the proposed development insofar as it extended outside the State. The claimant argued that the duty to have regard to the effects of the development outside the State was *ultra vires* but the Supreme Court held that the board was entitled to look beyond the boundaries of the State and to consider the possible effects of the development on other jurisdiction and that to do so was *intra vires*.

**[10.05]** PDA 2000, s 34(2)(b) puts the matter clearly, as follows:

> In considering its decision in accordance with paragraph (a), a planning authority shall consult with any other planning authority where it considers that a particular decision by it may have significant effect on the area of that authority, and the authority shall have regard to the views of that other authority and, without prejudice to the foregoing, it shall have regard to the effect a particular decision by it may have on any area outside its area (including areas outside the State).[8]

In *European Commission v Federal Republic of Germany*,[9] it was held that the Commission, given its role as guardian of the Treaty, is alone competent to decide whether it is appropriate to bring proceedings against a Member State for failure to fulfil its obligations.

**[10.06]** Article 12(2) of Directive 85/337/EEC, as amended, requires Member States to communicate the text of the provisions of national law which they adopt in the field covered by Directive 85/337/EEC to the Commission. All relevant provisions must be communicated. Article 4(2) of Directive 85/337/EEC, on the assessment of the effect of certain public and private projects on the environment, provides that projects of the classes listed in Annex II to the Directive are to be made subject to assessment where Member States consider that the characteristics so require and that, to that end, Member States may specify certain types of project as being subject to an assessment or may establish the criteria and/or thresholds necessary to determine which of the projects of the classes concerned are to be subject to any assessment. Articles 2(1) and 4(2) of Council Directive 85/337/EEC of 27 June 1985 are to be interpreted as not conferring on a Member State the power to exclude generally and definitively from possible assessment one or more of the classes in question. Consequently, if it does not include in

---

7.    *Keane v An Bord Pleanála* [1998] 2 ILRM 241, SC. Note that this case is also authority for the proposition that EIA is directed to assess both the beneficial and the harmful effects of a development proposal.
8.    PDA 2000, s 34(2)(a) deals with proper planning and sustainable development and the planning authority is restricted to considering the proper planning and sustainable development of the area regard being had to various matters not including transfrontier effects which are dealt with in PDA 2000, s 34(2)(a).
9.    *European Commission v Federal Republic of Germany* (Case C–301/95) [1995] ECR I–2189.

the scope of its implementing law all the subdivisions listed in Annex II to this Directive and thereby excludes, in advance, from the EIA required, whole classes of projects, a Member State fails to fulfil its obligations under arts 2(1) and 4(2) of the Directive.

**[10.07]** The operative part of the court's judgment in *Commission of the European Communities v Federal Republic of Germany*[10] delivered on 22 October 1998 reads as follows:

– by failing to take the necessary measures to comply with Council Directive 85/337/EEC of 27th June 1985 on the assessment of the effects of certain public and private projects on the environment within the prescribed period,

– by failing to communicate to the Commission all the measures which it has taken to comply with that Directive,

– by not requiring an environmental impact assessment for all projects on which such an assessment had to be carried out in compliance with that Directive, where the consent procedure was commenced after 3 July 1998, and

– by excluding in advance from the Environmental Impact Assessment requirement whole classes of project listed in Annex II to that Directive,

the Federal Republic of Germany has failed to fulfil its obligations under Articles 2(1), 4(2) and 12(1)&(2) of that Directive;

National authorities within the EU are bound to ensure compliance with the Directive.[11]

**[10.08]** The European Court of Justice (ECJ) in *Aannemersbedrijf PK Kraaijeveld BV EA v Gedeputeerde Staten Van Zuid-Holland*[12] held that where the discretion under arts 2(1) and (4) of Directive 85/337/EEC has been exceeded, national authorities must, according to their respective powers, take all general and particular measures necessary to ensure that projects are examined in order to determine whether or not they are likely to have significant effects on the environment. If such projects are likely to have significant effects on the environment they must be subject to EIA.

**[10.09]** In *Shannon Regional Fisheries Board v An Bord Pleanála*,[13] the decision of An Bord Pleanála to grant planning permission for a pig rearing installation was held to be *ultra vires* and was set aside on the grounds that such an installation required mandatory EIA by virtue of the EC (EIA) Regulations and no EIS was before the board when it considered the case and gave its decision. Barr J stated that a 'purposive approach'

---

10. *European Commission v Federal Republic of Germany* (Case C–301/95) [1995] ECR I–2189.
11. See EC, art 10 which provides that competent authorities are obliged to take, within the sphere of their competence, all general or particular measures for remedying the failure to carry out an assessment of the environmental effects of the project as provided for in Directive 85/337, art 2(1).
12. *Aannemersbedrijf PK Kraaijeveld BV EA v Gedeputeerde Staten Van Zuid-Holland* (Case C–72/95) [1996] ECR I–5403.
13. *Shannon Regional Fisheries Board v An Bord Pleanála* [1994] 3 IR 449, HC, Barr J.

should be adopted in the interpretation of the relevant regulations. The learned judge remitted the matter back for further consideration by the board when the requisite EIS had been submitted.

**[10.10]** In *Martin v An Bord Pleanála*,[14] Smyth J had, in the High Court, dismissed the applicant's application to strike down a permission granted by An Bord Pleanála on 3 March 2007 to permit a company called 'Indaver' to develop a waste management and incinerator development on its 25-acre site at Duleek, Co Meath. On the day that the board granted permission, the Environmental Protection Agency (EPA) had not granted a 'waste licence' which was a necessary requirement for the operation of the plant. The case was made on behalf of Mr Martin that the absence of the 'waste licence' meant that there had been no EIA of potential environmental pollution before planning permission was granted. It was Mr Martin's case that the permission granted had been granted on the basis of a partial consent only. The Supreme Court rejected the appellant's argument and held that Directive 85/337/EEC, as amended by Directive 97/11/EC, relating to EIAs should not be interpreted as meaning that there is only one body responsible for carrying out EIA. In effect, the combination of An Bord Pleanála's assessment and the assessment of the EPA together met the requirements of the Directive. It did not matter that the assessments were not made at the same time because, in any case, the Indaver project needed to acquire both planning permission and a waste licence before it could commence its operation.

**[10.11]** Some flexibility was demonstrated, albeit *obiter*, by the Supreme Court in *McBride v Galway Corporation*[15] in refusing to dismiss a case where no EIS had been submitted with an application for a foreshore lease which application was made to the Minister for the Marine by Galway Corporation. The court noted that the Minister had already considered an EIS for the same project in the course of a different EIA which had been submitted to him by Galway Corporation. The Supreme Court held that there had been substantive compliance with the Directive. Keane J (as he then was) pointed out that the obligation to undertake EIA and to provide an EIS (as and if required) rests with the Member State. It does not specifically rest with the Minister. Although the Minister was an organ of the administration he could not be regarded as being in breach of any requirement of the Directive during the relevant period. The court concluded that Ireland, as a Member State, had complied with its EIA/EIS obligation through an EIS undertaken by the local authority on a different occasion but for the same project. The court admitted that it was influenced by the pressing nature of the case, namely that the local authority wished to urgently commence a new and comprehensive drainage scheme for Galway City and for its outskirts in order to control and to attempt to prevent continuing pollution and ongoing pollution of Galway Bay. The court's clear preference was to encourage these drainage works rather than delay them which preference, it must be said, is clearly related to the primary objective of the EIA Directive. Standing back a little from the Supreme Court judgment in *McBride v Galway Corporation*,[16] some

---

14. *Martin v An Bord Pleanála* [2007] IESC 23 (10 May 2007), Smyth J.
15. *McBride v Galway Corporation* [1998] 1 IR 485, SC.
16. *McBride v Galway Corporation* [1998] 1 IR 485, SC.

commentators would agree that Keane J's reasoning may have been incorrect especially since the judgment of the ECJ in *Kraaijeveld*,[17] which was not available at the time this case was before the High Court, was opened to the Supreme Court in the course of hearing.

**[10.12]** In summary, the objective of the EIA Directive is that where 'projects' are likely to have significant effects on the environment such projects must be subjected to EIA before any decision is made to grant 'development consent'.

**[10.13]** Article 3 of the EIA Directive, in defining the objective of the EIA provides:

> The environmental impact assessment shall identify, describe and assess in an appropriate manner, and in the light of each individual case and in accordance with Articles 4 and 11, the direct and indirect effects of a project on the following factors:
>
> - Human beings, fauna and flora,
> - Soil, water, air, climate and landscape,
> - Material assets and cultural heritage,
> - Interaction between the factors mentioned in the first, second and third indents.

## DIRECT EFFECT

**[10.14]** The ECJ has held, on a mainly consistent basis, that Directive 85/337/EEC, as amended,[18] has 'direct effect', that is to say that it can be relied on directly in proceedings before the courts dealing with the planning authorities and with appeals before An Bord Pleanála.[19]

**[10.15]** In the *Kraaijeveld*[20] case, the ECJ held that in interpreting the various classes of 'project', national courts should have regard to the purpose and general scheme of the Directive. To date, the ECJ has held that arts 1(1), 2(1), 4(2), 5 and 6(1) have direct effect. For 'direct effect' to apply in relation to the articles above numbered, the subject matter of the Directive must be sufficiently precise and it must also be unconditional.

---

17. *Aannemersbedrijf PK Kraaijeveld BV EA v Gedeputeerde Staten Van Zuid-Holland* (Case C–72/95) [1996] ECR I–5403.
18. Directive 85/337/EEC has been amended by Directive 97/11/EC, Directive 2003/35/EC and by Directive 2009/31/EC. The consolidated version is what appears in this chapter when reference is made to the EIA Directive.
19. See *World Wildlife Fund (WWF) and Others v Autonome Provinz Bozen and Others* (Case C–435/97) [1998] ECR I–5613 and more particularly *Aannemersbedrijf PK Kraaijeveld BV and Others* (Case C–72/95) [1996] ECR I–5403.
20. *Aannemersbedrijf PK Kraaijeveld BV EA v Gedeputeerde Staten Van Zuid-Holland* (Case C–72/95) [1996] ECR I–5403.

**[10.16]** Article 1 of the EIA Directive, as amended, reads as follows:[21]

**Article 1**

1. This Directive shall apply to the assessment of the environmental effects of those public and private projects which are likely to have significant effects on the environment.

2. For the purposes of this Directive:

'project' means:

- the execution of construction works or other installations or schemes,
- other interventions in the natural surroundings and landscape including those involving the extraction of mineral resources;

'developer' means:

the applicant for authorisation for a private project or the public authority which initiates a project.

'development consent' means:

the decision of the competent authority or authorities which entitles the developer to proceed with the project.

'public' means:

- one or more natural or legal persons and, in accordance with national legislation or practice, their associations, organisations or groups.

'public concerned' means:

- the public affected or likely to be affected by, or having an interest in, the environmental decision-making procedures referred to in Article 2(2);
- for the purposes of this definition, non-governmental organisations promoting environmental protection and meeting any requirements under national law shall be deemed to have an interest.

3. The competent authority or authorities shall be that or those which the Member States designate as responsible for performing the duties arising from this Directive.

---

21. EU Directives are less familiar to many practitioners than Irish State law and regulations. The EIA Directive is an important piece of legislation which has 'direct effect' in Ireland. At the risking of irritating some readers the entire Directive and its Annexes have been included here. Compared with some of the torturous language contained in some of the more convoluted sections in our planning legislation (not to mention other legislation) the EIA Directive is simply and clearly written and it is easily readable. To read the EIA Directive is to understand it. Could that be said of PD(A)A 2010, say, particularly Pts XA and XAB? There is scope in Ireland for a new breed of parliamentary draftsmen who would simplify sections such as PDA 2000, ss 177A to 177AE inclusive. This comprises 31 sections of the PD(A)A 2010 and the last section is nine pages long. Our draftsmen either lack confidence in the manner in which they express themselves by complicating statutory provisions with torturous and indigestible sentences or, perhaps they set out to confuse us all! It must be conceded that this author has advised himself on several occasions to take a long course on EU draftmanship but to date he has not heeded his own advice.

4. Member States may decide, on a case-by-case basis if so provided under national law, not to apply this Directive to projects serving national defence purposes, if they deem that such application would have an adverse effect on these purposes.

5. This Directive shall not apply to projects the details of which are adopted by a specific act of national legislation, since the objectives of this Directive including that of supplying information, are achieved through the legislative process.

**[10.17]** Article 2 of the EIA Directive, as amended, reads as follows:

### Article 2

1. Member States shall adopt all measures necessary to ensure that, before consent is given, projects likely to have significant effects on the environment by virtue, inter alia, of their nature, size or location are made subject to requirement for development consent and an assessment with regard to their effects. These projects are defined in Article 4.

2. The environmental impact assessment may be integrated into the existing procedures for consent to projects in the Member States, or failing this, into other procedures or into procedures to be established to comply with the aims of this Directive.

2.(a) Member States may provide for a single procedure in order to fulfil the requirements of this Directive and the requirements of Council Directive 96/61/EC of 24 September 1996 on integrated pollution prevention and control.

3. Without prejudice to Article 7, Member States may, in exceptional cases, exempt a specific project in whole or in part from the provisions laid down in this Directive.

In this event, the Member States shall:

(a) consider whether another form of assessment would be appropriate;

(b) make available to the public concerned the information obtained under other forms of assessment referred to in (a), the information relating to the exemption decision and the reasons for granting it;

(c) inform the Commission, prior to granting consent, of the reasons justifying the exemption granted, and provide it with the information made available, where applicable, to their own nationals.

The Commission shall immediately forward the documents received to the other Member States. The Commission shall report annually to the Council on the application of this paragraph.

**[10.18]** Article 3 of the EIA Directive, as amended, reads as follows:

### Article 3

The environmental impact assessment shall identify, describe and assess in an appropriate manner, in the light of each individual case and in accordance with

Articles 4 to 11, the direct and indirect effects of a project on the following factors:

- Human beings, fauna and flora;
- Soil, water, air, climate and the landscape;
- Material assets and the cultural heritage;
- The interaction between the factors mentioned in the first, second and third indents.

**[10.19]** Article 4 of the EIA Directive, as amended, reads as follows:

### Article 4

1. Subject to Article 2(3), projects listed in Annex I shall be made subject to an assessment in accordance with Articles 5 to 10.

2. Subject to Article 2(3), for projects listed in Annex II, the Member States shall determine through:

(a) a case-by-case examination, or

(b) thresholds or criteria set by the Member State

whether the project shall be made subject to an assessment in accordance with Articles 5 to 10.

Member States may decide to apply both procedures referred to in (a) and (b).

3. When a case-by-case examination is carried out or thresholds or criteria are set out for the purpose of para 2, the relevant selection criteria set out in Annex III shall be taken into account.

4. Member States shall ensure that the determination made by the competent authorities under para 2 is made available to the public.

**[10.20]** Article 5 of the EIA Directive reads as follows:

### Article 5

1. In the case of projects which, pursuant to Article 4, must be subjected to an environmental impact assessment in accordance with Articles 5 to 10, Member States shall adopt the necessary measures to ensure that the developer supplies in an appropriate form the information specified in Annex III inasmuch as:

(a) the Member States consider that the information is relevant to a given stage of consent procedure and to the specific characteristics of a particular project or type of project and of the environmental features likely to be affected;

(b) the Member States consider that a developer may reasonably be required to compile this information having regard inter alia to the current knowledge and methods of assessment.

2. Member States shall take the necessary measures to ensure that, if the developer so requests before submitting an application for development consent, the competent authority shall give an opinion on the information to be supplied by the developer in accordance with paragraph 1. The competent authority shall consult

the developer and authorities referred to in Article 6(1) before it gives its opinion. The fact that the authority has given an opinion under this paragraph shall not preclude it from subsequently requiring the developer to submit further information.

Member States may require the competent authorities to give such an opinion, irrespective of whether the developer so requests.

3. The information to be provided by the developer in accordance with paragraph 1 shall include at least:

- a description of the project comprising information on the site, design and size of the project,
- a description of the measures envisaged in order to avoid, reduce and, if possible, remedy significant adverse effects,
- the data required to identify and assess the main effects which the project is likely to have on the environment,
- an outline of the main alternatives studied by the developer had an indication of the main reasons for his choice, taking into account the environmental effects,
- a non-technical summary of the information mentioned in the previous indents.

4. Member States shall, if necessary, ensure that any authorities holding relevant information, with particular reference Article 3, shall make this information available to the developer.

**[10.21]** Article 6 of the EIA Directive reads as follows:

### Article 6

1. Member States shall take the measures necessary to ensure that the authorities likely to be concerned by the project by reason of their specific environmental responsibilities are given an opportunity to express their opinion on the information supplied by the developer and on the request for development consent. To this end, Member States shall designate the authorities to be consulted, either in general terms or on a case-by-case basis. The information gathered pursuant to Article 5 shall be forwarded to these authorities. Detailed arrangements for consultation shall be laid down by the Member States.

2. The public shall be informed, whether by public notices or other appropriate means such as electronic media where available, of the following matters early in the environmental decision-making procedures referred to in Article 2(2) and, at the latest, as soon as information can reasonably be provided;

(a) the request for development consent;

(b) the fact that the project is subject to an environmental impact assessment procedure and, where relevant, the fact that Article 7 applies;

(c) details of the competent authorities responsible for taking the decision, those from which relevant information can be obtained, those to which comments or questions can be submitted, and details of the time schedule for transmitting comments or questions;

(d) the nature of possible decisions or, where there is one, the draft decision;

(e) an indication of the availability of the information gathered pursuant to Article 5;

(f) an indication of the times and places where a means by which the relevant information will be made available;

(g) details of the arrangements for public participation made pursuant to paragraph 5 of this Article.

3. Member States shall ensure that, within reasonable time-frames, the following is made available to the public concerned:

(a) any information gathered pursuant to Article 5;

(b) in accordance with national legislation, the main reports and advice issued to the competent authority or authorities at the time when the public concerned is informed in accordance with paragraph 2 of this Article;

(c) in accordance with the provisions of Directive 2003/4/EC of the European Parliament and of the Council of 28th January 2003 on public access to environmental information, information other than that referred to in paragraph 2 of this Article which is relevant for the decision in accordance with Article 8 and which only becomes available after the time the public concerned was informed in accordance with paragraph 2 of this Article.

4. The public concerned shall be given early and effective opportunities to participate in the environmental decision-making procedures referred to in Article 2(2) and shall, for that purpose, be entitled to express comments and opinions when all options are open to the competent authority or authorities before the decision on the request for development consent is taken.

5. The detailed arrangements for informing the public (for example by bill posting within a certain radius or publication in local newspapers) and for consulting the public concerned (for example by written submissions or by way of a public enquiry) shall be determined by the Member States.

6. Reasonable time-frames for the different phases shall be provided, allowing sufficient time for informing the public and for the public concerned to prepare and participate effectively in environmental decision making subject to the provisions of this Article.

**[10.22]** Article 7 of the EIA Directive reads as follows:

### Article 7

1. Where a Member State is aware that a project is likely to have significant effects on the environment in another Member State or where a Member State likely to be significantly affected so requests, the Member State in whose territory the project is intended to be carried out shall send to the affected Member State as soon as possible and no later than when informing its own public, inter alia:

(a) a description of the project, together with any available information on its possible transboundary impact;

(b) information on the nature of the decision which may be taken, and shall give the other Member State a reasonable time in which to indicate whether it wishes to participate in the environmental decision-making procedures referred to in Article 2(2), and may include the information referred to in paragraph 2 of this Article.

2. If a Member State which receives information pursuant to paragraph 1 indicates that it intends to participate in the environmental decision-making procedures referred to in Article 2(2), the Member State in whose territory the project is intended to be carried out shall, if it has not already done so, send to the affected Member State the information required to be given pursuant to Article 6(2) and made available pursuant to Article 6(3)(a) and (b).

3. The Member States concerned, each insofar as it is concerned, shall also:

(a) arrange for the information referred to in paragraphs 1 and 2 to be made available, within a reasonable time, to the authorities referred to in Article 6(1) and the public concerned in the territory of the Member State likely to be significantly affected; and

(b) ensure that those authorities and the public concerned are given an opportunity, before development consent for the project is granted, to forward their opinion within a reasonable time of the information supplied to the competent authority in the Member State in whose territory the project is intended to be carried out.

4. The Member State concerned shall enter into consultations regarding, inter alia, the potential transboundary effects of the project and the measures envisaged to reduce or eliminate such effects and shall agree on a reasonable time frame for the duration of the consultation period.

5. The detailed arrangements for implementing this Article may be determined by the Member States concerned and shall be such as to enable the public concerned in the territory of the affected Member State to participate effectively in the environmental decision-making procedures referred to in Article 2(2) for the project.

**[10.23]** Article 8 of the EIA Directive reads as follows:

### Article 8

The results of consultations and the information gathered pursuant to Articles 5, 6 and 7 must be taken into consideration in the development consent procedure.

**[10.24]** Article 9 of the Directive reads as follows:

### Article 9

1. When a decision to grant or refuse development consent has been taken, the competent authority or authorities shall inform the public thereof in accordance with the appropriate procedures and shall make available to the public the following information:

- the content of the decision and any conditions attached thereto,
- having examined the concerns and opinions expressed by the public concerned, the main reasons and considerations on which the decision is based, including information about the public participation process,

- a description, where necessary, of the main measures to avoid, reduce and, if possible, offset the major adverse effects.

2. The competent authority or authorities shall inform any Member State which has been consulted pursuant to Article 7, forwarding to it the information referred to in paragraph 1 of this Article.

The consulted Member State shall ensure that information is made available in appropriate manner to the public concerned in their own territory.

**[10.25]** Article 10 of the EIA Directive reads as follows:

### Article 10

The provisions of this Directive shall not affect the obligation on the competent authorities to respect the limitations imposed by National Regulations and administrative provisions and accepted legal practices with regard to commercial and industrial confidentiality, including intellectual property, and the safeguarding of public interest.

Where Article 7 applies, the transmission of information to another Member State and the receipt of information by another Member State shall be subject to the limitations in force in the Member State in which the project is proposed.

**[10.26]** Article 10(A) of the EIA Directive reads as follows:

### Article 10(A)

Member States shall ensure that, in accordance with the relevant national legal system, members of the public concerned:

(a) having a sufficient interest, or alternatively,

(b) maintaining the impairment of a right, where administrative procedural law of a Member State requires this as a pre-condition,

have access to a review procedure before a court of law or another independent and impartial body established by law to challenge the substantive or procedural legality of decisions, acts or omissions subject to the public participation provisions of this Directive.

Member States shall determine at what stage the decisions, acts or omissions may be challenged.

What constitutes a sufficient interest and impairment of a right shall be determined by the Member States, consistently with the objective of giving the public concerned wide access to justice. To this end, the interest of any non-governmental organisation meeting the requirements referred to in Article 1(2), shall be deemed sufficient for the purpose of sub-paragraph (a) of this Article. Such organisation shall also be deemed to have rights capable of being impaired for the purpose of sub-paragraph (b) of this Article.

The provisions of this Article shall not exclude the possibility of a preliminary review procedure before an administrative authority and shall not affect the requirement of exhaustion of administrative review procedures prior to recourse to judicial review procedures, where such a requirement exists under national law.

Any such procedure shall be fair, equitable, timely and not prohibitively expensive.

In order to further the effectiveness of the provision of this Article, Member States shall ensure that practical information is made available to the public on access to administrative and judicial review procedures.

**[10.27]** Article 11 of the EIA Directive reads as follows:

### Article 11

1. The Member States and the Commission shall exchange information on the experience gained in applying this Directive.

2. In particular, Member States shall inform the Commission of any criteria and/or thresholds adopted for the selection of the projects in question, in accordance with Article 4(2).

3. Five years after notification of this Directive, the Commission shall send the European Parliament and the Council a report on its application and effectiveness. The report shall be based on the aforementioned exchange of information.

4. On the basis of this exchange of information, the Commission shall submit to the Council additional proposals, should this be necessary, with a view to this Directive's being applied in a sufficiently coordinated manner.

**[10.28]** Article 12 of the EIA Directive reads as follows:

### Article 12

1. Member States shall take the measures necessary to comply with this Directive within three years of its notification.

2. Member States shall communicate to the Commission the texts of the provisions of national law which they adopt in the field covered by this Directive.

**[10.29]** Article 13 has been removed.

**[10.30]** Article 14 of EIA Directive reads as follows:

### Article 14

This Directive is addressed to the Member States.

**[10.31]** Annexes I, II and III shall be replaced by Annexes I, II, III and IV as they appear in the Annex. Although it is tedious to set out Annexes I, II, III and IV, they deal with the classifications of various private and public projects which are likely to have significant effects on the environment and they must be read to be understood.

**[10.32]** ANNEX 1

**PROJECTS SUBJECT TO** ARTICLE 4(1)

1. Crude -oil refineries (excluding undertakings manufacturing only lubricants from crude oil) and installations for the gasification and liquefaction of 500 tonnes or more of coal or bituminous shale per day.

**[10.32]** Planning and Environmental Law in Ireland

2. Thermal power stations and other combustion installations with a heat output of 300 megawatts or more, and nuclear power stations and other nuclear reactors including the dismantling or decommissioning of such power stations or reactors* (except research installations for the production and conversion of fissionable and fertile materials, whose maximum power does not exceed 1 kilowatt continuous thermal load).

3.(a) Installations for the reprocessing of irradiated nuclear fuel.

   (b) Installations designed:

- for the production or enrichment of nuclear fuel,
- for the processing of irradiated nuclear fuel or high –level radioactive waste,
- for the final disposal of irradiated nuclear fuel,
- solely for the final disposal of radioactive waste,
- solely for the storage (planned for more than 10 years) of irradiated nuclear fuels or radioactive waste in a different site than the production site.

4. Integrated works for the initial smelting of cast -iron and steel;

Installations for the production of non-ferrous crude metals from ore, concentrates or secondary raw materials by metallurgical, chemical or electrolytic processes.

5. Installations for the extraction of asbestos and for the processing and transformation of asbestos and products containing asbestos: for asbestos-cement products, with an annual production of more than 20 000 tonnes of finished products, for friction material, with an annual production of more than 50 tonnes of finished products, and for other uses of asbestos, utilization of more than 200 tonnes per year.

6. Integrated chemical installations, ie those installations for the manufacture on an industrial scale of substances using chemical conversion processes, in which several units are juxtaposed and are functionally linked to one another and which are:

(i) for the production of basic organic chemicals;

(ii) for the production of basic inorganic chemicals;

(iii) for the production of phosphorous-, nitrogen- or potassium-based fertilizers (simple or compound fertilizers);

(iv) for the production of basic plant health products and of biocides;

(v) for the production of basic pharmaceutical products using a chemical or biological process;

(vi) for the production of explosives.

7.(a) Construction of lines for long-distance railway traffic and of airports[22] with a basic runway length of 2100m or more;

---

22. For the purposes of this Directive, 'airport' means airports which comply with the definition in the 1944 Chicago Convention setting up the International Civil Aviation Organization (Annex 14).

(b) Construction of motorways and express roads;[23]

(c) construction of a new road of four or more lanes, or realignment and/or widening of an existing road of two lanes or less so as to provide four or more lanes, where such new road, or realigned and/or widened section of road would be 10 km or more in a continuous length.

8.(a) Inland waterways and ports for inland -waterway traffic which permit the passage of vessels of over 1350 tonnes;

(b) Trading ports, piers for loading and unloading connected to land and outside ports (excluding ferry piers) which can take vessels of over 1350 tonnes.

9. Waste disposal installations for the incineration, chemical treatment as defined in Annex IIA to Directive 75/442/EEC[24] under heading D9, or landfill of hazardous waste (ie waste to which Directive 91/689/ EEC[25] applies).

10. Waste disposal installations for the incineration or chemical treatment as defined in Annex IIA to Directive 75/442/EEC under heading D9 of non-hazardous waste with a capacity exceeding 100 tonnes per day.

11. Groundwater abstraction or artificial groundwater recharge schemes where the annual volume of water abstracted or recharged is equivalent to or exceeds 10 million cubic metres.

12.(a) Works for the transfer of water resources between river basins where this transfer aims at preventing possible shortages of water and where the amount of water transferred exceeds 100 million cubic metres/year;

(b) In all other cases, works for the transfer of water resources between river basins where the multi -annual average flow of the basin of abstraction exceeds 2 000 million cubic metres/year and where the amount of water transferred exceeds 5% of this flow.

In both cases transfers of piped drinking water are excluded.

13. Waste water treatment plants with a capacity exceeding 150,000 population equivalent as defined in Article 2 point (6) of Directive 91/271/EEC.[26]

14. Extraction of petroleum and natural gas for commercial purposes where the amount extracted exceeds 500 tonnes/day in the case of petroleum and 500,000m$^3$/day in the case of gas.

15. Dams and other installations designed for the holding back or permanent storage of water, where a new or additional amount of water held back or stored exceeds 10 million cubic metres.

---

23. For the purposes of the Directive, 'express road' means a road which complies with the definition in the European Agreement on Main International Traffic Arteries of 15 November 1975.
24. [1975] OJ L194/39. Directive as last amended by Commission Decision 94/3/EC ([1994] OJ L5/15).
25. [1991] OJ L377/20. Directive as last amended by Directive 94/31/EC ([1994] OJ L168/28).
26. [1991] OJ L135/40. Directive as last amended by the 1994 Act of Accession.

16. Pipelines with a diameter of more than 800 mm and a length of more than 40 km,
    – for the transport of gas, oil, chemicals and,
    – for the transport of carbon dioxide ($CO_2$) streams for the purposes of geological storage, including associated booster stations.

17. Installations for the intensive rearing of poultry or pigs with more than:
    (a) 85,000 places for broilers, 60 000 places for hens;
    (b) 3,000 places for production pigs (over 30 kg); or
    (c) 900 places for sows.

18. Industrial plants for the
    (a) production of pulp from timber or similar fibrous materials;
    (b) production of paper and board with a production capacity exceeding 200 tonnes per day.

19. Quarries and open-cast mining where the surface of the site exceeds 25 hectares, or peat extraction, where the surface of the site exceeds 150 hectares.

20. Construction of overhead electrical power lines with a voltage of 220 kV or more and a length of more than 15 km.

21. Installations for storage of petroleum, petrochemical, or chemical products with a capacity of 200 000 tonnes or more.

22. Any change to or extension of projects listed in this Annex where such a change or extension in itself meets the thresholds, if any, set out in this Annex.

23. Storage sites pursuant to Directive 2009/31/EC of the European Parliament and of the Council of 23rd April 2009 on the geological storage of carbon dioxide.

24. Installations for the capture of $CO_2$ streams for the purpose of geological storage pursuant to Directive 2009/31/EC from installations covered by this Annex, or where the total yearly capture of $CO_2$ is 1.5 megatonnes or more.

**[10.33]** ANNEX II

**PROJECTS SUBJECT TO ARTICLE 4(2)**

**1. Agriculture, silviculture and aquaculture**

(a) Projects for the restructuring of rural land holdings;
(b) Projects for the use of uncultivated land or semi-natural areas for intensive agricultural purposes;
(c) Water management projects for agriculture, including irrigation and land drainage projects;
(d) Initial afforestation and deforestation for the purposes of conversion to another type of land use;
(e) Intensive livestock installations (projects not included in Annex I);
(f) Intensive fish farming;
(g) Reclamation of land from the sea.

## 2. Extractive industry

(a) Quarries, open-cast mining and peat extraction (projects not included in Annex I);

(b) Underground mining;

(c) Extraction o f minerals by marine or fluvial dredging;

(d) Deep drillings, in particular:
- geothermal drilling,
- drilling for the storage of nuclear waste material,
- drilling for water supplies,

with the exception of drillings for investigating the stability of the soil;

(e) Surface industrial installations for the extraction of coal, petroleum, natural gas and ores, as well as bituminous shale.

## 3. Energy industry

(a) Industrial installations for the production of electricity, steam and hot water (projects not included in Annex I);

(b) Industrial installations for carrying gas, steam and hot water; transmission of electrical energy by overhead cables (projects not included in Annex I);

(c) Surface storage of natural gas;

(d) Underground storage of combustible gases;

(e) Surface storage of fossil fuels;

(f) Industrial briquetting of coal and lignite;

(g) Installations for the processing and storage of radioactive waste (unless included in Annex I);

(h) Installations for hydroelectric energy production;

(i) Installations for the harnessing o f wind power for energy production (wind farms);

(j) Installations for the capture of $CO_2$ streams for the purposes of geological storage pursuant to Directive 2009/31/EC from installations not covered by Annex I of this Directive.

## 4. Production and processing of metals

(a) Installations for the production of pig iron or steel (primary or secondary fusion) including continuous casting;

(b) Installations for the processing of ferrous metals:

   (i) hot-rolling mills;

   (ii) smitheries with hammers;

   (iii) application of protective fused metal coats;

(c) Ferrous metal foundries;

(d) Installations for the smelting, including the alloyage, of non-ferrous metals, excluding precious metals, including recovered products (refining, foundry casting, etc);

- (e) Installations for surface treatment of metals and plastic materials using an electrolytic or chemical process;
- (f) Manufacture and assembly of motor vehicles and manufacture of motor vehicle engines;
- (g) Shipyards;
- (h) Installations for the construction and repair of aircraft;
- (i) Manufacture of railway equipment;
- (j) Swaging by explosives;
- (k) Installations for the roasting and sintering of metallic ores.

### 5. Mineral industry

- (a) Coke ovens (dry coal distillation);
- (b) Installations for the manufacture of cement;
- (c) Installations for the production of asbestos and the manufacture of asbestos-products (projects not included in Annex I);
- (d) Installations for the manufacture of glass including glass fibre;
- (e) Installations for smelting mineral substances including the production of mineral fibres;
- (f) Manufacture of ceramic products by burning, in particular roofing tiles, bricks, refractory bricks, tiles, stoneware or porcelain.

### 6. Chemical industry (Projects not included in Annex I)

- (a) Treatment of intermediate products and production of chemicals;
- (b) Production of pesticides and pharmaceutical products, paint and varnishes, elastomers and peroxides;
- (c) Storage facilities for petroleum, petrochemical and chemical products.

### 7. Food industry

- (a) Manufacture of vegetable and animal oils and fats;
- (b) Packing and canning of animal and vegetable products;
- (c) Manufacture of dairy products;
- (d) Brewing and malting;
- (e) Confectionery and syrup manufacture;
- (f) Installations for the slaughter of animals;
- (g) Industrial starch manufacturing installations;
- (h) Fish-meal and fish-oil factories;
- (i) Sugar factories.

### 8. Textile, leather, wood and paper industries

- (a) Industrial plants for the production of paper and board (projects not included in Annex I);
- (b) Plants for the pretreatment (operations such as washing, bleaching, mercerization) or dyeing of fibres or textiles;

- (c) Plants for the tanning of hides and skins;
- (d) Cellulose-processing and production installations.

## 9. Rubber industry

Manufacture and treatment of elastomer based products.

## 10. Infrastructure projects

- (a) Industrial estate development projects;
- (b) Urban development projects, including the construction of shopping centres and car parks;
- (c) Construction of railways and intermodal transshipment facilities, and of intermodal terminals (projects not included in Annex I);
- (d) Construction of airfields (projects not included in Annex I);
- (e) Construction of roads, harbours and port installations, including fishing harbours (projects not included in Annex I);
- (f) Inland-waterway construction not included in Annex I, canalization and flood-relief works;
- (g) Dams and other installations designed to hold water or store it on a long term basis (projects not included in Annex I);
- (h) Tramways, elevated and underground railways, suspended lines or similar lines of a particular type, used exclusively or mainly for passenger transport;
- (i) Oil and gas pipeline installations for the transport of $CO_2$ streams for the purpose of geological storage (projects not included in Annex I);
- (j) Installations of long-distance aqueducts;
- (k) Coastal work to combat erosion and maritime works capable of altering the coast through the construction, for example, of dykes, moles, jetties and other sea defence works, excluding the maintenance and reconstruction of such works;
- (l) Groundwater abstraction and artificial groundwater recharge schemes not included in Annex I;
- (m) Works for the transfer of water resources between river basins not included in Annex I.

## 11. Other projects

- (a) Permanent racing and test tracks for motorized vehicles;
- (b) Installations for the disposal of waste (projects not included in Annex I);
- (c) Waste-water treatment plants (projects not included in Annex I);
- (d) Sludge-deposition sites;
- (e) Storage of scrap iron, including scrap vehicles;
- (f) Test benches for engines, turbines or reactors;
- (g) Installations for the manufacture of artificial mineral fibres;
- (h) Installations for the recovery or destruction of explosive substances;
- (i) Knackers' yards.

**12. Tourism and leisure**

(a) Ski-runs, ski-lifts and cable-cars and associated developments;

(b) Marinas;

(c) Holiday villages and hotel complexes outside urban areas and associated developments;

(d) Permanent camp sites and caravan sites;

(e) Theme parks.

13. Any change or extension of projects listed in Annex I or Annex II, already authorized, executed or in the process of being executed, which may have significant adverse effects on the environment (*change or extension not included in Annex 1*);

*Projects in Annex I, undertaken exclusively or mainly for the development and testing of new methods or products and not used for* more than two years.

## [10.34] ANNEX III

### SELECTION CRITERIA REFERRED TO IN ARTICLE 4(3)

**1. Characteristics of projects**

The characteristics of projects must be considered having regard, in particular, to:

- the size of the project,
- the cumulation with other projects,
- the use of natural resources,
- the production of waste,
- pollution and nuisances,
- the risk of accidents, having regard in particular to substances or technologies used.

**2. Location of projects**

The environmental sensitivity of geographical areas likely to be affected by projects must be considered, having regard, in particular, to:

- the existing land use,
- the relative abundance, quality and regenerative capacity of natural resources in the area,
- the absorption capacity of the natural environment, paying particular attention to the following areas:

    (a) wetlands;

    (b) coastal zones;

    (c) mountain and forest areas;

    (d) nature reserves and parks;

    (e) areas classified or protected under Member States 'legislation; special protection areas designated by Member States pursuant to Directive 79/409/EEC and 92/43/EEC;

(f) areas in which the environmental quality standards laid down in Community legislation have already been exceeded;

(g) densely populated areas;

(h) landscapes of historical, cultural or archaeological significance.

### 3. Characteristics of the potential impact

The potential significant effects of projects must be considered in relation to criteria set out under and 2 above, and having regard in particular to:

- the extent of the impact (geographical area and size of the affected population),
- the transfrontier nature of the impact,
- the magnitude and complexity of the impact,
- the probability of the impact,
- the duration, frequency and reversibility of the impact.

## [10.35] ANNEX IV INFORMATION REFERRED TO IN ARTICLE 5(1)

1. Description of the project, including in particular:

- a description of the physical characteristics of the whole project and the land-use requirements during the construction and operational phases,
- a description of the main characteristics of the production processes, for instance, nature and quantity of the materials used,
- an estimate, by type and quantity, of expected residues and emissions (water, air and soil pollution, noise, vibration, light, heat, radiation, etc) resulting from the operation of the proposed project.

2. An outline of the main alternatives studied by the developer and an indication of the main reasons for this choice, taking into account the environmental effects.

3. A description of the aspects of the environment likely to be significantly affected by the proposed project, including, in particular, population, fauna, flora, soil, water, air, climatic factors, material assets, including the architectural and archaeological heritage, landscape and the inter-relationship between the above factors.

4. A description[27] of the likely significant effects of the proposed project on the environment resulting from:

- the existence of the project,
- the use of natural resources,
- the emission of pollutants, the creation of nuisances and the elimination of waste,

and the description by the developer of the forecasting methods used to assess the effects on the environment.

---

27. This description should cover the direct effects and any indirect, secondary, cumulative, short, medium and long-term, permanent and temporary, positive and negative effects of the project.

5. A description of the measures envisaged to prevent, reduce and where possible offset any significant adverse effects on the environment.

6. A non-technical summary of the information provided under the above headings.

7. An indication of any difficulties (technical deficiencies or lack of know-how) encountered by the developer in compiling the required information.

## Irish courts and direct effect

**[10.36]** At first, the Irish courts appeared to be unsympathetic to the notion that the Directive should have 'direct effect' in Ireland. In *McBride v Mayor, Alderman & Burgesses of Galway*,[28] Quirke J stated that he was satisfied that the requirements imposed by art 4(2) of Directive 85/337/EEC did not have direct effect. The *McBride* High Court decision was delivered prior to the judgment in the *World Wildlife Fund (WWF) and Others v Autonome Provinz Bozen and Others*.[29] The *'Bozen'* judgment, which was handed down on 16 September 1999, in the summary stated:

> Article 4(2) of Directive 85/337 on the assessment of the effects of certain public and private projects on the environment provides that projects of the classes listed in Annex II to the Directive are to be made subject to an assessment where Member States consider that their characteristics so require and that to that end Member States may specify certain types of project as being subject to an assessment or may establish the criteria and/or thresholds necessary to determine which of the projects of the classes concerned are to be so subject. The limits of that discretion are to be found in the obligation, set out Article 2(1) of the Directive, under which projects likely, by virtue inter alia of their nature, size or location, to have significant affects on the environment must be subject to an impact assessment.[30]

The above provisions must be interpreted as not conferring on a Member State the power either to exclude, from the outset and in their entirety, from the EIA procedures established by the Directive, certain classes of project falling within Annex II of the Directive, including modifications to those projects, or to exempt from such a procedure a specific project, either under national legislation or on the basis of an individual examination of that project, unless the specific project, or those classes of project in their entirety, could be regarded, on the basis of a comprehensive assessment, as not being likely to have significant effects on the environment.

**[10.37]** Where the discretion conferred by arts 2(1) and 4(2) has been exceeded by the legislative or administrative authorities of a Member State, individuals may rely on those provisions before a court of that Member State against the national authorities and thus obtain from the latter the setting aside of the national rules or measures incompatible

---

28. *McBride v Mayor, Alderman & Burgesses of Galway* (unreported, 31 July 1997) HC, Quirke J.
29. *World Wildlife Fund (WWF) and Others v Autonome Provinz Bozen and Others* (Case C–435/97) [1998] ECR I–5613.
30. *World Wildlife Fund (WWF) and Others v Autonome Provinz Bozen and Others* (Case C–435/97) [1998] ECR I–5613, at para 3.

with those provisions. In such cases, it is for the authorities of the Member State to take, according to the relevant powers, all the general or particular measures necessary to ensure that projects are examined in order to determine whether they are likely to have significant effects on the environment and, if so, to ensure that they are subject to an impact assessment.

**[10.38]** In *Browne v An Bord Pleanála*,[31] scant, if any, attention was paid to Directive 85/337/EEC. Barron J held that it is solely for the planning authority to determine the adequacy of an EIS where an application for planning permission was accompanied by an EIS. *Browne v An Bord Pleanála* was heard in 1989 before the decisions in *'Kraaijeveld'*[32] and *'Bozen'*.[33]

**[10.39]** It is now clearly accepted that the courts in Ireland will adopt what is described as a 'purposive approach' in interpreting Irish law in the context of the EIA Directive. In *Maher v An Bord Pleanála*,[34] the facts were that An Bord Pleanála had granted a permission on appeal for a 200 sow integrated pig rearing installation. No EIA was undertaken although it was clear that the development exceeded the prescribed threshold. Kelly J held that an EIS was required and that without an EIA the permission granted was fatally flawed. That must be described as a 'purposive approach'.

**[10.40]** Scannell concludes:

> Nonetheless, it is now more or less accepted that these (articles 2(1) & (4) of Directive 85/337/EEC) have direct effects, though this is probably not quite the same thing as saying that they are directly effective. Consequently, it is not enough for a competent regulatory authority to comply with national requirements on EIA: it must also comply with these articles of the Directive even if it has not been properly transposed into Irish law. In so doing, it must take a purposive approach when dealing with projects that might be subject to EIA and must ensure that an EIS is submitted with any application for development consent if the Directive requires this – even if it is not required by domestic legislation.[35]

## ANNEX I PROJECTS DISTINGUISHED FROM ANNEX II PROJECTS

**[10.41]** Article 2 of the EIA Directive requires Member States to adopt all measures necessary before consent is given for development to ensure that any projects which are likely to have significant effects on the environment by virtue of their nature, size or location will require EIA. EIA is mandatory in respect of Annex I projects unless they have been exempted from EIA under art 2(3), which allows Member States, in

---

31. *Browne v An Bord Pleanála* [1991] 2 IR 209, HC, Geoghegan J.
32. *Aannemersbedrijf PK Kraaijeveld BV EA v Gedeputeerde Staten Van Zuid-Holland* (Case C–72/95) [1996] ECR I–5403.
33. *World Wildlife Fund (WWF) and Others v Autonome Provinz Bozen and Others* (Case C–435/97) [1998] ECR I–5613.
34. *Maher v An Bord Pleanála* [1999] 2 ILRM 198, Kelly J.
35. Scannell, *Environmental and Land Use Law* (Thomson Round Hall, 2006) pp 384–385, para 5.13.

'exceptional circumstances', to exempt a specific project in whole or in part from mandatory EIA. Annex II projects do not require mandatory EIA but instead art 4(2) provides that the question as to whether or not EIA is required shall be determined through:

(a) a case-by-case examination, or

(b) thresholds or criteria set by the Member State or both.

**[10.42]** Article 4(3) provides that when a case-by-case examination is carried out or if thresholds or criteria are set for Annex II projects account must be taken of the relevant selection criteria set out in Annex III to include:

(1) characteristics of projects;

(2) location of projects; and

(3) characteristics of the potential impact.

**[10.43]** Although Pt X of PDA 2000 (as amended) is headed 'Environmental Impact Assessment', Pt X also deals with environmental impact statements. If Annex II projects are likely to have significant effects on the environment, Member States must take the necessary steps to require EIA.

**[10.44]** In summary, an EIA will be required in the following circumstances.

As seen, the Directive contains an Annex I list and that list is similar (nearly identical) to the list contained in Sch 5, Pt 1 of PDR 2001. Section 176(1) of PDA 2000, as amended by PD(A)A 2010, s 56, provides that:

> The Minister shall for the purpose of giving effect to the Environmental Impact Assessment Directive, make regulations–
>
> (a) identifying development which may have significant effects on the environment, and
>
> (b) specifying the manner in which the likelihood of such development would have significant effects on the environment is to be determined.

**[10.45]** PDA 2000, s 176 provides:

> (2) Without prejudice to the generality of subsection (1), regulations under that subsection may provide for all or any or more of the following matters:
>
> (a) The establishment of thresholds or criteria for the purpose of determining which class of development are likely to have significant effects on the environment;
>
> (b) The establishment of different such thresholds or criteria in respect of different classes of areas;
>
> (c) The determination on a case-by-case basis in conjunction with the use of thresholds or criteria, of the developments which are likely to have significant effects on the environment;

(d) Where thresholds or criteria are not established, the determination on a case-by-case basis of the developments which are likely to have significant effects on the environment;

(e) The identification of selection criteria in relation to–

    (i) The establishment of thresholds or criteria for the purpose of determining which classes of development are likely to have significant effects on the environment, or

    (ii) The determination on a case-by-case basis of the developments which are likely to have significant effects on the environment,

(3) Any reference in an enactment to development of a class specified under Article 24 of the European Communities (Environmental Impact Assessment) Regulations 1989 (SI No 349 of 1989) shall be deemed to be a reference to a class of development prescribed under this section.

As seen, art 93 of the 2001 Regulations states that the prescribed classes of development for the purposes of s 176 are set out in Sch 5.

[10.46] The Directive contains a list of what are called 'Annex II projects' and these are similar (but not identical) to PDR 2001, art 93 comprising Sch 5. Pt 2, listing activities in the following categories, namely:

(1) Agriculture, silviculture and aquaculture.
(2) Extractive industry.
(3) Energy industry.
(4) Production and processing of metal.
(5) Mineral industry.
(6) Chemical industry.
(7) Food industry.
(8) Textiles, leather, wood and paper industries.
(9) Rubber industry.
(10) Infrastructure projects.
(11) Other projects.
(12) Tourism and leisure.
(13) Changes, extensions, development and testing.

An EIA will only be required for Annex II and or Pt 2 development where the thresholds set out in Pt 2 of Sch 5 are exceeded.

[10.47] Where the project is a Sch 5, Pt 2 project but is sub-threshold, an EIA may nevertheless be required if the planning authority or the board requires one. Article 103 of PDR 2001, as amended by art 25 of PDR 2006, permits a planning authority to require an EIS by notice even though the application is for a Pt 2 sub-threshold development in circumstances where the planning authority considers that the development will have significant effects on the environment. If the sub-threshold development is not accompanied by an EIS and if the development proposal is to locate the development on any of the following:

- (a) a European site,
- (b) an area the subject of a notice under s 16(2)(b) of the Wildlife (Amendment) Act 2000 (No 38 of 2000),
- (c) an area designated as a natural heritage area under s 18 of the Wildlife (Amendment) Act, 2000,
- (d) land established or recognised as a nature reserve within the meaning of s 15 or s 16 of the Wildlife Act, 1976 (No 39 of 1976) as amended by s 26 and s 27 of the Wildlife (Amendment) Act 2000, or
- (e) land designated as a refuge for flora or as a refuge for fauna under s 17 of the Wildlife Act, 1976 as amended by s 28 of the Wildlife (Amendment) Act 2000,

the planning authority shall decide whether the development would or would not be likely to have significant effects on the environment of such site, area or land as appropriate.

**[10.48]** In *Waddington v An Bord Pleanála*,[36] the board granted permission for the extension of a riverside quay in 1999. The applicant's case was that the board did not undertake a new EIA although one had been carried out in 1999 when the site was a special protection area (SPA). Butler J recognised that the court might have formed an opinion as to whether or not the development was likely to have 'a significant effect' on a European site but the learned judge rejected that claim. Butler J also rejected the claim that the board had acted irrationally and in breach of natural justice.

**[10.49]** In *O'Connor v Dublin Corporation (No 2)*,[37] permission was granted by An Bord Pleanála subject to a number of significant conditions dealing with the protection of the environment. When the conditions were not adhered to the planning authority sought enforcement. O'Neill J held that the significance of the matters which the planning authority sought to enforce were such as to require the planning authority to insist upon an EIS in the first instance.

**[10.50]** PDR 2001, art 104 provides that a written notice served by a planning authority requiring an EIS under PDR 2000, art 103 will cease to have effect where the board grants exemption from the requirement to submit an EIS in circumstances where a request is made for such exemption. If the board, in granting exemption, imposes additional requirements the applicant must be notified of such additional requirements by the planning authority. PDA 2000, s 172, as amended by PD(A)A 2010, s 54, provides the statutory requirement in Ireland for an EIS. Application for planning permission must be accompanied by an EIS where the development proposal is a development or a class of development referred to in the regulations made under PDA 2000, s 176. PDA 2000, s 176, as amended by PD(A)A 2010, s 56, makes regulations in

---

36. *Waddington v An Bord Pleanála* [2000] IEHC 110, Butler J.
37. *O'Connor v Dublin Corporation (No 2)* [2000] IEHC 68, O'Neill J.

connection with the EIA Directive and those regulations are made and contained in PDR 2001, Pt X, art 92 to 132 inclusive, as amended by arts 23 to 132 of PDR 2006. For the purpose of considering, in each individual case of Annex II developments, as to which particular developments shall be deemed to have significant effect on the environment and if so shall require EIA, the regulations must be consulted and examined.

## RULING OF ECJ IN RELATION TO RETENTION PERMISSION

[10.51] The ECJ had ruled in Case C–215/06, entitled *Commission v Ireland*,[38] that the provisions made under PDA 2000 for the granting of retention planning permission were inconsistent with the requirements of the EIA Directive. The ECJ ruling was correct in judging that Ireland's enforcement regime did not guarantee effective application of the EIA Directive. The Commission gave a list of examples where enforcement action was not taken against unauthorised development in Ireland but rather than relying on the individual cases the ECJ based its decision on the fact that EIA, where it is required, must be carried out before the development works pursuant to a development consent are commenced. Ireland accepted that principle but argued that the retention permission procedure represented a reasonable fallback mechanism to take account of the fact that some projects will, inevitably, proceed before the grant of development consent. The ECJ's measured response made the case that retention permission procedures should only apply in 'exceptional circumstances' but that the procedure should never be available in cases where the EIA Directive required EIA prior to the granting of development consent.

[10.52] In the course of delivering its judgment the ECJ had this to say:

> It is undisputed that, in Ireland, the absence of an environmental impact assessment required by Directive 85/337 as amended can be remedied by obtaining a retention permission which makes it possible, in particular, to leave projects which were not properly authorised undisturbed, provided that the application for such permission is made before the commencement of enforcement proceedings.[39]

Although the ECJ also complained of the Irish retention procedure in cases where no EIA is required, retention permission can still be obtained in Ireland in particular cases where there is no requirement for EIA. The ECJ strongly made the point in relation to the surviving retention procedures in Ireland that a distinction should be made between retention permission and conventional permission. The purpose of the distinction would be to try to dissuade developers from relying on the parachute escape alternative offered by retention permission, by making it an unattractive option. The fees collected in Ireland for an application for retention permission are slightly higher than the fees payable for a conventional development consent but the difference was not considered by the ECJ to be an adequate deterrent. The ECJ judgment highlighted the fact that there was no requirement in Irish law to establish 'exceptional circumstances' before an

---

38. *Commission of European Communities v Ireland* (Case C–215/06) [2008] ECR I–4911.
39. *Commission of European Communities v Ireland* (Case C–215/06) [2008] ECR I–4911.

application for retention permission can be applied for. The ECJ concluded that retention permission in Ireland was commonplace. The ECJ took the view that permission should be confined to exceptional cases only. PDA 2000, s 34(12), as amended by PD(A)A 2010, s 23(c) by substituting the following new sub-s (12), provides:

> (12) A planning authority shall refuse to consider an application to retain unauthorised development of land where the authority decides that if an application for permission had been made in respect of the development concerned before it was commenced the application would have required that one or more than one of the following was carried out–
>
> (a) an environmental impact assessment,
>
> (b) a determination as to whether an environmental impact assessment is required, or
>
> (c) an appropriate assessment.

**[10.53]** PD(A)A 2010 provides a new s 34(12A) for PDA 2000 which reads:

> For the purposes of subsection (12), if an application for permission had been made in respect of the following development before it was commenced, the application shall be deemed not to have required a determination referred to at subsection (12B):
>
> (a) development within the curtilage of a dwellinghouse, for any purpose incidental to the enjoyment of the dwellinghouse as dwellinghouse;
>
> (b) modifications to the exterior of a building.

Where a planning authority refuses to consider a planning application for permission under the provisions of s 34(12) (that is to say an application for retention permission) it shall return the fee to the applicant and shall give stated reasons to the applicant for its decision.[40]

**[10.54]** PDA 2000, s 34(12B) reads:

> Where a planning authority refuses to consider an application for permission under subsection (12) it shall return the application to the applicant, together with any fee received from the applicant in respect of the application, and shall give reasons for its decision to the applicant.

Apart from cases where the planning authority has decided that (a) EIA is required, (b) a determination as to whether EIA is required must be made, or (c) an appropriate assessment is required and subject to the provisions of sub-ss (12) and (12A), an application for development of land in accordance with the permission regulations may be made for the retention of unauthorised development and the section shall apply to such application, subject to any necessary modification.[41]

---

40. PD(A)A 2010, s 23(12B).
41. PD(A)A 2010, s 23(12C).

**[10.55]** PDA 2000, s 34(12C) reads:

> (12C) Subject to subsections (12) and (12A), an application for development of land in accordance with the permission regulations may be made for the retention of unauthorised development, and this section shall apply to such an application, subject to any modifications.

**[10.56]** In *Commission v Ireland*,[42] the ECJ appears to have recognised that Member States should be allowed to regularise unauthorised development by the grant of a retrospective retention consent permission but, as already highlighted, it expected that the regularisation would be confined to exceptional circumstances. In the course of the judgment the ECJ stated that:

> While Community law cannot preclude the applicable national rules from allowing, in certain cases, the regularisation of operations or measures which are unlawful in the light of Community law, such a possibility should be subject to the conditions that it does not offer the persons concerned the opportunity to circumvent the Community rules or to dispense with applying them, and that it should remain the exception.

It is not absolutely clear that Ireland has legislated for all that was asked of it by the ECJ. An application for development consent will be sent back where there is any question of EIA but there is nothing in PD(A)A 2010, s 23(12C) which indicates that an application for retention permission can only be made in 'exceptional circumstances'. The penalties for offences provided by s 156 of PDA 2000 have been substantially increased. Also, development within the operation of a quarry or dealing with the extraction of peat is singled out for special attention. Where the development other than the operation of a quarry or the extraction of peat has been carried out for more than seven years prior to the date of the commencement of s 47, no warning letter or enforcement notice may issue. Injunctions and enforcement proceedings in relation to unauthorised development in the operation of a quarry or in the extraction of peat may be applied for at any time *sine die*.

**[10.57]** PDA 2000, s 162 provides that the onus of proving the existence of a planning permission where proceedings are taken for an offence rests with the defendant. The section also provides that it will not be a defence to a prosecution under this part for the defendant to prove that he/she has applied for or has been granted planning permission under s 34(12):

(a) Since the initiation of proceedings under this Part,

(b) Since the date of the sending of a warning letter under section 152, or

(c) Since the date of service of an enforcement notice in the case of urgency in accordance with section 155.

No enforcement action or application for injunction under s 160 may be served or applied for, as the case may be, if an application for retention permission or a grant of

---

42. *Commission v Ireland* (Case C–215/06) [2008] ECR I–4911.

retention permission is made or granted under the provisions of PD(A)A 2010, s 23(12C).[43]

**[10.58]** The ECJ judgment was critical of the fact that the taking of enforcement action to include s 160 injunctions is entirely discretionary. There is nothing in the amending sections of PD(A)A 2010 to indicate that any action has been taken to address the criticism of discretionary enforcement.

**[10.59]** An *Irish Times* report of 7 October 2008 recorded that the Minister had indicated at that time that he intended to revoke the current seven-year time limit on the taking of enforcement action. With the exception of development within the operation of a quarry, and development by way of extraction of peat, all other classes of development had been spared from the abolition of the seven-year time limit for taking enforcement proceedings. It is entirely reasonable that there should be a seven-year time limit. Indeed, if a planning authority or a member of the public allows unauthorised development to sit there for seven years or, in the case where planning permission was granted but not strictly adhered to, for the life of the planning permission plus seven years, without taking any action, the right to take such action should not be preserved indefinitely. The extraction of peat is a very special case and a very sensitive environmental issue but it is suggested that there really is no reason why the seven-year time limit should not be re-established in quarry cases once the new statutory regime provided in s 261A[44] has worked its way through the system.

## OBJECTIVES OF EIA

**[10.60]** EIA is a procedure which is designed to assess environmental impact and to pass that assessment on to competent authorities to make a decision with all available information concerning the significant effects which a development may have on the environment.[45] If the significant effects cannot be controlled, the competent authority might decide that the project should not proceed. If the significant effects on the environment can be rectified, altered, controlled or mitigated to such an extent that those significant effects on the environment no longer have adverse impacts, the project might proceed subject to the required controlling conditions being imposed. Although there are similarities between the examination and assessment of a planning application and the examination and assessment of the significance of the environmental impact in relation to a particular development or project, they are two distinct and separate disciplines. Much more information is presented to the decision-maker in the EIA process. The decision-maker in EIA is bound to consider alternatives and to consider mitigation measures. Also, the extent of the public participation and the rules governing public participation are both more developed and more demanding than the requirement for public participation in a planning appeal. EIA is policed by a specific judicial review

---

43. PDA 2000, s 162(1), (2) and (3) as amended by PD(A)A 2010, s 49.
44. PD(A)A 2010, s 75.
45. See Directive 85/337/EEC as replaced by Directive 97/11/EC, arts 1 to 5.

procedure which has been inserted into Directive 85/337/EC as art 10(a)[46] by Directive 2003/35/EC. The article requires Member States to provide access within their legal system to a review procedure for members of the public concerned who have a sufficient interest or who maintain the impairment of a right. The administrative procedural law of the Member State requires this as a precondition in order to challenge the substantive or procedural legality of decisions, acts or omissions subject to public participation procedures contained in this Directive. Another additional burden attaching to the decision-maker in EIA cases, which does not apply to decisions on planning applications, is contained in art 9[47] of the Directive which requires the competent authority, in refusing development consent, to inform the public of the decision and to make the following information available:

- the content of the decision and any conditions attached thereto,
- having examined the consensus and opinions expressed by the public concerned, the main reasons and considerations on which the decision is based, including information about the public participation process,
- a description, where necessary, of the main measures to avoid, reduce and, if possible, off-set the major adverse effects.

## IMPLEMENTATION OF THE EIA DIRECTIVE INTO IRISH LAW

[10.61] For the main part, the EIA Directive has been implemented into Irish law through planning legislation and regulations, specifically by PDA 2000[48] and by the European Communities (Environmental Impact Assessment) (Amendment) Regulations 1999.

[10.62] PDA 2000, s 172[49] deals with the requirement for environmental impact statement.

[10.63] Pt X of PDA 2000 is headed 'Environmental Impact Assessment'. Pt X also deals with environmental impact statemens. EIA is a process carried out by the decision-maker whereas EIS is a document submitted by the developer which, as will be seen below, is rarely either comprehensive or completely definitive.

[10.64] Pt X of PDA 2000 comprises ss 172 to 177 inclusive. PDA 2000, ss 172, 174 and 176 have been amended respectively by PD(A)A 2010, ss 54, 55, 56 and 57.

[10.65] Specifically, s 172 (as amended) concerns applications for planning permission for which EIS is required.

---

46. See Directive 2003/35/EC, art 3(7) which inserts Directive 85/337/EC, art 10a.
47. Directive 85/337/EEC, art 9 is amended by Directive 2003/35/EC, art 1(6).
48. See PDA 2000, Pt X (as amended) dealing with EIA in PDA 2000, ss 172 to 177 and PDR 2001, Pt X (as amended) dealing with EIA in PDR 2001, arts 92 to 123 and dealing with transboundary environmental effects PDR 2001, Ch 5, arts 124 to 132.
49. PDA 2000, s 172 has been substantially amended by PD(A)A 2010, s 54.

Section 172 (as amended) now reads:

> (1) An environmental impact assessment shall be carried out by a planning authority or the Board, as the case may be, in respect of an application for consent for proposed development, or a class of such proposed development, prescribed by regulations under section 176.

**[10.66]** A new sub-s (1A) defines the terms used in sub-s (1) namely 'proposed development' and 'consent for proposed development' as follows:

(a) a proposed development' means–

    (i) a proposal to carry out one of the following:

        I. development to which Part III applies;

        [Part III of PDA 2000 as amended by PD(A)A 2010 deals with control of development.]

        II. development that may be carried out under Part IX;

        [Part IX deals with strategic development zones.]

        III. development by a local authority or a State authority under Part XI;

        [Part XI deals with development by local and State authorities, etc.]

        IV. development on the foreshore under Part XV;

        V. development under section 43 of the Act 2001;

        [The Act of 2001 is the Transport (Railway Infrastructure) Act 2001];

        VI. development under section 5(1) of the Roads Act 1993;

And

    (ii) Notwithstanding that development has been carried out, development in relation to which an application for substitute consent is required under Part XA.

(b) 'consent for proposed development' means as appropriate–

    (i) A grant of permission;

    (ii) A decision of the Board to grant permission on application or on appeal;

    (iii) Consent to development under Part IX;

    (iv) Consent to development by a local authority or a State authority under Part XI;

    (v) Consent to development on the foreshore under Part XV;

    (vi) Consent to development under section 43 of the Act of 2001;

    (vii) Consent to development under section 51 of the Roads Act 1993; or

    (viii) Substitute consent under Part XA.

(1B) An applicant for consent to carry out a proposed development referred to in subsection (1) shall furnish an environmental impact statement to the planning authority or to the Board, as the case may be, in accordance with the permission regulations.

(1C) A planning authority or the Board, as the case may be, shall refuse to consider an application for planning permission in respect of a development referred to in subsection (1) if the applicant fails to furnish an environmental impact statement under subsection (1B).

PDA 2000, s 33(2) permits the Minister to make regulations regarding applications for planning permission and sub-s (2) sets out in paras (a) to (l) inclusive the circumstances for which regulations may be made. Those regulations have been made and are dealt with in **Ch 3**.

# EXEMPTIONS FROM EIA

**[10.67]** The EIA Directive permits exemptions from EIS in certain circumstances. The first of these is referred to in art 1(4) and (5) of the Directive. Article 1(4) allows Member States to decide, on a case-by-case basis if it is so provided under national law, not to apply the EIA Directive to projects serving national defence purposes if the Member State deems that the application would have an adverse effect on such purposes. In *WWF v Autonome Provinz Bozen*,[50] the ECJ ruled that the exemption in respect of projects serving national defence purposes must be construed narrowly and that the exemption would only apply to genuine projects serving national defence purposes. They would not apply to projects in which national defence is only a small part of the project. In that case, the exemption was not granted where a military airport was being extended to allow its use for commercial purposes.

**[10.68]** Secondly, EIA Directive, art 1(5) provides that the Directive shall not apply to projects, the details of which are adopted by a specific Act of national legislation. In that case, also, the possibility of exemption must be interpreted in a restrictive manner. Effectively, the exemption will not be granted if the project adopted by a specific Act of national legislation does not provide full information which would be at least equivalent to the information required to be submitted to a competent authority in normal procedures where EIA is required. In effect, therefore, the full environmental impact of the proposal together with the measures to be taken to deal with those impacts must be fully disclosed in the legislative authorisation.

**[10.69]** Thirdly, art 2(3) of EIA Directive provides for another possibility of exemption from EIS by allowing Member States, in 'exceptional cases', to exempt a specific project either in whole or in part from the provisions of the Directive. In order to achieve exemption the Member State shall:

(a) Consider whether another form of assessment would be appropriate;

---

50. *WWF v Autonome Provinz Bozen* (Case C–435/97) [1999] ECR I–5613.

(b) Make available to the public concerned the information obtained under other forms of assessment referred to in (a), the information relating to the exemption decision and the reasons for granting it;

(c) Inform the Commission, prior to granting consent, of the reasons justifying the exemption granted, and provide it with the information made available, where applicable, to their own nationals.

**[10.70]** Fourthly, exemption is also provided for in PDA 2000, s 172(3) (as amended) by the European Communities (Environmental Impact Assessment) Regulations 2006, reg 4, which permits An Bord Pleanála to exempt a developer of a project from a requirement to submit an EIS where the board is satisfied that 'exceptional circumstances' so warrant but no exemption will be granted where another Member State of the EU or a party to the Transboundary Convention or a State Party to the Espoo Convention, having been informed about the proposed development and its likely effects on the environment in that state, has indicated that it wishes to make a submission in relation to the effects of the proposed development in that state.

**[10.71]** PDA 2000, s 175(8) provides that the board may in exceptional circumstances grant exemption from the requirement to submit an EIS in relation to a development proposed to be carried out by a local authority unless another Member State or other party to the Transboundary Convention or a party to the Espoo Convention has indicated that it wishes to furnish views on the effects on the environment in that State. PDA 2000, s 175(8)(b), as inserted by the European Communities (Environmental Impact Assessment) (Amendment) Regulations 2006 (reg 62), requires the board in granting a sub-s (8) exemption to:

(i) consider whether the effects, if any, of the proposed development on the environment should be assessed in some other form, and

(ii) make available to members of the public the information relating to the exemption decision referred to under paragraph (a), the reasons for granting such exemption and the information obtained under any other form of assessment referred to in paragraph (i),

and the Board may apply such requirements regarding these matters in relation to the application for approval as it considers necessary or appropriate.

## MEANING OF 'EXCEPTIONAL CASES'

**[10.72]** The term 'exceptional cases' will be interpreted narrowly by the ECJ. In *WWF v Autonome Provinz Bozen*,[51] an exemption *'for projects serving national defence purposes'* had to be construed narrowly in the sense that the exemption would only apply to projects which mainly served national defence purposes. The exemption will not apply where the national defence purpose is only a small part of the project.

---

51. *WWF v Autonome Provinz Bozen* (Case C–435/97) [1999] ECR I–5613.

**[10.73]** In *Luxemburg v Linster*,[52] the ECJ ruled that:

> Article 1(5) of the Directive should be interpreted having regard to the objectives of the Directive and to the fact that since it is a provision limiting the Directive's field of application, it must be interpreted restrictively.

It is not enough to demonstrate the case in question is exceptional in order to justify the art 2(3) exemption and, in order to cross over into 'exceptional case' territory, the following criteria would have to be in existence:

(a) That there is an urgent and substantial need for the project.

(b) That it was not possible to undertake the project at an earlier stage.

(c) That the project is one which produces an inability to meet the full requirements of the Directive in the sense that it would not be possible to achieve full compliance within the Directive. Also it must be shown that the case is exceptional.

(d) The project, if it is to achieve exemption status, would have to be such that failure to proceed would be likely to cause a serious threat to:

   (i) life, health or human welfare.

   (ii) the environment in the sense of, for example, causing flooding or contamination of land, water or air.

   (iii) political, administrative or economic stability.

   (iv) security.

Specifically, art 3(8) of the Strategic Environmental Assessment (SEA) Directive 2001/42/EC contains an exemption, the sole purpose of which is to provide for cases of unforeseen civil emergency.

**[10.74]** To illustrate how the SEA exemption works in the case of anti-flooding measures, the situation is that the exemption could be used for a project to contain or divert water as an anti-flooding measure in order to avoid the possibility of a flood emergency. If, however, the area to be protected has a history of flooding, because it will be a predictable emergency, the exemption is unlikely to work. The disaster or emergency must be an unpredictable event but where a disaster could have been anticipated but could not have been prescribed, the exemption may very well be appropriate for works of containment or for works of reconstruction. Where the requirements of the EIA Directive quite simply cannot be met because of overriding or overpowering circumstances, the exemption provisions may apply. For example, damage may occur as a result of an unpredicted natural disaster which requires immediate mitigation works in circumstances where there is no time to prepare and provide all the environmental information required by art 5(1) of the Directive. In such a case an overwhelming necessity to proceed with the works will allow the exemption to operate.

---

52. *Luxembourg v Linster* (Case C–287/98) [2000] ECR I–6917.

## PROJECT SPLITTING

[10.75] It is important that a planning authority or the board ensures, when examining an application for development consent, that the entire project is included in the application. The danger is that if what is in reality a single project is presented as a series of applications for several separate projects, the series of separate projects, when examined separately, may each be sub-threshold and may not require EIA. Most commonly, the fragmenting of development proposals has arisen in road building cases where, in order to keep expenses under control, different sections of a roadway or of a motorway are constructed to completion before work is commenced on the next stage. At times, the 'project splitting' of a development is put into effect for genuine reasons. At other times, the clear intention of the developer, in dividing the applications for development, is to avoid EIA by keeping each section below the Annex II threshold. Where a series of separate applications is submitted the planning authority or other regulatory authority should always ensure that the series is not in fact separate pieces of the same whole where the separate pieces, in reality, combine to make up one single project. The objective of the EIA Directive is to ensure that the cumulative effects of a development which makes up the entirety of the development do not either separately or, more particularly, together, make a development, the effects of which are likely to have significant effects on the environment.

[10.76] Member States cannot take advantage of the EIA Directive by exempting a number of separate projects which, individually, do not exceed the threshold set and, therefore, do not require impact assessment in circumstances where if the cumulative effect of a project was such that, taken together, the project would have significant environmental effects. Also, Member States cannot defeat the requirement for assessment by setting absolute thresholds at a level which means that it is not possible to ensure that every project likely to have significant effects on the environment is subject to impact assessment. In *Commission of the European Communities v Ireland*,[53] the Commission brought an action under art 169 of EC Treaty (now art 226 EC) for a declaration that, by failing to adopt all necessary measures to ensure the correct transposition of Council Directive 85/337/EEC on the assessment of the effects of certain public and private projects on the environment, Ireland had failed to fulfil its obligations under the Directive and, in particular, art 12 thereof and under the EC Treaty. In the first place, an assessment is always required for certain projects set out in Annex I to the Directive but secondly, assessment of projects listed in Annex II is only required where Member States consider that their characteristics demand EIA. Member States may select criteria and/or thresholds in order to determine whether or not projects listed in Annex II should be subject to an assessment but they cannot choose the thresholds at will. Threshold levels must be set strictly in accordance with the provisions of arts 5 to 10 of the EIA Directive. In setting out the grounds for the action taken by the Commission against Ireland in this case para 19 reads:

> The Commission alleges that Ireland has transposed Article 4(2) of the Directive incorrectly by setting absolute thresholds for the classes of projects covered by

---

53. *European Communities v Ireland* (Case C–392/96) [1999] ECR I–5901.

points 1(b) (use of uncultivated land or semi-natural areas for intensive agricultural purposes), 1(d) (initial afforestation/land reclamation) and 2(a) (extraction of peat) of Annex II to the Directive. The absolute nature of the thresholds means that it is not possible to ensure that every project likely to have significant effects on the environment is subject to an impact assessment because the mere fact that the project does not reach the threshold is sufficient for it not to be subjected to such assessment, regardless of its other characteristics. Under Article 4(2) of the Directive, however, account must be taken of all the characteristics of a project, not the single factor of size or capacity. Furthermore, Article 2(1) refers also to a projects nature and location as criteria for assessing whether it is likely to have significant effects. The Commission considers that this analysis is consistent with the judgments of the Court in Case C–133/94 *Commission v Belgium* [1996] ECR 1–2323 and in Case–72/95 *Kraaijeveld and Others V Gedeputeerde Staten van Zuid-Holland* [1996] ECR 1–5403.[54]

**[10.77]** It is clear that projects which do not exceed thresholds set may, nevertheless, have significant environmental effects and therefore it is possible that certain sites (to include European sites) which have a particular value and sensitivity may be damaged by projects which do not exceed the thresholds set. Also, the legislation intended to take account of the cumulative effect of projects and in practice the cumulative effect of projects is taken into account. Thus, individual projects may not, on their own, have significant environmental effects and, therefore, may not require impact assessment but, when a number of separate projects are taken together they may indeed have significant environmental effects. Ireland, therefore, in separately assessing uncultivated land or semi-natural areas which were to be used for intensive agricultural purposes, initial afforestation/land reclamation and the extraction of peat as three distinct units was in breach of the EIA Directive. The ECJ held that Ireland had failed to correctly transpose its obligations under Directive 85/337/EEC of 27 June 1985.

**[10.78]** PDA 2000, s 173(1) provides that a planning authority, in determining a planning application which requires an EIS, will have regard, in addition to the requirements of s 34(3),[55] to the EIS lodged and any additional information required and/or any submissions or observations regarding the effect of the development on the environment as may be made.

**[10.79]** In *BAA plc v Secretary of State for Transport, Local Government and the Regions*,[56] two separate applications were made in respect of a link road development which was, in fact, a single development. Turner J held that the combined environmental effects of both applications should have been considered in deciding whether or not an EIA was required.

---

54. *European Communities v Ireland* (Case C–392/96) [1999] ECR I–5901, para 19.
55. PDA 2000, s 34(3) lists the matters which the planning authority shall have regard to in considering an application for planning permission to include the application itself, and any information furnished with the application and written submissions or observations made to it in accordance with the permission regulations by persons or bodies other than the applicant.
56. *BAA plc v Secretary of State for Transport, Local Government and the Regions* [2003] JPL 610.

**[10.80]** The case of whether assessment of roadway projects should be a single or multiple assessment has not been satisfactorily determined. It may not always be possible, particularly in road development, to identify the full extent of the project. If EIA is undertaken at too early a time it may be impossible to make the assessment in a comprehensive manner. Parts of the route which are, so to speak, further down the road, may not have been accurately identified. There has, on occasions, been a reluctance to conclude an EIA on what, at the particular time, was considered to have been the full extent of the project. Some road projects have lasted for 10 years or more. Changes may occur in that period of time. Advocate General Gulmann recognised the difficulties in identifying what comprises the 'entire project' in a road building case where the construction of the sections was staggered over relatively long periods. In that case, Advocate General Gulmann stated:

> Nor can it be excluded that there might be cases where such significant changes are made to the project or the consent procedure for the project is postponed for such long periods that it might be right in order to ensure compliance with the directive to hold that a new consent procedure should be initiated accompanied by an obligation to carry out an environmental impact assessment.[57]

**[10.81]** In *Commission v Spain*,[58] although the development being carried out related to a 13.2km section of railway, the court held that the project in question was part of 'a long distance railway traffic' being the railway line between Valencia and Tarragona linking the Spanish region of Levante to Catalonia and to the French border.

**[10.82]** Paragraph 48 of the opinion of Advocate General Poiares Maduro in *Commission v Spain* reads as follows:

> As a railway line 251km long is constructed in stages, if Spain's reasoning were followed it would mean that a specific project would never be regarded as involving long-distance traffic because the successive sections of the line would all cover small distances and would connect neighbouring places. Adopting this interpretation of the Directive would be likely to restrict its scope considerably and to jeopardise the attainment of its objective.[59]

**[10.83]** The prohibition against project splitting is designed to prevent applicants from splitting various features of the development as a means of avoiding EIA. Road cases may be in a slightly different category and there are circumstances where it is permissible to seek a series of development consents where major road development is involved. Where there are separate consents in these circumstances, there may also be separate EIAs but only if each individual EIS would give some indication of the cumulative effect of the projects.

---

57. *Bund Naturschutz in Bayern BV and Others v Freistaat Bayern* [1994] ECR I–3717.
58. *Commission v Spain* (Case C–227/01) [2004] ECR I–8253.
59. *Commission v Spain* (Case C–227/01) [2004] ECR I–8253.

## SCOPING

**[10.84]** Article 5(2) of the EIA Directive requires Member States to provide an opinion on the information to be supplied by a developer in accordance with art 5(1) if a request is made by the developer before submitting an application for permission. Member States are also permitted to require competent authorities to give a scoping opinion even if the developer has not requested it. Before giving its opinion, a competent authority is obliged to consult with the developer and the authorities likely to be concerned with the project by virtue of their particular environmental responsibilities. PDA 2000, s 173(2)[60] and (3) provides the 'scoping' statutory provisions permitting an applicant to seek a written opinion from the planning authority or from the board on appeal in advance of submitting an EIS. Subsection (2) deals with scoping requests submitted to the planning authority while sub-s (3) deals with scoping requests submitted to the board. Subsection (2) has been amended by PD(SI)A 2006, s 32 and the planning authority must consult with the board before giving a written opinion in response to a scoping request.

**[10.85]** In preparing a scoping request reference should be made to PDR 2001, art 95, as amended by PDR 2006, art 24.

## TRANSBOUNDARY ENVIRONMENTAL IMPACTS

**[10.86]** Article 7 of EIA Directive provides that where a Member State is aware that a project is likely to have significant effects on the environment of another Member State or where a Member State likely to be significantly affected so requests, the Member State in whose territory the project was intended to be carried out must send a description of the project together with any available information on its possible transboundary impacts together with information on the nature of the decision which may be taken. The Member State, which is to develop the project, shall give the other Member State a reasonable opportunity in which to indicate whether it wishes to participate in the environmental decision-making procedure. If the Member State indicates that it intends to participate then the Member State in which the development is to take place will send the other Member State the information referred to in art 5 of the EIA Directive. Article 6 also provides that the public concerned will be given early and effective opportunities to participate in the environmental decision-making procedures and that for that purpose they will be entitled to express comments and opinions when all options are open to the competent authority or authorities and before the decision on the request for development is taken. The public must be informed by displaying bill posting within a certain radius of the development or by publication of a notice in a local newspaper.

**[10.87]** PDA 2000, s 174 provides that the Minister may make regulations in respect of applications for development which require submission of EIS where either the planning authority or the board, in dealing with the application or appeal, is aware that the

---

60. PDA 2000, s 173(2) was substituted by PD(SI)A 2006, s 32.

development is likely to have significant effects on the environment in another Member State of the European Communities or a State which is party to the Transboundary Convention. Section 174(2) requires that the planning authority or the board, as the case may be, shall have regard, where appropriate, to the views of any Member State of the EU or other party to the Transboundary Convention in relation to the effects on the environment of the proposed development. Section 174(3) provides that either the planning authority or the board on appeal may impose conditions on any grant of permission or approval in order to reduce or eliminate potential transboundary effects of any proposed development. Section 174(4) deals with a situation where another Member State of the EC or other party to the Transboundary Convention sends notice to another Member State to the effect that a development which it is undertaking may have effects on the environment in the notified State. Section 174(4)(b) (as amended) provides that a planning authority or a State authority or the Minister may request another member of the EC or other party to the Transboundary Convention to forward information in respect of any development which is subject to the EIA Directive or transboundary convention and which is likely to have significant environmental effects.[61] Submissions and observations may be made by the affected State through the Minister or planning authority and the affected State may enter into discussions with the State involved in the development regarding the potential transboundary effects of that development and the measures envisaged to reduce or eliminate those effects. Section 174(6) provides that the Minister may enter into an agreement with any other Member State of the EC or other party to the Transboundary Convention regarding the detailed procedures to be followed in respect of consultations regarding proposed developments which are likely to have significant transboundary effects.

**[10.88]** The requirements of art 7 of the EIA Directive and the regulations made under PDA 2000, s 174 (as amended) are implemented under Pt X, Ch V of PDR 2001, as substituted by arts 124 to 132 inclusive of PDR 2006. The procedure, as substituted, applies both to applicants for planning permissions and to applications in respect of strategic infrastructure. The 2006 Regulations also apply to applications for the approval/assessment of local authority and State authority development.

## TRANSBOUNDARY ENVIRONMENTAL EFFECTS – NOTIFICATION TO THE MINISTER

**[10.89]** PDR 2006, art 124(1)(a) requires a planning authority to notify the Minister as soon as may be after receipt of a planning application where, in the planning authority's opinion, the proposed development referred to in the application is one which is likely to have significant effects on the environment in a transboundary State.

**[10.90]** PDR 2006, art 124(1)(b) imposes the same obligation on the board after receipt of an appeal or an application for approval to which this part applies or an application, in the first instance, for strategic infrastructure development. The Board will notify the

---

61. This subsection has been amended by PD(A)A 2010, s 55.

Minister where it is of the opinion that the application for approval or the application for strategic infrastructure development relates to development which would be likely to have significant effects on the environment in a transboundary State or art 124(2) where the application is for strategic infrastructure or a request for alteration under s 146(c) of PDA 2000, either the applicant or the requestor, as appropriate, has notified a transboundary State of the proposed development or alteration. Full details in accordance with art 124(c)(i), (ii), (iii), (iv) and (v) must be furnished in the notice to the Minister and art 124(2) requires that the notice must be accompanied with a copy of any relevant EIS.

**[10.91]** PDR 2006, art 124(3) requires that when the Minister is so notified he/she will consult with the relevant planning authority or the board as appropriate in relation to the proposed development.

## TRANSBOUNDARY ENVIRONMENTAL EFFECTS – INFORMATION TO THE MINISTER

**[10.92]** PDR 2006, art 125 allows the Minister to require detailed information or documents as he or she may specify from the planning authority or the board as appropriate relating to such application, appeal, application for approval or application for a strategic infrastructure development, as appropriate, once the Minister has formed an opinion that the development is one which is likely to have significant effects on the environment in a transboundary State or where a transboundary State considers that the development would be likely to have significant effects on its environment and where it has requested information on the proposed development.

## TRANSBOUNDARY CONSULTATION

**[10.93]** PDR 2006, art 126 requires the relevant planning authority or the board as appropriate to provide information on a proposed development referred to in arts 124 or 125, such information to be provided to the transboundary State concerned (except in a case for an application for strategic infrastructure or in a case of a request for an alteration referred to in s 146C and the applicant or requestor as appropriate has already notified the transboundary State of the proposed development or alteration). The relevant planning authority or the board shall then enter into consultations with the State in relation to potential transboundary effects of the proposed development and at the same time the planning authority or the board shall notify the Minister under art 124(1) or upon a request for such information by the transboundary State under art 125. The information to be provided by the relevant planning authority or the board as appropriate includes:

    (a)    A description of the project, together with any available information on its possible transboundary impact,

    (b)    An indication that the project is subject to an environmental impact assessment procedure,

    (c)    An indication that the planning authority or the Board, as the case may be, is the competent authority responsible for taking the decision,

**[10.94]** Planning and Environmental Law in Ireland

    (d)    An indication of the types of decision the planning authority or the Board, as the case may be, may make in relation to the application, appeal, application for approval or application for strategic infrastructure,

    (e)    An indication that a decision will not be taken on the proposed development until the views, if any, of the transboundary State had been received or the consultations are otherwise completed, and

    (f)    An indication that where the transboundary State indicates that it wishes to take part in the decision-making procedures in relation to the proposed development, a copy of the EIS will be sent to it.

**[10.94]** The planning authority or the board, as appropriate, is then required to enter into consultations with that State in relation to potential transboundary effects which the proposed development may have. The other parties to the application or to the appeal are to be notified by the planning authority or the board of that fact, as appropriate, in relation to the proposed development.

## NOTIFICATION OF BOARD BY PLANNING AUTHORITY

**[10.95]** PDR 2006, art 127 provides that where notice of a planning application or details, information or documents in relation to a planning application have been given to the Minister by the planning authority under art 124 or 125, the planning authority when complying with the requirements of PDA 2000, s 128[62] shall notify the board of that fact.

## REQUEST FOR FURTHER INFORMATION

**[10.96]** The general provision for a request for further information is that one request for further information only can be made. PDR 2006, art 128, however, provides, in relation to transboundary environmental effects, that notwithstanding art 33(2) a planning authority may, having regard to the views of a transboundary State, require an applicant to submit further information in respect of the application. If the further information supplied contains 'significant additional data' on the effects on the environment of the development proposal, the planning authority may require the applicant to give further public notice and to send a copy of the further information to the prescribed bodies, the Minister and the transboundary State.[63] The planning authority may also require the applicant to publish a notice containing the further information in a newspaper notice marked 'Environmental Impact Statement – Further Information'. Further details as to what is to be included in the newspaper notice are set out in PDR 2006, art 128(2)(c)(i) to (v). If the planning authority considers that the notice published in the newspaper in accordance with sub-art 2(c) is inadequate the planning authority may require a further notice to be published in terms to be specified by the authority.

---

62.    PDA 2000, s 128 provides for the documents which must be sent by a planning authority to the board in the event of an appeal. The section has been substituted by PD(SI)A 2006, s 21.

63.    PDR 2006, art 128(2).

**[10.97]** If the requirement for further information is not complied with by the applicant the planning application shall be deemed to be withdrawn after a period of six months from the date when the further information was first sought.

**[10.98]** Where an application for permission is made, in the first instance, to An Bord Pleanála under the provisions of the strategic infrastructure development legislation or where an application for approval/assessment of a local authority or State authority development is made, An Bord Pleanála similarly has a power to request the submission of further information or evidence in respect of the application or, indeed, in respect of any appeal. An Bord Pleanála must also notify the Minister and the transboundary State if the further information received contains 'significant additional data' on the effects on the environment of the development proposal.[64]

## MINIMUM PERIOD FOR DETERMINATIONS

**[10.99]** PDA 2000, s 34(8), as amended by PD(A)A 2010, s 23, sets out the various time limits in relation to making decisions. However, notwithstanding s 34(8), a planning authority shall not decide to grant or refuse permission in respect of a planning application to which **Ch 5** (dealing with transboundary environmental effects) applies or the board shall not determine an appeal or an application for approval to which **Ch 5** applies or an application for strategic infrastructure development until after:

(a) the views, if any of any relevant transboundary State have been received in response to consultations under Article 126(1), or

(b) the consultations are otherwise completed.

**[10.100]** This is an unsatisfactory situation in that the time limit may have no limit. However, although the planning authority or the board may not make a determination within the normal eight-week period required under s 34(8), it is clear that no default planning permission will apply. Presumably neither the planning authority nor the board is required to delay its determination indefinitely in circumstances where the transboundary State has not expressed its views. It is probable that a 'reasonable period' must be allowed to the transboundary State to convey its views but if the time limit extends beyond what is considered to be a 'reasonable period' the board or the planning authority should proceed with its determination. There may well be cases where objections to transboundary environmental effects have more to do with preventing competition than to do with purely objective environmental issues.

## INCLUSION OF NOTICE OF TRANSBOUNDARY EFFECTS IN WEEKLY LIST

**[10.101]** PDR 2006, art 27 provides that a planning authority shall publish a weekly list not later than the fifth working day following a particular week listing the planning applications received by the authority during that week. PDR 2006, art 130(a) requires

---

64. PDR 2006, art 128(4) to (7).

that the art 27 list shall include any proposed development which may have transboundary environmental effects where that is the case. Also PDR 2001, art 72 provides that the board shall not later than the third working day following a particular week make available a list of appeals and referrals received by the board and a list of appeals and referrals determined, dismissed or withdrawn or in relation to which a direction is given by the board pursuant to s 139 of the Act during that week. The art 72 weekly list under the provisions of PDR 2006, art 130 shall also indicate that proposed development may have transboundary environmental effects, where that is the case.

## NOTICE OF DECISION

[10.102] PDR 2006, art 31 provides that any notice of decision on the application, appeal or application for approval or an application for strategic infrastructure development must be sent to the Minister and to any relevant transboundary State.

## PUBLIC NOTICE OF INFORMATION RECEIVED PURSUANT TO REQUEST UNDER PDA 2000, S 174(4)[65]

[10.103] PDR 2006, art 132(1) provides that where the Minister receives information from a transboundary State in respect of any development which is subject to the EIA Directive or the Transboundary Convention and which is likely to have significant effects on the environment, the Minister shall, as soon as may be, following receipt of such information, notify any planning authority likely to be affected by the proposed development and send a copy of the information to any such authority. PDR 2000, art 132(2) requires a planning authority which receives information under sub-art (1) or otherwise receives information from a transboundary State in respect of any development subject to the EIA Directive or to the Transboundary Convention which is likely to have significant effects on the environment, as soon as may be, following receipt of the information, to publish notice in an approved newspaper and give notice to the prescribed bodies listed under art 28 of the PDR 2001.

[10.104] PDR 2006, art 132(3) gives a list of the matters which must be stated in the sub-art 2 notice namely as follows:

(i) That information has been received in relation to the proposed development in such transboundary State,

(ii) The nature of the information received,

(iii) That the proposed development is subject to an Environmental Impact Assessment procedure and has potential transboundary effects,

(iv) The nature of possible decision, or where there is one, the draft decision,

(v) That the information is available for inspection, or purchase at a fee not exceeding the reasonable cost of making a copy, during office hours at the offices of the authority, and

---

65. PDA 2000, s 174(4) as amended by PD(A)A 2010, s 55.

(vi) That a submission or observation in relation to the proposed development may be made in writing to the authority within a specified period.

**[10.105]** PDR 2006, art 132(4) requires the planning authority to consult with the Minister as soon as may be following receipt of any observations referred to in sub-art 3 in relation to consultation with the state concerned on the potential transboundary effects of the proposed development.

**[10.106]** PDR 2006, art 132(5) provides that following the consultation between the Minister and the planning authority under sub-art 4 the planning authority shall enter consultations with the state concerned in relation to the potential transboundary effects of the proposed development.

**[10.107]** PDR 2006, art 132(6) requires the Minister, as soon as may be, following receipt of information to send such information to the planning authority likely to be affected by the decision where the Minister has received information from a transboundary State in relation to a decision to grant or refuse a development which is likely to have transboundary effects on all or any of the 32 counties of Ireland.

**[10.108]** PDR 2006, art 132(7) requires a planning authority on receipt of information referred to in sub-art 6 or otherwise to publish notice in an approved newspaper stating that it has received such information, giving an outline of the nature of the decision and stating that the information is available for inspection or purchase for a fee not exceeding the reasonable cost of making a copy during office hours at the office of the planning authority.

## EIA DISTINGUISHED FROM EIS

**[10.109]** PDA 2000 provided no definition of EIA, but PD(A)A 2010, s 2 defines 'environmental impact assessment' as having the meaning given to it by s 171(A), namely:

(1) In this Part–

'environmental impact assessment' means an assessment carried out by a planning authority or the Board, as the case may be, in accordance with this Part and regulations made thereunder, that shall identify, describe and assess in an appropriate manner, in light of each individual case and in accordance with Articles 4 to 11 of the Environmental Impact Assessment Directive, the direct and indirect effects of a proposed development on the following:

(d) human beings, flora and fauna,
(e) soil, water, air, climate and the landscape,
(f) material assets and the cultural heritage, and
(g) the interaction between the factors mentioned at paragraphs (a), (b) and (c).

(2) Subject to this Part, a word or expression that is used in the Part and that is also used in the Environmental Impact Assessment Directive has, unless the context

otherwise requires, the same meaning in this Part as it has in the Environmental Impact Assessment Directive.

'Environmental impact statement' is defined in s 2 of PDA 2000 as meaning a statement of the effects, if any, which proposed development, if carried out, would have on the environment.

**[10.110]** An EIS is a document submitted by a developer and it is distinguished from EIA which is an ongoing process of assessment carried out by the decision-maker in relation to developments which may or may not have significant environmental effects. McMahon J in *Klohn v An Bord Pleanála*[66] had this to say on the distinction between an EIS and an EIA:

> Although the EIS is intended to be comprehensive, it is rarely definitive. As the first document in the investigation process, it is, at most, the point of departure in an ongoing process. It is intended to launch a process which will attract comment and submissions from other parties including observations from those with entitlements to participate in the process. The intention is that, as a seminal document, it sets the agenda for further discussion and deliberation which will, finally, provide a body of information which will enable the decision-maker to make its assessment in full possession of the relevant environmental factors. It is also worth emphasising that the EIS is a *document* submitted by the developer, the terms of which are set when it is submitted. In contrast, the EIA *is a process* which is an ongoing exercise undertaken by the decision-maker. A great deal can happen, and a great deal of information can be accumulated, between the lodging of the EIS by the developer and the final decision by the planning authority or by An Bord Pleanála. Two further points should be noted. First, the content of the EIS is primarily determined by the wording of the relevant regulations (article 9(4) and Schedule 6, of Planning & Development Regulations 2001 (SI No 600 of 2001)) ('the 2001 Regulations') whereas its *adequacy* is determined by the decision-maker (article 111 of the 2001 Regulations). Failure to supply the minimum contents as mandated by the Regulations may threaten the process, for example, where clear mandatory provisions are ignored. The *adequacy* of the information supplied in the EIS, however, is primarily a matter for the decision-maker and is thus much more difficult to challenge. Second, the interval between the making of the EIS and the EIA will, inevitably, mean that the decision-maker will have gathered information from many other sources by the time a decision is called for by it. Moreover, the assessment process which it is obliged to carry out, the EIA, will no doubt be greatly informed by its own expert knowledge and its expertise in this area, an input that undoubtedly will, in many cases, fill any remaining information deficit in the documents submitted to it. In these circumstances, it is not surprising that a great deal of discretion is left to the decision-maker in making this call. From this, it can also be seen that a flaw or deficiency in the EIS submitted by the developer does not invariably inflict a fatal wound on the assessment process, which is carried out at a later phase in the process, with the benefit of additional submissions and observations and informed by its own

---

66. *Klohn v An Bord Pleanála* [2008] IEHC 111 *per* McMahon J.

expertise. The effect of a flaw in the EIS has on the subsequent assessment will, of course, depend greatly on the facts of each case.

EIA is required as a process for assessing the environmental impact of a development proposal before a decision is made on the application for planning permission. EIA is mandatory in some cases and may be required in other cases of specified classes of development prescribed by regulations made under PDA 2000, s 176, as amended by s 56 of PD(A)A 2010.

**[10.111]** Specifically, EIS is a statement prepared and submitted by the developer with prescribed information to be contained in an EIS by virtue of art 94 of the 2001 Regulations. The requirements of contents of an EIS are mandatory, and non-compliance will invalidate the process.

**[10.112]** The EIS shall contain:

> The information specified in paragraph 1 of Schedule 6.
>
> Paragraph 1 of Schedule 6 PDR 2001 reads:
>
> (a) a description of the proposed development comprising information on the site, design and size of the proposed development.
>
> (b) a description of the measures envisaged in order to avoid, reduce and, if possible, remedy significant adverse effects.
>
> (c) the date required to identify and assess the main effects which the proposed development is likely to have on the environment.
>
> (d) an outline of the main alternatives studied by the developer and an indication of the main reasons for his or her choice, taking into account the effects on the environment.

**[10.113]** PDR 2001, art 94(b) provides that further information contained in an EIS is the information specified in para 2 of Sch 6 to the extent that:

> (i) such information is relevant to a given stage of the consent procedure and to the specific characteristics of the development or type of development concerned and of the environmental features likely to be affected, and
>
> (ii) the person or persons preparing the EIS may reasonably be required to compile such information having regard, among other things, to current knowledge and method of assessment and

**[10.114]** PDR 2001, art 94(c) provides as follows:

> (c) a summary in non technical language of the information required under paragraphs (a) and (b).

**[10.115]** PDR 2001, Sch 6, para 2 lists the further information, by way of explanation or amplification, which is required to be furnished in addition to the requirements of para 1 and this further information is on the following matters:

> (a) (i) a description of the physical characteristics of the whole proposed development and the land-use requirements during the construction and operational phases;

(ii) a description of the main characteristics on the production processes, for instance, nature and quantity of materials used;

(iii) an estimate, by type and quantity, of expected residues and emissions (including water, air and soil pollution, noise, vibrating, light, heat and radiation) resulting from the operation of the proposed development;

(b) a description of the aspects of the environment likely to be significantly affected by the proposed development, including in particular:

- human beings, flora and fauna;
- soil, water, air, climatic factors and the landscape;
- material assets, including the architectural and archaeological heritage and the cultural heritage, – the inter-relationship between the above matters;

(c) a description of the likely significant effects (including direct, indirect, secondary, cumulative, short, medium and long-term, permanent and temporary, positive and negative) of the proposed development on the environment resulting from:

- the existence of the proposed development,
- the use of natural resources,
- the emission of pollutants, the creation of nuisances and the elimination of waste,

and a description of the forecasting methods used to assess the effects on the environment;

(d) an indication of any difficulties (technical deficiencies or lack of know-how encountered by the development in compiling the required information).[67]

**[10.116]** The Environmental Protection Agency has published two detailed documents to assist with the preparation of an EIS. The first of these is titled 'Guidelines on the information to be contained in Environmental Impact Statements'. The second is a detailed document titled '**Advice notes on current practice** (in the preparation of Environmental Impact Statements)'. This second document is an extraordinarily useful document particularly in signposting the environmental affects which are likely to have significant impact on human beings, flora, fauna, soils, water, air, climate, the landscape, material assets, cultural heritage and the interaction of the foregoing. The document lists 33 different project types and in each case lists the principal impacts arising from each project type. By way of example the following project types are dealt with, namely:

(i) thermal power stations or other combustion installations;

(ii) nuclear power stations or other nuclear reactors including dismantling or decommissioning such a station or reactor;

---

67. PDR 2001, Sch 6 is identical to the European Communities (Environmental Impact Assessment) (Amendment) Regulations 1999, Sch 2 in setting out information which is required to be included in an EIS.

(iii) installation designed solely for permanent storage or final disposal of radioactive waste;

(iv) installations for the extraction of asbestos;

(v) railway lines, tramways, elevated and underground railways;

(vi) airports;

(vii) seawater and freshwater marinas;

(viii) restructuring of rural landholdings;

(ix) replacement of broadleaf species with conifers;

(x) deforestation for the purpose of conversion to another type of land use;

(xi) reclamation of land from the sea;

(xii) flood relief works;

(xiii) works to combat coastal erosion;

(xiv) pig rearing and poultry rearing installations;

(xv) peat extraction;

(xvi) mineral extraction;

(xvii) quarries;

(xviii) petroleum and natural gas;

(xix) pipelines for gas, oil, chemical, steam and hot water transport;

(xx) petrol and chemical storage;

(xxi) knackers yard in built up areas;

(xxii) cellulous processing;

(xxiii) industrial estates, construction of dwelling units, car parks, shopping centres, holiday villages, hotel complexes, permanent camp sites and caravan parks. Industrial estates will usually only be affected if chemical-based industries are sited there. In relation to the remainder listed in this section the most significant impact of these would tend to be landscape and infrastructural impacts;

(xxiv) waterways treatment plants;

(xxv) installations for the disposal of waste to include sludge deposition sites;

(xxvi) waste disposals for incineration chemical treatment or landfill or hazardous and non-hazardous waste;

(xxvii) installations for harvesting wind power for energy.

There is an overwhelming necessity to check developments to see if there is any potential for EIA. If there is any such potential and the matter proceeds without assessment or permission it will never be possible to obtain retention permission and the completed development may or will have to be deconstructed. With so much at risk the need for professional and very careful and thorough screening is an essential element of the planning process and of the environmental process.

## PROJECTS FOR WHICH EIA IS NECESSARY

**[10.117]** As already seen, EIA is mandatory in respect of all Annex I projects. Some Annex I projects require EIA without qualification. Others, as will be seen when Annex I is examined, will only require EIA if the specified Annex I threshold is exceeded.

**[10.118]** An example of where a threshold is involved includes dams and other installations designed to hold back or provide permanent storage of water. Such dams or other installations will automatically require EIA if the new or additional amount of the water to be held back exceeds 10 million cubic metres. Paragraph 1 of Annex I gives examples of an unqualified mandatory requirement to undertake EIA in relation to crude oil refineries and an example of a case where EIA is required only if the threshold figure of, in that case, 500 tonnes or more of coal or bituminous shale *per* day is put through a process of gasification and liquefaction. In number 16 of Annex I pipelines for transport of gas, oil or chemicals will not require EIA if the diameter of the pipe is less than 800mm and the length is less than 40km.

**[10.119]** Annex II projects may not always require EIA. Bearing in mind that the objective of EIA and the EIA Directive is to ensure that development projects which are likely to have significant effects on the environment should be subject to EIA, Annex II projects may have significant effects on the environment or indeed they may not. Article 4(2) of the EIA Directive requires Member States to determine whether EIA is required for Annex II projects through a case-by-case examination and/or through thresholds or criteria set by the Member State in order to establish which Annex II projects should be subject to EIA. In making the case-by-case examination and in identifying thresholds or criteria set by Member States, the EIA Directive further requires, under art 4(3), that account must be taken of the relevant selection criteria set out in Annex III of the EIA Directive, under the headings in Annex III, namely:

1. characteristics of projects;
2. location of projects;
3. characteristics of potential impact.[68]

**[10.120]** Article 4(4) obliges Member States to make the determination on Annex II projects available to the public. There is an express obligation to make a decision as to whether an Annex II project requires or does not require EIA but there does not appear to be any express obligation to require that the decision made is a reasoned decision. Although there is no obligation to make a reasoned decision, nevertheless the ECJ, in *Commission v Italy*,[69] stated that a decision as to whether an Annex II project's characteristics, etc, do or do not require EIA must be accompanied by all the information that makes it possible to check that it is based on adequate screening, carried out in accordance with the requirements of Directive 85/337/EEC, as subsequently amended.

---

68. EIA Directive, Annex III; see para **10.34**.
69. *Commission v Italy* (Case C–87/02) [2005] ENV LR 21, (unreported, 10 June 2004).

**[10.121]** The judgment in *Commission v Italy*[70] gives a very good insight as to a Member State's responsibility in determining whether or not EIA is necessary in an Annex II project. The project in that case was the construction of an outer ring road at Teramo. The project was known as the 'lotto zero project' or, in its full title, 'Lotto Zero-Variante, Tra Teramo (Italy) e Giulianova, Alla Strada Statale SS 80'. The project was a type listed in Annex II of Council Directive 85/337/EEC on the assessment of the effects of certain public and private projects on the environment. The summary of the judgment in this case reads as follows:

> 1. The fact that a Member State has conferred on its regions the responsibility for giving effect to Directives cannot have any bearing on the application of art 226 EC. A Member State cannot plead conditions existing within its own legal system in order to justify its failure to comply with obligations and time-limits resulting from community directives. While each Member State may freely allocate internal legislative powers as it sees fit, the fact remains that it alone is responsible towards the community under art 226 EC for compliance with obligations arising under Community law.
>
> 2. The fact that proceedings had been brought before a national court to challenge the decision of a national authority which is the subject of an action for failure to fulfil its obligations and decisions of that court not to suspend implementation of that decision cannot effect the admissibility of the action for failure to fulfil obligations brought by the Commission. The existence of remedies available through the national courts cannot in anyway prejudice the bringing of an action under art 226 EC, since the two procedures have different objectives and effects.
>
> 3. The second sub-para of art 4(2) of Directive 85/337 on the assessment of the effects of certain public and private projects on the environment mentions, by way of indication, methods to which Member States may have recourse when determining which of the projects falling within Annex II are to be subject to an assessment within the meaning of the Directive.

Consequently, Directive 85/337/EEC confers a measure of discretion on the Member States and does not, therefore, prevent them from using other methods to specify the projects requiring an EIA under the Directive. The Directive does not exclude the method consisting in the designation, on the basis of individual examination of each project concerned or pursuant to national legislation of a particular project falling within Annex II to the Directive, as not being subject to the procedure for assessing its environmental effects.

**[10.122]** However, the fact that the Member State has discretion is not in itself sufficient to exclude a given project from the assessment procedure under the Directive. If that were not the case, the discretion accorded to the Member States by art 4(2) of the Directive could be used by them to take a particular project outside the assessment obligation when, by virtue of its nature, size or location, it could have significant environmental effects. Consequently, whatever the method adopted by a Member State to determine whether or not a specific project needs to be assessed, be it by legislative

---

70. *Commission v Italy* (Case C–87/02) [2005] ENV LR 21, (unreported, 10 June 2004).

designation or following an individual examination of the project, the method adopted must not undermine the objective of the Directive, which is that no project likely to have significant effects on the environment, within the meaning of the Directive, should be exempt from assessment, unless the specific project excluded could, on the basis of a comprehensive screening, be regarded as not likely to have such effects.

**[10.123]** In that regard, a decision by which the national competent authority takes the view that a project's characteristics do not require it to be subjected to an assessment of its effects on the environment must contain or be accompanied by all the information that makes it possible to check that it is based on adequate screening, carried out in accordance with the requirements of Directive 85/337/EEC.

**[10.124]** The operative part of the ECJ's findings in *Commission v Italy*[71] reads as follows:

> The Court (First Chamber) declares that since the Abruzo region failed to ascertain whether the project to construct an outer ring road at Teramo (a project known as Lotto Zero – Variante, Tra Teramo a Giullianova, Alla Strada Statale SS 80), of a type listed in Annex II to Council Directive 85/337/EEC of 27th June 1985 on the assessment of the effects of certain public, private projects on the environment, required an environmental impact assessment in accordance with Articles 5 to 10 of that directive, the Italian Republic has failed to fulfil its obligations under Article 4(2) of that directive.

## DEFINITION OF 'PROJECT'

**[10.125]** From reading the EIA Directive it becomes clear that the word 'project' is an important concept within the Directive. Article 1(2) defines 'project' as meaning:

- The execution of construction works or of other installations or schemes,
- Other interventions in the natural surroundings and landscape including those involving the extraction of mineral resources

In the context of the EIA Directive, the real significance of a project is whether or not it is likely to have significant effects on the environment. If the project is likely to have such effects on the environment, the effects must be fully described in an EIS. The meaning of 'project' is narrower than the meaning of 'development'. Development combines the carrying out of physical works and perhaps a material change in use. Development also includes an activity which is licensed under the Environmental Protection Agency Acts 1992/2003. Project, on the other hand, as defined in art 1(2) of the Directive, is narrowly limited to the execution of construction works other installation schemes. It includes other interventions in natural surroundings and landscape and extraction of mineral resources. The definition does not include material change of use and neither does it include an activity licensed under the Environmental Protection Agency Acts 1992/2003.

---

71. *Commission v Italy* (Case C–87/02) [2005] ENV LR 21, (unreported, 10 June 2004).

**[10.126]** As already noted, both the ECJ and the Irish courts have and will continue to adopt a 'purposive' approach in interpreting Irish law in the context of the EIA Directive and in the context of making an assessment of the effects of certain projects on the environment. *Aannemersbedrijf PK Kraaijeveld BV EA v Geduputeerde Staten van Zuid-Holland*[72] concerned repair and modification including dyke reinforcements to be undertaken by the Sliedrechgt Municipal Council pursuant to a regional development law in the Netherlands. Annex II, in listing a number of projects, includes infrastructure projects, and canalisation and flood relief. Although the EIA Directive had been adopted into national law in the Netherlands, no EIA was made because the size of the works was less than the minimum laid down by the national legislation. Point 3 of the ECJ's ruling reads as follows:

> Article 4(2) of Directive 85/337 and point 10(e) of Annex II must be interpreted as meaning that a Member State which establishes the criteria or thresholds necessary to classify projects relating to dykes at a level such that, in practice, all such projects are exempted in advance from the requirement of an impact assessment exceeds the limit of its discretion under Articles 2(1) and 4(2) of the directive unless all projects excluded could, when viewed as a whole, be regarded as not being likely to have significant effects on the environment.

> Where under national law a court must or may raise of its own motion pleas in law based on a binding national rule which have not been put forward by the parties, it must, for matters within its jurisdiction, examine of its own motion whether the legislative or administrative authorities of the Member State have remained within the limits of their discretion under Articles 2(1) and 4(2) of the directive, and take account thereof when examining the action for annulment.

> Where the discretion has been exceeded and consequently the national provisions must be set aside in that respect, it is for the authorities of the Member State, according to their respective powers, to take all the general or particular measures necessary to ensure that projects are examined in order to determine whether they are likely to have significant effects on the environment and, if so, to ensure that they are subject to an impact assessment.

In *Ó Nualláin v Dublin Corporation*,[73] the planning authority proposed the construction of what is now the 'spire' in O'Connell Street, Dublin. The suggestion made by a senior planner in the planning authority was that there should be public consultation to take place under the provisions of LG(PD)R 1994, Pt X. The purpose of the public consultation was to enable members of the public to express their opinions. Clearly, the public consultation suggested did not amount to EIA which could only be brought into being by a managerial order. The High Court, *per* Smyth J, decided that the decision to proceed with the public consultation under LG(PD)R 1994 was invalid. The learned judge held that the development of the spire was likely to have significant effects on the environment and in those circumstances EIA was required for this Annex II project.

---

72. *Aannemersbedrijf PK Kraaijeveld BV EA v Geduputeerde Staten van Zuid-Holland* (Case C–72/95) [1996] ECR I–5403.
73. *Ó Nualláin v Dublin Corporation* [1999] 4 IR 137, HC per Smyth J at 137.

**[10.127]** *Commission v Kingdom of Spain*[74] is another case where the Member State did not consider that EIA was required for the Valencia to Tarragona railway project. The facts in the pre-litigation procedure in this case may be summarised as follows: The Commission of the European Communities received a complaint that the Spanish authorities had misapplied Council Directive 85/337/EEC by constructing a 13.2km railway line crossing the Communes of Castellòn, Benicassim and Oropesa in that no public enquiry was held and no EIA was undertaken. The railway project provided for a second set of railway tracks on what had been an existing single track line over a distance of 13.2km. Spain argued that EIA was not necessary because the route adopted had been included in a 1992 railway reservation which had been subject to an environmental impact report. The 1992 project had been approved by the Director-General for the Quality of the Environment of the Autonomous Government of Valencia. The Commission replied by pointing out that the environment assessment of 1992 did not cover the whole route.

**[10.128]** The Commission's case in the legal context was that the object of the Directive is to prevent pollution and other damage to the environment by subjecting certain public and private projects to preliminary assessment of their effects on the environment. The Directive distinguishes between two classes of project. The first comprises projects which are likely to have significant effects on the environment and are listed in Annex I of the Directive. EIA is mandatory in respect of Annex I cases. The second class is listed in Annex II to the Directive and Member States have a discretion to decide whether or not to carry out a prior EIA. It was the Commission's view that the project for the Las Palmas–Oropesa section of the Valencia–Tarragona line should be classified as a railway line within the meaning of point 7 of Annex I of the Directive. Spain argued that that part of the project was a modification of an existing project and that it could be classified as being subject to point 12 of Annex II of the Directive because the project did not entail the construction of a new line in the sense of a new route between destinations, but merely the duplication of tracks. Spain argued that point 7 of Annex I refers only to the construction of new railway routes.

**[10.129]** The sixth recital of the preamble and art 2 claim that the Directive's fundamental objective is that, before consent is given, projects likely to have significant effects on the environment should be subjected to EIA. More generally, the objective of the Directive is that no project likely to have significant effects on the environment should be exempt from assessment. If the interpretation proposed by Spain were accepted, an EIA would be required only for the construction of railway lines entailing a new route. The construction of new tracks or the conversion of tracks for regional use into tracks for long distance travelling would not be subject to environmental assessment, even though they could have significant effects on the environment. The Commission argued that to interpret the Directive in that way would be contrary to its fundamental objective.

---

74. *Commission v Kingdom of Spain* (Case C–227/01) [2004] ECR I–8253.

**[10.130]** The Commission pointed out that the project in question included the construction of a new double railway track suitable for speeds of 200 to 220km/h. The previous tracks were suitable for trains which travelled at just 90km/h. The Commission maintained that the duplication of tracks falls within point 7 of Annex I of the Directive and, therefore, requires EIA. There are two reasons why point 7 of Annex I is appropriate. Firstly, the Commission pointed out that the duplication of a track entails the construction of a new track, even though it is parallel to an existing track. Secondly, a different interpretation of the Directive would be contrary to its objectives, because the impact assessment provided by Spain showed that duplication of tracks on the section concerned was likely to have significant effects on the environment. In answer to the Commission's point, Spain pointed out that including the duplication of tracks in the definition of 'construction of railway lines' would be absurd because point 10(d) of Annex II to the Directive does not require that the construction of roads is subject to a mandatory assessment of the environmental impact.

**[10.131]** In considering all the arguments before it, the ECJ found that the Kingdom of Spain had failed to fulfil its obligations arising from arts 2, 3, 5(2) and 6(2) of Council Directive 85/337/EEC by reason of the fact that it did not carry out an EIA of the 'Valencia-Tarragona railway project, Las Palmas-Oropesa section roadbed'.

**[10.132]** *Maher v An Bord Pleanála*,[75] is an important decision where Kelly J held that the interpretation of thresholds is a matter of law which must be decided by the court. In that case, the learned judge held that the omission of 'weaners' and 'finishers' should have been included in the calculation of what was a 'pig' for the purpose of deciding whether or not an EIS was required. In fact, no EIS was submitted and no EIA was undertaken in circumstances where such assessment should have been undertaken. Kelly J struck down the board's decision to grant planning permission because no EIS had been submitted.

**[10.133]** *Paul Abraham and Others v Règion Wallone and Others*,[76] concerned a former military airport at Liege-Bierset where numerous individuals objected to noise pollution brought about by the establishment of an airfreight centre at that airport. Extracts from the summary of the *Abraham* case read as follows:

> Although an agreement signed between the public authority, a company in charge of the development and promotion of an airport and airfreight company which provides for certain modifications to the infrastructure of that airport in order to enable it to be used 24 hours per day and 365 days per year is not a project within the meaning of Directive 85/337 on the assessment of the effects of certain public and private projects on the environment, it is for the national court to determine, on the basis of the applicable national legislation, whether such an agreement constitutes development consent within the meaning of Article 1(2) of that directive. It is necessary, in the context, to consider whether the consent forms part of a procedure carried out in several stages involving a principal decision and implementing decisions and whether account is to be taken of the cumulative

---

75. *Maher v An Bord Pleanála* [1999] 2 ILRM 198 per Kelly J at 198.
76. *Paul Abraham and Others v Région Wallonne and Others* (Case C–2/07) [2008] ECR I–1197.

effects of several projects whose impact on the environment must be assessed globally.

**[10.134]** In its original version, point 12 of Annex II in Directive 85/337/EEC on the assessment of the effects of certain public and private projects on the environment, which refers to 'modifications to development projects included in Annex I', read in conjunction with point 7 of Annex I, which encompass the 'construction ... of airports with a basic runway length of 2100m or more', also encompasses works to modify the infrastructure of an existing airport, without extension to the runway, where they may be regarded, in particular because of their nature, extent and characteristics, as a modification of the airport itself. That is the case, in particular, for works aimed at significantly increasing the activity of the airport and air traffic. It is for the national court to establish that the competent authority has correctly assessed whether the works at issue in the main proceedings were to be subject to an EIA.

**[10.135]** The scope of Directive 85/337/EEC is wide in its purpose and it is very broad. It would be contrary to the very objective of that Directive to exclude works to improve or extend the infrastructure of an existing airport from the scope of Annex II on the ground that Annex I of that Directive covers the 'construction of airports' and not 'airports' as such. Such an interpretation would allow all works to modify a pre-existing airport, regardless of their extent, to fall outside the obligations resulting from Directive 85/337/EEC and would, in that regard, thus deprive Annex II of that Directive of all effect.

**[10.136]** As regards a project covered by point 12 of Annex II in the Directive 85/337/EEC on the assessment of the effects of certain public and private projects on the environment, the competent authorities have an obligation to take account of the projected increase in the activity of an airport in determining the environmental effect of modifications made to its infrastructure with a view to accommodating that increase in activity. In *Ecologistas en Acciòn – CODA v Ayuntamiento de Madrid*,[77] the issue once again was whether a category of project referred to 'construction' would extend to development which involved refurbishment and improvement of an existing road.

**[10.137]** The ECJ ruled as follows:

> Council Directive 85/337/EC of 27 June 1985 on the assessment of the effects of certain public and private projects on the environment, as amended by Council Directive 97/11/EC of 3 March 1997, must be interpreted as meaning that it provides for environmental impact assessment of refurbishment and improvement projects for urban roads, either where they are projects covered by point 7(b) or (c) of Annex I to the directive or where they are projects covered by point 10(e) of Annex II or the first indent of point 13 thereof, which are likely, by virtue of their nature, size or location and, if appropriate having regard to their interaction with other projects, to have significant effects on the environment.[78]

---

77. *Ecologistas en Acciòn – CODA v Ayuntamiento de Madrid* (Case C–142/07) [2008] ECR I–6097.
78. *Ecologistas en Acciòn – CODA v Ayuntamiento de Madrid* (Case C–142/07) [2008] ECR I–6097.

**[10.138]** *R (on application of Edwards) v Environmental Agency*,[79] is an interesting case which usefully illustrates the definition of 'project'.

**[10.139]** The town of Rugby in England has had a long and significant history in the manufacture of cement. The firm Ruby Ltd was acquired by the Mexican multinational Cemex. The cement factory at Lawford Road is a 'state of the art' cement works built some 13 years ago, and at the time of its construction it received authorisation under the UK Environmental Protection Act 1990. In 1999/2000 a new pollution prevention control regime was put into place in the UK both by statute and by regulation to enable Britain to give effect to Directive 96/61/EC (the IBBC Directive) concerning integrated pollution prevention and control. All operators of cement plants were required to obtain a permit from the environment agency. The purpose of the regulations is to ensure that all appropriate preventative measures are taken against pollution through the application of best avail techniques ('BAT') and to ensure that no significant pollution is caused. BAT provide a number of bench marks dealing with emission limits and also provide 'indicative standards' which must not be exceeded. If BAT cannot prevent significant pollution, the activity concerned should not be licensed. 'Significant pollution' is pollution which causes the breach of an environmental quality standard or standards (EQS).

**[10.140]** Cemex applied for a permit from the Environment Agency, and from all reports it appears that the new state of the art plant was causing fewer adverse effects on the environment when compared with the operation of the old plant. However, Cemex had a new proposal in relation to the power source. The old plant was fired exclusively by coal and petroleum coke. That exclusive fuel source was replaced in the new plant by a mix of the old power source and by an additional fuel source, namely shredded vehicle tyres. The company gave assurances that the new fuel source would cause less pollution in terms of smoke and in terms of smell than the old fuel source but not all of the citizens of Rugby believed those claims and Mr David Edwards made an application to the courts for judicial review.

**[10.141]** The partial change of fuel source, namely, the burning of vehicle tyres, supplemented the original fuel source. Burning fuel is not the only potential source of pollution from a cement plant. Cement powder is made by mixing chalk, limestone and clay and also some sand and some iron oxide. That cocktail is then fired in the kiln at very high temperatures and the resultant clinker is cleared out and ground down in a mill in order to make cement powder. What is emitted from a cement factory chimney during the firing operation is a mixture including oxides of sulphur and nitrogen, water vapour and dust. Apart from chimney emissions, the raw materials which are delivered to the factory and moved about on the site are, inevitably, a source of dust which is raised into the atmosphere by wind or by movement of heavy machinery on the site. This is referred to as low level point sources ('LLPS') which can be inhaled and which may be/is a source of respiratory diseases.

---

79. *R (on application of Edwards) v Environmental Agency* [2008] UKHL 22 on appeal from [2006] EWCA Civ 877.

**[10.142]** The particulates matter within the LLPS has a very real potential of causing damage to human health. By definition, the particulates are smaller than 10 microns (millionths of a metre in diameter – referred to as PM10). Because of the minute size of particulates they can be inhaled. It is the particulates which are most likely to cause respiratory disease.

**[10.143]** Mr Edwards's main grounds of complaint related to the PM10 emissions and to the fact that the Environment Agency had failed to properly discharge its statutory obligation to consult the public before reaching a decision as to whether the plant would or would not cause significant pollution. Cemex made the case that they had complied with BAT.

**[10.144]** An EIS had been submitted by Cemex to the Environment Agency. Mr Edwards claimed that the gap in the information about the environmental effects of PM10 was so great that the Environment Agency could not really have judged the application made by Cemex to be a valid application. PM10s, by their very nature, were likely to have significant effects on the environment.

**[10.145]** Dealing with the content and substance of the EIS, Lord Hoffmann quoted Sullivan J in *R (Blewett) v Derbyshire County Council*[80] as follows:

> In an imperfect world it is an unrealistic counsel of perfection to expect that an applicant's environmental statement would always contain the 'full information' about the environmental impact of a project. The Regulations are not based upon such an unrealistic expectation. They recognise that an environmental statement may well be deficient, and make provision through the publicity and consultation process for any deficiencies to be identified so that the resulting 'environmental information' provides the local planning authority with as full as picture as possible. There will be cases where the document purporting to be an environmental statement is so deficient that it could not reasonably be described as an environmental statement as defined by the Regulations...but they are likely to be few and far between.[81]

Lord Hoffmann held that the Environment Agency was entitled to find that the Cemex application was valid. The plant was an existing installation. The only change made to the operation of the plant was the use of tyres as a partial fuel source which was combined with the traditional firing of coal and petroleum coke. A 'project' is not limited to the construction of undertakings and it may include changes of one kind or another which, in planning terms, fall short of a material change in use. In environmental terms the relevant question is whether or not the changes to be effected, no matter what the scale of the change is, may have significant adverse effects on the environment.

**[10.146]** In the *Edwards* case, the Environment Agency, in granting a permit for the partial change in fuel source, inserted a condition to enable it to consider further

---

80. *R (Blewett) v Derbyshire County Council* [2004] Env LR 29.
81. *R (on application of Edwards) v Environmental Agency* [2008] UKHL 22 on appeal from [2006] EWCA Civ 877.

whether additional abatement measures might be justified on BAT grounds. The condition read as follows:

> The operator shall complete a comprehensive audit of all particulate emissions from the site including point source and fugitive emissions. The audit will then be used to assess the combined impact of the emissions on air quality for both short term and long term scenarios. The operator shall develop BAT proposals for any remedial work required. A report outlining the assessment, its conclusions and measures to address any issues raised is to be forwarded to the agency.

The Environment Agency had produced a somewhat inconclusive report on the question of the predicted effect of LLPS emissions of PM10. The report was produced by a unit within the Environment Agency known as the Air Quality Modelling Assessment Unit (AQMAU).

[10.147] In August 2004, Cemex produced a report as required by its license from the agency. Rugby Borough Council also commissioned a report from experts. Both reports concluded that the EQS was not being exceeded. Rugby Borough Council accepted the advices that they should not designate an Air Quality Management Area around the Cemex works, for PM10. In November 2007, Rugby Borough Council published a draft Air Quality Action Plan. That plan concluded that studies had shown that there were no exceedances of the PM10 National Air Quality Objectives resulting from the operation of the Cemex plant. Mr Edwards's application was unanimously dismissed in the House of Lords.

## MITIGATING MEASURES

[10.148] Where a development proposal is sub-threshold the planning authority or the board, as appropriate, would usually require an EIS where it is of the opinion that the development proposal is likely to have significant effects on the environment. In order to avoid the necessity of submitting an EIS a developer may take steps to ensure that there are no significant effects on the environment and these are referred to as 'mitigating measures'.

[10.149] If, at screening stage, a planning authority can make a clear judgment that there is not any likelihood of any significant effect on the environment it is absolutely permissible for the planning authority to conclude that there is no requirement for an EIA.[82]

[10.150] Developers, in contemplating the question as to whether or not, for example, a particular Annex II project requires EIA, are always faced with an important question and that is whether or not their project proposal is or is not likely to have significant effects on the environment. In the UK, Council Directive 85/337/EEC of 27 June 1985 on the assessment of the effects of certain projects on the environment was implemented by the provisions of the Town and Country Planning (Assessment of Environmental

---

82. See *R (On the application of Dickens) v Aylesbury DC* [2008] JPL 1575.

Effects) Regulations 1988. The combined effects of reg 2 and 4 in the 1988 Regulations is that EIA procedures must be followed, but only if, the 'proposed development' would be likely to have significant effects on the environment by virtue of factors such as its nature, size or location. That wording reflects the language of art 2.1 of Council Directive 85/337/EEC which provides that projects listed in Annex II shall be made subject to an assessment 'where Member States consider that their characteristics so require'.

**[10.151]** The principles involved were comprehensively dealt with in the English case of *Bellway Urban Renewal Suthern v Gillespie*.[83] The project for development was a 3.5 hectare site in Stepney which had old gas storage tanks on about 20% of the site. The Save Stepney Campaign ('SSC') objected to the proposal.

**[10.152]** The planning inspector hearing an appeal by the developer noted the planning benefit which would result from a development of affordable housing to include a community health centre, and a community employment training centre. The SSC objected on the grounds that four nationally significant gas holders were on the site and that it was both government policy and a requirement of the development plan to preserve such archaeologically important features. On the other hand, it was acknowledged that regeneration was an aspiration particularly for the provision of houses on a brownfield site in an area of London where more homes were needed. Another plus which favoured the community based housing proposal was the fact that the contaminated land, if the development were to proceed, would be remediated and brought back into beneficial use.

**[10.153]** The inspector recommended that the developer's appeal should be dismissed but the Secretary of State disagreed on the grounds that the appellant's development proposal outweighed the presumption in favour of the preservation of archaeological remains and the conflict with the development plan. The Secretary of State's decision was challenged before Richards J in the Queens Bench Division Administrative Court. The learned judge quashed the permission granted on the grounds that it was an undisputed fact that the site or at least a substantial part of it was seriously contaminated. In those circumstances, the learned judge held that EIA was required before the application for planning permission could be considered. In effect, the Secretary of State was required to make a judgment as to whether this urban development project would be likely to have 'significant effects on the environment by virtue of factors such as its nature, size or location'. The Secretary of State did make a judgment to the effect that the development would not be likely to have significant effects on the environment. Richards J held that the Secretary of State erred in the test which he applied.

---

83. *Bellway Urban Renewal Suthern v Gillespie* [2003] EWCA Civ 1408 Court of Appeal (Civil Division) on appeal from the Queens Bench Division Administrative Court (Richards J) before Pill, Laws and Arden LJJ.

**[10.154]** The applicant's planning consultant, a Mr Painting, stated:

> The difficulty in regenerating the site lies in the nature of the previous use of the site, which as demonstrated by Mr Edwards, has resulted in extensive contamination of the land. This presents a considerable barrier to ensuring the development of the site. Remediation, in my view, would therefore represent considerable planning benefit in its own right, as recognised by government guidance ...

Accordingly, any redevelopment proposals must account for this additional and abnormal requirement. The Secretary of State had decided that it was unlikely that the development would have significant effects on the environment and that decision was made in the full knowledge of the facts which were that the site was contaminated to a significant degree because of its previous use.[84]

**[10.155]** The Court of Appeal acknowledged that the site or at least a substantial part of the site was extensively contaminated. The Court of Appeal also acknowledged the view of the Council as planning authority and the view of the Environment Agency (which is equivalent to the Environmental Protection Agency in Ireland), that remediation strategies to address the contamination *in situ* could be dealt with by planning conditions. A planning authority granted permission having decided that the development would not give rise to significant effects upon the environment. The planning authority also conditioned the developer to decontaminate the site. The condition contained in the planning authority's permission (no VI) reads as follows:

> Before any development commences a detailed site investigation shall be undertaken to establish the nature, extent and degree of the contamination present on the site. The scope, method and extent of this site investigation shall be submitted to and approved by the local authority prior to the commencement of the site investigation. The site investigation work shall also propose a scheme for remediation on this contamination, including measures to be taken to minimise risk to the public, the environment and prevention of contaminated ground and surface water from escaping during the remediation, together with provisions for monitoring during and after remediation. The detailed site investigation shall be submitted to and approved in writing by the local planning authority prior to the commencement of the remediation works on site and no remediation or development works on site shall proceed other than in accordance with the approved measures.

**[10.156]** In the *Bellway* case Pill LJ had this to say at para 36:

> When making his screening decision, the Secretary of State was not in my judgment obliged to shut his eyes to the remedial measures submitted as a part of the planning proposal. That would apply whatever the scale of development and whether (as in BT)[85] some harm to the relevant environmental interest is inevitable

---

84. Some readers may recall the amount of earth which was removed from the gasometer site on Dublin's south quays prior to the redevelopment of that site. The earth was transported by ship to mainland Europe where it was dumped into a disused coalmine.
85. This refers to *British Telecommunications plc v Gloucester City Council* [2001] EWHC Admin 1001.

or whether (as is the plain in the present case) the development will actually produce an improvement in the environment. As stated in *Bozen*,[86] it is the elements of the specified project which must be considered and all the elements of the project relevant to the EIA. In making its decision, the Secretary of State is not required to put into separate compartments the development proposal and the proposed remedial measures and consider only the first when making his screening decision. If the judges in the cases cited took a contrary view, I respectfully disagree, though it appears to me that both Sullivan J in *Lebus*[87] and Richards J in the present case did not require all remedial or mitigating measures to be ignored.[88]

The Court of Appeal held, that on the facts, although a decontamination condition had been put in place the gas containers were still on site and had not been disassembled. No assessment of the extent of the contamination of the site had been undertaken. The Court of Appeal held that the wrong test had been applied in determining whether or not EIS was required. Consequently, the Court of Appeal quashed the High Court decision but it did not go so far as to say that an EIS was required. In dismissing the appeal, Laws LJ gave guidance as to circumstances in which an EIS should be required:

> I would express my reasons for dismissing the appeal very shortly as follows. Where the Secretary of State is contemplating an application for planning permission for development which, but for remedial measures, may or will have significant environmental effects, I do not say that he must inevitably cause an EIA to be conducted. Prospective remedial measures may have been put before him whose nature, availability and effectiveness are already plainly established and plainly uncontroversial; though I should have thought there is little likelihood of such a state of affairs in relation to a development of any complexity. But if prospective remedial measures are not plainly established and not plainly uncontroversial then, as it seems to me the case calls for an EIA. If then the Secretary of State were to decline to conduct an EIA, as it seems to me he would pre-empt the very form of enquiry contemplated by the Directive and Regulations; and to that extent he would frustrate the purpose of the legislation.[89]

Subsequent to the Court of Appeal's decision in *Bellway*, in *R (On the application of Jones) v Mansfield District Council*[90] the Court of Appeal held that a planning authority cannot rely on conditions and undertakings as a surrogate for the EIA process. In making a decision as to whether or not EIA is required a planning authority cannot decide not to call for EIA on the grounds that proposed mitigation measures, when put in place, would eliminate any significant effects which the development might have on

---

86. See *World Wildlife Fund v Autonome Provinz Bozen* (Case C–435/97) [1998] ECR I–5613.
87. See *R (Lebus) v South Cambridgeshire District Council* [2002] EWHC 2009 Admin, where the planning authority did not require EIA for a 12,000 free range chicken farm. Sullivan J held that a decision could be made as to whether or not such a development would have significant effects on the environment but that the planning authority should require an EIS so that they could make an informed decision.
88. *Bellway Urban Renewal Suthern v Gillespie* [2003] EWCA Civ 1408.
89. *Bellway Urban Renewal Suthern v Gillespie* [2003] EWCA Civ 1408.
90. *Bellway Urban Renewal Suthern v Gillespie* [2003] EWCA Civ 1408.

the environment. In that case, the court held that a planning authority must be fully and sufficiently informed about the impact of a project in order to make a decision as to whether or not the development proposal is likely to have a significant effect on the environment. Looking at the facts in *Bellway*, the council did not know what remedial action was required in order to be able to state definitively that the development proposal would not have significant effects on the environment. The gas work tanks were in place and clearly boreholes and excavation and other examinations would have to take place before the council would be adequately informed to make the decision.

## DEVELOPMENT CONSENTS

[10.157] Planning permission, in the sense of a notification of grant of permission, issued by a planning authority is not always an indication that the development may commence after service of a commencement notice on the planning authority. Other permissions or licenses may be required, or perhaps a precondition may require compliance before development can be commenced.

[10.158] The comprehensive term used in the EIA Directive is 'development consent' which is defined in art 1(2) of EIA Directive as:

> The decision of the competent authority or authorities which entitles the developer to proceed with the 'project'.[91]

[10.159] In *Dunne v Minister for the Environment, Heritage and Local Government (No 2)*,[92] the principal question to be determined was whether a new section, specially introduced to facilitate the completion of works on the South Eastern Route (SER) of the M50 motorway in the area where that motorway is adjacent to an archaeological site at Carrickmines Castle was in breach of Arts 5, 10, 15 and 40 of the Constitution and also whether the provision affected the requirements of Council Directive 85/337/EEC, as amended by Council Directive 97/11/EC. If neither the Constitution nor the EIA Directives were offended by the provisions of s 8 of the National Monuments (NM) Amendment Act 2004 the plaintiff further required to know whether certain directions issued by the Minister for the Environment, pursuant to s 8, were null and void having regard to the EIA Directive. The plaintiff asked whether the ministerial directions under s 8 of the National Monuments (Amendment) Act 2004 form part of the 'development consent', and alternatively, whether the Minister's ministerial directions were separate and distinct from the principal consent, namely, the statutory approval given in the first instance under the Roads Acts 1993 to 1998.

[10.160] Murray CJ, in a comprehensive judgment, examined the principles which determined whether or not a particular decision constitutes a 'development consent'. Previously, in the High Court, Laffoy J, in giving judgment in the same matter, held (1) that the relevant development project for the purposes of the Directive was the road

---

91. See definition of 'project' at para **10.125**.
92. *Dunne v Minister for the Environment, Heritage and Local Government (No 2)* [2006] IESC 49, [2007] ILRM 264.

development and not the archaeological works, and (2) that the ministerial directions did not constitute 'development consent' within the meaning of the Directive.

**[10.161]** The Chief Justice supported Laffoy J's view that ministerial directions do not constitute 'development consent' in their own right. Murray CJ had this to say:

> The Ministerial directions regulate works of excavation and, in some instances, of removal. They do not constitute a project for the purposes of the environmental impact assessment. The requirement for environmental impact assessment only applies to a limited class of development projects as prescribed under Annex I and Annex II of the Directive. It is manifestly clear that these prescribed projects do not include works of the type permitted under the directions of August 2004. The project subject to environmental impact assessment is the road development itself. The road development is authorised under the decisions of 1998, not under the directions of August 2004.
>
> The concept of 'development consent' has been considered in a number of cases, including *R (Wells) v Secretary of State for Transport, Local Government and the Regions* (Case C–201/02) [2004] ECR 1–723, *R v North Yorkshire County Council ex parte Browne* [2000] 1 AC 397; and *R (on the application of Porkopp) v London Underground Limited* [2004] 1 P&C R 479, and some of these case are more fully explored in the judgment of the learned trial judge.
>
> What emerges clearly from these judgments is that the question as to whether or not a particular decision constitutes a 'development consent' cannot be determined simply by the application of a 'but for' test; in other words, the fact that the development might not be permitted to proceed 'but for' the particular decision in issue cannot per se be conclusive. As Lord Justice Buxton stated in *Porkopp* (at para 60):
>
> 'In our case both in law and in common sense the 'project' is the whole of the ELLX. For that reason, as Mr Gordon pointed out, the fact that by a rule of the domestic law of a particular member state further permission is required in the course of the project, though for reasons unconnected with its environmental impact, does not mean that the granting of such permission must be treated as a 'development consent'. Indeed, quite the reverse, the relevant and only such consent in terms of the Directive was the original decision that permitted the project to go forward in the first place'.[93]

**[10.162]** In *Dunne v Minister for Environment*, the Chief Justice was clear in stating that the principal development consent was the consent of October 1998. The Chief Justice gave reasons as to why the ministerial directions given in August 2004 did not constitute a 'development consent':

a.  Firstly, the Minister does not have the power under section 8 to embark upon a reconsideration of the environmental issues arising for the road development and, more importantly, does not have power to modify the road development. All that is left for the Minister is a power to regulate the

---

93. *Dunne v Minister for the Environment, Heritage and Local Government (No 2)* [2006] IESC 49, [2007] ILRM 264 *per* Murray CJ.

manner in which the works which are necessary to allow the road to proceed are carried out.

b. Secondly, the project is prescribed for the purposes of the environmental impact assessment Directive as the road development, the subject matter of the 1998 consent. Excavation works of the type the subject matter of the ministerial directions under section 8 are not a prescribed project.[94]

Further on, the learned Chief Justice commented that 'it is the construction of the road development which gives rise to the environmental impact, not the archaeological resolution measures contained in the ministerial directions'.

**[10.163]** Generally, a notification of grant of permission is the 'development consent' but a developer may not be able to commence development when other environmental authorisations are required. It is not uncommon for environmental authorisation to issue from two separate regulatory authorities operating under separate legislation. The environmental assessment of a development proposal might very well be carried out by the Environmental Protection Agency (EPA) dealing with its specific environmental responsibilities to include, for example, licenses or permissions relating to such matters as discharge of water, control of particulates in the atmosphere, waste management licences or radioactive substances discharged authorisations.

**[10.164]** The planning authority will impose general conditions in its grant of permission. The most important point is that all impacts which have significant effects on the environment must be assessed by a competent authority and the competent authority must aim to eliminate or at least control the significant impacts before the developer is allowed to commence development. It does not matter which competent authority assesses the significant impacts so long as the significant impacts are assessed. The developers may need a whole host of additional environmental consents before work can proceed but the question is, are these ancillary lists or requirements development consents or is the development consent the notification of grant of planning permission?

**[10.165]** In *R (on the application of Delena Wells) v Secretary of State for Transport, Local Government and the Regions*,[95] the ECJ strongly emphasised that EIA must be carried out at the first stage in the process if that is possible. In *Wells*, an old mining permission was granted in 1947 to Conygar Quarry. The applicant, Mrs Wells, lived in a house which was located between the two sections of the Conygar Quarry. Mrs Wells purchased her house in 1984 some 37 years after the 1947 permission was granted. In 1984, the quarry was dormant and had been dormant for some time. In June 1991, operations recommenced for a short period. The site is recognised to be environmentally extremely sensitive and it is located in an area which is subject to several designations of nature and environmental conservation importance. At the beginning of 1991, Conygar

---

94. *Dunne v Minister for the Environment, Heritage and Local Government (No 2)* [2006] IESC 49, [2007] ILRM 264 *per* Murray CJ.
95. *R (on the application of Delena Wells) v Secretary of State for Transport, Local Government and the Regions* (Case C–201/02) [2004] ECR I–723.

Quarry applied to the competent authority being the mining planning authority for registration of the old mine, under a scheme similar to the scheme set up in PDA 2000 for the registration of quarries. Registration was completed on 24 August 1992 but no development was authorised to commence until new planning conditions had been attached by the Mineral Planning Authority (MPA). Conygar Quarry made a submission concerning conditions to the MPA and in December 1994 the MPA issued a note of their conditions which were more stringent than the conditions submitted by Conygar Quarry. Conygar Quarry appealed to the Secretary of State. Subsequent to the appeal the Secretary of State added some more conditions making a total of 54 conditions and leaving some matters to be decided by the MPA. The MPA made its final decision as competent authority on 8 July 1999 but, at the time, neither the MPA nor the Secretary of State made any enquiries as to whether quarry operations were likely to have a significant impact on the environment and no decision was taken to request an EIA. Delena Wells requested revocation or modification of the planning permission but the Secretary of State declined. The High Court, Queens Bench Division, stayed the proceedings and referred a number of questions to the ECJ for interpretation.

[10.166] In answer to the questions referred to by the High Court of Justice of England and Wales the ECJ ruled as follows:

> 1. Article 2(1) of Council Directive 85/337/EEC of 27th June 1985 on the assessment of the effects of certain public and private projects on the environment, read in conjunction with Article 4(2) thereof, is to be interpreted as meaning that, in the context of applying provisions such as section 22 of the Planning and Compensation Act 1991 and Schedule 2 of that Act, the decisions adopted by the competent authorities, whose effect is to permit the resumption of mining operations, comprise, as a whole, a development consent within the meaning of Article 1(2) of that Directive, so that the competent authorities are obliged, where appropriate, to carry out an assessment of the environmental effects of such operations. In a consent procedure comprising several stages, that assessment must, in principal, be carried out as soon as it is possible to identify and assess all the effects which the project may have on the environment.
>
> 2. In circumstances such as those of the main proceedings, an individual may, where appropriate, rely on Article 2(1) of Directive 85/337, read in conjunction with Articles 1(2) and 4(2) thereof.
>
> 3. Under Article 10 EC the competent authorities are obliged to take, within the sphere of their competency all general or particular measures for remedying the failure to carry out an assessment of the environmental effects of a project as provided for in Article 2(1) of Directive 85/337. The detailed procedural rules applicable in that consent are a matter for the domestic legal order of such Member State, under the principle of procedural autonomy of the Member States, provided that they are not less favourable than those governing similar domestic situations (principle of equivalence) and that they do not render impossible in practice or accessibly difficult the exercise of rights conferred by the Community legal order (principle of effectiveness). In that regard it is for the national courts to determine whether it is possible under domestic law for a consent already granted to be revoked or suspended in order to subject the project to an assessment of its

environmental effects, in accordance with the requirements of Directive 85/337, or alternatively, if the individual so agrees, whether it is possible for the latter to claim compensation for the harm suffered.

In summary, the approval of new conditions by the MPA was a 'development consent' for which EIA was required because it had the same effect, as the second consents replaced not just the terms but the very substance of a prior consent.

**[10.167]** In Ireland, the Supreme Court decision in *Dunne v Minister for Environment Heritage and Local Government (No 2)*[96] held that Ministerial directions regulating archaeological works did not form part of the 'development consent' for a road development. The Supreme Court further held that the 'development consent' was the statutory approval given under the Roads Act. The Ministerial directions which followed dealt with the regulation of activities and in doing so it raised substantial environmental issues but those regulations were not 'development consent'.

**[10.168]** The ECJ decision in *Wells* clearly indicates that the *Dunne* decision may have to be looked at again. In *Wells*, the MPA considered that the earlier permission was the 'development consent' and because it was the 'development consent' there would be no requirement to carry out EIA at the time of the subsequent application for registration or at the time when the MPA imposed its regulatory conditions.

**[10.169]** Simons[97] in commenting on the *Wells* decision had this to say:

> The ECJ regarded the decision determining new conditions and the decision approving matters reserved by the new conditions as representing principal consents. With respect, this must be correct: it would have been artificial to suggest – in circumstances where the previous planning permission would have lapsed but for the application for registration and the determination of the new conditions, and where the very substance of the old planning permission was replaced – that the more recent decisions were merely ancillary to the old planning permissions.

**[10.170]** The English and Welsh decisions generally indicated that the EIA Directive did not apply to decisions which guided activities for which the fundamental consent ('development consent') had already been granted. The main thrust of the English and Welsh case law indicated that what were described as ancillary or implementing decisions were not development consents. However, Lord Hoffmann, in *R v North Yorkshire County Council, ex parte Browne and Another*[98] held that when a mineral planning authority (MPA) set conditions on the continued operation of a quarry which had been in operation since pre-1947, that decision was a 'development consent' which required to be supported by an EIA because, in the circumstances of that case, it was clear that the development had significant effects.

---

96. *Dunne v Minister for Environment Heritage and Local Government (No 2)* [2007] 1 ILRM 264.
97. See Simons, *Planning and Development Law* (2nd edn, Thomson Round Hall, 2007) at para 13.121, p 775.
98. *R v North Yorkshire County Council, ex parte Browne and Another* [2000] 1 AC 397.

**[10.171]** Lord Hoffmann's decision in *Browne* must be distinguished from the ECJ's decision in *Wells*. In *Browne*, Lord Hoffman accepted that the MPA's conditions did amount to development consent, but, he was emphatic in making a distinction between principal and subsidiary consents. The MPA conditions were principal conditions and as such amounted to development consent but decisions which list detailed regulation of activities, subsequent to a principal decision, would not amount to development consent which requires EIA. That finding raises an immediate conflict with the ECJ judgment in *Wells* which allows for a multi-stage development consent which may be taken together to comprise a single development consent. Allowing for the fact that the EIA Directive has 'direct effect' throughout the EU it is likely that the principles set out in the ECJ's judgment in *Wells* will prevail.[99]

## EIA AND OUTLINE PERMISSION

**[10.172]** In Ireland, any development which requires an EIS has been expressly excluded from the possibility of obtaining outline permission and this has been the case since 1994.[100] The exclusion is now covered by PDR 2001, art 96. If, in the relevant circumstances, an assessment is made either by a planning authority on an application for outline permission or by the board on appeal in respect of a decision on an outline permission to the effect that an EIS is required because the development proposal is likely to have significant effects on the environment, the planning authority or the board, as the case may be, shall send a notice to the applicant refunding any fee paid and informing the applicant for an outline permission which requires an EIS that the application is deemed to be withdrawn. Persons who have made submissions or observations on an application for outline permission which requires an EIS will be similarly informed by notice.

**[10.173]** In England, the courts upheld outline permission in cases where the development proposal would have significant effects on the environment and where EIA was necessary, notably in *R v Rochdale Metropolitan Borough Council ex parte Milne*[101] where Sullivan J recognised the problem which developers have in adequately describing the full extent of environmental impacts on large or complex developments. The learned judge concluded that those difficulties could be overcome by the imposition of conditions.

**[10.174]** On 4 May 2006, the ECJ in *Commission v United Kingdom*[102] the House of Lords sought a reference for a preliminary ruling from the ECJ arising out of proceedings between Diane Baker and the London Borough Council of Bromley. The

---

99. See *Commission v United Kingdom* (Case C–508/03) (4 May 2006). In that case, a reserved matters approval meant that the project could not proceed on a 'but for' basis. The 'but for' approval was sufficient to make it part of the development consent.
100. See Local Government (Planning and Development) Regulations 1994, art 20(2). See also PDR 2001, art 96 and see also PDR 2001, art 21.
101. *R v Rochdale Metropolitan Borough Council ex parte Milne* [2001] JPL 470.
102. *Commission v United Kingdom* [2000] Env LR 1.

reference for a preliminary ruling concerned the interpretation of arts 1(2), 2(1) and 4(2) of the EIA Directive (Council Directive 85/337/EEC) on the assessment of the effects of certain public and private projects on the environment. The development concerned comprised a proposal to develop a leisure complex at Crystal Palace Park in London, without any EIA being carried out. The developer sought permission from Bromley Council to develop:

(i) on the ground floor, 18 cinemas, a leisure area and an exhibition area;

(ii) at the gallery level, restaurants and cafes, two leisure areas and public toilets;

(iii) at roof level, a roof-top car park with a maximum of 950 spaces, four viewing areas and areas enclosing plant and equipment;

(iv) the addition of a mezzanine floor of 800m$^2$; and

(v) changes to the construction of the external walls.

Bromley Council issued a notice of approval on 10 May 1999 in circumstances where no EIA was either requested or furnished. When the matter came before the House of Lords doubts arose as to the compatibility with EU law of English rules which provided that an EIA can be carried out only at the outline planning permission stage and not when the reserved matters are subsequently approved. In those circumstances it was decided to stay the proceedings and to refer three questions to the ECJ for a preliminary ruling, namely:

> (1) Is identification of 'the decision of a competent authority or authorities which entitles the developer to proceed with the project' (Article 1(2) of Directive 85/337/EEC ('the Directive')) exclusively a matter for the national court applying national law?
>
> (2) Does the Directive require an EIA [Environmental Impact Assessment] to be carried out if, following the grant of outline planning permission subject to conditions that reserved matters to be approved, without an EIA being carried out, it appears when approval of reserve matters is sought that the project may have significant effects on the environment by virtue inter alia of its nature, size or location (Article 2(1) of the Directive)?
>
> (3) In circumstances where:
>
> (a) national planning law provides for the grant of outline planning permission at an initial stage of the planning process and requires consideration by the competent authority at that stage as to whether an EIA is required for purposes of the Directive; and
>
> (b) the competent authority then determines that it is unnecessary to carry out an EIA and grants outline planning permission subject to conditions reserving specified matters for later approval; and
>
> (c) that decision can then be challenged in the national courts;
>
> may national law, consistently with the Directive preclude a competent authority from requiring that an EIA be carried out at a later stage of the planning process?

The courts answered questions 1, 2 and 3 as follows:

> The answer to the first question must therefore be that classification of a decision as a 'development consent' within the meaning of Article 1(2) of Directive 85/337 must be carried out pursuant to national law in a manner consistent with Community law.
>
> The answer to the second and third questions must be that Articles 2(1) and 4(2) of Directive 85/337 are to be interpreted as requiring an environmental impact assessment to be carried out if, in the case of grant of consent comprising more than one stage, it becomes apparent, in the course of the second stage, that the project is likely to have significant effects on the environment by virtue of its size and location.

On those grounds, the ECJ ruled as follows:

> 1. Classification of a decision as a 'development consent' within the meaning of Article 1(2) of Council Directive 85/337/EEC of 27 June 1985 on the assessment of the effects of certain public and private projects on the environment must be carried out pursuant to national law in a manner consistent with Community laws.
>
> 2. Articles 2(1) and 4(2) of Directive 85/337 are to be interpreted as requiring an environmental impact assessment to be carried out if, in the case of grant of consent comprising more than one stage, it becomes apparent, in the course of the second stage, that the project is likely to have significant effects on the environment by virtue inter alia of its nature, size or location.

In effect, the ECJ held that the two decisions (planning and environmental) constitute a multi-stage development consent. In failing to provide for the possibility of assessment at the stage of approval of reserved matters, the UK legislative scheme was not consistent with the requirements of the Directive.

## DECISIONS NOT TO TAKE ENFORCEMENT ACTION AGAINST UNAUTHORISED DEVELOPMENT

**[10.175]** In *R (on the application of Prokopp) v London Underground Limited*,[103] the subject matter of the case concerned the proposed East London Underground extension and the demolition of Bishopsgate Goods Yard. In that case, the planning permission had expired and the Court of Appeal concluded that failure to take enforcement action in those circumstances did not represent a development consent. Buxton LJ held that a failure to take a decision not to take enforcement proceedings did not amount to a development consent and the failure did not entitle the developer to proceed; if the developer decided to proceed he did so at his own risk. Schiemann LJ held that a decision not to take enforcement action where EIA development was concerned was capable of amounting to a development consent but where national authorities allowed development falling within the Directive to proceed without EIA that inaction might well amount to a breach of the Member States' obligations under the EIA Directive.

---

103. *R (on the application of Prokopp) v London Underground Limited* [2003] EWCA Civ 961.

## EIA FOR MODIFICATION OR EXTENSION TO PROJECTS

**[10.176]** Clearly, Annex I projects require EIA and EIA is also required for modifications and/or extensions of Annex I projects. In *Aannemersbedrijf PK Kraaijeveld BV v Gedeputeerde Staten van Zuid – Holland*,[104] the ECJ ruled that modifications of Annex II projects must also be subject to EIA where the assessment carried out demonstrates that the modification of the Annex II project is likely, by reason of its nature, size or location to have significant effects on the environment.

**[10.177]** In *Commission v Germany*,[105] complaint was made against the Federal Republic of Germany by the Commission when development consent was granted for the construction of a new block at Groskotzenbur Power Station without an acceptable preliminary EIA. The Commission's case was that Germany had failed to comply with its obligation under arts 5 and 189 of the EEC Treaty read in conjunction with Council Directive 85/337/EEC (the EIA Directive). The new generating block was designed with a heat output of 500 megawatts which is 200 megawatts in excess of the heat output threshold determined by art 2 of Annex I. Germany made 11 submissions to the ECJ which were not accepted by the court. Supported by the United Kingdom, Germany submitted that the new block was not a project but rather it was a modification to a project. On that particular point the ECJ ruled as follows:

35. By virtue of paragraph 2 of Annex I to the directive, projects for thermal power stations with heat output of 300 megawatts or more must undergo systematic assessment. For the purpose of that provision, such projects must be assessed irrespective of whether they are separate constructions, are added to a pre-existing construction or even have close functional links with a pre-existing construction. Links with an existing construction do not prevent the project from being a 'thermal power station with a heat output of 300 megawatts or more' so as to bring it within the category headed 'Modifications to development projects included in Annex I', mentioned in paragraph 12 of Annex II.

36. In this case, it is common ground that the construction at issue is a block of a thermal power station with a heat output of 500 megawatts. It is therefore a project within the meaning of Article 4(1) of, and Annex I to the directive. The project was required to undergo an assessment of its effects on the environment in accordance with that directive.

Dealing with the obligation to carry out an assessment in accordance with the Directive the ECJ ruled that the EIA which had been submitted by the Federal Republic of Germany to the relevant competent authority and which was favourably assessed on the basis of the national legislation then enforced, did not satisfy the requirements of the Directive which are stricter than the national legislation then in force.

---

104. *Aannemersbedrijf PK Kraaijeveld BV v Gedeputeerde Staten van Zuid–Holland* (Case C–72/95) [1996] ECR 1–5403.
105. *Commission v Germany* (Case C–431/92) [1995] ECJ I–2189.

**[10.178]** The competent authority was the Regierungspraesidium Darmstadt. That competent authority made all information available to the public concerned who had an opportunity to express an opinion. The ECJ ruled that, in those circumstances, the objective of making the public aware of the environmental implications of the project on the basis of specific information provided by the developer was attained. It was also clear to the ECJ that the developer had provided full information on the environmental impact of the project and that information was considered by the Commission itself, as sufficient from the point of view of the requirements of art 5 and Annex III to the Directive. Regierungspraesidium Darmstadt integrated the information gathered and the reactions of the sectors concerned in the consent procedure and took all of that into account in making its decision to approve the modification of the project.

**[10.179]** Ultimately the ECJ ruled as follows:

> 45. In the light of those considerations, the Commission should have specified on what specific points the requirements of the Directive were not complied with during the procedure for consent for the project at issue and should have provided appropriate evidence of non compliance. Its application does not include such details backed by specific evidence. It must therefore be dismissed as unfounded.[106]

**[10.180]** Scannell makes the following useful comment:

> One advantage of the requirement for EIA of modifications of projects listed in Annexes I and II is that pre–1988 projects that were never subject to EIA may be required to undergo the procedure if they are significantly expanded.[107]

## 'SIGNIFICANT EFFECTS ON THE ENVIRONMENT'

**[10.181]** A competent authority (usually a planning authority or An Bord Pleanála on appeal) is bound to require EIA in respect of a project which is likely to have significant effects on the environment. Significant effects do not include every possible environmental effect. The term 'significant effect' is directed towards 'main effects' or 'likely significant effects', but this does not immediately exclude small scale projects. Significant effects have the potential of being identified in any project irrespective of its size or scale. Projects on any scale may have significant effects on the environment if, for example, it is to be located close to an environmentally sensitive area. In *Commission v Ireland*,[108] the Commission alleged that Ireland had failed to effectively transfer the EIA Directive into national law. It was the Commission's case that transposition in this instance was defective or insufficient. In particular, the complaint related to afforestation on Pettigo Plateau and it also concerned peat extraction, in particular, from Clonfinane Bog in County Tipperary. The Commission's case was that projects which do not exceed the threshold set may nonetheless have significant

---

106. *Commission v Germany* (Case C–431/92) [1995] ECR I–2189.
107. See Scannell, *Environmental and Land Use Law* (2nd edn, Thomson Round Hall, 2006) at p 413, para 5–68.
108. *Commission v Ireland* (Case C–392/96) [1999] ECR I–5901.

environmental effects and the Commission highlighted two factors of importance in that regard, namely:

1. That certain sites which are particularly sensitive or valuable may be damaged by projects which do not exceed thresholds set. That particularly related to areas identified as valuable and important for nature conservation and areas of particular archaeological or geomorphological interest.

2. That the Irish legislation failed to take account of the cumulative effect of projects. A number of separate projects which individually do not exceed the threshold set and therefore do not require an impact assessment may, taken together, have significant environmental effects.

Dealing with the scale of the development it was recorded at para 66 in this *Commission v Ireland*[109] case as follows:

66. Even a small-scale project can have significant effects on the environment if it is in a location where the environmental factors set out in Article 3 of the Directive such as fauna and flora, soil, water, climate or cultural heritage, are sensitive to the slightest alteration.

**[10.182]** The EIA Directive was amended by Directive 97/11/EC which set out guidance notes for competent authorities within Member States to assist them in making a decision as to whether or not a development was likely to have 'significant effects on the environment'. The guidance is set out in Annex III of the 1997 amending Directive and is set out below.

**SELECTION CRITERIA REFERRED TO IN ART 4(3)**

1. Characteristics of projects

The characteristics of projects must be considered having regard, in particular, to:

- the size of the project,
- the cumulation with other projects,
- the use of natural resources,
- the production of waste,
- pollution and nuisances,
- the risk of accidents, having regard in particular to substances or technologies used.

2. Location of projects

The environmental sensitivity of geographical areas likely to be affected by projects must be considered, having regard, in particular, to:

- the existing land use,
- the relative abundance, quality and regenerative capacity of natural resources in the area,

---

109. *Commission v Ireland* (Case C–392/96) [1999] ECR I–5901.

**[10.183]** Planning and Environmental Law in Ireland

- the absorption capacity of the natural environment, paying particular attention to the following areas:

    (a) wetlands;

    (b) coastal zones;

    (c) mountain and forest areas;

    (d) nature reserves and parks;

    (e) areas classified or protected under Member States' legislation; special protection areas designated by Member States pursuant to Directive 79/409/EEC and 92/43/EEC;

    (f) areas in which the environmental quality standards laid down in Community legislation have already been exceeded;

    (g) densely populated areas;

    (h) landscapes of historical, cultural or archaeological significance.

3. Characteristics of the potential impact

The potential significant effects of projects must be considered in relation to criteria set out under 1 and 2 above, and having regard in particular to:

- the extent of the impact (geographical area and size of the affected population),
- the transfrontier nature of the impact,
- the magnitude and complexity of the impact,
- the probability of the impact,
- the duration, frequency and reversibility of the impact.[110]

In making a decision as to whether or not a sub-threshold development is likely to have significant effects on the environment a competent authority within a Member State must have regard to the Annex III criteria.

**[10.183]** The most important and perhaps the most difficult task in making screening decisions as to whether or not a sub-threshold development is likely to have significant effects on the environment is the interpretation of what is or is not 'significant'. The Department's guidance document offers the following advice to competent authorities at para 5.5:

> Each decision has to be taken on its own merits. Those responsible for making the decision must exercise their best professional judgment taking account of consideration such as the nature and size of the proposed development, the environmental sensitivity of the area in which it is proposed to locate the development and the nature of the potential effects of the development. Each decision on the need for EIA must be taken on the basis of a global assessment of all these factors. In general, it is not intended that special studies or technical

---

110. EIA Directive, Annex III above has been transposed into Irish legislation in the European Communities (Environmental Impact Assessment) (Amendment) Regulations 1999, Sch 3 and in PDR 2001, Sch 7.

evaluations will be necessary for the purpose of making a decision. The guidance below is designed to assist decision-making by people with the qualifications and experience typically found in competent/consent authorities.

It is the competent authority who must make the decision as to whether or not a project is likely to have significant effects on the environment. The competent authority's decision on that question could only be challenged by judicial review where it was seen to be unreasonable.

**[10.184]** The likeliest significant effects of a proposed project on the environment are not limited to negative effects only. The positive or beneficial effects must also be taken into account. The reason why significant effects include both adverse and beneficial effects was outlined by Elias J in *British Telecommunications plc v Gloucester City Council*[111] as follows:

> In my judgment an important feature of this democratic process, as the part of the Government publication which I have emphasised notes, is that individuals 'should form their own judgments on the significance of the environmental issue raised by the project'. This involves a recognition that it is not always clear whether an impact is beneficial or not. In particular, where the development of sites of historic or architectural interest are concerned, there will generally be a range of views held about the artistic and aesthetic features of the scheme and whether they best preserve the true character of the area which is the subject of the development. It would frustrate the process of debate about the merits of such a development if the planning authority could determine that the impact was beneficial and as a consequence rule that no environmental impact statement was needed.

**[10.185]** The European Commission guidance document on art 6 of the Habitats Directive concludes at s 4.4.1 that:

> The notion of what is 'significant' needs to be interpreted objectively. At the same time, the significance of effects should be determined in relation to the specific features and environmental conditions of the protected site concerned by the planning or project, taking particular account of the sites conservation objectives ... it is clear that what may be significant in relation to one site may not be in relation to another. For example, a loss of a 100 square metres of habitat may be significant in relation to a small rare orchid site, while a similar loss in a large steppic site may be insignificant.

**[10.186]** The Department of the Environment, Heritage and Local Government guidance documents supplies a checklist at para 5.39. The purpose of the checklist is to assist competent authorities in deciding whether the effects of a project are likely to be significant and in consequence of that decision whether an EIA is or is not required.

---

111. *British Telecommunications plc v Gloucester City Council* [2002] JPL 993 at 69. See also *Ó Nualláin v Dublin Corporation* [1999] 4 IR 137 at 148.

This checklist is helpful in understanding the criteria used by a competent authority when evaluating the significance of environmental effects:[112]

1. Will there be a large change in environmental conditions?
2. Will new features be out-of-scale with the existing environment?
3. Will the effect be particularly complex?
4. Will the effect extend over a large area?
5. Will there be any potential for transfrontier impact?
6. Will many people be affected?
7. Will many receptors of other types (fauna and flora, businesses, facilities) be affected?
8. Will valuable or scarce features or resources be affected?
9. Is there a risk that environmental standards will be breached?
10. Is there a risk that protected sites, areas, features will be affected?
11. Is there a high probability of the effect occurring?
12. Will the effect continue for a long time?
13. Will the effect be permanent rather than temporary?
14. Will the impact be continuous rather than intermittent?
15. If it is intermittent will it be frequent rather than rare?
16. Will the impact be irreversible?
17. Will it be difficult to avoid, or reduce or repair or compensate for the effect?

## EIA OF CERTAIN DEVELOPMENTS CARRIED OUT BY OR ON BEHALF OF LOCAL AUTHORITIES

**[10.187]** Because the local authority is frequently the competent authority which will make the assessment as to whether or not EIA is required in circumstances where, as competent authority, it concludes that a sub-threshold project proposal would be likely to have significant effects on the environment it would not be appropriate for the local authority to adjudicate its own cause. In such cases the local authority is obliged to prepare an EIS and to submit it for approval to An Bord Pleanála. The provision applies to a local authority that is a planning authority and to other persons on behalf of or jointly in partnership with such local authority pursuant to a contract entered into by that

---

112. The checklist is extracted from Guidance on EIA – Screening; June 2001; prepared for the European Commission by ERM (UK).

local authority.[113] All projects prescribed by the Minister under PDA 2000, s 176 must be subjected to EIA except for proposed road development under the Roads Act 1993. Sections 50 and 51 of the Roads Act 1993 (as amended) provide a separate procedure for the submissions of an EIS and the carrying out of an EIA in respect of certain road developments.

[10.188] Local authority development cannot be commenced until An Bord Pleanála approves the development with or without modifications.[114]

[10.189] Before submitting application to An Bord Pleanála a local authority must publish a notice in one or more newspapers circulating in the area in which it is proposed to carry out the development indicating the nature and location of the proposed development. The notice also states that the local authority is seeking approval of the board for the proposed development and that environmental impact statement has been prepared. If the development is likely to have transboundary effects that fact will also be disclosed in the notice. Members of the public must be given at least six weeks to allow them to participate in the process by the making of submissions or observations to the board relating to the implications of the development proposal for proper planning and sustainable development in the area concerned and the likely effects on the environment of the proposed development if carried out. Similar notices must be served on the prescribed authorities inviting submissions from them. Article 121 of PDR 2001, as amended by PDR 2006, lists the prescribed authorities and they will vary depending on the nature of the development. The notice must also specifically state that the board may give approval with or without conditions or that it may refuse the application.[115]

[10.190] PDA 2000, s 175(5)(a), as amended by s 34(a) of PD(SI)A 2006, permits the board to request a planning authority to furnish further information in relation to its application for approval for a proposed development to be undertaken by the local authority. The further information which may be sought under the section, as amended, relates to the effects on the environment of the proposed development or the consequences for proper planning and sustainable development in the area in which it is proposed to locate the development.

[10.191] Section 175(5)(a)(ii) permits the board to inform the local authority that it is provisionally of the view that it would grant approval if certain alterations are made. The subsection invites the local authority to submit further information regarding the suggested alterations and, if necessary, to submit a revised EIS. If alterations are submitted by the local authority they must be made available for public inspection and an invitation must be offered to the public to make submissions within three weeks. Prescribed authorities must also be notified of the proposed alterations and they too must be given an opportunity to make submissions within three weeks. If the board concludes that the response to the request for further information includes significant

---

113. PDA 2000, s 175(1)(a) and (b).
114. PDA 2000, s 175(2).
115. PDA 2000, s 175(4).

additional information concerning the likely effects on the environment or the improper planning and sustainable development of the area a notice must be published in a newspaper circulating in the area concerned stating that the further information as submitted by the local authority may be inspected by members of the public who may also make submissions in relation to such further information within a period of not less than three weeks.

**[10.192]** The assessment of whether additional information contains 'significant additional data' is carried out by the planning authority and not by the court. In Ireland, in the planning area at least, the courts have a marked reluctance to interfere with a decision of the appropriate authority and they will normally only do so where the decision made by the appropriate authority is, in the *O'Keefe* sense, irrational. McMahon J in *Klohn v An Bord Pleanála*[116] commented on this point as follows:

> It is recognised in cases such as this that the court in reviewing the Board's decision will not interfere with the bona fide exercise of its discretion in these matters. It is not the court's function to second-guess the Board and substitute its own decision for that of the Board. The legislature, in its wisdom, vested the power to make such a decision in a body which has expertise and experience in these matters. Such a body is much better qualified and in a much better position to make such technical decisions in this specialised area then the court, which has to rely on expert evidence to inform it in these cases. The courts will only interfere in such decisions where they appear so irrational that no reasonable authority or decision maker in this position would have made such a determination. Although the attitude has been criticised as being over-deferential, this judicial restraint is now well established in our juris prudence.

**[10.193]** PDA 2000, s 175(6), as amended by PD(SI)A 2006 and s 34, requires the board to consider the following matters in making its decision in respect of the proposed development, namely:

(a) the environmental impact assessment submitted and any submissions or observations made together with any other information furnished which relates to the likely effects on the environment of the proposed development and the likely consequences for proper planning and sustainable development in the area where the development is to take place.

(b) the views of the Member States of the EU and any State which is a party to the Transboundary Convention which has received a copy of the environmental impact assessment.

(c) the report and any recommendations of the person conducting a hearing in relation to compulsory purchase of land which relates wholly or partly to a proposed development under this section, where the evidence heard relates to (i) the likely effects on the environment of the proposed development, and (ii) the likely consequences for proper planning and sustainable development in the area where it is proposed to locate the development.

---

116. *Klohn v An Bord Pleanála* [2008] IEHC 111.

**[10.194]** PDA 2000, s 175(7) provides that a person conducting the oral hearing in relation to compulsory purchase of land which relates wholly or partly to a proposed development under this section is entitled to hear evidence relating to the likely effects on the environment or the proper planning and sustainable development of the area.

**[10.195]** PDA 2000, s 175(8)(a) provides that the board may, in exceptional circumstances, grant exemption from the requirement to submit an EIS in relation to a development proposed to be carried out by a local authority unless another Member State or another party to the Transboundary Convention has indicated that it wishes to furnish views on the effects of the environment in that State. Section 175(8)(b), as inserted by the European Communities (Environmental Impact Assessment) (Amendment) Regulations 2006 (reg 6(2)), requires the board in granting any exemption under para 8 to:

    (i) consider whether the effects, if any, of the proposed development on the environment should be assessed in some other form, and

    (ii) make available to members of the public the information relating to the exemption decision referred to under paragraph (a), the reasons for granting such exemption and the information obtained under any other form of assessment referred to in paragraph (i),

and the Board may apply such requirements regarding these matters in relation to the application for approval as it considers necessary or appropriate.

**[10.196]** Section 175(8)(c) requires that an exemption granted and the reasons for granting the exemption and any requirements applied under para (b) must be published in Iris Oifigiúil and in at least one daily newspaper published in the State. Exemption notices granted under para (a) must also be given to members of the public when requested and to the Commission of the European Communities.

**[10.197]** PDA 2000, s 175(9) and (9A) has been added by PD(SI)A 2006 s 34. Subsection (9)(a) permits the board to approve a proposed development but it has discretion to approve with modification also; it may approve part only of the proposal with or without modifications. It may also refuse approval or it may attach conditions to an approval. Subsection (9)(b) permits the board to impose a condition which will amount to a facility or service which could, in the opinion of the board, constitute a substantial gain to the community. The substantial gain must benefit the entire community and not just a selected part of it. It is not, however, a community gain without limit and sub-s (9)(c) requires that the conditions providing the community gain must not seek an amount of financial resources to be committed as would substantially deprive the person in whose favour the approval operates, of the benefits likely to accrue from the grant of approval. The amount to be spent by the developer in providing this is, in the first instance, determined by the board. The imposition of a condition allowing for a community gain can be justified by the fact that it is for the common good and that it would be proportionate to its objective.

**[10.198]** Subsection (9A) is also a new insert which allows the board to charge the local authority concerned for the costs and expenses incurred by it in determining the application for approval to include costs of the oral hearing, consultants' and/or advisors' fees and proportioned payments to staff members of the board for the time spent by them in dealing with the application. Any 'reasonable expenses' incurred in dealing with the application would also be covered by sub-s (9A).

**[10.199]** PDA 2000, s 175(10) provides that if the proposed development is one in respect of which an integrated pollution control licence or a waste licence is required, the board cannot impose conditions for the purpose of controlling emissions either from the operation of the activity or following its cessation. The Board may also decide to refuse permission for a proposed development for which an IPC licence or a waste licence is required or even where a licence or licences have been issued, where it considers that the development, notwithstanding the licensing of the activity, is unacceptable on environmental grounds, having regard to proper planning and sustainable development of the area in which the development is or will be situated.

**[10.200]** Before making a decision the board may request the Environmental Protection Agency (EPA) to make observations and the board must have regard to any such observations made and received. The making of observations by the EPA will not prejudice any other function of the EPA under PDA 2000. The Board may approve the development or approve the development subject to conditions (other than conditions concerning emissions) or it may refuse the permission for development.

**[10.201]** PDA 2000, s 175(11) provides that the Minister is given power to make regulations as to administrative matters in relation to the applications by the planning authority to the board for approval under PDA 2000, s 175(11). Those regulations may allow for a scoping request by the local authority to the board on matters of procedure regarding observations from the EPA, notification of other Member States of the European Union or other parties to the Transboundary Convention, and requiring the board to give information in respect of its decision regarding the proposed development for which approval is sought.

**[10.202]** PDA 2000, s 175(12) provides that in considering any information received by it relating to the likely consequences for proper planning and sustainable development, the board shall have regard to:

- the provisions of the development plan for the area,
- the provisions of any special amenity area order relating to the area,
- if the area or part of the area is a European site or an area described in the development plan for conservation or protection of the environment (and in particular archaeological and natural heritage),
- where relevant, the policies of the government, the Minister for the Environment, Heritage and Local Government or any other Minister,
- the provisions of PDA 2000 and the regulations made thereunder.

**[10.203]** PDA 2000, s 175(13) provides that any person contravening a condition imposed by the board under this section shall be guilty of an offence.

**[10.204]** PDA 2000, s 175(14) provides that s 175 does not apply to a proposed road development within the meaning of the Roads Act 1993 by or on behalf of a road authority. It should be noted, however, that PDA 2000, s 175 provides generally for EIA of development carried out by a local authority within its own functional area.

## EIA AND STATE AUTHORITY DEVELOPMENT

**[10.205]** PDA 2000, s 181, as amended by PD(SI)A 2006, s 35(a), provides that if the Minister is of the opinion that certain development is required in connection with or for the purposes of public safety or order, the administration of justice or national security or defence, regulations may be made exempting that class of development from the requirements of the Act of 2000. The Minister in dealing with this class of exempted development has further discretion to require that, if specified, it should be made subject to a form of public consultation as provided in s 181. There is a separate requirement for approval of certain State development requiring EIA.

**[10.206]** PDA 2000, s 181(a), as amended by PD(SI)A 2006, s 36 and by PD(A)A 2010, s 60, deals with the approval of certain State developments requiring EIA.

**[10.207]** State authority development, since the decision in *Howard v Commissioner of Public Works*,[117] unlike local authority development is not generally exempted development save, as seen, in respect of developments concerning public safety or order, the administration of justice or natural security or defence. Regulations have been drawn up to provide a procedure to deal with these exempted developments to include such things as development of garda stations, prisons, courthouses, barracks, offices relating to the legislature and ministerial departments and other similar developments and public notice requirements provided in PDR 2001, art 87, as amended by PDR 2006, art 20. The amended art 87 requires that public notice of the proposed State authority development must be given by publishing a notice in an approved newspaper and erecting or fixing a site notice on the land or structure where the proposed development would be situated. Article 87(1), as amended, applies to the classes of development specified in art 86(1)(a), (b) or (c) other than:

(a) development consisting of the construction or erection of such temporary structures for the purpose of or in connection with the operations of the Defence Forces or An Garda Síochána as are urgently required for reasons of national security, or

(b) development identified as likely to have significant effects on the environment in accordance with section 176 of the Act, and the development to which this Article applies is hereafter in this part referred to as 'proposed development'.

**[10.208]** Article 88 of PDR 2001, as amended by art 21 of PDR 2006, provides that notice of the proposed development will be given to the planning authority for the area

---

117. *Howard v Commissioner of Public Works* [1994] 1 IR 101.

and also to the Minister for Arts, Heritage, Gaeltacht and the Islands where the proposed development consists of or comprises the carrying out of works:

- (a) which would materially affect the character of a protected structure or proposed protected structure, or
- (b) to the exterior of a structure which is within an architectural conservation area.

**[10.209]** All classes of development specified under s 31 are bound by the s 181(1)(b) public consultation procedure with the exception of construction or erection of temporary structures which are urgently required for reasons of national security for purposes of or in connection with the operations of the Defence Forces or An Garda Síochána. The notices published in the newspaper and exhibited on the site must contain the following information:

- (a) the location, town land or postal address of the proposed development;
- (b) the nature and extent of the proposed development;
- (c) copies of the drawings and particulars of the development are to be made available for inspection in accordance with PDR 2001, art 89;
- (d) if the proposed development consists or comprises the carrying out of works which would materially affect the character of a protected structure or a proposed protected structure or would materially affect the exterior of the structure which is within an architectural conservation area that fact must be indicated in the notice;
- (e) invite submissions or observations in relation to the proposed development dealing with the proper planning and sustainable development of the area in which the development would be situate to be submitted in writing to the State authority within a period of six weeks from the date of the publication of the notice.

The relevant State authority must also send a copy of the notice of the proposed development to the relevant planning authority for the area and to the Minister for Environment, Heritage and Local Government in cases where the development would materially affect the character of a protected structure or of a proposed protected structure or where the development would materially alter the character of an architectural conservation area.

**[10.210]** PDR 2001, art 89, as amended by art 22 of PDR 2006, requires the State authority to make the following documents available for inspection for a period of six weeks beginning on the date in which the newspaper notice is published, namely:

- (a) a document describing, in outline, the nature and extent of the proposed development,
- (b) a location map, drawn to scale of not less than 1;1000 in built up areas and 1;2500 in all other areas (which shall be identified thereon) and marked or coloured so as to identify clearly the land on which it is proposed to carry out the development,

(c) in the case of proposed development referred to in Article 86(1)(a) or (b), drawings or particulars describing, in outline, the external appearance of the building, or other premises or installation, or other structure or facility, to be provided or extended (as the case may be), and

(d) in the case of proposed development referred to in Article 86(1)(c) such drawings or particulars as are necessary to show how the development would affect the character of a structure.

**[10.211]** PDR 2000, art 90 requires that the State authority shall have regard to the submissions or observations received from either a planning authority or from any other person or body in accordance with this Part. In taking these submission into account the State authority may decide that the proposed development will be carried out with our without variations of modifications or that it will not be carried out.

## APPROVAL OF CERTAIN STATE DEVELOPMENTS REQUIRING EIA

**[10.212]** Where a development to be carried out by a State authority is likely to have significant effects on the environment, EIA must be carried out.[118] The assessment to be made is carried out by An Bord Pleanála. The assessment procedure replaces the public consultation procedure. In effect, development specified in PDR 2001, art 86, such as garda stations, prisons, courthouses, barracks, certain office buildings used for the purposes of the President, the Oireachtas, the Department of the Taoiseach and the Office of the Tánaiste, and the Departments of Defence, Foreign Affairs, Justice, Court Service, the Attorney General Office, the Office of the Chief State Solicitor and the Office of the Director of Public Prosecutions will require EIA where the development is likely to have significant effects on the environment even though they are exempt from the necessity to apply for formal planning permission. Whereas assessment as to whether an EIS is required under the EU Directive is limited to development projects which come within the scope of Annex I and Annex II, all development specified in art 86 of PDR 2001, as amended, will require EIA without further query, if it is a development which is likely to have significant effects on the environment. The requirement for assessment in relation to EIA under Irish national law is broader than the requirement for assessment under the EIA Directive.

**[10.213]** Unless An Bord Pleanála has carried out the assessment and unless the board has approved the State's development proposal with or without modifications, the development cannot proceed.

**[10.214]** A State authority is defined as and referred to as 'a prospective applicant' but, in fact, both terms are used in PDA 2000, ss 181A, 181B and 181C (as inserted and as amended).

---

118. PDA 2000, s 181A(2) as inserted by PD(SI)A 2006, s 36.

**[10.215]** Before making an application for approval under s 181B a prospective applicant (State authority) must enter into consultations with the board in relation to the proposed development.[119]

**[10.216]** Both screening and scoping are available to a prospective applicant when applying for approval under PDA 2000, s 181B (as inserted and as amended) on application to the board to request it:

(a) to make a determination of whether a development of a class specified in regulations made under section 181(1)(a) which it proposes to carry out or have carried out is likely to have significant effects on the environment in accordance with section 176 (and inform the applicant of the determination), or

(b) to give the applicant an opinion in writing prepared by the Board on what information will be required to be contained in an environmental impact statement in relation to the proposed development.[120]

The Board is obliged to keep a written record of any consultations held with the perspective applicant in relation to the proposed development and to keep a record of the names of the persons who participated in the consultations. A copy of the record must be placed with the documents to which any application in respect of the proposed development relates.[121]

## STATE AUTHORITY'S APPLICATION FOR APPROVAL TO AN BORD PLEANÁLA

**[10.217]** Where a State authority proposes to carry out development which is for the purpose of public safety or order, the administration of justice or national security or defence in accordance with the regulations[122] and where the development is identified as likely to have significant effects on the environment or adverse effects on the integrity of a European site as the case may be, the authority shall prepare or cause to be prepared an application for approval of the development under s 181B and an EIS or a Natura impact statement or both of those statements as the case may be in respect of the development and shall apply to the board for such approval.[123]

**[10.218]** Before making the application for approval the State must publish a public notice in a newspaper circulating in the area where the development is to take place indicating the nature and location of the proposed development and stating that:

(I) it proposes to seek the approval of the Board for the proposed development,

---

119. PDA 2000, s 181C as inserted by PD(SI)A 2006, s 36.
120. PDA 2000, s 181C(3) as inserted by PD(SI)A 2006, s 36. 3(a) is 'screening' and 3(b) is 'scoping'.
121. PDA 2000, s 181C(7) as inserted by PD(SI)A 2006.
122. PDA 2000, s 181A(1) as inserted by PD(SI)A 2006, s 36 and as amended by PD(A)A 2010, s 60.
123. See specifically PDA 2000, s 181A(3) as inserted by PD(SI)A 2006, s 36 and as amended by PD(A)A 2010, s 60.

(II) an environmental impact statement or a Natura impact statement or both of these statements, as the case may be, has been prepared in respect of the proposed development,

(III) where relevant, the proposed development is likely to have significant effects on the environment in another Member State of the European Communities or other party to the Transboundary Convention.[124]

The notice must also specify the times and places where the documents may be inspected free of charge or purchased at a fee not exceeding the reasonable cost of making a copy during a period of six weeks from the date of the notice. The notice invites members of the public during the six week period to make submissions or observations to An Bord Pleanála relating to:

(I) the implications of the proposed development for proper planning and sustainable development in the area or areas concerned, and

(II) the likely effects on the environment or adverse effects on the integrity of a European site as the case may be of the proposed development if carried out,[125]

and specifying the types of decision the Board may make, under section 181B in relation to the application.

[10.219] The State authority is required to send a copy of the application and the EIS or Natura impact statement or both, as the case may be, to the local authority or to each local authority in whose functional area the proposed development would be located and to any prescribed bodies together with a note stating that submissions or observations may be made during the six-week period in writing to the board in relation to:

(i) the implications of the proposed development for proper planning and sustainable development in the area concerned, and

(ii) the likely effects on the environment or adverse effects on the integrity of a European site as the case may be of the proposed development, if carried out.[126]

Where the proposed development is likely to have significant effects on the environment of a Member State of the European Communities or on a State which is a party to the Transboundary Convention the State authority must also send copies of the application and the EIS to the prescribed authority of the relevant State advising it that submissions or observations may be made to An Bord Pleanála.[127]

[10.220] The Board may require the State authority to furnish further and better information in relation to the effects on proper planning and sustainable development or

---

124. See specifically PDA 2000, s 181A(3) as inserted by PD(SI)A 2006, s 36 and as amended by PD(A)A 2010, s 60.
125. See PDA 2000, s 181A(3)(iii) as inserted by PD(SI)A 2006, s 36 and as amended by PD(A)A 2010, s 60.
126. PDA 2000, s 181A(3)(b)(i) and (ii) as inserted by PD(SI)A 2006 and as amended by PD(A)A 2010, s 60.
127. PDA 2000, s 181A(3)(c) as inserted by PD(SI)A 2006.

the environment of the proposed development as the board may specify. If the board is provisionally of the view that the State authority's proposal should be approved subject to certain alterations it may notify the State authority of that view and invite the State authority to make the alteration specified in the notification. If the alterations require submission of a further EIS or the submission of a Natura impact statement or both the board shall request same from the State authority.[128]

**[10.221]** If the board considers that further information received contains significant additional data relating to the likely effects on the environment of the proposed development and the likely consequences for proper planning and sustainable development in the area or areas in which it is proposed to situate the said development, where the State authority has made the alterations specified in the notice given to it by the board the board shall require the State authority to give further public notice and further notice to the prescribed bodies allowing them a period of at least three weeks for the making of further submissions and observations.

## APPROVAL OF STATE AUTHORITY'S PROPOSED DEVELOPMENT

**[10.222]** In making a decision to approve or not to approve the State authority's development proposal An Bord Pleanála must consider the following matters:

    (a)    the environmental impact statement or a Natura impact statement or both of those statements as the case may be submitted pursuant to section 181A(1) or (4), any submissions or observations made in accordance with sections 181A(3) or (7) and any other information furnished in accordance with section 181A(4) relating to–

        (i)    the likely consequences for proper planning and sustainable development in the area in which it is proposed to situate the proposed development of such development, and

        (ii)    the likely effects on the environment or adverse effects on the integrity of a European site as the case may be of the proposed development and,

    (b)    the report and any recommendations of a person conducting any oral hearing relating to the proposed development.[129]

Where the board is satisfied that exceptional circumstances so warrant it may grant the State authority an exemption from the requirement to prepare an EIS or a Natura impact statement or both of those statements as the case may be but the exemption cannot be granted where another Member State of the EU or a State which is party to the Transboundary Convention has indicated that it wishes to furnish views on the effects of

---

128. PDA 2000, s 181A(4)(a) and (b) as inserted by PD(SI)A 2006 and as amended by PD(A)A 2010, s 60.
129. PDA 2000, s 181(B)(1).

the environment in that Member State.[130] In granting an exemption the board shall consider whether:

    (a)    the effects, if any, of the proposed development on the environment or adverse effects, if any of the proposed development on the integrity of a European site should be assessed in some other manner and,

    (b)    the information arising from such an assessment should be made available to the members of the public and it may apply such requirements regarding these matters in relation to the application for approval as it considers necessary or appropriate.[131]

The Minister for Defence is empowered to grant an exemption from the requirement to prepare and submit an EIS or a Natura impact statement or both statements where the development proposed is for the purposes of national defence where the Minister is satisfied that the assessment procedure for the preparation of the EIS or the Natura impact statement would have adverse effects on those national defence purposes.[132]

**[10.223]** Where notice of exemption is granted by An Bord Pleanála in exceptional circumstances or by the Minister for the purposes of national defence, notice of the exemption must be published in Iris Oifigiúil and in at least one daily newspaper as soon as may be and notice must also be given together with a copy of the information, if any, made available to members of the public, to the Commission of the European Communities.[133]

**[10.224]** In dealing with an application under PDA 2000, s 181A (as inserted) for the approval of a proposed development the board may:

    (a)    approve the proposed development,

    (b)    make such modifications to the proposed development as it specifies in the approval and approve the proposed development as so modified,

    (c)    approve, in part only, the proposed development (with or without specified modifications of it of the foregoing kind),

           or

    (d)    refuse to approve the proposed development,

and may attach to an approval under paragraph (a), (b) or (c) such conditions as it considers appropriate.[134]

Without prejudice to the generality of the board's power to attach conditions, the board may expressly attach a condition obliging the State authority to provide:

    (a)    the construction or financing, in whole or in part, of the construction of a facility or

---

130. PDA 2000, s 181B(2) as inserted by PD(SI)A 2006 and as amended by PD(A)A 2010, s 61.
131. PDA 2000, s 181B(3) as inserted by PD(SI)A 2006.
132. PDA 2000, s 181B(4) as inserted by PD(SI)A 2006 and as amended by PD(A)A 2010, s 61.
133. PDA 2000, s 181B(5) as inserted by PD(SI)A 2006.
134. PDA 2000, s 181B(6) as inserted by PD(SI)A 2006.

(b) the provision or the financing, in whole or in part, of the provision of a service;

in the area in which the proposed development would be situated being a facility or service that, in the opinion of the Board would constitute a substantial gain to the community.

The power of An Bord Pleanála to provide a planning gain is subject to a restriction to the effect that a condition shall not require such an amount of financial resources to be committed for the purposes of the condition being complied with as would substantially deprive the person in whose favour the approval under this section operates of the benefits likely to accrue from the grant of the approval.[135]

## *European Commission v Ireland* C–50/09

**[10.225]** The Commission complained that Ireland had failed to fulfil its obligations under Council Directive 85/337/EEC of 27 June 1985[136] on the assessment of the effects of certain public and private projects on the environment as amended by Council Directive 97/11/EC of 3 March 1997[137] and by Directive 2003/35/EC of the European Parliament and of the Council of 26 May 2003[138] referred to as 'Directive 85/337' by its failure to transpose art 3 of Directive 85/337. The Commission also complained that Ireland, by failing to ensure that, where Irish planning authorities and the Environmental Protection Agency (EPA) both have decision-making powers on a project, there should be complete fulfilment of the requirements of arts 2–4 of that Directive. The Commission further complained that by excluding demolition works from the scope of its legislation on transposing that Directive, Ireland has failed to fulfil its obligation under that Directive.

**[10.226]** As seen in this Chapter, Pt X comprises s 172 to s 177 inclusive. Pt X of PDA 2000 is amended by PD(SI)A 2006 is further amended by PD(A)A 2010.

**[10.227]** By letter dated 19 November 1998 Ireland was formally put on notice that it had not correctly transposed arts 2–6, 8 and 9 of Directive 85/337/EEC. The letter was accompanied by a reasoned opinion. Ireland's response was that it needed more time but that legislative amendments were being prepared to ensure that the relevant article would be correctly transposed. Nothing occurred for some four years and almost nine months later when a further letter was sent by the Commission which was replied to by Ireland by making the case that Irish legislation did constitute an adequate transposition of the Directive. The Commission did not agree with Ireland's submission and it commenced proceedings at the European Court of Justice (ECJ).[139]

---

135. PDA 2000, s 181B(7) and (8) as inserted by PD(SI)A 2006.
136. [1985] OJ L175.
137. [1997] OJ L73.
138. [2003] OJ L156.
139. *Commission v Ireland* (Case C–50/09) (3 March 2011).

[10.228] The first complaint was the allegation that Ireland had failed to transpose art 3 of the Directive 85/337 into its national legislation.[140]

[10.229] The Commission argued that art 3 is of pivotal importance in setting out what constitutes an EIA and that accordingly art 3 must be transposed 'explicitly'. PDA 2000, s 173(1) to (3)[141] requires the planning authority and the board to have regard to the statement and to any supplemental information furnished to include any submissions or observations concerning the effect on the environment of the proposed development. The sections in Irish legislation do not 'explicitly' require that the EIA which is carried out must specifically identify, describe and assess all of the matters referred to in art 3 which include effects, either direct or indirect, of the development on human beings, fauna, flora, soil, water, air, climate, the landscape, material assets and cultural heritage. It also includes the interaction between all of those factors.

[10.230] Articles 94, 108 and 111 of Sch 6 of PDR 2001[142] are confined, in the Commission's view, firstly to the setting out of matters on which the developer must supply information in his/her EIS and secondly to specifying the obligation on the competent authority to establish that the information is complete. The obligations laid down by those provisions are different from the obligations imposed on the competent authority by art 3 of Directive 85/337, namely the carrying out of a full EIA.[143]

[10.231] By way of defence Ireland made the case that art 3 of Directive 85/337 was transposed fully by PDA 2000, s 172(1)[144] and s 173[145] and by PDR 2000 as amended by PDR 2008 Sch 6, art 94 and by art 108, respectively.

[10.232] Ireland also argued that two Supreme Court judgments had ruled that planning authorities and the EPA are required to assess all other factors referred to in art 3 and the interaction between them.[146] It was Ireland's case that these judgments should be taken into consideration when assessing the scope of national provisions at issue. Not surprisingly, the Commission correctly made the case that while the courts may interpret ambiguous provisions so as to ensure their compatibility with the Directive, the judgments of the courts are interpretive and are not legislative. What counts is the real meaning of Directive 85/337/EEC itself.[147]

---

140. Directive 85/337, art 3.
141. Note PDA 2000, s 173(2) was substituted by PD(SI)A 2006, s 32.
142. Note PDR 2001 specifies the information to be contained in an EIS, details measurements for implantation of PDA 2000 and it has been amended by PDR 2008.
143. See *Commission v Ireland* (Case C–50/09) (3 March 2011) judgment of the Court (First Chamber), para 28, p 6.
144. PDA 2000, s 172(1) and (1A) a substituted by PD(A)A 2010, s 54(a).
145. PDA 2000, s 173(2) as substituted by PD(SI)A 2006, s 32.
146. *O'Connell v Environmental Protection Agency* [2003] 1 IR 530 and *Martin v An Bord Pleanála* [2007] IESC 23 (10 May 2007).
147. See *Commission v Ireland* (Case C–50/09) (3 March 2011) judgment of the Court (First Chamber), paras 31 and 32, p 6.

**[10.233]** Ireland further made the case that the concepts of 'proper planning' and 'sustainable development' referred to in PDA 2000, s 34[148] together with all the criteria referred to in PDA 2000, s 34 have fully and explicitly transposed arts 2–6, 8 and 9 of Directive 85/437 into Irish law.

**[10.234]** Ireland complained that the Commission did not respect the discretions enjoyed by Member States under art 249 EC as to the form and methods for transposing a Directive. By requiring the literal transposition of art 3 of Directive 85/337 the Commission has disregarded the body of legislation and case law built up in Ireland over 45 years surrounding the concepts of 'proper planning' and 'sustainable development'.[149]

**[10.235]** A difference emerged between Ireland and the Commission on the interpretation of art 3 Directive 85/337. The Commission's view is that art 3 clearly lays down obligations which go beyond the requirements of arts 4 to 11. Ireland, on the other hand, held the view that art 3 is no more than a provision drafted in general terms but that arts 4 to 11 set out the details of the process of EIA.

**[10.236]** Article 3 clearly does not make the competent environmental authority responsible for carrying out an EIA which assessment must be carried out before any consent is granted, being the consent which would enable the project to proceed. The EIA to be made must also include a description of the project's direct and indirect effects on human beings, flora and fauna, soil, water, air, climatic factors, the landscape, material assets including architectural and archaeological heritage and cultural heritage, and the interaction between those factors.[150]

**[10.237]** The Commission's clear interpretation was that the assessment obligation is distinct from the obligations laid down in arts 4, 7, 10 and 11 of Directive 85/337. These latter obligations are obligations to collect and exchange information, consult, publicise and guarantee the possibility of challenge before the courts. These are procedural provisions which do not cover the implementation of the substantial obligation laid down in art 3 of that Directive.[151]

**[10.238]** The assessment obligation and the obligation to take into consideration all of the information gathered by a planning authority or by other competent body are quite distinct processes and the assessment process must be undertaken before the decision making process.[152]

---

148. PDA 2000, s 34 as respectively inserted and substituted by PD(SI)A 2006, by the Protection of the Environment Act 2003 and by PD(A)A 2010.
149. See *Commission v Ireland* (Case C–50/09) (3 March 2011) judgment of the Court (First Chamber), para 33, p 7.
150. *Commission v Spain* (Case C–332/04) [2006] ECR I–40, para 33.
151. See *Commission v Ireland* (Case C–50/09) (3 March 2011) judgment of the Court (First Chamber), paras 34–38, p 7.
152. *Commission v United Kingdom* (Case C–508/03) [2006] ECR 1–3969 para 103.

**[10.239]** The ECJ found that art 3 is a fundamental provision and further that the transposition of arts 4–11 alone cannot be regarded as transposing art 3.[153] In examining PDA 2000, s 172 and s 173 together with art 94 and with the Sixth Schedule of PDR 2001, as amended by PDR 2008, the ECJ concluded that the obligation imposed by that legislation does not correspond to the broader obligation imposed by art 3 of the Directive 85/337 on the competent environmental authority, namely, the obligation for the planning authority or the board to carry out an EIA. However, this has been rectified and s 172(1) has been substituted and s 172(1A) has been inserted by PD(A)A 2010, s 54(a).[154] In the meantime, the ECJ ruled that national provisions invoked by Ireland did not (at least prior to the amendments made) attain the result required pursuant to art 3 of Directive 85/337.

**[10.240]** Paragraph 46 of the judgment of the Court (First Chamber) handed down on 3 March 2011 in Case–50/09 reads:

> Whilst it is true that, according to settled case-law, the transposition of a directive into domestic law does not necessarily require the provisions of the directive to be enacted in precisely the same words in a specific, express provision of national law and a general legal context may be sufficient if it actually ensures the full application of the directive in a sufficiently clear and precise manner (see, in particular, Case C–427/07 *Commission v Ireland* [2009] ECR 1–6227, paragraph 54 and the case-law cited), the fact remains that according to equally settled case-law, the provisions of a directive must be implemented with unquestionable binding force and with the specificity, decision and clarity required in order to satisfy the need for legal certainty, which requires that, in the case of a directive intended to confer rights on individuals, the persons concerned must be enabled to ascertain the full extent of their rights (see, in particular, Commission v Ireland, at paragraph 55 and the case-law cited).[155]

**[10.241]** The ECJ also considered *O'Connell v Environmental Protection Agency*.[156] The court agreed that the judgment in that case contained an interpretation of domestic law which was consistent with Directive 85/337. However, the ECJ ruled that even if a consistent interpretation of the provisions of domestic law was outlined, that interpretation by the Supreme Court in Ireland cannot achieve the clarity and precision needed to meet the requirements of legal certainty.

**[10.242]** The ECJ held that *Martin v An Bord Pleanála*[157] did not assist Ireland's case because the Supreme Court decision in that case has no bearing on the question, which is decisive for the purposes of determining the first complaint, and which alleged failure

---

153. See *Commission v Ireland* (Case C–50/09) (3 March 2011) judgment of the Court (First Chamber), para 41, p 18.
154. Interestingly the amendments made by PD(A)A 2010, s 54(a) were commenced on 19 August 2010 in advance of the decision of Case C–50/09 which judgment was handed down on 3 March 2011.
155. *Commission v Ireland* (Case C–50/09) (3 March 2011), at para 46.
156. *O'Connell v Environmental Protection Agency* [2003] 1 IR 530.
157. *Martin v An Bord Pleanála* [2007] IESC 23 (10 May 2007).

**[10.243]** to transfer art 3 of Directive 85/337, on what the examination of the factors by the competent national authority should comprise.[158]

**[10.243]** The ECJ also rejected Ireland's argument that the concept of 'proper planning' and 'sustainable development' did not mean that art 3 had been correctly transposed as it does not establish that the requirement is that those criteria be taken into account in all cases for which EIA is required.[159]

**[10.244]** The Commission's first complaint was held to be well founded.

**[10.245]** The second complaint alleged failure to ensure compliance with arts 2–4 of Directive 85/337 because, in relation to certain projects requiring EIA, the process comprises two separate decision-making processes. The first process involves a decision-making on land use aspects of the project by the planning authority or by An Bord Pleanála. The second process involves decision-making by the Environmental Protection Agency (EPA) on pollution aspects. The Commission made no objection to the fact that there were two decision-making processes as such but it criticised the fact that Irish legislation failed to impose any obligation on the planning authority, or on An Bord Pleanála, or on the EPA to coordinate their activities. Ireland objected both to the admissibility of the second complaint and to the substance of that complaint. Ireland's plea of inadmissibility was rejected by the ECJ.

**[10.246]** The Commission made the case that it had identified, in the Irish legislation, a gap arising from the combination of two factors. The first factor is the fact that the EPA has no statutory entitlement to require EIA when it receives an application from a prospective licensee to cover the pollution aspects of the proposed development.

**[10.247]** The second factor is the probability that an application for a licence dealing with pollution aspects of the proposed development may, under the Irish legislative regime, be received before application is made to the planning authority and before any application for planning permission is made. There is nothing in the EPA Regulations which gives the EPA the right to advise a planning authority of any application for a licence which it receives. The EPA is not bound to notify the planning authority. The conclusion must be that the EPA, as the authority responsible for licensing a project as regards pollution aspects, may make a decision as to whether or not to grant the licence without any EIA having been carried out in accordance with arts 2–4 of Directive 85/337.

**[10.248]** The ECJ held that the Commission's second complaint, in support of its action for failure to fulfil obligations, is well founded.[160]

---

158. See *Commission v Ireland* (Case C–50/09) (3 March 2011) judgment of the Court (First Chamber), para 47, at p 8.
159. See *Commission v Ireland* (Case C–50/09) (3 March 2011) judgment of the Court (First Chamber), para 48, at p 8.
160. See *Commission v Ireland* (Case C–50/09) (3 March 2011) judgment of the Court (First Chamber), paras 50–85, at pp 9 to 13.

[10.249] The third complaint made was that the Commission alleged that Ireland failed to apply Directive 85/337 to demolition works. It was the submission of the Commission that demolition work may constitute a 'project' within the meaning of art 1(2) of Directive 85/337, which reads:

> For the purpose of this Directive:
>
> 'Project' means:
>
> - the execution of construction works or of other installations or schemes.
> - Other interventions in the natural surroundings and landscape including those involving the extraction of mineral resources.
>
> 'developer' means:
>
> - The applicant for authorisation for a private project or the public authority which initiates a project.
>
> 'development consent' means:
>
> - The decision of the competent authority or authorities which entitles the developer to proceed with the project.

Because 'demolition work' falls within the concept of 'other intervention in natural surroundings and landscape', Ireland had excluded demolition works from the scope of the national legislation transposing Directive 85/337. At the time that the complaint was made by the Commission, and at the date that the Commission lodged its additional reasoned opinion, demolition works were not, as a general rule, subject to EIA and, indeed, such demolition was, in principle, entitled to exemption from EIA.

[10.250] Demolition of a national monument under the provisions of the National Monuments Act 1930, s 14(1)(a) and (b) takes no account of the possibility that such demolition work might constitute a 'project' within the meaning of art 1(2) of the Directive 85/337 and as such it would require EIA.

[10.251] The Commission's third complaint was held to be well founded.

[10.252] Paragraph 107 of the judgment of the Court (First Chamber) in Case C–50/09 reads:

> Accordingly, it must be declared that:
>
> – by failing to transpose Article 3 of Directive 85/337;
>
> – by failing to ensure that, where planning authorities and the agency both have decision-making powers concerning a project, there will be a complete fulfilment of the requirements of Article 2 to 4 of that directive; and
>
> – by excluding demolition works from the scope of its legislation transposing that directive,
>
> Ireland has failed to fulfil its obligation under that directive.

Ireland was ordered to pay the costs of the case.

**[10.253]** In anticipation of the judgment in Case C–50/09 going against Ireland (as it did on the 3 March 2011), PDA 2000, s 172(1) was substituted by and sub-s (1A) was inserted by PD(A)A 2010, s 54(a), and the subsections were commenced on 19 August 2010 by SI 405/2010. The substituted and amended s 172(1) now makes examination and scrutinisation of applications a compulsory part of the process to establish whether or not EIA and EIS are necessary.

**[10.254]** The Commission's second complaint related to the split decision-making where the planning authority or the board grant permission but a licence is necessary from the EPA or other body, for example, for the discharge of water or dealing with pollution in one way or another. The Commission had alleged failure to ensure full compliance with arts 2–4 of Directive 85/337 where more than one authority is involved in the decision making. Effectively, the second complaint, in the Commission's view, required to be remedied so that the EPA or other licensing body would have the power to request EIA, particularly in circumstances where the application for an EPA licence or other licence was made before the application for planning permission.

**[10.255]** The situation giving rise to that complaint has now been remedied by the Planning and Development (Amendment) Regulations 2008 (SI 256/2008). Article 9 of PDR 2001 dealing with restrictions on exemption has been amended by the insertion after sub-art (2) of a new article which reads:

> (3) For the avoidance of doubt, sub-article 1(a)(vii) shall not apply to any operation or activity in respect of which a Minister of the Government has granted consent or approval in accordance with the requirements of regulation 31 of the Habitats Regulations 1997, and where Regulation 31(5) does not apply.

The explanatory note appearing on SI 256/2008 reads as follows:

> The purpose of these Regulations is to amend Article 9 of the Planning & Development Regulations 2001 to provide for the reinstatement of an exemption where an appropriate assessment has been concluded satisfactorily.

At the date of going to press no legislation has been introduced to deal with the third complaint, which held that Ireland failed to apply Directive 85/337 to demolition works, but it is understood that that legislation is now in the course of preparation.

# Chapter 11

# STRUCTURAL INFRASTRUCTURE DEVELOPMENT

## INTRODUCTION

[11.01] The Planning and Development (Strategic Infrastructure) Act 2006 (PD(SI)A 2006) provides a special planning application procedure for strategic infrastructure development whereby the planning authority is bypassed and the planning application is made directly to An Bord Pleanála. PD(SI)A 2006 required the board to set up a new division within the board to be known as the strategic infrastructure division.[1] The purpose of the strategic infrastructure division within the board is to deal directly with applications for strategic infrastructure projects. The need to streamline the planning process in relation to applications for permission to develop strategic infrastructure was recognised and after the PD(SI)B had passed through the Senate the Act was commenced on 16 July 2006. Details of the 'application process' are contained in the Planning and Development Regulations (PDR 2001–2008).

[11.02] The term 'strategic infrastructure' has specific meaning given to it in PDA 2000, as amended by PD(SI)A 2006 and amended by PD(A)A 2010. Strategic infrastructure includes the following:

(i) Development listed as infrastructure development in the Seventh Schedule of PDA 2000 for the purposes of ss 37A and 37B.[2]

(ii) Development belonging to a class of development, identified for the purposes of s 176,[3] proposed by a local authority or by some other person on behalf of or jointly in partnership with such local authority to be carried out within the area of the local authority and which is referred to in PDA 2000, s 175(1), requiring an environmental impact assessment (EIA).[4]

---

1. PDA 2000, ss 112 and 112A. PDA 2000, s 112(4) inserted by PD(SI)A 2006, s 18 and PDA 2000, s 112A inserted by PD(SI)A 2006, s 19.
2. The Seventh Schedule has been inserted by PD(SI)A 2006, s 5. The types of infrastructural development projects listed (many of which are referenced to thresholds) may qualify as 'strategic infrastructure' development for the purposes of the Act but to do so they must (a) be of strategic economic or social importance to the State or, (b) contribute significantly to the fulfilment of the objectives of the National Spatial Strategy or, (c) have a significant effect on an area of more than one planning authority.
3. PDA 2000, s 176(1) is amended by PD(A)A 2010, s 56. PDA 2000, s 176 deals with prescribed classes of development requiring assessment and, particularly, s 176 allows the Minister to make regulations in relation to EIA. See PDR 2000, Pt 10, Schs 5, 6 and 7.
4. PDA 2000, s 175 which deals with the requirement for EIA of certain development carried out by or on behalf of a local authority.

(iii) Development proposed by a local authority or by some other person on behalf of or jointly in partnership with such local authority to be carried out within the area of the local authority and which comprises development on the foreshore which will be likely to have significant effects on the environment.[5]

(iv) Development proposed by State authorities requiring EIA to include, specifically, development which has been exempted from the necessity to obtain planning permission but which development is likely to have significant effects on the environment. The State authority, unlike all other applicants seeking approval from the board in respect of strategic infrastructure developments, is not required to consult with the board before making an application.[6]

(v) Where an undertaker intends to carry out development for the purposes of electricity transmission, the application is made, in the first instance, to An Bord Pleanála.[7]

(vi) Where an undertaker intends to develop strategic gas infrastructure[8] the application is made, in the first instance, to An Bord Pleanála.

## SYNOPSIS OF THE SEVENTH SCHEDULE

**[11.03]** What is probably the most common form of a direct strategic infrastructure planning application relates to development which falls within one of the four categories listed in PDA 2000, Seventh Schedule[9] under the headings:

(1) energy infrastructure;

(2) transport infrastructure;

(3) environmental infrastructure;

(4) health infrastructure.[10]

There are 13 categories of energy infrastructure, four categories of transport infrastructure, 11 categories of environmental infrastructure and one category of health infrastructure.

**[11.04]** The heading beneath the Seventh Schedule reads:

Infrastructure Developments for the purposes of Sections 37A and 37B.

---

5. PDA 2000, s 226(6). The developments listed at (ii) and (iii) are developments to be carried out by or in partnership with a local authority which would be normally be exempt from the requirement to obtain ordinary planning permission.
6. PDA 2000, s 181A inserted by PD(SI)A 2006, s 36.
7. PDA 2000, s 182A as inserted PD(SI)A 2006, s 4 and amended by PD(A)A 2010, s 63(a).
8. PDA 2000, s 182C inserted by PD(SI)A 2006, s 4 and amended by PD(A)A 2010, s 65(a), (b), (c), (d), (e) and (f).
9. PDA 2000, Sch 7 as inserted by PD(SI)A 2006, s 5.
10. Paragraph 4 as amended by PD(A)A 2010, s 78(c).

For a full understanding of these schedules it is well worth reading the entire Schedule but set out below is a synopsis of the contents of the four categories listed:

1. Energy infrastructure deals with onshore extraction of petroleum or natural gas, crude oil refineries, thermal power stations, electricity generating stations, oil pipelines and associated terminals, surface storage of natural gas, underground storage of combustible gases, surface storage of oil or coal, hydroelectric energy production stations, windfarms, onshore thermal installations for storage of natural gas and LNG facilities (this means a thermal used for liquefaction of natural gas). In each case a threshold is specified.

2. Transport infrastructure to include intermodal transhipment facilities for passengers or for goods, terminal buildings or installations for railways, tramways, surface, elevated or underground railway or railway supported by suspended lines made for the purpose of passenger transport, large airports, runways, taxiways, piers, car parks, terminals and all facilities whether for air passengers or for cargo and certain harbours and port installations.[11] Thresholds are specified for each different category of transport infrastructure listed in this paragraph.

3. Environmental infrastructure to include waste disposal by incineration, landfill or chemical treatment for hazardous waste and for non-hazardous waste and generally in dealing with waste water treatment, transfer of water resources between river basins, waste water treatment plants, sludge disposal, flood relief schemes, dams for water storage, aquaducts and coastal erosion schemes.[12]

4. Health infrastructure in the Seventh Schedule includes development of a healthcare centre providing inpatient services but excluding a development which is predominantly for the purpose of providing care service within the meaning of s 3 of the Nursing Home Support Scheme Act 2009.[13]

## Thresholds in the Seventh Schedule

**[11.05]** Some examples of thresholds in the Seventh Schedule are:

1. Crude oil refineries or installations for gasification and liquefaction are subject to a 500 tonnes or more of coal or bituminous shale per day.

2. Thermal power station and industrial installations for production of electricity are subject to an output of 300 megawatts or more.

3. An oil pipeline with its associates terminals, buildings and installations requires that the length of the pipeline would need to exceed 20 kilometres.

---

[11]. The part of para 2 dealing with Harbours and Ports is the result of an amendment made by PD(A)A 2010, s 78(b).
[12]. The Seventh Schedule was inserted by PD(SI)A 2006, s 5 and it generally covers large scale environmental infrastructure. A reading of the Schedule is advisable particularly to note the various thresholds imposed in each case.
[13]. Paragraph 4 as amended by PD(A)A 2010, s 78(c).

4. An installation for underground storage of combustible gases requires that the storage capacity would need to exceed 200 tonnes.

5. Hyrdoelectric installations must have 300 megawatt output or more or where the new or extended superficial area of water impounded would be 30 hectares or more or where there would be a 30 per cent change in maximum, minimum or mean flows in the main river channel.

6. Windfarms for harnessing wind power for energy production with more than 25 turbines must have a total output greater than 50 megawatts.[14]

7. Only large airports with not less than two million instances of passenger use *per annum* to include any runway, taxiway, pier, car park, terminal or other facilities or installations relating to it are covered.

8. A waste disposal installation for the incineration or chemical treatment of non-hazardous waste must have a capacity for annual intake which is greater than 100,000 tonnes.

9. A groundwater abstraction or artificial groundwater re-charge scheme requires that the annual volume of water abstracted or re-charged must be equivalent to or exceed two million cubic metres.

10. A sludge/deposition site must have a capacity per annum of the deposition of 500,000 tonnes of sludge (wet).

11. A dam or any installation designed for holding back water for permanent or long term storage, where the new or extended area of water impounded would be thirty hectares or more or where a new or additional amount of water held back or stored would exceed ten million cubic metres.

If the thresholds are exceeded EIA and the subsequent preparation of an environmental impact statement (EIS) is mandatory. Even if the thresholds are not exceeded, if it can be shown that the project, or plant, etc, is likely to have a significant effect on the environment then EIA and the preparation of an EIS will also be mandatory.

## CASES OF STRATEGIC INFRASTRUCTURE OTHER THAN THOSE LISTED IN THE SEVENTH SCHEDULE

**[11.06]** Apart from the infrastructure developments listed in the Seventh Schedule for the purposes of ss 37A and 37B, strategic infrastructure includes the following:

1. Development proposed by a local authority or by some other person on behalf of, or jointly in partnership with, such a local authority to be carried out within the area of the local authority's boundaries and which requires an EIA.[15]

2. Development proposed by a local authority or by some other person on behalf of, or jointly in partnership with, such local authority to be carried out within

---

14. This threshold used to refer to 50 turbines or a windfarm with an output in excess of 100 megawatts. This has been amended by PD(A)A 2010, s 78(a).
15. PDA 2000, s 175(1).

the area of the local authority's boundaries comprising development of the foreshore which would be likely to have significant effects on the environment.[16]

3. Development proposed by a State authority requiring EIA (or Natura impact statement or both of those statements as the case may be)[17] to include, specifically, development which has been exempted from the necessity to obtain ordinary planning permission but where the development is likely to have significant effects on the environment or adverse effects on the integrity of a European site, as the case may be.[18] The State authority, unlike other applicants, in seeking approval from the board in respect of strategic infrastructure development is not required to consult with the board before making its application.[19]

4. Where an undertaker intends to carry out development comprising, or for the purposes of electricity transmission the application is made to An Bord Pleanála under PDA 2000, s 182B.[20] 'Electricity transmission' includes the transport of electricity by means of a high voltage line (110kv) and the interconnector (regardless of ownership) is defined with reference to the Electricity Regulation Act 1999 which defines 'transmission' to mean:

> the transport of electricity by means of a transmission system, that is to say, a system which consists, wholly or mainly, of high voltage lines and electric plant and which is used for conveying electricity from a generating station to a substation, from one generating station to another, from one substation to another or to or from any interconnector or to final customers but shall not include any such lines which the Board may, from time to time, with the approval of the Commission, specify as being part of the distribution system but shall not include any interconnector owned by the Board.[21]

PDA 2000, s 182B sets out a number of matters which the board must consider in relation to any application made to it under s 182A to include:

1. Any EIS or Natura impact statement or both of these statements as the case may be or any revised EIS or revised Natura impact statement.[22]

2. Any submissions or observations made by any person(s) or body/bodies on the application for permission for structural infrastructure development under PDA 2000, s 182A(4) and/or (8) and any other

---

16. PDA 2000, s 226(6). Note that the developments listed at (i) and (ii) are developments to be carried out by or in partnership with a local authority which would be usually exempt from the requirement to obtain planning permission.
17. PDA 2000, s 181A(3)(a)(ii) as amended by PD(A)A 2010, s 60(b).
18. PDA 2000, s 181A(1)(b) as amended by PD(A)A 2010, s 60(a).
19. PDA 2000, s 181A as inserted by PD(A)A 2006, s 36.
20. PDA 2000, s 182B as inserted by PD(SI)A 2006, s 4 and amended by PD(A)A 2010, s 64(a)(i) and (ii) dealing with the criteria for decision, and with certain exemptions, etc.
21. See Electricity Regulation Act 1999, s 2(1).
22. PDA 2000, s 182A(1) and (5) as amended by PD(A)A 2010, s 63(a), (b) and (c).

**[11.06]** Planning and Environmental Law in Ireland

information furnished in accordance with the provisions of s 182A(5)[23] relating to:

    (i)    The likely consequences for proper planning and sustainable development in the area in which it is proposed to situate the said development of such development, and

    (ii)    The likely effects on the environment or adverse effects on the integrity of a European site as the case may be of the proposed development.

3.    The report and any recommendations of the person who conducted the oral hearing.[24]

The Board, if it is satisfied that exceptional circumstances exist, may grant exemption from the requirement to furnish an EIS provided that no EU Member State nor any State which is a party to the Transboundary Convention have indicated that they may wish to furnish views on the effects on the environment in that State which may result from the structural infrastructure development proposed.

In granting an exemption, in exceptional circumstances, from the requirement to lodge an EIS the board shall consider:

(a)    the effects, if any of the proposed development on the environment or adverse effects, if any, of the proposed development on the integrity of a European site should be assessed in some other manner, and

(b)    the information arising from such an assessment should be made available to the members of the public, and it may apply such requirements regarding these matters in relation to the application for approval as it considers necessary or appropriate.[25]

If granted, notices of exemption must be published in Iris Oifigiúil and in at least one daily newspaper published in the State. Notice of exemption must also be made available to members of the public and any such notice must be sent to the Commission of the EC.[26]

In deciding an application for approval under s 182 the board has the following options:

(a)    approve the proposed development,

(b)    make such modifications to the proposed development as it specifies in the approval and approve the proposed development as so modified,

(c)    approve, in part only, the proposed development (with or without specified modifications of it of the foregoing kind), or

---

23.    PDA 2000, s 182A(4), (5) and (8) as amended by PD(A)A 2010, s 63(a), (b) and (c).
24.    PDA 2000, s 182B(1)(b).
25.    PDA 2000, s 182B(3)(a) and (b) as amended by PD(A)A 2010, s 64(b).
26.    PDA 2000, s 182B(4)(a) and (b).

(d) refuse to approve the proposed development, and may attach to an approval under paragraph (a), (b) or (c) such conditions as it considers appropriate.[27]

Any decision made by the board shall state:

(5A)(a) the main reasons and considerations on which the decision is based,

(b) where conditions are attached under subsection (5) or (6) the main reasons for attaching them,

(c) the sum and direct payment of the sum to be paid to the Board towards the costs incurred by the Board of–

(i) giving a written opinion in compliance with a request under section 182E(3) (inserted by section 4 of the Act of 2006),

(ii) conducting consultations under section 182E, and

(iii) determining the application made under section 182A (inserted by section 4 of the Act of 2006) under this section,

and, in such amount as the Board considers to be reasonable, state the sum to be paid and direct the payment of the sum to any planning authority that incurred costs during the course of consideration of that application and to any other person as a contribution to the costs incurred by that person during the course of consideration of that application (each of which the sums the Board may, by virtue of this subsection, require to be paid).

(5B) A reference to costs in subsection (5A)(c) shall be construed as a reference to such costs as the Board in its absolute discretion considers to be reasonable costs, but does not include a reference to so much of the costs there referred to as have been recovered by the Board by way of a fee charged under section 144.

(5C) A notice of a decision given under subsection (5) shall be furnished to the applicant as soon as may be after it is given but shall not become operative until any requirement under subsection (5A)(c) in relation to the payment by the applicant of a sum in respect of costs have been compiled with.

(5D) Where an applicant for permission fails to pay the sum in respect of costs in accordance with a requirement under subsection (5A)(c), the Board, the planning authority or any other person concerned (as may be appropriate) may recover the sum as a simple contract debt in any court of competent jurisdiction.[28]

In approving a structural infrastructure development the board may attach a condition requiring the construction or financing, in whole or in part, of the construction of a facility or the provision or financing, in whole or in part, of the provision of a service in the area where the strategic infrastructure development is to be carried out.

The facility or service to be constructed or provided must be such as would constitute a substantial gain to the community.[29] There is a cautionary limit set on the amount of a financial contribution or the cost of providing a facility or a

---

27. PDA 2000, s 182B(5)(a), (b), (c) and (d).
28. PDA 2000, s 182B(5A)–(5D) as inserted by PD(A)A 2010, s 64(c).
29. PDA 2000, s 182B(6) as inserted by PD(SI)A 2006, s 4.

**[11.06]** Planning and Environmental Law in Ireland

service in that the amount of resources to be committed by the developer must not deprive the developer of the benefits likely to accrue from the grant of approval.[30]

The Board, before making its decision, must also consider the matters set out in PDA 2000, s 182B(1)(a) and (b) and in doing so the board shall have regard to the following matters also, namely:

(a) the provision of the development plan for the area,

(b) the provision of any special amenity area order relating to the area,

(c) if the area or part of the area is a European site or an area prescribed for the purposes of section 10(2)(c),[31] that fact,

(d) if the proposed development would have an effect on a European site or an area prescribed for the purposes of section 10(2)(c), that fact,

(e) the mattes referred to in section 143,[32] and

(f) the provisions of this Act and regulations under this Act where relevant.[33]

PDA 2000, s 182B(11)(a) provides that permission under ss 34 or 37G is not required for any development which is approved under this section. Furthermore, Pt VIII of PDA 2000 (which deals with enforcement) shall apply in any case where development referred to in s 182A(1) is carried out otherwise than in compliance with an approval under this section. Part VIII will also apply if conditions imposed in an approval are not complied with.

5. Where an undertaker intends to carry out development comprising strategic gas infrastructure development and where, subsequent to a consultation with the board under PDA 2000, s 182E[34] which determines that the development is one which if carried out would fall within one or more of the following paragraphs of s 37A(2), namely:

(a) the development would be of strategic economic or social importance to the State or the region in which it would be situate,

(b) the development would contribute substantially to the fulfilment of any of the objectives of the National Spatial Strategy or in any regional planning

---

30. PDA 2000, s 182B(7) as inserted by PD(SI)A 2006, s 4.
31. PDA 2000, s 10(2)(c) deals with the content of development plans and, in particular, the conservation and protection of the environment including archaeology, natural heritage and the conservation and protection of European sites and any other sites which may be prescribed.
32. PDA 2000, s 143 was substituted by PD(SI)A 2006, s 26 requires the board to have regard to policies and objective for the time being of the government, State authorities, the Minister, planning authorities and other bodies and have regard to the national interest and any effect the performance of the board's functions may have on issues of strategic economic or social importance to the State and have regard to the National Spatial Strategy and any regional planning guidelines for the time being in force.
33. The matters to which the board shall have regard to para (a) to (f) is provided by PDA 2000, s 182B(10) as inserted by PD(SI)A 2006, s 4.
34. PDA 2000, ss 182A–182E were all inserted by PD(SI)A 2006, s 4.

guidelines in force in respect of the area or areas in which it would be situate,

(c) the development would have a significant effect on the area of more than one planning authority,[35]

the undertaker must then either prepare or cause to be prepared:

(a) an application for approval of the development under Section 182D, and

(b) an environmental impact statement or Natura impact statement or both of those statements as the case may be in respect of the development, and shall apply to the Board for such approval accordingly, indicating in the application whether the application relates to a strategic upstream gas pipeline or a strategic downstream pipeline.[36] The downstream pipeline must be longer than 20km and be designed to operate at 16 bar pressure or greater.

The upstream pipeline must be within the functional area of the planning authority and be part of the gas production project or for the purposes of conveying unprocessed natural gas to a processing plant, terminal or final coastal landing terminal.

**[11.07]** An application for strategic gas infrastructure development which relates to a pipeline must be accompanied by a certificate under s 26 of the Gas Act 1976 (as amended) or s 20 of the Gas (Amendment) Act 2000 by:

(a) in the case of a strategic upstream gas pipeline, the Minister for Communications, Marine and Natural Resources, or

(b) in the case of a strategic downstream gas pipeline, the Commission.

The proposed strategic gas infrastructure development cannot be carried out unless the board has approved it with or without modifications.[37]

**[11.08]** The procedure in s 182C is analogous to the procedure provided in s 182A which deals with electricity transmission development. It will not be repeated here save for PDA 2000, s 182C(9), (9A), (9B), (9C), (9D), (9E) and (9F)[38] which has been entirely substituted by PD(A)A 2010, s 65(e).

**[11.09]** PDA 2000, s 182C(9) has been entirely substituted by PD(A)A 2010, s 65(e). PDA 2000, s 182C(9) provides that where application is made for strategic gas infrastructural development to the board, the board is required to request the Commission for Energy Regulation to make observations on safety or operational matters including safety advice and/or specific recommendations which the

---

35. PDA 2000, s 37A(2)(a), (b) and (c) as inserted by PD(SI)A 2006, s 3.
36. PDA 2000, s 182C as inserted by PD(A)A 2010, s 4 and particularly PDA 2000, s 182C(1)(a) and (b).
37. PDA 2000, s 182C as inserted by PD(SI)A 2006, s 4(3).
38. PDA 2000, s 182C(9) substituted by PD(A)A 2010, s 65E and PDA 2000, s 182C(9A)–(9F) as inserted by PD(A)A 2010, s 65(f).

Commission for Energy Regulation considers appropriate. The Commission for Energy Regulation recommendations can be made at any time that the Commission considers appropriate provided they are made later than three weeks after the date of the request.

**[11.10]** PDA 2000, s 182C(9A) to (9E) set out the manner in which the board must react to the observations of the Commission for Energy Regulation. The Board is not bound to follow the observations but if it does not do so the board shall, before it makes a decision not to accept the Commission's observations, give reasons for not doing so and request the Commission for Energy Regulation to respond to those reasons within three weeks. The Board must then consider the Commission's response before making its decision. If the board's decision either in whole or in part does not follow the observations of the Commission it shall give reasons for not doing so.

**[11.11]** PDA 2000, s 182C(9E) deals with the making of observations on the part of the Commission for Energy Regulation pursuant to a request from the board to do so. Section 182C(9E) reads as following:

> In making observations on safety or operational matters including any relevant safety advice or specific recommendations which the Commission[39] considers appropriate under this section, the Commission may, without prejudice to the generality of the entitlement to make such observations, refer to such matters as it considers appropriate, including–
>
> (a) a safety framework established under section 13I of the Act of 1999,[40]
>
> (b) directions made by the Minister for Communications, Energy and Natural Resources under section 13J[41] of the Act of 1999,
>
> (c) guidelines issued under section 13L of the Act of 1999,[42]

---

39. 'Commission' in this section refers to the Commission for Energy Regulation.
40. Any reference to the Act of 1999 in PDA 2000, s 182C(9E)(a) to (k) is a reference to the Electricity Regulation Act 1999, s 13I, as amended by the Petroleum (Exploration and Extraction) Safety Act 2010, s 3, which deals with the establishment and implementation of a risk-based petroleum safety framework.
41. The Electricity Regulation Act 1999, s 13J, as amended by the Petroleum (Exploration and Extraction) Safety Act 2010, s 3, deals with directions which the Minister may give in writing to the Commission concerning measures to be taken with regard to petroleum incidents and reviewing or amending the safety framework where the Minister considers it is the public interest to do so. The Commission is bound to comply with any directions given by the Minister under this section and most of the direction is published in Iris Oifigiúil as soon as practicable thereafter.
42. The Electricity Regulation Act 1999, s 13L, as amended by the Petroleum (Exploration and Extraction) Safety Act 2010, s 3, requires that the Commission shall from time to time prepare guidelines relating to the preparation and contents of a safety case applicable to all designated petroleum activity or activities and in doing so may consult various bodies to include the Health and Safety Authority, the Environmental Protection Agency, the Irish Aviation Authority, the National Standards Authority of Ireland, the Minister for Transport and such other persons as prescribed by the Minister.

(d) a safety case as defined by section 13A(1) of the Act of 1999,[43]

(e) a revised safety case within the meaning of section 13N of the Act of 1999,[44]

(f) a safety permit issued pursuant to section 13P of the Act of 1999,[45]

(g) an improvement notice issued under section 13Z of the Act of 1999,

(h) a prohibition notice issued under section 13AA of the Act of 1999,[46]

(i) safety standards referred to in guidelines issued under section 13L of the Act of 1999,[42]

(j) standards and codes of practice referred to in section 13L(3)(c),[47] and

(k) conditions relating to petroleum authorisations.

[11.12] In summary, the provisions of PDA 2000 (as inserted) by s 182A to s 182E provide that any strategic infrastructure development for electricity transmission and/or strategic gas infrastructure development require Board approval. Before seeking such approval under s 182B or 182D, PDA 2000, s 182E[48] provides that a person shall enter into consultations with the board in relation to the proposed development. The purpose of the consultations are to enable the board to give advice to the perspective applicant regarding the proposed application and the procedures involved in making the application together with the considerations which must be taken account relating to proper planning and sustainable development particularly in relation to the environment. Where an EIS is required a prospective applicant may obtain an opinion in writing from the board indicating the contents to be contained in an EIS for the proposed development. All consultations under s 182E shall be recorded in writing by the board and the board may, in its absolute discretion, consult with any person who may have

---

43. The Electricity Regulation Act 1999, s 13A(1) is a detailed section providing a number of important interpretations of terms used in Part II A providing for regulation of petroleum activities.
44. The Electricity Regulation Act 1999, s 13N, as amended by the Petroleum (Exploration and Extraction) Safety Act 2010, s 3, provides that a safety case is regarded as a working document to ensure the safety management system in the safety case is properly implemented and reviewed at least every five years or whenever new facts or technology etc. come into being.
45. The Electricity Regulation Act 1999, s 13P, as amended by the Petroleum (Exploration and Extraction) Safety Act 2010, s 3, provides that the Commission prepares the safety case or revised safety case for the purpose of issuing a safety permit to the petroleum undertaken. This is a detailed section and would require further reading for full understanding of it.
46. The Electricity Regulation Act 1999, s 13AA, as amended by the Petroleum (Exploration and Extraction) Safety Act 2010, s 3, requires the Commission to issue a prohibition notice if it is of the opinion that an activity being, or likely to be, carried out involves substantial risk to safety.
47. The Electricity Regulation Act 1999, s 13L, as amended by the Petroleum (Exploration and Extraction) Safety Act 2010, s 3, provides that the safety case guidelines may include the standards and codes of practice applicable to designated petroleum activities including standards and codes of practice that have been formulated or recommended by the National Standards Authority of Ireland.
48. PDA 2000, s 182E was inserted by PD(SI)A 2006, s 4.

information which is relevant for the purposes of consultation under the section in relation to the proposed development.

## RAILWAY ORDERS AND ROADS

[11.13] Apart from electricity transmission lines and approval for gas infrastructure development, railway projects requiring a railway order are also subject to the new strategic infrastructure procedures. Any proposed railway infrastructural development has, since the passing of PD(SI)A 2006, to be determined by the board which has replaced the Minister for Transport. There is in fact no change in relation to road development and PDA 2000, s 215 has transferred the functions under the Roads Acts 1993 and 1998 to An Bord Pleanála.

## BOARD'S JURISDICTION IN RELATION TO CERTAIN PLANNING APPLICATIONS

[11.14] PDA 2000, s 37A sets out the planning application procedure where an application is made for a strategic infrastructure development. The initial application is made directly to An Bord Pleanála and the planning authority in whose area the strategic infrastructure project is to be developed, is bypassed. Strategic infrastructure developments are now determined by a special strategic infrastructure division which has been established within An Bord Pleanála.

[11.15] If an application is to be made for a development which is listed in one of the four classes of development specified in the Seventh Schedule the application to be made to An Bord Pleanála must, as a pre-requisite, satisfy the conditions listed in PDA 2000, s 182B(10)(a) to (f) inclusive:[49]

- (a) The development would be of strategic economic or social importance to the State or the region in which it would be situate,
- (b) The development would contribute substantially to the fulfilment of any of the objectives in the National Spatial Strategy or in any regional planning guidelines in force in respect of the area or areas in which it would be situate,
- (c) The development would have significant effect on the area of more than one planning authority.[50]

[11.16] The public sector projects which are within the definition of 'strategic infrastructure development' include:

1. Local authority development or local authority development in partnership with a private undertaker which requires EIS including development wholly or partly on the foreshore.

---

49. PDA 2000, s 182B inserted by PD(SI)A 2006, s 4. Note that paras (a) to (f) are listed at para **11.11**.
50. PDA 2000, s 37A(2)(a), (b) and (c).

2. State authority development that is exempt from planning control but requires EIS.

3. Railway authority development that requires an EIS.

4. Road authority development that requires an EIS and any motorway, bus way or protected road scheme.

**[11.17]** The private sector projects which come within the definition of strategic infrastructure development are:

1. Development for the purposes of electricity transmission.

2. Strategic gas infrastructure development.

3. Transport, energy and environmental infrastructure that comes within one of the following pre-conditions, namely:

   (a) That the development proposal is of strategic economic or social importance to the State or region;

   (b) That the development amounts to a substantial contribution to objectives or to certain national or regional development guidelines or

   (c) That the development amounts to a significant effect on the area of more than one local planning authority.

However, some important potential developments are excluded from the benefits of strategic infrastructure development to include building of schools and sports fields. It also correctly excludes iron and steel production, pharmaceutical and chemical production and the off-shore extraction of petroleum or gas. Nuclear energy is also excluded.

**[11.18]** Looking again at the provisions of PDA 2000, s 37A it should be noted that a new sub-s (4)(a), (b) and (c) has been inserted[51] which provides that if a planning application is made for a development listed in the Seventh Schedule which is to be located in an SDZ, the prospective applicant may elect to make the application directly to the relevant planning authority under PDA 2000, s 34 (as amended) and under the relevant regulations which apply. If such an application is made directly to the planning authority the provisions of PDA 2000, s 170 (as amended) which deal with applications in a SDZ are applicable and the provisions of s 37B are not applicable.

## PRE-APPLICATION CONSULTATION WITH AN BORD PLEANÁLA

**[11.19]** PDA 2000, s 37B requires a person who proposes to apply for permission for any development specified in the Seventh Schedule, or relating to electricity transmission, gas infrastructure and rail projects, to enter into consultations with the board in relation to the proposed development prior to making any application. Such person is referred to in ss 37B, 37C and 37D as a 'prospective applicant'.

---

51. PDA 2000, s 37A(4) as inserted by PD(A)A 2010, s 25.

**[11.20]** The main purpose of the consultation is to identify whether the development would or would not meet the relevant pre-conditions in relation to being entitled to make an application for permission under the strategic infrastructure system. A second purpose of these pre-application consultations is to allow the board an opportunity to give advice to a prospective applicant regarding the proposed application. It is, therefore, a screening process and the board will, in the first instance, determine whether the project falls within one or more of the following three paragraphs:

> (a) whether the proposed development would, if carried out, fall within one or more of the paragraphs (a) to (c) of Section 37A(2).[52]
>
> (b) the procedures involved in making a planning application and in considering such application, and
>
> (c) what considerations, related to proper planning and sustainable development or the environment, may, in the opinion of the Board, have a bearing on its decision in relation to the application.[53]

The Board may give advice and that advice is specified in PDA 2000, s 37B(3)(a), (b) and (c) as highlighted above.

**[11.21]** Another purpose of the consultation is to offer the prospective applicant an opportunity to supply sufficient information to the board in relation to the proposed development so that the board may be put in a position to make an assessment of the proposed development in terms as to whether or not it will fall within the 'strategic infrastructure' provisions.[54]

**[11.22]** The Board is required to keep a written record of any consultations held under s 37B including the names of those who participated in the consultation and a copy of the record shall be placed on the relevant planning file.

**[11.23]** An obligation is also placed on the board under PDR 2006, art 219(2) to indicate as follows:

> (i) the plans, particulars or other information which the Board will require for the purposes of consideration of the application;
>
> (ii) the time frames and sequencing to be applied to the application process;
>
> (iii) any other matters in relation to the application process as the Board considers appropriate; and
>
> (iv) where transboundary impacts are likely, the bodies, in which States that must be notified and how many copies of the application and EIS should be sent with this notification. The Board may also give advice to a

---

52. As seen these are: (a) the development would be of strategic economic or social importance to the State or the region in which it would be situate, (b) the development would contribute substantially to the fulfilment of any of the objectives of the National Spatial Strategy or in any regional planning guidelines in force in respect of the area or areas in which it would be situate, (c) the development would have a significant effect on the area of more than one planning authority.
53. PDA 2000, s 37B(3)(a), (b) and (c).
54. PDA 2000, s 37C(1).

perspective applicant as to the prescribed bodies which should be notified of the application.[55]

Other topics which may be discussed at the consultation meeting with the board include the following:

(a) whether or not the proposed development would be likely to come within the scope of the Major Accident (Seveso) Directive;

(b) whether or not the proposed development might give rise to likely significant effects on the environment in a transboundary State;

(c) whether the proposed development might or might not require an IPPC or waste licence and if such is required it would be mandatory that the EPA be notified at once.

**[11.24]** Section 37C(2)[56] provides that the holding of consultations under s 37B will not prejudice the performance by the board of any other of its functions under the Act or under the Regulations and that the consultation cannot be relied upon in the formal planning process or in any legal proceedings.

**[11.25]** When the consultation has been concluded under this section the board must form its opinion and if it is of the opinion that the application does fall within one or more of paras (a) to (c) of s 37A(2) it shall serve notice on the prospective applicant stating that it is of that opinion.

**[11.26]** Alternatively, if the board forms an opinion that the application does not fall within any of those paras (a) to (c) of s 37A(2) is shall serve notice in writing on the prospective applicant stating that it is of that opinion.

## EIA OF STRATEGIC INFRASTRUCTURE DEVELOPMENT APPLICATIONS

**[11.27]** PDA 2000, s 37E[57] provides that if application for permission for development is made subsequent to a consultation and pursuant to a notice from the board stating that it is of the opinion that the development would, if carried out, fall within one or more of paras (a) to (c) of s 37A(2), that application must be accompanied by an EIS in respect of the proposed development.[58]

**[11.28]** If the application for permission or the EIS lodged with it is considered by the board to be either inadequate or incomplete, having regard to the regulations and to any consultation held under PDA 2000, s 37B, the board may refuse to deal with the application.[59]

---

55. PDR 2001, art 210 as inserted by PDR 2006.
56. PDA 2000, s 37C(2) as inserted by PD(SI)A 2006, s 3.
57. PDA 2000, s 37E as inserted by PD(SI)A 2006, s 3.
58. PDA 2000, s 37E(1) as inserted by PD(SI)A 2006, s 3.
59. PDA 2000, s 37E(2) as inserted by PD(SI)A 2006, s 3.

**[11.29]** All applications for permission for strategic infrastructure development, if they are lodged with the board subsequent to a consultation, which has indicated the necessary compliance requirements, must be accompanied by the EIS. Prior to lodging it, however, the prospective applicant may seek a 'scoping' opinion in writing from the board as to what information will be required in the EIS in relation to the development.[60]

**[11.30]** If the board requires further information in relation to the 'scoping' request made by the prospective applicant, it may apply to the applicant for it and the applicant is required to supply the board with sufficient information relating to the proposed development to enable the board to assess it.[61]

**[11.31]** The provision of a scoping opinion in relation to an EIS under s 37D will not prejudice the performance by the board of any other of its functions under the Act or regulations under the Act and it cannot be relied upon in the formal planning process or in legal proceedings.[62]

## PUBLIC NOTICE

**[11.32]** Public notice must have been given before the application is lodged. It is a requirement of the board that all information lodged must be made available on a dedicated website. The applicant must ensure that the exact same information lodged with the board is available on that website.

**[11.33]** The Board requires that the fullest information is made available to all interested parties so that they may examine the issues and ensure that all information is made available in a clear and unambiguous manner.

**[11.34]** The requirements for public notice are set out in PDA 2000, s 37E(3)(a) to (d).[63] In practice, the board advises the applicant on the steps to be taken in publishing a public notice and the board's advice is almost invariably prescribed at the pre-application consultation. Although there is no statutory requirement for a site notice the board may nevertheless require one where it considers that a site notice is necessary. Notice, however, must be published in one or more newspapers circulating in the area or areas where the development is to occur. The notice must indicate the nature and location of the development and it must also state that:

    (I)    the person proposes to make an application to the Board for permission for the proposed development,

    (II)   an environmental impact statement has been prepared in respect of the proposed development, and

---

60.    PDA 2000, s 37D(1) as inserted by PD(SI)A 2006, s 3.
61.    PDA 2000, s 37D(3) as inserted by PD(SI)A 2006, s 3.
62.    PDA 2000, s 37D(4) as inserted by PD(SI)A 2006, s 3.
63.    As inserted by PD(SI)A 2006, s 3.

(III) where relevant, the proposed development is likely to have significant effects on the environment of a Member State of the European Communities or other party to the Transboundary Convention,[64]

The public notice published in the newspaper must also contain details of the times and places at which and the period of display (being not less than six weeks), where the application and the EIS may be inspected free of charge or purchased for a fee not to exceed the reasonable cost of making a copy.[65]

**[11.35]** Before an application is made by a prospective applicant to the board the applicant must send a prescribed number of copies of the application and of the EIS to the planning authority or authorities where the development straddles two local authority areas. Similarly, a prescribed number of copies of the application and of the EIS with a notice stating that submissions or observations made during the six week period specified in clause s 37E(3)(a)(ii) must be sent to An Bord Pleanála.

**[11.36]** The planning authority or planning authorities who have received the planning application and the EIS have a period of 10 weeks from the date the application was made to the board by the prospective applicant, or such longer period as may be specified by the board, to prepare and submit to the board a report stating its views on the effects of the proposed development on the environment and on the proper planning and sustainable development of the area having regard to:

(i) the provisions of the development plan,
(ii) the provisions of any special amenity area order relating to the area,
(iii) any European site or other area prescribed for the purposes of Section 10(2)(c), (of the 2000 Act)
(iv) where relevant, the policy of the Government, the Minister or any other Minister of the Government,
(v) the matters referred to in subsection (4), (subsection (4) deals with the imposition of conditions), and
(vi) any other relevant provision or requirement of this Act, and any regulations made thereunder.[66]

## SUBMISSIONS AND OBSERVATIONS IN RELATION TO APPLICATIONS TO THE BOARD FOR STRATEGIC INFRASTRUCTURE DEVELOPMENT

**[11.37]** The public notice invites the making of submissions and observations to the board during a six-week period, which submissions and observations will relate to:

(I) the implications of the proposed development for proper planning and sustainable development, and

---

64. PDA 2000, s 37E(3)(a)(i)(I), (II) and (III) as inserted by PD(SI)A 2006, s 3.
65. PDA 2000, s 37E(2) as inserted by PD(SI)A 2006, s 3.
66. PDA 2000, s 37E(4) as inserted by PD(SI)A 2006. Note that paras (i) to (vi) are taken from PDA 2000, s 34(2)(a).

(II) the likely effect on the environment of the proposed development, if carried out.[67]

(d) where the proposed development is likely to have significant effects on the environment of a Member State of the European Communities or a State which is a party to the Transboundary Convention, send a prescribed number of copies of the application and the environmental impact statement to the prescribed authority of the relevant State or States together with a notice stating that the submissions or observations may, during the period referred to in paragraph (a)(ii), be made in writing to the Board.[68]

Although the planning authority is excluded from the process of granting or refusing strategic infrastructure approval, s 37E invites the planning authority to make submissions and observations, within a ten-week period in the case of a Seventh Schedule (of the Act of 2000) application and a six-week period in all other cases. Those time limits may be extended by the board but only in exceptional cases. The planning authority's admissions and observations to the board set out the planning authority's views on the effects which the proposed development may have on the environment and its views in relation to the proper planning and sustainable development of the area. The Board is bound to send copies of both the application and the EIS to the relevant planning authority/authorities in whose area the strategic infrastructure development is to occur.

**[11.38]** Apart from inviting members of the public to make submissions and observations to the board, the public notice must also specify the types of decision the board may make, under s 37G, in relation to the application.[69]

**[11.39]** The role of the planning authority in the strategic infrastructure process is significant in that the manager of the planning authority is required to prepare a report, having first sought the views of the members of the authority. Section 37E(6) provides that the members of the authority may decide to attach recommendations specified in the resolution to the report of the authority. The views of the elected members must be sought in the case of a Seventh Schedule application and in any other case, although no formal input is required from the elected members, the manager's report may include the views of the elected members for consideration by the board. The Board may require a planning authority or planning authorities to confer with and seek the views of adjoining or other planning authorities where areas may be significantly affected by the proposed development. The Board may require a planning authority or planning authorities to furnish any information obtained from those other planning authorities to the board dealing with any significant effects on the environment (if any) and/or any effects which the proposed development might have on the proper planning and sustainable development of the area concerned. The members of a planning authority may decide,

---

67. PDA 2000, s 37E(3)(a)(iii), (I) and (II) as inserted by PD(SI)A 2006.
68. PDA 2000, s 37E(3)(d) as inserted by PD(SI)A 2006.
69. PDA 2000, s 37E(3)(a)(iv) as inserted by PD(SI)A 2006, s 3.

on their own initiative, by resolution, to attach recommendations. In fact, s 37E(6) is non-specific as to the nature of the recommendations which elected members can make. Dodd[70] suggests with good reason that the recommendations of the elected members which must be appended to the manager's report are open ended 'and so could involve a recommendation to grant or refuse the application or to attach conditions to deal with some aspect of the development'. It is, of course, always open to the elected members to make no recommendations whatsoever.

## APPLICATION TO THE BOARD FOR STRUCTURAL INFRASTRUCTURE PERMISSION

[11.40] PDA 2000, s 37E(1)[71] leaves an applicant in no doubt about the compulsory requirement to lodge an EIS with the planning application to the board in all cases of strategic infrastructure with a small exception in respect of some electricity works for which no EIS is required.

[11.41] PDA 2000, s 37E(2)[72] permits the board to refuse to deal with an application for permission and/or to refuse to deal with an EIS when either or both of these documents are incomplete or inadequate or where the permission regulations or any regulations made under PDA 2000, s 177[73] (which permits the Minister to prescribe information regarding environmental impact statements) have not been complied with. The use of the phrase in s 37E(2) *'refuse to deal'* indicates that the board may return the application and the EIS rather than retaining the application and the EIS, and seek further information from the applicant. The Board may, of course, entirely at its own discretion, seek further information. The application for strategic infrastructure permission is made by filling in a standard An Bord Pleanála application form to be lodged with the EIS and with a fee of €100,000.

### Supplemental provisions relating to the application[74]

[11.42] PDA 2000, s 37F(1) allows the board a discretion at any time before determining a strategic infrastructure application for permission to:

    (a)    require the applicant for permission to submit further information, including a revised environmental impact statement,

---

70. See Dodd, *Planning Acts 2000–2007 Annotated and Consolidated* (Round Hall, 2008) at para 1.52, p 163.
71. PDA 2000, s 37E as inserted by PD(SI)A 2006, s 3.
72. PDA 2000, s 37E as inserted by PD(SI)A 2006, s 3.
73. PDA 2000, s 177 permits the Minister to prescribe information regarding environmental impact statements or in relation to any consultations held under PDA 2000, s 37B (which latter section deals with discussions with the board before making the application).
74. PDA 2000, s 34F(1) to (8) as inserted by PD(SI)A 2006, s 3.

[11.43]      Planning and Environmental Law in Ireland

> (b) indicate that it is considering granting permission, subject to the applicant for permission submitting revised particulars, plans or drawings in relation to the development,
>
> (c) request further submissions or observations from the applicant for permission, any person who made submissions or observations, or any other person who may, in the opinion of the Board, have information which is relevant to the determination of the application,
>
> (d) without prejudice to subsection (2) and (3), make any information relating to the application available for inspection, notify any person or the public that the information is so available and, if it considers appropriate, invite further submissions or observations to be made to it within such period as it may specify, or
>
> (e) hold meetings with the applicant for permission or any other person–
>
>> (i) where it appears to the Board to be expedient for the purpose of determining the application, or
>>
>> (ii) where it appears to the Board to be necessary or expedient for the purpose of resolving any issue with the applicant for permission or any disagreement between the applicant and any other party, including resolving any issue or disagreement in advance of an oral hearing.[75]

Clearly, in exercising its discretion, as the board is entitled to do under the Act, the board must exercise its discretionary powers in accordance with fair procedures. This point was recognised in *Ballintuber Heights Ltd v Cork County Council*,[76] where it was held that members of the public are entitled to make submissions and observations in circumstances where post planning application meetings are held with officials from either the planning authority or the board and where additional information is sought. To exclude the public from making further submissions and observations in those circumstances would indicate an absence of fair procedures. The main thrust of the *Ballintuber Heights* case was that the applicant sought a judicial review of a Cork County Council planning decision to grant permission. In those circumstances, Ó Caoimh J held that the application for judicial review did not have sufficient *locus standi*.

[11.43] The matter of 'fair procedures' in these circumstances is covered by s 37F(2), which reads:

> (2) Where an applicant submits a revised environmental impact statement to the Board in accordance with sub-section (1)(a) or otherwise submits further information or revised particulars, plans or drawings in accordance with subsection (1), which, in the opinion of the Board, contains significant additional

---

75.    PDA 2000, s 37F(1)(a) to (e) as inserted by PD(SI)A 2006, s 3.
76.    *Ballintuber Heights Ltd v Cork County Council* (unreported, 21 June 2002) HC, Ó 'Caoimh J.

information on the effect of the proposed development on the environment to that already submitted, the Board shall–

(a) make the information, particulars, plans or drawings, as appropriate, available for inspection,

(b) give notice that the information, particulars, plans or drawings are so available, and

(c) invite further submissions or observations to be made to it within such period as it may specify.[77]

The same provisions apply where any other additional further information or revised particulars, plans or drawings are submitted by an application which in the opinion of the board contains significant additional information on the effect of the proposed development on the environment.

**[11.44]** Where the board hold meetings with the applicant or with any other person a written record of the meeting must be kept.[78]

**[11.45]** The Board or any authorised employee of the board may appoint any person to hold a meeting with the applicant for permission or with any other person.[79]

**[11.46]** PDA 2000, s 37F(5) and (6) provide that before An Bord Pleanála makes its decision on an application under s 37G in relation to a strategic infrastructure development which requires either an integrated pollution control licence or a waste licence from the Environmental Protection Agency (EPA) the board may request the EPA to make observations thereon within three weeks from the date of the request or as may be specified by the board in relation to the proposed development.[80] When making its decision, the board is required to have regard to the observations (if any) made by the EPA.[81]

**[11.47]** The Board or an employee of the board duly authorised by the board may assign a person to report on a file and to prepare a report on any matter on behalf of the board which shall include a recommendation and the board shall consider the report and recommendation before determining the matter.[82] A person appointed could include an inspector charged with the inspection of a site. In *Killiney and Ballybrack Development Association Limited v Minister for Local Government (No 2)*,[83] it was held that since evidence was not disclosed at the public hearing but was sent to the board as part of the report of the inspector, the decision must be presumed to have been based on materials

---

77. PDA 2000, s 37F(2) as inserted by PD(SI)A 2006, s 3.
78. PDA 2000, s 37F(3) as inserted by PD(SI)A 2006, s 3.
79. PDA 2000, s 37F(4) as inserted by PD(SI)A 2006, s 3.
80. As inserted by PD(SI)A 2006, s 3.
81. As inserted by PD(SI)A 2006, s 3.
82. PDA 2000, s 146(1) and (2).
83. *Killiney and Ballybrack Development Association Limited v Minister for Local Government (No 2)* [1978] ILRM 78.

other than those disclosed at the oral hearing. In consequence, the decision was held to be invalid.

**[11.48]** PDA 2000, s 146 also provides that all relevant material or information must be made available for inspection by the public both at the offices of the board or other nominated cases and by electronic means. PDA 2000, s 146(3)[84] reads:

> Where, during the consideration by it of any matter falling to be decided by it in performance of a function under or transferred by this Act or any other enactment, the Board either–
>
> (a) is required by or under this Act or that other enactment to supply to any person documents, maps, particulars or other information in relation to the matter, or
>
> (b) considers it appropriate, in the exercise of its discretion, to supply to any persons such documents, maps, particulars or information ('relevant material or information'),
>
> subsection (4) applies as regards compliance with that requirement or such supply in the exercise of that discretion.

**[11.49]** Section 146(4) states that it is sufficient compliance with the requirements of s 146(3) for the board to both make relevant material information available for inspection at the offices of the board or other places and by electronic means and the board shall notify persons concerned that the relevant material or information is so available for inspection.

**[11.50]** Section 146(5) provides that within three days after making the decision on any matter falling to be decided by the board all documents relating to the matter shall be made available for inspection at the offices of the board to members of the public and they may also be made available for such inspection at any other place or by electronic means as the board considers appropriate.

**[11.51]** It is the board's policy to hold oral hearings as a general rule in major infrastructure project applications. It is also the policy of the board to hold the oral hearings within five weeks of the date when the planning authority submits its final submissions to the board. Although it is the board's policy to hold oral hearings, PDA 2000, s 134 gives the board an absolute discretion in determining whether or not an oral hearing of an appeal or referral will take place. A request may be made under PDA 2000, s 134 for an oral hearing and, in theory at least, a decision of the board to refuse an oral hearing could be challenged on grounds of unreasonableness.

**[11.52]** The power of the board to hold a meeting with the applicant for permission or with other persons as provided in s 37F(i) and (ii) is a new feature of the consent

---

84. As substituted by the PD(SI)A 2006, s 29.

process. John O'Connor, Chairperson of An Bord Pleanála, had this to say about these meetings:

> Here I might refer briefly to the Board's power to hold meetings with any of the parties to the process during the course of consideration of the formal application. It is the Board's intention that this power would be used sparingly and, in fact, it has not been used to date. I would see it as being used solely to obtain specific information that might be necessary for proper assessment of the project including clarification of details, apparent errors, etc. Conceivably, meetings may also have a limited use in relation to CPO's, eg in facilitating the withdrawal of an objection. These meetings would not be a vehicle for applicants to put forward arguments in support of their proposals and will in no way be a substitute for an oral hearing. A record will be kept of any such meetings and will form part of the file documentation on the case. When a meeting has taken place before an oral hearing, the record of the meeting will be made available before the hearing and would also be available at the hearing.[85]

If a revised EIS is submitted to the board, the board must make it available for inspection and invite submissions and observations. In assessing whether the information submitted does contain 'significant additional information on the effects of the development on the environment' the board, as an expert body, will be using its expertise to make a planning judgment which would only be reviewable by the courts under the notoriously high standard of irrationality set in *O'Keefe v An Bord Pleanála*.[86]

## THE BOARD'S DECISION ON APPLICATION UNDER S 37E[87]

**[11.53]** In making its decision on an application for strategic infrastructure development the board may consider any relevant information before it or any other matter to which, by virtue of this Act, it can have regard. Neither the term 'relevant information' nor 'other matters' is defined but it may be assumed that if the board does not stray outside the bounds of proper planning and sustainable development it will not be acting *ultra vires*. Specifically, it must consider the following matters:

(a) the environmental impact statement submitted under section 37E(1), any submissions or observations made, in response to the invitation referred to in section 37E(3), within the period referred to in that provision, the report (and the recommendations and record, if any, attached to it) submitted by the planning authority in accordance with section 37E(4), any information furnished in accordance with section 37F(1) and any other relevant information before it relating to—

　　(i) the likely consequences of the proposed development for proper planning and sustainable development in the area in which it is proposed to situate the development, and

　　(ii) the likely effects on the environment of the propose development,

---

85. Extracted from a paper delivered by John O'Connor, Chairman of An Bord Pleanála, at the fifth Round Hall Planning and Environmental Law conference, 8 November 2008.
86. *O'Keefe v An Bord Pleanála* [1993] 1 IR 39.
87. PDA 2000, s 37G(1) to (11).

**[11.54]** Planning and Environmental Law in Ireland

- (b) any report or recommendation prepared in relation to the application in accordance with section 146, including the report of the person conducting any oral hearing of the proposed development and the written record of any meeting referred to in section 37F(3),
- (c) the provisions of the development plan or plans for the area,
- (d) the provisions of any special amenity area order relating to the area,
- (e) if the area or part of the area is a European site or an area prescribed for the purposes of section 10(2)(c), that fact,
- (f) if the proposed development would have an effect on a European site or an area prescribed for the purposes of section 10(2)(c), that fact,
- (g) the matters referred to in section 143,
- (h) any relevant provisions of this Act and of any regulations made under this Act.[88]

If a decision relates to an application for strategic infrastructure where the proposed development requires an integrated pollution control licence or a waste licence the board is not entitled to insert conditions in any grant of permission for the purpose of controlling emissions emanating from the operation of the proposed activity including prevention, limitation, elimination, abatement or reduction of those emissions. The Board is also not permitted to impose conditions controlling emissions relating to or following the cessation of the operation or activity.[89] The imposition of those conditions is a matter for the EPA.

**[11.54]** It is specifically provided that the board is entitled to refuse an application for permission to develop strategic infrastructure development which is unacceptable on environmental grounds, having regard to the proper planning and sustainable development of the area in which the development would be situated, even though the strategic infrastructure development comprises an activity for which an integrated pollution control licence or a waste licence is required.[90]

**[11.55]** An Bord Pleanála is entitled to grant permission for any development even though the development materially contravenes the development plan. Provision is made allowing the board to materially contravene the development plan in its decisions on normal planning applications in PDA 2000, s 37(2)(a). Specifically, the constraints imposed in PDA 2000, s 37(2)(b) do not apply to a decision on a strategic infrastructure application. Although the board may grant a permission even though the permission contravenes materially the development plan where the development falls within the definition of strategic infrastructure, nevertheless the board, in making its decision, must have regard to the provisions of the development plan and, presumably, it must also indicate in its decision the main reasons and considerations for contravening materially the development plan as is provided in PDA 2000, s 37(2)(c).[91]

---

88. PDA 2000, s 37G(2) as inserted by PD(SI)A 2006, s 3.
89. PDA 2000, s 37E(4)(a) and (b) as inserted by PD(SI)A 2006, s 3.
90. PDA 2000, s 37G(5) as inserted by PD(SI)A 2006, s 3.
91. PDA 2000, s 37G(6) as inserted by PD(SI)A 2006, s 3.

**[11.56]** An uncomprehensive sample of the type of conditions which the board may impose in granting permission for development for strategic infrastructure is listed in PDA 2000, s 37G(7).[92] The conditions listed in sub-s (7) are as follows:

(a) a condition with regard to any matters specified in section 34(4),[93]

(b) a condition requiring the payment of a contribution or contributions of the same kind as the appropriate planning authority could require to be paid under section 48 or 49 (or both) were that authority to grant the permission (and the scheme or schemes referred to in section 48 or 49, as appropriate, made by that authority shall apply to the determination of such contribution or contributions),

(c) a condition requiring the applicant to submit further information to it or any other local or state authority, as the Board may specify before commencing development, or

(d) a condition requiring–

(i) the construction or the financing, in whole or in part, of the construction of a facility, or

(ii) the provision or financing, in whole or in part, of the provision of a service,

in the area in which the proposed development would be situated, being a facility or service that, in the opinion of the Board, would constitute a substantial gain to the community.

The power of the board to impose a planning gain condition which may be either a facility or a service which must be of 'substantial gain' to the community is limited by the provisions of s 37G(8) which provide that the financial commitment must not be so onerous as to substantially deprive the person in whose favour the permission operates of the benefits likely to accrue from the grant of permission.[94]

**[11.57]** Simons[95] comments as follows:

> The power under s 37G(7)(d), in contrast, is open ended.[96] The objective justifying the abstraction of a planning gain, namely a substantial gain to the community, is vague, and is not necessarily confined to pressing or substantial social objectives such as the provision of social and affordable housing. The section might therefore have to be 'read down' by applying the double-construction rule.

---

92. As inserted by PD(SI)A 2006, s 3.
93. PDA 2000, s 34(4) lists sixteen conditions which may be imposed in a grant of permission other than permission for strategic infrastructure.
94. PDA 2000, s 37G(7)(d) as inserted by PD(SI)A 2006, s 3.
95. Simons, *Planning and Development Law* (2nd edn, Thomson Round Hall, 2007) at 10–89 and 10–90.
96. Garrett Simons here is contrasting the Supreme Court decision in *Re Article 26 and Part V of the Planning and Development Bill 1999* [2000] 2 IR 321 which held that the State entitlement to recoup some part of an enhanced value of development plan (whether deriving from its zoning or from the grant of planning permission) was constitutional.

**[11.58]**

The extent of the planning gain is delimited only by reference to the imprecise standard that it not 'substantially deprive' the applicant of the benefit of the planning permission. In the absence of a clear statement of the principle or policy in this regard, it will be almost impossible for a developer to challenge the imposition of such condition. This offends against legal certainty, and may well render the subsection unconstitutional.

**[11.58]** Section 37G(8) provides that where a condition is attached under s 37G(7)(d) the condition must not require the use of financial resources or the payment of a financial amount as would substantially deprive the person in whose favour the permission operates of the benefit likely to accrue for the grant of such permission. In other words, the construction or part financing of a construction or the provision of finance for the provision of services must not be so large as to leave no profit for the developer who has obtained a grant of permission.

**[11.59]** Section 37G(9) defines the meaning of 'appropriate planning authority' as used in sub-s (7)(b) as meaning whichever planning authority would, but for the enactment of s 3 of the PD(SI)A 2006, be the appropriate planning authority to grant the permission referred to in this section. It may happen that a strategic infrastructure development could very well be located in several local authority areas and where that occurs the board is entitled to impose contributions under the local authority scheme which are proportioned to the extent to which development is located within the area of such local authorities.

**[11.60]** Section 37G(10) permits the board to impose planning conditions to provide that points of detail may be determined between the planning authority and the developer. The matter as to whether such condition constitutes an application by the board of its decision-making powers was considered in *Boland v An Bord Pleanála*.[97] In that case, it was held that the board in imposing such conditions must have regard to the need to allow for some flexibility in a complex development where technical matters can be left for agreement with the local authority particularly where such matters are the responsibility of the local authority. The Board must also have regard to the practicability of imposing such conditions. In the High Court, Blayney J enunciated a further criterion, namely, could any member of the public have reasonable grounds for objecting to the work to be carried out pursuant to the condition.

**[11.61]** The matter was also considered in *O'Connor v Dublin Corporation*,[98] where the High Court was asked to decide whether compliance orders issued by the planning authority in respect of conditions attached to the planning permission were *ultra vires*. O'Neill J held that the test to be applied in such cases was not the test of 'reasonableness' of the decision as it would be in a review of a decision to grant or refuse permission. Instead, the test is whether the planning authority has correctly interpreted the meaning of the conditions so that a compliance order will adhere to, and implement those conditions. If, as was the case in *O'Connor v Dublin Corporation*, the

---

97. *Boland v An Bord Pleanála* [1996] 3 IR 435, HC (Blayney J) and SC.
98. *O'Connor v Dublin Corporation* [2000] IEHC 68, O'Neill J.

agreement is beyond the scope of the condition, the agreement will be *ultra vires*. Clearly, it is only points of detail which can be left over for agreement between the developer and the board. Where a condition is imposed leaving points of detail for subsequent agreement the condition should clearly state the reasons for its imposition and it should also lay down the ground rules by which the developer and the planning authority can reach agreement.

**[11.62]** Section 37G(11) reads:

> (11) Without prejudice to the generality of section 18(a) of the Interpretation Act, 2005 a reference, however expressed, in this section or sections 37H to 37J to the area in which the proposed development would be situated includes, if the context admits, a reference to the 2 or more areas in which the proposed development would be situated and cognate references shall be construed accordingly.

**[11.63]** Interpretation Act 2005, s 18(a) provides that the word importing the singular shall be read as also importing the plural and vice a versa.

## COSTS

**[11.64]** PDA 2000, s 37H[99] outlines the steps to be taken by An Bord Pleanála after it has made its determination on the application.

Once the decision has been made the board will send a copy to the applicant, the planning authority in whose area the development will be situate and to any persons who made submissions or observations on the application for permission.[100]

**[11.65]** Section 37H(2) requires that the decision given under s 37G and the notification of the decision must state the main reasons and considerations on which the decision is based and, where conditions are imposed in relation to the grant of any permission, the main reasons for the imposition of any such conditions.

**[11.66]** Section 37H(2)(c) is a new subsection inserted by PD(A)A 2010, s 26. This new subsection clears up some of the uncertainties that were created by the previous s 37H(2)(c) by specifying headings as to how the sum due to be paid to the board is calculated, namely as follows:

> (c) the sum due to be paid to the Board towards the cost incurred by the Board of–
>
>> (i) conducting consultations entered into by the applicant under section 37B,
>>
>> (ii) compliance by the Board with a request by an applicant for an opinion of the Board under section 37D, or
>>
>> (iii) determining an application under section 37E,

---

99. PDA 2000, s 37H(1) to (6) as inserted by PD(SI)A 2006, s 3.
100. PDA 2000, s 37H(1) as inserted by PD(SI)A 2006, s 3.

and, in such amount as the Board considers to be reasonable, state the sum to be paid and direct the payment of the sum to any planning authority that incurred costs during the course of consideration of that application and to any other person as a contribution to the costs incurred by that person during the course of consideration of that application (each of which sums the Board may, by virtue of this subsection, require to be paid).

The costs will be payable irrespective of the outcome of the application and the same costs are payable if permission is granted, if it is granted with conditions or if it is refused. The Board has complete discretion as to what it considers to be reasonable costs; nevertheless the board must act judicially and in doing so it must be assumed that the discretion would require the board to act in a reasonable manner in assessing costs.[101]

**[11.67]** Section 37H(4) provides that no grant of permission will become operative until the applicant has paid the costs specified in the notice of decision. Although the permission issues (as soon as may be), it cannot be implemented until the costs have been discharged.

**[11.68]** Any person entitled to costs may recover those costs as a simple contract debt in any court of competent jurisdiction.[102]

**[11.69]** The grant of planning permission under s 37G does not necessarily mean that the person entitled to permission can commence the development and where there are other legal requirements to include other licensing requirements those requirements must be dealt with before the commencement of the development.[103]

**[11.70]** In *Weir v Dublin Corporation*,[104] a condition in a planning permission required the provision of a bus lane. The design of the bus lane was approved and carried out with the knowledge of the local authority. In fact, the bus lane was constructed two inches lower than the surface of the road and, when the Plaintiff tripped and was injured, the Supreme Court awarded personal injuries in respect of the injuries caused by tripping in the bus lay-by. In *Convery v Dublin County Council*,[105] the Supreme Court overruled a High Court decision[106] where it was held that Dublin County Council in allowing extensive residential development without a corresponding requirement that developers contribute to a bypass, had caused a public nuisance in terms of serious traffic congestion, and was obliged to abate that nuisance within a reasonable time. In the Supreme Court, the High Court decision was overruled on the basis that:

(a) The local authority was not in a sufficient relationship of proximity with the local residents to owe them a duty of care; and

---

101. Please refer to PDA 2000, s 144(1), (1A) and (1B). Section 144(1) was substituted by and s 144(1A) and (1B) inserted by PD(A)A 2010, s 44.
102. PDA 2000, s 37H(5) as inserted by PD(SI)A 2006, s 3.
103. PDA 2000, s 37H(6) as inserted by PD(SI)A 2006, s 3.
104. *Weir v Dublin Corporation* [1983] IR 242.
105. *Convery v Dublin County Council* [1996] 3 IR 161.
106. *Convey v Dublin County Council* [1996] 3 IR 153, HC.

(b) That motorists rather than the local authority had caused the nuisance complained of and that the local authority was not liable in negligence as no duty of care could be established between the parties pursuant to the respondent exercising his powers under the planning legislation.

The Supreme Court decision in *Convery* overruled the Supreme Court decision in *Weir v Dun Laoghaire Corporation*.[107] See also *Cablelink Limited v An Bord Pleanála*,[108] where an appeal was taken to An Bord Pleanála in respect of a grant of planning permission regarding a television deflector system. In the course of the appeal it was established that Cablelink Limited did not have a licence to operate the deflector system and a licence was a requirement under the Wireless Telegraphy Acts. Carroll J held that An Bord Pleanála was entitled to refuse to overturn the grant of permission in that the permission to the third party did not authorise any illegal activity on the land to which it referred. Enforcement of the Wireless Telegraphy Acts was a matter for the government and was one which was quite separate to and distinct from the grant of planning permission.

[11.71] PDA 2000, s 37I[109] permits the Minister to make regulations to provide for matters of procedure and administration as appear to be necessary or expedient in respect of the following specified matters:

(a) consultation under section 37B,

(b) the giving of an opinion under section 37D,

(c) applications for permission under section 37E, and

(d) decisions under section 37G.

Regulations may also be made in relation to matters of procedure and in relation to making the application for permission under s 37E, including the giving of public notice and the making of applications in electronic form and regulations may also be made in relation to matters of procedure concerning the making of observations by the EPA under s 37F(5).[110]

# TIME LIMITS

[11.72] On the one hand, developers complain about the use of aspirational time limits, that is, eight weeks for a planning authority and 18 weeks for An Bord Pleanála, on the basis that if the time limits are not met in the case of the board, no sanctions are imposed. Thus, the general duty of An Bord Pleanála to ensure that a decision on an application is made within 18 weeks beginning on the last day for making submissions

---

107. *Weir v Dublin Corporation* [1983] IR 242.
108. *Cablelink Limited v An Bord Pleanála* [1999] 1 IR 596, HC, Carroll J.
109. As inserted by PD(SI)A 2006, s 3.
110. PDA 2000, s 37I(2)(a) and (b).

**[11.73]**

and observations is heavily qualified. PDA 2000, s 37J(2)(b)[111] provides that the 18-week period may be changed and the period between application and decision may be such other period as the Minister may prescribe either generally or in respect of a particular class or classes of matter. This adds a further qualification to the 18-week time limit. Section 37J(3) reads:

> Where it appears to the Board that it would not be possible or appropriate, because of the particular circumstances of the matter with which the Board is concerned, to determine the matter which the period referred to in paragraph (a) or (b) of subsection (2) as the case may be, the Board shall, by notice in writing served on the applicant for permission, any planning authority involved and any other person who submitted submissions or observations in relation to the matter before the expiration of that period, inform the authority and those persons of the reasons why it would not be possible or appropriate to determine the matter within that period and shall specify the date before which the Board intends that the matter should be determined.[112]

**[11.73]** The general duty is also heavily qualified by further s 37J(4), (5), (6) and (7). On the one hand, the Chairman of the board, John O'Connor, speaking of oral hearings had this to say:

> However, if the Board is to have a realistic prospect of meeting the statutory time objective it is imperative that hearings are, in the words of the Act, conducted 'expeditiously' and 'without undue formality'. The Act contains provisions strengthening the powers of the inspector holding the hearing. I would make a plea to those participating in hearings to cooperate fully in this respect. There is some concern that some lawyers participating in hearings are engaging in court room histrionics which may be good for the odd headline but have no place in a planning hearing. While not denying that lawyers can make a valuable input to hearings, this conduct tends to prolong hearings unduly and distract from the real purpose of the hearing and they can even hinder the inspector in getting to the root of the real planning and environmental issues involved and reporting the facts to the Board.[113]

On the other hand, Garrett Simons SC robustly defended the work that lawyers do at all hearings stressing the importance of putting on record, in the course of the hearing, points which need to be recorded as a matter of law and upon which any potential application for judicial review will be based. If some who attended that conference experienced even a small degree of Saturday morning drowsiness the exchanges between Garrett Simons SC and Chairman John O'Connor, delivered in firm but dignified language, were quite simply electrifying. There is, of course, middle ground between the two points of view and there must be occasions when 18 weeks is too short a period to deal with the complexities of large strategic infrastructural developments.

---

111. As inserted by PD(SI)A 2006, s 3.
112. PDA 2000, s 37J(3) as inserted by PD(SI)A 2006, s 3.
113. See Chairman John O'Connor's paper presented at the fifth Round Hall Planning and Environmental Conference 2008 on 8 November 2008.

## NUCLEAR INSTALLATIONS

**[11.74]** PDA 2000, s 37K[114] reads as follows:

> Nothing in this Act shall be construed as enabling the authorisation of development consisting of an installation for the generation of electricity by nuclear fission.

The prohibition against the generation of electricity by nuclear fission is Irish Government policy and the Planning Acts cannot be implied to authorise a development of this nature. It is not, however, clear for how long we can continue to use carbon fuels for the generation of electricity and at the present time by far the greater part of the electricity consumed in Ireland is generated by carbon fuel with some small assistance from hydroelectric schemes, windmills and solar panels. Generation of electricity by nuclear power stations is, almost, a carbon free operation but, as we are all too well aware after Chernobyl, and more particularly, after the explosion at the Fukushima Daiichi plant in Japan and other nuclear stations in that country, it is a particularly and seriously dangerous industrial hazard.

**[11.75]** Even if present day nuclear generating stations can be rendered completely safe in terms of the highest health and safety standards, radioactive nuclear waste remains a problem. Radioactive nuclear waste does diminish with time. At one end of the scale 'spent' fuel remains hazardous to humans and to other creatures and plants for hundreds and thousands of years while other radioisotopes remain hazardous for millions of years. Energy produced from fossil fuels has catastrophic side effects in terms of carbon emissions and the consequent global warming factor. It is unlikely that the world will agree to turn off all the lights, silence the electric engines and mothball the Dart and the Luas.

**[11.76]** The problem with renewable sources of energy, to include wind, hydro, solar and photovoltaic is that adequate storage facilities are not available. Although renewable energy makes a valuable contribution to the national grid it is unlikely to provide all the answers. The requirement is for a gigawatt-scale electricity generator and the solution is likely to be a nuclear solution. Undeniably, the present generation of nuclear fuel power stations carry with them high hazard levels coupled with waste disposal problems which may remain problems for millions of years into the future.

**[11.77]** Laser Inertial Fusion Engines (LIFEs) have been developed by the National Ignition Facility (NIF) in the United States. A LIFE has been placed by the NIF within a ten storey building with a footprint the size of three football pitches. The engine emits 192 laser beams which travel 1,500 metres to a target chamber. The target chamber contains targets filled with a mix of deuterium, which is a stable isotope of hydrogen found in abundance in seawater and with tritium, which is a radioactive isotope of hydrogen which is not found naturally in earth but which may be produced by the transmutation of lithium. Lithium is a common element in soil.

---

114. As inserted by PD(SI)A 2006, s 3.

**[11.78]** As the lasers travel along the 1,500 metre path they are amplified and the energy increases from one billionth of a joule to four million joules – a multiplication factor of more than a quadrillion. The entire 1,500 metre journey along the path takes just a five millionth of a second. The projected outcome of these experiments will result in the production of gigawatts scale electricity, at least equivalent to the coal, oil, gas and nuclear power stations of today. The LIFE engines output will be produced with no greenhouse gas emissions and with controllable radioactive by-products as a consequence of resultant short lived radioactive by-products. A LIFE powerhouse would offer no danger of a meltdown.

**[11.79]** These developments should come on stream during the 2030's. There is, already, a need to acknowledge and prepare for the advent of LIFE, which may sustainably and safely replace the nuclear power plants and the fossil fuel power plants which are in use around the world today. The nuclear power plants split heavy atoms such as uranium in order to generate energy and that is why they are high risk and it is also the reason why the radioactive waste produced in those stations remains a potential danger to life on earth for such a very long time.

**[11.80]** The next Planning and Development Act, which hopefully, for the sake of this volume's shelf life, will be a good many years away, should consider the removal or at least the amendment of PDA 2000, s 37K (as inserted) to accommodate LIFE and other containable forms of fusion-based generation which are in the pipeline now. For the present, at least, Ireland should postpone any decisions on present generation nuclear plants and await the outcome of the NIF experiments in the United States. It is certain that a far less volatile nuclear solution is just around the corner.

## ALTERATION BY AN BORD PLEANÁLA OF STRATEGIC INFRASTRUCTURE DEVELOPMENT

**[11.81]** PDA 2000, s 146B(1)[115] reads as follows:

> Subject to subsections (2) to (8) and section 146C, the Board may, on the request of any person who is carrying out or intending to carry out a strategic infrastructure development, alter the terms of the development the subject of a planning permission, approval or other consent granted under this Act.

The section, in contrast to s 146A, which permits amendment of a planning permission or of a planning condition, allows the board to alter the terms of the strategic infrastructure development which has already received permission, approval or consent. Such a request must be made to the board preferably prior to the commencement of the development but it may also be made during the time that the strategic infrastructure development is being carried out. No application for amendment can be made once the strategic infrastructure development has been completed.

---

115. As inserted by PD(SI)A 2006, s 30.

**[11.82]** Under s 146B(2)(a), the board must make a decision as to whether the alteration requested will amount to a material alteration of the terms of the development concerned. The term 'material alteration' is not defined.

**[11.83]** Before making a decision under s 146B(2)(a), the board, entirely at its own discretion, may invite submissions either from the public in general or from a more limited class of person to include persons who made submissions on the original permission, approval or consent. The Board shall have regard to any such submissions made to it.[116]

**[11.84]** Two possible alternatives arise under s 146B(3)(a) and (b). Firstly, if the board decides that the making of the alteration sought would not amount to a material alteration of the development concerned the board shall alter the permission, approval or consent as requested and notify both the requester and the planning authority or planning authorities concerned. Secondly, if the board decides that the making of the alteration sought would amount to a material alteration of the development concerned it has three alternatives, namely:

(3)(i) Make the alteration,

(ii) Make an alteration of the terms of the development concerned, being an alteration that would be different from that which the request relates (but which would not, in the opinion of the Board, represent, overall, a more significant change to the terms of the development than that which would be represented by the latter alteration), or

(iii) Refuse to make the alteration.[117]

(4) Before making a determination under subsection (3)(b), above the Board must determine whether the extent and character of–

(a) the alteration requested under subsection (1), and

(b) any alternative alteration it is considering under subsection (3)(b)(ii),

are such that the alteration, were it to be made, would be likely to have significant effects on the environment (and, for this purpose, the Board shall have reached a final decision as to what is the extent and character of any alternative alteration the making of which it is so considering).

(5) If the Board determines that the making of either kind of alteration referred to in subsection (3)(b)–

(a) is not likely to have significant effects on the environment, it shall proceed to make the determination under subsection (3)(b), or

(b) is likely to have such effects, the provisions of section 146C shall apply.

PDA 2000, s 146C[118] as inserted by PD(SI)A 2006, s 30 deals with the preparation of an EIS for the purposes of s 146B.[119]

---

116. PDA 2000, s 146B(2)(b) as inserted by PD(SI)A 2006, s 30.
117. PDA 2000, s 146B(3)(a) and (b) as inserted by PD(SI)A 2006, s 30.
118. As inserted by PD(SI)A 2006, s 30.
119. Fuller details of PDA 2000, s 146C are provided below.

**[11.85]** Where the board decides that the alteration does have significant effects on the environment it must publish a notice under s 146. If, however, the board decides that the alteration is not likely to have significant effects on the environment the board then makes its determination to make the alteration being one of the alternatives set out in s 146B(3)(b)(i), (ii) or (iii). Having altered the planning permission, approval or consent the board will notify the requester and the planning authority or planning authorities concerned.[120]

**[11.86]** The Board is required to have regard to the general criteria for assessing significant effects on the environment under PDA 2000, s 176 and also to the content of the Seventh Schedule of PDR 2001.

**[11.87]** Dodd,[121] who made a good effort to avoid the somewhat torturous language used in s 146B, has set out the steps required for this process in a simple and understandable way, namely as follows:

1. Request for alteration received by the Board.
2. The Board must require persons making a request to make the information available for inspection and notify certain classes of persons and to invite submissions from such persons.
3. The Board considers whether to invite submissions from certain classes of persons.
4. The Board determines whether the alteration or alterative alteration would be likely to have significant effects on the environment.
5. If it has significant effects on the environment, the procedures set out in s 146C must be followed.
6. The Board has regard to the submissions received.
7. The Board makes its determination which may be:
    (a) To make the alteration
    (b) To make a different alteration or
    (c) To refuse to make the alteration
8. The Board notifies its determination to the person making the request, to the planning authority for the area concerned and to any person who made submissions on the proposed alteration.

## PREPARATION OF EIS FOR PURPOSES OF S 146B

**[11.88]** PDA 2000, s 146C(1) to (9)[122] applies where the board's determination indicates that the amendment to the development is likely to have significant effects on the environment and, in consequence, there is a requirement to carry out an EIA and to prepare an EIS. The requester is required by the board to prepare an EIS in relation to

---

120. PDA 2000, s 146B(6) as inserted by PD(SI)A 2006. s 30.
121. Dodd, *The Planning Acts 2000–2007 Annotated and Consolidated* (Round Hall, 2008) at pp 379 and 380, para 1–174.
122. As inserted by PD(SI)A 2006, s 30.

the alteration of the terms of the development concerned where the board has determined that the alteration will have significant effects on the environment. The information required for the EIS is set out in sub-s (3) of s 146C. Apart from the EIS, the requester must also prepare a summary, in non-technical language, of the information referred to in s 146C(3)(a) and (b), namely:

- (a) any information that any regulations made under section 177 require to be contained in environmental impact statements generally under this Act, and
- (b) any other information prescribed in any regulations made under section 177 to the extent that–
    - (i) Such information is relevant to–
        - (I) the given stage of the consent procedure and to the specific characteristics of the development or type of development concerned, and
        - (II) the environmental features likely to be affected, and
    - (ii) the person or persons preparing the statement may reasonably be required to compile it having regard to current knowledge and methods of assessment.

[11.89] Section 146C(4) requires the requester to submit a copy of the EIS to the board along with a proposed or published newspaper notice which notice must state that the EIS has been submitted and that it is available for inspection for a period of not less than four weeks and that it may be purchased. The newspaper notice must also invite submissions or observations to be made and sent to the board. A copy of the EIS and the prescribed notice must also be sent to the relevant planning authority and to any Member State of the European Communities or any State which is a party to the Transboundary Convention where the board considers that the proposed alteration of the terms of the development is likely to have significant effects on the environment of that State.

[11.90] Section 146C(5) provides that once the preceding subsections have been complied with the board shall, subject to s 146C(6) and (7), proceed to make its determination under s 146B(3)(b) or (c).

[11.91] Section 146C(6) details the matters which the board is to have regard to in making its determination on whether or not to permit the alteration. The Board, in making its determination, shall have regard to the following:

- (a) the environmental impact statement submitted pursuant to subsection (4)(a), any submissions or observations made in response to the invitation referred to in subsection (4)(b) or (c) before the date specified in the notice concerned for that purpose and any other relevant information before it relating to the likely effects on the environment of the proposed alteration of the terms of the development concerned.
- (b) where such alteration is likely to have significant effects on the environment in another Member State of the European Communities, or a

(c) the development plan or plans for the area in which the development concerned is proposed to be, or is being, carried out (referred to subsequently in this section as 'the area');

(d) the provisions of any special amenity area order relating to the area;

(e) if the area or part of the area is a European site or an area prescribed for the purposes of section 10(2)(c), that fact;

(f) if the development concerned (where it to be carried out in the terms as they are proposed to be altered) would have an effect on a European site or an area prescribed for the purpose of section 10(2)(c), that fact;

(g) the matters referred to in section 143;

(h) any social or economic benefit that would accrue to the State, a region of the State or the area where the development concerned to be carried out in the terms as they are proposed to be altered;

(i) commitments entered into and the stage at which the development concerned has progressed under the permission, approval or other consent in the terms as originally granted; and

(j) any relevant provisions of this Act and of any regulations made under this Act.

**[11.92]** PDA 2000, s 146C(7)[123] provides that the board may not make its determination until the period allowed for making submissions has expired.

**[11.93]** The Seventh Schedule has been referred to and its contents need to be recognised and understood as it sets out the types of strategic infrastructural development which may potentially come within the strategic infrastructure development regime. To come within that regime the developments listed in the Seventh Schedule must also be of strategic economic or social important to the State and must contribute significantly to the fulfilment of the objectives of the National Spatial Strategy or have a significant effect on the area of more than one planning authority.

---

123. As inserted by PD(SI)A 2006, s 30.

# Chapter 12

# PLANNING AND ENVIRONMENTAL LAW FOR CONVEYANCERS

## PLANNING HISTORY OF THE DEVELOPMENT

### [12.01] Questioning a client

It is advisable to send out a pre-contract questionnaire, with a written fee quotation, to learn as much about the property as possible and to anticipate replies that are required to requisitions of which a solicitor acting in a property transaction has no knowledge or information. In planning matters, the vendor should be able to assist, to some degree at least, in relation to planning matters but a purchaser too could help by examining the property and advising if there is any evidence of newly built structures or additions or alterations in the premises which may have required planning permission or which may be an exempted development. If acting for the vendor, as a minimum, a solicitor will need to establish the following:

A. (i) Have there been any developments (including change of use) on any part of the premises for sale within the meaning of the Planning Acts since 1 October 1964? If there have been any such developments, to include change of use, the solicitor must obtain a copy of the planning permission and bye-law approval (if applicable) or Fire Safety Certificate (if applicable). A commencement notice is required for all development where the Building Regulations apply and so too is a copy of the Fire Safety Certificate save and except for dwelling houses other than apartments.

(ii) If any development has taken place since 1 January 1970 in respect of which planning permission and bye-law approval (if applicable) exist, or if planning permission, commencement notice and (where applicable) Fire Safety Certificates exist, it will be necessary to obtain an architect's certificate of compliance or opinion on compliance, in relation to the planning permission and bye-law approval (where bye-law approval was required) and in relation to the Building Regulations. A Law Society recommendation indicates that no certificate of compliance is required for planning permission or bye-law approvals which are pre-1970.

(iii) If there have been any exempted developments at the side or to the rear of the house, the vendor's solicitor should ask the client to advise of these. If there is evidence of exempted development and if there is no certificate of compliance one will have to be obtained to ensure that the exempted development was, at the time it was built, compliant with the exempted development regulations. A solicitor should not rely on the client's judgment nor on the vendor's auctioneer's representations as to what is or

**[12.01]** Planning and Environmental Law in Ireland

is not 'exempt development' but should, in all cases, seek expert advice from an architect or other qualified person such as an engineer to be provided, signed and dated in a report or sworn in a statutory declaration. This applies whether the solicitor is acting for a vendor or a purchaser.

(iv) The dates on which any development was carried out are of great importance and the solicitor acting should try and establish the date, where known, of any building operations or change of use which affect the premises. If any development was completed before 1 October 1964, then neither planning permission nor bye-law approval is required. Bye-law approval is no longer required since 1 June 1992. All developments carried out prior to 13 June 1989 are deemed to have bye-law approval even in cases where no bye-law approval was obtained. Note that bye-law approvals are required in relation cases where development takes place between the 13 June 1989 and 1 June 1992. Bye-laws have been replaced by the Building Control Regulations and a commencement notice must be served before any development takes place if development started after 1 June 1992. In all cases, remember that 'development' includes 'change of use'.

(v) A solicitor acting for either a vendor or a purchaser must enquire as to whether any unauthorised structures exist on any part of the premises within the meaning of the Planning Acts.

(vi) A solicitor must enquire as to whether any applications have been made for planning permission, and if so, a request must be made for details of same, even if no development has been carried out on foot of these applications. Details of all applications, permissions and refusals should be obtained. A purchaser is entitled to know if applications for permission have been refused as the reasons for any such refusal may be significantly relevant to a purchaser.

(vii) Enquires should be made as to whether any application for outline permission was made and if permission was granted. It should be noted that the life of outline permission, as opposed to planning permission, is three years and not five years (save in special circumstances where additional time is allowed).

(viii) A solicitor should also ask the client to check and see if there are any unauthorised uses on the premises or uses which appear to be unauthorised so that the matter can be investigated.

(ix) When acting for a vendor, it is most important to establish whether any notices have been served on the vendor by the planning authority and in particular to make specific enquiries as to any warning letters or enforcement notices which may have been served under the Planning Acts.

(x) Enquires should be made of the vendor or purchaser as to whether they are aware of any road widening proposals which might affect the property. The solicitor should in any case conduct a pre-contract planning search whether acting for a vendor or for a purchaser.

(xi) An enquiry should be made as to whether any sterilisation agreements – now called 'planning agreements' under s 47 of PDA 2000, have been entered into with the local authority. These agreements are used to restrict or regulate the development or use of land either permanently or for the specified period. Clearly this would have a bearing on the value of the property. Local Authorities may also impose conditions compelling an applicant for development permission to enter into a s 47 planning agreement, restricting or regulating the use of lands or portion of lands. These planning agreements are enforceable against successors on title. They are somewhat akin to restrictive covenants but while they may not be terminated by the landowner, they may, however, be terminated by the local authority.

(xii) Enquiries should be made as to whether any compulsory purchase notice has been served in relation to any part of the property under the Planning Acts or under any other act.

(xiii) Apart from warning letters and planning enforcement notices under PDA 2000, enforcement notices may also be served under the provisions of the Building Control Act 1990 and a solicitor should ask if any such notices have been served.

(xiv) In a case where there is a non-conforming or non-compliant development, the safe course, in advising a purchaser, is to recommend that the contract is made conditional upon the vendor obtaining retention permission bearing in mind that retention permission is no longer available in cases where an EIS is available or where an EIA should have been undertaken in the first instance. Even if there is a non-conforming development which has gained immunity from enforcement after the relevant seven-year period has elapsed, the proper course is to at least consider retention permission (if available), or if that is not an option, it would be prudent for a solicitor to give written advice to the client and to request his/her written instructions to proceed (if he/she should wish to proceed) in spite of that advice. At first, a view was taken by many planners that if an application for retention permission was applied for, the risk that the applicant was taking, where immunity from enforcement had been gained, was that that immunity would be waved. If, for example, an applicant had carried out a development to build a hotel although the application had been for a very large mansion and, without permission, had developed the hotel in say, 1990, that permission had a five-year life span and prior to the PDA 2000 if a further five-year time span elapsed without any prosecution being taken then after 10 years from the date of

**[12.01]** Planning and Environmental Law in Ireland

the permission no enforcement proceedings could be taken by the local authority. When PDA 2000 was enacted in March 2002 the period for immunity was the life of the permission where application was made for permission, namely five years plus seven years. If, however, a development took place in respect of which no application for permission existed then enforcement proceedings could not be taken seven years after the completion of the development. Developments which had no permission but which had obtained immunity were still non-conforming developments and if somebody wished to rectify that they would have to make an application for retention permission, if appropriate. The danger with the retention permission was that it opened up the question of enforcement and if, for example, application for retention permission was refused many planners felt that the local authority could then start enforcement proceedings against the non-complying/non-conforming development. *Fingal Co Co v William P Keeling & Sons Ltd*[1] held that a developer is not estopped from claiming that a development is in fact an exempted development, by reason only of having made an application for planning permission for retention of that development. This decision was made on the basis that to allow the estoppel would deprive the developer of a right at law simply because he had exercised a different right. It is the case, therefore, that once the immunity against enforcement has been obtained (12 years in the case of a development with permission which infringes the permission or seven years in the case of a development with no permission) that immunity cannot be withdrawn. The planning authority cannot commence enforcement proceedings even though it refuses a subsequent application for retention permission. Apart from planning enforcement notices, enforcement notices may also be served under the provisions of the Building Control Act 1990 and the solicitor should ask if any such notices have been served.

(xv) A solicitor should enquire as to whether the vendor or any person on behalf of the vendor has made any application for compensation under the Planning Acts and whether any award of compensation has been made under the Acts and if so, full details and all relevant documentation should be requested.

(xvi) A solicitor should enquire as to whether the development or any part of the development is a protected structure. This is an important enquiry. While there are some surprising omissions in the list of protected structures, there are also some very surprising inclusions. A planning search will disclose a protected structure.

(xvii) A solicitor will have to try and establish the 'use history' of the premises to ensure that it is a conforming use.

---

1. *Fingal Co Co v William P Keeling & Sons Ltd* [2005] 2 IR 108.

Planning and Environmental Law for Conveyancers [12.01]

B. (i) A solicitor will need to carefully examine the planning documentation submitted with the title, bearing in mind that there is no requirement for a Fire Safety Certificate for a dwelling house other than an apartment. A Fire Safety Certificate is necessary for an apartment and for other developments other than dwelling houses, and commencement notice must be served in all cases of development carried out after 1 June 1992. Local Authorities now issue a letter of receipt once the commencement notice is served and both a copy of the commencement notice and a copy of the letter of receipt should be sought.

(ii) Copy of the planning permission should be sought and if the development has been completed you will need an architect's certificate of compliance with planning and an architect's certificate of compliance with the Building Regulations. The solicitor will need to check the Architect's Certificate, be it in draft form or in completed form, to ensure that it is not unduly qualified and that the architect or engineer giving the certificate is adequately qualified. Many certificates are qualified to such an extent that the development is not in compliance with the relevant planning permission or Fire Safety Certificate. The extent of the qualification must never be overlooked.

(iii) A solicitor will also need to check to see that all financial contributions have been discharged and that financial receipts are available. The architect's certificate of compliance, if it is unqualified, will normally offer satisfactory evidence of compliance with the planning permission and with the conditions in the planning permission which by implication includes financial contributions. Nevertheless, it is normal practice to obtain separate evidence of compliance with financial contributions. An architect's certificate will not be evidence of the service of a commencement notice and this must be separately proven. Under PDA 2000 it is a requirement that the local authority must enter the service of its commencement notice in its planning register. Evidence in the planning register would be evidence that a commencement notice was served, even though, the commencement notice itself might not be available. At the same time, it must be remembered that, planning registers are not always kept fully up to date.

C. It is essential, whether a solicitor is acting for a vendor or a purchaser, to carry out a pre-contract planning search. This is a *must*. It is a protection against actions in negligence. The results of the search, if it requires explanation, must be sent to the vendor client and to the purchaser's solicitors, or vice versa as the case may be with a request to explain the acts thereon. As stated, the planning search is not an absolute guarantee because planning registers are not always up to date.

D. If necessary (and this would not usually be necessary in most cases of residential sales) a solicitor may have to make an inspection of the premises being sold or purchased to seek out whether any hidden planning or environmental lacunas, which may not be evident from the documentation, affect the property. It is good practice for a solicitor either to inspect industrial premises and other more complex development. Although it may not be obligatory in every case, it is advisable for a solicitor to have industrial premises or more complex development with environmental issues inspected by an expert.

## PLANNING WARRANTY

**[12.02]** When the full implications of Special Condition 36 of the Law Society Contract are realised it is easy to understand why the condition is so frequently deleted in conveyancing transactions. The warranty which the vendor offers in General Condition 36 is now so wide and it goes back for so many years, that it is almost impossible to stand over it except in cases of recent development or developments with a complete record of the planning and environmental history.

**[12.03]** Condition 36 provides great comfort to the purchaser where it is not deleted but in many cases it might be asked whether the vendor realises the full extent of the warranty. The Condition 36 warranty is the vendor's warranty. It is not the vendor's solicitor's warranty.

**[12.04]** In effect, by allowing Condition 36 to stand in a contract, the vendor warrants:

1. That no development has taken place since 1 October 1964 in respect of which planning permission or Bye–Law Approval was required.

2. That where development did take place since 1 of October 1964 planning permission and bye-law approvals were obtained (save in respect of matters of trifling materiality), the conditions in the permissions were complied with substantially in relation to development on the site.

3. The vendor warrants (1) and (2) above but the warranty does not extend to Bye-Law approvals in respect of development or works carried out prior to 13 December 1989 because of the amnesty contained in the Building Control Act 1990 which requires no proof of Bye-Laws prior to 13 December 1989 even if no Bye-Law approval was obtained in areas where it was required.

4. The vendor's warranty, unless altered by special condition, warrants, in relation to the design or development of any property or any use, that it is in substantial compliance with the Building Control Act 1990.

5. The vendor warrants that all permissions and approvals under the Planning Acts and, if relevant, under the Building Bye-Laws will be made available to the purchaser.

6. The vendor warrants that Fire Safety Certificates and (if available) commencement notices under the Building Control Act 1990 referable to the property will be furnished.

7. Save for any developments intended to be carried out between the date of sale and the date on which the sale should be completed, the vendor will, prior to completion, furnish to the purchaser written confirmation from the local authority in respect of payment of all financial contributions or the furnishing of bonds contained in planning permissions or Fire Safety Certificates (if any) but this only applies in cases where the consents relate to a residential development which forms part of a residential housing estate.

8. The vendor will furnish to the purchaser a certificate or opinion from an architect or an engineer or other professionally qualified person competent to certify and confirm in relation to all planning permissions, Bye–Law Approvals (if applicable) and Building Regulations that the same relate to the subject property and, where applicable, that the design of the buildings is in substantial compliance with the Building Control Act 1990 and the Regulations made thereunder and that the development of the property has been carried out in substantial compliance with the planning permission and in compliance with the provisions of the Building Control Act 1990 and the Regulations made thereunder.

Tracking the planning history of a development back to 1 October 1964 has, in many cases, become an impossibility. The records of the planning authority are often patchy, to say the least. Memories fade and since 1964 a very large percentage of property in Ireland has changed hands many times. It is impossible in many cases, or almost impossible, to build a complete picture which will enable a vendor to give a Condition 36 warranty and that is why it is frequently deleted. There are also too many cases where the Condition 36 warranty should have been deleted in circumstances where it was not, in fact, deleted.

[12.05] Solicitors frequently overlook the fact that the Condition 36 warranty is the vendor's warranty. It is, after all, the vendor who signs the contract. It is essential that the vendor realises the implications of the warranty which she is giving to a purchaser. On occasions, contracts are sent out by a Solicitor on a vendor's behalf and the vendor has either no idea of the extent of the warranty being given or, more commonly, she is not aware that any warranty whatsoever is being given. There is only one safe way to deal with this. In preparing a contract and collecting details from the vendor, the vendor should be advised (preferably in writing) of the extent of the warranty which is being given. A letter containing paragraphs 1 to 8 above would be a very comprehensive explanation but it could be shortened and made more user-friendly. It might be sufficient to say that, in signing a contract for sale, the vendor is warranting that all matters relating to planning, bye-laws (where applicable), Building Regulations and all environmental law issues are in perfect order and that there is no unauthorised development affecting any part of the property in sale. If the warranty which the vendor is asked to give in all Law Society contracts is not explained then it is open to the vendor to say that she did not know about it and that, if she had known, she could not possibly have given such a warranty. She would say that he certainly would not have given any warranty without notice of it. If a vendor denies that she was advised of the warranty

**[12.06]** contained in Condition 36 then, in the event of the warranty being seriously defective, it is the vendor's solicitor who will be liable for the consequences.

**[12.06]** In many cases it is likely that the warranty required by Condition 36 is unsafe unless the vendor is personally aware of the full planning history of the development back to its 'development date' or unless it was developed prior to 1 October 1964 and no development has taken place since that date. If Condition 36 is not deleted, the vendor warrants an absolutely clean bill of health in relation to planning and building control legislation. When a vendor's solicitor deletes Condition 36 the burden in relation to a planning investigation and in relation to planning compliance is shifted from the vendor to the purchaser.

**[12.07]** Where a purchaser's solicitor sees that the planning warranty has been struck out, he/she will be immediately suspicious. The purchaser's solicitor will expect that there may be some serious planning defects. The purchaser *must* be advised by his/her Solicitor that Condition 36 has been deleted, where that is the case, and the implications of that deletion must be fully explained. Where a planning warranty has been deleted it is often (but not always) a danger signal. Invariably, it will be necessary to employ an architect or planning consultant to examine the planning history of the premises and to scrutinise the planning files. If any planning defects are found (no matter how trivial) a solicitor must advise his/her client in writing. A solicitor must seek written instructions confirming that the client has been so advised and, if it is the case, the instruction should state that the client intends to proceed with the transaction. A solicitor must *never* take responsibility for other people's planning defects. Most importantly, where planning defects are disclosed or where they are detected, they should always be included in the 'qualifications' section of a certificate of title where the purchaser is obtaining a loan from a financial institution and that information should be communicated to the financial institution at the earliest possible occasion and certainly before the loan cheque is bespoken.

**[12.08]** The client should be advised that General Condition 36 relates only to developments carried out on the property since 1 October 1964 but it does not protect a purchaser against restrictions which may affect the potential for future development of the property such as:

(i) The Wildlife Act 1976 and the Wildlife (Amendment) Act 2000 which updates many of the provisions of the Wildlife Act 1976. It places Natural Heritage Areas (NHA's) on a statutory basis for the first time;

(ii) Council Directive 79/409EEC of 7 April 1979 on the conservation of wild birds ('the Birds Directive');

(iii) Council Directive 92/43/EC of 21 May 2002 on the conservation of natural conservation of Natural Habitats and Wild Flora and Fauna ('the Habitats Directive');

(iv) In addition to the above there are also the Water Pollution Acts 1977 to 1990, the Air Pollution Act 1987, the Fisheries Acts 1959–1990, the Environmental

Protection Agency Act 1992–2003, the Derelict Sites Acts 1990–2000, the Building Control Act 1990–2007 and the regulations made thereunder and the Waste Management Act 1996–2003.

Each of these Acts contains provisions which can restrict or inhibit the development potential of property.

## NEED FOR A PLANNING AMNESTY

[12.09] All of this indicates that there is a pressing need for a 'planning amnesty'. Both the Law Society and the Law Reform Commission have advocated a planning amnesty but, so far, the Oireachtas has not listened to these recommendations. It is, of course, quite possible that the ECJ would not give its blessing to a planning amnesty particularly in cases where EIA should have been undertaken in the first instance and/or where an EIS was required but was not provided with the original application.

[12.10] At the same time we cannot continue to look back over the past 47 years+, to 1 October 1964. A planning amnesty which might, for example, provide that no investigation is required in respect of any development completed more than 15 years ago, is an immediate requirement. If a development contains planning defects, that development should be deemed by the amnesty to be in full compliance with all planning and building regulations and legislative requirements once, say, a 15 year period has passed since the development was completed. Development which requires/ required EIA and/or EIS and, where none were provided, should be excluded from the proposed planning amnesty.

[12.11] Until the amnesty becomes a reality solicitors and planners are left in a limbo situation. In summary, and while solicitors and planners remain in limbo, the following guidelines must be followed as a minimum:

1. Fully explain the meaning of the warranty offered by Condition 36 to a vendor client.

2. Always think before deleting Condition 36. In a spirit of co-operation solicitors should all try to assist a transaction so that it closes quickly and without difficulty. If a vendor's solicitor is satisfied from the investigations made that there are no planning defects and that the vendor is happy to warrant such, then Condition 36 should not be deleted. If, on the other hand, a vendor's solicitor is not so satisfied, then Condition 36 must be deleted.

3. If Condition 36 is deleted the onus shifts in relation to all planning and building regulations matters from the vendor to the purchaser. The purchaser must therefore make all enquiries necessary which, in all but the simplest cases, will involve employing an architect, engineer or town planner to inspect the property and to inspect the local authority files.

4. A solicitor should never take responsibility for other people's planning defects. If a development, or part of a development, does not have planning permission

then the only advice which can be given to a client is that retention permission must be obtained where that is possible. It is a matter for the client, and not for the solicitor, to decide whether or not to proceed with the application for retention permission in appropriate cases. The client should be advised of the circumstances in which retention permission may or may not be applied for.

5. Always include planning defects in the 'qualifications' section of a financial institution's certificate of title.

## CONSEQUENCES OF PLANNING DEFECTS

**[12.12]** All planning defects must be notified and explained by a solicitor to his/her client and the consequences must be spelt out whether the solicitor is acting for the purchaser or the vendor, to include such relevant matters as:

(i) Where a purchaser is obtaining a loan from a financial institution, the financial institution will require a certificate of title, which certificate of title will have to be qualified by highlighting any planning defects which appear. This opens up the possibility that the financial institution will not proceed with the loan. All too frequently, planning defects are not included in the schedule of qualifications in a certificate of title. This can be, and invariably is, a dangerous omission. Solicitors must declare any defects or suspected defects into the qualification section of the certificate of title. Most banks, building societies and other financial institutions now insist that all qualifications are approved by them before the loan cheque issues.

(ii) That the life of a planning permission is generally five years from the date of notification of grant of permission or the date of the Bord Pleanála decision (whichever is relevant) or such other period as may be specified. If there is still outstanding work to be done after the life of the planning permission has expired, a new permission must be obtained.

(iii) A planning authority has a period of seven years in which to commence proceedings. *The seven years starts from the expiration of the life of the permission, in a case where permission has been obtained.* If the permission has a five-year life (which is normal) then the planning authority cannot take enforcement proceedings after 12 years. Sometimes a permission may have a longer life, for example 10 years, and, in that case, it will be 17 years before a planning authority is precluded from taking enforcement action. In a case where no permission has been granted, time for the seven-year period runs from the date that the development is deemed to have been completed. There may be argument both about the date of completion and whether or not the development has been completed. 'Completed' in this context does not mean 'fully completed'.

(iv) Although unauthorised developments are immune from general enforcement proceedings after the relevant seven year period, where there is no planning permission, or after the expiration of the life of a planning permission plus seven years where there is planning permission, those unauthorised developments remain unauthorised developments and suffer from a number of disadvantages as non-conforming developments to include the following:

(a) the possibility that under PDA 2000, s 258 conditions will be applied by the sanitary authority before permitting a connection to a sanitary authority's sewer to the effect that retention permission (where obtainable) must be obtained in respect of any unauthorised development which is seeking a connection as of a right;

(b) PDA 2000, s 259, denies a right of supply of water for unauthorised developments comprising a house;

(c) in the event of subsequent compulsory acquisition, unauthorised elements would not attract compensation;

(d) there is an almost automatic entitlement to compensation under the planning legislation in circumstances where premises have been destroyed by fire and, for some reason, planning permission to reinstate is refused. However, this is only the case where the premises were, in the first instance, authorised by a grant of planning permission;

(e) in a situation where an original development was an unauthorised development, it may be difficult to obtain permission for further development or redevelopment of that property. For example, a planning authority may impose a condition requiring the applicant to obtain retention permission (where applicable) for the unauthorised development before granting a permission or before allowing a grant of permission to become effective for the development, redevelopment or extension of that property;

(f) a development which would otherwise be an 'exempted development' will not be such if the same would 'consist or comprise' an extension, alteration, repair or renewal of an unauthorised structure, or structure the use of which is an unauthorised use;

(g) most importantly, it is the 'discomfort factor' experienced by banks and building societies when they are told that the property, or perhaps part of it, which represents a significant part of the purchase price, is a non-conforming development – a development which does not have planning permission and will not have such permission unless retention permission (where appropriate) is obtained. Unauthorised development, even if the seven-year period prohibiting enforcement has passed, should always be disclosed in a certificate of title, and the consequences of unauthorised development, which has been there for seven years and upwards, should always be explained by a professional advisor to his client;

(h) the importance of PDA 2000, s 246, regarding the power of the Minister to make regulations for additional fees payable to the planning authority for various matters must be stressed. These include fees for the making of submissions or observations in respect of planning permissions, fees for requesting declarations under PDA 2000, s 5, fees for granting of licences or certificates under PDA 2000, ss 231, 239 and 254. Most importantly, the Minister, under PDA 2000, s 246(2), may prescribe that the fee payable to a planning authority for an application for permission for the retention of an unauthorised development shall be an amount which shall be related to the estimated cost of the development, or the unauthorised part thereof, as the case may be.

(v) Where there are planning defects, the property, inevitably, becomes less marketable and unless the defects can be satisfied there is always a possibility that a well advised purchaser may refuse to proceed. It must be said that, in most conveyancing transactions, minor planning lacunas are ignored but whether the decision to ignore them is conscious or unconscious may be relevant in a potential negligence action against a solicitor.

## BUILDING ENERGY RATING CERTIFICATES

[12.13] A common and understandable definition of BER is that it is a calculation of a dwelling's energy performance which is similar to a litre *per* kilometre rating for a motor car. BER certificates must be furnished to a purchaser of a dwelling house and other premises before contracts are exchanged and, in the case of a letting of a dwelling or other premises, the BER certificates must be furnished to the tenant before the lease is signed. A BER certificate is a document of increasing significance and although it may not yet have happened, purchasers, in looking for a dwelling or other premises, will come to attach as much importance to a BER rating as they now do to the litre *per* kilometre rating of a motor car. It will not be many years before a low energy rating will amount to a positive disincentive to buy a building because of potential for extra cost. Apart from the certificate, which gives both a written and a graphic assessment of the energy performance of a dwelling ranging from 'A1' (most efficient) to 'G' (least efficient), a detailed report is also provided which states whether or not the dwelling is compliant with Building Regulations in terms of energy efficiency and which specifies details of the assessment made. The report provides advice and information on the steps which must be taken to improve energy efficiency in a dwelling or other unit. A BER certificate has a ten year life-span and any BER certificate which is more than ten years old is an invalid certificate. The date of the certificate must be carefully checked.

[12.14] There are two types of BER, namely (1) provisional BER and (2) full BER. The provisional BER is used where the vendor is selling property by reference to plans in circumstances where the house/building has not yet been built. The provisional BER for an un-built house/building must be available to a purchaser before the building contract is exchanged. When the building of the dwelling has been completed, a full BER must be provided to the purchaser.

**[12.15]** Although a BER certificate was, in the first instance, only required for dwellings, the EU Energy Performance in Buildings Directive[2] applies to all buildings in the EU and the BER requirement was introduced on a phased basis as follows:

1. New dwellings for which planning permission was applied for, on or before 1 January 2007 require BER certificates.

2. New non-domestic buildings for which planning permission was applied for after 1 July 2008 require BER certificates.

3. Existing buildings which include both dwellings and other buildings which are offered for sale or letting on or after 1 January 2009 require BER certificates.

**[12.16]** In effect, a vendor is required to provide a BER certificate for all buildings to the purchaser or to the tenant as the case may be. For the immediate future, this means that purchasers and tenants will inevitably take into account the energy performance of a building as a competitive element before deciding whether or not to purchase or rent a building. vendors and landlords will have to ensure that their building's have an acceptable rating in terms of 'marketplace comparatives' if they wish to remain competitive when the time comes for the sale or letting of the building.

## SPECIAL PRECAUTIONS WHEN DEALING WITH EXEMPTED DEVELOPMENT

**[12.17]** Exempted development, where it occurs, should raise a danger flag. Very often, the most difficult task is in obtaining information as to whether or not exempted development has taken place. Apart from taking great care, when you are put on notice of exempted developments, solicitors should be very wary indeed in furnishing replies to planning requisitions. Allowing for the fact that the planning history of the premises may go back to 1 October 1964, it is possible that your own client will not know the planning history of the premises. Because of some inadequacies in the maintenance and upkeep of the planning register in some counties, searches may not reveal all of what has occurred in many cases. Searches, in any case, will not reveal anything about exempted development or development which is claimed to be exempted although it is not in fact exempt from the requirement to obtain planning permission. It is most important, when acting for a vendor, that you ask your client whether he/she is aware of any exempted developments on any part of the premises. Similarly, in acting for a purchaser, a solicitor should specifically request the purchaser to check the premises being purchased to see if there is any evidence of any additions or extensions which might conceivably come within the exempted development provisions or, which may, indeed, have required

---

2. EU Directive 2001/91/EC of the European Parliament and Council of 16 December 2002 on energy performance of buildings.

planning permission. Some important points to remember in connection with exempted development include the following:

(i) Where there is exempted development, a solicitor must make sure that a qualified person certifies that the development is in fact exempted development. Solicitors should not rely on their own judgment or on the judgment of their client.

(ii) Exempted development never required planning permission but it did require bye-law approval. Section 22 of the Building Control Act 1990 provides that no further bye-laws shall be made under the Public Health Acts or the Dublin Corporation Act 1890 except in relation to roads and drainage outside the curtilage of the site, which is comparatively rare. However, new housing developments commenced after 1 June 1992 still require bye-law approval in respect of roads and drainage outside the curtilage of the site and this is still relevant to conveyancers, architects, engineers, contractors, etc.

Any works carried out prior to 13 December 1989, in respect of which building bye-law approval ought to have been obtained, but was not obtained, are now deemed to have building bye-law approval. Thus, an effective bye-law amnesty has been prescribed by statute, but a problem has been left for all time (unless changed), which relates to buildings or portions of buildings developed between the period 13 December 1989 and 1 June 1992, in respect of which bye-law approval was not obtained, in areas where bye-law approvals were required. Retrospective bye-law approval cannot be obtained, so that unless an architect's certificate is forthcoming to certify that the premises were built in substantial compliance with bye-laws, the premises may be unsaleable unless works are carried out to make them comply with the old building bye-law provisions. If, for example, the ceiling is too low (and this is not uncommon), rectification may be difficult, if not impossible. There can be no logical reason why the bye-law amnesty should not be extended, at this stage, to include the period 13 December 1989 to 1 June 1992. At present, this often overlooked lacuna is still around to worry us.

(iii) A protected structure does not qualify for exempted development and planning permission must be obtained for all development affecting protected structures.

(iv) A search is necessary to establish whether or not the development, the subject matter of a sale, is located in an area of special amenity. Much of Howth Head would be an example of an area which is controlled by a special amenity area order and no development can take place within the boundaries of that area without permission, even though it might otherwise be exempted development.

(v) Any development which requires an EIS is not 'exempted development' no matter what is stated in the Act of 2000 (as amended) or in the Regulations made under that Act.

(vi) The question as to whether or not there are any exempted developments on any property which is the subject matter of any conveyancing transaction, should always be asked of a vendor or purchaser client in the solicitor's pre-contract questionnaire submitted to the client. If there is doubt about the answer, the client should employ an architect or planning expert.

## SPECIAL PRECAUTIONS WHEN DEALING WITH PROTECTED STRUCTURES

**[12.18]** The Law Society requisitions do not make any specific reference to protected structures although questions are asked about notices served under various Acts including the Planning Acts. If the legislation is analysed, it is apparent that there are a number of requisitions which should be raised where the property or any part of the property, which is the subject matter of a conveyancing transaction, is a protected structure or a proposed protected structure. It is good practice, whether acting for a vendor or for a purchaser, to make a pre-contract planning search. Such searches will reveal whether or not the relevant premises is or is not a protected structure or a proposed protected structure and, if the premises is either protected or proposed to be protected, the questions to be asked by way of requisitions are set out below by way of example:

(i) Is the property or any part thereof to include the attendant grounds part of a 'protected structure' or 'proposed protected structure' under the Planning and Development Act 2000 (as amended)?

(ii) If the property or any part thereof is a 'proposed protected structure' when was notification of proposal to include the item in the record of protected structures served? Make a request for the vendor to furnish copies of any submissions or observations submitted to the Planning Authority by the vendor or any other person in this regard.

(iii) Have any declarations (declaration as to the type of works which would not affect the character of the structure) been made or sought under s 57(2) of PDA 2000?[3] If so, give details and furnish copies of any declaration.

(iv) Has any declaration, referred to at paragraph (iii), been reviewed by the local authority?

(v) Has a notice under s 59 of PDA 2000 (prevention of endangerment of protected structure) been served in respect of the property? If so, please furnish copies of the notice.

(vi) If a notice under s 59 has not yet become effective, provide details of the current status of the matter (including any appeals, objections or representations or discussions with the planning authority including details of any assistance which the local authority has agreed or refused to provided)?

---

3. The planning authority may receive a written request from an owner or an occupier of a protected structure to issue a declaration as to the type of works which it considers would or would not materially affect the character of the structure or any element which contributes to a special architectural, historical, archaeological, artistic, cultural, scientific, social or technical interest.

(vii) Has a notice under s 60 of PDA 2000 (restoration of protected structures) been served in respect of the property? If so, please furnish a copy of the notice?

(viii) If a notice under s 60 has not yet become effective, give details of the current status of the matter (including any appeals, objections or representations or discussions with the planning authority (including details of any assistance which the local authority has agreed or refused to provide)).

(ix) Have all works required to be effected pursuant to any of the aforementioned notices been carried out to the satisfaction of the Planning Authority?

(x) Has an order under s 67 of PDA 2000 (an order directing that all, or part, of the costs of work to prevent the endangerment of a protected structure or of a proposed protected structure be borne by another person) been made against the vendor or against any predecessor on title? Has an application for such an order been proposed by any person?

(xi) Has the Planning Authority indicted an intention to acquire the premises or any part thereof for the protection of a protected structure or has a notice of intention to compulsorily acquire the property for such purposes been served in accordance with s 72 of PDA 2000?

(xii) If notice of intention to compulsorily acquire the property or any part thereof has been served and a vesting order has not yet been made, give details of the status of the compulsory acquisition process including the date of the notice of intention to acquire and any objection made on any decisions of An Bord Pleanála and any discussions regarding compensation.

## DECLARATIONS AND REFERRALS FOR INFORMATION

**[12.19]** PDA 2000, s 5 replaced s 5 of the 1963 Act which permitted references to be made to the board on what was or was not development or exempted development. If any question arises as to what is or is not exempted development within the meaning of the Act, a person may request the relevant planning authority, in writing, on payment of a fee to prepare a declaration dealing with the circumstances of the applicant's request and stating whether or not the applicant's proposal is or is not exempted development. The submission to the planning authority requesting the declaration should be as full as possible and it should give as many details as possible because, if the planning authority requires further information, it will delay the issue of the declaration.

**[12.20]** Section 5 provides that the planning authority must issue a declaration on the questions raised and give reasoned decisions in the declaration within four weeks of the receipt of the request. If the planning authority does not have sufficient information, it may seek further information, and in that case, the planning authority is given another three weeks from the date of receipt of the information to issue its declaration.

**[12.21]** If the person who receives the declaration is not satisfied with the contents or interpretation contained, the planning authority's declaration may be referred to An Bord Pleanála on payment of a fee for review by the board. The Board has a four-week period to conclude its review. If a person does not receive the declaration from the planning authority within the prescribed time limit, that person can submit the declaration and refer the questions submitted to the planning authority for a decision by the board within four weeks of the date on which the declaration was due to issue.

**[12.22]** A planning authority itself may, on payment of a fee, refer a question as to what is or is not exempted development, to An Bord Pleanála by way of referral.

**[12.23]** The details of any declaration issued by a planning authority or the details of the decision of An Bord Pleanála on referral must be entered into the local authority's planning register. The Board is bound to keep a record of any decision made by it on referral including the main reasons and considerations on which its decision is based and these are available by purchase and inspection, to the public. At least once a year, An Bord Pleanála is compelled to forward to each planning authority, a copy of the record of the decision made by it on referral.

**[12.24]** Declarations and referrals under s 5 are matters which should properly be covered by requisitions on title in appropriate cases. Suggested requisitions are as follows:

1. Has the vendor or his or her agent made any application to the local authority for a declaration under s 5 of the Planning and Development Act 2000? And if so, please furnish the date of the application and copy of the application. State whether any notice requiring any further information was received from the local authority.

2. Has any declaration been issued by the local authority under s 5 of the Planning and Development Act of 2000? And if so, please furnish copy of same.

3. Has any referral been made on any declaration furnished by the local authority under s 5 of the Planning and Development Act 2000 to An Bord Pleanála, and if so has any decision been issued by the Board? Please state if the referral was made on the basis of a disagreement with the contents of the Planning Authority's declaration or alternatively whether the referral was made because the Planning Authority did not issue a declaration within the prescribed time.

4. Please furnish copy of An Bord Pleanála's decision on the referral.

# REQUISITIONS RELATING TO ENFORCEMENT PROCEDURES AND PLANNING INJUNCTIONS

**[12.25]** If specific requisitions in relation to enforcement procedures and planning injunctions are required the suggested wording might be as follows:

1. Is the vendor or her agent aware of any representations in writing made to the Planning Authority by any person claiming that an unauthorised development may

have been, is being or may be carried out on any part of the property on sale? If so, please give details.

2. Have any warning letter or letters been served by the Planning Authority under s 152 of the Planning and Development Act 2000 and if so, please furnish copies and confirm full compliance with the matters referred to in the warning letter together with certificate of compliance completed by a competent person?

3. Is the vendor or her agent aware of any decision on the part of the Planning Authority to issue an enforcement notice as having been taken, notwithstanding the failure of the Planning Authority to issue a warning letter?

4.(a) Is the vendor, or her agent aware of the service of any enforcement notice or notices?

(b) If so, please furnish copies of same stating the date of service and the names and addresses of the persons served. Furnish now evidence that all matters complained of in the enforcement notice have now been rectified and furnish certificate of compliance made by a competent person.

(c) Please confirm, in relation to the enforcement notice, that there are no other proceedings in being, under Pt VIII of the Planning and Development Act 2000.

5. Please confirm that there are no prosecutions pending for non-compliance with any enforcement notice.

6.(a) Please confirm, if such is the case, that neither the vendor nor her agents are aware of any threatened or actual proceedings under s 160 of the Planning and Development Act 2000 as amended by s 48 of the Planning and Development (Amendment) Act 2010 seeking a planning injunction against any party connected with the property in sale either on the High Court or Circuit Court.

(b) If there are either documents threatening the issue of a planning injunction or if proceedings have been served, please furnish copies of same and confirm that prior to closing, all matters complained of or all matters in respect of which an application has been made to the court under the said s 160 (as amended) have been fully remedied and furnish certificate of compliance made by a competent person, or confirm that such proceedings have been conclusively withdrawn and do not in any way, adversely affect the property in sale.

## REQUISITIONS RELATING TO TREE PRESERVATION ORDERS

**[12.26]** It is important to enquire, in appropriate cases (and this may include relatively small dwelling houses) as to whether the property, the subject of any sale, is subject to a tree preservation order (TPO). This topic is dealt with by s 205 of PDA 2000. If it appears to the planning authority that it is expedient, in the interest of amenities or the environment, to make provisions for the preservation of any tree, trees, group of trees or woodlands, it may, for that purpose, and the stated reasons, make a TPO with respect to any such tree, trees, group of trees or woodlands as may be specified in the order. TPO's are generally not applicable to small residential homes but the question must always be asked in any case where there is evidence of mature trees, groups of trees or woodlands. The importance of the question is emphasised by the fact that it is an offence to contravene a TPO or a proposed TPO and fines in excess of €12,000,000 plus imprisonment, not exceeding two years, may be imposed for breaches of the order.

**[12.27]** The appropriate requisitions are as follows:

1. Has a TPO been served or has the Planning Authority served a notice of a proposal to make a TPO which would affect any part of the subject property? If so please furnish a copy immediately.

2. Has there been any breach of any TPO or proposed TPO?

## REQUISITIONS RELEVANT TO PUBLIC RIGHTS OF WAY CREATED BY ORDER

**[12.28]** Apart from s 207 of PDA 2000 (dealt with below in para **12.30**), the question should be asked as to whether any public rights of way have been included in the development plan under s 14 of PDA 2000. Examples of such public rights of way which are included in development plans include the Wicklow Way, the Kerry Way, the Sheep Head Way, the Howth Hill Walk, the Killiney Hill Walk, the Killarney to Kenmare Walk and so on. Enquiries should be made as to whether any notice has been served of an intention to include a specific public right of way in a local authority's development plan. If notice is served there is a right of appeal to the Circuit Court. The fact that a public right of way is not included in the development plan does not affect the existence or validity of such right of way.

**[12.29]** PDA 2000, s 206 permits the planning authority to enter into agreements for dedication by persons of public rights of way and, in the case of such an agreement, it is the duty of the planning authority to take all necessary steps to ensure that the creation of the right of way is effected in accordance with the agreement. Particulars of any such agreement must be entered in the planning register.

**[12.30]** Section 207 gives the planning authority compulsory powers for creation of public rights of way. A planning authority may, by resolution, make an order creating a public right of way over land, subject to conditions or without conditions. The order can be appealed to An Bord Pleanála and particulars of the right of way, when created, shall be entered in the register. No compensation provisions are provided. Since there are circumstances in which the creation of such a public right of way, even though it cannot be made without public notice and notice to the landowner, could drastically reduce the value and amenity of a person's land in circumstances where PDA 2000, Sch 5, para 26 specifically excludes compensation, it is important to know whether or not such a right of way affects the property. The exclusion of compensation relating to the creation of public rights of way under s 207 is manifestly unjust and probably worthy of a constitutional challenge.

[12.31] Suggested requisitions dealing with public rights of way are as follows:

1. Has any agreement been made by the Planning Authority regarding dedication of a public right of way over any part of the property (and if so, please furnish same) or is there any proposal for the Planning Authority to create a public right of way over the property or any part thereof?

2. Is the property or any part of the property affected by public rights of way created by either or both s 206 and/or 207 of PDA 2000?

## REQUISITIONS RELEVANT TO OUTLINE PERMISSION

[12.32] Outline permission is provided for under s 36 of PDA 2000. The grant of an outline permission does not authorise the carrying out of development until such time as a subsequent permission has been granted. The word 'approved' is no longer used in connection with outline permission. The application for subsequent permission must be made under s 36(3) of PDA 2000 within three years of the date of grant of the outline permission but the planning authority under that section does have the right to extend the outline permission from three years to five years. Outline permissions are nevertheless in a special category in relation to time limits or duration of the permission. Under s 40 PDA 2000 a normal planning permission has a life of five years. Under s 41, An Bord Pleanála may, having regard to the nature and extent of the development and other material considerations, specify a period in excess of five years during which the permission will be effective. That additional period will be stated on the planning permission. Section 42 allows a planning authority, in relation to an application, to extend the normal five years period by such additional period not exceeding five years as the authority considers appropriate in order to enable the development to be completed. Section 42 has been extensively altered by the s 28 amendment in PD(A)A 2010 to the extent that one extension only is permitted and that such an extension shall not exceed five years. The application for the extension must still be made before the permission previously granted expires. Before any single extension, which must not exceed five years, is granted the planning authority must be satisfied on the following points:

1. That substantial works have been carried out pursuant to the original grant of permission which was due to expire and that such an application was made before the expiry of that permission.

2. That the development can be completed within a reasonable time.

3. That the development has not proceeded because commercial, economical or technical considerations, beyond the control of the applicant, have substantially militated against the commencement of the development or against the carrying out of substantial works pursuant to the planning permission.

4. The planning authority must be satisfied that there are no changes in the development plan or in any regional planning guidelines which would render the development proposal inconsistent with proper planning and sustainable development of the area.

5. The planning authority must also be satisfied that the development would not offend any guidelines issued by the Minister under s 28 of PDA 2000 (as amended) by PD(A)A 2010, s 20 and it must also be satisfied that an EIA, or an appropriate assessment (if required), was carried out before the permission was granted.[4]

If a s 42 extension is allowed a planning authority is entitled to attach an additional condition requiring adequate security for the satisfactory completion of the proposed development and it may also vary any of the conditions which were imposed by the original permission.[5]

## Special characteristics applying to outline permissions

[12.33] There are special characteristics that apply to outline permissions:

1. Outline permissions cannot be applied for retention of a development.

2. Outline permissions cannot be applied for in relation to works to be carried out on a protected structure or a proposed protected structure.

3. Outline planning permission cannot be applied for development comprising an activity requiring an IPC licence or a waste licence.

4. Outline permission cannot be applied for the provision or modification of an 'establishment' within the meaning of the Major Accidents Directive.

5. The decision to grant planning permission consequent upon a grant of outline permission cannot be appealed to An Bord Pleanála. The time for making of submissions in relation to outline planning permission is within five weeks of the date of application for outline planning permission and if there is to be an appeal, the appeal must be lodged within four weeks of the date of the decision on the outline permission.

6. A planning authority will not be able to refuse permission on a subsequent application for permission on the basis of a matter agreed by the planning authority when the outline permission was granted, provided that the authority is satisfied that the proposed development is within the terms of the outline permission.

[12.34] Requisitions relating to outline permission will include the following:

(i) Furnish now (where applicable) copy Outline Permission and, if applicable, copy notification of grant of permission granted pursuant to the Outline Permission.

(ii) Please state whether any appeal has been lodged or is pending against the grant of Outline Permission and if so, please furnish full details.

---

4. PD(A)A 2010, s 28(1)(a)(i) and (ii), and (b), (c) and (d).
5. PD(A)A 2010, s 28(2).

(iii) If Outline Permission has been granted have any extensions been sought or granted and if so then:
- (a) for how long?
- (b) have any additional conditions been attached?

## REQUISITIONS RELATING TO STRATEGIC DEVELOPMENT ZONE

**[12.35]** It is obviously important to establish whether, if you are buying land or sites, the land or sites are affected by any SDZ and the following requisitions may be suggested in appropriate cases:

1. Is the property located within a SDZ as defined in s 105 of the 2000 Act or is there any proposal to make an SDZ which would include the property or any neighbouring property?
2. Has a planning scheme been adopted for the SDZ and if so has there been:
   - (i) any appeal against the making or deemed making of the planning scheme.
   - (ii) any revocation or amendment of the scheme.
   - (iii) any proposal to revoke or amend the scheme.
3. Has any person entered into an agreement with a development agency for the purpose of facilitating the development of the property pursuant to s 167 of the 2000 Act? If so, please furnish a copy and give details of the extent of compliance with same.

## REQUISITIONS RELEVANT TO ARCHITECTURAL CONSERVATION AREAS AND AREAS OF SPECIAL PLANNING CONTROL

**[12.36]** It is suggested that the following requisitions on title might be raised in relation to architectural conservation areas and areas of special planning control, namely as follows:

1. Is the property or any part thereof within an 'Architectural Conservation Area' or is the vendor aware of any proposal to designate the area in which the property is situate as an 'Architectural Conservation Area'.
2. If so, has the planning authority indicated an intention to acquire the premises or any part thereof for the purposes of preserving land situated in an architectural conservation area, etc, under s 183 of PDA 2000?
3. If notice of intention to compulsorily acquire the property or any part thereof has been served and a vesting order has not yet been made give details of the status of the compulsory acquisition process including the dates of the notice of intention to acquire and any objection made on any decisions of An Bord Pleanála and any discussions regarding compensation.
4. If the property or any part thereof is in a city or town, is the property or a part thereof within an area of 'Special Planning Control' under the 2000

Act (as amended) or is the vendor aware of proposals to designate the area which the property is situate as an area of 'special planning control'. If so:

(i) Has the vendor or any predecessor in title been served with a notice under s 85(4) (objectives or provisions or Special Planning Control relating to specific properties)?

(ii) Has a declaration been sought under s 87(3) of PDA 2000 (declaration as to what type of development would be contrary to the special planning control scheme, the objectives of the scheme which apply to the land and the measures to be undertaken to comply with the objectives or provisions) in respect of the property? If so, please furnish a copy of any declarations and state whether or not same have been rescinded or varied.[6]

(iii) Has a notice under s 88 of PDA 2000 (notice specifying measures to be undertaken for the restoration, demolition, removal, alterations, replacement, maintenance, repair or cleaning of a structure, or the discontinuance of any use or the continuance of a use subject to conditions) been served in respect of the property or is the vendor aware of any intention to serve such a notice? If a notice has been served, please indicate the current status of the matter including any agreements or offers negotiated with the planning authority in respect of compensation or any appeals of the notice.

(iv) Has the notice referred to at 4(iii) been complied with to the satisfaction of the planning authority?

(v) Has the planning authority indicated an intention to enter the property to carry out the works themselves or to seek a court order?

## REQUISITIONS RELEVANT TO LANDSCAPE CONSERVATION ORDERS

[12.37] A planning authority is entitled to designate an area as a landscape conversation area for the purposes of preserving the landscape and this was introduced by PDA 2000, s 204 with a view to preventing removal of hedges and ditches and the division of commonage, afforestation and land reclamation which would normally be exempted development. It is suggested that the question which should be asked is as follows:

1. Is the property or any part thereof within a landscape conservation area or has a notice proposing to make a landscape conservation area Order which would affect the subject property (or to amend or revoke any existing Landscape Conservation Area Order) been published?

---

6. PDA 2000, s 87(3) is similar to PDA 2000, s 57(2) which permits an owner or occupier of a protected structure to make a written request to the relevant planning authority as to the type of works which would be considered by that planning authority to affect the character of the protected structure.

## REQUISITIONS RELATING TO ADVERTISEMENT STRUCTURES

**[12.38]** Clearly, permission for any relevant advertising structure must be produced together with a certificate of compliance (where applicable) signed by a qualified person. PDA 2000, s 209 allows the planning authority to require the repairing and tidying of advertisement structures and advertisements. It is suggested, in appropriate cases, that a requisition might be raised in relation to this as follows:

1. Furnish a copy of planning permission and certificate of compliance relating to the advertisements structure.

2. Has any notice been served by the planning authority regarding the repair, tidying or removal of an advertisement structure or an advertisement pursuant to s 209 of PDA 2000?

## REQUISITIONS RELATING TO CABLES, WIRES, PIPELINES AND APPLIANCES

**[12.39]** PDA 2000, s 254 requires that a licence be obtained for the following:

> Vending machines, town or landscape map for indicating directions or places, hoarding, fences or scaffolding, an advertisement structure, a cable, wire or pipeline, a telephone kiosk or pedestal or any other appliance, apparatus or structure prescribed by regulation on, under, over or along a public road unless:
> 
> (i) planning permission has been obtained;
> 
> (ii) it is erected on a temporary basis in accordance with a condition of a planning permission;
> 
> (iii) it comprises a cable, wire or pipeline constructed by a statutory undertaker eg gas, electricity or telecommunications services.

In other words, development carried out in accordance with the licensing provisions under s 254 shall be exempted development for the purpose of the Act. It is suggested that there may be at least two requisitions which could be raised under this heading, namely:

(1) Has the local authority indicated an intention to place, construct or lay any cable, wire or pipeline or attach any bracket or other fixture to support or carry same on the property? If so, give details including whether there is any agreement or dispute with the local authority.

(2) Are there any items which are licensed or required to be licensed under s 254 of PDA 2000? If so, furnish copies of the relevant licence.

## REQUISITIONS RELATING TO MAJOR ACCIDENTS DIRECTIVE

**[12.40]** PDA 2000, s 2, as amended by PD(A)A 2010, s 4(1)(b)(iv), defines The Major Accidents Directive as Council Directive 96/82/EC of 9 December 1996 ([1997] OJ

L10/13), amended by Directive 2003/105/EC of the European Parliament Council of 16 December 2003 ([2003] OJ L345/97–105). The Directives were designed to identify major accident hazards of certain industrial activities and are concerned with the prevention of such major accidents which might result from particular industrial activities. The Directives also seek to limit the consequences of major accidents for humans and the environment. Some tragic consequences have been demonstrated by hazards which arise when dangerous sites and dwelling houses are placed close together, eg, a fireworks factory in Mexico, a nuclear generation station in Russia, a chemical factory in Bhophal, India, etc. The Directives apply to establishments where dangerous substances are present in quantities equal to, or in excess of, quantities listed in an annex to the Directive. If production or an activity is affected by the Major Accidents Directive, safety reports will be required by operators demonstrating that a major accident prevention policy and a safety management system are in place. As these are EU Directives, they apply to all Member States, who must ensure that the objectives of preventing major accidents and limiting the consequences of such accidents are taken into account in their land use policies and/or other relevant policies.

**[12.41]** Part XI of The Planning and Development Regulations of 2001 provides regulations dealing with The Major Accident Directives. If acting as a solicitor for a purchaser in connection with an establishment to which the Major Accidents Directive might apply, special inquiries will have to be made or if the client intends to develop an establishment which will be affected by the Major Accidents Directive, advice in relation to EIA, notices and other matters in accordance with the regulations should be given. This is a complicated and highly specialised area and if you suspect that a Major Accidents Directive may apply, the question should be asked as to whether the requirements of the Major Accidents Directives have been met.

**[12.42]** General requisitions should be raised asking, for example, for a copy of the up-to-date safety report and seeking full details of major accident prevention policies. A check should the made to see what major accident prevention policies are in place together with details of the safety management system in place. The question should be asked as to whether any accidents have occurred in the premises.

**[12.43]** Solicitors do not have the knowledge or the training to deal with serious requisitions dealing with premises affected by the Major Accidents Directives. In particular, it is not a solicitor's discipline to understand the intricacies of safety management systems and accident prevention policies and those matters, together with relevant questions to be asked relating to the potential of controlling accident hazards, are, most certainly, best left to experts who are familiar with the legislation.

**[12.44]** A question has been asked by some politicians and by environmental groups in Ireland, as to effectiveness of the Major Accidents Directive in the light of additions to establishments at the MOX plant at Sellafield/Windscale in Cumbria on the north east coast of England.

## REQUISITIONS RELATING TO SOCIAL AND AFFORDABLE HOUSING

**[12.45]** The following list comprises suggested requisitions dealing with social and affordable housing:

(1) Is the planning permission a permission to which s 96(2) of PDA 2000, as amended by s 3 of P&D (Amendment) Act 2002 (agreement with planning authority for social and affordable housing), applies? If so furnish:

   (a) a certified copy of the agreement (including a map of the property affected by the agreement) entered into with the planning authority;

   (b) confirmation (if applicable) from an architect that the property in sale is not comprised within the property, the subject of the agreement;

   (c) the information, if any, given by the planning authority of its intention, in relation to the provision of housing on the lands to be transferred pursuant to the agreement.

(2) Please confirm that the property, the subject of the agreement with the local authority, is subject to an obligation by the owners or occupiers thereof to comply with the same obligations (including payment of service charges) as the owners or occupiers of other units in the development.

(3) (a) Is the permission a permission which would have withered but for the provisions of s 4 of PD (Amendment) Act 2002?

   (b) If the same permission is a permission which would have withered in the circumstances outlined in para (a) above, please state whether a levy has been paid or is still payable in the sum of 1% of the sale price if equal to or in excess of €270,000 or 0.5% of the sale price if less than that amount.

   (c) Please furnish local authority's receipt for payment of the levy (if applicable).

   (d) If it is stated that no levy is payable, please state the reasons.

(4) If a certificate has issued pursuant to s 97 of PDA 2000 (as amended) (a certificate that s 96 does not apply because the property consists of the provision of four or fewer houses or for housing on land of 0.1 hectares or less) furnish:

   (a) a certified true copy of the certificate and an extract from the planning register showing the registration of the certificate;

   (b) where development of the property has not completed, confirmation that the certificate has not been revoked by the applicant or the owner of the land to which the certificate relates; or any person acting with the permission of such owner; or by the authority;

   (c) please confirm that the information provided in the application for the s 97 certificate was not false or misleading and the vendor is not aware of any circumstances which could give rise to the revoking of the certificate by the local authority.

(5) If the property is social and affordable housing which is being resold on the first occasion, please state the amount repayable under s 99 of PDA 2000.

## REQUISITIONS RELATING TO TAKING ESTATES IN CHARGE

**[12.46]** PDA 2000, s 180[7] contains the provision for taking charge of building estates including apartment blocks by a local authority. Planning Authorities are required under this section, to take these estates in charge where requested to do so by the person carrying out the development or by a majority of the owners of the houses involved on the estate once the estate has been completed and the relevant requisitions would be as follows:

1. Has any request been made by the person carrying out the development or by the owners or a majority of the owners of the houses to have the roads, open spaces, etc, taken in charge? If so, please state the result of that request.

2. In the alternative, has the Planning Authority expressed dissatisfaction with the manner in which the estate is being completed and have any enforcement proceedings been commenced by the Planning Authority within seven years beginning on the expiration, with respect to the permission authorising the development, of the appropriate period, or has any order been made under s 11(1) of the Roads Act 1993?

Note that it is a matter for the purchaser to check whether enforcement proceedings may or may not be taken on any particular estate. This is done by looking at the date of the planning permission and, assuming there have been no extensions, the life of the planning permission is five years and immunity from enforcement occurs seven years after that date.

## GENERAL REQUISITIONS RELATING TO ENVIRONMENTAL MATTERS

**[12.47]** The requisitions in the Law Society Requisitions on Title may, just about, be adequate for a residential purchase but further and more searching environmental requisitions are required for the purchase of industrial property and other more complex developments. Below are relevant definitions and a comprehensive list of general enquiries to be made concerning environmental matters, some of which may also be relevant to the purchase of residential premises.

### Definitions

**[12.48]** 'Owner' includes, where the context so admits or requires, any predecessor in title of the owner of the property.

---

7. PDA 2000, s 180 as amended by PD(A)A 2010, s 59(a)–(e) and as inserted by PD(A)A 2010, s 59(c) and as substituted by PD(A)A 2010, s 59(f) and (g).

**[12.48]** Planning and Environmental Law in Ireland

'Hazardous materials' means any pollutants, contaminants, radioactive, explosive, oxidising, flammable, toxic, harmful, corrosive, irritant, dangerous, hazardous, infectious, carcinogenic, teratogenic, etiologic, or mutagenic substances, materials, constituents, chemicals, preparations or wastes (including without limitation, petroleum or any by-products or fractions thereof, any form of natural gas, asbestos and asbestos-containing materials, or any derivations thereof, polychlorinated biphenyls ('PCB's') and PCB-containing equipment, radon or other radio-active elements, pesticides and defoliants) or any other meanings ascribed to such terms by any Environmental Laws.

'Hazardous substance' means any substance or material regulated, controlled, prohibited or defined under any Environmental Laws.

'Hazardous waste' means hazardous waste as defined by the Waste Management Acts 1996–2003.

'Environment' means all or any of the following media, namely air (including the air within buildings or other natural or man-made structures above or below ground), water (including groundwater, aquifers and water in pipes, drains and conduits) or land (including soil and sub-surface strata) and includes all such media located within and outside of the properties.

'Environmental consents' means any permit, licence, authorisation, approval or consent required under or in relation to all Environmental Laws by the vendor relating to the use of, or any activities or operations carried out at, the Properties.

'Environmental laws' means all international, European Union, national, State, federal, regional or local laws (including common law, statute law, civil and criminal law), which are in force and binding as at the date of completion relating to environmental matters and this definition shall include, in particular, without limitation, the following Acts: the Public Health (Ireland) Act 1878; the Air Pollution Act 1987; the Local Government (Water Pollution) Act 1977, as amended by the Local Government (Water Pollution) (Amendment) Act 1990; the Fisheries (Consolidation) Acts 1959–2003; the Dangerous Substances Acts 1972–1979; the Litter Act 1982; the Safety Health and Welfare at Work Acts 1989–2005; the Safety in Industry Act 1980; the Factories Act 1955; the Local Government (Planning and Development) Acts 2000–2010 together with Regulations made thereunder; the Building Control Acts 1990–2007 together with Regulations made thereunder; the Waste Management Acts 1996–2008; and the European Communities Acts 1972–2007 and all regulations, bye-laws, orders and codes made thereunder.

'Environmental licences' means any permit, licence, approval, consent, registration or other authorisation required by or pursuant to any applicable Environmental Laws or relating to environmental matters.

'Environmental matters' means any matter arising out of, relating to, or resulting from the pollution, contamination, protection of the environment, human health and safety, health and safety of employees, health and safety of animal and plant life, sanitation and any matters in relation to emissions, discharges, disseminations, releases or threatened releases of hazardous materials into the environment or otherwise arising out of, or relating to, or resulting from the manufacture, processing, distribution, use, treatment, storage, disposal, transport or handling of hazardous materials.

'The property' means the premises the subject matter of these enquiries.

'Waste' means waste as defined by the Waste Management Acts 1996–2003.

## GENERAL PRE-CONTRACT ENQUIRIES/REQUISITIONS CONCERNING ENVIRONMENTAL MATTERS

### Enquiries

**[12.49]** This is a comprehensive list of environmental requisitions which should be carefully scrutinised before settling requisitions to ensure that all requisitions are relevant to the actual property being purchased:

1. Has the owner, or to the best of the owner's knowledge has any third party ever used, generated, manufactured, treated, stored, emitted, released, discharged or disposed of, on, under or about the property, or transported to or from the property, any hazardous materials? If so please furnish full details now.

2. Are the materials which were used in the construction of the buildings on the property free from contamination by any hazardous materials, particularly, is there any asbestos used in any part of the structures on the site? If asbestos has been used and if the property is not treated for contamination by hazardous materials please furnish full details now.

3. Does the owner have all requisite environmental licences? Please furnish copies of each such environmental licence now.

4. Are any environmental licences required in force at the date of these requisitions? Please state the date when they expire or require to be renewed.

5. Are any such environmental licences presently the subject of review by the competent authority or has any notice or communication been received that such a review is proposed? If so please furnish full details now.

6. Has the owner ever been in breach of any Environmental Laws or any notice served on the owner pursuant to such Environmental Laws? If so please furnish full details now.

7. Has the owner ever been in breach of any environmental licences or any condition of same or any notices served on the owner pursuant to such environmental licences? If so please furnish full details now.

8. Has the owner ever received any notice or communications alleging that it has been, is or may be in breach of any Environmental Laws or any environmental licences or any conditions of same? If so, please furnish full details now.

9. Are there, or have there ever been any underground or above ground storage tanks, incinerators, or surface impoundments at, on, under or within the property? If so please furnish full details now.

10. Is the owner aware of any breach of Environmental Laws or environmental licences or any conditions of same by any third party or any circumstances relating to environmental matters, which have resulted or may result in damage or injury to the property or any persons thereon from time to time? If so please furnish full details now.

11. Does the owner:

   (i) discharge trade effluent or dispose of waste substances on or from the property?

   (ii) handle, store or keep waste hazardous materials on the property?

   (iii) discharge pollution into the environment?

And if so, please supply details of or any of the above.

12. Has the owner been involved in or been threatened with any claim, either as plaintiff or defendant, in any litigation concerning environmental matters or is any such claim now pending? If so please furnish full details now.

13. Has the owner claimed under any policy of insurance in relation to environmental matters? If so please furnish full details now.

14. Please supply copies of all environmental impairment insurance policies and related documentation.

15. Has the owner an internal environmental audit procedure and/or has it ever engaged the services of an environmental surveyor or consultant? If so, please provide a copy of such procedures and/or reports from such persons.

16. Has the owner ever received any complaint from members of the public, adjoining landowners or other groups or organisations concerning environmental matters? If so, please furnish full details now.

17. Has the owner been required by the local authority or such other body as may be appropriate to carry out an environmental impact study? If so please furnish a copy of same now.

18. Please supply copies of all audits, action plans, reports, impact statements, site or remedial investigations, feasibility studies or assessments prepared by the owner, environmental consultants or other agent of the owner, insurance carriers of the owner and of the owner's predecessors, or by any local or governmental authority regarding the existence of or liability for, any potential or actual environmental contamination or any material non-compliance with Environmental Laws:

   (i) at the property;

   (ii) at any location (including any real property owned by persons other than the owner) used by the owner for disposal of hazardous materials or any waste substances; and

   (iii) at any location allegedly resulting from the spill or the release of any substances from the property or any facility used by the company or its predecessors.

19. Has any notice been served or agreement entered into pursuant to the Wildlife Acts 1976 and the Wildlife (Amendment) Act 2000 or the European Communities (Natural Habitat) Regulations 1997–2005 affecting any part of the property?

20. Does the property or any part of it host a priority natural habitat type or a priorities species, as defined in the European Communities (Natural Habitat) Regulations 1997–2005?

21. Has any part of the property been classified as a special protection area under the Birds Directive?

22. (i) Is the property situated in any area which may be regarded as being of archaeological significance or is there any feature on or in the property of archaeological significance?

   (ii) In particular, has any part of the property been designated as a national monument under the National Monuments Acts 1930–2004 or has notice of any intention to so designate been served on the vendor?

23. Is there any 'protected structure' or 'proposed protected structure' (as defined in the Planning and Development Act 2000) on any part of the property'?

# PRE-CONTRACT ENQUIRIES/REQUISITIONS RE HABITATS DIRECTIVE

## Wildlife Acts 1976–2000

**[12.50]**

1. Has any order been made under s 16 (recognition of a nature reserve) of the Act as amended by s 27 of the Wildlife (Amendment) Act 2000 affecting the property or any part thereof?

2. Has any notice been served under s 17 (refuge for fauna) of the Act as amended by s 28 of the Wildlife (Amendment) Act 2000 affecting the property or any part thereof?

3.(a) Has any agreement been made under s 11 or 18 of the Act or reg 12 of the European Communities (Natural Habitats) Regulations 1997 for the management of the property or any part thereof?

  (b) Has any negotiation or correspondence been entered into with the Minister with a view to entering into an agreement under s 11 or 18 or reg 12?

4.(a) Is the vendor aware of the presence of any wild birds or animals specified in the Fourth or Fifth Schedule to the Act on any part of the property?

  (b) Is the vendor aware of the presence of any protected species of flora under s 21 of the Act as amended by s 29 of the Wildlife (Amendment) Act 2000 on any part of the property?

(c) Has any part of the property been specified in any order made by the Minister pursuant to s 21(1)(b) as amended by s 29 of the Wildlife (Amendment) Act 2000 with regards a species of flora?

5. Has any purchase order been made, or is the vendor aware of any proposal or intention to make a purchase order, under Pt IV of the Act?

6.(a) With regard to any lake or inland waters in the property, has the Minister published a notice pursuant to s 57 of the Act requiring persons who claim an interest in the lake or inland waters to furnish details of their interest?

(b) Has the Minister made any declaration pursuant to s 57 of the Act vesting the fee simple in any lake or inland waters in the State?

7. Has any right of way used or enjoyed as appurtenant to the property been extinguished, or has any application been made by the Minister to extinguish such a right of way, under s 19 of the Forestry Act 1946 or s 61 of the Act?

8. Has any right of way been created, or has any application been made by the Minister to create a right of way over any part of the property pursuant to s 21 of the Forestry Act 1946 or s 60 of the Act?

## Birds Directive

[12.51] 9. Is any part of the property designated as a special protection area pursuant to art 4 of the Birds Directive?

10(a) Does the property form the natural habitat of any birds listed in Annex 1 to the Birds Directive?

(b) Do any migratory species listed in Annex 1 of the Birds Directive visit any part of the property on a regular basis?

## Natural Heritage Areas

[12.52] 11(a) Has any Natural Heritage Area Order been made in respect of the property or any part of it pursuant to s 18(1) of the Wildlife (Amendment) Act 2000? If so please furnish copy of such order.

(b) Has any notice of intention to make an order designating the property or any part of it a Natural Heritage Area been served under s 16 of the Wildlife (Amendment) Act 2000? If so please furnish copy of such notice.

(c) Have any 'works'[8] (within the meaning of s 15 of the Wildlife (Amendment) Act 2000) been carried out on the property or any part of it

---

8. 'Works' as defined in the Wildlife (Amendment) Act 2000, s 15 includes any activity which destroys or which significantly alters, damages or interferes with the integrity of (a) a site, or (b) any of its species, communities or habitats either intentionally or unintentionally or any activity which has a significant impact on the site or any of its species, communities or habitats, or on its land forms of geological or geomorphological features or on its diversity of natural attributes, other than a development by a local authority or a development which is not exempted development for the purposes of the Planning and Development Acts 2000–2010.

since the date of the service of a notice of intention to make an order designating the property or any part of it, a Natural Heritage Area? If so please furnish full details.

(d) Has any application been made to the Minister for Arts, Heritage, Gaeltacht and the Islands for consent to the carrying out of works (as defined as aforesaid) on the property or any part of it? If so please furnish full details including copy of the decision of the Minister.

(e) Has any direction been given by the Minister for Arts, Heritage, Gaeltacht and the Islands requiring the carrying out of any restoration works pursuant to s 21 of the Wildlife (Amendment) Act 2000?

(f) Please give details of the use to which the land has been put in the last five years.

## Habitats Directive and European Communities (Natural Habitats) Regulations 1997

[12.53] 12. Does the property or any part of it host a 'priority natural habitat type' or a 'priority species' as defined in the Regulations?[9]

13.(a) Has the Minister notified the owner or any occupier of the property or is the vendor otherwise aware of any proposal to include any part of the property in a candidate list of European sites as defined in the Regulations?[10] If so, please furnish copy of the notice.

(b) Has any objection been made to such an inclusion pursuant to art 5 of the Regulations?

(c) Is the vendor aware of any consultation procedure initiated in respect of the property or any part of it pursuant to reg 6 with a view to adding it to the candidate list of European sites?

14. Has any authorised officer inspected, or sought to inspect any part of the property pursuant to reg 7(5)(a) or requested any assistance or information in respect of the property pursuant to reg 7(5)(b)?[11]

15. Has the Minister served any notice pursuant to reg 8 that it is proposed to designate the property or any part of it as a special area of conservation?

16. Has the property or any part of it being designated as a special area of conservation?

17.(a) Has any licence approval consent or other authorisation relating to the property been modified or revoked pursuant to reg 15(2)?

(b) Has any assessment been requested by the Minister in relation to any such licence approval, consent or other authorisation pursuant to reg 15(2)?

---

9. European Communities (Natural Habitats) Regulations 1997, reg 10.
10. European Communities (Natural Habitats) Regulations 1997, reg 4 as substituted by the European Communities (Natural Habitats) (Amendment) Regulations 2005, reg 3(1).
11. European Communities (Natural Habitats) Regulations 1997, reg 7 as amended by the European Communities (Natural Habitats) (Amendment) Regulations 2005, reg 3(3).

18.(a) Has any assessment of any operation or activity, on the property, or any part of it, been required by the Minister pursuant to reg 17?[12]

(b) If so, has any application been made to court in respect thereof pursuant to reg 17(3)?[13]

(c) Has any assessment of any operation or activity on lands other than the property, but which is liable to have an adverse effect on the integrity of the property, been required by the Minister pursuant to reg 18?

(d) If so, has any application been made to court in respect thereof pursuant to reg 17(3)?

19.(a) Has any direction been issued by the Minister to restore the property or any part of it pursuant to reg 19(1)(a)?[13] If so, please furnish copy of the direction.

(b) Has the direction been complied with?

20. Has the Minister requested a review of any existing planning permission affecting the property or any part of it pursuant to reg 27(11)?

21.(a) Has any assessment been carried out in connection with an application for a licence or a revised licence or the review of a licence relating to the property or any part thereof pursuant to reg 32?

(b) Is any such assessment currently being carried out, or has such an assessment been required?

22. Is the vendor aware of any lands being a European site or appearing on a candidate list of European sites the existence of which, by reason of its proximity to, or relationship with the property, might

(a) prevent or restrict any operation or activity on the property;

(b) require an assessment to be carried out on foot of the Regulations in connection with any proposed development of the property, to establish whether the integrity of the European site, or site appearing on a candidate list of European sites would be adversely affected and which would:

(i) result in the modification or revocation of any licence, approval, consent or other authorisation relating to the property, under reg 15(2), or

(ii) require an assessment of the environmental implications prior to the grant or review of a licence or revised licence relating to the property, under reg 32?

## LIFE SPAN OF PLANNING PERMISSION

**[12.54]** Where no period is specified in the planning permission the development must be substantially completed within a period of five years from the date of notification of

---

12. European Communities (Natural Habitats) Regulations 1997, reg 17 as substituted by the European Communities (Natural Habitats) (Amendment) Regulations 2005, reg 3(6).
13. European Communities (Natural Habitats) Regulations 1997, reg 19(1)(a) as amended by the European Communities (Natural Habitats) (Amendment) Regulations 2005, reg 4(8).

grant of planning permission. If the development is of such a scale that it would, in any case, take more than five years to complete, the planning permission will specify another appropriate period which would be equivalent to the time that it would take to finish the development

**[12.55]** PDA 2000, s 42,[14] as amended and substituted, offers a single opportunity to apply for an extension of a planning permission provided substantial works have been carried out. The application must be made before the expiry of the original planning permission. Apart from the 'substantial works' extension allowed by the old PDA 2000, s 42 which required that the development would be completed within a reasonable time, an amended version of s 42 extends the basis in which an extension can be obtained. An extension may be given where the authority is satisfied:

    (I)    that there were considerations of a commercial, economic or technical nature beyond the control of the applicant which substantially militated against either the commencement of the development or the carrying out of substantial works pursuant to the planning permission,

    (II)    that there have been no significant changes in the development objectives in the development plan or in regional development objectives in the regional planning guidelines for the area of the planning authority since the date of the permission such that the development would no longer be consistent with the proper planning and sustainable development of the area,

    (III)    that the development would not be inconsistent with the proper planning and sustainable development of the area having regard to any guidelines issued by the Minister under section 2(8), notwithstanding that they were so issued after the date of the grant of permission in relation to which an application is made under this section, and

    (IV)    where the development has not commenced, that an environmental impact assessment, or an appropriate assessment, or both of those assessments, if required, was or were carried out before the permission was granted.

If the appropriate period is extended a planning authority can attach conditions requiring adequate security to ensure that the development to be carried out during the period of the extended time limit is satisfactorily completed within the extended time limit specified. This is a once-only opportunity and the maximum extension is five years. Under the unamended version of PDA 2000, s 42 it was possible to apply for a second and further extension if the applicant could satisfy the planning authority that failure to complete the development was outside the control of the person carrying out the development.

**[12.56]** The possibility of a default extension permission decision has been removed by PDA 2000, s 42.

---

14.    As substituted by PD(A)A 2010, s 28.

**[12.57]** PDA 2000, s 42, as substituted by PD(A)A 2010, s 28(3), reads as follows:

(a) Where an application is duly made under this section to a planning authority and any requirements of, or made under, regulations under section 43 are complied with as regards the application, the planning authority shall make its decision on the application as expeditiously as possible.

(b) Without prejudice to the generality of paragraph (a) it shall be the objective of the planning authority to ensure that it shall give notice of its decision on an application under this section within a period of eight weeks beginning on–

(i) in case all of the requirements referred to in paragraph (a) are complied with on or before the day of receipt by the planning authority of the application, that day, and

(ii) in any other case, the day on which all of those requirements stand complied with.

The requisition to be raised dealing with the life span of a planning permission is printed in the Law Society's Objections and Requisitions on Title at requisition 27. Requisition 27.3 asks:

27.3 In respect of developments completed after the 1st November 1976 furnish now evidence by way of Statutory Declaration of a competent person that each development was completed prior to the expiration of the Permission/Approval.[15]

## RADON GAS REQUISITIONS

**[12.58]** Radon gas is a natural occurring radioactive gas. It is produced when uranium decays in rocks and soil. The gas wafts up through the earth and through the foundations of older homes. It cannot be detected by humans in a house because it has neither smell nor colour. It can, however, be detected by specialist equipment.

**[12.59]** All houses built since July 1998 are required to have a radon sump in place.

**[12.60]** Radon gas has been linked to an estimated 200 lung cancer deaths *per annum* and purchasers do need to know what, if any, tests have been carried out to determine whether or not radon has been detected or, if not detected, to decide whether a test for radon gas is required in order to check the level. High radon areas in Ireland include Wicklow, Carlow, Wexford, Waterford, Galway, Mayo and Sligo but no county is completely free of it. The high risk counties require that a radon barrier is put in place.

---

15. Law Society's Requisition 27.3 is in group of requisitions with a title printed in bold print which reads: 'Local Government (Planning and Development) Act 1963 ('the Planning Acts')' which heading indicates just how old and out of date the Law Society's planning requisitions are. The Law Society's environmental requisitions are equally, if not more inadequate than its planning requisitions. Until updated (this note was written in April 2011), the Law Society's Planning and Environmental Requisitions should be used with care and added to to take account of new legislation in force since the Society's requisitions were published.

Each of these counties also requires that a radon barrier is incorporated in the foundations of any premises being developed. The presence of granite in an area is often a warning sign which should encourage testing in cases where no testing has previously been carried out. Radon gas can, and has been measured in terms of levels which, exceed the recommended safety margin although no trace of granite was found in the area.

[12.61] The most thoroughly tested county in Ireland to date is Sligo where over one thousand properties have been tested. The result disclosed that 24% of the houses and premises tested had measurements which were in excess of 'safe' levels. It is suggested that, from a conveyancing point of view, the only safe way of dealing with the potential of an unsafe radon gas measurement is to put a special condition in the contract to provide that if no measurements or readings are available at the date of the contract that the contract is subject to obtaining a test which is minimum of, say, 20% below the safe level and if such a higher result is found the purchaser reserves the right to withdraw from the contract and to obtain a refund of any deposit paid.

[12.62] The wording of a requisition which should be raised as a pre-contract requisition is suggested as follows:

> Has the premises been tested for the presence of radon gas? If so, furnish copies of the results. If not, will the vendor agree to have the premises tested and the results disclosed prior to exchange contract?

A prudent conveyancer might be well advised to insert a condition in a contract particularly for premises which are located in the higher risk areas above listed. The contract special condition would require the vendor to produce the results of any test carried out prior to the exchange of contract and if there are no tests they should be carried out by the vendor but if the vendor refuses the purchaser may be well advised to carry out the test in any case and to carry it out before the exchange of contract. Such a clause may not be acceptable to a vendor or to the vendor's advisors but, where there is the slightest hint of radon, or even where there is none, it may, in view of the potential fatal consequences, be advisable to establish the true position. In terms of providing a comprehensive service to a purchaser a solicitor should, at least, mention the radon issue and particularly in high risk counties.

[12.63] To assist in finding out whether or not premises have been tested there is a good website which is kept up to date by the Radiological Protection Institute of Ireland (RPII). Information as to the premises which have been tested may be found on the RPII website at www.rpii.ie. That website allows users to search for the address of the premises which have been tested and where radon levels have been found. There is also a free phone information number at 1800 300 600. The website contains a useful map giving a general indication of the high risk areas. The RPII has conceded that just 5% of all Irish homes believed to have high levels of gas have been identified. It appears that 10 of the 15 highest individual measurements have been found in Kerry around Tralee and the Castleisland area.

## ENVIRONMENTAL WARRANTIES

**[12.64]** Environmental warranties would not usually be required in a routine purchase of a dwelling, shop or office in an urban area and selective pre-contract planning and environmental requisitions should suffice.

**[12.65]** Where Condition 36 has been deleted in the Law Society Contract the purchaser's solicitor may, in certain circumstances, have to advise a purchaser that an environmental warranty should be obtained before signing the contract. This would not normally apply to the ordinary dwelling house purchase/sale transaction but it may apply in specific cases. Where the vendor has refused to provide warranties, the consequences are that, apart from endeavouring to obtain an environmental warranty, detailed pre-contract planning and environmental requisitions must be raised. If a satisfactory environmental warranty can be obtained prior to contract many of the requisitions listed in this chapter dealing with environmental issues will be become superfluous. An example of a draft environmental warranty is as follows:

## Draft environmental warranty

**[12.66]** The warranty should start with the same definitions that are set out at para **12.48**. After the definitions have been inserted the subject matter of the warranty is set out as follows:

### 1. No Hazardous Materials

The vendor to the best of his/her knowledge, warrants that neither he/she nor any previous owner, tenant, occupier or user of the property nor any other person has engaged in or permitted any operations or activities upon, or in connection with, the use of the property or any portion thereof for the purpose of or in any way involving the handling, manufacture, treatment, storage, use, generation, recycling, release, discharge, refining, dumping or disposal of any Hazardous Materials under, in or about the property or has transported any Hazardous Materials to, from or across the property or has permitted any Hazardous Materials to be used in any construction, or to be deposited or stored or otherwise located on, under, in or at the property or has permitted any Hazardous Materials to migrate from the property upon or beneath other properties or has any knowledge of any Hazardous Materials migrating or threatening to migrate from other properties on, about or beneath the property.

### 2. No unsuitable building materials

There is no material used in the construction of any buildings or works located on the property likely to cause any environmental hazard or harm to health. All works erected after 26 December 1991 comply with the European Communities (Construction Products) Regulations 1992.[16] No unsafe or unsound materials have been used in construction of any buildings or works. The property is not affected by any nuisance or pollution. There has been no landfill on the property or any adjoining properties. No polluting activity has been carried out on the property.

---

16. These regulations implement Council Directive 89/106/EEC of 21 December 1988.

The vendor has caused surveys and environmental audits to have been carried out at least annually and no problems have been revealed concerning the property.

### 3. Compliance with Environmental Laws

The condition, use, maintenance and operation of the property and every part thereof and all activities and conduct of business related thereto comply, and have at all times complied, with all Environmental Laws pertaining to the property and its use. The vendor has complied with and the vendor is aware of no previous breach of any Environmental Laws relating to environmental matters. The use of the property and the property itself is not causing breach of any regulations designed to protect third parties.

### 4. No notice of non-compliance or litigation

Neither the vendor, nor any prior owner or occupier of the property has received notice or other communication concerning any alleged non-compliance or contravention of Environmental Laws or notice of other communication concerning alleged liability for damages in connection in any way with the property. The vendor has not received any written or oral communication from a Governmental agency, authority, citizens group, employee or other person; alleging that the company or the vendor is not in full compliance with Environmental Laws. To the best of the vendor's knowledge and belief having made due enquiries, there are no circumstances known to the vendor that may prevent or interfere with full compliance with Environmental Laws in the future. There is no environmental claim pending or threatened against the vendor or to the best of the vendor's knowledge, after due enquiry, against any personal entity whose liability for any environmental claim the vendor has or may have retained or assumed either contractually or by operation of law. The vendor is not aware of any actions, claims or proceedings whether actual or potential relating in any way to the environmental matters nor has he/she any reason to believe that they have or is likely to have any liability in relation to such matters.

### 5. All required licences issued and in effect

The vendor has all registrations, permits, authorisations, licences and consents required to be issued by any relevant authority on account of any or all of its activities on the property and is in full compliance with the terms and conditions of such registrations, permits, authorisations, licences and consents. No change in the facts or circumstances reported or assumed in the application or granting of the same exists and all the same are in full force and effect. The vendor is in full compliance with all applicable Environmental Laws. The vendor has obtained all necessary permits, licences and Government authorisations under applicable Environmental Laws all of which are in full force and effect. No notification or prosecution has been received in respect of breaches of regulations and a protection of third parties and no claims have been received from any third parties in respect of nuisance. There is and has been no breach of Regulations governing operating standards for the industry carried on by the vendor, there is and has been no breach of regulations regarding health and safety relating to the operation of the vendor's business and there is and has been no claim from employees regarding working practices.

## 6. Liabilities

The company and the vendor have no liability (actual or contingent), and there are no circumstances which would give rise to any such liability on the part of the vendor to make good, repair, reinstate, or clean up any property now, or previously owned or used by the vendor, to re-dispose of or re-process any waste, or to remedy any effects of a disposal, spillage, leak or emission of any waste or hazardous or polluting matter.

## 7. Use

7.1 The vendor occupies and uses the property solely for the purpose of conducting its business and has quiet enjoyment thereof and the activities of the vendor and of every tenant and licensee of the vendor carried on at the property and the use to which the property is and has been put do not contravene the provisions of the Planning Acts or the Environmental Laws or other legislation or any requirement of any local or other relevant authority.

7.2 No consent has been refused or granted subject to unusual or onerous terms in respect of the property or any part thereof and there is no agreement with any Planning Authority relating to the use or development of the property or any part thereof or the modification of any consent in respect thereof.

7.3 The property has not been and is not affected by any nuisance, pollution, noise or other factors adversely affecting the vendor's use or other rights in respect thereof.

7.4 There is in force an appropriate licence or permit in respect of all activities carried on or at the property and all materials, substances or wastes kept or used on or at the property or any part thereof and all conditions therein contained are now being and have at all times been, complied with.

7.5 The property had not been polluted or otherwise adversely affected as the result of any process carried out, or substance kept or used thereon nor have the atmosphere, soil, services or watercourses on or in the vicinity of the property been so polluted.

7.6 The property has not been used in a manner which has adversely affected the value, use or enjoyment of any adjoining or neighbouring property.

7.7 No application for authorisation consent or permission under the Environmental Laws have been refused or granted subject to unusual or onerous conditions and the vendor is not in breach of any condition of any such authorisation and no enforcement proceedings have been taken under that legislation.

7.8 No landfill or mining operation or any act or omission capable of giving rise to a liability under Environmental Laws have been carried out on or in the immediate vicinity of the property or any part thereof.

## 8. Surveys

8.1 All necessary soil and site investigations and environmental surveys have been carried out from time to time with regard to the property and the use thereof as necessary to establish the accuracy of the warranties set out above.

8.2 The vendor has not commissioned nor is aware of any survey, inspection, report or audit which has revealed any matter which would be a contravention of any of the provisions of this paragraph and the vendor has carried out a full investigation and, survey of the property in this respect within the last 12 months.

## 9. Enquiries

The replies to written enquiries made by the purchaser's solicitor concerning the property have been given after making due and diligent enquiry and are completely true and accurate in all respects.

## 10. Insurance

The vendor's Environmental Impairment Insurance and General Accident Liability Insurance cover the risks specified in Schedule [...], are valid and properly obtained. The vendor has not done anything to vitiate such insurance policies. Such insurance policy covers past activities on the property. All information given to insurers is produced at the date of this agreement and is listed in Schedule [...] hereto.

## 11. Remedial Action

11.1 The vendor shall upon demand, and at his/her sole cost and expense, promptly take all actions and undertake all such works which, in the reasonable opinion of the purchaser, are necessary to mitigate any environmental harm or damage and to allow full economic use of property provided that such action and works are necessary to and take due to the presence upon, above or beneath the property Hazardous Materials or any non-compliance with or contravention of Environmental Laws.

11.2 The action to be undertaken by the vendor shall include but not be limited to investigation of any environmental claim relating to the property, the commissioning of feasibility studies, reports remedial plans as appropriate and the-monitoring and supervision.

11.3 All such action shall be performed by one or more contractors selected by the vendor and approved in advance in writing by the purchaser

11.4 The vendor shall not proceed continuously and diligently in such investigatory and remedial actions. Any such actions shall be performed in a good, safe and workmanlike manner to minimise the impact on the business conducted at the property.

11.5 The vendor shall promptly provide to the purchaser copies of testing results and the reports that are generated in connection with remedial action taken.

11.6 Within seven days of demand therefor, the vendor shall provide the purchaser with a bond evidencing that the necessary funds are available to perform the obligations established by this clause in relation to remedial action.

## ENVIRONMENTAL INDEMNITIES

**[12.67]** Provided a purchaser is satisfied that the vendor is in good standing and able to indemnify the purchaser, another approach to dealing with environmental matters would be to obtain an indemnity from the vendor to keep the purchaser indemnified against any claims, charges, losses, liabilities or expenses (including any depletion or reduction in the value of the purchaser). This indemnity could start off with the same definitions that are set out at para **12.48**. A list of suggested matters to which the indemnity might apply is as follows:

(i) The condition of the properties prior to or on the date of completion;

(ii) Any soil contamination at the properties the presence of which arose prior or on the date of completion;

(iii) The presence of or release or migration on or from the properties of any contamination or polluting substances or Hazardous Substance prior to or on the date of completion;

(iv) Any breach of Environmental Laws or environmental consents occurring prior to or on the date of completion;

(v) The cost of clearing, removing, replacing or remediating any contamination or polluting substances or Hazardous Substance present at or on the properties prior to or on the date of Completion;

(vi) The release, escape, movement or migration from the properties after the date of completion of any contamination or polluting substances or Hazardous Substance present at or on the properties prior to on the date of completion;

(vii) The holding, storage, transport, recovery or disposal of any waste or hazardous waste generated or held at any of the properties on or prior to the date of completion.

## SUGGESTED LIMITED INDEMNITY IN RESPECT OF ENVIRONMENTAL ISSUES GIVEN BY VENDOR AND COUNTER-INDEMNITY GIVEN BY PURCHASER

**[12.68]** 1. Subject to the provisions of Clause 2 hereunder the vendor undertakes to indemnify the purchaser in respect of any facility and legally sustainable claims under Environmental Law against the purchaser by third parties arising out of the migration of any Hazardous Substance present on the property prior to the completion from the property on or after completion.

2. It shall be a pre-condition of the purchaser's right to claim under this indemnity that:

(i) The purchaser shall use all reasonable endeavours to avoid and, if impossible to avoid, to minimise the size or extent of any liabilities which are the subject of this indemnity.

(ii) Any liability the subject of this indemnity shall not have been aggravated or increased or caused in any way by the purchaser or by any third party subsequent to Completion or at the direction of the purchaser prior to Completion or by any matter subsequent to Completion and outside the vendor's control.

    (iii)    Written notification of the liquidated liability is received by the vendor no later than the [...] anniversary of the date of this agreement.

3. The purchaser shall, to enable the vendor to assess its liabilities (if any) and to determine appropriate courses of action under this indemnity and to take such action as it considers appropriate in the circumstances to minimise its liabilities under the terms of this indemnity:

    (i)    keep the vendor at all times fully informed of any circumstances that give rise or may give rise, to or otherwise relate to any liabilities which are the subject of this indemnity whether existing or potential;

    (ii)    supply to the vendor such information (including copies of relevant documents) as the vendor reasonably requires;

    (iii)    permit the vendor and its representatives access to the property for the purpose of undertaking tests and taking samples from the property and carrying out such preventative or other remedial work as it may reasonably think fit subject to the vendor making good after completion of such work and taking reasonable steps to minimise disturbance to the purchaser;

    (iv)    give such co-operation as is reasonably requested by the vendor (including but without limitation) meeting with and reviewing matters with the vendor.

4. The purchaser shall consult fully with the vendor and comply with the vendor's reasonable requirements as to whether and how any matter which may be the subject of this indemnity shall be defended, satisfied, remedied, settled, compromised or in any way dealt with.

5. The purchaser shall not acknowledge the validity of quantum of any claim or settle or compromise any claim or proceedings without the prior approval (not to be unreasonably withheld or delayed) of the vendor.

6. The vendor's liability under this indemnity shall be limited as follows:

    (i)    This indemnity does not apply in any case where the property is used for a purpose other than that of (   );

    (ii)    This indemnity does not extend to loss of profits or any form of consequential loss;

    (iii)    The vendor's liability shall be limited to an aggregate of (€ );

    (iv)    The vendor shall not be liable in respect of any claim the value of which is less than (€ );

    (v)    The vendor's liability shall be limited to that part of any claim which exceeds the sum specified in Clause 6(iv);

    (vi)    The vendor's liability in respect of any individual claim shall be limited to the minimum amount required to undertake remediation works to prevent any further material migration of the relevant Hazardous Substance from the part of the property in respect of which the claim shall have arisen to any land outside the boundaries of the property.

7. Subject to the preceding provisions of this Clause the purchaser undertakes to indemnify the vendor in respect of all and any liabilities and expenses which may be incurred by the vendor arising out of or in connection with the presence of any Hazardous Substance in or under the property or the migration of any Hazardous Substance from the property on or after Completion.

8. The provisions of Clause [ ] *mutatis mutandis* apply to any claim by the vendor against the purchaser under the terms of Clause [ ].

## SUGGESTED LIST OF TENANT'S COVENANTS DEALING WITH ENVIRONMENTAL ISSUES TO BE CONTAINED IN A LEASE

**[12.69]** The Tenant covenants with the Landlord during the Term as follows:

1. To maintain the property in no worse state and condition then that at the commencement of the Lease as evidenced by the Environmental Report.

2. Not to commit or allow to be committed any act or make or allow to be made any omission which would or may cause any Hazardous Substance to escape, leak or be spilled or deposited on the property or discharged from the property or migrate to or from it and to notify the Landlord immediately of any such occurrence.

3. Not to store in, on or under the property any petrol or other specifically inflammable explosive or combustible substance or any other Hazardous Substance (excluding any Hazardous Substance in general use for domestic purposes) except any such which are approved in writing by the Landlord and/or which is used in connection with the Tenant's business on the property.

4. Not to discharge or cause or permit to be discharged into any pipe, drain or sewer serving the property any Hazardous Substance or without limitation any deleterious matter (including without limitation oil or grease) but to keep thoroughly cleaned the property and the pipes, drains and sewers serving the property whenever necessary.

5. Not to use the property:
    (i) Except for the business of [    ] or such other purpose as the Landlord shall, entirely at its discretion, approve;
    (ii) In any manner which would cause or may lead to a breach of the provisions of Clause [ ].

6. Not to erect nor install in or on the property any engine, furnace, plant or machinery which would or may cause noise, fumes or vibration which can be heard, smelled or felt outside the property or may lead to a breach.

7. Not to carry out or cause or permit to be carried out in, on or under the property any excavations, tunnelling, engineering or building works or exploratory works or without limitation other operations involving the disturbance or penetration of the surface or subsoil of the property.

8. To obtain and maintain all the permits necessary to carry out the permitted use and on the termination of the Lease (for whatever cause or reason) to take all steps available to the Tenant to ensure that all such permits are (at the direction of the Landlord) duly transferred to the Landlord or to other persons or that they are surrendered.

9. To comply with good industrial practice in relation to any activity carried on at the property which may affect the environment and/or the health and comfort of human beings and/or other organisms.

10. Prior to commencing the permitted use to obtain a report from a suitably qualified environmental consultant and to comply with his/her/its recommendations in relation to any activity carried on at the property.

11. To notify the Landlord forthwith of any complaint from any person or any notice or proceedings against the Tenant relating to any matters affecting the property concerning the Environment or the health or comfort of human beings or other organisms and to provide the Landlord with copies of any correspondence, notices, proceedings or other documents relating thereto.

12. At the termination of the Lease for whatever reason to obtain a report from a suitably qualified environmental consultant as to the steps required to put the property including, without limitation, the subsoil, back into such condition as is:

    (i) Suitable for the permitted use;

    (ii) Necessary to ensure that no Hazardous Substance will migrate from the property;

    (iii) Comply with the recommendations of any report furnished and to obtain a further report from such environmental consultant stating that all requirements of this Clause have been complied with.

13. To ensure that any plant and equipment on the property are capable of functioning so as to comply with applicable environmental laws.

14. To permit the Landlord and its employees or agents at all reasonable times after giving the Tenant 48 hours written notice (except in case of emergency) to enter the premises to:

    (i) inspect, view and examine its condition and to undertake investigations (including without limitation the taking of samples) in, on and/or under the property to ascertain the condition of the property without limitation the nature, extent and mobility of Hazardous Substances in, on and/or under the property;

    (ii) undertake any works which the Landlord deems necessary and (for which the Tenant is not responsible) to avoid or minimise the risk of any Hazardous Substance in, on or under the property polluting the Environment causing harm to human health or to any other living organism or damaging property provided that the Landlord shall make good after the completion of such works and take all reasonable steps to minimise disturbance to the Tenant provided further that the Tenant shall not be entitled to any compensation in respect of the exercise by the Landlord of the rights in this Clause.

15. Where, by reason of breach by the Tenant of its obligations under the terms of the Lease, works are required to be remedied such breach and such works relate in any way to any Hazardous Substance the Landlord shall be permitted to carry out and complete at the expense of the Tenant to the satisfaction of the Landlord and in accordance in all respects with the Landlord's specifications and under the Landlord's supervision all remediation and works as shall be required by the Landlord by notice to the Tenant and within such reasonable period as is specified in the notice provided that the Landlord may himself, herself or itself or by his/her/its employees or agents enter and remain on the property (with plant equipment and materials) as necessary to execute such remediation and works.

16. The Landlord in the notice to the Tenant shall incorporate notification of its election to carry out the works or shall notify the Tenant that if the Tenant fails to comply with the notice the Landlord shall carry out the said works.

17. To pay the Landlord on demand all expenses and costs directly or indirectly incurred by the Landlord under Clause [ ] (such expenses and costs and any interest on them calculated from the date the expenditure is incurred to be recoverable as if they were rent in arrears).

18. To keep the Landlord indemnified in respect of all and any actions, losses, damages, liabilities, charges, claims, costs and expenses which may be paid, incurred, suffered or sustained by the Landlord arising (directly or indirectly) by reason of breach by the Tenant of its obligations under this Lease.

## SUGGESTED LANDLORD'S CONVENANTS DEALING WITH ENVIRONMENTAL ISSUES CONTAINED IN A LEASE

**[12.70]** These clauses could start with the same definitions that are set out at para **[12.48]**.

1. The Landlord shall treat or remove any Hazardous Substance present in, on or under the property at the commencement of the Lease in accordance with the recommendations of the Environmental Report.

2. The Landlord shall indemnify the Tenant in respect of all or any actions, losses, damages, liabilities, charges, claims, costs (including without limitation legal and consultancy fees) and expenses (including without limitation the costs of any work reasonably required to avoid or mitigate any such actions, losses, damages, liabilities, charges, claims, costs or expenses) which may be paid, incurred, suffered or sustained by the Tenant arising (directly or indirectly) out of or in connection the presence of any Hazardous Substance in or under the property at the commencement of the Lease.

3. It is hereby agreed and declared that no covenant by the Tenant in this Lease shall extend to any Hazardous Substance present in or under the property at the commencement of the Lease.

# SUGGESTED LOAN AGREEMENT CLAUSES COVERING ENVIRONMENTAL ISSUES

**[12.71]** These clauses should start with the same definitions are set out at para **12.48**. After the definitions have been inserted the subject matter of the loan agreement clauses are set out as follows:

1. The borrower has obtained all permits requisite for the operation of its business and has at all times fully complied in all material respects with the terms of those permits and all other applicable Environmental Laws.

2. So far as the borrower is aware there are no Hazardous Substances in, on or under the property which are likely to give rise to liabilities on the borrower or any owner or occupier of the property.

3. No notification has been received by the borrower suggesting that the borrower or any other owner or occupier of the property is in breach of any Environmental Law in relation to the property or that a claim may be made against the borrower in relation to any such matter.

4. The borrower is unaware of any circumstances which may give rise to a claim in relation to the property against the borrower or any owner or occupier of the property under any Environmental Law.

5. The borrower has complied with all lawful requirements of any environmental regulatory authority relating to the property.

6. The borrower shall comply with all Environmental Laws relating to the property and the borrowers business.

7. The borrower shall obtain and maintain in force all permits relating to the property and the borrowers business and fully comply in all material respects with the terms and conditions of all such permits.

8. The borrower shall promptly upon receipt of the same notify the lender of any claim, notice or other communication served on it in respect of any alleged breach of any Environmental Law which might reasonably be expected, if substantiated, to have a material adverse effect on the ability of the borrower to perform its obligations under the agreement.

9. The borrower shall provide to the lender on request all information relating to the borrower's compliance with Environmental Law including without limitation compliance with the conditions of any permit.

10. The borrower shall obtain and maintain in full force and effect, environmental insurance on terms acceptable to the lender (provided, that such insurance is obtainable on reasonable terms and at commercially reasonable rates) in relation to the condition of the property and liabilities resulting from the operation of the borrower's business.

11. The borrower shall comply with environmental best practice in operating its business.

12. The borrower shall not keep hazardous substances at the property unless they are required for carrying on the borrower's business and they are kept in compliance with all applicable environmental laws.

# APPENDIX OF PLANNING FORMS

## [NAME OF FORM]

SCHEDULE
SCHEDULE 3
PRESCRIBED NOTICES

Form no. 1                                                                                                         Article 19
Site notice.

NAME OF PLANNING AUTHORITY.

SITE NOTICE[a]

I, _____, intend to apply for permission / retention permission / outline permission/ permission consequent on the grant of outline permission (Ref. No. of outline permission) for development at this site

_____

_____

The development will consist/consists of _____.

The planning application may be inspected or purchased at the offices of the planning authority during its public opening hours. A submission or observation in relation to the application may be made in writing to the planning authority on payment of the prescribed fee within the period of 5 weeks beginning on the date of receipt by the authority of the application.

Signed:_____

Date of erection of site notice_____

    Directions for completing this notice.

1. The name of the planning authority to which the planning application will be made should be inserted here.
2. The name of the applicant for permission (and not his or her agent) should be inserted here
3. Delete as appropriate. The types of permission which may be sought are—
    (a) permission,
    (b) retention permission,
    (c) outline permission,
    (d) permission consequent on the grant of outline permission. If this type of permission is being sought, the reference number on the planning register of the relevant outline permission should be included.
4. The location, townland or postal address of the land or structure to which the application relates should be inserted here.
5. Delete as appropriate. The present tense should be used where retention permission is being sought.

6. A brief description of the nature and extent of the development should be inserted here. The description shall include—
   (a) where the application relates to development consisting of or comprising the provision of houses, the number of houses to be provided. 'Houses' includes buildings designed as 2 or more dwellings or flats, apartments or other dwellings within a building,
   (b) where the application relates to the retention of a structure, the nature of the proposed use of the structure and, where appropriate, the period for which it is proposed to retain the structure,
   (c) where the application relates to development which would consist of or comprise the carrying out of works to a protected structure or proposed protected structure, an indication of that fact,
   (d) where an environmental impact statement has been prepared in respect of the planning application, an indication of that fact,
   (e) where the application relates to development which comprises or is for the purposes of an activity requiring an integrated pollution control licence or a waste licence, an indication of that fact, or
   (f) where a planning application relates to development consisting of the provision of, or modifications to an establishment within the meaning of Part 11 of these Regulations (Major Accidents Directive), an indication of that fact.
7. Either the signature of the applicant or the signature and contact address of the person acting on behalf of the applicant should be inserted here.
8. The date that the notice is erected or fixed at the site should be inserted here.

a. PDR 2001, Sch 3, Form no 1 as substituted by PDR 2006.

## Appendix of Planning forms

# [NAME OF FORM]

**Form No. 2 Schedule 3**  **Article 22 PDR 2006**

*Planning Application Form.*

**BEFORE FILLING OUT THIS FORM PLEASE NOTE THE FOLLOWING:**
**STANDARD PLANNING APPLICATION FORM AND ACCOMPANYING DOCUMENTATION:**

*Please ensure that each section of this application form is fully completed and signed. The applicant should enter n/a (not applicable) where appropriate.*

*Please ensure that all necessary documentation is attached to your application form.*

Failure to complete this form or attach the necessary documentation, or the submission of incorrect information or omission of required information will lead to the invalidation of your application.

### ADDITIONAL INFORMATION

*It should be noted that each planning authority has its own development plan, which sets out local development policies and objectives for its own area. The authority may therefore need supplementary information (i.e. other than that required in this form) in order to determine whether the application conforms with the development plan and may request this on a supplementary application form.*

*Failure to supply the supplementary information will not invalidate your planning application. However, if it is not supplied, the planning authority may not be able to reach a decision on whether or not to grant permission on the basis of the information available to it. Therefore failure to supply this information could delay the decision on an application or lead to a refusal of permission.*

*Applicants should therefore contact the relevant planning authority to determine what local policies and objectives would apply to the development proposed and whether additional information is required*

PLANNING APPLICATION FORM

**1. Name of Relevant Planning Authority:**

**2. Location of Proposed Development:**

*Postal Address*

*or*

*Townland or Location (as may best identify the land or structure in question)*

*Ordnance Survey Map Ref No (and the Grid Reference where available)*

**3. Type of planning permission (please tick appropriate box):**

☐ Permission

1083

☐ Permission for retention
☐ Outline Permission
☐ Permission consequent on Grant of Outline Permission

**4. Where planning permission is consequent on grant of outline permission:**

Outline Permission Register Reference Number:

Date of Grant of Outline Permission:        /    /

**5. Applicant:**

*Name (s)*

*Address(es)*

*Telephone No.*

*Mobile No. (if any)*

*Email Address*

*(if any)*

*Fax No. (if any)*

**6. Where Applicant is a Company (registered under the Companies Acts 1963 to 1999):**

*Name(s) of company director(s)*

*Registered Address (of company)*

*Company Registration No.*

*Telephone No.*

*Email Address (if any)*

*Fax No. (f any)*

**7. Person/Agent on behalf of the Applicant if any):**

*Name*

*Address*

*Telephone No.*

*Mobile No. (if any)*

*Email Address (if any)*

*Fax No. (f any)*

**Should all correspondence be sent to the above address? (please tick appropriate box)**

(Please note that if the answer is 'No', all correspondence will be sent to the Applicant's address)

Yes  [  ]            No  [  ]

## Appendix of Planning forms

**8. Person responsible for preparation of Drawings and Plans:**

*Name*

*Address*

*Telephone No.*

*Mobile No. (if any)*

*Email Address (if any)*

*Fax No. (f any)*

**9. Description of Proposed Development:**

*Brief description of nature and extent of development*

**10. Legal Interest of Applicant in the Land or Structure:**

*Please tick appropriate box to show applicant's legal interest in the land or Structure*

A. Owner    B. Occupier

C. Other

*Where legal interest is 'Other', please expand further on your interest in the land or Structure*

*If you are not the legal owner, please state the name and address of the owner and supply a letter from the owner of consent to make the application as listed in the accompanying documentation*

**11. Site Area:**

*Area of site to which the application relates in hectares*

**12. Where the application relates to a building or buildings:**

*Gross floor spaces of any existing building(s) in $m^2$*

*Gross floor space of proposed works in $m^2$*

*Gross floor space of work to be retained in $m^2$ (if appropriate)*

*Gross floor space of any demolition in $m^2$ (if appropriate)*

**13. In the case of mixed development (e.g. residential, commercial, industrial, etc), please provide breakdown of the different classes of development and breakdown of the gross floor area of each class of development:**

Class of Development          Gross floor area in $m^2$

**14. In the case of residential development please provide breakdown of residential mix:**

Number of      Studio    1 Bed    2 Bed    3 Bed   4 Bed    4+ Bed    Total
Houses
Apartments

Number of car-parking spaces to be provided      Existing:   Proposed:   Total:

**15. Where the application refers to a material change of use of any land or structure or the retention of such a material change of use:**

*Existing use (or previous use where retention permission is sought)*

*Proposed use or use it is proposed to retain)*

# Appendix of Planning forms

*Nature and extent of any such proposed use (or use it is proposed to retain)*

## 16. Social and Affordable Housing

*Please tick appropriate box*     Yes          No

*Is the application an application for permission for development to which Part V of the Planning and Development Act 2000 applies?'*

If the answer to the above question is 'yes' and the development is not exempt (see below), you must specify, as part of your application, the manner in which you propose to comply with section 96 of Part V of the Act.

If the answer to the above question is 'yes' but you consider the development to be exempt by virtue of section 97 of the Planning and Development Act 2000, a copy of the Certificate of Exemption under section 97 must be submitted (or, where an application for a certificate of exemption has been made but has not yet
been decided, a copy of the application should be submitted).

If the answer to the above question is 'no' by virtue of section 96(13) of the Planning and Development Act 2000, details indicating the basis on which section 96(13) is considered to apply to the development should be submitted.

## 17. Development Details

*Please tick appropriate box*                                    *Yes*          *No*

Does the proposed development consist of work to a
protected structure and/or its curtilage or proposed
protected structure and/or its curtilage?

Does the proposed development consist of work to the
exterior of structure which is located within an
architectural conservation area (ACA) ?

Does the application relate to development which
affects or is close to a monument or place recorded
under section 12 of the National Monuments
(Amendment) Act, 1994?

Does the application relate to work within or close to a
European Site (under SI No 94 of 1997) or a Natural
Heritage Area?

Does the proposed development require the preparation
of an Environmental Impact Statement?

Does the application relate to a development which
comprises or is for the purposes of an activity requiring
an integrated pollution prevention and control licence?

Does the application relate to a development which
comprises or is for the purposes of an activity requiring
a waste licence?

Do the Major Accident Regulations apply to the
proposed

development?

Does the application relate to a development in a
Strategic

Development Zone?

Does the proposed development involve the demolition
of any habitable house?

## 18. Site History

Details regarding site history (if known)

Has the site in question ever, to your knowledge, been flooded?

Yes [ ]     No [ ]

If yes, please give details e.g. year, extent.

Are you aware of previous uses of the site e.g. dumping or quarrying?

Yes [ ]     No [ ]

If yes, please give details.

Are you aware of any valid planning applications previously made in respect of this land/structure?

Yes [ ]     No [ ]

## Appendix of Planning forms

If yes, please state planning reference number(s) and the date(s) of receipt of the planning application(s) by the planning authority if known:
Reference No.: _____ Date: _____

If a valid planning application has been made in respect of this land or structure in the 6 months prior to the submission of this application, then the site notice must be on a yellow background in accordance with article 19(4) of the Planning and Development Regulations 2001 as amended.

**Is the site of the proposal subject to a current appeal to An Bord Pleanála in respect of a similar development?**
Yes [ ]   No [ ]
*An Bord Pleanála Reference No.:* _____

### 19. Pre-application Consultation
**Has a pre-application consultation taken place in relation to the proposed development**
Yes [ ]   No [ ] If yes, please give details:
Reference No. (if any): _____
Date(s) of consultation: _____ /_____ /_____
Persons involved: _____

### 20. Services
*Proposed Source of Water Supply*

Existing connection [ ]
New connection [ ]
Public Mains    [ ]
Group Water Scheme [ ]
Private Well    [ ]
Other (please specify):
*Name of Group Water Scheme (where applicable)*

*Proposed Wastewater Management/Treatment*
Existing [ ]   New [ ]
Public Sewer [ ]  Conventional septic tank system [ ]
Other on-site treatment system [ ] Please specify

*Proposed Surface Water Disposal*
Public Sewer/Drain [ ]  Soakpit [ ]
Watercourse [ ]  Other [ ]
Please specify

## 21. Details of Public Notice

*Approved newspaper in which notice was published*

*Date of publication*

*Date on which site notice was erected*

## 22. Application Fee

Fee payable

*Basis of calculation*

**I hereby declare that, to the best of my knowledge and belief, the information given in this form is correct and accurate and fully compliant with the Planning and Development Act 2000, as amended, and the Regulations made thereunder:**

*Signed*

*(Applicant or Agent as appropriate)*

*Date*

> An applicant will not be entitled solely by reason of a planning permission to carry out the development. The applicant may need other consents, depending on the type of development. For example, all new buildings, extensions and alterations to, and certain changes of use of existing buildings must comply with building regulations, which set out basic design and construction requirements.
>
> *This form should be accompanied by the following documentation:*
>
> Please note that if the appropriate documentation is not included, your application will be deemed invalid.
>
> **ALL Planning Applications**
>
> - ☐ The relevant page of newspaper that contains notice of your application
> - ☐ A copy of the site notice
> - ☐ 6 copes of site location map
> - ☐ 6 copies of site or layout plan
> - ☐ 6 copies of plans and other particulars required to describe the works to which the development relates (include detailed drawings of floor plans, elevations and sections— except in the case of outline permission)
> - ☐ The appropriate Planning Fee
>
> **Where the applicant is not the legal owner of the land or structure in question:**
>
> - ☐ The written consent of the owner to make the application

# Appendix of Planning forms

**Where the application is for residential development that is subject to Part V of the 2000 Act:**

- [ ] Specification of the manner in which it is proposed to comply with section 96 of Part V

Or

- [ ] A certificate of exemption from the requirements of Part V

Or

- [ ] A copy of the application submitted for a certificate of exemption.

**Where the application is for residential development that is not subject to Part V of the 2000 Act by virtue of section 96(13) of the Act:**

- [ ] Information setting out the basis on which section 96(13) is considered to apply to the development.

**Where the disposal of wastewater for the proposed development is other than to a public sewer:**

- [ ] Information on the on-site treatment system proposed and evidence as to the suitability of the site for the system proposed.

**Where the application refers to a protected structure/ proposed protected structure/ or the exterior of a structure which is located within an architectural conservation area (ACA):**

- [ ] Photographs, plans and other particulars necessary to show how the development would affect the character of the structure.

**Applications that refer to a material change of use or retention of such a material change of use:**

- [ ] Plans (including a site or layout plan and drawings of floor plans, elevations and sections which comply with the requirements of article 23) and other particulars required describing the works proposed.

**Where an application requires an Environmental Impact Statement:**

- [ ] An Environmental Impact Statement

**Applications that are exempt from planning fees:**

- [ ] Proof of eligibility for exemption

**Directions for completing this form.**

1. Grid reference in terms of the Irish Transverse Mercator.
2. 'The applicant' means the person seeking the planning permission, not an agent acting on his or her behalf.
3. Where the plans have been drawn up by a firm/company the name of the person primarily responsible for the preparation of the drawings and plans, on behalf of that firm/company, should be given.
4. A brief description of the nature and extent of the development, including reference to the number and height of buildings, protected structures, etc.

5. Gross floor space means the area ascertained by the internal measurement of the floor space on each floor of a building; i.e. Floor areas must be measured from inside the external wall.

6. Where the existing use is 'vacant', please state most recent authorised use of the land or structure.

7. Part V of the Planning and Development Act 2000 applies where—

   - the land is zoned for residential use or for a mixture of residential and other uses;
   - there is an objective in the Development Plan for the area for a percentage of the land to be made available for social and/or affordable housing; and
   - the proposed development is not exempt from Part V.

8. Under section 97 of the Planning and Development Act 2000, applications involving development of 4 or fewer houses or development on land of less than 0.1 hectare may be exempt from Part V.

9. Under section 96(13) of the Planning and Development Act 2000, Part V does not apply to certain housing developments by approved voluntary housing bodies, certain conversions, the carrying out of works to an existing house or the development of houses under an agreement made under section 96 of the Act

10. The Record of Monuments and Places, under section 12 of the National Monuments Amendment Act 1994, is available, for each county, in the local authorities and public libraries in that county. Please note also that if the proposed development affects or is close to a national monument which, under the National Monuments Acts 1930 to 2004, is in the ownership or guardianship of the Minister for the Environment, Heritage and Local Government or a local authority or is the subject of a preservation order or a temporary preservation order, a separate statutory consent is required, under the National Monuments Acts, from the Minister for the Environment, Heritage and Local Government. For information on whether national monuments are in the ownership or guardianship of the Minister for the Environment, Heritage and Local Government or a local authority or are the subject of preservation orders, contact the National Monuments Section, Department of the Environment, Heritage and Local Government (1890 20 20 21).

11. An Environmental Impact Statement (EIS) is required for classes of development prescribed by article 93 and Schedule 5 of the Planning and Development Regulations 2001–2006. In accordance with article 103 of the Planning and Development Regulations 2001, an EIS may also be required for developments below the prescribed threshold if the planning authority considers that the development is likely to have significant effects on the environment or, where the development would be located on or in an area, site, etc. set out in article 103(2), it considers that the development would be likely to have significant effects on the environment of that area, site, etc.

12. Demolition of a habitable house requires planning permission.

**Appendix of Planning forms**

13. The appeal must be determined or withdrawn before another similar application can be made.

14. A formal pre-application consultation may only occur under Section 247 of the Planning and Development Act 2000. While it is not mandatory, a pre-planning consultation is recommended. The applicant should contact the planning authority to arrange specific times and locations. In the case of residential development to which Part V of the 2000 Act applies, applicants are advised to avail of the pre-application consultation facility in order to ensure that a Part V agreement in principle can be reached in advance of the planning application being submitted.

15. The list of approved newspapers, for the purpose of giving notice of intention to make a planning application, is available from the planning authority to which the application will be submitted.

16. All plans, drawings and maps submitted to the planning authority should be in accordance with the requirements of the Planning and Development Regulations 2001–2006.

17. The location of the site notice(s) should be shown on site location map.

18. See Schedule 9 of Planning and Development Regulations 2001. If a reduced fee is tendered, details of previous relevant payments and planning permissions should be given. If exemption from payment of fees is being claimed under article 157 of the 2001 Regulations, evidence to prove eligibility for exemption should be submitted.

## [NAME OF FORM]

*Articles 28 and 35*

*Form No. 3*

ACKNOWLEDGEMENT of RECEIPT of SUBMISSION or OBSERVATION on a PLANNING APPLICATION

**THIS IS AN IMPORTANT DOCUMENT**

KEEP THIS DOCUMENT SAFELY. YOU WILL BE REQUIRED TO PRODUCE THIS ACKNOWLEDGEMENT TO AN BORD PLEANÁLA IF YOU WISH TO APPEAL THE DECISION OF THE PLANNING AUTHORITY. IT IS THE ONLY FORM OF EVIDENCE WHICH WILL BE ACCEPTED BY AN BORD PLEANÁLA THAT A SUBMISSION OR OBSERVATION HAS BEEN MADE TO THE PLANNING AUTHORITY ON THE PLANNING APPLICATION.

**PLANNING AUTHORITY NAME**_____ *(insert name)*
**PLANNING APPLICATION REFERENCE No.** _____ *(insert ref no.)*
**A submission/observation in writing, has been received from**_____
*(insert name of person or body who made submission)* on _____
*(insert date received)* **in relation to the above planning application.**
**The appropriate fee of**_____ *(insert amount)* **has been paid.** *(Fee not applicable to prescribed bodies)*

The submission/ observation is in accordance with the appropriate provisions of the Planning and Development Regulations 2001 and will be taken into account by the planning authority in its determination of the planning application.

_____
Official's Name          Planning Authority Stamp
Date_____

# [NAME OF FORM]

*Form no. 4* *Article 35*

## NAME OF PLANNING AUTHORITY
SITE NOTICE OF FURTHER INFORMATION/ REVISED PLANS

Name of applicant_____

Reference number of the application _____

The development applied for consisted of_____

---

Significant Further Information/ Revised Plans has/have been furnished to the planning authority in respect of this proposed development, and is/are available for inspection or purchase at the offices of the authority during its public opening hours.

A submission or observation in relation to the further information or revised plans may be made in writing to the planning authority within the statutory time limit. A submission or observation must be accompanied by the prescribed fee, except in the case of a person or body who has already made a submission or observation.

Signed:

Date of erection of site notice:_____

### Directions for completing this notice.

1. The name of the planning authority to which the planning application was made should be inserted here.
2. The name of the applicant for permission (and not his or her agent) should be inserted here.
3. Reference number of the planning application on the register of the planning authority.
4. This description should be identical to that used on the site notice (Form no. 1).
5. Delete as appropriate.
6. Either the signature of the applicant or the signature and contact address of the person acting on behalf of the applicant should be inserted here.
7. The date that the notice is erected or fixed at the site should be inserted here.

# [NAME OF FORM]

## PLANNING COMPLAINT FORM NOTES
## PLEASE READ CAREFULLY BEFORE COMPLETING FORM.

1. All of the questions on the form must be fully answered to enable the Planning Authority to decide whether the complaint has substance and foundation and to enable a valid Warning Letter to be issued, if considered appropriate. If incorrect/incomplete addresses are given, the issuing of a valid Warning Letter will not be possible. Where information is inadequate the matter complained of may not be investigated and/or returned for further elaboration.

2. Please note that a Warning Letter will be issued to the person(s) named by you in the Planning Complaint Form based on the information given in the form. Therefore it is important that the information given is accurate and detailed.

3. Where possible a site location map should be attached.

4. If an application for Planning Permission has been applied for/granted you should quote relevant Planning Number. Please note that where the City Council's decision is appealed to An Bord Pleanála, the ABP decision supersedes that of the City Council. In such cases it is the conditions of the ABP decision that are relevant.

5. The Planning and Development Act, 2000 places statutory time limits on the taking of Enforcement action by the Council. Therefore, should legal proceedings be instituted in this matter, the person making the complaint may be required to give evidence in court as to the date of commencement of the unauthorised development. If this evidence is not forthcoming the Council may not be able to fully deal with this complaint.

6. Freedom of Information Act, 1997–2003 – Complaints regarding unauthorised development constitute part of the Council's records for the purposes of the above acts. The Council will endeavour to maintain as confidential any complaints made to it in confidence and in good faith. The Council cannot however, give absolute guarantees on this as requests under the Freedom of Information Act can be appealed by requesters to the Information Commissioner.

7. In the case of legal proceedings, it is possible that the nature of the complaint and your name/address may be requested by the Court or developer's solicitors and you may be required to appear in Court to give evidence in support of any enforcement proceedings which may arise.

8. The Planning Authority will not investigate complaints of a civil nature, such as those relating to encroachment, private rights of way, trespass, private nuisance and civil boundary disputes etc

9. Before making a written complaint, you should ensure that the matter is one within the scope of planning control. Certain matters, such as complaints relating to roads (parking), water, drainage, Council housing, dangerous structures, environment (litter, noise levels) may be within the remit of other Council Directorates and should be referred directly to same.

10. Unless the information furnished is decipherable, the form is signed and the name and address of the person making the complaint is given, the said complaint will not be investigated.

# Appendix of Planning forms

Below is a copy of Cork City Council's Enforcement Complaint Form:

*Cork City Council – Planning Enforcement Section*
*Written Complaints regarding alleged unauthorised developments*

The Planning Authority welcomes written complaints from persons who are concerned about unauthorised developments. Such complaints can and do serve a valuable role in the identification and control of breaches of the Planning code.

Under Planning Legislation and due to possible criminal proceedings being initiated as a result of complaints received, the Planning Authority must ensure that all complaints are received in writing.

Where the Planning Authority determines that a written complaint is vexatious, frivolous, without substance/foundation, trivial or of a minor nature, further enforcement action will not proceed.

In order to ensure that effective action is taken on both the receipt and investigation of such complaints, persons making written complaints are required to fully comply with the following.

1. The complaint must contain sufficient substance to enable the Planning Authority to issue a Warning Letter if considered appropriate. Complaints therefore should indicate:
   (i) The name and address of the person(s) carrying out the alleged unauthorised development and/or
   (ii) The name/address of the owner and/or occupier of the land in question, if different from the above.
   (iii) A clear description of the address/location where the development is taking place. A map outlining the location of the site is usually helpful for this purpose.
   (iv) A clear description of the alleged works/ development in question.
   (v) A clear indication of when the alleged unauthorised development commenced.
   (vi) In the case of non-compliance with a Planning Permission, the relevant reference number (Planning Authority/An Bord Pleanala) and relevant condition(s).

   The above details are the *minimum* considered necessary by the Planning Authority in order for a written complaint to be deemed to have substance. Such details will allow the Planning Authority (if considered necessary/appropriate in the circumstances) to issue a Warning Letter within the six week period required by Planning Legislation. Please note that if a Warning Letter is issued it will be on the basis of the information and details supplied by you.

   If complaints received are incomplete, those making them will be asked for additional information and/or clarification, as appropriate to be furnished in writing. The case will then be considered for the issuing of a Warning Letter (in accordance with the general procedure outlined above) within the six weeks following receipt of such written further information details.

2. You are requested to refrain from ongoing complaints on the matter which is subject of the investigation -- The Planning Authority has a six week period, following receipt of written complaints, within which to issue a Warning Letter and carry out an investigation subsequent to the service of the Warning Letter. Once complaints are acknowledged we would ask persons concerned to refrain, during this 6 week period from regularly calling to, phoning or writing to the Enforcement Section, regarding progress on the complaint. This inevitably delays enforcement action because finite staff time and resources tend to be consumed in multiple dealings with persons making complaints. This situation is neither in the interests of those making complaints nor the Planning Authority itself, and ultimately the general public.

    We would therefore request that you allow the Planning Authority to process complaints within this six week period. If however, during this period you become aware of *significant* further details/information on the case (eg in regard to identity of developers/ owners etc) then please feel free to bring such information to our notice, in *writing*.

3. Freedom of Information Act, 1997–2003 – Complaints regarding unauthorised development constitute part of the Council's records for the purposes of the above Acts. The Council will endeavour to maintain as confidential any complaints made to it in confidence and in good faith. The Council cannot however, give absolute guarantees on this as requests under the Freedom of Information Act can be appealed by requesters to the Information Commissioner.

    Due to possible criminal proceedings being initiated as a result of complaints received, the Council would like to point out that where complaints transpire to have been made in bad faith or maliciously, then the person making such written complaints cannot expect that the record(s) of his/her complaint will be treated in confidence.

4. Feedback from Planning Authority – Having processed a complaint the Council may or may not decide to issue a Warning Letter and/or Enforcement Notice. Where it is decided not to issue an Enforcement Notice, you will be notified by the Planning Authority within two weeks of the decision.

    Where an Enforcement Notice is served you will be notified of the fact.

Specific provision for the above notifications is provided for under the enforcement provisions of the Planning and Development Act. The Planning Authority however, also undertakes to notify you if a Warning Letter is issued or if it is decided that a Warning Letter is not warranted.

Enforcement Section,
Cork City Council,
Planning & Development Directorate.
June, 2006.

## [NAME OF FORM]

**Comhairle Cathrach Chorcai**
**Cork City Council**
**Planning & Development Directorate**
**City Hall, Anglesea Street, Cork**

**ENFORCEMENT COMPLAINT FORM**

**PLEASE READ THE NOTES BEFORE COMPLETING THIS FORM**

1(a) Location of alleged unauthorised development:
(see note 3)


1(b) Is the development to front, side or rear of the property:


2(a) Details of the complaint: (nature of the alleged unauthorised development – additional information and/or sketches may be provided on a separate sheet)
(See notes 8 & 9)


2(b)
Reasons for complaint:(specify particular issues which in your opinion might justify the issue of a Warning Letter)


3 If related to a planning permission/approval, quote planning reference no. and specify conditions or term (drawings etc) not complied with: (see note 4)

In relation to items 4, 5 and 6 below additional contact addresses and business addresses may be provided where known:

4(a) Name of person(s) carrying out alleged unauthorised development: (see note 2)

4(b) Address at which this/these person(s) ordinarily reside:

5(a) Name of landowner(s)/ Landlords(s): (see note 2)

5(b) Address at which this/these person(s) ordinarily reside:

6(a) Name of occupier(s): (see note 2)

7   Date development commenced: Specify how you can state this date with certainty. (see note 5)

8   If an unauthorised use/change of use is alleged, state previous use:

9   In the event that court proceedings are considered necessary please confirm that you would be willing to give evidence in court on behalf of the Council: (see note 5 & 7)    Yes: ☐ Please tick box

10  Do you have an objection to the disclosure of your identity: (see note 6)    Yes: ☐ No: ☐

11  Name, address and telephone no.(s) of person making complaint: (see note 10)

## Appendix of Planning forms

I HAVE READ THE NOTES RELATING TO THIS FORM AND
UNDERSTAND THE IMPLICATIONS OF SAME

12   SIGNATURE:        Signed: _____

Note: Any complaint will NOT be investigated unless name and address are given and the form is signed. (see note 10)    Date: _____

# INDEX

*[all references are to paragraph number]*

**Abandonment of permission**
    development, and, 2.26

**Abdication of jurisdiction**
    planning conditions, and, 3.228–3.229

**Abandonment of permission for use and/or for works**
    development, and, 2.27–2.38

**Access to public road**
    restrictions on exempted development, and, 2.240

**Acquiescence**
    injunctions, and, 5.127

**Acquisition of structure or other land**
    architectural conservation areas, and, 1.224–1.225

**Adjoining local authority areas**
    strategic development zones, and, 1.201

**Advertisements**
    'advertisement', 2.386
    'advertisement structure', 2.387
    agricultural demonstrations, 2.421–2.422
    airports, 2.403
    building sites, 2.408–2.409
    bus stations, 2.403
    business premises, 2.388–2.390
    business premises where ads not visible from outside, 2.393
    carnivals, 2.419–2.420
    compensation, and, 8.06
    conveyancing requisitions, and, 12.38
    cultural events, 2.417–2.418
    cultural institutions, 2.399–2.400
    definition, 8.01
    derelict advertisements, 8.04–8.05
    'development', 8.02
    educational events, 2.417–2.418
    educational institutions, 2.399–2.400
    election posters, 2.413–2.415
    enclosed land, 2.401–2.402
    exempted development, and
        generally, 2.385–2.422
        introduction, 8.07–8.08
    flags, 2.394–2.396
    funfairs
        generally, 2.419–2.420
        introduction, 8.181
    generally, 8.01–8.14
    guesthouses, 2.399–2.400
    identification, direction or warning as to land or structures, 2.412
    illuminated behind a window, 2.391–2.392
    introduction, 8.07–8.08
    letting of structure or land, 2.404–2.405
    name plates, 2.397–2.398
    overnight accommodation provision, 2.399–2.400
    planning notices, 2.416
    political events, 2.417–2.418
    public works, 2.410–2.411
    railway land, 2.401–2.402
    railway stations, 2.403
    religious events, 2.417–2.418
    religious institutions, 2.399–2.400
    repair and tidying, 8.03
    road signs, 2.410–2.411
    sale of goods, 2.406–2.407
    sale of land, 2.404–2.405
    sale of livestock, 2.406–2.407
    sale of structure, 2.404–2.405
    sporting events, 2.417–2.418
    statutory notices, 2.416
    travelling circuses, 2.419–2.420

**Aerodrome**
    definition, 2.235

**Aerodrome licensees**
PDR exempted development, and, 2.326–2.327

**Affordable housing**
conveyancing requisitions, and, 12.45
development control, and, 3.197–3.198
development plans, and, 1.95–1.97
planning conditions, and, 3.255–3.259
strategic development zones, and, 1.200

**Agreements regulating development or use of land**
generally, 8.348–8.356
planning conditions, and, 3.262–3.269

**Agricultural demonstrations**
advertisements, and, 2.421–2.422

**Agricultural use development**
'agriculture', 2.125
generally, 2.124–2.137
'osier land', 2.126
turbary, 2.128
use of land, 2.129
woodlands, 2.128

**Aids to navigation**
PDR exempted development, and, 2.342–2.343

**Air quality measurement**
PDR exempted development, and, 2.355–2.356

**Airport**
definition, 2.235

**Airport operational building**
definition, 2.235

**Airports**
advertisements, and, 2.403

**Alteration of structure**
compensation, and
generally, 7.86–7.87
introduction, 7.01
time limits, 7.09
generally, 8.332–8.347

**Amenity purposes**
PDR exempted development, and, 2.328–2.338

**Amusement arcade**
definition, 2.235

**Ancillary use**
development, and, 2.39–2.47

**Animal shelters**
rural exempted development, and
greyhounds, 2.447–2.448
larger animals, 2.437–2.438
smaller animals, 2.439

**Antenna**
PDR exempted development, and, 2.254

**Appeals to An Bord Pleanála**
appellants
generally, 4.07–4.10
landowner of adjoining lands, 4.14
non-governmental organisations, 4.13
prescribed body that is not notified, 4.11–4.12
applications, 4.35–4.48
appointment of inspector for oral hearing, 4.105–4.111
availability of documents, 4.54
calculation of time, 4.95–4.96
conditions, against
financial contribution, requiring, 4.22–4.24
generally, 4.20–4.21
*de novo* determination, 4.18
expenses, 4.104
fees
generally, 4.102–4.103
introduction, 4.36
financial contribution conditions, against, 4.22–4.24
frivolous appeals, 4.19
introduction, 4.01
jurisdiction, 4.02
major accident hazards, and, 8.208–8.211

# Index

**Appeals to An Bord Pleanála (contd)**
  material contravention of development plan, and, 4.16–4.17
  matters other than those raised by parties, 4.87–4.91
  notice of postponement of decision, 4.33
  oral hearings
    appointment of inspector, 4.105–4.111
    generally, 4.67–4.69
    matters other than those raised by parties, 4.87–4.91
    supplemental provisions, 4.70–4.86
  planning regulations, and, 4.117–4.135
  policies and objectives, and, 4.100–4.101
  prohibition against further applications, 4.25–4.28
  public availability of planning documents, 4.112–4.116
  regulation-making powers, 4.97–4.99
  *res judicata*, and, 4.28
  rules and procedures, 4.29
  submission of documents, 4.49–4.53
  submissions
    other parties, by, 4.55
    power of Board to request, 4.61–4.64
    power of Board to require, 4.65
    power of Board where notice is served, 4.66
    third parties, by, 4.56–4.60
  taking other matters into account, 4.87–4.91
  time limits for decision
    'appropriate period', 4.15
    calculation, 4.95–4.96
    generally, 4.30–4.32
    notice of postponement, 4.33
    variation by Minister, 4.34
  time limits for lodgment
    calculation, 4.95–4.96
    generally, 4.15
  vexatious appeals, 4.19
  withdrawal, 4.92–4.94

**Appeals to Supreme Court**
  statutory judicial review, and, 4.270–4.286

**Applications for planning permission**
  content
    generally, 3.53–3.56
    legal interest of applicant, 3.69–3.72
    requirements for accompanying particulars, 3.58–3.68
    specified additional information, 3.57
  default permission, 3.108–3.113
  determination
    maximum period, 3.101–3.107
    minimum period, 3.102
  electricity undertaking, and, 3.73
  environmental impact statements, 3.35
  further information
    generally, 3.121–3.125
    revised plans, 3.133–3.136
  introduction, 3.12
  legal interest of applicant, 3.69–3.72
  major accident hazards, and
    generally, 8.201–8.207
    introduction, 3.35
  modification of permission, 3.89–3.93
  newspaper notices, 3.37
  notice of intention, 3.36
  notices
    newspaper notices, 3.37
    notice of intention, 3.36
    site notices, 3.38–3.44
    statutory recipients, 3.86–3.88
  notification of decision, 3.114
  notification of planning applications, 3.86–3.88
  observations on applications
    generally, 3.94–3.99
    public holidays, and, 3.100–3.101
  Planning and Development Regulations 2001, and, 3.12
  pre-application consultations, 3.45–3.52
  procedure by LPA on receipt, 3.74–3.81

**Applications for planning permission (contd)**
  regulations, 3.12
  requirements for accompanying particulars, 3.58–3.68
  site notices, 3.38–3.44
  specified additional information, 3.57
  submissions
    generally, 3.94–3.99
    public holidays, and, 3.100–3.101
  types, 3.13–3.34
  weekly list, 3.82–3.85

**Appropriate assessment**
  candidate site of Community importance
    European site, and, 9.103
    generally, 9.89–9.95
  candidate special protection area
    European site, and, 9.103
    generally, 9.96–9.97
  compensatory measures, 9.98–9.99
  competent authority, 9.100–9.101
  consent for proposed development, 9.102
  definition, 9.70
  DEHLG Guidance for Planning Authorities, 9.78
  European site
    generally, 9.103
    hosts priority habitat or species, 9.124–9.126, 9.140–9.141
    not host priority habitat or species, 9.122–9.123, 9.135–9.139
  generally, 9.68–9.78
  imperative reasons of overriding public interest
    land use plans, and, 9.119–9.121
    proposed development, and, 9.131–9.134
  introduction, 9.05
  land use plans
    imperative reasons of overriding public interest, 9.119–9.121
    meaning, 9.104
    procedure, 9.127–9.130
  local authority development, 9.143–9.151
  meaning, 9.79–9.88
  Natura 2000, and
    impact report, 9.106–9.108
    impact statement, 9.108–9.112
    introduction, 9.69
    network, 9.105
  obligation to undertake, 9.73
  procedure, 9.75
  proposed development
    generally, 9.113
    imperative reasons of overriding public interest, 9.131–9.134
  regulations, 9.142
  screening, 9.114–9.115
  site of Community importance, 9.116
  special areas of conservation
    European site, and, 9.103
    generally, 9.79
    introduction, 9.09–9.12
    meaning, 9.117
  special protection areas
    European site, and, 9.103
    generally, 9.79
    introduction, 9.09–9.12
  wildlife sites, 9.118

**Archaeological areas**
  compensation for landowners, 8.25
  generally, 8.23–8.24

**Archaeological objects**
  definition, 8.15
  discovery
    compensation for finder, 8.21–8.22
    generally, 8.20
  excavation, 8.16–8.17
  generally, 8.15–8.25
  reporting obligations, 8.18

**Architectural conservation areas**
  acquisition of structure or other land, 1.224–1.225
  conveyancing requisitions, and, 12.36
  development control, and, 3.194
  development plans, and, 1.92

# Index

**Architectural conservation areas (contd)**
generally, 1.220–1.223
restrictions on exempted development, and, 2.240

**Areas of special amenity**
confirmation of order, 1.258–1.260
generally, 1.246–1.257
restrictions on exempted development, and, 2.240

**Areas of special planning control**
compensation, and
  generally, 7.91
  introduction, 7.01
  time limits, 7.09
development, and, 1.236–1.237
development control, and, 3.196
generally, 1.226–1.235
notices under s 88 PDA 2000
  appeals, 1.240–1.241
  enforcement, 1.243–1.245
  generally, 1.238–1.239
  implementation, 1.242
requisitions, and, 12.36

**Audience**
event and funfair licensing, and, 8.154

**Awnings**
PDR exempted development, and, 2.252–2.253

**Banners and flags**
PDR exempted development, and, 2.340–2.341

**Betting office**
definition, 2.235

**Biomass**
definition, 2.235

**Biomass boilers**
PDR exempted development, and, 2.381
rural exempted development, and, 2.465

**Birds**
conveyancing requisitions, and, 12.51
Natura 2000, and, 9.11

**Boat moorings**
rural exempted development, and, 2.426

**Boats**
PDR exempted development, and, 2.263

**'Bring-facility'**
PDR exempted development, and, 2.347

**Building energy rating certificates**
conveyancing requisitions, and, 12.13–12.16

**Building sites**
advertisements, and, 2.408–2.409

**Burial grounds**
PDR exempted development, and, 2.344

**Bus stations**
advertisements, and, 2.403

**Business premises**
advertisements, and
  generally, 2.388–2.390
  not visible from outside, 2.393
definition, 2.235

**Cables, wires and pipelines**
compensation, and
  generally, 7.92–7.93
  time limits, 7.09
conveyancing requisitions, and, 12.39

**Camper vans**
rural exempted development, and, 2.426

**Candidate site of Community importance**
European site, and, 9.103
generally, 9.89–9.95

**Candidate special protection area**
European site, and, 9.103
generally, 9.96–9.97

**Capping walls**
PDR exempted development, and, 2.265

**Caravans and camper vans**
  PDR exempted development, and, 2.263
**Care**
  definition, 2.235
**Carnivals**
  advertisements, and, 2.419–2.420
**Carrying out works**
  planning conditions, and, 3.240
**Case stated by arbitrator**
  compensation, and, 7.12–7.19
**Casual trading areas**
  exempted development, and, 2.226
**Challenging planning decisions**
  appeals to An Bord Pleanála
    *See also* **Appeals**
    appellants, 4.07–4.14
    applications, 4.35–4.48
    appointment of inspector for oral hearing, 4.105–4.111
    availability of documents, 4.54
    calculation of time, 4.95–4.96
    conditions only, against, 4.20–4.21
    *de novo* determination, 4.18
    expenses, 4.104
    fees, 4.102–4.103
    financial contribution conditions, against, 4.22–4.24
    frivolous appeals, 4.19
    introduction, 4.01
    jurisdiction, 4.02
    material contravention of development plan, 4.16–4.17
    oral hearings, 4.67–4.86
    planning regulations, and, 4.117–4.135
    policies and objectives, and, 4.100–4.101
    prohibition against further applications, 4.25–4.28
    public availability of planning documents, 4.112–4.116
    regulation-making powers, 4.97–4.99
    rules and procedures, 4.29
    submission of documents, 4.49–4.53
    submissions, 4.55–4.66
    taking other matters into account, 4.87–4.91
    time limits for decision, 4.30–4.34
    time limits for lodgment, 4.15
    vexatious appeals, 4.19
    withdrawal, 4.92–4.94
  referrals to An Bord Pleanála
    *See also* **Referrals**
    applications, 4.35–4.48
    appointment of inspector for oral hearing, 4.105–4.111
    availability of documents, 4.54
    calculation of time, 4.95–4.96
    definition, 4.136
    expenses, 4.104
    fees, 4.102–4.103
    frivolous referrals, 4.19
    introduction, 4.01
    jurisdiction, 4.03–4.06
    oral hearings, 4.67–4.86
    planning regulations, and, 4.117–4.135
    policies and objectives, and, 4.100–4.101
    public availability of planning documents, 4.112–4.116
    regulation-making powers, 4.97–4.99
    relevant referrals, 4.136–4.155
    rules and procedures, 4.29
    submission of documents, 4.49–4.53
    submissions, 4.55–4.66
    taking other matters into account, 4.87–4.91
    time limits for decision, 4.30–4.34
    vexatious referrals, 4.19
    withdrawal, 4.92–4.94
  statutory judicial review
    *See also* **Statutory judicial review**
    alternative remedies, 4.259–4.264
    appeals to Supreme Court, and, 4.270–4.286

# Index

**Challenging planning decisions (contd)**
  statutory judicial review (contd)
    application for leave to apply, 4.219–4.422
    application to stay proceedings, 4.197–4.201
    case law examples, 4.264
    EIA Directive, and, 4.155–4.170
    expeditious determination, 4.291–4.293
    extension of time, 4.211–4.218
    grounds, 4.242–4.258
    introduction, 4.171–4.178
    leave to apply, 4.179–4.196
    quashing part of decision or act, 4.289–4.290
    remittal, and, 4.287–4.288
    substantial interest, 4.223–4.241
    time limits, 4.202–4.210
    undertaking as to damages, 4.265–4.269

**Change of use**
  PDR exempted development, and
    development which is exempted under art 10 PDR 2001, 2.271
    generally, 2.269–2.270

**Childminding**
  definition, 2.235

**CHP**
  definition, 2.235

**Circuses**
  PDR exempted development, and, 2.238

**Classes of use**
  PDR exempted development, and
    art 10 PDR 2001, and, 2.284–2.289
    detailed listings, 2.273–2.283
    introduction, 2.272

**Codes of practice**
  event licensing, and, 8.171

**Combined heating power systems**
  PDR exempted development, and
    industrial buildings, for, 2.373
    light industrial buildings, for, 2.374
    rural exempted development, and, 2.461

**Company directors**
  injunctions, and, 5.183–5.188

**Compensation**
  alteration of structure, and
    generally, 7.86–7.87
    introduction, 7.01
    time limits, 7.09
  archaeological areas, and, 8.25
  archaeological objects, and, 8.21–8.22
  areas of special planning control, and
    generally, 7.91
    introduction, 7.01
    time limits, 7.09
  cables, wires and pipelines, and
    generally, 7.92–7.93
    time limits, 7.09
  case stated by arbitrator, 7.12–7.19
  Constitution, and, 7.02–7.03
  creation of rights of way, and
    generally, 7.94
    time limits, 7.09
  determination of claim, 7.10–7.11
  development control decisions, and
    assignment, 7.83
    determination of amount, 7.43–7.47
    excluded development, 7.49–7.63
    general right, 7.38
    generally, 7.36–7.42
    introduction, 3.170–3.172
    modification of permission, and, 7.84–7.85
    notice preventing compensation, 7.67–7.79
    prematurity, and, 7.57–7.58
    restriction, 7.48–7.66
    revocation of permission, and, 7.84–7.85
    rules for determination of amount, 7.43–7.47
    s 192 notices, 7.67–7.79

**Compensation (contd)**
- development control decisions, and (contd)
  - structures substantially replacing structures demolished or destroyed by fire, 7.80–7.82
  - time limits, 7.09
  - discontinuation of use, and
    - generally, 7.88–7.90
    - time limits, 7.09
  - double compensation, 7.26
  - entry on land, and
    - generally, 7.95–7.96
    - introduction, 7.01
    - time limits, 7.09
  - general provisions
    - determination of claim, 7.10–7.11
    - introduction, 7.01
    - prohibition of double compensation, 7.26
    - recovery by planning authority on subsequent developments, 7.29–7.35
    - recovery from planning authority, 7.27
    - registration, 7.28
    - regulation-making powers, 7.20–7.25
  - grant of permission subject to conditions, and
    - assignment, 7.83
    - determination of amount, 7.43–7.47
    - excluded conditions, 7.64–7.66
    - general right, 7.38
    - generally, 7.36–7.42
    - introduction, 3.170–3.172
    - modification of permission, and, 7.84–7.85
    - notice preventing compensation, 7.67–7.79
    - prematurity, and, 7.57–7.58
    - restriction, 7.48–7.66
    - revocation of permission, and, 7.84–7.85
    - rules for determination of amount, 7.43–7.47
  - s 192 notices, 7.67–7.79
  - structures substantially replacing structures demolished or destroyed by fire, 7.80–7.82
  - time limits, 7.09
- human rights, and, 7.40–7.41
- introduction, 7.01–7.08
- legislative basis
  - general provisions, 7.01
  - introduction, 7.01
- land transferred to local authority for affordable housing, and, 6.73–6.94
- mineral development, and, 8.247
- modification of permission, and, 7.84–7.85
- notice preventing compensation, 7.67–7.79
- pipelines, cables and wires, and
  - generally, 7.92–7.93
  - introduction, 7.01
  - time limits, 7.09
- prohibition of double compensation, 7.26
- protection of property, and, 7.40–7.41
- public rights of way, and
  - generally, 7.94
  - introduction, 7.01
  - time limits, 7.09
- recovery by planning authority on subsequent developments, 7.29–7.35
- recovery from planning authority, 7.27
- refusal of permission, and
  - assignment, 7.83
  - determination of amount, 7.43–7.47
  - excluded development, 7.49–7.63
  - general right, 7.38
  - generally, 7.36–7.42
  - introduction, 3.170–3.172
  - modification of permission, and, 7.84–7.85
  - notice preventing compensation, 7.67–7.79
  - prematurity, and, 7.57–7.58
  - restriction, 7.48–7.66
  - revocation of permission, and, 7.84–7.85

# Index

**Compensation (contd)**
refusal of permission, and (contd)
rules for determination of amount, 7.43–7.47
s 192 notices, 7.67–7.79
structures substantially replacing structures demolished or destroyed by fire, 7.80–7.82
time limits, 7.09
registration, 7.28
regulations, 7.20–7.25
removal of structure, and
generally, 7.86–7.87
introduction, 7.01
time limits, 7.09
revocation of permission, and, 7.84–7.85
s 192 notices, 7.67–7.79
special planning control schemes, and
generally, 7.91
introduction, 7.01
time limits, 7.09
statutory provisions, 7.01
structures substantially replacing structures demolished or destroyed by fire, and, 7.80–7.82
time limits, 7.09
tree preservation orders, and, 8.406–8.407
wires, cables and pipelines, and
generally, 7.92–7.93
introduction, 7.01
time limits, 7.09

**Compensatory measures**
appropriate assessment, and, 9.98–9.99

**Competent authority**
appropriate assessment, and, 9.100–9.101

**Completion of works**
planning conditions, and, 3.244

**Compulsory acquisition**
'acquisition of lands', 7.120
Air Navigation Act 1998, under, 7.145
amendment of s 10 Local Government (No 2) Act 1960, 7.194
appropriation of land for local authority purposes, and, 7.97–7.102
confirmation of order, 7.148–7.149
derelict sites, and, 8.138–8.139
development by local authority, and, 7.112–7.117
disposal of land by local authority, and, 7.103–7.111
Gas Act 1976, under, 7.144
Harbours Act 1996, under, 7.146–7.147
introduction, 7.97
judicial review, and, 7.139–7.140
jurisdiction, 7.97
making order, 7.118–7.132
meetings with local authority, 7.162–7.163
National Assets Management Agency Act 2009, under, 7.198–7.202
open spaces, for, 7.203–7.209
oral hearings
costs, 7.182–7.183
generally, 7.173–7.175
objective of Board, 7.186–7.192
supplemental provisions, 7.176–7.181
parallel procedures, 7.184–7.185
power to make decisions on transferred functions, 7.170–7.173
procedure
confirmation of order, 7.148–7.149
costs of hearings, 7.182–7.183
making order, 7.118–7.132
meetings with local authority, 7.162–7.163
objective of Board, 7.186–7.192
oral hearings, 7.173–7.181
parallel procedures, 7.184–7.185
power to make decisions on transferred functions, 7.170–7.173
request for further submissions or observations, 7.162

**Compulsory acquisition (contd)**
  procedure (contd)
    supplemental provisions, 7.161–7.169
    time limits, 7.150–7.160
  protected structures, and,
    generally, 8.308–8.310
    vesting orders, 8.311–8.317
  references to transferred functions in regulations, 7.195–7.197
  request for further submissions or observations, 7.162
  Roads Acts, under, 7.141–7.143
  statutory provisions, 7.97
  time limits, 7.150–7.160
  transfer of functions to An Bord Pleanála
    Air Navigation Act 1998, under, 7.145
    Gas Act 1976, under, 7.144
    generally, 7.133–7.138
    Harbours Act 1996, under, 7.146–7.147
    Roads Acts, under, 7.141–7.143
  use of acquired land, 7.125–7.128

**Conditions of permission**
  abdication of jurisdiction of planning body, and, 3.228–3.229
  affordable housing agreements, and, 3.255–3.259
  appeals, and
    financial contribution, requiring, 4.22–4.24
    generally, 4.20–4.21
  carrying out works, 3.240
  completion of works within specified period, 3.244
  co-operation of third party, and, 3.215
  deprivation of landowner of existing rights or uses, and, 3.216–3.220
  development of adjoining land, 3.237–3.239
  directly depart from application, which, 3.231
  enforceability, 3.222–3.225
  fire conditions, 3.232
  general conditions, 3.208–3.229
  introduction, 3.207
  landscaping, 3.243
  local authority's other duties, and, 3.214
  management of site, 3.245
  matters to be agreed, and, 3.233–3.235
  modification of existing permission not yet implemented, and, 3.221
  noise emissions, 3.241
  occupancy conditions, 3.270–3.276
  open spaces, 3.242
  operating hours of a business, 3.249
  planning agreements, and, 3.262–3.269
  planting and landscaping, 3.243
  points of detail to be agreed, 3.250–3.254
  precision, 3.226–3.227
  protected structures, 3.248
  quarries, and
    appeals, 8.66
    compensation, 8.59–8.65
    generally, 8.38–8.55
  reasonableness, 3.210–3.212
  relevance to planning policy, 3.213
  restriction of use of premises, 3.261–3.269
  roads and other facilities, 3.245
  security for satisfactory completion, 3.245
  signage, 3.247
  social housing agreements, and, 3.255–3.259
  standard conditions, 3.230
  statutory conditions under PDA 2000 s 34(4), 3.236–3.249
  sterilisation agreements, and, 3.262–3.269
  temporary permission, 3.246
  transboundary environmental impacts, 3.260
  use of adjoining land, 3.237–3.239

**Connection of premises to services**
  PDR exempted development, and, 2.357–2.358

# Index

**Consent for proposed development**
appropriate assessment, and, 9.102

**Conservatories**
PDR exempted development, and
declarations and referrals, 2.247–2.248
generally, 2.245–2.246

**Constitution**
compensation, and, 7.02–7.03
development plans, and, 1.30–1.37

**Construction or erection outside functional area**
PDR exempted development, and, 2.253–2.254

**Contravention of condition attached to a permission**
restrictions on exempted development, and, 2.240

**Control of development**
*See also* **Development control**
conditions in permissions, 3.207–3.276
content of planning applications, 3.53–3.73
default permission, 3.108–3.113
determination of planning applications, 3.102–3.107
development contribution schemes, 3.277–3.300
environmental impact statements, 3.35
further information, 3.121–3.125
generally, 3.01–3.02
irrelevant considerations, 3.169–3.206
legal interest of applicant, 3.69–3.72
major accident regulations, 3.35
modification of permission, 3.89–3.93
notices, 3.36–3.44
notification of decision, 3.114
notification of grant of permission, 3.115–3.116
notification of planning applications, 3.86–3.88
obligation to obtain permission, 3.03–3.11
planning gain, 3.164–3.165

pre-application consultations, 3.45–3.52
procedure of planning authority, 3.74–3.81
'proper planning', 3.136–3.159
refusal for past failure, 3.166–3.168
regulations, 3.12
*res judicata*, 3.160–3.163
revised plans, 3.126–3.136
revocation of permission, 3.89–3.93
submissions or observations, 3.94–3.101
sustainable development, 3.136–3.159
types of permission, 3.13–3.34
weekly list of planning applications, 3.82–3.85
weekly list of planning decisions, 3.117–3.119

**Conveyancing requisitions**
advertisement structures, 12.38
affordable housing, 12.45
architectural conservation areas, 12.36
areas of special planning control, 12.36
Birds Directive, 12.51
building energy rating certificates, 12.13–12.16
cables, wires and pipelines, 12.39
consequences of planning defects, 12.12
creation of rights of way, 12.28–12.31
declarations and referrals, 12.19–12.24
duration of planning permission, 12.54–12.57
enforcement procedures, 12.25
environmental matters
Birds Directive, 12.51
definitions, 12.48
general enquiries, 12.49
Habitats Directive, 12.53
introduction, 12.47
Natural Heritage Areas, 12.52
Wildlife Acts, 12.50
environmental indemnities
generally, 12.66
landlord's covenants in a lease, 12.70

**Conveyancing requisitions (contd)**
   environmental indemnities (contd)
      limited form, 12.68
      loan agreement clauses, 12.71
      tenant's covenants in a lease, 12.69
   environmental warranties
      draft precedent, 12.66
      generally, 12.64–12.65
   exempted development, 12.17
   Habitats Directive, 12.53
   injunctions, 12.25
   landscape conservation orders, 12.37
   major accidents Directive, 12.40–12.44
   Natural Heritage Areas, 12.52
   outline permission
      generally, 12.32
      special characteristics, 12.33–12.34
   pipelines, wires and cables, 12.39
   planning amnesty, 12.09–12.11
   planning history of the development, 12.01
   planning injunctions, 12.25
   planning warranty, 12.02–12.08
   pre-contract questionnaires, 12.01
   protected structures, 12.18
   public rights of way, 12.28–12.31
   radon gas, 12.58–12.63
   social housing, 12.45
   Special Condition 36 of Law Society Contract, 12.02–12.08
   special planning control areas, 12.36
   strategic development zones, 12.35
   taking estates in charge, 12.46
   tree preservation orders, 12.26–12.27
   Wildlife Acts, 12.50
   wires, cables and pipelines, 12.39

**Co-operation of third party**
   planning conditions, and, 3.215

**'Core strategy' principles**
   development control, and, 3.01
   development plans, and, 1.06–1.28

**Costs**
   injunctions, and, 5.174–5.182
   strategic infrastructure development, and, 11.64–11.71

**Creation of rights of way**
   compensation, and
      generally, 7.94
      time limits, 7.09
   conveyancing requisitions, and, 12.28–12.31

**Cultural events**
   advertisements, and, 2.417–2.418
   PDR exempted development, and, 2.338

**Cultural institutions**
   advertisements, and, 2.399–2.400

**Culvert maintenance and construction**
   rural exempted development, and, 2.428–2.430

**Curtilage of a house**
   exempted development, and, 2.221–2.225
   PDR exempted development, and
      declarations and referrals, 2.247–2.248
      generally, 2.245–2.246
   protected structures, and, 8.262–8.267

**Customs House Docks area**
   exempted development, and, 2.484

**Damages**
   injunctions, and, 5.163

**Day centre**
   definition, 2.235

**Declaration and referral**
   conveyancing requisitions, and, 12.19–12.24
   development, and, 2.507–2.527
   major accident hazards, and, 8.221–8.244

**De-exempted development**
   generally, 2.122

**Default permission**
   generally, 3.108–3.113

# Index

**DEHLG Planning Guidelines No 15**
   development plans, and, 1.29

**Demolition**
   PDR exempted development, and
      generally, 2.360–2.365
      restrictions, 2.240
   restrictions on exempted development, and, 2.240

**Deposit boxes**
   PDR exempted development, and, 2.324

**Deprivation of landowner of existing rights or uses**
   planning conditions, and, 3.216–3.220

**Derelict advertisements**
   generally, 8.04–8.05

**Derelict sites**
   compulsory acquisition, 8.138–8.139
   definition, 8.127
   derelict site notices
      generally, 8.132
      ministerial power, 8.140
   exempted development, and, 2.484
   generally, 8.125–8.126
   levy, 8.135–8.136
   obligations
      local authorities, of, 8.131
      owners and occupiers, of, 8.130
   offences, 8.133–8.134
   registration, 8.128–8.129

**Development**
   'abandonment of permission', 2.26
   'abandonment of permission for use and/or for works', 2.27–2.38
   'ancillary use', 2.39–2.47
   control of
      *See also* **Development control**
      conditions in permissions, 3.207–3.276
      content of planning applications, 3.53–3.73
      default permission, 3.108–3.113
      determination of planning applications, 3.102–3.107

      development contribution schemes, 3.277–3.300
      environmental impact statements, 3.35
      further information, 3.121–3.125
      generally, 3.01–3.02
      irrelevant considerations, 3.169–3.206
      legal interest of applicant, 3.69–3.72
      major accident regulations, 3.35
      modification of permission, 3.89–3.93
      notices, 3.36–3.44
      notification of decision, 3.114
      notification of grant of permission, 3.115–3.116
      notification of planning applications, 3.86–3.88
      obligation to obtain permission, 3.03–3.11
      planning gain, 3.164–3.165
      pre-application consultations, 3.45–3.52
      procedure of planning authority, 3.74–3.81
      'proper planning', 3.136–3.159
      refusal for past failure, 3.166–3.168
      regulations, 3.12
      *res judicata*, 3.160–3.163
      revised plans, 3.126–3.136
      revocation of permission, 3.89–3.93
      submissions or observations, 3.94–3.101
      sustainable development, 3.136–3.159
      types of permission, 3.13–3.34
      weekly list of planning applications, 3.82–3.85
      weekly list of planning decisions, 3.117–3.119
   declaration and referral, 2.507–2.527
   definition
      'abandonment of permission', 2.26
      'abandonment of permission for use and/or for works', 2.27–2.38
      'ancillary use', 2.39–2.47

**Development (contd)**
  definition (contd)
    'extinguishment of existing use rights', 2.48–2.55
    generally, 2.05
    'intensification of works/use', 2.56–2.73
    'material change in use', 2.09–2.20
    'planning unit', 2.21–2.25
    'resumption of existing use rights', 2.48–2.55
    'use', 2.08
    'works', 2.06–2.07
  definitions, 2.03
  event licensing, and, 8.143
  exempted development
    *See also* **Exempted development**
    advertisements, 2.387–2.422
    agricultural use development, 2.124–2.137
    casual trading areas, for, 2.226
    curtilage of a house, within, 2.221–2.225
    declaration and referral, 2.507–2.527
    definition, 2.92–2.93
    forest husbandry, 2.218–2.220
    generally, 2.121–2.122
    interior of structure, 2.213–2.217
    introduction, 2.92–2.93
    land reclamation, 2.227–2.230
    listed in PDR 2001–2010, 2.231–2.483
    local authority exempted development, 2.138–2.181
    other enactments, under, 2.484–2.490
    other sections in PDA 2000, provided by, 2.491–2.506
    prescribed for purposes of PDA 2000, s 179, 2.173–2.181
    rural areas, in, 2.423–2.466
    state authority development, 2.181–2.196
    statutory exempted development, 2.123–2.137
    subject to EIA, 2.153–2.156
    woodland husbandry, 2.218–2.220
  'extinguishment of existing use rights', 2.48–2.55
  'foreshore', 2.113–2.120
  funfairs, and, 8.143
  'intensification of works/use', 2.56–2.73
  'land', 2.90
  material change in use
    definition, 2.09–2.20
    generally, 2.74–2.88
  need for planning permission, 2.01–2.04
  'planning unit', 2.21–2.25
  'resumption of existing use rights', 2.48–2.55
  'retention permission', 2.94–2.106
  'structure', 2.89
  'substratum of land', 2.91
  'unauthorised development', 2.107–2.108
  'unauthorised structure', 2.109–2.110
  'unauthorised use', 2.111
  'unauthorised works', 2.112
  'use', 2.08
  'works', 2.06–2.07

**Development agencies**
  generally, 1.192

**Development of land by local authority**
  compulsory acquisition, and, 7.112–7.117

**Development control**
  affordable housing, 3.197–3.198
  aim, 3.02
  architectural conservation areas, and, 3.194
  compensation, and
    assignment, 7.83
    determination of amount, 7.43–7.47
    excluded development, 7.49–7.63
    general right, 7.38
    generally, 7.36–7.42
    introduction, 3.170–3.172
    modification of permission, and, 7.84–7.85

# Index

**Development control (contd)**
  compensation, and (contd)
    notice preventing compensation, 7.67–7.79
    prematurity, and, 7.57–7.58
    restriction, 7.48–7.66
    revocation of permission, and, 7.84–7.85
    rules for determination of amount, 7.43–7.47
    s 192 notices, 7.67–7.79
    structures substantially replacing structures demolished or destroyed by fire, 7.80–7.82
    time limits, 7.09
  conditions in planning permissions
    abdication of jurisdiction of planning body, and, 3.228–3.229
    affordable housing agreements, and, 3.255–3.259
    carrying out works, 3.240
    completion of works within specified period, 3.244
    co-operation of third party, and, 3.215
    deprivation of landowner of existing rights or uses, and, 3.216–3.220
    development of adjoining land, 3.237–3.239
    directly depart from application, which, 3.231
    enforceability, 3.222–3.225
    fire conditions, 3.232
    general conditions, 3.208–3.229
    introduction, 3.207
    landscaping, 3.243
    local authority's other duties, and, 3.214
    management of site, 3.245
    matters to be agreed, and, 3.233–3.235
    modification of existing permission not yet implemented, and, 3.221
    noise emissions, 3.241
    occupancy conditions, 3.270–3.276
    open spaces, 3.242
    operating hours of a business, 3.249
    planning agreements, and, 3.262–3.269
    planting and landscaping, 3.243
    points of detail to be agreed, 3.250–3.254
    precision, 3.226–3.227
    protected structures, 3.248
    reasonableness, 3.210–3.212
    relevance to planning policy, 3.213
    restriction of use of premises, 3.261–3.269
    roads and other facilities, 3.245
    security for satisfactory completion, 3.245
    signage, 3.247
    social housing agreements, and, 3.255–3.259
    standard conditions, 3.230
    statutory conditions under PDA 2000, s 34(4), 3.236–3.249
    sterilisation agreements, and, 3.262–3.269
    temporary permission, 3.246
    transboundary environmental impacts, 3.260
    use of adjoining land, 3.237–3.239
  content of planning applications
    generally, 3.53–3.56
    legal interest of applicant, 3.69–3.72
    requirements for accompanying particulars, 3.58–3.68
    specified additional information, 3.57
  'core strategy', and, 3.01
  default permission, 3.108–3.113
  determination of planning applications
    maximum period, 3.101–3.107
    minimum period, 3.102
  development plan, and, 3.02
  electricity undertaking, and, 3.73
  energy infrastructure, and, 3.09
  environmental impact assessments, and, 3.199
  environmental impact statements, 3.35
  environmental infrastructure, and, 3.09

1117

**Development control (contd)**
   European sites
   further information
      generally, 3.121–3.125
      revised plans, 3.133–3.136
   general obligation, 3.03–3.11
   generally, 3.01–3.02
   government policy, and, 3.187
   infrastructure development, and, 3.09
   irrelevant considerations
      compensation, 3.170–3.172
      licences required as pre-condition under other legislation, 3.173–3.176
      introduction, 3.169
      ownership of land, 3.177
      permission required as pre-condition under other legislation, 3.173–3.176
      personal circumstances, 3.179–3.181
   legal interest of applicant, 3.69–3.72
   major accident regulations, 3.35
   meaning, 3.01
   ministerial policy, and, 3.187
   modification of permission, 3.89–3.93
   notices
      newspaper notices, 3.37
      notice of intention, 3.36
      site notices, 3.38–3.44
      statutory recipients, 3.86–3.88
   notification of decision, 3.114
   notification of grant of permission, 3.115–3.116
   notification of planning applications, 3.86–3.88
   obligation to obtain permission, 3.03–3.11
   observations on applications
      generally, 3.94–3.99
      public holidays, and, 3.100–3.101
   outline planning permission
      duration, 3.17
      generally, 3.14–3.21
      regulations, 3.22–3.23
      restrictions, 3.24
   Planning and Development Regulations 2001, and, 3.12
   planning applications
      content, 3.53–3.73
      determination, 3.102–3.107
      electricity undertaking, by, 3.73
      environmental impact statements, with, 3.35
      further information requests, 3.121–3.125
      introduction, 3.12
      legal interest of applicant, 3.69–3.72
      major accident regulations, and, 3.35
      newspaper notices, 3.37
      notice of intention, 3.36
      notification, 3.86–3.88
      notification of decision, 3.114
      prior consultations, 3.45–3.52
      procedure by LPA on receipt, 3.74–3.81
      regulations, 3.10
      requirements for accompanying particulars, 3.58–3.68
      site notices, 3.38–3.44
      specified additional information, 3.57
      submissions or observations, 3.94–3.101
      types, 3.13–3.34
      weekly list, 3.82–3.85
   planning gain, 3.164–3.165
   planning permission
      conditions, 3.207–3.276
      default permission, 3.108–3.113
      extension, 3.19–3.20
      modification, 3.89–3.93
      notification of grant, 3.115–3.116
      obligation to obtain, 3.03–3.09
      outline permission, 3.14–3.24
      regulations, 3.10–3.11
      retention permission, 3.25–3.34
      revocation, 3.89–3.93
      types, 3.13–3.34
      weekly list, 3.117–3.120
   pre-application consultations, 3.45–3.52

# Index

**Development control (contd)**
  procedure of planning authority, 3.74–3.81
  'proper planning'
    alternative sites, 3.144–3.145
    amenity, 3.146–3.147
    common good, 3.148
    compulsory purchase orders, 3.149
    environmental pollution, 3.158
    generally, 3.136–3.142
    planning history of land, 3.150–3.151
    precedent, 3.153
    private interest, 3.154–3.155
    public health and safety, 3.156–3.157
    restraint on power to grant permission in material contravention of development plan, 3.152
    relevant considerations, 3.143–3.159
  protected structures, 3.191–3.193
  purpose, 3.02
  refusal for past failure, 3.166–3.168
  regard to policies and objectives, 3.200–3.206
  regulations, 3.12
  *res judicata*, 3.160–3.163
  retention permission
    generally, 3.25–3.31
    substitute consent, 3.32–3.34
  revised plans
    generally, 3.126–3.132
    notice of further information, 3.133–3.136
  revocation of permission, 3.89–3.93
  site notices, 3.38–3.44
  social housing, 3.197–3.198
  special amenity area orders, and, 3.182–3.185
  special planning control areas, and, 3.196
  standard planning permission, 3.18
  statutory planning conditions, 3.188
  strategic development zones, and, 3.195
  submissions on applications
    generally, 3.94–3.99
    public holidays, and, 3.100–3.101
  supplementary development contribution schemes
    generally, 3.296–3.300
    introduction, 3.277
  sustainable development
    alternative sites, 3.144–3.145
    amenity, 3.146–3.147
    common good, 3.148
    compulsory purchase orders, 3.149
    environmental pollution, 3.158
    generally, 3.136–3.142
    planning history of land, 3.150–3.151
    precedent, 3.153
    private interest, 3.154–3.155
    public health and safety, 3.156–3.157
    restraint on power to grant permission in material contravention of development plan, 3.152
    relevant considerations, 3.143–3.159
  transport infrastructure, and, 3.09
  types of permission
    introduction, 3.13
    outline planning permission, 3.14–3.24
    retention permission, 3.25–3.34
  weekly list of planning applications, 3.82–3.85
  weekly list of planning decisions, 3.117–3.120
  zoning, and, 3.01

**Development of adjoining land**
  planning conditions, and, 3.237–3.239

**Development plans**
  adoption, 1.105–1.111
  affordable housing, and, 1.95–1.97
  architectural conservation area, and, 1.92
  areas of special planning control, and, 1.93–1.94

**Development plans (contd)**
    Constitution, and, 1.30–1.37
    contents
        affordable housing, 1.95–1.97
        architectural conservation area, 1.92
        areas of special planning control, 1.93–1.94
        generally, 1.77–1.88
        introduction, 1.06–1.07
        protected structures, 1.89
        social housing, 1.95–1.96
        strategic development zones, 1.91
        waste management, 1.90
    copies, 1.77–1.79
    'core strategy' principles, 1.06–1.28
    definition
        case law, 1.04
        sustainability, and, 1.40
    DEHLG Planning Guidelines No 15, 1.29
    development control, and, 3.02
    environmental impact assessments, and, 1.97–1.100
    EU Directives, 1.39
    European Convention on Human Rights, 1.38
    frequency, 1.02
    generally, 1.01–1.05
    interpretation, 1.75–1.76
    land use plans, and
        *See also* **Land use plans**
        architectural conservation areas, 1.220–1.225
        areas of special amenity, 1.246–1.260
        areas of special planning control, 1.226–1.245
        landscape conservation areas, 1.261–1.268
        local area plans, 1.175–1.190
        meaning, 9.104
        strategic development zones, 1.191–1.219
    legal effects, 1.164–1.174
    local area plans, and, 1.02
    making, 1.112–1.135
    material contravention, 1.44–1.72
    ministerial directions, 1.143–1.160
    ministerial guidelines and directives, 1.316–1.327
    objectives
        discretionary objectives, 1.83
        generally, 1.80–1.88
        introduction, 1.08
        mandatory objectives, 1.81–1.82
    permission for development, 1.43
    preparation, 1.105–1.111
    protected structures, and, 1.89
    public right of way, 1.161–1.163
    regional planning guidelines, and, 1.269–1.315
    social housing, and, 1.95–1.96
    strategic development zones, and, 1.91
    strategic infrastructure development, and, 1.73–1.74
    sustainability, 1.40–1.42
    variation
        generally, 1.136–1.142
        ministerial directions, 1.143–1.160
    waste management, and, 1.90

**Discontinuation of use**
    compensation, and
        generally, 7.88–7.90
        time limits, 7.09

**Discretion**
    injunctions, and, 5.146

**Disposal of land by local authority**
    compulsory acquisition, and, 7.103–7.111

**Double compensation**
    generally, 7.26

**Drain maintenance and construction**
    rural exempted development, and, 2.428–2.430

**Drainage schemes**
    PDR exempted development, and, 2.477–2.478
    restrictions on exempted development, and, 2.239

# Index

**Drains**
    PDR exempted development, and, 2.259–2.261

**Dublin Docklands area**
    exempted development, and, 2.484

**Educational events**
    advertisements, and, 2.417–2.418

**Educational institutions**
    advertisements, and, 2.399–2.400

**EIA Directive**
    statutory judicial review, and
        case law, 4.162–4.170
        generally, 4.155–4.161

**Election posters**
    advertisements, and, 2.413–2.415

**Electricity transmission**
    exempted development, and, 2.488
    strategic infrastructure development, and, 11.08–11.12

**Electricity undertakers' development**
    PDR exempted development, and, 2.318–2.323

**Electricity undertaking**
    development control, and, 3.73

**Enclosed land**
    advertisements, and, 2.401–2.402

**Endangering public safety**
    restrictions on exempted development and, 2.240

**Endangerment notices**
    appeals, 8.293–8.294
    generally, 8.286–8.287
    procedure, 8.297–8.307

**Energy infrastructure**
    development control, and, 3.09
    exempted development, and, 2.485
    strategic infrastructure development, and, 11.04

**Enforcement**
    conveyancing requisitions, and, 12.25
    decision to proceed, 5.47–5.60

    development commenced more than seven years previously, 5.88
    enforcement notices
        appeals, 5.99
        challenges, 5.99–5.103
        contents, 5.66–5.71
        decision to proceed, 5.47–5.60
        effect of non-compliance, 5.73
        expiry, 5.75–5.77
        emergency situations, in, 5.78
        generally, 5.61–5.65
        judicial review, 5.100
        penalties for offences, and, 5.79–5.87
        service, 5.72
        warning letters, 5.30–5.46
        withdrawal, 5.74
    funfairs, and, 8.186
    injunctions
        acquiescence, 5.127
        attitude of planning authority, 5.137
        company directors, and, 5.183–5.188
        conduct of applicant, 5.128–5.130
        conduct of developer, 5.131–5.135
        costs, 5.174–5.182
        damages award, and, 5.163
        discretion, and, 5.146
        hardship to developer, 5.121–5.125
        hearing at discretion of court, 5.110–5.115
        hearsay evidence, 5.158
        introduction, 5.104–5.109
        laches, 5.126
        onus of proof, 5.147–5.157
        procedure for application, 5.138–5.145
        public interest, 5.136
        technical or trivial breach, 5.116–5.120
        time limits, 5.165–5.173
        undertakings as to damages, 5.159–5.162
    introduction, 5.01
    other provisions, 5.88–5.98
    penalties for offences, 5.79–5.87
    quarries, and, 8.67–8.68

## Enforcement (contd)

retention permission, 5.05–5.29
substitute consent, and, 9.53–9.56
unauthorised development
   decision on enforcement, 5.47–5.60
   development carried out pursuant to planning condition, 5.03–5.04
   enforcement notices, 5.61–5.78
   general offence, 5.02
   injunctions, 5.104–5.109
   penalties, 5.79–5.87
   retention permission, 5.05–5.29
   warning letters, 5.30–5.46
warning letters
   contents, 5.41–5.46
   general procedure, 5.30–5.40

## Enforcement notices

appeals, 5.99
challenges, 5.99–5.103
contents, 5.66–5.71
decision to proceed, 5.47–5.60
effect of non-compliance, 5.73
expiry, 5.75–5.77
emergency situations, in, 5.78
generally, 5.61–5.65
judicial review, 5.100
penalties for offences, and, 5.79–5.87
service, 5.72
warning letters, 5.30–5.46
withdrawal, 5.74

## Entry on land

compensation, and
   generally, 7.95–7.96
   introduction, 7.01
   time limits, 7.09

## Environmental assessment

strategic development zones, and, 1.199

## Environmental impact assessments

annex I projects, 10.41–10.50
annex II projects, 10.41–10.50
Council Directive
   annexes as amended, 10.31–10.35
   case law on direct effect, 10.36–10.40
   direct effect, 10.14–10.15
   generally, 10.03
   implementation into Irish law, 10.61–10.66
   text as amended, 10.16–10.30
decisions not to take enforcement action against unauthorised development, 10.175
definition of 'project', 10.125–10.147
development consents, 10.157–10.171
development control, and, 3.199
development plans, and, 1.97–1.100
distinguished from EIS, 10.109–10.116
'exceptional cases', 10.72–10.74
exemptions, 10.67–10.71
extension to projects, and, 10.176–10.180
introduction, 10.01–10.13
local authority developments, and, 10.187–10.204
minimum period for determining planning application, 10.99–10.100
mitigating measures, 10.148–10.156
modification of projects, and, 10.176–10.180
notice of decision, 10.102
notification of Board by planning authority. 10.95
objectives, 10.60
outline permission, and, 10.172–10.174
'project', 10.125–10.147
project splitting, 10.75–10.83
projects for which necessary, 10.117–10.124
public notice of information received pursuant to request, 10.103–10.108
quarries, and
   generally, 8.56–8.58
   introduction, 8.34
request for further information, 10.96–10.98

## Environmental impact assessments (contd)
retention permission, and
ECJ ruling, 10.51–10.59
generally, 9.01–9.04
scoping, 10.84–10.85
'significant effects on the environment', 10.181–10.187
state authority development, and
application for approval, 10.217–10.221
approval, 10.212–10.216
*Commission v Ireland* (C–50/09), 10.225–10.255
generally, 8.205–8.211
introduction, 2.197–2.212
making decision to approve or not to approve, 10.222–10.224
statutory judicial review, and
case law, 4.162–4.170
generally, 4.155–4.161
strategic infrastructure development, and, 11.27–11.31
substitute consent, and, 9.05
transboundary environmental impacts
consultation, 10.93–10.94
generally, 10.86–10.88
inclusion in weekly list, 10.101
information to Minister, 10.92
minimum period for determining planning application, 10.99–10.100
notification of Board by planning authority, 10.95
notification to Minister, 10.89–10.91
request for further information, 10.96–10.98
weekly list, 10.101

## Environmental impact statements
distinguished from EIA, 10.109–10.116
planning applications, and, 3.35
strategic infrastructure development, and, 11.88–11.93

## Environmental infrastructure
development control, and, 3.09
exempted development, and, 2.487
strategic infrastructure development, and, 11.04

## Environmental conveyancing requisitions
Birds Directive, 12.51
definitions, 12.48
general enquiries, 12.49
Habitats Directive, 12.53
indemnities
generally, 12.66
landlord's covenants in a lease, 12.70
limited form, 12.68
loan agreement clauses, 12.71
tenant's covenants in a lease, 12.69
introduction, 12.47
Natural Heritage Areas, 12.52
warranties
draft precedent, 12.66
generally, 12.64–12.65
Wildlife Acts, 12.50

## Environmental Protection Agency Act 1992, s 86(8)
restrictions on exempted development, and, 2.237

## EU Directives
development plans, and, 1.39

## European Convention on Human Rights
development plans, and, 1.38

## European site
generally, 9.103
hosts priority habitat or species, 9.124–9.126
not host priority habitat or species, 9.122–9.123

## Event licensing
*See also* **Licensing of funfairs**
applications
content, 8.161
determination, 8.168
further information, 8.167
introduction, 8.155

**Event licensing (contd)**
  applications (cond)
    notice of intention to apply, 8.159
    'prescribed bodies', 8.157
    timing, 8.160
  'audience', 8.154
  availability of documents, 8.163–8.165
  codes of practice, 8.171
  content of application, 8.161
  determination of application, 8.168
  'development', and, 8.143
  'event', 8.147
  exclusion from planning control, 8.144–8.145
  further information, 8.167
  generally, 8.141–8.154
  grant of licence, 8.169–8.170
  inspection powers, 8.174–8.175
  'licence', 8.151
  'local authority', 8.152
  notice of intention to apply, 8.159
  obligation of person holding event, 8.153
  observations by other parties, 8.165–8.166
  'outdoor events', 8.147
  pre-application procedure, 8.156–8.158
  'prescribed bodies', 8.157
  procedure
    availability of documents, 8.163–8.165
    content of application, 8.161
    determination of application, 8.168
    further information, 8.167
    introduction, 8.155
    notice of intention to apply, 8.159
    observations by other parties, 8.165–8.166
    pre-application procedure, 8.156–8.158
    'prescribed bodies', 8.157
    submissions by other parties, 8.165–8.166
    timing of application, 8.160
  regulation-making powers, 8.148
  safety obligations, 8.173
  service of notices, 8.172
  statutory provisions, 8.141
  submissions by other parties, 8.165–8.166
  timing of application, 8.160
  warning notices, and, 8.141

**Excavation**
  PDR exempted development, and
    research and discovery, for, 2.348
    surveying or prospecting, for, 2.351–2.352

**Excluded premises**
  definition, 2.235

**Exempted development**
  advertisements
    'advertisement', 2.386
    'advertisement structure', 2.387
    agricultural demonstrations, 2.421–2.422
    airports, 2.403
    building sites, 2.408–2.409
    bus stations, 2.403
    business premises, 2.388–2.390
    business premises where ads not visible from outside, 2.393
    carnivals, 2.419–2.420
    cultural events, 2.417–2.418
    cultural institutions, 2.399–2.400
    educational events, 2.417–2.418
    educational institutions, 2.399–2.400
    election posters, 2.413–2.415
    enclosed land, 2.401–2.402
    flags, 2.394–2.396
    funfairs, 2.419–2.420
    generally, 2.385
    guesthouses, 2.399–2.400
    identification, direction or warning as to land or structures, 2.412
    illuminated behind a window, 2.391–2.392
    letting of structure or land, 2.404–2.405
    name plates, 2.397–2.398
    overnight accommodation provision, 2.399–2.400

# Index

**Exempted development (contd)**
  advertisements (contd)
    planning notices, 2.416
    political events, 2.417–2.418
    public works, 2.410–2.411
    railway land, 2.401–2.402
    railway stations, 2.403
    religious events, 2.417–2.418
    religious institutions, 2.399–2.400
    road signs, 2.410–2.411
    sale of goods, 2.406–2.407
    sale of land, 2.404–2.405
    sale of livestock, 2.406–2.407
    sale of structure, 2.404–2.405
    sporting events, 2.417–2.418
    statutory notices, 2.416
    travelling circuses, 2.419–2.420
  agricultural use development
    'agriculture', 2.125
    generally, 2.124–2.137
    'osier land', 2.126
    turbary, 2.128
    use of land, 2.129
    woodlands, 2.128
  casual trading areas, and, 2.226
  contravenes materiality of local authority's own development plan, which, 2.157–2.159
  conveyancing requisitions, and, 12.17
  curtilage of a house, and, 2.221–2.225
  Customs House Docks area, 2.484
  declaration and referral, 2.507–2.527
  de-exempted development, and, 2.122
  definition, 2.92–2.93
  derelict sites, 2.484
  Dublin Docklands area, 2.484
  forest husbandry, and, 2.218–2.220
  'functional area', 2.143
  generally, 2.121–2.122
  interior of structure, and, 2.213–2.217
  introduction, 2.92–2.93
  land reclamation, and, 2.227–2.230
  light railway works, 2.484
  local authority exempted development
    contravenes materiality of its own development plan, which, 2.157–2.159
    'functional area', 2.143
    generally, 2.138–2.139
    prescribed for purposes of PDA 2000, s 179, which is, 2.173–2.181
    'proposed development', 2.162
    public consultation procedure, 2.160–2.172
    PDA 2000, s 4(1), under, 2.140–2.152
    'statutory undertaker', 2.141
    subject to EIA, which is, 2.153–2.156
  material change in use
  'osier land', 2.126
  other non-planning enactments, under
    examples, 2.484–2.490
    generally, 2.477–2.478
    introduction, 2.237–2.238
    overview, 2.122
  other sections in PDA 2000, provided by, 2.491–2.506
  Planning and Development Regulations 2001, under
    *See also* **Planning and Development Regulations 2001**
    advertisements, 2.387–2.422
    article 6, and, 2.240–2.242
    classes of use, 2.467–2.475
    definitions, 2.235
    general exempted development, 2.243–2.386
    interpretation of terms, 2.235
    introduction, 2.231–2.234
    overview, 2.122
    rural exempted development, 2.423–2.466
    summary, 2.236
    under other enactments, 2.237–2.238
    works specified in drainage schemes, 2.239
  prescribed for purposes of PDA 2000, s 179, which is
    generally, 2.173–2.181

**Exempted development (contd)**
  prescribed for purposes of PDA 2000, s 179, which is (contd)
    public consultation procedure, 2.160–2.172
    'proposed development', 2.162
  protected structures, and, 8.274–8.275
  Roads Acts 1993–1998, under, 2.484
  rural areas, in, 2.423–2.466
  state authorities, by
    'Commissioners', 2.181
    environmental impact assessment, 2.197–2.212
    generally, 2.181–2.196
    overview, 2.122
    'state authority', 2.181
  statutory exempted development
    agricultural use development, 2.124–2.137
    generally, 2.123
    local authority exempted development, 2.138–2.181
    'statutory undertaker', 2.141
    strategic infrastructure, 2.484
    subject to EIA, which is, 2.153–2.156
    woodland husbandry, 2.218–2.220

**Extensions to houses**
  PDR exempted development, and
    declarations and referrals, 2.247–2.248
    generally, 2.245–2.246

**External parts of buildings or structures**
  PDR exempted development, and, 2.267

**Extinguishment of existing use rights**
  development, and, 2.48–2.55

**Extraction licences**
  mineral development, and, 8.249–8.250

**Fairground equipment**
  *See also* **Funfairs**
  definition, 8.177

**Fees**
  appeals, and
    generally, 4.102–4.103
    introduction, 4.36

**Fences**
  exempted development, and
    Class 5 development, 2.255–2.258
    Class 9 development, 2.266
    land open etc to the public, and, 2.240

**Financial contribution conditions**
  appeals, and, 4.22–4.24

**Fire**
  planning conditions, and, 3.232

**Fish counter**
  definition, 2.235

**Flags**
  advertisements, and, 2.394–2.396
  PDR exempted development, and, 2.340–2.341

**Foreshore**
  development, and, 2.113–2.120

**Forest husbandry**
  exempted development, and, 2.218–2.220

**Frivolous appeals**
  generally, 4.19

**Functional area**
  exempted development, and, 2.143

**Funfairs**
  *See also* **Event licensing**
  advertisements
    generally, 2.419–2.420
    introduction, 8.181
  'audience', 8.154
  duty of care of organisers, 8.177–8.178
  enforcement, 8.186
  engineering issues, and, 8.146
  exclusion from planning control, 8.144–8.145
  exempted development, and
    generally, 2.338
    introduction, 8.145
  'fairground equipment', 8.177

# Index

**Funfairs (contd)**
'funfair', 8.177
generally, 8.176
health and safety, and
   generally, 8.179
   introduction, 8.146
introduction, 8.141
'licence', 8.151
'local authority', 8.152
obligations of organisers, 8.177–8.178
PDR exempted development, and, 2.338
regulation-making powers, 8.180–8.185

**Further information**
generally, 3.121–3.125
revised plans, 3.133–3.136

**Garage conversions**
PDR exempted development, and
   declarations and referrals, 2.247–2.248
   generally, 2.245–2.246

**Garages**
PDR exempted development, and, 2.252–2.253

**Gas infrastructure**
strategic infrastructure development, and, 11.07–11.12

**Gates**
PDR exempted development, and
   Class 5 development, 2.255–2.258
   Class 9 development, 2.264

**Golf courses**
PDR exempted development, and, 2.234–2.235

**Government policy**
development control, and, 3.187

**Greater Dublin Area**
definition, 2.235

**Greenhouses**
PDR exempted development, and, 2.252–2.253

**Ground source heat pump systems**
PDR exempted development, and
   generally, 2.249–2.251
   industrial buildings, for, 2.379
   light industrial buildings, for, 2.380
   rural exempted development, and, 2.464

**Guesthouses**
advertisements, and, 2.399–2.400

**Habitats Directive**
conveyancing requisitions, and, 12.53

**Harbour authority works**
PDR exempted development, and, 2.316

**Hardship to developer**
injunctions, and, 5.121–5.125

**Health infrastructure**
strategic infrastructure development, and, 11.04

**Health and safety**
funfairs, and
   generally, 8.179
   introduction, 8.146

**Hearsay evidence**
injunctions, and, 5.158

**Heating systems**
PDR exempted development, and, 2.249–2.251

**High water mark**
PDR exempted development, and, 2.370

**House**
definition, 2.235

**Housing supply**
affordable housing
   agreements, 6.41–6.72
   allocation, 6.124–6.133
   clawback on resale, 6.134–6.162
   compensation for land transferred to local authority, 6.73–6.94
   conditions, 6.41–6.72
   controls on resale, 6.134–6.162

**Housing supply (contd)**
   affordable housing (contd)
      definition, 6.13–6.20
      exemptions from conditions, 6.104–6.115
      'house', 6.42
      legislative basis, 6.10–6.12
      refusal of exemption certificates, 6.116–6.119
      strategies, 6.21–6.39
      'withering permissions', and, 6.96–6.103
   compensation for land transferred to local authority, 6.73–6.94
   conditions
      exemptions, 6.104–6.115
      generally, 6.41–6.72
   exemption certificates
      definitions, 6.106
      generally, 6.104–6.116
      offences for non-compliance, 6.120–6.123
      refusal, 6.116–6.119
   housing strategies
      development plans, and, 6.35–6.39
      generally, 6.21–6.34
   introduction, 6.01–6.12
   refusal of exemption certificates, 6.116–6.119
   regulations, 6.163–6.166
   residential integration, and, 6.02
   social housing
      agreements, 6.41–6.72
      compensation for land transferred to local authority, 6.73–6.94
      conditions, 6.41–6.72
      definition, 6.13–6.20
      exemptions from conditions, 6.104–6.115
      'house', 6.42
      legislative basis, 6.10–6.12
      refusal of exemption certificates, 6.116–6.119
      strategies, 6.21–6.39
      'withering permissions', and, 6.96–6.103
   strategies
      development plans, and, 6.35–6.39
      generally, 6.21–6.34
   'withering permissions', and
      generally, 6.96–6.103
      introduction, 6.10

**Human rights**
   compensation, and, 7.40–7.41

**Identification, direction or warning as to land or structures**
   advertisements, and, 2.412

**Illuminated**
   definition, 2.235

**Illumination behind a window**
   advertisements, and, 2.391–2.392

**Imperative reasons of overriding public interest**
   land use plans, and, 9.119–9.121
   proposed development, and, 9.131–9.134

**Industrial building**
   CHP systems, and, 2.373
   definition, 2.235
   ground heat pump systems, and, 2.379
   solar panels, and, 2.376
   wind turbines, and, 2.375

**Industrial process**
   definition, 2.235

**Industrial undertaker**
   definition, 2.235

**Infrastructure development**
   development control, and, 3.09

**Initial afforestation**
   rural exempted development, and, 2.450

**Injunctions**
   acquiescence, 5.127
   attitude of planning authority, 5.137
   company directors, and, 5.183–5.188
   conduct of applicant, 5.128–5.130
   conduct of developer, 5.131–5.135
   conveyancing requisitions, and, 12.25

# Index

**Injunctions (contd)**
costs, 5.174–5.182
damages award, and, 5.163
discretion, and, 5.146
hardship to developer, 5.121–5.125
hearing at discretion of court, 5.110–5.115
hearsay evidence, 5.158
introduction, 5.104–5.109
laches, 5.126
onus of proof, 5.147–5.157
procedure for application, 5.138–5.145
public interest, 5.136
technical or trivial breach, 5.116–5.120
time limits, 5.165–5.173
undertakings as to damages, 5.159–5.162

**Inland waterways**
PDR exempted development, and, 2.236

**Inspection powers**
event licensing, and, 8.174–8.175

**Intensification of works/use**
development, and, 2.56–2.73

**Intensive agriculture**
rural exempted development, and, 2.449

**Interference with character of landscape, etc**
restrictions on exempted development, and, 2.240

**Interior of structure**
exempted development, and, 2.213–2.217
protected structures, and, 8.276

**Irrelevant considerations**
compensation, 3.170–3.172
licences required as pre-condition under other legislation, 3.173–3.176
introduction, 3.169
ownership of land, 3.177
permission required as pre-condition under other legislation, 3.173–3.176
personal circumstances, 3.179–3.181

**Judicial review**
*See also* **Statutory judicial review**
*Commission v Ireland*
(Case C–427/07)
access to justice, 4.167–4.168
conclusion, 4.169–4.170
generally, 4.162–4.164
transposition of term 'the public concerned', 4.165–4.166
compulsory acquisition, and, 7.139–7.140
EIA Directive, and
case law, 4.162–4.170
generally, 4.155–4.161
introduction, 4.171

**Laches**
injunctions, and, 5.126

**Land**
development, and, 2.90

**Land reclamation**
exempted development, and, 2.227–2.230
rural exempted development, and, 2.445–2.446

**Land use plans**
architectural conservation areas
acquisition of structure or other land, 1.224–1.225
generally, 1.220–1.223
areas of special amenity
confirmation of order, 1.258–1.260
generally, 1.246–1.257
areas of special planning control
development, and, 1.236–1.237
generally, 1.226–1.235
notices under s 88 PDA 2000, 1.238–1.245
European site
generally, 9.103
hosts priority habitat or species, 9.124–9.126
not host priority habitat or species, 9.122–9.123

**Land use plans (contd)**
  imperative reasons of overriding public interest, 9.119–9.121
  landscape conservation areas
    generally, 1.261–1.262
    procedure, 1.263–1.268
  local area plans, 1.175–1.190
  meaning, 9.104
  procedure, 9.127–9.130
  strategic development zones
    adjoining local authority areas, in, 1.201
    affordable housing, and, 1.200
    applications for development, and, 1.213–1.217
    environmental assessment, 1.199
    generally, 1.191–1.196
    making, 1.202–1.212
    planning schemes, 1.197–1.198
    revocation of scheme, 1.218–1.219
    social housing, and, 1.200

**Landscape conservation areas**
  conveyancing requisitions, and, 12.37
  generally, 1.261–1.262
  procedure, 1.263–1.268

**Landscaping**
  planning conditions, and, 3.243
  PDR exempted development, and, 2.259–2.261

**Leave to apply**
  statutory judicial review, and
    appeals to Supreme Court, and, 4.270–4.286
    application, 4.219–4.422
    generally, 4.179–4.196
    substantial grounds, 4.242–4.258
    substantial interest, 4.223–4.241
    time limits, 4.202–4.218

**Legal interest of applicant**
  development control, and, 3.69–3.72

**Letterboxes**
  PDR exempted development, and, 2.324

**Letting of structure or land**
  advertisements, and, 2.404–2.405

**Licences required as pre-condition under other legislation**
  development control, and, 3.173–3.176

**Licensing of events**
  *See also* **Licensing of funfairs**
  applications
    content, 8.161
    determination, 8.168
    further information, 8.167
    introduction, 8.155
    notice of intention to apply, 8.159
    'prescribed bodies', 8.157
    timing, 8.160
  'audience', 8.154
  availability of documents, 8.163–8.165
  codes of practice, 8.171
  content of application, 8.161
  determination of application, 8.168
  'development', and, 8.143
  'event', 8.147
  exclusion from planning control, 8.144–8.145
  further information, 8.167
  generally, 8.141–8.154
  grant of licence, 8.169–8.170
  inspection powers, 8.174–8.175
  'licence', 8.151
  'local authority', 8.152
  notice of intention to apply, 8.159
  obligation of person holding event, 8.153
  observations by other parties, 8.165–8.166
  'outdoor events', 8.147
  pre-application procedure, 8.156–8.158
  'prescribed bodies', 8.157
  procedure
    availability of documents, 8.163–8.165
    content of application, 8.161
    determination of application, 8.168
    further information, 8.167
    introduction, 8.155

# Index

**Licensing of events (contd)**
  procedure (contd)
    notice of intention to apply, 8.159
    observations by other parties, 8.165–8.166
    pre-application procedure, 8.156–8.158
    'prescribed bodies', 8.157
    submissions by other parties, 8.165–8.166
    timing of application, 8.160
  regulation-making powers, 8.148
  safety obligations, 8.173
  service of notices, 8.172
  statutory provisions, 8.141
  submissions by other parties, 8.165–8.166
  timing of application, 8.160
  warning notices, and, 8.141

**Licensing of funfairs**
  *See also* **Licensing of events**
  advertisements, 8.181
  'audience', 8.154
  duty of care of organisers, 8.177–8.178
  enforcement, 8.186
  engineering issues, and, 8.146
  exclusion from planning control, 8.144–8.145
  'fairground equipment', 8.177
  'funfair', 8.177
  generally, 8.176
  health and safety, and
    generally, 8.179
    introduction, 8.146
  introduction, 8.141
  'licence', 8.151
  'local authority', 8.152
  obligations of organisers, 8.177–8.178
  regulation-making powers, 8.180–8.185

**Light industrial building**
  CHP systems, and, 2.374
  definition, 2.235
  ground source heat pump systems, and, 2.380
  solar panels, and, 2.377
  wind turbines, and, 2.375

**Light railway works**
  exempted development, and, 2.484

**Local area plans**
  development plans, and, 1.02
  generally, 1.175–1.190
  land use plan, and, 9.104
  ministerial directions, 1.143–1.160
  role and use, 1.11
  sustainability, 1.42

**Local authority development**
  appropriate assessment, and, 9.143–9.151
  major accident hazards, and
    not requiring EIA, 8.215–8.219
    requiring EIA, 8.212–8.214

**Local authority exempted development**
  contravenes materiality of its own development plan, which, 2.157–2.159
  generally, 2.138–2.139
  prescribed for purposes of PDA 2000, s 179, which is,
    generally, 2.173–2.181
    public consultation procedure, 2.160–2.172
  'proposed development', 2.162
  public consultation procedure, 2.160–2.172
  s 4(1) PDA 2000, under
    'functional area', 2.143
    generally, 2.140–2.152
    'statutory undertaker', 2.141
  subject to EIA, which is, 2.153–2.156

**Maintenance of drains, ponds and culverts**
  rural exempted development, and, 2.428–2.430

**Major accident hazards**
  conveyancing requisitions, and, 12.40–12.44
  Council Directives, 8.187–8.188
  declaration and referral, 8.221–8.244

**Major accident hazards (contd)**
 'establishment', 8.197
 generally, 8.187–8.200
 local authority development
  not requiring EIA, 8.215–8.219
  requiring EIA, 8.212–8.214
 Planning and Development
  Regulations 2001, and, 8.189
 planning appeals, 8.208–8.211
 planning applications
  generally, 8.201–8.207
  introduction, 3.35
 restrictions on exempted development, and, 2.240
 state authority development, 8.220

**Management of site**
 planning conditions, and, 3.245

**Material contravention of development plans**
 appeals, and, 4.16–4.17
 generally, 1.44–1.72

**Material change in use**
 definition, 2.09–2.20
 generally, 2.74–2.88

**Mineral development**
 compensation, 8.247
 extraction licences, 8.249–8.250
 generally, 8.245–8.253
 oil and petroleum, 8.252–8.253
 preservation of support orders, 8.251
 prospecting licences, 8.248
 rural exempted development, and, 2.434–2.436
 state mining permission, 8.250
 statutory provisions, 8.245

**Ministerial directions**
 development plans, and, 1.143–1.160

**Ministerial guidelines and directives**
 development plans, and, 1.316–1.327

**Ministerial policy**
 development control, and, 3.187

**Mobile telephony**
 definition, 2.235

**Modification of permission**
 compensation, and, 7.84–7.85
 planning conditions, and, 3.221

**Name plates**
 advertisements, and, 2.397–2.398

**Natura 2000 network**
 generally, 9.105

**Natura 2000 sites**
 appropriate assessment, and, 9.69
 compensatory measures, and, 9.98–9.99
 generally, 9.09–9.16

**Natura impact report**
 generally, 9.106–9.112

**Natura impact statement**
 generally, 9.108–9.112
 introduction, 9.12

**Natural Heritage Areas**
 conveyancing requisitions, and, 12.52

**Nature reserves**
 PDR exempted development, and, 2.237

**Navigation aids**
 PDR exempted development, and, 2.342–2.343

**Noise emissions**
 planning conditions, and, 3.241

**Notices**
 applications for permission, and
  newspaper notices, 3.37
  notice of intention, 3.36
  site notices, 3.38–3.44
  statutory recipients, 3.86–3.88
 compensation, and, 7.67–7.79
 endangerment notices
  appeals, 8.293–8.294
  generally, 8.286–8.287
  procedure, 8.297–8.307
 exempted development, 8.274–8.275
 interior works, 8.276

## Index

**Notices (contd)**
  endangerment of protected structures, and
    appeals, 8.293–8.294
    generally, 8.286–8.287
    procedure, 8.297–8.307
  restoration of character of protected structures, and
    appeals, 8.293–8.294
    effective date, 8.296
    form and content, 8.287
    generally, 8.288–8.291
    procedure, 8.297–8.307
    scope, 8.295

**Notification**
  planning applications, and, 3.86–3.88
  planning permission, and, 3.115–3.116

**Notification of decision**
  planning applications, and, 3.114

**Nuclear installations**
  strategic infrastructure development, and, 11.74–11.80

**Objectives**
  development plans, and
    discretionary objectives, 1.83
    generally, 1.80–1.88
    introduction, 1.08
    mandatory objectives, 1.81–1.82

**Observations**
  compulsory acquisition, and, 7.162
  event licensing, and, 8.165–8.166
  planning applications, and
    generally, 3.94–3.99
    public holidays, and, 3.100–3.101
  strategic infrastructure development, and, 11.37–11.39

**Occasional social or recreational purposes of schools, halls, etc**
  PDR exempted development, and, 2.291

**Occupancy conditions**
  planning conditions, and, 3.270–3.276

**Oil and petroleum**
  mineral development, and, 8.252–8.253

**On-site development by industrial undertakers**
  PDR exempted development, and, 2.307–2.309

**Onus of proof**
  injunctions, and, 5.147–5.157

**Open loose yards**
  rural exempted development, and, 2.440–2.441

**Open spaces**
  compulsory acquisition, and, 7.203–7.209
  planning conditions, and, 3.242

**Operating hours of a business**
  planning conditions, and, 3.249

**OPW drainage works**
  PDR exempted development, and, 2.366–2.367

**Oral hearings**
  appeals, and
    appointment of inspector, 4.105–4.111
    generally, 4.67–4.69
    matters other than those raised by parties, 4.87–4.91
    supplemental provisions, 4.70–4.86
  compulsory acquisition, and
    costs, 7.182–7.183
    generally, 7.173–7.175
    objective of Board, 7.186–7.192
    supplemental provisions, 7.176–7.181

**Ornamental gardens**
  PDR exempted development, and, 2.329–2.333

**Osier land**
  exempted development, and, 2.126

**Outdoor events**
  event licensing, and, 8.147

1133

**Outline planning permission**
   conveyancing requisitions, and
      generally, 12.32
      special characteristics, 12.33–12.34
   duration, 3.17
   generally, 3.14–3.21
   regulations, 3.22–3.23
   restrictions, 3.24

**Overnight accommodation provision**
   advertisements, and, 2.399–2.400

**Ownership of land**
   development control, and, 3.177

**Painting**
   definition, 2.235

**Parks**
   PDR exempted development, and, 2.329–2.333, 2.337

**Past failure to comply**
   refusal of permission, and
      generally, 8.318–8.331
      introduction, 3.166–3.168

**Paths**
   PDR exempted development, and, 2.259–2.261

**Peat extraction**
   rural exempted development, and, 2.453–2.457

**Permission required as pre-condition under other legislation**
   development control, and, 3.173–3.176

**Permitted development**
   *See also* **Exempted development**
   generally, 2.122

**Personal circumstances**
   development control, and, 3.179–3.181

**Petroleum prospecting**
   exempted development, and, 2.485
   mineral development, and, 8.252–8.253
   rural exempted development, and, 2.434–2.436

**Photo-voltaic solar panels**
   PDR exempted development, and, 2.378

**Pipelines, cables and wires**
   compensation, and
      generally, 7.92–7.93
      introduction, 7.01
      time limits, 7.09
   conveyancing requisitions, and, 12.39
   PDR exempted development, and, 2.317

**Pitch and putt courses**
   PDR exempted development, and, 2.234–2.235

**Places etc of archaeological, geological etc interest**
   restrictions on exempted development, and, 2.240

**Planning agreements**
   generally, 8.348–8.356
   planning conditions, and, 3.262–3.269

**Planning amnesty**
   conveyancing requisitions, and, 12.09–12.11

**Planning and Development Regulations 2001 (as amended)**
   *See also* **Exempted development**
   access to public road, and, 2.240
   advertisements, and
      'advertisement', 2.386
      'advertisement structure', 2.387
      agricultural demonstrations, 2.421–2.422
      airports, 2.403
      building sites, 2.408–2.409
      bus stations, 2.403
      business premises, 2.388–2.390
      business premises where ads not visible from outside, 2.393
      carnivals, 2.419–2.420
      cultural events, 2.417–2.418
      cultural institutions, 2.399–2.400
      educational events, 2.417–2.418
      educational institutions, 2.399–2.400
      election posters, 2.413–2.415

# Index

**Planning and Development Regulations 2001 (as amended) (contd)**
advertisements, and (contd)
  enclosed land, 2.401–2.402
  flags, 2.394–2.396
  funfairs, 2.419–2.420
  generally, 2.385
  guesthouses, 2.399–2.400
  identification, direction or warning as to land or structures, 2.412
  illuminated behind a window, 2.391–2.392
  letting of structure or land, 2.404–2.405
  name plates, 2.397–2.398
  overnight accommodation provision, 2.399–2.400
  planning notices, 2.416
  political events, 2.417–2.418
  public works, 2.410–2.411
  railway land, 2.401–2.402
  railway stations, 2.403
  religious events, 2.417–2.418
  religious institutions, 2.399–2.400
  road signs, 2.410–2.411
  sale of goods, 2.406–2.407
  sale of land, 2.404–2.405
  sale of livestock, 2.406–2.407
  sale of structure, 2.404–2.405
  sporting events, 2.417–2.418
  statutory notices, 2.416
  travelling circuses, 2.419–2.420
aerodrome licensees, 2.326–2.327
aids to navigation, 2.342–2.343
air quality measurement, 2.355–2.356
amenity purposes, 2.328–2.338
antenna, 2.254
appeals, and, 4.117–4.135
architectural conservation areas, and, 2.240
article 6, and
  generally, 2.467–2.475
  introduction, 2.236
  restrictions, 2.240–2.242
awnings, 2.252–2.253
banners and flags, 2.340–2.341

biomass boilers
  generally, 2.381
  rural exempted development, 2.465
boats, 2.263
'bring-facility', 2.347
burial grounds, 2.344
capping walls, 2.265
caravans and camper vans, 2.263
change of use, and
  development which is exempted under art 10 PDR 2001, 2.271
  generally, 2.269–2.270
CHP systems
  industrial buildings, for, 2.373
  light industrial buildings, for, 2.374
circuses, 2.238
classes of use
  art 10 PDR 2001, and, 2.284–2.289
  detailed listings, 2.273–2.283
  introduction, 2.272
connection of premises to services, 2.357–2.358
conservatories
  declarations and referrals, 2.247–2.248
  generally, 2.245–2.246
construction or erection outside functional area, 2.253–2.254
contravention of condition attached to a permission, and, 2.240
cultural events, 2.338
curtilage of house
  declarations and referrals, 2.247–2.248
  generally, 2.245–2.246
definitions, 2.235
demolition of buildings
  generally, 2.360–2.365
  restrictions, 2.240
deposit boxes. 2.324
development control, and, 3.12
drainage schemes, and
  generally, 2.477–2.478
  introduction, 2.239
drains, 2.259–2.261

**Planning and Development Regulations 2001 (as amended) (contd)**
    electricity undertakers' development, 2.318–2.323
    endangering public safety, and, 2.240
    Environmental Protection Agency Act 1992, s 86(8), and, 2.237
    excavation
        research and discovery, for, 2.348
        surveying or prospecting, for, 2.351–2.352
    extensions to houses
        declarations and referrals, 2.247–2.248
        generally, 2.245–2.246
    external parts of buildings or structures, 2.267
    fences
        Class 5 development, 2.255–2.258
        Class 9 development, 2.266
    fencing land open etc to the public, and, 2.240
    flags and banners
        advertisements, and, 2.394–2.396
        generally, 2.340–2.341
    funfairs
        generally, 2.338
        introduction, 8.145
    garage conversions
        declarations and referrals, 2.247–2.248
        generally, 2.245–2.246
    garages, 2.252–2.253
    gates
        Class 5 development, 2.255–2.258
        Class 9 development, 2.264
    general exempted development, 2.243–2.386
    golf courses, 2.234–2.235
    greenhouses, 2.252–2.253
    ground heat pump systems
        generally, 2.249–2.251
        industrial buildings, for, 2.379
        light industrial buildings, for, 2.380
    harbour authority works, 2.316
    heating systems, 2.249–2.251
    high water mark, and, 2.370
    inland waterways, 2.236
    interference with character of landscape, etc, and, 2.240
    interpretation of terms, 2.235
    introduction, 2.231–2.234
    landscaping, 2.259–2.261
    letterboxes, 2.324
    major accident hazards, and
        generally, 8.189
        introduction, 2.240
    miscellaneous matters, 2.339–2.384
    nature reserves, 2.237
    navigation aids, 2.342–2.343
    occasional social or recreational purposes of schools, halls, etc, 2.291
    on-site development by industrial undertakers, 2.307–2.309
    OPW drainage works, 2.366–2.367
    ornamental gardens, 2.329–2.333
    other enactments, and, 2.237–2.238
    overview, 2.122
    parks, 2.329–2.333, 2.337
    paths, 2.259–2.261
    photo-voltaic solar panels, 2.378
    pipelines by Irish Gas Board, 2.317
    pitch and putt courses, 2.234–2.235
    places, sites etc of archaeological, geological etc interest, and, 2.240
    plastering walls, 2.265
    political events, 2.338
    ponds, 2.259–2.261
    porches
        generally, 2.262
        restrictions, 2.240
    private street, road or footpath repairs, 2.268
    public rights of way, and, 2.240
    pump houses, 2.349–2.350
    railings, 2.255–2.258
    railway operators' development, 2.313–2.315
    reclamation of foreshore, 2.371
    recreational purposes, 2.328–2.338
    Regional Fisheries Board development, 2.368–2.369

# Index

**Planning and Development Regulations 2001 (as amended) (contd)**
  religious events, 2.338
  repair of private streets, roads or footpaths, 2.268
  restrictions, 2.479–2.481
  roadside shrines, 2.329–2.333
  rural exempted development
    animal shelters, 2.437–2.439, 2.447–2.448
    biomass boilers, 2.465
    boat moorings, 2.426
    camper vans, 2.426
    combined heating power systems, 2.461
    construction of drains, ponds and culverts, 2.428–2.430
    ground source heat pump systems, 2.464
    initial afforestation, and, 2.450
    intensive agriculture, and, 2.449
    introduction, 2.423–2.425
    land reclamation, 2.445–2.446
    maintenance of drains, ponds and culverts, 2.428–2.430
    mineral prospecting, 2.434–2.436
    open loose yards, 2.440–2.441
    peat extraction, 2.453–2.457
    petroleum prospecting, 2.434–2.436
    renewable technologies, 2.458–2.465
    replacement of broad-leaf forest by conifer species, 2.451–2.452
    roofed structures and yards for housing greyhounds, 2.447–2.448
    roofed structures for housing animals, 2.437–2.439
    roofless cubicles, 2.440–2.441
    scout camps, 2.427
    self feed silos, 2.440–2.441
    silage areas, 2.440–2.441
    solar panels, 2.463
    stores, barns, sheds and glass-houses, 2.442–2.243
    temporary masts for mapping meteorological conditions, 2.466
    tents, 2.426
    unroofed fenced areas for training horses. 2.444
    walls and fences, 2.431–2.433
    wind turbines, 2.462
  satellite dishes
    business premises, on, 2.372
    generally, 2.254
  school extensions, 2.382–2.384
  school grounds, 2.344
  shades, 2.252–2.253
  sheds, 2.252–2.253
  show grounds, 2.344
  side extensions to houses
    declarations and referrals, 2.247–2.248
    generally, 2.245–2.246
  solar panels
    generally, 2.249–2.251
    industrial buildings, for, 2.376
    light industrial buildings, for, 2.377
  special amenity area orders, and, 2.240
  sports fields, 2.329–2.333
  stamp machines, 2.324
  statutory requirements, 2.345–2.346
  statutory undertakers development
    electricity undertakers, 2.318–2.323
    generally, 2.312
    harbour authority works, 2.316
    pipelines by Irish Gas Board, 2.317
    Post Office, 3.324
    railway operators, 2.313–2.315
    'statutory undertakers', 2.312
    telecommunications services, 2.325
  storage within curtilage of industrial building not visible from road, 2.310–2.311
  summary, 2.236
  telecommunications services' development, 2.325
  temporary accommodation on building sites, 2.294–2.295
  temporary masts of mapping meteorological conditions, 2.301–2.302

**Planning and Development Regulations 2001 (as amended) (contd)**
    temporary plant and machinery
        building sites, 2.292–2.293
        mining operations, 2.296–2.297
    temporary structures
        building sites, 2.290
        mining operations, 2.296–2.297
        schools, 2.303
        visiting dignitaries, 2.298–2.299
    temporary uses
        building sites, 2.290
        elections, 2.300
        schools, 2.304–2.306
    tents, 2.252–2.253
    unauthorised structures, and, 2.240
    walls, 2.255–2.258
    Waste Management Act 1992, s 54(4)(a), and, 2.238
    wells, 2.349–2.350
    wind turbines
        generally, 2.249–2.251
        industrial buildings, for, 2.375
    wired broadcast relay, 2.359
    works specified in drainage schemes, 2.239
    works under public road, and, 2.240

**Planning appeals**
    appellants
        generally, 4.07–4.10
        landowner of adjoining lands, 4.14
        non-governmental organisations, 4.13
        prescribed body that is not notified, 4.11–4.12
    applications, 4.35–4.48
    appointment of inspector for oral hearing, 4.105–4.111
    availability of documents, 4.54
    calculation of time, 4.95–4.96
    conditions, against
        financial contribution, requiring, 4.22–4.24
        generally, 4.20–4.21

    *de novo* determination, 4.18
    expenses, 4.104
    fees
        generally, 4.102–4.103
        introduction, 4.36
    financial contribution conditions, against, 4.22–4.24
    frivolous appeals, 4.19
    introduction, 4.01
    jurisdiction, 4.02
    major accident hazards, and, 8.208–8.211
    material contravention of development plan, and, 4.16–4.17
    matters other than those raised by parties, 4.87–4.91
    notice of postponement of decision, 4.33
    oral hearings
        appointment of inspector, 4.105–4.111
        generally, 4.67–4.69
        matters other than those raised by parties, 4.87–4.91
        supplemental provisions, 4.70–4.86
    planning regulations, and, 4.117–4.135
    policies and objectives, and, 4.100–4.101
    prohibition against further applications, 4.25–4.28
    public availability of planning documents, 4.112–4.116
    regulation-making powers, 4.97–4.99
    *res judicata*, and, 4.28
    rules and procedures, 4.29
    submission of documents, 4.49–4.53
    submissions
        other parties, by, 4.55
        power of Board to request, 4.61–4.64
        power of Board to require, 4.65
        power of Board where notice is served, 4.66
        third parties, by, 4.56–4.60
    taking other matters into account, 4.87–4.91

# Index

**Planning appeals (contd)**
  time limits for decision
    'appropriate period', 4.15
    calculation, 4.95–4.96
    generally, 4.30–4.32
    notice of postponement, 4.33
    variation by Minister, 4.34
  time limits for lodgment
    calculation, 4.95–4.96
    generally, 4.15
  vexatious appeals, 4.19
  withdrawal, 4.92–4.94

**Planning applications**
  content
    generally, 3.53–3.56
    legal interest of applicant, 3.69–3.72
    requirements for accompanying particulars, 3.58–3.68
    specified additional information, 3.57
  default permission, 3.108–3.113
  determination
    maximum period, 3.101–3.107
    minimum period, 3.102
  electricity undertaking, and, 3.73
  environmental impact statements, 3.35
  further information
    generally, 3.121–3.125
    revised plans, 3.133–3.136
  introduction, 3.12
  legal interest of applicant, 3.69–3.72
  major accident hazards, and
    generally, 8.201–8.207
    introduction, 3.35
  modification of permission, 3.89–3.93
  newspaper notices, 3.37
  notice of intention, 3.36
  notices
    newspaper notices, 3.37
    notice of intention, 3.36
    site notices, 3.38–3.44
    statutory recipients, 3.86–3.88
  notification of decision, 3.114
  notification of planning applications, 3.86–3.88
  observations on applications
    generally, 3.94–3.99
    public holidays, and, 3.100–3.101
  Planning and Development Regulations 2001, and, 3.12
  pre-application consultations, 3.45–3.52
  procedure by LPA on receipt, 3.74–3.81
  regulations, 3.12
  requirements for accompanying particulars, 3.58–3.68
  site notices, 3.38–3.44
  specified additional information, 3.57
  strategic infrastructure development, and, 11.14–11.18
  submissions
    generally, 3.94–3.99
    public holidays, and, 3.100–3.101
  types, 3.13–3.34
  weekly list, 3.82–3.85

**Planning conditions**
  abdication of jurisdiction of planning body, and, 3.228–3.229
  affordable housing agreements, and, 3.255–3.259
  appeals, and
    financial contribution, requiring, 4.22–4.24
    generally, 4.20–4.21
  carrying out works, 3.240
  completion of works within specified period, 3.244
  co-operation of third party, and, 3.215
  deprivation of landowner of existing rights or uses, and, 3.216–3.220
  development of adjoining land, 3.237–3.239
  directly depart from application, which, 3.231
  enforceability, 3.222–3.225
  fire conditions, 3.232
  general conditions, 3.208–3.229
  introduction, 3.207
  landscaping, 3.243

1139

**Planning conditions (contd)**
    local authority's other duties, and, 3.214
    management of site, 3.245
    matters to be agreed, and, 3.233–3.235
    modification of existing permission not yet implemented, and, 3.221
    noise emissions, 3.241
    occupancy conditions, 3.270–3.276
    open spaces, 3.242
    operating hours of a business, 3.249
    planning agreements, and, 3.262–3.269
    planting and landscaping, 3.243
    points of detail to be agreed, 3.250–3.254
    precision, 3.226–3.227
    protected structures, 3.248
    reasonableness, 3.210–3.212
    relevance to planning policy, 3.213
    restriction of use of premises, 3.261–3.269
    roads and other facilities, 3.245
    security for satisfactory completion, 3.245
    signage, 3.247
    social housing agreements, and, 3.255–3.259
    standard conditions, 3.230
    statutory conditions under PDA 2000 s 34(4), 3.236–3.249
    sterilisation agreements, and, 3.262–3.269
    temporary permission, 3.246
    transboundary environmental impacts, 3.260
    use of adjoining land, 3.237–3.239

**Planning documents**
    interpretation, 1.75–1.76

**Planning gain**
    development control, and, 3.164–3.165

**Planning history of the development**
    conveyancing requisitions, and, 12.01

**Planning injunctions**
    acquiescence, 5.127
    attitude of planning authority, 5.137
    company directors, and, 5.183–5.188
    conduct of applicant, 5.128–5.130
    conduct of developer, 5.131–5.135
    conveyancing requisitions, and 12.25
    costs, 5.174–5.182
    damages award, and, 5.163
    discretion, and, 5.146
    hardship to developer, 5.121–5.125
    hearing at discretion of court, 5.110–5.115
    hearsay evidence, 5.158
    introduction, 5.104–5.109
    laches, 5.126
    onus of proof, 5.147–5.157
    procedure for application, 5.138–5.145
    public interest, 5.136
    technical or trivial breach, 5.116–5.120
    time limits, 5.165–5.173
    undertakings as to damages, 5.159–5.162

**Planning notices**
    advertisements, and, 2.416

**Planning permission**
    challenges to
        *See also* **Challenging planning decisions**
        appeals and referrals to An Bord Pleanála, 4.01–4.154
        statutory judicial review, 4.155–4.293
    conditions
        abdication of jurisdiction of planning body, and, 3.228–3.229
        affordable housing agreements, and, 3.255–3.259
        carrying out works, 3.240
        completion of works within specified period, 3.244
        co-operation of third party, and, 3.215
        deprivation of landowner of existing rights or uses, and, 3.216–3.220
        development of adjoining land, 3.237–3.239

# Index

**Planning permission (contd)**
  conditions (contd)
    directly depart from application, which, 3.231
    enforceability, 3.222–3.225
    fire conditions, 3.232
    general conditions, 3.208–3.229
    introduction, 3.207
    landscaping, 3.243
    local authority's other duties, and, 3.214
    management of site, 3.245
    matters to be agreed, and, 3.233–3.235
    modification of existing permission not yet implemented, and, 3.221
    noise emissions, 3.241
    occupancy conditions, 3.270–3.276
    open spaces, 3.242
    operating hours of a business, 3.249
    planning agreements, and, 3.262–3.269
    planting and landscaping, 3.243
    points of detail to be agreed, 3.250–3.254
    precision, 3.226–3.227
    protected structures, 3.248
    reasonableness, 3.210–3.212
    relevance to planning policy, 3.213
    restriction of use of premises, 3.261–3.269
    roads and other facilities, 3.245
    security for satisfactory completion, 3.245
    signage, 3.247
    social housing agreements, and, 3.255–3.259
    standard conditions, 3.230
    statutory conditions under PDA 2000, s 34(4), 3.236–3.249
    sterilisation agreements, and, 3.262–3.269
    temporary permission, 3.246
    transboundary environmental impacts, 3.260
    use of adjoining land, 3.237–3.239
  default permission, 3.108–3.113
  extension, 3.19–3.20
  modification, 3.89–3.93
  notification of grant, 3.115–3.116
  obligation to obtain, 3.03–3.11
  outline planning permission
    duration, 3.17
    generally, 3.14–3.21
    regulations, 3.22–3.23
    restrictions, 3.24
  regulations, 3.10–3.11
  retention permission
    generally, 3.25–3.31
    substitute consent, 3.32–3.34
  revocation, 3.89–3.93
  types
    introduction, 3.13
    outline planning permission, 3.14–3.24
    retention permission, 3.25–3.34
  weekly list, 3.117–3.120

**Planning unit**
  development, and, 2.21–2.25

**Planning warranty**
  conveyancing requisitions, and, 12.02–12.08

**Planting and landscaping**
  planning conditions, and, 3.243

**Plastering walls**
  PDR exempted development, and, 2.265

**Political events**
  advertisements, and, 2.417–2.418
  PDR exempted development, and, 2.338

**Ponds**
  PDR exempted development, and, 2.259–2.261
  rural exempted development, and, 2.428–2.430

**Porches**
  PDR exempted development, and, 2.262
  restrictions on exempted development, and, 2.240

**Pre-application procedure**
    event licensing, and, 8.156–8.158
    planning applications, and, 3.45–3.52
    strategic infrastructure development, and, 11.19–11.26

**Pre-contract questionnaires**
    conveyancing requisitions, and, 12.01

**Prescribed bodies**
    event licensing, and, 8.157

**Preservation of support orders**
    mineral development, and, 8.251

**Private street, road or footpath repairs**
    PDR exempted development, and, 2.268

**'Proper planning'**
    alternative sites, 3.144–3.145
    amenity, 3.146–3.147
    common good, 3.148
    compulsory purchase orders, 3.149
    environmental pollution, 3.158
    generally, 3.136–3.142
    planning history of land, 3.150–3.151
    precedent, 3.153
    private interest, 3.154–3.155
    public health and safety, 3.156–3.157
    restraint on power to grant permission in material contravention of development plan, 3.152
    relevant considerations, 3.143–3.159

**Proposed development**
    exempted development, and, 2.162
    generally, 9.113

**Prospecting licences**
    mineral development, and, 8.248

**Protected structures**
    'attendant grounds', 8.258
    causing damage to structure, 8.292–8.293
    compulsory acquisition
        generally, 8.308–8.310
        vesting orders, 8.311–8.317
    consequences of designation, 8.277–8.283
    conveyancing requisitions, and, 12.18
    curtilage of structure, 8.262–8.267
    definition, 8.258
    development control, and, 3.191–3.193
    development plans, and, 1.89
    duty of owners and occupiers, 8.284–8.285
    endangerment notices
        appeals, 8.293–8.294
        generally, 8.286–8.287
        procedure, 8.297–8.307
    exempted development, 8.274–8.275
    'have regard to', 8.272
    interior works, 8.276
    introduction, 8.254–8.257
    location, 8.261
    ministerial guidelines, 8.268–8.271
    notice to require restoration of character of structures
        appeals, 8.293–8.294
        effective date, 8.296
        form and content, 8.287
        generally, 8.288–8.291
        procedure, 8.297–8.307
        scope, 8.295
    notice to require works in relation to endangerment of structures
        appeals, 8.293–8.294
        generally, 8.286–8.287
        procedure, 8.297–8.307
    planning conditions, and, 3.248
    'proposed protected structure', 8.258
    'protection', 8.258
    record
        details, 8.260
        generally, 8.259
        location, 8.261
        ministerial guidelines, 8.268–8.271
        status, 8.263
    restoration notices
        appeals, 8.293–8.294
        effective date, 8.296
        form and content, 8.287
        generally, 8.288–8.291
        procedure, 8.297–8.307

**Protected structures (contd)**
  restoration notices (contd)
   scope, 8.295
   'structure', 8.258
   words affecting character, 8.273
   'works', 8.258

**Protection of property**
  compensation, and, 7.40–7.41

**Public interest**
  injunctions, and, 5.136

**Public notices**
  strategic infrastructure development, and, 11.32–11.36

**Public rights of way**
  compensation, and
   generally, 7.94
   introduction, 7.01
   time limits, 7.09
  conveyancing requisitions, and, 12.28–12.31
  development plans, and, 1.161–1.163
  restrictions on exempted development, and, 2.240

**Public works**
  advertisements, and, 2.410–2.411

**Pump houses**
  PDR exempted development, and, 2.349–2.350

**Quarries**
  conditions
   appeals, 8.66
   compensation, 8.59–8.65
   generally, 8.38–8.55
  definition, 8.72
  enforcement action, 8.67–8.68
  environmental impact assessments
   generally, 8.56–8.58
   introduction, 8.34
  existing use rights, 8.27
  failure to provide information, 8.67–8.68
  generally, 8.26–8.27
  guidelines, 8.70
  inspection and examination, 8.44–8.45
  interpretation, 8.71–8.72
  introduction, 8.26–8.27
  IPC licence, and, 8.53
  material changes in operation, 8.28–8.32
  registration, 8.37
  retention permission, and, 8.57
  s 261A controls, 8.88–8.124
  specified information
   failure to provide, 8.67
   further information requests, 8.36
   generally, 8.35
   registration, 8.33–8.34
  statutory provisions, 8.28
  substitute consent, and, 9.08

**Radon gas**
  conveyancing requisitions, and, 12.58–12.63

**Railings**
  PDR exempted development, and, 2.255–2.258

**Railway land**
  advertisements, and, 2.401–2.402

**Railway operators' development**
  PDR exempted development, and, 2.313–2.315

**Railway orders**
  strategic infrastructure development, and, 11.13

**Railway stations**
  advertisements, and, 2.403

**Reasonableness**
  planning conditions, and, 3.210–3.212

**Reclamation of foreshore**
  PDR exempted development, and, 2.371

**Recreational purposes**
  PDR exempted development, and, 2.328–2.338

**Referrals to An Bord Pleanála**
   applications, 4.35–4.48
   appointment of inspector for oral hearing, 4.105–4.111
   availability of documents, 4.54
   calculation of time, 4.95–4.96
   definition, 4.136
   development, and, 4.137–4.146
   exempted development, and, 4.137–4.146
   expenses, 4.104
   fees, 4.102–4.103
   frivolous referrals, 4.19
   introduction, 4.01
   jurisdiction, 4.03–4.06
   oral hearings, 4.67–4.86
   planning regulations, and, 4.117–4.135
   policies and objectives, and, 4.100–4.101
   public availability of planning documents, 4.112–4.116
   regulation-making powers, 4.97–4.99
   relevant referrals
      introduction, 4.136
      PDA 2000, s 5, under, 4.137–4.146
      PDA 2000, s 34(5), under, 4.147–4.148
      PDA 2000, s 37(5), under, 4.149
      PDA 2000, s 57(2)–(4), under, 4.150
      PDA 2000, s 96(5), under, 4.151–4.153
      PDA 2000, s 193(2), under, 4.154
   rules and procedures, 4.29
   submission of documents, 4.49–4.53
   submissions, 4.55–4.66
   taking other matters into account, 4.87–4.91
   time limits for decision, 4.30–4.34
   vexatious referrals, 4.19
   withdrawal, 4.92–4.94

**Refusal of permission**
   amenity, and, 3.147
   challenges to
      *See also* **Challenging planning decisions**
   appeals and referrals to An Bord Pleanála, 4.01–4.154
   statutory judicial review, 4.155–4.293
   compensation, and
   assignment, 7.83
   determination of amount, 7.43–7.47
   excluded development, 7.49–7.63
   general right, 7.38
   generally, 7.36–7.42
   introduction, 3.170–3.172
   modification of permission, and, 7.84–7.85
   notice preventing compensation, 7.67–7.79
   prematurity, and, 7.57–7.58
   restriction, 7.48–7.66
   revocation of permission, and, 7.84–7.85
   rules for determination of amount, 7.43–7.47
   s 192 notices, 7.67–7.79
   structures substantially replacing structures demolished or destroyed by fire, 7.80–7.82
   time limits, 7.09
   notification of decision, and, 3.114
   particulars to accompany applications, and, 3.59
   past failure to comply, and
      generally, 8.318–8.331
      introduction, 3.166–3.168
   precedent, and, 3.153

**Regional Fisheries Board development**
   PDR exempted development, and, 2.368–2.369

**Regional planning guidelines**
   development plans, and, 1.269–1.315
   land use plan, and, 9.104

**Registration**
   compensation, and, 7.28

**Religious events**
   advertisements, and, 2.417–2.418
   PDR exempted development, and, 2.338

# Index

**Religious institutions**
  advertisements, and, 2.399–2.400
**Remittal**
  statutory judicial review, and, 4.287–4.288
**Removal of structure**
  compensation, and
    generally, 7.86–7.87
    introduction, 7.01
    time limits, 7.09
  generally, 8.332–8.347
**Renewable technologies**
  rural exempted development, and, 2.458–2.465
**Repair of private streets, roads or footpaths**
  PDR exempted development, and, 2.268
**Replacement of broad-leaf forest by conifer species**
  rural exempted development, and, 2.451–2.452
**Repository**
  definition, 2.235
**Requisitions for conveyancing**
  advertisement structures, 12.38
  affordable housing, 12.45
  architectural conservation areas, 12.36
  areas of special planning control, 12.36
  Birds Directive, 12.51
  building energy rating certificates, 12.13–12.16
  cables, wires and pipelines, 12.39
  consequences of planning defects, 12.12
  creation of rights of way, 12.28–12.31
  declarations and referrals, 12.19–12.24
  duration of planning permission, 12.54–12.57
  enforcement procedures, 12.25
  environmental matters
    Birds Directive, 12.51
    definitions, 12.48
    general enquiries, 12.49
    Habitats Directive, 12.53
    introduction, 12.47
    Natural Heritage Areas, 12.52
    Wildlife Acts, 12.50
  environmental indemnities
    generally, 12.66
    landlord's covenants in a lease, 12.70
    limited form, 12.68
    loan agreement clauses, 12.71
    tenant's covenants in a lease, 12.69
  environmental warranties
    draft precedent, 12.66
    generally, 12.64–12.65
  exempted development, 12.17
  Habitats Directive, 12.53
  injunctions, 12.25
  landscape conservation orders, 12.37
  major accidents Directive, 12.40–12.44
  Natural Heritage Areas, 12.52
  outline permission
    generally, 12.32
    special characteristics, 12.33–12.34
  pipelines, wires and cables, 12.39
  planning amnesty, 12.09–12.11
  planning history of the development, 12.01
  planning injunctions, 12.25
  planning warranty, 12.02–12.08
  pre-contract questionnaires, 12.01
  protected structures, 12.18
  public rights of way, 12.28–12.31
  radon gas, 12.58–12.63
  social housing, 12.45
  Special Condition 36 of Law Society Contract, 12.02–12.08
  special planning control areas, 12.36
  strategic development zones, 12.35
  taking estates in charge, 12.46
  tree preservation orders, 12.26–12.27
  Wildlife Acts, 12.50
  wires, cables and pipelines, 12.39

***Res judicata***
  appeals, and, 4.28
  development control, and, 3.160–3.163

**Restoration notices**
    appeals, 8.293–8.294
    effective date, 8.296
    form and content, 8.287
    generally, 8.288–8.291
    procedure, 8.297–8.307
    scope, 8.295

**Resumption of existing use rights**
    development, and, 2.48–2.55

**Retention permission**
    development, and, 2.94–2.106
    environmental impact assessments, and, 9.01–9.04
    enforcement, and, 5.05–5.29
    generally, 3.25–3.31
    quarries, and, 8.57
    substitute consent, 3.32–3.34

**Revised plans**
    generally, 3.126–3.132
    notice of further information, 3.133–3.136

**Revocation of permission**
    compensation, and, 7.84–7.85

**Road signs**
    advertisements, and, 2.410–2.411

**Roads Acts 1993–1998**
    exempted development, and, 2.484

**Roads and other facilities**
    planning conditions, and, 3.245

**Roadside shrines**
    PDR exempted development, and, 2.329–2.333

**Roofed structures**
    rural exempted development, and
        greyhounds, 2.447–2.448
        larger animals, 2.437–2.438
        smaller animals, 2.439

**Roofless cubicles**
    rural exempted development, and, 2.440–2.441

**Rural exempted development**
    animal shelters
        greyhounds, 2.447–2.448
        larger animals, 2.437–2.438
        smaller animals, 2.439
    biomass boilers, 2.465
    boat moorings, 2.426
    camper vans, 2.426
    combined heating power systems, 2.461
    construction of drains, ponds and culverts, 2.428–2.430
    ground source heat pump systems, 2.464
    initial afforestation, and, 2.450
    intensive agriculture, and, 2.449
    introduction, 2.423–2.425
    land reclamation, 2.445–2.446
    maintenance of drains, ponds and culverts, 2.428–2.430
    mineral prospecting, 2.434–2.436
    open loose yards, 2.440–2.441
    peat extraction, 2.453–2.457
    petroleum prospecting, 2.434–2.436
    renewable technologies, 2.458–2.465
    replacement of broad-leaf forest by conifer species, 2.451–2.452
    roofed structures
        greyhounds, 2.447–2.448
        larger animals, 2.437–2.438
        smaller animals, 2.439
    roofless cubicles, 2.440–2.441
    scout camps, 2.427
    self feed silos, 2.440–2.441
    silage areas, 2.440–2.441
    solar panels, 2.463
    stores, barns, sheds and glass-houses, 2.442–2.243
    temporary masts for mapping meteorological conditions, 2.466
    tents, 2.426
    unroofed fenced areas for training horses. 2.444
    walls and fences, 2.431–2.433
    wind turbines, 2.462

**s 192 notices**
    compensation, and, 7.67–7.79

# Index

**Safety obligations**
event licensing, and, 8.173

**Sale of goods**
advertisements, and, 2.406–2.407

**Sale of land**
advertisements, and, 2.404–2.405

**Sale of livestock**
advertisements, and, 2.406–2.407

**Sale of structure**
advertisements, and, 2.404–2.405

**Satellite dishes**
PDR exempted development, and
business premises, on, 2.372
generally, 2.254

**School**
definition, 2.235

**School extensions**
PDR exempted development, and, 2.382–2.384

**School grounds**
PDR exempted development, and, 2.344

**Scout camps**
rural exempted development, and, 2.427

**Screening for appropriate assessment**
generally, 9.114–9.115

**Security for satisfactory completion**
planning conditions, and, 3.245

**Self feed silos**
rural exempted development, and, 2.440–2.441

**Seveso II Directive**
*See also* **Major accident hazards**
generally, 8.189

**Shades**
PDR exempted development, and, 2.252–2.253

**Sheds**
PDR exempted development, and, 2.252–2.253

**Shop**
definition, 2.235

**Show grounds**
PDR exempted development, and, 2.344

**Side extensions to houses**
PDR exempted development, and
declarations and referrals, 2.247–2.248
generally, 2.245–2.246

**Signage**
planning conditions, and, 3.247

**Silage areas**
rural exempted development, and, 2.440–2.441

**Site notices**
planning applications, and, 3.38–3.44

**Site of Community importance**
European site, and, 9.103
generally, 9.116

**Sites etc of archaeological, geological etc interest**
restrictions on exempted development, and, 2.240

**Social housing**
conveyancing requisitions, and, 12.45
development control, and, 3.197–3.198
development plans, and, 1.95–1.96
planning conditions, and, 3.255–3.259
strategic development zones, and, 1.200

**Solar panels**
PDR exempted development, and
generally, 2.249–2.251
industrial buildings, for, 2.376
light industrial buildings, for, 2.377
rural exempted development, and, 2.463

**Special amenity area orders**
development control, and, 3.182–3.185
PDR exempted development, and, 2.240

**Special areas of conservation (SACs)**
    appropriate assessment, and, 9.79
    European site, and, 9.103
    generally, 9.09–9.12
    meaning, 9.117

**Special Condition 36 of Law Society Contract**
    conveyancing requisitions, and, 12.02–12.08

**Special planning control areas**
    compensation, and
        generally, 7.91
        introduction, 7.01
        time limits, 7.09
    conveyancing requisitions, and, 12.36
    development, and, 1.236–1.237
    development control, and, 3.196
    generally, 1.226–1.235
    notices under s 88 PDA 2000
        appeals, 1.240–1.241
        enforcement, 1.243–1.245
        generally, 1.238–1.239
        implementation, 1.242

**Special protection areas (SPAs)**
    appropriate assessment, and, 9.79
    European site, and, 9.103
    generally, 9.09–9.12

**Sporting events**
    advertisements, and, 2.417–2.418

**Sports fields**
    PDR exempted development, and, 2.329–2.333

**Stamp machines**
    PDR exempted development, and, 2.324

**Standard planning conditions**
    generally, 3.230

**Standard planning permission**
    generally, 3.18

**State authority development**
    environmental impact assessment, 2.197–2.212
    generally, 2.181–2.196
    major accident hazards, and, 8.220
    'state authority', 2.181

**State mining permission**
    mineral development, and, 8.250

**Statutory exempted development**
    agricultural use development
        'agriculture', 2.125
        generally, 2.124–2.137
        'osier land', 2.126
        turbary, 2.128
        use of land, 2.129
        woodlands, 2.128
    contravenes materiality of its own development plan, which, 2.157–2.159
    generally, 2.123
    local authority exempted development
        contravenes materiality of its own development plan, which, 2.157–2.159
        generally, 2.138–2.139
        prescribed for purposes of PDA 2000, s 179, which is, 2.173–2.181
        'proposed development', 2.162
        public consultation procedure, 2.160–2.172
        s 4(1) PDA 2000, under, 2.140–2.152
        subject to EIA, which is, 2.153–2.156
    prescribed for purposes of PDA 2000, s 179, which is
        generally, 2.173–2.181
        public consultation procedure, 2.160–2.172
        'proposed development', 2.162
    s 4(1) PDA 2000, under
        'functional area', 2.143
        generally, 2.140–2.152
        'statutory undertaker', 2.141
    subject to EIA, which is, 2.153–2.156

# Index

**Statutory judicial review**
  alternative remedies available, 4.259–4.264
  appeals to Supreme Court, and, 4.270–4.286
  application for leave to apply, 4.219–4.422
  application to stay proceedings, 4.197–4.201
  case law examples, 4.264
  characteristics, 4.171
  EIA Directive, and
    case law, 4.162–4.170
    generally, 4.155–4.161
  expeditious determination, 4.291–4.293
  extension of time, 4.211–4.218
  grounds, 4.242–4.258
  introduction, 4.171–4.178
  leave to apply by *ex parte* motion
    appeals to Supreme Court, and, 4.270–4.286
    application, 4.219–4.422
    generally, 4.179–4.196
    substantial grounds, 4.242–4.258
    substantial interest, 4.223–4.241
    time limits, 4.202–4.218
  legislative basis, 4.174
  quashing part of decision or act, 4.289–4.290
  remittal, and, 4.287–4.288
  substantial grounds
    definition, 4.244
    examples, 4.245
    generally, 4.242–4.258
  substantial interest, 4.223–4.241
  time limits
    extension, 4.211–4.218
    generally, 4.202–4.210
  undertaking as to damages, 4.265–4.269

**Statutory notices**
  advertisements, and, 2.416

**Statutory planning conditions**
  generally, 3.236–3.249
  introduction, 3.188

**Strategic development zones**
  development control, and, 3.195

**Statutory requirements**
  PDR exempted development, and, 2.345–2.346

**Statutory undertakers development**
  electricity undertakers, 2.318–2.323
  exempted development, and, 2.141
  generally, 2.312
  harbour authority works, 2.316
  pipelines by Irish Gas Board, 2.317
  Post Office, 3.324
  railway operators, 2.313–2.315
  'statutory undertakers', 2.312
  telecommunications services, 2.325

**Sterilisation agreements**
  generally, 8.348–8.356
  planning conditions, and, 3.262–3.269

**Storage within curtilage of industrial building not visible from road**
  PDR exempted development, and, 2.310–2.311

**Stores, barns, sheds and glass-houses**
  rural exempted development, and, 2.442–2.243

**Strategic development zones**
  acquisition of site, 1.195–1.196, 8.365
  adjoining local authority areas, in, 1.201
  affordable housing, and, 1.200
  applications for development, and, 1.213–1.217, 8.377–8.380
  conveyancing requisitions, and, 12.35
  definition, 1.193, 8.358
  designation, 8.359–8.364
  'development agency', 1.192, 8.357
  development plans, and, 1.91
  effect, 8.383
  environmental assessment, 1.199
  generally, 8.357–8.76
  introduction, 1.191–1.196

**Strategic development zones (contd)**
  planning schemes
    adoption, 8.369–8.376
    generally, 1.197–1.198
    land use plan, and, 9.104
    making, 1.202–1.212
    preparation of draft, 8.366–8.368
    revocation, 1.218–1.219, 8.381–8.382
  social housing, and, 1.200

**Strategic Environmental Assessment (SEA)**
  sustainability, 1.41–1.42

**Strategic infrastructure development**
  alteration on request, 11.81–11.87
  applications for permission
    determination, 11.53–11.63
    EIA, and, 11.27–11.31
    generally, 11.40–11.41
    public notice, 11.32–11.36
    submissions by public, 11.37–11.39
    supplemental provisions, 11.42–11.52
    time limits, 11.72–11.73
  costs, 11.64–11.71
  definition, 11.02
  determination of applications, 11.53–11.63
  development plans, and, 1.73–1.74
  electricity transmission lines, 11.08–11.12
  energy infrastructure, 11.04
  environmental impact assessment, and, 11.27–11.31
  environmental impact statements, 11.88–11.93
  environmental infrastructure, 11.04
  exempted development, and, 2.484
  gas infrastructure, 11.07–11.12
  health infrastructure, 11.04
  introduction, 11.01–11.02
  nuclear installations, 11.74–11.80
  observations by public, 11.37–11.39
  other cases, 11.06–11.12

Planning and Development Act 2000, Schedule 7
  generally, 11.03–11.04
  threshold examples, 11.05
  planning applications, and, 11.14–11.18
  pre-application consultation, 11.19–11.26
  public notice, 11.32–11.36
  railway orders and boards, 11.13
  submissions by public, 11.37–11.39
  time limits for applications, 11.72–11.73
  transport infrastructure, 11.04

**Structure**
  development, and, 2.89

**Submissions**
  compulsory acquisition, and, 7.162
  event licensing, and, 8.165–8.166
  planning applications, and
    generally, 3.94–3.99
    public holidays, and, 3.100–3.101
  strategic infrastructure development, and, 11.37–11.39

**Substantial interest**
  statutory judicial review, and, 4.223–4.241

**Substitute consent**
  applications
    generally, 9.31–9.52
    supplementary provisions, 9.57–9.67
  applications for leave to apply
    notice not served by planning authority, where, 9.19–9.29
    notice served by planning authority, where, 9.17–9.18
  enforcement, 9.53–9.56
  generally, 9.05–9.06
  grounds, 9.07
  quarries, and, 9.08

**Substratum of land**
  development, and, 2.91

**Supermarket**
  definition, 2.235

# Index

**Supplementary development contribution schemes**
    generally, 3.296–3.300
    introduction, 3.277

**Sustainability**
    development plans, and, 1.40
    strategic environmental assessment, and, 1.41–1.42

**Sustainable development**
    alternative sites, 3.144–3.145
    amenity, 3.146–3.147
    common good, 3.148
    compulsory purchase orders, 3.149
    environmental pollution, 3.158
    generally, 3.136–3.142
    planning history of land, 3.150–3.151
    precedent, 3.153
    private interest, 3.154–3.155
    public health and safety, 3.156–3.157
    restraint on power to grant permission in material contravention of development plan, 3.152

**Taking estates in charge**
    application of security, 8.387
    conveyancing requisitions, and, 12.46
    generally, 8.384–8.396
    mandatory obligation, 8.386–8.389
    plebiscites, 8.390
    procedure, 8.394
    Roads Act 1993 s 11, and, 8.385
    statutory provision, 8.384
    Water Services Act 2007, and, 8.392
    wishes of owners of houses, 8.390

**Telecommunications network**
    definition, 2.235

**Telecommunications service**
    definition, 2.235

**Telecommunications services**
    PDR exempted development, and, 2.325

**Temporary accommodation on building sites**
    PDR exempted development, and, 2.294–2.295

**Temporary masts of mapping meteorological conditions**
    PDR exempted development, and, 2.301–2.302
    rural exempted development, and, 2.466

**Temporary permission**
    planning conditions, and, 3.246

**Temporary plant and machinery**
    PDR exempted development, and
        building sites, 2.292–2.293
        mining operations, 2.296–2.297

**Temporary structures**
    PDR exempted development, and
        building sites, 2.290
        mining operations, 2.296–2.297
        schools, 2.303
        visiting dignitaries, 2.298–2.299

**Temporary uses**
    PDR exempted development, and
        building sites, 2.290
        elections, 2.300
        schools, 2.304–2.306

**Tents**
    PDR exempted development, and, 2.252–2.253
    rural exempted development, and, 2.426

**Time limits**
    compensation, and, 7.09
    compulsory acquisition, and, 7.150–7.160
    injunctions, and, 5.165–5.173
    statutory judicial review, and
        extension, 4.211–4.218
        generally, 4.202–4.210
        strategic infrastructure development, and, 11.72–11.73

**Transboundary environmental impacts**
  planning conditions, and, 3.260

**Transport infrastructure**
  development control, and, 3.09
  exempted development, and, 2.486
  strategic infrastructure development, and, 11.04

**Travelling circuses**
  advertisements, and, 2.419–2.420

**Tree preservation orders**
  compensation, 8.406–8.407
  consequences, 8.398
  conveyancing requisitions, and, 12.26–12.27
  generally, 8.397–8.407
  procedures, 8.402–8.405
  registration, 8.399

**Unauthorised development**
  decision on enforcement, 5.47–5.60
  definition, 2.03
  development carried out pursuant to planning condition, 5.03–5.04
  enforcement notices, 5.61–5.78
  general offence, 5.02
  generally, 2.107–2.108
  penalties, 5.79–5.87
  retention permission, 5.05–5.29
  warning letters, 5.30–5.46

**Unauthorised structure**
  definition, 2.03
  generally, 2.109–2.110
  restrictions on exempted development, and, 2.240

**Unauthorised structures**
  PDR exempted development, and, 2.240

**Unauthorised use**
  definition, 2.03
  generally, 2.111

**Unauthorised works**
  definition, 2.03
  generally, 2.112

**Undertaking as to damages**
  injunctions, and, 5.159–5.162
  statutory judicial review, and, 4.265–4.269

**Unroofed fenced areas for training horses**
  rural exempted development, and, 2.444

**Use**
  development, and, 2.08

**Use of adjoining land**
  planning conditions, and, 3.237–3.239

**Variation**
  development plans, and
    generally, 1.136–1.142
    ministerial directions, 1.143–1.160

**Vexatious appeals**
  generally, 4.19

**Walls**
  PDR exempted development, and, 2.255–2.258
  rural exempted development, and, 2.431–2.433

**Warning letters**
  contents, 5.41–5.46
  general procedure, 5.30–5.40

**Waste management**
  development plans, and, 1.90

**Waste Management Act 1992, s 54(4)(a)**
  restrictions on exempted development, and, 2.238

**Weekly lists**
  planning applications, 3.82–3.85
  planning decisions, 3.117–3.120

**Wells**
  PDR exempted development, and, 2.349–2.350

**Wholesale warehouse**
  definition, 2.235

**Wildlife sites**
  generally, 9.118

# Index

**Wind turbines**
    PDR exempted development, and
        generally, 2.249–2.251
        industrial buildings, for, 2.375
    rural exempted development, and, 2.462

**Wired broadcast relay**
    PDR exempted development, and, 2.359

**Wires, cables and pipelines**
    compensation, and
        generally, 7.92–7.93
        introduction, 7.01
        time limits, 7.09

conveyancing requisitions, and, 12.39

**Woodland husbandry**
    exempted development, and, 2.218–2.220

**Woodlands**
    agricultural use development, and, 2.128

**Works**
    development, and, 2.06–2.07

**Works under public road**
    restrictions on exempted development, and, 2.24

**Zoning**
    development control, and, 3.01